D1161832

OUTDOOR RECREATION

OUTDOOR RECREATION

United States National Parks, Forests, and Public Lands

Charles I. Zinser
Professor of Geography
State University of New York—Plattsburgh

Mapping by Janice Millea

John Wiley & Sons, Inc.
New York · Chichester · Brisbane · Toronto · Singapore

This text is printed on acid-free paper.

Copyright © 1995 by John Wiley & Sons, Inc.

All rights reserved. Published simultaneously in Canada.

Reproduction or translation of any part of this work beyond
that permitted by Section 107 or 108 of the 1976 United
States Copyright Act without the permission of the copyright
owner is unlawful. Requests for permission or further
information should be addressed to the Permissions Department,
John Wiley & Sons, Inc., 605 Third Avenue, New York, NY
10158-0012.

This publication is designed to provide accurate and
authoritative information in regard to the subject
matter covered. It is sold with the understanding that
the publisher is not engaged in rendering legal, accounting,
or other professional services. If legal advice or other
expert assistance is required, the services of a competent
professional person should be sought.

Library of Congress Cataloging in Publication Data:
Zinser, Charles I.
    Outdoor recreation : United States national parks, forests, and
public lands / Charles I. Zinser ; mapping by Janice Millea.
      p.   cm.
    ISBN 0-471-05373-2 (cloth : acid-free paper)
    1. Outdoor recreation—United States—Management. 2. Public
lands—United States—Recreational use—Management. 3. Natural
resources—United States—Management. I. Title.
GV191.4.Z56 1995
350.858—dc20   94-38100

Printed in United States of America

10 9 8 7 6 5 4 3 2 1

To my daughters, Kiki and Sugar Bear,
who are the pride of my life.

Contents

Index   867

Maps

Preface

The use of natural resources for recreation has become a leading consideration in the allocation of natural resources in the United States. As a result, many new and challenging issues have arisen. Throughout much of our nation's history the commodity value of natural resources has dominated. But during the environmental movement of the 1960s and 1970s major interest evolved for amenity (noncommodity) resource valuation. While certain aspects of the preservation school of natural resource management can be traced to the creation of Yellowstone National Park in 1872, it was not until the 1960s that widespread application of this principle occurred outside of our national parks. The passage by Congress in the 1960s of preservation-oriented legislation such as the Wilderness Act (1964) and the Wild and Scenic Rivers Act (1968) did indeed mark a major watershed in national policy in which amenity resource value was given paramount importance in natural resource allocation. This legislation drastically altered the timber-cutting policies of the Forest Service and the building of dams by the Army Corps of Engineers and the Bureau of Reclamation.

In the 1950s and 1960s, concurrent with this increased emphasis on amenity resource valuation, there arose a tremendous increase in the recreational use occurring on our public lands. The attendance at national parks, national forests, state parks, and local parks skyrocketed. The physical facilities and their resource managers were not prepared for this tremendous influx of visitors. This "recreation explosion" was documented in the 1962 report of the federal Outdoor Recreation Resources Review Commission; no other federal report has impacted the use of lands for recreational purposes to such a degree. Congress enacted many of the recommendations of this commission into law. The Bureau of Outdoor Recreation in the Interior Department, created in 1962, was the first federal agency to have *recreation* in its title. The recreational land-use planning process at the federal level had reached maturity. The Bureau of Outdoor Recreation was not a land-managing agency; it had no public land under its jurisdiction. It was a planning agency. The Land and Water Conservation Fund, legislated by Congress in 1965 and managed by the Bureau of Outdoor Recreation, became a major funding source for recreational resource development. It serves as a source of funding for planning, land acquisition, and development on public recreation lands. Since this time many new recreational facilities have been built on public lands—federal, state, county, and local.

This book is about the allocation, location, planning and management of natural resources for recreational purposes. It is a spatial analysis of recreational resources. The importance of the legislation enacted by Congress as a primary factor determining the type of recreational land use that is permissible is stressed. It uses the case

study approach and does not intend to be all-encompassing. The main focus is on federal public lands in the United States. Chapter 1 provides background information and basic concepts of recreational land-use planning. Chapter 2 identifies the federal legislation that is responsible for current recreation programs and identifies the public and private recreation resource sectors and their roles in providing recreational services and facilities. The four principal land-managing agencies in the United States are the National Park Service, the Forest Service, the Fish and Wildlife Service, and the Bureau of Land Management. These four agencies have jurisdiction over 500,000,000 acres, or 25 percent of our total national territory. There is a spatial imbalance between population distribution and the geographic location of these lands. Chapters 3 through 6 focus on the National Park Service and the National Park System, and Chapters 7 through 10 center on the Forest Service and the National Forest System. Chapter 11 deals with the Fish and Wildlife Service and the National Wildlife Refuge System, and Chapter 12 chronicles the Bureau of Land Management. The Bureau of Land Management is the federal land-managing agency with more land under its jurisdiction than any other agency. The tremendous impacts on land use—and recreational land use in particular—that the Alaska National Interest Lands Conservation Act has on lands administered by these four agencies in Alaska is a major theme of this book.

There are several other federal land-managing agencies that also have important recreational lands under their administration. They are the Army Corps of Engineers, the Bureau of Reclamation, the Tennessee Valley Authority, and the Bureau of Indian Affairs. The recreational opportunities on lands managed by the first three of these are reservoir-oriented. Many people are surprised to learn that the most recreational use occurs within the National Forest System (ahead of the National Park System) and that the number two federal agency in terms of recreational use is the Army Corps of Engineers. Chapter 13 examines the recreational resources of these other federal agencies. The focus of the final chapter—Chapter 14—is on significant federal concepts for protecting amenity resources. Examples of these are the National Wilderness Preservation System, the National Trails System, and the National Wild and Scenic Rivers System. The legislation that established the National Wilderness Preservation System and the National Wild and Scenic Rivers System is extremely significant. For the first time, in a *de jure* manner, it was declared national policy that amenity resources could be protected from extractive resource utilization. Such legislation ensures their future availability for recreational, wildlife, and watershed values.

This book is for those who desire an introduction to the availability of recreational resources in the United States. Its function is to serve as a "one-source" document for information on our federal recreation system. It is not an all-encompassing treatise on single topics, such as our national parks or wildlife refuges; there are many other good guides that have this focus. Instead the purpose of this text is to whet your interest in further exploring the recreational resources of the United States. The reader can then consult the detailed field guides for precise trip planning. Other books cover recreation, but none have focused on recreational resources in the manner of this book. Its purpose is to introduce the reader to the great variety of recreational resources that exist in the United States. Its strongest suit is the large numbers of maps and statistical data that are available in no other source. An especially unique feature of this book is its coverage of the tremendous recreational potential that exists

on Bureau of Land Management lands. Not only is the historical evolution of each recreational system chronicled, but the recreational opportunities and resource management issues are analyzed. Environmental history and public land politics are interwoven in the entire book.

This book addresses a diverse audience. It is suitable as a text for university classes in geography, land use, environmental conservation, resource management, natural resources, recreation, and forestry. But the broader audience will be the recreating and touring public, both domestic and foreign. This book will introduce them to the diversity of recreational resources found on the public lands of the United States and serve as a major reference for helping them plan vacations and the use of their leisure time. It is not a purely scholarly book nor is it a purely popular book; I have tried to maintain a reasonable balance between the two, with the scale tipped toward the scholarly side. In particular, this book will serve as a valuable reference for the large number of foreign tourists who visit the public lands of the United States on vacation. During the field research for this book I became aware of the popularity of America's public land recreational resources as major destinations for foreign tourists from countries as diverse as Germany and Japan.

This book represents the culmination of 25 years of university teaching of a course entitled "Recreational Geography" at the State University of New York at Plattsburgh. For 25 years I have not had a suitable book to use for this course. I am deeply indebted to Jerry Van Meter at the University of Illinois at Champaign-Urbana, who first stimulated my interest in the subject in a course entitled "Recreational Use of Public Lands." I took this course as part of my cognate work in the Department of Parks and Recreation Administration for my Ph.D. in Geography.

Charles I. Zinser

Acknowledgments

This book could not have been written without the assistance of many individuals. Very special recognition and thanks go to my wife, Deborah A. Zinser, who typed all of the tables and appendixes and rendered dedicated proofreading assistance. Special recognition also is given to Janice Millea, who prepared all of the maps. Major assistance was also rendered by several hundred U.S. government employees. In addition to the federal government employees listed in the following paragraphs, there are seven individuals who warrant special recognition. Four Bureau of Land Management employees who rendered extraordinary help are Hal Hallett and Rob Hellie in the Washington, D.C. office, Steve L. Smith in the Nevada office, and David Wickstrom in the California office. In the National Park Service, extraordinary help was rendered by John Monroe in the North Atlantic regional office. Robert Marker in the Tennessee Valley Authority also provided major assistance. Wayne Nicholls, Public Affairs Director for the Tongass National Forest in Juneau, read and critiqued the portions of the manuscript pertaining to Alaska and the Tongass National Forest. Deb, Jan, Hal, Rob, Steve, Dave, John, Bob, and Wayne—Thanks! I could not have done it without your assistance.

Acknowledgment is given to the following National Park Service employees who provided research material and assistance: Cynthia Alvidres/Lattin, John M. Anderson, Joan M. Anzelmo, Liz Appling, Douglas A. Barnard, Gail Bennett, Gilbert E. Blinn, William J. Briggle, Joyce Brown, Tessy Chirakawa, Bobby L. Crisman, Denny Davies, Frank J. Deckert, Howard L. Dimot, Ellen Eberhardt, Bruce Edmonston, Steve Elkinton, Mark R. Flippo, L. Edward Gastellum, Steve Golden, Lou Good, Dana H. Harper, Pete Hart, John Haubert, Larry Henderson, Albert J. Hendricks, Susan Holly, Jeff Kartheiser, Valerie Kilthau, Al Klein, Carol M. Kruse, John D. Lancaster, H. Gilbert Lusk, James A. Mack, John Mangimeli, Renee Minnick, Gail C. Menard, John Monroe, David K. Morris, Irvin L. Mortenson, Jack Neckels, Dave Olson, Bruce Paige, William F. Paleck, Warren Rigby, Clair A. Roberts, Dave Roberts, Ann Sheppard, Harold Smith, Margie Steigerwald, Rolland R. Swain, Patricia Tolle, Richard Tourangeau, Kent Turner, Kim Valentino, Merle Van Horne, Tom Wade, Roy W. Weaver, Donald Weir, and Karen Whitney.

Also, the following Forest Service employees provided research material and assistance: James R. Abbott, Gary Adams, Stan Allgeier, Phil Barker, Carter Betz, Deborah Black, Homer R. Bowles, Kimberly Evart Bown, Paul Brewster, Caren F. Briscoe, Deborah Call, James L. Caswell, Jason H. Chase, Laura Conroy, Bob Cron, Barry Davis, Roger Deaver, Terri Denny, Cris Dinwiddie, Herbert E. Echelberger, Kathy Frank, Carl Gephardt, Charles Gill, Ed Gornowski, Richard E. Grace, Myrennia A. Harris, Jim Higgins, Joel D. Holtrop, Fred Kacprzynski, Clarence Krause, Lyle Laverty, Jim Lawrence, Jeanette Ling, Lori Long, John J. Maschi, Jay McConnell, Paula McMasters, Britta Morner, Sylvia Morrison, John Neeling, Susan B. Nelson, Wayne Nicholls, Susan Oderwald, George A. Olson, Don Palmer, Dennis Parker, Carole Patton, Mary H. Peterson, Lee Poague, Elbert O. Reed, Joe Robles, Karl Roenke, Bob Ross, Marie Sales, Rachel G. Schneider, Jerry Schumacher, Tina Sechler, Gary Sinclair, Samuel E. Stone, Denise Stuhr, Dave Tucci, Mark Van Every, Warren Williamson, Kathleen M. Winn, Greg Wright, Bob Wrightman, Tah Yang, Gaylord Yost, and Jose Zambrana.

In addition, the following Bureau of Land Management employees provided research material and assistance: Deanna Anderle, Oscar Anderson, Robin Bourke, Edward Bovy,

Paul Brink, DuShawn Brooks, Jennifer Callan, Mark Goldbach, Hal Hallett, Rob Hellie, Steve Knox, John A. Kwiatkowski, Frank Snell, David Vickery, Ken White, Bob Wick, David Wickstrom. Acknowledgment for research assistance is also given to: Jane Bechtold, David Hardt, Nancy A. Marx, Sue Oliveira, Catherine B. Sheppard, Bruce E. Weber, and Robert A. Zelley of the Fish and Wildlife Service; Cori Brown, Roland Davis, Brad Keshlear, and Kenneth Waldie of the Army Corps of Engineers; Jack G. Byers and Eugene Hertzog of the Bureau of Reclamation; Billy J. Bond and Homer D. Gray of the Tennessee Valley Authority; Patrick A. Hayes of the Bureau of Indian Affairs; Richard M. Hoppe and Ben Beach of the Wilderness Society; Susan A. Henley of the American Hiking Society; and Mary Shoshone of the Mammoth Mountain Ski Area.

OUTDOOR RECREATION

## CHAPTER 1

Recreational Resources: Basic Concepts and Use

Resources are the bases of both security and opulence; they are the foundations of power and wealth. They affect man's destiny in war and peace.

Erich Zimmermann (1951)

RECREATIONAL RESOURCES

Provision for outdoor recreation has become one of the major considerations in the nation's allocation of resources. This rise in priority of resource allocation for recreational use has developed many new and challenging resource management problems. Some of these issues are:

1. What kinds of recreational environments should be provided?
2. What is the exact nature of the responsibility of the federal, state, local, and private sectors?
3. Where should development take place?
4. How much access and development should take place?

This book focuses on the use of natural resources for recreational purposes. It is about recreational places, where people spend their leisure time, and provides a spatial analysis of recreational resources in the United States. The main focus is on federal recreational resources.

In 1933, and again in 1951, Erich Zimmermann defined resources using a functional interpretation, saying that the elements of the environment are not resources until they are capable of satisfying human needs. His concept is subjective: A *resource* is "neutral stuff" until humans (1) perceive their presence, (2) recognize their capacity to satisfy human wants, and (3) devise means to utilize them. "Resources are not, they become, they are not static but expand and contract in response to human wants and human actions" (Zimmermann, 1951, 15). According to Zimmermann, resources are culturally determined. The term *natural resource* will be used throughout this book to refer to elements of the natural environment that are perceived, satisfy human wants, and are utilized by humans.

During the environmental movement of the 1960s and 1970s a major interest evolved in amenity resource valuation. **Amenity resource value** refers to the non-monetary, intangible (noncommercial) value of natural resources. Amenity resource value contrasts with traditional commodity resource value, such as forests for timber or land for mining. It is easy to establish a value for a given number of board feet of timber to be harvested on a national forest, but the aesthetic value of preserving a wilderness forest presents valuation problems because aesthetic and spiritual qualities are very difficult to quantify. The recreational use of natural resources is considered amenity use. Isolated examples of amenity resource valuation did occur in the 19th century, such as preservation of the Yosemite Valley (1864) (Figure 1.1) and the creation of Yellowstone National Park (1872). The preservation of many natural environments for their amenity value assumed wide-scale proportion in the 1960s and 1970s with the passage of legislation such as the Wilderness Act (1964) and the Wild and Scenic Rivers Act (1968). This book is about the amenity use of natural resources.

It has been demonstrated that economic values can be determined for amenity resources. This is the subject of a classic environmental text by two scientists—John V. Krutilla and Anthony C. Fisher—doing research in the Resources for the Future natural environments research program. Their book, *The Economics of Natural Environments: Studies in the Valuation of Commodity and Amenity Resources,* was published in 1975 and revised in 1985. It includes a number of case studies that show how econometric analysis can be applied to natural resource decisions that concern amenity resources. The stated purpose of their book was to "bring the amenity resources of natural environments into an analytical valuation framework comparable to that for the extractive resources" (Krutilla and Fisher, 1975, vi). They accomplished this by applying the tools and concepts of conventional economic theory "in somewhat unconventional situations." For example, one of their case studies involved the White Cloud Peaks Mountains in Idaho's Challis National Forest. This area was evaluated

Figure 1.1 A view of Yosemite Valley (Yosemite National Park) as seen from Tunnel View.

for two greatly contrasting types of land uses: wilderness-type recreation and molybdenum mining. They concluded that the use of the White Cloud Peaks for recreation will exceed the value of the incompatible mining alternative. The issue was the potential massive degradation of a very scenic and ecologically attractive area.

The issue of amenity resource values is still very much in the headlines today. Probably the most familiar of these issues is the cutting of old-growth timber on the national forests of the Pacific Northwest. The preservation of habitat for an endangered species—the northern spotted owl—is the focus of this debate. A timber summit presided over by President Clinton and Vice President Gore was held in Portland, Ore., in April 1993, where these issues were discussed.

To define *recreational resources* it is necessary first to define recreation and leisure. **Recreation** is usually considered any type of conscious enjoyment that occurs during leisure time. There is no sharp line between recreation and other activities; the same activity may be work at some times and recreation at others. The distinguishing characteristic of recreation is not the activity itself but the attitude with which it is undertaken. **Leisure time** is the free or discretionary time available for people to use as they choose after meeting the biological requirements of existence and the subsistence requirements of work. There are four patterns in which leisure time occurs: daily, weekly, vacation, and retirement.

Daily leisure is usually defined as time after work or after school in which only a few hours are available for recreation. The recreational resources used are usually close to home, such as a neighborhood park, and activities of short duration dominate. *Weekly leisure* usually refers to the weekend, where a larger block of time allows the use of recreational resources located farther from home, such as a visit to a state park. This large block of time can become divided, thus impacting the type of recreational activity, due to interruption by daily chores postponed during the week. On many weekends the weekly leisure period is extended by a holiday thus allowing a three-day weekend. *Vacation leisure* provides an extended block of time, up to three to five weeks, in which it is possible to travel long distances to use distant recreational resources and undertake unusual and adventurous pursuits. *Retirement leisure* has shown the most striking change in recent years and provides much time for retirees to pursue recreational resources. Many retirees are now in excellent health and actively participate in recreation and travel.

Leisure is a time concept and recreation is an activity concept. **Recreational resources,** as used in this book, refers to natural resources that are used to obtain conscious enjoyment during leisure. Many broader definitions of a recreational resource have been used, such as "a source of supply of recreational opportunity," in which there is no distinction between human-made and natural resources. (Chubb and Chubb, 1981).

Many dualities exist when referring to recreation: indoor versus outdoor, resource oriented versus activity-oriented, developed versus undeveloped, urban versus extra urban, and spectator versus active participation. Some recreational activities cross the boundary of these duality's. Activities such as tennis, football, and baseball occur both indoors and outdoors. The focus of this book will be on outdoor, resource-oriented, extraurban recreational resources that are both developed and undeveloped and used by both spectators and active participants. There are some notable exceptions to this generalization. Many of the "historical" units in our National Park Sys-

tem are in urban areas. Private and commercial recreation are also strongly developed in urban areas. Finally, local recreational resources are aligned with population distribution. A recent study concluded that most recreation (60 percent) in the United States occurs in the parks and play areas of local communities (Cordell et al., 1990).

FACTORS THAT AFFECT THE USE OF RECREATIONAL RESOURCES

Outdoor recreation is only a part of the total life of the nation. Therefore, the demand for outdoor recreation is in many respects determined by factors external to recreation itself. We live in a highly automated and fast-moving society, in which *change* is the watchword. In his highly acclaimed book, *Future Shock,* Alvin Toffler pointed out the difficulty of living in the presence of constant and rapid change. The rapid changes in society have altered attitudes and formed a new philosophy of the importance of leisure. The President's Commission on Americans Outdoors in 1987 concluded that three major factors affect demand for outdoor recreation: leisure time, income, and mobility. Outdoor recreation demands on natural resources soared to peak levels in the mid-1970s and since this time have continued to grow, but at a much slower rate. Many factors have interacted in a synergistic manner to affect this demand for recreational resources.

The use of recreational resources occurs during leisure time. Recreation is only one activity that can occur during leisure time, but leisure time is a prerequisite before recreation can occur. Leisure and work are competitors for time; if one increases, the other decreases. Until the late 1970s the average American had about 125 days a year not devoted to earning a living. This increase in leisure time was made possible by shorter work weeks, time-saving devices, flextime, earned time, three-day weekends, and four-day work weeks. The most notable changes in demand for recreational resources are related to the larger blocks of time that became available during weekly, vacation, and retirement leisure. The President's Commission on Americans Outdoors did reveal that in the late 1980s a 30 percent loss of leisure time had occurred since the 1970s. This amounted to a loss of 8 hours per week. Factors that contributed to this loss included corporate consciousness about the economy, an increasing percentage of women entering the workforce, and adults returning to school.

Income is a major determinant of an individual's recreational activities. Real income has trended upward for a long time in the United States. This trend has been somewhat irregular, being broken by depressions and recessions, and becoming steeper in times of rising prosperity. *Disposable personal income* is that portion of the national product left to individuals, after taxes, for spending or saving. The portion of disposable personal income that is left after the normal costs of living is called *discretionary purchasing power*. From one's discretionary purchasing power the decision may be made to allocate funds for recreational pursuits or equipment. Discretionary purchasing power really suffered during the recession of the early 1990s, and when hard times hit it is often the recreation portion of the personal budget that is first cut. Many recreational activities require a substantial outlay of money for equipment

prior to actually undertaking the activity. For example, it is difficult to buy the necessary equipment for backpacking, even buying low-end gear, for under $500–$600, or in the case of downhill skiing, purchasing equipment for under $700–$800. Once one has equipment for backpacking, the additional cost per day can be quite low, but for an activity such as downhill skiing the average lift ticket is about $35–$45 per day. The President's Commission on Americans Outdoors found a bimodal pattern of income in the United States. The middle class in the $15,000–$35,000 income range was shrinking, resulting in an increase in the number of both low-income and high-income Americans. This trend has resulted in an increasing demand for private recreation for the rich and public recreation for lower-income Americans.

Mobility is one of the most distinctive features of American life. As a result, patterns of work and play have changed materially. There has been a tremendous expansion of the recreational environment: from 3 miles during daily leisure in the 19th century to 60 miles today, and from 10 miles to 200 miles during weekly and vacation leisure. Increased ownership of low-cost private automobiles and an expanded and improved highway system has been largely responsible for this increased mobility. Americans in some cities, such as New York City, do have a lower degree of ownership of private autos. This makes them rely on available mass transit, which in turn influences the nature of their recreational environment. The expansion and completion of the interstate highway system has had an especially noticeable impact on the use of recreational resources. It is now possible to drive nonstop on the interstate highway system, with the only limiting factor causing stops being the capacity of the fuel tank. Many driving times have been cut by 50 percent or more. Witness the impact of the completion of Interstate 70 in Colorado through the Eisenhower Tunnel. What was once a relatively slow trip on U.S. 6 over the 12,000-foot Loveland Pass, which would take an hour or more in winter conditions, is now completed in 5 minutes. Winter driving conditions on U.S. 6 over the Loveland Pass would often deteriorate enough to require closing the road. Closures are now much less common on I-70 through the "tunnel." Anyone who has experienced an eastward drive through the tunnel and "downhill" to Denver will bear witness to the huge volume of traffic that moves, *too fast,* on I-70.

Many other mobility-related changes have affected the use of recreational resources. The deregulation of the airlines has greatly changed the recreational range of moderate- and high-income Americans for sightseeing, skiing, hunting, and fishing. It is very easy for a person on the East Coast to leave on a 7:00 A.M. flight and be skiing in the Wasatch Range in Utah by early afternoon. Comfortable tour buses are the source of access for many Americans, especially retirees. The types of tours available on these buses are almost limitless, from a weekend gambling trip to Atlantic City, N.J., to an extended tour of national parks in the entire western United States. The resurgence of interest in cruise ships has been a major trend of the last decade. These cruises range from short daily trips, such as from Miami to Freeport, Bahamas, to extended cruises on the Inside Passage from Vancouver to Alaska (Figure 1.2). A sad occurrence is the semidisappearance of the passenger train. Anyone who has attempted to plan a major trip on Amtrak quickly becomes aware of the limited routes and inconvenient schedules. The President's Commission on Americans Outdoors has noted a decline in the "Chevy Chase Vacation" type of cross-country auto trip to "Wally World" in recent years. Many Americans do appear to be staying closer

Figure 1.2   Cruise ships anchored at Freeport, Grand Bahama Island, Bahamas.

to home in their recreational trips and activities. This has increased the pressure on local, state, and private recreation resources.

The geographic variable of **location** of recreational resources plays a major role in the demand for them. Recreational resources "do not become" until humankind not only perceives their presence but also recognizes their capacity to satisfy human wants and devises means to utilize them. All other things being equal, demand for recreational resources will be greatest when the resources are in close proximity to the using population. Yet certain valuable recreational resources receive heavy use, despite having a remote location, Yellowstone National Park being a good example. Such distant resources have to possess exceptional qualities not found elsewhere before individuals are willing to travel to their location.

Closely related to the geographic variable of location is the geographic variable of **physical geography.** The main aspects of physical geography used in analyzing recreational resources are climate, landforms, water, and biota. Climate is the basic limiting factor for many recreational activities. Chubb and Chubb (1981) attempt to define the "optimal climate," as "one which will permit participation in comfort for a maximum number of days each year in walking, playing games, or sitting out-of-doors relaxing in the sun." Using this definition, they identify the number 1 optimal climate as Koppen's dry summer subtropical (Cs) and the number 2 as Koppen's humid subtropical (Cfa). While these heliotrophic climates are indeed many people's definition of the optimal recreational climate, this definition fails to address the importance of different climates to different recreational activities. Neither of these two climates would be optimal for the skier or the snowmobiler; the latter would favor Koppen's humid continental climates (Dfa and Dfb). The attractiveness of even a favored climate varies with the weather in this climate. While *climate* refers to the long-term conditions of the atmosphere, *weather* refers to the day-to-day or minute-to-minute conditions of the atmosphere. Have you ever observed the activity and

amount of use at a beach on a sunny day in the 90s compared to a blustery, rainy day in the 50s? One is hard-pressed to find a variable of physical geography that determines use more than climate and weather. The "right weather" plays a major role in determining the quality of a given recreational experience.

Landforms refers to the general shape of the surface and the particular surface structure. Landforms may be classed as *major landforms* (mountains, hills, plateaus, plains, and plains with hills or mountains) or *minor landforms* (mountain peak, cliff, valley, beach, delta, and so on). Particular aspects of landforms that have high recreational value include: mountainous areas, canyons, caves, sand dunes, beaches—especially barrier beaches, islands, shorelines, volcanic landscapes, and thermal activity. Particularly, along the land-water interface, high recreational value exists. Figure 1.3 illustrates the attraction of beaches in a tropical climate on the island of St. John at Virgin Islands National Park, U.S. Virgin Islands. Some recreational activities are largely dependent on a particular landform characteristic. A major alpine ski area needs steep slopes with a vertical drop of at least 1000 to 2000 feet to succeed. Closely related to landforms is the **surface material.** The brilliant white coral sand of Virgin Islands National Park holds high recreational value.

Water holds a special quality eagerly sought after by recreationists. It is especially along shorelines at the land-water interface many recreational activities occur. Zinser (1974) found that the major factor governing leisure home location on private land in New York's Adirondack Mountains was a pond or lakefront location. Other researchers have drawn similar conclusions in other areas of the United States. The water we find can be either fresh or salt. Rivers, which are more widely distributed than ponds or lakes, hold great recreational attraction. Many artificial reservoirs have been constructed on rivers. Water is not only sought for swimming, boating, and fishing but also for snow skiing. Artificial snow making is now considered essential

Figure 1.3 The water is clear, the sand is brilliant, and the climate is sunny and tropical at Virgin Islands National Park, St. John Island, U.S. Virgin Islands.

for ski areas from Vermont to Colorado to California. Even a feature such as tides can have a major effect on recreational use, as anyone who has used the beaches around the Bay of Fundy in New Brunswick and Nova Scotia will attest.

Biota refers to not only the exotic and native plants but also to the animal life. Many of our national parks and national monuments have been created primarily for their biotic value, for example, Redwood National Park, Joshua Tree National Monument, Sequoia National Park, Saguaro National Monument, and Great Basin National Park. Other parks have several life zones; for example, Grand Canyon National Park has five of the seven life zones in North America. The chief recreational value of our National Wildlife Refuge System is viewing wildlife. Most major wildlife species of North America spend part or all of their time on units of the National Wildlife Refuge System. Some of these units are well known for individual species of wildlife, such as the elk of the National Elk Range in Jackson Hole, Wyo., or the bison of the National Bison Range in Montana. Sport hunting assumes great importance in most of our national forests during the fall, as does fishing in the spring, summer, and fall. Sections of Glacier National Park can be closed at times due to the presence of grizzly bears. Certain noxious forms of biota, such as insects, can ruin a recreational experience, as any hikers and campers in the Adirondacks will attest to during the end of May each year, when blackflies are at their peak.

Population—its nature, density, distribution, and age—plays a major role in the use of recreational resources. Population distribution is very uneven in the United States. Although the population center has moved westward, most people still live in the Northeast, the Lake States, the Far West and the South-Central parts of the country. Two-thirds of the population lives in the eastern third of the country. The spatial imbalance between population and resource-based recreation resources is one of the most distinctive features of the recreational geography of the United States and Canada. As population increases, more land is needed for other purposes, which subtracts from the recreational base. The United States is a nation that is over 80 percent urban. A distinctive feature of our urban landscape is that as cities grow, the evolving low-density residential areas are using much more land per capita than they did earlier in the century. A significant feature of this metropolitan pattern is one of low density for all land use. A century ago when a city expanded by 1000 people, it urbanized only 10 acres; 30 years ago, 30 acres were used, and 200 acres are required today. This type of development is not necessarily undesirable, but it does place great distances between the urban dwellers and the natural resources they use for outdoor recreation. It is only when land is dedicated to amenity resource purposes that this trend is reversed. Yet there are advantages to the economies of scale offered by contemporary urban systems. A given area must have a certain *threshold population*, which is the number of people needed to justify a recreational facility, program, or service—both economically and administratively. Many of the recreational opportunities that are commonplace in urban environments, such as major league sports and amusement parks, are nonexistent in rural areas.

As population increases, so does the use of recreational resources. The lines at ski areas increase, the waiting time to launch boats at boat ramps increases, and campsites at national parks are frequently filled by 9:00 A.M. We are having to share our recreational resources with more people each year. The number of public recreation acres per thousand people varies greatly, with low values in the Northeast (294),

South (578), and North Central states (672), high values in the West (8373), and extremely high values in Alaska (804,750). However, the factor of ready accessibility in Alaska limits the use of these resources, since roads are limited, and long winters shorten the season of use.

Age plays a major role in many recreational activities. The more active sports, such as skateboarding, snowboarding, and surfing, are practiced by younger people. The activities in which older Americans participate is surprising; it is quite common to find Americans in their sixties and seventies who still actively participate in downhill skiing. But there is probably no sport that is better suited for the entire life spectrum than golf.

The rapid growth in **technology** has tremendously affected outdoor recreation, resulting in entire new activities. It is the development of off-road vehicles (ORVs) that has really changed outdoor recreation use patterns. In the 1960s the growth in popularity of snowmobiles resulted in the use of back country in many areas that had seldom been visited in winter. In the 1980s ATVs (all-terrain vehicles) rose in popularity. These motorized, single-passenger "three-wheelers" and "four-wheelers" opened up in summer the same new country that snowmobiles opened up in winter. Although greatly expanding the recreational range of the users, ATVs have decreased the carrying capacity of the land to sustain recreational use. The development of comfortable four-wheel-drive passenger vehicles, such as the Jeep Cherokee, allowed a new class of clientele to pursue "four wheelin'." In the late 1980s and 1990s extremely strong, lightweight mountain bikes with wide knobby tires became popular, placing new challenges on the shoulders of land managers. The State Land Master Plan that regulates land use in New York's Adirondack Park Forest Preserve was rewritten in 1987 to regulate mountain bike use. Prior to 1987 only "motorized" vehicles were prohibited on the forest preserve, but this regulation was changed to prohibit "mechanically propelled" devices.

Technology has affected nonmotorized activities as well. Ski equipment, both alpine and cross-country, has changed radically. The appearance of the "metal" ski and plastic boot in the 1960s revolutionized downhill skiing, making it much easier to learn. By the 1980s, wooden cross-country skis had all but disappeared, to be replaced by lightweight, artificial-material skis with bottom designs that made the sometimes challenging task of waxing a thing of the past. The development of lightweight backpacking equipment in the 1960s and 1970s made extended hiking trips very feasible.

Technological changes have altered recreational use of water as well as of land. New designs of motorboats have contributed to increased family ownership. The sport of fishing has been revolutionized by the development in the 1980s of inexpensive "fish graphs." Anglers can now cruise the water in their power boats until their graphs indicate the location of fish. In the late 1980s a new kind of water vehicle, now referred to as PWCs (personal watercraft) and sometimes described as "snowmobiles built for water," was developed. Use of PWCs has gotten out of control on many lakes, and the State of New Hampshire has banned them on most lakes.

There has been tremendous social pressure for more **education,** with the result that a higher percentage of high school graduates now attend college than ever before. Education is the key to higher income, and higher income influences what people do for recreation and where they go to practice it. The higher-educated person

not only has more recreational interests but also more means with which to pursue them. A high percentage of the users of our rapidly expanding National Wilderness Preservation System are not only college graduates but also hold advanced degrees from American universities. These individuals have been strong supporters of environmental interest groups such as the Sierra Club, the Wilderness Society, and The Nature Conservancy. These groups have played a major role in lobbying for the protection of amenity resources like the Wild and Scenic Rivers System, the National Trails System, and the National Wilderness Preservation System.

Patterns of **ownership** and changes in the **policies** and **regulations** of the owners or controlling agencies have drastically altered recreational patterns. Private land accounts for 60 percent of the United States. Traditionally, private lands have served as a valuable recreational resource in many sections of the country. This has been especially true in the Midwest and Great Plains. Unfortunately, more and more private land is being posted and thus closed to use. This places increased pressures on already overburdened public recreation resources. On public lands many new policies and regulations place new restrictions on recreational land use. For example, as new wilderness areas are added to our National Wilderness Preservation System, restrictions on entry into heavily used areas, based on quotas or permits, are becoming more common. It is not unusual to find "wilderness closed" signs at the trailhead. Land-use regulations on some public lands place firm limits on use. A recent commission in New York State, for example, has recommended that a maximum party size of five be imposed on groups entering lands classified as "wilderness" on the Forest Preserve; in 1972 the implementation of the State Land Master Plan prohibited the landing of float planes and the use of motors on boats on this land. Even privately operated ski areas, especially in the East, now limit their sale of lift tickets. Increased regulations in the future are inevitable as we have to share our limited recreational resources with more and more users.

CLASSIFICATION OF RECREATIONAL RESOURCES

The classification of recreational resources is important to the planning process. Classification of recreational resources helps provide the consumer with information, helps the land manager with policy making and management decisions, and suggests a purpose and a dominant theme. No universally used method of classification has evolved. The commonly used scheme presented by Clawson and Knetsch in *Economics of Outdoor Recreation* (1966) will be the one used throughout this book. This scheme has three categories of recreational use: user-oriented, resource-based, and intermediate. Five criteria are used to differentiate one classification from the others: (1) general location, (2) major types of activities, (3) when major use occurs, (4) typical sizes of areas, and (5) common types of agency responsibility.

At one extreme in this system of classification is the **resource-based areas.** Physical resources are their dominant characteristic. Determining the resource quality for recreation is largely a subjective matter, yet most people will agree that some areas are inherently more attractive than others. There is only one Grand Canyon or Yel-

lowstone or Yosemite. The major areas in this class includes mountains, forests, sea-shores and lakeshores, and deserts. Because they are often located at considerable distances from the users, a great amount of travel can be involved, so recreational visits to these areas can require considerable expense in both time and dollars. As a result, the period of use correlates with vacation and retirement leisure. Major rec-reational activities associated with this category include sightseeing, hiking and mountain climbing, wildlife observation, fishing, and hunting. Except for historical sites, which are often fairly small, resource-based areas are usually at least several thousand acres in size. Many of the resource-based areas in Alaska are much larger; Wrangell–St. Elias National Park and Preserve is almost 13 million acres, and the Yukon Delta National Wildlife Refuge is 19 million acres. Typical of this group are most national parks and national monuments, national recreation areas, national for-ests and national grasslands, national wildlife refugees, large areas of national re-source lands managed by the Bureau of Land Management, some state parks, and some privately owned lands such as lakeshores, seashores, and large private estates. There is an access problem on these private lands unless either one is a friend or relative of the owner or it is operated commercially. When these resource-based areas are located in close proximity to major population centers, very heavy use takes place. Such is the case for beaches in the Northeast, such as the Cape Cod National Seashore (Mass.) and Fire Island National Seashore (New York). Forested areas in the North-east, such as New York's Adirondack Park, are heavily used, as are the national forests in California. Twenty-five percent of the recreational use of our entire National Forest System takes place in the national forests of California.

At the other extreme of this classification system are the **user-oriented areas.** Their most important characteristic is their ready accessibility to users. They are used during daily leisure: during the day by children (after school), retirees, and house parents, and after work hours by working adults. These areas also serve as important recreational resources for working adults whose weekend is divided into smaller blocks of time by the necessity of chores, such as cutting the grass or working on the house or car. User-oriented areas are located on whatever resources are available. Some of these recreational environments are artificially made, such as Chicago's Mount Trashmore—an alpine ski area crafted on a mound of sanitary landfill. The lakes of St. Louis' Forest Park are artificially created. City parks and playgrounds are the most common type of user-oriented areas. Activities such as golf, tennis, swim-ming, picnicking, walking, cycling, horseback riding, and visiting zoos and amuse-ment parks commonly occur. Such areas are frequently small, ranging from less than 1 acre in vest-pocket parks to several hundred acres, as in New York City's Central Park, which is 850 acres. A recent study has estimated that 60 percent of outdoor recreation occurs in the parks and play areas of local communities (Cordell et al., 1990). The main administering agencies of these areas are county, city, town, and village governments. The private sector also plays a major role in providing recrea-tional opportunities. It is in our urban areas where commercial recreation is best developed. Many of these forms of recreation are indoor recreation, a subject beyond the scope of this book. There are many types of outdoor recreation that the private sector provides in urban areas. Examples of these are golf courses, amusement parks, go-cart tracks, golf driving ranges, and racetracks for horses and cars. Perhaps none of these is more famous than New York City's Coney Island (Figure 1.4).

Figure 1.4 Coney Island, New York City.

Intermediate areas lie between user-oriented and resource-based areas in terms of both geographic location and use. They cannot be located too far from the users, in most cases within 1 or 2 hours' travel time. (Since traffic flow is variable in our cities, it is best to refer to driving time instead of mileage.) Intermediate areas are located on the best resources available within this distance limitation. Such areas are primarily used for all-day outings and during the weekends. Visits to them involve less travel time and expense than do visits to resource-based areas. Intermediate areas are usually much larger than user-oriented ones but much smaller than resource-based areas, with the typical size being several hundred acres. Representative outdoor recreation activities include camping, picnicking, swimming, hiking, hunting, and fishing. Most state parks fit into this class, as do most reservoirs administered by the Army Corps of Engineers, the Bureau of Reclamation, and the Tennessee Valley Authority. Some private areas are also included.

One other noteworthy recreational resource classification system is the one outlined by the Outdoor Recreation Resources Review Commission in its report *Outdoor Recreation for America* (1962). This system was adopted by the Bureau of Outdoor Recreation in 1962 to provide uniformity in nationwide and state agency recreational planning. These classes are:

> *Class I—High-Density Recreation Areas*   These areas are intensively developed and managed for mass use and are generally close to major urban areas. This group includes city, county, and regional parks and some state and national parks. Class I is similar to Clawson's user-oriented areas.
>
> *Class II—General Outdoor Recreation Areas*   These areas are subject to substantial development for a wide variety of specific recreational uses. They are usually located some distance from cities and include ski areas, developed state parks, and relatively highly developed portions of both state and national forests and fish and wildlife areas. This class resembles Clawson's intermediate category.

Class III—Natural Environment Areas   Various types of areas suitable for recreation in a natural environment fall into this group and are usually used in combination with other (nonrecreational) uses. It includes most areas in national parks, most state and national forests, and large areas in state parks. This class is also similar to Clawson's intermediate category.

Class IV—Unique Natural Areas   These are areas of outstanding scenic splendor, natural wonder, or scientific importance such as Carlsbad Caverns National Park, the Mammoth Hot Springs area of Yellowstone National Park, and the main valley of Yosemite National Park. This class would be comparable to Clawson's resource-based category.

Class V—Primitive Areas   These are undisturbed, roadless areas characterized by natural, wild conditions and they include wilderness areas. They are large and remote enough to provide a wilderness experience and include isolated sections of national parks, national forests, national wildlife refuges, Bureau of Land Management–administered public lands, and some state lands. This class is divided into two subclasses: V-A for *de jure* wilderness where established by the Wilderness Act, and V-B for *de facto* wilderness, which is usually remote from cities. All primitive areas are comparable to those in Clawson's resource-based category.

Class VI—Historic and Cultural Sites   These are places of major historic or cultural significance, whether local, regional, or national and include many historic buildings and archaeological sites. They are found in state parks, national parks, and local park systems and resemble Clawson's resource-based areas.

MEASUREMENT OF RECREATIONAL LAND USE AND VISITATION

Measuring the supply of available recreational opportunities is not a simple task, for there are several different systems in use. The key aspect of any measuring system should be to evaluate the number of recreational opportunities that are provided. The easiest way to measure recreational facilities is to count *facility units*, such as number of campsites, number of picnic tables, size of lakes or ponds, miles of hiking trails, acres of ski trails, or acres of beach. While this is relatively easy to do, it is not very useful in identifying the number of recreational opportunities available. By measuring *use units*, it is possible to determine the number of opportunities. For example, suppose a 100-facility-unit campground has an average of 4 users per site; then the number of opportunities at any one time would be $4 \times 100 = 400$. Unfortunately, the use of use units is not that simple.

There are a number of factors that influence the number of recreational opportunities, including but not limited to the mix of activities that occur, the turnover rate, the carrying capacity, the length of day, the availability of artificial lighting, the hours of use, and the availability of employees and an acceptable budget. It is ultimately the *turnover rate*, which varies greatly with activities, that determines the number of available recreational opportunities; it is defined as "the number of times per

day that the activity can be undertaken by a different group of users." Table 1.1 presents the turnover factors used by recreational planners in New York State. Some activities, such as tennis and handball, have a turnover rate of possibly 6 times per day or more. Others, such as camping, have a possible turnover rate of only 1 time per day. Even the turnover rate for these activities can vary; tennis courts can be open for a greater amount of time during the longer days of summer and if artificial lighting is available. Determining an acceptable number of experiences is more difficult for some activities since it involves setting an acceptable level of use, or *carrying capacity*. For a tennis court this is quite simple; it will be physically determined and is either 2, 3, or 4 users. But for a primitive hiking trail the task is more challenging. Should it be 5 users or 50 users per mile? Table 1.2 and Table 1.3 present the standards used by recreation planners in New York State to determine capacities, here referred to as *instant maximum user density* or *instant capacity*. In this system, an acceptable level of recreational experiences is set for each facility unit. By multiplying the number of facility units by the acceptable number of units of use, the instant maximum user density or instant capacity is determined. By multiplying the instant capacity by the turnover factor, the *total daily capacity* is determined.

The following example will illustrate the difference between instant maximum user density and total daily capacity. Assume a state park has the following recreational facilities and standards for users per facility unit: 300 campsites (4 users/campsite); 500 picnic tables (3.5 users/table); 1000 acres available for big-game hunting (1 hunter/5 acres); 10 miles of stream for fishing (5 users/mile); 100 tennis courts (4 users/court); 18-hole golf course (8 users/hole); and a 100-foot by 200-foot swimming pool (1 user/25 sq ft). The instant maximum user density of this park would be as follows: camping (1200), picnicking (1750), big-game hunting (200), stream fishing (50), tennis (400), golf (144), and pool swimming (800), for a total of 4544. In actuality the instant maximum user density would not be exactly this number since

Table 1.1 Turnover Factors by Activity—New York State

Activity	Turnover Rate*	Activity	Turnover Rate*
Picnicking	2.0	Fishing	2.0
Camping	1.0	Hiking/Ski Touring	2.0
Swimming		Biking	2.0
Pool	2.5	Horseback riding	2.0
Beach (ocean)	2.0	Snowmobiling	2.0
Beach (nonocean)	2.0	Skating*	3.0
Field games*	2.5	Sledding/Tobogganing	2.0
Tennis/Handball*	6.0	Shuffleboard	4.0
Boccie	4.0	Archery	4.0
Basketball/Volleyball	4.0	Amphitheater	1.0
Golf	3.0	Passive park	4.0
Boating		Nature area	1.5
Launch ramp	1.0	Horseshoes	4.0
Car top	1.0	Game tables	4.0
Berthings	1.2	Ski slopes	1.2
Tot lots	3.0		

*For lighted facilities add 1.0 to the rate.
Source: Bob Anderson, New York Office Parks, Recreation and Historic Preservation.

Table 1.2   Facility Development Standards—New York State

Facility Type	Instant Maximum User Density	Standard per 1000 Population	Comments
Skating areas (natural)	500 users/acre	1 site/2500	This category includes nonrefrigerated rinks also.
Camping	20 users/acre	Not applicable	Density figure based on 5 sites per acre, 4 users per site.
Picnicking	35 users/acre	Not applicable	Density figure based on 10 tables per acre, 3.5 users per table.
Boating	6–8 acres/boat	Not applicable	This figure is for both power and sail boating. There are generally 3 users in each boat.
Skiing	30 users/acre of developed slope	Not applicable	
Big-game hunting	1 hunter/5 acres	200 acres/1000	There are 770,000 hunters in N.Y. state or 1 in 25 of general pop.
Fishing (stream)	5 users/mile	0.5-mile stream/1000	One of 5 people in N.Y. go fishing.
Boating access	40 boats/launching ramp	1 ramp/2500	
Golf course	8 users/hole	0.5 holes/1000	
Field games	15 users/acre	3 acres/1000	The following may be provided through off-peak use of school facilities.
Swimming pool	1 user/25 sq. ft.	750 sq. ft./1000	The following may be enclosed to extend seasonal use.
Tennis courts	4 users/court	1 court/2000	The following can be lighted and converted for ice skating.
Basketball (courts)	16 users/court	1 court/1000	

Source: New York State Office of Parks, Recreation and Historic Preservation, *People, Resources, Recreation,* Albany, N.Y.: 1989, Appendix E.

there would be a certain mix of recreational activities occurring; for example, someone occupying a picnic table could also be at the pool swimming. Thus 4544 represents a theoretical upper limit. If the turnover rates from Table 1.1 are applied, the total daily capacity of this park changes to 9832.

Another measuring problem focuses on the development of *recreational opportunity standards.* This essentially entails determining "critical minimum population densities" (threshold population) and developing "standards per 1,000 population" for different types of recreational facilities. Table 1.4 presents the terminology used for facilities, the critical minimum population density, the approximate size in acres, the standards per 1000 population, maximum travel time, and means of access; it is from the New York State Comprehensive Outdoor Recreation Plan (SCORP).

A third measuring problem involves the actual tally of visits to the recreational site. The main problem is that for many recreational resources, measurements are not taken, particularly for local recreation areas, where fees are not charged. It is only at areas where fees are included that an accurate estimate of the volume of use is made. Measurement of recreational use at dispersed types of recreational resources, such as occurs on much of the National Forest System and Bureau of Land Management

Table 1.3 Recreation Way Capacity Standards—New York State

Facility Type	Instant Maximum User Density	Comments/Criteria
Hiking trail—"primitive area"	5 users/mile	Three-foot width; avoid wet areas where possible; build switchbacks on steep slopes; mark trails well; establish lean-tos or primitive tent camping areas for overnight use.
Hiking trail—"developed area"	30 users/mile	4–6 foot tread; bridges necessary to cross streams and wet areas; trails should be less steep then "primitive" and designed for day hiker; provide for overnight use only if part of long-distance trail or system.
Bikeway (class 1)	40 users/mile	Recommended 10–14-ft height, 8-ft width; completely separated travelway; best surface is asphalt or crushed stone pavement; gravel and packed earth is generally not acceptable for 10-speed bicycles; minimum of vehicular and pedestrian crossings; rest area/minipark "bubbles" should be spaced periodically depending on surface treatment. Walking, jogging, and ski touring, or snowmobiling may be permitted.
Horse trail	15 users/mile	Minimum 10-ft height required; parking for trailers must be provided; avoid areas susceptible to erosion.
Snowmobile trail	15 users/mile	Wildlife wintering areas must be avoided; parking for trailers must be provided and parking area plowed, 6–8-ft width; obstructions below snow should be removed; grooming is desirable.
Ski touring trail	30 users/mile	Excessively steep slopes should be avoided; tight turning radii are undesirable; trail must be well marked with marker that stands out against snow.
Trail bike	15 users/mile	Wildlife areas and recreational day-use areas must be avoided; soils susceptible to erosion are undesirable; other types of trail activities are not compatible.

Source: New York Office of Parks, Recreation and Historic Preservation, *People, Resources, Recreation,* Albany, N.Y.: 1989, Appendix E.

lands, represents the "best guess" of the land managers. Even where fees are collected, different measures of use are employed. A **recreation visit** is defined as "the entry of a person into an area of land and water for the purpose of engaging in one or more recreational activities." This could entail a visit to a national monument such as the Statue of Liberty for less than an hour, or an all-day and all-night stay at a national park such as Grand Teton. The National Park Service employs the *visit* as its basic unit of measurement. To complicate matters the National Park Service reports four kinds of annual visit totals: recreation visits by fiscal year; recreation visits by calendar year; total visits by fiscal year; and total visits by calendar year. *Total visits,* for both fiscal and calendar years, include both recreation and nonrecreation visits. The latter consists of entries by travelers and in holders passing through the park for transportation purposes and by persons (other than National Park Service and concessioner employees) visiting the park on commercial or government business. The other visitation unit is the **recreation visitor day** (RVD), a statistical reporting unit consisting of 12 visitor hours. A *visitor hour* is the presence of a person on an area of

Table 1.4 Recreational Opportunity Standards*—New York State

Facility Type	Critical Min. Pop. Density	Approx. Size in Acres	Standard per 1,000 Pop.	Maximum Travel Time	Means of Access	Comments
Playlot	2500/sq. mi.	1–2 acres	2 acres/ 1000	10 min	By foot or bicycle	Combined with residential development or school
Vest pocket park	2500/sq. mi.	0.25–0.50 acres	0.25 acres/ 1000	10 min	By foot or bicycle	For office workers, shoppers, neighborhood residents
Neighbor-hood park	2500/sq. mi.	4–7 acres	1 acres/ 1000	20 min	By foot or bicycle	Should contain passive areas with landscaping, as well as active areas such as playfields, court games, tot lots, etc.
District park	500/sq. mi.	20–100 acres	2 acres/ 1000	30 min	Automobile, mass transit, bike hiking trail	Should include comfort station, interests for all ages; 1/3 capacity for winter activities (e.g., ice skating, sledding)
City park	**	50–100 acres	5 acres/ 1000	30 min.	Automobile, mass transit, bike hiking trail	Should include comfort station, interests for all ages; 1/3 capacity for winter activities (e.g., ice skating, sledding)
Large regional parks	**	40+ acres	15 acres/ 1000	1–2 hr	Automobile, charter bus, mass transit, major trail	Extensive day use areas, camping, picnicking should include water access and selected winter activities ski touring, snowmobiling
Metroparks	10,000/sq. mi.	25 acres	25 acres/ 2,000,000	30 min.	Limited auto access and all nonauto modes	Urban parks emphasizing special recreational cultural or historic themes and activities; day and evening operation during all seasons

*Partially derived from National Recreation and Parks Association.
**Not applicable.
Source: New York Office of Parks, Recreation and Historic Preservation, *People, Resources, Recreation*, Albany, N.Y.: 1989, Appendix E.

land and water for the purpose of engaging in one or more recreational activities during a period or periods of time totaling 60 minutes. The Forest Service has traditionally used the visitor day as its statistical measure of use.

A final measurement problem focuses on setting development priorities and the actual size of the development. To establish development priorities the analysis of supply and demand is translated into a measure of facility need. The different facility needs are then evaluated in terms of service to be expected per dollar of development cost. The translation factor used is the **design day,** sometimes defined as "the highest use day." Facilities should not be planned to accommodate peak use at all times, nor should they be planned in complete disregard for fluctuations in use. Different activities have different degrees of **peaking** in use. Examples of high peaking activities are swimming, picnicking, and skiing; of medium peaking activities—boating, golfing, snowmobiling, and camping; and of low peaking activities—biking, court games, field games, tennis, fishing, hiking, and local winter activities. The approach of

focusing on annual use per dollar of resource investment emphasizes those activities with long seasons and consistently high use rates. While it is desirable to have uniform use and long seasons, some of the most popular activities are tied to high peaking and short seasons. Weather and climate in different sections of the country place strict limitations. For example, in New York State, snowmobiling has the shortest season (75 days), and court and field games have the longest season (270 days). The number of design days for snowmobiling is 15 and for court games is 67; facilities are designed for these number of days, and approximately 40 percent of the season's use is encompassed by them. Beyond these periods, ample capacity can be expected to exist if capacity is sufficient on the design days. The number of design days depends on both the degree of peaking and the length of season. While much of the use in certain recreational activities occurs at favorable times, *facilities should not be planned to accommodate this peak use*; it is not efficient. There will be some days on which peak demand cannot be met.

RECREATIONAL LAND-USE PLANNING AND PLANNING CONCEPTS

Recreation is only one type of land use that is competing for land in the allocation of scarce resources. *Recreational land-use planning* did not really emerge as a well-recognized subfield of the broader field of land-use planning until the early 1960s. Three major events occurred in this era that greatly stimulated the development of the field: (1) the Outdoor Recreation Resources Review Commission's (ORRRC) release of its report, *Outdoor Recreation for America* in 1962; (2) the establishment of the Bureau of Outdoor Recreation within the Interior Department in 1962; and (3) the establishment of the Land and Water Conservation Fund in 1965. "The ORRRC report (1962) was the basic trend-setting document for public recreational land management today. Most recent governmental policy and legislation on recreation can be traced back to that 1962 report of a citizens' committee" (Knudson, 1984, 2). This was the first comprehensive study of the nation's outdoor recreation resources, and it analyzed present and projected future recreational demands, supplies, and policies. No other document has impacted recreational land-use planning and development to the same degree.

The *Bureau of Outdoor Recreation* (BOR) was the first federal agency created principally for recreational purposes and the first one to carry *recreation* in its title. Its title was changed to *Heritage Conservation and Recreation Service* (HCRS) in 1978; this agency was abolished by Executive Order of President Ronald Reagan shortly after his inauguration in January 1981. The BOR was not a land-managing but a recreation planning agency that was concerned with planning, advising, and coordination. It also managed the *Land and Water Conservation Fund*, which provides the money, on a fifty-fifty basis, for technical and financial assistance for the development of public recreation facilities. This assistance is to federal agencies with principal roles in outdoor recreation, such as the National Park Service, the Forest Service, and the Fish and Wildlife Service. It also provides grants to states, and through them to political

subdivisions of states, for planning, acquisition, and development of public outdoor recreation areas and facilities. To be eligible for Land and Water Conservation Fund aid a state must develop a comprehensive statewide outdoor recreation plan (SCORP) and update and refine the plan on a continuing basis. All 50 states have approved SCORPs, but when federal subsidies were reduced in the early 1980s, some states greatly curtailed their planning efforts. The planning and administration functions of the HCRS were transferred to the National Park Service in 1981, when the agency was abolished. The budget cuts and staff shortages in the National Park Service have resulted in the former planning activities of HCRS being carried out at a much diminished rate.

The most outstanding book every written on the subject of outdoor recreation planning is *Outdoor Recreation Planning* by Alan Jubenville of the University of Wyoming in 1976. In this book he presents an outdoor recreation systems model adapted from S. S. Frissell of the University of Montana. The basic model components are people; resources; and management (planning). The resources are the natural resources, such as the land, water, air, fauna, and flora. The interrelationships of the resources determine the appearance and stability of the particular resource setting, which in turn affects the types of recreational experiences that can be provided. The people (users) component is the social subsystem for which planning is undertaken, and planning is the component that develops harmony between the people and the resource, that is, providing for the recreational needs of people while minimizing the impacts of the visitors on the resource. "In reality there is only a small degree of harmony between the visitor, the resource, and planning. . . . More sophisticated planning can improve the performance, but there will never be total harmony (a situation where there is no uncertainty or unknown in the planning process)" (Jubenville, 1976, 49). There are three basic steps to this user-resource relationship model: (1) identify recreational users and resources; (2) estimate recreation demand and supply; and (3) develop a proposed recreation plan.

There are five different levels of outdoor recreation planning for public lands: (1) nationwide, (2) state, (3) regional/local, (4) area, and (5) site. The first U.S. *Nationwide Outdoor Recreation Plan*, entitled *The Recreation Imperative*, was completed by the BOR in 1970 but impounded by the Office of Budget and Management and not released until 1974 as a Committee Report. Our first *published* nationwide plan, entitled *Outdoor Recreation: A Legacy for America*, was prepared by the BOR and released in 1973. This plan set forth the framework within which federal recreation programs should be developed and managed. The most recent plan, *The Third Nationwide Outdoor Recreation Plan*, was released in 1979. Its major objective was to provide an introduction to the broad range of recreational experiences available to the American public and the vast network of government and private organizations and individuals that provide such opportunities. The focus throughout is not on solving problems so much as on raising and exploring the numerous pertinent issues that affect recreation nationwide. The Land and Water Conservation Fund stimulated *state planning*, providing 50 percent of the funding. From 1965 until 1981, all 50 states prepared SCORPs. These plans described the states' priority for recreational facilities and indicated directions for the development of resources and programs. The SCORP is supposed to direct planning and development action on all outdoor recreation programs, both public and private. Some states greatly diminished their planning activities when

federal subsidies were reduced in 1981. The key feature of nationwide and state planning is that they are a publication of policies, programs, and priorities. This is also the principal feature of most *regional and local plans,* but regions can be defined in many ways. In some cases a region may be defined as a single city or urban area or county. It can also refer to a group of counties. In most cases, a regional plan does not correspond to any single administrative unit and has no total administrative or legal sanction. For example, in New York State the Lake George–Lake Champlain region, for which a Regional Recreation Plan has been prepared, consists of the five counties of Clinton, Hamilton, Essex, Warren, and Washington. Regional planning thrived until its major source of funding, Section 701 of the Housing Act of 1954, as amended, was terminated in the 1980s.

The purpose of *area planning* is to allocate space for recreational development. Such planning usually involves a single ownership and might involve from several hundred to several thousand acres, or more. An area plan is for a parcel of land and water that is large enough to provide a variety of outdoor recreation experiences. This is probably the most important level of planning to a given agency. This is how park and recreational systems are planned, how space is allocated for a certain use, how commitments of money and staffing are made, and how courses of action are periodically evaluated. This type of plan is often called a master plan, for it not only involves a site but also includes policies, programs, and priorities. The development of a state park master plan would be a good example of area planning. Regional and local planning agencies often prepare master plans as well as comprehensive policy plans.

Albert Rutledge (1981) has identified three phases of the master planning process. In the *survey* phase, program development, an inventory of on-site factors, and an inventory of off-site factors are undertaken. In the *analysis* phase, program relationships and site analysis are undertaken. Rutledge's final phase is the *synthesis* (often referred to as the *Master Plan Design*), in which the design concept and refined plan are drawn. Zinser (1982) has added the limitation-for-development maps to Rutledge's analysis phase. These maps are drawn by overlaying a *slope map* showing 3 percent, 8 percent, 15 percent, and 25 percent isarithms on a *soil series map.* The following limitation-for-development maps are constructed: septic tank filter fields, low buildings with basements, low buildings without basements, streets and parking lots, athletic fields, play and picnic areas, campsites for tents, campsites for trailers, and golf courses. Each map identifies three possible degrees of limitations for each land use. "Slight limitations" are colored green on the map and indicate the ideal location for specific site development for each recreational land use. "Moderate limitations" are colored in yellow and identify areas where certain environmental restrictions should raise caution about developing in this area; these areas are not the best but are also not the worst to develop. "Severe limitations" are colored in red on the map, and any development in these areas should be seriously questioned. This does not mean that it is impossible to build or develop these severe areas, but that serious engineering solutions, which can be expensive, are required to overcome the limitations. The environmentally ideal design would favor restricting all site development to the slight degree of limitations-for-development category. Because it is a far from ideal world in which we live, some areas might be developed where the limitations are severe or moderate. The important conclusion to be drawn about this

process is that the most economic design is the one that is environmentally sound. In some cases the point at which area planning stops and site planning begins is not clearly defined.

Site planning is where some development is designed according to some spatial arrangement within the framework of the area plan. Jubenville (1976, 141) has defined site planning as "a scale graphic representation of specific recreational site development, including the facility components and their spatial relationships." The specific sites to be developed (beach, marina, picnic area, campground, ski area) are first identified in the area plan and then fully developed in the site plan. A site plan should include a site map, which indicates the location and types of facilities for the site; a narrative report, which analyzes the resource base and expected behavioral patterns; a general development schedule, which identifies the time framework for each of the development phases; and construction plans, which show and identify construction details.

Four basic planning concepts that apply to outdoor recreation are carrying capacity, multiple use, dominant theme, and effective acres. The first two are quite complex and will be detailed in later paragraphs. **Dominant theme** refers to the basic use of any given recreation area. Once the proper recreational experience is decided, only complementary activities should be allowed. This helps preserve the quality of the recreational experience. For example, snowmobiles should be prohibited from an area designated for cross-country skiing, and motorized boats should be prohibited from areas designated as wilderness. Many types of recreational activities are incompatible with others. By following the principle of dominant theme, the resource manager not only has an easier job but the user/consumer of the resource is better informed when choosing the area.

Effective acres are those acres that meet predescribed objectives according to acceptable criteria and are designed to best serve the purpose for which they were intended. The questions Where are the acres located? and What is contained in the acres? are addressed. The role of the designer is critical in coming up with the best overall design. An example of the application of the principle of effective acres would be the road-and-parking-lot design for a picnic area. The tables used most often are those closest to the parking since it is difficult to carry coolers and grills long distances; as a result, tables that are remotely located are largely unused, except at certain peak times. Another example of effective acres would be the use made of picnic tables in a hot, sunny climate. In White Sands National Monument (New Mexico) the picnic tables have wind- and sunscreens on them; their use would be much less, if at all, if these features were not provided.

Carrying capacity is a basic natural resource management concept. In a broad, generic sense it refers to the amount of use a given resource can sustain before an irreversible deterioration in the quality of the resource begins to occur. The concept of carrying capacity was initially applied in the fields of range management and wildlife management. In these cases, it referred to the maximum number of animals a given unit of land can support on a sustained basis without destroying the resource base. While it is quite easy to identify the metabolic reserve that is essential for range plants to sustain themselves, applying this concept to recreational resources presents more serious problems. Chubb and Chubb (1981, 292) have defined **recreational carrying capacity** as "the number of recreational opportunities that a specific unit of a

recreation resource can provide year after year without appreciable biological or physical deterioration of the resource or significant impairment of the recreation experience." This is as good as any other definition of the term that exists, but defining recreational carrying capacity does raise several difficult questions. Terms such as *irreversible deterioration, appreciable deterioration,* and *significant impairment* are difficult to define. The large increase in users that were starting to crowd popular wilderness areas in the 1960s made wilderness management a problem for land managers. Some wilderness areas were therefore restricted to use (Snyder, 1966). In 1974 the Forest Service first rationed the use on the 10.7-mile Mount Whitney trail to only 75 persons per day. Prior to this quota, it was not unusual to have over 250 people per day on this trail (Knudson, 1984, 311). In 1974 there was a downturn in visitation by white-water floaters on the Grand Canyon after management instituted a quota of 14,253. The numbers of visitors per year reported in earlier years were: 1950, 7; 1960, 205; 1970, 9935; and 1972, 16,432. The waiting list to float through the Grand Canyon is now so long that new applicants must wait 10 years (Hammitt and Cole, 1987, 9, 10). Today, such restrictions are found in most areas of the United States. These restrictions are outgrowths of the carrying capacity concept. The Nationwide Outdoor Recreation Plan (Bureau of Outdoor Recreation, 1973), called for the identification of recreational carrying capacity for federal land management units.

Two aspects or kinds of carrying capacity are often referred to—biophysical and social or psychological. *Biophysical carrying capacity* refers to the ecological impact of recreational use; examples of studies that have been conducted to determine this type of carrying capacity include soil compaction, vegetation trampling, and water quality. Sometimes a distinction is made between *physical carrying capacity,* which refers to nonliving aspects of habitat such as trail compaction and the ability to absorb human-made objects, and *biological carrying capacity,* which refers to impact on ecological systems. *Social* or *psychological carrying capacity* refers to the quality of the recreational experience as perceived by users and involves items such as crowds, odors, noise, and even the quality of other users. When individuals undertake a certain recreational experience, they have certain expectations. If nothing occurs during the experience to diminish their expectations, they have probably had a quality recreational experience. However, if events or things occur to lessen the quality of the preconceived recreational experience, the users' psychological carrying capacity has been exceeded. Examples of this would be hiking into a remote wilderness pond to enjoy the solitude of nature only to find a wild party going on, or, at an alpine ski area that has just received 1 foot of new powder, having to wait in line 30 minutes to buy a lift ticket and then stand in another line for an hour to get on the lift. Defining the quality of a recreational experience is like defining art—it is very subjective. What is quality to one individual is not to another. The classic study that examined the perceptions of both users and managers was done by Lucas (1964) in the Boundary Waters Canoe Area in the Superior National Forest. He suggested that by identifying the different perceptions of users the carrying capacity could be increased.

A recreational opportunity is created by a combination of physical, social, and managerial factors. There are thus three basic components of carrying capacity: (1) management objectives, (2) visitor attitudes or perception, and (3) impact on the physical resource. Managers can do much to help increase the carrying capacity: reduce conflicts among competitive uses, reduce the destructiveness of people, in-

crease the durability of the physical resource, and provide opportunities for visitor enjoyment. These goals can be accomplished by three overlapping courses of action. Site management is the first course of action. Imaginative design is important, and access should be provided to underused areas, and irrigation, fertilization, and re-seeding can be undertaken. Regulating visitor behavior is a second course of action managers can undertake. They can determine where visitors may go, how long they may stay, and when they may enter the area. Specific procedures include zoning, rotating use, limits on party size, and reservations. A third course of action, more subtle and less obtrusive, is modifying visitor behavior by communication and interpretive services, implementing fees (including differential fees), and establishing eligibility requirements.

Hammitt and Cole (1987, 19) argue that, while it is possible to select a carrying capacity, this is in itself wasteful of legitimate recreational opportunities, in that the relationship between the amount of use and impact is not direct. If capacities are set, they must be set very low to allow for variation in all other factors affecting the amount of impact, or they must be only a small part of a management program. The amount of impact is affected by the timing, type, and distribution of use; the setting where it occurs; and mitigative actions taken by management. For example, most of the trail damage in mountainous areas of the Northeast caused by hikers and mountain bikes occurs during the "mud season" of spring immediately after snowmelt; during the dry season of late summer or fall the amount of trail damage is minimal.

Frissell and Stankey (1972) have stated that managers must set limits of acceptable change (LAC). Change beyond what is normal in nature is considered human-caused impact. A certain amount of change must be considered acceptable, even in wilderness areas. The limit of acceptable change, a management judgment, divides acceptable from unacceptable impact. Management must decide where to draw the line and then hold that line through management programs (Stankey et al., 1984).

Multiple use is a natural resource–land-use planning concept in which all land uses are given equal consideration in the planning process. Multiple-use planning increases the output of any given area, with the economic rationale being that the sum total of values created exceed the values from the dominance of any one single use. Codominance is the dominant theme. The major uses that are usually considered are timber, water, fish and wildlife, grazing, and water. To be effective multiple use planning must be done over a large area, such as a ranger district of a national forest. Not all of these uses might be compatible in any small section of the larger area, so it does permit a dominant use in such a smaller area. The emphasis is on the final mix of uses and outputs rather than on just one use, and on achieving maximum yields over the longer period of time rather than just for 1 year.

The two principal federal land-managing agencies for which multiple-use planning is applied are the Forest Service and the Bureau of Land Management. This policy was formalized for the Forest Service in 1960 by the passage of the Multiple-Use Sustained-Yield Act (Public Law 86-517). This law clarified and further defined the concept that national forests are to be administered on a multiple-use basis for five primary uses: outdoor recreation, watershed, range, timber, and fish and wildlife. For the first time, amenity resource values such as recreation and wildlife were recognized officially as having importance comparable to that of the commodity resources on the national forest. In the planning process it was mandated, for the first

time, that recreation be accorded equal consideration with timber as plans for land use allocations are made. Provisions of this act were further defined and strengthened in the Forest and Rangeland Renewable Resources Planning Act (P.L. 93-378) in 1974 and the National Forest Management Act (P.L. 94-588) in 1976. The Classification and Multiple Use Act (1964) and Federal Land Policy and Management Act (1976) extended the concept of multiple-use management to the land administered by the Bureau of Land Management.

Multiple use can be achieved by spatial zoning or temporal zoning. *Spatial zoning* is the zoning by space or geographic area; it is the most common way to achieve multiple use. *Temporal zoning* refers to zoning by time. An example of temporal zoning would be a lake or reservoir on which "no-wake" boating is allowed from 6:00 P.M. until 10:00 A.M. and "wake" boating is allowed from 10:00 A.M. until 6:00 P.M. This way the anglers would have calm water during their favored fishing times and the speed boaters and water-skiers would have their opportunity during the warmer middle of the day. Spatial zoning could also be applied to these bodies of water by zoning a certain section for no-wake boating for the entire day through the placement of marker buoys to indicate the protected section(s). Spatial zoning is applied to units, such as ranger districts, in our national forests. Under this scheme a 100,000-acre ranger district could have 50,000 acres designated for timber production, 40,000 acres as wilderness, 5000 acres for a reservoir, 4000 acres for a major ski area, and 1000 acres as a mining area. Such an application of multiple use would result in a greater total output as compared to the dominance of one use.

New York's **Adirondack Park** will be used as a case study of achieving multiple use by the use of spatial zoning. The park was created in 1892 and enlarged in 1912, 1931, 1956, and 1972 to reach its current size of 6,000,000 acres. It is a predominantly forested, mountainous area roughly the size of Vermont or New Hampshire. The park has a unique checkerboard pattern of 40 percent public and 60 percent private land. Virtually all of the public land is designated as forest preserve, which is declared "forever wild" and protected by the state constitution. A Temporary Study Commission, appointed by Governor Nelson Rockefeller in 1968, was charged to make recommendations to help solve growing land-use challenges in the region. Its report was issued in 1970 and made 181 recommendations, the most significant of which were (1) that an Adirondack Park Agency be created with power over the use of public and private land, and (2) that the Agency prepare a comprehensive plan for the park. The state legislature passed the Adirondack Park Agency Act in 1971, which established a superregional planning agency. This is the largest area in the United States today that is under the control of a regional land-use plan. Under the supervision of the Adirondack Park Agency, a State Land Master Plan was enacted by the legislature in 1972 and a more controversial Private Land Use and Development Plan was enacted in 1973.

The *Adirondack Park State Land Master Plan* zones the state-owned land into nine classifications. The classifications regulate the types of recreational use that are permissible on the forest preserve. Fifty-two percent of the forest preserve is classified as *wild forest,* defined as an area where the resources permit a somewhat higher degree of human use than in wilderness, primitive, or canoe areas, while retaining an essentially wild character. Motorboats and float planes are allowed on most lakes and ponds, and snowmobiles are allowed on designated trails in this classification.

Vehicles are allowed on some dirt roads. Forty-five percent of the forest preserve is designated *wilderness,* whose definition follows the federal wilderness classification definition, in which no motorized vehicles are allowed. Hiking, backpacking, snow-shoeing, and skiing are the main types of recreational activities. Figure 1.5 shows hikers in the High Peaks Wilderness Area. Less than 4 percent of the forest preserve is designated *primitive,* which is essentially wilderness in character but contains some non-conforming uses, such as a fire tower, a jeep road, a telephone line, or a ranger cabin. One *canoe area,* the St. Regis, is designated on 18,000 acres of land that contains closely spaced small ponds. It is managed under wilderness guidelines. A fifth classification is *intensive use,* in which the state provides facilities for intensive forms of outdoor recreation; included are 43 campgrounds, 22 boat launch sites, two ski centers (the 1980 Olympic alpine events were held at Whiteface Mountain), a bobsled run, a parkway, and a memorial highway. The sum total of these intensive-use areas occupy 6000 acres, of which only approximately 1500 acres are currently developed. A sixth classification is *wild, scenic, and recreational river,* a state-managed system modeled after the federal Wild and Scenic Rivers Act. The three other categories, which are limited in acreage, are not all located on forest preserve: they are: *travel corridors; historic sites,* of which there are only two; and *state administrative areas,* of which a significant number are prisons.

The *Adirondack Park Private Land Use and Development Plan* divides the park's 3,600,000 acres of private land into six types of land-use areas. The overall aim of the plan is to channel future development so as to minimize adverse environmental impact in the park. The protection of natural open space is fundamental to the plan, which has four major mechanisms for achieving these goals: (1) intensity guidelines and compatible-use lists; (2) a project review and permit system; (3) the designation of critical environmental areas; and (4) shoreline development restrictions. The *hamlet* classification occupies 1 percent of the private land in the park and has no average-

Figure 1.5 Hikers on Algonquin Mountain in New York's Adirondack Park (High Peaks Wilderness Area).

lot-size requirements; hamlets are to serve as the service and growth centers of the park, and are compatible with all land uses. The *moderate-intensity use areas* are located near or adjacent to the hamlets to provide for residential expansion. The average lot size requirement is 1.28 acres and this classification covers 3 percent of the private land. *Low-intensity use areas* are reasonably close to hamlets and moderate intensity areas and can withstand development at an intensity somewhat lower than these areas. The average lot size is 3.2 acres, and this classification occupies 8 percent of the private land. *Rural use areas* have natural resource limitations and public considerations that necessitate fairly stringent development constraints. This category requires an average lot size of 8.5 acres and covers 34 percent of the private land. While the compatible primary use for these first four classifications is single family dwellings, this is not the case for the most restrictive classification, *resource management area*. The three compatible primary uses for this category are agriculture, open-space recreation, and forestry. The average lot size in resource management areas is 42.7 acres, and this one category occupies 53 percent of the private land in the park. A sixth classification is *industrial* and has no specific guidelines for development; it occupies 1 percent of the private land. Zinser (1980) concluded that the main impact of the Private Land Use and Development Plan was to greatly impede the subdivision of land for recreational homes, especially large projects such as the failed Ton-da-lay (5000 homes) and Horizon (10,000 homes) developments and Loon Lake Estates and Valmont Village.

General Sources Consulted

Throughout the text the following general sources were used.

Brockman, C. Frank, and Lawrence C. Merriam, Jr. *Recreational Use of Wild Lands*. Third edition. New York: McGraw-Hill Book Co., 1979.

Chubb, Michael, and Holly R. Chubb. *One Third of Our Time?* New York: John Wiley & Sons, 1981.

Clawson, Marion, and Carlton Van Doren. *Statistics on Outdoor Recreation*. Washington, D.C.: Resources of the Future, 1984.

Cordell, H. Ken, John C. Bergstrom, Lawrence A. Hartman, and Donald B. K. English. *An Analysis of the Outdoor Recreation and Wilderness Situation in the United States 1989–2040. A Technical Document Supporting the 1989 USDA Forest Service RPA Assessment*. General Technical Report RM-189. Fort Collins, Colo.: Rocky Mountain Forest and Range Experiment Station, Forest Service, USDA, 1990.

Culhane, Paul C. *Public Lands Politics*. Baltimore: Published for Resources of the Future by Johns Hopkins University Press, 1981.

Fisher, Ron. *Our Threatened Inheritance*. Washington, D.C.: National Geographic Society, 1984.

Jensen, Clayne R. *Outdoor Recreation in America*. Fourth edition. Minneapolis: Burgess Publishing Co., 1985.

Jones, John Oliver. *The U.S. Outdoor Atlas & Recreation Guide*. New York: Houghton Mifflin Co., 1992.

Knudson, Douglas M. *Outdoor Recreation*. Revised edition. New York: Macmillan Publishing Co., 1984.

National Geographic Society. *A Guide to Our Federal Lands*. Washington, D.C.: National Geographic Society, 1984.

President's Commission on Americans Outdoors. *Americans Outdoors: The Legacy, the Challenge*. Washington, D.C.: Island Press, 1987.

Zaslowsky, Dyan, and the Wilderness Society. *These American Lands*. New York: Henry Holt and Co., 1986.

References

Bureau of Outdoor Recreation. *Outdoor Recreation for America*. Washington, D.C.: U.S. Government Printing Office, 1973.

Chubb, Michael, and Holly R. Chubb. *One Third of Our Time?* New York: John Wiley & Sons, 1981.

Clawson, Marion, and Jack L. Knetsch. *Economics of Outdoor Recreation*. Baltimore: Johns Hopkins University Press, 1966.

Cordell, H. Ken, John C. Bergstrom, Lawrence A. Hartman, and Donald B. K. English. *An Analysis of the Outdoor Recreation and Wilderness Situation in the United States 1989–2040. A Technical Document Supporting the 1989 USDA Forest Service RPA Assessment*. General Technical Report RM-189. Fort Collins, Colo.: Rocky Mountain Forest and Range Experiment Station, Forest Service, USDA, 1990.

Epperson, Arlin F. *Private and Commercial Recreation*. New York: John Wiley & Sons, 1977.

Frissell, S. S., and G. H. Stankey. "Wilderness Environmental Quality: Search for Social and Ecological Harmony" in *Proceedings, Society of American Foresters Annual Meeting*. Hot Springs, Ark., 1972.

Hammitt, William E., and David N. Cole. *Wildland Recreation: Ecology and Management*. New York: John Wiley & Sons, 1987.

Heritage Conservation and Recreation Service. *The Third Nationwide Outdoor Recreation Plan*. Washington, D.C.: U.S. Government Printing Office, 1979.

Jubenville, Alan. *Outdoor Recreation Planning*. Philadelphia: W. B. Saunders Co., 1976.

Knudson, Douglas M. *Outdoor Recreation*. Revised edition. New York: Macmillan Publishing Co., 1984.

Krutilla, John V., and Anthony C. Fisher. *The Economics of Natural Environments: Studies in the Valuation of Commodity and Amenity Resources*. Baltimore: Johns Hopkins University Press, 1975 (revised, 1985).

Lucas, Robert C. "Wilderness Perception and Use: The Example of the Boundary Waters Canoe Area." *Natural Resources Journal*, No. 3, 394–411, 1964.

National Park Service. *Federal Recreation Fee Report to Congress—1991*. Washington, D.C.: National Park Service.

Office of Budget and Program Analysis, USDA. *Natural Resources: Federal Spending and Resource Performance, 1940–1989*. Washington, D.C.: USDA, January 1993.

Outdoor Recreation Resources Review Commission. *Outdoor Recreation for America*. Washington, D.C.: U.S. Government Printing Office, 1962.

Outdoor Recreation Resources Review Commission. *Study Reports*. Washington, D.C.: U.S. Government Printing Office, 1962.

President's Commission on Americans Outdoors. *Americans Outdoors: The Legacy, the Challenge*. Washington, D.C.: Island Press, 1987.

Rutledge, Albert. *Anatomy of a Park*. Revised edition. New York: McGraw-Hill Book Co., 1981.

Snyder, A. P. "Wilderness Management: A Growing Challenge." *Journal of Forestry* 64(7): 441–446, 1966.

Stankey, G. H., S. F. McCool, and G. L. Stokes. "Limits of Acceptable Change: A New Framework for Managing the Bob Marshall Wilderness." *Western Wildlands,* Fall, 1984.

West, Terry L. *Centennial Mini-Histories of the Forest Service, FS-518.* Washington, D.C.: USDA, Forest Service, 1992.

Zimmermann, Erich W. *World Resources and Industries.* Revised edition. New York: Harper & Row, 1951.

Zinser, Charles I. *The Economic Impact of Leisure Homes on the Economy of the Area within the Blue Line of the Adirondack Park,* Published Ph.D. Dissertation in Geography at the University of Illinois at Champaign-Urbana, 1974.

Zinser, Charles I. *The Economic Impact of the Adirondack Park Private Land Use and Development Plan.* Albany: State University of New York Press, 1980.

Zinser, Charles I. *The Preparation of Limitation for Development Maps* (Mimeograph handout for Geography 431). Plattsburgh, N.Y.: State University of New York, 1982.

Recreational Resources: Background and Sectors

Conservation means the wise use of the earth and its resources for the lasting good of men.

Gifford Pinchot (1947)

RECREATION AND THE AMERICAN CONSERVATION MOVEMENT

The preservation and reservation of land in the United States for its amenity resource value preceded the development of the American conservation movement. An appreciation of the historical development of recreation helps us to understand present behavior and probable future trends. As Socrates was once purported to have said, "no wind is favorable if one does not know from what port he has departed and to what port he is heading." The *Boston Commons*, established in 1634, was the first city park established in the English Colonies. Although it was initially set aside as communal pasture land, it soon became a public meeting place and parkland. In 1640 the *Great Ponds Act* of the Massachusetts Bay Colony decreed 2000 bodies of water over 10 acres in size to be public resources open for "fishing and fowling"; these ponds became increasingly used for their recreational value. In 1832 the *Hot Springs Reservation* in Arkansas's Ouachita Mountains was reserved for the future to protect a number of mineral hot springs from private monopoly and exploitation. It was dedicated to public use as a park in 1880 and redesignated as a national park in 1921.

Although conservation as a well-recognized social issue in the United States was not initiated until the 20th century, some of the most important conservation efforts were made in the area of recreation during the second half of the 19th century. This period between 1850 and 1900 is referred to as the *twilight of the conservation movement*. During this time period the conservation movement began to take form. In 1853, New York City set aside 850 acres for *Central Park*. The design of Frederick L. Olmsted brought a rural landscape to the urban dweller. Central Park was the first "planned park" in the United States and is still noted for its scenic and recreational objectives. It has served as a model for similar passive retreats in many large urban centers. In the 1864 *Yosemite Grant*, Congress entrusted the Yosemite Valley and Mariposa Big Tree Grove to the State of California "upon the express condition that the premises

shall be held for public use, resort, and recreation; shall be inalienable for all time." This was the first area of undeveloped land to be reserved expressly for recreation. In 1890 a park was established and the federal government accepted the lands returned by the state of California in 1906. In 1864, George P. Marsh's *Man and Nature: Or Physical Geography as Modified by Human Action* deflated the illusion that the United States' resources were inexhaustible and put forth the concept of endangered resources resulting from long term use. *Yellowstone National Park* was established in 1872 as the world's first national park. This was the real beginning of the *national park movement;* it provided impetus to conservation and raised interest in later establishment of other national parks in the United States and the world. By 1900, four other national parks had been established: Yosemite (1890); General Grant (1890); Sequoia (1890), and Mt. Rainier (1899). Shortly thereafter, Crater Lake (1902) and Wind Cave (1903) were added as national parks. It would be 1916 before the National Park Service was established.

Several other isolated events occurred during this twilight of the conservation movement that involved the recreational use of land. In 1879, Major John Wesley Powell pushed for land reform in the arid Southwest; he also published *Lands of the Arid Region* and helped create the United States Geological Survey. The work of this one-armed Civil War veteran, who was the first to raft down the Colorado River through the Grand Canyon in 1869, eventually led to the passage of the Reclamation Act in 1902. In New York State, a leader in the conservation movement, the legislature created the New York Forest Preserve in 1885 and the Adirondack Park in 1892, considered the first state park in the United States. In 1889, Minnesota began its state park system. The passage of the *Forest Reserve Act* in 1891 culminated 20 years of congressional debate over public land policy. President Harrison established the Yellowstone Park Timber Land Reserve (renamed the Shoshone National Forest in 1908) and the River Plateau Timber Land Reserve in 1891. By 1900, 38 forest reserves existed on 46,000,000 (gross) acres. The Forest Reserve Act made these and later reserves possible; they were renamed national forests in 1907. This formed the nucleus of our current National Forest System.

During the second half of the 19th century, public awareness for all aspects of conservation developed: The first five national parks were established, initial state parks were created, forestry commissions and state forests were started, the first federal forest reserves were established, and natural area parks in large cities were created. The momentum that developed during this period continued beyond the turn of the century and, despite resistance and occasional reverses, lent its force to the expansion and refinement of the entire program of natural resource and environmental conservation in the United States.

Although the momentum for the *conservation movement* developed during the second half of the 19th century, it was not until the 20th century that conservation as a major social issue matured. Most of the great advances in the conservation movement were made in three waves of action that are associated with the terms of office of U.S. presidents. It is the enactment of federal legislation that is the best indicator of national magnitude. The management of natural resources for recreation and other land uses is largely dictated by the laws enacted by Congress, and supportive presidents can have a major effect on the enactment of such legislation. Accordingly, the legislation that particularly affects recreational land use will be highlighted in this section.

The *first wave* of the conservation movement is associated with the presidency of Theodore Roosevelt (1901–1909). A key player in Roosevelt's administration was Gifford Pinchot, who served as Chief Forester of the Forestry Division and then as Chief of the Forest Service when it was established in 1905. Pinchot coined the term *conservation* in 1907, basing it on the government forests in India that emphasized particular forestry practices and were known as "conservancies." To Pinchot the concept of conservation meant "use under systematic management." This interpretation of conservation contrasted sharply with that of John Muir, who founded the Sierra Club in 1892. Muir represented what came to be known as the *preservationist* school of natural resource management, while Pinchot represented the *utilitarian* (*sustained-yield*) school of natural resource management. Pinchot worked within the government for his interpretation of conservation, and Muir worked outside the government. This schism in the interpretation of natural resource management persists today. The original environmental battle occurred over building a dam on the Tuolumne River in the Hetch Hetchy Valley of Yosemite National Park for power generation and a water-supply reservoir for San Francisco, with Pinchot in favor and Muir opposed. On December 6, 1913, the preservationists were defeated when the Senate voted 43 to 25 in favor of the dam. Creation of the dam inundated a valley purported to be second only to the main Yosemite Valley in beauty. Figure 2.1 is an aerial photo of the Hetch Hetchy Reservoir. Muir died a dejected man on Christmas Eve, 1914. Such battles still occur today, as for example, the conflict between preserving northern spotted owl habitat and harvesting the ancient old-growth timber on the national forests of the Pacific Northwest. If Muir were alive today, he would be on the spotted owl's side and Pinchot, if he were alive, would be on the loggers' side.

Early in the Theodore Roosevelt administration the Reclamation Act (1902) was passed. It provided for the construction of reservoirs and other water-resource programs in the West. While these reservoirs, which are built by the Bureau of Reclamation, have the provision of water for irrigation as their primary objective, they have become extremely valuable recreational resources. The *Antiquities Act* (1906)

Figure 2.1   The Hetch Hetchy Reservoir in Yosemite National Park as seen from 35,000 feet.

gave the president the power to proclaim national monuments on public lands, which gave a degree of expediency to protecting important natural resources. Devil's Tower, Wyoming, was secured as our first national monument in 1906. Many national monuments would later become national parks. The Inland Waterways Commission, appointed by Roosevelt in 1907, in its first report emphasized the interrelated character of water, forest, transportation, and fuel problems. It was after the White House Conference on Natural Resources (1908) that the conservation movement assumed definite shape on a nationwide scale. This conference was attended by governors, congressional leaders, scientists, informed sports people, and foreign experts. A National Conservation Commission was formed, with Pinchot as chair, that completed the first complete natural resource inventory in the United States. President Roosevelt used this inventory as the basis to withdraw 200 million acres of public-domain land from further settlement and entry. Three-quarters of this land was added to the National Forest System, with the remaining quarter consisting of withdrawn mineral lands. Most of the governors who attended this meeting established conservation agencies in their states shortly after this meeting. The recommendation of creating a National Park Service sprang from this conference. At the time there was no one agency responsible for administering a growing number of national parks and national monuments. The *National Park Service Act* was passed in 1916.

The stimulus for passage of the Weeks Act (1911) was given by the T. Roosevelt presidency. The Weeks Act authorized the purchase of headwater areas to protect navigable streams. This marked a major change in the manner in which national forests were created. Most of the land added to our National Forest System prior to the Weeks Act was withdrawn from already-existing federal public-domain land. Most of the national forests in the eastern United States resulted from Weeks Act purchases of private land, for example the White Mountains; the Monongahela; the Nantahala; the Shawnee; and the Ouachita National Forests.

The *second wave* of the conservation movement occurred between 1933 and 1939 and coincided with the pre-World War II presidential terms of Franklin D. Roosevelt. F.D.R.'s New Deal is often referred to as the "golden age" of conservation. It was characterized by the passage of much legislation and the creation of numerous bureaus and agencies to transform legislation into meaningful action at the grassroots level. The primary focus was on land planning, with a special focus on soil improvement programs. Roosevelt's programs created employment opportunities while at the same time solving natural resource problems. Many recreation projects were carried out by programs such as the Civilian Conservation Corps, the Public Works Administration, and the Works Progress Administration. Many of the hiking trails and the state park infrastructure in the Northeast were constructed by workers in these programs. The *Tennessee Valley Authority Act* (1933) established the Tennessee Valley Authority (TVA) for the purpose of developing and managing water projects in the Tennessee Valley. This is the first time a river basin was recognized as the planning unit. The TVA region occupies parts of eight states and covers 50,000 square miles, an area the size of New York State. The reservoirs and flowing streams of the TVA system serve as a very valuable recreational resource in the southeastern United States. The TVA system is still hailed as the classic example of multiple-use planning, integrating resource development in an entire river basin. In 1934, the Natural Resources Board completed the second comprehensive national natural resource inven-

tory. The Migratory Bird Hunting Stamp Act (Duck Stamp Act) of 1934 has provided funds that are used to expand the National Wildlife Refuge System. The Soil Conservation Service (SCS) was established in 1935. Recreational land-use planners today are indebted to the SCS for their accurate soil maps, which allow environmentally sound plans to be made. The Historic Sites Act (1935) empowered the president to add historic sites to the National Park System by proclamation. The Wildlife Restoration (Pittman-Robertson) Act (1937) established an excise tax on sporting arms and ammunition, with the proceeds going to state wildlife agencies for wildlife management. In 1936, our first national recreation area (Lake Mead in Nevada and Arizona) and our first national parkway (the Blue Ridge spanning North Carolina and Virginia) were established. Our first national seashore, (Cape Hatteras, in North Carolina) was established in 1937.

The *third wave* of the conservation movement started in 1961 with John F. Kennedy assuming the presidency. During World War II and the Korean War national attention was focused on military victory, often at the expense of natural resource deterioration and depletion. Massive funding via the Marshall Plan was provided for economic recovery programs for our defeated enemies. At this time private participation in resource management began with the establishment of the Conservation Foundation (1948) and Resources for the Future (1952). The former sponsors research that is more ecology-oriented, while the latter focuses on the "economic engineering" approach to natural resource management. The Conservation Foundation has had a particularly dramatic impact on amenity resource protection, and Resources for the Future publications have also analyzed amenity resource valuation. Probably the most prominent recreation researcher of the century, Marion Clawson, is a fellow and past president of Resources for the Future. Clawson's classic article, "The Crisis in Outdoor Recreation," appeared in *American Forests* in 1959.

In this time period between the start of World War II and 1961 some significant events occurred that have impacted recreational resources. Congress passed the Flood Control Act in 1944, which revised the 1936 Flood Control Act, and authorized recreational developments at Army Corps of Engineer reservoirs. The large number of recreation projects constructed at these reservoirs since this time is responsible for making the Corps the number 2 federal agency in recreational visitation; the Forest Service is number 1, followed by the Park Service at the number 3 spot. The *Bureau of Land Management* (BLM) came into being when the General Land Office and the Grazing Service ceased to exist in 1946, the direct result of the Reorganization Plan No. 3 Act. Today, the BLM controls more land than any other federal agency, the recreational potential of which is just being discovered. The Fish and Wildlife Act (1956) established the Fish and Wildlife Service in basically its present form and enlarged the participation of the federal government in wildlife management. The National Wildlife Refuge System Administration Act (1956) described and refined federal policy with respect to the National Wildlife Refuge System. The National Park Service launched Mission 66 in 1956 to restore and improve its recreational facilities, with the Forest Service initiating a similar program, Operation Outdoors in the same year. The Outdoor Recreation Resources Review Act (1958) established the Outdoor Recreation Resources Review Commission to examine the nation's recreational needs. The impact of this federal commission is analyzed later in this book. The Federal Highway Aid Act (1958) provided massive funding to start constructing our interstate

highway system, which drastically cut travel time needed to reach recreational resources. Few other single pieces of federal legislation had a more significant impact on the use of recreational resources. The *Multiple Use-Sustained Yield Act* (1960) clarified and further defined the concept that national forests are to be administered on a multiple-use basis with five primary uses: outdoor recreation, watershed, range, timber, and fish and wildlife.

John F. Kennedy was the first charismatic president with a strong personal image since F.D.R. The third wave of conservation in the United States is recognized as beginning with his assumption of the presidency in 1961. Environmental historians are not in agreement as to the end date of this third wave. It is interpreted here that the third wave persisted through the Johnson, Nixon, Ford, and Carter presidencies and ended abruptly with Ronald Reagan assuming the office in January 1981. To appreciate the impact of Lyndon B. Johnson's presidency, one only has to visit Lyndon B. Johnson National Historical Park and State Park (Texas) and view the pens President Johnson used to sign into law a very large number of environmental and recreational pieces of legislation. Much of the legislation pushed by Johnson was actually initially proposed by J.F.K. The central focus of this phase of the conservation movement was environmental quality. In 1962, a White House conference was attended by 500 of the nation's leading conservationists to review the status of America's resources. The ORRRC's report, *Outdoor Recreation for America,* was released that year, and the BOR was established to coordinate, assist, and stimulate recreation. *The Public Land Law Review Act* (1964) established the Public Land Law Review Commission, whose purpose was to review United States federal land policies; this charge was undertaken from 1964 to 1970. In 1970 the commission's report, *One Third of the Nation's Land,* was released. It contained 452 recommendations, many of these were broad in nature.

One of the most significant and far-reaching pieces of legislation ever passed by Congress—*The Wilderness Act*—was signed into law by President Johnson on September 5, 1964. Although lands reserved for wilderness management can be traced to the declaration of the Gila primitive area in the Gila National Forest in 1924, such areas were only administrative creations that could be declassified at any time. The Wilderness Act provided for an initial Wilderness Preservation System of 54 areas occupying 9.1 million acres on the national forests; it further provided a review process for the study of additional national forest lands, national parks, and national wildlife refuges for possible inclusion into the system. The *Federal Land Policy and Management Act* (1976) not only clarified the land management policies for the BLM but also specified that these lands would also be reviewed for possible inclusion into the National Wilderness Preservation System. The Wilderness Act demonstrated that preserving areas of solitude "where the earth is untrammeled by man" was now a high-priority national goal. Organized in 1935 as a private environmental interest group, the Wilderness Society played a pivotal role in lobbying for the National Wilderness Preservation System.

Another extremely significant piece of legislation was the *Land and Water Conservation Fund Act* (1965). It served as a major source of funding for public outdoor recreation projects and stimulated the recreational land-use planning process. The Federal Water Project Recreation Act (1965) mandated that federal water-resource agencies, such as the Bureau of Reclamation, should give full consideration to rec-

reation and fish and wildlife enhancement in connection with their projects. The *National Trail System Act* (1968) established the framework for developing a National Trail System and designated two initial trails, the Appalachian and the Pacific Crest. This system has grown to now encompass eight national scenic trails, 11 national historic trails, and 801 national recreation trails. The *Wild and Scenic Rivers Act* (1968) established the Wild and Scenic Rivers System and designated its initial components. The system now totals over 10,000 miles and contains 150 rivers designated as wild, scenic, or recreational. The act established the fact that preservation of free-flowing rivers is now a high-priority national goal. It stopped largely single-purpose agencies, such as the Bureau of Reclamation and the Army Corps of Engineers, from damming most of our remaining free-flowing streams. The National Environmental Policy Act (1969) did establish the fact that preservation of environmental quality is also a high-priority national goal, and in establishing this fact has served to protect amenity resources with recreational value. The initial versions of Water Quality Act (1965) and Air Quality Act (1967) were also environmentally important legislation of this first decade of the third wave. The national seashore and lakeshore concept was renewed in the 1960s with the authorization of Cape Cod National Seashore (1961). Prior to this time Cape Hatteras (1937) was our only national seashore. Our first national lakeshore, Pictured Rocks on Lake Superior, was authorized in 1966.

Some environmental historians contend that the third wave of conservation ended when the Nixon presidency became mired in the Watergate incident but it is argued here that the third wave continued through the presidencies of Gerald Ford and Jimmy Carter. President Nixon was an environmentally committed president, and his support had a major impact on making amenity resources available for recreational use. The Endangered Species Act (1973) serves the function of slowing culturally induced biotic extinction thus ensuring that plant and animal life will remain for those people who recreate through observation. The *Forest and Rangeland Renewable Resources Planning Act* (1974) was passed to improve planning and management of the National Forests, including planning and management for recreation. The *National Forest Management Act* (1976) provided improved management guidelines and priorities for the national forests, by mandating the development of 50-year unit-by-unit management plans. The National Parks and Recreation Act (1978) provided massive funding for improving urban parks and the National Park System.

One of the last pieces of legislation signed into law by President Jimmy Carter was the *Alaska National Interest Lands Conservation Act* (1980), which basically settled the final disposition of public lands in Alaska. The disposition of this land had its origin in two other laws: the Alaska Statehood Act (1958) and the Alaska Native Claims Settlement Act (1971). The Alaska National Interest Lands Conservation Act altered the boundaries of previously established units and greatly enlarged the National Wildlife Refuge System and National Park System in Alaska; the Chugach National Forest was also enlarged. The Alaska National Interest Lands Conservation Act (1) doubled the size of the National Park System, (2) tripled the size of the National Wilderness Preservation System, (3) doubled the size of the National Wildlife Refuge System, and (4) doubled the size of the National Wild and Scenic River System. No previous law has had (nor will any future law have) the magnitude of impact on the public lands as the Alaska National Interest Lands Conservation Act. Future environmental historians will view this law as one of the most significant

pieces of environmental legislation ever enacted, for massive areas of amenity resources and natural ecosystems are now protected for posterity.

The third wave of conservation in the United States came to an abrupt end with the inauguration of Ronald Reagan on January 20, 1981. No blow to recreation was more severe than the Executive Order that abolished the Heritage Conservation and Recreation Service (formerly the BOR) very early in the Reagan Presidency. Members of the *sagebrush rebellion*, which gained the forefront in the news, wanted to return much of our federal public land to either the states or the private sector. This movement was particularly strong in the West, where many states have a high percentage of federal land ownership; for example, Nevada is 86 percent federally owned. Reagan's Secretary of the Interior, James Watt, and Director of the Budget, David Stockman, were sympathetic to this movement. It was public outcry at this possible loss of much of our public land that largely determined the ultimate outcome of this issue. An example of the public's success is the case of the Forest Service's Hector Land Utilization project in New York's Finger Lake Country. This valuable 13,000-acre recreational resource was proposed for sale to help solve the nation's budget deficit. However, the recreational users of this resource made their feelings known, and in 1985 the area was established as Finger Lakes National Forest.

It should not be assumed that the protection of amenity resources with high recreational value halted altogether during the Reagan presidency. During this time our National Park System was expanded, including the addition of a new national park, Great Basin National Park, in Nevada in 1986. Our National Wild and Scenic Rivers System saw the addition of 65 new rivers, and the National Wilderness Preservation System continued its growth, with 1984 being a particularly large growth year. Many BLM areas in Arizona were also added at this time. And our National Trails System continued to expand, especially in the type of trail designated "recreational." George Bush's policy in regard to the environment and amenity resources was essentially similar to that of Ronald Reagan.

Recreationists hold great hope for a reversal of this trend under President Bill Clinton. But after almost two years in office, few of his actions as president have supported his campaign rhetoric. President Clinton is finding that it is easy to make promises on the campaign trail but more difficult to translate these promises to action in Washington. The fourth wave of conservation has not yet started in the United States.

OUTDOOR RECREATION RESOURCES REVIEW COMMISSION

During the 1950s the growing public demand for the outdoors amid sharpening competition for outdoor recreation resources became matters of increasing concern. Recognizing the need for a nationwide study of these problems, the Outdoor Recreation Resources Review Commission (ORRRC) was created on June 28, 1958 (P.L. 85-470, 72 Stat. 238). The task assigned to the commission was to seek answers to the following basic questions:

- What are the recreation wants and needs of the American people now, and what will they be in the years 1976 and 2000?
- What are the recreational resources of the nation that are available to fill these needs?
- What policies and programs should be recommended to insure that the needs of the present and future are adequately met?

The commission's report *Outdoor Recreation for America,* was presented to the president and Congress on January 31, 1962. In addition, 27 volumes on many different subjects were presented, the titles of which are given in Table 2.1. These reports represented the most comprehensive study of outdoor recreation ever undertaken in the United States or the world. Study Reports Number 3, *Wilderness Recreation—A Report on Resources, Values, and Problems,* and Number 17, *Multiple Use of Land and Water Areas* are still accepted as important references on these subjects.

Some of the Outdoor Recreation Resources Review Commission findings are particularly significant:

- Adequate provisions were not being made for the rapidly expanding needs of outdoor recreation.

Table 2.1 Studies of the Outdoor Recreation Resources Review Commission

Number	Title
1	Public Outdoor Recreation Areas—Acreage, Use, Potential
2	List of Public Outdoor Recreation Areas—1960
3	Wilderness and Recreation—A Report on Resources, Values, and Problems
4	Shoreline Recreation Resources of the United States
5	The Quality of Outdoor Recreation: As Evidenced by User Satisfaction
6	Hunting in the United States—Its Present and Future Role
7	Sport Fishing—Today and Tomorrow
8	Potential New Sites for Outdoor Recreation in the Northeast
9	Alaska Outdoor Recreation Potential
10	Water for Recreation—Values and Opportunities
11	Private Outdoor Recreation Facilities
12	Financing Public Recreation Facilities
13	Federal Agencies and Outdoor Recreation
14	Directory of State Outdoor Recreation Administration
15	Open Space Action
16	Land Acquisition for Outdoor Recreation—Analysis of Selected Legal Problems
17	Multiple Use of Land and Water Areas
18	A Look Abroad: the Effect of Foreign Travel on Domestic Outdoor Recreation and a Brief Survey of Outdoor Recreation in Six Countries
19	National Recreation Survey
20	Participation in Outdoor Recreation: Factors Affecting Demand among American Adults
21	The Future of Outdoor Recreation in Metropolitan Regions of the United States
22	Trends in American Living and Outdoor Recreation
23	Projections to the Year 1976 and 2000: Economic Growth, Population, Labor Force and Leisure, and Transportation
24	Economic Studies of Outdoor Recreation
25	Public Expenditures for Outdoor Recreation
26	Prospective Demand for Outdoor Recreation
27	Outdoor Recreation Literature: A Survey

- The gap between supply and demand would widen if effective actions were not taken immediately.
- The gap was qualitative as well as quantitative, as many existing programs were not aimed at providing what people wanted and needed.
- It was projected that by the year 2000 the population would double and that the recreational demand would triple due to more free time, increased discretionary purchasing power, and increased mobility.
- The kinds of outdoor recreation most people participate in are quite simple: walking and driving for pleasure, outdoor games and sports, swimming, and so on.
- What people did then was not necessarily what they want to do in the future.
- Water was a focal point of outdoor recreation.
- The recreation problem involved not total acres but effective acres; the demand was not being met because of poor location and poor management.
- Most people wanted outdoor recreation close to home.
- Yet, as mobility continues to increase, more people would travel farther to enjoy outstanding scenic, wildlife, and wilderness areas.
- There were many overlooked outdoor recreation resources in urban areas; it is important to develop such resources since there was such tremendous demand within after-work and weekend leisure.

Several significant actions have resulted from the recommendations set forth by the commission:

1. *Bureau of Outdoor Recreation*   One of the first results of the ORRRC's recommendations was creation of the Bureau of Outdoor Recreation (BOR) in the Department of the Interior on April 2, 1962. This was the first federal agency created principally for recreational purposes and the first one to carry the word *recreation* in its title. It was not a land-managing agency, for it had no land directly under its jurisdiction. BOR responsibilities included:

- Coordinating related federal recreation programs
- Stimulating and providing for assistance to the states in outdoor recreation
- Sponsoring and conducting outdoor recreation research
- Encouraging interstate and regional cooperation in outdoor recreation
- Conducting surveys of recreational resources
- Formulating a nationwide outdoor recreation plan on the basis of state, regional, and federal plans
- Managing the Land and Water Conservation Fund

In 1978, Interior Secretary Cecil Andrus signed an order that abolished the BOR and created in its place the Heritage Conservation and Recreation Service (HCRS). While most of the responsibilities of the former BOR remained with the HCRS, the National Natural Landmarks Program and Office of Archaeology and Historic Preservation programs were transferred from the National Park Service. Secretary Andrus (Dept. of Interior Press Release) characterized the duties of this new agency as follows: "In general HCRS will establish and maintain registers for heritage resources; formulate policies and programs for their preservation; and coordinate federal, state and local resource and recreation policies and actions." The HCRS was abolished by

Executive Order shortly after Ronald Reagan assumed the presidency on January 20, 1981. Most of the programs were transferred to the National Park Service, but the staff was not available to equal the accomplishments of the BOR and its successor, the HCRS.

2. *Land and Water Conservation Fund*   The Land and Water Conservation Fund was established in 1965 by P.L. 88-578. Its purpose was to provide financial assistance to certain federal agencies with principal roles in outdoor recreation (National Park Service, Forest Service, Fish and Wildlife Service, and Bureau of Land Management), and to provide grants to states and through the states to political subdivisions of the states for:

- Planning of public outdoor recreation areas and facilities
- Acquisition of public outdoor recreation areas and facilities
- Development of public outdoor recreation areas and facilities

The grants usually covered 50 percent of the project. The basic eligibility requirement was that a state must develop, update, and refine comprehensive statewide outdoor recreation plans, which needed to be approved by the BOR and later by HCRS prior to their demise. To qualify, a project must meet high-priority public recreation needs identified in the state plan. Assistance can be given for projects in highly populated urban areas as well as more primitive areas, but priority consideration is usually given to:

- Projects serving urban populations
- Projects serving the general public over limited groups
- Projects that are basic rather than elaborate
- Projects for which other adequate financing is not available

The Land and Water Conservation Fund was based on a simple principle—that of reinvestment of a portion of the sale of oil and gas leases on the Outer Continental Shelf. The funding for the Land and Water Conservation Fund was greatly diminished in the 1980s and was especially cut back for nonfederal purposes. This resulted in much less activity among the states in planning for recreational land use. The President's Commission on Americans Outdoors (1987) concluded: In 1986, localities and states received just one-sixth of 1978 funding levels. The fund was initially authorized at $100 million annually, but reached its highest level of funding in 1978 with $900 million authorized by Congress. Since its inception the fund enabled localities and states to acquire almost 3 million acres of recreational lands and waters by providing $3 billion that was matched by local and state and some private-sector contributions. Another 3 million acres were added to national parks, forests, wilderness, refuges, and BLM recreation areas. The Land and Water Conservation Fund was scheduled to expire in 1989, but was reauthorized until 2015.

3. *Nationwide Outdoor Recreation Plan*   Our first published and released nationwide recreation plan, *Outdoor Recreation: A Legacy for America*, was released in November 1973. This plan:

- Takes into consideration the plans of the various federal agencies, states, and their political subdivisions

- Sets forth the needs and the demands of the public for outdoor recreation
- Identifies the current and foreseeable future availability of outdoor recreation resources to meet these needs
- Identifies crucial outdoor recreation problems, and recommends solutions at each level of government and by private interests
- States that federal departments and independent agencies shall carry out recreational responsibilities in general conformance with the plan
- Can serve as a guide for state and local governments and the private sector

4. Several states were stimulated by the ORRRC to authorize and help finance recreation-land acquisition programs.

5. *Section 704 of the Housing and Urban Development Act*   This legislation, enacted in 1965, established a Housing and Urban Development Open Space Program. It authorized the secretary of Housing and Urban Development to make grants to local public agencies to acquire sites needed for the future construction of public facilities, including recreation.

6. The ORRRC lent support to Congress finally establishing a *National Wilderness Preservation System* in 1964.

7. The ORRRC promoted a substantial expansion of our *National Park System*.

The Outdoor Recreation Resources Review Commission was thus a catalyst in the development of public interest in comprehensive national recreation planning and a major factor in implementing positive action toward that goal. Very few federal commissions have had the impact of the ORRRC. Many of the outdoor recreation facilities that Americans use during their leisure time have been developed and made available by this catalyst.

PRESIDENT'S COMMISSION ON AMERICANS OUTDOORS

Twenty years after the release of the Outdoor Recreation Resources Review Commission's reports, its chair, Laurance Rockefeller, recognized the need to reexamine the adequacies of our outdoor recreation resources. He convened a group of conservation and recreation leaders under the chair of New York's former commissioner of Environmental Conservation, Henry Diamond, and known as the Policy Review Group, to explore again the issues raised 20 years earlier. The group found (1) that retrenchments in government in the 1980s threaten the integrity of the country's recreational infrastructure; (2) that outdoor recreation is more important than ever in American life; and (3) that the private sector is doing more—and could do even—more with government cooperation. The Policy Review Group was unsuccessful in persuading Congress to enact a comprehensive appraisal of the nation's recreation policy and resources but did win over President Reagan's interest. On January 28, 1985, an Executive Order issued by President Ronald Reagan established the President's Commission on Americans Outdoors, a 15-member commission that was chaired by Governor Lamar Alexander of Tennessee.

In conducting its review the commission was charged by the Executive Order to examine:

- Existing outdoor recreation lands and resources and the land and resource base necessary for outdoor recreation
- The roles of the federal, state, county, and municipal governments in providing outdoor recreation opportunities, protecting outdoor recreation resources, and meeting anticipated outdoor recreation conditions
- The role of the private sector in meeting present and future outdoor recreation needs, and the potential for cooperation between the private sector and government in providing outdoor recreation opportunities and protecting outdoor recreation resources
- The relationship between outdoor recreation and personal and public health, the economy, and the environment
- The future needs of outdoor recreation management systems, including qualified personnel, technical information, and anticipated financial needs
- The relationship of outdoor recreation to the broader range of recreational pursuits and its implications for the supply of and demand for outdoor recreation resources and opportunities
- Underlying social, economic, and technological factors likely to affect the demand for and supply of outdoor recreation resources, including trends in disposable income and demographic characteristics of the United States

The commission's methodology was to solicit views from the American people about how current and future needs for recreation might be better met. It decided its report's primary purpose was to stimulate local action, as opposed to primarily influencing Washington policy makers. The commission concluded that

> outdoor recreation occurs close to home, in or near towns and cities where 80 percent of us will soon live. So, more and more, the solutions must be found close to home. . . . The best way to assure that Americans will have adequate outdoor recreation opportunities is through a prairie fire of concern and investment community by community.

The final report of the Commission on Americans Outdoors was presented to President Reagan on January 28, 1987. The commission issued 70 recommendations responding to the problems and opportunities it documented; these recommendations are listed in Appendix I.

Some of the findings of the President's Commission on Americans Outdoors are that:

- American's place a high value on the outdoors; it is central to the quality of our lives and the quality of our communities.
- Outdoor recreation provides significant social, economic, and environmental benefits. Because these benefits are difficult to assess in dollars, recreation and recreational resources protection suffer in competition with other programs for public and private dollars.
- High-quality resources—land, water, and air—are essential to fishing and boating, camping and hiking, skiing and bicycling, hunting and horseback riding, and every other outdoors activity.

- The quality of the outdoor estate remains precarious. People continue to misuse and abuse resources and facilities. However, we are becoming aware of more pervasive long-term threats, such as toxic chemicals, water pollution from nonpoint sources, groundwater contamination, and acid precipitation.
- The nation is losing valuable open space on the fringe of fast-growing urban areas and near water. Wetlands and wildlife are disappearing.
- Wild and free-flowing rivers are being dammed, while residential and commercial development is cutting off public access to rivers in urban areas.
- With more people doing many different things outdoors, competition for available lands and waters is increasing; to accommodate these pressures we will have to manage better what we have.
- The quality of recreational services delivery is inadequate. Though some services are improving, much remains to be done.
- Inadequate funding for staff, development of facilities, and maintenance limits recreational use of some public lands.
- People in central cities have a harder time experiencing the outdoors.
- Barriers to investment prevent the private sector from reaching its potential as a recreation provider.
- Resource management and recreation programs offered by public and private providers are not coordinated as well as they should be.
- The liability crisis is limiting our opportunities to enjoy the outdoors.
- We don't have a good overall picture of what we have, and we lack systematic monitoring of resource conditions and public needs.
- We take the outdoors for granted and assume it will always be there, not recognizing that its maintenance depends on each of us.
- Aggravating these problems is a population increase of about 2.2 million persons a year—the equivalent of a Houston and a New Orleans.

The commission also concluded that, since the 1960s, three factors beyond population level have significantly affected the demand for outdoor recreation: leisure time, income, and mobility. These factors were discussed in Chapter 1. Tables 2.2, 2.3, and 2.4 summarize why people choose recreation areas, the main reason they participate in outdoor recreation, and the rank order of participation of adults in outdoor recreation activities.

Group strategic planning sessions were held to elicit views of future trends, issues, and optimal solutions to determine a course of future action. The first group consisted of futurists, policy analysts from several fields, environmentalists, conservationists, industry representatives and other experts. These experts served as the primary identifiers of trends. The second group consisted of public and private recreation providers who supplied expert views on the supply of recreation and who identified additional trends. These sessions identified nearly 60 trends. The top ten trends the participants believed were the most significant are:

1. *Changing Social and Demographic Composition*   American society is aging, increasing its ethnic mix and its education level, changing its work patterns and creating new centers of population.

2. *Fluctuating Energy Availability and Cost*   Travel and tourism, and recreation activities depend on energy and will continually be faced by uncertainties based upon day-to-day changes in world market and political conditions.

Table 2.2 Why We Choose a Recreation Area: Attributes Adults Consider, in Rank Order, When Choosing Parks, Beaches, and Other Outdoor Recreation Areas

Rank	Attribute
1	Natural beauty
2	Amount of crowding
3	Restroom facilities
4	Parking availability
5	Available information
6	Picnic areas
7	Cultural events
8	Fees charged
9	Concessions
10	Organized sports
11	Guided activities

Source: 1986 Market Opinion Research Survey, "Participation in Outdoor Recreation among American Adults and the Motivations Which Drive Participation," in the President's Commission on Americans Outdoors, *Americans Outdoors* (1987).

Table 2.3 Main Reasons for Participating in Outdoor Recreation

Main Reasons (Top Mentions Only)	Total Sample (%)
Enjoy/Enjoyment/Fun	36
Exercise/Keep in shape	25
To be outdoors/Outside/Just to get out	22
Health/Healthier/For the health/Feel good	15
Fresh air	12
Be with people/Friends/Camaraderie/Socialize	8
Be with family/Son/Children/Spouse	6
Relax/Relaxation	5
Sunshine/Need the sun	5
Nature/Like nature	3
Claustrophobia/Hate to be confined in the house	3
Like sports	2
Pass time/Helps pass the time/Keep busy	2
Weather	2
Clear mind/Take mind off work	2
Scenery	2
Individualism/Be by myself	1
Always did/Grew up	1
Get away from work/Diversion from work	1
For work/Working/Work purposes	1
Enjoy wildlife/Animals	1
Competition	1
Nothing/I don't participate	3
Don't know/Refused	4
(Base)	(2000)

Source: President's Commission on Americans Outdoors, *Americans Outdoors* (1987).

Table 2.4   Rank Order of Adult Participation 1 or More Times in Past Year

1986 % Participation	Sometimes, Often, or Very Often	Often or Very Often
Walking for pleasure	84	(50)
Driving for pleasure	77	(43)
Sightseeing	77	(34)
Picnicking	76	(28)
Swimming outdoors	76	(43)
Ocean, lake, river	(63)	(30)
Outdoor pool	(58)	(28)
Visit zoos, fairs, amusement parks	72	(17)
Attend outdoor sports events	60	(22)
Visit historic sites	59	(14)
Fishing	51	(25)
Bicycling	46	(17)
Camping	45	(21)
Tent camping	(29)	(9)
Recreational vehicle	(22)	(8)
Other camping	(17)	(5)
Softball/baseball	43	(16)
Running or jogging	42	(17)
Attend outdoor plays/concerts	42	(11)
Bird watching, nature study	35	(15)
Tennis outdoor	30	(10)
Basketball	27	(10)
Motor boating, waterskiing	27	(15)
Day hiking	27	(12)
Driving off-road vehicles/snowmobiles	24	(11)
Canoeing/kayaking/rafting	22	(5)
Golfing	22	(10)
Football	21	(6)
Hunting	21	(11)
Backpacking	17	(5)
Sledding	17	(4)
Horseback riding	15	(3)
Sailing or windsurfing	15	(4)
Downhill skiing	14	(5)
Ice skating	12	(3)
Soccer	10	(3)
Cross-county skiing	8	(3)
(Base)	(2000)	

Source: President's Commission on Americans Outdoors, *Americans Outdoors* (1987).

3. *Technological Innovations*   New products and new ways of doing work greatly increase the choices for using leisure time, but can also change demands on recreation providers.

4. *Shifts in Political Power Closer to the People*   State and local governments have shown initiatives in problem solving and assuming responsibilities while the federal government has been reducing its regulatory and financial assistance roles.

5. *Increased Accountability of Institutions and Leaders*   People are increasingly participating in public processes to plan programs and formulate policies. Private institutions are being required to make available more information on products and plans.

6. *Concern for the Environment*   Public interest and involvement in environmental protection issues remains high, with more emphasis placed on threats to personal environmental health and safety than on threats to nature.

7. *Creation of Innovative Partnerships*   Cooperative efforts between and among public and private sectors are developing to more efficiently meet public demand for recreation and other services.

8. *Shifts in Economic Strengths and Weaknesses*   A domestic shift in employment from manufacturing to services and information is changing the time and the money available for recreation.

9. *Changes in Recreation and Leisure*   Development of new equipment, changes in lifestyles and the variability of the leisure fashion of the moment place strong pressures on the ability of providers to respond to these changing demands.

10. *Changes in Transportation Systems*   Near completion of the interstate highway system, deregulation of airline and bus travel, and smaller automobiles are changing how, when, and where we travel for pleasure.

The participants in eight field sessions verified these trends and listed issues relating to recreational and outdoor opportunities arising from these trends. They then voted on the top 10 issues, but no single issue finished in the top 10 for all eight field sessions. The rank order of issues varied widely among the eight sessions, reflecting the differences between large urban areas and smaller cities, the lack or presence of extensive federally managed lands, and many other factors. Table 2.5 lists the combined total votes from all eight sessions of the issues that were identified.

The commission compared national population trends in summer participation in 1960 and 1982 for various outdoor recreation activities for those age 12 and older. By 1982, swimming and walking for pleasure had replaced picnicking and driving for pleasure as the top two activities, with over 50 percent participating. There was a decrease in the percentage of people participating in picnicking, driving for pleasure, and boating. Participation rates (in percentage increase) increased for swimming, sightseeing, walking for pleasure, playing sports, fishing, attending sports, and bicycling. The nine activities showing the greatest percentage change for this time

Table 2.5   Major Issues Identified

Issue	Total Votes
1. Protection of natural resources and open space	131
2. Conflicting uses of recreational lands and waters	130
3. Roles of providers	110
4. Liability	88
5. Physical access to open space	85
6. Funding operations, maintenance, capital improvements	84
7. Alternative funding sources	69
8. Benefits of recreation	67
9. Acquisition of open space	67
10. Land-use planning	54
11. Social access to open space	52
12. Partnerships	50
13. Database needs	48

Source: President's Commission on Americans Outdoors, *Americans Outdoors* (1987).

period are canoeing (515 percent); bicycling (382 percent); attending outdoor cultural events (342 percent); camping, all styles (240 percent); sailing (211.5 percent); hiking and backpacking (199 percent); attending outdoor sports (144 percent); walking for pleasure (132 percent); and waterskiing (120 percent).

A comparison made of recreational trips, by outing type and one-way travel miles for 1972 and 1982 revealed some dramatic changes. For short outings there has been an increase in people staying within 10 miles of home (30 percent in 1972 versus 75 percent in 1982). For day outings there has been a major shift (with over 55 miles the leading category in 1972 and 0 to 10 miles the leading category in 1982). The same type of shift has occurred in the leading category of overnight trips (500 or more miles in 1972 and 0 to 100 miles in 1982). In short, Americans have been staying closer to home for outdoor recreation, which is placing increased pressures on already overused recreational resources.

There has also been a major change in time spent away from home for recreational use at public areas. The base years for comparison are 1960 and 1985, and the five time spans evaluated for being away from home were: 6 hours; 6 to 12 hours; 13 hours to 1 day; 2 to 4 days; and 5+ days. The leading category in 1960 was 5+ days (39 percent), followed by 6 hours (24 percent); 2 to 4 days (14 percent), 6 to 12 hours (13 percent), and 13 hours to 1 day (8 percent); in 1985 the leading category had changed to 6 hours (54 percent), followed by 6 to 12 hours (15 percent), 2 to 4 days (13 percent), 13 hours to 1 day (10 percent), and 5+ days (8 percent).

The President's Commission on Americans Outdoors 25 years later attempted to restore the impetus given to outdoor recreation by the Outdoor Recreation Resources Review Commission the 1960s. The budget cuts of the early 1980s and Ronald Reagan's New Federalism seriously curtailed recreational resource development. The basis for the "prairie fire" that the 1987 commission had hoped to ignite were 70 recommendations. As of 1994, this "prairie fire" was only mildly smoldering.

RECREATION RESOURCE SECTORS

The most common way to subdivide recreational resources into major groups or *sectors* is to classify them as either private or public. For the purpose of this book five major *recreation resource sectors* will be employed:

1. Public—federal recreation resource sector
2. Public—state recreation resource sector
3. Public—local and regional recreation resource sector
4. Private—noncommercial recreation resource sector
5. Private—commercial recreation resource sector

This book is devoted primarily to coverage of public federal recreation resources. However, throughout the entire book continual reference will be made to the other recreation resource sectors. Much of the developed infrastructure that supports many of our resource-based federal recreation resources occurs on private land. Even in our national parks, private concessioners provide many of the services. This is especially true for the noncamping type of lodging in the national parks. Some of the

campgrounds in the national parks, as in Yosemite National Park, are operated by private concessioners. The commercial recreation industry is well developed and supports the tourism that is attracted to our federal resource-based areas. Examples of tourist centers located in close proximity to federal areas are: Gatlinburg, Tenn. (Great Smoky Mountains National Park); Jackson, Wyo. (Grand Teton National Park); West Yellowstone, Mont. (Yellowstone National Park); Moab, Utah (Arches and Canyonlands National Parks); and Bar Harbor, Me. (Acadia National Park). Many visitors to national parks plan to camp for their overnight accommodations. Unfortunately, many of the national park campgrounds fill very early in the day. Such is the case for Devil's Garden Campground in Arches National Park (Figure 2.2). The commercial motels in nearby Moab, although more expensive, provide a welcome alternative to visitors who find the campground full. In many cases, state recreational resources support the use of federal recreational resources. Chadron State Park or Fort Robinson State Park, Nebraska, provide excellent camping experiences for visitors to Nebraska National Forest. Many visitors to Redwood National Park camp at adjacent California state parks.

Researchers have drawn different conclusions on the distribution of actual time usage for the different resource sectors. Part of the reason for these discrepancies relates to the definition for recreation that is employed. Chubb and Chubb (1981, 325), who use a very broad definition of recreation, estimated that 80 to 90 percent of people's recreation time in Western nations is spent at home, with media-related activities (TV, newspapers, and magazines) being the leading recreational activities. Using this definition, they further estimated that 5 to 10 percent of their recreation occurred at commercial recreation facilities (theaters, golf courses, and so forth). They conclude that only 10 to 15 percent of people's time is spent on public lands. It is difficult to measure the recreational use on much of the public sector since fees are not collected; this is especially true for recreational resources such as parks and play-

Figure 2.2 Devil's Garden Campground in Arches National Park (Utah) fills very early in the morning on most days.

grounds in the local sector. In the state sector, fees are usually collected at most state parks; this allows good use data to be collected. But many state recreation lands, such as state forests and wildlife areas, do not collect fees, and measuring attendance is more difficult.

The best use data for the public sector is for federal recreation lands. Each year the National Park Service prepares a publication, *Federal Recreation Fee Report to Congress,* which contains data on recreational use for the seven primary federal land-managing agencies (National Park Service, Forest Service, Fish and Wildlife Service, Bureau of Land Management, Army Corps of Engineers, Bureau of Reclamation, and Tennessee Valley Authority). It also contains statistics on use of state parks. The 1991 version of this report identified 652,430,700 total recreation visitor days or 1,642,683,900 visits for these seven federal agencies. For the same year there were 639,735,000 visitors to state parks. The problems in using the actual tallied unit of measurement (for example, visit versus visitor day) were covered earlier.

Figure 2.3 presents the estimates of Cordell et al. (1990, 31) on overall outdoor recreation land use in the United States. They estimated that most outdoor recreation occurs in the parks and play areas of local communities, with local recreational opportunities accounting for about 60 percent of all outdoor recreation participation. Federal lands receive about 12 percent of all outdoor recreation participation. State and private lands and enterprises each serve about 14 percent of the participation. Figures 2.4 and 2.5 summarize the findings of the President's Commission on Americans Outdoors for "where people recreate 'often' on public areas and private areas." Surprisingly, the percentage of people who recreate "often" on public local areas (39 percent) is only slightly ahead of state areas (33 percent). The importance of "streets/lots" is revealed in that this category was identified as being where people recreate "often," 8 percent of the time. Federal areas were identified as the areas of recreation choice 18 percent of the time. For private lands, the two leading categories where

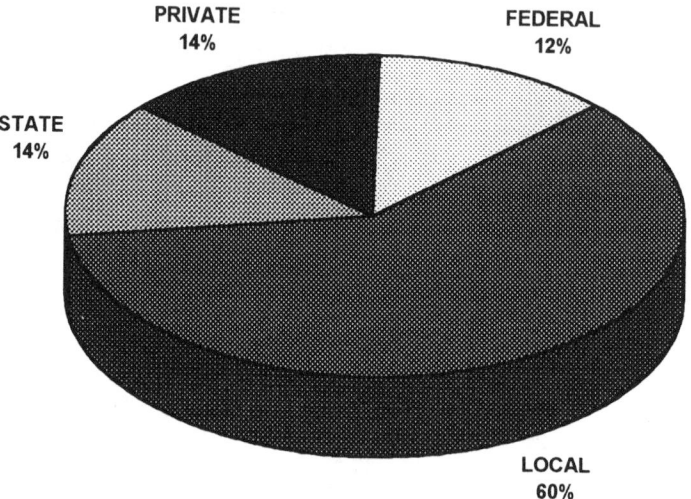

Figure 2.3   Participation in outdoor recreation. (After Cordell et al. 1990, 31)

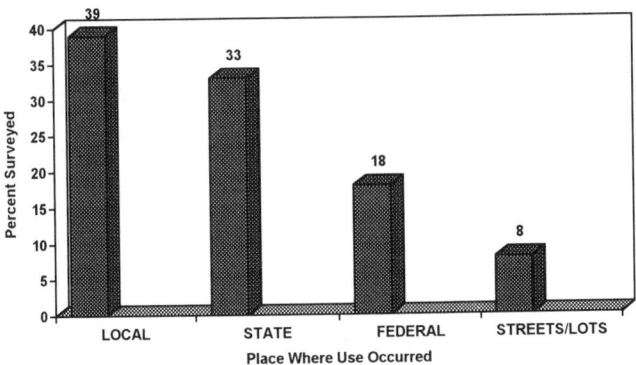

Figure 2.4 Public areas where people "often" recreate. (*Source:* President's Commission, 1987)

people recreate "often" are private lands (21 percent) and clubs and pools (20 percent). The third leading category was private commercial (15 percent).

The following conclusions about the use of outdoor recreation resources can be reached after analyzing the results of these different studies:

- No definitive conclusions can be reached about the true magnitude of actual outdoor recreation use that occurs on private lands. This is related primarily to a problem in defining outdoor recreation that was referred to earlier. Private commercial recreation is highly developed in urban areas, since it is market-driven.
- The amount of recreational use made of public federal lands is approximately equal to the use made of state parks—650,000,000 visits per year. When overall public

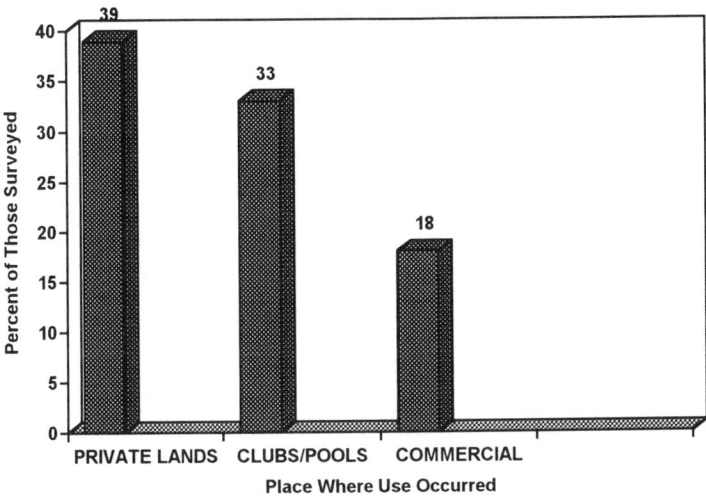

Figure 2.5 Private areas where people "often" recreate. (*Source:* President's Commission, 1987)

state recreation land use is included, this overall figure is considerably more than the public federal category, perhaps 750,000,000 or more visits per year.

- The amount of recreational use made of public local recreation lands cannot be precisely determined, but one can infer that its magnitude is at least double the combined total of state and federal land, or close to 3 billion visits per year.

Public Recreation Resource Sectors

The lion's share (91 percent, or 707,700,000 acres) of the 778,400,000 acres of public recreation lands in the United States occurs on federal lands, while the larger portion of the actual number of public recreation areas (62 percent, or 67,685) is found on municipal lands. The average size of a federal recreation area is 398,929 acres, and the average size of a municipal recreation area is 44.3 acres. Between these two extremes the average size for state recreation areas is 3042 acres and for regional recreation areas is 286.6 acres; a small number of very large state recreation areas magnifies this value. The average federal size is greatly enlarged by the huge size of some national parks, especially in Alaska. Table 2.6 and Figures 2.6 and 2.7 summarize the acreage and number of recreation areas for the various public sectors.

The President's Commission on Americans Outdoors (1987, 63), concluded: "Public acreage totals are a better measure of *potential* than of *actual* outdoor recreation opportunity." Four factors affect whether people can use a recreation area:

1. Can they get to it (accessibility)?
2. Are necessary facilities present?
3. Are there necessary services, including information?
4. Do other areas offer similar opportunities?

Distance from where people live is only one measure of accessibility, but the fact that almost half of all federal lands are located in Alaska does present accessibility problems. Figure 2.8 identifies the distribution of public recreation lands by geographic region in the United States. Accessibility is also affected by the availability of roads, other means of transportation, and access points. Much of the public land is relatively remote from population centers and difficult to reach, and some parcels are blocked by private land. Public recreation sites in urban areas may not be accessible due to lack of public transportation. While some activities (such as wilderness hiking and camping) may not require facilities, for others (boating, swimming, golf, or tennis) developed facilities are essential. A better measure for identifying regional variations of public recreation resources is to relate the acreage to the population Figure 2.9

Table 2.6   Public Recreation Lands

	Federal	State	Regional	Municipal
Number of areas	1,774	20,375	19,884	67,685
Percent of areas	1.6%	18.6%	18.1%	61.7%
Size	707,700,000 acres	62,000,000 acres	5,700,000 acres	3,000,000 acres
Percent of acres	90.9%	8.0%	0.7%	0.4%
Average size	398,929 acres	3,042 acres	286.6 acres	44.3 acres

Source: Adapted from the President's Commission on Americans Outdoors, *Americans Outdoors* (1987).

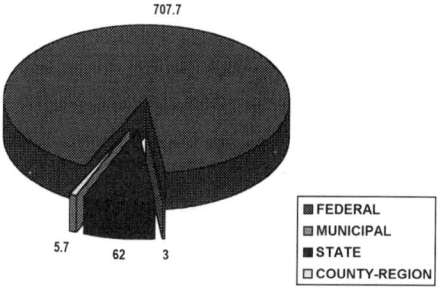

Figure 2.6 Public recreation lands (million acres). (*Source:* President's Commission, 1987)

presents the amount of public recreation acres per 1000 people. Alaska's share of public recreation resources becomes even more dominant when this is done: 804,750 acres per 1000 people. A logarithmic scale was needed to construct Figure 2.9. The West has a much greater acreage per 1000 people (8373) than the Northeast (294), with the North-Central region (672) and the South (587) falling between these two values.

Public Federal Recreation Resource Sector   A dominant factor of the land ownership geography of the United States is the vast acreage controlled by the federal government. Over one-quarter of the country's land area is under control of this sector. In five states, over half of the state area is controlled by the federal government: Nevada (82.3 percent); Alaska (67.8 percent); Utah (63.8 percent); Idaho (62.6 percent); and Oregon (52.42 percent). Other states with exceptionally high percentages of federal ownership are Wyoming (48.7 percent); California (44.45 percent); and Arizona (43.32 percent). It was this dominance of federal ownership that provided fuel for the "sagebrush rebellion" of the 1980s. Four federal agencies manage 94 percent of the overall acreage: the Bureau of Land Management, the Forest Service, the Fish and Wildlife Service, and the National Park Service. These four agencies are the main federal *land-managing agencies.* Most of their recreational lands would be classified as resource-based. Table 2.7 summarizes the land under the control of these agencies for each state. The land of each of these agencies has valuable recreational

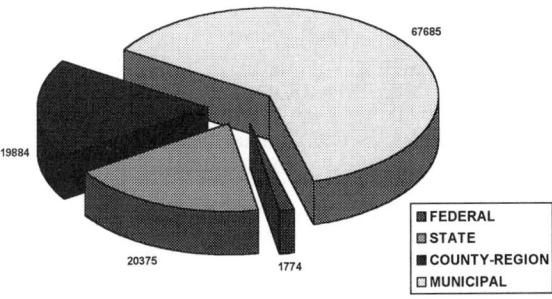

Figure 2.7 Numbers of public recreation areas. (*Source:* President's Commission, 1987)

Table 2.7   Federal Land Acreage, by Agency and by State

State	BLM*	FS*	NPS*	FWS*	Total Federal	Total Acreage of State	Federal % of Total State Area
Alabama	111,003	658,164	2,359	53,309	549,858	32,678,400	1.68%
Alaska	90,437,842	22,219,636	53,727,972	76,385,060	247,802,245	365,481,600	67.80%
Arizona	14,257,623	11,238,606	1,745,104	1,715,329	31,491,365	72,688,000	43.32%
Arkansas	291,166	2,508,594	101,344	233,250	3,421,061	33,599,360	10.18%
California	17,240,275	20,618,936	4,684,864	348,304	44,541,202	100,206,720	44.45%
Colorado	8,309,528	14,461,517	647,963	61,596	22,647,838	66,485,760	34.06%
Connecticut		24		347	13,910	3,135,360	0.44%
Delaware				25,182	30,360	1,265,920	2.40%
D.C.			8,806		10,872	39,040	27.85%
Florida	25,277	1,127,977	2,253,622	531,457	3,355,544	34,721,280	9.66%
Georgia		859,228	40,411	476,039	2,292,379	37,295,360	6.15%
Hawaii		1	245,327	271,517	676,824	4,105,600	16.49%
Idaho	11,859,423	20,437,559	66,167	87,990	33,121,959	52,933,120	62.57%
Illinois	5,003	266,439	12	122,297	493,878	35,795,200	1.38%
Indiana	200	188,365	9,912	8,056	469,794	23,158,400	2.03%
Iowa	1,400		1,663	78,429	159,134	35,860,480	0.44%
Kansas	42	108,175	696	51,560	689,845	52,510,720	1.31%
Kentucky		670,374	71,979	2,060	1,391,208	25,512,320	5.45%
Louisiana	920	600,674	9,651	428,453	745,257	28,867,480	2.58%
Maine		52,860	1	43,207	152,678	19,847,680	0.77%
Maryland			47,177	36,596	196,921	6,319,360	3.12%
Massachusetts			28,146	13,052	82,563	5,034,880	1.64%
Michigan	74,854	2,816,329	631,942	117,048	3,564,777	36,492,160	9.77%
Minnesota	153,409	2,810,181	132,893	491,788	2,386,684	51,205,760	4.66%
Mississippi	58,177	1,149,932	122,495	168,752	1,670,524	30,222,720	5.53%
Missouri	2,575	1,475,132	63,420	57,801	2,030,505	44,248,320	4.59%
Montana	8,066,927	16,806,196	1,084,273	1,197,922	25,862,496	93,271,040	27.73%
Nebraska	7,613	352,004	5,854	166,921	718,604	49,031,680	1.47%
Nevada	47,998,825	5,797,357	1,546,052	2,375,433	57,803,208	70,264,320	82.27%
New Hampshire		720,016	141	1,863	754,411	5,768,960	13.08%
New Jersey			1,691	54,843	135,461	4,813,440	2.81%
New Mexico	12,878,826	9,321,181	346,550	383,343	25,747,308	77,766,400	33.11%
New York		13,232	30,335	25,045	223,283	30,680,960	0.73%
North Carolina		1,231,743	135,479	411,234	1,140,931	31,402,880	3.63%
North Dakota	66,484	1,105,789	71,387	1,330,764	1,964,786	44,452,480	4.42%
Ohio		203,151	16,757	8,433	321,730	26,222,080	1.23%
Oklahoma	2,630	296,639	9,517	153,467	874,004	44,087,680	1.98%
Oregon	15,714,236	15,651,020	194,716	574,546	32,289,422	61,598,720	52.42%
Pennsylvania		513,103	65,513	9,923	640,939	28,804,480	2.23%
Rhode Island			5	1,489	4,686	677,120	0.69%
South Carolina		607,222	25,214	173,995	433,771	19,374,080	2.24%
South Dakota	279,150	1,995,694	263,549	637,455	2,743,763	48,881,920	5.61%
Tennessee		627,696	544,647	110,363	1,322,215	26,727,680	4.95%
Texas		753,354	1,159,191	399,858	2,844,943	168,217,600	1.69%
Utah	21,937,273	8,098,589	2,015,616	102,591	33,611,396	52,696,960	63.78%
Vermont		340,130		6,014	354,917	5,936,640	5.98%
Virginia		1,645,209	244,031	109,147	1,918,344	25,496,320	7.52%
Washington	327,284	9,151,460	1,930,604	192,813	12,373,150	42,693,760	28.98%
West Virginia		1,025,080	39,269	764	1,027,814	15,410,560	6.67%
Wisconsin	160,208	1,516,726	77,412	225,588	3,528,845	35,011,200	10.08%
Wyoming	18,399,710	9,254,728	2,561,543	79,485	30,407,259	62,343,040	48.77%
Other		27,978	14,785	234,734			
U.S. TOTAL	268,976,599	191,324,090	77,028,057	90,766,512	662,158,201	2,271,343,000	29.15%

*BLM, Bureau of Land Management; FS, Forest Service; NPS, National Park Service; FWS, Fish and Wildlife Service.
Source: Bureau of Land Management, Public Land Statistics, 1991 and 1992; Fish and Wildlife Service, Annual Report of Lands under Control of U.S. Fish & Wildlife Service, Sept. 30, 1991; Forest Service, Land Areas of the National Forest System, Sept. 30, 1991; National Park Service, The National Parks: Index 1991.

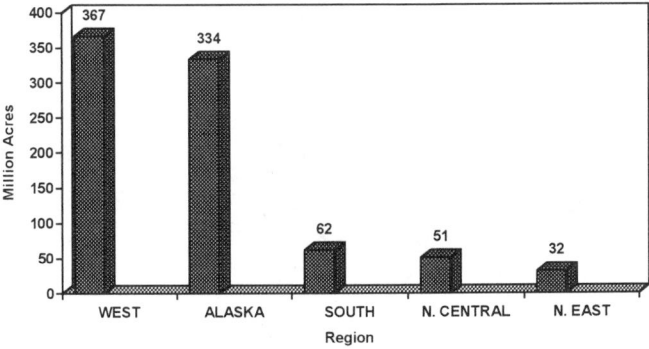

Figure 2.8 Public recreation land by region (local, state, and federal). (*Source:* Adapted from President's Commission, 1987)

opportunities. The recreational potential of the BLM lands is just beginning to be realized. In addition to these, lands of three other federal agencies offer outdoor recreation opportunities: the Army Corps of Engineers, the Bureau of Reclamation, and the Tennessee Valley Authority (TVA). There is one other federal agency whose administration is associated with lands having valuable recreational resources—the Bureau of Indian Affairs (BIA). Native Americans own 90 million acres of land. While the BIA has some administrative responsibility for federal Indian reservations, it is up to the tribe or the pueblo to decide whether their land will be opened for public use.

Of the seven major federal land-managing agencies, the greatest amount of outdoor recreation use takes place on the National Forest System—278,849,000 visitor days, which accounts for 42 percent of the federal total. Surprisingly, the Army Corps of Engineers tallies the second most visitor days (192,166,500, or 29 percent). The National Park Service receives the third most visitor days (111,998,600, or 17 percent). The other 10 percent of visitor days are accounted for by the BLM (44,981,600, or 7 percent), the Bureau of Reclamation (23,365,200, or 4 percent), the Fish and Wildlife Service (4,410,300, or 0.7 percent), and the TVA (1,069,800, or 0.2 percent). Figure 2.10

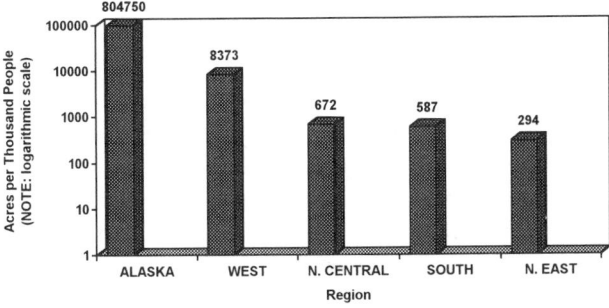

Figure 2.9 Public recreation acres per 1000 people. (*Source:* Adapted from President's Commission, 1987)

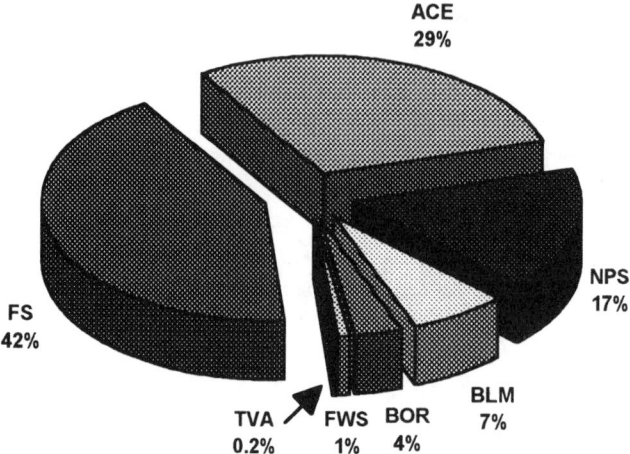

Figure 2.10   Recreation visitor days on federal lands, 1991. (*Source:* National Park Service, *Federal Recreation Fee Report to Congress,* 1991)

presents this recreational use graphically. Except near urban areas, much of the use in federal areas occurs during vacation or retirement leisure.

Bureau of Land Management   The BLM, an agency of the Interior Department, is the largest land manager in the United States, having jurisdiction over 268,976,599 acres. The bulk of these public lands, which are sometimes referred to as national resource lands, are located in the 11 western states and Alaska. The Federal Land Policy and Management Act mandates these lands to be managed under the principles of multiple use and sustained yield. Much of this land is the lower-elevation and drier portions of the western United States; it is the land that was "left over"—not allocated to other purposes such as national parks, national forests, or national wildlife refuges. One-half of this land is classified as grazing districts. The most valuable forested land administered by the BLM is on the western slope of the Cascade Range in Oregon— the larger revested Oregon and California Railroad Lands and the smaller revested Coos Bay Wagon Road Lands. The 12-million-acre California Desert Conservation Area is on BLM land. Since 1978, BLM lands have started to be added to our growing National Wilderness Preservation System. To date, Alaska has been excluded from these allocations because of a directive by former Secretary of the Interior James Watt.

Forest Service   The Forest Service, in the Department of Agriculture, manages the 191,324,000-acre National Forest System. The largest amount of the acreage in the system is classed as national forest (186,995,764 acres) and national grassland (3,848,690 acres). While the majority of the 155 national forests are in the West and Alaska, national forests are well distributed in the Southeast also. The Forest Service manages these lands for multiple use: outdoor recreation, timber, range, watershed, fish and wildlife, and minerals. Included in the National Forest System are 17 congressionally designated national recreation areas, 21 game refuges and national wildlife preserves, two national volcanic monument areas, and one national historic area.

Much of our National Wilderness Preservation System is also in the National Forest System, with 80 percent of the Forest Service's share in the lower 48 states, and much of the resource base of our national trails and wild and scenic rivers is also in the National Forest System. Forty-two percent of all outdoor recreation visitor days are counted in the National Forest System. Most of the major alpine ski areas in the United States are located either totally or partially on national forest land. Twenty-five percent of the recreational use of the national forests occurs in one state—California.

Fish and Wildlife Service   The Fish and Wildlife Service, in the Interior Department, manages the 90,400,000-acre National Wildlife Refuge System, which has over 500 units. The system includes wildlife refuges, wildlife ranges, game ranges, wildlife management areas, and waterfowl production areas. The management focuses on protection of wildlife habitat. The Refuge Recreation Act of 1962 authorizes recreational use when it does not interfere with a refuge's primary purpose. Hunting is permitted if it is compatible with the major purpose for which the refuge was established. Most of the recreational use of the system involves wildlife observation, with scenic road loops and observation towers along their route. There are some day-use areas with picnic tables and boat launches that allow picnicking and fishing. Developed interpretive centers are a focal point of some refuges. A large percentage of our National Wilderness Preservation System is located in these lands, 90 percent of which is in Alaska. The system was greatly enlarged by the Alaska National Interest Lands Conservation Act in 1980. Over half of the acreage of the system is in Alaska; two refuges, the Arctic and Yukon Delta, are just under 20 million acres each. Although the total visitor days of 4,410,300 in 1990 accounted for less than 1 percent of the federal total, in some areas of the United States the wildlife refuges are one of the main recreation resources available for public use.

National Park Service   The National Park Service, in the Interior Department, manages the 357 units occupying 80,155,984 acres known as the National Park System, which is the most varied of all the federal land systems. It includes the great national parks like Grand Canyon, Yellowstone, and Yosemite; national monuments, which may have either natural or cultural value; numerous historic and prehistoric sites; and national recreation areas in urban as well as extraurban areas. Figure 2.11 shows the view from Cape Royal on the north rim of Grand Canyon National Park. The National Park Service Act of 1916 mandated that the lands are to be managed "to conserve the scenery and the natural and the historic objects therein and to provide for the enjoyment of the same in such a manner and by such means as will leave them unimpaired for future generations." The mandate to preserve but still allow use is difficult to implement. Although the National Park System was not established expressly for recreation, recreation and tourism are the chief reasons most people, many of them foreign tourists, visit the system today. Only at the federal level could resources of such outstanding national significance be protected. Important portions of our protected amenity resources are located within the national parks, including portions of the Wild and Scenic Rivers System, the National Trails System, and the National Wilderness Preservation System. The National Park Service administers more of our National Wilderness Preservation System than any other agency, and 85

Figure 2.11   Tourists from Germany viewing the scenery from Cape Royal on the north rim of Grand Canyon National Park.

percent of the National Park Wilderness acreage is in Alaska. The National Park System accounts for 17 percent of the recreation visitor days on federal lands, which puts it in third place behind the Forest Service and Army Corps of Engineers.

Army Corps of Engineers   The Army Corps of Engineers, in the Defense Department, manages 10 million acres of lands and waters at 460 hydropower dams, navigation projects, and flood-control projects. The corps has no explicit recreational mandate, but it provides recreation at the reservoirs it manages under provisions of the Flood Control Act of 1944, which allows the corps to operate recreational facilities at its projects, and the Federal Water Project Recreation Act of 1965. Recreation accounts for the greatest dollar value of benefits in cost-benefit analyses of potential projects. Many of these water development projects (reservoirs) are located close to major population centers in the Northeast and Great Plains and serve as the major recreational resource for a large number of Americans. It is for this reason that the Army Corps of Engineers accounts for the second greatest number of recreation visitor days of any federal agency—192,166,500, or 29 percent.

Bureau of Reclamation   The Bureau of Reclamation, in the Department of the Interior, administers 4,707,340 acres of land and 1,707,450 acres of water for recreation around its 330 dams and reservoirs in the 17 westernmost states. These reservoirs, with a combined shoreline of 12,994 miles, are fairly widespread westward from the area between Texas and North Dakota. The 1902 Reclamation Act authorized the constructions of these reservoirs. There is no legislation that gives the agency *comprehensive* recreational authority, so it manages its land and water under a combination of acts: the Reclamation Act, the Federal Water Project Recreation Act of 1965, and the Fish and Wildlife Coordination Act of 1946. During the early years of reclamation, recreation was not considered important in planning these water projects. Many of the dams and reservoirs, however, became major recreational attractions. Since 1936,

when the bureau entered into agreements with the National Park Service to provide recreational facilities at Hoover Dam's Lake Mead and Grand Coulee Dam's Roosevelt Lake, the bureau has made agreements for transferring responsibility for managing recreation areas to other federal agencies or to state, county, or municipal governments or to water-user organizations. One-third of these recreation areas are managed by state agencies. Four percent of the visitor days at federal recreation areas were counted at bureau facilities.

Tennessee Valley Authority   The TVA manages 1 million acres of lands and waters around its hydropower, flood-control, and navigation dams and reservoirs in the Southeast. The Tennessee Valley Authority Act of 1933 was created to plan the entire multiple-use development of an eight-state region of 50,000 square miles that encompassed the drainage basin of the Tennessee River. Although the original legislation made no specific reference to recreation, TVA planners, recognizing early the reservoirs' potential for recreation, were able to acquire adjacent lands to provide access for recreation. Eighteen major dams with over 11,000 miles of shoreline serve as the sites for 44 TVA-administered recreation sites. Next to the reservoirs there also exists over 500 access points, 20 state parks, and over 100 county and municipal parks. The TVA has transferred over 100,000 acres to the National Park Service, the Forest Service, and the Fish and Wildlife Service. There are a large number of private recreation businesses and over 20,000 privately owned leisure homes on the reservoir shorelines. Lands have been sold or leased to private clubs and to service organizations such as the Boy Scouts and the YMCA. The TVA administers the 170,000-acre Land Between the Lakes National Recreation Demonstration Area. This area between Lake Barkley (an Army Corps of Engineers project on the Cumberland River) and Kentucky Lake on the Tennessee River forms the focal point of a major tourist industry based on these human-made lakes. Although the TVA's recreational facilities account for only a fraction of 1 percent of the total federal recreation visitor days, it is regionally a very important recreational resource.

Bureau of Indian Affairs   The BIA jointly administers with the Native American tribes over 52 million acres of land. This is, in a sense, private land, since the land is held in trust or has restricted status. There are also state reservations and other lands owned by Native Americans that add up to 90 million acres of land (President's Commission on Americans Outdoors, 1987). These lands are regarded as private lands, and decisions to develop public recreation facilities rest exclusively with the tribe or pueblo. The opening of Indian Lands for tourism and public access is a relatively recent phenomena. The President's Commission on Americans Outdoors (1987) estimated that these Indian lands support approximately 10.5 million recreation days a year, including 8.5 million days of public use. Most of this recreation is water-based, especially fishing. Many Native American tribes and pueblos are now recognizing the economic benefits of tourism and recreation and are actively developing their resources for such use.

The President's Commission on Americans Outdoors (1987, 124) has concluded:

> The recreation potential of our federal lands, which encompasses nearly a third of our nation's land base, is not fully realized. We must search for ways to resolve competing demands on our public lands, to more effectively utilize and manage them for the full spectrum of uses for which they are capable of supporting. Rec-

reation does not have to conflict with the traditional uses of multiple use lands. The American people tell us that management of the public estate should reflect the high premium which Americans give to outdoor recreation.

Public State Recreation Resource Sector   States administer 61.8 million acres of state parks and recreation areas, forests, and wildlife areas. These include 5300 state parks, 721 state forests, and 7400 wildlife areas, as well as a variety of natural, historic, and cultural areas and river-and-reservoir recreation sites. There are 10 million acres in these park systems. The visitation to state parks and related areas in 1991 was 639,735,000 recreation visits; 90 percent of this was day use. State parks are usually located in rural areas, and most have developed campgrounds and other facilities (see, for example, Figure 2.12). Caution must be exercised when comparing the numbers of state parks in one state against another. For example, Oregon's 250 state parks comprise much less acreage than Michigan's 100, which not only are larger but also more developed with large campgrounds. Many of Oregon's parks are roadside picnic areas administered by the state highway department. While 10 percent of the states have some parks that contain rather elaborate resort hotels or lodges, most of the parks offer primarily basic campgrounds. Kentucky has the best-developed state park system that contains elaborate state resort parks.

Thirty-nine states have their own forest systems totaling 20 million acres. Most of these are quite small, with only 12 systems exceeding 200,000 acres. The largest state forest systems are in Michigan, Idaho, Minnesota, Pennsylvania, Arizona, Alaska, and Wisconsin. The state forests are managed for multiple-use purposes, which includes recreation, just like the national forests. The recreational use of most state forest systems tends to be distributed more evenly during the year than that at state parks. Forty-six states have designated fish and game areas totaling 19.9 million acres, many of which are larger than the average state park system. It is especially for hunting and fishing that recreational use is made of these areas, but activities

Figure 2.12   The campground at Blackhawk Lake State Park in western Iowa.

such as hiking, wildlife observation, and canoeing also occur, dependent on the degree of accessibility and development (President's Commission on Americans Outdoors, 1987).

These state recreation lands serve a purpose midway between the generally more remote federal lands and the readily accessible municipal and county areas. They serve as the ideal recreational outlet for people who desire a more natural setting than is available in local areas but do not demand unmodified primitive surroundings or cannot afford the time or expense of a longer visit to remote federal lands. Most of these state recreation areas would be classified as intermediate. The usual recreational activities include picnicking, camping, hiking, walking, bicycling, scenic drives, beach swimming, sailing, canoeing, boating, fishing, hunting, and nature study. The use of many of these state areas can be quite high, especially when large urban areas are nearby.

Public Local and Regional Recreation Resource Sector   Providing parks and recreational facilities has been an accepted function of local governments for over a century. The first large area to be acquired for park purposes by a municipality was New York City's Central Park in 1853. Central Park allows for a sylvan outdoor recreation setting in the heart of Manhattan Island (Figure 2.13). Essex County, N.J., was the first county to purchase a park site, in 1895. As municipal park systems expanded, this led to the development of parkways and the acquisition of municipally owned and administered parks outside of cities such as Denver and Phoenix. County and regional or district park systems are now of great importance in more densely populated portions of the United States. These local recreation lands affect more people to a greater degree than recreational opportunities provided by any other type of land. Since there is no practical way of determining attendance, no accurate records of use exist. It is estimated that the recreational use of these local

Figure 2.13 Central Park provides open space in the midst of New York City.

lands is probably close to 3 billion visits per year, which is greater than use on the combined sum of federal and state public lands. These areas are important because they are located near concentrations of people and so are readily available for daily leisure. Classified as user-oriented, these local areas are vital units of open space in crowded urban areas. These areas provide the only contact with the outdoors for many Americans who lack either the time, money, or experience necessary to pursue more distant intermediate or resource-based recreational resources.

Figures 2.6 and 2.7 showed that municipal, county, and regional parks and forests account for the largest number of recreation sites but a much smaller number of acres in the public sectors. Small parks comprise many of the sites in urban areas, with 67,685 municipal parks totaling more than 3 million acres. Counties administer over 17,000 recreation areas of various types covering 5.1 million acres. These municipal and county parks account for a large portion of America's daily recreation, close to home. While county parks are distributed throughout the nation, county forests are found only in Illinois, Wisconsin, Minnesota, and Alaska. There are 2780 regional park, forest, and recreation areas on 500,000 acres. The regional authorities that administer these recreational facilities often include more than one county and sometimes as many as five counties, as in the Huron-Clinton Metropark Authority in the Detroit urban area. These multicounty regional authorities have a special influence on maintaining open space under the pressures of urban growth: They often manage large areas on the urban fringe, and they focus on protection of key regional resources, such as river valleys or forested areas (President's Commission Americans Outdoors, 1987).

Private Recreation Resource Sectors

We know less about the private sector than any other sector in outdoor recreation. Private lands constitute nearly two-thirds of our nation's land base and host many types of outdoor recreation land use. As the demand for outdoor recreation grows, the private sector will increasingly help meet this demand. It is estimated that over 50 percent of this private land has some outdoor recreation potential, and most of this is available to the public under certain circumstances. Yet many landowners have concerns, ranging from liability to vandalism and littering, that prevent them from opening their lands to the public for recreational use. Ownerships of small farms and forests are increasingly acquired for personal recreation space, and these owners are less inclined to open their lands to other people. Moreover, these smaller tracts of land often preclude certain types of recreation. The future availability of private lands for outdoor recreation is difficult to determine because of the lack of consistent information for determining these trends.

There are several pressures on using private lands for recreation. First of all, large portions of these lands are located near population centers, causing people to seek them out. Conversely, most public lands in the United States are located far from where people live. This makes private lands particularly important in certain regions of the country, notably the East and South. Second, some private lands provide the only access to public lands. Third, the overcrowding and overuse at many public areas causes people to seek out private land. Fourth, private lands are often the most logical sites for the more elaborate recreational facilities, such as hotels, trailer parks,

and highly developed campgrounds. The development of these more elaborate facilities on private land helps to minimize the disturbance of high-quality public land. The cost of these more elaborate facilities is appropriately borne by their patrons, which frees public funds for investment in more basic areas. Fifth, present budget limitations at the federal, state, and local levels make dramatic increases in public recreation land holdings unlikely.

Although a healthy arrangement can be worked out between the role of the private sector and the public sector, overdevelopment at certain private sites can detract from scenic public land resources. Such is the case near the entrance to Zion National Park, where the private sector is proposing to install a huge movie screen that will mar the scenic beauty first viewed when approaching the park. Both public and private planners and administrators now recognize the need to consider the private-sector contribution in developing responsive recreational facilities in order to avoid unnecessary duplication, unfair competition, and imbalance between supply and demand.

The availability of private lands, recreational facilities, and services is a major factor in determining actual recreational opportunity. The private sector has the ability to respond to the diverse recreational demands of the public rapidly, and it performs many services that make public lands accessible and more enjoyable to the public. We know that the private lands and facilities are an important and integral part of the overall supply of outdoor recreation resources, but we do not know the extent of private recreation opportunities. The rapidly changing state of the private recreation supply makes a comprehensive inventory of private areas and services difficult.

A simple twofold division of the private sector's involvement in outdoor recreation is presented here: noncommercial and commercial. The primary difference between the two sectors is the profit motive. Most *commercial recreation* enterprises will cease to operate if sufficient profit is not generated. There are some exceptions to this generalization, such as the case when tax advantages can make a money-losing operation an asset. *Noncommercial recreation* activities and ventures are generally provided either for personal or group enjoyment and/or education. There are some recreational land uses that can straddle the fence between these two categories. Such an example would be a privately owned leisure home. Owners often use one of three management schemes for their leisure homes: (1) using it exclusively for personal family recreation, (2) renting it out for a portion of the year to generate just enough revenue to cover the actual costs of ownership; and (3) renting it for a long-enough period during the year to turn a profit (an option that also include using it for some personal recreation). Such a recreational land use could thus be considered either noncommercial or commercial, depending on the motive of the owner. Table 2.8 presents a classification system that lists the principal private noncommercial and commercial recreation resources.

Private Noncommercial Recreation Resource Sector   Many Americans own second, or leisure, homes that are the focus of their outdoor recreation. Leisure homes take many forms. They may be shoreline homes on the ocean or lakes, a hunting cabin in the mountains, or a chalet at a ski resort. Figure 2.14 illustrates a private leisure home (locally called a camp) in New York's Adirondack Mountains. Leisure

Table 2.8   Classification of Private Recreation Resources

Private Noncommercial	Private Commercial
Personal resources	Participating sport facilities
Second home (leisure home)	Amusement parks
Dual-purpose home	Traditional parks
Farms and ranches	Theme parks
Other personal resources	Stadiums and Racetracks
Private organization resources	Marinas
Private recreation organizations	Camps, hotels, resorts
Environmental interest groups	Campgrounds
Quasi-public organization resources	Resorts (self-contained)
Youth-oriented organizations	Cruise ships
Social welfare organizations	Farms and ranches
Preservation organizations	Camps and schools
Industrial resources	Exhibits, shows, and tours
Resources used by general public	Commodities and Delivery Systems
Resources for employees	Commodities
	Delivery systems

Source: Modified from Chubb and Chubb, *One Third of Our Time?* (1981).

homes in the form of condominiums have appeared in many areas of the country, especially since the advent of time sharing. The small number of Americans fortunate enough to live on large parcels of land, such as farms and ranches, use these for their personal recreation. Increasingly, more families have purchased relatively small tracts of land outside of the cities where they locate their residence and commute to work. These holdings of typically 50 to 100 acres are used for personal recreation since they might contain a pond for fishing, hiking and ski trails, ATV trails, or wildlife habitat.

Private recreation organizations are a focal point of some people's outdoor recreation. These may include sportsperson clubs (such as hunting and fishing clubs),

Figure 2.14   A private lakeside leisure home in Franklin County, in New York's Adirondack Mountains.

boat or vehicle clubs, hiking or travel clubs, and sports (such as tennis) or athletic clubs. Some of these organizations are environmental interest groups that sponsor outings and nature walks. It is a common practice for some sportsperson clubs to rent land from the commercial forest industry for their exclusive private interest, and in some cases they own the land outright.

Quasi-public organization resources include youth-oriented organizations, social welfare organizations, and preservation organizations. They may be group- or program-oriented, such as the Scouts, or 4-H or facility-based, such as Y's, Boys' Clubs, or hostels. Some of the Scout camps located around the country are quite large and provide a resource-based experience for the users. Social welfare organizations can have camping organizations and resident camps. Preservation organizations, such as The Nature Conservancy and the Land Trust Exchange, have the ability to act quickly to protect important recreation and wildlife habitat lands. Five hundred local land trusts have been established in the last decade. Organizations such as The Nature Conservancy sometimes establish nature trails on their property. Many times they resell the land they acquire to the public sector.

Industrial resources may be available for use by the general public or for the exclusive use of their employees. As part of their public relations programs, power companies and some timber companies open their land free of charge to the public. These facilities include picnic areas, campgrounds, and boat-launching ramps. Industrial tours are major attractions, although many of these tend to be indoors. Powerline rights-of-way are made available for ATVs in the warm season and for snowmobiles in places where there is a snow season. Some industrial companies offer as a fringe benefit to their employees developed outdoor recreation facilities such as sports fields, campgrounds, picnic areas, swimming areas, or golf courses.

Private Commercial Recreation Resource Sector   Many types of private commercial enterprises forming the basis of the recreation and tourist industry will not be discussed in this book, although they are important to the total recreation experience. These include shopping facilities and food and drink services. It is the outdoor recreation facilities that will be the focus of this section. As pointed out earlier, it is sometimes difficult to identify the dividing line between indoor and outdoor recreation. Many a tourist or recreationist who has driven or hiked to the height of Glacier Point in Yosemite National Park appreciates the small concession stand located there, which provides a tasty drink or ice cream bar (for a fee of course).

Participatory sports facilities include ski areas (both alpine and cross country), golf courses, and shooting preserves. It is particularly for these types of facilities that the private sector is a major provider. Six hundred privately operated ski areas, some located on leased public land (primarily the national forests), provide almost all of the downhill skiing opportunities in the nation. The number of commercial private cross-country ski areas is rapidly growing; the largest in the United States is Royal Gorge, near Donner Summit in California's Sierra Nevada Mountains. The National Golf Foundation reports 4789 private golf courses, which makes the private sector a major provider of this activity. In New York State there are 703 regulation golf courses, 43.4 percent of them being commercial and another 41.1 percent private clubs. Traditional amusement parks are still alive and well in some parts of the United States, but the greatest growth of amusement parks in the last few decades has been

the theme type. Coney Island in New York City is the most famous of these traditional amusement parks. Many of the large traditional amusement parks have disappeared over the years. In the author's home city—St. Louis, Mo.—the famous Forest Park Highlands burned to the ground and was not replaced, and the Westlakes and Chain-of-Rocks amusement parks were lost to urban expansion for homes, businesses, and highways. The first megatheme park was Disneyland, which opened at Anaheim, Calif., in 1955. The theme amusement parks are built close to, or between, major urban centers. They are usually located on or very close to the interstate highway system. Most major league baseball and professional football stadiums are outdoors, or at least have a removable roof. Probably the two most famous racetracks are the Indianapolis Motor Speedway and Churchill Downs, but virtually every fairground across the country has a racetrack where a variety of outdoor activities are held.

Marina and associated boating facilities are largely provided by the private commercial sector. In New York State, 89 percent of the 281 places with boat moorings are either at private clubs or commercial sites. These private facilities account for 84 percent of the 10,947 moorings in New York. Approximately the same percentages hold for places in New York with boat docks: 88 percent of the 1278 places with docks and 86 percent of the 71,315 dock slips are either private clubs or commercial.

Camps and hotels form a group of commercial private recreation facilities in which the participant stays overnight at a recreational resource. About 70 percent of the available campsites in the United States are found on 10,000 private campgrounds. Hotels, motels, and cabins provide overnight accommodations for recreationists who find camping not to their liking—or who find national park campgrounds filled. The Grand Canyon Lodge is operated by private concessioners and is located on the very edge of the North Rim of the Grand Canyon. Chubb and Chubb (1981) have identified four types of *self-contained resorts:* warm-weather recreation; winter sports; health and beauty; and sports instruction and practice. Caneel Bay Plantation on the island of St. John in the U.S. Virgin Islands is one of the finest self-contained resorts in the Caribbean. The complex of hotels and other tourist facilities at Waikiki Beach is one of the world's most famous warm-weather attractions (Figure 2.15). Two Rocky Mountain ski resorts are world-famous: Aspen arose in an already-existing mining town, and Vail was built from the ground up in a former sheep-grazing pasture in a high mountain valley. At Vail the ski slopes, lifts, and restaurants are built on the White River National Forest under permit from the Forest Service. The elegant Two Elk Restaurant on the ridge between the Northeast Bowl and China Bowl at Vail is the finest in U.S. ski country; the view of the Gore Range to the north and the Mountain of the Holy Cross to the south is awesome.

The cruise-ship industry has shown phenomenal growth during the last decade. Most of the facilities of a large resort are now found aboard cruise ships. Most Americans take their cruises in the Caribbean, but short day cruises to the Bahamas from ports such as Miami and Fort Lauderdale are growing in popularity. Cruises through the Inside Passage of British Columbia and Alaska have long been favorites. Cruises departing from San Diego to the west coast of Mexico have become extremely popular in recent years. Sternwheeler ships, such as the elaborate Mississippi Queen, even provide cruises on the Mississippi River.

Farms and ranches also contribute recreational opportunities. There are over 500 vacation farms in the United States, most of which are in the Northeast. Some of

Figure 2.15 Tourist development along Waikiki Beach in Honolulu, Hawaii as seen from Diamondhead Crater.

these farms accept only a few guests at a time and the guests can take part in the farm work or relax at their leisure. There are two types of ranches that cater to recreationists. The first is an actual working ranch, which operates similarly to a vacation farm. The second is a guest ranch, which is more like a resort than an actual working ranch. These guest ranches especially cater to fishing and hunting activities, and on many the facilities are quite elaborate.

Children's camps are probably the best-known type of camps and schools. Very few day camps are operated on a commercial basis; most are run by church or religious organizations. Commercial residential camps are especially common in the Northeast. Outdoor recreation activities usually include swimming, canoeing, boating, sailing, fishing, horseback riding, hiking, and sports. Special camps have resources and programs similar to residential camps but cater to children with special needs. Travel camps can provide long distance canoe, horse, backpack, or bicycle trips. In recent years, more camps for adults have been established.

Many Americans are attracted to commercial exhibits, shows, and tours. Traveling carnivals are a prominent feature of rural America in the warmer months. Cave tours are major attractions in certain sections of the country, such as Missouri. Private boat tours and plane tours allow many Americans to view sights that would not be available without them. Two of the most famous tours in the United States are the boat tour to the base of Niagara Falls and plane or helicopter rides over the Grand Canyon. Strategically placed towers, such as the tower in Hot Springs National Park, allow, for a fee, magnificent views.

The final classification of private commercial recreation resources is commodities and delivery systems. The commodities needed to partake in outdoor recreation are sometimes very expensive. Examples of commodities are power boats, ATVs, snowmobiles, canoes, rifles and shotguns, fishing rods, backpacking equipment, mountain bikes, and ski equipment. Many outdoor recreation activities could not be undertaken

without this equipment, the sum of production of which forms a major industry in the United States and the world. Many Americans depend on delivery systems to provide the commodities since for many activities they are too expensive to buy. Canoes can be rented to float down Ozark National Scenic Riverways, and power boats can be rented to travel on Lake Powell behind Glen Canyon Dam (Arizona) to Rainbow Bridge National Monument and other points on the reservoir. Charter flights can be booked to fly into the interior of Alaska. And guided or package tours have shown tremendous growth in popularity in recent years. In New York's Adirondack Mountains outfitters will for a charge provide a guide, a canoe, camping equipment, clothing, and food for a weekend or a week. Many ways of experiencing the Grand Canyon also depend on commercial services: due to a limited number of openings, one must pay for a commercial raft tour down the Colorado River in Grand Canyon National Park.

References

Chubb, Michael, and Holly R. Chubb. *One Third of Our Time?* New York: John Wiley & Sons, 1981.

Clawson, Marion. "The Crisis in Outdoor Recreation." *American Forests,* 1959.

Cordell, H. Ken, John C. Bergstrom, Lawrence A. Hartman, and Donald B. K. English. *An Analysis of the Outdoor Recreation and Wilderness Situation in the United States 1989–2040. A Technical Document Supporting the 1989 USDA Forest Service RPA Assessment.* General Technical Report RM-189. Fort Collins, Colo.: Rocky Mountain Forest and Range Experiment Station, Forest Service, USDA, 1990.

Marsh, George P. *Man and Nature: or Physical Geography as Modified by Human Action.* New York: Charles Scribner, 1864.

National Park Service. *Federal Recreation Fee Report to Congress 1991* (and earlier years). Washington, D.C.: U.S. Department of the Interior, National Park Service.

Outdoor Recreation Resources Review Commission. *Outdoor Recreation for America.* Washington, D.C.: U.S. Government Printing Office, 1962.

Pinchot, Gifford. *Breaking New Ground.* New York: Harcourt, Brace and Company, 1947, p. 505.

Public Land Law Review Commission. *One Third of the Nation's Land.* Washington, DC: U.S. Government Printing Office, 1970.

Powell, John Wesley. *Report on the Lands of the Arid Region of the U.S.* Cambridge: Belknap Press of Harvard University Press, 1962 (republished from 1879 original version).

President's Commission on Americans Outdoors. *Americans Outdoors: The Legacy, the Challenge.* Washington, D.C.: Island Press, 1987.

Public Land Law Review Commission. *One-Third of the Nation's Land.* Washington, D.C.: U.S. Government Printing Office, 1970.

## CHAPTER 3

National Parks: Concept and System

. . . Preserved in their pristine beauty and wildness, in a magnificent park, where the world could see for ages to come, the native Indian in his classic attire, gallop his wild horse amid the fleeting herds of elks and buffaloes. What a specimen for America to preserve for her refined citizens and the world, in future ages. A nation's park, containing man and beast, in all the wild and freshness of their nature's beauty.

George Catlin (1833)

EARLY PARKS

The national park idea is credited to the artist George Catlin, who was best known for his paintings of American Indians. The above-captioned statement, published in the *New York Daily Commercial Advertiser* in 1833, was based on Catlin's observations during a trip to the Dakota country in 1832 and reflected a change from negative attitudes toward nature. Four decades would pass before the world's first national park was established at Yellowstone. The oldest nonurban area in our present National Park System was set aside as the Hot Springs Reservation in 1832, but not until 1921 would it become classified as a national park. Some claim that the Yosemite Grant, which deeded the main valley and Mariposa Big Trees Grove to the state of California in 1864, constituted our first national park, but it was not until 1890 that Yosemite was established as a national park and not until 1906 that the federal government accepted the lands returned from the state of California.

On March 1, 1872, President Ulysses S. Grant signed into law an act that established **Yellowstone National Park** in the territories of Montana and Wyoming. The *Yellowstone Act* withdrew more than 1 million acres of the public domain from settlement, occupancy, or sale to be "dedicated and set apart as a public park or pleasuring-ground for the benefit and enjoyment of the people." The park was placed under the exclusive control of the Secretary of the Interior, who was charged to "provide for the preservation, from injury or despoilation, [*sic*] of all timber, mineral deposits, natural curiosities, or wonders within said park, and their retention in their natural condition." He was also charged with preventing the "wanton destruction and commercial taking of fish and game." The founding of Yellowstone National

Park gave a dramatic new meaning to the term *national park* and began a worldwide national park movement. Today, there are over 2000 national parks or equivalent preserves in 120 nations of the world, and it all started at Yellowstone.

The first white man who attempted to make the world aware of the geological wonders of Yellowstone was John Colter. A member of the Lewis and Clark expedition in 1805 and 1806, Colter explored Yellowstone in 1807 and 1808. He told the outside world of Yellowstone's geothermal activity (Figure 3.1), and the area became known as "Colter's Hell." Significant explorations of the region did not occur until 1869–1871, when a group of Montana Territory citizens led by David Folsom, Henry Washburn, Nathaniel Langford, and Ferdinand Hayden suggested that Yellowstone should be reserved for public use rather than allowing it to fall into private hands. The suggestion of a national park is credited to a Helena, Mont., lawyer named Cornelius Hedges. This event allegedly occurred at a campfire at the junction of the Firehole and Gibbons River. The park idea received influential support from the Northern Pacific Railroad, whose projected main line through Montana would benefit from a major tourist destination. The land was in the public domain, so anyone could make a claim in accordance with the law and eventually gain ownership. At this time, the main park supporters were from Montana, which, like Wyoming, was still a territory. The Yellowstone bill encountered some opposition from congressmen who

Figure 3.1   The Old Faithful Geyser is the best-known geothermal feature at Yellowstone National Park.

questioned such a large reservation, but it did pass Congress, and the park became a reality when President Grant signed the bill into law.

Once Yellowstone was established, the precedent was now set to create other natural reserves under federal jurisdiction. By the turn of the century national parks were established at Sequoia (1890), General Grant (1890; made part of King's Canyon National Park in 1940), and Yosemite (1890) all in California, and Mt. Rainier (1899) in Washington. At the time these early parks were being considered for national park status, a separate movement to preserve prehistoric cliff dwellings, pueblo ruins, and early missions was forming. Congress took a step in this direction in 1889 by authorizing the president to reserve from settlement or sale the land in Arizona containing the Casa Grande Ruins; three years later it was designated as Casa Grande Ruins Reservation by President Harrison and redesignated a national monument in 1918. The ruins remained under the Department of Interior's General Land Office until 1918, when it was reassigned to the National Park Service (Figure 3.2). Other early national parks created during the "first wave" of the conservation movement were Crater Lake (Oregon, 1902); Wind Cave (South Dakota, 1903); Sullys Hill (North Dakota, 1904); Platt (Oklahoma, 1906); and Mesa Verde (Colorado, 1906). Sullys Hill was declassified as a national park in 1931 and today is a unit in our National Wildlife Refuge System. Sulphur Springs Reservation, created in 1902 around 32 mineral springs, was enlarged in 1904 and renamed Platt National Park in 1906. In 1976, the 500-acre Platt National Park was incorporated into the new Chickasaw Nation National Recreation Area. Mesa Verde was our first national park designated as an archaeological site.

The move to protect prehistoric archaeological sites in the Southwest led to the passage of the *Antiquities Act,* signed into law by President Theodore Roosevelt on June 8, 1906. This act gave Presidents blanket authority to proclaim and reserve "historic landmarks, historic and prehistoric structures, and other objects of historic or

Figure 3.2 Casa Grande Ruins National Monument (Arizona) was one of the first units set aside for preservation (1889) in what became later known as the U.S. National Park System in 1916.

scientific interest" on lands owned by the United States as national monuments. An extremely significant piece of legislation, the Antiquities Act was used to protect natural features as well as cultural features. Before he left office in 1909, President Roosevelt proclaimed a total of 18 national monuments—six cultural and 12 natural. Our first national monument, Devils Tower (Wyoming, 1906), is a massive 867-foot shaft of volcanic origin. Three other national monuments were proclaimed in 1906: El Morro (New Mexico), Montezuma Castle, and Petrified Forest (both in Arizona). Petrified Forest National Monument was redesignated a national park in 1962. Between 1906 and 1978, 12 Presidents used the Antiquities Act to proclaim 99 national monuments, of which 38 were mostly historic or prehistoric and 61 were natural. By 1990, 52 of them were still designated national monuments. Of the others, 28 became or contributed to 25 national parks or preserves, four became national historical parks, one was labeled a national battlefield and one a national historic site, two were incorporated into a national parkway, and 11 were abolished. *Nearly a quarter of today's National Park System can trace its origin to the Antiquities Act.* National monuments were proclaimed on lands administered by the Departments of Agriculture and War, as well as the Interior, remaining under their jurisdiction until 1933, except where Congress made it a national park. Such was the case for Grand Canyon National Monument, proclaimed in 1908, which remained under the Agriculture Department until it was incorporated into a larger Grand Canyon National Park in 1919 and transferred to the Interior Department. Similarly, Lassen Peak and Cinder Cone National Monuments, proclaimed under Forest Service jurisdiction, were transferred to the Interior in 1916, when Lassen Volcanic National Park was established.

Other early National Monuments are Chaco Canyon (New Mexico, 1907), Muir Woods and Pinnacles (both in California, 1908), Natural Bridges (Utah, 1908), Lewis and Clark Cavern (Montana, 1908; abolished 1937), Tumacacori (Arizona, 1908; incorporated into Tumacacori National Historical Park in 1990), Navaho (Arizona, 1909), Mukuntuweap (Utah, 1909; incorporated into Zion National Park in 1919), Shoshone Cave (Wyoming, 1909; abolished 1954), Gran Quivira (New Mexico, 1909; incorporated into Salinas National Monument in 1980), Sitka (Alaska, 1910; redesignated a national historical park in 1972), Rainbow Bridge (Utah, 1910), Colorado (Colorado, 1911), Papago Saguaro (Arizona, 1914; abolished 1930), Dinosaur (Colorado and Utah, 1915), Sieur de Monts (Maine, 1916; incorporated into Lafayette National Park in 1919; redesignated Acadia National Park in 1929), and Capulin Mountain (New Mexico, 1916; redesignated Capulin Volcano in 1987).

National parks designated between 1907 and 1916 included Glacier (Montana, 1910), Rocky Mountain (Colorado, 1915), Hawaii (Hawaii, 1916; split into Haleakala National Park and Hawaii National Park in 1960; Hawaii National Park was redesignated Hawaiian Volcanoes National Park in 1961), and Lassen (California, 1916; incorporated in 1907 into Cinder Cone and Lassen Peak National Monuments from the Agriculture Department).

NATIONAL PARK SERVICE ACT

By August 25, 1916, the Department of the Interior had under its control 14 national parks, 21 national monuments, the Hot Springs Reservation, and the Casa Grande Reservation. This collection of areas was not yet a true park system, due to the lack

of any systematic management: There were no provisions for financial support, administration, or protection, and the relationships between the various parks were disjointed. This lack of a cohesive administrative authority threatened to undermine the concept on which the parks had been founded. The Army was called on to protect Yellowstone and the California parks. Law enforcement is still a major function of Park Service Rangers (Figure 3.3). The Army Corps of Engineers built the basic highway system of Yellowstone at this time. Most of the national monuments received minimal care. The Forest Service administered parks such as Mt. Rainier. A major threat to the parks at this time was the conservationists of the utilitarian school, who championed the construction of dams for water supplies, irrigation, and power production. The two major schools of conservation—utilitarian and preservation—came to blows over the construction of a dam in the Grand Canyon of the Tuolumne River in Yosemite National Park. John Muir was a major spokesperson for the preservationists. This dam was sought by the City of San Francisco for a water-supply source. Congress approved in 1913 what historian John Ise later called "the worst disaster ever to come to any national park." The utilitarianists won, and the Hetch Hetchy Dam was constructed on the Tuolumne River in Yosemite National Park.

The "rape of Hetch Hetchy," as the preservationists called it, pointed out the institutional weakness of the park movement. The need for an organization to operate the parks and advocate for their interest was now clear. The first suggestion for a national parks bureau was made by Dr. Horace McFarland (president of the American Civic Association) and Governor Charles Evans Hughes (governor of New York) during the 1908 White House Conservation Conference. In 1912, President Taft sent a message to Congress recommending the establishment of a national parks bureau. Although Congress failed to take action on the President's suggestion, the idea continued to ripen. On June 21, 1915, *Stephen T. Mather* was sworn in as Assistant Sec-

Figure 3.3 Law-enforcement activities are a major function of National Park Service Rangers. Shown is a ranger at the Madison Campground at Yellowstone National Park.

retary to the Secretary of the Interior, Franklin Lane. Mather, a successful Chicago business person, assumed responsibility for administering the national parks. *Horace Albright* became Mather's top aide. Mather and Albright worked skillfully to prepare a Park Service bill and lobby for its passage. The Forest Service resisted the establishment of a national parks bureau because it was concerned that the creation of new national parks would mean the loss of national forests.

On August 25, 1916, President Woodrow Wilson signed legislation creating the National Park Service. The **National Park Service Act** stated in part:

> ... The service thus established shall promote and regulate the use of the Federal areas known as national parks, monuments and reservations hereinafter specified by such means and measures as conform to the fundamental purpose of the said parks, monuments and reservations, which purpose is to conserve the scenery and the natural and historic objects and the wildlife therein and to provide for the enjoyment of the same in such manner and by such means as will leave them unimpaired for the enjoyment of future generations.

The National Park Service became responsible for 14 national parks, 21 national monuments, and the Hot Springs Reservation. Secretary Lane appointed Mather as its first director. He was a strong, dedicated leader who attracted supporters and was able to organize a loyal and supportive staff. During the first three years of the new agency, Mather was initially incapacitated by illness, so Albright organized the new bureau, obtained its first appropriations from Congress, and prepared its first park policies. In 1919, Albright moved to Yellowstone National Park to serve as its superintendent and succeeded Mather as director of the Park Service in 1929.

Mather's influence in the development of our National Park Service was crucial. Although he was interested in the preservation of the parks as natural preserves, he also felt the need for the development of roads and adequate hotels in the parks to encourage travel. He was also concerned with educating the visitor and encouraged the establishment of interpretive services. The first policies, issued in a May 13, 1918, letter from Secretary of the Interior Lane to Mather, elaborated on the Park Service's dual mission of conserving park resources and providing for their enjoyment by the public. Automobiles were to be allowed in all parks; they had been prohibited from Yellowstone until 1915. "Low-priced camps . . . as well as comfortable and even luxurious hotels" would be provided by concessionaires. Many of the "Grand Hotels," such as the Ahwahnee (Figure 3.4) at Yosemite National Park, owe their origins to this policy. Acceptable activities would include mountain climbing, horseback riding, swimming, boating, fishing, winter sports, natural history museums, exhibits, and other activities supporting the educational use of the parks. Lane's policy letter also sought to guide further expansion of the park system.

> In studying new park projects, you should seek to find scenery of supreme and distinctive quality or some natural feature so extraordinary or unique as to be of national interest and importance. You should seek distinguished examples of typical forms of world architecture; such, for instance, as in the Grand Canyon, as exemplifying the highest accomplishment of stream erosion, and the high, rugged portion of Mount Desert Island as exemplifying the oldest rock forms in America and the luxuriance of deciduous forests. . . . The national park system as now constituted should not be lowered in standard, dignity, and prestige by the inclusion of areas which express in less than the highest terms the particular class or kind of exhibit which they represent.

Figure 3.4 The Ahwahnee Hotel in Yosemite National Park is operated by a private concessionaire.

EXPANSION OF THE NATIONAL PARK SYSTEM

Since its establishment on August 25, 1916, our National Park System has grown to include 357 different units covering 80,155,984 acres in 49 states, the District of Columbia, American Samoa, Guam, Puerto Rico, Saipan, and the Virgin Islands. Appendix II presents a complete chronology of the status of every unit that is or was part of our National Park System, and Appendix III lists all units of the system, giving the size and use statistics for each unit. Figure 3.5 shows the location of each unit of the National Park System and is keyed to Appendix III. Since it is not the author's intent to mention in the text the date and name of every addition to the National Park System, the appendices should be consulted for details on each of the units comprising the system. This section will identify and give examples of major trends that have occurred as the National Park System developed. In addition, it will also describe how the best-known units of our National Park System—the national parks, of which there are 50 today—got established. This section will also cover the development of units that provide especially great outdoor recreation opportunities: national seashores and lakeshores, national recreation areas, national preserves, national rivers, national parkways, and national trails. Of necessity, this treatment will exclude the mention of many units of our National Park System that are historical in nature.[1]

---

[1]The author does not intend to demean historical units, for his undergraduate degree was in history; each and every unit of our National Park System is of equal importance. However, the focus of this book is on outdoor recreation resources, and many of the historical units of our National Park System do not have this focus or at best their recreational opportunities are limited.

1916–1933

Through the 1920s the National Park System was really a western park system. Acadia (Maine) was the only national park located east of the Mississippi. Natural areas meeting national park standards were less common in the East, and most eastern lands were privately owned. National parks established in the period between 1916 and 1933 included Mount McKinley (Alaska, 1917; expanded and renamed Denali in 1980), Grand Canyon (Arizona, 1919; incorporated the national monument of the same name), Lafayette (Maine, 1919; incorporated Sieur de Monts National Monument; redesignated Acadia in 1929), Zion (Utah, 1919; incorporated Mukuntuweap National Monument), Great Smoky Mountains (North Carolina and Tennessee, 1926), Shenandoah (Virginia, 1926), Mammoth Cave (Kentucky, 1926), Bryce Canyon (Utah, 1928; incorporated the national monument of the same name), Grand Teton (Wyoming, 1929), and Isle Royale (Michigan, 1931). Bryce Canyon National Park is one of the major attractions for both foreign and domestic visitors (Figure 3.6). Two Alaska national monuments proclaimed at this time—Katmai (1918) and Glacier Bay (1925)—were each larger than any national park and until 1978 were the two largest units in the entire National Park System; in 1980 they became redesignated national parks. Other national monuments established in this time period, and that would later become national parks, were Carlsbad Cave (New Mexico, 1923; reclassified Carlsbad Caverns National Park in 1930), Badlands (South Dakota, 1929; redesignated as a national park in 1978), and Arches (Utah, 1929; redesignated as a national park in 1971). Three unique natural areas that have varying degrees of recreational potential and that have been national monuments since this time are Great Sand Dunes (Colorado, 1932), White Sand Dunes (New Mexico, 1933), and Death Valley (California and Nevada, 1933). Death Valley National Monument today is over 2 million acres in size and is the second largest unit (after Yellowstone) in our National Park System

Figure 3.6 Visitors from Belgium at Bryce Canyon National Park.

in the lower 48 states. Albright, who succeeded Mather as director of the National Park Service in 1929, argued that the Park Service's greatest opportunity in the East was in the realm of history and historic sites. Table 3.1 lists the directors of the National Park Service. Albright persuaded Congress to establish three new historical parks in the East under Park Service administration: George Washington Birthplace National Monument (Virginia, 1930), Colonial National Monument (Virginia, 1930; redesignated a national historical park in 1936); and Morristown National Historical Park (New Jersey, 1933). Morristown was the first area in the system designated a national historical park.

1933–1951

The *Reorganization of August 10, 1933,* was the most significant event in the evolution of the National Park System. President Franklin D. Roosevelt issued two orders, signed June 10 and July 28, both effective August 10, that

- Transferred administrative responsibility of the War Department's parks and monuments to the National Park Service;
- Transferred the Forest Service's national monuments to the National Park Service;
- Made the National Park Service responsible for almost all future national monuments;
- Transferred the responsibility for the national capital parks to the National Park Service.

There was now a single federal system of park lands, national in scope, that embraced historic as well as natural places. The Park Service was not constrained to limiting new parks to military history but could focus on all aspects of America's past. Today, *national capital parks* officially denotes only those miscellaneous park lands in the District of Columbia and nearby Maryland not classed as discrete units of the National Park System. This designation thus excludes the National Mall, the Washington

Table 3.1 National Park Service Directors

Stephen T. Mather	May 16, 1917–January 8, 1929
Horace M. Albright	January 12, 1929–August 9, 1933
Arno B. Cammerer	August 10, 1933–August 9, 1940
Newton B. Drury	August 20, 1940–March 31, 1951
Arthur E. Demaray	April 1, 1951–December 8, 1951
Conrad L. Wirth	December 9, 1951–January 7, 1964
George B. Hartzog, Jr.	January 9, 1964–December 31, 1972
Ronald H. Walker	January 7, 1973–January 3, 1975
Gary Everhardt	January 13, 1975–May 27, 1977
William J. Whalen	July 5, 1977–May 13, 1980
Russell E. Dickenson	May 15, 1980–March 3, 1985
William Penn Mott, Jr.	May 17, 1985–April 16, 1989
James M. Ridenour	April 17, 1989–June 1, 1993
Roger Kennedy	June 1, 1993–

Source: National Parks Service, *The National Parks: Shaping the System* (1991).

Monument and other major memorials, Rock Creek Park, and areas of similar status. National memorials in and outside Washington, D.C., formed the most distinctly different class of areas added in the reorganization.

Before the 1933 reorganization, 21 national monuments had been proclaimed in the national forests. One of these Forest Service national monuments was Mount Olympus in Olympic National Forest; it formed the nucleus for Olympic National Park (Washington, established in 1938). Four Forest Service national monuments were caves: Jewel Cave (South Dakota), Oregon Caves (Oregon), Lehman Caves (Nevada), and Timpanogos Cave (Utah). Lehman Caves National Monument was incorporated into Great Basin National Park in 1986. Archaeological monuments on Forest Service land, that were transferred, included Gila Cliff Dwellings (New Mexico), Tonto (Arizona), Walnut Canyon (Arizona), and Old Kasaan (Alaska, abolished in 1955). President Hoover enlarged Bandelier National Monument in 1932 and reassigned it to the Park Service. A limited revision to Agriculture Department administration of national monuments occurred on December 1, 1978, when President Jimmy Carter proclaimed the Admiralty Island and Misty Fjords National Monuments within the Tongass National Forest. In 1982, Congress established Mount St. Helens National Volcanic Monument in the Gifford Pinchot National Forest (Washington) and in 1990, the Newberry National Volcanic Monument in the Deschutes National Forest (Oregon). Since 1975 the Forest Service has administered Gila Cliff Dwellings under an agreement with the Park Service, which retains formal jurisdiction.

With the 1933 reorganization, historic preservation became a primary mission of the National Park Service. The *Historic Sites Act* of 1935 established the Park Service as the lead agency at the federal level. The Act declared "a national policy to preserve for public use historic sites, buildings and objects of national significance for the inspiration and benefit of the people of the United States." The first secretarial designation under the Historic Sites Act was the Jefferson National Expansion Memorial in St. Louis, Mo. (1935). This project was the first extensive urban responsibility of the Park Service outside of Washington, D.C. Most of the area was bulldozed, and the 630 foot Gateway Arch was erected in the 1960s. The justification for the project was to use federal monies for urban renewal and a modern memorial to westward expansion rather than historic preservation. A 3000-acre Saratoga National Historical Park, N.Y. was established in 1938 to commemorate a battle that marked the turning point in the Revolutionary War.

From the reorganization through 1951, 60 of today's units were added to the National Park System. Forty-one of these were historic areas, 11 were predominantly natural in character, and eight were classified as recreational. *Arno Cammerer* succeeded Horace Albright as the third director of the Park Service and served until 1940. He was replaced by *Newton B. Drury*, who served until 1951. Another mission assigned to the Park Service in 1933 was supervision of the new Civilian Conservation Corps (CCC). At the program's peak in 1935, the Service oversaw 600 CCC camps; 118 of them were in national park lands and 482 were in state parks. In addition to many park improvements, the CCC had lasting effects on Park Service organization and personnel. In 1937 the regional offices established in the state parks to coordinate the CCC evolved into a permanent regional structure for management of the National Park System.

Between 1933 and 1951 two entirely new national parks, one national memorial park later designated a national park, and eight national monuments protecting natural features were added to the system, and three essentially new national parks were formed or expanded from previous holdings. Five of the national monuments were later incorporated or turned into four national parks and a national seashore. The new national parks were the Everglades (Florida, 1934) and Big Bend (Texas, 1935). Theodore Roosevelt National Memorial Park (North Dakota, 1947) was redesignated a national park in 1978. Other national parks formed were Olympic (Washington, 1938), and Kings Canyon (California, 1940). Natural-area national monuments established in this time period were Cedar Breaks (Utah, 1933), Joshua Tree (California, 1936), Organ Pipe Cactus (Arizona, 1937), Capitol Reef (Utah, 1937; redesignated a national park in 1971), Channel Islands (California, 1938; redesignated a national park in 1980), and Zion (Utah, 1937; incorporated into Zion National Park in 1956). After sufficient lands were acquired from nonfederal sources, national parks were formally established at Great Smoky Mountains, (North Carolina and Tennessee, 1934), Shenandoah (Virginia, 1935), Isle Royale (Michigan, 1940), and Mammoth Cave (Kentucky, 1950).

A controversy arose over the land acquisition procedures of John D. Rockefeller's Snake River Land Company, which acquired land adjacent to Grand Teton National Park; President Roosevelt declared a Jackson Hole National Monument in 1943, to accept this donated land. Part of this national monument was added to Grand Teton National Park in 1950. Legislation abolishing the national monument was passed by Congress in 1944 but was vetoed by Roosevelt. The act that allowed for the expansion of Grand Teton National Park in 1950 contained special provisions for tax-revenue compensation and hunting in the park and prohibited the establishment of national monuments or enlargement of national parks in Wyoming in the future, except for congressional action. Jackson Lake is the largest body of water in Grand Teton National Park. Withdrawal of water from this human-made lake can lower water levels so much that recreational boating is limited (Figure 3.7). After the Jackson Hole controversy, Presidential proclamations of national monuments virtually ceased. Only five more national monuments were established between 1943 and 1978: Buck Island Reef (Virgin Islands, 1961), Marble Canyon (Arizona, 1969), Effigy Mounds (Iowa, 1949), Chesapeake and Ohio Canal (Maryland, 1961), and Russell Cave (Alabama, 1961). President Jimmy Carter's proclamation of 11 national monuments in Alaska in 1978 was the last use of the Antiquities Act. As a rule, the Executive branch deferred responsibility to Congress when it came to expanding the National Park System.

The accelerated development of river basins by the Army Corps of Engineers and the Bureau of Reclamation after World War II brought new threats to the National Park System. The proposed Bridge Canyon Dam on the Colorado River would have impounded the river in Grand Canyon National Monument, causing it to back up into the adjacent National Park; Glacier View Dam on the Flathead River in Montana threatened to flood 20,000 acres of Glacier National Park; the reservoir behind the proposed Mining City Dam on Kentucky's Green River would have periodically flooded the underground Echo River in Mammoth Cave National Park; and dams on the Potomac above and below Great Falls would have submerged 40 miles of the historic Chesapeake and Ohio Canal. The most controversial dam projects, however,

Figure 3.7 The downstream release of water in the Snake River for irrigated agriculture in Idaho lowered the level of water in Jackson Lake in Grand Teton National Park to the point where recreational boating was drastically curtailed. Shown here are docks on the lake bottom at Colter Bay, with the Teton Range in the background.

were those proposed at Echo Park and Split Mountain on the Green and Yampa Rivers in Dinosaur National Monument. Congress refused to fund the Dinosaur dams, and most other proposals affecting park lands were dropped.

In the period between 1933 and 1951, another new group of areas came under control of the National Park Service. One of the new categories added to the Service's responsibility was *parkways*. Colonial Parkway (Virginia, 1930) was the first parkway brought under jurisdiction of the Park Service outside of the capital area. The major parkways, however, were the Blue Ridge (North Carolina and Virginia; authorized in 1933; land acquired in 1936) and the Natchez Trace (Mississippi, Alabama, and Tennessee; authorized in 1934; land acquired in 1938). In 1936 the National Park Service, under an agreement with the Bureau of Reclamation, assumed responsibility for all recreational activity on Lake Mead behind Boulder Dam on what was first called Boulder Dam National Recreation Area and in 1947 renamed Lake Mead National Recreation Area. In 1952, Davis Dam created Lake Mohave downstream from Boulder Dam and was included in the area. This was the first designated *national recreation area* in the National Park System and clearly established the role of the Park Service as having recreational responsibility. A second national recreation area, Coulee Dam, was established in 1946 under a similar agreement with the Bureau of Reclamation. The Service's other major recreational initiative addressed *national seashores*. In 1934, the Service surveyed the Atlantic and Gulf coasts and identified 12 significant areas worthy of federal protection. Cape Hatteras, North Carolina, was designated in 1937 our first national seashore, through the help of a private foundation that provided the funds to acquire the needed lands. Although it would be a quarter of a century before the next national seashore would be established, the

precedent was now set for the National Park Service to take a more active role in providing outdoor recreation opportunities.

1951–1972

Visits to the National Park System rose from 6 million in 1942 to 33 million in 1950 to 72 million in 1960. In 1951, *Conrad Wirth* assumed the directorship of the National Park Service and in 1956 launched *Mission 66* to improve deteriorating conditions in the parks. Mission 66 was a 10-year program to upgrade facilities, staffing, and resource management throughout the National Park System in time for the 50th anniversary of the Park Service in 1966. *George Hartzog, Jr.*, assumed the director's position in 1964 and continued until 1972. Of the 100 permanent additions to the system from 1952 through 1972, 69 were made during Hartzog's tenure. Historical additions were the leading category at 56, with 32 in the recreational category and 12 classed as natural. Additions in all categories were aided by the Land and Water Conservation Fund Act (1965). The Bureau of Outdoor Recreation (BOR), which administered the fund, took away from the Park Service its responsibilities for recreation planning and assistance—and some of its staff and funds also shifted. The Park Service regained these functions at a diminished capacity when the BOR, reconstituted as the Heritage Conservation and Recreation Service (HCRS) in 1978, was cut by Executive Order in 1981. In 1964, Secretary of the Interior Stewart Udall signed a management policy memorandum prepared by Hartzog and his staff that identified three categories of Park Service units: natural, historical and recreational. Each category required a separate management concept and principles. Separate policy manuals were developed for each category and published in 1968. The *National Historic Preservation Act* (1966) authorized the Park Service to maintain a comprehensive National Register of Historic Places. In 1970 the *General Authorities Act* redefined the Park System to include all areas managed "for park, monument, historic, parkway, recreational, or other purposes" by the National Park Service. Hartzog ordered the preparation of a National Park System plan, which was published in 1972.

In the two decades between 1952 and 1972 there were 12 additions in the natural area category; seven were national parks and five were national monuments. A 13th area, Marble Canyon National Monument (1969), was incorporated into Grand Canyon National Park in 1975. Two preexisting national monuments, Arches and Capitol Reef, were upgraded to national park status with the same names in 1971. The new national parks included Virgin Islands (U.S. Virgin Islands, 1956), Haleakala (Hawaii, 1960; from Hawaii National Park, which was renamed Hawaiian Volcanoes National Park in 1961), Canyonlands (Utah, 1964), North Cascades (Washington, 1968), Redwoods (California, 1968), and Voyageurs (Minnesota, 1971). Long and bitter controversies over timber and mining interests surrounded the establishment of both Redwoods and North Cascades National Parks. Redwood's establishment and enlargement in 1978 entailed the taking of valuable private timberlands and compensatory benefits to affected loggers. It was by far the most expensive park ever created, costing $1.5 billion for land acquisition alone. New national monuments established were Buck Island Reef (Virgin Islands, 1961), Biscayne (Florida, 1971; redesignated a national park in 1980), Agate Fossil Beds (Nebraska, 1965), Florissant Fossil Beds (Colorado, 1969), and Fossil Butte (Wyoming, 1972). The *Wilderness Act* (1964) was of

great importance in preserving natural values in the Park System; this topic will be covered in Chapter 14.

From 1952 to 1972, 32 permanent additions to the National Park System were in the recreational category. More than half were reservoir-related areas and seashores and another parkway. The rest were new kinds of areas and included lakeshores, rivers, a trail, performing arts facilities, and two major urban recreation complexes. Areas established as national recreation areas were Shadow Mountain (Colorado, 1952; transferred to the Forest Service in 1978), Glen Canyon (Arizona and Utah, 1958), Whiskeytown-Shasta-Trinity, Whiskeytown Unit (California, 1961), Flaming Gorge (Utah and Wyoming, 1963; transferred to the Forest Service in 1968), Arbuckle (Oklahoma, 1965; incorporated into Chickasaw National Recreation Area in 1976), Curecanti (Colorado, 1965), Sanford (Texas, 1965; redesignated Lake Meredith Recreation Area in 1972; redesignated Lake Meredith National Recreation Area in 1990), Delaware Water Gap (Pennsylvania and New Jersey, 1965), Amistad Recreation Area (Texas, 1965; redesignated Amistad National Recreation Area in 1990), Bighorn Canyon National Recreation Area (Montana and Wyoming, 1966), Lake Chelan (Washington, 1968), and Ross Lake (Washington, 1968). Two new types of national recreation areas were created in urban areas in 1972: Gateway (New York City and New Jersey) and Golden Gate (San Francisco and Marin County, Calif.). Before Gateway and Golden Gate, nearly all the units of the National Park Service in major urban areas that were outside the national capital region had been small historic sites. These two acquisitions placed the Park Service squarely in the business of urban mass recreation for essentially local populations. *This was a major departure in Park Service policy and assumption of federal responsibility.*

The national seashore movement, which had started in 1937 at Cape Hatteras, was revived in the 1960s and 1970s. National seashores were established at Cape Cod (Massachusetts, 1961), Point Reyes (California, 1962), Padre Island (Texas, 1962), Fire Island (New York, 1964), Assateague Island (Maryland and Virginia, 1965), Cape Lookout (North Carolina, 1966), Gulf Island (Florida and Mississippi, 1971), and Cumberland Island (Georgia, 1972). A new category, that of national lakeshores, was established at Pictured Rocks (Michigan, 1966), Indiana Dunes (Indiana, 1966), Sleeping Bear Dunes (Michigan, 1970), and Apostle Islands (Wisconsin, 1970). Our first national river, Ozark National Scenic Riverways (Missouri, 1964), was established four years prior to the passage of the Wild and Scenic Rivers Act (1968). Two other rivers that were added to the National Park System are the St. Croix National Scenic River (Minnesota and Wisconsin, 1968) and Buffalo National River (Arkansas, 1972). The Appalachian National Scenic Trail, designated an initial component of our National Trails System (1968), is part of the Park System. The one parkway added during this time was the John D. Rockefeller Memorial Parkway (Wyoming, 1972). The Park Service became involved with another new type of area in the form of two performing arts centers: the Wolf Trap Farm Park for the Performing Arts (Virginia, 1966) and the John F. Kennedy Center for the Performing Arts (Washington, D.C., 1972).

1973–1990

Between 1973 and 1990, 97 new or essentially new parks were added to the system. Especially large additions in Alaska in 1978 and 1980 more than doubled the size of

the entire system. The frequent turnover of directors in the 1970s reversed the stability previously given by longer terms of office held by directors. This negatively impacted the expansion of the system—excepting for the large additions in Alaska. *Ronald Walker* replaced George Hartzog, Jr., in 1973 as director, but served only until the end of 1973. *Gary Everhardt* served as director from 1974 until 1977, and *William Whalen* served from 1977 until 1980. Five years of stability were added by the tenure of *Russell Dickinson* as director, from May 1980 until March 1985; however, with the exception of the Alaskan additions of 1980, the only substantive addition to the system was the Harry S. Truman National Historic Site (designated 1982; established 1983). The system did see some significant additions, including Great Basin National Park (1986), during *William P. Mott*'s directorship from 1985 until 1989. A more conservative attitude toward National Park System expansion reappeared in 1989 with President Bush's appointment of *James M. Ridenour* as director. On June 1, 1993, President Clinton's appointee, *Roger Kennedy,* assumed the directorship of the National Park Service. If President Clinton and Vice President Gore follow through with their campaign promises, the National Park System should benefit and prosper. By the mid-1970s the categorization of each National Park System unit as natural, historical, or recreational was causing planning and management problems. In 1975, the Park Service responded to these problems by replacing the three separate policy manuals with a single policy manual, and in 1977 the area categories were officially abolished. The current management policies manual, *Management Policies* is dated 1988.

From 1973 through 1990, over half (51 out of 97) of additions to the system were historic in nature. A third of these were military and presidential sites, and the remainder addressed themes less represented in the system. The Bicentennial theme of the 1970s saw the establishment of Boston National Historical Park (Massachusetts, 1974), and the Vietnam Veterans Memorial (D.C., 1980) was a memorial to an American war. Presidential site additions included reclassification of the Lyndon B. Johnson National Historic Site (1969) to a national historical park of the same name (Texas, 1980). Other new historical themes represented by additions to the system were: literature, art, and drama; social and human movements; and industrial and transportation history. Examples of units added in these classes include the Frederick L. Olmsted National Historic Site (Massachusetts, 1979), the Women's Rights National Historical Park (New York, 1980), the Martin Luther King, Jr. National Historic Site (Georgia, 1980), and Lowell National Historical Park (Massachusetts, 1978).

Between 1973 and 1990, 29 natural units were added to the National Park System. This figure is diluted by the huge additions in Alaska, which accounted for 17 of the areas added. A detailed discussion of the impact of the Alaska National Interest Lands Conservation Act and the new parks created by it in Alaska in 1980 is reserved for Chapter 4. Three new national parks outside of Alaska were created from preexisting national monuments: Channel Islands (California, 1980) and Biscayne Bay (Florida, 1980) were created from national monuments of the same name. Great Basin National Park (Nevada, 1986) incorporated Lehman Caves National Monument (established 1922 under Forest Service administration; transferred to the Park Service in 1933) and annexed surrounding land in the Snake Range from Humboldt National Forest. A new classification was added to the Park System called *national preserve;* the first two national preserves were Big Cypress (Florida, 1974) and Big Thicket (Texas, 1974). City of Rocks National Reserve (Idaho, 1988) represents the second such clas-

sified unit in the system; the intent of the reserve classification is to transfer the administration of these lands to the local or state governments once they establish zoning or other land protection measures. Other natural areas added to the system include Congaree Swamp (South Carolina, 1976), Timacuan Ecological and Historic Preserve (Florida, 1988), and National Park of American Samoa (American Samoa, 1988).

Seventeen areas designated as recreational in character were added to the National Park System between 1973 and 1990. One addition was our most recent national seashore—Canaveral (Florida, 1975). A reservoir area, Chickasaw National Recreation Area (Oklahoma, 1976), combined Arbuckle National Recreation Area (1965) and Platt National Park (1906; incorporated as the Sulphur Springs Reservation). Three urban recreation areas were added to the system: Cuyahoga Valley National Recreation Areas (Ohio, 1974), Chattahoochee National Recreation Area (Georgia, 1978), and Santa Monica National Recreation Area (California, 1978). Santa Monica National Recreation Area was established by the *National Parks and Recreation Act* (1978), which also added five rivers to the System: (1) Delaware National Scenic River (Pennsylvania and New Jersey); (2) Upper Delaware Scenic and Recreational River (Pennsylvania and New York); (3) Missouri National River (Nebraska and South Dakota), (4) New River Gorge National River (West Virginia), and (5) the Rio Grande Wild and Scenic River (Texas). Other rivers added to the system in this time period were Big South Fork National River and Recreation Area (Tennessee and Kentucky, 1974), Obed Wild and Scenic River (Tennessee, 1976), Mississippi National River and Recreation Area (Minnesota, 1988), Bluestone National Scenic River (West Virginia, 1988), and Gauley River National Recreation Area (West Virginia, 1988). Two national scenic trails were also added to the system: the Natchez Trace (Mississippi, Alabama, and Tennessee, 1983) and the Potomac Heritage (Pennsylvania, Maryland, Virginia, and D.C., 1983).

NATIONAL PARK SYSTEM TODAY

Classification of Units

The diversity of our National Park System becomes apparent in examining the variety of names given to the different kinds of areas. These include such designations as national park, national recreation area, national monument, national preserve, national seashore, national lakeshore, national memorial, national historic site, national historical park, national battlefield park, national river, and national parkway. Although some terms are self-explanatory, others have been used in different ways. The title *national monument* has been applied to areas as diverse as Death Valley and the Statue of Liberty. In recent years both the National Park Service and Congress have attempted, with some success, to simplify the nomenclature and to establish basic criteria for use of the different titles.

Areas that have been added to the system for their natural values are usually large areas of land and water that have great scenic and scientific value. These areas

are usually classified as national parks, national monuments, national preserves, national seashores, national lakeshores, or national rivers. They may contain one or more distinctive attributes such as biota, landforms, or geology. The term *national park* is generally applied to an area that contains a variety of resources and encompasses large land or water areas to help protect the resource. A *national monument* is intended to preserve at least one nationally significant resource; it is usually smaller than a national park and lacks the diversity of attractions. The title *national preserve* is applied to an area primarily for the protection of certain resources; activities such as hunting and fishing or the extraction of minerals and fuels may be permitted if they do not jeopardize the resource values. *National reserves* are similar to national preserves, except that management of the former is by local or state authorities. *National seashores* and *national lakeshores* preserve shorelines and off-shore islands, while at the same time providing water-oriented recreation. *National rivers* and *wild and scenic rivers* preserve ribbons of land bordering free-flowing streams that have not been dammed, channeled, or altered by humans. Besides preserving these rivers in their natural state, these areas provide opportunities for hiking, canoeing, and hunting. *National scenic trails* are generally long-distance footpaths that wind through areas of scenic beauty.

Although the National Park System is best known for its great scenic parks, over one-half of the units preserves places and commemorates persons, events, and activities important in our nation's history. In recent years, *national historic site* has been the most common term used by Congress in authorizing such areas to the system. Probably the most confusing terms applied in the past and that still persist today have been used for units associated with American military history, for example, *national military park, national battlefield park, national battlefield site,* and *national battlefield*. Other areas such as national monuments and national historical parks may include features associated with military history. *National historical parks* are commonly areas of greater physical extent and complexity than national historic sites. The one *international historic site* refers to a site relevant to both United States and Canadian history. The title *national memorial* is most often used for areas that are commemorative but need not be on sites associated with their subjects. Several units administered by National Capital Region, whose titles do not contain the words *national memorial,* are nevertheless classified as such.

Originally, *national recreation areas* in the Park System were units surrounding reservoirs impounded by dams built by other agencies such as the Bureau of Reclamation. The Park Service manages these areas under cooperative agreements. The concept of national recreation areas has grown to encompass other lands and waters set aside by acts of Congress and now includes major areas in urban centers. There are also national recreation areas outside the National Park System managed by the Forest Service. *National parkways* are ribbons of land flanking roadways that offer an opportunity for leisurely driving through scenic areas. They are not designed for high-speed travel. Two areas have also been set aside as the *National Center for the Performing Arts*. Most of the public parks in Washington, D.C., are administered by the National Capital Region of the National Park Service, a responsibility transferred to it by the Reorganization Act of 1933. Most park lands in the city are included in the federal holdings, although the District of Columbia also operates parks, playgrounds, and recreational facilities. The National Capital Region also administers several units of the National Park System in Maryland, Virginia, and West Virginia.

Our National Park System consists of 357 areas on 80,155,984.18 acres. Table 3.2 presents a statistical summary, by classification, for these units. It must be stressed, however, that all units are considered "parks." The leading classification in numbers is national monument (78 units), followed by national historic site (69 units) and national park (50 units). Overall, about 193 (54 percent) units of the system are primarily historical in nature. In addition to the 69 units designated national historic sites, the following units are primarily historical, as opposed to natural or recreational: international historic site (1), national battlefield (11), national battlefield park (3), national battlefield site (1), national historical park (31), national military park (9), national memorial (26), national monument (41), and national park (1). In addition, it was determined that 41 of the national monuments are primarily historical in nature and 32 are primarily natural. There are a few, such as Cape Krusenstern (Alaska), for which it could not be determined if they were primarily historical or natural since both elements are strongly represented. Most of the national monuments determined to be primarily historical are Indian ruins and forts; only a few, such as the Statue of Liberty (New York) are monuments in the traditional sense. Most of the national monuments that are primarily natural are either ecological or palaeontological, although a few, for example, Saguaro, Arizona, and Congaree Swamp, South Carolina, are based on biological characteristics. The one national park that is primarily historical is Mesa Verde (Colorado).

The 63 units classified as primarily recreational in scope (18 percent of the total) are national recreation areas (18), national seashores (10), other parks (11), national

Table 3.2   National Park System Statistical Summary 1991

Classification	Number	Acreage[1]
International historic sites	1	35.39
National battlefields	11	12,843.31
National battlefield parks	3	8,725.30
National battlefield sites	1	1.00
National historic sites	69	18,551.19
National historical parks	31	150,616.70
National lakeshores	4	227,306.73
National memorials	26	7,949.16
National military parks	9	35,873.21
National monuments	78	4,848,652.27
National parks	50	47,436,577.18
National parkways	4	168,619.32
National preserves	13	22,152,181.34
National recreation areas	18	3,697,315.38
National reserves	1	14,407.19
National rivers[2]	5	360,113.07
National scenic trails	3	172,376.55
National seashores	10	592,508.65
National wild and scenic river and riverways[3]	9	212,612.45
Parks (other)	11	38754.00
Totals	357	80,155,984.18

[1]Acreages as of December 31, 1990.
[2]National Park System units only.
[3]National Park System units and components of the Wild and Scenic Rivers System. On December 11, 1991, President George Bush signed legislation changing the name of Custer Battlefield National Monument to Little Bighorn Battlefield National Monument.
Source: National Park Service, *The National Parks: Index 1991* (1992).

wild and scenic rivers (9), national rivers (5), national parkways (4), national lake-shores (4), and national scenic trails (3). The categories that are primarily natural contain almost 100 units (28 percent of the total): national parks (49), national pre-serves (13), and national reserve (1). While this latter group of national park units is primarily natural, it also possesses a great diversity of recreational opportunities—skiers at Badger Pass Ski Area in Yosemite National Park would attest to this.

The true scope of the classifications in the National Park System is better revealed by assessing the acreage in each. Eighty-eight percent of the acreage of the entire system falls into just two classifications. The leading classification in acreage is na-tional parks (47.4 million acres, which is 60 percent of the entire system) and the second is national preserves (22.2 million acres, or 28 percent of the entire system). Most of this acreage is in Alaska. The 10 largest units in the system are national parks and national preserves in Alaska. Later in this chapter and in Chapter 4 the domi-nance of Alaska will be presented and analyzed. The other two largest classifications in terms of acreage are national monuments (4.8 million acres, or 6 percent of the system) and national recreation areas (3.7 million acres, or 5 percent of the system). It is noteworthy that one lone, large national monument, Death Valley (2.07 million acres), accounts for 43 percent of the entire national monument classification.

Geographic Distribution

The basic geographic distribution of the National Park System is uneven, with some areas of the country being well represented and other areas underrepresented. When evaluating the geographic distribution there are several factors that have to be con-sidered: the number of parks, the size of parks, the size of states, and the population of states. Complicating this analysis is the fact that Park visitors are often from other states and even foreign countries. To account for this interstate movement, the states have been grouped into regions for spatial distribution analysis. Table 3.3 presents the regional grouping employed and the results of this analysis. Alaska is considered to be a separate region, and the "other" category is for the Virgin Islands, Puerto Rico, Guam, and American Samoa. The basic input data for each state were the number of parks, the acreage of park lands, the acreage of states, and the population of states. These data were aggregated for each of the 10 regions. This data was used to calculate average park size, percentage of park land, acres of park per capita, and population for each park. Some park units are in one or more states; for example, the Appalachian Trail passes through 14 states, and Yellowstone National Park is in three states. These multiple-state units are double-counted here, giving a number to each unit in each state. The total of column 2 (the number of parks), though not shown in the table, will therefore add up to approximately 10 percent more than the actual of number of park units reported in Table 3.2.

The most obvious aspect of the geographic distribution of our National Park System is the dominance of Alaska. The 10 largest units are located in Alaska and occupy over half of the acreage of the total system. The combined area of our largest National Park—Wrangell–St. Elias—combined with the adjacent Wrangell–St. Elias National Preserve, is over 13 million acres. A major section of Chapter 4 is devoted to the Alaska National Interest Lands Conservation Act and the Alaskan parks. Table 3.4 presents the 20 largest parks in the system—each one over 1 million acres. These

Table 3.3   National Park System Regional Analysis

State	No.	Acres Park	Acres State	Population	Average Park Size	% Park Land	Acres Park per Capita	Population per Park
Alaska Region								
	23	53,727,971.70	385,296,000.00	550,043.00	2,335,998.77	13.94%	97.68	23,914.91
Pacific Region								
California	21	4,684,863.50	101,563,520.00	29,760,021.00	223,088.74	4.61%	0.16	1,417,143.86
Hawaii	7	245,327.10	4,128,000.00	1,108,229.00	35,046.73	5.94%	0.22	158,318.43
Oregon	4	194,715.80	62,067,840.00	2,842,321.00	48,678.95	0.31%	0.07	710,580.25
Washington	10	1,930,604.30	43,642,880.00	4,866,692.00	193,060.43	4.42%	0.40	486,669.20
Region	42	7,055,510.70	211,402,240.00	38,577,263.00	167,988.35	3.34%	0.18	918,506.26
Mountain Region								
Arizona	22	1,754,103.80	72,901,760.00	3,665,228.00	79,322.90	2.39%	0.48	166,601.27
Colorado	11	647,962.70	66,718,080.00	3,294,394.00	58,905.70	0.97%	0.20	299,490.36
Idaho	5	66,167.10	53,476,480.00	1,006,749.00	13,233.42	0.12%	0.07	201,349.80
Montana	7	1,084,272.70	94,168,320.00	799,065.00	154,896.10	1.15%	1.36	114,152.14
New Mexico	14	346,549.80	77,866,240.00	1,515,069.00	24,753.56	0.45%	0.23	108,219.21
Nevada	3	1,546,052.20	70,745,600.00	1,201,833.00	515,350.73	2.19%	1.29	400,611.00
Utah	13	2,015,615.60	54,346,240.00	1,722,850.00	155,047.35	3.71%	1.17	132,526.92
Wyoming	7	2,561,542.50	62,664,960.00	453,588.00	365,934.64	4.09%	5.65	64,798.29
Region	82	10,013,266.40	552,887,680.00	13,658,776.00	122,113,00	1.81%	0.73	166,570.44
West North-Central Region								
Iowa	2	1,662.50	36,025,600.00	2,776,755.00	831.25	0.00%	0.00	1,388,377.50
Kansas	2	696.40	52,648,960.00	2,477,574.00	348.20	0.00%	0.00	1,238,787.00
Minnesota	6	132,892.70	53,803,520.00	4,375,099.00	22,148.78	0.25%	0.03	729,183.17
Missouri	6	63,420.00	44,599,040.00	5,117,073.00	10,570.00	0.14%	0.01	852,845.50
North Dakota	3	71,387.30	45,219,200.00	638,800.00	23,795.77	0.16%	0.11	212,933.33
Nebraska	4	5,853.90	49,425,280.00	1,578,385.00	1,463.48	0.01%	0.00	394,596.25
South Dakota	5	263,549.20	49,310,080.00	696,004.00	52,709.84	0.53%	0.38	139,200.80
Region	28	539,462.00	331,031,680.00	17,659,690.00	19,266.50	0.16%	0.03	630,703.21
West South-Central Region								
Arizona	5	101,344.30	33,986,560.00	2,350,725.00	20,268.86	0.30%	0.04	470,145.00
Louisiana	2	9,651.00	31,054,720.00	4,219,973.00	4,825.50	0.03%	0.00	2,109,986.50
Oklahoma	2	9,517.40	44,748,160.00	3,145,585.00	4,758.70	0.02%	0.00	1,572,792.50
Texas	13	1,159,191.30	171,128.320.00	16,986,510.00	89,168.56	0.68%	0.07	1,306,654.62
Region	22	1,279,704.00	280,917,760.00	26,702,793.00	58,168.36	0.46%	0.05	1,213,763.32
East North-Central Region								
Illinois	1	12.00	36,096,000.00	11,430,602.00	12.00	0.00%	0.00	11,430,602.00
Indiana	3	9,912.40	23,226,240.00	5,544,159.00	3,304.13	0.04%	0.00	1,848,053.00
Michigan	3	631,941.80	37,258,240.00	9,295,297.00	210,647.27	1.70%	0.07	3,098,432.33
Ohio	5	16,756.90	26,382,080.00	10,847,115.00	3,351.38	0.06%	0.00	2,169,423.00
Wisconsin	3	77,412.10	35,938,560.00	4,891,769.00	25,804.03	0.22%	0.02	1,630,589.67
Region	15	736,035.20	158,901,120.00	42,008,942.00	49,069.01	0.46%	0.02	2,800,596.13
East South-Central Region								
Alabama	5	2,358.80	33,029,760.00	4,040,587.00	471.76	0.01%	0.00	808,117.40
Kentucky	4	71,979.20	25,852,800.00	3,685,296.00	17,994.80	0.28%	0.02	921,324.00
Mississippi	7	122,494.90	30,538,240.00	2,573,216.00	17,499.27	0.40%	0.05	367,602.29
Tennessee	12	544,646.80	27,036,160.00	4,877,185.00	45,387.23	2.01%	0.11	406,432.08
Region	28	741,479.70	116,456,960.00	15,176,284.00	26,481.42	0.64%	0.05	542,010.14

Table 3.3   (continued)

State	No.	Acres Park	Acres State	Population	Average Park Size	% Park Land	Acres Park per Capita	Population per Park
			South Atlantic Region					
D.C.	17	8,806.20	64,000.00	606,900.00	518.01	13.76%	0.01	35,700.00
Delaware		0.00	1,316,480.00	666,168.00		0.00%	0.00	
Florida	11	2,253,621.90	37,478,400.00	12,937,926.00	204,874.72	6.01%	0.17	1,176,175.09
Georgia	11	40,410.80	37,680,640.00	6,478,216.00	3,673.71	0.11%	0.01	588,928.73
Maryland	16	47,177.10	6,769,280.00	4,781,468.00	2,948.57	0.70%	0.01	298,841.75
North Carolina	10	135,478.50	33,655,040.00	6,628,637.00	13,547.85	0.40%	0.02	662,863.70
South Carolina	6	25,214.10	19,875,200.00	3,486,703.00	4,202.35	0.13%	0.01	581,117.17
Virginia	20	244,030.80	26,122,880.00	6,187,358.00	12,201.54	0.93%	0.04	309,367.90
West Virginia	6	39,268.70	15,475,840.00	1,793,477.00	6,544.78	0.25%	0.02	298,912.83
Region	97	2,794,008.10	178,437,760.00	43,566,853.00	28,804.21	1.57%	0.06	449,142.81
			Middle Atlantic Region					
New Jersey	7	1,691.10	5,015,040.00	7,730,188.00	241.59	0.03%	0.00	1,104,312.57
New York	21	30,334.60	31,728,640.00	17,990,455.00	1,444.50	0.10%	0.00	856,688.33
Pennsylvania	17	65,513.32	29,013,120.00	11,881,643.00	3,853.72	0.23%	0.01	698,920.18
Region	45	97,539.02	65,756,800.00	37,602,286.00	2,167.53	0.15%	0.00	835,606.36
			New England Region					
Connecticut	2	0.00	3,205.760.00	3,287,116.00	0.00	0.00%	0.00	1,643,558.00
Rhode Island	1	4.60	776,960.00	1,003,464.00	4.60	0.00%	0.00	1,003,464.00
Massachusetts	13	28,145.90	5,284,480.00	6,016,425.00	2,165.07	0.53%	0.00	462,801.92
Vermont	1	0.00	6,149,760.00	562,758.00	0.00	0.00%	0.00	562,758.00
New Hampshire	2	141.20	5,954,560.00	1,109,252.00	70.60	0.00%	0.00	554,626.00
Maine	3	141,084.00	21,257,600.00	1,227,928.00	47,028.00	0.66%	0.11	409,309.33
Region	22	169,375.70	42,629,120.00	13,206,943.00	7,698.90	0.40%	0.01	600,315.59
			Other					
	5	14,732.00	267,520.00	274,900.00	2,946.40	5.51%	0.05	54,980.00

Source: 1990 Census of the United States; Microsoft Bookshelf—1992; National Park Service, 1991 Annual Abstract (1992).

parks occupy 61 million acres, or 76 percent of the total area of the National Park System. Only seven of them are located in the lower 48 states: Yellowstone National Park (Wyoming, Montana, and Idaho; 2.2 million acres), Death Valley National Monument (California and Nevada; 2.1 million acres), Lake Mead National Recreation Area (Nevada and Arizona; 1.5 million acres), Everglades National Park (Florida; 1.4 million acres), Glen Canyon National Recreation Area (Arizona and Utah; 1.2 million acres), and Glacier National Park (Montana; 1.0 million acres).

Table 3.3 reveals that Alaska has the most units (23) and greatest acreage (54 million) of any state. The next-ranked states—Arizona (22), California (21), New York (21), and Virginia (20)—come close in number of areas to Alaska, but only California and Arizona have substantial park acreages. California has far more acres than any other state in the lower 49 states: 4.7 million acres. States and districts that have the highest percentage of their total state area designated national parks are Alaska (13.9 percent), the District of Columbia (13.8 percent), Florida (6 percent), Hawaii (5.9 percent), California (4.6 percent), and Wyoming (4.1 percent). The states with the lowest percentages are Iowa, Kansas, Nebraska, Illinois, Oklahoma, Louisiana, Alabama, New Jersey, Connecticut, Vermont, New Hampshire, and Rhode Island—all of which

Table 3.4   Largest National Park System Units

Park Unit	State	Map Number	Gross Acres	Park Acres
Wrangell–St. Elias National Park	AK	18	9,141,604.00	8,905,970.00
Gates of the Arctic National Park	AK	9	7,523,888.00	7,281,654.50
Noatak National Preserve	AK	16	6,574,481.00	6,569,710.00
Denali National Park	AK	8	4,716,726.00	4,715,200.10
Wrangell–St. Elias National Preserve	AK	18	4,856,721.00	4,349,564.00
Katmai National Park	AK	11	3,716,000.00	3,575,000.00
Glacier Bay National Park	AK	10	3,225,284.00	3,224,938.00
Bering Land Bridge National Preserve	AK	6	2,784,960.00	2,690,179.00
Lake Clark National Park	AK	15	2,636,839.00	2,573,724.00
Yukon-Charley Rivers National Preserve	AK	19	2,523,509.00	2,249,071.00
Yellowstone National Park	WY, ID, MT	351	2,219,790.70	2,219,772.70
Death Valley National Monument	CA, NV	48	2,067,627.70	2,048,928.90
Kobuk Valley National Park	AK	14	1,750,421.00	1,726,463.00
Lake Mead National Recreation Area	NV, AZ	198	1,495,665.50	1,468,952.20
Everglades National Park (4)	FL	99	1,506,499.40	1,398,613.60
Denali National Preserve	AK	8	1,311,365.00	1,310,565.00
Lake Clark National Preserve	AK	15	1,407,293.00	1,288,259.60
Glen Canyon National Recreation Area	UT, AZ	307	1,236,880.00	1,193,671.00
Grand Canyon National Park (4)	AZ	26	1,218,375.20	1,179,194.10
Glacier National Park	MT	191	1,013,572.40	1,012,995.70
Total				60,982,426.40

Source: National Park Service, *The National Parks: Index 1991* (1992).

have 0.03 percent or less of their state area in national parks. Delaware has the distinction of being the only state without any designated units in our National Park System. Regionally, the west North-Central and the Mid-Atlantic regions have the smallest portions of their areas designated as park land—0.15 percent; close behind at the bottom of the list are the West South-Central and East North-Central regions.

The average park size varies substantially, by both state and region. Again, Alaska is dominant, with an average size of over 2 million acres. The average Park sizes in the Pacific and Mountain regions are 168,000 and 122,000 acres, respectively. The largest average park sizes are found in the West in California, Washington, Montana, Nevada, Utah, and Wyoming and in the East in Florida and Michigan. The parks are extremely small in Illinois, Vermont, Connecticut, and New Hampshire. Illinois's only national park unit—Lincoln Home National Historic Site—is only 12 acres.

The acreage of national parks per capita is probably one of the best indicators of geographic disparity. Alaska is again first with 98 acres per person. In the lower 48 states, Wyoming (at 6 acres per capita) is the leader. The only other states with over 1 acre per capita are Montana, Nevada, and Utah. After Alaska, the Mountain states region has the most acres of parks per person—0.7 acres. The Pacific region, with large acreages, has a low acres-per-capita value (0.18), which is accounted for by the large populations in this region of almost 40 million people. At the most unfavorable position on the list are New England and the Middle Atlantic regions, closely followed by the East North Central and West North-Central regions.

The following conclusions have been reached about the geographic distribution of our National Park System:

- A spatial disparity exists in many parts of the country between supply (parks) and demand (population).
- Most of the acreage of the system is accounted for by a relatively few number of very large parks in Alaska and the West.
- There is a large number of relatively small historical units in the East, especially concentrated between Virginia and Massachusetts; these are usually within 100 miles of the coast.
- There are very few units in the system in New England, with the exception of Massachusetts.
- West of the Appalachians and east of the Rockies, there are very few units.
- There are very few units in the Great Plains between Texas and North Dakota; Badlands National Park is the only large unit found in this area.
- The only really large park in the East is Everglades National Park.
- Over 500 miles of continuous national park units are found along the Colorado River—from Lake Mead National Recreation Area, to Grand Canyon National Park, to Glen Canyon National Recreation Area, to Canyonlands National Park.
- There are a few very large parks in the northern Rockies and the Northwest: Glacier, North Cascades, Mt. Rainier, and Olympic National Parks.
- California has large parks, especially in the Sierra Nevada—for example, Sequoia, Yosemite, and Kings Canyon National Parks.
- There is a large number of national park units in Arizona and New Mexico, most of which are national monuments and preserve historic and prehistoric Indian ruins; this is the densest concentration of national park units outside of the East Coast.
- There are relatively few park lands in the Intermountain area between the Rocky Mountains and the Sierra Nevada and Cascade Ranges.
- Alaska is the most "park-rich" state.
- Delaware is the most "park poor" state.
- The most underrepresented states in terms of both acreage and numbers of national parks are Iowa, Illinois, Kansas, Nebraska, Oklahoma, and Louisiana.

Recreational Use

There has been a steady growth in the use made of our National Park System, with the exception of World War II (1941–1945) and the energy crisis of the mid-1970s. Accurate records were first kept in 1904 and showed 121,000 visitors. In 1920 the number of visitors increased to over 1 million and in 1930 to 3.3 million. Attendance in the system increased dramatically in the 1930s with the addition of many new units; it was 6.3 million in 1934 and 12 million in 1936. By 1941 it had increased to 21 million visits but dropped to 6.9 million in 1943. In 1946 the visits were again up to 22 million, increasing to 33 million in 1950. It was during the recreation explosion in the 1950s and 1960s that recreational use of the National Park System started to skyrocket. In 1950 the system accounted for 33 percent of the recreation visits on federal land, but this decreased to 21 percent in 1960, when the visitation reached 72

million. This relative decrease was accounted for by a dramatic rise in recreation visits at newly constructed Army Corps of Engineers reservoirs. By 1971, visits to the park system had increased to 190 million. In the 1970s the National Park Service started to differentiate between "recreation visits" and "nonrecreation visits." When use data are evaluated it is important to distinguish between these two categories. A *nonrecreation visit* includes persons going to and from inholdings, through traffic, tradespeople with business in the park, and government personnel (other than Park Service employees) with business in the park. The term *inholding* will be used in many places in this book. It refers to other land ownerships within national parks, national forests, national wildlife refuges, and national resource lands. To further complicate data analysis, the National Park Service revises and adjusts the manner in which visits are tallied. For example, the *1981 National Park Statistical Abstract* lists 220 million recreation visits and 80 million nonrecreation visits for 1980, while the *1991 Annual Abstract* lists 198 million recreation visits for 1980.

In 1991, the number of recreation visits to the National Park System was 267,841,000, and the number of nonrecreation visits was 88,027,400. These figures reflect a steady growth in recreation visits during the 1980s, except for 1985, when this upward trend was temporarily reversed. In recent years this increase in use has averaged about 3 percent per year. The equivalent recreation hours for 1991 were 359,016,200 (45,378,600 nonrecreational hours) and recreation visitor days were 113,251,300 (3,781,600 nonrecreation visitor days). This represents 17 percent of the recreation visitor day total for all federal agencies. While the visitor day is the most useful statistical unit for comparison purposes, most of the National Park System data are tallied by the recreation visit.

The National Park Service region that receives the heaviest use is the Southeast, with nearly 62 million recreation visits in 1991. This regional total is skewed by very heavy use on the Blue Ridge Parkway, the Great Smoky Mountains National Park, the Natchez Trace Parkway, and the Gulf Islands National Seashore. The second ranking region is the Western, with over 56 million recreation visits in 1991. Lake Mead National Recreation Area is the most heavily visited western region park. The National Capital Region's 32 million recreation visits in 1991 is extremely high, when the small size of the region is accounted for. At the low end of the scale is the Alaska region with 1.2 million recreation visits in 1991. One park, Denali National Park, accounts for almost 50 percent of the Alaska region total. Table 3.5 identifies the recreation visits for 1991 for all 10 national park regions. Eight National Park Service regions showed an increase in visits from 1990 to 1991, and two showed a decrease. Those regions showing an increase from 1990 to 1991 (with rate of increase in paren-

Table 3.5   1991 Recreation Visits to National Park Service Areas by National Park Service Region (In Thousands)

Region	Visits	Region	Visits	Region	Visits
Alaska	1216.8	North Atlantic	29,962.6	Southeast	61,923.1
Mid-Atlantic	20,992.2	Pacific Northwest	8,656.7	Southwest	13,649.1
Midwest	13,513.6	Rocky Mountains	29,611.6	Western	56,484.9
National Capital	31,830.8				

Source: National Park Service, *1991 Statistical Abstract* (1992).

theses) are the Pacific Northwest (9 percent), Alaska (7.8 percent), the North Atlantic (6.7 percent), the Rocky Mountains (6.5 percent), the Midwest (5.7 percent), the West (3.3 percent), the Southeast (1.5 percent), and the Mid-Atlantic (0.8 percent). Those showing a decrease in recreation visits were the National Capital (−4.5 percent) and the Southwest (−0.3 percent).

Table 3.6 lists the recreation visits for 1991 by state—California is clearly the leading state with 36 million recreation visits. Other states or districts with very high numbers of recreation visits include the District of Columbia (21 million), Virginia (21 million), North Carolina (17 million), New York (15 million), Arizona (11 million), and Massachusetts (10 million). The only state with no use is Delaware, due to a total lack of units. Very low state totals exist for Vermont, New Hampshire, Rhode Island, Kansas, Nebraska, Wisconsin, Iowa, Idaho, and Illinois.

National parks, with its 50 units, is the leading category in the entire National Park System, accounting for the most recreation visits (57 million), but close to this category is the "national recreation area" category, whose 18 areas account for 50 million recreation visits. Lake Mead National Recreation Area and Gateway National Recreation Area have more recreation visits than any national park except the Great Smoky Mountains. The third-ranking category, with just four units, is "national park-ways," with 29 million visits. Other categories with high numbers of recreation visits are national monuments (26 million), national historical parks (23 million), and national seashores (20 million). The 14 national preserves have the least visitor use of any category—just 231,000. Table 3.7 lists the recreation visits for all classifications.

As recounted earlier in this chapter and in Chapter 1, the National Park Service uses several different methods of reporting use. A *recreation visit* is defined as "the entry of a person into an area of land and water for the purpose of engaging in one or more recreational activities." A *recreation visitor day* is "a statistical reporting unit consisting of 12 visitor hours." A *recreation visitor hour* is "the presence of a person

Table 3.6   1991 Recreation Visits to National Park Service Areas by State (In Thousands)

State	Visits	State	Visits	State	Visits
Alabama	890.0	Louisiana	875.4	Ohio	1,604.6
Alaska	1,216.8	Maine	2,475.9	Oklahoma	1,453.0
Arizona	11,483.1	Maryland	3,834.5	Oregon	939.7
Arkansas	2,445.9	Massachusetts	10,087.8	Pennsylvania	8,519.8
California	36,309.2	Michigan	1,973.2	Puerto Rico	2,345.3
Colorado	5,968.6	Minnesota	644.3	Rhode Island	107.6
D.C.	21,338.6	Mississippi	6,778.0	South Carolina	752.4
Florida	8,309.2	Missouri	5,224.2	South Dakota	4,312.3
Georgia	6,865.9	Montana	4,219.5	Tennessee	7,620.5
Guam	60.0	Nebraska	241.1	Texas	4,805.0
Hawaii	4,474.8	Nevada	6,397.6	Utah	8,888.3
Idaho	460.0	New Hampshire	39.8	Virginia	20,847.0
Illinois	509.5	New Jersey	5,113.9	Virgin Islands	872.3
Indiana	2,396.1	New Mexico	2,139.9	Washington	7,256.9
Iowa	423.8	New York	15,278.9	West Virginia	1,378.8
Kansas	121.3	North Carolina	17,481.1	Wisconsin	375.4
Kentucky	3,770.9	North Dakota	512.6	Wyoming	5,400.5

Source: National Park Service, *1991 Statistical Abstract* (1992).

Table 3.7   1991 Recreation Visits, Areas Administered, and Areas Reporting Recreation Visits in the National Park System by Classification

Classification*	Recreation Visits	Areas Administered	Areas Reporting Visits
International historic sites	Not reporting	1	0
National battlefields	1,612,533	11	9
National battlefield parks	2,168,671	3	3
National battlefield sites	Not reporting	1	0
National historical parks	22,617,194	31	28
National historic sites	16,516,217	70	64
National lakeshores	4,151,066	4	4
National memorials	13,299,926	26	26
National military parks	4,750,255	9	9
National monuments	25,752,855	78	73
National parks	57,460,610	50	49
National parkways	28,828,545	4	4
National preserves	230,867	14	11
National recreation areas	49,781,806	18	17
National rivers	4,918,783	5	4
National seashores	20,264,632	10	10
National trails**	Not reporting	3	0
National wild and scenic rivers	778,469	10	5
Parks—other***	14,708,570	11	10
National Total	267,840,999	359	326

*Does not include 31 affiliated areas not reporting public use to the NPS.
**Public-use records of the Appalachian National Scenic Trail are kept by the Appalachian Trail Commission.
***Parks without national designation include National Capital Park, the National Mall, and the White House.
Source: National Park Service, *1991 Statistical Abstract* (1992).

on an area of land and water for the purpose of engaging in one or more recreational activities during a period or periods of time aggregating 60 minutes." The rank order of the most heavily visited National Park System Units changes, depending on the measure of use that is employed. Table 3.8 identifies the top 20 national park units in terms of recreation visits for 1991, while Table 3.9 identifies the top 20 national park units in terms of recreation visitor days for 1991. Notice that the rank order using these two different units of measurement drastically changes from one table to the other. Only the Blue Ridge Parkway maintains the number 1 position in each table—16.4 million recreation visits and 8.7 million recreation visitor days in 1991. *The special case of Golden Gate National Recreation Area should be noted here; the reporting of data in 1991 was suspended pending completion of studies to verify validity of data.* In 1990 the Golden Gate National Recreation Area reported 14.7 million visits and 3.4 million visitor days; these data would have made this unit the second-ranking one for recreation visits and the eighth-ranking unit for recreation visitor days. See Appendix III for the complete visitor use statistics for each National Park System unit.

In terms of recreation visits, as reported in Table 3.8, the Blue Ridge Parkway's use (16.4 million) is close to double the next two entries on the list, Great Smoky Mountains National Park (8.7 million) and the Lake Mead National Recreation Area (8.4 million). Only three national parks, in addition to Great Smoky Mountains, ap-

Table 3.8   Top 20 National Park Units: Recreation Visits—1991

Park Unit	Recreation Visits
Blue Ridge Parkway	16,414,300
Great Smoky Mountains National Park	8,654,500
Lake Mead National Recreation Area	8,445,000
National Capital Parks	7,530,400
Gateway National Recreation Area	6,643,900
Natchez Trace Parkway	5,832,700
Cape Cod National Seashore	5,442,400
George Washington Memorial Parkway	5,004,700
Gulf Islands National Seashore	4,988,000
Statue of Liberty National Monument	4,343,000
San Francisco Maritime National Historic Park	4,317,600
Delaware Water Gap National Recreation Area	4,275,800
Grand Canyon National Park	3,886,000
Yosemite National Park	3,423,100
John F. Kennedy Center for the Performing Arts	3,401,900
Castle Clinton National Monument	3,344,100
Independence National Historical Park	3,200,400
Glen Canyon National Recreation Area	3,181,100
Yellowstone National Park	2,920,500
Martin Luther King, Jr., National Historic Site	2,870,600

Source: National Park Service, *1991 Annual Abstract* (1992).

Table 3.9   Top 20 National Park Units: Recreation Visitor Days—1991

Park Unit	Recreation Visitor Days
Blue Ridge Parkway	8,677,700
Yellowstone National Park	8,435,400
Yosemite National Park	7,675,300
Lake Mead National Recreation Area	6,761,100
Glen Canyon National Recreation Area	5,706,400
Grand Canyon National Park	5,703,700
Great Smoky Mountains National Park	5,539,500
Sequoia National Park	3,099,600
Kings Canyon National Park	2,963,100
Natchez Trace Parkway	1,958,400
Mount Rainier National Park	1,875,500
Gateway National Recreation Area	1,822,300
Rocky Mountain National Park	1,663,100
Delaware Water Gap National Recreation Area	1,556,200
Assateague Island National Seashore	1,539,600
Glacier National Park	1,481,300
Grand Teton National Park	1,366,300
Joshua Tree National Monument	1,334,100
Shenandoah National Park	1,319,900
Gulf Islands National Seashore	1,285,700

Source: National Park Service, *1991 Annual Abstract* (1992).

pear in the top 20 on this list (#13, Grand Canyon; #14, Yosemite; and #19, Yellowstone). Three other national recreation areas appear on this list (#5, Gateway; #12, Delaware Water Gap; and #18, Glen Canyon). Two Parkways are also ranked (#6, Natchez Trace; and #8, George Washington Memorial). The two national seashores ranked on this list are Cape Cod (#7) and Gulf Islands (#9). The other units ranked in Table 3.8 include three historical units, two historically related national monuments, one performing arts center, and the National Capital Parks.

When the top 20 units are ranked by recreation visitor days (RVD), as is done in Table 3.9, some significant changes occur. *Recreation visitor days is a far superior method for assessing the actual magnitude of use on site.* In this ranking, 11 of the top 20 are national parks. While the Blue Ridge Parkway (8.7 million RVD) still retains its number 1 position, Yellowstone National Park (8.4 million RVD) jumps in rank from number 19 to number 2, and Yosemite National Park (7.7 million RVD) jumps from 14 to 3. Lake Mead National Recreation Area (6.7 million RVD) keeps its relatively high ranking at number 4, and Glen Canyon National Recreation Area (5.7 million RVD) jumps from position 18 to position 5. While Grand Canyon National Park (5.7 million RVD) skips from number 13 to number 6, Great Smoky Mountains National Park (5.5 million RVD) moves from position 2 to position 7. This latter change in position is caused by shorter visits due to a major highway passing through the park. Seven national parks appear on this list that were not in the top 20 list by recreation visits: Sequoia (3.1 million RVD), Kings Canyon (3.0 million RVD), Mount Rainier (1.9 million RVD), Rocky Mountain (1.7 million RVD), Glacier (1.5 million RVD), Grand Teton (1.4 million RVD), and Shenandoah (1.3 million RVD). Assateague Island National Seashore (1.5 million RVD) and Joshua Tree National Monument (1.3 million RVD) are also on the RVD top 20 list but not on the recreation-visit top 20 list. Nine units on the top 20 list for recreation visits are deleted from the RVD top 20 list: National Capital Parks, George Washington Memorial Parkway, Statue of Liberty National Monument, San Francisco Maritime National Historical Park, John F. Kennedy Center for the Performing Arts, Castle Clinton National Monument, Independence National Historical Park, and Martin Luther King, Jr., National Historic Site; the only nonurban unit to disappear in this manner is the Cape Cod National Seashore. The prime reason for this change in rank order is the longer on-site visits at the remote western national parks, a major component of which is overnight stays at campgrounds and lodges.

The National Park Service identifies recreation visits by five kinds of locations: urban, suburban, outlying, rural, and remote. An *urban park area* is a park located in the central city of a Metropolitan Statistical Area. A *suburban park area* is a park located outside the central city but still within a Metropolitan Statistical Area of greater than 1 million population. An *outlying area park* is a park located within a Metropolitan Statistical Area of less than 1 million population. A *rural area park* is a park located outside of any Metropolitan Statistical Area and accessible by paved highway or by scheduled air or marine transportation service. A *remote area park* is a park located outside of any Metropolitan Statistical Area and requiring special travel arrangements to reach. Parks are also classed as *mixed area parks* if located in a mixture of outlying, rural, suburban, and urban areas. Figure 3.8 identifies the recreation visits to the five

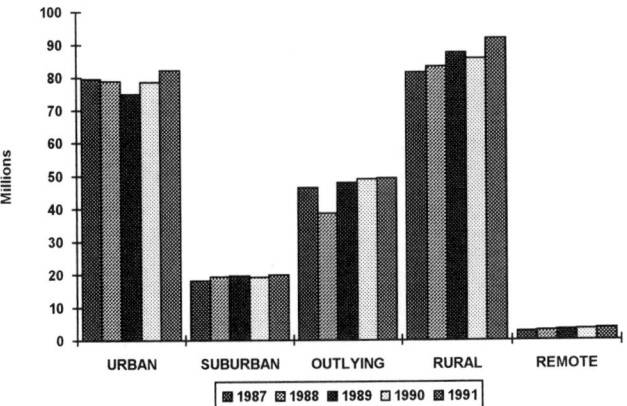

Figure 3.8 National Park Service recreation visits by type of location, 1987–1991. (*Source: National Park Service, 1991 Annual Statistical Abstract*)

major kinds of locations for 1987 to 1991. The "urban" and "rural" categories have shown an increase in recreation visits, while visits in the other three have remained rather flat.

While July (slightly over 15 percent), closely followed by August (slightly under 15 percent), are still the most frequent months for recreation visits to the entire National Park System, a change in the seasonality of visits has occurred when the period 1979–1981 is compared to the period 1988–1990. These two months, along with June, have shown a decrease in the relative percentage of overall use occurring for the entire system. All other months of the year have shown an increase in the relative percentage for the period 1988–1990 compared to the period 1979–1981. December is the only month that has remained rather flat for the two time periods. Interviews conducted by the author during the fall of 1992 with Park Service personnel at Yellowstone National Park indicate that attendance for September for the last several years has been as strong as for July and August. Prior to this time, September marked the start of the slow season at Yellowstone. There are seasonal variations at some parks that have climatic extremes; for example, Everglades National Park is busier in January than in July due to the rain, heat, and insects of July and at parks in the Southwest the spring and fall are favored over the heat of summer. For the entire system, January, February, and December are still the least-visited months, each accounting for about 3 to 4 percent of the total number of recreation visits in the system.

Appendix IV details the nature of overnight stays for each unit of the National Park System. For 1991 there was a total of 17.8 million overnight recreational stays; the leading category of accommodation was National Park Service "campground tent sites" (4.2 million), closely followed by "concession lodging" (4.0 million) and National Park Service "campground recreational vehicle sites" (3.6 million). National Park Service "group and miscellaneous," accounted for another 3.1 million visits in 1991; this category includes any other overnight stay that is not otherwise defined, such as sleeping aboard boats, camping in organized groups; inholders are not reported in this category. National Park Service "backcountry" accounted for 2.0 million overnight stays in 1991; this category consists of primitive or wilderness areas in

parks that are reached primarily by hiking, boating, or horseback. Figure 3.9 shows the trends and details for each of these types of overnight accommodations for the years 1983 and 1991. Note that there has been an increase in "miscellaneous," National Park Service "tent," and "concession lodging" during this time period. The greatest decrease is for National Park Service "recreational vehicle camping," "backcountry," and "concession camping." Figure 3.10 compares the percentage distribution of overnight accommodations from 1987 to 1991. For this time period the most dramatic changes in overnight accommodations included a decrease in "recreational vehicle camping" and an increase in the "miscellaneous," "tent camping," "backcountry," and "concession lodging" categories.

Certain National Park System units account for a sizable portion of the overnight stays. For the "concession lodging" category, Yosemite National Park accounts for over 25 percent of the entire National Park System total, and Grand Canyon National Park accounts for another 16 percent. When the next five leaders (Grand Teton National Park, Glen Canyon National Recreation Area, Shenandoah National Park, Sequoia National Park, and Glacier National Park) for this category are tallied in, these seven units alone account for 60 percent of the overnight stays at concession-operated lodges. The same can be said about "concession camping," where two-thirds of the overnight stays occur at just four national park units: Lake Mead National Recreation Area (31 percent of total), Yellowstone National Park (15 percent of total), Glen Canyon National Recreation Area (11 percent of total), and Grand Teton National Park (7 percent of total).

For National Park Service "tent" and "recreational vehicle" overnight camping, the distribution among the parks is more even, but some parks do dominate. For overnight "tenting," Yosemite National Park (647,698 stays) is the leader followed by Yellowstone National Park (257,824 stays) and Great Smoky Mountains National Park (190,879 stays). But 13 other parks also have over 100,000 overnight "tent" stays: Acadia and Glacier National Parks; Glen Canyon National Recreation Area; Grand Canyon and Grand Teton National Parks; Joshua Tree National Monument; Kings Canyon National Park; Lake Mead National Recreation Area; Olympic National Park;

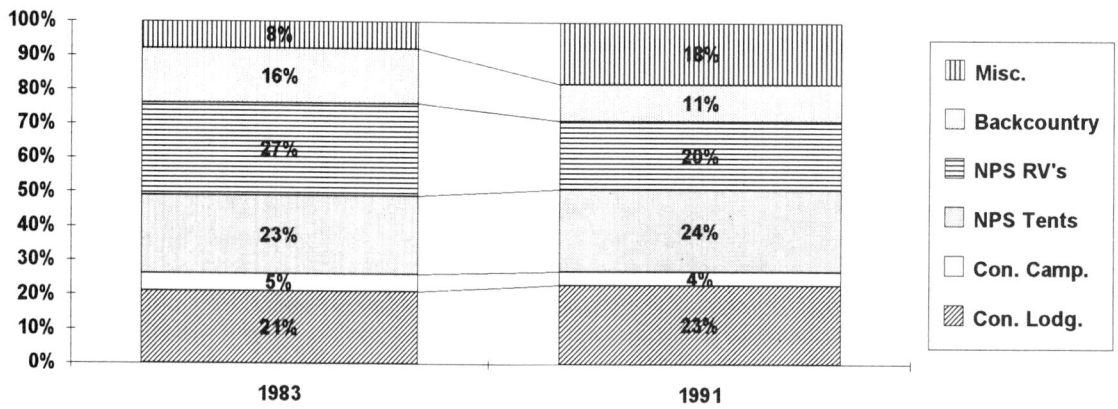

Figure 3.9   National Park Service recreation overnight stays by type of accommodation and by percentage, 1983–1991. (*Source:* National Park Service, *1991 Annual Statistical Abstract*)

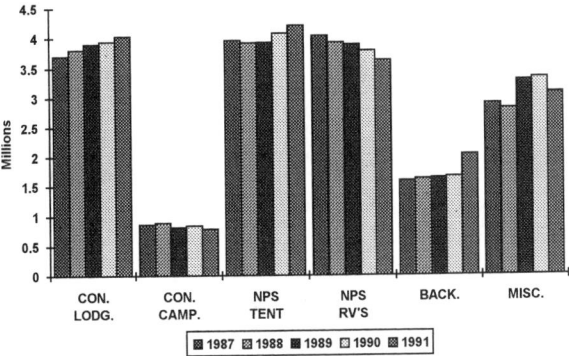

Figure 3.10 National Park Service recreation overnight stays by type of accommodation, 1987–1991. (*Source:* National Park Service, *1991 Annual Statistical Abstract*)

Ozark National Scenic Riverways; and Sequoia, Shenandoah, and Zion National Parks. The dominant three parks for "recreational vehicle" overnight camping are Yosemite (355,184 stays), Lake Mead National Recreation Area (348,070 stays), and Yellowstone (312,592 stays), but five other parks record over 100,000 stays (Glacier, Grand Canyon, Grand Teton, Great Smoky Mountains, and Zion).

For overnight recreational stays at National Park Service "backcountry" sites, one area dominates the statistics: Lake Mead National Recreation Area accounts for 504,972 stays, which is 25 percent of the total for the entire National Park System. Grand Canyon National Park is ranked number 2 in this category, with 225,781 stays (11 percent of total) and Yosemite is number 3 with 121,913 stays (6 percent of total). The next-ranking parks are Great Smoky Mountains, Olympic, Sequoia, Canyonlands, Kings Canyon, Delaware Water Gap National Recreation Area, and Yellowstone.

For overnight stays at National Park Service "group and miscellaneous" sites, one national recreation area—Glen Canyon—accounts for 55 percent (1,706,150 out of 3,108,053) of the stays. Two other national recreation areas each account for another 5 percent of the stays: Lake Mead (166,429) and Lake Meredith (Texas, 155,665). Virgin Islands National Park receives 131,119 overnight stays. The popularity of these areas is accentuated by the boating opportunities, and it is assumed most of the stays are overnight on boats. Three other areas having relatively high overnight stays in this class are Hawaii Volcanoes National Park (66,073), Joshua Tree National Monument (56,578), and Ozark National Scenic Riverways (46,912).

Appendix V details by state the recreational facilities and opportunities available at each National Park Service unit. The following information on availability is provided for each area in the system: entrance fee; visitor center; museum/exhibit; picnic area; campground; hiking; mountain climbing; horseback riding; swimming; bathhouse; boating; boat rental; fishing; hunting; bicycle trail; snowmobile route; cross-country ski trail; cabin rental; hotel, motel or lodge. Many parks charge entrance fees, and these fees vary. An annual entrance permit called the *Golden Eagle Pass* ($25), provides admittance to all federal fee areas and may be bought at all parks that charge fees. Annual park-specific passes are also available. Two other special

passes are *Golden Age Passports,* available to United States citizens or permanent residents 62 years or older and *Golden Access Passports,* available to qualifying disabled persons; both of these latter passports are free.

At campgrounds, campsites may be for recreational vehicles, tents, or both. Most are available on a first-come, first-served basis. Reservations can be made ahead of time through Mistix of San Diego for the following popular parks: Acadia National Park, Assateague Island National Seashore, Cape Hatteras National Seashore, Death Valley National Monument, Grand Canyon National Park, Great Smoky Mountains National Park, Joshua Tree National Monument, Ozark National Scenic Riverways, Rocky Mountain National Park, Sequoia-Kings Canyon National Park, Shenandoah National Park, Whiskeytown National Recreation Area, Yellowstone National Park, and Yosemite National Park. Camping fees vary. Reservations may be required for group campsites; some sites are only for educational and other organized groups. Many parks require free *backcountry permits;* some require reservations. State and federal regulations may apply for hunting and fishing.

PLANNING AND MANAGEMENT

The basic management scheme that has guided the National Park Service was specified in the National Park Service Act of 1916 and has remained the same until the present. The exact wording of this legal mandate was quoted earlier in this chapter. In part, this mandate is: "to conserve the scenery and the natural and historic objects and the wildlife therein and to provide for the enjoyment of the same in such manner and by such means as will leave them unimpaired for the enjoyment of future generations." The key phrasing in this mandate are "conserve;" "provide for enjoyment;" and "leave them unimpaired." The National Park Service has been challenged to balance the preservation concept with the use concept. Increasingly, because most of the resources of our National Park System are not renewable, the aspect of preservation must dominate over the use aspect. A recent example of the domination of the preservation concept over the use concept is at Sunset Crater National Monument (Arizona). Hiking to the summit of Sunset Crater is no longer allowed because of the increasing damage done to the crater by hikers. Another example in which the preservation aspect dominates is the institution in 1971 of a maximum number of river-rafting experiences on the Colorado River in Grand Canyon National Park. The fragile gravel bars used for camping in the park are limited in size, and their character was being degraded. Resource managers in many National Park System units are finding that they are having to implement use limitations to protect the resources of the parks.

Criteria for Inclusion in the System

Proposals for inclusion in the System may come from the public, state and local officials, Native American tribes, members of Congress, or the National Park Service.

To be eligible for favorable consideration as a unit of the National Park Service, an area must:

1. Possess nationally significant natural, cultural, or recreational resources
2. Be a suitable and feasible addition to the system
3. Require direct National Park Service management instead of alternative protection by other agencies or the private sector

A proposed unit is considered *nationally significant* if it meets all four of the following standards:

1. It is an outstanding example of a particular type of resource.
2. It possesses exceptional value or quality in illustrating or interpreting the natural or cultural themes of our nation's heritage.
3. It offers superlative opportunities for recreation, for public use and enjoyment, or for scientific study.
4. It retains a high degree of integrity as a true, accurate, and relatively unspoiled example of the resource.

Examples of *nationally significant natural areas* may include:

- An outstanding site illustrating the characteristics of a landform or biotic area that is still widespread
- A rare remnant natural landscape or biotic area of a type that was once widespread but is now vanishing due to human settlement and development
- A landform or biotic area that has always been extremely uncommon in the region or nation
- A site possessing exceptional diversity of ecological components (species, communities, habitats) or geological features (landforms or observable manifestations of geologic processes)
- A site containing biotic species or communities whose natural distribution at that location makes them unusual (a relatively large population at the limit of its range, or an isolated population)
- A site harboring a concentrated population of a rare plant or animal species, particularly one officially recognized as threatened or endangered
- A critical refuge necessary for the continued survival of a species
- A site containing unusually rare or unusually abundant fossil deposits
- An area with outstanding scenic qualities, such as dramatic topographic features, unusual contrasts in landforms or vegetation, spectacular vistas, or other special landscape features
- A site that is an invaluable ecological or geological benchmark due to an extensive and long-term record of research and scientific discovery

Nationally significant cultural resources include districts, sites, buildings, structures, or objects that possess exceptional value or quality in illustrating or interpreting our heritage and that possess a high degree of integrity of location, design, setting, materials, workmanship, feeling, and association. Examples of such would include those that:

- Are associated with events that have made a significant contribution to and are identified with, or that outstandingly represent, the broad national patterns of U.S. history and from which an understanding and appreciation of those patterns may be gained
- Are associated with the lives of persons nationally significant in the history of the United States
- Represent some great idea or ideal of the American people
- Embody the distinguishing characteristics of an architectural type specimen that is exceptionally valuable for study of a period, style, or method of construction; or that represent a significant, distinctive, and exceptional entity whose components may lack individual distinction
- Are composed of integral parts of the environment that are not sufficiently significant by reason of historical association or artistic merit to warrant individual recognition but that collectively compose an entity of exceptional historic or artistic significance; or that outstandingly commemorate or illustrate a way of life or culture
- Have yielded or may be likely to yield information of major scientific importance by revealing new cultures or by shedding light on periods of occupation over large areas of the United States

Ordinarily, cemeteries, birthplaces, graves of historic figures, properties owned by religious institutions or used for religious purposes, structures that have been moved from their original locations, reconstructed historic buildings, and properties that have achieved significance within the last 50 years are not considered appropriate for addition to the National Park System unless they have transcendent importance, unless they possess inherent architectural or artistic significance, or unless no other site associated with that theme remains.

Examples of *nationally significant recreational resources* include:

- A natural or cultural feature providing a special setting for a variety of recreational activities different from those available at the local or regional level
- A spacious area located near a major population center with the potential to provide exceptional recreational opportunities and to serve visitors from around the nation rather than solely from the immediate vicinity
- An area that protects a unique recreational resource that is scarce and disappearing in a multistate region, such as an outstanding recreational river, a unique maritime environment or coastline, or a unique scenic area
- A unique combination of natural, cultural, and recreational resources that collectively offer outstanding opportunities for public use and enjoyment even though each feature might not individually be considered nationally significant

An area that is nationally significant also must meet criteria for suitability and feasibility to qualify as a potential addition to the system. To be *suitable* for inclusion an area must represent a natural or cultural theme or type of recreational resource that is not already adequately represented in the National Park System or is not comparably represented and protected for public enjoyment by another land-managing entity. Adequacy of representation is determined on a case-by-case basis by comparing the proposed area with other units in the system for differences or simi-

larities in the character, quality, or combination of resources and in opportunities for public enjoyment. To be *feasible* as a new unit in the system, an area's natural systems and/or historic settings must be of sufficient size and appropriate configuration to insure long-term protection of the resources and to accommodate public use. It must have potential for efficient administration at a reasonable cost. Important feasibility factors include land ownership, acquisition costs, access, threats to the resource, and staff or development requirements.

Alternative management options to National Park Service management might adequately protect resources even if they are significant, suitable, and feasible additions to the system. Additions to the National Park System will not usually be recommended if another arrangement can provide adequate protection and opportunity for public enjoyment. Congress decides if an area should be added to the National Park System or if some other action might be appropriate. Congressional committees usually hold hearings on proposed additions to the system and ask the Secretary of the Interior for recommendations. Studies by the National Park Service provide information to help the secretary develop a position and to help Congress decide what action to take.

Park Planning Process

Each park is to prepare a *statement for management,* which is to be evaluated by the superintendent and the regional director every 2 years and revised as necessary. This document compiles information about the park's purpose, the nature and significance of its resources, the existing uses of its lands and water, its regional context and adjacent land considerations, the legislative and administrative requirements for its management, the influences on park resources and the experience of park visitors, and nonrecreational park use by Native Americans and others. This information is used to identify major issues and problems that need to be addressed, to determine the need for additional information, and to establish park management objectives, all of which will also be included in the statement for management. The statement for management assesses existing conditions without identifying solutions. An analysis of the plans and tasks needed to address issues, gather information, and achieve objectives is included in the *outline of planning document.* This programming document, evaluated annually by the superintendent and regional director and updated as necessary, contains a priority listing of the studies and surveys needed to produce an adequate information base for planning and compliance; it also includes the plans and designs needed for the park.

A sufficient *information base* is needed before a plan is initiated. Each park must develop, gather, compile, store, analyze, and update information about natural and cultural resources and regional demographic, ethnographic, and socioeconomic data relevant to planning and management. These data serve as an information base for formulating proposals, evaluating alternatives, and making decisions during planning. Opportunities are to be provided for ample public participation throughout the entire planning process. These opportunities for public participation may include public workshops and meetings, informal work sessions on particular issues, and public review and comment on draft documents.

Each park is to have an approved *general management plan* (GMP), which sets forth a management concept for the park; establishes a role for the unit within the context of regional trends and plans for conservation, recreation, transportation, economic development, and other regional issues; and identifies strategies for resolving issues and achieving management objectives, usually within a period of 15 years. Until a GMP is completed and approved, the management objectives established by the statement for management are to guide day-to-day operations. No new development or major rehabilitation may take place without an approved GMP. The GMP components will be reviewed periodically and revised or amended as necessary to reflect new issues or changes in management objectives. General management planning will be conducted by an interdisciplinary team of planning professionals and park managers. The superintendents will have the major planning responsibility in their own parks. This planning team may include staff from the Denver Service Center, the regional office, the Harpers Ferry Center, and other field offices. As required by the National Environmental Policy Act, during the planning process a range of alternatives will be formulated to evaluate distinct management approaches for dealing with the issues. All GMPs and their accompanying environmental documents will consider "no action" and other reasonable alternatives. If the actions proposed in the plan constitute a major federal action significantly affecting environmental quality, an environmental impact statement is to be filed. Specific guidelines are provided in the *National Environmental Policy Act Guideline* (NPS—12).

The general management plan is to provide a system of *management zoning* for park lands and waters to designate where various strategies for management and use will best fulfill management objectives and achieve the purpose of the park. The delineation of management zones is based on an evaluation of the congressionally established purposes of the park; the nature of the park's natural and cultural resources; all past, existing, and anticipated uses; and park management objectives. The management zoning system recognizes that different types of parks have different purposes and consequently should be managed differently. There are four primary management zones: natural, cultural, park development, and special use. Within this framework, subzones may be further delineated for any park where it serves a useful purpose. The zones and their basic management strategies are described as follows:

Natural Zone   The land and water in this zone is managed in order to conserve natural resources and ecological processes and to provide for their use and enjoyment by the public in ways that do not adversely affect these resources and processes. Development in this zone is limited to dispersed recreational and essential management facilities that have no adverse effect on scenic quality and natural processes and that are essential for management, use, and appreciation of natural resources. Examples of typical facilities include trails, signs and trailside information displays, walk-in primitive shelters, walk-in storage facilities, stream-gauging devices, weather stations, and small-boat docks. Types of natural subzones include "outstanding natural area," "natural environment," "protected natural area," "wilderness," "research natural area," and "special management."

Cultural Zone   This zone includes lands managed for the preservation, protection, and interpretation of cultural resources and their settings in order to

provide for their use and enjoyment by the public. Cultural resources key to the purposes of the park are classed in this category. Other cultural resources—including properties listed or eligible for listing in the National Register of Historic Places, along with resources not eligible for the register but worth preserving for interpretive or other management purposes—are included in the zone that best reflects the primary management emphasis of their particular area of the park. Development in the cultural zone must be compatible with preservation and interpretation of cultural values. Consistent with policies for preservation and use of cultural resources, historic structures may be adaptively used for utilitarian or other purposes. Types of cultural subzones include "preservation," "adaptive use," and "commemoration."

Park Development Zone   This zone includes land that is managed to provide and maintain facilities serving park managers and visitors. It includes areas where park development or intensive use may substantially alter the natural environment or the setting for culturally significant resources. The development zone includes the facilities themselves and all associated lands directly modified as a result of their continuing management and use. Each development zone should be restricted to the smallest area necessary, and impacts associated with such development should be mitigated to the greatest extent possible. New development zones are to be established only after considering alternative sites, including sites outside the park. Types of park development subzones include "administrative development," "visitor support," and "landscape management area."

Special-Use Zone   This zone includes lands and waters that the National Park Service anticipates will continue to be used for activities not appropriate in other zones. Types of special-use subzones include "commercial," "exploration and mining," "grazing," "forest utilization," and "reservoir."

Every general management plan should include interrelated proposals for resource protection and management; land protection; cooperation with associated local interests; interpretation; visitor use; Native American activities; accessibility for disabled visitors; carrying capacities; park operations; and a general indication of the location, size, capacity, and function of physical developments. A plan implementation schedule and cost estimate are also required. Other elements that may be added to GMPs include development concept plans; land protection plans; boundary studies; land suitablility analyses; wilderness suitability reviews; and detailed strategies for access, circulation, resource management, mineral management, and interpretation. Such planning guidance may be incorporated into the GMP or separated into individual studies or implementation plans.

Following the approval of a general management plan, the park's outline of planning requirements are updated to guide plan implementation. The GMP is a comprehensive plan that varies in detail with the size and complexity of a given park. In most instances, more detailed plans and studies are prepared for subjects that are addressed only generally in the GMP. All implementation plans should be consistent with the GMP. Examples of implementation plans include development concept plans, land protection plans, wilderness management plans, resource management plans, mineral management plans, concession management plans, backcountry management plans, historic structure reports, and exhibit plans. These plans

are prepared in accordance with guidelines developed by staff in their respective program areas.

Recreational Management

The management policies for each of the nine major sections of the National Park Service's *Management Policies* (1988) are presented in Table 3.10. This section will focus on the management policies that pertain especially to recreational land uses:

Table 3.10   National Park Service Summary of Management Policies

Park System Planning
The National Park Service will conduct planning activities to evaluate possible additions to the national park system; to identify how park resources will be preserved and how parks will be used and developed to provide for public enjoyment; to facilitate coordination with other agencies and interests; and to involve the public in decision making about park resources, activities, and facilities. NPS plans will represent the Park Service's commitment to the public and to Congress of how parks will be managed.

Land Protection
The National Park Service will use all available authorities to ensure that lands within park boundaries are protected. Where parks contain nonfederal lands, the Park Service will identify the minimum interest that needs to be acquired to carry out park purposes and will use cost-effective protection methods.

Natural Resource Management
The National Park Service will manage the natural resources of the national park system to maintain, rehabilitate, and perpetuate their inherent integrity.

Cultural Resource Management
The National Park Service will preserve and foster appreciation of the cultural resources in its custody through appropriate programs of research, treatment, protection, and interpretation.

Wilderness Preservation and Management
The National Park Service will manage wilderness areas for the use and enjoyment of the American people in such manner as will leave them unimpaired for future use and enjoyment as wilderness. Management will include the protection of these areas, the preservation of their wilderness character, and the gathering and dissemination of information regarding their use and enjoyment as wilderness. Public purposes of wilderness will include recreation, scenic preservation, scientific study, education, conservation, and historical use.

Interpretation and Education
The National Park Service will conduct interpretive programs in all parks to instill an understanding and appreciation of the value of parks and their resources; to develop public support for preserving park resources; to provide the information necessary to ensure the successful adaptation of visitors to park environments; and to encourage and facilitate appropriate, safe, minimum-impact use of park resources.

Use of the Parks
The National Park Service will promote and regulate the use of parks, and it will provide those services necessary to meet the basic needs of park visitors and to achieve each park's management objectives.

Park Facilities
The National Park Service will provide appropriate facilities necessary for resource protection and required for visitor enjoyment of parks. The visitor and management facilities provided by the Park Service and its concessioners will be harmonious with park resources, compatible with natural processes, aesthetically pleasing, functional, as accessible as possible to all segments of the population, energy-efficient, and cost-effective.

Concessions Management
The National Park Service will provide, through the use of concessions, those commercial facilities and services within the parks necessary for visitors' use and enjoyment. Concession development will be limited to that necessary and appropriate for public use and enjoyment of the parks and be consistent, to the highest degree possible, with their preservation and conservation.

Source: National Park Service, *Management Policies* (1988).

Recreational Use—General   The National Park Service encourages recreational activities that are consistent with applicable legislation, that promote visitor enjoyment of park resources through a direct association or relation to those resources, that are consistent with the protection of resources, and that are compatible with other visitor uses. Recreational uses that may be allowed include, but are not limited to, boating, camping, bicycling, fishing, hiking, horseback riding and packing, outdoor sports, picnicking, scuba diving, cross-country skiing, caving, mountain and rock climbing, and swimming. General regulations addressing aircraft use, off-road bicycling, hang-gliding, hunting, off-road vehicle use, and snowmobiling require that special regulations be developed before these uses may be authorized in parks. Appropriate tools for managing recreational activities may include general or special regulations; permit and reservation systems; and local restrictions, public use limits, closures, and designations implemented under the discretionary authority of the superintendent. Any restrictions on recreational use will be limited to the minimum necessary to protect park resources and values and to promote visitor safety and enjoyment. The National Park Service will consider the park's purposes and the effects on park resources and visitors when determining the appropriateness of a specific recreational activity in a specific park. Unless the activity is mandated by statute, the Park Service will not allow a recreational activity in a park or in certain locations within a park if it would involve or result in any of the following:

- Inconsistency with the park's enabling legislation or proclamation, or derogation of the values or purposes for which the park was established
- Unacceptable impacts on visitor enjoyment due to interference or conflict with other visitor use activities
- Consumptive use of park resources (does not apply to certain traditional activities specifically authorized by National Park Service general regulations)
- Unacceptable impacts on park resources or natural processes
- Unacceptable levels of danger to the welfare or safety of the public, including participants in the activity under consideration.

Wilderness   Public use of any motorized equipment or any form of mechanical transport, including bicycles, is prohibited outside of Alaska. The use of hand-propelled watercraft is allowed but must be removed at the end of each trip. Mobility-impaired persons may use wheelchairs. The Wilderness Act does authorize the use of aircraft and motorboats where their use had been established prior to wilderness designation. Activities such as guide services for outfitted horseback riding, hiking, mountain climbing, and river trips or similar activities may be authorized and appropriate if conducted under the terms and conditions outlined in the park's wilderness management plan and in documents authorizing concessions or commercial use. The only structures allowed to support such commercial services are temporary shelters, such as tents, which are to be removed from the wilderness after each trip.

Backcountry Use   The National Park Service uses the term *backcountry* to refer to primitive, undeveloped portions of parks. This is not a special management zone but refers to a general condition of land that may occur in any appropriate zone or subzone. Backcountry use is managed to avoid unacceptable

impacts on park resources or adverse effects on visitor enjoyment of appropriate recreational experiences. The Park Service identifies acceptable limits of impacts, monitors backcountry use levels and resource conditions, and takes prompt corrective action when unacceptable impacts occur. Management strategies designed to guide the preservation, management, and use of the backcountry and to achieve the park's management objectives are integrated into the park's backcountry management plan. The number and types of facilities to support visitor use, including sanitary facilities, are limited to the minimum necessary to achieve a park's backcountry management objectives and to provide for the health and safety of park visitors. Refuse may not be disposed of in backcountry areas, except that combustibles may be burned where authorized.

River Use   A river management plan is developed for each park having significant levels of river use or the potential for such use. Public use is to be managed to prevent unacceptable impacts on aquatic or riverine resources or adverse effects on visitor enjoyment. Each river management plan includes specific procedures for disposing of refuse and human waste.

Fishing   Recreational fishing is allowed in parks where it is authorized by federal law or where it is not specifically prohibited and does not interfere with the functions of natural aquatic ecosystems or riparian zones. Where fishing is allowed, it is conducted in accordance with applicable federal laws and treaty rights and state laws and regulations. However, the National Park Service may restrict fishing activities whenever necessary to achieve the management objectives outlined in a park's resource management plan.

Hunting and Trapping   Hunting, trapping, and any other method of harvesting wildlife by the public are allowed in parks only where specifically authorized by federal law. Where such an activity is authorized on a discretionary basis under federal law, it may take place:

- Only after the Park Service has determined that the activity will not compromise public safety and enjoyment and that the proposed use is consistent with sound resource management principles.
- Only pursuant to special regulations.
- Only if conducted in accordance with federal laws and applicable laws of the state or states where the park is located.

The National Park Service may establish regulations or closures that are more restrictive than applicable state regulations if it finds that such restrictions are necessary for public safety, resource protection, or visitor enjoyment.

Off-Road Vehicle Use   The use of motor vehicles is limited to park roads and parking areas and to routes and areas designated for off-road motor vehicle use by special regulation and only in national preserves, national seashores, national lakeshores, and national recreation areas. Routes and areas are designated only in locations where there will be no significant adverse impacts on the area's natural, cultural, and scenic resources and values and in consideration of other visitor uses.

Snowmobiles   The use of snowmobiles is prohibited except on designated routes and frozen water surfaces that are used during other seasons by motor vehicles and motorboats, respectively, or as otherwise specifically provided by federal

statute. Routes and water surfaces are designated for snowmobile use only where there will be no significant adverse impacts on the park's natural, cultural, or scenic resources and values relative to other visitor uses. Routes and water surfaces designated for snowmobile use are identified in special regulations.

Hiking Trails and Walks   Trail design will vary to accommodate a range of users. Heavily used trails and walks outside the backcountry may be surfaced as necessary for visitor safety, accessibility to persons with impaired mobility, resource protection, and erosion control. Wetlands are generally avoided, but where necessary they may be spanned by a boardwalk or other means that will not disturb hydrologic processes. Backcountry trails are unsurfaced and modest in character, except where a more durable surface is needed. Artificiality in the form of nonnative materials is avoided in the backcountry.

Equestrian Trails   Equestrian trails and related support facilities, such as feed boxes and hitch rails, can be provided where consistent with park objectives and where site conditions are suitable.

Bicycle Trails   To encourage and facilitate bicycle use, bicycle travel ways may be integrated with park roads where safe, feasible, and appropriate. Bicycle trails can be provided where appropriate and where site conditions are suitable; they may be paved or stabilized for the safety and convenience of the users.

Interpretive Trails   Interpretive trails and walks, both guided and self-guiding, may be used for purposes of visitor appreciation and understanding of park values.

Trailheads   Trailheads and trail access points, from which trail use can begin, should be carefully tied into other elements of the park development and circulation system to facilitate trail use and management.

Trail Bridges   Trail bridges can be used for crossing swift waters, areas prone to flash flooding, and other places constituting a safety hazard. Less obtrusive alternatives such as culverts, fords, and trail relocation, should be considered before building a bridge. If a bridge is determined to be appropriate, it should be kept to a minimum size needed to serve trail users, designed to be in harmony with the surrounding natural scene, and as unobtrusive as possible.

Signs   Signs should be carefully planned and designed to fulfill their important roles of conveying an appropriate park image and of providing information and orientation to visitors. Each park is to have an approved parkwide sign plan that establishes design criteria based on that park's unique resources and values. Entrance and other key signs should be distinctively designed to reflect the character of the park. Signs are held to the minimum number, size, and wording required to serve their intended functions, so as to minimally intrude on the natural or historic setting.

Entrance Stations   Entrance and fee collection stations should be harmonious with the park environment and should reflect the architectural character of the park.

Visitor Centers   Where necessary to provide information and interpretive services, visitor centers can be constructed at locations identified in approved plans. To minimize visual intrusions and harm to major park features, visitor centers should not be located near such features. They will be constructed only

where it has been determined that indoor media are the most effective means of communicating major elements of the park story and that a central public contact point is needed. A visitor center, where appropriate, may include information services, sales of educational materials and theme-related items, audiovisual programs, museums, artifact storage, exhibits, and other staffed or self-help programs and spaces necessary for a quality visitor experience.

Amphitheaters Amphitheaters may be provided at campgrounds and other locations where formal interpretive programs are desirable. Campfire circles may be provided in campgrounds to accommodate evening programs and informal social gatherings.

Wayside Exhibits Wayside exhibits may be provided along roads and heavily used walks and trails to interpret resources on site.

Viewing Devices Viewing devices (pedestal binoculars or telescopes) may be provided at appropriate locations when the superintendent determines such viewing devices to be desirable for meaningful interpretation or understanding of park resources. Viewers may be provided by the National Park Service or by others under a concession permit or contract.

Overnight Accommodations and Food Services In many cases overnight accommodations and food services are not needed within a park. However, visitors need these services in the park when the distance and travel time to accommodations outside the park are too great to permit reasonable use. Furthermore, certain activities, such as backcountry use, may require overnight stays. Overnight facilities and food services are restricted to the kinds and levels necessary to achieve each park's purposes and are provided only when other public agencies or the private sector cannot adequately provide them in the park vicinity. Overnight accommodations may vary from unimproved backcountry campsites to motel- or hotel-type lodging, as appropriate. Where adequate facilities exist or can feasibly be developed by private enterprise to serve park visitors' needs for commercial services outside park boundaries, such facilities are not expanded or developed within parks.

Campgrounds Where campgrounds are determined to be necessary, their design should accommodate the differences between recreational vehicle camping and tent camping and should consider terrain, soils, vegetation, climate, special needs of users, visual and auditory privacy, and other relevant factors. The National Park Service generally does not provide a full range of amenities and utility hookups. Portable generators are allowed, but their use may be limited to designated areas. Shower facilities may be provided where feasible. Modest-sized play areas for small children are permissible, as are informal areas for field sports. Wherever wood fires at individual sites must be restricted or prohibited because of fire danger, air pollution, or other hazards, alternatives such as facilities for use of charcoal or other fuels or central cook sheds may be provided. Sanitary dump stations are provided at or near campgrounds for recreational vehicles when a need exists. Campgrounds intended to accommodate large recreational vehicles or buses are located only where existing roads can safely accommodate them and an increased traffic load. Campgrounds will not exceed 250 sites unless a larger number of sites has been approved by the director of the National Park Service. Where desirable

for purposes of management, tent camping may be accommodated in separate campgrounds or in separately designated areas within campgrounds. Provision may also be made for accommodating organized groups in separate campgrounds or in separately designated areas. Boaters' campgrounds may be provided in parks with waters used for recreational boating. The need for campgrounds and their size, location, and number is determined by (1) the type of water body (river, lake, reservoir, or saltwater area); (2) the availability and resiliency of potential campsites; (3) the feasibility of providing and maintaining docking, beaching, mooring, camping, and sanitary facilities; and (4) the potential impacts on park natural and cultural resources.

Backcountry Campsites   Backcountry and wilderness campsites are permitted but only within the acceptable limits of use determined by the park's resource management plan or other pertinent planning document.

Hostels and Shelters   Hostels are low-cost, supervised accommodations that encourage and facilitate energy-efficient, nonmotorized enjoyment of parks and their surrounding regions by individuals and families. Such facilities, along with hostellike accommodations, such as huts and shelters, are considered in the planning process if overnight use is determined to be an appropriate use of the park, particularly as a means of encouraging use of trails and backcountry areas. The National Park Service cooperates with other agencies, nonprofit organizations, park concessioners, and others to plan and develop hostels, where appropriate, as part of hostel systems. Hostels are to be managed by others under the provisions of concession policies and guidelines or by the National Park Service where management by others is not prudent or feasible. At a minimum, hostels should contain sheltered overnight accommodations and sanitary facilities, and they will usually contain cooking, eating, and recreation spaces. Hostels may be used for other park programs, such as environmental education or interpretation. Although nonmotorized access to hostels is emphasized, motorized transportation may also be available.

Comfort Stations   Comfort stations should have waste disposal systems that meet public health standards. Levels of use will determine the size and nature of utility systems provided. Low-water-use or waterless (oil and composting) toilets are to be considered where water supply and wastewater disposal problems exist. Chemical toilets in portable enclosures may be used for temporary purposes where necessary. Pit privies, vault toilets, and other alternatives that meet public health standards may suffice in little-used areas where utility services are not readily available.

Picnic and Other Day-Use Areas   Picnic areas and other day-use areas to be used for specific purposes (such as play areas) are provided on a limited basis as appropriate to meet existing visitor needs.

Facilities for Water Recreation   Boating facilities (such as courtesy docks, boat ramps, floating-sewage pump-out stations, and marinas), breakwaters, and fish cleaners are provided as appropriate for safe visitor enjoyment of water recreation resources and to protect natural resources.

Skiing Facilities   Because downhill skiing is an active sport activity that requires extensive development and can be provided outside park areas, it will generally not be provided for in parks. The National Park Service will not permit

new downhill skiing facilities or associated structures in any unit of the National Park System. Where such facilities were provided based on previous policy, their use may continue. Any proposal to eliminate or increase the capacity of such existing facilities will be accomplished through the National Park Service planning process and involve public participation and an environmental assessment of effects.

Other Visitor Facilities   Other visitor facilities may be provided where necessary for visitor enjoyment of the area and where consistent with the protection of park values. Visitor facilities determined to be detrimental to park values are not permitted.

Planning Criteria for Park Concessions   Any building program or service authorized in a concession contract or permit must conform with the appropriate approved plan(s) for the area in consideration. A decision to authorize a park concession is based on a determination that the following conditions are met:

- The facility or service is necessary and appropriate for public use and enjoyment of the park in which it is located.
- The use of the facility or service will enhance the use and enjoyment of the park without resulting in impairment of park resources and values.
- The facility or service will be located where the least impact on park resources and values will occur.
- The number of sites and the locations and sizes of the tracts of land assigned for necessary facilities will be the minimum essential for proper and satisfactory operation of the facilities, consistent with proper spacing and preservation of aesthetic values. Moreover, such developments as are permitted will be constructed to be as harmonious as possible with their surroundings.

References

Albright, Horace, as told to Robert Cahn. *The Birth of the National Park Service: The Founding Years, 1913–33.* Salt Lake City, Utah: Howe Brothers, 1985.

Catlin, George. *The Manners, Customs, and Conditions of the North American Indians.* London: 1841, Vol. 1, 261–262 (originally published as a series of letters in 1833 in the *New York Daily Commercial Advertiser*).

Darling, F. Frazer and Noel D. Eichhorn. *Man and Nature in the National Parks.* Washington, D.C.: The Conservation Foundation, 1971.

Everhardt, William C. *The National Park Service.* Boulder, Colo.: Westview Press, 1983.

Foresta, Ronald A. *America's National Parks and Their Keepers.* Washington, D.C.: Resources for the Future, 1984.

Ise, John. *Our National Park Policy: A Critical History.* Baltimore: Johns Hopkins Press, 1961.

National Park Service. *Criteria for Parklands.* Washington, D.C.: National Park Service, "not dated."

National Park Service. *Management Policies.* Washington, D.C.: National Park Service, 1988.

National Park Service. *National Park Statistical Abstract.* Denver: National Park Service, 1991 and earlier.

National Park Service. *The National Parks: Shaping the System.* Washington, D.C.: National Park Service, 1991.

National Park Service. *1991 Annual Statistical Abstract.* Denver: National Park Service, 1992.

National Park Service. *The National Parks: Index 1991*. Washington, D.C.: U.S. Government Printing Office, 1992.

Runte, Alfred. *The National Parks: An American Experience*. Lincoln: University of Nebraska Press, 1979.

Shankland, Robert. *Stephen Mather of the National Parks*. New York: Alfred A. Knopf, 1951.

Swain, Donald C. *Wilderness Defender: Horace M. Albright and Conservation*. Chicago: University of Chicago Press, 1970.

Tilden, Freeman. *The National Parks*. New York: Alfred A. Knopf, 1951.

## CHAPTER 4

National Parks: Alaska

> .... *preserving the priceless heritage of Alaska's natural resources is my own number-one environmental priority. . . . We owe our children and their children and our nation our best.*
>
> President Jimmy Carter (1980)

Alaska is being given special attention in this book for two primary reasons: (1) the vast geographic space it occupies; and (2) the huge amount of land that was afforded protection for amenity resource purposes by the Alaska National Interest Lands Conservation Act in 1980. Chapter 3 focused on the National Park System as an entity. The present chapter will focus on the National Park System in Alaska. Alaska's land ownership patterns—and resulting recreational geography—have changed in a shorter period of time than in any other place in the United States. It was legislation passed in Washington, D.C. that brought about these changes. This drastic change in land ownership and land management practices started with the Alaska Statehood Act (1958) and it continued with the passage by Congress of the Alaska Native Claims Settlement Act (1971). However, the Alaska National Interest Lands Conservation Act (1980) affected more land than the combined change brought about by both the previous two acts. No single piece of public land legislation has ever impacted public lands to the degree of the Alaska National Interest Lands Conservation Act. This "gift to the American people" and to the world was the last major piece of environmental legislation signed by outgoing President Jimmy Carter. When environmental historians in the future write the history of the American conservation movement, they will most likely identify this act as one of, if not the most, important pieces of federal environmental/land-use legislation enacted in the 20th century. It added over 100 million acres of land to the national conservation system, protecting most of this land for its amenity resource value.

GEOGRAPHY

In terms of size—591,004 square miles—if Alaska were a country it would rank as the 21st largest in the world. Within the United States, Alaska is larger than the combined areas of the next three largest states—Texas, California, and Montana.

Geographically, Alaska extends from longitude 130°W to 173°E and from latitude 52°N to 71°N. If one were to superimpose a map of Alaska on the "lower 48," as Alaskans refer to the 48 conterminous states, its southeastern corner would be on the Georgia coast, the Aleutian Islands would extend through southern coastal California, and the North Slope would be on the U.S.-Canadian border in northern Minnesota and Wisconsin. The Aleutian Island chain alone extends for 1700 miles. Twenty-five percent of the state lies poleward of the Arctic Circle. This high latitude location makes for long hours of daylight in the summer but for long hours of darkness in the winter. At the latitude of the Arctic Circle (66½°N), and poleward, on the summer solstice (June 21) there are 24 hours of continual daylight; conversely, on the winter solstice (December 21) the entire 24-hour-period is dark. The long, heavily indented Alaskan coastline is longer than the entire coastline of the lower 48 states.

Alaska is a land of great contrasts in terms of geomorphology, climate, flora, and fauna. The highest mountain in North America, Mt. McKinley (20,320 ft.), lies in the Alaska Range in south-central Alaska. To the southeast lie the Wrangell Mountains (14,163 ft.) and Mt. St. Elias (18,008 ft.). To the north of these high mountains of the south lies a central plateau and lowland drained by the Yukon and Kuskokwim Rivers. In the north the high mountains of the Brooks Range (8500 ft.) extend east-west. The Brooks Range serves as a major climatic divide, with the area to the south having much hotter summers and much colder winters. In summer, temperatures can reach 85°F or hotter but in winter can reach −60°F or colder. The summers in this central region are short and warm to hot and the winters are very long and extremely cold. The vegetation to the north of the Brooks Range on the North Slope of Alaska is tundra and is treeless. Here, winters are not as cold and summers are not as hot as the region to the south of the Brooks Range. The wind-swept cool marine climate of the Aleutians is the cause for an absence of trees. Between the Alaska Range and the Brooks Range the vegetation is dominated by taiga—northern coniferous forest—whose trees are small in size and have little commercial timber value. This is the area of subarctic climate—the most continental climate in the world. But in southern and southeastern coastal Alaska the temperate, marine west coast climate with its copious rainfall is the reason for "big trees," such as the Sitka spruce and western hemlock. This area has Alaska's only two national forests—the Chugach and Tongass—and the largest trees. Some of the largest tidewater glaciers in the world are found in southeastern Alaska. Precipitous mountains which rise as much as 9000 feet from the sea isolate the coastal settlements from the Canadian mainland. Among the settlements clinging to the coast of the Inside Passage is the capital city Juneau. The fog-bound Aleutian Islands are barren tundra and divide the Bering Sea from the Pacific Ocean.

Alaska was purchased in 1867 from Russia for $7.2 million and was referred to as *"Seward's Folly,"* after Secretary of State William Seward. Two gold rushes in the 1890s—the Klondike (1896) and the Alaskan (1899) at Nome—opened up the interior to settlement. In 1912, Alaska received territorial status. Alaska became the site of major military bases after the Japanese invaded Attu and Kiska in the Aleutian Islands in 1942. On January 3, 1959, Alaska became the 49th state. The 1968 discovery of a major oil field at Prudhoe Bay on the northern coast resulted in the construction of the Alaskan pipeline between 1974 and 1977 to Valdez on the southern coast. This set the stage for a period of rapid population growth. There was a price to be paid for this tremendous period of economic growth. In 1989 the largest oil spill in the

history of the United States occurred in Prince William Sound when the *Exxon Valdez* struck Bligh Reef. Even though Alaska saw a 47 percent rate of population growth between 1980 and 1990, its population of 550,043 is still the second smallest in the nation—even less than Vermont's 562,758 people (Wyoming = 453,588). The three largest cities are Anchorage (224,392), Fairbanks (30,345), and Juneau (26,696).

CHANGES BROUGHT BY FEDERAL LEGISLATION

Congress divided Alaska's public domain by passing three major pieces of legislation: (1) the *Alaska Statehood Act* (1958), (2) the *Alaska Native Claims Settlement Act* (*ANCSA*) (1971), and (3) the *Alaska National Interest Lands Conservation Act* (*ANILCA*) (1980). Figure 4.1 graphically depicts the Alaskan land status that has resulted from this federal legislation. Table 4.1 presents a detailed summary of these changes for each owner/classification of land. In 1958, over 80 percent of Alaska's 375 million acres were open, public domain, under the jurisdiction of the Bureau of Land Management (BLM). At this time, 96 percent of the entire state was under federal ownership. Passage of the acts of 1958, 1971, and 1980 resulted in great changes in the land ownership and management policies. Of the four major federal land-managing agencies, the BLM lost the greatest amount of land under its jurisdiction from 309 million acres in 1958 to 47 million acres today. The federal agencies that gained the most from these land transfers were the Fish and Wildlife Service (from 22.2 million acres to 75.4 million acres, a gain of 53.2 million acres), the National Park Service (from 7.5 million acres to 52 million acres, a gain of 44.5 million acres), and the Forest Service (from 20.7 million acres to 23 million acres, a gain of 2.3 million acres). The other land gainers, at the expense of the BLM, were the state of Alaska, which gained 105 million acres, and the Alaskan natives, who gained 44 million acres.

The division of the public domain took place slowly and with much controversy during the first 20 years after Alaska became a state. Many interest groups and in-

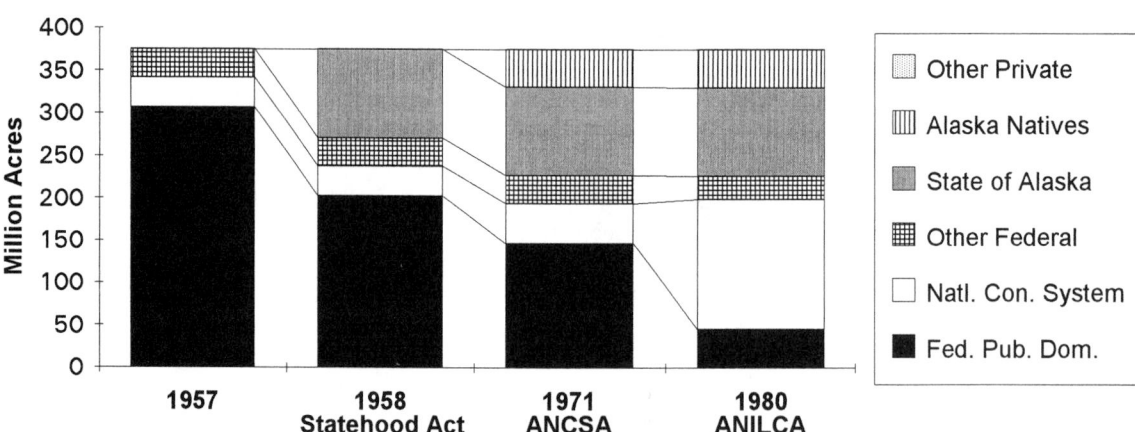

Figure 4.1   Alaska land status resulting from federal legislation. (*Source:* Leask, Linda. "Changing Ownership and Management of Alaska Lands." *Alaska Review of Social and Economic Conditions.* Vol. XXII, No. 2, October, 1985.)

Table 4.1 Changes in Alaska Landownership, 1965–1985 (in millions of acres)

Owner/Classification	1965	1985	Ultimate Entitlement	1985 as Percent of Ultimate	% Change, 1965 to Ultimate*	Ultimate* Ownership
Federal lands						
Public domain	274	80.0	45	173%	−83%	
Conservation and Recreation Areas						
Wildlife refuges	22.2	75.4	75.4	100	+240%	
Parks, preserves, monuments	7.5	52.0	52.0	100	+593%	
Forests, monuments	20.7	23.0	23.0	100	+11%	
National petroleum reserve	23.0	23.0	23.0	100		
Native reserves[a]	4.1	0.09	0.09	100		
Military reserves	2.6	1.8	1.8	100	−28%	
Other	7.5	2.6	2.6	100	−66%	
All federal lands	361	260	225	115%	−38%	60%
State lands						
Parks	0.9	3.2	N/A			
Game refuges, sanctuaries, CHAs[b]	0.3	2.0	N/A			
Forest		1.8	N/A			
Other	12.3	73.0	N/A			
All state lands[c]	13.5	+80.0	105.1	76%	+678%	28%
Municipal lands						
Transfers from state[d]		0.4	+.77			
Transfers from native Corps.[e]	N/A	N/A	N/A			
Other[f]	N/A	N/A	N/A			
All municipal lands	N/A	+0.4	+.77			0.2%
University of Alaska[g]	0.15	0.15	0.15	100%		0.04%
Private lands						
Native						
Corporations	0.015	33.2	44	75%		
Allotment[h]	0.0005	0.13	±1.2			
Townsite[i]		+0.0005	N/A			
All Native[j]	0.0155	33.3	+44			11.7%
Other private						
Land disposal programs (state)		0.35[k]	N/A			
Other	0.5	1.0[l]	+1.0			
All other private	+0.5	1.35[l]	+1.35[m]			+0.4%[m]
All private lands	0.515	34.6	+45.35		+8800%	+12.1%
Total, Alaska Lands	375	375	375			100%

Table 4.1 Changes in Alaska Landownership, 1965–1985 (in millions of acres) (continued)

*"Ultimate" here means land transfers from the federal government to the state and the native corporations are complete.

[a]All native reserves in Alaska except for the Metlakatla Reserve on Annette Island were revoked by the 1971 Alaska Native Claims Settlement Act.

[b]CHAs = critical habitat areas.

[c]The 1965 and 1985 figures include not only lands to which the state government had patent, but also those that the federal government had "tentatively approved" for state ownership; this tentative approval in effect gives the state legal rights to lands that have not yet been surveyed and therefore cannot be patented.

[d]These are lands the state government is transferring to borough and city governments under the Municipal Entitlement Act, which allows municipal governments to select some of the state land within their boundaries. The existing boroughs and cities outside boroughs will ultimately receive 774,000 acres; new boroughs formed in the future could be entitled to more land.

[e]The claims settlement act requires native village corporations to reconvey some of their lands within communities to local governments for various public purposes; in places where there are no organized local governments, the state takes the land in trust. Originally, corporations were each required to transfer 1280 acres under this provision, but that requirement was recently changed to allow the corporations and local governments to decide acreages through negotiation. Almost no land has actually been conveyed to local governments so far, and it is not possible to say right now how many acres the village corporations will ultimately convey to local governments.

[f]Municipal governments do own some additional lands, acquired through purchase or other means, but figures on such lands are not readily available.

[g]The University of Alaska owns 150,000 acres that it received from the federal government because it is a land-grant college. This land is considered separate from state land; it is managed by the university and is not subject to the state's land-use plans.

[h]The Native Allotment Act of 1906 allowed Alaskan natives to apply for title to up to 160 acres; the act was revoked by the 1971 Alaska Native Claims Settlement Act, but the thousands of applications pending at that time were considered valid existing rights and are still being processed by the BLM. Figures cited here are rough estimates, based on approved and pending applications and average size of allotments approved in 1984. As of October 1984, 1029 allotments had been approved; the authors of this table multiplied that figure by 127 acres—the average size allotment approved in 1984—to reach an estimate of 131,000 acres conveyed under the program from 1906 through 1984. As of early 1985, the BLM had under consideration 9400 applications; to arrive at a rough estimate of how much land could be transferred if all these applications were approved, the authors multiplied 9400 by 127 acres. It is impossible right now to say just how many acres will ultimately be transferred to Alaska natives under the allotment program; there have been over the years a number of changes in standards for approving allotment applications, which have resulted in reconsideration of applications that were once rejected. There are also pending court suits that could substantially increase the number of allotments ultimately approved, including one case involving 535 allotment petitions.

[i]The Native Townsite Act of 1926 allowed native communities to apply for title to their townsite lands, although very little land was actually transferred under this act through 1971, when it was revoked by the Claims Settlement Act. However, the Department of the Interior took the position that applications pending in 1971 were valid existing rights, and village corporations were not able to apply for lands that had been applied for under the Town Site Act. The BLM continues to process townsite applications. Several native village groups have gone to court to try to have lands under townsite applications opened for selection by village corporations. The outcome of these court suits will largely determine how much more land will ultimately be conveyed under the Townsite Act.

[j]The 1985 figures include not only lands that have been patented to the village and regional corporations, but also lands that have been "interim conveyed"; these are lands to which the corporations have been awarded ownership but which are not yet patented because they have not been completely surveyed.

[k]The figure cited here is a very rough estimate of acreage that the state sold or otherwise disposed of under its various public land disposal programs, from statehood through 1984. More exact figures are difficult to get. The land disposal program is complex and has changed a number of times over the years. It is not possible to say right now how much land the state might ultimately offer for private ownership.

[m]How much private, nonnative land there will be in Alaska in the future is impossible to say right now; it depends on future public land disposal programs and other factors. Estimates.

Source: Adapted from Linda Leask, "Changing Ownership and Management of Alaska Lands," *Alaska Review of Social and Economic Conditions* 22(2):10–11, October 1985.

dividuals saw great opportunities in these huge acreages, which made up the largest undeveloped areas left in the United States. The chief claimants on the public domain were the new state government, which needed lands as an economic base; Alaskan natives, who had aboriginal claims to lands; industrial groups, which wanted Alaskan lands left open for exploration and development; and environmental organizations, which wanted large amounts of land added to the national conservation systems. The primary cause for this slow transfer of land was that the Interior Department withheld much of the public domain from state and native selection while Congress debated which lands to add to the national conservation systems. While there was enough public domain in Alaska to cover state and native land grants, not all lands were equally desirable due to resources having an uneven spatial distribution. In Alaska, the best lands for development and settlement are generally under 1000-ft elevation. One-third of Alaska's lands are above 2000 feet, and almost 10 percent are covered with glaciers. "And so over 20 years, there were many battles over who would get which lands. At base the bitterest fights came down to this: were certain Alaska lands most valuable for their beauty and wildlife habitats, or for their minerals and other resources" (Leask, 1985, 2). Through the three big land acts, all the parties got some of what they wanted, but none were entirely satisfied.

Although it was the acts of 1958, 1971, and 1980 that had the major impact on the geography of Alaska's land ownership and land management, the efforts to protect distinct areas of Alaska began more than a century ago. In 1869, Congress passed special legislation to protect seals in the Pribilof Islands. In 1892, President Harrison proclaimed the Afognak Forest and Fish Culture Reserve on Afognak Island, off Alaska's southwestern coast. During the first wave of conservation, President Theodore Roosevelt proclaimed the Alexander Archipelago and the Tongass Forest Reserve. In 1908 these two reserves were combined to form the 6.7-million-acre Tongass National Forest. Harrison also proclaimed a 4.9-million-acre Chugach National Forest in 1907. In 1910 President Taft fired Gifford Pinchot as Chief of the Forest Service because of controversy arising over the creation of these national forests in Alaska. In 1909 and 1912 Taft issued Executive Orders that established five national wildlife refuges along the Alaskan coast, and in 1913 he established the Aleutian Islands National Wildlife Refuge. In 1910 he also proclaimed the first site in Alaska to become part of our National Park System: a 107-acre national monument marking the site of the 1804 fort and battle at New Archangel commemorating the last major Tlingit Indian resistance to Russian colonization. This national monument was designated Sitka National Historical Park in 1972. In 1916, Old Kasaan was declared a national monument by President Wilson, put under the supervision of the Forest Service in the Agriculture Department, and later abolished in 1955. Eight of the totem poles from Old Kasaan were moved from the site and restored in the village of New Kasaan. The rest of Old Kasaan was so badly deteriorated that it was abolished.

In 1917, largely through the efforts of naturalist Charles Sheldon, Alaska's first national park—Mt. McKinley—was created (see Figure 4.2). In 1918, President Wilson proclaimed Katmai National Monument, and in 1925 President Coolidge created Glacier Bay National Monument. John Muir increased our knowledge about Glacier Bay as the result of several visits he made there during the 19th century. Mt. McKinley National Park, Katmai National Monument, Glacier Bay National Monument, and the 107-acre Sitka National Monument were the only National Park Service–admin-

Figure 4.2   Mount McKinley (20,320 ft.) dominates the landscape of Denali National Park and is the highest point in North America. (National Park Service photo)

istered areas in Alaska until 1976, when the Klondike Gold Rush National Historical Park was added to the system. The largest withdrawal of land from Alaska's public domain, made by President Harding in 1923, was a petroleum reserve on the North Slope of the Brooks Range named Navy Petroleum Number 4. Explorations of the Brooks Range by Robert Marshall in the 1930s inspired conservation organizations, such as the Wilderness Society, to work for preservation of the area. Marshall named the "Gates of the Arctic" in the central Brooks Range; this area was declared a Gates of the Arctic National Park in 1980. A 9-million-acre Arctic National Wildlife Range was established in the northeastern corner of the state in 1960. During the 1950s and 1960s the National Park Service conducted studies that identified 39 areas as potential additions to the National Park System in Alaska.

Alaska Statehood Act (1958)

Statehood was slow to come for Alaska. It was not until 2500 Americans were killed in combat on the Aleutian Islands of Attu and Kiska in 1942 that the bonds between the lower 48 states and Alaska started to mature. Military installations were constructed there, which introduced 300,000 American troops to Alaska's beauty. New momentum was gained in the quest for statehood after World War II, and in 1958 Congress passed the Alaska Statehood Act. This act set the stage for the first big reduction in Alaska's public-domain lands. It allowed the new state government the right to select 104 million acres from unreserved lands administered by the BLM. The state was given 25 years to make its selection. Table 4.1 and the second bar in Figure 4.1 indicate the shifts in landownership that resulted. The percentage distribution of land now was: federal public domain, 53 percent; state government, 27 percent; national conservation systems, 10 percent; other federal reserves, nearly 10 percent; and private lands, less than 1 percent. No other state government owns as much, or as

large a part of the lands within its borders. This grant surpassed the total acreage transferred to 17 western states on their admission to the Union. This large land grant was intended to give the state of Alaska an economic base. Other federal laws brought the state's entitlement to more than 105 million acres. The law also gave the state government ownership of the beds of most navigable rivers and lakes and of submerged lands up to 3 miles off its coasts. A major economic boost for the new state was that it would be allowed to retain 90 percent of the royalties generated from oil and mineral leases on the remaining public domain.

The state began its land selection in the 1960s, but those selections had barely started when the Department of the Interior stopped all land transfers to the state, and almost all other federal land transfers in Alaska, pending settlement of the land claims of Alaskan natives. The federal government had long recognized the rights of the natives to claim land as legitimate, but it never agreed on what land might be claimed. The Alaskan natives did not organize and press these land claims, except for the Court of Claims case of the Tlingit-Haida natives, until the state government began choosing its land. In 1964, they formed the Alaskan Federation of Natives, which gave them the political clout they had always lacked. By the end of the 1960s the natives had made claims totaling all of the land in Alaska. This is why the Interior Department implemented what was known as the *"land freeze,"* imposed by Secretary of Interior Udall in 1966, which virtually stopped all transfers of federal lands to the state of Alaska. The state had received only 14 million acres out of its entitlement. At this time (1968), a group of oil companies discovered the Prudhoe Bay oil field on the North Slope, proclaimed the largest discovery ever found in North America. This oil field lay under lands the federal government had already approved for state ownership. Within a month, a consortium of oil companies proposed building an 800-mile pipeline from Prudhoe Bay to Valdez, a small fishing village on Prince William Sound. Much of the land the pipeline would cross was under claim by Alaskan natives. *Suddenly the settlement of native claims became urgent—to the natives, the oil companies, and the state of Alaska.* The state government had two strong reasons for wanting native claims settled: (1) to end the freeze on land transfers, and (2) to clear the way for the pipeline to be built. The state would have a substantial income, since it owned the lands at Prudhoe Bay.

The state government now owns lands throughout Alaska, with most of its holdings concentrated in large blocks in south-central, southwestern, and interior regions. It also owns substantial acreages at and near Prudhoe Bay on the North Slope. The ownership of these lands has brought billions of dollars in royalties and other income from development of the Prudhoe Bay oil field. State holdings include lands with a number of known or suspected resources, including coal, petroleum, timber, and minerals. The state has chosen lands that can be (as some are) used as lands for home sites or farms. Some state lands are set aside for parks and wildlife sanctuaries. State parks covered 1 million acres in the late 1960s but increased to 3.2 million acres by 1985. Game refuges and sanctuaries were established on about 300,000 state acres in 1965, and by 1985, they covered 2 million acres. State forests, a category that did not exist in the 1960s, became estabished on almost 2 million acres by 1985. In a few instances, the state government owns lands within national conservation units created in 1980. Among the largest of these state holdings are those in Wrangell–St. Elias

National Park. The state plans to sell some of the lands within the park to private interests—a plan the National Park Service opposes. By 1985, the state had received more than 80 million acres of its entitlement. In recent years, municipalities have received more than 400,000 acres of state land under the municipal entitlement program, which allows municipalities to select up to 10 percent of the unreserved state lands within their boundaries.

Alaska Native Claims Settlement Act (1971)

The discovery of oil at Prudhoe Bay was the primary factor that set the stage for a fairly rapid passage by Congress in 1971 of the Alaska Native Claims Settlement Act. This act awarded Alaskan natives 40 million acres plus a cash payment of $962 million for renouncing all claims to the rest of the state. The act defined Alaskan natives as any Alaskan-born person at least one-quarter Eskimo, Aleut, or Indian. Half of the financial compensation was to be paid by the federal government and the other half from oil royalties. The native selections were to come largely from designated areas of federal land, mostly around villages. Villages on preexisting reserves were given the option of taking title to those lands; several did so, and that brought the native entitlements under the settlement to about 44 million acres. The act mandated the natives to form corporations for ownership of the land and management of the money. Only natives could hold shares in these corporations, and the shares could not be sold or exchanged for a period of 20 years. Twelve regional and more than 200 village corporations were established. These corporations began choosing their lands in the early 1970s.

Some natives were sardonic about their good fortune. Joe Upicksoun, president of the North Slope Native Association, remarked: "*Without intending to belittle your land, the real reason for the entire settlement is oil, which by accident is on our land, not yours.*" Despite this cynicism on the part of some natives, most groups were happy with the settlement. Dyan Zaslowsky summed it best:

> The discovery of mammoth oil reserves in Alaska carried with it something for everybody. The Natives secured their birthright (presumably), Alaskan boosters achieved their ultimate boom, and oil companies found something to sell. Conservationists found a way to save some land for the future, too (Zaslowsky and Wilderness Society, 1986, 268).

The 44 million acres awarded to Alaskan natives changed the picture of landownership in Alaska as shown in bar 3 of Figure 4.1 and in Table 4.1: state government, 27 percent; federal public domain, 40 percent; national conservation systems, 13 percent; Alaskan natives, almost 12 percent; other private land, less than 1 percent.

Far from clearing the way for resuming land transfers to the state, the Settlement Act added another layer of complication that hampered state and native selections for years to come because, once the state and natives selected their lands, something had to be done with the lands that remained in the public domain. The solution to

the disposition of the unreserved public domain lands was addressed by *Section 17(d)(2)* of the act:

> The Secretary ... is directed to withdraw from all forms of appropriations under the public land laws, including the mining and mineral leasing laws, and from selection under the Alaska Statehood Act, and from selection by Regional Corporations ... up to, but not to exceed, eighty million acres of unreserved public lands ... deemed suitable for addition or creation as units of the National Park, Forest, Wildlife Refuge, and Wild and Scenic Rivers Systems.

This provision was added to the act to keep claims from being made on it by the state and Alaskan natives while Congress decided whether to include them in the national conservation systems. The act specified that the Secretary of the Interior had 2 years to make his recommendations, and furthermore, that if Congress did not act within 5 years, the withdrawn lands would revert back to public domain status and claims could be made against them.

Most of the 35 million acres of private land in Alaska in 1985 belonged to the native corporations. Individuals owned less than 2 million acres at this time. Prior to the passage of the Alaska Native Claims Settlement Act, Alaskan natives could get title to land under two federal laws—the Native Allotment Act of 1906 and the Native Townsite Act of 1926. The Claims Settlement Act revoked both of these laws but did recognize as valid, applications pending under them in 1971. The native corporation lands are in smaller, more scattered blocks than are state government lands, since most land the federal government opened for selection was either around or near the roughly 200 villages. Native holdings include a mix of traditional subsistence lands and lands with resources that may become marketable, including timber, minerals, coal, and possibly petroleum. In a number of cases, corporations have inholdings on national conservation lands—particularly wildlife refuges—because some native villages are in areas added to the conservation system in 1980. Among the most publicized of such inholdings are those near Kaktovik in the Arctic National Wildlife Refuge, where a native corporation is exploring for oil.

Political Debate over the Alaska National Interest Lands Conservation Act

The fight in Congress over which lands should be put into the conservation system went on until 1980. In 1972 and 1973, Secretary of the Interior Rogers C. B. Morton oversaw the land-use planning process by having to make a series of withdrawals from the public domain, and then by December 18, 1973, come up with recommendations to guide Congress. In March, 1972 he withdrew nearly 80 million acres of d-2 [Section 17(d)(2), or national interest] lands and 45 million acres of d-1 [Section 17(d)(1), or public interest] lands. These were refined to a total of 79 million acres in the political arena, amidst a lawsuit brought by the state of Alaska. Morton ran into tough negotiating with Secretary of Agriculture Earl Butz, who wanted 42 million acres added to the National Forest System. Morton offered 18.8 million acres to Butz, in a compromise. Morton finally recommended 83.5 million acres for the four

national conservation systems. His proposal reached Congress at the end of 1973, when attention was focused on President Nixon and Watergate. Congress was in no hurry to act, since it had until December 1978 to decide. It was not until after Jimmy Carter assumed the presidency in 1977 that the d-2 lands began to assume more importance. The state government, industrial groups, and others argued that putting large areas of essentially unexplored lands into classifications that prohibited or sharply limited development would restrict the state's economic growth and cost the nation valuable resources. Environmental groups and others argued that the large wilderness areas of Alaska offered the nation its last chance to keep undisturbed lands for the enjoyment of future generations.

As expected, Congress started to pay more attention to the d-2 matter for Alaska when Jimmy Carter assumed the presidency in January, 1977. Morris Udall, who was elected to chair the Interior Committee in the House of Representatives, introduced the first version of *H.R. 39* in January 1977. Several versions of this bill were proposed in different congressional sessions, and in modified form it was finally approved in the Senate in August 1980 as an amendment 1961 and in the House as the new *H.R. 39*. From January 1977 until August 1980, much lobbying occurred. A key role was play by the *Alaska Coalition,* a consortium of 55 organizations and interest groups, the key organizations being: The Wilderness Society, the Sierra Club, Friends of the Earth, and the National Audubon Society. The coalition kept Congressional hearings on Alaska well stocked with testimony from citizens all over the country.

In 1978, as the deadline neared for congressional decisions on the d-2 lands, President Carter and Interior Secretary Cecil Andrus fulfilled promises they had made if Congress failed to act. At the last minute in October 1978, H.R. 39 dissolved, as the Senate adjourned, which ended the 95th Congress. The issue was killed at this time by Alaska Senator Mike Gravel's opposition to a last-minute 1-year extension bill. On November 16, 1978, Andrus used his emergency authority under the 1976 Federal Land Policy and Management Act to withdraw from mining claims or state selection 110 million acres of land in Alaska. This was the area under consideration for inclusion in the four national conservation systems; these withdrawals would remain effective for 3 years but could be made permanent by later secretarial action. He used his secretarial powers in February 1980 when he permanently protected 37 million of these acres as wildlife refuges. At the request of Agriculture Secretary Bob Bergland, 11 million acres covering 22 areas in the Tongass and Chugach National Forests were withdrawn for 2 years. On December 1, 1978, President Carter used the 1906 Antiquities Act and designated 17 new national monuments in Alaska, covering 56 million acres of additions to the National Park System, the National Forest System, and the National Wildlife Refuge System. These national monuments proclaimed by Carter gave protection to the most critical areas proposed for legislative designation— 13 proposed national parks, two proposed national wildlife refuges, and two proposed National Forest System wilderness areas. President Carter defended this decision by stating, "Because of the risks of immediate damage to these magnificent areas, I felt it was imperative to protect all of these lands and preserve for the next Congress an unhampered opportunity to act next year."

In the 96th Congress (1979), a weakened H.R. 39 in the Senate proved unacceptable, so again the d-2 land issue remained in limbo. But in 1980 the issue again rose to the forefront. A strongly worded H.R. 39 was introduced by Morris Udall, and a

substitute bill was passed in May 1980. A diluted compromise bill emerged from the Senate (Amendment 1961), which reduced the acreage of parks and refuges to 104.3 million acres. Alaska's Senators, Mike Gravel and Ted Stevens, who fought vociferously for the emphasis of multiple use over preservation for their state, could no longer delay the passage of such a bill in the Senate. The conservationists were disturbed by several provisions of this bill, most notably that (1) it mandated an annual cut of 450 million board feet of timber from the Tongass National Forest; (2) it allowed exploration for oil and gas in the Arctic National Wildlife Refuge; (3) it reduced the land corridor for Alaskan Wild and Scenic Rivers from 2 miles on either side to ½ a mile; and (4) it severely cut lands designated as wilderness. The stunning political victory of Ronald Reagan over incumbent Carter in November 1980 and the gain of control of the House of Representatives by the Republicans in the elections forced the Alaska Coalition and House leaders to take the Senate's bill, rather than risk getting a worse bill in years to come. On November 12, the day Congress returned after the election, Udall introduced the Senate substitute bill on the House floor, and it passed by voice vote. The situation was best described by Dyan Zaslowsky and the Wilderness Society (1986, 273): "The greatest conservation act ever passed by any government had, at the last instant, become hostage to political expediency."

Alaska National Interest Lands Conservation Act (1980)

On December 2, 1980, President Jimmy Carter signed into law the Alaska National Interest Lands Conservation Act, also known as the d-2 lands bill or the compromise H.R. 39 bill. By the stroke of his pen an area larger than California was designated for conservation. This act placed 104.5 million acres into national conservation systems in Alaska. It doubled the size of both the National Park System and National Wildlife Refuge System, doubled the size of the Wild and Scenic Rivers System by protecting 25 free-flowing rivers in the natural state, and tripled the size of the National Wilderness Preservation System by classifying 56 million acres as wilderness.

The Alaska d-2 lands bill broke new ground in a number of ways. A deliberate effort was made to include entire ecosystems in protected status. Along the Alaska peninsula an effective continuity of wildlife habitat lands was created, utilizing a variety of land classifications. In the Brooks Range, the protected habitat now extends from the Canadian boundary to near the Bering Sea. Most of the Porcupine caribou herd's migration is now protected, and attempts are being made to establish similar protection on the Canadian side. A desire to maintain cultural integrity for native communities and rural lifestyles within the newly created national parks generated provisions to continue subsistence activities including hunting, fishing, and trapping by using motorized vehicles (such as snowmobiles and motorboats) where traditionally practiced. In addition, the means of access to wilderness areas for all includes traditional methods such as airplanes and motorboats. Provisions for retaining, maintaining, and building new shelter cabins where required for public safety are also included. Mineralized zones and areas with known oil and gas potential are excluded from designated areas to permit development, when economically feasible. Cooperative management agreements between the state and federal agencies are being ne-

gotiated in areas where such agreements will provide better fulfillment of management guidelines.

Passage of the Alaska Lands Act altered land ownership in Alaska, as illustrated in bar 4 of Figure 4.1 and detailed in Table 4.1: national conservation systems, 41 percent; federal public domain, 12 percent; other federal reserves, 7 percent; state government, 27 percent; Alaskan natives, nearly 12 percent; and other private lands, less than 1 percent. The 1980 addition of 104.5 million acres, together with conservation lands established before 1980, brought to 154 million acres the total national conservation acres in Alaska. Figure 4.3 shows the geographic location of Alaska's national interest lands. This map is keyed to Table 4.2, which identifies, by land-managing agency, the national interest lands. The term *national interest lands* is used synonymously with the term *national conservation systems*, and refers to the National Park System, National Forest System, National Wildlife Refuge System, and two specially designated BLM areas—the White Mountains National Recreation Area and the Steese National Conservation Area. The BLM oversees these last two areas, in addition to the remaining unreserved public-domain land in Alaska.

Over a period of 20 years, Alaska shifted from a territory with most of the country's remaining unreserved public-domain lands to a state with most of the U.S.'s national parks, national wildlife refuges, national forests, and designated wilderness areas. Between 1958 and 1980, the federal government agreed to give up ownership of about 40 percent of Alaska lands; it kept 60 percent. Upon the completion of all transfers to the state government and native corporations, federal public-domain land will make up about 12 percent of the acreage in Alaska—down from 80 percent in 1958. When Alaska became a state, it had about 60 percent of the nation's unreserved federal lands; ultimately, it will have about 10 percent. As the public-domain lands declined, the conservation system grew. The national conservation systems in Alaska grew from 50 million acres at the time of the land freeze in 1966 to 154 million acres in 1985. Alaska today has a very large share of the nation's protected lands: 70 percent of the national parks, 84 percent of the national wildlife refuges, and 12 percent of the national forests. Almost three-quarters of the land designated "wilderness" in the United States is in Alaska.

The largest land gainer as a result of the Alaska National Interest Lands Conservation Act was the National Wildlife Refuge System, which increased from 22.2 million acres to 75.4 million acres; there are now 16 refuges. The details of the changes in the National Wildlife Refuge System in Alaska will be highlighted in Chapter 11. About 25 percent of the land in the Alaskan refuges is designated wilderness. Two of the refuges contain almost half of the total acreage of the entire National Wildlife Refuge System—the 19.6-million-acre Yukon Delta National Wildlife Refuge and the 18-million-acre Arctic National Wildlife Refuge. The latter, located on the northeastern corner of the North Slope, has gained notoriety in recent years, for analysts believe there may be commercial quantities of oil in a caribou calving area. The second largest federal land gainer was the National Park Service. The National Park System in Alaska is the subject of the next section of this chapter.

National forests in Alaska changed less dramatically, at least by Alaskan standards, from 20.7 million acres to 23 million acres. Alaska's two national forests, the Tongass and the Chugach, cover 23 million acres in southeastern Alaska and along the south-central coast. These lands include much of the commercial timber in Alaska.

Table 4.2   National Interest Lands—Alaska*

National Park System

1. Aniakchak National Monument and Preserve
2. Bering Land Bridge National Preserve
3. Cape Krusenstern National Monument
4. Denali National Park and Preserve
5. Gates of the Arctic National Park and Preserve
6. Glacier Bay National Park and Preserve
7. Katmai National Park and Preserve
8. Kenai Fjords National Park
9. Kobuk Valley National Park
10. Lake Clark National Park and Preserve
11. Noatak National Preserve
12. Wrangell–Saint Elias National Park and Preserve
13. Yukon-Charley Rivers National Preserve

National Wildlife Refuge System

14. Alaska Maritime National Wildlife Refuge
15. Alaska Peninsula National Wildlife Refuge
16. Arctic National Wildlife Refuge
17. Becharof National Wildlife Refuge
18. Innoko National Wildlife Refuge
19. Izembek National Wildlife Refuge
20. Kanuti National Wildlife Refuge
21. Kenai National Wildlife Refuge
22. Kodiak National Wildlife Refuge
23. Koyukuk National Wildlife Refuge
24. Nowitna National Wildlife Refuge
25. Selawik National Wildlife Refuge
26. Tetlin National Wildlife Refuge
27. Togiak National Wildlife Refuge
28. Yukon Delta National Wildlife Refuge
29. Yukon Flats National Wildlife Refuge

National Forest System

30. Chugach National Forest
31. Tongass National Forest

Bureau of Land Management

32. Steese National Conservation Area
33. White Mountain National Recreation Area

*Numbers keyed to Figure 4.3.
Source: Alaska Geographic Society, "Alaska National Interest Lands," *Alaska Geographic* 8(4), 1981.

The Chugach National Forest received a 2.3-million-acre addition, which has very little timber. While logging is a central use of the Tongass National Forest, substantial areas are closed to logging—two national monuments and 6 million acres designated as wilderness. The Lands Conservation Act allows an average annual cut of 450 million board feet of timber from the Tongass National Forest. Chapter 10 will examine in more detail Alaska's national forests.

The Alaska National Interest Lands Conservation Act also created one national recreation area (the White Mountains) and one national conservation area (the Steese, on 2 million acres). These areas are under the control of the BLM and are managed

Table 4.3   Federal Lands Potentially Open to Various Uses, 1985

	Acres (thousands)	% of Federal Lands Open
Total federal acreage	255 Million	
Acreage open to:		
Sport fishing	255,000	100
Sport hunting	223,000	87
Subsistence hunting and fishing	245,000	96
New mining claims	62,000	24
Petroleum leasing	141,000	55
Settlement programs	40	0.02
Commercial timber harvest	—	—
Recreation	255,000	100
Motorized access	255,000	100

Source: University of Alaska, Linda Leask, *Alaska Review of Social and Economic Conditions* 22(2): 18, October 1985.

less strictly than park or refuge lands but more rigorously than other public-domain lands managed by the same agency. These areas are northeast of Fairbanks and are in a mineralized area where there are a number of existing claims. They will be discussed in more detail in Chapter 12.

The biggest federal reserve in Alaska outside the conservation systems is the national petroleum reserve on the North Slope. Its size—23 million acres—has not changed since it was created as Navy Petroleum Number 4 in 1923 by President Harding. Other federal lands in the state include military reserves and holdings of various other agencies. These holdings declined from about 10 million acres in 1965 to less than 5 million acres in 1985.

Several tables summarize the status of lands transferred to the state and native corporations and the land uses that are permissible on various categories of land in Alaska. Table 4.3 identifies the federal land that is potentially open for various land uses, and Table 4.4 does the same for state lands. Table 4.5 illustrates the status of

Table 4.4   State Lands Potentially Open to Various Uses, 1985

	Acres (millions)	% of State Lands Open
Total state acreage	+80	
Acreage open to:		
Sport fishing	80	100
Sport hunting	80	100
Subsistence hunting and fishing	80	100
New mining claims	73.5	92
Petroleum leasing	76.8	96
Land disposal programs	0.7	<1
Commercial timber harvest	N/A	—
Recreation	80	100
Motorized access	<80	<100

Source: University of Alaska; Linda Leask, *Alaska Review of Social and Economic Conditions* 22(2):15, October 1985.

Table 4.5   Status of Land Transfers to State Government and Native Corporations, 1985 (in millions of acres)

	Entitlement	Selections	Lands Transferred		
			Patented	I.C./T.A.*	Total
State of Alaska	105	110.7	23.1	56.9	80.0
Native corporations	44	66.6	3.3	29.9	33.2
Village	26	—	3.2	18.6	21.8
Regional	18	—	0.1	11.3	11.4

*I.C.—interim conveyed, T.A.—tentatively approved.
Source: University of Alaska; Linda Leask, *Alaska Review of Social and Economic Conditions* 22(2):21, October 1985.

land transfers to state government and native corporations, Table 4.6 shows the allowable land uses in 1965 and 1985 for federal public domain, and Table 4.7 does the same for the national petroleum reserve.

CHARACTERISTICS OF THE NATIONAL PARK SYSTEM IN ALASKA

The National Park System in Alaska contains 53,727,972 acres, which is 70 percent of the total acreage of the entire U.S. National Park System. Most of the land in the system is classified as national park, national monument, or national preserve. National parks are managed to preserve the scenic, wildlife, and recreational values for which they were set aside. Mining, logging, and other forms of resource exploitation

Table 4.6   Federal Public Domain in Alaska, Allowable Land Uses, 1965 and 1985

	1965	1985
Total Acreage:	274 million acres	± 80 million acres
Sport fishing	All open	All open
Sport hunting	All open	All open
Subsistence hunting and fishing	All open	All open
New mining claims	All open	10.4 million open; 45 million potentially open
New petroleum leasing	All open	8.1 million open; 45 million potentially open
Settlement	All open	40,000 open
Commercial timber harvest[a]	N/A	N/A
Recreation	All open	All open
Motorized access	All open	All open[b]

[a]Technically, public-domain lands could be opened for commercial timber harvest, but in fact almost all commercial timber on federal lands in Alaska is within the Tongass and Chugach National Forests.
[b]Although there are no general restrictions on use of motorized vehicles (including airplanes, snow machines, off-road vehicles, and motorboats) on public domain, there are restrictions in specific areas.
Source: University of Alaska; Linda Leask, *Alaska Review of Social and Economic Conditions* 22(2):32, October 30, 1985.

Table 4.7   National Petroleum Reserve in Alaska Allowable Land Uses, 1965 and 1985

	1965	1985
Total Acreage:	21 million acres	23 million acres
Sport fish	All open	All open
Sport hunting	All open	All open
Subsistence hunting and fishing	All open	All open
New mining claims	All closed	All closed
New petroleum leasing	All closed	8.8 million open, 23 million potentially open
Settlement all closed	All closed	All closed
Timber harvest	N/A	N/A
Recreation	All open	All open
Motorized access	All open	All open

Source: University of Alaska; Linda Leask, *Alaska Review of Social and Economic Conditions* 22(2):32, October 1985.

are not permitted, nor is hunting allowed under ordinary park regulations. Motorized access is restricted to automobile traffic on authorized roads. The two national monuments are relatively small by Alaskan standards. However, in all new parks, monuments, and preserves and in the additions to older parks, subsistence hunting, fishing, and gathering activities by natives are allowed. They may use such motorized vehicles as snowmobiles, motorboats, and airplanes, where such activities have been customary. The category national preserve was added to recognize traditional uses of certain areas. The Alaska National Interest Lands Conservation Act established that national preserves would be managed as national parks, except that sport hunting would be allowed. Some trapping may also be undertaken in the national preserve category.

Several of Alaska's largest parks are in mountainous country: in the Brooks Range to the north, the Alaska Range in the interior (which includes Mt. McKinley), the southeastern corner of mainland Alaska (where several mountain ranges come together and there are many glaciers), and the area around Lake Clark on the west side of Cook Inlet. Other parks include areas with tidewater glaciers and coastal fjords. Over 62 percent of lands in the National Park System are classified as wilderness.

Table 4.8 summarizes the status of the National Park System in Alaska before the Alaska Native Claims Settlement Act (1971) and after the Alaska National Interest Lands Conservation Act (1980). Prior to 1971 there were only three major parks in Alaska: Mt. McKinley National Park and the Glacier Bay and Katmai National Monuments. There was also the 108-acre Sitka National Historical Park. The Conservation Act renamed Mt. McKinley National Park as Denali National Park and tripled the acreage for a combined national park and national preserve. Glacier Bay and Katmai were upgraded to national park status and each also had an adjacent National Preserve added. Two other national parks were created (Kenai Fjords and Kobuk Valley) along with three other national parks/national preserves (Gates of the Arctic, Lake Clark, and Wrangell–St. Elias). Three national preserves were established (Bering Land Bridge, Noatak, and Yukon-Charley Rivers). One combined national monument/national preserve (Aniakchak) and one national monument (Cape Krusenstern) were also established. Table 4.9 summarizes the uses that were allowed on national parks, monuments, and preserves in Alaska in 1965 and in 1985.

Table 4.8 National Park Service Units in Alaska

Before 1971[a]		As of December 2, 1980[b]					
			Total	Acreage by Classification			
Name	Acreage	Name (numbers refer to Figure 4.3)	Acreage	Monument	Park[c]	Preserve[c]	Wilderness[d]
		1. Aniakchak National Monument and Preserve	514,000	138,000		376,000	
		2. Bering Land Bridge National Preserve	2,457,000			2,457,000	
		3. Cape Krusenstern National Monument	560,000	560,000			
Mount McKinley National Park	1,940,000	4. Denali National Park and Preserve	5,696,000[e]		4,366,000	1,330,000	1,900,000
		5. Gates of the Arctic National Park and Preserve	7,952,000		7,052,000	900,000	7,052,000
Glacier Bay National Monument	2,748,000	6. Glacier Bay National Park and Preserve	3,328,000[e]		3,271,000	57,000	2,770,000
Katmai National Monument	2,923,000	7. Katmai National Park and Preserve	4,268,000[e]		3,960,000	308,000	3,473,000
		8. Kenai Fjords National Park	567,000		567,000		
		9. Kobuk Valley National Park	1,710,000		1,710,000		190,000
		10. Lake Clark National Park and Preserve	3,653,000		2,439,000	1,214,000	2,470,000
		11. Noatak National Preserve	6,460,000			6,460,000	5,800,000
		12. Wrangell–St. Elias National Park and Preserve	12,318,000		8,147,000	4,171,000	8,700,000
		13. Yukon-Charley Rivers National Preserve	1,713,000			1,713,000	
Total Acreage	7,611,000		51,196,000	698,000	31,512,000	18,986,000	32,355,000

[a]1971–Section 17(d)(2) of the Alaska Native Claims Settlement Act (ANCSA) authorized the withdrawal of unreserved public lands by December 1978. However, Congress failed to meet the deadline, so late in 1978 that these lands were withdrawn by the Secretary of the Interior under emergency authority prescribed by the Federal Land Policy and Management Act of 1976, and designated national monuments by the president.

[b]In December 1980, the Alaska National Interest Lands Conservation Act established these lands as monuments, parks, and preserves.

[c]Includes acreage classified as wilderness.

[d]Lands within parks and preserves that are maintained as natural areas.

[e]Includes pre-1971 acreage.

Source: Alaska Geographic Society, "Alaska National Interest Land." *Alaska Geographic* 8(4), 1981.

Table 4.9   National Parks and Preserves in Alaska: Allowable Land Uses, 1965 and 1985

	1965	Parks/Monuments	1985	Preserves
Total acreage	7.5 million acres	32 million	52 million[a]	20 million
Sport fishing	All open	All open		All open
Sport hunting	Closed	Closed		All open
Subsistence hunting and fishing[b]	Closed	9.7 million closed		All open
New mining claims[c]	All open	Closed		Closed
New petroleum leasing	Closed	Closed		Closed
Settlement	Closed	Closed		Closed
Timber harvest	Closed	Closed		Closed
Recreation	All open	All open		All Open
Motor access[d]	All open	All open		All open

[a]Of the 52 million acres of parks and preserves, more than 32 million acres are designated as wilderness; in general, most uses that are prohibited in wilderness areas are already prohibited in the park system, so it is not necessary to separate wilderness areas here.
[b]The original Glacier Bay, Katmai, and Mt. McKinley National Parks were closed to subsistence hunting and fishing; those same areas, plus the 1980 additions to Katmai and Glacier Bay Parks and the new Kenai Fjords are now closed to subsistence hunting and fishing. Within parks open to subsistence hunting and fishing, such uses may be restricted to specific areas.
[c]National parks in Alaska were open for mineral location and mining until passage of the Mining in Parks At in 1976, which closed the parks to new entry.
[d]In general, all parks and preserves in Alaska, including areas designated as wilderness, are open to some motorized vehicles but closed to others. Snow machines and motorboats are essentially allowed throughout the parks and preserves, whereas off-road vehicles are not. Planes can be flown into parks and preserves for recreational uses but not for use in subsistence hunting. Helicopters are prohibited except under special permit from the park superintendent.
Source: University of Alaska; Linda Leask, *Alaska Review of Social and Economic Conditions* 22(2):30, October 1985.

The National Park Service has always had the dual mission of both preserving the value of parks lands and providing for their use and enjoyment by people. Alaska's new national park lands have added another dimension to National Park Service management. The areas established as parks under the Alaska National Interest Lands Conservation Act contain lands that have been traditionally used and occupied by indigenous peoples. To help preserve the culture of these people, which often depends on the use of natural resources for subsistence and survival, the new park areas are directed by the Conservation Act to permit subsistence activities to continue. Thus, on the new parks, rural Alaskans are allowed to hunt and fish, to trap for their own use, to cut firewood and house logs, and to gather berries and other products used in handicrafts. Traditional methods of transportation for subsistence activities are allowed, including the use of mechanized equipment such as snowmobiles and motorboats.

Aniakchak National Monument and Preserve

The Aniakchak Caldera, covering some 30 square miles in area and 6 miles across, is one of the great dry calderas of the world (Figure 4.4). Located in southwestern Alaska, 400 miles southwest of Anchorage in the volcanically active Aleutian Mountains, the Aniakchak last erupted in 1931. The crater includes lava flows, cinder cones, and explosion pits as well as Surprise Lake, which is a landing spot for seaplanes and a source of the Aniakchak Wild River. The area was proclaimed a national monument on December 1, 1978, and a combined national monument (137,176 acres), and national preserve (454,151 acres), on December 2, 1980. This park is difficult to visit because air travel is essential and there are no accommodations in the park. The

Figure 4.4 Cinder Cone in Aniakchak Caldera, Aniakchak National Monument and Preserve. (National Park Service photo)

nearest overnight accommodations are in King Salmon, 150 miles distant. From the top of the crater's walls above Surprise Lake, an expanse of snow- and ice-covered peaks and uninhabited rolling hills and plains overlook both the Bering Sea and Pacific Ocean—when the air is clear. Violent wind storms can make camping in the caldera difficult. Very few people visit this park, and its prime attraction is an opportunity to explore on foot a wilderness area seldom visited. However, there are no hiking trails. Other possible recreational activities include primitive camping, fishing, photography, observing natural history, and river rafting. The western Alaska Peninsula, into which part of the monument and preserve extends, is treeless tundra with brushy thickets along riverbeds. Wildlife includes brown and grizzly bears, caribou, fox, moose, and wolf on land; eagles, migratory waterfowl, and seabirds above; sea lions, sea otters, and seals in coastal waters; and salmon and trout in the streams.

Bering Land Bridge National Preserve

Located on the central and northwestern Seward Peninsula in northwestern Alaska just below the Arctic Circle, the Being Land Bridge National Preserve is a remnant of the land bridge that once connected Asia with North America more than 13,000 years ago and was at times up to 900 miles wide. The area was declared a national monument on December 1, 1978, and a national preserve on December 2, 1980. It is 621,592 acres in size and lies 50 miles south of Kotzebue, 90 miles north of Nome, and 60 miles east of Siberia. Air travel is the only way to reach this isolated preserve. There are no accommodations, roads, or hiking trails in the preserve; only primitive camping is available. This preserve is different from others in that, except Cape Krusenstern, it has no spectacular features such as high mountains, glaciers, gorges, or

forests. However, paleontological and archeological resources abound, and the area is rich with wildlife. Large populations of migratory birds nest here; an inventory lists 137 species of birds. Fifteen species of marine mammals, including seals, walrus and whales, swim offshore. Larger mammals include polar bear, brown or grizzly bear, Arctic fox, and moose. Caribou, which were once plentiful, have been replaced by domesticated reindeer, owned and tended by Eskimos who have permits to graze their herds within the preserve. A part of the attraction of the preserve is to observe Eskimos pursuing subsistent lifestyles by tending reindeer herds and producing handicrafts and art objects. There are no trees in the preserve; only tundra. The coastal area is flat, marshy, and filled with ponds. The interior topography, even in the Bendeleben Mountains with elevations reaching 3700 feet, is rolling. Recreational opportunities include wilderness hiking and camping, photography, fishing, river floating, canoeing, and observing natural history.

Cape Krusenstern National Monument

Cape Krusenstern National Monument, which contains 621,592 acres, was proclaimed on December 1, 1978, and received a boundary change on December 2, 1980. It is located in northwestern Alaska along the Chukchi Sea coast above the Arctic Circle and 450 miles northwest of Fairbanks. The area is quite featureless, with a terrain consisting of ponds and endless ridges of treeless tundra. The large mammals and marine mammals are similar to those found at Bering Land Bridge National Preserve. Archeological sites located along a succession of 114 lateral beach ridges illustrate Eskimo communities of every known cultural period in Alaska, dating back 4000 years. Older sites (dated back to 6,000 BC) are located inland, along foothills.

Air or boat access is necessary to reach the monument. There are no accommodations in the monument, but Kotzebue, 10 miles to the south, has hotels, restaurants and stores. Much of the river and beach front land (38,215 acres) is owned by local residents and should be respected as private property. Recreational activities include primitive camping, hiking, bird watching, fishing, and experiencing the sense of human history.

Denali National Park and Preserve

Within the present-day area of Denali is the former Mt. McKinley National Park, established in 1917. The park contains North America's highest mountain, 20,320-foot Mount McKinley. A separate Denali National Monument was established on December 1, 1978. On December 2, 1980 the national park and national monument were incorporated into the present Denali National Park and Preserve. The national park is 4,715,200 acres and the national preserve is 1,310,565 acres; the combined total of 6,025,765 acres is more than triple the size of the original Mt. McKinley National Park (1,940,000 acres). The area designated as wilderness is 1,900,000 acres. The national preserve is located in two sections, one on the northwestern side of the park and the other on the southwestern side. There is also a Denali State Park bisected by Alaska Highway 3 on the southeastern side of the national park. The national park was designated a biosphere reserve in 1976. The national park is fairly accessible for Alaska, with the main entrance along Alaska Highway 3, which connects Anchorage

(240 miles to the south) and Fairbanks (120 miles to the north) and is open all year. The Alaska Railway provides daily passenger and freight service from both cities in the summer, but the schedule is more limited in the winter.

The dominant feature is the Alaska Range, which trends southwest to northeast in the southern half of the national park. Mt. McKinley is the highest peak at 20,320, but there are numerous peaks over 10,000 feet, including Mt. Foraker (17,400 ft.), Mt. Hunter (14,573 ft.), and Mt. Silverthrone (13,220 ft.). Mt. McKinley rises an astounding 18,000 feet vertically above the 2000-foot elevation of Wonder Lake. There are many large glaciers in the Alaska Range, including the 35-mile Muldrow Glacier; it comes within one-half mile of the main park road. Much of the area is covered with ice and snow the entire year, but mixed spruce and birch are found in stream valleys and uplands up to the 2700-foot timberline. Tundra dominates between 3000 and 4000 feet. Wildlife is especially abundant, with caribou, Dall sheep, moose, grizzly bears, and timber wolves.

Traffic on the main park road is restricted to protect wildlife viewing. This main road runs for 85 miles to Wonder Lake; it is a 5½-hour trip each way. The highest elevation on the road is 3980 feet, at Highway Pass. The Eielson Visitor Center is at mile 66. During snow season the park road is not plowed beyond headquarters at mile 3.5; the only access beyond this point is for skiers or dogsledders. During the summer, free shuttle buses and tour buses move through the park (Figure 4.5). Visitors are encouraged to get off and on these buses along the road but are warned they may have to wait a while, when they desire to reboard. Private vehicles are restricted beyond Savage River (mile 12), due to limited bus space; the only visitors allowed beyond this point are those with special access permits for campsites at Teklanika or for lodges at Wonder Lake. Buses are required for access beyond Savage River. Coupons may be obtained at the Visitor Access Center up to 2 days in advance. Visitors are warned that they may have to wait a day or two at the entrance before

Figure 4.5 Shuttle bus at Denali National Park. (National Park Service photo)

bus space and/or campsites become available. A new reservation system for the shuttle buses is planned for 1995 and there will be a fee charged.

There are commercial lodges and private campsites near the entrance, but no food or gasoline service is available beyond the hotel area inside the park. The largest campsite is Riley Creek (102 sites), which is located at the entrance. Only it and Savage River (mile 12.0 with 34 sites) and Teklanika River (mile 29.0, 50 sites) can accommodate tents, trailers, and campers. The other four campsites—Morino (mile 1.5, 60 sites), Sanctuary River (mile 22.0, 7 sites), Igloo Creek (mile 34.0, 7 sites), and Wonder Lake (mile 85, 28 sites)—are for tents only; buses are the only means of access to the last three sites. Inside the park, commercial lodging is available at Denali Park Hotel (100 units, 1 mile inside park), Camp Denali (18 cabins, 3 miles west of Wonder Lake), and North Face Lodge (15 rooms, 1 mile west of Wonder Lake).

Recreational opportunities include camping (primitive and developed), wildlife watching, interpretive talks and walks, hiking, limited fishing due to silted glacial streams, dog sledding, and cross-country skiing. Hunting is allowed in the preserve. Excellent ice and rock climbing can be found. Mountaineering on the higher peaks requires special equipment and skills. Free backcountry permits are required, but there is a quota system for backcountry units. Most units require the use of a bear-resistant food container, which is available free of charge. Campfires are not permitted in the backcountry. Some areas of the Park may be temporarily closed due to bear and other wildlife activity. Denali is by far the most heavily used national park unit in Alaska, receiving 276,200 visitor days in 1991 which compares to a state total visitation of 716,900 for all parks. Most of this use occurs primarily along the main park road.

Gates of the Arctic National Park and Preserve

This extremely remote park, which lies entirely north of the Arctic Circle and is 200 miles northwest of Fairbanks, is about as close as one can come to the ultimate wilderness experience. Hundreds of square miles of pristine wilderness, almost untouched by humans, allow the user to encounter nature on its own terms. Gates of the Arctic National Park and Preserve preserves a portion of the Central Brooks Range, which extends for 200 miles and is the northernmost extension of the Rocky Mountains (Figure 4.6). This second largest unit of our National Park System (and in the world) is characterized by jagged peaks that reach 8510 feet at Mount Igikpak, gentle Arctic valleys, deep glaciated valleys, wild rivers, and numerous lakes. On the southern side of the Brooks Range the forest extends up to timberline at 2100-foot elevation, but the rest of the park is tundra. Initially, the area within this park was proclaimed a national monument on December 1, 1978, and established as a national park and preserve on December 2, 1980. The national park acreage is 7,281,655 acres, and the national preserve acreage is 948,504 acres, for a combined total of 8,230,159 acres. A portion was designated a biosphere reserve in 1984. Wilderness has been designated on 7,052,000 acres. The Gates of the Arctic National Preserve comes in two discontinuous tracts, one adjoining the northeastern corner and the other adjoining the southwestern corner of the national park. Noatak National Preserve borders the national park on the west, and Kobuk Valley National Park adjoins Noatak Na-

Figure 4.6 West Ridge Cirque, Arrigetch Peaks, Gates of the Arctic National Park. (National Park Service photo)

tional Preserve on the south. The park takes its name from two peaks in its eastern portion, that Bob Marshll named the "Gates of the Arctic" when he explored the area between 1929 and 1939. The two peaks are Frigid Crags (5501 ft.) and Boreal Mountain (6654 ft.).

Access to the park allows only a few options. Bettles, 50 miles to the south, has guides and outfitters. Most visitors fly to Bettles/Evansville and then catch a smaller charter plane into the park's interior. One can also fly to Anatuvuk, a Nunamiut Eskimo village in the north (the only one in the park). The only two ranger stations for the park are at these two villages. The unpaved, gravel Alaska Highway 11 (Dalton Highway) follows the Alaskan pipeline on the eastern side of the park and can be driven to Dietrich Field Camp, 40 miles north of Wiseman. There are no visitor centers or established campgrounds or facilities in the park. There are two small private establishments in the park's interior: the three-room Alatna Lodge near the headwaters of the Alatna River and the Alatna River Wilderness Cabins (two cabins) near the Arrigetch Peaks.

Backpacking and river trips are the dominant way to visit the park, with the rivers serving as the best travel routes. Six rivers in the National Wild and Scenic Rivers System flow through the park: the Alatna, John, Kobuk, Noatak, North Fork Koyukuk, and Tinayguk. The Noatak can be floated for 350 miles through the park and through Noatak National Preserve. There are no established hiking trails. Hunting is allowed in the national preserve, with fishing allowed in both the park and the preserve. Exceptional opportunities exist for wildlife watching. Species present include the western Arctic caribou, grizzlies, black bears, Dall sheep, moose, wolves, lynx, and wolverines. Total self-sufficiency is needed to visit this park. Good equipment is essential, since any visit will entail extended backpacking or canoeing and rafting. It may snow during any month of the year. The actual use of the park is light, and only 11,700 visitor days were reported in 1991, which is just 4 percent of

the use at Denali National Park. Local native and nonnative residents use the park and preserve resources to support their subsistent ways of life; such camps, fishnets, traps, and equipment are private property. There are both small and large tracts of private land in the park and preserve that should be respected as private property.

Glacier Bay National Park and Preserve

The glaciers that flow from the snowclad peaks of the Fairweather Range to fjordlike inlets make Glacier Bay National Park and Preserve one of the most scenic spots in Alaska. It contains Mt. Fairweather (15,300 ft.), the highest peak in southeastern Alaska. The Brady Icefield dominates the portion of the park between Glacier Bay and the Gulf of Alaska. Great tidewater glaciers, a dramatic range of plant communities from rocky terrain recently covered by glaciers to lush temperate rain forest, and a large variety of animals, including brown and black bears, mountain goats, whales, seals, and eagles, are found.

President Harding proclaimed Glacier Bay National Monument in 1925, and it was reclassified a national park (3,224,938 acres) and national preserve (55,439 acres) on December 2, 1980. The relatively small area of national preserve is located in the extreme northwestern corner of the park. A large portion of the park (2,770,000 acres) is classified as wilderness. The park extends from Cross Sound for 50 miles to the Canadian border; in the west it extends for another 50 miles to the north, lying west of the Canadian border. This park is a living laboratory for the study of glacial retreat and biotic succession. John Muir publicized this area in 1879, and the Muir Glacier is named in his honor (Figure 4.7). At the southern end of Glacier Bay temperate rain

Figure 4.7   The Muir Glacier in 1971, Glacier Bay National Park and Preserve. (National Park Service photo)

forest is found in an area that was covered with ice 200 years ago. Forty miles up the bay is bare land that receding glaciers have just uncovered. Sixteen major tidewater glaciers exist, with those in the east and southwest receding, and those in the western portion advancing. Twenty-five miles north of its mouth, the Bay, which averages 10 to 15 miles in width, divides into two "arms", which continue to the north: the West Arm, with the highest mountains and most active glaciers, and Muir Inlet, which extends for another 25 miles to the base of the Takhinsha Mountains.

Air or boat is the only means of access for visiting this park, which lies 50 miles west of Juneau. Most visitors see the park from the deck of cruise ships or tour boats (Figure 4.8). Many cruise ships sail the Inside Passage north from Seattle and Vancouver to visit this park. The main center of activity is at Bartlett Cove, near the southern entrance to Glacier Bay. Here the 55-room Glacier Bay Lodge is concessionaire operated. There is also a restaurant here, and day and overnight tour boats depart from this area. A free campground is located at Bartlett Cove, which is also park headquarters. There is an airport 10 miles away at Gustavus. The vegetation is temperate rain forest in this part of the Park. The major recreational activities include glacier watching, natural history study, boating, camping, hiking, fishing, and wildlife and bird watching. Muir Inlet is a kayaker's delight, since cruise ships seldom ply its waters. Access to the backcountry usually requires a boat or float plane, and drop-off permits are required.

Glacier Bay National Park and Preserve is the second-most-visited national park in Alaska, with 245,500 visitor days in 1991. Most of this visitation occurs on the cruise ships and tour boats that sail the water of Glacier Bay and the West Arm. In 1993, cruise lines applied to the National Park Service for a 75 percent increase in visitor quotas.

Figure 4.8   Cruise ship in Tarr Inlet viewing Margerie Glacier, Glacier Bay National Park and Preserve. (National Park Service photo)

Katmai National Park and Preserve

Katmai National Park and Preserve is located 300 miles southwest of Anchorage at the beginning of the Alaska Peninsula. It was the scene of the violent eruption in 1912 of Novarupta Volcano, forming the ash-filled Valley of Ten Thousand Smokes (40 sq. mi.) where steam once rose from countless fumaroles. Today only a few active vents remain. There are still 15 active volcanoes that line the Shelikof Strait, which make this park one of the world's most active volcanic centers today. Originally established as a national monument in 1918, Katmai was enlarged and reclassified a national park (3,575,000 acres) and national preserve (374,000 acres) on December 2, 1980. The national preserve lies in the northern portion of the park. The McNeil River State Game Sanctuary borders the park on the north. The Becharof National Wildlife Refuge adjoins the southwestern border of the park. Most of the park (3,473,000 acres) is classified as wilderness. This large park includes a variety of features: lakes, forest, mountains, volcanoes, and marshlands. Glacier-covered mountains of the Aleutian Range are found in the eastern portion of the park, with Mt. Dennison (7606 feet) the highest point. Katmai is located in the part of Alaska where tundra vegetation approaches sea level, but some spruce and birch trees are found in the lower elevation.

The main access point is at King Salmon, 6 miles from the park's western boundary. From here charter flights provide access to the park's interior. There is an unimproved road from King Salmon to the park's western boundary. Most use of the park takes place at Brooks Camp on Nahnek Lake; it can become rather crowded here at times. Located here is a campground, ranger station, and visitor center, as well as the concessionaire-operated Brooks River Lodge (16 cabins). This is also the starting point for a 23-mile bus or van tour to the Valley of Ten Thousand Smokes, which is also the most popular portion of the park for hiking. There is also concessionaire-operated lodging at Grosvenor Lake Lodge (9 cabins). Other private lodging is at Kulik Lodge (9 cabins), Enchanted Lake Lodge (7 cabins), and Battle River Wilderness Retreat (3 cabins). The lodging costs at these private lodges are quite high—$1500 to $5000 per person per week. There are 141,000 acres of private inholdings and native corporation lands. Some of the best sport fishing in Alaska is found here, and wildlife viewing is exceptional, with brown and grizzly bears, marine mammals, and salmon. A popular activity from late July until September is to watch the amusing antics of the brown bears as they feed on sockeye salmon in the streams. The 750 bears are protected in the park. In addition to observing natural history, fishing, and wildlife watching, the main recreational opportunities are canoeing, kayaking, and backpacking. The Alagnak Wild River starts in the western part of the park. Only 45,000 visitor days were recorded in 1991.

Kenai Fjords National Park

This smallest of Alaska's national parks (649,946 acres) is located on the southeastern side of the Kenai Peninsula, 130 miles south of Anchorage. It was established as a

national monument on December 1, 1978, and reclassified a national park on December 2, 1980.

Glacial ice covers much of the park. This Park contains the major portion of one of the four major icecaps in the United States—the 700-square-mile Harding Icefield—and magnificent coastal fjords. The Harding Icefield feeds 30 glaciers, eight of which extend to tidewater. The ice is up to 5000 feet thick, and numerous *nunataks* (mountain peaks) thrust above the ice and dominate the skyline. This icefield is the remnant of a much larger ice cap that once covered the Kenai, Chugach, and St. Elias Mountains during the Pleistocene.

Deep fjords thrust into the coastline. McCarthy Fjord is 23 miles long, and its walls rise 4000 feet above sea level. Coastal hemlock and Sitka spruce dominate the rain forest on the lower elevations and are replaced by tundra on higher ground. The coastal fjord system has an abundant supply of marine mammals, with 14 species of whales visiting the coastline. Other species include Dall sheep, mountain goats, black and brown (or grizzly) bears, and seabirds.

The gateway community of Seward is 130 miles south of Anchorage. It may be accessed via the Seward Highway year-round or the Alaska Railway and cruise ships in the summer. Motels, restaurants, and campgrounds are located here, as well as the Park headquarters. The most popular access to the park is a 8.5-mile gravel road—the only road in the park—which enters 13 miles northwest of Seward at Exit Glacier. Ten walk-in campsites are also located here. The rest of the park must be accessed by charter air and boat. There are no overnight or food accommodations in the park. With the exception of the road, ranger station, and small walk-in campsite at Exit Glacier, the only other public-use facility is a cabin on Aialik Bay, the most visited fjord in the park.

In addition to wildlife, fjord, and ice observation, the major recreational activities are fishing, sailing, sea kayaking, hiking, skiiing, snowmobiling, dog sledding, snowshoeing, flight-seeing via small planes, and charter boating. Because of its relative accessibility, Kenai Fjords National Park is the third-most-visited national park unit in Alaska, with 53,800 visitor days tallied in 1991. But this use represents only 20 percent of the use that occurs at Denali or Glacier Bay.

Kobuk Valley National Park

This remote national park, which lies north of the Arctic Circle, has the distinction of being the least visited of all national parks—1,800 visitor days in 1991. When the visitor days are related to actual number of visitors, this number drops considerably. It is estimated by the author that perhaps 300 people visit the park each year—on the ground, that is.

Kobuk Valley was proclaimed a national monument on December 1, 1978, and a national park on December 2, 1980. A relatively small proportion (190,000 acres) out of the total park size (1,750,421 acres) is classed as wilderness. The park is a blend of biological, geological, and cultural resources. The Kobuk River flows for 300 miles

from the Brooks Range to the Chukchi Sea; 50 of those miles pass through this park (Figure 4.9). It is a wide and pleasant stream whose current is hardly detectable. The Kobuk Valley forms a transition zone between the taiga and tundra. Here in the northern reaches of the boreal forest, a rich array of Arctic wildlife can be found, including caribou, grizzly and black bear, wolf, and fox. The Selawik National Wildlife Refuge adjoins the entire southern border. The Great Kobuk Sand Dunes cover 25 square miles and rise as much as 100 feet. They are found on the south bank of the river against the base of the Waring Mountains and are the result of windblown glacial outwash. Mt. Angayukaqsraq reaches 4760 feet in the Baird Mountains of the northern portion of the park.

The park is located about 75 miles east of Kotzebue, where the park information center is located, and 350 miles northwest of Fairbanks. There are no roads into the park, so visitors must fly to Kotzebue and then catch another charter flight to one of two Eskimo villages: either Ambler (east of the park) or Kiana (west of the park); in most cases it is Ambler, since it is located upstream. A leisurely float downstream from Ambler to Kiana takes about a week and is the most common use made by the few visitors to the park. Planes or boats can also be chartered from these villages. The only ranger stations are at Onion Portage (summer only) and Kallarichuk (sometimes staffed in summer). Archeological sites in the park are extensive. Onion Portage is an important archeological site, as well as the site on a riverbend where migrating caribou cross the Kobuk River. The park contains no trails or river crossings. The Salmon Wild River flows south from the Baird Mountains for its entire course to join the Kobuk. Rafting, canoeing, kayaking, hiking, camping, sport fishing, and aerial sightseeing are the principal recreational activities. Eskimos own much of the land along the river and engage in subsistence hunting and fishing.

Figure 4.9 The Kobuk River gently flows through Kobuk Valley National Park, the least visited of our national parks. (National Park Service photo)

Lake Clark National Park and Preserve

Located on the west side of Cook Inlet, 150 miles west of Anchorage, Lake Clark is the most diverse national park in Alaska and possibly the United States. The spine of the park is the Chigmit Mountains, which join the Alaska and Aleutian Ranges (Figure 4.10). The climate on the Cook Inlet side differs markedly from the northwestern slopes and plains. Maritime climatic patterns dominate the former, and drier continental patterns dominate the latter. There are four distinct physiographic regions: (1) a coastal region along Cook Inlet, with luxuriant alder thickets and Sitka spruce; (2) the rugged Chigmit Mountains; (3) a foothill-lake region of boreal forest; and (4) a tundra plain. Glacier-carved peaks, large icefields and glaciers cover the Chigmits, which were created by the collision of the North American plate and the Pacific plate. This geological collision is the cause for two active volcanoes: Iliamna (10,016 ft.) and Redoubt (10,197 ft.). Redoubt Volcano started erupting again in 1989. A large number of glacial-carved lakes lie to the west of the Chigmit Mountains, the largest of which is the 40-mile-long Lake Clark. The park was created to protect the spawning grounds for red salmon in Lake Clark and its tributaries.

A national monument was established on December 1, 1978, which became a national park (2,573,724 acres) and preserve (1,288,260 acres) on December 2, 1980. The national preserve is located in the western part of the park, where more recreational use occurs; sport hunting is allowed here. Wilderness classification has been given to 2,470,000 acres.

Aircraft is the primary means of access to the park and preserve. Port Alsworth, a small community in the preserve portion and on Lake Clark, is the most common air access point. There is no road access to the park. This accessibility problem ac-

Figure 4.10 A portion of the Alaska Range in Lake Clark National Park and Preserve. (National Park Service photo)

counts for the low number of visitor days (2600 in 1991). There are no National Park Service facilities, but there is a field office in Port Alsworth. There is only one developed hiking trail—2 miles long—which starts here. Hiking can be difficult below 2000 feet elevation in the western part of the park and below 700 feet elevation in the eastern part due to thick underbrush. There are a number of private lodges and cabins in the park that specialize in hunting and fishing, primarily on Lake Clark. Their precipitous prices reflect this specialization. The rivers and lakes in the western part of the park yield trophy salmon, Arctic grayling, and trout. Three rivers designated wild—the Chilikadrotna, Mulchatna, and Tlikakila—provide float-trip opportunities. Any camping is primitive in nature. Wildlife within the park includes caribou, moose, Dall sheep, brown or grizzly and black bears, and seals and whales offshore along the coastal eastern boundary.

Noatak National Preserve

The Noatak River basin—site of Noatak National Preserve—is the largest mountain-ringed river basin in the nation still virtually unaffected by humans. Gates of the Arctic National Park borders this preserve on the east, and Kobuk Valley National Park borders it on the south. This huge, 6,569,710-acre preserve was initially proclaimed a national monument on December 1, 1978, and established as a national preserve on December 2, 1980; 5,800,000 acres are designated wilderness. It was designated a biosphere reserve in 1976. The major portion of the Noatak River lies inside this preserve, with most of the rest (upstream) in Gates of the Arctic National Park. Only a single settlement (Noatak, population 261) lies along its course, and this is outside of the protected section on the lowermost course of the river. The mountainous headwaters of the river, in Gates of the Arctic National Park, are in deeply scoured canyons with precipitous walls. It then opens up in the great Noatak basin, which is 40 miles wide and 75 miles long. Below the basin is the 65-mile Grand Canyon of the Noatak, and farther downstream is the more spectacular Noatak Canyon. Much of the preserve is treeless, with only alder and willow along streambeds, although cottonwood and spruce appear in the lower canyons. The preserve is a transition zone and migration route (especially for caribou) for plants and animals between Arctic and subarctic environments, and an array of flora among the most diverse anywhere in the earth's northern latitudes is found. Besides the 200,000-head Arctic caribou herd, there are also moose, brown or grizzly and black bears, wolves, wolverines, foxes, Dall sheep, and a variety of birds.

There is no road access to the preserve, so chartered air is the only means of access. The preserve is 350 miles northwest of Fairbanks, but its westernmost section is close to Kotzebue. Access is from Kotzebue on the west or from Bettles on the east (if the visitor wants to float the Upper Noatak in Gates of the Arctic National Park). Within the preserve only primitive camping is available, and there are no commercial accommodations. Visitors are on their own and should have enough supplies to be self-sufficient. Floating down the Noatak can be done in rubber raft, canoe, or kayak. Float trips and fishing and primitive camping are therefore the dominant recreational uses made of the preserve. Sport hunting is allowed, since this is a national preserve.

The preserve is lightly used, with only 7100 visitor days in 1991, and almost 100 percent of this use is restricted to the immediate corridor along the Noatak River.

Wrangell–St. Elias National Park and Preserve

This national park and preserve is the premier mountain wilderness of North America. The Chugach, Wrangell, and St. Elias mountain ranges converge here in what is often referred to as the "mountain kingdom of North America." This area holds the continent's largest collection of glaciers, which extend into Kluane National Park in adjacent Canada. Nearby Mt. Logan (19,850 ft.), in Kluane National Park, is the second highest mountain in North America. This park contains nine of the 16 highest peaks in the United States, four of them over 16,000 feet: Mt. St. Elias (18,008 ft.) and Mt. Bona (16,421 ft.) in the St. Elias Mountains, and Mt. Blackburn (16,390 ft.) and Mt. Sanford (16,237 ft.) in the Wrangell Mountains. The east end of the Alaska Range extends into the northern portion of the park in the Mentasta and Nutzotin Ranges. The St. Elias range has the tallest coastal mountains in the world. The Wrangell Mountains are volcanic in origin, and three of the peaks are still considered active: Mt. Wrangell (14,163 ft.), Mt. Sanford (16,237 ft.), and Mt. Drum (12,010 ft.). Vents of steam still issue from the summit of Mt. Wrangell, which last erupted in 1930. The Wrangells are a major geothermal area. This whole region is a major collision zone of two tectonic plates. One of the most active faults in Alaska, the Totshunda, lies in the northern part of the park. A major earthquake in 1964 did much damage here.

This park, which extends 130 miles in an east-west direction and 170 miles in a north-south direction, is the largest in the United States and the world: 8,905,970 acres are national park, and 4,349,564 acres are national preserve, for a combined total of 13,255,534 acres. With 8,700,000 acres classified as wilderness, it is the largest unit of our entire National Wilderness Preservation System. The national preserve is located mainly in the northern half of the park, to the north, west, and south of the Wrangell Mountains. President Carter proclaimed the area a national monument on December 1, 1978, and the Alaska National Interest Lands Conservation Act established it a national park and national preserve on December 2, 1980. Wrangell–St. Elias National Park and Preserve and the adjacent Canadian Kluane National Park were declared a 20-million-acre world heritage site in 1979.

The high country of this park is covered with ice and snow the entire year— there are over 150 glaciers (Figure 4.11). Bagley Icefield, near the coast, is the largest subpolar icefield in North America and spawns such giant glaciers as the Tana, Miles, Guyot, and Hubbard. Climatologists have estimated that the world's heaviest precipitation, over 600 inches of water equivalent, may fall on the Bagley Icefield and other Chugach mountain peaks. The Malaspina Glacier, which is larger than the State of Rhode Island, flows off the St. Elias Mountains between Icy Bay and Yakutat Bay. The only lowlands are found in the Chitina River Valley between the Chugach and Wrangell Mountains, the Copper River Valley along the western boundary, and in the northeastern corner of the park. The Copper River is the park's largest river.

Three ecosystems are represented within the park: northern coniferous, alpine tundra, and coastal coniferous. Treeline in the Park's interior occurs between 3000 and 4000 feet. In the lower elevations white spruce and balsam poplar dominate,

Figure 4.11   Root Glacier near Kennicott, in Wrangell–St. Elias National Park and Preserve. (National Park Service photo)

while in the upper-elevation range aspen, birch, and balsam poplar prevail. Dall sheep are found on the higher slopes of the Wrangell Mountains and on the northern slopes of the Chugach Mountains. Mountain goats prefer the coastal mountains. Three caribou herds are found in the northern part of the Park. Other major wildlife species includes moose, brown or grizzly and black bears, and two introduced bison herds in the Copper River and Chitina River Valleys. A major salmon run occurs on the Copper River. In Yakutat Bay, seals, sea lions, sea otters, dolphins, and killer whales may be observed.

The impact of humans has been greater in Wrangell–St. Elias than in many of the other Alaskan national parks. A road provided access to the Kennecott Copper Mine, which produced ore from 1911 until 1938. The ruins of this mine may be observed today near the small town of McCarthy. The 62-mile-long road that runs up the Chitina River Valley from the park's western boundary at Chitina to McCarthy is one of two roads that penetrate the park; the other is the 46-mile Nabesna Road in the northern reach of the Park. The area around each road is classed largely as preserve. With the exception of these two roads, the only access to the park is by the air. The western margin of the park at Glennallen, 190 miles northeast from Anchorage, can be reached via Alaska Highway 1. The park's headquarters and visitor center is 5 miles north of Copper Center on the Old Richardson Highway. The Richardson Highway (Alaska Highway 4) ends at Valdez, which is also accessible via the Alaska Ferry. There are two private campgrounds within the park on the McCarthy Road (near mile 10). The BLM and the state of Alaska run campgrounds along the Richardson Highway. Rustic accommodations are provided at privately operated fishing camps, guide cabins, and full-service lodges in various parts of the park; two of these are in McCarthy and Kennecott, and the other is on Tanada Lake in the northern part of the park. There is still mining activity on private land in the park.

Despite the imprint of humans, this is still a park for wilderness-oriented activities. Travel services and facilities are limited. Visitors are mostly on their own here and thus must be highly motivated and self-sufficient (Figure 4.12). Besides sightseeing, major activities consist of backpacking, hiking, camping, hunting, fishing, mountaineering, river running, kayaking along the coast, and cross-country skiing. Most backpackers and day hikers start from points along the McCarthy or Nabesna Roads. There are few designated trails. The Copper and Chitina Rivers offer excellent rafting and kayaking opportunities. Kayakers are starting to discover the bays and inlets in the Yakutat and Icy Bay areas. Wrangell–St. Elias is the fourth-most-visited national park unit in Alaska, recording 39,000 visitor days in 1991. Within the park, residents may carry out traditional subsistence activities such as hunting, trapping, and fishing. Within the preserve, the same local subsistence uses are permitted, as are sports hunting, fishing and trapping for nonresidents.

Yukon-Charley Rivers National Preserve

Located along the Canadian border in east-central Alaska, the Yukon-Charley Rivers National Preserve protects 115 miles of the 1800-mile Yukon River and the entire Charley River basin. This 2,249,071-acre-area was declared a national monument on December 1, 1978, and established as a national preserve on December 2, 1980. The landscape is not spectacular, but it represents the intermountain plateau region between the Brooks and Alaska Ranges. Numerous old cabins and relicts are reminders of the importance of the Yukon River during the 1899 gold rush. Paleontological and archeological sites have added much to our knowledge. Peregrine falcons nest in the bluffs overlooking the river, and abundant wildlife is found on the rolling hills. Bot-

Figure 4.12 Backpacker in Chitistone Pass, which divides the Wrangell Mountains and the St. Elias Mountains in Wrangell–St. Elias National Park and Preserve. (National Park Service photo)

tomland spruce and poplar are the dominant vegetation along the Yukon River, changing to spruce, aspen, and birch along the Charley River. The Charley, an 88-mile Wild River, is considered by many to be the most spectacular river in Alaska.

The Taylor and Steese Highways are the primary summer access routes, terminating respectively in Eagle and Circle City on the Yukon River, just outside the preserve's boundaries. There are no accommodations in the preserve, so camping is required. Accommodations are found in Eagle and Circle City. During the gold rush in 1899 the Yukon was a busy highway, with 56 sternwheelers plying the water. Remnant historic towns and mining camps can be observed along the Yukon today. Sightseeing river tours travel from Dawson City, Canada, to Fort Yukon, Alaska. These river tours pass through the portion of the preserve traversed by the Yukon River and make stops at Eagle and Circle City. Recreational opportunities focus on the rivers, with river floating, canoeing and kayaking as the major activities. Helicopter access is needed to access the Charley River for floating. The overall use of the preserve is very light, with just 3900 recreation visitor days in 1991.

References

Alaska Geographic Society. "Alaska National Interest Lands." *Alaska Geographic* (*Alaska National Interest Lands*) 8(4), 1981.

Alaska National Interest Lands Conservation Act of 1980. Public Law No. 96-487. *94 Stat.* 2371.

Alaska Native Claims Settlement Act of 1971. Public Law No. 92-203. *85 Stat.* 688.

Cahn, Robert. *The Fight to Save Wild Alaska.* National Audubon Society, 1982.

Frome, Michael. *National Park Guide—1992.* New York: Prentice Hall Travel, 1992.

Leask, Linda. "Changing Ownership and Management of Alaska Lands." *Alaska Review of Social and Economic Conditions* 22(2):1–32, October 1985.

National Geographic Society. *National Geographic's Guide to the National Parks of the United States.* Washington, D.C.: National Geographic Society, 1992.

National Park Foundation. *The Complete Guide to America's National Parks, 1990–1991 Edition.* New York: Prentice Hall, 1990.

National Park Service. *Cape Krusenstern, Noatak, Kobuk Valley—Northwest Alaska Areas.* Gridmap Official Map and Guide. Washington, D.C.

National Park Service. *Denali National Park and Preserve.* Gridmap Official Map and Guide. Washington, D.C.

National Park Service. *Gates of the Arctic National Park and Preserve.* Gridmap Official Map and Guide. Washington, D.C.

National Park Service. *Glacier Bay National Park and Preserve.* Gridmap Official Map and Guide. Washington, D.C.

National Park Service. *Katmai National Park and Preserve.* Gridmap Official Map and Guide. Washington, D.C.

National Park Service. *Kenai Fjords National Park and Preserve.* Gridmap Official Map and Guide. Washington, D.C.

National Park Service. *Lake Clark National Park and Preserve.* Gridmap Official Map and Guide. Washington, D.C.

National Park Service. *Wrangell–St. Elias National Park and Preserve.* Gridmap Official Map and Guide. Washington, D.C.

Simon, David J., Editor. *Our Common Lands: Defending the National Parks.* Washington, D.C.: Island Press, 1988.

Williss, Frank G. *Administrative History: The National Park Service and the Alaska National Interest Lands Conservation Act of 1980.* Washington, D.C.: National Park Service, 1985.

Zaslowsky, Dyan, and the Wilderness Society. *These American Lands.* New York: Henry Holt and Co., 1986.

## CHAPTER 5

National Parks: The Lower 49 States

As to my attitude regarding the proposed use of Hetch Hetchy by the City of San Francisco ... I am fully persuaded that ... the injury ... by substituting a lake for the present swampy floor of the valley ... is altogether unimportant compared with the benefits to be derived from its use as a reservoir.

Gifford Pinchot (1913)

These temple destroyers, devotees of ravaging commercialism seem to have a perfect contempt for Nature, and instead of lifting their eyes to the God of the Mountains, lift them to the Almighty Dollar.

John Muir (1912)

The National Park System contains 357 units; 22 of these units are in Alaska, and the other 335 are in the lower 49 states. Chapter 3 of this book focused on the National Park System as a whole, and Chapter 4 focused on Alaska. All of the National Park units of Alaska, except Sitka National Historical Park and Klondike Gold Rush National Historical Park, were the subject of discussion in the previous chapter. The present chapter and the following one will focus on the National Park System in the lower 49 states. Carefully selected case studies representing the diversity of units comprising the National Park System have been chosen. By necessity, they detail only about 15 percent of the units in the system for the lower 49 states. Emphasis has been equally given to topical themes and to geographic distribution, with a focus on the recreational value of the National Park System.

The present chapter uses 15 of the national parks in the lower 49 states for case studies. These 15, together with the eight Alaskan national parks, comprise almost half of the national parks in the system. (Remember, however, that the national parks, although the best-known units of the National Park System and accounting for 60 percent of its acreage, are not the only units in the system.) Appendix III is a complete list of all National Park System units, their acreage, geographic location, and recreational-use statistics. Appendix IV details the types of overnight stays for those park

units that have overnight facilities. Appendix V summarizes the facilities, recreational and other, for every unit in the system. Figure 3.5, which is keyed to Appendix III, shows the location of each unit of the National Park System. Table 5.1 contains an analysis of data for the 50 national parks, including the size in federal acres, the number of recreation visits for 1991, the number of recreation visitor days for 1991, and the ratio of recreation visits to recreation visitor days. This ratio is a meaningful index for assessing the length of recreation visitation: Stays are shorter in the parks with the higher ratios and longer in the parks with the lower ratios. Thus this ratio is a good measure for identifying day-use parks as opposed to more extended-stay parks. The final statistic gives the number of acres for each recreation visitor day for each park. This index is significant for assessing the intensity of use for each national park; the larger the number the lower the intensity of use and vice versa. In most parks a large percentage of the use is concentrated in a few locations, but even in the parks with low acreages per recreation visitor day, uncrowded locations can still be found. It is also important to emphasize that these statistics do not reflect seasonal variation in use; visitors to Yellowstone or Yosemite in August, for example, will find crowds.

NATIONAL PARKS

Acadia

Acadia National Park is a magnificent blend of ocean and mountains along the northern Maine coast 50 miles southeast of Bangor (Figure 5.1). Its 40,728 acres place it among the smallest of our national parks; only Bryce Canyon, Wind Cave, Haleakala, Virgin Islands, and Hot Springs are smaller. It is the only national park in the Northeast and the first national park created east of the Mississippi. The sea sets the mood here, uniting the rugged coastal area of Mount Desert Island, picturesque Schoodic Peninsula on the mainland, and the spectacular cliffs of Isle au Haut—it can be foggy at times. It was proclaimed as Sieur de Monts National Monument in 1916, established as Lafayette National Park in 1919, and renamed Acadia National Park in 1929. Its establishment is unusual in that it was neither carved out of the public domain nor bought with public funds but rather was envisioned and donated through the efforts of private citizens, mostly summer residents of the area. Among others, John D. Rockefeller, Jr., played a critical role, as he built the carriage roads and donated over 11,000 acres. A fire in 1947 destroyed 10,000 acres. Because of this evolutionary growth, a permanent boundary was not established until 1986. Today, over 97 percent of the area within the boundaries is national park land.

Geographically, the larger portion of the park is on Mt. Desert Island, which is almost attached to the mainland at Mt. Desert Narrows. Somes Sound, the only true fjord on the East Coast, comes close to dividing the island in two. About two-thirds of the park lies to the east of Somes Sound, and the other third lies west of it. Approximately 50 percent of Mount Desert Island is private land. While the island only extends about 15 miles in a latitudinal direction and 13 miles in a longitudinal di-

Table 5.1   National Park Analysis

Park	State	Size (Acres)	Recreation Visits (000's)	Recreation Visitor Days (000's)	Visit/ Visitor Day Ratio	Acres Visitor Day
Wrangell–St. Elias National Park	AK	8,905,970.00	39.00	39.00	1.00	228.36
Gates of the Arctic National Park	AK	7,281,654.50	1.20	11.70	0.10	622.36
Denali National Park	AK	4,715,200.10	558.90	276.20	2.02	17.07
Katmai National Park	AK	3,575,000.00	41.40	45.00	0.92	79.44
Glacier Bay National Park	AK	3,224,938.00	203.70	245.50	0.83	13.14
Lake Clark National Park	AK	2,573,724.00	4.10	2.60	1.58	989.89
Yellowstone National Park	WY, ID, MT	2,219,772.70	2,920.50	8,435.40	0.35	0.26
Kobuk Valley National Park	AK	1,726,463.00	2.80	1.80	1.56	959.15
Everglades National Park	FL	1,398,613.60	1,292.00	704.90	1.83	1.98
Grand Canyon National Park	AZ	1,179,194.10	3,886.00	5,703.70	0.68	0.21
Glacier National Park	MT	1,012,995.70	2,097.00	1,481.30	1.42	0.68
Olympic National Park	WA	912,870.00	2,759.70	1,217.40	2.27	0.75
Big Bend National Park	TX	764,608.10	296.50	745.50	0.40	1.03
Yosemite National Park	CA	759,463.70	3,423.10	7,675.30	0.45	0.10
Kenai Fjords National Park	AK	649,946.00	107.00	53.80	1.99	12.08
Isle Royale National Park	MI	539,281.90	22.00	114.30	0.19	4.72
Great Smoky Mountains National Park	TN, NC	520,003.80	8,654.50	5,539.50	1.56	0.09
North Cascades National Park	WA	504,554.80	22.80	30.10	0.76	16.76
Kings Canyon National Park	CA	461,845.00	1,071.00	2,963.10	0.36	0.16
Sequoia National Park	CA	402,298.70	1,120.30	3,099.60	0.36	0.13
Canyonlands National Park	UT	337,570.40	339.30	309.00	1.10	1.09
Grand Teton National Park	WY	307,616.60	1,625.80	1,366.30	1.19	0.23
Rocky Mountain National Park	CO	264,747.10	2,751.80	1,663.10	1.65	0.16
Mount Rainier National Park	WA	235,612.50	1,549.40	1,875.50	0.83	0.13
Badlands National Park	SD	232,742.20	1,518.40	510.10	2.98	0.46
Capitol Reef National Park	UT	222,753.40	618.10	86.40	7.15	2.58
Hawaii Volcanoes National Park	HI	217,298.10	1,238.70	689.70	1.80	0.32
Shenandoah National Park	VA	195,403.70	1,939.50	1,319.90	1.47	0.15
Crater Lake National Park	OR	183,223.80	456.90	218.60	2.09	0.84
Biscayne National Park	FL	169,345.30	488.10	172.50	2.83	0.98
Zion National Park	UT	143,040.40	2,237.00	868.70	2.58	0.16
Voyageurs National Park	MN	131,900.90	221.90	137.60	1.61	0.96
Lassen Volcanic National Park	CA	106,366.50	463.20	454.60	1.02	0.23
Petrified Forest National Park	AZ	93,532.60	874.50	111.80	7.82	0.84
Great Basin National Park	NV	77,100.00	63.90	66.30	0.96	1.16
Guadalupe Mountains National Park	TX	76,293.00	200.40	54.10	3.70	1.41
Redwood National Park	CA	75,341.80	366.30	219.40	1.67	0.34
Theodore Roosevelt National Park	ND	69,701.70	468.90	110.60	4.24	0.63
Arches National Park	UT	66,343.50	705.90	292.30	2.41	0.23
Channel Islands National Park	CA	64,254.60	149.30	127.70	1.17	0.50
Mesa Verde National Park	CO	51,890.70	678.10	504.70	1.34	0.10
Mammoth Cave National Park	KY	51,592.10	2,158.20	332.30	6.49	0.16
Carlsbad Caverns National Park	NM	46,435.30	679.50	199.80	3.40	0.23
Acadia National Park	ME	40,728.10	2,475.90	1,099.90	2.25	0.04
Bryce Canyon National Park	UT	35,832.60	929.10	571.50	1.63	0.06
Wind Cave National Park	SD	28,295.00	597.10	51.50	11.59	0.55
Haleakala National Park	HI	27,468.30	1,228.30	240.50	5.11	0.11
Virgin Islands National Park	VI	12,909.60	710.20	367.30	1.93	0.04
Hot Springs National Park	AK	4,853.10	1,203.90	69.00	17.45	0.07
National Park of American Samoa		0.00	0.00	0.00	—	—
Total		46,898,590.60	57,461.10	52,476.40	1.09	0.89

Figure 5.1 Acadia National Park preserves a section of the Maine coast.

rection, its rugged, deeply indented and embayed coastline makes it seem much larger. Small fragments of Acadia National Park are on islands: Baker, 4 miles south of Mount Desert Island; Bar, Sheep Porcupine, and Bald Porcupine, each less than 1 mile off the east coast of Mount Desert Island in Frenchman Bay; and Isle au Haut, 20 miles to the southwest. Isle au Haut is the hardest to reach but well worth the effort. The only portion of Acadia on the mainland is the Schoodic Peninsula, which is just seven air miles to the east of Mount Desert Island, but 45 miles by road. A one-way road leads around the peninsula, and a gravel road winds to the summit of Schoodic Head (440 ft.). Primarily because of geographic location and accessibility, most of the visitation occurs on Mount Desert Island. Acadia's 1,099,900 visitor days in 1991 made it the 13th most visited national park (2,475,900 visits ranked it seventh in number of visits). The great volume of visitors is not really apparent except when visited in July or August or when comparing the number of visitors with its relatively small size. Acadia had the least number of acres per visitor day in 1991 of all national parks except the Virgin Islands. This index of magnitude of use is calculated by dividing the park's acreage by the number of visitor days. In 1991, Acadia had 0.037 acres per visitor day compared with a median of 0.5 acres per visitor day for all the national parks and a high of 990 acres per visitor day for Lake Clark National Park (Alaska).

Part of the attraction of Acadia is its poetic blend of glacially scoured mountains and seacoast, combined with picturesque seaport towns and harbors. The largest town is Bar Harbor, a thriving tourist center and resort community that bustles with activity in summer and fall and where parking spots are hard to find. Other nearby towns include Northeast Harbor, Southwest Harbor, and Bass Harbor. These towns provide deep-sea fishing and boat access and tours to the insular park property. The park's visitor center is 3 miles north of Bar Harbor at Hull's Cove. Many visitors to the park either day-trip as passengers or take their car on the *MV Bluenose*, a ferry

that runs from Bar Harbor to Yarmouth, Nova Scotia. Somesville, at the head of Somes Sound, was the site of the first permanent settlement on Mt. Desert Island in 1761. Numerous mountains rise within a mile or two of the coast to well over 1000 feet. Samuel Champlain named Mt. Desert Island in 1604 for its barren-looking summits. These summits are largely devoid of vegetation and are smoothly rounded due to glacial action in the area during the Pleistocene. The highest point in the park, Cadillac Mountain, is 1531 feet above sea level, and there is a paved road to the summit, where there is a gift shop and snack bar. There are also four hiking trails that reach the summit. The congestion on the summit of Cadillac Mountain can rival that of Bar Harbor. The embayed nature of the submerged New England Coast can be readily viewed from Cadillac Mountain looking down into Frenchman's Bay.

Most of the visitors to the park drive the scenic 27-mile Park Loop Road, which is one-way traffic in the east and south, where is is known as Oceanside Drive. The 110-foot Otter Cliffs along Oceanside Drive are outstanding. The only ocean swimming allowed in the park is found north of Otter Cliffs at Sand Beach. Very few people venture more than knee-deep into the water at Sand Beach; and those that do, quickly retreat. The water is very cold (low 50s) due to the Labrador Current, which brings cold water from the north. The other principal swimming site is Echo Lake Beach, which is freshwater and located to the west of Somes Sound. On a warm summer day this beach can be extremely congested. The two National Park Service campgrounds are at Blackwoods (in the southeastern part of the park) and at Seawall (in the extreme southwestern part of the park) which also has a picnic area. The Ship Harbor Nature Trail, which is 1¼ miles long, is also nearby. Reservations are necessary for Blackwoods, and sites are hard to find at Seawall in July and August. Many visitors who plan to camp at Acadia usually end up at one of a dozen private campsites outside the park on Mt. Desert Island.

An especially scenic location is the site of the Jordan Pond House, on Jordan Pond. (The Park Loop Road is two-way here.) The original Jordan Pond House was founded as a restaurant in the 1870s, destroyed by fire in 1979, and rebuilt in 1982. Views of the Bubbles (low mountains) and Jordan Pond are extremely resplendent. The complex includes a restaurant, a gift shop, a garden, and an outside deck. The local specialty is popovers, a type of pastry. Those on a limited budget will probably avoid eating at the Jordan Pond House. Nearby is the National Park Service authorized concessioner, Wildwood Stables. Horses can be rented and carriage rides taken to the top of nearby Day Mountain. Between 1915 and 1933, John D. Rockefeller, Jr., financed and directed the building of 57 miles of carriage roads—a network of woodland roads free of motor vehicles—for hikers, bicyclists, horseback riders, and carriages. This carriage-road network has 16 ornate granite bridges and two magnificent gatehouses. Eagle Lake Loop Road is especially graded for bicycles. There are 120 miles of hiking trails in the park—for day use only, since no backcountry camping is allowed in Acadia. The only camping allowed within the park is at the two National Park Service campgrounds at Seawall and Blackwoods. In the winter all but 2 miles of Park Loop Road and Cadillac Mountain Road are closed. This, combined with the carriage roads, provides ample opportunities in the winter for cross-country skiing, snowshoeing, and snowmobiling.

Big Bend

Big Bend National Park is remotely located in the empty country of West Texas, over 400 miles west of San Antonio and over 300 miles southwest of El Paso. Mountains contrast with desert in this great U-shaped bend of the Rio Grande River. This park was authorized in 1935 and established in 1944. The Park was designated a biosphere reserve in 1976. The most recent boundary adjustment reflects the inclusion of the 64,000-acre Harte Brothers' Ranch, which was donated in 1989 and added to the northern portion of the park.

Its 764,608 acres rank it the 13th-largest national park. In the lower 49 states, only Yellowstone, Everglades, Grand Canyon, Glacier, and Olympic National Parks are larger. The 745,500 recreation visitor days in 1991 ranked it in 15th place among the Parks in terms of use. Its magnitude of use of 1.03 acres per visitor day indicates an uncrowded park, but much of this use is concentrated in relatively small areas, such as the Chisos Basin and Rio Grande Village. Due to the park's remote location, only dedicated visitors reach it; there is no public transportation to or through the park. The northern entrance is 40 empty miles south of the small town of Marathon on U.S. 385, and it is another 30 miles across desert flatland to park headquarters at Panther Junction. The western entrance is 80 miles south of Alpine on Texas Highway 118.

Three distinct environments exist in Big Bend: river canyons, deserts, and mountains. The Rio Grande, which forms the border with Mexico, is a Wild and Scenic River for 191.2 miles, 107 of which form the park's southern boundary. Three major canyons are found within the park on the Rio Grande: Santa Elena, Mariscal, and Boquillas. These canyons are a major attraction for river rafters. Willows and cottonwoods are found long the river, and this is the best location for bird watching. More birds are found in Big Bend—over 400—than in any other national park, among them the rare Colima warbler and the peregrine falcon. The volcanic Chisos Mountains, in the south-central part of the park, are the dominant topographic feature. The most interesting geology is found in the Chisos Mountains and along the Ross Maxwell Scenic Drive, where numerous dikes are exposed. The Terlingua Fault rises abruptly 1500 feet and forms the Sierra de Santa Elena, most of which is on the Mexican side of the Rio Grande; this imposing fault scarp extends into Texas north of Santa Elena Canyon. The Chihuahuan Desert vegetation consisting of bunchgrasses, creosote bush, cacti, lechuguillas, yucca, and sotols dominates most of the park's territory outside of the Chisos Mountains and the river canyons. Usually, if rainfall is favorable, the desert plants and wildflowers bloom profusely in March and also in September. Wildlife of the desert includes coyote, ringtail, kit fox (very rare), mule deer, and peccary (javelina). The Chisos Mountains, which may be 20° cooler than the desert floor, reach 7835 feet at Emory Peak. Mountain lions and bears may be found at these higher elevations, where the vegetation changes to juniper, pine, and oak.

The park headquarters and visitor center is at Panther Junction, 29 miles into the park from the north entrance. The short Panther Pass Nature trail is an excellent introduction to the desert vegetation of the park. The most unique portion of the park is the Chisos Basin, on the north side of the Chisos Mountains. The road to this area climbs from the desert 3 miles west of Panther Junction over Panther Pass (5770

Figure 5.2   The higher-elevation Chisos Basin in Big Bend National Park is a major attraction because it contrasts with the lower-elevation desert that covers most of the park. Shown here is the National Park Service campground.

ft.) and then follows hairpin turns down to the 5400-ft elevation of the Basin. The Chisos Mountain Lodge (rooms and cabins) is located here, as well as a 62-unit National Park Service campsite (Figure 5.2). This is the best hiking area in the Park. For those who do not wish to hike, saddle horses, pack animals, and guides are available. The 13-mile (round) trip to the South Rim (7400 ft.) offers the best views in the park. Another major campsite area is at Rio Grande Village, where there are 99 sites, the only full hookups for RVs, and a supply store. Due to lower elevation, this is the hottest part of the park. The only Mexican settlement across from the park is the small village of Boquillas, located 1 mile up a hill from the river. A boat ride can be hired to cross the Rio Grande at Rio Grande Village. A smaller National Park Service campsite is near Castolon, on the Rio Grande in the southwestern corner of the park. Castolon has a small store and is a historic district remnant from an old pioneer settlement and U.S. Cavalry post. There are also designated backcountry campsites on some roads, but high clearance and four-wheel drive is required for access to some of these. There are no rafts for rent in the park, but outfitters are located west of the Park at Terlingua and Lajitas. The dominant recreational activities in the park include walking and hiking, camping, river running, bird watching, flower gazing, and river fishing (for catfish).

Canyonlands

Canyonlands National Park is a geological showcase in southeast Utah consisting of plateaus, steep-walled mesas, spires, arches, and other various rock formations cut by the deep canyons of the Colorado and Green Rivers, which have their confluence here. Prehistoric Native American rock art and ruins dot the redrock landscape. It is in the heart of the Canyonlands subdivision of the Colorado Plateau physiographic

province. The park was established in 1964, and there was a boundary change in 1971. Today, the park is 337,570 acres, all of which are federally owned, and it is completely surrounded by federal land. The Bureau of Land Management (BLM) administers land bordering on the north, east, and south, and Glen Canyon National Recreation Area (administered by the National Park Service) borders on the west. Over 500 miles of continuous National Park System–protected lands extend downstream on the Colorado River from the northeastern corner of Canyonlands to below Davis Dam at Bullhead City, Ariz. This corridor of national park units represents the longest lineal extent of any national park lands found anywhere in the world. Lake Mead National Recreation Area extends upstream from Bullhead City to Grand Canyon National Park. The Colorado is placid for most of this distance since 67-mile Lake Mohave lies behind Davis Dam and 110-mile Lake Mead is formed behind Hoover Dam. The Colorado River races undammed throughout all of Grand Canyon National Park. Glen Canyon National Recreation Area continues the national park lands upstream from Grand Canyon National Park. Glen Canyon Dam tames the Colorado for almost another 200 miles in the form of Lake Powell, the principal feature of Glen Canyon National Recreation Area. Canyonlands National Park begins where the foaming water of Cataract Canyon ends in Lake Powell. The Colorado flows undammed for 45 miles through Canyonlands. Twenty miles upstream from Canyonlands, another 10 miles on the north side of the river is protected by Arches National Park.

This 500-mile stretch of the Colorado River has been one of the most formidable geographic barriers in the United States. Even today, there are only five bridges and one ferry that cross this extent of the Colorado: U.S. 191 at Moab, Utah; Utah 95 at Hite; Utah 276 at Lake Powell Ferry (Hall's Crossing/Bullfrog); U.S. 89 at Glen Canyon Dam, Arizona; U.S. Alternate 89 at Marble Canyon, Arizona; and U.S. 93 at Hoover Dam. The isolation caused by the Grand Canyon is the principal reason the North Rim of Grand Canyon National Park receives much less use than the South Rim, where 90 percent of the use occurs. Though the rims are only 10 miles apart as the crow flies, by road they are more than 215 miles apart.

Geologically, Canyonlands is typical Colorado Plateau country, which consists primarily of horizontal sedimentary rock strata that have been dissected by running water and represents 300 million years of geological history. The oldest rocks are in the inner gorges and from the Pennsylvanian Period and the youngest are on the upper surfaces, and Jurassic in age. It is a stair-step type of landscape, with sheer cliffs and broad, flat benches. The sandstones, such as the Wingate and Cedar Mesa, are the cliff formers. The White Rim Sandstone caps most of the bench that lies at intermediate elevations in the park. The White Rim section takes its name from the color of this rock and forms a distinctive white band above the inner canyons. More poorly cemented and softer layers of sand and shale tend to be slope formers such as the Organ Rock Shale and the Chinle Formation. Most of the elevations on the canyon rims are 5500 to 6500 feet, while those on the benches are usually between 4500 and 5500 feet in elevation. Elevations range from 6987 feet at Cedar Mesa to 3720 feet at the lower end of Cataract Canyon. Canyonlands is a broad desert plain with low structural anticlines and deep canyons. The climate is arid, averaging only 8 inches of rain per year. The sparse vegetation is dominated by blackbush, juniper–pinyon woodlands, semidesert grasslands, and sagebrush shrubland. Wildlife that

may be observed includes bald eagle, peregrine falcon, desert bighorn sheep, badger, mountain lion, bobcat, mule deer and river otter. One of the principal resource management problems faced by park managers is how to prevent and repair damage done to the cryptobiotic crust (cryptogamic soil) by hikers, bikers, horses, and four-wheel-drive vehicles. This black crust, which is so impacted by use, consists of living plants that protect the desert from erosion.

The physiography and the confluence of the Green and Colorado Rivers geographically isolate Canyonlands National Park into four distinct districts, each reached by separate access. The most accessible district, called Island in the Sky, is found in the northern part of the park between the confluence of the Colorado and Green Rivers. It is readily accessible from park headquarters in Moab (32 miles away) and nearby Arches National Park.

Island in the Sky is one of only two places in the park where a paved road penetrates. This road extends 14 miles to Grand View Point Overlook, which is the best overall single view in the park. From here one can see The Maze and The Needles (two areas in the park, to be described shortly), and the Henry, LaSal, and Abajo Mountains. A spur road that is paved for 5 miles runs to nearby Upheaval Dome, whose bowl-shaped depression—1-mile in diameter and 1000 feet deep—is believed to have been caused by a meteorite. Upheaval Dome is the park's most unusual geological phenomena. A side road heads east and south to Dead Horse Point Overlook in Dead Horse Point State park before the Canyonlands park entrance is reached. This overlook is an outstanding one, and the state park contains 21 campsites.

The other three districts, to varying degrees, are less accessible. A second distinct district, The Needles, is located in the southeastern corner of the park; it is 75 miles from park headquarters at Moab to the Needles Visitor Center. The paved road extends for only 8 miles into the park here. The Needles consists of a variety of interesting geological formations: weathered spires of sandstone, steep sandstone walls, grabens, arches, and potholes. The third district, The Maze, while only a few miles across the Colorado River from The Needles district and a few miles across the Green River from the Island in the Sky district, is a long distance by road from the rest of the park. Four-wheel drive and hiking are the only means of accessing this district. To reach The Maze it is necessary to travel 20 miles north from Moab on U.S. 191 to I-70, 31 miles west on I-70, 23 miles south on Utah 24, and then another 80 miles on a dirt road. The Maze consists of an intricate network of box canyons. The Hans Flat Visitor Center, which serves the Maze, is located outside the Park in Glen Canyon National Recreation Area and requires 46 miles of travel along a dirt road to reach it. A detached portion of Canyonlands National Park, called Horseshoe Canyon, part of The Maze district, lies to the northwest and can be reached by two-wheel-drive vehicles in dry weather along the road leading to The Maze. Horseshoe Canyon is noted for spectacular pictographs. The fourth, or River, district is comprised of the Colorado and Green Rivers.

Canyonlands is an adventurer's park—you have to work to really see it. There are few visitor facilities and only two places where paved roads penetrate the park. It is virtually roadless, except for miles of jeep trails; 85 percent of it is backcountry; and there is no overnight lodging, food, or gas. It is a park to explore on your own. Paved and two-wheel-drive dirt roads exist in Island in the Sky and The Needles, which lead to interesting natural features, overlooks, trailheads, picnic areas, and developed campgrounds. These developed campgrounds are small and quite prim-

itive. Squaw Flat Campground (26 tent and RV sites) is located in The Needles district and has the only seasonally available water in the entire park. Willow Flat Campground (12 tent and RV sites) is located in the Island in the Sky districts. The view from the picnic area just north of Grand View Point Overlook in the Island in the Sky district has an awesome view. The visitation to Canyonlands has increased dramatically, from 36,700 in 1970 to over 300,000 in 1991. While the 309,000 recreation visitor days recorded in 1991 place Canyonlands at the midpoint for the 50 national parks, its 1.1 acres per visitor day rank it as the seventh least-used park in the lower 49 states.

Four-wheel-drive roads wind throughout the park, offering trips as short as a day or as long as a week. One of the more popular is the 100-mile White Rim Trail Road, which is accessed by the steep and winding Shafer Trail Road, which begins near the Island in the Sky visitor center (Figure 5.3). This route is also a favorite for mountain bikers. The White Rim Trail Road follows along a "bench" 1200 feet below Island in the Sky but above the inner gorge of the rivers. Primitive campsites, which require backcountry permits, are located along many of these roads. There are 20 campsites along the White Rim Trail Road. Motorboats, rafts, and canoes can navigate the quiet, upper waters of the Green and Colorado Rivers, but persons boating above the confluence of the two rivers are required to have a backcountry permit. Anyone planning a trip below the confluence through Cataract Canyon must obtain a permit at park headquarters. A limited number of individuals are allowed to run this 14-mile stretch of dangerous white-water each year. Boat launch sites are at locations north of the park, including the towns of Moab and Green River. There are no services along the rivers. Commercial tours that operate out of Moab and Green River may be hired for four-wheel-drive tours, hiking trips, horseback rides, and river float trips.

Everglades

Everglades National Park, located 50 miles south-southwest from Miami at the southern tip of the Florida peninsula, is the largest remaining subtropical wilderness in the conterminous United States. The park is characterized by (1) extensive fresh- and saltwater areas that cover half of the park, (2) open Everglade prairies of sawgrass with hardwood hammocks that rise like islands, and (3) mangrove forests along the coast. From Cape Sable the park extends 45 miles north along the Gulf of Mexico and 30 miles east along Florida Bay. Its 1,398,614 acres rank it as the ninth-largest national park; 1,296,500 acres are designated wilderness. Yellowstone is the only national park larger in the lower 49 states. Abundant wildlife includes rare and colorful birds, such as the roseate spoonbill. The park was authorized in 1934 but did not become established until 1947. The hard work of conservation-minded citizens was responsible for the creation of the park. In 1916, a 1920-acre Royal Palm State Park was established in the Royal Palm area, and was expanded to 4000 acres in 1921. This state park was donated to the National Park Service to serve as a nucleus for Everglades National Park. Boundary changes to the park occurred in 1958, 1959, 1960, 1964, 1969, and 1989. The park was designated a biosphere reserve in 1976 and a world heritage site in 1979.

The Everglades ecosystem is essentially a slowly moving freshwater river that is only a few inches deep (never more than 2 ft.) and 40 to 50 miles wide that runs from Lake Okeechobee south for 100 miles to Florida Bay. Lake Okeechobee is fed

Figure 5.3 The Shafer Trail Road descends in a steep and winding manner in Canyonlands National Park.

from central Florida's Kissimmee River basin's lakes and streams. The Indian name for the Everglades was "Pa-hay-okee," or river of grass. Development, agriculture, and human-made canals have drastically altered this natural system. Four Army Corps of Engineers floodgates/spillways (the "S12 structures") control the entire flow of fresh water that reaches the park. One is hard-pressed to find any other major ecosystem in the United States that has been impacted by humans to the degree of South Florida. The current amount (millions of dollars) being spent to return the original bends to the human-straightened Kissimmee River is testimony to human folly and destructiveness. The present-day park protects only a small portion of this ecosystem. Agricultural land extends to the east boundary of the park. In 1974, Big Cypress National Preserve (along with Big Thicket) was added as a new classification in the National Park System. Big Cypress adjoins Everglades National Park in the northwest and, supposedly, provides a freshwater supply crucial to the park's survival. Field investigations have revealed that only a small portion of the water flowing through Everglades National Park originates in the Big Cypress National Preserve. The 1989 expansion that added the 107,600-acre tract known as East Everglades to the northeastern corner of the park was an attempt to restore natural conditions to the full width of Shark River Slough, the main watershed of the park. This expansion involved buying land from 8000 landowners. The Army Corps of Engineers scheme of levees, canals, and spillways was designed to route water around the East Everglades. The Park Service is working with the Corps to return some of this flow to the East Everglades.

Because of this multitude of water-related problems, Everglades National Park is considered the most threatened of all U.S. national parks. The interruption of the natural drainage flow has had dramatic effects. Nesting wading birds (herons, egrets, ibis, and wood storks) have declined 90 percent. High concentrations of mercury have been found in fish, Florida panthers, and egrets. Seagrass die-off has occurred in

Florida Bay, and cattails have taken over thousands of acres of former sawgrass marsh. Alligator nests are sometimes flooded by excess summer water that would normally spread over a larger area with little damage.

An elevation change of only a few inches can dramatically affect the landscape in the Everglades. Nowhere in the park does the level of the land above sea level exceed 8 feet. On the better-drained land in the park, the largest slash pine forest left in South Florida is located in the *pinelands. Freshwater slough* is the location of the main water flow; Shark River Slough is the main slough, and Taylor Slough is also significant. Much of the interior of the park that is not slough is *freshwater marl prairie*. In both the freshwater sloughs and freshwater marl prairie, are found *hardwood hammocks,* which occur on slight rises of land above "seas of grass" and are composed of hardwood trees characteristic of the West Indies such as the mahogany, strangler fig, and gumbo-limbo. Dwarf *cypress* trees, more characteristic of Big Cypress National Preserve to the northwest, are found in the southeastern interior of the park in depressions in the limestone. At Rock Reef Pass (elevation 3 ft. above sea level) the main park road cuts a limestone ridge that separates the drainage of Shark River Slough from that of Taylor Slough. Trees and shrubs grow distinctly on this feature, compared with the sawgrass prairie that is found on either side. Solution of the limestone bedrock can be observed on the hammocks, pinelands, and cypress forest. Closer to the coast, *mangrove* dominates with islands of *coastal prairie* rising above in places. This mangrove ecosystem is most widespread in the southwestern corner of the park, surrounds Whitewater Bay, and occupies most of the northwestern corner of the park, including the Ten Thousand Islands. Three species of mangrove and the closely related buttonwood are found in this ecosystem, where the fresh water from the sloughs and rivers mixes with salt water from the ocean. This is the largest mangrove forest in the world. Over 1000 species of plants and 300 bird species are found in Everglades National Park, along with the endangered and rare manatee, crocodile, and Florida panther.

Everglades National Park is essentially a wilderness park, but there are three main places of cultural intrusion that offer access from the land. Ten miles southwest of Florida City, Highway 9336 turns into the main park road, which runs for 38 miles to Flamingo. On Florida Bay, Flamingo is the main developed portion of the park. A number of short walking trials along this main road introduces the visitor to the principal ecosystems of the park. The main visitor center is located just inside the entrance. Probably the best views in the park are located at the Royal Palm Visitor Center. Here the Anhinga Trail crosses a human-made canal in Taylor Slough via an elevated boardwalk. Along this trail one may view alligators, anhingas, turtles, herons, egrets, and river otter. Also at Royal Palm is a short trail, the Gumbo-Limbo, that passes through a hammock. At the Pa-hay-okee Overlook there is an excellent view of the glades and hammocks. The two campgrounds in the park—Long Key Pine and Flamingo—are found along this road. (Figure 5.4 shows the hosts at the National Park Service Flamingo Campground in Everglades National Park.) Also at Flamingo are concessioner-operated facilities known as the Florida Lodge, Marina and Outpost. This complex consists of a motel, housekeeping cabins, dining room, lounge, and screened-in pool and offers full service from November 1 to April 30. From the marina, boats may be rented or tours hired for sport fishing, sightseeing, or bird watching. The Buttonwood Canal leads into Coot Bay and Whitewater Bay.

Figure 5.4   John and Jean Ratcliff are campground hosts at Flamingo Campground in Everglades National Park.

Several marked canoe trails start at Flamingo, including the 100-mile Wilderness Waterway, which runs from Flamingo to Everglades City. Backcountry campsites are available along these canoe trails, either on beaches or on raised wooden platforms called "chickees."

Other access points are at Shark Valley and Everglades City. Shark Valley is located in the northern part of the park, 30 miles west of Miami on U.S. 41 (the Tamiami Trail). Open-air tram tours are available, or bicycles may be rented for the 15-mile-loop trip, which includes a 65-foot observation tower at the midpoint. At Everglades City in the extreme northwestern corner of the park, which has a visitor center, one may take boat tours and charter fishing trips (for snapper, sea trout, tarpon, and redfish). This is also the location of the Ten Thousand Islands mangrove region of the park.

Everglades National Park's tourist seasons are related to the weather. The main season, which corresponds to the dry season, extends from mid-December to mid-April. Wildlife observation is best during the dry season because it congregates at the limited waterholes. The off-season runs from mid-April until mid-December, when the weather is hot and humid with numerous thunderstorms, and the mosquitoes are almost unbearable. One needs to be a dedicated outdoors person to camp in the backcountry during the wet season. During the off-season some facilities and services are limited or not available. Everglades was the 16th-most-visited national park in 1991, with 704,900 visitor days. Its 1.98-acres-per-visitor-day magnitude of use was among the most favorable of all national parks, with only Capitol Reef, Isle Royale, and North Cascades having more space in the lower 49 states.

Glacier

Precipitous peaks rise to over 10,000 feet in elevation in this glacially carved portion of the Northern Rocky Mountains in northwestern Montana. This ruggedly beautiful

land, which straddles the Continental Divide for 50 miles, includes nearly 50 glaciers, many picturesque alpine and glacially carved lakes and troughs, numerous streams, a wide variety of wildlife, and bountiful displays of wildflowers. The park extends for 40 miles of longitude, from the Great Plains in the east to the Flathead River in the west. Elevations range from 10,448 feet (Mount Cleveland) to 3150 feet (Flathead River). Glacier was established as a national park in 1910 and received boundary changes in 1912, 1915, 1939, 1944, 1972, and 1978. The park was authorized and proclaimed in 1932 as part of Waterton-Glacier International Peace Park and designated a biosphere reserve in 1976. It was the world's *first international peace park*. Waterton Lakes National Park, which adjoins Glacier along the Canadian border, was established in 1895. It is just a fraction of the size of Glacier, and lies in extreme southwestern Alberta and British Columbia. The same glacially carved landscape of Glacier continues in Waterton. The main lake of Waterton, Upper Waterton Lake, straddles the U.S.-Canadian border. Although the two parks are administered separately, they do cooperate in wildlife management and scientific research and some visitor services. Glacier's 1,012,996 acres rank it the 11th-largest national park in the U.S. system; in the lower 49 states, only Yellowstone, Everglades, and Grand Canyon are larger. Although 95 percent of Glacier is managed as wilderness, none of it has yet been included in our National Wilderness Preservation System.

The Northern Rocky Mountain Province abruptly rises from the glaciated Missouri Plateau Section of the Great Plains Province at the eastern edge of Glacier National Park. The Lewis Range on the east and the Clark Range on the west form the sides of a broad synclinal structure that moved eastward along the Lewis overthrust fault 100 million years ago. This overthrust area reaches the surface at the eastern side of the park. This thrust is at least 135 miles and perhaps as much as 300 miles long. It has been traced for 50 miles south of the international boundary and 85 miles north of it (Thornbury, 1965, 389). In Glacier National Park, the Precambrian Altyn Formation has been thrust over Cretaceous shales and sandstones. Chief Mountain (9066 ft.) is the easternmost remnant of the overthrust. Throughout its length the trace of the Lewis thrust has an irregularly scalloped plan. While these ranges are not as high as those in the Southern and Middle Rockies, they exhibit some of the finest glacial topography to be seen in the Rocky Mountain system. Their much lower snow line accounts for their extensive glaciation. The rocks here are layered sedimentary rocks that range from 1600 million to 800 million years in age, which gives the glacial topography a unique aspect not found in the granite ranges of the Middle and Southern Rockies. Most of the erosional landforms produced by mountain glaciation can be viewed here, ranging from glacial cirques, tarns, horns, and aretes along the range crests, to trough lakes in the lower portions of the glaciated valleys. Clements Mountain and Reynolds Mountain are examples of classic glacial horns and may be viewed from Logan Pass. The Garden Wall, which is part of the Continental Divide, forms as fine an example as can be found of an *arete* (a steep, serrated, knifelike ridge cut by glaciation in mountains). The main valleys contained glaciers over 2000 feet thick 20,000 years ago. The 50 or so remnant glaciers in the park, while still extremely spectacular, are but small reminders of the once much larger glaciers that recently impacted the landscape. For example, the Jackson Glacier, which may be viewed from Going-to-the-Sun Road, retreated 4800 feet between 1850 and 1980 (Raup et al., 1983, 25), losing 76 percent of its surface area.

This landscape is a wilderness full of wildlife and wildflowers with distinct local variations. The western side of the Continental Divide serves as a major climatic divide. It receives significantly more rainfall and snowfall than the leeward eastern slope and has trees such as Douglas fir, larch, hemlock, and western red cedar. Glacier National Park is a biotic treasure chest with over 1000 species of flowering plants: The alpine areas provide some of the best wildflower displays in North America, and wildflowers are also present on the prairie in the eastern part of the park. Wildlife is equally spectacular, with 60 native mammals and over 200 bird species. Wildlife that may be observed in the park includes elk, bighorn sheep, mountain goat, grizzly bear, moose, mule deer, gray wolf, bobcat, and lynx. There are fewer than 900 grizzlies in the lower 49 states, and 300 of them roam at least part of the year through Glacier. These bears can be dangerous and should be observed from a great distance.

Although Glacier is remotely located from major population centers, visitors are well set up to experience it once they arrive. Amtrak provides rail service with stops at both Belton (West Glacier) and East Glacier. U.S. 2 skirts the southern boundary of the park. The spectacular Going-to-the-Sun Road provides ready access to the heart of the park by passing through its middle, roughly dividing the park in two. This 50-mile narrow, steep, and winding road skirts Lake McDonald (10 miles long and 472 ft. deep) in the west, then climbs to the high country along the Garden Wall, crosses the Continental Divide at Logan Pass (6646 ft.), and descends to St. Mary Lake. The completion of this road in 1932 opened up the interior of Glacier. The road is usually open from about mid-June until mid-October for its entire length. There, vehicle length-and-width limitations become increasingly restrictive each year, and bicycles are not allowed during the middle of the day. In 1994 a maximum vehicle length of 20 feet and a maximum width (including mirrors) of 7.5 feet was allowed. The Chief Mountain International Highway, which is open mid-May to mid-September, passes through the extreme northeastern corner of the park and offers road access to Waterton. It provides magnificent views of Chief Mountain and Mount Cleveland.

A visitor-friendly network of over 700 miles of hiking and riding trails fan out in all directions from hotels, chalets, and campgrounds. There are visitor centers at Apgar, Logan Pass, and St. Mary. On the western side of the park the main hub of activity is at Apgar. Several comfortable hotels and lodges are located within the park's boundary, the largest being the 208-unit Many Glacier Hotel in the area of the park with the same name. This grand hotel was built in 1915 by the Great Northern Railroad to promote tourism. Two hike-to-only chalets in the high country—Granite Park Chalet and Sperry Chalet—were also built by the Great Northern Railroad. Both serve meals as well as provide overnight accommodations for hikers. Reservations well ahead of time are necessary.

Glacier is a hiker's paradise, and there are 70 backcountry campsites. The lower-elevation trails open up by mid-June, and the higher elevation trails by mid-July. One of the finest hikes for motorists is the 3-mile round-trip Hanging Garden Walk in Logan Pass at the visitor center, where spring does not arrive until August. Alpine flowers and other vegetation may be observed along a paved and boardwalk trail that leads to an excellent view of Hidden Lake. An 11-mile round-trip hike leads to one of the most accessible glaciers in the Many Glacier area, the Grinnell. Saddle horses are available at Apgar, Lake McDonald Lodge, and Many Glacier Hotel. Boat tours are operated on Lakes McDonald, Two Medicine, St. Mary, Swiftcurrent, and

Josephine. There are several styles of camping for the visitor. Paved roads lead to campgrounds at Apgar (196 sites), Avalanche Creek (87 sites), Fish Creek (180 sites), Many Glacier (114 sites), Rising Sun (83 sites), St. Mary (156 sites), Two Medicine (99 sites), and Sprague Creek (25 sites). Trailer space is available at all but Sprague Creek, which is closed to towed vehicles. For more adventurous and remote camping, graveled roads lead to campsites at Bowman Lake, Kintla Lake, Cut Bank, Logging Creek, and Quartz Creek. The first two are remotely located in the northwestern corner of the Park. In the winter, cross-country skiing is increasing in popularity. Glacier's 1,481,300 visitor days in 1991 ranked it ninth in use among national parks; 0.68 acres per recreation visitor day placed Glacier at about the midpoint of national park intensity of use.

Great Basin

Located in eastern Nevada near the Utah border, Great Basin is one of the newest of our national parks. In 1986 Lehman Caves National Monument was added to a portion of the Humboldt National Forest to create the 77,100-acre park. Lehman Caves was originally proclaimed a national monument in 1922 in a small portion of what is now the present-day park. The monument was transferred from the Forest Service to the Park Service in 1933. Major features of the park are a remnant small glacier beneath 13,063-foot Wheeler Peak (Nevada's second highest), ancient bristlecone pine trees and other forest types, alpine plants, alpine lakes, abundant wildlife, the 75-foot limestone Lexington Arch, and tunnels and decorated galleries in Lehman Caves. This park represents a much needed addition to an underrepresented ecosystem in our National Park System. It represents the "mountain islands" in the Great Basin region, which stretches between the Sierra Nevada and the Wasatch Range. In these mountain ranges of the Great Basin Section of the Basin and Range Province, the higher elevations intercept moisture, and the vegetation changes from the desert sagebrush of the lower elevations (at 4000 to 5000 feet) to forest as elevation increases (to 10,000 feet and higher). The park includes much of the southern Snake Range, which provides a good example of biogeography, the relationship between living things and the landscape: As elevation increases, the climate changes, creating habitats for different plants and animals.

Wheeler Peak Scenic Drive provides good views of the Snake Range and its ecosystems and is an excellent introduction to mountain microclimatology and biogeography. The road climbs 3400 feet in elevation in 12 miles and passes through a variety of habitats: from desert sagebrush to pinyon-juniper woodlands; along a creekbed lined with aspen trees; through a zone of shrubby mountain mahogany and manzanita; into Englemann spruce and Douglas fir; to meadows and subalpine forest of limber pine, spruce, and aspen at Wheeler Peak campground (9800 ft.). Thirteen peaks rise above 11,000 feet, and snow can fall in any month of the year—even July. The trees found highest in the Snake Range, limber and bristlecone pines, appear between 9000 and 11,000 feet. While both species are fairly hardy, the bristlecones are the masters of longevity. Near the end of the scenic drive one can take a 3.5-mile (round-trip) trail among bristlecone pines that are 2000 to 3000 years old. A bristlecone pine found here was declared the world's oldest living tree until 1964. In this year "Prometheus," as the 4950-year-old tree was called, was cut to obtain an accurate

reading of its growth rings. The honor today falls to a bristlecone pine over 4600 years old in the White Mountains of the Inyo National Forest. Three main stands of bristlecone pines occur in the park: on the northeastern slopes of Wheeler Peak, on Mount Washington, and on Peak 10,842. Figure 5.5 illustrates the vegetation, small glacier, and 13,063-ft. summit of Wheeler Peak, as seen from the 10,000-foot elevation on Wheeler Peak Scenic Drive.

The other major resource of the park is found underground—Lehman Caves. This is a single cavern (despite its plural name) extending a quarter mile into the limestone and low-grade marble that flank the base of the Snake Range. Discovered in 1885, this cavern is one of the most richly decorated in the country. It started forming millions of years ago when the climate was more humid. As the climate turned drier, the water drained from the cave, leaving smooth walls and hollow rooms. In the second stage of cave development, small amounts of water trickled in but, instead of enlarging the cave, started to fill it in. The result is a rich display of cave formations (*speleothems*), such as stalactites, stalagmites, columns, draperies, and flowstone. Lehman Caves is most famous for its rare and mysterious structures called *shields,* which consist of two roughly circular halves, almost like flattened clamshells. A half-mile guided walking tour through the cavern is conducted for a fee by the National Park Service. There are other wild caves in the park that can be explored, but a permit is needed; of these, Muddy Cave is the best known.

The main park entrance and visitor center is 5 miles west of the tiny hamlet of Baker, Nev. The nearest cities are Ely, Nev., 70 miles to the west, and Delta, Utah, 100 miles to the east. Las Vegas is 286 miles to the south, Salt Lake City is 234 miles to the northeast, and Reno is 385 miles to the west. The cave entrance, a lovely picnic area, and a cafe and gift shop are located at the visitor center. A small grocery store, limited motel accommodations, and gasoline are available in Baker. All park roads

Figure 5.5 Wheeler Peak (13,063 ft.) and a small glacier as seen from the 10,000-ft. elevation along Wheeler Peak Scenic Drive in Great Basin National Park.

except the Wheeler Peak Scenic Drive are unpaved and infrequently traveled. Four developed campgrounds (Baker Creek, Lower Lehman Creek, Upper Lehman Creek, and Wheeler Peak) provide water and restrooms. Two primitive campgrounds (Snake Creek and Shoshone) have pit toilets but no water. The Wheeler Peak campground (elevation 9800 ft.), is especially pleasant and scenic, as tame mule deer walk right up to you! Because this park was previously a national forest, open-range livestock grazing is still permitted. Often the "wildlife" observed is domestic cattle, and "cow pies" frequently dot the drive. Backcountry opportunities abound, but there are few maintained trails. Wildlife such as bighorn sheep or mountain lions may be seen. The cross-country skiing in the winter can be very good. Great Basin's 66,300 visitor days in 1991 make it among the least-visited national parks in the system. Only nine national parks have fewer visitors, and in the lower 49 states the only parks with fewer visitors are North Cascades, Wind Cave, and Guadaloupe Mountains. A relatively large 1.16 acres per recreation visitor day makes Great Basin among the least crowded of our national parks. The few visitors to this relatively unknown national park are very pleasantly surprised with a high-quality experience.

Great Smoky Mountains

The Great Smoky Mountains are the majestic southern climax of the Appalachian Highlands. Here in this national park are preserved the world's finest examples of temperate deciduous forest and other luxuriant plant life in the loftiest range east of the Black Hills. Besides the exquisite flora and fauna, the park also preserves structures representing Southern Appalachian Mountain culture. The word *Smoky* comes from the smokelike haze that often envelopes the mountians. This 520,004-acre park equally straddles the North Carolina—Tennessee border for 70 miles and was gradually created from purchased private land. It was authorized in 1926, established for administration and protection only in 1930, and established for full development in 1934. Boundary changes occurred in 1930, 1932, 1934, 1940, 1944, 1950, 1958, 1963, 1964, and 1969. It was designated a biosphere reserve in 1976 and a world heritage site in 1983. It is located 25 miles southeast of Knoxville, Tenn., and 40 miles west of Asheville, N.C. In the eastern United States, only Everglades and Isle Royale National Parks are larger. The Blue Ridge Parkway starts at Great Smoky Mountains National Park and runs north for 469 miles to Shenandoah National Park. In North Carolina, the Pisgah and Nantahala National Forests and in Tennessee, the Cherokee National Forest, border the Park.

The Great Smoky Mountains are in the Southern Section of the Blue Ridge Province of the Appalachian Highlands and are the easternmost range of the Unakas. The Great Smoky overthrust pushed rocks of the Blue Ridge northwest over carbonate rocks of the Ridge and Valley Province, thus forming the mountains. Most of the rocks are Cambrian and Upper Precambrian sedimentary and Precambrian gneisses and plutonics. There are 16 peaks in the park over 6000 feet, and the main ridge remains above 5000 feet for 36 miles. Occurring on some of the highest peaks are *grass balds*, which are unexplained, yet very distinctive features. *Coves*, found in the northwestern part of the park, are smooth-floored, oval-shaped valleys underlain by Ordovician limestone and shale that do not exceed 10 square miles in size. The coves, of which Cades Cove is the most famous, are windows and thus inliers (areas of

different geologic structure) of Great Valley topography in the Great Smoky Mountains thrust sheet. The park is a meeting ground of southern and northern forest types, with 130 different tree species, which range from luxuriant temperate deciduous species at the lower and middle elevations, to red spruce and Fraser fir at the higher elevations. Over 1500 species of flowering plants occur, the most famous being the rhododendron and flame azaleas, which burst into color in June and July. The park has over 200 species of birds and abundant numbers of mammals, including black bear. The 735 miles of streams in the park provides excellent fishing for rainbow and brown trout and bass; possession of brook trout is prohibited.

Great Smoky Mountains is the leading national park in terms of number of recreation visits—8,654,500 in 1991. The park's ranking drops to number 4 when considering recreation visitor days—5,539,500 in 1991—which is the more meaningful measure of recreational use (only Yellowstone, Yosemite, and Grand Canyon have more visitor days). This high recreational use is attributable to its favorable location close to large population centers of the Southeast. Much of this high use occurs along the only highway that crosses the park, U.S. 441. This scenic road, which is closed to commercial vehicles, crosses the mountain spine at the 5048-foot Newfound Gap in the heart of the park (Figure 5.6). It connects the bustling tourist centers of Cherokee, N.C., and Gatlinburg, Tenn. This through-road, which allows people to pass through the park on other business, also accounts for the park's overwhelming lead position among national parks for nonrecreation visits (9,267,000) and nonrecreation visitor days (386,100, both in 1991). The park headquarters and Sugarlands Visitor Center are on U.S. 441 on the northern side of the park, 2 miles south of Gatlinburg, while the Oconoluftee Visitor Center is in the southern part of the park, 2 miles north of Cherokee. Figure 5.7 illustrates farm buildings at Pioneer Farmstead at the Oconoluftee Visitor Center. At Newfound Gap a 7-mile road runs west through spruce and

Figure 5.6 The Newfound Gap Road (U.S. 441) climbs through the heart of Great Smoky Mountains National Park to an elevation of 5048 ft. Commercial traffic is not allowed.

Figure 5.7 The Pioneer Farmstead at the Oconaluftee Visitor Center in Great Smoky Mountains National Park preserves historic farm buildings that were gathered from their original locations within the park.

fir forest to a half-mile trail that leads to spiral stairs and an observation tower at the highest point in both Tennessee and the Park: 6643-foot Clingmans Dome. The time of heaviest use is during the summer and the fall foliage season.

Another popular and heavily visited portion of the park is Cades Cove, which is located in the western part in Tennessee. Here, pioneer life is depicted along an 11-mile one-way-loop road that passes fields, churches, and pioneer homesteads. The cultural heritage of the Southern Appalachians is preserved here. In 1850, almost 700 people lived in Cades Cove. Today there is an operating gristmill, and demonstrations of pioneer activities are performed. The park's third visitor center is also located here. Cades Cove is an excellent location for bicycling, and on Saturdays the road is closed until 10:00 A.M. for exclusive bicycle use.

Recreational opportunities in Great Smoky Mountain National Park are diverse, including hiking, camping, interpretive programs, horseback riding, fishing, picnicking, pioneer exhibits and demonstrations, nature walks, auto tours, and wildflower and bird watching. The park contains 170 miles of paved roads and 100 miles of gravel roads, and there are over 900 miles of foot and horse trails. The Appalachian Trail follows the mountain crest for the full 70-mile length of the park, and includes 13 backcountry shelters, each a day's hike apart. There is a one-day limit for these shelters, and permits are required.

Ten developed campgrounds are scattered throughout the park, the three major ones being Elkmont, Smokemont, and Cades Cove. All ten contain basic National Park Service tent and RV sites with no hookups. Seven of the ten campgrounds have sites for groups. Two alternatives to camping are offered by private concessioner-operated lodgings. One is the 27-unit Wonderland Club Hotel at Elkmont, which was a private club prior to creation of the national park. The other, LeConte Lodge atop

6593-foot Mount LeConte, is for hikers only. Here, meals are served, and there are 10 cabins that have no electricity. A half-day hike is required to arrive at LeConte Lodge. A wide variety of commercial accommodations, restaurants, shops, and attractions are found in the two gateway tourist centers at either main entrance to the park: Gatlinburg, Tenn., and Cherokee, N.C. The Eastern Cherokee Indian Reservation borders the southeastern entrance of the park around Cherokee.

Haleakala

Located on the island of Maui in the Hawaiian Islands, Haleakala National Park preserves the outstanding features of Haleakala Crater and protects the unique and fragile ecosystems of Kipahulu Valley, the scenic pools along 'Ohe'o Stream, and many rare and endangered species. It was originally created as one of three sections of Hawaii National Park in 1916 (the other two being Kilauea and Mauna Loa), and was redesignated Haleakala National Park in 1961. Boundary changes took place in 1922, 1928, 1938, 1940, 1961, and 1978. Designation as a biosphere reserve occurred in 1980 and as a world heritage site in 1987. The 27,468-acre park has over two-thirds of its area (19,270 acres) designated as part of the National Wilderness Preservation System. Only Virgin Islands and Hot Springs National Parks are smaller in size. The 240,500 recreation visitor days recorded in 1991 place Haleakala near the median for the national parks, but its relatively small size ranks it the eighth most crowded, with 0.11 acres per recreation visitor day.

Maui is shaped like an assymmetrical figure-eight on its side, with the larger portion in the east. After making the long flight across the Pacific to the Hawaiian Islands, usually landing at Honolulu on Oahu, visitors must then take another flight to Kahului on Maui. Haleakala National Park is in the eastern part of Maui, and road access only reaches it at the extreme eastern and western ends. The nature of the road access geographically isolates the park into two sections: Crater Rim Road in the west and Kipahulu Valley in the east. Better roads make the western part of the park the most easily reached. From Kahului in west-central Maui it is 37 miles to the crater rim and 62 miles to the Kipahulu section of the park. Hawaii Highway 378 climbs to the western park entrance, and a steep road steadily climbs for 10 miles from the park entrance to the House of the Sun Visitor Center on the crater rim. Just inside the entrance, a side road leads to Hosmer Grove and the only drive-to campsite in this part of the park. Here, in 1910, Ralph Hosmer planted an experimental tract with temperate-climate tree species, including Douglas fir, California redwood, and eucalyptus. Less than a mile from the Hosmer turnoff, at the 7000-foot level, is park headquarters. As the road climbs to the crater rim, the Leleiwi and Kalahaku Overlooks provide two views of Haleakala Crater. The road ends at the crater rim, at 10,000 ft. of elevation. Haleakala (which means "house of the sun") is a moonlike landscape on a giant dormant volcano whose crater is 7.5 miles long, 2.5 miles wide, and 21 miles in circumference. The floor of the crater, where 600-foot cinder cones rise, is 3000 feet below the rim (Figure 5.8). The last volcanic eruption on Maui occurred in 1790, outside of the park area. The Hawaiian Islands formed where mantle plumes rose in "hot spots" in the middle of the Pacific Plate as the plate moved to the northwest. Therefore the islands to the northwest are older than those to the

Figure 5.8   Haleakala Crater in Haleakala National Park.

southeast. Hawaii is the youngest and most volcanically active of the Hawaiian Islands, and Maui is the next youngest.

There are no overnight accommodations or meals served in Haleakala National
Park. Three cabins (Hoalua, Kapalaoa, and Paliku) in the crater can be booked ahead
of time, and two primitive tent campsites (Hoalua and Paliku) can only be reached
by hiking or horseback. There are 30 miles of trails in the park. The highest point on
the rim is Puu Ulaula (10,023 ft.), and nearby is a closed area called Science City,
which has observatories and labs. On the crater rim there are interpretive exhibits
and guide talks and walks. The rare silversword, found nowhere else in the world,
occurs on the rim. The weather can be decidedly chilly on the rim due to its 10,000-
foot elevation—up to 40° colder than at sea level; there is more rain, clouds, and fog
in the winter. During the 38-mile trip from near sea level at Kahului to the rim one
moves from the humid tropical rain forest to subalpine desert.

The Kipahulu Valley supports a rain forest where the valley drops from the east
rim of the crater. Many rare and endangered species occur here, among them the
endangered Maui *nukupu'u* (parrotbill) and the nene goose. In the higher elevations
of the valley native *koa* and *'ohi'a* rain forest are found. Hiking, camping, picnicking,
and swimming are the recreational opportunities in this part of the park, which
touches the ocean. There is no potable water, gas, food, or lodging in Kipahulu Valley,
and the campground here is more primitive than those in the crater. The ocean shore
is rugged with harsh waves, so most swimming takes place in the pools of 'Ohe'o
Stream. The Pipiwai Trail follows this stream, which is noted for its pools and waterfalls, some as high as 300 feet. The big problem with this section of the park is
getting there. Hawaii 36 to Hana on the wet northern side of the island is a rough
road, although paved; the same road on the dry, southern side is paved only part of
the way, and rental cars are not allowed.

Hot Springs

Hot Springs has the distinction of being the first federal land in the United States reserved for the future (1832), the smallest national park (4853 acres), and our only urban, highly developed national park (in the small city, population 37,000, of Hot Springs National Park). The Hot Springs Reservation was originally set aside in 1832 to protect 47 thermal springs and four sections of land from private monopoly and exploitation. It was not until 1880 that it was dedicated as a public park and in 1921 redesignated a national park. Boundary changes occurred in 1892, 1906, 1924, 1930, 1931, 1936, 1938, 1939, 1954, 1958, and 1959. It is located 55 miles southwest of Little Rock, Ark., in the Zig Zag Mountains on the eastern edge of the exposed Ouachita Range. The mountaintops are erosion-resistant remnants of folded layers of novaculite and sandstone. Music Mountain in the southwestern part of the park is the highest point (1405 ft.) in this small mountain system and is the center of a great horseshoe-shaped ridge whose ends are Sugarloaf and West Mountains. Other mountains in the park are Hot Springs, North, Blowout, and Indian Mountains. The valley floors are about 600 feet in elevation. The hot springs emerge from the Hot Springs Sandstone on the lower western side of Hot Springs Mountain. Opposite the southern end of the horseshoe is the heart of the urban area. The water initially penetrates the earth in the fractured Bigfork Chert and Arkansas Novaculite in the mountains to the northeast and is heated by the natural thermal gradient—it takes 4000 years for the water to reach the faults and joints of the Hot Springs sandstone beneath the west flank of Hot Springs Mountain. Then, in about 1 year the heated water rises and emerges at the hot springs. Dense forests of oak, hickory and shortleaf pine dominate this region. Flowering trees are common, and rosebud and dogwood bloom in the early spring, gracing the understory of the pine and hardwood woodlands. Flowering Southern magnolias lend historic Bathhouse Row a special beauty, particularly in early summer. Songbirds and small animals are abundant in the forest.

Visitors quickly become confused as to exactly where the national park is and where the City of Hot Springs National Park is, since both have the same name. One would need a detailed map in hand to differentiate the boundaries, for the city surrounds part of the national park, and the park surrounds part of the city. Most visitors enter the park on Central Avenue, and if they know where they are, they might spot the Fordyce Bathhouse Visitor Center. While the restored Fordyce Bathhouse is exquisite, its locational choice as the visitor center is poor. Traffic is heavy on Central Avenue, parking spaces are rare, and turning around in the heavy traffic is dangerous. Hot Springs National Park is, in this author's opinion, the most confusing of our national parks—at least at the initial arrival and orientation stage. The park ranked number 18 among all national parks in recreation visits in 1991 (1,203,900) but number 39 in recreation visitor days (69,000). This tremendous difference between the two statistics reflects the short duration of the visits to this essentially urban park; no other national park has such a wide variation between the two statistics. Only three national parks have fewer acres per recreation visitor day than Hot Spring's 0.07: Bryce Canyon, Acadia, and Virgin Islands. Hot Springs is also noteworthy for receiving the greatest number of nonrecreation visits for all national parks (4,289,700) except for Great Smoky Mountains (9,267,000).

Figure 5.9 Looking north on Central Avenue in Hot Springs National Park; the bathhouses and hot springs are on the right side of the Avenue. (National Park Service photo)

The City of Hot Springs National Park is a year-round health and pleasure resort. In addition to the hot springs, there are golf courses and nearby water-oriented recreation on Lakes Hamilton and Ouachita. The city's main street, Central Avenue (Bathhouse Row), passes right between Hot Springs and West Mountains. Across from businesses on the west side of Central Avenue are the bathhouses of the park. The original Hot Springs Creek now flows under this street. Most of the hot springs are on the immediate east side of Central Avenue and extend up the lower west side of Hot Springs Mountain to, and past, the Grand Promenade (Figure 5.9). The grand bathhouses started to fall into a state of disrepair in the 1950s, but a restoration program has been quite successful. The restored Fordyce Bathhouse now serves as the visitor center for the park, having reopened in 1989. Only six of the bathhouses are now operating: two in the park and four are in hotels. All but two of the 47 hot springs are covered today while the water is collected for distribution in one central system. The water that flows from these springs remains a uniform 143°F.

In addition to the traditional baths, other recreational opportunities at the park include naturalist-led activities, bathhouse tours, walking, hiking, horseback riding, and auto tours. The park has 10 miles of roads with scenic overlooks. The 2.5-mile auto road to the top of Hot Spring Mountain was originally built for horse-drawn vehicles in 1884. There is a picnic area near the top of this drive and a 216-foot observation tower that is concessioner-operated. In this tower an elevator transports the visitor to a lofty view—for a fee. There is also a 2-mile road to an overlook on West Mountain. The second picnic area is at the entrance to the Gulpha Gorge campsite 2 miles northeast of downtown. There are 47 tent and RV sites for camping here but no hookups. Once the confusion of Central Avenue is left behind, very pleasurable experiences may be had at places such as Gulpha Gorge and Hot Springs Mountain. It is ironic that the hot springs, which attracted development in the first place,

are now the reason for the crowds and congestion in downtown Hot Springs National Park.

Mammoth Cave

Mammoth Cave National Park (Kentucky) is one of the two parks in the system whose primary purpose is to protect outstanding enormous cave resources; the other is Carlsbad Caverns (New Mexico). Other caves are protected in the National Park System, such as Lehman Caves (Great Basin National Park, Nevada), Timpanogos Cave National Monument (Utah), and Oregon Caves National Monument (Oregon), but they are not of the same order of magnitude as the extensive caves at Carlsbad Caverns and Mammoth Cave. Mammoth Cave National Park protects a huge cave system, including Mammoth Cave proper, the scenic river valleys of the Green and Nolin Rivers, and a section of the hilly country north of the Green River. This is the longest recorded cave system in the world, with more than 330 miles explored and mapped on five different levels. There is archaeological evidence of human habitation dating back approximately 4000 years. The park was authorized in 1926 but did not become fully established until 1941. Boundary changes occurred in 1934, 1937, 1940, and 1942. Designation as a world heritage site transpired in 1981 and as a biosphere reserve in 1990. The surface area of the park is 51,592 aces, which ranks Mammoth Cave as one of the smaller national parks (44th in size); but the 332,300 recreation visitor days in 1991 rank it at the 23rd position in terms of use. The relative crowded use intensity of 0.155 acres per visitor day does not reveal the fact that much of the use recorded is below ground.

Mammoth Cave National Park is located in the Interior Low Plateaus physiographic province, in west-central Kentucky. It is 30 miles northeast of Bowling Green. The Park is located on the gently sloping Dripping Springs Cuesta, which has a thin layer of Cypress Sandstone on top of soluble Saint Genevieve Limestone. These sedimentary strata are Mississippian in age. The porous sandstone, instead of protecting the limestone, has favored percolation at the expense of surface runoff. The topography that has developed is a classic karst landscape. Numerous dolines several hundred feet deep are aligned dendritically toward Green River Gorge. The Green River is the master stream toward which the subterranean drainage flows. The great cavern systems lie under the uplands between the steep-walled valleys. The solution work of groundwater has been responsible for forming the multitude of limestone caves, underground rivers, springs, and sinkholes. The dry upper levels of the cave system were hollowed out thousands of years ago, while the lower passages are still being enlarged by the flowing waters of Echo River and other underground streams. The huge vertical shafts, called pits (Bottomless Pit is 105 ft. deep) and domes (Mammoth Dome is 192 ft. from floor to ceiling), have been created by water percolating through the roofs of sinkholes and cracks in the protective sandstone.

There are two worlds to explore in the park. In addition to the extraordinary world of the underground is the more familiar surface world of oak-hickory forests, meandering rivers, and woodland wildlife. Much of the park is in its natural state, providing shelter to a large variety of birds and other wildlife. The scenic Green River traverses the well-forested terrain for 24 miles, and along the western boundary of the park flows the Nolin River. Both rivers are tributaries of the Ohio River. Sev-

enty miles of woodland trails follow the rivers' bluffs, ridges and valleys. These afford attractive vistas and access to the backcountry. There are no bridges in the park; only two ferries cross the Green River. There is one commercial lodging establishment in the Park (the Mammoth Cave Hotel) and three campgrounds—at headquarters, Houchin's Ferry, and Dennison Ferry (tent-only sites). On the surface the main recreational activities are nature walks, hiking, fishing, horseback riding, boat trips, and bicycling. An interesting commercial boat cruise traverses the Green River. The Joppa Ridge Motor Trail is a 2-mile dirt and gravel road that affords a scenic drive through part of the park.

Most visitors, however, are attracted to the park by the cave tours. The ranger-guided tours offered range from ¼ mile and 1¼ hours long to 5 miles and 6 hours. Five tours are offered all year, while three others are offered only in the summer. Twelve miles of passages are available for tours. Tour members meet at the visitor center and then walk or take a bus to one of five different cave entrances, where their tour begins. Some passages and rooms are decorated with sparkling white gypsum crystals, while others are filled with the colorful sculptured shapes of stalactites, stalagmites, and other cave formations. In the cave's absolute blackness dwell many rare and unusual animals, including eyeless fish, eyeless crayfish, white spiders, blind beetles, and cave crickets. The "Historic Tour" (2 miles, 2 hours) begins at the Historic Entrance and traces the cave's long and colorful history. It passes through the Rotunda, which was a source of nitrates to make gunpowder for the War of 1812. The "Half Day Tour" (4 miles, 4.5 hours) explores many of Mammoth's natural features, with a stop for lunch at the Snowball Dining Room. Lint from visitors' clothing is responsible for a fungus that has degraded the white color of the "Snowballs." The latter part of this tour follows the "Frozen Niagara Tour" route. The "Frozen Niagara Tour" (0.75 miles, 2 hours) begins at New Entrance and ends at Frozen Niagara Entrance; along its route are colorful stalactites, stalagmites, and massive flowstone formations. The "Travertine Tour" (0.25 miles, 1.25 hours) is a less strenuous version of the "Frozen Niagara Tour," and so is better suited for the elderly. The "Disabled Tour" (0.5 miles, 1.5 hours) is for physically impaired persons and their assistants. This tour begins with a ride on the service elevator to Snowball Dining Room and includes part of Cleaveland Avenue. These five tours are offered year-round.

Three other tours are offered in the summer only. The "Lantern Tour" (3 miles, 3 hours) recreates an old-time tour of Mammoth, when guides led the way with kerosene lanterns. It starts at the Historic Entrance, follows the first part of the "Historic Tour" route, continues into Main Cave and Chief City, and exits at Violet City Entrance. The "Echo River Tour" (3 miles, 3 hours) begins and ends at the Historic Entrance. It descends to the cave's deepest passages, where Echo River and the River Styx flow, and includes a boat ride on the Echo River. The "Wild Cave Tour" (5 miles, 6 hours) is a strenuous investigation of a wild portion of Mammoth Cave, beginning at Carmichael Entrance and ending at Frozen Niagara Entrance. The trip requires stooping and belly crawling through tight passages with hard hats and head lamps.

Mesa Verde

Mesa Verde is our only national park established primarily for its archaeological resources. Its pre-Columbian cliff dwellings and other works of early native people

are the most notable and best preserved in the United States. The park was established in 1906, but not until 1913 when the Ute Indians traded this land for a larger parcel, were the best ruins added to the park. Other boundary changes occurred in 1932 and 1963. Its 51,891 acres make it one of the smaller parks; 8100 acres are designated wilderness. It became designated a world heritage site in 1978. In 1991 there were 504,700 visitor days, which is in the middle position for the parks, but its relatively small acreage yields a crowded use of 0.1 acres per recreation visitor day. People work hard to reach this remote area in the southwestern corner of Colorado. The park is located where the Canyonlands Section of the Colorado Plateaus Province meets the Navaho Section of the same Province. The regional name for this part of the country is "Four Corners," named for the corners of the four states (Colorado, Utah, New Mexico, and Arizona) that meet here.

Mesa Verde is Spanish for "green table," referring to the comparatively level upper topographic surface, which is heavily forested with juniper and pinon pine. This plateau rises 1800 to 2000 feet above the Montezuma and Mancos Valleys. On this plateau and in the alcoves in the canyon cliffs below this surface are 4000 prehistoric sites, dating back to between 550 and 1270 A.D. Between 750 and 1100 the Anasazi ("ancient ones") perfected their living quarters mainly on the mesa tops, building *kivas* (ceremonial rooms) and *pueblos* (courts). Their highly decorative arts and crafts (elaborately decorated pottery and cloth) reached a peak between 1100 and 1300. Around 1200 they moved their structures into the alcoves of the cliffs for unknown reasons, and then, mysteriously, in the last quarter of the 13th century, left the area. It is speculated that drought, depleted soils, overpopulation, or a combination of these factors was responsible for their disappearance from Mesa Verde.

The entrance to the park is in its extreme north, 10 miles east of Cortez and 8 miles west of Mancos. The main road extends through the entire north-south extent of the park, but one must backtrack to exit. The Ute Indian Reservation borders on the south and west; thus, there is no access to the park here. The only campground in the park is located at Morefield Village 4 miles from the entrance. Groceries, food, gas, showers, and laundry facilities are found at Morefield Village. One must drive another 11 miles along a narrow, winding road, which passes through a tunnel before arriving at the Far View Visitor Center. Overnight accommodations, dining, cafeteria eating, gifts, and gas can be obtained here. A spur road 6 miles after Morefield Village leads to the Park Point Fire Lookout, the highest point in the Park at 8571 feet. The view from this point is a spectacular one of the Four Corners region. Paved roads lead to all of the major ruins. Several areas are closed in the winter due to snow. The 12-mile road to Wetherill Mesa is closed each winter, and the Ruins Road loops may also close due to snow. Only the Museum and the Spruce Tree Ruins can be counted on to be open in winter. It is 6 miles from the Far View Visitor Center to the Museum at park headquarters on Chapin Mesa. The Ruins Road has two 6-mile loops here that provide views of about 40 cliff dwellings from canyon-rim lookout points. Cliff Palace, the largest and most famous of the cliff dwellings with 200 rooms, is located on the eastern loop road, but it is closed during the winter. Spruce Tree Ruin, located just behind the Museum at park headquarters, is the best preserved and one of the largest ruins in the park. In addition to auto tours, archaeological walks, and camping, other recreational opportunities at Mesa Verde include limited hiking on five trails, photography, and cross-country skiing, and snowshoeing in winter. Interesting

visits outside the park include Ute Tribal Park, which borders on the south and west, and the San Juan National Forest to the north.

Olympic

This spectacular National Park occupies much of the Olympic Peninsula in the extreme northwest of Washington. Puget Sound and Hood Canal are to the east, the Straight of Juan de Fuca to the north, the Pacific Ocean to the west, and the Chehalis River to the south. Most of the forested land on the peninsula was added to Olympic Forest Reserve in 1897 by the proclamation of President Cleveland. This became the Olympic National Forest in 1907. In 1909, President Theodore Roosevelt proclaimed Mount Olympus National Monument within the national forest, to protect the summer range and breeding ground of the Olympic elk, now called the Roosevelt elk in his honor. This national monument was transferred from the Forest Service to the Park Service in the 1933 reorganization, and in 1938 it was established as Olympic National Park. Boundary changes occurred in 1940, 1943, 1953, 1976, 1986, and 1988. Status as a biosphere reserve was awarded in 1976 and as a world heritage site in 1981. Ninety-six percent (876,669 acres) of the park's 912,870 acres have been added to the National Wilderness Preservation System. As Olympic National Park evolved and expanded, Olympic National Forest diminished in size; all of today's park was once part of Olympic National Forest, except for the Pacific Coast strip added in 1953. Olympic National Forest is still the park's most common neighbor bordering on the east, south, southwest, and northwest sides of the park and covering a total of 627,213 acres. The Quinault Indian Reservation borders the park in the southwest, and the Makah Indian Reservation occupies the extreme northwestern corner of the Olympic Peninsula and borders the Pacific Coast strip of the park on the north. Sizable areas of Washington State Forest border the park on the west. Olympic is one of our largest national parks, being exceeded in size in the lower 49 states only by Yellowstone, Everglades, Grand Canyon, and Glacier.

The Olympic Mountains are the highest and most beautiful of any of the coastal ranges in the Pacific Border Province. Many of the ridges rise to 4500 to 5000 feet, giving a nearly level or gently undulating horizon. Above this horizon rise exceedingly steep-sided, jagged ridges, many of them between 7000 and 8000 feet, the highest, Mount Olympus, is 7965 feet. Most of the higher mountains form a circle 40 miles in diameter in the center of the park. The oldest rocks belong to the lower Cretaceous Soleduck Formation and consist of metamorphosed sedimentary and volcanic rocks that are now argillites, slates, phyllites, and greenstones. These rocks underlie most of the mountain mass. Several of the peaks along the margin of the uplift have rocks of the Lower Eocene Metchosen Formation, which consists of basalts, volcanic tuffs and breccias, and interbedded marine beds. The youngest rocks are Oligocene marine sediments. Uplift of the mountains began in late Cretaceous or early Tertiary time and culminated during the Pliocene-Pleistocene (Cascadian) orogeny, which raised the Cascade Mountains and depressed Puget Trough. Pleistocene glaciers were numerous, and their topographic effects are conspicuous. While there are no granite outcrops in the Olympics, granite boulders are found on the north side of mountains up to 3000 feet. Today, 60 major glaciers up to 4 miles long are found. Blue Glacier on Mount Olympus moves 5 inches a day, and an estimated 500 inches of snow fall

in these higher elevations each year. Six other glaciers are found on Mount Olympus. After declining to levels of 2000 feet, the mountains fall off very abruptly to the surrounding lowlands. Over a dozen rivers flow radially outward in a spokelike pattern from the high country of the central portion of the peninsula.

The wettest climate in the lower 49 states occurs here, with 200 inches of water equivalent falling each year in the high country around Mount Olympus. Even in the western valleys, up to 140 inches of rain fall each year. However, pronounced rain shadows do occur; Sequim, outside the northeastern corner of the park, averages only 17 inches of rain per year. In all cases, 75 percent of the precipitation occurs between October and April. Many climatologists claim this region of the United States has the finest weather in the country during June, July, and August. This is when the northeast extending limb of the Hawaiian Anticyclone provides ample sunshine and the marine air is pleasant. One is well advised, however, to have rain gear handy for most of the year.

The park can be divided into six major biological zones. The first is a narrow 57-mile strip of wild and scenic ocean shore that extends from the Quinault Indian Reservation in the south to the Makah Indian Reservation in the north. Three other very small Indian reservations—the Hoh, the Quileute, and Ozette Reservations—slightly break up this coastal zone. Seals, sea otters, and Pacific gray whales may be observed along this shoreline. The beaches are rocky in the north, but sand becomes more prevalent to the south. Sea stacks (erosional remnants that rise above the sea water surface) are frequent along this coast. A second major zone, found in the coastal valleys on the west side of the peninsula, has the finest remaining Pacific Northwest temperate rain forest. The dominant tree species on the lower elevation slopes of this zone are Sitka spruce, western red cedar, and Douglas fir. The mosses and ferns in this temperate rain forest are rich and luxuriant. The Douglas fir can reach 300 feet high and 450 inches in circumference; the Sitka spruce can be 200 feet in height, but their girth is especially impressive—up to 700 inches. Exceptional old-growth forest can be observed in the valleys of the Hoh, Quinault, Bogachiel, and Queets Rivers. Somewhat offsetting the reverent experiences of viewing this ancient temperate rain forest are the ugly scars of clear-cutting on private and national forest land. Richly diverse lowland forest continues up to about 3000 feet, where western hemlock and Alaska cedar become more prevalent in a third zone that is snowier but still biolog-ically dense montane forest. At 4500 to about 6000 feet a fourth zone of less dense subalpine forest of fir occurs. Above 5500 to 6000 feet subalpine fir mixes in a park-land landscape and mingles with the grasses of the alpine meadows in a fifth zone. The snow and ice of the some 60 glaciers of the highest peaks constitute the sixth zone.

Besides the rare Roosevelt elk, other wildlife in the park include black bear, blacktail deer, cougar, and coyote. Mountain goats were introduced in the 1920s, but since they have inflicted damage to the alpine meadows, the Park Service in 1988 started a reduction program. Rare species include the Olympic magenta painted cup, the Olympic marmot, the Olympic Mazama pocket gopher, and the Beardslee trout. The northern spotted owl, which was listed in 1990 as endangered, has been a species of concern during the last few years; 45 percent of the park has suitable habitat for this species. While logging is not permitted in the park, it is allowed in parts of the adjacent spotted owl habitat in the Olympic National Forest.

Puget Sound and adjoining waters effectively isolate the Olympic Peninsula from Seattle and other urban areas. The Washington State Ferry System provides good service across this geographic barrier. However, there are no roads that pass through the interior of Olympic National Park. The 15 roads penetrate no more than 20 miles into the park. As a result, the park is rather isolated from these urban areas. Even if the ferry is utilized, it is still 3 hours of travel time and 135 miles from Seattle to Forks on the northwestern side of the park. If the ferry is not taken, this trip becomes over 4 hours of travel time and 236 miles. U.S. 101 forms a horseshoe around the east, north, and west sides of the park. U.S. 12 and Washington Route 8 extend east-west in the south. The overall design of Olympic National Park is a fine one. While much of the interior is preserved in its natural state with minimal development, the circumferential road pattern, with access points that penetrate partially to the interior, allows motoring visitors to experience all aspects of the park's environment except the glaciers—which must be viewed from the distance. Olympic's 1,217,400 visitor days in 1991 ranked it number 12 among the national parks; its size ranking is also number 12. Its intensity of use of 0.75 acres per recreation visitor day in 1991 indicates it is about average for the 50 national parks in terms of crowds. Olympic allows the best of both worlds for all visitors, which has been the mandate of the National Park Service Act since 1916—"to allow use . . . but conserve the resources."

Most visitors spend much of their driving time making the circular trip around the park. There are visitor centers at Port Angeles, Hoh Rainforest, Kalaloch, and Storm King (Lake Crescent). Among the 15 roads that partially penetrate the park's interior, a few are worth special mention. One is the 18-mile paved road that rises to the 5200-foot elevation at Hurricane Ridge, if not the most, then one of the most scenic spots that can be driven to in the entire national park system (Figure 5.10). Alpine meadows with numerous hiking trails radiate from this spot. There is a visitor center and a nearby picnic area. The view from the picnic tables on Hurricane Ridge

Figure 5.10 Park ranger giving interpretive talk at Hurricane Ridge Visitor Center in Olympic National Park. Mt Olympus (7965 ft.) with glaciers is in the background.

to the wilderness and high peaks and glaciers of the interior is absolutely superb (Figure 5.11). *The author rates this picnic area the number 1 such drive-to area in the entire National Park System.* Blacktail deer walk right up to your table and beg for food— but feeding the wildlife is prohibited in the National Parks. The only other place in this high country that can be accessed by motor vehicles is to the east at Deer Park, where a 17-mile unpaved road accesses subalpine meadows. The ancient temperate rain forest can be accessed by several roads along the western side of the park, among them the 19-mile Hoh Road that leads to the Hoh Rainforest and Visitor Center. Here, one may walk a nature trail among the ferns, mosses, and giant Sitka spruce and Douglas fir of the temperate rain forest. A nature trail at the Quinault Rainforest leads to one of the finest remaining Douglas fir groves in the world.

In addition to auto tours on the roads that penetrate to park attractions, a variety of other recreational opportunities abound at Olympic National Park: interpretive programs, camping, picnicking, bird and wildlife watching, nature walks, hiking, horseback riding, mountain climbing, fishing, swimming, skiing, and snowshoeing. The park has 15 drive-to and two walk-in developed campgrounds and four commercial lodges within its borders. Thirteen of the campgrounds are open all year, three (Altaire, Deer Park, and Dosewallips) are closed from October to May, and one (Soleduck) is closed if it snows. There are many other campsites in surrounding Olympic National Forest. Hunting is allowed in the national forest. There are almost 600 miles of hiking trails in the park, although one has to note that parts of the high country can be closed from fall to July due to heavy snow. Raft and guide service are available on the Elwha, Hoh, and Queets Rivers, and (non-motorized) boats may be rented at Crescent Lake, which is 10 miles long and over 600 feet deep. The Pacific Ocean portion of Olympic is special: Here are found the only wilderness beaches left in the United States. The two most accessible beaches are at Kalaloch and Ruby. Ruby Beach is wilder and requires a hike to access; sea stacks and offshore islands add to

Figure 5.11   Picnic site at Hurricane Ridge in Olympic National Park.

the scenery here. A large National Park Service campsite is located at Kalaloch Beach. The sunsets over the Pacific are a very special part of the Olympic experience. Olympic is indeed one of the crown jewels of our National Park System.

Virgin Islands

Virgin Islands National Park occupies over half of the relatively undeveloped island of St. John in the U.S. Virgin Islands. The other two major islands—St. Thomas and St. Croix—are much more developed and congested, especially St. Thomas. St. John is a completely different world from the crowded St. Thomas. The park is characterized by steep mountain slopes that rise as high as 1277 feet from the crystal-clear blue-green water of the sea, white coral sand beaches, lush green tropical vegetation, and quiet coves. Here are found early Carib Indian relics and the remains of Danish colonial sugar plantations. With the exception of The National Park of American Samoa and Hot Springs National Park, Virgin Islands' 12,160 acres (of which 5650 acres are water) rank it as our smallest national park. The park was authorized by Congress in 1956, with impetus being given by the donation of 5000 acres by Laurance Rockefeller. Boundary changes occurred in 1960, 1962, and 1978, with the park designated as a biosphere reserve in 1976. The 367,300 recreation visitor days recorded in 1991 indicate heavy use in this small park. The 0.035 acres per visitor days make Virgin Islands our most crowded national park, even more crowded than Acadia, Bryce Canyon, or Hot Springs.

These volcanic islands were formed as they started to rise above sea level 100 million years ago. The latitudinal location of 17° N makes the Virgin Islands more tropical than Hawaii. The U.S. Virgin Islands consist of three larger and 50 smaller islands and cays in the south and west of the Virgin Islands group, 70 miles east of Puerto Rico. The Anegada Passage lies between Puerto Rico and the Virgin Islands, the Caribbean Sea lies to the south, and the Atlantic Ocean is located to the north. The British Virgin Island colony is located to the north and east. Although St. John is only 9 by 5 miles in extent, a variety of landscapes are found over relatively short distances due to varying rainfall in the prevailing northeast trade winds. Lush, almost tropical rain forest vegetation exists on the northern coast, but the rain shadow effect is responsible for xerophytic cactus woodland on parts of the southern shore. All of the modern forest vegetation is second or third growth. The highest elevation is Bordeau Mountain (1277 ft.). Most of St. John consists of steep, lofty hills. Because of the ocean barrier surrounding St. John, practically all of the mammals on the island are nonnative, introduced by humans. One of the more interesting is the mongoose, brought in to control the black rat, itself an unwanted introduction. Birds account for a large percentage of the island fauna.

Passenger ferries run between Cruz Bay, St. John, and St. Thomas. Cars, jeeps, and motorbikes can be rented in Cruz Bay. The roads are steep and curving, and local rules require driving on the left-hand side. One is well advised to listen to the vehicle rental people and avoid certain roads, expecially after rain.[1] A great deal of

---

[1]The author did not heed this advice and became stuck in the mud in a four-wheel-drive jeep on the east side of the Bordeaux Mountain Road below the summit of Bordeaux Mountain. This is the only time he has ever been stuck in a four-wheel-drive vehicle.

visitor pressure is put on the park by hordes of tourists who arrive at Cruz Bay via cruise ships. The park's visitor center is located here. Regular taxi and "safari bus" transportation is available to north-shore beaches. A favorite destination of the safari bus procession is Trunk Bay and Beach, where snorkeling gear can be rented to follow an underwater snorkeling trail. Many colorful fish are attracted to the beauty of the coral reefs of St. John. This is the most congested spot on the island. Hawksnest Beach is even closer than Trunk Bay to Cruz Bay. The glistening white coral sand is beautiful at all beaches, and the water is crystal-clear and turquoise, but if one wants to avoid the most congestion, the beaches to the east (Cinnamon Bay, and Maho Bay) are better choices. The eastern side of the island, around Coral Bay, is the least-congested part of the park. The busiest season is from December through March.

Overnight accommodations on St. John are limited. Ironically, the Rockefellers are responsible for this situation: Although they donated 5000 acres to the National Park Service to serve as the nucleus of the national park, they kept ownership of a few choice parcels in their corporation, RockResorts. The largest portion of the national park land is in the center of the island, running from the south shore to the north shore. The Rockefellers own Maho Bay Campground and Caneel Bay Plantation. Maho Bay Campground, on the north side of the island, is a camp with "tent-cabins" containing cooking facilities. There is a camp store and central dining area where meals are served. The prices are quite expensive for "tents." Caneel Bay Plantation is on the west side of the island, north of Cruz Bay. It is a beautiful resort with excellent food and facilities and beaches. One of the outdoor dining areas is built around the remains of an old sugar mill. However, it is very expensive.[2] The law of supply and demand is alive and well in Virgin Islands National Park. Those on a tight budget are restricted to the one National Park Service campsite—Cinnamon Bay Campground. Accommodations include bare tent sites, sites with tent-covered platforms already set up, and cottages; the latter two types of units come equipped with cooking supplies and linens. There is a camp store with food, other supplies, and a cafeteria.

Besides swimming, snorkeling, and camping, other recreational activities include interpretive walks, talks, and exhibits, hiking, fishing, boating, and auto tours. The U.S. and British Virgin Islands contain a multitude of hidden harbors, beaches, and dive spots to cruise and explore. Charter operations provide excursions lasting from a half day to several weeks. Powerboats may be rented in Red Hook on St. Thomas. Charter boats for world-class deep-sea fishing are also available in Red Hook, although prices for these ocean excursions are equal to those at Caneel Bay Plantation. Several historic sites are available to tour on St. John. One of the most famous is the Annaberg Ruins, the remains of a Danish colonial sugar plantation. Virgin Islands National Park is truly a beautiful place, but unfortunately most Americans will not be able to afford to visit it.

Voyageurs

Voyageurs is a north-country lake park: One must get out on the water to experience it. It protects a 56-mile stretch of the historic waterway route of the French-Canadian

---

[2]Caneel Bay is the most expensive place this college professor ever stayed and it is definitely out of his price range—but it was a truly memorable stay!

voyageurs along the Minnesota-Canadian border. The voyageurs paddled birch-bark canoes between Montreal and the Canadian Northwest along this route in the late 18th and 19th century for fur trading companies. The interconnected northern lakes are dotted with islands covered with northern forest (fir, spruce, aspen, and birch), signs of recent glaciation, and boreal forest wildlife (wolf, deer, black bear, moose, beaver, loon, and bald eagle). The park is in the heart of the only region of the continental United States where the eastern timber wolf survives. Over one-third (83,789 acres) of the park's gross area is water. The park was authorized in 1971 and established in 1975; there was a boundary change in 1983. Only 131,901 acres, or 61 percent of the park's gross area (218,035 acres), are federally owned. The only other national park that has a lower percentage of federal land within its boundary is Channel Islands (26 percent). Most of the inholdings in Voyageurs are privately owned recreational cottages. Voyageurs is not a very heavily used park, receiving 137,600 visitor days in 1991. Its 0.96 acres per recreation visitor day rank it the 18th least crowded of the national parks.

The park is located on a watery stretch of the border on the Canadian Shield, where the Superior Uplands grade imperceptibly into the West Lakes Section of the Central Lowlands geomorphic province. The ancient rocks of the shield represent some of the oldest rock formations exposed anywhere in the world. At least four times in the last 1 million years continental glaciers 2 miles thick bulldozed the land-scape. They removed previous features, leaving mostly level, pockmarked rock up to 2.7 billion years old. Hundreds of ponds, lakes, and streams now nestle in the depressions, and some rock surfaces bear the scrape marks. Although there are over 100 lakes and ponds in the park, four large ones dominate: Sand Point, Namakan, Kabetogama, and Rainey. At one-quarter million acres (much of its acreage in Canada), Rainey Lake is by far the largest. Between the lakes and adjacent rocky knobs and ridges extend bogs, marshes, and beaver ponds. These waters play a major role in one's experience at the park.

The park is located 160 miles north of Duluth, Minn., and 10 miles east of International Falls. Four private resort areas not part of the park nevertheless serve as entrances to the park: Crane Lake, Ash River, Kabetogama, and Rainey Lake, with visitor centers at the last three of these. In addition to the accommodations provided by the over 60 commercial lodges at these resort areas, one can hire guides and rent canoes, motorboats, and houseboats, the last being quite popular. There are no roads into the interior of the park. After arriving at one of the four main entry points, you leave your car behind and set out by water, traveling much like the voyageurs. This park is primarily a boating area, with the interior and its primitive campsites accessible only by boat. Motorboats are allowed, and seaplanes fly some visitors into the interior of the park. There are 120 primitive boat-in campsites scattered throughout the Park; most of these campsites are on islands or along the lakeshore. Hiking trails can be reached by boat. One can cross over Kabetogama Lake and hike a nature trail to Locator Lake, where a National Park Service canoe is cached for free use (after obtaining a key for the lock at the visitor center). Narrated boat tours are offered on the larger lakes. In the interior of the park is "Minnesota's most remote hotel," Kettle Falls Hotel, located on the channel between Namakan and Rainey Lakes. It was built in 1910 and restored in 1988. Its 12 rooms are the only commercial lodging within the park. From December through March, winter sports are popular and include cross-country skiing, snowshoeing, snowmobiling, winter camping, and ice fishing.

The park is inaccessible in November, when the ice starts to form, and in April, when the ice goes out. The Boundary Waters Canoe Area is nearby to the east in the Superior National Forest.

Yosemite

Yosemite National Park is located near California's eastern border, in the central part of the state. It extends from the crest of the Sierra Nevada, where elevations reach 13,000 feet, down the western slope of the range to 2000 feet in elevation. Yosemite is a land of glacially scoured deep valleys and granite peaks and domes that rise above broad meadows in the heart of the Sierra Nevada. It is world renowned for its groves of giant sequoias, lakes, and plunging waterfalls. Parts of the present-day park were among the earliest parcels of federal land set aside for amenity resource values—only the Hot Springs Reservation (1832) was set aside sooner. In 1864, during the Civil War, President Lincoln oversaw the transfer of the main Yosemite Valley and the Mariposa Big Tree Grove to the state of California. The park was established in 1890, but it was not until 1906 that California returned the original Yosemite Grant lands. Boundary changes occurred in 1905, 1906, 1913, 1928, 1930, 1931, 1932, and 1937. The El Portal administrative site of 1398 acres was authorized in 1958. The park was also designated a world heritage site in 1984. Of the Park's 759,464 acres, 677,600 have been designated wilderness as part of the National Wilderness Preservation System. Yosemite is one of our largest national parks, with only six exceeding its size in the lower 49 states.

Four hundred million years ago the region lay submerged beneath an ancient sea where deposited sediments hardened into rock. These sedimentary rocks were later folded into mountain ranges, and heat from molten rock rising within the earth beneath them metamorphosed them. Most of the metamorphic rocks have worn away, but remnants may still be seen in the western foothills and on some of the peaks in the eastern part of the park. Between 25 and 15 million years ago the exposed granite (the Sierra Nevada Batholith) was uplifted and tilted, causing a long slope westward to the Central Valley and a steep escarpment to the east. About 2 million years ago (during the Ice Age), local mountain icecaps formed, from which flowed great valley glaciers. These valley glaciers changed V-shaped, stream-cut valleys into U-shaped ones. The combined Merced-Yosemite Glacier extended for 15 miles. After the glaciers receded, deposits formed level floors in these valleys. The main Yosemite Valley, which is 7 miles long and 1 mile wide, has deposits 2000 feet deep (Thornbury, 1965, 512). The glaciers were responsible for smoothing the granite domes and carving the basins that now dot Yosemite with lakes. Today only a few small glaciers remain in the park (the MacLure and Lyell glaciers being the best examples). The process of exfoliation by load relief is important today in the production and maintenance of cliffs and domes where the original granite rock is unfractured. El Capitan's 3000-foot rise make it the largest single granite rock in the world, and Half Dome rises majestically for 4733 feet.

The park has a wide range in elevation, from 2000 to 13,114 feet (at Mt. Lyell), resulting in a great variety in environmental landscape: Five out of seven life zones in the continental United States are found in Yosemite. The landscape is vertically zoned, ranging from semiarid foothills, to oak woodland, to mixed forest, to boreal

forest, to alpine meadow, and to the snow-capped alpine crest. Within the park are found 37 different native tree species, 1400 flowering species, 242 bird species, 29 species of amphibians and reptiles, 77 species of mammals, and 11 species of fish (6 of them natural). The most unusual tree species is the giant sequoia, which grows at 4500 to 7000 feet on the west slope of the Sierras. There are three groves in Yosemite. The best known is the Mariposa Grove, located at the South Entrance. One must take a tram or hike to access this grove. There are 500 giant sequoias in this grove, 200 of which are over 10 feet in diameter. The Grizzly Giant is 209 feet tall, has a diameter of 32 feet, and is estimated to be 2700 years old. This grove also includes the Wawona Tunnel Tree, whose trunk straddled the road and had a drive-through tunnel cut through it; this tree fell in 1969. There are two other groves with easy accessibility: the Tuolumne Grove (25 trees) and the Merced Grove (20 trees). The huge sugar pines of the Rockefeller Tract are another splendid vegetation marvel.

The two principal rivers of the park are the Merced and Tuolumne. The Merced River flows through Yosemite Valley and is a popular swimming spot. The Tuolumne River begins in the meadows of the same name and flows through the Grand Canyon of the Tuolumne until it is impounded in the Hetch Hetchy Reservoir behind O'Shaughnessy Dam. This dam was authorized by Congress in 1913 as a water supply for San Francisco; a bitter controversy pitched John Muir (opposed) against Gifford Pinchot (in favor). Hetch Hetchy Reservoir is the largest water body in the park. Before the dam was built, the Hetch Hetchy Valley was purported to have been equal in scenery to the Yosemite Valley. The Hetch Hetchy Dam is a classic example of an irreversible natural resource decision. The water flow in the streams and over the waterfalls of the park varies greatly during the seasons. The climate is one of dry summers and winter rainfall and snowfall. The average precipitation at Yosemite Valley (elevation 4000 feet) is 36.51 inches, and average snowfall here is 29 inches. These amounts decrease in lower elevations and increase greatly in the higher elevations. Extremely heavy snow falls in the high country, so roads are closed in winter. Above 6000 feet in elevation the snowfall increases rapidly. The main high-country road, the Tioga Road, is the only access point from the east and closes in winter. This road reaches 9945 feet elevation in Tioga Pass at the Park's East Entrance. The most extensive meadow in the Sierras (Tuolumne Meadows) is found along this road. The flow over the park's famed waterfalls varies, with the most spectacular displays occurring during snowmelt in the spring, slowing to a trickle in fall. The three combined falls (Upper, 1430 ft.; Middle, 675 ft.; and Lower 320 ft.) of Yosemite Falls make it the highest in North America—2425 ft. Many other spectacular falls leap downward from the granite cliffs.

The park has four entrances, three of which are open all year. The Tioga Road from the east is closed during winter. The Arch Rock Entrance is 70 miles from Merced, the South Entrance is 60 miles from Fresno, and the North Entrance is 70 miles from Oakdale. It is a 4- to 5-hour drive from San Francisco, which is located to the west, and a 6-hour drive from Los Angeles, located to the south. Once at the park, visitors are afforded easy access to most sections since there are 360 miles of paved roads and 94 miles of graded roads. An excellent hiking trail system of over 800 miles fans out in all directions. The Pacific Crest National Scenic Trail passes through the park, and the 185-mile John Muir Trail to Mt. Whitney begins here. Saddle trips by mule and horseback lead into the wilderness backcountry from Tu-

olumne Meadows. The backcountry is limited to 4000 users at one time. A more civilized way of enjoying the backcountry is to stay at one of five commercially run High Sierra camps (May Lake, Merced Lake, Sunrise, Vogelsang, and Glen Aulin), which have tent-cabins, showers, and dining rooms, and are spaced about 5 miles apart in the backcountry. The park is surrounded by four national forests: the Inyo on the east, the Sierra on the south and west, the Stanislaus on the west and north, and the Toiyabe on the north and east. Several small campsites in the Inyo National Forest just outside the park's East Entrance provide accommodations for many visitors who find the "all full" sign posted at Yosemite.

Yosemite is a very heavily used park, but much of this use is concentrated in the Yosemite Valley, which occupies only 7 square miles out of 1189. With 7,675,300 recreation visitor days in 1991 Yosemite was exceeded only by Yellowstone (8,435,400), among the national parks. The use intensity of 0.099 acres per recreation visitor days ranks Yosemite among the most crowded parks, with only Great Smoky Mountains, Hot Springs, Bryce Canyon, Acadia, and Virgin Islands being more crowded. Yosemite has one of the lowest ratios of recreation visits to recreation visitor days (0.45), which indicates that once the visitors arrive, they stay. The only national parks with lower ratios are Big Bend (0.40), Sequoia (0.36), Yellowstone (0.35), Isle Royale (0.19), and Gates of the Arctic (0.10). Yosemite is not a day-use park, such as Hot Springs (17.44), Wind Cave (11.49), Capitol Reef (7.88), Petrified Forest (7.82), Mammoth Cave (6.49), or Haleakala (5.10). However, finding lodging in Yosemite can be difficult, especially in the Yosemite Valley—reservations are a necessity. Many disappointed visitors, who have not planned ahead, have to make the long drive to find the nearest lodging outside of the park.

Traffic jams and air pollution are common in the Yosemite Valley. In its upper portion, Yosemite Village is a small city in its own right. This area is the main attraction in the park and thus is the most urban like, congested portion. The lower-elevation view of the Valley from the Wawona Overlook at the Wawona Tunnel on CA 41 (Wawona Road) is nothing short of spectacular. The higher-elevation view of the upper valley and the high country from Glacier Point (3214 ft. above the valley floor) is one of the most impressive views in the entire National Park System (Figure 5.12). Yosemite has shops, stores, lodging, campgrounds, stables—even a fire department and jail. The finest hotel is the 123-room Ahwahnee, built in 1927, and any visitor to the Valley should admire its interior, especially the entrance area and the elegant dining room. The Ahwahnee and the Victorian Wawona Hotel (105 units, built 1879) at Wawona are both designated national historic sites. There is a golf course at the Wawona. The 495-room Yosemite Lodge and the unattractive tent slum of Curry Village are also located in Yosemite Village. The latter has 18 rooms, 183 cabins, and 427 tent cabins and is definitely the most economical commercial lodging in Yosemite, but the old adage, "you get what you pay for," is ever so true. The commercial concessioner that oversees these lodging facilities is the Yosemite Park and Curry Company, whose contract with the National Park Service expired in 1993. In addition, five of the 17 National Park Service campgrounds are located in Yosemite Village. The National Park Service is continually making changes in the Valley, attempting to mitigate the congestion and pollution caused by visitors here. Many of the roads are now one-way, a shuttle bus system exists, 7 miles of bikeways have been built, campsites at the five campgrounds have been reduced in number, and the

Figure 5.12 View of Upper Yosemite Valley and the Sierra high country from Glacier Point in Yosemite National Park. Half Dome soars almost 5000 feet above the valley floor.

golf course at the Ahwahnee Hotel has be removed. The 250-vehicle asphalt parking lot, which was in front of the visitor center, has been removed and the space converted to a pedestrian plaza and revegetated with 40 species of native plants. Also, the 400-strip parking spaces along valley roadways have been removed. Morning and afternoon wood fires are prohibited in the Yosemite Valley; fires are permitted only between 5 P.M. and 11 P.M.

The park has a total of 1900 campsites in 17 campgrounds, three of them walk-in; three of them are open all year (two at Yosemite Valley and one at Wawona). The largest single campsite is the 314-unit site at Tuolumne Meadows. Black bears are a serious nuisance at this campsite. Upon arrival, when one views the steel food lockers, the seriousness of the bear problem is made apparent.[3]

The recreational opportunities at Yosemite are outstanding. The view along the roads are magnificent, especially along the Tioga Road, from Glacier Point (a short hike from parking lot) and Wawona Tunnel. One of the most disconcerting experiences at Yosemite is the inability of the entrance stations to collect the entrance fee. Waits of 30 to 60 minutes are common at these entry stations. It is recommended that the Park Service try to do something about this irritating experience, especially for patrons with Golden Eagle or Golden Age passes. The Sierra backcountry of Yosemite is outstanding for hiking and backpacking. Other recreational opportunities include climbing, horseback riding, swimming, fishing, rafting, boating, and a myriad of in-

[3]The author's one camping experience at this campsite in September 1992 was a memorable one. As soon as the campers quieted down and turned in, the bears arrived. They were quite persistent and could not be shooed away. They banged and tried to open the steel food lockers most of the night. When they tired, they would stand next to the tent and pant awhile, until they started banging on the food lockers again. Despite their gallant attempts to break open the food lockers, however, they were unsuccessful!

terpretive activities. The fishing is not especially noteworthy. To improve fishing, a new catch-and-release-only policy for native rainbow trout was implemented in 1992 in the Merced River from Happy Isles footbridge to Pohono bridge. Only artificial lures or flies with barbless hooks may be used. Brown trout may be kept, subject to a daily limit of 5 fish per day, with a 10-fish possession limit. Other commercial lodging is found in the park outside the Valley and Wawona areas. On the Tioga Road at White Wolf are 4 cabins and 24 tent cabins, and at Tuolumne Meadows Lodge there are 69 tent cabins. In winter, 350 miles of the park's roads are suitable for cross-country skiing, including the Glacier Point Road above the Badger Pass Ski Area, which is groomed. There is an ice-skating rink at Curry Village. The Badger Pass Ski Area, on the Glacier Point Road, is California's oldest, and still one of only a few, alpine ski areas in national parks. Built in 1935, today it has four chairs, two surface lifts, and nine slopes and is also a draw for cross-country skiing.

References

Bedinger, M. S. *Valley of the Vapors—Hot Springs National Park*. Philadelphia: Eastern National Parks and Monument Association, 1974.

Fenneman, Nevin. *Physiography of the Western United States*. New York: McGraw-Hill Book Co., 1931.

Fenneman, Nevin. *Physiography of the Eastern United States*. New York: McGraw-Hill Book Co., 1938.

Florida National Parks and Monuments Association. *Motorists Guide to Everglades National Park*. Homestead, Fla.: Florida National Parks and Monuments Association, 1988.

Fodor's Travel Publications. *National Parks of the West*. New York: Fodor's Travel Publications, 1992.

Hanor, Dr. Jeffrey S. *Fire in Folded Rocks—Geology of Hot Springs National Park*. Philadelphia: Eastern National Park and Monument Association, 1991.

Jadan, Doris. *A Guide to the Natural History of St. John*. St. John, U.S. Virgin Islands: Environmental Studies Program, 1979.

Jones, Holway. *John Muir and the Sierra Club: The Battle for Yosemite*. San Francisco: Sierra Club, 1965.

National Park Service. *Acadia National Park*. Gridmap Official Map and Guide. Washington, D.C.

National Park Service. *Big Bend National Park*. Gridmap Official Map and Guide. Washington, D.C.

National Park Service. *Canyonlands National Park*. Gridmap Official Map and Guide. Washington, D.C.

National Park Service. *Everglades National Park*. Gridmap Official Map and Guide. Washington, D.C.

National Park Service. *Great Basin National Park*. Gridmap Official Map and Guide. Washington, D.C.

National Park Service. *Great Basin National Park: Draft General Management Plan, Development Concept Plans, Environmental Impact Statement*. 1991.

National Park Service. *Great Smoky Mountains National Park*. Gridmap Official Map and Guide. Washington, D.C.

National Park Service. *Haleakala National Park*. Gridmap Official Map and Guide. Washington, D.C.

National Park Service. *Hot Springs National Park.* Gridmap Official Map and Guide. Washington, D.C.

National Park Service. *Internal Memorandum* To: Superintendent, Yosemite National Park. From: Public Affairs Officer. Subject: General Management Plan Accomplishments. Date: February 13, 1990.

National Park Service. *Mammoth Cave National Park.* Gridmap Official Map and Guide. Washington, D.C.

National Park Service. *Mesa Verde National Park.* Gridmap Official Map and Guide. Washington, D.C.

National Park Service. *Olympic National Park.* Gridmap Official Map and Guide. Washington, D.C.

National Park Service. *Summary: Yosemite General Management Plan.* November 1980.

National Park Service. *Virgin Islands National Park.* Gridmap Official Map and Guide. Washington, D.C.

National Park Service. *Voyageurs National Park.* Gridmap Official Map and Guide. Washington, D.C.

National Park Service. *Waterton/Glacier International Peace Park.* Gridmap Official Map and Guide. Washington, D.C.

National Park Service. *Yosemite—1992 Fact Sheet.*

National Park Service. *Yosemite National Park.* Gridmap Official Map and Guide. Washington, D.C.

Raup, Omer B., Robert L. Earhart, James W. Whipple, and Paul E. Carrara. *Geology along Going-to-the-Sun Road—Glacier National Park, Montana.* West Glacier, Mont.: Glacier Natural History Association, 1983.

Robinson, Alan H. *Virgin Islands National Park—The Story Behind the Scenery.* Las Vegas, Nev.: KC Publications, 1974.

Stevenson, George B. *Trees of the Everglades National Park and the Florida Keys.* Miami: Banyan Books, 1988.

Thornbury, William D. *Regional Geomorphology of the United States.* New York: John Wiley & Sons, 1965.

Yandell, Michael, Editor in Chief. *A Photographic and Comprehensive Guide to Glacier and Waterton Lakes National Parks.* Casper, Wyo.: World-Wide Research and Publishing Co., 1974.

Yosemite Association. *Yosemite Road Guide.* El Portal, Calif.: Yosemite Association, 1989.

## CHAPTER 6

National Parks: Other Areas—The Lower 49 States

The nation behaves well if it treats the natural resources as assets which it must turn over to the next generation increased, and not impaired, in value.

Theodore Roosevelt

Recall that Chapter 3 covered the National Park System as an entity, Chapter 4 focused on the system in Alaska, and Chapter 5 covered the units classified as national parks in the lower 49 states. The present chapter will emphasize the other units of the National Park System that have primarily recreational value.[1] These include areas classified as national preserve, national recreation area, national seashore, national lakeshore, national river, national trail, and national parkway. Many national monuments also have recreational value, and they will be covered in this chapter. Case studies of five historical units will be included. Finally, 12 other areas that have recreational value but do not neatly fit into the major categories used by the National Park Service will be detailed.

NATIONAL MONUMENTS

"National monument" is the most nonhomogeneous category within the National Park System. According to the Park Service, "A National Monument is intended to preserve at least one nationally significant resource. It is usually smaller than a

---

[1]This focus necessitates placing a lesser emphasis on the historical- and cultural-theme units of the system. The intent is not to demean the significance of the historical and cultural units—many of these areas provide fine outdoor recreational experiences. An example might be a day trip from San Antonio to picnic at Lyndon B. Johnson State Park and then a tour of adjacent Lyndon B. Johnson National Historical Park on the banks of the Perdernales River. All this makes for a moving and educational day outing. However, most of the historical and cultural units do not have recreation as their main focus, and recreation is the subject of this book.

National Park and lacks its diversity of attractions." The author has determined that there are 81 national monuments on 4,651,622 acres. They range in size from Death Valley's 2,048,929 acres to Castle Clinton's 1.0 acre. Only seven national parks are larger than Death Valley, and six of these are in Alaska. This makes Death Valley National Monument the second largest National Park System unit in the lower 49 states, after Yellowstone. Six other national monuments are over 100,000 acres, but the median size is 841 acres. A diverse complex of units characterize this category. Twenty-four are primarily natural, 23 are primarily historical, 22 are primarily archaeological, and five are primarily palaeontological. Another dozen have mixed characteristics: four are natural and archaeological; one is historical and archaeological; one is natural and historical; and one is natural and palaeontological. Geographically, the most national monuments are located in the Southwest. The states with the greatest number are Arizona (15), New Mexico (10), Colorado (7), California (7), and Utah (7).

Although the "national monument" category has the most units in the National Park System, the amount of recreational use that occurs at them is relatively small when compared with recreational use of the total system. In 1991, the national monuments received 25,521,700 recreation visits, which is 10.1 percent of the system total. When this figure is converted to recreation visitor days, it decreases to 6,090,000, which is 5.5 percent of the recreational use of the system. In terms of recreation visits, five national monuments received over 1 million visitors in 1991: Statue of Liberty (4.3 million), Castle Clinton (3.3 million), Muir Woods (1.5 million), Cabrillo (1.2 million), and Joshua Tree (1.1 million). In terms of the more meaningful measure of recreation visitor day, the ranking changes; 10 units have over 100,000 recreation visitor days: Joshua Tree, 1,334,100; Statue of Liberty, 1,085,800; Death Valley, 603,100; Canyon de Chelly, 467,400; Dinosaur, 168,900; Muir Woods, 168,700; Cabrillo, 144,100; Castle Clinton, 139,400; Bandelier, 126,600; and Organ Pipe Cactus, 101,200.

For illustrative purposes, four national monuments, each representing a different type, will be used here as case studies: Death Valley; Montezuma Castle; Saguaro; and Statue of Liberty.

Death Valley

This large desert area is part of the Mohave Desert and is nearly surrounded by high mountains. It is mostly in eastern California with a small part extending into Nevada. Elevations range from -282 feet at Badwater, the lowest spot in the Western Hemisphere, to 11,049 feet on Telescope Peak. Its 2,048,929 acres stretch for 125 miles from north to south and 40 miles from east to west. A large area that is below sea level and that roughly follows the shape of the national monument boundary runs for 75 miles from north to south and is 5 miles wide. This below-sea-level depression is the site of North America's highest officially recorded temperature: 134°F in 1913 at Greenland Ranch. The lower Armagosa Range is to the east of this central depression, and the higher Panamint Range is to the west; both are faulted mountain ranges. Prominent cultural features include Scotty's Castle, the grandiose home of a wealthy midwesterner, and other remnants of gold and borax mining. Death Valley, the largest of our national monuments, was proclaimed in 1933, with boundary changes in 1937 and 1952. Congress is deliberating renaming the monument Death Valley National

Park, enlarging its boundaries, and classifying a large portion of it as wilderness. The California Desert Protection Act (S-21) passed the Senate on April 14, 1994. This action on Death Valley is only part of what this bill proposes.

Death Valley is part of the Great Basin Section of the Basin and Range Province. This region is one of the least alluviated parts of the Great Basin Section and is excellent for the study of basin-range structure. Death Valley is essentially a fault trough or *graben*, formed in late Pliocene or Pleistocene time. The mountain ranges on both side of the graben are quite rugged. Recency of faulting is evidenced by numerous alluvial scarps and displacement of Pleistocene basalt flows. Rocks are Precambrian, Paleozoic, Mesozoic, and Tertiary in age. Present are granitic intrusions of uncertain age (Thornbury, 1965, 489), and Quaternary fanglomerates, playa and lake deposits, dunal sands, and basalt cinder cones and flows. The Ubehebe Craters at the north end of Death Valley are almost perfect examples of craters and are so recent they have undergone little erosion. A former large Pleistocene lake, Lake Manly, was approximately 90 miles long and 6 to 11 miles wide (Blackwelder, 1933). This large lake has evaporated and left alkali flats. An interesting evaporative landscape feature is the Devil's Golf Course on the Death Valley Salt Pan. Here the salt pan surface is covered with jagged salt spikes.

Death Valley is the hottest spot in America and is a place to avoid in the summer. This is why the main season of use is from November through April. Between May and September the temperature regularly reaches at least 100–115°F each day and can stay above 100°F for a week at a time. The average daily highs for the warmer months are May, 99.5°F; June, 109.7°F; July, 116.2°F; August, 113.5°F; and September, 106.0°F. In December (average high, 65.9°F; av. low, 40.3°F), January (av. high, 64.6°F; av. low 39.3°F), and February (av. high, 72.9°F; av. low, 46.2°F) the climate is much more tolerable. It is possible to drive to elevations of 5000 to 7000 feet, where the temperatures can be up to 25° cooler.

Death Valley is also one of the driest spots in North America. The mean annual precipitation in the valley floor is under 2 inches. There are a few oases created by springs, which is where most of the cultural settlement occurs. The vegetation is largely xerophytic desert vegetation, but the higher elevations change to pinon, juniper, and even bristlecone pine above 10,000 feet. There are more than 900 species of plants and trees, 21 of which are unique to the valley. Wildlife that may be observed include desert bighorn sheep, coyote, cougar, deer, bobcat, and badger. There are over 250 species of birds. Four species of fish are relics from former Pleistocene Lakes, including the desert pupfish, which may be observed at the Salt Creek Nature Trail. There are still several hundred feral (wild) burros, but many burros have been removed.

This is a desolate, isolated location, and a car is necessary for traveling the great distances between the major features. The national monument is 140 miles west and northwest of Las Vegas and 125 miles northeast from Los Angeles. Death Valley takes its name from a group of gold seekers who in 1849 became lost and perished in this area. In 1881, borax discoveries were made near Furnace Creek. From 1883 to 1889, 20-mule teams hauled loads of borax over the Panamint Range to the railroad at Mohave. There is an interpretive trail at Harmony Borax Works, the first successful borax plant in Death Valley. Death Valley contains hundreds of abandoned mines and associated structures that are potentially dangerous. The Park Service has closed

many of these mine openings, but it will be many years before the job is completed. Forgotten caches of explosives are occasionally found in mine areas. The limited facilities (including gas) in the monument are found only at Furnace Creek, Scotty's Castle, and Stovepipe Wells. Due to the isolated desert environment, it is essential that one's vehicle be in sound mechanical condition, and any visits during May to October require air conditioning.

Most recreational activities at Death Valley are related to scenic drives. Artists Drive is a 9-mile, one-way loop through colorful badlands and canyons in the foothills of the Black Mountains. From the vicinity of the Furnace Creek Visitor Center a road leads 24 miles through the colorful badlands of Furnace Creek Wash to Dantes View. Points of interest along the way include the overlook at Zabriskie Point and the loop drive through Twenty Mule Team Canyon. From the overlook at Dantes View, one has spectacular views of the lowest point in the Western Hemisphere plus the Panamint Range and surrounding mountains (Figure 6.1). On clear winter days it is possible to see 14,375-foot Mount Williamson in the Sierra Nevada. In the northern part of the monument are Ubehebe Crater and Scotty's Castle. Ubehebe Crater is 2400 feet in diameter and was created 1000 years ago in a violently destructive volcanic eruption. Eight miles away in Grapevine Canyon is Scotty's Castle, a Mediterranean-style hacienda that was the desert retreat of Albert Johnson. It takes its name from "Death Valley Scotty," a friend and frequent guest of the Johnson's who lived here for 6 years after Johnson's death in 1948. Another scenic drive is Emigrant Canyon Road in the western part of the monument. From here one can reach Wildrose Canyon, where there is a row of abandoned charcoal kilns. Death Valley has a 150-mile network of primitive roads that can be used by jeeps or light trucks for day use and camping. Four-wheeling and mountain biking are recreational attractions in the monument. There are a number of short and long hiking opportunities. A trail up

Figure 6.1 Death Valley National Monument as viewed from Dante's View. Panamint Range is on far side of the valley.

Telescope Peak from the Mahogany Flat campground provides an all-day hike to a stand of bristlecone pines atop the monument's highest elevation at 11,049 feet.

Two resorts provide lodging and other commercial services within the monument. Furnace Creek Inn and Ranch (at Furnace Creek) and Stovepipe Wells Village Motel (at Storepipe Wells) are operated by the Fred Harvey Company and together have 369 rooms. Furnace Creek is an oasis, with palms and cottonwood trees where people golf, swim, and dine. The more deluxe Furnace Creek Inn was built in 1927 at the Greenland Ranch, and from May to October its services are limited. This oasis attracts motor homes during the winter. In addition to the two resorts, the monument has nine campgrounds with 1600 sites. Three are open all year: Furnace Creek, Mesquite Spring, and Wildrose. Three others are open from October to April: Texas Spring, Sunset, and Stovepipe Wells. Three other campgrounds are open April to October: Emigrant, Thorndike, and Mahogany. Death Valley is the 14th-most-visited national monument in terms of recreation visits (743,600 recorded in 1991) but is the third-ranking one when recreation visitor days are tallied (603,100 in 1991). The only national monuments with higher recreation-visitor-day totals are Joshua Tree and Statue of Liberty.

Montezuma Castle

This national monument has one of the best-preserved cliff dwellings in the United States: Its five-story, 20-room castle is still 90 percent intact. It is also one of the most accessible units of the National Park System, being only 2.5 miles off I-15, 75 miles north of Phoenix, and 50 miles south of Flagstaff. The pueblo ruin was given its name by the early European settlers in the Verde Valley, who believed it had been built by Aztec refugees fleeing from central Mexico at the time of the Spanish conquest. Actually, the pueblo had nothing to do with Montezuma. A 150-foot cliff protects the "castle," which was the home of the Sinagua people, who farmed, hunted, and gathered here between 1150 and 1400 A.D. The national monument was one of the first in the nation proclaimed the same year the Antiquities Act was passed—1906. In this year, 160 acres were set aside, and in 1937, another 366 acres were added to give better protection to the entrance and the area in the foreground of the monument. In 1947, Montezuma Well, a detached portion of the monument located 10 miles north of the castle, was acquired from private owners. Boundary changes in 1959 and 1978 brought the monument to its present size of 841 acres.

Montezuma Well is an amazing sight in the dry desert. The limestone sinkhole is 470 feet wide and 55 feet deep, and it is rimmed by pueblos and cliff dwellings. Its spring has a discharge of over a 1 million gallons a day. A self-guiding trail and picnic facilities are available at the Well portion. In terms of visits, Montezuma Castle is the seventh-most-visited national monument, with 876,100 recreation visits in 1991. The relatively short duration of the visits is reflected by the much lower number of recreation visitor days for the same year—72,200.

Montezuma Castle and Tuzigoot National Monument (20 miles to the west) preserve remnants of two distinctive cultures that once flourished in the Verde Valley. In the 1400s the Sinagua abandoned the entire valley for reasons unknown. The landscape of the Verde Valley drops from forested mountains and high mesas down to sparsely vegetated desert valleys with ribbons of dense growth bordering the

stream valleys. The monument is situated on the northern limit of the Lower Sonoran plant zone but exhibits plants more typical of the Upper Sonoran zone, which begins a few miles to the north. The self-guiding nature trail provides a good introduction to many of these plants and offers good views of the castle. There are 167 species of plants, including creosote bush, mesquite, cactus, yucca, agave, cottonwood, syca- more, and willow. A morning stroll in the shade along the ⅓-mile trail is a very pleasant experience. The oasis on Beaver Creek, a tributary of the Verde, is an at- traction to cattle that graze nearby, and visitors are occasionally startled by their crashing through the brush. Visitors are not allowed to climb in the castle, but a scale model is on exhibit at the visitor center along with other artifacts. There is a very pleasant picnic area at the castle. A short distance downstream from the castle are the ruins of what was once a six-story, 40-room building built by the Sinagua people against the base of a cliff. Most visitors spend an hour or less at this monument, but all declare it a very worthwhile stop. Visitors to the monument are usually either heading to or coming from national park units to the north (such as Grand Canyon National Park, Glen Canyon National Recreation Area, or the Utah National Parks). This is strictly a day-use park: There are no camping, lodging, or food services within the national monument, but lodging and food are available at the exits of I-15.

Saguaro

Saguaro National Monument is located in southeastern Arizona. It is divided into two districts 25 miles apart, with the Santa Cruz Valley and Tucson metropolitan area lying between them. These two districts are the smaller Saguaro West (Tucson Moun- tain District) and the larger Saguaro East (Rincon Mountain District). Both districts contain giant saguaro cactus, from which the name of the monument is derived. This giant cactus, unique to Arizona and Mexico, grows to 35 feet (occasionally as high as 50 feet) and lives as long as 200 years (Figure 6.2). It produces beautiful creamy white flowers (the state flower of Arizona) that are up to 4 inches in diameter and bloom most profusely in late May and early June. This region is the northeastern corner of the Sonoran Desert in what is referred to as the Arizona Upland. The temperatures here are not as hot as the lower elevation portion of the desert and the precipitation is higher (11 inches) because of the 2400-foot elevation in the floor of the Santa Cruz Valley. The area has the "Arizona type" of biannual rainfall regime: a maximum in summer and winter, and much less in spring and fall.

The national monument was proclaimed on March 1, 1933, under jurisdiction of the Forest Service, but later in the same year (August 10) was transferred to the National Park Service. Boundary changes occurred in 1961 and 1976. The monument is the ninth largest, with 81,958 acres, 71,400 of which are designated part of the National Wilderness Preservation System.

The monument is located in the extreme northeastern corner of the Sonoran Desert Section of the Basin and Range Province. The geology of the area is quite complex, with igneous, metamorphic, and sedimentary rocks present. There are more granite and volcanic rocks in the lower-elevation Saguaro West district, and meta- morphic gneiss dominates in the higher-elevation Saguaro East district. Elevations in the Saguaro West district range from 2200 feet, to 4687 feet at Wasson Peak. Vegetation in this section is limited to desert scrub, with some desert grassland on Wasson Peak.

Figure 6.2   Saguaro National Monument is named after the giant saguaro cactus, which is a prominent feature along Cactus Forest Drive.

There is dense saguaro forest here as well. A wider variety of vegetation is altitudinally zoned in the Saguaro East district, where elevations extend from 2700 feet, to 8666 feet at Mica Mountain. The giant saguaro cactus forest and *paloverde* (a spiny, nearly leafless shrub that has showy yellow flowers) occurs in the Lower Sonoran life zone in the western part of this section up to about 4000 feet. Between 3500 and 4500 feet the Upper Sonoran grassland transition dominates. From 4500 to 7000 feet, oak woodland grades to oak-pine woodland in the Upper Sonoran life zone. In the higher elevation east and northeast of the Saguaro East unit, a transition to coniferous forest starts. The largest trees in the monument, Ponderosa pine, are found at 6000 feet. On the highest elevations is the start of the Canadian life zone, where restricted areas of Douglas fir and white fir grow. Temperatures can be 30°F cooler in the highest elevations, and rainfall increases from 10–12 inches to 18–25 inches. A wide variety of wildlife can be observed: coyote, gray fox, javelina, mule and whitetail deer, mountain lion, red-tailed hawk, gila monster (the only poisonous lizard in the United States), roadrunner, great horned owl, short horned lizard, and scorpion. The giant saguaro cacti are important nesting sites for gilded flicker, cactus wren, Gila woodpecker, and elf and screech owls.

The park headquarters and visitor center are located at the entrance of the Rincon Mountain (Saguaro East) section. Visitors should explore the excellent display of vegetation that is interpreted immediately outside the visitor center (Figure 6.3). An 8-mile-long scenic Cactus Forest Drive winds through the heart of an extensive saguaro forest and offers a close look at a variety of Sonoran Desert life. This one-way paved road begins and ends at the visitor center. The 0.25-mile paved Desert Ecology Trail starts on Cactus Forest Drive and is accessible for the disabled. Several longer hiking trails, totaling 75 miles, and requiring foot or horse travel, penetrate the wilderness area. Camping in the wilderness is allowed only at six designated campgrounds, each with only three sites and a limit of six people per site. Many of the trails intersect

Figure 6.3   Ranger Jeff Kartheiser gives the author a guided tour of the vegetation found in Saguaro National Monument at park headquarters and visitor center at the Rincon Mountain (East) unit.

each other, thus allowing hikes of various lengths. This is a part of the monument few people visit. It has scrub oak and pine and forests of ponderosa pine and Douglas fir. Horseback riding is permitted on all trails except the Tanque Verde Ridge, Miller Creek, and Rincon Peak Trails. There are two picnic areas in Saguaro East, each located along Cactus Forest Drive. Each picnic area has picnic tables, fire grills, and pit toilets but no drinking water. The Coronado National Forest, which surrounds Saguaro East on the north, east, and south, has campgrounds, hiking trails, and picnic areas.

The Red Hills Information Center introduces the visitor to Saguaro West against the backdrop of the Tucson Mountains. At the center is the paved Cactus Garden Trail that passes through a variety of desert plants. The 6-mile Bajada Loop Drive, a graded dirt road beginning 1.5 miles from the information center, passes through dense saguaro forests. Within 1 mile of the information center are two short nature trails. The Desert Discovery Nature Trail loops for 0.5 miles along gently sloping *bajadas* (land surface) at the foot of the Tucson Mountains. The Valley View Overlook Trail is a 1.5-mile round-trip that has spectacular views and extensive cactus forests. Longer trails penetrate the wild country. Horseback riding is allowed on all trails in the Saguaro West district, but camping is not permitted. Four picnic areas are located along the roads; a fifth, in the backcountry, can be reached only by trail. South of Saguaro West are two places of interest: the Arizona-Sonora Desert Museum, which has a live collection of about 200 desert animal species and 300 kinds of plants, and the Tucson Mountain County park, which has hiking and horse trails and a campground.

Saguaro National Monument in 1991 ranked 16th among the national monuments for both recreation visits (679,000) and recreation visitor days (74,200). This high ratio of visits to visitor days (almost 10 to 1) reflects the domination of day

visits, most of which are limited to a few hours. The main recreational opportunities are scenic pleasure driving, wildlife and bird watching, hiking, nature walks, picnicking, photography, wilderness backpacking (Saguaro East district only), and horseback riding.

Statue of Liberty

The Statue of Liberty is one of the best known human-made objects in the world (Figure 6.4). It is a symbol of the United States to much of the world. The famous 152-foot copper statue bearing the torch of freedom was a gift of the French people in 1886 to commemorate the alliance of the two nations during the American Revolution. The idea for the statue was conceived by French Republicans, to help keep the republican ideal alive in France. They viewed New York Harbor as a very visible location for preserving this ideal. The statue was designed and built by Frederic Auguste Bartholdi, using 2.5-mm copper sheets. A condition of this gift was that the Americans were to provide the foundation. Bartholdi completed the statue in 1884, and it stood in Paris for almost a year before being moved to Liberty Island in Upper New York Bay. It was dedicated on October 28, 1886, but was not proclaimed a national monument until 1924. It was initially under the jurisdiction of the War Department, but in the 1933 reorganization the National Park Service gained jurisdiction. There were boundary changes in 1937 and 1965; the monument now contains 58.4 acres. It was designated a world heritage site in 1984.

Boat is the only means of access to the monument. The Circle Line Statue of Liberty Ferry provides access from Battery Park in New York City and Liberty State Park in New Jersey. The Ferry slip in New York is right next to another national monument, Castle Clinton, which was a defense fort for New York Harbor and served as an immigration depot. It is a 15 minute ferry ride from Battery Park to Liberty

Figure 6.4 Statue of Liberty National Monument, located on Liberty Island in New York Harbor, is one of the best-known human-made objects in the world.

Island. Stairs and elevators access the upper level of the 156-foot pedestal, from which one can see excellent views of the New York Harbor. One must climb a spiral staircase equivalent to 22 stories to reach the crown; access to the torch is not available. Waits can be as long as 2 to 3 hours for this climb. The statue was completely refurbished for its centennial celebration in 1986. The American Museum of Immigration is in the pedestal. The only service available is a refreshment stand. Ellis Island, an immigration port from 1892 to 1954, is also part of the monument. The Statue of Liberty is the leader among national monuments in terms of recreation visits—4,343,000 were recorded in 1991. This figure converts to 1,085,800 recreation visitor days, a value exceeded only by Joshua Tree's 1,334,100.

NATIONAL PRESERVES

The classification "national preserve" was first applied to units of the National Park System in 1974, when Big Thicket (Texas) and Big Cypress (Florida) were added as the first two units in this category in the system. The establishment of the "national preserve" category created a new management concept for the National Park Service, since this classification allows higher degrees of resource consumption. Activities such as hunting, trapping, fishing and the extraction of minerals and fuels are permitted if they do not jeopardize the natural values. In 1980, most of the present national preserve acreage was added by the Alaska National Interest Lands Conservation Act. This act created three separate national preserves (Noatak, Bering Land Bridge, and Yukon-Charley Rivers), one combined national preserve and national monument (Aniakchak), and six combined national preserves and national parks (Wrangell–St. Elias, Denali, Lake Clark, Gates of the Arctic, Katmai, and Glacier Bay). The employment of the less restrictive national preserve category was a necessary compromise to allow the Alaska National Interest Lands Conservation Act to move through Congress. (Recall that these units of the National Park Service in Alaska, which total 20,317,271 acres, were discussed in Chapter 4.) The overwhelming majority of the national preserve acreage is in Alaska (97 percent).

Big Thicket (83,270 acres) and Big Cypress (535,191) acres) are still the only two units so classified in the lower 49 states. Big Cypress differs from Big Thicket in that it is much larger and its geographic area is one contiguous tract. Big Thicket, however, has a dozen tracts that are noncontiguous. Big Cypress National Preserve does have 25 percent inholdings, while Big Thicket National Preserve, in its fragmented holdings, only has 3 percent inholdings. Two other National Park System units have "preserve" in their title: Jean Lafitte National Historical Park and Preserve (Louisiana) and Timucuan Ecological and Historical Preserve (Florida). As their names imply, these two units are more historical in nature. The recreational use statistics for the combined Alaskan units are not broken down between preserve and park or preserve and monument but instead are combined. Big Cypress and Big Thicket are the leaders for the reported recreational use of national preserves. Big Cypress received 159,200 recreation visits (37,800 recreation visitor days) in 1991, and Big Thicket received 64,100 recreation visits (19,000 recreation visitor days) in 1991.

Big Thicket

A great number of plant and animal species coexist in this "biological crossroads" of North America, the Big Thicket. This 83,270-acre preserve was established in 1974 to protect the remnant of its complex biological diversity. What is extraordinary is not the rarity or abundance of its life forms, but how many species coexist here. It is located in the West Gulf Coastal Plain Section of the Coastal Plain physiographic province. The Big Thicket once extended from the Sabine River on the east to beyond the Trinity River on the west. Less than 10 percent of the original, almost impenetrable, combination of woodlands and swamps of the Big Thicket remains. This thicket of woods resulted from the unusual intermingling of five different biological habitats: southeastern swamps, eastern forests, central plains, southwestern deserts, and the Appalachians. Here, bogs sit near arid sandhills and Eastern bluebirds nest near roadrunners. There are 85 tree species, 60 shrubs, nearly 1000 flowering plants (including 20 orchids), and four of North America's five species of insect-eating plants. Nearly 300 species of birds live or move through this area. Fifty reptile species include a small population of alligators. Its preserve status prevents further timber harvesting but allows oil and gas exploration, hunting, and trapping to continue. Only low-impact visitor facilities will be built. The preserve was designated a biosphere reserve in 1991. The protected area will provide a standard for measuring human impact on the environment. A bill in Congress as of January 1995 proposes to increase the size of the preserve.

The 12 fragmented units of Big Thicket National Preserve are widely scattered over a 2000-square-mile area of southeastern Texas north of Beaumont. This area extends for 43 miles in a latitudinal direction and 48 miles in a longitudinal direction. The preserve has four land units and eight river-corridor units, which range in size from the Loblolly Unit's 550 acres to the Lance Rosier Unit's 25,024 acres. The Beaumont Unit adjoins the northern boundary of the City of Beaumont. A 40-mile lineal stretch of the preserve follows the Neches River from the Army Corps of Engineers' dam (which creates B. A. Steinhagen Lake) south to the Beaumont city limits. The development of the preserve is currently minimal, with few visitor facilities, but there are plans for more development in the future as funds become available. There are no accommodations, but food and lodging are available in nearby communities. The preserve's information center is located in the southern part of the centrally located Turkey Creek Unit. The greatest plant diversity is also found in this unit, which has a 15-mile trail that provides access for viewing this biological diversity. The Kirby Nature Trail introduces many plants and explores Village Creek's floodplain. In the northeast of this unit is a disabled-access boardwalk that allows exploration of the carnivorous pitcher plant area. Nearby and to the west is the Hickory Creek Savannah Unit, which consists of dry sandy uplands and wetter lowlands resulting in a diversity of flowers and grasses. Longleaf pine forests and wetlands mix here. There is a 1-mile loop trail and a 0.5-mile disabled-access boardwalk. A 1-mile loop trail through the Beech Creek Unit to the northeast affords the opportunity to observe biotic succession in an area where the loblolly pines were decimated by southern pine beetles in the mid-1970s. In the west is the Big Sandy Creek Unit, a sloping forest of beech, magnolia, and loblolly pine that descends into dense stands of hardwoods in the Big Sandy Creek floodplain. There are two looped hiking trails here: a 5.4-mile trail fol-

lows the sloping forest to the creek, and a 1.5-mile trail loops around a series of ponds formed by old beaver dams. Another, 18-mile trail in this unit is the only trail on which horseback riding and ATVs are allowed.

The principal recreational activities in the preserve are day-oriented. Day hikes and interpretive nature walks are the most common recreational opportunities. Small watercraft may be launched at locations along the Neches River, Pine Island Bayou, and along Village and Turkey Creeks. Fishing is allowed in all waters, and there are picnic sites in many of the units. The most popular swimming area is the Lakeview Sandbar area in the Beaumont Unit on the Neches River. It is designated a no-wake zone for boaters. Hunting and trapping are allowed only in specific areas at certain dates and times. Only backcountry camping is allowed in certain sections. There are no developed campgrounds. Several private and public campgrounds are located nearby. Camping is available at the Alabama-Coushutta Indian Reservation, which adjoins the Big Sandy Creek Unit. The B. A. Steinhagen Lake, which adjoins the Upper Neches River Corridor Unit on the north, is managed by the Army Corps of Engineers and has boating, swimming, fishing, and camping. The Big Thicket Museum in Saratoga has a slide show and exhibits of the natural and cultural history of the area.

NATIONAL RECREATION AREAS

"National recreation area" is the only category in the National Park System nomenclature that uses *recreation* in its name. The first such units were areas that surrounded reservoirs impounded by dams built by other federal agencies. These early areas were located in the West and managed under cooperative agreements with the other agency, which was usually the Bureau of Reclamation. Lake Mead National Recreation Area (first called Boulder Dam National Recreation Area) was established in 1936, and Coulee Dam National Recreation Area was established in 1946. A quarter of a century passed before additional national recreation areas were added to the National Park System. Since this time the concept has grown to encompass other lands and waters set aside for recreational use by acts of Congress, and it now includes major areas in urban centers in the East as well as in the West. There are also national recreation areas outside the National Park System that are administered by the Forest Service. These areas will be discussed in Chapters 7–10.

Table 6.1 summarizes the 20 national recreation areas that comprise 3.4 million acres in the National Park System. Two of these units are much larger than the others and comprise 80 percent of the national recreation area acreage: Lake Mead National Recreation Area (1.5 million acres) and Glen Canyon National Recreation Area (1.2 million acres). Other units are very small. The Chattahoochee River National Recreation Area has a gross area of 9257 acres, but only 4,005 acres are federal. All of the Gauley River National Recreation Area's 10,300 acres are nonfederal, and the federal facilities are very limited. In terms of both recreation visits and recreation visitor days, Lake Mead is the most-used national recreation area. Two of the urban/near-urban areas are among the most visited: Gateway and Delaware Water Gap. Golden

Table 6.1   National Recreation Area Analysis

National Recreation Area	State	Size (Acres)	Recreation Visits (000's)	Recreation Visitor Days (000's)	Visit/Visitor Day Ratio	Acres/ Visitor Day
Lake Mead National Recreation Area	NV, AZ	1,468,952.20	8,445.00	6,761.10	1.25	0.217
Glen Canyon National Recreation Area	UT, AZ	1,193,671.00	3,181.10	5,706.40	0.56	0.209
Ross Lake National Recreation Area	WA	115,857.40	298.90	157.90	1.89	0.734
Coulee Dam National Recreation Area	WA	100,390.30	1,771.40	587.60	3.01	0.171
Bighorn Canyon National Recreation Area	MT, WY	68,484.60	481.10	247.30	1.95	0.277
Lake Chelan National Recreation Area	WA	59,293.90	58.10	47.60	1.22	1.246
Amistad National Recreation Area	TX	57,292.40	1,215.70	761.90	1.60	0.075
Delaware Water Gap National Recreation Area	PA, NJ	54,600.80	4,275.80	1,556.20	2.75	0.035
Lake Meredith National Recreation Area	TX	44,977.60	1,280.00	414.50	3.09	0.109
Whiskeytown-Shasta-Trinity National Recreation Area	CA	42,448.20	1,537.10	468.60	3.28	0.091
Curecanti National Recreation Area	CO	42,114.50	1,090.90	459.50	2.37	0.092
Golden Gate National Recreation Area	CA	28,749.70	NA	NA	NA	NA
Gateway National Recreation Area	NY, NJ	20,375.90	6,643.90	1,822.30	3.65	0.011
Big South Fork National River and Recreation Area	TN, KY	16,860.00	860.00	468.60	1.84	0.036
Santa Monica Mountains National Recreation Area	CA	16,667.40	334.30	99.00	3.38	0.168
Cuyahoga Valley National Recreation Area	OH	16,544.30	1,359.00	233.90	5.81	0.071
Chickasaw National Recreation Area	OK	9,517.40	1,453.00	399.10	3.64	0.024
Chattahoochee River National Recreation Area	GA	4,005.00	1,660.60	553.50	3.00	0.007
Gauley River National Recreation Area	WV	0.00	NA	NA	NA	NA
Mississippi National River and Recreation Area	MN	Undetermined	NA	NA	NA	NA
Total		3,360,802.60	35,945.90	20,745.00	1.73	0.162

Source: Calculated by the author.

Gate would be near the top of the list, but reporting of use for this national recreation area was suspended pending completion of studies to verify the use data. The ratio of recreation visits to recreation visitor days varied from Glen Canyon's 0.56 to Cuyahoga Valley's 5.81; the average for the national recreation areas is 1.73. The remote location of Glen Canyon necessitates overnight use, while Cuyahoga Valley is very much day-use-oriented. The degree of "crowdedness" is related to geographic accessibility, and varies from Lake Chelan's roomy 1.25 acres per recreation visitor day to Chattahoochee River's very crowded 0.007 acres per recreation visitor day. The close proximity of the latter's relatively small area to Atlanta accounts for its high degree of use. The average value for the national recreation areas is 0.162 acres per recreation visitor day.

Prior to 1972, the units of the National Park System were primarily site-oriented and only secondarily demand-oriented, but the establishment of two national recreation areas in large urban areas marked a major departure in this policy. In this year, Gateway National Recreation Area was established in four units surrounding the entrance to the New York Harbor in New York (3 units) and New Jersey (1 unit). Golden Gate National Recreation Area was established in parts of San Francisco, Marin, and San Mateo Counties and includes Alcatraz Island. Two years later the Cuyahoga National Recreation Area, which links the urban centers of Cleveland and Akron, was established. Three other units are very close to large urban areas: Delaware Water Gap, Santa Monica Mountains, and Chattahoochee River National Rec-

reation Areas. The Delaware Water Gap National Recreation Area is on the border of New Jersey and Pennsylvania and within a short drive of a large number of people. Santa Monica Mountains National Recreation Area covers a large rugged area of chaparral mountains, which front on the sandy beaches north of Los Angeles. The federal facilities are limited, and less than 10 percent of the acreage within the boundary is federally owned.

The most recently created national recreation areas focus on rivers: Mississippi National River and Recreation Area (Minnesota), Gauley River (W. Virginia), Big South Fork (Tennessee and Kentucky), and Chattahoochee River (Georgia). An interesting national recreation area is the small Chickasaw, located in southern Oklahoma. In its present-day area is the former Sulphur Springs Reservation (designated 1902), which was redesignated Platt National Park in 1906 and then in 1976, combined with Arbuckle National Recreation Area as Chickasaw National Recreation Area. It is 9517 acres in size, of which 2409 are water. In the Whiskeytown-Shasta-Trinity National Recreation Area, only the Whiskeytown Unit is administered by the National Park Service; the Shasta and Trinity Units are administered by the Forest Service.

For illustrative purposes, two different types of national recreation area are used here as case studies: a large, nonurban national recreation area (Lake Mead) and a smaller, urban-centered one (Gateway).

Lake Mead

Lake Mead (formed by Hoover Dam) and Lake Mohave (formed by Davis Dam) on the Lower Colorado River comprise this first national recreation area established by an act of Congress. The Bureau of Reclamation completed Hoover Dam, then called Boulder Dam, on the Colorado River in 1935. The next year, under an agreement with the Bureau of Reclamation, the National Park Service assumed responsibility for all recreational activities on this reservoir, which was first called Boulder Dam National Recreation Area. The responsibility became a major one; Lake Mead is 110 miles long with 550 miles of shoreline, and affords extensive opportunities for boating, swimming, and camping. In 1947 the name was changed to Lake Mead National Recreation Area. In 1953, 67-mile long Lake Mohave, formed behind Davis Dam, was added to the area. The Bureau of Reclamation controls the release of water from both dams. Guided tours for Hoover Dam and self-guided tours for Davis Dam may be taken. Congress officially established the National Recreation Area, the nation's first and largest, in 1964. There was a boundary change in 1975. Today the area is 1,468,952 acres—1,348,076 (87 percent) of which are land. The other 186,700 acres (13 percent) is the water surface of Lake Mead and Lake Mohave. This national recreation area is the lowermost stretch of over 500 miles of the Colorado River that is continuously protected as National Park System land, which begins with Canyonlands National Park, includes Glen Canyon National Recreation Area, and then Grand Canyon National Park, whose western end abuts against the national recreation area. The national recreation area straddles the state border in southern Nevada and northwestern Arizona. Las Vegas is located 25 miles west of Lake Mead. Las Vegas would not be "Las Vegas" without Hoover Dam and Lake Mead, for they are the source of the water for the fountains, green lawns, and swimming pools and of the electricity for the colorful lights so extravagantly used in this city.

The location of Lake Mead National Recreation Area is in the area where four sections of two physiographic provinces meet: the Great Basin, Sonoran Desert, and Mexican Highland Sections of the Basin and Range Province, and the Grand Canyon Section of the Colorado Plateau Province. The elevations range from 517 feet at Davis Dam to 7072 feet in pinyon-juniper forests of the Shivwits Plateau (Arizona). The geological history from 1.8 billion years ago to the last ice age can be seen within the area. This is the junction of three of the four American deserts—Mohave, Great Basin, and Sonoran—which provide a wide variety of plant and animals, some of which are at the extreme of their range (for example, the gila monster and the smoke tree). Wildlife that may be observed includes bighorn sheep, mule deer, coyote, kit fox, bobcat, ring-tailed cat, desert tortoise, numerous lizards and snakes, and a wealth of bird species such as herons, grebes, and eagles. Fourteen species are under consideration for listing or are now listed as threatened or endangered species. The desert tortoise, the peregrine falcon, and two ancient Colorado River fish species—the bonytail chub and the razorback sucker—are examples. There are 40 desert springs that attract wildlife. One of the park's major management problems is located at these springs, where damage is caused by feral burros. In this desert climate summer temperatures regularly rise above 100°F daily. From October through May, temperatures are less extreme; winter highs average 50°F and nighttime lows seldom drop below 32°F.

The two dams that form Lakes Mead and Mohave are major attractions for visitors. Hoover Dam, named for President Herbert Hoover, is 726.4 feet high (the highest dam in the Western Hemisphere), 45 feet thick at the crest, which is 1244 feet long (over which passes U.S. 93), and 660 feet thick at the bottom (Figure 6.5). It contains 17 generators with a capacity of 1,920,000 kilowatts. It is an arch-gravity concrete

Figure 6.5 Hoover Dam is the reason for the existence of Lake Mead National Recreation Area. This 726-ft-high dam has formed the largest human-made reservoir in the United States—Lake Mead.

construction type of dam. Lake Mead is the largest human-made reservoir in the United States: It has a surface area of 157,900 acres and a capacity of 28,537,000 acre-feet, reaches a depth of 500 feet and averages 200 feet deep, contains 550 miles of shoreline, and is 8 miles at its widest point. It is named for Dr. Elwood Mead, the Commissioner of Reclamation from 1924 to 1936. Davis Dam is named in honor of the Director of Reclamation from 1914 to 1932—Arthur Powell Davis. It is 200 feet high, 50 feet thick at the crest (whose length is 1600 feet), and 1400 feet thick at the base. Its construction type is earth-and-rock-fill embankment with concrete spillway, intake, and power plant (five generating units produce 240,000 kilowatts). Lake Mohave is 67 miles long, has 150 miles of shoreline and 28,800 acres of surface area, and is 4 miles at its widest point. Its capacity is 1,818,300 acre-feet (National Park Service).

Most recreational activities focus on the water and include dam tours, swimming, fishing, boating (including houseboats), waterskiing, camping, picnicking, and scenic drives. There are also a variety of camping and hiking opportunities. The Alan Bible Visitor Center is located on U.S. 93, 4 miles east of Boulder City, where park headquarters are located. Boaters can travel up narrow, steep-walled canyons (Iceberg Canyon in Lake Mead or Black Canyon in Lake Mohave) and investigate hundreds of coves on the two lakes. Many of these coves have sandy beaches that are excellent for picnicking or camping. There are six concession-operated marinas on Lake Mead, three on Lake Mohave, and free public launches and parking are located at each. (Figure 6.6 shows the Callville Bay Marina.) Marinas rent fishing boats, ski boats, houseboats, and equipment. A variety of boat tours are run by concessioners on both lakes. The lakes offer some of the best sport fishing in the United States. The large striped bass of Lake Mead and the rainbow trout in the upper reaches of Lake Mohave in Black Canyon are popular. Both desert lakes are clear, clean, and ideal for swimming, snorkeling and diving, although the cold tail water released into upper

Figure 6.6 Callville Bay Marina at Lake Mead National Recreation Area. (E. Hertzog, Bureau of Reclamation photo)

Lake Mohave from Hoover Dam discourages most swimmers. Boulder Beach on Lake Mead and Katherine Beach on Lake Mohave are the principal designated swimming areas.

Several paved roads wind through 237 miles of the dramatic desert scenery of Lake Mead country. One popular drive follows the Lakeshore and Northshore Scenic Drives along the shore of Lake Mead. From these roads there are panoramas of the blue lake set against a backdrop of the browns, blacks, reds, and grays of the desert mountains. At the northern end of the Northshore Drive is Nevada's Valley of Fire State Park, a spectacular display of brilliant red sandstone formations. The road to Pearce Ferry crosses one of the world's finest Joshua tree forests. There are 800 miles of graded backcountry roads that pass through remote desert canyons and plateaus. No off-road use is permitted. Shaded picnic areas with tables, water, fire grills, and restrooms are found at the six areas listed in Table 6.2 and along Northshore Road.

There are nine developed areas on Lake Mead and Lake Mohave that offer a wide range of accommodations year-round. Table 6.2 highlights the major ones at each site. All lodges, trailer villages, and marinas are run by concessioners. Each developed area is easily accessible by car and boat. For overnight stays there are six motels with 214 rooms and 1148 campsites. Backcountry camping is allowed along the shores of both lakes and at designated sites along unpaved backcountry roads. Lake Mead is the leading national recreation area in terms of both recreation visits (8,445,000) and recreation visitor days (6,761,000) in 1991. It is a little less crowded than average for a national recreation area, with 0.22 acres per recreation visitor day.

Gateway

This 20,376-acre national recreation area is comprised of four units which surround the entrance to Lower New York Harbor: The Breezy Point Unit on the Rockaway

Table 6.2 Developed Facilities—Lake Mead National Recreation Area

	Ranger Station	Lodging	Trailer Village (fee)	Campground	Marina	Restaurant	Picnic Area
Lake Mead							
Boulder Beach (3 km/2 mi)	x	x	x	x	x	x	x
Las Vegas Wash (16 km/10 mi)	x			x	x	x	x
Callville Bay (43 km/27 mi)	x		x	x	x	x	x
Echo Bay (79 km/49 mi)	x	x	x	x	x	x	
Overton Beach (101 km/63 mi)	x		x		x	x	
Temple Bar (81 km/50 mi)	x	x	x	x	x	x	
Lake Mohave							
Willow Beach (35 km/22 mi)	x	x	x		x	x	x
Cottonwood Beach (87 km/54 mi)	x	x	x	x	x	x	x
Katherine (130 km/81 mi)	x	x	x	x	x	x	x

Source: National Park Service. *Lake Mead National Recreation Area.* Gridmap Official Map and Guide. Washington, D.C.

Peninsula in Brooklyn, the Jamaica Bay Unit also in Brooklyn, the Staten Island Unit (which lies across the harbor from these first two units), and the Sandy Hook Unit in the northeast corner of New Jersey. The area takes its name from the natural gateway formed by two of these arms of land (Sandy Hook and Rockaway Peninsula), which stretch across the water toward each other. This natural gateway was the entrance to America for millions of immigrants who came to the new world. Open space is preserved for future generations in the midst of one of the world's largest urban areas. With beaches, marshes, islands, historic structures, military installations, airfields, a lighthouse, and adjacent waters in New York Harbor, this area offers urban residents a wide range of recreational opportunities and historical perspectives. This park was created from a collection of various preexisting lands and facilities. Former military bases have been added to the park, and large areas were donated by the City of New York and the states of New York and New Jersey. In the Rockaways, citizens halted the building of a high-rise complex to preserve the natural quality of a rare stretch of ocean beach. Gateway, established in 1972 (along with Golden Gate), was among the first large urban parks to be added to the National Park System. With this addition, the National Park Service went into the urban, mass recreation business. At Gateway the total area is 26,311 acres, 20,376 acres of which are federal.

The unique aspect of Gateway is its ready access via a well-developed mass-transit (bus and subway) system. A diversity of outdoor recreation opportunities abound at Gateway: swimming, picnicking, sunbathing, sports, interpretive programs, biking, fishing, boating, birdwatching, crabbing, and horseback riding. Visitor facilities include a marina, a boathouse, beaches, sport facilities, restrooms, parking areas, a wildlife refuge, a bicycle trail, and picnic areas. The only overnight facilities are primitive campsites at Ecology Village at Floyd Bennett Field and are available for organized youth groups on a reservation basis. Since the park opened in 1974, there has been an ongoing cleanup of beaches and community involvement. Through educational programs, thousands of schoolchildren have discovered Gateway's historic sites and natural beauty. Gateway is one of the most heavily visited units of the National Park System, with 6,643,900 recreations visits in 1991. (Lake Mead is the only national recreation area with a higher number.) In terms of visitor days, the high degree of day use is reflected in its 1,822,300 recreation visitor days for the same year; the ratio of visits to visitor days is 3.65. Gateway is the most-crowded national recreation area, with only 0.011 acres per visitor day.

Jamaica Bay is essentially a 6000-acre wildlife refuge that attracts over 300 species of birds, especially ducks and geese. Large and noisy big silver birds of another nature regularly fly over Jamaica Bay and "nest" at John F. Kennedy International Airport on the east side of the bay. A visitor center is located on an island in the bay and is accessible by subway and bus. Park headquarters are at Floyd Bennett Field. On the other side of Flatbush Avenue are tennis courts, a driving range, baseball batting cages, miniature golf, and a marina at Dead Horse Bay. A riding stable is located at Bergen Beach. Excellent fishing may be had at Canarsie Pier and North Channel Bridge. Frank Charles Memorial Park and Hamilton Beach Park are located on the northeastern corner of this unit.

One of the major attractions of the Breezy Point Unit is Jacob Riis Park, which has one of the best ocean beaches in the New York area. Swimming and surf fishing

(in designated areas), along with team sports, are major activities here. Historic Fort Tilden has served a strategic role since 1812; tours are offered. This is also the site of the Rockaway Naval Air Station, another historic site. The Staten Island Unit lies on the western side of the Lower Harbor. Great Kills Park was once the site of an Algonquin Indian Village. Its topography was changed by massive land filling in the 1940s, when Crookes Island became Crookes Point, a choice spot for fishing. There is a beach and marina at Great Kills Park. To the northeast is Miller Field, a spot of historic and recreational interest. It was built after World War I to serve hydroplanes of the U.S. Air Service.

The Sandy Hook Unit is in the extreme northeastern corner of New Jersey. Because it dominates a major channel into New York Harbor, it has been the site of a lighthouse and a series of forts since colonial times. The Sandy Hook Lighthouse was built in 1764 and is the oldest in the United States. The last of the great forts, Fort Hancock, is largely intact, as are the great gun emplacements that once guarded the harbor. The remains of the Sandy Hook Proving Grounds, where new U.S. Army weapons were tested from 1874 until 1919, may still be seen. Beaches on the Atlantic provide exceptional swimming and surf-fishing opportunities. On the Sandy Hook Bay side are superb resources for exploring history and nature, including the Holly Forest.

NATIONAL SEASHORES

The purpose of national seashores is to preserve the natural values of shoreline areas and off-shore islands, while at the same time providing water-oriented recreation. In 1934, the National Park Service surveyed the Atlantic and Gulf Coasts and identified 12 significant areas deserving federal protection. Among them was Cape Hatteras, (North Carolina), which Congress authorized as the first national seashore in 1937. Land acquisition lagged until after World War II. The Mellon family foundations then made substantial grants to help North Carolina purchase and donate the needed lands. This national seashore encompasses almost 100 miles of barrier islands and beaches, which provide an outstanding natural resource base for swimming, surfing, sunbathing, sport fishing, nature study, and other recreational activities.

Further development of national seashores did not take place until a revival of the concept in 1961, when Congress authorized Cape Cod (Massachusetts). It was 1966 before the land was acquired and the seashore established. Cape Cod was the first large natural or recreational area for which Congress at the outset permitted the use of appropriate funds for land acquisition.

The legislation that established Cape Code National Seashore prohibited the Secretary of Interior from using eminent domain condemnation proceedings for private improved properties, once the local jurisdictions had approved zoning ordinances. Private development was closing out many Americans from ocean access. The Outdoor Recreation Resources Review Commission recognized this and recommended that national seashores and national lakeshores be added to the National Park System. In the 1960s Congress authorized the following National Seashores: Point Reyes (Cal-

ifornia; authorized 1962, established 1972), Padre Island (Texas; authorized 1962, established 1968), Fire Island (New York, 1964), Assateague (Maryland, Virginia; 1965), and Cape Lookout (N. Carolina; 1966). In the 1970s the last three national seashores were established: Gulf Islands (Florida, Mississippi; 1971); Cumberland Island, (Georgia; 1972), and Canaveral, (Florida; 1975). Point Reyes is the only national seashore on the Pacific coast.

All of the national seashores are on barrier islands except for Point Reyes, which is on a peninsula. Some of them have no road access, such as the Mississippi portion of Gulf Islands and Cumberland Island. Even those with road access have long stretches of beach that are distant from the nearest road. Units of the National Wilderness Preservation System are located in three of the seashores: Gulf Islands (1800 acres), Cumberland Island (8840 acres), and Fire Island (1363 acres). Table 6.3 presents the analysis for the national seashores. The 10 national seashores cover almost 0.5 million acres. Padre Island, selected for the case study in this section, is the largest, and Fire Island is the smallest. Yet even Fire Island is a world apart from the nearby large urban area, and wilderness experiences may be had. The 20.3 million recreation visits in 1991 at the national seashores accounted for 8 percent of the National Park Service total, and the 6.8 million recreation visitor days accounted for 6.2 percent of the total. In terms of recreation visits, Cape Cod (5.4 million) and Gulf Islands (5.0 million) are the clear leaders, but their ratios of visits to visitor days (6.06 and 3.88) indicate relatively short duration visits. Canaveral also had a very high visit-to-visitor-day ratio of 4.74. In terms of recreation visitor days in 1991, Assateague (1.5 million) and Gulf Islands (1.3 million) received the most total use. The least-used and least-crowded of the seashores is Cumberland Island, with 0.271 acres per recreation visitor days. Padre Island (0.241) and Canaveral (0.236) are also relatively uncrowded. Assateague, with 0.012 acres per visitor day, is the most crowded, followed by Fire Island (0.026), Cape Cod (0.030), and Cape Hatteras (0.032). Among the National Seashores, Cumberland Island is the most primitive and most undeveloped, and the plans are to keep it that way.

Table 6.3   National Seashore Analysis

National Seashore	State	Size (Acres)	Recreation Visits (000's)	Recreation Visitor Days (000's)	Visit/Visitor Day Ratio	Acres/ Visitor Day
Padre Island National Seashore	TX	130,355.50	972.10	541.10	1.80	0.241
Gulf Islands National Seashore	FL, MS	98,125.80	4,988.00	1,285.70	3.88	0.076
Point Reyes National Seashore	CA	64,505.10	2,396.90	896.70	2.67	0.072
Canaveral National Seashore	FL	57,626.70	1,159.00	244.40	4.74	0.236
Cape Hatteras National Seashore	NC	30,318.90	2,098.90	949.70	2.21	0.032
Cape Cod National Seashore	MA	27,386.40	5,442.40	898.60	6.06	0.030
Cape Lookout National Seashore	NC	25,173.60	320.20	178.60	1.79	0.141
Cumberland Island National Seashore	GA	18,698.10	36.50	68.90	0.53	0.271
Assateague Island National Seashore	MD, VA	17,774.90	2,087.50	1,539.60	1.36	0.012
Fire Island National Seashore	NY	6,220.60	763.20	241.90	3.16	0.026
Total		476,185.60	20,264.70	6,845.20	2.96	0.070

Source: Calculated by the author.

Padre Island

Padre Island is noted for its wide, white sand-and-shell beaches, excellent fishing, and abundant bird and marine life. It is the longest barrier island in the United States and extends along the Texas Gulf Coast for 113 miles; 66 miles of it is preserved as Padre Island National Seashore. This is the largest stretch of undeveloped ocean beach in the United States (Weise, 1980, 6). It was authorized in 1962 and became established in 1968. This, the largest of our national seashores, has only 78.8 acres of nonfederal inholdings in its 130,434-acre total. Padre Island is broken only by the human-made Mansfield Channel and extends southward from Corpus Christi almost to Mexico. Corpus Christi Pass, a natural pass to the north, once separated Padre Island from Mustang Island but is now filled so that the two islands are joined. The northern portion of the seashore may be accessed by two approaches, but a paved road extends for only 8.5 miles into the seashore. There is no through road, since the Mansfield Channel prohibits even four-wheel-drive passage. Four-wheel-drive vehicles may drive for 60 miles on the beach through the seashore to the Mansfield Channel. The island may be accessed from the south, where a causeway passes from Port Isabel to South Padre Island and Cameron County Parks, but this part of the island is not in the seashore. South Padre Island is a very popular attraction for college students on spring break. Brownsville, the southernmost city in South Texas, is located nearby.

Geologically, Padre Island is among the youngest land found in the United States; its oldest deposits are estimated to be only a few thousand years old. The waves and currents of the Gulf of Mexico have formed this barrier island, which is separated from the mainland by Laguna Madre. Part of the Intracoastal Waterway passes through the Laguna Madre and is sheltered by Padre Island. Most of Padre Island is less than 20 feet above mean sea level; however, the highest point is reached at 50 feet, along the fore-island dune ridge. The island varies from about 0.6 miles to 2.5 miles in width. A common sequence of environments from the Gulf of Mexico to Laguna Madre include the sand-and-shell beach; a stable ridge of fore-island dunes; vegetated flats with scattered, stabilized, grass-covered dunes; the barren, shifting sands of back-island dune fields; and the featureless plains of wind-tidal flats. The beach changes from a sandy gentle slope in the north to the steeper Little Shell and Big Shell beaches on central Padre, to the mixed shell-and-sand beaches on south Padre. The fore-island dune ridge is highest and most continuous adjacent to the shell beaches. Laguna Madre is as wide as 10 miles and is extremely salty because there is no circulation exchange with the Gulf; its extent changes with the tides. The climate of Padre Island is subtropical and semiarid. Mean annual precipitation varies from 29 inches in the north to 26 inches in the south. Most of it comes in early and late tropical storm and hurricane seasons (June–October). The summers are long and hot, and the winters are short and mild. Afternoon and evening sea breezes help to moderate summer temperatures with temperatures in the summer being 10° to 15° cooler than a short distance inland.

Over 300 species of plants and 380 species of birds are found, including the only marine nesting colony of white pelicans on the Gulf Coast. Five sea turtle species (loggerhead, green, hawksbill, leatherback, and Kemp's ridley) have been observed on Padre Island, all threatened or endangered. An international effort is underway

to try and establish a second nesting area for the Kemp's ridley sea turtle in this national seashore. Its principal nesting area is to the south in Mexico; it is estimated that less than 2000 adults remain in the world (National Park Service). Other species that may be seen in the seashore include: coyotes, blacktailed jackrabbits, lizards, Western diamondback rattlesnakes, and ghost crabs. Fish that may be caught in the surf on the Gulf side of the island include redfish, speckled sea trout, black drum, whiting, and sand trout.

Padre Island National Seashore offers a diversity of outdoor recreation opportunities: beach driving, swimming, fishing, picnicking, wind surfing, surfing, sailing, boating, shelling, nature study, and bird and wildlife watching. The Malaquite Beach complex serves as the center of visitor services for the seashore. It is accessed via a paved road that runs 8.5 miles into the northern part of the seashore. This complex includes a visitor center, an observation deck, a snack bar and gift shop, restrooms, rinse-off showers, and changing rooms. Shaded tables for picnics are also available here. Visitor services are very limited outside of Malaquite Beach. The Malaquite Beach campground has more than 40 sites suitable for campers with tents or recreational vehicles. It is open year-round, and no reservations may be made (Figure 6.7). There are no electrical, water, or sewage hookups. The beach is closed to vehicles for 5 miles at Malaquite Beach, with barriers indicating the limits of closure. There is a self-guiding 0.75-mile-loop Grasslands Nature Trail near Malaquite Beach, but watch out for Western diamondback rattlesnakes! To the west of Malaquite Beach, on Laguna Madre at Bird Island Basin, there is a primitive campground and the seashore's only boat-launching ramp. All vehicles can travel on the 8.5-mile paved park entrance road and for the first 5 miles to South Beach. Five miles south of Malaquite Beach there are 55 miles of Gulf beach that are open to four-wheel driving, primitive camping, and other recreational pursuits. Driving and camping here are restricted to the beach. This portion of the seashore is remote and primitive, and visitors are on their

Figure 6.7 Beachfront campground at Malaquite Beach, Padre Island National Seashore.

own—there are no visitor services. It is easy to become stuck here, even in four-wheel drive. There is a primitive campsite at Yarborough Pass on the Laguna Madre that is accessible via a loose shell road. Padre Island National Seashore is relatively lightly used and recorded 541,000 recreation visitor days in 1991. Its 0.241 acres per recreation visitor days ranked it among the least crowded of the national seashores. When driving down the beach in a four-wheel-drive vehicle south of South Beach, it is possible to travel a considerable distance without seeing another person.

NATIONAL LAKESHORES

The same concern about the loss of public access to the oceanfront that resulted in the revival of the national seashore concept in the 1960s also existed for the loss of public access to the Great Lakes' shorelines. As a result, the four national lakeshores authorized in 1966 and 1970 generally followed the national seashore pattern. Our first national lakeshore was Pictured Rocks (Michigan, 1966). Multicolored sandstone cliffs, broad beaches, dunes, waterfalls, inland lakes, ponds, marshes, and hardwood and coniferous forests with a multitude of wildlife comprise this scenic area on the Upper Peninsula of Michigan on Lake Superior. Two months later in the same year (1966), Indiana Dunes became a national lakeshore. On the southern shore of Lake Michigan between Gary and Michigan City, Indiana, Indiana Dunes had been proposed as a national park as early as 1917. Here dunes rise as much as 180 feet above Lake Michigan's southern shore, and there are beaches, bogs, marshes, swamps, prairie remnants, and historic sites. It is the most urban of the national lakeshores. In 1970, Apostle Islands (Wisconsin) became the third national lakeshore. Here, 21 picturesque islands and an 11-mile strip of the adjacent Bayfield Peninsula, along the southern shore of Lake Superior, comprise this national lakeshore. Five days later our fourth, and most recent, national lakeshore was established on 34 miles of shoreline and islands at Sleeping Bear Dunes (Michigan). Sleeping Bear Dunes is the case study that will be used in this section.

Table 6.4 presents the analysis for the national lakeshores. These four units comprise 144,490 acres of the National Park System. A total of 4.1 million (1.6 percent of total) recreation visits and 1.2 million (1.0 percent of total) recreation visitor days were recorded in 1991. Indiana Dunes' 2.1 million visits clearly rank it the leader among the lakeshores, but in terms of recreation visitor days, Sleeping Bear Dunes

Table 6.4   National Lakeshore Analysis

National Lakeshore	State	Size (Acres)	Recreation Visits (000's)	Recreation Visitor Days (000's)	Visit/Visitor Day Ratio	Acres/ Visitor Day
Sleeping Bear Dunes National Lakeshore	MI	56,868.5	1,246.30	504.00	2.47	0.113
Apostle Islands National Lakeshore	WI	42,124.2	141.00	62.60	2.25	0.673
Pictured Rocks National Lakeshore	MI	35,791.4	704.90	287.80	2.45	0.124
Indiana Dunes National Lakeshore	IN	9,705.4	2,058.80	343.10	6.00	0.028
Total		144,489.5	4,151.00	1,197.50	3.47	0.121

Source: Calculated by the author.

is ahead. Apostle Islands receives much less use than the other three lakeshores, with 0.673 acres per recreation visitor day in 1991. Indiana Dunes, being the most crowded, had only 0.028 acres per recreation visitor day. Indiana Dunes' recreation-visit-to-recreation-visitor-day ratio of 6.0 is caused by its urban location and shorter stays. Varying amounts of inholdings are found within the boundaries of these lakeshores: Pictured Rocks, 51 percent; Apostle Islands, 38 percent; Indiana Dunes, 30 percent; and Sleeping Bear Dunes, 20 percent. The land use around Indiana Dunes is quite interesting. This lakeshore is divided into two halves, with an industrial complex consisting of Midwest Steel, Bethlehem Steel, Northern Indiana Public Service Company, and the Port of Indiana located between the two sections; U.S. Steel borders the lakeshore on the west.

Sleeping Bear Dunes

This is a diverse landscape with massive sand dunes, quiet birch-lined streams, white sand beaches, dense beech-maple forests, clear lakes, and rugged bluffs towering as high as 460 feet above Lake Michigan. Two offshore wilderness islands, the Manitou Islands, offer tranquility and seclusion. The national lakeshore is located on the northwestern corner of Michigan's Lower Peninsula, west of Traverse City. Although authorized in 1970, it was not established until 1977. Twenty percent of its gross area of 71,188 acres are inholdings; the land area is 58,473 acres. The area takes its name from an Indian legend about a mother bear and her cubs: A forest fire in Wisconsin forced the bears into the water, where they swam toward the Michigan shore. The mother made it to shore first and waited for her cubs on top of a bluff now called the "Sleeping Bear Dune." North and South Manitou Islands represent the cubs, who drowned. Today, Sleeping Bear Dunes is not only our largest national lakeshore; it is also the most used, recording 504,000 recreation visitor days in 1991.

This region is a product of the Ice Age and the great continental glaciers that advanced and retreated over the area. They deposited huge piles of sand and rock debris when they melted, leaving behind the hilly terrain seen today. The last glaciers retreated from this area 12,000 years ago. The sandy coast with westerly winds was ideal for dune building. There are two kinds of sand dunes in Sleeping Bear Dunes. *Beach dunes* develop on low-lying shores of Lake Michigan and are built from beach sand. The Aral Dunes, along Platte Bay's north shore, are good examples of beach dunes. *Perched dunes* sit high above the shore on flat surfaces and are composed of glacial sands. The Sleeping Bear Dune is a perched sand dune. Some dunes migrate, and as they do, bury trees. The remains of these dead trees are called "ghost forests." Beach grass and sand cherry are among the first plants to grow on newly built dunes. Their roots hold the sand in place and stabilize the dunes. Vehicles are prohibited from the dune areas because of the damage they do to this vegetation.

Recreational opportunities include bird and wildlife watching, fishing, boating, camping, picnicking, primitive camping, hiking, interpretive activities, canoeing, swimming, horseback riding, scenic drives, and hunting. Visitor centers are at Empire (where park headquarters are also) on the mainland and on South Manitou Island. There are also exhibits at Sleeping Bear Dune Coast Guard Station Maritime Museum. The Pierce Stocking Scenic Drive is 7.1 miles and offers panoramic views of Sleeping Bear Dunes, Glen Lake, and Lake Michigan. There are several trails and hiking op-

portunities at Sleeping Bear Dunes, which cover 4 square miles. The lakeshore's lakes and rivers offer opportunities for swimming, boating, and fishing. Canoes can be rented on the Platte and the Crystal Rivers, and anglers can fish for trout, salmon, pike, and bass. There are two developed campgrounds—Platte River and D. H. Day—and a group camping area near the Glen Lake Picnic Area. Backcountry camping is allowed at walk-in campgrounds on the mainland and on the Manitou Islands. Free backcountry permits are required. Most of the area's private cottages and motels are only open in summer. Ferry service is available to both North and South Manitou Islands. Points to visit on South Manitou Island are the Valley of Giants, with its huge white cedar trees, lighthouse, and other historic sites. There is 15,000 acres of wilderness for hikers to explore on North Manitou Island. Hunting is allowed in season for deer, rabbit, squirrel, ruffed grouse, and waterfowl. About 55 miles of trails are marked in the winter for cross-country skiing.

NATIONAL RIVERS

National rivers and wild and scenic rivers preserve ribbons of land bordering on free-flowing streams that have not been dammed, channeled, or otherwise altered by humans. Besides preserving rivers in their natural state, these areas provide opportunities for outdoor activities such as hiking, canoeing, rafting, fishing, and hunting. The first of the national rivers was Ozark National Scenic Riverways in southeastern Missouri, authorized by Congress in 1964. This enactment foreshadowed the Wild and Scenic Rivers Act of 1968. Today, there are two different groups of rivers administered by the National Park Service. These two groups of rivers are identified and analyzed in Table 6.5. The first group consists of rivers designated by Congress as specific units of the National Park System; there are five of these. The second group is rivers designated by the Wild and Scenic Rivers Act to be administered by the National Park Service; there are seven of these. (The Wild and Scenic Rivers System will be covered in Chapter 14 of this book.) In terms of recreational visits, Ozark National Scenic Riverways, with 2.3 million, is the leader, but in terms of recreation visitor days the Saint Croix National Scenic Riverway (Minnesota and Wisconsin, 583,600) and Buffalo National River (Arkansas, 493,900) receive more use than Ozark (396,600).

Ozark National Scenic Riverways

The 140 miles of the Current and Jacks Fork Rivers provide canoeing, tubing, fishing, and swimming opportunities in this first Congressionally designated national scenic river component of the National Park System. Nearly 100 springs pour thousands of gallons of clear, cold, blue water into the streams. Ozark culture is preserved throughout the area, and demonstrations are given. Ozark National Scenic Riverways was authorized in 1964 and established in 1972. It is located in the Salem Plateaus Section

Table 6.5   National River Analysis

	State	Size (Acres)	Recreation Visits (000's)	Recreation Visitor Days (000's)	Visit/Visitor Day Ratio	Acres/ Visitor Day
National Park System Units Only						
Bluestone National Scenic River	WV	3,032.0	NA	NA	NA	NA
Buffalo National River	AR	91,788.3	981.80	493.90	1.99	0.186
Missouri National Recreational River	NE, SD		NA	NA	NA	NA
New River Gorge National River	WV	34,103.2	772.20	77.40	9.98	0.441
Ozark National Scenic Riverways	MO	61,368.4	2,304.80	396.60	5.81	0.155
Total		190,291.9	4,058.80	967.90	4.19	0.197
National Park System Units—Wild and Scenic River System Components						
Alagnak Wild River	AK	24,038.0	NA	NA	NA	NA
Delaware National Scenic River	PA, NJ, NY	0.0	NA	NA	NA	NA
Lower Saint Croix National Scenic Riverway	WI, MN	8,143.4	NA	NA	NA	NA
Obed Wild and Scenic River	TN	3,109.0	86.40	32.90	2.63	0.094
Rio Grande Wild and Scenic River	TX	0.0	0.60	9.40	0.06	
Saint Croix National Scenic Riverway	WI, MN	27,144.5	468.80	583.60	0.80	0.047
Upper Delaware Scenic and Recreational River	PA, NY	14.5	222.60	89.90	2.48	0.000
Total		62,449.4	778.40	715.80	1.09	0.087

Source: Calculated by the author.

of the Ozark Plateau Province of the Interior Highlands. The widespread distribution of limestones and dolomites of Ordovician age, along with the deep dissection, are responsible for the large number of springs and caves in the area. The Current River begins at Montauk Spring in Montauk State Park. Big Spring, near the lower course of the riverway, flows out of Eminence Dolomite and is one of the largest in the United States, with an average daily flow of 286 million gallons a day.

Most of the recreational opportunities are water-related: canoeing, swimming, hiking, camping, fishing, picnicking, float trips, boating, cave tours, hunting, craft demonstrations, and interpretive talks. The ambiance of an Ozark float trip on the Current River is made by a combination of the clear water and numerous springs, scenic bluffs, caves to explore, excellent fishing, and gravel-bar camping. (As a Boy Scout, the author grew to love the outdoors and eventually became a recreational geographer because of his early experiences on this river.) Unfortunately, the publicity gained when the river became a unit of the National Park System has greatly added to the crowds that now use the river. In the 1950s, canoeing on this river was almost a wilderness experience. Today, one is always within either sight or sound of other canoes, at least during the summer. The National Park Service has authorized 19 concessioners to rent canoes and provide shuttle service. Fish that may be caught include largemouth and smallmouth bass, goggle-eye, and trout. Five poisonous snakes occur in the riverway: cottonmouth, copperhead, and pygmy, massasauga, and timber rattlesnakes. Campgrounds are located at Akers (81 sites), Pulltite (55 sites), Round Spring (60 sites), Two Rivers (12 sites), Powder Mill (10 sites), Big Spring (195 sites), and Alley Spring (187) sites). Headquarters for the riverway are located at Van Buren. Private property does occur within the boundaries, with 25 percent of

the riverway consisting of inholdings. The Mark Twain National Forest is nearby on all sides of the riverway.

NATIONAL SCENIC TRAILS

National scenic trails are generally long-distance footpaths winding through areas of natural beauty. Three of these trails have been designated as part of the National Park System: the Appalachian National Scenic Trail, the Natchez Trace National Scenic Trail, and the Potomac Heritage National Scenic Trail. Since the passage in 1968 of the National Trails System Act, a number of other trails have been designated national scenic trails. The National Trails System Act provides for the creation of four different categories of trails—scenic, historic, recreational, and side and connecting trails. (Chapter 14 will detail the National Trails System, which was established by the National Trails System Act.)

Of the three national scenic trails that are designated units of the National Park System, only one—the Appalachian—is presently developed for public use. It will serve as the case study for this classification.

The Potomac Heritage Trail recognizes and commemorates the unique mix of history and recreation along the Potomac River. While it was authorized to be included in the National Park System in 1983, the trail route has not yet been formally designated and is therefore not yet developed for public use. A comprehensive management plan is being developed that will result in ultimate designation of trail segments. The general trail corridor will begin at the mouth of the Potomac River and follow both banks of the Potomac to the District of Columbia and west through Virginia to Harper's Ferry, where it will cross into Maryland and follow the Chesapeake and Ohio towpath to Cumberland. The entire 184-mile length of the Chesapeake and Ohio Canal in the District of Columbia and Maryland is a segment of the 704-mile trail. From Cumberland, the trail will continue through Maryland into Pennsylvania to Conemaugh Gorge, just west of Johnstown. The 18-mile Mount Vernon Trail in Virginia and the 75-mile Laurel Highlands Trail in Pennsylvania will be included in the trail's route.

The Natchez Trace National Scenic Trail, which lies within and parallels the boundaries of the Natchez Trace Parkway (described later in the chapter) extends for 694 miles from Natchez, Miss., to Nashville, Tenn. It also passes through the northwestern corner of Alabama. Although designated a national scenic trail in 1983, it is not yet developed for public use. It contains 10,995 acres, all of which are nonfederal. The Natchez Trace is a historic route that began as animal and Native American trails that were later used by explorers. In the trail's 1987 comprehensive plan, four segments near Nashville, Jackson, and Natchez were selected for development as hiking and horseback trails.

Appalachian

The Appalachian National Scenic Trail is a public footpath across 2146 miles of Appalachian ridgelines from Mount Katahdin (Maine) to Springer Mountain (Georgia).

Along the way it passes through the states of New Hampshire, Vermont, Massachusetts, Connecticut, New York, New Jersey, Pennsylvania, Maryland, West Virginia, Virginia, Tennessee, and North Carolina. It was established in 1968 as one of the two initial units of the National Trails System (the other being the Pacific Crest National Scenic Trail, which is administered by the Forest Service). The acreage included in the trail is 161,382 acres, of which 100,334 are federal. The trail was first envisioned in 1921 by regional planner and forester Benton MacKaye, who wanted to preserve the Appalachian crests as an accessible, multipurpose wilderness and belt, a retreat from eastern urban life. Roads that cross it for all but the 100 northernmost miles provide ready access. It was designed, constructed, and marked in the 1920s and 1930s by 32 volunteer hiking clubs that joined together in 1925 to form the *Appalachian Trail Conference.* In the 1930s the Civilian Conservation Corps helped speed up trail construction. When it was completed and opened in August 1937, it connected two national parks and eight national forests across a lot of private land. Later development, land sales, and other problems have forced changes: More than 200 miles of the trail were moved from the forest to the roads, and the southern end had to be moved from Mt. Oglethorpe (Georgia), 20 miles north to Springer Mountain, its current southern terminus.

The 1968 National Trails System Act made the Appalachian Trail a linear unit of the National Park System and authorized funds to surround the entire route with public lands (either federal or state) that were protected from incompatible uses. This legislation made the National Park Service a major partner with the Appalachian Trail Conference, whose headquarters are at Harper's Ferry, Va. In the summer of 1993, the trail was nearly 98 percent protected, with only 47.3 miles left to go. David N. Startzell, executive director of the Appalachian Trail Conference, reported in July 1993 that only about 430 tracts of land remained to be acquired, of which about 40 would have to go to eminent domain condemnation proceedings to be acquired. Only in New Jersey is the trail completely protected. In Maryland, 20 percent of the trail's right-of-way is threatened by encroaching residential development. The other state with a sizable portion of the unprotected trail is Connecticut.

The trail hugs the crest of the Appalachian Mountains and is open only to hikers. The main recreational uses are short- and long-term hiking, camping, backcountry use, and bird and wildlife watching. About 175 people each year hike the entire trail, while millions find inspiration and adventure on shorter trips. Most long-distance hikers start in late March or April and take 5 to 6 months to hike the entire trail, usually from south to north. (One is ill-advised to go the opposite direction, for the snow in Maine, New Hampshire, and Vermont reaches its greatest depths at this time.) The only visitor facilities on the trail are lean-to-shelters, fire pits, and picnic tables. Shelters are spaced at convenient distances for overnight stays. Camping permits are needed in Great Smoky Mountains and Shenandoah National Parks. There are youth hostels, church-related hostels, and other sleeping accommodations along certain sections of the trail. The only meals served along the trail are provided in some national parks and in the unique hut system operated in the White Mountain National Forest, where both shelter and food is provided.

The trail starts on Mt. Katahdin (5267 ft.) in north-central Maine and passes through its most remote section of 120 miles without a road crossing. Hikers should

be aware of the insect pests[2] and deep snows that can occur along much of the trail. In New Hampshire, a lot of the trail is above timberline and passes over the spectacular Presidential Range (Mt. Washington, at 6288 ft.). In Vermont the trail follows the lower 101.3 miles of the Long Trail along the crest of the Green Mountains south of Sherburne Pass (Killington Peak, 4241 ft.). In Massachusetts the trail passes over Mt. Greylock (3491 ft.) and follows the Taconic Range into Connecticut. In Connecticut, New York, and New Jersey the trail is less wild than to the north and frequented more. It crosses the Hudson River at the Bear Mountain Bridge. Along New Jersey's Kittatinny Ridge the trail becomes more primitive again. As far west as the Susquehanna River the trail follows the easternmost ridge of the Alleghenies in Pennsylvania. Ten miles beyond this river it crosses the Cumberland Valley, where much cultivation occurs. In Maryland it follows the ridge crest of South Mountain and joins the Chesapeake and Ohio Canal towpath at the Potomac River.

At Harper's Ferry it crosses the Potomac River into West Virginia, and then shortly crosses the Shenandoah River back into Virginia. The trail passes through 100 miles of Shenandoah National Park and crosses Skyline Drive 32 times. South of Shenandoah National Park the trail roughly parallels the Blue Ridge Parkway and crosses it twice. Remote stretches occur in the Jefferson and George Washington National Forests. The trail touches West Virginia again, near the Bluestone National Scenic River. Shortly after passing over 5729-foot Mt. Rogers, it passes into the Cherokee National Forest of Tennessee. The trail then passes back and forth along the Tennessee–North Carolina border (Pisgah National Forest). The highest-elevation portion of the trail occurs in the 70-mile section through Great Smoky Mountains National Park. Upon leaving Great Smoky Mountains, it passes through North Carolina's Nantahala National Forest in a very rugged and high-elevation section. In Georgia the trail is entirely within the Chattahoochee National Forest to its end (or beginning) at Springer Mountain (elevation 3782 ft.).

NATIONAL PARKWAYS

National parkways encompass ribbons of land flanking roadways and offer an opportunity for leisurely driving through areas of scenic interest. They are not designed for high-speed travel. Besides the areas set aside as national parkways, other units of the National Park System include parkways within their boundaries, such as the Skyline Drive in Shenandoah National Park. The Skyline Drive served as the prototype for the Blue Ridge Parkway. Automobile parkways originated in Westchester County, N.Y., during the second decade of the century. Early parkways on federal land in the Capital District were the 4-mile Rock Creek and Potomac Parkway (classified now as a component of National Capital Parks) and Mount Vernon Parkway

---

[2]In early June 1972, the author gave a ride to one of his students from the University of Illinois to Plattsburgh, N.Y. This student was headed to Mt. Katahdin to hike the entire Appalachian Trail, and he had never heard of black flies. The poor fellow was chewed into raw meat at the end of the first 120-mile section of the trail when he emerged at Monson, Me. He dejectedly headed back to Champaign-Urbana at this point.

(incorporated into George Washington Memorial Parkway). Colonial Parkway (now part of Colonial National Historical Park) was a scenic 23-mile drive between Jamestown and Yorktown, Virginia. These parkways primarily served local traffic. Authorization of the Blue Ridge Parkway in 1933 and the Natchez Trace Parkway in 1934 marked a new type of parkway, one that protected recreational roads and traversed long stretches of scenic and historic rural landscapes. Both parkways were begun as New Deal works projects and were soon made units of the National Park System. Table 6.6 presents statistical analyses of the four national parkways, which comprise 161,355 acres of the National Park System.

The George Washington Memorial Parkway runs along the Potomac River front from Mount Vernon to Great Falls and links landmarks in the life of George Washington. The parkway was authorized in 1930 and transferred to the National Park Service in 1933. In 1989 the Maryland portion between I-495 and Chain Bridge was renamed the Clara Barton Parkway. Boundary changes occurred in 1947, 1965, and 1976. The parkway occupies 7089 acres. In 1991 there were 5.0 million recreation visits or 0.6 million recreation visitor days. The high ratio of visits to visitor days (8.37) indicates that it is primarily a drive-through road. Most of the visitors are heading from the nation's capital to Mount Vernon. There are picnic tables, walkways, and bike paths along the way.

The Natchez Trace Parkway generally follows the old Indian trace (trail) between Nashville, Tenn., and Natchez, Miss., passing through the northwestern corner of Alabama. Of its estimated 445 miles, 415 are completed. It is an especially pleasant bicycle route. Construction funds were authorized in 1934, and it was established as a parkway under National Park Service administration in 1938. It contains 51,651 acres and recorded 5.8 million recreation visits (2.0 million recreation visitor days) in 1991. It is the least crowded of the parkways, with 0.026 acres per recreation visitor day.

The scenic, 82-mile corridor of the John D. Rockefeller Memorial Parkway links West Thumb in Yellowstone National Park and the South Entrance of Grand Teton National Park. It commemorates Rockefeller's role in establishing many national parks, including Grand Teton. The parkway was authorized in 1972, and all 23,777 acres are federal. Its primarily drive-through nature is indicated by a ratio of 6.97 for recreation visits to recreation visitor days in 1991 (1.6 million recreation visits and 0.23 million recreation visitor days). There is a campsite at Snake River and a concessioner-operated resort at Flagg Ranch.

Table 6.6   National Parkway Analysis

Parkway	State	Size (Acres)	Recreation Visits (000's)	Recreation Visitor Days (000's)	Visit/Visitor Day Ratio	Acres/ Visitor Day
Blue Ridge Parkway	NC, VA	78,837.80	16,414.30	8,677.70	1.89	0.009
Natchez Trace Parkway	MS, AL, TN	51,651.10	5,832.70	1,958.40	2.98	0.026
John D. Rockerfeller, Jr., Memorial Parkway	WY	23,777.20	1,576.80	226.10	6.97	0.105
George Washington Memorial Parkway	VA, MD	7,088.60	5,004.70	598.10	8.37	0.012
Total		161,354.70	28,828.50	11,460.30	2.52	0.014

Source: Calculated by the author.

The fourth national parkway, the Blue Ridge Parkway, will be the case study in this section.

Blue Ridge

This scenic, 469-mile parkway follows the crest of the Blue Ridge Mountains and averages 3000 feet above sea level. It links Shenandoah National Park (Virginia) with Great Smoky Mountains National Park (North Carolina) and is the longest scenic drive in the world. Along its way it embraces several large recreational and historical areas and Appalachian cultural sites. The initial construction funds were authorized in 1933, and in 1936 it was established by act as a unit of the National Park System. Boundary changes occurred in 1961 and 1968. It contains 78,838 federal acres. *This is the most visited unit of the National Park System.* In 1991 the number of recreation visits (16.4 million) was double that of the next most visited unit, Great Smoky Mountains National Park. This parkway was also the leading unit in 1991 in terms of recreation visitor days; its 8.7 million recreation visitor days exceeded even those for Yellowstone and Yosemite. Of the national parkways, it receives the longest period of use per visitor, with a 1.89 ratio of recreation visits to recreational visitor days. It is the most heavily used of the parkways not only in terms of total recreational use but also in terms of density of recreational use, with only 0.009 acres per recreation visitor day in 1991.

The parkway follows the Appalachian Mountain chain and provides seemingly endless views of many parallel ranges connected by cross ranges and scattered hills. It starts immediately south of I-64 near Waynesboro, Va., at Rockfish Gap (mile 0, elevation 1900 feet) and follows the Blue Ridge—the eastern rampart of the Appalachians—for 355 miles, 217 of which are in Virginia. For the last 114 miles it skirts the massive Black Mountains, passes through the Craggies, the Pisgahs, and the Balsams, and ends in the Great Smokies, at U.S. 441 in Great Smoky Mountains National Park (mile 469). Elevations range from 649 feet at the James River (mile 64) to 6053 feet at Richland Balsam (mile 431) (Figure 6.8). Large areas of the southern section of the parkway are especially impressive with their continual high elevation: Long sections stay above 5000 feet. Heavy snows at the high elevations in the south can close the parkway in the winter. At Black Mountain Gap (mile 355, elevation 5160 ft.), a side road leads to Mt. Mitchell State Park. At 6684 feet, Mt. Mitchell is the highest point east of the Mississippi River. Because of the large altitudinal differences along the parkway, the vegetation and wildlife varies. While most of the parkway is essentially deciduous forest, a dark green forest of spruce and fir occurs in the higher elevations of North Carolina. Flowering shrubs, such as rhododendron and flame azalea, put on remarkable displays, with peak displays occurring in mid-June in the higher elevations of North Carolina and a month earlier in Virginia's lower elevations. Craggy Gardens (miles 363–370) has an especially superb display of purple rhododendron in mid-June. At Devil's Courthouse (mile 422, elevation 5462 ft.) a short walk takes you to a bare rock summit from which a spectacular view of the mountains of the Pisgah National Forest may be seen. In the fall the varied hardwood deciduous forest puts on a dazzling display of color. A variety of wildlife may be observed including black bear, deer, bobcat, fox, and raccoon.

Recreational opportunities along the parkway are varied: auto tours, wildlife and wild flower observations, camping, exhibits, picnicking, hiking, camping, fishing, in-

Figure 6.8 The highest elevation (6053 ft.) on the Blue Ridge Parkway occurs at mile 431 at Richland Balsam. A boreal forest vegetation (spruce and fir) occurs here.

terpretive walks and talks, and craft demonstrations and sales. Around every bend there is a scenic pull-off. Although the maximum speed limit is 45 miles per hour, the scenic views and mountainous terrain dictate slow travel. Averaging 30 miles an hour, even when the traffic is light, for through-driving with no stops is considered good time.[3] The history of the southern highland culture is told at many overlooks and facilities along the parkway, including Humpback Rocks (miles 5–9), Peaks of Otter (miles 84–87), Mabry Mill (mile 176), Brinegar Cabin (mile 239), Northwest Trading Post (mile 259), and the Parkway Craft Center at Moses Cone Memorial Park (miles 292–295). Year-round lodging is offered on the parkway at Peaks of Otter Lodge and from May through October at four other lodges. There are nine campgrounds located along the parkway that are open from May 1 until late October or early November, depending on the weather. Along the parkway there are several picnic grounds with tables, fireplaces, drinking water, trash cans, and comfort stations. Several parking overlooks also have picnic tables. There are endless walking and hiking trails along the parkway. Many miles of excellent trails are at Peaks of Otter, Rocky Knob, Doughton Park, and at Cone and Price Memorial Parks.

HISTORICAL UNITS

Nearly half (47 percent) of the 357-unit National Park System is comprised of units that are either classified as "historical" or are historical national monuments. The first group (142 units) includes: an international historic site (1 unit), national battlefields

[3]On the author's first visit to the Parkway in 1968 he averaged 5 miles per hour. The Blue Ridge Parkway is a road designed for low speed, leisurely driving. If you are in a hurry, don't drive the Parkway. Use I-81 instead, which is nearby to the west and parallels the parkway.

(11 units), national battlefield parks (3 units), a national battlefield site (1 unit), national historic sites (69 units), national historical parks (31 units), and national memorials (26 units). Geographically, a disproportionate number of these 142 relatively small historical units are located in the East. The second group consists of 25 of the 81 national monuments that are not classified as historical but nevertheless are historical in nature; many of these are in the West. The total acreage of the 142 units is only 170,435 acres (0.2 percent of the National Park System total), and the total acreage of historical national monuments is 80,098 acres (0.1 percent of the system). The average size of a classified historical unit is 1200 acres, and the average size of a historical national monument is 3204 acres. The recreational use made of these historical areas, however, is disproportionately large relative to size. The 142 units classified as historical received 59.1 million recreation visits (23 percent of the system) or 6.5 million recreation visitor days (6 percent of the system) in 1991. The 25 historical national monuments received 13.7 million recreation visits (5.4 percent of the system) or 1.9 million recreation visitor days (1.7 percent of the system) in 1991. Visits to both kinds of historical areas are primarily short, with recreation-visit-to-recreation-visitor-day ratios of 9.1 and 7.2, respectively. The 142 historical areas received a high intensity of use. Their acres per recreation visitor day statistic is 0.026, compared with 0.042 for the historical national monuments.

Five case studies will be employed here to characterize the historical units: Lyndon B. Johnson National Historical Park; Saratoga National Historical Park; Gettysburg National Military Park; Jefferson National Expansion Memorial; and Jimmy Carter National Historic Site. National historical parks are commonly areas of greater physical extent and complexity than national historic sites. In recent years, "national historic site" has been the title most commonly applied by Congress in authorizing the addition of such areas to the national Park System. Table 6.7 presents the statistics for these five case studies.

Lyndon B. Johnson National Historical Park

This park consists of the birthplace, boyhood home, and ranch of our 36th President (1963–1969) along with his grandparents' log cabin and the Johnson family cemetery. It is located in the Texas Hill Country, 60 miles north of San Antonio and 50 miles west of Austin. It was designated a national historic site in 1969 and redesignated a

Table 6.7   Historical Area Analysis

Historic Site	State	Size (Acres)	Recreation Visits (000's)	Recreation Visitor Days (000's)	Visit/Visitor Day Ratio	Acres/ Visitor Day
Jimmy Carter National Historic Site	GA	0.00	34.30	1.40	24.50	0.000
Jefferson National Expansion Memorial	MO	91.00	2,622.40	218.50	12.00	0.000
Saratoga National Historical Park	NY	2,847.70	169.90	23.70	7.17	0.120
Gettysburg National Military Park	PA	3,699.20	1,415.80	356.40	3.97	0.010
Lyndon B. Johnson National Historical Park	TX	550.10	194.20	45.50	4.27	0.012
Total		7,188.00	4,436.60	645.50	6.87	0.011

Source: Calculated by the author.

national historical park in 1980. The park consists of two distinct areas: the LBJ Ranch and Johnson City, which is 15 miles east of the ranch. Of the park's 1572 total acres, only 550 acres are federal. This park has a unique relationship with the adjacent Lyndon B. Johnson State Historical Park. The state park consists of 700 acres and is on the south side of the Pedernales River, while the LBJ Ranch is on the north side of the river (Figure 6.9). The visitor center for both parks is located in the state park, and the bus tours for the LBJ Ranch unit of the national historical park start at the state park. Together, the two parks interpret the Texas Hill Country, its influence on Lyndon Johnson, and the life of the President. To a degree unparalleled among presidential parks, they are a physical documentation of the origins, ancestry, and full life span of a president. There were 194,200 recreation visits, or 45,500 recreation visitor days, in 1991.

In Johnson City, the principal points of interest are the Boyhood Home of Lyndon Johnson and the Johnson Settlement. A visitor center provides information about the park, exhibits, and publications. It is a short walk from the Boyhood Home to the nearby Johnson Settlement. This complex of restored historic structures traces the evolution of the Texas Hill Country from the open- range cattle kingdom of Lyndon Johnson's grandfather, Sam Early Johnson, to the local ranching and farming of more recent times.

To visit the LBJ Ranch unit, which is 15 miles west of Johnson City on U.S. 290, one must first go to the Lyndon B. Johnson State Historical Park Visitor Center. Access to the LBJ Ranch unit is only by National Park Service guided tour bus, which departs from and returns to the state park. There are two stops along the ranch tour, where visitors can depart from the bus (Figure 6.10). The tour includes the one-room country school first attended by Lyndon at age 4, his reconstructed birthplace, the Johnson family cemetery, where the president is buried, and various views of the ranch and

Figure 6.9 The LBJ Ranch House is located in the grove of trees on the far side of the Pedernales River in Lyndon B. Johnson National Historical Park.

Figure 6.10   National Park Service–operated trams at one of the stops at Lyndon B. Johnson National Historical Park.

its registered Hereford cattle. In the summer of 1994, Mrs. Johnson was still alive and living at the ranch, which is guarded by the Secret Service. The tour bus passes next to the ranch house, but does not stop. Along the tour the Park Service personnel play tapes of segments of famous speeches made by President Johnson.[4] The humble nature of Lyndon Johnson is reflected in the simple cemetery under the live oaks on the banks of the Pedernales River, with his pet beagles buried nearby.

On the adajcent state park of the same name, there is a visitor center with exhibits and programs. On display here also are the pens President Johnson used to sign a large number of public laws. Particularly impressive is the large number of signing pens for amenity resource–related laws, many of which form the basis for the amenity resources that are protected and used for recreation and the subject of this book. Among them are the Wilderness Act (1964), the Land and Water Conservation Fund Act (1965), the National Trails System Act (1968), and the Wild and Scenic Rivers Act (1968). Attached to the visitor center is the Behrens Cabin, a two-room dogtrot cabin built by a German immigrant in the 1870s. A nature trail includes a Hill Country botanical exhibit and winds past wildlife enclosures stocked with bison, white-tailed deer, wild turkey, and other native wildlife and Texas longhorn cattle. The Sauer-Beckmann Farmstead, located east of the visitor center and off the nature trail, is an operating historical farm. Life on the farmstead is depicted as it was during the time of World War I. Park interpreters in period clothing do the farm and household chores as they were done 80 years ago and also conduct tours for the visitors.

---

[4]The most moving experience this author has had at any National Park System unit was listening to portions of one of these speeches, in which, the president expressed his love for the ranch on the Pedernales; Johnson recounted how he could "think more clearly, where the air is cleaner and the stars are brighter."

Recreational facilities are available at the state park for swimming, hiking, picnicking, and nature study. An Olympic-sized swimming pool, covered pavilion, and children's wading pool create an entertainment complex for warm-weather recreation. Two picnic areas have been built with native limestone, and some of the tables are covered by cedar-shingled roofs. The picnic tables along the bank of the Pedernales are in a particularly scenic location. Also available to the park visitor are two tennis courts, a lighted baseball diamond, one enclosed group picnic area, and an open-air picnic area.

Saratoga National Historical Park

The American victory in Old Saratoga, N.Y., over the British in the fall of 1777 was the turning point of the American Revolution and one of the most decisive battles in world history. This victory earned the support of France, Holland, and Spain for the cause of the American Revolution. The park was authorized in 1938, and there was a boundary change in 1983. It is located on U.S. 4, 30 miles north of Albany, N.Y. Eight miles north of the main portion of the park, at Schuylerville (Old Saratoga), is Maj. Gen. Philip Schuyler's 25-acre country home and the 155-foot Saratoga Monument. The park contains 2848 acres. In 1991, 169,900 recreation visits or 23,700 recreation visitor days were recorded.

The Hudson River was the centerpiece of British General John Burgoyne's campaign in 1777, which called for his army of 4200 British "redcoats," 4000 German "blue coats," and several hundred Canadians and Indians to move south from Canada to Albany. His army crossed the Hudson and arrived at Saratoga (now Schuylerville) on September 13. Support he had expected from Col. Barry St. Leger failed to materialize, so he began marching south again. Four miles north of the village of Stillwater he came upon a Colonial force of 9000 under the command of Gen. Horatio Gates. The Americans were entrenched on Bemis Heights, a strong position where the road to Albany squeezed through a defile between the hills and the river, as does today's U.S. 4. Thaddeus Kosciuszko, a Polish military engineer serving with the Americans, had chosen and fortified the site. In a series of battles fought on the site of the present-day park between September 19 and October 7, the British situation deteriorated. On the night of October 8 the British began their retreat northward and took refuge in a fortified camp on the heights of Saratoga. Here the American force grew to 20,000 and surrounded the exhausted British army. Faced with such overwhelming numbers, Burgoyne surrendered on October 17, 1777. Thus was gained one of the most decisive victories in U.S. and world history. The 155-foot Saratoga Monument commemorates Burgoyne's surrender to Gates. It was erected in 1883 and stands within what was Burgoyne's entrenched camp during the final days of the campaign. A panoramic view exists from the top floor, although it was closed in 1994 because of structural deterioration.

The visitor center is located in the northwestern corner of the park. It may be accessed by the park entrance road, which runs west from U.S. 4, or from N.Y. 32 on the western side. The visitor center sits on Fraser Hill, which is the highest point in the park. There are visual programs, talks, exhibits, and picnic facilities here. Craft and weapon demonstrations are given by park employees in period dress during the summer at various locations. A 10 mile driving-and-walking interpretive tour begins

Figure 6.11 Bicyclers at the Great Redoubt above the Hudson River at Saratoga National Historical Park.

at the visitor center. There are 10 stops alone this one-way route that interpret the battles of Saratoga, which occurred between September 19 and October 17, 1777: Freeman Farm Overlook, Neilson Farm (Bemis Heights), American River Fortifications, Chatfield Farm, Barber Wheatfield, Balcarres Redoubt (Freeman Farm), Breymann Redoubt, Burgoyne's Headquarters, The Great Redoubt Camp, and Fraser Burial Site and Trail. There is a steep 1-mile-loop hiking trail and picnic facilities at the Fraser Burial Site stop. The historic 1777 road system is gradually being turned into hiking trails. The park is very popular among cyclists (Figure 6.11). The park is open for skiing in the winter; snowmobiles are not allowed.

Gettysburg National Military Park

This park commemorates the greatest battle of the Civil War, which was fought near Gettysburg, Penn., on July 1–3, 1863. The second Confederate invasion of the North under Gen. Robert E. Lee was repulsed in this battle, in which more men fell than in any battle ever fought in North America (51,000 men were killed, wounded, or missing). The victorious Union general was George G. Meade. Many of the Union solders who died here are buried in the adjoining 20.6-acre National Cemetery, which was dedicated by President Abraham Lincoln's 2-minute, 272-word *Gettysburg Address* on November 19, 1863. This cemetery contains 7000 interments from this battle, 1668 of which have been unidentified. The park was established in 1895 and transferred from the War Department to the National Park Service in the 1933 reorganization. There were boundary changes in 1948, 1953, and 1974. The park contains 3699 acres and had 1,415,800 recreation visits (356,400 recreation visitor days) in 1991. The park virtually surrounds the town of Gettysburg on all sides except the northeast. The East Cavalry Battlefield Site is detached and lies 1.5 miles to the east. The 690-

acre Eisenhower National Historic Site adjoins the park on the southwest. This farm was the only home ever owned by General Dwight D. Eisenhower and his wife, Mamie. It served as a refuge when he was president and as a retirement home after he left office.

Recreational opportunities here include auto tours, Ranger-conducted walks and talks, living history and campfire programs, hiking, biking, jogging, picnicking, and cross-country skiing in winter. Camping is available only for organized groups from mid-April to mid-October. An 18-mile self-guided auto tour traces the 3-day battle in chronological order. It begins at the visitor center, passes through Gettysburg, and takes about 3 hours to complete. At most of the numbered stops, markers describe significant action during the 3 days of battle. Auto tours conducted for a fee by licensed battlefield guides also begin at the visitor center. The visitor center and the Gettysburg Museum of the Civil War have orientation displays, Civil War exhibits, and the famous Electric Map, which shows, through the use of colored lights, troop movements during the battle. The Cyclorama Center has exhibits, a free film, and the Gettysburg Cyclorama, a spectacular painting by Paul Philippoteaux of Major Gen. George E. Pickett's charge, displayed with a light-and-sound program inside the large circular auditorium. The use of bicycles is encouraged in the park, and there is a variety of hiking trails. The best way to see the land is to walk the battlefield. The High Water Mark Trail is about 1 mile long and begins at the Cyclorama Center. It includes regimental monuments, part of an artillery battery, the ground defended by Union soldiers who repulsed Pickett's charge, and General Meade's headquarters. On the 1-mile Big Round Top Loop Trail the plants, animals, and rocks of the Pennsylvania hardwood forest are revealed. Stone breastworks are still visible along this trail. Longer trails include the 9-mile Billy Yank and 3.5-mile Johnny Reb Trails. There is a wide selection of food and lodging establishments in the town of Gettysburg.

Jefferson National Expansion Memorial

This memorial on St. Louis' Mississippi riverfront commemorates Thomas Jefferson and others who directed territorial expansion of the United States. Westward expansion and pioneers are commemorated by Eero Saarinen's prize-winning stainless steel Gateway Arch. The 91-acre memorial sits on the original site of the first settlement in St. Louis. The arch is the tallest human-made monument in the United States, being 75 feet higher than the Washington Monument. This memorial was the first secretarial designation (1935) under the Historic Sites Act of 1935. The designated area, encompassing 37 blocks on the riverfront, was the first extensive urban responsibility of the Park Service outside of Washington, D.C. It is ironic that the designation was made to justify federal expenditures for urban renewal and a modern memorial to western expansion, rather than historic preservation. It was not until 1954 that the memorial was authorized. Most of the area was bulldozed and the soaring Gateway Arch was erected from 1962 to 1965. Of the gross area of 191 acres, only 91 are federal. There was a boundary change in 1969. The memorial received 2,622,400 recreation visits (218,500 recreation visitor days) in 1991. The ratio of 12.0 for visits to visitor days indicate that the average visit is quite short.

The 630-foot arch is the dominating structure of the memorial (Figure 6.12). It traces the lines of a catenary curve, and is constructed of stainless steel equilateral

Figure 6.12   The Gateway Arch towers above the St. Louis skyline at Jefferson National Expansion Memorial.

triangles that range in size from 54 feet on a side (at the base) to 17 feet (at the top).[5] The Museum of Westward Expansion is located in a vast chamber beneath the arch. The exhibit is organized by themes that fan out chronologically from a central bronze statue of Thomas Jefferson. Two passenger trams, one in each leg, carry visitors to the top of the arch. Each tram has eight capsules that hold five passengers each. Passengers board the trams in the base of each leg for the 4-minute ride to the top. A jerky, self-adjusting system keeps the capsule level as they ascend and descend. In the top of the arch there is an observation room 6'9" high, 7'2" wide, and 65 feet long; it can hold 100 people. From it may be seen a panoramic view of St. Louis and the Mississippi riverfront. One should be cautioned that waits of an hour or more to ride the tram are common. Also included in the memorial is the Old Courthouse (built 1839), where Dred Scott sued for freedom in the historic slavery case, and the Old Cathedral (built 1831). The green lawns of the memorial provide a very pleasant open space within walking distance of downtown St. Louis and is the sight of many events and concerts.

Jimmy Carter National Historic Site

The rural southern culture of Plains, Ga., which evolves around farming, church, and school, had a large influence in molding the character and in shaping the political policies of the 39th president of the United States (1977–1981). This site, which was authorized in 1987, includes President Carter's residence, boyhood home, and high

---

[5]It was an amazing sight to watch the construction of this arch between 1962 and 1965. The north and south legs of the arch were each raised independently, remaining at the same height. The author, and most other residents of St. Louis, wondered how they would ever meet.

school. The railroad depot, which served as campaign headquarters during the 1976 election, is now the site's visitor center. The Jimmy Carter National Preservation District, separate from the historic site, includes part of the town of Plains and its environs. The area surrounding the Carter residence is under the protection of the Secret Service, and no attempt should be made to enter. There are limited federal facilities, and the 70 acres of the site are all nonfederal. The site is not heavily visited, with only 34,300 visits (1400 visitor days) in 1991, although this number does increase the traffic significantly in a town of 700 people. A self-guiding tour begins at the railroad depot at the corner of Hudson and Main Streets. The depot contains original furniture, photographs, and other memorabilia and presents a 15-minute video. Additional stops on the tour include the former president's boyhood homes, his high school, and the softball field where he and his brother Billy played on rival teams during the White House years. The Carters still live in Plains, but their home is not open to the public.

OTHER AREAS

There are 13 units of the National Park System that do not fit into the major classification categories that have been discussed earlier in this chapter and in Chapters 3, 4 and 5. Table 6.8 lists these areas and presents their statistical analysis. This last section of this chapter will highlight these areas. Six are in the District of Columbia, of which three are relatively small parks, one is a large park, one consists of a complex of parks, and one is a performing arts center. Four other areas are parks close by in Maryland, and two others (a large park and a performing arts center) are nearby in Virginia. The final "other" unit is a scenic area in Idaho. Collectively, these 13 areas comprise 44,572 acres of the National Park System and received 15,371,800 recreation

Table 6.8   Other Areas in the National Park System

Areas	State	Size (Acres)	Recreation Visits (000's)	Recreation Visitor Days (000's)	Visit/Visitor Day Ratio	Acres/ Visitor Day
Catoctin Mountain Park	MD	5,770.20	581.40	199.30	2.92	0.029
City of Rocks National Reserve	ID	7,001.20	NA	NA	NA	NA
Constitution Gardens	DC	52.00	NA	NA	NA	NA
Fort Washington Park	MD	341.00	349.70	111.10	3.15	0.003
Greenbelt Park	MD	1,176.00	249.20	80.30	3.10	0.015
John F. Kennedy Center for the Performing Arts	DC	17.50	3,401.90	547.00	6.22	0.000
National Capital Parks	DC	6,467.90	7,530.40	969.10	7.77	0.007
National Mall	DC	146.40				
Piscataway Park	MD	4,216.50	164.50	27.40	6.00	0.154
Prince William Forest Park	VA	17,410.30	290.70	217.30	1.34	0.080
Rock Creek Park	DC	1,754.40	2,155.80	319.40	6.75	0.005
Theodore Roosevelt Island	DC	88.50	50.70	7.60	6.67	0.012
Wolf Trap Farm Park for the Performing Arts	VA	130.30	597.50	170.30	3.51	0.001
Total		44,572.20	15,371.80	2,648.80	5.80	0.017

Source: Calculated by the author.

visits (2,648,800 recreation visitor days) in 1991. Most of this recreational use occurs at just three of these units.

Six of these "other areas" are in the District of Columbia. *Constitution Gardens* is a 52-acre park constructed during the American Revolution Bicentennial and authorized in 1978. On an island in a lake is a memorial to the 56 signers of the Declaration of Independence. *Theodore Roosevelt Island* is an 88.5-acre wooded island sanctuary of the Potomac River, where a trail leads to an imposing statue of Roosevelt, the conservation-minded 26th president. His tenets on nature, manhood, youth, and the state are inscribed on tablets. This unit was transferred to the National Park Service in 1933 and was authorized in 1932. The *National Mall* is a 146-acre landscaped park extending from the Capitol to the Washington Monument. It was delineated in Pierre L'Enfant's plan for the city of Washington and approved in 1790, except for 42 acres which were transferred later from other agencies. The National Park Service assumed jurisdiction in 1933. *Rock Creek Park* contains 1754 acres and is one of the largest urban parks in the United States. This wooded preserve contains a wide range of natural, historical, and recreational features in the midst of Washington. It was authorized in 1890 and transferred to the National Park Service in 1933. It is an important recreational resource in the nation's capital, with 2,155,800 recreation visits (319,400 recreation visitor days) in 1991. The park system of *National Capital Parks* comprises 300 parks, parkways, and reservations in the District of Columbia. It includes such properties as the Battleground National Cemetery, the President's Parks (Lafayette Park north of the White House and the Ellipse south of the White House), a variety of military fortifications, and green areas. The Park Service assumed administrative responsibility for these areas in 1933. Heavy recreational use is made of its total acreage of 6468 acres. There were 7,530,400 recreation visits (969,100 recreation visitor days) in 1991. The *John F. Kennedy Center for the Performing Arts* occupies 15.5 acres and was authorized as a natural cultural center in 1958, but had it name changed in 1964. Plays, concerts, films, opera, and ballet are featured. In 1972 the nonperforming arts functions were transferred from the Smithsonian Institution to the National Park Service. Again, heavy recreational use is made of this unit, with 3,401,900 recreation visits (547,000 recreation visitor days) in 1991. The *White House* which occupies 18 acres, is also a unit of the National Park System in Washington.

Four of the other units are in Maryland. *Catoctin Mountain Park* is located 50 miles northwest of Washington, D.C. It is part of the forested ridge that forms the eastern rampart of the Appalachian Mountains in Maryland. This mountain park of 5770 acres has sparkling streams and panoramic vistas of the Monocacy Valley. It was originally called Catoctin Recreation Demonstration Area and was transferred to the National Park Service in 1936. It was given its present name in 1954, when a boundary change also occurred. *Fort Washington Park*, across the Potomac from Mount Vernon, was built to protect the city of Washington. Construction on this fort was begun in 1814 to replace a previous one destroyed during the War of 1812. This 341-acre site has recreational facilities. Transfer to the National Park Service was authorized in 1930 and became effective in 1940. *Greenbelt Park* is just 12 miles from Washington, D.C. This 1176-acre woodland park offers urban dwellers access to many forms of outdoor recreation, including camping all year. Its administration was transferred to the National Park Service in 1950. *Piscataway Park* is a pilot project in the

use of easements to protect park lands from obtrusive urban expansion; its 4216 acres protect the view of the Maryland shore seen from Mount Vernon. It was authorized in 1961, with boundary changes occurring in 1966 and 1976.

Two vastly different types of "other" units are located in Virginia. *Prince William Forest Park* is located 25 miles south-southwest of Washington, D.C. The pine and hardwood forests of this 17,410-acre park in the Quantico Creek watershed have hiking trails, campgrounds, playing fields, and five Civilian Conservation Corps–era cabins. It was originally called the Chopawamsic Recreation Demonstration Area and was transferred to the National Park Service in 1936; it assumed its present name in 1948. *Wolf Trap Farm Park for the Performing Arts* is located 15 miles west of Washington, D.C. Here, the Filene Center can accommodate an audience of 6786, including 3000 on the sloping lawn in a setting of rolling hills and woods. The stage house is 13 stories high, and the stage itself is 125 feet wide and 60 feet deep. Wolf Trap is a showcase for opera, jazz, modern dance, ballet, and symphony concerts. When it was authorized in 1966 on 130 acres, it was our first national park for the performing arts. Top-name artists have performed here; for example, in August 1993, Reba McEntire, Dionne Warwick, the Temptations, Anne Murray, and Willie Nelson, among others, were featured.

The last of these "other" areas in the National Park System is in Idaho—*City of Rocks National Reserve*. "National reserve" was a new category in the system when it was authorized in 1988, and to date it is the only one so classified. This category is similar to "national preserve," except that management is by local or state authorities. In City of Rocks National Reserve scenic granite spires and sculptured rock formations dominate the landscape. It is located in extreme southern Idaho, 50 miles southeast of Twin Falls, near the point where Idaho, Nevada, and Utah meet. Remnants of the California Trail are still visible in the area. Recreatonal opportunities include rock climbing and camping; the federal facilities are limited. Of its 14,407 acres, 7001 acres are federal. It is administered cooperatively by the National Park Service and the Idaho Department of Parks and Recreation.

References

National Park Service. *Appalachian Trail.* Gridmap Official Map and Guide. Washington, D.C.

National Park Service. *Big Thicket National Preserve.* Gridmap Official Map and Guide. Washington, D.C.

National Park Service. *Blue Ridge Parkway.* Gridmap Official Map and Guide. Washington, D.C.

National Park Service. *Death Valley National Monument.* Gridmap Official Map and Guide. Washington, D.C.

National Park Service. *Gateway National Recreation Area.* Gridmap Official Map and Guide. Washington, D.C.

National Park Service. *Gettysburg National Military Park.* Gridmap Official Map and Guide. Washington, D.C.

National Park Service. *Jefferson National Expansion Memorial.* Gridmap Official Map and Guide. Washington, D.C.

National Park Service. *Lake Mead National Recreation Area.* Gridmap Official Map and Guide. Washington, D.C.

National Park Service. *Lyndon B. Johnson National Historical Park.* Gridmap Official Map and Guide. Washington, D.C.

National Park Service. *Montezuma/Tuzigoot National Monuments.* Gridmap Official Map and Guide. Washington, D.C.

National Park Service. *Ozark National Scenic Riverways.* Gridmap Official Map and Guide. Washington, D.C.

National Park Service. *Padre Island National Seashore.* Gridmap Official Map and Guide. Washington, D.C.

National Park Service. *Saguaro National Monument.* Gridmap Official Map and Guide. Washington, D.C.

National Park Service. *Saratoga National Historical Park.* Gridmap Official Map and Guide. Washington, D.C.

National Park Service. *Sleeping Bear Dunes National Lakeshore.* Gridmap Official Map and Guide. Washington, D.C.

National Park Service. *Statue of Liberty National Monument.* Gridmap Official Map and Guide. Washington, D.C.

National Park Service. *Wolf Trap Farm Park for the Performing Arts Brochure.* 1993.

Schroeder, Albert H., and Homer F. Hastings. *Montezuma Castle.* Washington, D.C.: Division of Publications, National Park Service, 1954 (Reprint 1985).

Shelton, Napier. *Saguaro National Monument.* Washington, D.C.: U.S. Government Printing Office, 1985.

Texas Parks and Wildlife Department. *Lyndon B. Johnson State Historical Park.*

Thornbury, William D. *Regional Geomorphology of the United States.* New York: John Wiley & Sons, 1965.

Weise, Bonnie R., and William A. White. *Padre Island National Seashore: A Guide to the Geology, National Environments, and History of a Texas Barrier Island.* Austin: University of Texas, 1980.

## CHAPTER 7

National Forest System: Evolution and Extent

So great is the value of the national forest area for recreation, and so certain is this value to increase with the growth of the country and the shrinkage of the wilderness, that even if the forest resources of wood and water were not to be required by the civilization of the future, many of the forests ought certainly to be preserved, in the interest of national health and well-being, for recreation use alone.

Treadwell Cleveland, Jr. (1910)

The National Forest System is the largest single supplier of public outdoor recreation in the nation, with recreational use amounting to 287.7 million recreation visitor days in 1992. This represented more than two-fifths of all recreational use on federal lands. The Forest Service has been referred to by some as the largest provider of recreation in the world. In 1992 the total recreational capacity within the National Forest System at one time was 1,844,821 people on 19,429 sites (Washington Office Computerized Data). The National Forest System covers 191,453,345 acres, making the Forest Service the second-largest land manager in the United States. Only the Bureau of Land Management (BLM) has more land under its administration (268,976,599 acres). The National Forest System covers 8.4 percent of the acreage of the entire United States and accounts for 28.9 percent of the federal total.

A broad range of outdoor recreation opportunities may be experienced on this land. The goal of recreational management on National Forest System lands is to provide outdoor recreation opportunities as a major component among the multiple uses of the forest, range, and related resources on these federal lands. This objective is accomplished by providing a wide range of recreational uses and facilities, including wilderness, dispersed recreation areas, developed recreation areas, visitor information services, and management of visual resources. Although the bulk of this system consists of lands that are designated "national forest," there are almost 4 million acres of land designated "national grassland." The remaining acreage is in land utilization projects, research and experimental areas, and other areas. Furthermore, there are a number of special categories; special management guidelines are applied to these lands. Thirty-four million acres of the National Wilderness Preservation System are also part of the National Forest System. Sixteen areas in the National Forest Sys-

tem have been designated national recreation areas. Thirty-eight rivers on National Forest System lands have been added as components to the Wild and Scenic Rivers System. There are 21 national game refuges and wildlife preserves. Other special categories include: two national monuments; two national volcanic monuments; one national primitive area; one national historic area; and one national scenic-research area. Table 7.1 presents selected statistics for the Forest Service and the National Forest System.

The lands of the National Forest System are found in 44 states, Puerto Rico, and the Virgin Islands. (Only Delaware, Iowa, Maryland, Massachusetts, New Jersey, and Rhode Island have no lands in the system.) This acreage is not evenly distributed, ranging from New York's 13,327 acres to Alaska's 22,193,395 acres. Seventy-five percent of the system is found in the Pacific and Mountain census regions, with most of the acreage in the Sierra Nevada, the Cascade Range, the Rocky Mountains, and southeastern Alaska. In the East, most of the acreage is in the Appalachians, the Northern Great Lakes, the Ouachitas, and the Ozarks. The Forest Service does not control all land within the boundaries of the system. Within the gross area boundaries of 231,501,923 acres are located 40,048,578 acres of inholdings of state, private, and other nonfederal land.

More controversy has focused on National Forest System lands than on the lands of any other federal agency in recent years. Much of this controversy today is focused on the old-growth forests of the Pacific Northwest. The basic argument stems from different philosophies of resource management and interpretation of multiple use–

Table 7.1   Forest Service—Selected Fiscal Year 1992 Statistics

National Forest System	191 million acres
Recreational use	288 million visitor days
Trail system	120,284 miles
National scenic byways	6000 miles
National Wild and Scenic Rivers System	4316 miles of National Forest System
Lands burned by wildfire	530,000 acres
Insect and disease suppression	1.7 million acres
Wilderness	34 million acres
Watershed improvements	36,201 acres
Wildlife and fish habitat improvements	242,761 acres
Reforestation	492,000 acres
Livestock grazing	9.4 million animal unit months
Grazing allotments administered	9940 permits
Mineral cases processed	26,539
Timber sold	4.4 billion board feet
Timber harvested	7.2 billion board feet
Road system	369,000 miles
Woodland owners assisted	190,211
Research results published	2673 publications
Permanent and excepted full-time employees	36,137
Human resource programs	142,468 persons served
Expenditures	$3.87 billion
Receipts	$1.39 billion

Source: Forest Service, *Report of the Forest Service—Fiscal Year 1992*, Washington, D.C.: U.S. Government Printing Office, February 1993.

sustained yield management. *Amenity resource protection legislation* has been at the forefront of this debate and includes the Endangered Species Act and the Wilderness Act. Throughout much of the history of the National Forest System, while the official policy was multiple use, the principle of dominant use was actually followed. This resulted in commodity resource values, such as timber and grazing, dominating most resource management decisions. As a result, amenity resource values that did not have measurable economic value—such as outdoor recreation and wildlife management—would oftentimes be the loser in land-use decisions. Many land-use decisions have been irreversible. There have been some notable exceptions to this generalization; one is the establishment of areas to be managed as wilderness, a movement that can be traced back to the 1920s. However, throughout much of the history of the National Forest System, timber has dominated over aesthetics, but this is changing today.

It was the action of Congress that changed this situation. The *Multiple-Use Sustained Yield Act* (1960) officially recognized that outdoor recreation and fish and wildlife have equal importance to timber, range, and watershed resource values. The *Forest and Rangeland Renewable Resources Planning Act* (1974) and the *National Forest Management Act* (1976) provided for a meaningful public participation process for National Forest System resource management decisions. The *Wilderness Act* (1964) has been the legal basis for preserving 34 million acres of the National Forest System for its inherent natural values. The *Endangered Species Act* (1973) has directed attention to the issue of species extinction and habitat preservation. The *Wild and Scenic Rivers Act* (1968) declared it is national policy to preserve some of our remaining free-flowing streams.

Major changes have occurred in the last few years in timber-cutting policies for national forests. Washington's Olympic National Forest is an example of this change. Between 1981 and 1989, the Olympic National Forest timber harvest averaged 328 million board feet per year. In 1990, annual timber harvest dropped to 117 million board feet, and in 1991 it was down to 83 million board feet. Predictions for the future range between 12 and 26 million board feet (Forest Service, 1993b). These reductions of up to 90 percent reflect changes taking place in federal court–mandated management direction for northern spotted owl habitat and the shift in public ethics and values relating to balancing commodity production and amenity preservation. In 1993, it was announced that timber sales in the Green Mountain National Forest (Vermont) and White Mountain National Forest (New Hampshire and Maine) might possibly cease in the near future. This management decision, if it transpires, will be made because of the heavy demand placed on these national forests for recreational use. While the public at large will benefit from this emphasis on the National Forest System for its amenity resource values, there will also be many losers in this change of land-use allocations. The rapid cutback in timber harvest, especially in the Pacific Northwest, has wrought economic havoc in small timber-oriented communities.[1]

---

[1]This point really hit home for the author during a conversation with an unemployed logger at a restaurant in the northern California town of Willow Creek in the fall of 1992. This individual was "hoping for a major forest fire" as a source of income to support his family. He recounted that "fighting forest fires was the only employment opportunity available to him." There are losers in the resource management decision process, as well as winners.

This change in Forest Service policy was succinctly stated by Chief F. Dale Robertson in the *Report of the Forest Service—Fiscal Year 1992* (Forest Service, 1993b):

> My June 4 announcement of the ecosystem management approach to managing the national forests and grasslands, along with the elimination of clearcutting as a standard timber harvest practice, was a major policy change for the Forest Service. By ecosystem management, we mean that an ecological approach will be used to achieve multiple-use management of the National Forest System. Through this, we will better blend the needs of people and environmental values in ways that sustain diverse, healthy, and productive ecosystems.

HISTORICAL BACKGROUND

Beginnings

The origins of the National Forest System and the Forest Service can be traced to the 1870s. At this time American forests were being ravaged. The devastating Peshtigo, Wisc., fire of October 8, 1871, attracted national attention by burning nearly 1.5 million acres and killing close to 1500 people. This fire occurred on the same day as the Great Chicago Fire of 1871. J. Sterling Morton, a member of the Nebraska Board of Agriculture, proposed Arbor Day, and on April 10, 1872, over 1 million trees were planted in Nebraska; 20 years later there were 100,000 acres of trees, where there had previously been none. The *Timber Culture Act* (1873) offered 160 acres to homesteaders who would plant 40 acres of trees. The act failed in its purpose and was repealed in 1891. In 1876 the first modern professional forestry organization, the *American Forestry Association*, was formed. In this year the first bill was introduced in Congress to establish national forest reserves, but it failed.

The Forest Service started as a research agency. In 1876, Congress appointed *Dr. Franklin B. Hough* to be the first federal forestry agent and assigned him to the Department of Agriculture. His duty was to compile a statistical inquiry on the conditions of U.S. forests. In 1881, Hough was named chief of the Division of Forestry within the Department of Agriculture, and he worked until 1885 to increase the government's role in forestry. The multivolume *Report on Forestry (1878–1884)* called for management of federal timber lands, creation of federal forest experiment stations, tree planting, and public education on the need for forest conservation. Hough was credited with writing the first book of practical forestry in the United States in 1882—*Elements of Forestry*. Gifford Pinchot referred to Hough as "the chief pioneer in forestry in the U.S."

In 1886, the Division of Forestry was confirmed by an act of Congress and came under the direction of German-born and -trained *Bernard Fernow,* the first professional forester in the federal government. Fernow was the driving force behind the act that in 1891 gave the president the authority to establish forest reserves. Creation of the Adirondack and Catskill Forest Preserves in New York in 1885 served as a model for advocates of federal forest reserves. Some of Fernow's experimental plantings in the Adirondacks are important parts of the landscape today. Large Norway spruce, exotic to the Adirondacks and planted by Fernow, have overgrown the trail from Long Pond

to Mountain Pond in New York's Adirondack Mountains. They are a living memorial to Bernard Fernow.

Forest Reserves

Passage of the *Forest Reserve Act* (1891) followed two decades of Congressional debate over public land policy. The purpose of this bill was to repeal the Timber Culture Act of 1873. President Benjamin Harrison signed the bill on March 3, 1893. *Section 24* of this act gave the president the authority to:

> . . . set apart and reserve, in any State or Territory having public land bearing forests, any part of the public lands wholly or in part covered with timber or undergrowth, whether of commercial value or not, as public reservations. . . .

This act simply allowed forest land to be set aside; it failed to call for any affirmative regulatory program. On March 30, 1891, President Harrison established the Yellowstone Park Timber Land Reserve, renamed the Shoshone National Forest in 1908 (Figure 7.1). The next forest reserve was the White River Plateau Timber Land Reserve, established on October 18, 1891. The forest reserves were first administered by the General Land Office in the Department of Interior. Almost 40 million acres in 29 forest reserves had been proclaimed by President's Harrison and Cleveland by 1897, when Congress finally decided their purpose in the *Organic Administrative Act* (1897). The act stated that forest reserves were to be established only to secure favorable water-flow conditions and to furnish a continuous timber supply. This act also gave the Secretary of the Interior authority to regulate occupancy and use within the reserves, develop mineral resources, provide for fire protection, and permit the sale of

Figure 7.1 The present-day Shoshone National Forest is the site of the first forest reserve, the Yellowstone Park Timber Land Reserve, proclaimed by President Harrison in 1891. It was renamed the Shoshone National Forest in 1908.

timber. This Organic Act remained essentially unchanged until the passage of the Multiple-Use Sustained-Yield Act of 1960.

In 1898, *Gifford Pinchot* was appointed chief of the Division of Forestry. That same year he organized the *Society of American Foresters*. Pinchot then rapidly expanded the USDA Division of Forestry. He offered to prepare working plans, free of charge, for owners of private timberlands. These early timber management plans were based on Pinchot's experience managing the Biltmore Forest on the Vanderbilt Estate in North Carolina. Pinchot oversaw the development of both forest and range planning for the forest reserves. The title Division of Forestry was changed to Bureau of Forestry in 1901, but the role of Pinchot's agency was still advisory: Department of Interior personnel patrolled the forest reserves, and Department of Agriculture foresters provided technical management plans. There were four principal features of Pinchot's conservation planning: (1) prepare detailed inventories, (2) monitor the condition of the reserves, (3) determine sustainable use levels, and (4) exclude use from specific areas where necessary to protect the watershed and other resources. This system of planning was utilized by the Forest Service after Pinchot was forced from office in 1910 and has continued to guide Forest Service thinking today.

U.S. Forest Service Established

Pinchot used his personal association with Theodore Roosevelt and members of Congress to lobby for transferring the administration of the forest reserves from the General Land Office of the Department of the Interior to the Department of Agriculture's Bureau of Forestry. Pinchot was successful, and on February 1, 1905, Congress passed the *Forest Transfer Act*. On March 3, 1905, by act of the Secretary of Agriculture, the Bureau of Forestry became the *Forest Service,* and the forest reserves became known as *national forests* under the Act of March 4, 1907. Pinchot was the first chief forester of the Forest Service. He not only had a personal bond with Roosevelt but also served as his advisor on conservation policy. The guidebook of the agency was Pinchot's *The Use of the National Forest Reserves* (1905). Controversy arose over regulations and fees the Forest Service imposed on sheep ranchers and mining interests. Western Congressmen were angered by Roosevelt's reserve-making tendencies. As a result, Congress passed a law in 1907 requiring congressional review and approval of reserve proclamations by the president. Before Roosevelt signed the agriculture bill that would prevent him and every future president from proclaiming national forests, he signed into existence another 21 new national forests on 16 million acres in Arizona, California, New Mexico, Nevada, and Utah. Pinchot and his staff did the necessary work to prepare these proclamations for Roosevelt.

"By 1908 the Forest Service had a staff of 1,500 in charge of 150 million acres of National Forest; under Pinchot the agency was a far different one than the modest forestry information division vacated by Fernow in 1898" (West, 1992, 39). Roosevelt added 132 million acres of forest reserves from 1901 until 1908. Table 7.2 chronicles the growth of the National Forest System. When Roosevelt left office in 1909, the National Forest System had grown to 90 percent of its present extent. Pinchot's tenure as chief of the Forest Service ended in 1910, shortly after Roosevelt left office. Pinchot had become snarled in a dispute with Secretary of the Interior Richard Ballinger's policy of exploitive coal leases in Alaska. Pinchot's outspoken criticism of Ballinger

Table 7.2   National Forest Lands—Annual Acreage (1891–1992)

Year	Total Number of Forests	NFS Acreage	Year	Total Number of Forests	NFS Acreage	Year	Total Number of Forests	NFS Acreage
1891*	1	1,239,000	1925	159	158,395,056	1959	148	180,468,001
92*	6	3,254,000	26	160	158,759,210	1960	151	180,843,513
93*	15	13,417,000	27	159	158,800,424	61	154	181,050,808
94*	17	17,928,000	28	151	159,480,856	62	154	181,635,371
1895*	17	17,928,000	29	150	159,750,520	63	154	181,974,887
96*	17	17,928,000	1930	149	160,090,817	64	154	182,078,340
97*	29	39,103,000	31	151	160,787,687	1965	154	182,138,750
98*	31	40,866,000	32	148	161,360,691	66	154	182,272,997
99*	37	46,168,000	33	148	162,009,145	67	154	182,507,377
1900*	38	46,515,000	34	145	162,591,124	68	154	182,615,576
01*	41	46,324,000	1935	142	163,310,002	69	154	182,340,141
02*	54	51,896,000	36	147	165,978,691	1970	154	182,571,102
03*	53	63,211,000	37	157	171,403,306	71	154	182,578,296
04*	59	62,611,000	38	158	172,451,394	72	155	182,773,942
1905*	83	75,352,000	39	158	173,225,983	73	155	183,014,294
06	106	94,159,000	1940	160	174,769,543	74	155	182,045,476
07	159	132,732,000	41	160	175,763,793	1975	155	183,280,072
08	165	147,820,000	42	160	176,593,251	76	154	183,380,761
09	150	172,230,000	43	160	176,925,027	77	154	183,447,427
1910	149	168,029,000	44	158	177,422,436	78	154	183,554,842
11	153	168,165,000	1945	155	177,641,903	79	154	183,186,893
12	163	165,027,000	46	152	177,768,552	1980	155	183,060,464
13	163	165,516,518	47	153	178,165,104	81	155	186,441,602
14	163	163,848,524	48	152	178,595,882	82	155	186,559,221
1915	162	162,773,280	49	152	179,339,893	83	155	186,531,949
16	153	155,399,809	1950	151	179,685,328	84	156	183,383,802
17	152	155,166,619	51	151	179,947,794	1985	156	186,315,499
18	151	155,374,602	52	153	180,168,800	86	156	186,463,004
19	151	153,933,460	53	153	180,386,928	87	156	186,454,781
1920	152	156,032,053	54	152	180,358,491	88	156	186,245,659
21	149	156,666,045	1955	149	180,302,398	89	156	186,905,252
22	148	156,837,282	56	149	180,354,267	1990	156	187,083,200
23	146	157,236,807	57	149	180,335,417	91	156	186,996,286
24	146	157,502,793	58	148	180,378,544	92	156	187,114,116

*Gross acreage for 1891–1905.
Source: Forest Service, *Land Areas of the National Forest System—As of Sept. 30, 1992* (1993).

as mismanaging public lands caused President Taft to force him from the position of chief. This dismissal of Pinchot led to congressional investigations of the matter.

The *Weeks Act* (1911) authorized the Forest Service to expand the National Forest System by acquiring private forest lands in the headwater areas of navigable streams in the East, for the stated purpose of watershed protection. The Pisgah National Forest (North Carolina) was the first in the East, established in 1916. The first "Weeks Act" national forest in the Northeast was New Hampshire's White Mountain National Forest (Figure 7.2). This marked a new departure in national forest origins, since all of the earlier land in the system was reserved from the public domain. The *Clark-McNary Act* (1924) extended the Weeks Act, allowing the Forest Service to purchase lands valuable for timber production in their own right. Under the authority of these

Figure 7.2   The Swift River in New Hampshire's White Mountain National Forest is an important "headwater stream" for the Saco River. The Weeks Act authorized the establishment of such national forests in the East.

two acts the Forest Service acquired most of the remainder of its land, adding some 20 million acres to the lands previously reserved from the public domain. The last of the major acquisitions in the National Forest System were acquired under the *Bankhead–Jones Farm Tenant Act* (1937). These lands were primarily in the "dust bowl" of the Great Plains. They were later transferred to the Forest Service and have been classified as national grasslands since 1960. The Soil Conservation Service worked to restore these submarginal farmlands. Some of these lands are classified as Land Utilization Projects even today.

Growth of Recreation Management

It was not until after world War I that the Forest Service started to plan for recreational resources. The Forest Service was originally pushed into recreational activities in self-defense. People gradually discovered the recreational values of the forests and began to use them accordingly. The Forest Service found itself attempting to manage recreation in order to minimize fire hazards, stream pollution, and hazards to the recreationists themselves. As early as 1910, a few forestry leaders started to call attention to the growing public interest and use of the national forests. There was a negative attitude on the part of many foresters toward recreational use. At this time national forests were not developed, their boundaries were not clearly defined, the nature and abundance of resources were not fully inventoried or understood, road and trail development was limited, and there were personality clashes between forestry leaders and preservationists. There was much controversy over the withdrawing of national forest land for national park purposes, yet as early as 1912 an annual report recognized for the first time the recreational value of the national forests.

Congress first recognized recreation as a use of the national forests in 1915, when it authorized the Forest Service to grant permits to build summer homes, stores, and hotels in the national forests (Wilkinson, 1987, 318). In 1918 the first official Forest Service study of recreation was published, and in 1922 the first tangible support ($10,000) was given, primarily to improve existing campgrounds. In 1921 the *Forest Service Manual* stated: "No plan of national forest administration would be complete which did not conserve and make [recreation resources] fully available for public use." Also in 1921, *Aldo Leopold*, an assistant forester in the Southwest Region, proposed setting aside a vast area of 700,000 acres as wilderness in New Mexico's Gila National Forest. This proposal was antithetical to Gifford Pinchot's policies but was adopted in 1924 and applied later in other parts of the country.

During the 1930s, recreation and wilderness planning expanded through the efforts of Leopold, *Arthur Carhart*, and *Robert Marshall*. In 1933, Robert Marshall identified seven "distinct types of recreational forest areas." While Marshall was chief of the Division of Recreation, the Forest Service enlarged the wilderness system to 14 million acres by 1939. Marshall's "U-Regulations" established guidelines for wilderness management. In the 1930s, Roosevelt's "Forest Army," the *Civilian Conservation Corps* (CCC) had a major impact on recreation in the national forests. CCC labor built many of the campgrounds, fire towers, rustic office buildings, and trails that are still valuable recreation assets today. By the 1940s many elements of the Forest Service's current recreation planning system were already in place, including visual management of highway and water corridors, limitations on motorized recreation, and classification of land areas for various types of recreational use. With the exception of the 1915 law that governed permits for summer homes and resorts, the only statutory authority or guidance for these policy decisions was the 1897 Organic Act (Wilkinson and Anderson, 1987, 320–321).

"The history of the Forest Service can be simplified into two fundamental stages: the custodial era (1905 to 1942) and the commodity production era (1942 to present)" (West, 1992, 69). In this first era the Forest Service's job was relatively uncomplicated because management of range, timber, and noncommodity resources did not often interfere with each other. During the 1950s this harmonious planning framework began to break down because of the increased demand for timber and other resources. Even during the high-demand time of World War II, only 2 percent (2.2 billion board feet) of the national supply of timber came from national forests. The timber harvest increased from 3 billion board feet in 1950 to 9 billion board feet in 1960. This volume peaked at 12.7 billion board feet in 1987, which accounted for 13 percent of the wood harvest in the Nation (West, 1992, 69–70). "The massive road building and timber sales during the postwar stage of Forest Service history signified a major change in an agency image that not all the public accepted" (West, 1992, 70). The road-building budget soared, and hiring civil engineers became a priority. "Today, more than 350,000 miles of roads run through the National Forest, making it the most extensive road system in the world, and civil engineers, the next largest professional group after foresters, number about 3,500" (Zaslowsky, 1986, 89).

After a temporary decline in use during World War II, the use of national forests for recreational purposes also accelerated. As early as the 1950s recreationists were beginning to seriously compete with the timber industry for choice national forest lands. For the first time Congress began to appropriate substantial sums of money

for campgrounds and other recreational facilities. In 1957 the Forest Service launched *Operation Outdoors,* a 5-year program designed to improve maintenance of existing recreational facilities and to develop new facilities. The Forest Service leased many high-elevation sites to private operators for alpine ski operations, with the result that recreation became a year-round activity. There were many diverse groups now competing for the natural resources of the National Forest System.

Legislative Mandates

During the 1950s the Forest Service attempted to use the multiple-use concept to balance competing pressures on the national forests. The agency was under increasing pressure to change its management policies. Lumber interests sought further increases in allowable timber cuts, and preservation interests urged legislation to prohibit the agency from harvesting or developing the remaining wilderness in the national forests. Congress responded to this situation by passing three pieces of legislation that specifically applied to the Forest Service and mandated how the Forest Service would address these issues: (1) the Multiple-Use Sustained-Yield Act (1960), (2) the Forest and Rangeland Renewable Resources Planning Act (1974), and (3) the National Forest Management Act (1976). In addition to these three laws, which were specifically directed at the Forest Service and the National Forest System, several other pieces of legislation also had a major impact on Forest Service resource management decisions: (1) the Wilderness Act (1964), (2) the Wild and Scenic Rivers Act (1968), (3) the National Environmental Policy Act (1970), and (4) the Endangered Species Act (1973).

Multiple-Use Sustained Yield Act (1960)   "Passage of the Multiple-Use Sustained-Yield Act of 1960 marked the beginning of a new and unsettled era of Forest Service Planning" (Wilkinson and Anderson, 1987, 29). This act recognizes officially that recreation has comparable importance to four other national forest resource values—range, timber, watershed, and fish and wildlife. Two key points of the law are that no resource has statutory priority and that each resource is to receive equal consideration in determining the best combination of uses. The problem is, Who would determine the mix, and on what basis? Section 528 of this law states: "It is the policy of the Congress that the national forests are established and shall be administered for *outdoor recreation, range, timber, watershed,* and *wildlife and fish* purposes." Section 531(a) defines *multiple use* as:

> ... the management of all the various renewable surface resources of the national forests so that they are utilized in the combination that will best meet the needs of the American people; making the most judicious use of the land for some or all of these resources or related services over areas large enough to provide sufficient latitude for periodic adjustments in use to conform to changing needs and conditions; that some land will be used for less than all of the resources; and harmonious and coordinated management of the various resources, each with the other, without impairment of the productivity of the land, with consideration being given to the relative values of the various resources, and not necessarily the combination of uses that will give the greatest dollar return or the greatest unit output.

Section 531(b) defines *sustained yield* as:

... the achievement and maintenance in perpetuity of a high-level annual or regular periodic output of the various renewable resources of the national forests without impairment of the productivity of the land.

The expansion of planning after passage of the Multiple-Use Sustained-Yield Act took two forms: (1) the Forest Service began to write separate functional plans for recreation, wildlife, and other resources, and (2) the Forest Service began to experiment with land zoning. In 1961 the Forest Service initiated a two-stage planning process to divide the National Forests into management zones. In the first stage, each of the nine regional offices wrote a Multiple-Use Planning Guide. The second stage required each district ranger to prepare a District Multiple-Use Management plan. These plans were the Forest Service's first systematic attempt to resolve problems of conflicting use. "However, the plans suffered from chronically poor inventory data concerning soil stability, wildlife habitats, and other site-specific data. Consequently, district rangers were reluctant to establish management guidelines that were any more concrete than those stated in the regional guides" (Wilkinson and Anderson, 1987, 32).

Controversy arose over multiple use and its relationship to the issue of clear-cutting, which had become standard procedure by the 1960s. "By 1969, 61 percent of the harvest from the Western national forests was clear-cut, while about 50 percent of the Eastern national forest harvest was obtained this way" (Zaslowsky, 1986, 92). It was the clear-cutting schemes in the Bitterroot (Montana) and the Monongahela (West Virginia) National Forests that really brought the interpretation of multiple use to a head. Senator Frank Church of Idaho, chair of the Senate Subcommittee on Public Lands, held hearings on this matter. More legislation would be shortly passed by Congress.

Wilderness Act (1964)   The Wilderness Act prompted an increase in wilderness planning. The subject of national forest wilderness will be discussed in Chapters 8–10, and the broader topic of the entire National Wilderness Preservation System is reserved for Chapter 14. As early as 1924, the first national forest "wilderness" area was established, on 700,000 acres in New Mexico's Gila National Forest; Aldo Leopold worked for its establishment. In the 1920s and 1930s Leopold, Carhart, and Marshall worked to add to this administrative "wilderness" system. However, this wilderness system on the national forests existed because of administrative policy and not because of statutory directives. Prior to passage of the Wilderness Act, there were four types of wilderness areas in the national forests: "wilderness" (over 100,000 acres); "wild" (5000–100,000 acres); "primitive," which were subject to the same restrictions as wild and wilderness areas, pending further study of whether they should be classified as wild or as wilderness or should revert to the status of ordinary forests; and canoe, which had the same restrictions as wilderness and wild areas, with the exception that timber cutting was permitted outside of no-cut zones. Prohibited on all four areas were logging, roads, residences, and commercial enterprises. In the one canoe area—Boundary Waters in the Superior National Forest (Minnesota)—a certain amount of cutting was allowed. Hunting and fishing (subject to state law) and grazing, prospecting, and mining were permitted in all four classifications.

The Wilderness Act established an *Initial Wilderness Preservation System* by immediately classifying as "wilderness" all wilderness, wild, or canoe areas in the na-

tional forests. This initial system was exclusively national forest land and included 54 different areas on 9.1 million acres. Only three of these areas were located east of the Rockies: Boundary Waters Canoe Area (Minnesota), Linville Gorge (North Carolina), and Great Gulf (New Hampshire) (Figure 7.3). The act specified that the 34 national forest areas, designated as "primitive" (totaling 5.4 million acres) were to be reviewed within 10 years for possible addition to the National Wilderness Preservation System. The act also specified that all roadless areas over 5000 acres in the National Park System and similar-size holdings and every roadless island within the National Wildlife Refuge System were to be reviewed within 10 years for possible inclusion in the Wilderness System.

During the early 1970s the Forest Service voluntarily conducted a *Roadless Area Review and Evaluation (RARE)* to identify areas for suitable inclusion in the Wilderness System. Roadless area planning came under intense public and judicial scrutiny, with many environmental interest groups critical of RARE I. The initial inventory identified 1449 roadless areas, containing 56 million acres, with wilderness potential. Only two of these areas were in the East, and one of these was in Puerto Rico. The lack of areas in the East was a point of controversy with environmentalists. As a result of this criticism, the Forest Service commenced a second RARE (II) in 1977. The basic objective of RARE II was to accelerate the planning process mandated by the Forest and Rangeland Renewable Resources Planning Act of 1974 and the National Forest Management Act of 1976. As a result of public comments in the RARE II process, the number of roadless areas to be considered for addition to the Wilderness System rose to 1921 (65.7 million acres).

The final RARE II *environmental impact statement* (EIS) was published on January 4, 1979. It called for: (1) wilderness allocation of 624 areas totaling 15,008,838 acres; (2) nonwilderness designation of 1981 areas totaling 36,151,558 acres; and (3) further planning for 314 areas totaling 10,796,508 acres (Hendee et al., 1990, 138). A contro-

Figure 7.3 The Great Gulf Wilderness Area in the Presidential Range of New Hampshire's White Mountain National Forest was only one of three such areas in the Initial Wilderness Preservation System (1964) located east of the Rocky Mountains.

versy in the Shasta-Trinity National Forest became a test of the RARE II process. The director of the California Natural Resources Agency sued the Forest Service and sought a court injunction against the release of 46 California study areas to nonwilderness uses. The district court on January 8, 1980, sided with the state of California, enjoining the 46 areas from development, saying that an EIS would have to be prepared for each area before their status could change. In October 1982, the Ninth Circuit Court of Appeals upheld the lower court ruling (Hendee et al., 1990, 139). In the summer of 1984, after a great deal of negotiations during the previous years, 18 National Forest Wilderness bills were passed, adding 6.6 million acres to the National Wilderness Preservation System. This was the largest national forest addition in a single session of Congress since the Wilderness Act was passed in 1964. Despite a troubled process, national forest lands designated as "wilderness" have increased from the initial 54 areas on 9.1 million acres in 1964, to 386 areas on 34 million acres in 1994. Thirty-eight states have varying amounts of designated wilderness in national forests. Five states have over 3 million acres each: Alaska (5.8 million acres), California (4.4 million acres), Idaho (4.0 million acres), Montana (3.4 million acres), and Wyoming (3.1 million acres).

National Environmental Policy Act (1970)   The *National Environmental Policy Act* (NEPA) of January 1, 1970, declared that the preservation of environmental quality was a high-priority national goal. It directed *all* federal agencies to consider the environmental impacts of any proposed action and to prepare EISs to insure compliance with this goal of environmental quality. NEPA had several important effects on the Forest Service: Participation by the public and other government agencies in the planning process increased substantially. Roadless area planning assumed greater significance because an EIS was now required before any roadless area could be developed. The Forest Service was encouraged to apply environmental planning requirements to regulate mining. Most importantly, NEPA's requirements spurred the Forest Service to develop vastly more complete natural resource inventories.

In 1973, local land-use plans (*Unit Plans*) replaced the multiple-use plans and became the Forest Service's principal means of complying with the EIS requirements of NEPA. A major objective of Unit Planning was to ensure greater consistency between national and local land-use priorities. The basic purpose of the Unit Plans was to classify national forests into land-use zones. To do this each regional forester prepared *Area Planning Guides* for geographic subdivisions of their region, which provided the general direction for *Forest Land-Use Plans* for each national forest. The Forest Plans guided the preparation of local Unit Plans within each National Forest. In the early 1970s the Forest Service developed another planning effort, the "Environmental Program for the Future." This process included a comparison of resource outputs predicted for a 10-year period under low, moderate, and high funding. Much of the Forest and Rangeland Renewable Resources Planning Act of 1974 was based on these planning concepts.

Forest and Rangeland Renewable Resources Planning Act (1974)   Historically, Congress seldom intruded into Forest Service resource planning or management. Prior to 1974, the Forest Service conducted its land and resource planning under the terms of the 1897 Organic Act. Two statutes of the 1970s changed this: the Forest and

Rangeland Renewable Resources Planning Act (Resources Planning Act, 1974) and the National Forest Management Act (1976). The Resources Planning Act (RPA) established a process for periodically assessing the nation's public and private forest and rangeland renewable resources. Mainly concerned with national planning, it requires the Forest Service to develop a long-range program to help ensure the supply of these resources and the maintenance of a quality environment. The Forest Service must periodically prepare three planning documents: (1) every 10 years an *assessment* describing the renewable resources of all the nation's forest and rangelands; (2) every 5 years a *program* proposing long-range objectives, with a planning horizon of at least 45 years, for all Forest Service activities; and (3) an *annual report* evaluating Forest Service activities in comparison with the objectives proposed in the program. The RPA has not significantly altered the budgetary process as expected, but it has had an important impact on the way the Forest Service has structured the planning process required by the National Forest Management Act.

The First RPA annual report was submitted in 1975 and recommended increasing the supply of recreational opportunities and services, with emphasis on dispersed recreation, as opposed to developed recreation. The 1980 resource planning assessment (RPA) maintained the primacy of dispersed recreation. Developed sites would still be maintained but the private and state sectors could offer better concentrated uses.

The current national strategic plan, the 1990 RPA program, outlines the agency's long-term direction and provides general policy guidelines for 5 years based on a 50-year projection. The next RPA program will be published in 1995. The 1990 program defined the major policy roles of the Forest Service and analyzed its relationship with and responses to contemporary issues. Four major themes emerged from these roles and issues. These themes have guided Forest Service actions and policies since 1990 and were instrumental in the evaluation of agency performance in FY92 (fiscal year 1992). These four themes are:

1. Enhancing recreation, wildlife, and fisheries
2. Producing environmentally acceptable commodities
3. Improving scientific knowledge about natural resources
4. Responding to global resource issues

National Forest Management Act (1976)   The National Forest Management Act, which replaced and clarified the original Organic Act of 1897, requires that the Forest Service involve the public more in its decision making and hire people trained in disciplines other than forestry. It also required that standards and guidelines be developed for resource planning within the National Forest System. "The 1976 Act amounted to a bitterly-contested referendum on Forest Service timber harvesting practices" (Wilkinson and Anderson, 1987, 40). During the 1960s the Forest Service continued to increase timber sales and expanded the use of clear cutting. This practice generated severe criticism, especially on the Bitterroot National Forest (Montana) and Monongahela National Forest (West Virginia). The matter was decided by the ruling of the Court of Appeals for the Fourth Circuit in the *Monongahela case* on August 21, 1975. It was ruled that the 1897 Organic Act effectively prohibited clear cutting in the national forest. Congress recognized that Forest Service timber practices needed

revision, and on October 22, 1976, President Ford signed the National Forest Management Act into law.

This act placed great importance on the preparation of local land and resource management plans. This was accomplished by directing the Secretary of Agriculture to prepare regulations for Forest Service planning, modeled on guidelines in the act. A committee of scientists was appointed by the Secretary to provide advice on the regulations. The act also required all contracts, permits, and other legal instruments allowing use of a national forest to conform to that forest's management plan. It imposed numerous ceiling limitations on timber harvesting, including limits on the amount that could be sold each year. Finally, the act required the Forest Service to "attempt" to complete the new plans by the end of FY85. The final planning regulations were adopted in 1979 and revised in 1982.

The National Forest Management Act also provided authorization and guidelines for inclusion of recreation in multiple-use management. The program has three major parts:

Recreation Management   The purpose of recreation management is to provide and protect the natural resources and facilities that accommodate the public's need for outdoor recreation, emphasizing opportunities to know and experience nature. It is also directed at maintaining, repairing, and restoring existing facilities necessary to meet the demands for public outdoor recreation in natural settings. Private sector capital through concession permits, challenge cost-share projects, and other partnerships are used when appropriate.

Wilderness Management   Wilderness management is directed at protecting and preserving resources and values while providing for the uses permitted by law. Wilderness is managed for scenic, scientific, educational, conservation, historical, and recreational use. Although people enjoy visiting wildernesses and experiencing the primitive environment, these lands are not primarily recreation areas. About 5 percent of recreational use on the national forests occurs in 386 wilderness areas in 38 states with a total of 34 million acres. One acre in 6 in the National Forest System is now in the National Wilderness Preservation System.

Cultural Resource Management   The purpose of the cultural resource program is to protect, manage, and interpret the cultural resources on the National Forest System lands in accord with the requirements of the National Historic Preservation Act of 1980, the National Environmental Policy Act of 1970, and the Archeological Resources Protection Act of 1979. The program also includes field surveys to identify cultural resources properties, the preparation of nominations to the National Register of Historic Places, and the enforcement of laws protecting cultural resources.

ORGANIZATION OF THE FOREST SERVICE

The Forest Service has always been an agency within the Department of Agriculture, and it is the largest agency in this department. The organizational structure of the

Forest Service includes six subdivisions: (1) National Forest System, (2) Research, (3) State and Private Forestry, (4) International Forestry, (5) Administration, and (6) Legislation and Programs. Because the focus of this book is on the National Forest System, this is the only subdivision that will be discussed here. Around 85 percent of the staff and appropriations for the Forest Service are for this subdivision, which is most central to the main mission, to manage the National Forest System. At the top of this organizational structure is the *chief*, formerly called the chief forester. The current chief of the Forest Service is *Jack Ward Thomas*, who replaced F. Dale Robertson in 1993. The chief has always been appointed from among professional ranks and is headquartered in the Washington office. There are nine functional divisions in the National Forest System: (1) Engineering; (2) Lands; (3) Land Management Planning; (4) Minerals and Geology Management; (5) Range Management; (6) Recreation, Cultural Resources and Wilderness Management; (7) Timber Management; (8) Watershed and Air Management; and (9) Wildlife and Fisheries.

There are four main levels of administration for the National Forest System: (1) the Washington office, (2) regions, (3) national forests, and (4) the ranger districts. At the top is the relatively small *Washington office*, which has had under 5 percent of the Forest Service employees in recent years. (In FY92 there were 36,137 employees in the entire Forest Service.) The chief presides over the Washington office, and this office is responsible for most major policy directives. Divisions of the Washington office coordinate specific activities and programs, working with the chief and deputy chiefs, the Agriculture Department, other federal agencies, and the field offices. The Washington office is mainly concerned with forestry activities on a national level, including forest research and cooperative federal-state forest management programs for nonfederal lands.

While the Washington office is responsible for general policy directives, most Forest Service operations are delegated to the field offices. The Forest Service is a very decentralized agency. The National Forest System is divided into nine *regions*, each of which is in the charge of a *regional forester*, who with staff has regional administrative responsibilities. For the system as a whole, the average number of national forests is 17, and the average acreage is 21 million for each region. The Alaska region (region 10) has only two national forests, and the Southern region (region 8) has 35 national forests. Figure 7.4 delineates the geographic area covered by each region and shows the location of each region's headquarters. The regional boundaries generally follow state lines except in the Northern Rocky Mountains in Idaho and Wyoming and the Great Plains in South Dakota. The regions are identified by the numbers 1 through 10, with the exception of 7. The former region 7 was made part of region 9 in 1966 to form an Eastern region. Appendix VII lists each of these regions and their address and phone numbers. As director for all activities in his or her region, the regional forester is delegated broad authority.

Immediately below the regional level is the *national forest*, headed by a *forest supervisor*. Presently there are 156 designated national forests, for which there are 133 administrative units, each managed by a forest supervisor. Joint administration for separate congressionally designated national forests is the reason for this discrepancy in numbers. In all but two cases, the joint administration is for two national forests. The Idaho Panhandle National Forest supervisor administers the Coeur d'Alene, Kaniksu, and St. Joe National Forests. The Grand Mesa, Uncompahgre, and Gunnison

Figure 7.5 District rangers are good sources of detailed information for national forests. Shown here is the district ranger station for the Carson Ranger District of the Toiyabe National Forest.

National Forests are administered by one supervisor, based at Delta, Colo. The *national grasslands* are administered like ranger districts by the nearest national forest; for example, the Nebraska National Forest supervisor is responsible for the Oglala National Grassland in Nebraska and the Fort Pierre and Buffalo Gap National Grass-

Figure 7.6 Fire tower observer in Kaibab National Forest south of Jacobs Lake, Arizona.

lands in South Dakota. The national forest is regarded as the central functional planning level of the field organization. "The supervisor has "line authority" to protect, develop, and utilize the resources in his care. Being a supervisor is one of the most desirable assignments in the Forest Service—close to the resource and policy" (Frome, 1984, 43). The Supervisor's office has a variety of specialists to aid in resource management plans and to form interdisciplinary teams: timber, engineering, recreation, wildlife, hydrology, soils, planning, landscape architecture, fire control, and occasionally archaeology.

Each national forest is divided into *ranger districts,* which serve as the basic administration units of the Forest Service. A *district ranger* is in charge of each ranger district. "The 600-plus ranger districts are the basic line units for administration of the national forest. The Chief is at the apex of the pyramid, but the ranger supports it from the base" (Frome, 1984, 43). The district ranger may administer more than 1 million acres in his (or her) district and supervise a staff of 30 to 150 during the summer. The average ranger district size is 290,000 acres. Whereas the forest supervisor's office is usually found in a principal city near the national forest, the district ranger's office is generally found in a small town in the heart of the district. The district ranger knows the district well and is an excellent source of information for persons seeking recreational opportunities there (Figure 7.5). Another excellent source of information is fire tower observers (Figure 7.6).

GEOGRAPHIC DISTRIBUTION OF THE NATIONAL FOREST SYSTEM

To understand the National Forest System it is necessary to define several terms. (All definitions are quoted from Forest Service, 1993a, ii.) The *National Forest System* is:

> A nationally significant system of Federally owned units of forest, range, and related land consisting of national forests, purchase units, national grasslands, land utilization project areas, experimental forest areas, experimental range areas, designated experimental areas, other land areas, water areas, and interests in lands that are administered by the USDA Forest Service or designated for administration through the Forest Service.

A *national forest* is "a unit formally established and permanently set aside and reserved for National Forest purposes." A *purchase unit* is "a unit designated by the Secretary of Agriculture or previously approved by the National Forest Reservation Commission for purpose of Weeks Law acquisition." A *national grassland* is "a unit designated by the Secretary of Agriculture and permanently held by the Department of Agriculture under Title III of the Bankhead-Jones Farm Tenant Act." A *land utilization project* is "a unit designated by the Secretary of Agriculture for conservation and utilization under Title III of the Bankhead-Jones Farm Tenant Act." A *research and experimental area* is defined as "a unit reserved by the Secretary of Agriculture for forest or range research and experimentation." In addition, there are seven special designations given to portions of the National Forest System: *national forest wilderness*

areas, national forest primitive areas, national wild and scenic river areas, national recreation areas, national scenic-research areas, national game refuges and wildlife preserve areas, and national monument areas.

Appendix VIII is a complete listing of all national forests and national grasslands, their gross and net acreage, recreation visitor day use, and wilderness recreation visitor day use. Figure 7.7, whose numbers correspond to Appendix VIII shows the location of the national forests and national grasslands. An examination of this map reveals that the geographic distribution of National Forest System areas is spatially imbalanced. The lands of the National Forest System are found in 44 states, Puerto Rico, and the Virgin Islands. Only Delaware, Iowa, Maryland, Massachusetts, New Jersey, and Rhode Island have no lands in the system. Some of the system acreage in eastern states is quite small; for example, Connecticut only has 24 acres. The lion's share of the National Forests are found in the mountains and higher elevations of the West. Particularly large concentrations are located in the Northern Rocky Mountains, Southern Rocky Mountains, Sierra Nevada, and Cascade Mountains. The two national forests of Alaska are located in the south-central and southeastern areas of the state. Most of the national grasslands are located in the western Great Plains. In the East, the much smaller proportion of the national forests are also found primarily in mountainous or highland areas. These areas include the Southern Appalachians, the Ozarks, and the Ouachita Mountains. Major eastern national forests are also located in the northern Great Lakes, but scattered national forests occur on the low-lying Gulf-Atlantic coastal plain from East Texas to North Carolina.

Table 7.3 presents a regional analysis of the national forest component of the national forest system; this table is organized by census regions, which are different than Forest Service Regions. The Mountain Census Region, which is also the largest geographic region, contains 50 percent of the acreage. It is also the leading region in terms of numbers of national forests (76). Another 25 percent of the acreage is in the Pacific Census Region, with 46 national forests. The Atlantic Census Region contains the least acreage and the least number of national forests (2). The average size of national forest in the Pacific and Mountain Census Regions is almost 1 million acres, while the average national forest size in the eastern Census Regions (with the exception of Minnesota and Missouri) is less than ½ million acres. Twenty-one percent of the Pacific Census Region and 17 percent of the Mountain Census Region are covered with national forest. Alaska, California, and Idaho each have over 20 million acres of national forest.

Acres of national forest per capita is the most meaningful statistical measure for assessing recreational potential. Alaska far exceeds the other states, with 40.4 acres per capita. In the lower 49 states, the Mountain region is the leader, with 6.9 acres per capita. The three leading states in the lower 49 are Montana (21.0 acres per capita), Idaho (20.3 acres per capita), and Wyoming (19.1 acres per capita). The only other region with over 1 acre of national forest per capita is the Pacific (1.2 acres per capita). Although California's 20.6 million acres of national forest rank it second among the states, its large population of 30 million dilutes the acres per capita to 0.7. The Middle Atlantic region has only 0.01 acres of national forest per capita; state lands in this region are much more important as recreational resources.

Table 7.4 gives a statistical summary of the National Forest System in four parts: U.S. totals; eastern regional totals; western regional totals; and Alaska regional totals.

Table 7.3   National Forests Regional Analysis

Region State	No.	Acres of Natl. Forest	Acres in State	Population	Average Forest Size	% Natl. Forest Land	Acres of Forest per Capita	Population per Forest
Alaska	2	22,193,395	385,296,000	550,043	11,096,698	5.76	40.35	275,022
Pacific								
CA	22	20,584,450	101,563,520	29,760,021	935,657	20.27	0.69	1,352,728
HI	0	0	4,128,000	1,108,229	—	0.00	0.00	—
OR	15	15,541,932	62,067,840	2,842,321	1,036,129	25.04	5.47	189,488
WA	9	9,158,904	43,642,880	4,866,692	1,017,656	20.99	1.88	540,744
Region	46	45,285,286	211,402,240	38,577,263	984,463	21.42	1.17	838,636
Mountain								
AZ	7	11,246,668	72,901,760	3,665,228	1,606,667	15.43	3.07	523,604
CO	12	13,838,233	66,718,080	3,294,394	1,153,186	20.74	4.20	274,533
ID	16	20,392,815	53,476,480	1,006,749	1,274,551	38.13	20.26	69,922
MT	11	16,805,969	94,168,320	799,065	1,527,815	17.85	21.03	72,642
NM	7	9,082,195	77,866,240	1,515,069	1,297,456	11.66	5.99	216,438
NV	4	5,801,183	70,745,600	1,201,833	1,450,296	8.20	4.83	300,458
UT	9	8,043,014	54,346,240	1,722,850	893,668	14.80	4.67	191,428
WY	10	8,682,526	62,664,960	453,588	868,253	13.86	19.14	45,359
Region	76	93,892,603	552,887,680	13,658,776	1,235,429	16.98	6.87	179,721
West North Central								
IA	0	0	36,025,600	2,776,755	—	0.00	0.00	—
KS	0	0	52,648,960	2,477,574	—	0.00	0.00	—
MN	2	2,730,013	53,803,520	4,375,099	1,365,007	5.07	0.62	2,187,550
MO	1	1,462,348	44,599,040	5,117,073	1,462,348	3.28	0.29	5,117,073
ND	0	0	45,219,200	638,800	—	0.00	0.00	—
NE	2	257,347	49,425,280	1,578,385	128,674	0.52	0.16	789,193
SD	2	1,144,793	49,310,080	696,004	572,397	2.32	1.64	348,002
Region	7	5,594,501	331,031,680	17,659,690	799,214	1.69	0.32	2,522,813
West South Central								
AR	3	2,528,906	33,986,560	2,350,725	842,969	7.44	1.08	783,575
LA	1	601,398	31,054,720	4,219,973	601,398	1.94	0.14	4,219,973
OK	1	254,257	44,748,160	3,145,585	254,257	0.57	0.08	3,145,585
TX	4	637,109	171,128,320	16,986,510	159,277	0.37	0.04	4,246,628
Region	9	4,021,670	280,917,760	26,702,793	446,852	1.43	0.15	2,966,977
East North Central								
IL	1	260,133	36,096,000	11,430,602	260,133	0.72	0.02	11,430,602
IN	1	189,166	23,226,240	5,544,159	189,166	0.81	0.03	5,544,159
MI	4	2,838,968	37,258,240	9,295,297	709,742	7.62	0.31	2,323,824
OH	1	210,783	26,382,080	10,847,115	210,783	0.80	0.02	10,847,115
WI	2	1,518,140	35,938,560	4,891,769	759,070	4.22	0.31	2,445,885
Region	9	5,017,190	158,901,120	42,008,942	557,466	3.16	0.12	4,667,660
East South Central								
AL	4	658,775	33,029,760	4,040,587	164,689	1.99	0.16	1,010,147
KY	2	529,959	25,852,800	3,685,296	264,980	2.05	0.14	1,842,648
MS	6	1,152,466	30,538,240	2,573,216	192,078	3.77	0.45	428,869
TN	1	627,405	27,036,160	4,877,185	627,405	2.32	0.13	4,877,185
Region	13	2,968,585	116,456,960	15,176,284	228,353	2.55	0.20	1,167,406

Table 7.3   (continued)

Region State	No.	Acres of Natl. Forest	Acres in State	Population	Average Forest Size	% Natl. Forest Land	Acres of Forest per Capita	Population per Forest
South Atlantic								
DC	0	0	64,000	606,900	—	0.00	0.00	—
DE	0	0	1,316,480	666,168	—	0.00	0.00	—
FL	4	1,135,306	37,478,400	12,937,926	283,827	3.03	0.09	3,234,482
GA	2	860,132	37,680,640	6,478,216	430,066	2.28	0.13	3,239,108
MD	0	0	6,769,280	4,781,468	—	0.00	0.00	—
NC	5	1,233,114	33,655,040	6,628,637	246,623	3.66	0.19	1,325,727
SC	2	608,710	19,875,200	3,486,703	304,355	3.06	0.17	1,743,352
VA	2	1,647,670	26,122,880	6,187,358	823,835	6.31	0.27	3,093,679
WV	3	1,019,151	15,475,840	1,793,477	339,717	6.59	0.57	597,826
Region	18	6,504,083	178,437,760	43,566,853	361,338	3.65	0.15	2,420,381
Middle Atlantic								
NJ	0	0	5,015,040	7,730,188	—	0.00	0.00	—
NY	1	13,327	31,728,640	17,990,455	13,327	0.04	0.00	17,990,455
PA	1	511,838	29,013,120	11,881,643	511,838	1.76	0.04	11,881,643
Region	2	525,165	65,756,800	37,602,286	262,583	0.80	0.01	18,801,143
New England								
CT	0	0	3,205,760	3,287,116	—	0.00	0.00	—
RI	0	0	776,960	1,003,464	—	0.00	0.00	—
MA	0	0	5,284,480	6,016,425	—	0.00	0.00	—
VT	1	344,482	6,149,760	562,758	344,482	5.60	0.61	562,758
NH	1	697,142	5,954,560	1,109,252	697,142	11.71	0.63	1,109,252
ME	1	42,183	21,257,600	1,227,928	42,183	0.20	0.03	1,227,928
Region	3	1,083,807	42,629,120	13,206,943	361,269	2.54	0.08	4,402,314
Puerto Rico	1	27,831	2,192,000	3,522,037	27,831	1.27	0.01	3,522,037

Source: 1990 Census of the United States: Microsoft Bookshelf—1992; Forest Service, Land Areas of the National Forest System—As of Sept. 30, 1992 (1993).

The category "national forest," which is the main focus of this book, accounts for the largest number of units (156) and the greatest amount of the acreage (98 percent) in the system. Most of the rest of the acreage is occupied by 20 national grasslands on almost 4 million acres. Note that the Forest Service does not control all land within the boundaries of the system: Within the gross area boundaries of 231,501,923 acres are located 40,048,578 acres of inholdings of state, private and other nonfederal land. For the system as a whole, these inholdings represent 17.3 percent of the gross acreage. This situation results from a fragmentary historical pattern of land ownership, especially in the East, where the land was acquired through Weeks Act purchases. Regionally, regions 8 and 9, which occupy the eastern half of the country, average 47 percent inholdings. This decreases to 10 percent inholdings for the western half of the country and Alaska. The Wayne National Forest (Ohio) has the distinction of being the forest with the highest percentage of inholdings (75 percent). Several of the national grasslands and a few very small national forests, such as the Calaveras Big Tree (380 acres), Choctawhatchee (1199 acres), and Finger Lakes (13,327 acres), have no inholdings. Appendix VIII presents these values for the entire system. There is a

Table 7.4   National Forest System—National and Regional Areas Summary

Area Kind	No. of Units	Gross Acreage	NFS Acreage	Other Acreage
National Totals				
National Forests	156	224,966,052	187,114,116	37,851,936
National Grasslands	20	4,243,823	3,854,184	389,639
Purchase Units	35	2,092,851	294,723	1,798,128
Land Utilization Projects	9	15,937	15,937	0
Research and Experimental Areas	20	73,152	64,869	8,283
Other Areas	33	110,108	109,516	592
Total	273	231,501,923	191,453,345	40,048,578
Eastern Regional Totals (Regions 8 & 9)				
National Forests	52	44,664,895	24,340,692	20,324,203
National Grasslands	2	184,099	38,093	146,006
Purchase Units	26	1,938,740	290,340	1,648,400
Land Utilization Projects	5	14,103	14,103	0
Research and Experimental Areas	14	12,554	4,271	8,283
Other Areas	3	221	221	0
Total	102	45,814,612	24,687,720	22,126,892
Western Regional Totals (Regions 1–6)				
National Forests	104	155,955,792	140,580,029	15,375,763
National Grasslands	18	4,059,724	3,816,091	243,633
Purchase Units	9	154,111	4,383	149,728
Land Utilization Projects	4	1,834	1,834	0
Research and Experimental Areas	6	60,598	60,598	0
Other Areas	30	109,887	109,295	592
Total	171	160,341,946	144,572,230	15,769,716
Alaska Regional Totals (Region 10)				
National Forests	2	24,345,365	22,193,395	2,151,970
National Grasslands		0	0	0
Purchase Units		0	0	0
Land Utilization Projects		0	0	0
Research and Experimental Areas		0	0	0
Other Areas		0	0	0
Total	2	24,345,365	22,193,395	2,151,970

Source: Forest Service, *Land Areas of the National Forest System—As of Sept. 30, 1992* (1993).

continuing program of land exchange and purchase to help alleviate administrative difficulties arising from this land ownership pattern.

The eastern regions (regions 8 and 9) contain only 13 percent of the acreage in the system. The western regions (regions 1–6) account for 75 percent of the acreage, and the Alaska region (region 10) contains 12 percent of the system in only two forests. Although 52 national forests are found in the eastern regions, the average-size forest is 468,000 acres. The 104 national forests of the western regions average over 900,000 acres each. Alaska has only two national forests, but they are the two largest in the system: the Tongass (16.7 million acres) and the Chugach (5.5 million acres).

Table 7.5 summarizes the National Forest System by Forest Service region. Figure 7.4 identified the geographic extent of these regions. Their boundaries generally follow state boundaries, except where region 4 meets region 1 in Idaho and Wyoming and where region 2 meets region 1 in South Dakota. The average size of each region is 21 million acres, but this varies from 11.9 million acres in the Eastern region and

Table 7.5   National Forest System—Regional Areas Summary

Area Kind	No. of Units	Gross Acreage	NFS Acreage	Other Acreage
Northern Region (1)				
National Forests	15	26,915,014	24,046,206	2,868,808
National Grasslands	4	1,260,118	1,260,118	0
Purchase Units	2	707	803	4
Land Utilization Projects	1	240	240	0
Research and Experimental Areas	1	40	40	0
Other areas	3	157	157	0
Total	26	28,176,276	25,307,464	2,868,812
Rocky Mountain Region (2)				
National Forests	17	22,194,198	19,949,414	2,244,784
National Grasslands	7	2,261,016	2,116,306	144,710
Purchase Units		0	0	0
Land Utilization Projects		0	0	0
Research and Experimental Areas	1	144	144	0
Other areas		0	0	0
Total	25	24,455,358	22,065,864	2,389,494
Southwestern Region (3)				
National Forests	12	22,006,685	20,328,863	1,677,822
National Grasslands	4	271,288	262,141	9,147
Purchase Units		0	0	0
Land Utilization Projects	1	240	240	0
Research and Experimental Areas		0	0	0
Other areas	7	103,724	103,132	592
Total	24	22,381,937	20,694,376	1,687,561
Intermountain Region (4)				
National Forests	18	34,112,216	31,773,956	2,338,260
National Grasslands	1	75,248	47,749	27,499
Purchase Units		0	0	0
Land Utilization Projects		0	0	0
Research and Experimental Areas	1	55,630	55,630	0
Other areas		0	0	0
Total	20	34,243,094	31,877,335	2,365,759
Pacific Southwestern Region (5)				
National Forests	19	23,563,370	19,984,015	3,579,355
National Grasslands	1	18,425	18,425	0
Purchase Units	3	145,992	2,299	143,693
Land Utilization Projects		0	0	0
Research and Experimental Areas	3	4,784	4,784	0
Other areas	20	6,006	6,006	0
Total	46	23,738,577	20,015,529	3,723,048
Pacific Northwestern Region (6)				
National Forests	21	27,164,309	24,497,575	2,666,734
National Grasslands	1	173,629	111,352	62,277
Purchase Units	4	7,412	1,381	6,031
Land Utilization Projects	2	1,354	1,354	0
Research and Experimental Areas		0	0	0
Other Areas		0	0	0
Total	28	27,346,704	24,611,662	2,735,042

Table 7.5   (continued)

Area Kind	No. of Units	Gross Acreage	NFS Acreage	Other Acreage
Southern Region (8)				
National Forests	35	23,692,342	12,626,381	11,065,961
National Grasslands	2	184,099	38,093	146,006
Purchase Units	8	988,027	144,861	843,166
Land Utilization Projects	1	40	40	0
Research and Experimental Areas	8	228	228	0
Other Areas		0	0	0
Total	54	24,864,736	12,809,603	12,055,133
Eastern Region (9)				
National Forests	17	20,972,553	11,714,311	9,258,242
National Grasslands		0	0	0
Purchase Units	18	950,713	145,479	805,234
Land Utilization Projects	4	14,063	14,063	0
Research and Experimental Areas	6	12,326	4,043	8,283
Other Areas	3	221	221	0
Total	48	21,949,876	11,878,117	10,071,759
Alaska Region (10)				
National Forests	2	24,345,365	22,193,395	2,151,970
National Grasslands		0	0	0
Purchase Units		0	0	0
Land Utilization Projects		0	0	0
Research and Experimental Areas		0	0	0
Other Areas		0	0	0
Total	2	24,345,365	22,193,395	2,151,970

Source: Forest Service, *Land Areas of the National Forest System—As of Sept. 30, 1992* (1993).

12.8 million acres in the Southern region to 31.9 million acres in the Intermountain region. The regional average is 17 national forests, but this varies from 2 in the Alaska region to 35 in the Southern region. The 25 largest national forests are listed in Table 7.6. All of these forests are close to 2 million acres or larger. Only one of these, the Superior National Forest, is in the eastern half of the country. The two largest national forests are in Alaska. The Toiyabe (Nevada and California) is the largest national forest in the lower 49 states. Table 7.7 identifies all 20 national grasslands. Seventeen of these grasslands are located in the western Great Plains, scattered from Texas and New Mexico to North Dakota. The Little Missouri National Grassland (N. Dakota) is by far the largest at over 1 million acres. The national grasslands located outside of the Great Plains are Curlew (Idaho), Crooked River (Oregon), and Butte Valley (California).

NEW DIRECTIONS FOR THE FOREST SERVICE

America's Great Outdoors Initiative

The *America's Great Outdoor Initiative* was developed to restore and improve outdoor recreation opportunities in the national forests and grasslands. It is a response to national trends that indicate a need to invest in programs and facilities near large

Table 7.6   Largest National Forests

Name	State(s)	Map No.	Gross Acreage	NF Acreage	% NF Acreage
Tongass	AK	6	17,446,595	16,724,169	95.9
Chugach	AK	5	6,898,770	5,469,226	79.3
Toiyabe	NV, CA	37	3,365,253	3,206,471	95.3
Tonto	AZ	13	2,969,542	2,874,896	96.8
Gila	NM	111	2,797,628	2,704,814	96.7
Boise	ID	61	2,958,665	2,648,636	89.5
Humboldt	NV	108	2,618,166	2,477,904	94.6
Challis	ID	64	2,488,105	2,464,679	99.1
Shoshone	WY	173	2,466,555	2,432,990	98.6
Flathead	MT	100	2,629,088	2,354,281	89.5
Payette	ID	70	2,424,892	2,323,195	95.8
Nez Perce	ID	69	2,258,542	2,223,993	98.5
Beaverhead	MT	97	2,198,815	2,128,753	96.8
Lolo	MT	104	2,621,695	2,112,127	80.6
Superior	MN	89	3,260,634	2,065,788	63.4
White River	CO	51	2,088,227	1,961,667	93.9
Inyo	CA, NV	21	2,003,110	1,900,543	94.9
Dixie	UT	154	1,967,190	1,883,955	95.8
San Juan	CO	49	2,107,592	1,875,877	89.0
Rio Grande	CO	45	1,958,787	1,855,196	94.7
Coconino	AZ	8	2,010,797	1,845,659	91.8
Lewis and Clark	MT	103	1,999,229	1,843,286	92.2
Kootenai	MT, ID	68	2,144,857	1,823,283	85.0
Apache	AZ, NM	7	1,876,891	1,808,457	96.4
Sawtooth	ID, UT	72	1,894,780	1,803,602	95.2

Source: Forest Service, *Land Areas of the National Forest System—As of Sept. 30, 1992* (1993).

Table 7.7   National Grasslands

Name	State	Map No.	Gross Acreage	NG Acreage	% NG Acreage
Little Missouri	ND	122	1,028,058	1,028,058	100.0
Buffalo Gap	SD	143	667,021	597,109	89.5
Thunder Basin	WY	175	583,116	572,211	98.1
Comanche	CO	52	460,211	435,319	94.6
Pawnee	CO	53	214,328	193,060	90.1
Grand River	SD	145	155,075	155,075	100.0
Kiowa	NM	114	143,497	136,417	95.1
Fort Pierre	SD	144	124,758	115,997	93.0
Crooked River	OR	138	173,629	111,352	64.1
Cimarron	KS	79	116,319	108,175	93.0
Oglala	NE	107	95,263	94,435	99.1
Rita Blanca	TX, OK	126	93,229	92,989	99.7
Sheyenne	ND	123	70,268	70,268	100.0
Curlew	ID	76	75,248	47,749	63.5
Black Kettle	OK, TX	125	33,113	31,286	94.5
Lyndon B. Johnson	TX	151	115,438	20,309	17.6
Butte Valley	CA	39	18,425	18,425	100.0
Caddo	TX	150	68,661	17,784	25.9
Cedar River	ND	121	6,717	6,717	100.0
McClelland Creek	TX	152	1,449	1,449	100.0

Source: Forest Service, *Land Areas of the National Forest System—As of Sept. 30, 1992* (1993).

populations, to respond to diversifying and aging populations, and to respond to a growing awareness and concern for the environment. Primary areas of focus are facilities and trails maintenance and construction, including providing accessibility for all people and reducing maintenance backlogs; management of special areas, with an emphasis on congressionally designated areas; and conservation education and interpretation and information services to meet the changing needs of an increasing urban-based population. The initiative provides $625 million over a 4- to 5-year period to restore and improve national forest and grassland recreational opportunities. Total funding for FY92 was $55 million, and $109 million was allocated for FY93. Federal funding is being supplemented with contributions of materials, labor, time and funds by nonfederal partners. During 1992, forests near urban locations, particularly those that incorporate special designated areas, received the most funding. Work was accomplished with a variety of partnerships and volunteers as well as with Forest Service personnel and contracts. Funding was devoted primarily to development of plans and guidelines. Major maintenance and construction programs will be implemented in the succeeding years of the initiative.

Hundreds of projects were accomplished during the first year of the America's Great Outdoors Initiative, among them:

- The 1992 Kirkwood Ranch Living History Program was established at Hell's Canyon National Recreation Area (Idaho and Oregon), which reached 20,000 people.
- Interpretive kiosks were constructed along the Mt. Baker Scenic Byway on the Mt. Baker National Forest (Washington). This scenic byway is traveled by over 200,000 people each year.
- Trail repair was conducted at a bear-viewing site on the Stikine Area of Alaska's Tongass National Forest.
- The water system at a campground at Lake Conasauga on the Chattahoochee National Forest (Georgia) was reconstructed.
- The Gallatin National Forest (Montana) conducted an accessibility survey with input from people with disabilities in the community.

Ecosystem Approach

On June 4, 1992, Chief F. Dale Robertson announced the *ecosystem management approach* to managing national forests and grasslands, along with the elimination of clear cutting as a standard timber harvest practice. This was a major policy change for the Forest Service. Ecosystem management refers to an ecological approach that will be used to achieve multiple-use management of the National Forest System. This approach is designed to better blend the needs of people and environmental values in ways that sustain diverse, healthy, and productive ecosystems. Ecosystem management emphasizes the value of all forest resources and the need to manage lands holistically, rather than for individual resources. This approach provides diverse and productive habitat for wildlife and fisheries, clean water and air, recreational opportunities, forest products, and long-term ecosystem sustainability that benefits both the land and the people living on it. The ecosystem approach is a continuation of the directions set in earlier statements, particularly the 1990 RPA program. The Forest

Service's research program is being significantly reoriented as a result of the ecosystem management policy. Research priorities are being changed to reflect the land manager's strong need for additional scientific information to implement ecosystem management. Forest Service scientists are spending more time working directly with land managers to ensure that the best available scientific information is used when land management decisions are made.

Scenic Byways

Driving for pleasure and viewing scenery is the most popular recreational activity in the national forests, accounting for one-third of the total recreational use. The recreating public heavily uses the 105,000 miles of roads in the national forests maintained for passenger vehicles. The *National Scenic Byways Program*, which was initiated by the Forest Service in 1988, identifies travel routes that traverse scenic corridors with outstanding aesthetic, cultural, or historical values. These byways offer motorists a spectrum of unique forest settings ranging from dense rain forests, to northern hardwoods, to mountain tundra and alpine forests—and an opportunity to pass through some of America's most spectacular scenery. The Forest Service designated its first scenic byway in 1988. Since then, the program has grown to 114 scenic byways extending over 6000 miles, in 33 states, in January 1993. In FY92, 14 new byways were added to the program. The Scenic Byways Program is focused on road corridors that contain scenic vistas and the facilities for enjoying them. Scenic byway corridors contain outstanding aesthetic, cultural, and interpretive values and offer many opportunities to provide visual and physical access; showcase Forest Service multiple-use management; interpret outstanding resource values; and strengthen service to urban residents, ethnic minorities, the physically challenged, the elderly, and the young.

The establishment of scenic byways in partnership with local communities can help stimulate the local tourism industry and diversify economies. Partnerships encompass other agencies, user groups, private industry, and nonprofit organizations. The Plymouth Division of Chrysler Motors was the first major partner for the Scenic Byways Program. Plymouth and two other key partners, Falcon Press and the Forest Education Foundation, worked to provide information to the driving public about the opportunities for viewing and enjoying the national forests. On June 27, 1992, the Forest Service dedicated the 100th national forest scenic byway—The Sawtooth Scenic Byway. This 61-mile byway is located on the Sawtooth National Forest in Idaho.

Challenge Cost-Share Program

The *Challenge Cost-Share Program* is a means to extend federal monies for recreation management by entering into cost-sharing partnerships with other agencies and with volunteers, private business, nonprofit organizations, and service clubs. In FY88, the first year of the Challenge Cost-Share effort, 30 projects were initiated nationwide. The total Forest Service funding level was $500,000, which was matched by $908,000 in partner contributions (of money, materials, and labor). In FY92, $15,496,000 in Forest Service funding was matched by almost $24,000,000 in partner contributions. In FY93, $15.2 million in Forest Service funding was matched by an estimated $24 to

30 million in partner contributions. Challenge Cost-Share projects represent more than dollars and cents; they are people working toward common goals. Following are some examples of successful, completed projects:

- The Williams Fork Boardwalk Construction Project (Colorado) included 14 different groups and agencies in cooperation with the Middle Park Ranger District and Routt National Forest employees. In just one weekend, 200 volunteers constructed a 1650-foot walkway access to a beaver pond wetland area. Preplanning required 140 hours of staff time by Volunteers for Outdoor Colorado and other volunteer labor. Physically challenged people were involved in the design and construction of the boardwalk; they are just one of the many groups of people who will benefit from this project.
- The Pot Creek Cultural Interpretive Site Project, in its third year on the Camino Real Ranger District in the Carson National Forest (New Mexico), has developed 1 mile of accessible trail with interpretive signs that tell the story of how the Anasazi lived over 1000 years ago. A small pueblo and kiva have been reconstructed and are open to the public for viewing. Partners include the New Mexico Volunteers for the Outdoors and the Taos Archaeological Society.
- Eight states and local organizations are working in cooperation with the Cohutta Ranger District on the Chattahoochee National Forest (Georgia) to recycle Christmas trees to improve fish habitat in Murray and Conasauga Lakes. The discarded trees now provide spawning sites as well as structures for fish cover.

Heritage Program

The public is keenly interested in heritage resources as evidenced by recreational use research that places visiting historic and archaeological sites second only to day hiking and by the overwhelming public response to such programs as "Passport in Time." The National Historic Preservation Act and the 1988 amendments to the Archeological Resources Protection Act call for programs to enhance the general public's understanding and appreciation of Heritage Program resources. The *Heritage Strategy*, released in December 1992, seeks to address the intent of those laws and to address the broad goals of heritage management. This not only includes protection from other resource developments, but also protection from vandalism and looting, investigation of important sites and areas outside of other resource project areas, preservation for present and future generations, and public interpretation and participation. The Heritage Program attempts to balance support responsibilities with larger program responsibilities. It includes 5 strategies:

1. Clarify or change existing programs and direction, through inclusion of heritage elements in forest planning, RPA, NEPA, and so forth.
2. Foster internal and external support by building partnerships with other Forest Service staffs, academia, and other interest groups.
3. Enhance recreational experiences through presentation of heritage values, via interpretation, education, and public participation.
4. Show that the past is relevant to contemporary issues and environmental concerns.
5. Develop a quality workforce to achieve a quality program by providing training that reflects the Heritage Program goals.

Passport in Time

Passport in Time is entering its fifth year as a national program dedicated to a partnership with the public in the management of Heritage Program resources. It has revitalized the Heritage Program workforce, accomplished valuable research and enhancement projects, and drawn rave reviews from the public. Passport in Time began in the Eastern region in 1989. In 1990, 66 volunteers contributed 4500 hours on seven projects in three regions. Today, over 1700 volunteers have contributed nearly 77,000 hours. There are currently 88 projects in 56 national forests in 23 states in eight of the nine regions. Passport in Time helps fill a growing recreational niche—that of *ecotourism*. The recreating public wants opportunities to become involved and to help in caring for the environment. They are getting older and healthier and have valuable skills to share. There are numerous instances where projects would not have been accomplished without the help and talent of the volunteers. Passport in Time is helping the Forest Service accomplish such deferred management tasks as wilderness survey, site stabilization, protection and monitoring of sensitive sites, and site evaluation.

Campground Reservation System

In response to requests by national forest campground users, an advance reservation service for campsites is now available. Reservations can be made year-round through a toll-free telephone number or by mail-in application. Initiated in 1989, the system was first operated under contract by Mistix, Inc., a reservations company in San Diego, Calif. They took the reservations, issued camping permits, and forwarded daily reports to all ranger districts on the system. Mistix also made reservations for some national parks and Army Corps of Engineers campgrounds. In 1992, Mistix made 80,980 reservations and collected $2,826,626 for the Forest Service and its concessionaires. A reservation fee of $6 for family units and $10 for group units was charged, in addition to the normal user fee for each reservation made. Mistix's 5-year contract ended December 31, 1993. A new contract was given to National Recreation Reservations of Cumberland, Md., effective January 1, 1994. The new reservation fee is $7.50 for family units and $15.00 for group units, in addition to the regular use fee. First-come, first-served sections are still available in the campgrounds participating in the program or in adjacent campgrounds.

Access America's Great Outdoors

To ensure that everyone has the opportunity to enjoy recreation in national forests, the chief of the Forest Service established an agency goal of "becoming the leading provider of accessible outdoor recreation opportunities in America." For millions of Americans, choices for a desired recreational experience are limited, as the majority of existing facilities were developed through traditional design, which has generally excluded people with disabilities. *Universal design* is a relatively new approach that considers the needs of all users, including children, older people, and people with sensory, cognitive, and mobility disabilities. The goal of universal design is to design facilities, programs, and services that provide all visitors with a sense of dignity,

independence, and social integration. It links customer expectations with accessibility across diverse recreation settings ranging from urban to primitive. Costs are estimated to exceed $300 million for a minimum level of accessibility. *Access America's Great Outdoors* invested $10 million in FY92 and the same in FY93 toward this facility rehabilitation effort.

References

Cleveland, Treadwell Jr. *National Forests as Recreation Grounds*. Annals of the American Academy of Political and Social Science 35:2(Mar., 1910), 25–26, 29–31.

Culhane, Paul J. *Public Lands Politics*. Baltimore: Published for Resources for the Future by Johns Hopkins University Press, 1981.

Fedkiw, John. *The Evolving Use and Management of the Nation's Forests, Grasslands, Croplands, and Related Resources*. A Technical Document Supporting the 1989 USDA Forest Service RPA Assessment—General Technical Report RM-175. Forest Service, USDA, September 1989.

Forest Service, USDA. *A Description of Forest Service Programs and Responsibilities*. A Technical Document Supporting the 1989 USDA Forest Service RPA Assessment—General Technical Report RM-176. September 1989.

Forest Service, USDA. *Land Areas of the National Forest System as of Sept. 30, 1992*, February 1993a.

Forest Service, USDA. *Report of the Forest Service—Fiscal Year 1992*. February 1993b.

Frome, Michael. *Whose Woods These Are: The Story of the National Forests*. Garden City, N.Y.: Doubleday & Co., 1962.

Frome, Michael. *The Forest Service*. Second edition. Boulder, Colo.: Westview Press, 1984.

Hendee, John C., George H. Stankey, and Robert C. Lucas. *Wilderness Management*. Golden, Colo.: North American Press, 1990.

Hilts, Len. *National Forest Guide*. Chicago: Rand McNally, 1978.

Ise, John. *The United States Forest Policy*. New Haven: Yale University Press, 1920.

Norse, Elliott A. *Ancient Forests of the Pacific Northwest*. Washington, D.C.: Island Press, 1990.

Pinchot, Gifford. *Breaking New Ground*. New York: Harcourt, Brace & Co., 1947.

Robinson, Glen O. *The Forest Service: A Study in Public Land Management*. Baltimore: Published for Resources for the Future by Johns Hopkins University Press, 1975.

Steen, Harold K. *The U.S. Forest Service: A History*. Seattle: University of Washington Press, 1977.

West, Terry L. *Centennial Mini-Histories of the Forest Service*. Forest Service, USDA, July 1992.

Wilkinson, Charles F., and H. Michael Anderson. *Land and Resource Planning in the National Forests*. Washington, D.C.: Island Press, 1987.

Zaslowsky, Dyan, and the Wilderness Society. *These American Lands*. New York: Henry Holt and Co., 1986.

National Forest System: Recreational Planning and Management

The earth and its resources belong of right to its people.

Gifford Pinchot

This chapter focuses on the topic of recreation planning and management in the National Forest System. Chapter 7 identified the historical evolution of planning and management policies that have been implemented internally by the Forest Service, as well as the role of new legislation passed by Congress. The most dramatic impact on planning and management was a result of this legislation enacted by Congress. It all started with the Multiple-Use Sustained Yield Act (1960) and continued with the Wilderness Act (1964), the Wild and Scenic Rivers Act (1968), the National Environmental Policy Act (1970), the Forest and Rangeland Renewable Resources Planning Act (1974), and the National Forest Management Act (1976). A new trend that emerged in the 1970s was the beginning of widespread public participation in the planning process. Public participation was required in the newly passed legislation that mandated the preparation of environmental impact statements (EISs). In the allocation of resources in the National Forest System, the Forest Service historically has favored the Gifford Pinchot concept of conservation. This philosophy of natural resource management often favored commodity utilization of natural resources at the expense of amenity resources.

The passage of the Multiple Use Act (1960) for the first time recognized recreation as one of the five principal resource values for which the National Forest System was to be managed. The amenity resource values (outdoor recreation and fish and wildlife) now had equal status with the traditional commodity resource values (timber and grazing) as planning and management decisions were made for the National Forest System. Increasing demand generated by the recreation explosion of the 1950s and 1960s set the stage for conflicts over allocation of resources in the National Forest. Many recreationists now clamored for National Forest land to be used for its amenity value, as opposed to commodity value. Membership in environmental interest groups such as the Sierra Club, the Wilderness Society, and the Audubon Society grew dra-

matically as more Americans increased their environmental awareness. Much of this environmental awareness can be attributed to increasing contact with natural environments during recreational experiences. These environmental interest groups became major players in the National Forest planning and management process. The legislation of the 1960s and 1970s provided the basis for legal suits brought against the Forest Service by these environmental interest groups. While almost all management decisions had once been made internally by the Forest Service, the courts were now deciding certain aspects of management direction.

This chapter uses the *Forest Service Manual* as its principal source. The *Manual* is an extremely large and complex document and is not available in libraries.[1] The format of this chapter will differ from the others in that in many places lists of objectives and policies will be the principal text. This is such an important topic that it should be included up front, in a chapter, rather than buried in an appendix. Because of the large amount of material contained in this chapter, a list format is used to save space.

RECREATION PLANNING

Objectives, Policy, and Responsibilities

Recreation planning on National Forest System lands is an integral part of Forest land and resource management planning, as required by the Forest and Rangeland Renewable Resources Planning Act (RPA) of 1974 and amended by the National Forest Management Act (NFMA) of 1976. The objective of recreation planning is to inventory, analyze, and propose levels and types of uses to meet the nation's outdoor recreation needs as established through RPA program and assessment, regional guides, and forest plans.

Objectives   Specific objectives of recreation resource planning are to:

- Inventory existing and potential recreational opportunities, determine future needs for those opportunities, analyze the issues and current management situation, and propose management activities to integrate the recreational needs of the public into planning for other resource needs.
- Determine levels, standards, and types of recreational opportunities needed to achieve recreational goals and to resolve issues and concerns identified in the *Forest*

---

[1]The author is extremely disappointed with the difficulty encountered in securing the sections of the *Manual* pertaining to recreation planning and management. He received the impression that it was a top-secret document that the Forest Service Washington office did not want to release. Even when most of the needed sections of the *Manual* were finally obtained, the material contained therein was often obsolete and not current. It is probably the enormity and complexity of the *Manual* that makes it extremely difficult to update and keep current. This problem in obtaining the *Forest Service Manual* was similar to a general lack of cooperation from many offices of the Forest Service in obtaining data that was only available from them. Dealing with the bureaucracy of the Forest Service has been the most demanding research endeavor this author has undertaken in his 28-year academic career.

Service Manual, section 2300, the RPA program, regional guides, and forest land resource management plans.

- Collect, store, use, and distribute recreational resource inventory data to better manage the resource and keep managers and the using public aware of the size and diversity of the Forest Service recreation program.
- Coordinate with other federal, state, and local agencies and the private sector in order to avoid competition with the private sector, duplication of recreational facilities and programs, and land-use conflicts.

Policy   To meet these objectives, the policy of the Forest Service is to:

- Use the Recreation Opportunity Spectrum (ROS, described later in the chapter) to establish planning criteria, generate objectives for recreation, evaluate public issues, integrate management concerns, project recreational needs and demands, and coordinate management objectives.
- Use the ROS system to develop standards and guidelines for proposed recreational resource use and development.
- Use the ROS system guidelines to describe recreational opportunities and coordinate with other recreational suppliers.
- Recognize that individual national forests need not provide recreational opportunities in each ROS class.
- Not provide urban opportunities with appropriated or other public funds, but rather, to channel urban opportunities provided by private-sector funds to private land if available.

Responsibilities   The responsibilities for working to achieve these objectives, for the various tiers of administrative responsibility, are as follows:

> *Director, Recreation Management Staff, Washington Office*   The director of Recreation Management at the Washington office is responsible for ensuring that recreation planning is coordinated with other agencies and that the Washington office staff are involved in land and resource management planning.
>
> *Regional Forester*   The regional forester, with the assistance of the Recreation Management staff, is to coordinate planning activities with external organizations and other government agencies to establish regional standards, and to ensure the integrity of the recreational resource in the national forest plan.
>
> *Forest Supervisor*   The forest supervisor, with the assistance of the Forest Recreation Management staff, shall:
>
> 1   Ensure that the recreational resource is integrated into the national forest plan.
> 2   Monitor the implementation schedule.
> 3   Ensure that Recreation Opportunity Spectrum (ROS) settings for recreational opportunities are presented in the national forest plan.
> 4   Assure the availability and accuracy of national forest recreation data.
> 5   Recommend recreation representatives to the forest supervisor to serve on interdisciplinary teams.
>
> *District Ranger*   The district ranger, with the assistance of the District Recreation staff, shall coordinate recreational objectives and road standards, coordinate

with the Forest Engineering staff to assure that strategies for access management are commensurate with recreational experience levels, and establish and implement the recreational portion of the forest plan implementation schedule.

Recreation Opportunity Spectrum

Zoning of land and water for various recreational uses is a traditional function of Forest Service planning that has assumed even greater importance in the NFMA planning process. The NFMA requires that "a broad spectrum of . . . outdoor recreation opportunities shall be provided" in the forest plans. This requirement has been implemented by the Forest Service through the *Recreation Opportunity Spectrum* (ROS). The ROS system and the *ROS Users Guide* (Forest Service) are used to delineate, define, and integrate outdoor recreation opportunities in land and resource management planning. Recreation integration and coordination provides for integrated management prescriptions and associated standards to deal with the recreational resource. The basic objective of ROS planning is to provide a diverse set of recreational opportunities to satisfy the wide range of public tastes and preferences, both now and in the future.

The ROS is an indispensable tool for recreation planning. It can be used to:

- Inventory existing opportunities
- Analyze the effects of other resource activities
- Estimate the consequences of management decisions on planned opportunities
- Link user desires with recreational opportunity
- Identify complementary roles of all recreational suppliers
- Develop standards and guidelines for planned settings and monitoring activities
- Help design integrated project sites for forest plan implementation

Setting Indicators   The end product of recreation management is the experiences people have. The key to providing most experience opportunities is the setting and how it is managed. In the ROS system, the land managers of the Forest Service can facilitate (or hamper) many desired experiences in how they manage seven *setting indicators*. Appendix IX presents a series of matrices that establish limits of acceptable change and interprets these setting indicators for the six ROS classes. Four terms are used to evaluate these setting indicators. The *norm* in the matrices describes normal conditions found in the setting. *Fully compatible* describes conditions that meet or exceed the norm. *Inconsistent* represents conditions that are not generally compatible with the norm but may be necessary under some circumstances to meet management objectives. *Unacceptable* defines conditions that, under any circumstances, do not permit the creation or maintenance of a given setting. Where unacceptable conditions are unavoidable, a change in setting will often result, which must be handled appropriately in the forest planning National Environmental Policy Act (NEPA) process. These seven setting indicators are as follows:

1. *Access* Access includes type and mode of travel. Highly developed access generally reduces the opportunities for solitude, risk, and challenge. It can enhance, however, opportunities for socializing, and feelings of safety and comfort. Accessibility for persons with disabilities can be organized along the

ROS framework. Access in "rural" and "urban" settings should be completely barrier-free. Increasing difficulty should be designed into travel ways as one moves toward the "primitive" end of the spectrum to elicit greater feelings of challenge and achievement.

2. *Remoteness*   This refers to the extent to which individuals perceive themselves as being removed from the sights and sounds of other human activity. A lack of remoteness is important for some setting experiences.

3. *Social Encounters*   This factor refers to the number and types of other recreationists met along travel ways, or camped within sight or sound of others. This setting indicator measures the extent to which an area provides opportunities for solitude or social interaction. Increasing the number of visitors to an area changes the kind of recreational experience offered, attracting new users and causing others to leave.

4. *Visitor Management*   This includes the degree to which visitors are regulated and controlled as well as the level of information and services provided for visitor enjoyment. In some opportunity settings, controls are expected and appropriate. For instance, people sometimes seek developed settings for security and safety. Elsewhere, on-site controls such as on-site interpretation and directional signing may detract from desired experiences, such as independence, self-discovery, self-reliance, and risk taking. Thus the type and level of information, and where it is provided to the visitor, may facilitate or hinder a desired experience. Generally, on-site information is more appropriate at the developed end of the spectrum, while off-site sources are preferable at the primitive end.

5. *On-site Development and Site Management*   This indicator refers to the level of site development. A lack of facilities and site modifications can enhance feelings of self-reliance and independence and can provide experiences with a high degree of naturalness. Highly developed facilities can add feelings of comfort and convenience, and increase opportunities for socializing.

6. *Visitor Impacts*   This factor refers to the impacts of visitor use on the environment. The relevant question for managers is not how impacts can be prevented, but rather, how much change will be allowed and which actions are appropriate for control. These impacts include soil and vegetation; wildlife habitat; and air, water, and sound quality. Maintaining air, water, and noise quality standards in the face of visitor impacts is important in all ROS classes.

7. *Naturalness*   This setting indicator refers to the degree of naturalness of the setting; it affects psychological outcomes associated with enjoying nature. This indicator is portrayed by using a compatible visual quality objective (VQO) for each setting. There are five VQOs: preservation, retention, partial retention, modification, and maximum modification. These will be described later in the chapter.

Classes   ROS defines six recreational opportunity classes that provide different settings for recreational use: "urban," "rural," "roaded natural," "semiprimitive motorized," "semiprimitive nonmotorized," and "primitive." Each class is defined in terms of its combination of activity, setting, and experience opportunities. Subclasses may be established to reflect local or regional conditions, as long as aggregations can

be made back to the six major classes for regional or national summaries. Table 8.1 lists some of the subclasses that have been used. ROS classes are used to describe all recreational opportunity areas—from natural, undisturbed, and undeveloped to heavily used, modified, and developed. The criteria involving the physical, social, and managerial environments found in the *ROS Users Guide* are applied to delineate the different ROS classes of land. Providing "urban" class areas is not normally an appropriate management objective for national forest lands. The ROS system provides a framework for dividing land into specific recreation zones and for establishing standards for future management of those zones. By zoning an area as a particular ROS class the Forest Service must exclude activities from the area that are inconsistent with providing the features associated with that ROS class. The ROS system allows for highly individualized land classification for recreation.

Urban   "Urban" class settings are characterized by high levels of human activity and by concentrated development, including developments for recreational opportunities. In urban settings levels of recreation use vary and can be extremely high or dense. There is a preponderance of signs and other indications of regulations on the user's behavior. The landscape is dominated by human structures, and green space is only sporadically dominant. Structures and structural complexes predominate and may include major resorts and marinas, national and regional ski areas, towns, industrial sites, condominiums, or second-home developments. An extremely wide variety of land-based, water-based, and snow- and ice-based recreational activities are also available in this setting. The vegetative cover is often exotic and manicured, although the background may have natural-appearing elements. Large numbers of users can be expected, both on-site and in nearby areas. This category has no re-

Table 8.1   Recreation Opportunity Spectrum Subclasses

Pristine	A subclass of "primitive" used to describe areas having high-quality solitude and where use is generally not encouraged by the construction of trails.
Motorized primitive	Used in Alaska to designate very remote lightly used settings where access is traditionally by float plane or power boat.
Portal, Transition	These two subclasses have been used to describe heavily used unmodified settings such as gateways to the more popular wilderness areas. They are in the "semiprimitive nonmotorized" ROS class; however, the social setting is more toward "roaded natural."
Roaded modified	Used to subdivide that part of "roaded natural" that has been heavily modified. Modification is generally more like rural except that the social setting is semiprimitive. Many feel this should be a separate ROS class.
Roaded scenic	A subclass of roaded natural that describes areas very sensitive to modification, such as along scenic highways.
Roaded natural nonmotorized	Areas that are closed to motorized use, yet have been heavily modified or are not large enough to be set aside as semiprimitive nonmotorized.
Roaded natural appearing	Another name for "roaded natural."

Source: Forest Service, *1986 ROS Book.*

moteness distance or size criteria. The concept of capacity coefficient ranges measured in PAOT per acre, where PAOT = persons at one time, is not applicable to this class.

Rural   In the "rural" class settings, the sights and sounds of human activity are readily evident, though less pronounced and less concentrated than in the "urban" class. The levels of use vary but do not reach the concentrations found in the "urban" class except at specialized and developed sites. While the characteristic landscape is often dominated by human-caused geometric patterns, there is also a dominant sense of open green space. Structures are readily apparent and may range from scattered clusters to small dominant clusters including power lines, microwave installations, local ski areas, minor resorts, and recreation sites. The same wide variety of land-based, water-based, and snow- and ice-based recreational activities of the "urban" class are available in the "rural" class. A considerable number of the facilities are designed for use by a large number of people. The frequency of contact with other people is moderate to high on developed sites, roads and trails, and water surfaces, and becomes moderate when away from developed sites. There are no remoteness distance or size criteria for this class. Regimentation and controls are obvious, numerous, and largely in harmony with the human-made environment. The capacity coefficient ranges range from 0.830 to 7.500 PAOT/acre.

The principles adopted by the ROS system to assess the visual attractiveness of the urban and rural settings dictate that human-caused visual patterns dominate the landscape. However, this should not be interpreted to mean that these areas are visually unattractive. On the contrary, there are many examples of beautiful cities, quaint villages, and the pastoral beauty of farm and ranch lands.

Roaded Natural   The "roaded natural" class is characterized by predominately natural-appearing settings, with moderate sights and sounds of human activities and structures. The overall perception is one of naturalness. Evidence of human activity varies from area to area and includes improved highways, railroads, developed campgrounds, small resorts and ski areas, livestock grazing, timber-harvesting operations, watershed restoration activities, and water diversion structures. Roads and motorized equipment are common in this setting. Density of use is moderate except at specific developed sites, and regulations on user behaviors are generally less evident than in the urban or rural setting. A wide range of land-based, water-based, and snow- and ice-based recreational activities are still common. There is an opportunity to have a high degree of interaction with the natural environment, as well as an opportunity for both motorized and nonmotorized forms of recreation. The interaction between users may be low to moderate, but evidence of other users is prevalent. Conventional motorized use is provided for in construction standards and design of facilities. Remoteness criteria do apply to this class. This is an area designated to be within 0.5 mile from better-than-primitive roads and from railroads. There are no size criteria. Structures are generally scattered and may include power lines and microwave installations. The frequency of contact is moderate to high on roads but low to moderate on trails and away from roads. The capacity coefficient ranges range from 0.083 to 7.500 PAOT/acre.

In some regions, a distinct subclass of setting features exists within the "roaded natural" class. This subclass occurs where human modification is locally dominant

or codominant with a natural-appearing landscape, much like the rural setting. However, the recreational opportunities provided are significantly different from the rural setting. For example, although numerous, highly improved roads might exist in this subclass, yet there is a sense of remoteness because of the distances from major travel ways. In addition, the density of recreation is often low compared with that in the "rural" class. Also, users have the opportunity for exploration and to use both on-road recreational vehicles and ORVs. Camping is not confined to developed campsites, so users have considerable autonomy in choosing sites and using equipment.

Semiprimitive   Both the "semiprimitive motorized" and "nonmotorized" classes are characterized by predominately natural or natural-appearing landscapes. Structures are rare or isolated in these areas. The moderate to large size of these areas gives a strong feeling of remoteness from the more heavily used and developed areas. The concentration of users is low, but there is often evidence of other users. The area is managed in such a way that minimum on-site controls and restrictions may be present but are subtle. Within these settings, there are ample opportunities to practice wild land skills and to achieve feelings of self-reliance. An environment is provided that offers challenge and risk. The number of land-based, water-based, and snow- and ice-based recreational activities is considerably less than in the "roaded natural," "rural," or "urban" settings. *The most significant difference between the semiprimitive motorized and nonmotorized settings is the presence or absence of motorized vehicles.* In the nonmotorized settings, the presence of roads is tolerated, provided that: they are closed to public use, that they are used infrequently for resource protection and management, and that the road standards and locations are visually appropriate for the physical setting. In many cases, old roads are acceptable as nonmotorized travel ways as long as they do not reflect misuse or poor stewardship of the land. These roads would have motorized use in the "semiprimitive motorized" class, especially by ORVs. The size criterion for both classes is 2500 acres. The capacity coefficient ranges from a low of 0.008 to a high of 0.083 PAOT/acre.

The "motorized" and "nonmotorized" classes are distinguished as follows:

Motorized   Here there is a moderate probability of experiencing isolation from the sights and sounds of humans, while still having the opportunity to use motorized equipment when in the area. Remoteness criteria apply to this class: A semiprimitive motorized area must be within 0.5 mile of primitive roads or trails used by motor vehicles, but not closer than 0.5 mile from better-than-primitive roads. The social setting is one of low to moderate contact frequency.

Nonmotorized   Here there is a high, but not extremely high, probability of experiencing isolation from the sights and sounds of humans. Remoteness criteria also apply to this class: A semiprimitive nonmotorized area must be at least 0.5 mile but not more than 3 miles from all roads, railroads, or trails with motorized use and can include the existence of primitive roads and trails if usually closed to motorized use. The social setting criteria are usually 6 to 15 parties per day encountered on trails and 6 or fewer visible at campsites.

Primitive   Primitive settings are characterized by essentially unmodified natural environments. Their size (over 5,000 acres) and configuration assure remoteness from the sights and sounds of human activity. The use of motorized vehicles and equip-

ment is not permitted except in extreme emergencies, such as saving someone's life or protecting the resource. In the "primitive" class the user is forced to be self-reliant and expects low levels of user density. The range of land-based, water-based, and snow- and ice-based recreational activities is much more restricted than in the other settings. The only activities allowed are those based on human power. The area is managed to be essentially free from evidence of human-induced restrictions and controls. A remoteness criterion applies to this class: A primitive area must be at least 3 miles from all roads, railroads, or trails with motorized use. Structures are extremely rare. The social setting criteria specify that usually fewer than six parties per day are encountered on the trails and fewer than three parties are visible at campsites. On-site regimentation is low, with controls primarily off-site. The capacity coefficient ranges from a low of 0.002 to a high of 0.025 PAOT/acre.

In primitive and semiprimitive settings, the use of the visual management system plays a critical role in assessing and maintaining conditions that support the naturalness of the area. For example, it may not be enough to forbid motorized use in the "nonmotorized" ROS classes. The character of any roads or other structures, such as buildings, bridges, or fences, must also be in harmony with the natural landscape.

Visual Resource Management

The National Forest Management Act regulations provide, as part of the forest planning process, for consideration of "the landscape's visual attractiveness and the public's visual expectations." The objective of the Forest Service is to manage all National Forest System lands to attain the highest possible visual quality commensurate with other appropriate public uses, costs, and benefits. The policy to achieve this objective is to:

- Inventory, evaluate, and manage the visual resource as a fully integrated part of the National Forest System land management process.
- Employ a systematic, interdisciplinary approach in this effort to ensure the integrated use of the natural and social sciences and the environmental design arts.
- Ensure that the visual resource is treated equally with other resources.
- Apply landscape management principles routinely in all National Forest System activities.

The *visual resource management system* consists of the following:

- Visual quality objectives, inventories, and direction
- Existing visual conditions inventory
- Visual absorption capability
- Future visual condition assessment

Visual quality objectives (VQOs) are to be used when developing or modifying forest plans, environmental assessments, environmental impact statements, and project-level decisions. The five visual quality objectives, each representing a different degree of acceptable alteration of the natural appearing landscape, are as follows:

1. *Preservation* This VQO allows ecological changes only. Management activities, except for very low visual-impact recreational facilities, are prohibited.

2. *Retention*   This VQO provides for management activities that are not visually evident. Under retention, activities may only repeat the form, line, color, and texture that are frequently found in the characteristic landscape. Changes in their size, amount, intensity, direction, pattern, and so forth, should not be evident.

3. *Partial Retention*   Management activities are visually evident but subordinate to the characteristic landscape when managed according to the partial retention VQO. Activities may repeat form, line, color, or texture common to the characteristic landscape but changes in their size, amount, intensity, direction, pattern, and so forth, remain visually subordinate to the characteristic landscape.

4. *Modification*   Under this VQO, management activities may visually dominate the original characteristic landscape. However, alterations of vegetation and landform must borrow from naturally established form, line, color, and texture so completely and at such a scale that visual characteristics of natural occurrences within the surrounding area or character type are retained.

5. *Maximum Modification*   Management activities that alter vegetation and landform may dominate the characteristic landscape. However, when viewed as background, the visual characteristics must be those of natural occurrences within the surrounding area or character type. When viewed as foreground or middle ground, the visual characteristics do not have to completely borrow from naturally established form, line, color, or texture. Alterations may also be out of scale or contain detail that is incongruent with natural occurrences as seen in foreground or middle ground areas.

Table 8.2 presents the VQOs for each ROS class, and Table 8.3 presents the visual access strategies for each ROS class.

Table 8.2   Visual Quality Objectives (VQOs) for Each ROS Class

| | Visual Quality Objectives | | | | |
ROS Class	Preservation	Retention	Partial Retention	Modification	Maximum Modification
Primitive	Norm[1]	Inconsistent[2]	///////////////////////// /////////////////////////	///////////////////// ///////////////////// /////////////////////	///////////////////// ///////////////////// /////////////////////
Semiprimitive nonmotorized		Norm	Inconsistent	/////////////Unacceptable[3]///////////// /////////////////////	///////////////////// /////////////////////
Semiprimitive motorized	—Fully Compatible—		Norm[4]	Inconsistent	/////////////////////
Roaded natural			Norm	Norm[5]	Inconsistent
Rural				Norm	Norm
Urban[6]	Acceptable				Norm

[1]Norm: the typical objective for the physical setting.
[2]Inconsistent: Objectives that are not generally compatible with the physical setting but may be necessary under certain circumstances.
[3]Unacceptable: Objectionable VQOs under any circumstances.
[4]Partial retention is desirable as viewed from sensitive roads and trails (Forest Service, USDA, *National Agriculture Handbook* 462. 1974).
[5]Modification acceptable where not visually dominant from sensitive roads and trails.
[6]Urban setting is normally inappropriate on national forest land.
Source: Forest Service, *Forest Service Manual*, section 2311.11.

Table 8.3   Visual Access Strategies for Each ROS Class

ROS Class	Cross-Country Travel & Trails[1]	Easy Trails[2]	Access Strategies Primitive Roads[3]	Controlled Access Roads[4]	Full Access Roads[5]
Primitive	Norm[6]	Inconsistent[7]	///////////////////// /////////////////////	///////////////////////// ///////////////////////// /////////////////////////	/////////////////// /////////////////// ///////////////////
Semiprimitive nonmotorized		Norm	Inconsistent	//////////////Unacceptable[8]////////////// /////////////////////////	/////////////////// /////////////////// ///////////////////
Semiprimitive motorized			Norm	Inconsistent	///////////////////
Roaded natural	Acceptable[9]			Norm	
Rural					Norm
Urban					

[1]Cross-country travel to difficult trails.
[2]Trails, easy to most difficult.
[3]Low-standard primitive roads (Traffic Service Level D roads).
[4]Controlled-access Traffic Service Levels B and C roads (Forest Service Handbook 7709.11, Transportation Engineering Handbook).
[5]Full-access Traffic Service Levels A, B, and C roads (Forest Service Handbook 7709.11).
[6]Norm: Acceptable strategies for the physical setting.
[7]Inconsistent: Strategies that are not generally compatible with the physical setting but may be necessary under certain circumstances to meet the management objectives.
[8]Unacceptable: Objectionable strategies under any circumstances.
[9]Acceptable: A range of acceptable strategies. Some may restrict access more than is necessary.
Source: Forest Service Manual, section 2311.11.

RECREATION MANAGEMENT

Objectives, Policy, and Responsibilities

Recreational opportunities in the national forests must only respond to demonstrated national public needs for natural resource–based outdoor recreation. These needs are distinguished from local or public regional needs, which are the responsibility of other suppliers. No precise distinction can be drawn. However, it is clear that each level of government has the responsibility to provide for its citizens. The national forest responsibilities and opportunities are further distinguished from those of other suppliers by the size of the land base. For the most part and in the long run, only the federal estate will be able to provide opportunities for unconfined outdoor recreation free of the urban influence. This is the principal feature that sets national forest recreation apart from most other suppliers since the converse, of highly modified and/or artificial environments, can be supplied by many. Therefore, national forest recreation focuses primarily on activities that require a large land base and provide a contrast to urbanization.

Objectives   Because of the nature of recreation itself, recreation management is a unique challenge to the Forest Service. Recreation is more socially oriented than the other Forest Service resource activities. The product, the recreational experience, is a personal value. Consequently, recreational targets, goals, and direction are more dif-

ficult to describe in precise terms, since they deal with people's experiences, their perception of those experiences, and the quality of those experiences. The objective is quality, not quantity. The Forest Service's objectives are therefore defined within the context of these intangibles:

- To provide nonurbanized outdoor recreation opportunities in natural-appearing forest and rangeland settings
- To protect the long-term public interest by maintaining and enhancing open-space options; public accessibility; and cultural, wilderness, visual, and natural resource values
- To promote public transportation and/or access to national forest recreational opportunities
- To shift landownership patterns as necessary to place urbanized recreation settings into other ownerships to create more public open space and/or natural resource values
- To provide outdoor recreation opportunities and activities that (a) encourage the study and enjoyment of nature, (b) highlight the importance of conservation, (c) provide scenic and visual enjoyment, and (d) instill appreciation of the nation's history, cultural resources, and traditional values

Policy   The policy to help achieve these recreation management objectives is to:

- Be sure public-use facilities provided by the Forest Service contrast with urbanization and harmonize and complement the natural environment. Facilities provided by the private sector should meet this policy as much as possible.
- Not provide facilities for urban-type sports, such as swimming pools, tennis courts, playground equipment, and golf courses, on national forest lands with public funds. Occasionally the private sector may receive approval to provide such facilities on National Forest System lands if they are a minor part of an overall complex. Any private-sector proposal to locate a new urban-type sports facility or complex on national forest lands requires review and approval by the chief. Proponents of such facilities should be advised that approval is granted only in rare circumstances.
- Use volunteers and cooperative workforce enrollees (*Forest Service Manual,* section 1800) to accomplish recreational objectives.
- Enhance the quality of the recreational experience through interpretive services, programs, and professional development of recreation managers.
- Ensure high-quality experiences, through facility location, design, and maintenance, that affords reasonably safe and healthy facilities and that are accessible to as many people as possible, including the handicapped, who will be integrated with the able-bodied.
- Encourage compatible off-season use of recreation areas.
- Enhance recreational experiences through a minimum of regulation and law enforcement.
- Plan and develop facilities to complement unconfined, nonfacility recreational opportunities; to manage National Forest recreational facilities and programs to provide natural resource-based outdoor recreation; and to strive for natural unmani-

cured atmospheres even when sophisticated facilities are necessitated by local conditions.

- Where feasible and economic, shift management of high-cost, highly developed, or nontraditional areas or facilities to other government and/or private entities, if the public will be well served.
- Manage recreational uses of national forest lands to meet the national needs rather than the needs of individuals or nearby communities. Local needs should usually be met by state and local governments.
- Coordinate, rather than compete, with private, other federal, state, county, and local entities to provide recreational facilities and programs in forest and rangeland settings, including both harvest and nonconsumptive enjoyment of wildlife; to not provide facilities that the private sector could provide, but rather openly encourage the private sector; and to not duplicate the role of other levels of government to provide urban and local facilities and programs.

Responsibilities   The responsibilities for implementing these policies are allocated among the different administrative levels as follows:

Chief   The chief reserves the authority to review and approve any proposal for new urban-type sport facilities or complexes on national forest land.

Director, Recreation Management Staff, Washington Office   The director of the Recreation Management staff provides staff advice and assistance to the deputy chief for the National Forest System on national recreation, wilderness, and related resource management issues by:

1 Recommending long- and short-range program targets, goals, and objectives.
2 Coordinating recreation, wilderness, and related resource management activities with other Washington office staff groups and Regional Recreation staff directors.
3 Coordinating cooperation with other federal agencies on recreational activities and with national organizations on recreation issues and programs.
4 Monitoring regional recreation, wilderness, and related resource management programs.
5 Overseeing the development of training in recreation, wilderness, and related resource management.

Regional Foresters   Regional foresters, with the advice and assistance of their Recreation Management staff directors, shall:

1 Establish long- and short-range targets, goals, and objectives for the regional recreation management program.
2 Coordinate cooperation with other regional office staff groups and Forest Recreation staff directors.
3 Coordinate cooperation with state, regional organizations, and private entities on recreation, wilderness, and related resource management issues.
4 Monitor forest recreation, wilderness, and related resource management programs.
5 Ensure that recreation management staff are trained in recreation, wilderness, and related resource management issues.

Forest Supervisors   Forest supervisors, with the advice and assistance of their Recreation Management staff officers, shall:

1   Set long- and short-range targets, goals, and objectives for recreation, wilderness, and related resource forest management programs through the forest planning, program development, and budgeting processes.
2   Coordinate with other Forest staff groups.
3   Coordinate cooperation on recreation, wilderness, and related resource management programs with other national forests; with state, county, and local agencies; with private organization entities; and with the public.
4   Monitor Ranger District Recreation, wilderness, and related resource management programs.
5   Provide opportunities for practical recreation management training to ensure that Forest Recreation management staff are trained.

District Rangers   District rangers are responsible for administering, scheduling, and assuring the quality of recreation, wilderness, and related resource programs.

Information Gathering

The information-gathering system and its distribution by the Forest Service, at least for recreation data, was in a sorry state of affairs in 1992 and 1993. Anyone who needs to acquire recreation data from the Forest Service is advised that it will be a long, arduous, frustrating, and only partially successful process—at best. There are two basic problems in obtaining data: (1) the often rude, unhelpful and incompetent staff of the Forest Service; and (2) a poor information retrieval system.[2]

Part of the lack of information availability is that the Forest Service is "in-between" two information-gathering systems. The *Recreation Information Management* (RIM) system was dropped in 1986 as a mandatory national database. In its place the Washington office established a relatively brief list of national reporting requirements and a set of spreadsheets that were to be filled in by the individual regions and forests. This system became known in 1989 as *WO-RIM*, and its primary purpose was to provide annual compilations of information on recreational use, recreational facilities, trails, and directory information of interest to publishers of travel guides.

---

[2]A disproportionate amount of the research time for this book was expended attempting to gather recreational use information on the National Forest System. A large number of letters sent and phone calls made were not answered. A big problem with the Forest Service staff answering the phones is that they do not know who to refer one to for basic recreational use data. The most serious problem, however, was the rudeness of the staff who answered the phones at certain locations, particularly the Pacific Northwest—at the regional headquarters in Portland and at the Gifford Pinchot National Forest. This discourteous behavior of public employees is totally inexcusable. Staff in other regions were much more helpful and informed, most notably in the Alaska, Pacific Southwest, Southern, and Intermountain regions. Although there are a lot of Forest Service employees who are very knowledgeable, professional in their work, and a pleasure to talk to, locating them was difficult. The second part of the problem was that once the author located someone on the staff who knew what a recreational visitor day (RVD) was (no small undertaking), it was very difficult and often impossible for the staffperson to retrieve the data. It is unbelievable that with the state of computers in 1993 the Forest Service has such difficulty providing basic data as RVDs by activity by forest, capacities by forest, and RVDs by wilderness areas.

WO-RIM is not an interactive database and is no longer capable of generating other reports because the original basic data from the field units are no longer stored in a national database. The RIM database is no longer available since the system was removed from the Fort Collins Computer Center in Colorado. Unfortunately, even the more limited data from WO-RIM is extremely difficult to come by. The *Forest Service Manual* still contains detailed information on the RIM system, which is no longer functional. The new information system the Forest Service is currently working on—hopefully to be implemented in the next few years—is called the *Recreation Resource Information System* (RRIS). It appears that this system holds potential.[3] In the meantime the Forest Service must make do with its current data retrieval system, which is abysmal for the world's largest recreation land manager. It makes one wonder on what basis decisions are made.

RIM   It was a mistake to suspend the RIM system prior to having another information system in place. The RIM system, in use from 1965 through 1986, was far superior when compared with the interim system of the last 8 years. The RIM system provided information on the facilities, description of the facilities, and use of all recreation areas on the National Forest System. RIM was developed because it was impossible before to keep track of the numbers, kinds, conditions, costs, and uses of the things and places that comprise the recreational resources. The basic input into the system was information from the recreation sites on the location, description, condition, cost, and use at the individual recreation sties.

The RIM system was designed to simultaneously cope with information about places, people, and things over periods of time. It coped with information about places (lands and waters) in terms of acres, sites, areas, counties, states, ranger districts, national forests, regions, and census divisions. It provided information about people (customers) who visit, view, harvest, and generally enjoy the benefits of the places. It coped with information about things that grew on the land or that were added to the land in other forms of improvements and/or investments to promote the beneficial use of places by people. It managed information about time relationships (present and future) between the people, the places, and the things. The data were systematized so that bits of information could be aggregated several different ways. The most common aggregations were by administrative units (region, national forest, ranger district), by political subdivisions (states, counties, congressional districts), and by classification of some type of physical attribute (wilderness, national recreation area, river basin). Summaries often required combinations of these three types of aggregates.

The beauty of the RIM system was that it could yield an almost limitless variety of reports in any array to meet data needs and requests—both internal and external—and to do it without extra, unscheduled impacts on field offices. These capabilities were lost when the system was suspended in 1986.

WO-RIM   In 1989 instructions accompanied the National Recreation Information Requirements and were sent to the forest supervisors, to be reported annually. These instructions mandated the reporting of the following *recreational use data* (in

---

[3]Numerous Forest Service employees told the author, "If only you were doing this project a few years from now."

RVDs): camping, picnicking and swimming; mechanized travel and viewing scenery; hiking, horseback riding, and water travel; winter sports; resorts, cabins, and organization camps; hunting; fishing; nonconsumptive fish and wildlife use; all other activities; and wilderness included in the above list. Also required were *recreation site and area data* by fee and nonfee status for the following kinds of areas: boating sites, swimming sites, campgrounds, picnic grounds, recreation residences, ski areas, major interpretive sites, and all other developed sites. *Recreational facility-condition data* were also to be reported in terms of backlog, reconstruction, replacement, elimination, addition, and resource treatment. *Recreation trail mileage* in terms of total length, wilderness, national recreation trails, national scenic trails, national historic trails, national side/connecting trails, constructed/reconstructed, and maintained were also to be reported. A National Recreation Information Directory was to contain data elements to serve as a central repository for furnishing service-wide information to the many publishers of campground directories.[4] However, this information is not available in an interactive database and is no longer capable of generating other reports—as RIM could—because the original basic data from the field units are no longer stored in a national database. In most cases, it is necessary to find the appropriate person in the individual national forests, and this in itself can be a major undertaking. You would never know the Forest Service was on the Data General Computer System. This current system (in 1994) is a very sad situation.

RRIS   To help solve the current information-gathering difficulties the Forest Service is in the midst of developing a new system, called the Recreation Resource Information System (RRIS). The material contained herein is based on the current status of the system, which is still in the evolutionary process. The Forest Service hopes to have the final version operational within the next few years.

RRIS has been prepared in response to an identified need for information concerning the lands, facilities, and people that comprise the recreational resources of the national forests. From 1965 through 1986, the RIM system was the method by which recreation information was collected, aggregated, and stored for use. In 1986, the RIM system was abandoned as being obsolete and unresponsive to the needs of recreation managers. RRIS is a new program designed to be responsive to the informational needs of recreation managers and to provide a means of inventorying the recreational resources available in the national forests. Managers can utilize the total capabilities of this system or only that portion needed to provide the minimal information required for effective management.

The "Recreation Resource Inventory" uses the ranger district as the basic inventory unit. All recreational resource characteristics and attributes are keyed to this basic unit. Both the "Recreation Resource Inventory" and "Recreation Use" are linked to each other by a unique site code. RRIS inventory data provide the attribute elements to *geographic information systems* (GISs). This inventory is directly tied to the spatial elements (the maps) of a GIS through the site code for a given site and/or general forest area. RRIS is structured so as to be compatible with national data standards. Through a complete and thorough set of data definitions, RRIS elements

---

[4]The author has two words to offer to anyone who attempts to locate these data—Good luck!

can be used throughout the National Forest System in a host of other relational database applications. Within RRIS itself, the system will be linked to the proposed RRIS-Trails and RRIS-Accessibility subsystems, to the Recreation Capital Investment database, and to other subsystems such as Code-A-Site and a Wild and Scenic Rivers Planning database. The one common data element linking all of these together is the site code, which can be "cross-walked" to all data elements.

Outdoor recreation in the National Forest System is both people- and resource-oriented. Although the environment is developed, enhanced, maintained, or modified for the benefit of the people, recreational opportunity is an attribute of the lands and waters that comprise the recreational resource. RRIS relates all information to specific places where opportunities exist, management efforts are directed, facilities have been placed, and the capacity to support recreation has been recognized. These individual places or managed units are treated as *elements* of the resource. For statistical purposes, the sum of all elements is the recreational resource population.

RRIS is designed to meet a wide array of data needs without repetitive information gathering by districts. The system has a tie to the forest land resource management plans, which allows information to be gathered for decisions within specific management areas. This system will respond to requests for information at all levels through the Integrated Data Base (IDB), which is accessible to all management levels. RRIS will also serve as the attribute elements for GISs. The Recreation Resource Information System utilizes the Oracle Relational Data Base Management System (version 6), which is available at all levels of the Forest Service organization on the Data General computer system. Information can be updated at any time as the database is initialized, updated, stored, and retrieved from the supervisor's office and/or the ranger district.

There are five existing and potential components or subsystems within RRIS:

- RRIS-Sites and Areas
- RRIS-Trails
- RRIS-Accessibility
- RRIS-Cultural Resources
- RRIS-Demand

Only RRIS-Sites and Areas currently exists as a fully documented component of RRIS. These components are linked together by a series of shared tables containing a set of common codes and through a unique set of site and area identifiers called the *site codes*.

Specific Recreation Management Policies

Site Development

Objectives

- To maximize opportunities for visitors to know and experience nature while engaging in outdoor recreation
- To develop and manage sites consistent with the available natural resources to provide a safe, healthful, aesthetic, and nonurban atmosphere

- To provide a maximum contrast with urbanization at national forest sites

Policy   The basic recreation policies as set forth in *Forest Service Manual*, section 2303 and the following supplementary policies shall govern the development and administration of sites and facilities. Where it is not possible to achieve the objectives to the degree defined in this chapter, close sites and facilities to public use. These policies are to:

- Use ROS guidelines (*Forest Service Manual*, Section 2310) when developing sites.
- Develop sites and facilities that will provide recreational experiences toward the primitive end of the spectrum, and not to provide urban class facilities.
- Use the land and resource management planning process to reach decisions to develop recreation sites.
- Develop sites and facilities to enhance natural resource-based activities normally associated with a natural environment.
- Seriously consider the element of cost efficiency when developing and operating sites and facilities.
- Establish priorities for the development and management of sites in the following order:

    1 Ensure public health and safety.
    2 Protect the natural environment of the site.
    3 Manage and maintain sites and facilities to enhance users' interaction with the natural resource.
    4 Provide new developments that conform to the National Forest recreational role.

- Allow concession operation of national forest campgrounds and related recreational facilities.
- Strive to make it possible for the handicapped to be included in the mainstream of life when pursuing outdoor recreation opportunities.
- Prepare site designs and environmental assessmets for all sites before undertaking construction or major rehabilitation efforts.

Table 8.4 identifies the permissible levels of site modification for each ROS class.

Fees   Established fees must cover, as nearly as possible, the costs of operating and maintaining the fee sites and facilities. In establishing rates, the following criteria, based on the Land and Water Conservation Fund Act (*Forest Service Manual*, Section 2330.1), should be considered:

- The amount charged for use of comparable facilities and services offered by the private sector in similar settings.
- The amount charged for use of comparable facilities and services administered by federal, state, and local agencies in similar settings.
- The benefits received by the user, including the quality and variety of recreational opportunities offered at or near the site and special services such as the use of amphitheaters, boat launching ramps, and swimming sites.
- The direct and indirect costs to the United States of developing, maintaining, and operating the site, facilities, and equipment and of providing services.
- The cost of collection versus the amount collected.

Table 8.4   Levels of Site Modification

ROS Class	Development Scale	
Primitive	1	Minimum site modification. Rustic or rudimentary improvements designed for protection of the site rather than comfort of the users. Use of synthetic materials excluded. Minimum controls are subtle. No obvious regimentation. Spacing informal and extended to minimize contacts between users. Motorized access not provided or permitted.
Semiprimitive (motorized and nonmotorized)	2	Little site modification. Rustic or rudimentary improvements designed primarily for protection of the site rather than the comfort of the users. Use of synthetic materials avoided. Minimum controls are subtle. Little obvious regimentation. Spacing informal and extended to minimize contacts between users. Motorized access provided or permitted. Primary access over primitive roads. Interpretive services informal, almost subliminal.
Roaded natural	3	Site modification moderate. Facilities about equal for protection of site and comfort of users. Contemporary or rustic design of improvements is usually based on use of native materials. Inconspicuous vehicular traffic controls usually provided. Roads may be hard-surfaced and trails formalized. Development density about 3 family units per acre. Primary access may be over high-standard roads. Interpretive services informal, but generally direct.
Rural	4	Site heavily modified. Some facilities designed strictly for comfort and convenience of users. Luxury facilities not provided. Facility design may incorporate synthetic materials. Extensive use of artificial surfacing of roads and trails. Vehicular traffic control usually obvious. Primary access usually over paved roads. Development density 3–5 family units per acre. Plant materials usually native. Interpretive services often formal or structured.
Urban	5	High degree of site modification. Facilities mostly designed for comfort and convenience of users and usually include flush toilets; may include showers, bathhouses, laundry facilities, and electrical hookups. Synthetic materials commonly used. Formal walks or surfaced trails. Regimentation of users obvious. Access usually by high-speed highways. Development density 5 or more family units per acre. Plant materials may be foreign to the environment. Formal interpretive services usually available. Designs formalized, and architecture may be contemporary. Mowed lawns and clipped shrubs not unusual.

Source: Forest Service Manual.

Variable fees by camping unit may be established within a site based on capacity and desirability of the individual unit. Fee rates may be raised during heavy-demand periods or reduced when there is a reduction in facilities and services. Self-service pay stations are found at many national forest campgrounds (Figure 8.1).

Hosts   Volunteer hosts are to be used in campgrounds as directed in *Forest Service Manual*, Section 1830. The host's camping site is to be situated prominently so that visitors to the site are aware of the host's presence. Signs are to be placed at both the entrance and at the host unit informing the public that a host is in attendance

Figure 8.1   Self-service pay station at Zealand Campground in New Hampshire's White Mountain National Forest.

(Figure 8.2). The hosts are to be provided with a nameplate and volunteer patch so they are identifiable to the public. The hosts are to be encouraged to present a clean, neat appearance at all times and to wear uniform vests.

Campgrounds and Picnic Grounds

Policy

- Separate camping and picnicking activities whenever practicable.
- Avoid intermingling facilities for large-group use with those designed for family-type use.
- Roads must conform to the terrain wherever possible, with a minimum of cuts and fills.
- Do not provide sports and play facilities such as swings, teeter-totters, formal horseshoe pits, and baseball diamonds at campgrounds and picnic grounds. However, open, level areas may be provided for impromptu sports such as Frisbee throwing, volleyball, and softball.
- Normally, do not provide showers at national forest campgrounds. In isolated instances where showers are provided, charge a fee for their use.
- Do not provide individual utility hookups at national forest campgrounds except when the following criteria are met and documented:

  1 There is no opportunity for private-sector development or expansion.
  2 A contrast with urbanization can be maintained.
  3 Daily fees can be set at a rate that will pay for the additional construction cost and for operation and maintenance.
  4 Nighttime heat and humidity conditions render sleep unrealistic without air-conditioning.

Figure 8.2 It is Forest Service policy that the campground host's site be clearly identified, as here at the Lone Pine Campground in the Inyo National Forest (California).

- Firewood may be provided by the Forest Service or by vendors under permit where it is necessary to protect the site and surroundings. Otherwise, encourage visitors to gather their own firewood as an important part of the recreational experience.

Trails, Rivers, and Other Low-Density Recreational Use

General   Trail, river, and similar recreational experience opportunities are characterized by activities that involve relatively low-density use and that occur over broad expanses of land and/or water. These activities include hiking, caving, mountaineering, snowmobiling, horseback riding, ORV driving, driving for pleasure, boating, hunting, and fishing. Two conditions make these types of recreational experience opportunities challenging to plan and manage for. First, the manager must manage the recreational user's entire environment. The components of this environment are stated in the ROS settings—physical, social, and managerial. All resource management activities affect these settings. The second condition is the pervasive nature of these recreational activities in the national forest. The activities occur in varying degrees throughout the forest in all seasons. The challenge, therefore, is to manage all resources on the entire forest with a sensitivity to their contribution to these recreational experiences and to skillfully combine settings in such a manner as to take maximum advantage of the forest's attributes and provide activities to meet public demands.

Objectives

- Provide recreational opportunities for users of the general forest, water, and cave resources.

- Provide opportunities for a variety of recreational pursuits with emphasis on activities that are in harmony with the natural environment and consistent with the recreational role of the national forest.
- Mitigate adverse impacts of users on the natural resources, cultural and historical resources, and on other users.

Policy

- Manage the general forest, water, and underground areas with their recreational access and support facilities under the principles defined in *Forest Service Manual*, Section 2303.
- Emphasize opportunities, in all ROS classes, that require minimal supporting facilities for the convenience of users, more self-reliance by the users, and less intrusion by constructed facilities upon the natural environment.
- Coordinate management of trail, river, and similar recreational opportunities with recreation sites and facilities so as to provide adjunct opportunities for users of these sites. Such sites and facilities include campgrounds, picnic areas, ski areas, resorts, and, as appropriate, recreation developments on other ownerships.
- Coordinate management of trail, river, and similar recreational opportunities with other resource management activities to take advantage of supportive relationships to the extent possible.
- Regulate users only to the extent necessary to provide for user safety; to protect the natural, cultural, and historical resources; and to achieve the recreational experience objectives.
- Emphasize user assistance (for example, low-impact use) in management and provide user information accordingly.

Trails

Objectives

- Provide trail-related recreational opportunities that serve public needs and meet land management and recreation policy objectives.
- Provide trail recreational opportunities that emphasize the natural setting of the national forest and are consistent with land capability.
- Provide trail access for national forest management and protection.

Policy

- Manage the Forest Development Trail System to carry out the objectives and direction established in the forest plans.
- Provide a diversity of trail opportunities for experiencing a variety of environments and modes of travel consistent with the national forest recreation role (*Forest Service Manual*, sections 2302 and 2303) and land capability.
- Designate the more outstanding and qualified trails or network of trails as components of the National Trails System.
- Emphasize long-term cost-effectiveness and need when developing or rehabilitating trail facilities.
- Where needed, provide trail access for resource management and protection.
- Inventory and include all forest development trails in the Forest Development Transportation System plan.

Rivers

Objective   Provide river and similar water recreation opportunities to meet the public needs in ways that are appropriate to the national forests' recreational role and are within the capabilities of the resource base. Protect the free-flowing condition of designated wild and scenic rivers and preserve and enhance the values for which they were established. Table 8.5 presents the guidelines for river recreation opportunities management.

Policy

- Plan and manage river recreation in a context that considers the resource attributes, use patterns, and management practices of nearby rivers. Consider both designated and nondesignated rivers managed by the Forest Service and/or other federal, state, and local management entities.
- Emphasize activities that harmonize with the natural setting of the national forest. Normally, limit river recreation opportunities to the primitive-to-rural portion of the ROS (*Forest Service Manual*, section 2310).

Table 8.5   Guidelines for River Recreation Opportunities Management

ROS Category	River Classification Management Objective	Facilities	Access	Compatible With
Primitive	Wild river	None except where absolutely necessary for health, safety, and resource protection. Very primitive where provided.	Water or trails.	Wilderness and primitive areas, national recreation areas, roadless areas, administratively established areas in forest plants. Trails remote.
Semiprimitive, nonprimitive	Wild and scenic river	Primitive. Facility emphasis is on health, safety, and resource protection plus some degree of user convenience.	Water, trails, and unobtrusive traffic service level C or D; roads closed to motorized use.	Watershed, range, wildlife, and timber management activities. Grazing. Perception of remoteness.
Semiprimitive motorized	Scenic river	Same as above.	As above. Opened to motorized use.	As above. Perception of remoteness.
Roaded natural	Recreational river	Nonurban as necessary and cost-efficient.	Water, roads, railroads, and powerboats. Traffic service levels A–D.	As above. Perception of development in a natural environment.
Rural	Recreational river	As authorized and existing.	As above.	As above.
Urban	Recommend adjustments where appropriate	As above.	As above.	Generally not compatible with Forest Service resource management.

[1]Some noted exceptions occur to the guidelines as a result of specific designation act language.
Source: Forest Service Manual, section 2311.11.

- Manage the use of rivers by establishing as few regulations as possible. Ensure that established regulations are enforceable.
- Emphasize user education and information. Educate users before they enter a river area. When necessary, prescribe direct management techniques (*Forest Service Manual*, section 2354.41a) that are sensitive to the values users seek. Impose only that level of direct management necessary to achieve management objectives.
- Coordinate river management with other federal, state, or local agencies having primary or concurrent jurisdiction. Where appropriate, enter into memorandums of understanding or cooperative agreements. Encourage the participation of state and local governments in planning and administering river management.
- Ensure that proposed and ongoing projects and activities conform with the purposes of the Wild and Scenic Rivers Act.
- Establish use limits and other management procedures that best aid in achieving the prescribed objectives for a river and in providing sustained benefits to the public.
- Acquire water rights needed to ensure sufficient water to achieve management objectives.

Off-Road Vehicles (ORVs)

Objective   Provide ORV recreational opportunities that are in concert with the environmental setting, minimize ORV effects on the land and resources, promote public safety, and control conflicts with other uses of National Forest System lands.

Policy

- Provide a diversity of ORV recreational opportunities when:

    1 The use is compatible with established land and resource management objectives.
    2 The use is consistent with the capability and suitability of the resources.
    3 The type of ORV opportunity is an appropriate national forest recreational activity (*Forest Service Manual*, sections 2302 and 2303).
    4 There is a demonstrated demand.

- Allow competitive use of ORVs only when it is determined, through an environmental analysis (Forest Service Manual, section 1950), that the event is appropriate for the national forest setting and that the conditions of the event meet the criteria set out in Forest Service Manual, section 2355.14. This analysis may be conducted during forest planning, during development of the forest ORV implementation program, or as a special analysis. Events appropriate to the national forest setting are prescribed by national forest recreation objectives and policies (*Forest Service Manual*, sections 2302, 2303, and 2355.35).
- Designate all National Forest System lands for ORV use in one of three categories: open, restricted, or closed (*Forest Service Manual*, section 2352.11). Figure 8.3 illustrates an open ORV trail on the Tongass National Forest (Alaska).
- Use signing to identify either the areas that are open to ORV use or the areas that are closed to ORV use. Select the method that better informs the public and that is easier to administer. Coordinate signing policy with adjacent federal, state, and local ORV managers.

Figure 8.3 All terrain vehicle on a trail in the Tongass National Forest (Alaska). (Forest Service photo)

- Provide public information that, as a minimum, includes maps describing the areas and trails where use is permitted, prohibited, or restricted and that explains the condition of such use.
- Close areas or trails to the type of ORV causing, or likely to cause, considerable adverse effects. The areas or trails shall remain closed until the adverse effects have been eliminated and until measures have been implemented to prevent recurrence. Take action to provide alternate use areas where feasible and where consistent with the forest plan.
- Use the monitoring activities established in the forest plan and the management review procedures to monitor and evaluate ORV use, its effects, and enforcement of restrictions and closures.

Interpretive Services

Objectives   The objectives of interpretive services are:

- To assist those visitors to the national forests, research projects, and state and private forestry locations in gaining a greater appreciation of the role of conservation in the development of the nation's heritage and culture.

- To promote visitor understanding of the Forest Service, the National Forest System, forestry research, and state and private forestry programs.
- To inform visitors of recreational opportunities and facilities in the national forests (Figure 8.4).
- To help visitors know and experience the natural environment.
- To implement an interpretive program that helps solve management problems and aids in the development of public understanding of Forest Service management.
- To expand the number of interpretive associations that contribute to public understanding of Forest Service practices, support interpretive services objectives, increase public awareness, and aid in management of national forest resources.
- To increase visitor understanding of natural, cultural, and historical principles and their relation to land management techniques.

Policy   In addition to general recreation policy in *Forest Service Manual,* section 2303, the following policies guide interpretive services:

- Use interpretive services as a management tool in the development of public and in-service understanding of Forest Service programs and practices.
- Encourage expansion of interpretive associations throughout the National Forest System.
- Ensure that National Forest lands be clearly identified along with national and regional sites of natural, historic, archaeological, and cultural interest.
- Ensure that a representative selection of interpretive service facilities and opportunities is available to the handicapped visitors.
- Ensure that all facilities, activities, and media of interpretive services are in character with the forest environment and exemplify concern for the ecosystem and energy conservation principles. Avoid nonconforming intrusions like visual distractions and noise pollution.

Figure 8.4   Red Canyon Visitor Center in Dixie National Forest (Utah).

- Use every reasonable situation to tell the multiple-use management message in Forest Service interpretive programs, signs, and exhibits.

Interpretation Associations   Interpretive associations may be formed to support and enhance the interpretation and management of natural resources of the national forests and to further the goals and objectives of the National Forest System. Their purpose is to make available to forest visitors the interpretive, educational, and informational materials and services that would add to the visitor's enjoyment and understanding of the natural, cultural, historical, and recreational resources of the national forests.

Wilderness

General

Objectives

- Maintain and perpetuate the enduring resource of wilderness as one of the multiple uses of National Forest System land.
- Maintain wilderness in such a manner that ecosystems are unaffected by human manipulation and influences so that plants and animals can develop and respond to natural forces.
- Minimize the impact of those kinds of uses and activities generally prohibited by the Wilderness Act but specifically excepted by the act or subsequent legislation.
- Protect and perpetuate wilderness character and public values including, but not limited to, opportunities for scientific study, education, solitude, physical and mental challenge and stimulation, inspiration, and primitive recreational experiences.
- Gather information and carry out research in a manner compatible with preserving the wilderness environment to increase understanding of wilderness ecology, wilderness uses, management opportunities, and visitor behavior.

Policy

- Where there are alternatives among management decisions, wilderness values shall dominate over all other considerations except when limited by the Wilderness Act, subsequent legislation, or regulations.
- Manage the use of other resources in wilderness in a manner compatible with wilderness resource management objectives.
- In wildernesses in which the establishing legislation permits resource uses and activities that are nonconforming exceptions to the definition of wilderness as described in the Wilderness Act, manage these nonconforming uses and activities in such a manner as to minimize their effect on the wilderness resource.
- Cease uses and activities and remove existing structures not essential to the administration, protection, or management of wilderness for wilderness purposes or not provided for in the establishing legislation.
- Because wilderness does not exist in a vacuum, consider activities on both sides of wilderness boundaries during planning, and articulate management goals and the blending of diverse resources in forest plans. Do not maintain buffer strips of undeveloped wild land to provide an informal extension of wilderness. Do not

maintain internal buffer zones that degrade wilderness values. Use the ROS as a tool to plan adjacent land management.

- Manage each wilderness as a total unit, and coordinate management direction when they cross other administrative boundaries.
- Use interdisciplinary skills in planning for wilderness use and administration.
- Gather necessary information and carry out research programs in a manner that is compatible with preservation of the wilderness environment.
- Whenever and wherever possible, acquire nonfederal lands within wildernesses, as well as nonfederal lands within those areas recommended for inclusion in the system.
- In all publications and personal contacts, inform wilderness visitors that they face inherent risks of adverse weather conditions, isolation, physical hazards, and lack of rapid communications, and that search and rescue may not be as rapid as would be expected in an urban setting.
- Manage primitive areas as wilderness areas consistent with 36 CFR (Code of Federal Regulations) 293.17 until their designation as wilderness or to other use is determined by Congress.

Recreation

Objectives

- Provide, consistent with management of the area as wilderness, opportunities for public use, enjoyment, and understanding of the wilderness, through experiences that depend on a wilderness setting.
- Provide outstanding opportunities for solitude or a primitive and unconfined type of recreation.

Policy

- Maximize visitor freedom within the wilderness. Minimize direct controls and restrictions. Apply controls only when they are essential for protection of the wilderness resource and after indirect measures have failed.
- Use information, interpretation, and education as the primary tools for the management of wilderness visitors.
- Manage for recreational activities that are dependent on the wilderness environment so that a minimum of adaptations within wilderness are necessary to accommodate recreation.
- Consistent with management as wilderness, permit outfitter or guide operations where they are necessary to help segments of the public use and enjoy wilderness areas for recreational or other wilderness purposes.

Special Recreation Management Designations   Certain limited areas of National Forest System lands not designated as wilderness and containing outstanding examples of plant and animal communities, geological features, scenic grandeur, or other special attributes merit special management. These areas are designated by law, or may be designated administratively, as special areas. Areas so designated are managed to emphasize recreational and other specific related values. Other uses are permitted in the areas to the extent that these uses are in harmony with the purpose for

which the area was designated. The law or order designating each area provides specific objectives and guidelines for management of that area.

Areas Designated by Law   Laws establishing special recreation management areas are:

National Recreation Areas

Area Name	Law
Spruce Knob–Seneca Rocks	16 U.S.C. 460p
Whiskeytown-Shasta-Trinity	16 U.S.C. 460q
Mount Rodgers	16 U.S.C. 460r
Flaming Gorge	16 U.S.C. 460v
Oregon Dunes	16 U.S.C. 460z
Sawtooth	16 U.S.C. 460aa
Hells Canyon	16 U.S.C. 460gg
Arapaho	16 U.S.C. 460jj
Rattlesnake	16 U.S.C. 460ll
White Rocks	16 U.S.C. 460nn
Mount Baker	16 U.S.C. 460pp
Allegheny	16 U.S.C. 460qq

National Monuments

Admiralty Island	16 U.S.C. 431 note
Misty Fiords	16 U.S.C. 431 note
Mount St. Helens	16 U.S.C. 431 note

National Scenic Areas

Mono Basin	16 U.S.C. 543
North Cascades Scenic Highway	Sec. 8(a) P.L. 98-339 (not codified)

National Scenic Research Areas

Cascade Head	16 U.S.C. 541

National Management Emphasis Areas

Lake Tahoe	Sec. 1, 2, 3 P.L. 96-586 (not coded)
Lee Metcalf	Sec. 2(c) P.L. 98-140 (not coded)
Oregon Cascade	16 U.S.C. 460oo
Antone Bench	Sec. 306(a) P.L. 98-428 (not coded)

Objectives   Each law states the specific management objectives for the area. General objectives for managing special areas established by law are to:

- Provide a showcase for national forest management standards.
- Provide for public enjoyment of the area for outdoor recreation or other benefits.
- Protect the special values and attributes of the area (that is, scenic, cultural, historical, wilderness, wildlife, or other values) that contribute to public enjoyment.
- Manage for any other resource values present in the area, in a manner that does not impair the public recreation values or the special attributes of the area.

Policy

- Manage each special area as an integral part of the National Forest System with emphasis on the primary values and resources as directed by the law that established the area.
- Manage values or resources not emphasized or prohibited in the law in a manner that complements or enhances the primary values of the area and is compatible with overall national forest management objectives.
- Manage each special area as a showcase to demonstrate national forest management standards for programs, service, and facilities.
- Except for portions of special areas designated as wilderness, provide interpretive services to enhance visitor enjoyment of the area.
- Manage each special area as a separate unit of national forest land in harmony with the other units as outlined in the forest plan.
- Incorporate management direction in the forest plan, or prepare a comprehensive management plan if directed by the law for each area, that gives specific management direction for all resource values within the area.
- Where wilderness and special area designation overlap, follow wilderness management direction (*Forest Service Manual*, sections 2320 and 2309.19).

Definitions

1. *National recreation areas*—Areas that have outstanding combinations of outdoor recreation opportunities, aesthetic attractions, and proximity to potential users. They may also have cultural, historical, archaeological, pastoral, wilderness, scientific, wildlife, and other values contributing to public enjoyment.
2. *National monuments*—Areas of unique ecological, geological, historical, prehistoric, cultural, and scientific interest.
3. *National scenic areas*—Areas that contain outstanding scenic characteristics, recreational values, and geological, ecological, and cultural resources.
4. *National scenic research areas*—Areas that contain outstanding scenic values for research, scientific, and recreational purposes.
5. *National management emphasis areas*—All other areas that contain unique or outstanding physical features and that contain specific physical, cultural, or political characteristics receiving specific emphasis in the legislation.

Areas Designated Administratively   The authority for administratively designating, preserving, and managing special areas within national forests is found in the principal acts from 1897 to the present that authorize multiple-use management and in 36 CFR 294.1.

Objective   To protect and manage for public use and enjoyment, special recreation areas with scenic, geological, botanical, zoological, paleontological, archaeological, or other special characteristics or unique values.

Policy

- Designate or recommend administrative designation of special areas with outstanding natural characteristics or unique recreational or cultural values (36 CFR 294.1 and *Forest Service Manual*, section 2372.2).

- Rescind the designation of areas when the designation is no longer appropriate (*Forest Service Manual,* section 2372.2).
- Manage each special area as an integral part of the National Forest System with emphasis on its unique values.
- Manage other values or resources in the area to a level compatible with the area's primary values and with overall national forest management objectives.
- Include management direction for each area in the forest plan. Amend the forest plan with management area direction for areas established after the forest plan was approved (*Forest Service Manual,* sections 2372.2, 1922, and 1950).

Definitions

1. *Scenic area*—A unit of land with outstanding natural beauty that requires special management to preserve this beauty.
2. *Geological area*—A unit of land with outstanding formations or unique features of the earth's development, such as caves, fossils, dikes, cliffs, or faults (Figure 8.5).
3. *Botanical area*—A unit of land that contains plant specimens, plant groups, or plant communities that are significant because of their form, color, occurrence, habitat, location, life history, arrangement, ecology, rarity, or other features.
4. *Zoological area*—A unit of land that contains animal specimens, animal groups, or animal communities that are significant because of their occurrence, habitat, location, life history, ecology, rarity, or other features.
5. *Paleontological areas*—A unit of land that contains fossils of plants and animals, shellfish, early vertebrates, coal swamp forests, early reptiles, dinosaurs, and other prehistoric plants or animals.
6. *Historical area*—A unit of land possessing a significant site or a concentration of sites, buildings, structures, or objects unite historically or prehistorically by plan or physical development. Memorial areas are included in this definition.

Figure 8.5 Gros Ventre Slide Geological Area in Teton National Forest (Wyoming).

7. *Recreational area*—A unit of land that has been administratively designated for particular recreational opportunities or activities such as hiking, rock hounding, recreational mining, photography, or other special activity.

Development, Occupancy, and Public Use

- Place campgrounds or other overnight recreational developments outside of special areas whenever possible.
- Locate roads, trails, sanitary facilities, picnic grounds, and parking spaces without disturbing the special features of the established area.
- Allow no resorts or other high-impact special uses within the area unless needed for public enjoyment of the principal features of the area.
- Keep developments such as roads, trails, and other facilities to the minimum necessary for public enjoyment of that area.
- Build no roads or other improvements on or through geological formations unless it is the only way to meet management objectives for the area.
- Encourage public use and enjoyment of each administratively designated special area up to the level that will ensure protection of the special values for which the area was established.
- Provide interpretive services to enhance the visitor's understanding and appreciation of the area's special features (Figure 8.4).
- Allow other occupancy and use of the area's resources to the extent they neither interfere with the primary values for which the area was established nor negatively affect the visitor's experience.

Private, State, and Local Recreational Use

General

Objectives

- Under special-use authorization, to provide sufficient suitable facilities and services to supplement or complement those provided by the private sector, state, and local government on private land and by the Forest Service on national forest land to meet public needs, as determined through land and resource management planning.
- To facilitate the use, enjoyment, understanding, and appreciation of the national forest natural resource setting.

Policy

- Issue special-use permits authorizing state, county, or municipal agencies to develop or manage recreation developments on national forest land only for (1) lands that over a long period should be dedicated to that purpose or (2) lands that could logically be conveyed to state or local governments through land-exchange procedures without detriment to national forest administration or programs. In either case, national forest lands eligible for such use *must meet at least two of the following conditions:*

  1 Be adjacent to exterior national forest boundaries
  2 Be small tracts associated with adjacent, larger, other-agency, or privately owned lands not suitable for acquisition for national forest purposes

3   Be adjacent to lands owned by the applicant agency and needed to complete a unit for development as a park or recreation area

- Deny special-use permit applications by state and local agencies proposing to develop parks or recreation areas that do not qualify under item 1 above, except in unusual circumstances or when the authorization is clearly in the public interest. Obtain the review and advice of the chief before approving permits based on these exceptions. Review by the chief is not required for roadside rest and picnic developments by county or state agencies if no suitable private or other-agency-owned land is available for such purposes.
- Deny applications by the private sector to construct or provide outdoor recreation facilities and services on National Forest System lands if these facilities and services are reasonably available or could be provided elsewhere in the general vicinity. Encourage business enterprises engaged in providing such facilities and services to locate on private lands or in nearby communities, by publicly promising not to compete.
- Normally, do not use appropriated funds to construct recreational facilities for operation by others under special-use authorization. Use appropriated funds, when necessary, to restore existing government-owned recreational improvements that have been operated under special-use authorization.
- Require holders to protect soil, vegetation, and other resources within the authorized area to perpetuate a condition suitable for recreational purposes.
- Prohibit gambling devices or activities at any facility or any area authorized for special recreation uses on national forest land.
- Ensure that all services and facilities provided by private individuals or public entities under special-use permits are equally available to all members of the public. Include antidiscrimination clauses in special-use permits (*Forest Service Manual*, section 2710), and revoke the permits if discriminatory practices occur.

Concessions

Objective   To provide a diversity of recreational activities that emphasize the forest setting and rustic, natural resource–based recreational opportunities.

Policy   Manage concession sites, activities, and programs according to the following policies:

- Authorize concession developments only where there is a demonstrated public need. Do not permit concession development either solely for the purpose of establishing a profit-making commercial enterprise or where satisfactory public service is or could be provided on nearby private or other public lands.
- Issue prospectuses to solicit proposals for development of concession sites, when it is in the public interest or when competition exists or may be created. Give existing concessionaires an opportunity to expand their operation to meet increasing public needs before offering new sites for development.
- Give priority to developments offering moderately priced accommodations and services as opposed to luxurious accommodations and services affordable only by the affluent.
- Encourage year-round recreational use at privately developed concession sites.

- Allow permit holders to provide only those services and facilities and to conduct only those activities specified in the special-use authorization. Some services may be allowed in conjunction with a resort that would not be allowed as a separate enterprise.
- Require concessionaires to provide all of the improvements and services needed by the public and specified by the special-use authorization. Under normal circumstances, issue only one authorization for each site and allow subleasing of facilities and services only where the holder can prove this would provide a clear public benefit.
- Periodically analyze use at concession sites to determine whether the services being provided are still necessary. If not, either require holders to change the services over time to meet public needs or terminate the authorization.
- For concession sites receiving limited patronage as evidenced by use records, low sales revenue, and low fee payments, require one of the following:

  1 Change of facilities, services, or activities
  2 Relocation
  3 Termination

- Restrict advertising outside of buildings to attractive and approved signs that simply state the services and accommodations available in each building. Do not allow other exterior advertising on national forest land.
- Clearly define the permit holders' responsibilities for the safety of their employees and the public within the boundaries of the authorization and while participating in activities covered by the authorization in the prospectus, special-use authorization, and site operating plans.
- Ensure that literature, brochures, and other advertising that permit holders distribute, with respect to a concession enterprise, do not contain misleading statements or indicate that discrimination is practiced against any prospective patron because of race, color, gender, or creed. Also ensure that such literature identifies the facility as being authorized on National Forest land.

Winter Sports   This category includes sites provided by and developed on national forest land by private individuals to accommodate alpine skiing, nordic skiing, snow play, tobogganing, snowmobiling, helicopter skiing, and other snow- and ice-related winter outdoor recreation activities. Winter recreation permit holders are encouraged to provide outdoor recreation opportunities during other seasons.

Policy   Manage winter recreation sites through application of the following general policies.

- Encourage summertime use of ski area facilities where that use is compatible with or enhances natural resource–based recreational opportunities and does not require additional specialized facilities. Ensure that permit holders provide for development of facilities and protection of environmental values as an integral part of the development plan for the area.
- Encourage privately operated nordic ski touring centers.

  1 Authorize high-investment, permanent facilities under a term-limit special-use authorization; base the length of the term on the permit holders' anticipated investment in the operation.

2 Allow permit holders to charge for the use of permitted trails when they make capital investments or incur expense directly for trail maintenance, grooming, and patrolling. Do not allow permit holders to charge for use of national forest land where they have made limited or no investment or provide only limited trail services.

- Plan for development of new winter recreation sites or expansion of existing sites in such a way that the location of ski runs, trails, lifts, and other facilities avoids terrain inherently prone to frequent and extensive or severe avalanche activity.
- Deny development and use of terrain that requires military ordnance for avalanche control, until the permit holders can own or operate the necessary equipment.

Recreation Residences   This section deals with noncommercial, recreational use, privately built and owned structures allowed on national forest land under special-use authorization. These structures are maintained for the use and enjoyment of concession holders and their guests. As recreational facilities, they are vacation sites and may not be used on a permanent basis. (See *Forest Service Manual*, section 2721.23.)

Policy

- Manage noncommercial recreation-use sites in accordance with basic recreation policy in *Forest Service Manual*, section 2303 as important and valid components of the overall national forest recreation program.
- Maintain in place those existing facilities now occupying national forest land under special-use authorization that (a) are at locations where the need for a higher public purpose has not been established, (b) do not constitute a material, uncorrectable off-site hazard to national forest resources, and (c) do not endanger the health or safety of the permit holder or the public.
- Deny applications for construction of new facilities except where they would replace similar existing facilities.
- Deny any proposal for commercial activity at permitted, noncommercial recreation-use sites.
- Require noncommercial recreation-use holders to maintain their sites to protect the natural forest environment. Do not allow construction or placement of nonauthorized facilities on these sites.
- Recreation residences are a very important use of National Forest System lands (Figure 8.6). They are an important component of the overall national forest recreation program and have the potential of supporting a large number of RVDs. The Forest Service is to work in partnership with the holders of these permits to maximize the recreational benefits of these residences.
- Administer recreation residence special-use permits to ensure proper use of the site for family and guest recreational purposes.
- Although a few full-time residences are currently authorized by special-use permit, do not approve any new authorizations for such uses, except in special situations to provide caretaker or other similar services where there is a strongly demonstrated need (*Forest Service Manual*, section 2347.12). Do not approve in-lieu sites for full-time residence use.
- Issue 20-year term permits unless the need for a higher public use at the same location has been documented or a renewal study is planned.

Figure 8.6 Private recreation residences under permit located in the middle of the Alta Ski Area, Wasatch National Forest (Utah).

- Give permit holders at least 10 years' written advance notice if the use is not to be continued, except when the permit is to be terminated when (a) it is in the public interest, particularly when the final-decision authority does not rest with the Forest Service; (b) there is an uncorrected breach of the permit; or (c) the site has been rendered unsafe by catastrophic events such as flood, avalanche, or massive earth movement. In these exceptions, give as much advance notice as possible.
- Termination of a recreation residence permit within the term of the permit should not be undertaken unless there are appropriations to pay for the improvements and there is an urgent need to use the site before it could be recaptured for public use by nonrenewable procedures.

Private Clubs   This category includes camps or other facilities developed for the use and enjoyment of members of a club, group, or organization. Such facilities are not available to the general public. Examples of this type of use may be alumni association ski lodges, organization camps that provide facilities and services only to organization members, and ski areas where only ski club members may ski.

Policy

- Issue no new authorizations for private-club-type uses. Reserve property with high outdoor recreation resource values for future use by the general public.
- Where conflict exists between currently permitted private-club use and the recreational needs of the general public, always consider the public's needs first.
- As opportunity presents, phase out private-club use unless forest plans indicate there will be no public need for the land involved. If this is the case, consider exchanging the land.
- Where permit-holder organizations have allowed individual members to construct cabins or erect other lodging accommodations and this use has been approved in

writing by the Forest Service, continue to allow the use until the term of the current permit expires. Upon expiration of the term permit, require holders either to remove the personal-use facilities or to convert ownership and control to the holder organization rather than to individual members.

References

Clark, Roger N., and George H. Stankey. *The Recreation Opportunity Spectrum: A Framework for Planning, Management, and Research.* General Technical Report PNW-98, December 1979.

Forest Service, USDA. *Draft—RRIS Handbook: Chapter 200—Recreation Resource Inventory.* April 1991.

Forest Service, USDA. *Forest Service Manual* (Recreation Sections).

Forest Service, USDA. *1986 ROS Book.*

Forest Service, USDA. *Recreation Settings Component—Recreation Opportunity Spectrum (ROS) Theme.*

Forest Service, USDA. *ROS Primer and Field Guide.* April 1990.

Forest Service, USDA. *ROS Users Guide.*

Pollock, James W. *Interpretation in the Recreation Opportunity Spectrum (ROS).* Forest Service January 1989.

National Forest System: Recreational Facilities and Use

Barring love and war few enterprises are undertaken with such abandon, or by such diverse individuals, or with so paradoxical a mixture of appetite and altruism, as that group of avocations known as outdoor recreation.

Aldo Leopold

National forests currently accommodate a wide spectrum and large quantity of outdoor recreation activities and visitors. These recreational opportunities vary from wilderness to urban experiences, from organized activities to individual boating and hunting, and from guided auto tours along forest roads to white-water rafting on waterways. In fiscal year 1992 the national forests hosted more than 691 million visitors. These visits equated 288 million recreation visitor days (RVDs), which represent a 3 percent increase from the previous year. The emphasis is mostly on traditional uses, such as sightseeing, camping, and hiking. National forest campgrounds and other developed sites have tended toward the less-developed end of the facility spectrum. The Forest Service has generally sought to control new uses so as to limit possible adverse effects on the resource and on the traditional uses. The general policy has been to avoid recreational developments and facilities that introduce urbanization into the forest. This has generally been consistent with the desires of traditional national forest users. However, the demands for less traditional national forest activities, such as trail biking, river rafting, and skiing, are growing fast. Moreover, many people, particularly in urban areas, do not use national forests—for many different reasons. A new recreation initiative, the "National Recreation Strategy—America's Great Outdoors," has been implemented by the Forest Service in an attempt to be more responsive to the public's outdoor recreation demands and to accommodate both nontraditional and traditional uses.

To meet the public's preferred demand for outdoor recreation opportunities, high rates of opportunity expansion (about 1 percent per year) will be needed for some activities. The largest shortages are predicted for undeveloped backcountry as well

as near-road opportunities. The most severe predicted shortages are for wildlife observation, day hiking, nature photography, pleasure driving, sightseeing, and similar activities. The greatest shortages anticipated for wilderness opportunities are for non-recreational uses. Downhill skiing capacity must expand 40 percent in the next 50 years to meet the predicted demand. National forests cannot offer unlimited recreational expansion because the Forest Service is a multiple-use agency and must accommodate many uses. Increased publicity about opportunities, more conveniences (such as modern toilets, better signing, stores, vistas, fitness trails, educational offerings), and improved access would better meet modern recreation demands (Cordell et al., 1990, 104).

National forests are quite different in character, availability, and concentration between west and east. Major distinctions also exist among Forest Service regions. Wet coastal forests, for example, differ dramatically from drier interior forests, and the two environments cannot equally accommodate the same uses. Many sections of the national forests in the West are very dry and do not have trees (Figure 9.1). Other national forest uses, such as timber, grazing, and wildlife habitat, also vary substantially between and within regions. Some national forests, particularly in New England, the Appalachians, the Rockies, and the Pacific coast, are closer to urban populations. They provide highly attractive natural settings and are very popular. These forests near the big cities and campgrounds close to main roads receive the heaviest use. But back from the main roads and in remote areas they are lightly used. It has been estimated that existing campgrounds can easily accommodate twice the number of campers currently using them. These more-accessible forests have different constituent groups than the more-remote forests. Resource and optimal-use differences, urban proximity, and different constituency interests strongly imply that some differences in recreation and wilderness policies among and within Forest Service

Figure 9.1   The lower elevations of the Toiyabe National Forest in western Nevada are desert with no trees.

Figure 9.2   At Granite Hot Springs Pool in the Teton National Forest (Wyoming), it is possible not only to swim on a fine June day, but also to trout fish in Granite Creek and to alpine ski (no lifts) on the higher slopes of the Gros Ventre Mountains.

regions may be desirable. Different policies imply emphasizing different uses in different places. For the future and in a few forests, a need now exists to emphasize recreation and education more than commodity production. This is especially true in the Appalachians, along Colorado's Front Range, and in California.

Climate plays a major role in determining the recreational activities and the season for recreational use and its length in the national forests. In extreme cases, in sections of the West, severe dryness leads to fire danger and can even close the national forests to recreational use. Due to the large size of the United States, a wide variety of climates occur. Camping is possible for much of the year in the warmer climates of the lower elevations in the Southern Region. In many other regions of the country, snow cover restricts the campground season from May until September. Some of the higher elevation campgrounds in the western mountains are open only for July and August, due to snow depth the remainder of the year. Many national forest roads are closed for the winter in snow country, and this restricts access by conventional vehicles. However, a durable winter snow cover is essential for recreational activities such as snowmobiling and cross-country and downhill skiing. In the higher western mountains that have considerable differences in elevation, the seasons vary dramatically.[1] Major differences in weather and climate occur in the same national forest at the same elevation where there is a pronounced rain-shadow effect, such as in Olympic National Forest. In some of the lower elevations of forests in the Southwest Region, fall, winter, and spring are the times of heavier recreational

---

[1]One of the author's favorite national forest locations is Granite Hot Springs Pool in the Teton National Forest (Wyoming). Here, on a fine June day, due to altitudinal differences in the Gros Ventre Mts., it was possible to swim, fish for trout, and ski on the same day (Figure 9.2).

use due to the severity of summer heat. Alpine skiers in California are grateful for the winter precipitation regime of the Mediterranean climate that, in most years, provides the snow. Boating is possible year-round in the forests of the Southern Region, but ice in many other regions brings this activity to a halt in winter. Swimming is another recreational activity closely tied to warm weather and water: The season is much longer in the Southern Region than elsewhere in the country. The climate of the marine west-coast climate of Alaska in the lower elevations is extremely mild for its high latitudinal location. All of these aspects of climate govern recreational use.

RECREATIONAL USE PATTERNS

Total Recreational Use

In 1992 a total of 287,690,500 recreation visitor days (691,180,286 visits) were recorded for the entire National Forest System. This is a tremendous increase from the 4.7 million visits in 1924, when recreational use data were first collected. The recreation visits in 1941 were 18.0 million (26.1 million person-days), in 1950 were 27.4 million (38.9 million person-days), and in 1955 were 45.7 million. The late 1950s saw a tremendous increase in use, which reached 92.6 million visits in 1960 and 133.8 million visits in 1964. In 1965 the Forest Service started using the recreation visitor day (RVD) to measure recreational use. In this year there were 160.3 million RVDs, which increased to 172.6 million in 1970, 199.2 million in 1975, and 233.5 million in 1980 (Clawson and Van Doren, 1984).

Table 9.1 presents the total recreational use in the national forests by states for 1988 through 1992. In this time period the number of RVDs for the entire United States increased from 242.3 million in 1988 to 287.7 million in 1992. Table 9.1 indicates that California receives far more recreational use in its national forests than any other state: 23.5 percent of the total recreational use for the entire National Forest System. Our most populous state has national forests located in close proximity to, or within a relatively short distance of, major urban areas. Colorado ranks second among the states, accounting for another 10.1 percent of the total recreational use of the national forests. Much of this use occurs in the Front Range, which are conveniently located next to the large urban centers at the base of the Great Plains and Rocky Mountains. Nonresidents make a major contribution to the winter-sports component of this figure, as several of the major ski areas in the country are located on national forests in Colorado (for example, Vail, Breckenridge, and Winter Park). Arizona ranks third, with 8.9 percent of the total RVDs; the Phoenix and Tucson metropolitan areas are in close proximity to national forests. Oregon ranks fourth, with 6.9 percent of the national total; Portland and other cities of the Willamette Valley are located very close to several national forests. Washington ranks fifth, with 6.5 percent of the total RVDs; the communities in the Seattle area around Puget Sound are located close to the national forests. Utah ranks sixth, with 6.4 percent of the total RVDs in national forests; Salt Lake City and other cities along the front of the Wasatch Range provide the majority of the users. *These six states accounted for 179 million RVDs (62 percent)*

Table 9.1   Total Recreational Use on National Forest System Lands by State, 1988–1992 (thousand RVDs[1])

State, Commonwealth, or Territory[2]	1992	1991	1990	1989	1988
Alabama	700.6	676.7	698.1	685.5	741.4
Alaska	5,887.5	5,717.9	5,413.6	4,636.2	4,354.5
Arizona	25,543.7	21,548.8	19,038.5	18,997.5	18,831.2
Arkansas	2,153.0	2,109.0	2,440.9	2,377.0	2,358.5
California	67,614.1	65,220.8	61,006.6	63,685.3	59,516.9
Colorado	29,053.0	25,998.0	25,204.2	23,238.2	21,484.0
Florida	3,104.4	3,080.8	2,961.2	2,851.5	2,787.5
Georgia	2,993.3	2,839.1	2,833.3	2,715.1	2,707.0
Idaho	13,086.8	12,908.5	11,819.1	11,738.3	10,736.3
Illinois	899.5	843.4	1,637.7	950.1	891.5
Indiana	551.8	594.0	568.8	587.6	430.1
Kansas	75.5	66.1	61.3	48.0	38.2
Kentucky	2,112.5	2,111.5	2,446.5	2,327.0	2,301.3
Louisiana	507.1	486.4	527.3	512.7	502.3
Maine	60.7	60.7	57.7	52.8	47.6
Michigan	4,755.0	8,153.0	4,916.4	4,725.4	4,319.6
Minnesota	5,738.5	4,956.4	5,399.3	5,147.6	4,449.6
Mississippi	1,297.5	1,285.1	1,177.1	1,236.9	1,240.4
Missouri	1,803.4	1,742.3	1,712.6	1,704.8	1,705.0
Montana	11,046.3	10,595.3	9,703.6	9,412.5	8,843.7
Nebraska	200.1	147.1	148.7	142.0	181.1
Nevada	3,360.0	3,283.1	3,277.9	3,081.5	2,656.8
New Hampshire	3,036.9	4,013.5	2,675.6	2,683.7	2,783.0
New Mexico	8,602.6	8,065.3	7,704.2	7,465.6	7,227.5
New York	31.2	45.0	71.5	22.4	25.6
North Carolina	5,767.3	5,691.8	5,472.0	5,036.2	4,973.2
North Dakota	142.2	198.6	168.5	184.3	186.7
Ohio	671.7	521.6	504.4	429.5	410.7
Oklahoma	368.8	373.0	386.8	341.4	331.4
Oregon	19,898.0	21,036.5	21,035.7	18,231.1	19,598.1
Pennsylvania	2,942.0	2,976.5	2,631.2	2,605.1	2,621.4
Puerto Rico	289.3	280.1	185.6	396.0	399.7
South Carolina	950.3	942.8	816.1	974.5	916.5
South Dakota	3,243.7	3,095.4	2,965.5	2,737.3	2,734.9
Tennessee	2,977.5	2,923.8	2,826.0	2,655.3	2,561.7
Texas	2,273.4	2,253.1	2,154.8	2,057.1	1,863.6
Utah	18,413.2	13,336.7	12,744.1	13,312.8	14,454.8
Vermont	1,564.7	1,570.5	1,368.9	1,352.3	1,154.1
Virginia	4,268.8	4,173.4	3,900.1	3,946.3	3,804.0
Washington	18,739.9	22,458.0	22,451.1	18,017.7	15,477.6
West Virginia	1,264.1	1,339.8	1,234.4	1,146.3	1,152.1
Wisconsin	2,185.1	2,215.3	2,094.9	1,978.6	2,000.1
Wyoming	7,515.5	6,914.3	6,608.8	6,068.0	6,514.5
Total	287,690.5	278,849.0	263,050.6	252,495.0	242,315.7

[1]One recreation visitor day (RVD) is the recreational use of national forest land or water that aggregates 12 visitor hours. This may entail 1 person for 12 hours, 12 persons for 1 hour, or equivalent combinations of individual or group use, either continuous or intermittent.
[2]States not listed have no forest program.
Source: Forest Service, *Report of the Forest Service-Fiscal Year 1992*, February, 1993.

out of the national total of 288 million for 1992. Puerto Rico and twelve of the states that have National Forest System lands within their boundaries had under 1 million RVDs in 1992. Among these units, New York had the least number, at 31,200. Not only are the national forests asymmetrically located, but their intensity of use is also very asymmetric.

Changes in Recreational Use Patterns

As mentioned in the last section, prior to 1965 the Forest Service used the visit to tally recreational use, and starting in 1965 the recreation visitor day was used to measure recreational use. The categories of recreational use also changed in 1965. Prior to 1965 "general enjoyment of the forest environment" was consistently the leading recreational activity in national forests since use data were first estimated in 1941. In this period between 1941 and 1965, "picnicking" was consistently the second-ranked recreational activity, and fishing was the third, growing in relative importance and almost equaling picnicking in 1964. Hunting consistently ranked fourth and camping fifth, although by 1964 camping almost equaled hunting. Starting in 1965, with use of the RVD, camping moved into first place as the most popular recreational activity in national forests and held this position through 1982. This change was accounted for by the greater amount of on-site time demanded by camping as an activity. Between 1965 and 1982 "mechanized" recreational travel was in a close second place. Fishing ranked third, and hunting ranked fourth from 1965 until 1982. Winter sports showed the greatest percentage increase in this time period. (Clawson and Van Doren, 1984). In 1992, the ranking of recreational activities were as follows:

1. Mechanized travel and viewing scenery (35 percent)
2. Camping, picnicking, and swimming (27 percent)
3. Hiking, horseback and water travel (8.4 percent)
4. Winter sports (6.27 percent)
5. Hunting (5.90 percent)
6. Resorts, cabins, and organization camps (5.73 percent)
7. Fishing (5.65 percent)
8. Other recreational activities (5.24 percent)
9. Nonconsumptive fish and wildlife use (0.87 percent).

Since the Recreational Information Management (RIM) system was suspended in 1986, several categories of recreational use are now aggregated for reporting purposes. This method of reporting, and thus the lack of fineness in the data, precludes more detailed analysis of recreational use patterns in the national forests. Figure 9.3 reveals that over half of the RVDs in 1992 were accounted for by dispersed recreation (mechanized travel and viewing scenery; hiking, horseback, and water travel; hunting; fishing; and nonconsumptive fish and wildlife use).

Forest Region Recreational Use

Table 9.2 summarizes the recreational use by activity for the nine Forest Service regions. Region 5 (Pacific Southwest) is by far the leading region, with over 23 percent of the national total. Although Region 5 includes California, Hawaii, Guam, and the

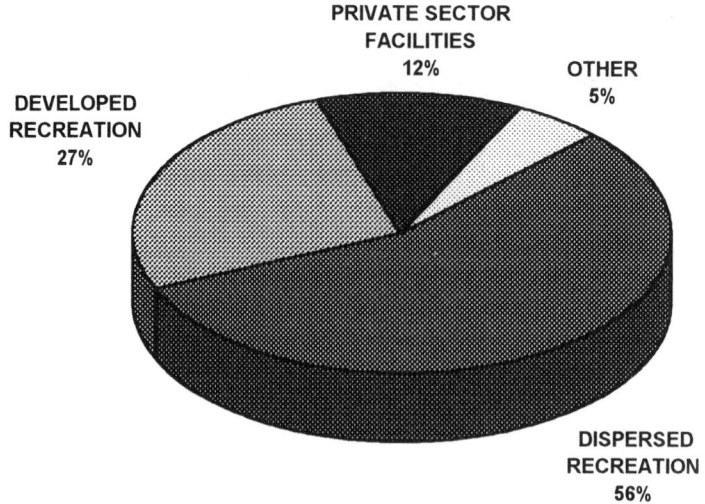

DEVELOPED RECREATION 27%

PRIVATE SECTOR FACILITIES 12%

OTHER 5%

DISPERSED RECREATION 56%

Figure 9.3 National forest recreation visitor days, 1992. (*Source:* Forest Service: *Report of the Forest Service Fiscal Year 1992,* February.)

Trust Territories of the Pacific Islands, all of the recreational use occurs in California. Six of the regions each receive within a few percent of 10 percent of the total national use: Region 6 (Pacific Northwest), 13.5 percent; Region 2 (Rocky Mountain), 12.7 percent; Region 4 (Intermountain), 12.3 percent; Region 3 (Southwestern), 11.9 percent; Region 8 (Southern), 10.5 percent; and Region 9 (Eastern), 8.7 percent. The two regions with the lightest use are the most remote—Region 1 (Northern, 5.3 percent) and Region 10 (Alaska, 2.1 percent). Geographic location plays a major role in the

Table 9.2 National Forest System Recreational Use Report Servicewide by Region—1992 (thousand visitor days)

	Camping, Picnicking, Swimming	Mechanized Travel and Viewing Scenery	Hiking, Horseback and Water Travel	Winter Sports	Resorts, Cabins, and Organi- zation Camps	Hunting	Fishing	Noncon- sumptive Fish and Wildlife Use	Other Recrea- tional Activities	Total	Per- centage of Total States
Region 1	3,412.4	4,869.0	1,729.0	768.2	506.2	1,566.2	1,120.5	165.3	1,221.6	15,358.4	5.34%
Region 2	7,345.4	12,406.0	2,916.7	6,781.7	1,382.3	2,235.8	2,031.1	206.1	1,282.7	36,587.8	12.72%
Region 3	9,379.6	13,433.5	2,245.8	1,200.8	1,222.2	1,552.2	1,259.3	585.3	3,284.7	34,163.4	11.88%
Region 4	10,259.6	11,672.6	3,202.9	2,112.8	1,643.0	1,999.6	2,005.0	198.0	2,158.6	35,252.1	12.25%
Region 5	17,647.1	24,457.3	4,536.3	4,100.0	7,593.4	1,554.7	2,911.5	481.4	3,146.7	66,428.4	23.09%
Region 6	12,756.2	14,502.2	3,516.3	1,258.6	2,434.2	1,245.3	1,520.8	368.0	1,160.4	38,762.0	13.47%
Region 8	9,253.4	8,548.2	3,131.7	25.6	584.6	4,337.2	2,616.2	280.1	1,318.2	30,095.2	10.46%
Region 9	6,836.4	7,374.6	2,578.6	1,661.1	943.3	2,323.9	2,358.5	174.6	904.2	25,155.2	8.74%
Region 10	320.9	3,652.2	381.4	135.8	170.7	148.0	445.3	37.3	595.9	5,887.5	2.05%
Total	77,211.0	100,915.6	24,238.7	18,044.6	16,479.9	16,962.9	16,268.2	2,496.1	15,073.0	287,690.0	100.00%
Percentage	26.84%	35.08%	8.43%	6.27%	5.73%	5.9%	5.65%	0.87%	5.24%	100.00%	

Source: Forest Service, Washington office.

recreational use that is made of the National Forest System. Figure 9.4 graphically depicts the share of each Forest Service region's recreational use.

Two categories of use account for 62 percent of the recreation visitor days on the National Forest System. Figure 9.5 shows the relative importance of the different categories of recreational use. The leading category of use for the entire country is "mechanized travel and viewing scenery," which accounts for 35 percent of the RVDs and a disproportionate 62 percent of the total recreational use in Region 10 (Alaska). The second-ranking category of use for the country is "camping, picnicking, and swimming," accounting for 27 percent of the RVDs. In Region 10 (Alaska), this category accounts for far fewer RVDs than in the rest of the regions—only 5 percent. In Region 2 (Rocky Mountain), 20 percent of the use is below the national average. As is shown in Table 9.2 and Figure 9.5, six of the other categories account for 5 to 10 percent of the RVDs. "Hiking, horseback riding, and water travel" ranks third and accounts for over 8 percent of the RVDs, reaching its greatest relative importance in Region 1 (Northern). "Winter sports" ranks fourth and is disproportionately important in Region 2 (Rocky Mountain). While this category accounts for 6 percent of the RVDs for the country, it accounts for 19 percent of the RVDs in this region. "Winter sports" is relatively insignificant in Region 8 (Southern), accounting for only 0.09 percent of the RVDs. While some skiing does occur in the "banana belt," it is limited to a few high-elevation areas. The category "resorts, cabins, and organization camps" is most important in Region 5 (Pacific Southwest). "Hunting" assumes greater significance in Regions 8 (Southern), 1 (Northern), and 9 (Eastern) and lesser significance in Regions 5 (Pacific Southwest), 6 (Pacific Northwest), and 10 (Alaska). "Fishing" is also of greater relative importance in Regions 8 (Southern) and 9 (Eastern).

State Recreational Use

The overwhelming importance of the national forests as a recreational resource in California, where 25 percent of the total use in the system takes place, was covered earlier in this chapter. The large number of RVDs in Colorado, Arizona, Washington,

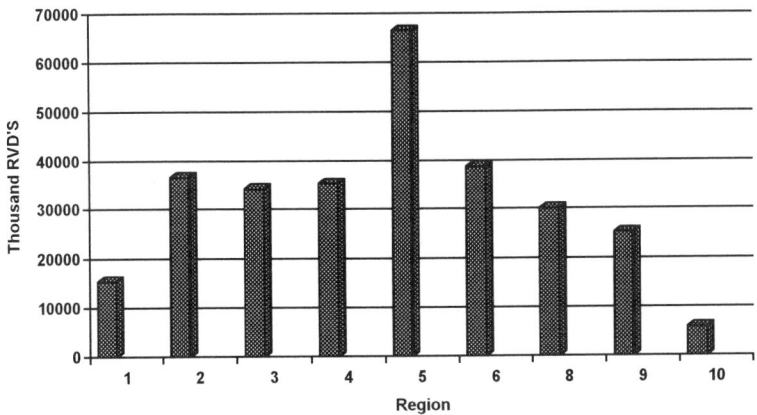

Figure 9.4 National forest recreation visitor days by region, 1992. (*Source:* Forest Service, Washington Office.)

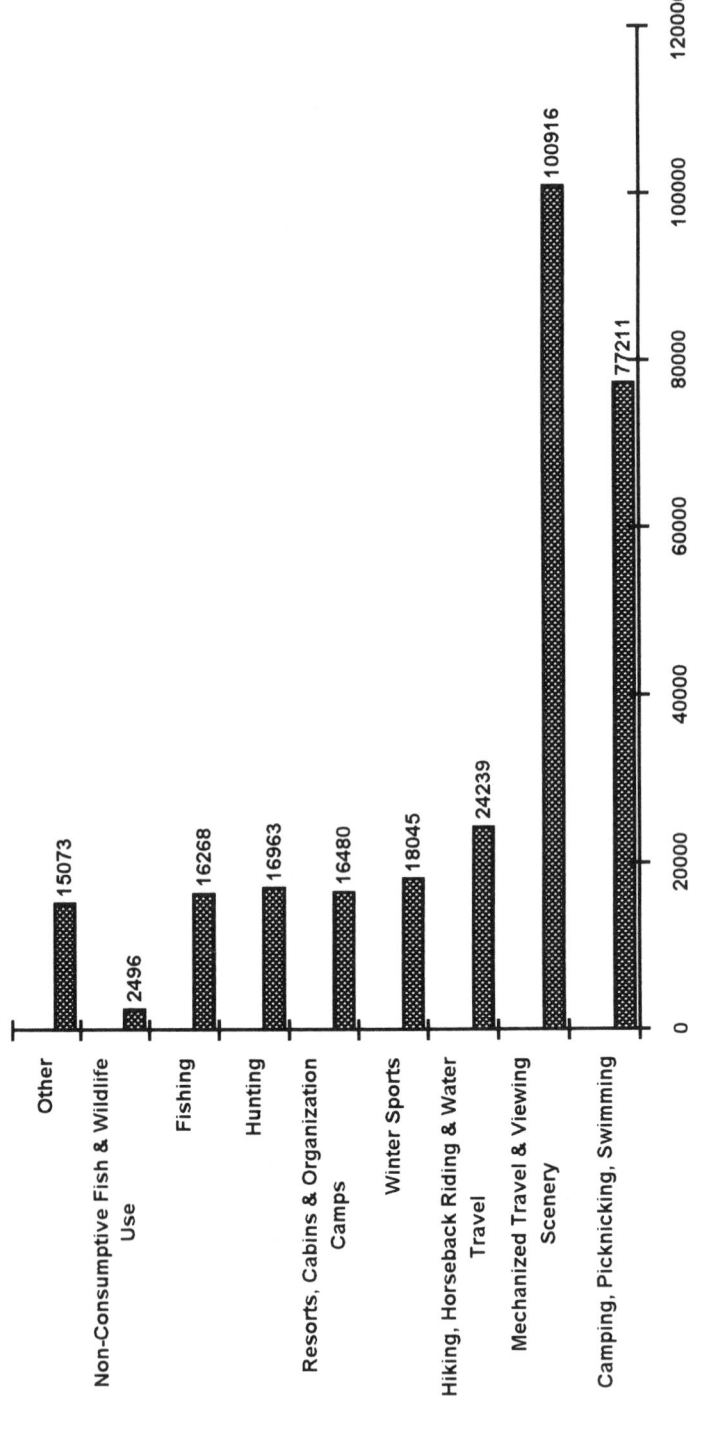

Figure 9.5 National forest recreation visitor days by activity, 1992. (*Source:* Forest Service, Washington Office.)

Oregon, and Utah were also discussed. Table 9.3 details the amount of recreational use by activity groupings for each state. The leading recreational activity for the entire National Forest System is "mechanized travel and viewing scenery," accounting for 35 percent of the RVDs. In addition to viewing scenery and automobile travel, this group includes the following uses: spectator viewing, motorcycle travel, ice and snowcraft travel, specialized landcraft travel, train and bus touring, using power boats and motorized aircraft, using aerial trams and lifts, bicycling, and nature study, hobbies, and education. In eight states this category accounts for an exceptionally low percentage of the total RVDs: New York (8 percent), Indiana (13 percent), Maine (14 percent), Florida (15 percent), Alabama (16 percent), West Virginia (17 percent), and Minnesota and Vermont (each 18 percent). Exceptionally high proportions for this category of use were tallied in South Dakota (76 percent) and Alaska (62 percent). California, with 24.9 million, and Arizona, with 11.4 million, are the leaders in total RVDs; also significant are: Colorado (8.6 million), Oregon (7.5 million), Utah (7.1 million), and Washington (7.0 million).

The other major category of use is "camping, picnicking, and swimming," which accounts for 27 percent of the total recreational use in the system. It is unfortunate that these categories were not broken into separate groups for reporting purposes. Forest Service personnel have estimated that about 75 percent of this RVD figure is accounted for by general day camping, automobile camping, trailer camping, and tent camping. Diving and water sports are included along with swimming. Swimming plays a greater role in the warmer climates of the Southwest and Southeast and a lesser role in the more northern states. A disproportionately high percentage of the use is accounted for in this category by Florida (55 percent), New York (52 percent), Indiana (44 percent), and Tennessee (40 percent). At the other end of the spectrum, very low use occurs in Alaska (6 percent), South Dakota (6 percent), Vermont (7 percent), North Dakota (11 percent), and Oklahoma (13 perent). The leaders in terms of RVDs are California (18.3 million), Arizona (6.6 million), Oregon (6.4 million), Washington (6.3 million), Colorado (6.2 million), and Utah (5.1 million).

"Hiking, horseback riding, and water travel" is the third-ranking category of recreational use and accounts for a little over 8 percent of the RVDs. This category includes canoeing, sailing, using other watercraft, and mountain climbing. It is particularly important in Minnesota, New York, and Wyoming (accounting for 15 percent of the total RVDs in each). A less significant role is played by this category in Kansas and Louisiana (each 3 percent) and Vermont and Wisconsin (each 4 percent). California (4.6 million) and Colorado (2.4 million) account for the greatest number of RVDs.

"Winter sports" shows more geographic variation than any of the other categories of recreational use. In 10 states, with all except Indiana and Kansas in the "Deep South," winter sports are nonexistent. In another nine states, winter sports account for less than 0.2 percent of the recreational use in the national forests. In Vermont, 53 percent of the total recreational use is accounted for by this category. The Green Mountain is the only national forest in Vermont. In the bordering state of New Hampshire, whose only national forest is the White Mountain, 21 percent of the RVDs are accounted for by winter sports. The comparable figure for Colorado in 23 percent. Colorado's 6.63 million "winter sports" RVDs are far ahead of Vermont's 0.83 million or New Hampshire's 0.63 million. Winter sports are also above average in significance

Table 9.3   State Summary of Total Recreational Use on National Forest System Land by Activity—1992 (thousand RVDs[1])

State, Commonwealth, or Territory[2]	Camping, Picnicking, and Swimming	Mechanized Travel and Viewing Scenery	Hiking, Horseback Riding and Water Travel	Winter Sports	Resorts, Cabins, and Organization Camps	Hunting	Fishing	Nonconsumptive Fish and Wildlife Use	Other Recreational Activities	Total
Alabama	204.0	114.6	65.0	0.0	0.4	166.5	70.4	5.4	74.3	700.6
Alaska	320.9	3,652.2	381.4	135.8	170.7	148.0	445.3	37.3	595.9	5,887.5
Arizona	6,626.4	11,413.6	1,451.2	421.9	943.7	916.7	937.1	434.6	2,398.5	25,543.7
Arkansas	609.6	533.9	203.0	0.1	24.2	518.5	110.5	25.3	127.9	2,153.0
California	18,261.9	24,875.2	4,582.6	3,956.9	7,621.5	1,582.6	3,145.2	482.4	3,153.8	67,614.1
Colorado	6,179.6	8,598.1	2,404.4	6,632.0	744.8	1,791.9	1,648.2	138.2	915.8	29,053.0
Florida	1,718.2	478.8	175.0	0.0	215.3	233.0	177.1	20.4	86.6	3,104.4
Georgia	899.7	955.9	384.9	0.8	44.9	380.5	192.4	36.8	97.4	2,993.3
Idaho	3,867.0	3,597.1	1,160.0	759.8	672.9	1,024.3	913.8	115.4	976.5	13,086.8
Illinois	180.9	348.9	140.8	0.8	7.5	123.3	40.0	14.1	43.2	899.5
Indiana	242.9	69.4	66.1	0.0	0.0	69.1	81.4	5.2	17.7	551.8
Kansas	15.5	26.5	2.5	0.0	1.9	6.9	11.0	2.0	9.2	75.5
Kentucky	644.3	666.3	260.0	2.3	21.4	207.0	206.7	10.0	94.5	2,112.5
Louisiana	152.2	130.9	16.1	0.0	26.7	103.6	39.0	1.5	37.1	507.1
Maine	19.4	8.6	13.0	1.2	2.4	8.7	4.4	1.4	1.6	60.7
Michigan	1,230.2	1,662.6	315.8	72.4	150.7	623.9	490.7	15.7	193.0	4,755.0
Minnesota	1,888.2	1,004.4	883.8	82.1	459.0	349.0	881.1	37.6	153.3	5,738.5
Mississippi	245.2	337.7	121.4	0.0	8.3	383.0	86.4	29.5	86.0	1,297.5
Missouri	524.2	532.5	239.3	0.0	10.6	266.9	112.4	19.3	98.2	1,803.4
Montana	2,227.0	3,465.9	1,361.8	663.4	369.8	1,073.0	877.4	121.1	886.9	11,046.3
Nebraska	45.6	45.7	16.6	0.5	38.7	18.6	5.2	0.2	29.0	200.1
Nevada	987.7	990.9	386.9	310.7	151.9	197.7	69.9	70.9	193.4	3,360.0
New Hampshire	698.4	1,139.5	346.6	629.7	120.3	36.1	27.6	12.8	25.9	3,036.9
New Mexico	2,748.4	2,017.4	793.5	778.9	278.1	631.0	320.5	150.4	884.4	8,602.6
New York	16.2	2.5	3.6	1.5	0.0	4.1	1.3	0.6	1.4	31.2
North Carolina	1,466.1	2,090.7	842.3	8.0	96.9	690.9	330.6	33.0	208.8	5,767.3
North Dakota	15.2	37.7	12.4	0.9	0.0	64.1	2.6	4.0	5.3	142.2
Ohio	109.7	145.3	73.8	0.8	0.0	231.9	48.5	5.0	56.7	671.7
Oklahoma	49.5	173.8	27.2	0.2	0.1	65.5	20.3	14.2	18.0	368.8
Oregon	6,393.0	7,524.3	1,585.8	612.4	1,333.5	699.4	993.6	179.4	576.6	19,898.0
Pennsylvania	843.7	1,310.2	258.8	9.3	68.8	199.0	156.9	21.3	74.0	2,942.0
Puerto Rico	109.1	100.1	23.3	0.0	7.0	0.0	0.0	1.9	47.9	289.3
South Carolina	254.1	219.8	135.1	0.0	0.4	208.7	52.2	15.8	64.2	950.3
South Dakota	200.9	2,455.6	161.2	16.6	115.4	96.3	58.3	6.5	132.9	3,243.7
Tennessee	1,176.7	865.9	325.7	4.9	94.1	237.3	180.2	27.4	65.3	2,977.5
Texas	621.5	425.1	98.2	0.0	22.6	233.1	784.2	17.1	71.6	2,273.4
Utah	5,130.6	7,190.0	1,169.9	1,076.2	789.0	895.0	903.4	56.3	1,202.8	18,413.2
Vermont	107.5	284.6	68.5	832.8	58.1	87.3	21.3	30.9	73.7	1,564.7
Virginia	1,025.9	1,364.0	426.9	9.3	20.7	815.6	346.1	38.8	221.5	4,268.8
Washington	6,288.5	6,982.2	1,915.5	650.5	1,100.7	543.9	497.5	177.7	583.4	18,739.9
West Virginia	525.6	212.0	110.5	1.7	47.6	194.6	118.7	6.7	46.7	1,264.1
Wisconsin	531.6	747.2	86.7	28.8	20.3	228.5	396.0	8.3	137.7	2,185.1
Wyoming	1,808.3	2,166.0	1,142.1	341.4	618.9	607.3	462.8	64.3	304.4	7,515.5
Total	77,211.1	100,915.6	24,239.2	18,044.6	16,479.8	16,962.3	16,268.2	2,496.7	15,073.0	287,690.5

[1]One recreation visitor day (RVD) is the recreational use of national forest land or water that aggregates 12 visitor hours. This may entitle 1 person for 12 hours, 12 persons for 1 hour, or any equivalent combination of individual or group use, either continuous or intermittent.
[2]States not listed have no Forest Service recreation program.
Source: Forest Service: *Report of the Forest Service Fiscal Year 1992*, February 1993.

in New Mexico and Nevada, where 9 percent of the RVDs in each state are accounted for by this category. In terms of recreation visitor days in this category, California's 4.0 million and Utah's 1.1 million rank after Colorado. No single recreational activity is so dependent on the national forests as alpine skiing. Much of the nation's "big-mountain skiing" is wholly or partly on land leased from the Forest Service.

"Resorts, cabins, and organization camps" is the category of recreational use that shows the greatest amount of geographic variation after winter sports. The specific recreational uses in this category include: general day organization camping, night organization camping, general resort and commercial public service, resort lodging, and recreational cabin use. Collectively, these uses account for almost 6 percent of the total recreational use on the National Forest System. Nebraska records the highest percentage of its RVDs in this category—19 percent—but the RVDs only total 38,700. This category is also significantly important in California, where 7.6 million or 11 percent of the total is measured. Oregon ranks second (1.3 million) and Washington ranks third (1.1 million). In four states (Indiana, New York, North Dakota, and Ohio) no use takes place in this category. In another 11 states, all but one of which are in the Deep South, less than 1 percent of the recreational use occurs in this category.

The category "hunting" includes big-game, small-game, upland-bird, and water-fowl hunting. In only four states are over 1 million RVDs achieved in this category: Colorado (1.8 million), California (1.6 million), Montana (1.1 million), and Idaho (1.0 million). In North Dakota, 45 percent of the state's 142,200 RVDs are accounted for by hunting. Other states with very high percentages of their total RVDs accounted for by hunting are Ohio (34 percent), Mississippi (30 percent), Alabama and Arkansas (24 percent each), South Carolina (22 percent), Louisiana (20 percent), Virginia (19 percent), and Oklahoma (18 percent). New Hampshire has the distinction of being the state with the lowest percentage of its national forest RVDs occurring as hunting—1 percent. Other low percentages are California (2 percent), and Washington and Alaska (3 percent each). The National Forest System serves as a major recreational resource for hunting, especially in the Southern Region.

Within the "fishing" category, there are four possible types of fishing tallied, depending on geographic circumstances: (1) cold-water, (2) warm-water, (3) saltwater, and (4) ice. Fishing, like hunting, accounts for just a little under 6 percent of the nationwide recreational use on the National Forest System. The greatest totals of RVDs measured are in California (3.1 million) and Colorado (1.6 million). Fishing accounts for 35 percent of the total RVDs in Texas. Other states with high percentages are Wisconsin (18 percent); and Minnesota, Indiana, and Kansas (15 percent each). Puerto Rico (Caribbean National Forest) receives no fishing. Fishing is also relatively insignificant in New Hampshire and Vermont (1 percent each); North Dakota, Nevada, and South Dakota (2 percent each); and Nebraska and Washington (3 percent each).

"Nonconsumptive fish and wildlife use" is the smallest category of recreational use, contributing less than 1 percent of the total RVDs in the National Forest System. This category includes nature study (plants), and study of wildlife, birds, and fish. Throughout most states there is not a great variation in the relative importance of this category. The exceptions to this generalization, where the percentage of RVDs is significantly above the national average of 1 percent are Oklahoma, Kansas, and North Dakota (3 percent each), while South Dakota has the distinction of having the least significance (0.2 percent).

The final category of recreational activity—"other recreational activities"—contains a variety of subcategories that include team sports, individual sports, games and play, gathering forest products, viewing interpretive exhibits, attending talks and programs, guided touring, unguided touring, guided walking, unguided walking, viewing interpretive signs, listening to audio programs, and general information. This mixture of activities accounts for 5 percent of the RVD totals. California (3.2 million), Arizona (2.4 million), and Utah (1.2 million) account for the greatest amount of RVDs, but percentage-wise this category is most important in Puerto Rico (17 percent), Nebraska (15 percent), and Kansas (12 percent).

Individual Forest Recreational Use

Much of the data analyzed in this section are contained in Appendix X. This appendix identifies the region each national forest is in, the number of RVDs in the nine major categories for each national forest, the total amount of recreational use for each national forest, and the number of RVDs in wilderness areas within each national forest. All of the tables in this section were constructed from the data in this appendix. The information in Appendix X is available from no other single source, not even from the Forest Service. (The author painstakingly assembled it from data provided by the offices of individual national forests.)

Total Recreation Visitor Days   The top 25 national forests, which represent 17 percent of the reporting units, account for 45 percent of the total recreational use. Seven of the 15 most-used national forests are in California. The mean RVD value for the 143 reporting national forests units was 2.01 million, and the median was 1.52 million. Table 9.4 lists in rank order the upper 50 percent of the national forests that received the most use. The Tonto National Forest (#1, 9.25 million RVDs) and the Angeles National Forest (#2, 9.16 million RVDs) are significantly ahead of the next two ranking national forests (the Inyo, #3, 8.38 million RVD, and the White River, #4, 8.23 million RVDs). There is a 25 percent decrease in RVDs between the White River and the Dixie (#5, 6.18 million RVDs) and another 6 percent decrease from the Dixie to the Coconino (#6, 5.79 million RVDs).

The Tonto and the Angeles National Forests accounted for 3.2 percent each of the total RVDs in the National Forest System. Both national forests are located very close to large urban centers—the Tonto north and east of Phoenix, Ariz., in the Superstition and other mountains, and the Angeles in the San Gabriel Mountains immediately north of Los Angeles. In the Tonto National Forest two categories—"camping, picnicking, and swimming" (39 percent) and "mechanized travel and viewing scenery" (44 percent)—accounted for 83 percent of the toal use, while "winter sports" and "nonconsumptive fish and wildlife use" played a very insignificant role. Table 9.2 identifies the following national average percentages by category of recreational use: "camping, picnicking, and swimming," 27 percent; "mechanized travel and viewing scenery," 35 percent; "hiking, horseback riding, and water travel," 6 percent; "winter sports," 6 percent; "resorts, cabins, and organization camps," 6 percent; "hunting," 6 percent; "fishing," 6 percent; "nonconsumptive fish and wildlife use," 1 percent; and "other recreational activities," 5 percent. The specific recreational activities in each of these categories were listed earlier in this chapter. These average

Table 9.4   National Forests: Most Heavily Used-1992 Recreational Use by Forest (thousand RVDs)

National Forest	RVDs	National Forest	RVDs	National Forest	RVDs
Tonto	9247.4	Eldorado	3304.9	Ocala	2122.4
Angeles	9158.0	Black Hills	3137.5	Daniel Boone	2111.1
Inyo	8376.3	White Mountain	3097.6	Boise	2093.0
White River	8232.3	Cherokee	2977.5	Nantahala	2034.0
Dixie	6175.6	Bridger-Teton	2960.4	Huron-Manistee	2021.9
Coconino	5788.4	Allegheny	2942.0	Umpqua	1883.8
Pike–San Isabel	5590.3	Cleveland	2875.0	Bighorn	1880.7
Mt. Baker–Snoqualmie	5511.3	Gifford Pinchot	2816.1	Chugach	1866.6
San Bernardino	5501.1	Gallatin	2797.9	Ashley	1852.5
Arapaho-Roosevelt	5437.7	Pisgah	2757.3	Prescott	1832.3
Tahoe	5175.4	Stanislaus–Calaveras Bigtree	2707.8	Mark Twain	1803.4
Wasatch-Cache	4866.0	Chattahoochee	2614.9	Chippewa	1720.3
Shasta-Trinity	4814.2	Santa Fe	2595.3	San Juan	1713.9
Los Padres	4749.1	Plumas	2562.9	Carson	1704.7
Sierra	4671.1	Apache-Sitgreaves	2482.9	Mt. Hood	1688.7
Grand Mesa–Gunnison–Uncompahgre	4644.8	George Washington	2444.1	Targhee	1627.0
		Idaho Panhandle	2424.9	Lassen	1596.5
Coronado	4607.5	Sawtooth	2291.1	Kootenai	1593.8
Tongass	4020.5	Siuslaw	2235.1	Kaibab	1585.3
Superior	4018.3	Olympic	2230.7	Lolo	1577.6
Wenatchee	3885.9	Routt	2189.6	Green Mountain	1564.7
Toiyabe	3789.9	Jefferson	2174.5	Hiawatha	1542.2
Deschutes	3728.4	Willamette	2172.1	Gila	1517.9
Uinta	3532.1	Wallowa-Whitman	2153.5		
Sequoia	3530.9				

Source: Forest Service.

values for the entire nation can be used for comparison to assess the relative importance of the categories of use in individual national forests. In the Angeles National Forest, "camping, picnicking, and swimming" accounted for 26 percent of the RVDs, "mechanized travel and viewing scenery" accounted for another 37 percent, while "resorts, cabins, and organization camps" accounted for a noteworthy 16 percent.

In the Inyo National Forest (2.9 percent of total national RVDs), "camping, picnicking, and swimming" accounted for a low 19 percent of the RVDs, but "mechanized travel and viewing scenery" (40 percent), "resorts, cabins, and organization camps" (12 percent), and "winter sports" (8 percent) were above average in importance. The Mammoth Mountain Ski Area, located in the Inyo, is one of the most heavily used in the country. The Inyo National Forest is remotely located on the eastern side of the Sierra Nevada Mountains and not near any large urban areas. Nevertheless, this forest is a popular recreation destination. Los Angeles, to the south, is a major provider of users; from there it is 200 miles and close to four hours' driving time to the southernmost part of the Inyo National Forest. Las Vegas is 275 miles to the southeast and 5 hours' driving time away. San Francisco is 300 miles and 5.5 hours' driving time away in the summer, when California Highway 120 over Tioga Pass in Yosemite National Park is open, but this becomes a 425-mile, 8-hour drive for the 8 months of the year the road is closed. The Sierra Nevada has a major impact on transportation patterns. In winter, for over 200 miles south from the Lake Tahoe area to south of Sequoia National Park, no road is open. Even in summer there is no

trans-Sierra road south of California 120 in Yosemite National Park for a distance of over 150 miles. The Eastern Escarpment of the Sierra Nevada is one of the most formidable geographic barriers in the United States. The Inyo National Forest will be case studied in Chapter 10.

The 8.23 million RVDs in the White River National Forest in Colorado account for another 2.9 percent of the national total. This forest is unique in that 47 percent of the RVDs are explained by one activity—"winter sports." The White River National Forest is located on the western side of the Continental Divide and western side of the Gore Range. The only towns of any size nearby are Glenwood Springs and Aspen. It takes recreationists from Denver 2 hours to drive more than 100 miles to reach the closest location in the White River National Forest, which is where Interstate 70 reaches the Vail Pass. Six major ski areas account for much of this use: Vail, Beaver Creek (10 miles west of Vail at Avon), and the four Aspen Mountains—Aspen Mountain, Aspen Highlands, Tiehack, and Snowmass. Moderate-sized ski areas are also located at Ski Cooper in the Tennessee Pass north of Leadville and Sunlight, ten miles south of Glenwood Springs. Both "camping, picnicking, and swimming" (16 percent) and "mechanized travel and viewing scenery" (21 percent) play a below-average role in recreational use in the White River National Forest. The completion of I-70, which passes through the heart of the forest—through Glenwood Canyon immediately east of Glenwood Springs—in the fall of 1992 has increased the accessibility of the Aspen ski areas.

The Dixie National Forest's 6.18 million RVDs rank it in fifth place, with 2.1 percent of the national total RVDs. The heavy recreational use made of this forest is one of the more surprising recreational use patterns discovered in the research for this book. The Dixie is remotely located at the northwestern corner of the Colorado Plateau Physiographic Province, where it meets the Great Basin Province. A disproportionately large percentage (59 percent) of the RVDs in the Dixie are credited to "mechanized travel and viewing scenery." Only 16 percent of the RVDs in the Dixie are credited to camping. Two primary factors explain the high recreational use of the Dixie National Forest: a major highway and several nearby popular national parks.

In the first place, I-15 passes close to different units of the Dixie. The nearest urban center is Las Vegas, 165 miles or 2.5 hours to the southwest of Cedar City. Los Angeles is 450 miles (7 hours' driving time) from Cedar City. Salt Lake City is 250 miles north of Cedar City, a driving time of 4 hours. Also, the recent upgrading and construction of Utah Highway 12 south of Torrey to Escalante, over Boulder Mountain in the Dixie National Forest, has become one of Utah's most scenic routes. This road over Boulder Mountain serves as the travel route from nearby Capitol Reef National Park and from Arches and Canyonlands National Parks, located farther east, to Bryce Canyon and Zion National Parks. The views to the east and south as the road climbs Boulder Mountain are among the best in Utah—to the east Capitol Reef National Park lies below the overlooks, and the Henry Mountains are in the distance. Bryce Canyon and Zion National Parks and Cedar Breaks National Monument are located in or close to the Dixie. Glen Canyon National Recreation Area is located a short distance to the southeast of the Dixie National Forest, and Grand Canyon National Park is located to the south. It is less than 100 miles to the more lightly used North Rim of Grand Canyon National Park, but over 200 miles to the more popular

South Rim. This particular section of the United States attracts a disproportionate share of foreign tourists. Tour buses, belching clouds of black exhaust, are a popular means of access for these visitors. The Dixie National Forest is one of the detailed case studies in Chapter 10.

Most of the other heavily used national forests are in close proximity to major urban areas. Flagstaff is in the middle of the Coconino National Forest (#6, 5.79 million RVDs), and Phoenix is 100 miles and 2 hours' driving time to the south. Most visitors to the more heavily used South Rim of Grand Canyon National Park pass through the Coconino. The Pike and San Isabel National Forests are jointly administered; their combined recreational use ranks them #7 with 5.59 million RVDs. These forests are located immediately west of the large Colorado cities of Denver, Colorado Springs, and Pueblo. The eighth-ranking, jointly administered Mt. Baker and Snoqualmie National Forests (5.51 million RVDs) are located immediately east of Seattle, Olympia, and other urban centers on the eastern side of Puget Sound. The close proximity of the Los Angeles urban area immediately west of the San Bernardino National Forest contributes to its #9 rank with 5.50 million RVDs. The tenth-ranked, jointly administered Arapaho and Roosevelt National Forests tallied 5.44 million RVDs in 1992. The Arapaho is located immediately west of Denver, and the Roosevelt is immediately west of Boulder. One of the most scenic drives in the national forests is Colorado Routes 103 and 5 to the summit of Mt. Evans (elevation 14,264 feet) through the Arapaho National Forest (Figure 9.6). "Mechanized travel and viewing scenery" accounts for a disproportionate share of use in the Coconino (58 percent), Mt. Baker–Snoqualmie (64 percent), and San Bernardino (50 percent). "Winter sports" play an above-average role in the Mt. Baker–Snoqualmie (10 percent), San Bernardino

Figure 9.6   One of the most scenic drives in the entire National Forest System results from exiting Colorado Route 103 at Echo Lake and following Colorado Route 5 through the Arapaho National Forest to the summit of Mt. Evans, (elevation 14,264 ft.). This is possible in summer only.

(9 percent), and Arapaho-Roosevelt (15 percent) National Forests. Some of the most heavily used ski areas in the country are in the Arapaho National Forest and include Winter Park, Copper Mountain, Breckenridge, Keystone, and Arapaho Basin.

"Winter sports" plays a significant role in several others of the most heavily used national forests. This is the case in 11th-ranked Tahoe National Forest (California; 5.18 million RVDs, with "winter sports" = 21 percent), 12th-ranked Wasatch-Cache National Forest (Utah; 4.87 million RVDs, "winter sports" = 17 percent) and 16th-ranked Grand Mesa–Uncompaghre–Gunnison National Forests (Colorado; 4.64 million RVDs, "winter sports" = 16 percent). In the Tahoe National Forest there are several major and moderately sized ski areas in the Donner Summit area. Interstate 80 provides a direct route from Sacramento (100 miles, 1.5 hours), San Francisco (175 miles, 3 hours), and Reno (30 miles, 0.5 hours). For much of the winter Interstate 80 is closed or chain regulations are in effect in the Donner Summit area due to heavy snow, but this does not deter skiers. The major ski areas on the east side of Donner Summit include Squaw Valley, Alpine Meadows, and Northstar at Tahoe. The world's largest cross-country ski area is located at Royal Gorge, just west of Donner Summit. The Wasatch and Cache National Forests are located immediately east of Salt Lake City and Ogden. Within a 45-minute drive of Salt Lake City are seven major alpine ski areas: Alta, Snowbird, Solitude, and Brighton on the west side of the Wasatch Crest and Park City, Deer Valley, and Park West to the east of the Crest. No other area in the United States has so many large ski areas less than an hour's drive away as occurs at Salt Lake City. Alta and Snowbird are especially renowned for their heavy falls of deep powder, each averaging close to 500 inches of snow per winter. The U.S. Forest Service perfected their avalanche control techniques and *snow ranger* training at Alta. Grand Mesa, Uncompaghre, and Gunnison National Forests are remotely located in western Colorado. The largest community in their proximity is Grand Junction; Montrose is a smaller community. The largest ski area is in the Gunnison National Forest at Crested Butte. Crested Butte has the world's best ski deal—free skiing from opening until Christmas!

Winter sports play a minor role in the 13th-ranked Shasta-Trinity National Forests (California; 1 percent), 14th-ranked Los Padres National Forest, (California; 1 percent), and 15th-ranked Sierra National Forest (California; 2 percent). "Resorts, cabins, and organization camps" were a major use in the Sierra National Forest, accounting for a disproportionately high 17 percent of its RVDs. The Coronado National Forest, which ranks 17th with 4.61 million RVDs, is located in southeastern Arizona, and the most heavily used sections are at Tucson's backdoor. Especially above average participation in "nonconsumptive fish and wildlife use" (7 percent) and "other recreational activities" (30 percent) occurs in the Coronado. The leading specific categories within the "other" category included gathering forest products, guided touring, unguided walking, viewing interpretive signs, and viewing interpretive exhibits. The southernmost ski area in the United States—Mount Lemmon—is located in the Coronado National Forest.

Alaska's Tongass National Forest ranks 18th in total use, with 4.02 million RVDs in 1992. This magnitude of recreational use was unexpected, given the Tongass' remote location and lack of any nearby major cities. The dominant category of use in the Tongass was "mechanized travel and viewing scenery," accounting for 62 percent of the total RVDs. The two leading subcategories in this broader group, which alone

accounted for over half of the total use, are "viewing scenery" (1.22 million RVDs) and "tour boat, ship, and ferry" (0.86 million RVDs). The category "camping, picnicking and swimming" was underrepresented, with only 4 percent of the RVDs. The Tongass National Forest is one of the case studies in Chapter 10.

It is obvious that the national forests are a much more important recreational resource in the West than in the East. This is a consequence of both their size and the availability of other recreational resources. Not only are the eastern national forests smaller, but there is also wider availability of state recreation resources. Among the top-30-ranked national forests, only four are in the East. The Superior, in the northeastern corner of Minnesota, is the East's most heavily used national forest, ranking 19th in national use with 4.02 million RVDs. Users from much of the Midwest travel to the Superior. "Hiking, horseback riding, and water travel" are disproportionately important in the Superior National Forest, accounting for 20 percent of the RVDs. One-third of the total use in the Superior National Forest occurs in the nation's most heavily used wilderness area—the Boundary Waters Canoe Area (1.4 million RVDs). The White Mountain National Forest (New Hampshire and Maine) is the East's second most heavily used national forest, ranking 27th nationally with 3.1 million RVDs; "Winter sports" accounts for 20 percent of its use. Interstate 93 offers a convenient access to this forest from the Boston metropolitan area, 100 miles to the south. The Cherokee National Forest, located in Tennessee along the Appalachian Mountain crest where it borders North Carolina, is the East's third-most-visited national forest but is ranked 28th nationally with 2.98 million RVDs in 1992. Interstate 75 provides direct access from Atlanta, 100 miles and 2 hours to the south, and Chattanooga and Knoxville. Its proximity to Great Smoky Mountains National Park is a major factor in its use. The fourth most heavily used national forest in the East in the Allegheny, which ranks number 30 nationally, with 2.94 million RVDs. It is located in northwestern Pennsylvania, within a 2 to 3-hour drive from the major urban centers of Buffalo, N.Y., Pittsburgh and Erie, Pa., and Cleveland and Akron, Ohio.

Table 9.5 identifies, by rank order, the national forests that in 1992 received less than the median value of 1.52 million RVDs. Among these 71 lesser-used national forests the following number of RVDs were recorded: 27 had less than 500,000 RVDs, 24 had 500,000 to 1,000,000 RVDs, and 19 had 1,000,000 to 1,500,000 RVDs. The 27 national forests with less than 500,000 RVDs, share certain dominating characteristics: They are primarily in the South (19 out of 27), they are usually relatively small for national forests (18 out of the 27 were under 250,000 acres in size), hunting and fishing are disproportionately important, and winter sports are nonexistent. Among these small southern national forests, especially high percentages of total RVDs are accounted for by hunting: Delta (48 percent), Homochitto (47 percent), Bienville (42 percent), and Conecuh (37 percent)—the first three in Mississippi and the last in Alabama.

There are some notable exceptions to these generalizations. The least-used national forest—New York's Finger Lakes—is in the Northeast, receiving only 31,200 RVDs in 1992. This 13,327-acre forest is located on the upland between two of New York's Finger Lakes—Cayuga Lake and Seneca Lake. It was formerly called the Hector Land Utilization Project and was under Forest Service jurisdiction before it was designated a National Forest in 1985. The area was one of the public land areas that

Table 9.5   National Forests: Least-Used-1992 Recreational Use by Forest (thousand RVDs)

National Forest	RVDs	National Forest	RVDs	National Forest	RVDs
Finger Lakes	31.2	Winema	462.2	Shawnee	899.5
Delta	43.8	DeSoto	494.6	Medicine Bow	905.7
Tuskegee	46.0	Siskiyou	498.5	Monongahela	915.7
Choctawhatchee	94.9	Kisatchie	507.1	Klamath	1000.5
St. Francis	95.7	Hoosier	551.8	Lewis and Clark	1009.4
Tombigbee	121.7	Angelina	553.3	Umatilla	1045.0
Conecuh	137.1	Uwharrie	590.6	Chequamegon	1056.4
Francis Marion	155.2	Salmon	667.1	Deerlodge	1092.1
Homochitto	182.3	Wayne	671.7	Nicolet	1128.7
Ochoco	199.1	Sam Houston	689.2	Ozark	1134.2
Holly Springs	211.2	Sabine	701.6	Okanogan	1158.7
Davy Crockett	226.7	Custer	738.9	Six Rivers	1161.5
Bienville	243.9	Nez Perce	748.1	Ottawa	1201.1
William B. Bankhead	248.3	Challis	748.4	Shoshone	1210.4
Talladega	269.2	Malheur	752.6	Fishlake	1275.8
Fremont	269.3	Humboldt	755.0	Ouachita	1284.7
Caribbean	289.3	Sumter	795.1	Lincoln	1289.4
Nebraska-McKelvie	349.2	Beaverhead	800.3	Rio Grande	1295.8
Oconee	378.4	Modoc	834.4	Rogue River	1316.2
Helena	394.0	Caribou	860.7	Colville	1488.4
Croatan	394.1	Manti–La Sal	865.0	Mendocino	1488.5
Bitterroot	401.1	Flathead	881.5	Cibola	1495.3
Apalachicola	436.2	Payette	897.3		
Osceola	450.9	Clearwater	898.8		

Source: Forest Service.

Director of the Budget, David Stockman, had proposed to dispose of to help solve the budget deficit. Public outcry stopped this from happening, resulting in its "national forest" designation by Congress. "Camping, picnicking, and swimming" is extremely important in this forest, accounting for 52 percent of the RVDs, and hunting is also important, with 13 percent of the RVD. The Choctawhatchee is the smallest national forest (1199 acres) that reports recreational use data. It was the fourth-least-used national forest, with 94,900 RVDs in 1992. Camping accounted for 58 percent of the RVDs in the Choctawhatchee. It is worth noting that the Choctawhatchee has the distinction of being the most intensively used national forest—0.013 acres per RVDs. (Intensity of use is the subject of the next section.) It is located in northwestern Florida and is administered as a part of the Apalachicola National Forest.

Six national forests, among the least-used 27, have some differences for these generalizations of southern location and size. Four of these forests that differ are in Oregon, and two are in Montana. Besides having a different geographic setting, these six forests are much larger; most are close to 1 million acres in size. The Ochoco National Forest in central Oregon is the 10th least used, with 199,100 RVDS in 1992; 56 percent of the recreational use was accounted for by "camping, picnicking, and swimming," and "hunting" was 15 percent of the use. The Fremont National Forest, in south-central Oregon, is the 16th-least-used national forest, with 269,300 RVDs; "camping, picnicking, and swimming" was the category for 42 percent of the RVDs. The next section will show that the Fremont (4.459 acres/RVD) and the Ochoco (4.259 acres/RVD) National Forests are the least intensively used in the entire system. West

of the Fremont is the Winema National Forest, which ranks 26th, with 462,200 RVD. The Siskiyou National Forest, located in extreme southwestern Oregon and extending into California, ranks 27th, with 498,500 RVDs. "Camping, picnicking, and swimming" are disproportionately important in both the Winema (49 percent of RVD total) and Siskiyou (41 percent of RVD total). In Montana, the Helena National Forest ranks 20th (394,000 RVDs) and the Bitterroot ranks 22nd (401,100 RVDs)—both among the least-used of national forests. "Hiking, horseback riding, and water travel" are disproportionately represented, accounting for 21 percent of the RVDs in the Bitterroot and 15 percent of the RVDs in the Helena.

Intensity of Use   The previous section highlighted the number of recreation visitor days for individual national forests. While this was a meaningful and useful exercise, this analysis did not relate the recreational use to the size of the areas. The national forests vary in size from the 380-acre Calaveras Bigtree National Forest (which is administered jointly with the Stanislaus National Forest) to the 16,724,169-acre Tongass National Forest. The best method of assessing the intensity of use in the National Forest System is to relate the recreational use (in RVDs) to area (in net acres of national forest). This is accomplished by dividing the net acreage of each forest by its RVDs for the year. The result is the number of acres in each forest for each RVD, and is referred to here as the *intensity-of-use index*. This index allows one to compare the intensity of use in different national forests. For several national forests, the recreational use data are available only for combined Forests (such as the Grand Mesa–Gunnison–Uncompaghre National Forests). This index was therefore calculated for 141 national forests instead of 156. The Southern Region (Region 8) does the best job of collecting recreational use data, and the Pacific Northwest Region (Region 6) does the poorest job. A similar analysis was undertaken to assess the intensity of use at the 50 national parks in Chapter 5.

The mean intensity-of-use index (0.662 acres/RVD) for the national forests is close to the median (0.631 acres/RVD). These values vary from 0.013 acres/RVD in the most intensely used Choctawhatchee National Forest (Florida) to 4.459 acres/RVD in the least intensely used Fremont National Forest (Oregon). There is a considerable difference between the *mean* intensity of use (0.89 acres/RVD) and the *median* (0.50 acres/RVD) for the 50 national parks. This difference is skewed by very large Alaskan parks that are extremely lightly used. Large portions of these parks are units of the National Wilderness Preservation System. As a result, four Alaskan Parks had anomalous intensity-of-use indexes: Lake Clark National Park, the least intensely used (989.89 acres/RVD); Kobuk Valley National Park (959.15 acres/RVD); Gates of the Arctic National Park (622.36 acres/RVD); and Wrangell–St. Elias National Park (228.36 acres/RVD). Virgin Islands National Park was the most intensely used, having an intensity-of-use index of 0.040. Five other national parks had higher indexes, (indicating less intensive use) than the Fremont National Forest whose 4.459 acres/RVD made it the least intensely used national forest. The four other very lightly used Alaskan national parks and their indexes are Katmai (79.44), Denali (17.07), Glacier Bay (13.14), and Kenai Fjords (12.08). In the lower states, North Cascade National Park, with an index of 16.76 acres/RVD, is less intensely used than any national forest. However, it has no road access. Many national parks have much lower intensities of use than any national forest, but most national parks are used more intensely

than the national forests for recreational purposes. This conclusion has been reached by comparing the median value of the intensity-of-use index for national parks (0.50) with the comparable value for national forests (0.631).

Caution in applying these index numbers is stressed, since several factors can cause seasonal and locational variation in recreational use. Foremost is the seasonality of use and the impact of climate. In national forests for which a high percentage of their RVD is accounted for by "winter sports," most of this use occurs during December, January, February, and March. For example, in the White River National Forest, 3.9 million out of a total 8.2 million RVDs are accounted for by "winter sports." Likewise, in Vermont's Green Mountain National Forest, 0.83 million out of a total 1.56 million RVDs are accounted for by "winter sports." Activities that are warm-weather-related will occur primarily in June, July, and August, especially in northern forests. The camping, picnicking, and swimming season in Montana's Flathead National Forest, for example, will be much shorter than in Florida's Ocala National Forest. Many of the scenic backcountry gravel roads are closed for much of the year in the West due to heavy snow. Accessibility is another factor that affects recreational use—one finds the majority of users on the paved roads. If one travels a short distance from paved roads, there is a better chance of encountering fewer users. Many expansive areas of designated wilderness have been established in the National Forest System, and here it is possible to experience extreme solitude. For example, while the Sierra National Forest receives 4.67 million total RVDs/year, the wilderness areas in the Forest account for only 0.22 million RVDs. New Hampshire and Maine's White Mountain National Forest receives a total of 3.01 million RVDs, but only 0.12 million are measured in the wilderness areas. Even in wilderness areas there are underused and overused sections. And finally, peaking of use within seasons occurs. At ski areas, Christmas week is the busiest of the year. While January is a slow month, following the frenzy of Christmas week at ski areas, the Martin Luther King holiday weekend in mid-January has become a major peak in weekend use. For summer activities such as camping, peak use occurs on the July 4th weekend. Because of the school year most Americans still take their vacations in July and August, which is when the largest crowds are encountered at most national forests.

Nevertheless, despite taking these precautions of interpretation into consideration, the intensity-of-use index is the best method for identifying the relative degree of use for different national forests. Table 9.6 presents intensity-of-use indexes for the 70 most intensively used national forests; all have indexes below the median value of 0.631 for the entire National Forest System. It can be concluded that a disproportionate share of the national forests with the most intense use are located in the eastern half of the country. Of the 25 forests with the lowest indexes, 16 are located in the East. Remember, a low index number indicates high intensity of use. No correlation exists between size of national forests and intensity of use: The size of the 25 forests with the lowest index numbers varies from the 1199-acre Choctawhatchee National Forest to the 1,961,667-acre White River National Forest. Many of the most intensively used national forests (such as Angeles, Caribbean, San Bernardino, and Cleveland) are in close proximity to urban areas, but many others are not (for example, Inyo, White River, Siuslaw, etc.).

The Choctawhatchee National Forest is by far the most intensively used national forest, with an intensity-of-use index of 0.013 acres/RVD. On its 1199 acres in 1992

Table 9.6   National Forests: Highest Intensity of Use—1992 (acres per RVD)

National Forest	Acres/ RVD	National Forest	Acres/ RVD	National Forest	Acres/ RVD
Choctawhatchee	0.013	Sierra	0.280	Wenatchee	0.429
Angeles	0.071	Siuslaw	0.281	Deschutes	0.431
Uwharrie	0.081	Olympic	0.281	George Washington	0.435
Caribbean	0.096	Chattahoochee	0.286	Sumter	0.451
San Bernardino	0.122	Shawnee	0.289	Plumas	0.457
Cleveland	0.147	Oconee	0.293	Mt. Baker–Snoqualmie	0.457
Tahoe	0.160	Dixie	0.305	Shasta-Trinity	0.458
Allegheny	0.174	Tonto	0.311	Gifford Pinchot	0.464
Ocala	0.181	Wayne	0.314	Huron-Manistee	0.477
Pisgah	0.182	Coconino	0.319	Rogue River	0.478
Eldorado	0.205	Wasatch-Cache	0.321	Superior	0.514
Cherokee	0.211	Sequoia	0.323	Routt	0.514
Green Mountain	0.220	Jefferson	0.325	Umpqua	0.523
St. Francis	0.222	Stanislaus–Calaveras Bigtree	0.332	Tombigbee	0.547
Inyo	0.227	Arapaho-Roosevelt	0.333	Hiawatha	0.579
Sabine	0.229	Hoosier	0.343	Nicolet	0.586
Sam Houston	0.234	Los Padres	0.369	Bighorn	0.589
White River	0.238	Chippewa	0.386	Mendocino	0.595
White Mountain	0.239	Coronado	0.388	Santa Fe	0.605
Tuskegee	0.241	Black Hills	0.397	Conecuh	0.606
Uinta	0.246	Pike–San Isabel	0.398	Gallatin	0.624
Daniel Boone	0.251	Croatan	0.401	Mt. Hood	0.631
Nantahala	0.258	Osceola	0.415		
Angelina	0.277	Finger Lakes	0.427		

Source: Forest Service.

there were 94,900 RVDs. "Camping, picnicking, and swimming" accounted for 58 percent of the recreational use. The Choctawhatchee National Forest is located in the western part of Florida's panhandle, east of Pensacola; it has an interesting history. This National Forest was proclaimed by President Theodore Roosevelt in 1908 and covered a gross area of 473,600 acres within its boundary (*35 Stat. 2209*). Legislation in 1940 allowed acquisition of all private land within its boundary:

> . . . Provided, that all Government-owned land in the Choctawhatchee National Forest, Florida is hereby transferred from the control and jurisdiction of the Forest Service, Department of Agriculture, to the control and jurisdiction of the War Department for use for military purposes; Provided further, that in the event the area hereby transferred, together with any land hereafter acquired by the War Department within or adjacent to said national forest, shall cease to be needed for military purposes it may, by proclamation or order of the President, be restored to a national forest status . . . (*54 Stat. 655*).

Today, the geographic extent of Eglin Air Force Base, the largest military base in the world, occupies almost all of the area that was originally designated as the Choctawhatchee National Forest in 1908. Eglin Air Force Base is 52 miles across from east to west and over 17 miles in a north-south direction. It is the home of the 33rd Fighter Wing of F-16s and is a major testing and development center. Gradually, as mandated by law, the land that is no longer needed for military purposes is reverting back to

national forest status and is being transferred to the Forest Service. By 1981, 675 acres had reverted back to national forest. This increased to the current 1199 acres in 1992, when President George Bush issued the Executive Order that permitted six tracts totaling 512 acres to be transferred from the Department of Defense to the Forest Service (43 U.S.C.A. §141). This most recent transfer consisted of noncontiguous tracts of 61, 40, 49, 50, 265, and 47 acres in the western and northern parts of Eglin Air Force Base (personal communication with Civil Engineering Dept., Eglin Air Force Base, 1993).

The index number for the second most intensively used national forest, the Angeles (654,723 acres), jumps considerably to 0.071 acres/RVD. Its geographic location—immediately next door to the Los Angeles metropolitan area—explains its heavy use. The third- and fourth-ranking national forests, the Uwharrie (0.081 acres/RVD) and the Caribbean (0.096 acres/RVD) are both small and have large urban centers close by. The 47,954-acre Uwharrie National Forest is located in central North Carolina and is surrounded by the urban areas of Charlotte, Winston-Salem, Greensboro, Durham–Chapel Hill, Raleigh, and Fayetteville, each only a 30-minute to one-hour drive away. Hunting accounted for 31 percent of the recreation visitor days in 1992. The 27,831-acre Caribbean National Forest, located in the northeastern corner of Puerto Rico, is close to the large urban centers of San Juan, Carolina, Trujillo, and Caguas. "Camping, picnicking, and swimming" accounted for 38% of its RVDs. The fifth- and sixth-ranking national forests are the San Bernardino (0.122 acres/RVD) and the Cleveland (0.147 acres/RVD). The San Bernardino (670,100 acres) is east of Los Angeles, and the Cleveland (421,974 acres) is east of San Diego. In both forests "mechanized travel and viewing scenery" and "resorts, cabins, and organization camps" are disproportionately important recreational activities, accounting for 50 and 12 percent, respectively, of the recreation visitor days in the San Bernardino, and 53 percent and 17 percent of the RVDs in the Cleveland.

The seventh-ranking Tahoe (California; 0.160 acres/RVD), eighth-ranking Allegheny (Pennsylvania; 0.174 acres/RVD), ninth-ranking Ocala (Florida; 0.181 acres/RVD), and tenth-ranking Pisgah (North Carolina; 0.182 acres/RVD) national forests are not immediately next to large urban areas but are within a 1 to 3-hour drive of such areas. In the Tahoe, "winter sports" play a much above average role; in the Ocala, "camping, picnicking, and swimming" play a disproportionate role; and "hiking, horseback riding, and water travel" play a significantly above average role in the Pisgah. The El Dorado (0.205 acres/RVD), Inyo (0.227 acres/RVD), and Sierra (0.280 acres/RVD) are other national forests in California that have high intensities of use. Other national forests in the Southeast with high intensities of use include the Cherokee (Tennessee; 0.211 acres/RVD), the Tuskegee (Alabama; 0.241 acres/RVD), the Daniel Boone (Kentucky; 0.251 acres/RVD), the Nantahala (N. Carolina; 0.258 acres/RVD), the Chattahoochee (Georgia; 0.286 acres/RVD), and the Oconee (Georgia; 0.293 acres/RVD). In the Northeast, the Green Mountain National Forest (Vermont; 0.220 acres/RVD) and White Mountain National Forest (N. Hampshire and Maine; 0.239 acres/RVD) are very important and intensively used recreational resources. "Winter sports" are especially important in these forests, being responsible for 53 percent of the recreational use in the Green Mountain and 20 percent of the recreational use in the White Mountain National Forests. The small, 21,201-acre St. Francis National Forest in eastern Arkansas on the Mississippi River is very inten-

sively used (0.222 acres/RVD). Three national forests in southeastern Texas have high intensity-of-use indexes: the Sabine (0.229 acres/RVD), the Sam Houston (0.234 acres/ RVD), and the Angelina (0.277 acres/RVD). Fishing is the dominant recreational activity in the Angelina and the Sabine, accounting for 50 percent of the recreation visitor days in each. In the Rocky Mountains the White River (Colorado) is the most intensively used national forest (0.238 acres/RVD); "winter sports" account for 47 percent of the RVDs. In the Intermountain Region the Uinta National Forest (Utah) has the most intensive use (0.246 acres/RVD). In the Pacific Northwest Region the Siuslaw (Oregon; 0.281 acres/RVD) and Olympic (Washington; 0.281 acres/RVD) are most intensively used. Illinois' Shawnee National Forest (0.289 acres/RVD) is also intensively used. The Shawnee National Forest is one of the case studies of Chapter 10.

Table 9.7 presents, in rank order, the intensity-of-use indexes for the 71 least intensively used national forests, those above the median value of 0.631 acres/RVD for the entire system. The differences in intensity of use among these national forests are considerably greater than among the most intensively used ones discussed previously. While the 70 most intensively used forests have indexes ranging from 0.013 to 0.631 acres/RVD, the spread for the least intensively used forests range from 4.459 to 0.636 acres/RVD. Twenty-three of these forests have an index between 0.631 and 1.0, 33 between 1.0 and 2.0, 10 between 2.0 and 3.0, three between 3.0 and 4.0, and four above 4.0 acres/RVD. The four least intensively used national forests—the Fre-

Table 9.7   National Forests: Lowest Intensity of Use—1992 (acres per RVD)

National Forest	Acres/ RVD	National Forest	Acres/ RVD	National Forest	Acres/ RVD
Fremont	4.459	Manti–La Sal	1.463	Targhee	1.010
Ochoco	4.259	Rio Grande	1.432	Ozark	0.991
Tongass	4.160	Talladega	1.429	Kaibab	0.983
Bitterroot	3.938	Delta	1.359	Monongahela	0.978
Challis	3.293	Umatilla	1.346	Lincoln	0.856
Humboldt	3.282	Lolo	1.339	Six Rivers	0.851
Nez Perce	2.973	Idaho Panhandle	1.324	Toiyabe	0.846
Chugach	2.930	Okanogan	1.294	Ottawa	0.817
Flathead	2.671	Apalachicola	1.293	Carson	0.816
Beaverhead	2.660	Ouachita	1.275	Chequamegon	0.811
Salmon	2.656	Boise	1.265	Mark Twain	0.811
Payette	2.589	Medicine Bow	1.207	Sawtooth	0.787
Helena	2.479	Kisatchie	1.186	Willamette	0.776
Winema	2.248	Bridger-Teton	1.148	Ashley	0.747
Siskiyou	2.195	Caribou	1.147	Nebraska-McKelvie	0.737
Shoshone	2.010	Kootenai	1.144	Bienville	0.731
Modoc	1.994	Fishlake	1.117	Holly Springs	0.729
Malheur	1.947	San Juan	1.095	William B. Bankhead	0.725
Clearwater	1.856	Deerlodge	1.093	Davy Crockett	0.714
Lewis and Clark	1.826	Cibalo	1.090	Prescott	0.676
Gila	1.782	Apache-Sitgreaves	1.057	Lassen	0.664
Klamath	1.708	Wallowa-Whitman	1.051	Colville	0.640
Francis Marion	1.610	Homochitto	1.042	Grand Mesa–Gunnison–	
Custer	1.605	DeSoto	1.019	Uncompahgre	0.636

Source: Forest Service.

mont (Oregon), the Ochoco (Oregon), the Tongass (Alaska), and the Bitterroot (Montana)—are separated from the others by a large margin in their indexes. While the most intensively used forests are primarily in the East, the reverse is the case for the least intensively used forests—76 percent are in the West. Another characteristic of the least intensively used forests is that they are remotely located, distant from major urban centers. A final characteristic of these forests is that they are very large: Among the 25 least intensively used forests, all of which have indexes above 1.500, two are over 5 million acres, eight are 2 to 5 million acres, and 11 are 1 to 2 million acres. Only three are below 1 million acres: the Ochoco (Oregon; 847,898 acres), Helena (Montana; 976,656 acres), and Francis Marion (S. Carolina; 249,870).

The Fremont National Forest has the distinction of being the least intensively used in the system for recreational use, having an intensity-of-use index of 4.459 acres/RVD. This means that it has 343 times more elbow room than the most intensely used forest (the Choctawhatchee), 63 times the elbow room of the second most intensely used National Forest (the Angeles), or 7 times the elbow room of the median-ranked national forest (the Mt. Hood). The Fremont National Forest has a remote geographic location on the eastern side of the Cascade Range in south-central Oregon. Klamath Falls, Ore., is the nearest settlement of any size and is 75 miles to the closest portion of the forest—and its population is only 17,000. "Camping, picnicking, and swimming," is the leading category of recreational use, accounting for 42 percent of the recreation visitor days in 1992. "Hunting" is also disproportionately important in the Fremont, accounting for 13 percent of the recreational use.

The second least intensively used National Forest—the Ochoco—is similarly located in Oregon east of the Cascade Range in the central part of the state. It is even more removed from population centers than the Fremont National Forest. The Ochoco's intensity-of-use index is a sparse 4.259 acres/RVD. Its recreational use pattern is similar to that of the Fremont, with "camping, picnicking and swimming" accounting for a much above average 56 percent of the recreational use and "hunting" for an above-average 15 percent.

The Tongass National Forest ranks as the third least intensively used national forest, with an intensity-of-use index of 4.160 acres/RVD. A large percentage of the recreational use (22%) on the Tongass is attributed to "tour boat, ship, and ferry use" (Figure 9.7). If this recreational use factor, during which the users do not step on land, were subtracted from the Tongass's 4.02 million RVDs, it would be the least intensively used national forest, with an Index of 5.292 acres/RVD. This large amount of recreational use, which ranks this forest number 18 among the 156 national forests, is quite surprising when the geographic location, highway access, and population centers are analyzed. Juneau, the most populous borough, has a population of only 27,000. The remote Haines Highway is the only year-round access point, and this is in the northern part of the forest. Twenty percent of the total recreational use in the Tongass occurs in the many units designated part of the National Wilderness Preservation System. Only three other national forests have a higher percentage of their total recreational use taking place in wilderness areas. "Mechanized travel and viewing scenery" account for 62 percent of the total RVDs. Alaska's other national forest, the Chugach, has a low intensity of use, ranking eighth in least intensity of use with an intensity of use index of 2.930 acres/RVD. Anchorage's population of 175,000—

Figure 9.7 Tour boat in Tracy Arm, Tongass National Forest (Forest Service Photo)

making it Alaska's largest city—offers ready access to the Chugach, but the Chugach's large size easily absorbs the users.

The Bitterroot National Forest, with an intensity of use index of 3.938 acres/RVD, is the last in this group of four national forests with exceedingly low intensities of use. It is located west of Butte and south of Missoula and straddles the Montana-Idaho border, with the larger portion in Montana. Its remote location is reflected in the recreational use statistics. A low 22 percent of the recreational use is credited to "mechanized travel and viewing scenery," a high 21 percent is credited to "hiking, horseback riding, and water travel," and an above-average 10 percent is accounted for by "hunting." A very high 25 percent of the total recreational use takes place in wilderness areas. Idaho's Challis National Forest has an even higher percentage of the total recreational use occurring in wilderness areas—31 percent. This is more than in any other national forest, except the Superior (Minnesota), whose similar value is 35 percent. The Challis is the fifth-ranked least intensively used national forest, with an intensity of use of 3.293. Other large, remote national forests in Idaho with low intensities of use include the Nez Perce (2.973 acres/RVD), the Salmon (2.656 acres/RVD), the Payette (2.589 acres/RVD), and the Clearwater (1.856 acres/RVD).

Nearby in Montana the Beaverhead (2.660 acres/RVD) receives low-intensity use, and farther to the north in Montana the Helena (2.479 acres/RVD), the Lewis and Clark (1.826 acres/RVD), and Flathead (2.671 acres/RVD) National Forests receive low-intensity recreational use. The low intensity of use in the Flathead contrasts greatly with the intensity of use that occurs in nearby Glacier National Park, which borders it on the north and east. In Chapter 5 it was pointed out that Glacier National Park had an intensity of use of 0.680 acres/RVD, four times that of the Flathead National Forest. The recreational use pattern is scattered more evenly during the year in the Flathead, with a major ski area at Big Mountain. In contrast, the recreational

use pattern is extremely seasonal in Glacier, with almost all of it occurring in June, July, and August and most of it concentrated in a few favored locations, such as the Going-to-the-Sun Road, the Many Glacier area, and the Lake MacDonald area. In southeastern Montana the Custer National Forest has a low intensity of use (1.605 acres/RVD).

There are eight other national forests with use intensities above 1.5 acres/RVD. The Humboldt National Forest (3.282 acres/RVD) is scattered over several mountain ranges in eastern and northern Nevada. With the exception of Alaska, this would be the most remote section of the United States if it were not for I-80 crossing the region. "Hiking, horseback riding, and water travel" and "hunting" are the recreational activities that are much above average in significance, accounting for 14 and 18 percent, respectively, of the RVDs. In Oregon, two National Forests have low intensities of recreational use: The Winema (2.248 acres/RVD) and Malheur (1.947 acres/RVD) have geographic positions and circumstances similar to the low-intensity-use Fremont and Ochoco National Forests. In the Winema National Forest, which is located along the crest of the Cascade Range and to the east of the range in south-central Oregon, "camping, picnicking, and swimming" are exceptionally important, accounting for 49 percent of the recreation visitor days. The Winema National Forest borders Crater Lake National Park on the south, east, and northeast. The Malheur National Forest is located in east-central Oregon, to the east of the Ochoco National Forest. Its intensity-of-use index is 1.947 acres/RVD; like the Fremont and Ochoco National Forests, "hunting" is above average in importance in the Malheur, accounting for 15 percent of the RVDs. "Mechanized travel and viewing scenery" are responsible only for an extremely low 6 percent of the RVDs, but the "other recreational activities" category accounts for an exceptionally high 43 percent of the RVDs.

In Wyoming the Shoshone National Forest, which is located east of Grand Teton and Yellowstone National Parks, has a low intensity of use—2.010 acres/RVD. "Resorts, cabins, and organization camps" account for a high 13 percent of the RVDs in the Shoshone. In California, two national forests have low intensities of use. The Modoc National Forest, located in the remote northeastern corner of California, has an intensity-of-use index of 1.994 acres/RVDs. "Hunting" accounts for a disproportionate 20 percent of the RVDs. The Klamath National Forest is located in the remote northern part of California, with 26,334 acres extending into Oregon, and has an intensity-of-use index of 1.708 acres/RVD. The Gila National Forest in southwestern New Mexico has a low intensity of use of 1.782 acres per RVD; "hiking, horseback riding, and water travel" are especially important in this forest, accounting for 16 percent of the RVDs.

Low intensities of use are notably absent from the national forests in the eastern half of the United States. The eastern national forest with the lowest intensity of use is the Francis Marion, with an index of 1.610 acres/RVDs. It is located on the central coast of South Carolina, northeast of Charleston. The Intracoastal Waterway separates it from Cape Romain National Wildlife Refuge, which fronts on the Atlantic Ocean. "Hunting" is especially important, accounting for 27 percent of the recreation visitor days. There are seven other eastern national forests that have relatively low intensities of use (over 1.0 acre/RVD)—at least for the East: the Talladega (Alabama; 1.429 acres/RVD), the Delta (Mississippi; 1.359 acres/RVD), the Apalachicola (Florida; 1.293

acres/RVD), the Ouachita (Arkansas and Oklahoma; 1.275 acres/RVD), the Kisatchie (Louisiana; 1.186 acres/RVD), the Homochitto (Mississippi; 1.042 acres/RVD), and the DeSoto (Mississippi; 1.019 acres/RVD). In all seven of these forests, "hunting" accounts for 20 to 50 percent of the total recreation visitor days. In the Apalachicola National Forest, "camping, picnicking, and swimming" account for a high 45 percent of the RVDs.

Patterns of Recreational Use by Activity   Appendix X identifies the number of recreation visitor days for national forests listed by recreational activity for 1992. The specific amount of use for each activity, in each national forest can be obtained from this appendix. This section will identify the national forests that have the most recreational visitor days in each of the nine major reporting activities. It will also identify the national forests in which certain categories of recreational use are significantly above and below national averages. The following percentages are the national averages of recreation visitor days by activity for the entire National Forest System: "camping, picnicking, and swimming," 27 percent; "mechanized travel and viewing scenery," 35 percent; "hiking, horseback riding, and water travel, 8 percent; "winter sports," 6 percent; "resorts, cabins, and organization camps," 6 percent; "hunting," 6 percent; "fishing," 6 percent; "nonconsumptive fish and wildlife use," 1 percent; and "other recreational activities," 5 percent. A series of tables in this section will identify both the individual national forests in which the greatest number of RVDs are tallied in each category and the individual national forests in which the percentage of use for the activity is significantly above the national average value. In this manner, variations in recreational use patterns can be identified for specific national forests in different regions of the country. The national forests having low numbers of RVDs for each category and the smaller percentage importance of total use will also be identified.

Camping, Picnicking, and Swimming   Table 9.8 summarizes the results for the category "camping, picnicking and swimming." The specific recreational activities tallied within this category include general day camping, automobile camping, trailer camping, tent camping, picnicking, swimming and water play, diving, waterskiing, and other water sports. Forest Service personnel have estimated that about 75 to 80 percent of the use across the country in this broad category is attributable to camping. For example, in Region 8 (Southern) the distribution of use among the subcategories in this major category is camping, 67 percent; picnicking, 18 percent; swimming and water play, 12 percent; waterskiing and other water sports, 2.5 percent; and diving, 0.3 percent. In Region 5 (Pacific Southwest) camping accounted for almost 75 percent of the recreation visitor days, and swimming for 13 percent, and picnicking for 12 percent. A few forests in Region 3 (Southwest) show extremes in both picnicking and camping. In the Cibola (New Mexico), picnicking accounts for 60 percent and in the Coronado (New Mexico and Arizona), picnicking accounts for 38 percent of this category. In the Kaibab (Arizona) camping accounts for 98 percent of the recreation visitor days, and in most national forests in Region 2 (Rocky Mountain) camping accounts for over 90 percent of the recreation visitor days. In the Routt National Forest (Colorado) only 1.3 percent of the RVDs in this category are accounted for by

Table 9.8 Camping, Picnicking, and Swimming—1992

Leading National Forests in Category—RVDs (000s) and % of Use

Tonto	3565.3	38.6%	Uinta	1418.6	40.2%
Angeles	2378.1	26.0%	Pike and San Isabel	1399.3	25.0%
Sequoia	1650.9	46.8%	White River	1327.2	16.1%
Inyo	1625.5	19.4%	Wasatch-Cache	1232.1	25.3%
Superior	1619.1	40.3%	Deschutes	1187.0	31.8%
Wenatchee	1567.3	40.3%	Cherokee	1176.7	39.5%
Arapaho-Roosevelt	1515.1	27.9%	Wallowa-Whitman	1157.2	53.7%
Shasta-Trinity	1468.8	30.5%	Ocala	1131.5	53.3%
Sierra	1466.2	31.4%	Santa-Fe	1107.6	42.7%
Toiyabe	1428.7	37.7%	Los Padres	1074.7	22.6%

National Forests with High % of Use in Category

Osceola	74.6%	Umatilla	47.5%	Siskiyou	41.3%
Choctawhatchee	58.5%	Sequoia	46.8%	Fishlake	41.2%
William B. Bankhead	57.8%	Mt. Hood	45.1%	Ashley	41.1%
Ochoco	56.1%	Apalachicola	44.6%	Wenatchee	40.3%
Wallowa-Whitman	53.7%	Hoosier	44.0%	Superior	40.3%
Ocala	53.3%	Mendocino	43.5%	Uinta	40.2%
Finger Lakes	51.9%	Santa Fe	42.7%	Klamath	40.1%
Winema	49.0%	Caribou	42.6%	Cherokee	39.5%
Monongahela	48.4%	Fremont	42.4%	Willamette	39.5%

Source: Forest Service.

picnicking. In all of the Eastern Region (Region 9) national forests camping is the overwhelming contributor (83 percent) to this category, while picnicking and swimming are each 8 percent.

The mean number of RVDs in this classification (camping, picnicking and swimming) is 524,583 per national forest, while the median is 363,000. The mean is skewed to the high side of the median by the very high use made of a relatively few national forests. A breakdown of the use data for this category into intervals yields: 1 forest over 3 million RVDs; 1 forest between 2 and 3 million RVDs; 5 forests between 1.5 and 2 million RVDs; 13 forests between 1 and 1.5 million RVDs; 35 forests between 0.5 and 1.0 million RVDs; 71 forests between 0.1 and 0.5 million RVDs and 18 forests under 0.1 million RVDs. The Tonto National Forest has 3.57 million RVDs in this category, which is significantly higher than the second-ranked Angeles National Forest (2.38 million RVDs). Both hold the same numbers 1 and 2 positions for total RVDs. While this category accounts for 39 percent of the total recreational use in the Tonto National Forest, it accounts for 26 percent in the Angeles National Forest. The third-ranked Sequoia National Forest has 1.65 million RVDs (this category accounts for 47 percent of the total recreational use). In terms of total recreational use, it is ranked 24th. The Inyo National Forest ranks fourth in this category, with 1.63 million RVDs, which was 19 percent of its total recreational use. The fifth-ranked Superior and sixth-ranked Wenatchee National Forests are ranked numbers 19 and 20 for total recreational use. This category accounts for 40 percent of the RVDs in each. Notably absent from the top of this category are the Dixie and Coconino National Forests; in terms of total use these forests rank fifth and sixth, but in terms of this category they rank 22nd and 27th. National forests that are ranked high in this category, but are ranked

much lower in total recreational use are the Wallowa-Whitman (#17 this category, and #48 total), Ocala (#18 this category, and #49 total), and Santa Fe (#19 this category and #37 total). Almost 54 percent of the total use in both the Wallowa-Whitman and Ocala occur in this classification. In 12 national forests an extremely small number of recreation visitor days—under 50,000—are measured in this category. All 12 of these forests are in the South except for the Finger Lakes National Forest (New York, 16,200 RVDs) and the Nebraska–Samuel R. McKelvie National Forests (Nebraska, 47,600 RVDs). The Tuskegee National Forest has the distinction of having the least number of RVDs in this classification (3000). Next to it at the bottom of the ranking is the Conecuh (Alabama) with 4800 RVDs, and the Delta (Mississippi) has the third least amount of recreational use in this category (11,400 RVDs).

The lower half of Table 9.8 identifies the national forests in which an exceptionally high percentage of their total recreational use is attributed to this category. Several of the national forests in the East stand out in this group. The mean of this value for the entire National Forest System is 26.8 percent, and the median is a close 26.5 percent. In seven forests, over 50 percent of the total RVDs are accounted for by this category; in 18 others it is 40 to 50 percent; in 27 it is 30 to 40 percent; in 54 it is 20 to 30 percent; in 31 it is 10 to 20 percent; and in 10 it is under 10 percent. Florida's climate plays a major role in this group, as three of the top six forests are in this state. The Osceola National Forest stands out as the prominent leader, with 75 percent of its total use in this category. This prominence seems almost anomalous in that in no other national forest—other than the Black Hills National Forest (N. Dakota) in the "mechanized travel and viewing scenery" category, where 75 percent of the use occurs—is there such a dominance in use by one activity. The Black Hills National Forest is at the bottom of the list, for "camping, picnicking and swimming" accounts for only 7 percent of the total recreation visitor days. The Osceola National Forest is located in extreme northern Florida, west of Jacksonville; the southern end of the Okefenokee Swamp extends from Georgia into its northern portion. The Osceola National Forest also has the distinction of having the lowest portion of its recreational use attributable to "mechanized travel and viewing scenery"; this value is an exceptionally low 3.2 percent. It is surprising that more use was not recorded in this category since I-10 passes through the forest. There is no "winter sports" or "noncomsumptive fish and wildlife use" in the Osceola. The Osceola is unusual for an eastern national forest in that it is 98 percent federal land.

The William B. Bankhead National Forest has a use pattern similar to that of the Osceola National Forest: A high 58 percent of the use is in "camping, picnicking, and swimming," and an extremely low 10.6 percent is in "mechanized travel and viewing scenery." The dominance of this category in the Choctawhatchee National Forest (59 percent of use) was previously discussed. Florida's Ocala National Forest (53 percent) and New York's Finger Lakes National Forest (52 percent) have especially high values. This category occupies a high percentage of total use in several national forests in Oregon: the Ochoco (56 percent), the Wallowa-Whitman (54 percent), the Winema (49 percent), the Umatilla (48 percent), the Mt. Hood (45 percent), the Fremont (42 percent), and the Siskiyou (41 percent). Other eastern forests with high values are the Monongahela (W. Virginia, 48 percent), the Apalachicola (Florida, 45 percent), the Hoosier (Indiana, 44 percent), the Superior (Minnesota, 40 percent), and the Cherokee (Tennessee, 40 percent). Exceptionally low percentages of total RVDs exist for the

following National Forest units: the Columbia River Gorge (Oregon and Washington), 2 percent; the Conecuh (Alabama), 4 percent; the Tongass (Alaska), 4 percent; the Tuskegee (Alabama), 7 percent; the Black Hills (Wyoming and S. Dakota), 7 percent; the Green Mountain (Vermont), 7 percent; and the Chugach (Alaska), 8 percent. The relative importance of hunting and lack of developed facilities explain the low values for the Conecuh and Tuskegee National Forests. In both the Tongass and Chugach almost two-thirds of the recreational use is occupied by "mechanized travel and viewing scenery." In the Green Mountain National Forest 53 percent of the RVDs are accounted for by "winter sports."

Mechanized Travel and Viewing Scenery   Table 9.9 summarizes the leading recreational use patterns in the category of "mechanized travel and viewing scenery." A wide variety of recreational activities is included within this category: viewing scenery; viewing activities (spectators); viewing works of humankind; automobile travel; motorcycle and scooter travel; ice and snowcraft travel; specialized landcraft travel; train and bus touring; tour boat, ship, and ferry use; power boating; motorized aircraft; aerial trams and lifts; nonmotorized aircraft; bicycling; and nature study, hobbies, and education. It is extremely unfortunate that the Forest Service lumps so many diverse categories of recreational use into one category for reporting purposes. In most national forests, automobile travel accounts for most of the RVDs, and in most viewing scenery is second in importance to this category total. Since most viewing of scenery in the National Forest System, outside of Alaska, is done from an automobile, it makes a person wonder how one category is separated from the other. In the Eastern Region the leading subcategories are automobile travel, 54 percent; viewing scenery, 14 percent; powered boat, 10 percent; ice and snowcraft travel, 7.6 percent; and motorcycle and scooter travel, 5 percent. In the Southern Region the leading subcategories are automobile travel 56 percent; viewing scenery, 19 percent; powered boats, 8 percent; and ice and snowcraft travel, 7 percent.

Table 9.9   Mechanized Travel and Viewing Scenery—1992

Leading National Forests in Category—RVDs (000s) and % of Use					
Tonto	4076.4	44.1%	Arapaho-Roosevelt	2244.9	41.3%
Dixie	3635.8	58.9%	Pike and San Isabel	2190.9	39.2%
Mt. Baker–Snoqualmie	3536.4	64.2%	Columbia R. Gorge	2106.4	63.7%
Angeles	3373.1	36.8%	Los Padres	2044.1	43.0%
Coconino	3355.2	58.0%	Shasta-Trinity	1979.6	41.1%
Inyo	3328.2	39.7%	White River	1708.4	20.8%
San Bernardino	2771.6	50.4%	Wasatch-Cache	1679.4	34.5%
Tongass	2483.4	61.8%	Cleveland	1532.4	53.3%
Tahoe	2402.3	46.4%	Coronado	1376.0	29.9%
Blackhills	2343.7	74.7%	Olympic	1320.5	59.2%

National Forests with High % of Use in Category					
Blackhills	74.7%	Olympic	59.2%	Cleveland	53.3%
Mt. Baker–Snoqualmie	64.2%	Dixie	58.9%	Nebraska–Samuel R. McKelvie	53.2%
Columbia R. Gorge	63.7%	Coconino	58.0%	Colville	52.6%
Chugach	62.6%	Kaibab	54.8%	Okanogan	52.6%
Tongass	61.8%	Prescott	54.6%	San Bernardino	50.4%

Source: Forest Service.

There are some very notable exceptions to this generalization about the dominance of auto travel. In the Chippewa National Forest (Minnesota), power boat RVDs exceed those for automobile travel, and the same is almost the case in the Superior National Forest (Minnesota). In the Green Mountain National Forest (Vermont), ice and snowcraft travel (actually snowmobiles) equals automobile travel. In the Routt National Forest (Colorado), viewing scenery outnumbers automobile travel at a 13:1 ratio, and the same is the case in the Shoshone National Forest (Wyoming) with a 7:1 ratio and the Nebraska National Forest (Nebraska) with a 4:1 ratio. In the Chugach National Forest (Alaska) viewing scenery accounts for 20 percent more recreation visitor days than automobile travel. In the Tongass National Forest (Alaska) the number of recreation visitor days for the leading subcategories within this major category are viewing scenery, 1,218,900 RVDs; automobile travel, 158,000 RVDs; and tour boat, ship and ferry, 857,300 RVDs. In the Coronado National Forest (Arizona and N. Mexico) within this broader category the leading subcategories of recreation visitor days are automobile travel, 538,300 RVDs; viewing scenery , 482,000 RVDs; and viewing works of humankind, 212,300 RVDs. In the Mendocino National Forest (California) motorcycle and scooter use is almost the equal of automobile travel, and a strong showing is also made by this category in the Cleveland and Los Padres National Forests, both in California. In the Los Padres, viewing scenery is almost equal to auto travel, and in the Shasta-Trinity National Forests viewing scenery accounts for over 3 times the number of RVDs that auto travel does. In the Sawtooth National Forest (Idaho and Utah), viewing scenery outnumbers auto travel, and in the Bridger-Teton National Forests (Wyoming) and the Humboldt National Forest (Nevada) the two are almost equal in importance. In the Croatan National Forest (N. Carolina) viewing scenery accounts for three times the RVDs as auto travel.

The mean number of RVDs per national forest in this category for 1992 was 705,763, and the median number was 426,000. This extreme skewing of the mean to the high side of the median is caused by very high values in a relatively small number of the national forests and small values of use in a large number of national forests. The breakdown of forests into intervals of use is as follows: over 4 million RVDs, 1; 3 to 4 million RVDs, 5; 2 to 3 million RVDs, 8; 1 to 2 million RVDs, 16; 0.5 to 1 million RVDs, 34; 0.1 to 0.5 million RVDs, 54; and under 0.1 million RVDs, 26. As was the case for both total recreational use and "camping, picnicking, and swimming," the Tonto ranks number 1 in this current category, with 4.76 million RVDs. The Dixie National Forest, which is fifth-ranked in terms of total use, ranks second in this category, with 3.64 million RVDs. A very large 59 percent of the total recreational use in the Dixie is accounted for by this category. The attracting force of National Park System units in close proximity to the Dixie National Forest was discussed earlier in this chapter. The closely third-ranked Mt. Baker–Snoqualmie National Forest has 3.53 million RVDs in this category. An exceptionally high 64 perent of the overall recreation visitor days were accounted for by this use. The fourth-ranked Angeles National Forest recorded 3.37 million RVDs in this category and ranked number 2 in overall use. The fifth-ranked Coconino National Forest, and the sixth-ranked Inyo National Forest, and the seventh-ranked San Bernardino National Forest were also closely ranked near the same positions in overall use. An extremely high 58 percent of the total recreational use in the Coconino is occasioned by this category. National forests that are ranked high in this category but are ranked lower in overall use are the

Tongass, the Black Hills, the Cleveland, and the Olympic. The Olympic National Forest showed a significantly different ranking—number 20 in this category but number 44 in total use. Seventeen of the 26 national forests in which under 100,000 RVDs were recorded are in the Southern Region. Exceptionally small totals of recreation visitor days in this category were recorded in the Finger Lakes National Forest (New York, 2500), the Delta (Mississippi, 4100), the Tuskegee (Alabama, 11,000), and the Osceola (Florida, 14,500).

The 15 national forests for which over 50 percent of their total recreation visitor days are accounted for by the "mechanized travel and viewing scenery" category are listed in the bottom half of Table 9.9. The mean value of this group for the entire country is 35.1 percent, which is close to the median value of 34 percent. The distribution of national forests by intervals of percent of use for this category are as follows: over 50 percent, 15; 40 to 50 percent, 13; 30 to 40 percent, 39; 20 to 30 percent, 48; 10 to 20 percent, 25; and under 10 percent, 4. The Black Hills National Forest (S. Dakota and Wyoming) has an amazing 75 percent of its total recreational use in this category. In no other national forest does one category account for such a large percentage of use. Several national park units are located within the boundary of the Black Hills National Forest and serve as attractions for visitors who drive the scenic roads: Wind Cave National Park, Jewel Cave National Monument, and Mount Rushmore National Memorial. The Black Hills ponderosa pine forest and rugged topography greatly contrasts with the surrounding grassland of the Great Plains. Interstate 84 passes through the Columbia River Gorge National Scenic Area (Oregon and Washington) and is a major contributing factor to the high use in this category. The contributing role of water travel to the high use in this category in the Tongass and Chugach National Forests in Alaska has been previously discussed in this section. The Olympic National Forest's (Washington) 59 percent of use in this category is in part related to the fact that it surrounds Olympic National Park on all sides. The location of the Coconino (58 percent in this catagory), the Kaibab (55 percent in this category), and the Prescott (55 percent in this category) between Phoenix and Flagstaff and in close proximity to the Grand Canyon provides a pleasant contrast to the lowland desert country. The popularity of the Nebraska–Samuel R. McKelvie National Forests is related to the contrast offered to the surrounding Great Plains—a situation similar to the Black Hills. The Osceola National Forest has less percentage of its use in this category than any national forest—3 percent. The role of "camping, picnicking, and swimming" accounting for 75 percent of the recreational use in this forest has already been discussed. Other national forests with less than 10 percent of their recreation visitor days in this category are the Malheur (Oregon), 6 percent; the Finger Lakes, 8 percent; and the Delta, 9 percent. Two other national forests in Florida—the Apalachicola (13 percent) and Ocala (18 percent)—have very low percentages of the use in this category. While many of these forests with very low percentages of use in this category are in the South, they are also found in other widely scattered sections of the country.

Hiking, Horseback Riding, and Water Travel   Table 9.10 summarizes the dominant recreational use patterns for the category "hiking, horseback riding, and water travel." The specific recreational activities included within this section are hiking and walking, horseback riding, canoeing, sailing, other watercraft, and mountain climbing. In

Table 9.10 Hiking, Horseback Riding, and Water Travel—1992

Leading National Forests in Category—RVDs (000s) and % of Use					
Superior	797.6	19.8%	Wenatchee	466.0	12.0%
Columbia R. Gorge	789.5	23.9%	Inyo	461.4	5.5%
Bridger-Teton	756.9	25.6%	Gallatin	453.7	16.2%
Angeles	736.8	8.0%	Grand Mesa–Gunnison–		
Pike and San Isabel	672.5	12.0%	Uncompaghre	449.5	9.7%
Los Padres	539.3	11.4%	White River	436.1	5.3%
Gifford Pinchot	528.5	18.8%	Coronado	382.0	8.3%
Tonto	526.3	5.7%	Nantahala	375.7	18.5%
Sierra	512.2	11.0%	Chattahoochee	366.3	14.0%
Uinta	498.4	14.1%	White Mountain	359.6	11.6%
			Pisgah	358.9	13.0%

National Forests with High % of Use in Category					
Bridger-Teton	25.6%	Challis	17.0%	Bienville	14.3%
Columbia R. Gorge	23.9%	Sumter	16.2%	Uinta	14.1%
Bitterroot	21.5%	Gallatin	16.2%	Chattahoochee	14.0%
Salmon	21.3%	Shawnee	15.7%	Klamath	13.5%
Superior	19.8%	Gila	15.6%	Humboldt	13.5%
Gifford Pinchot	18.8%	Payette	15.2%	Mark Twain	13.3%
Nantahala	18.5%	Lewis and Clark	15.2%	Willamette	13.3%

Source: Forest Service.

most national forests, hiking and walking account for the larger portion of the recreation visitor days in this category. In the Southern Region the percentage breakdown into subcategories is as follows: hiking and walking, 60 percent; horseback riding, 16 percent; and canoeing and other watercraft, each 10 percent. In the Eastern Region canoeing accounts for a very high 39 percent, hiking and walking for 46 percent, and horseback riding for 9 percent. The dominance of canoeing in the Eastern Region is caused by 82 percent of the region's total recreation visitor days being tallied in just one national forest—the Superior, where it is by far the leading subcategory within the larger category. Canoeing also accounts for more recreation visitor days than hiking in the Chippewa (Minnesota), the Huron-Manistee (Michigan), and the Ocala (Florida) National Forests. In the Ozark National Forest (Arkansas) the two are equal. In the Finger Lakes, the Shawnee (Illinois), the St. Francis (Arkansas), the Kisatchie (Louisiana), the Bienville (Mississippi), the Delta (Mississippi), and the Angelina (Texas) National Forests, horseback riding accounts for more recreation visitor days than hiking and walking. In the Rocky Mountain Region, horseback riding significantly exceeds hiking and walking in all but the Shoshone (Wyoming), where the two are almost equal. It does rank in a strong second place in the Grand Mesa–Gunnison–Uncompaghre, the Rio Grande (all in Colorado), the Bighorn (Wyoming), the Black Hills (S. Dakota and Wyoming), and the Nebraska National Forests. In Region 5 (Pacific Southwest) hiking accounts for 70 percent of the recreation visitor days, horseback riding for 14 percent, and canoeing and other watercraft each for 7 percent. In the Intermountain Region, recreational horseback riding is greater than hiking in the Caribou (Idaho, Utah, and Wyoming), and the two activities are almost equal in the Boise, the Payette (both Idaho), the Salmon (Idaho), the Dixie (Utah), and the Fishlake (Utah).

The mean number of recreation visitor days for each national forest in this category for 1992 was 171,169, and the median number was 115,100. A relatively few very high values and a larger number of small values account for the skewing of the mean. The following is a breakdown into intervals of recreation visitor days and numbers of national forests in each category: above 500,000, 9; 400,000 to 500,000, 6; 300,000 to 400,000, 9; 200,000 to 300,000, 17; 100,000 to 200,000, 40; 50,000 to 100,000, 27; and under 50,000, 26. In this category only 10 of the national forests most heavily used in terms of total recreational use are included in the ranking for "hiking, horseback riding, and water travel." The Superior National Forest is the leader in this category, with 0.80 million RVDs, closely followed by the Columbia River Gorge (0.79 million RVDs), the Bridger-Teton (0.76 million RVDs), and the Angeles (0.74 million RVDs). Significant changes in position occur for the Superior, the Columbia River Gorge, and the Bridger-Teton (ranked 19th, 26th, and 29th, respectively, for total RVDs). Other forests that show a significant shift in position and where high amounts of use in this category are the: Gifford Pinchot (32nd to seventh), the Gallatin (33rd to 13th), the Nantahala (52nd to 17th), the Chattahoochee (36th to 18th), and the Pisgah (34th to 20th).

The lower half of Table 9.10 identifies the national forests in which an exceptionally high percentage of their recreation visitor days are accounted for by this category. Notably absent from this group are national forests in the Pacific Southwest and the Southwest Regions. One-third of the leading forests in this ranking are in the Northern Rockies. The median of 8 percent is very close to the mean of 8.4 percent for the role played by this category in terms of total recreation visitor days. Only four national forests have over 20 percent of their total RVDs attributed to this category; another 10 have between 15 and 20 percent; 36 between 10 to 15 percent; 63 between 5 and 10 percent; and 31 under 5 percent. The Bridger-Teton (Wyoming) is the leader at 26 percent of the total. Hiking and walking account for 64 percent of the RVDs and horseback riding for another 24 percent. Ranking second is the Columbia River Gorge (Oregon and Washington), whose total RVDs in this category also ranked it second. Ninety-six percent of the use in this category in the Columbia River Gorge is accounted for by hiking and walking. The Bitterroot (Montana and Idaho) and Salmon (Idaho) National Forests are ranked third and fourth (21 percent each). Fifth-ranked is the Superior National Forest, which is the leader in the category "hiking, horseback riding, and water travel" for total recreation visitor days. In the Superior, "hiking, horseback riding, and water travel" account for more RVDs than does "mechanized travel and viewing scenery." This is related to the fact that the Boundary Waters Canoe Area occupies almost half of this national forest. At the bottom of the list with very low percentages of total recreation visitor days are the Kaibab (Arizona, 1.0 percent), Angelina (Texas, 1.3 percent), the Choctawhatchee (Florida, 2.2 percent), the Dixie (Utah, 2.4 percent), and the Ochoco (Oregon, 2.5 percent).

Winter Sports   Table 9.11 summarizes the category of "winter sports." The specific recreational activities included within this category are ice skating, tobogganing and sledding, downhill skiing, snow play, and cross-country skiing and snowshoeing. The national mean for all national forests in "winter sports" was 128,020 RVDs in 1992 and the median was 187,00 recreation visitor days. The mean is skewed significantly to the low side of the median because of the large number of forests within which

Table 9.11   Winter Sports—1992

Leading National Forests in Category—RVDs (000s) and % of Use					
White River	3894.2	47.3%	San Bernardino	517.0	9.4%
Tahoe	1072.0	20.7%	Angeles	488.8	5.3%
Green Mountain	832.8	53.2%	Lake Tahoe Basin	412.4	14.1%
Wasatch-Cache	824.9	17.0%	Coconino	318.1	5.5%
Arapaho-Roosevelt	821.0	15.1%	Eldorado	296.5	9.0%
Grand Mesa–Gunnison– Uncompaghre	760.0	16.4%	Deschutes	292.1	7.8%
			Pike and San Isabel	289.0	5.2%
Inyo	709.5	8.5%	Sawtooth	283.2	12.4%
White Mountain	630.9	20.4%	Mt. Hood	273.5	16.2%
Routt	603.7	27.6%	Carson	272.5	16.0%
Mt. Baker–Snoqualmie	541.0	9.8%			

National Forests with High % of Use in Category					
Green Mountain	53.2%	Wasatch-Cache	17.0%	Lake Tahoe Basin	14.1%
White River	47.3%	Grand Mesa–Gunnison–		Flathead	13.0%
Routt	27.6%	Uncompaghre	16.4%	Sawtooth	12.4%
Tahoe	20.7%	Mt. Hood	16.2%	Lincoln	12.3%
White Mountain	20.4%	Carson	16.0%	Boise	11.2%
		Arapaho-Roosevelt	15.1%		

Source: Forest Service.

there are either few or no winter sports. This relationship between the median and mean contrasts with the other recreational activity groups. The number of national forests in different numbers of use intervals are as follows: over 1 million, 2; 500,000 to 1,000,000, 9; 100,000 to 500,000, 23; 50,000 to 100,000, 14; under 25,000, 79. In 30 national forests there are no winter sports, as defined here.

This category of use shows more regional variation than any other, and climate plays a major role in this variation, especially in the Southern Region. "Winter sports" in Region 2 (Rocky Mountain) account for 38 percent of the total recreation visitor days in this category for the entire National Forest System, and Region 5 (Pacific Southwest) accounts for another 23 percent. All national forests in Region 2 have downhill ski areas except the Nebraska. In all forests except the Ashley (Utah and Wyoming) and the Bighorn, downhill skiing RVDs are far greater than those for cross-country skiing. In the Pacific Southwest Region, 63 percent of the recreaton visitor days in this category are attributable to downhill skiing, 18 percent to snow play, and 16 percent to cross-country skiing and snowshoeing. Five national forests in this region do not have downhill ski areas. Two-thirds of the downhill skiing RVDs in the Pacific Southwest Region are recorded in just three national forests: the Tahoe, the San Bernardino, and the Inyo. Only three forests in the Eastern Region out of 17 have downhill ski areas: the Green Mountain (742,000 RVDs), the White Mountain (499,600 RVDs), and the Ottawa (7300 RVDs). Ski areas in these three forests account for 75 percent of the total recreation visitor days in this category in the entire Eastern Region. In the Intermountain Region the Wasatch-Cache National Forest is the greatest contributor to this category, and two National Forests—the Ashley and the Fishlake—have no downhill ski areas. Cross-country skiing is responsible for more recreation visitor days than downhill skiing in the Challis (Idaho), the Humboldt (Nevada), the Salmon (Idaho), and the Uinta (Utah) national forests. In the Southwest

Region, snow play generates more recreation visitor days than downhill skiing, and there are no downhill ski areas in four national forests: the Gila (N. Mexico), the Apache-Sitgreaves (Arizona and N. Mexico), the Prescott (Arizona), and the Tonto (Arizona). In the Pacific Northwest Region, 68 percent of the total "winter sports" RVDs are accounted for by downhill skiing, and the Mt. Baker–Snoqualmie National Forest was the clear leader. In seven national forests in this region there are no downhill ski areas, and in the Umpqua and Okanogan, cross-country skiing RVDs exceed those for downhill skiing. Three regions each account for less than 5 percent of the national total: Region 8 (Southern), 0.1 percent; Region 10 (Alaska), 0.8 percent; and Region 1 (Northern), 4 percent. The Jefferson is the only national forest in the Southern Region with downhill skiing. Isolated snow play, sledding, and cross-country skiing account for the small number of recreation visitor days in "winter sports" in the Southern Region. The remote location of the national forests away from major population centers in the Northern Region plays a role in the low number of recreation visitor days generated and the relatively few major ski areas. "Winter sports" play a relatively minor role in Alaska, and in the Tongass National Forest cross-country skiing generates far more recreation visitor days than any other subcategories. Most of the visitors to Alaska come during the summer.

The dominance of the White River National Forest is the most outstanding geographic aspect of winter sports use and distribution in the National Forest System (3.89 million RVD). Twenty-two percent of the entire "winter sports" in the system occurs in this one national forest. The large amount of winter sports use plays a major role in the White River National Forest's number 4 ranking in total recreational use. Ninety-five percent of the "winter sports" RVDs are related to downhill skiing and 3 percent to cross-country skiing. The bulk of the recreational use in this forest occurs at Vail/Beaver Creek and in the Aspen area. The Vail ski area is located on the mountain of the same name, on I-70 on the western side of the Vail Pass, and is 125 miles west of Denver. The completion of the Eisenhower Tunnel in the 1970s made Vail within reach for the day-tripper from Denver, but the Vail Pass can still close at times due to snow-related problems (Figure 9.8). More lift tickets are sold at Vail than any other U.S. ski area. Vail is also the largest ski area in the country, with 4,014 acres of ski terrain. From the Mongolia surface lift in the east to the Cascade Village lift in the west, Vail stretches an impressive 7 miles and has 25 lifts. The "back bowls" have always been Vail's big attraction, but the only chairlift providing an exit from the bowls would often be extremely crowded. This crowding was significantly alleviated in 1988 with the construction of a new high-speed quad-chair in China Bowl and a surface lift in Siberia and Mongolia Bowls. (The author's fondest alpine skiing memories are of breaking new powder in Siberia Bowl at Vail with his daughter.) In 1991, a new restaurant, Two Elk, was built at the top of China Bowl to replace the small and often extremely crowded Far East Restaurant/Shelter. The Two Elk restaurant is not only one of the most magnificent in the world at a ski area on top of a mountain; it also has an overwhelming view. The restaurant sits at over 11,000 feet of elevation, with the Gore Range towering to the north and the Mountain of the Holy Cross and other Sawatch Range peaks on the southern horizon. The town of Vail is styled like an alpine village and is on land that was previously used for sheep pasture. Vail Associates also owns the Beaver Creek Ski Area, located 10 miles west on I-70 at Avon. Beaver Creek is a large ski area but only about half the size of Vail.

Figure 9.8   The Eisenhower Tunnel, where I-70 passes under the Continental Divide, has expanded the day-trip range of Denver skiers. Most of them drive right past one of Colorado's finer ski areas at Loveland, whose slopes on the Arapho National Forest are immediately above the tunnel.

Both areas have over 3000 feet of vertical rise. Beaver Creek is much less crowded than Vail and is recommended to visitors to Vail who become disillusioned with the crowds. There is an excellent cross-country ski area at the top of the Strawberry Park lift on the western side of Beaver Creek. Beaver Creek will be discussed in more detail later in this chapter in the "ski area" section.

The other major contributors to the high winter sports use in the White River National Forest are the four major ski areas in the Aspen area. Aspen is only 38 air miles from Vail but 107 road miles. To reach Aspen in winter (when the Independence Pass is closed), it is necessary to take I-70 west to Glenwood Springs and then take Colorado 82 to the southeast. This trip has become a little faster with the completion of I-70 through Glenwood Canyon. The best-known ski area is Aspen Mountain, often called Ajax, which rises immediately above the old mining town of Aspen. The resort town of Aspen contrasts greatly with Vail. Aspen arose in a preexisting town in which many structures built in the 19th century were active, while Vail was built as a new resort. The greatest vertical rise among the Aspen ski areas, and the greatest in Colorado (3800 ft.), is at Aspen Highlands. It was the maverick of the four Aspen ski areas but finally fell under the control of the Aspen Ski Corporation in 1993. To the north of Aspen Highlands is Buttermilk/Tiehack Ski Area, with a more modest 2000-foot vertical rise. Beginning in the 1993–1994 ski season, "Buttermilk" was dropped from its name, and it is now known as the Tiehack Ski Area. This ski area has been known as Aspen's learning mountain, but it is also excellent for intermediate skiers who want to cruise its exceptionally well groomed trails. The biggest Aspen ski area, Snowmass, is located 10 miles north and west of Aspen. (In the author's opinion, Snowmass is the finest intermediate cruiser's ski area in the country.) To most skiers, the names Aspen and Vail are associated with the ultimate skiing experience. Skiers travel from all over the world for the ambience of the "Vail" or the "Aspen experience."

The Tahoe National Forest in California's Sierra Nevada Mountains is second ranking in terms of "winter sports" use, and its position in total recreational use in 1992 was number 11. However, its 1.07 million recreation visitor days in 1992 was only one-quarter that of the White River National Forest. Cross-country skiing plays a greater role than in other leading national forests, accounting for 14 percent of the recreation visitor days. Alpine skiing still dominates, however, with 83 percent of the category total. Interstate 80 passes through the heart of this forest. The two largest ski areas are Squaw Valley and Alpine Meadows, both on the eastern side of the Donner Summit. This location is convenient for skiers from Reno, Nev., just 30 miles to the east. Snowstorms raise havoc with the access routes of most users, who travel over the Summit from Sacramento and San Francisco. These skiers can more easily reach Boreal Ridge and Sugar Bowl, which are located immediately to the western side of the Donner Summit. The world's largest cross-country ski area—Royal Gorge—is located near Sugar Bowl and Boreal Ridge.

Green Mountain National Forest (Vermont), Wasatch-Cache National Forest (Utah, Wyoming, and Idaho), and Arapaho-Roosevelt National Forests (Colorado) are closely ranked at positions 3, 4, and 5 with 0.833, 0.825, and 0.821 million RVDs in "winter sports." The Green Mountain National Forest was ranked relatively low in total recreational use (#69) but ranked third in "winter sports" use. The larger ski areas in the Green Mountain National Forest are Sugarbush in the north and Mount Snow in the south. Several years ago the Sugarbush Ski Area acquired Glen Ellen Ski Area and has been trying to get permission from the Forest Service to connect the two ski areas with lifts and trails in the Slide Brook area. In the Green Mountain National Forest 89 percent of the winter sports use is accounted for by downhill skiing and another 7 percent by cross-country skiing. Major ski areas in the Wasatch-Cache National Forest, which is located immediately east of Salt Lake City, include Alta, Snowbird, and Park City. Eighty-eight percent of the use in this forest is downhill skiing and 7 percent is cross-country skiing. The Roosevelt National Forest is located between Boulder and Rocky Mountain National Park, but the Arapho National Forest, located west of Denver on both sides of the Continental Divide, is where the greatest portion of the "winter sports" recreational use occurs. Major ski areas include Breckenridge, Keystone/Arapaho Basin, Copper Mountain, and Winter Park. All of these ski areas have base elevations above 9000 feet, the highest in the United States, and it is essential for flatlanders to acclimatize themselves before skiing. Breckenridge Ski Area is usually the second or third leading ski area in lift tickets sold in the United States, after the perennial leader Vail. Winter Park is located on the western side of the Continental Divide, right where the Moffat Tunnel emerges at West Portal, and is owned by the city of Denver. On weekends, ski trains may be used as a method of transportation to and from Winter Park, the only such possibility in the national forest. The main lodge and lifts are only a few hundred feet from where one departs the train. The ski train offers a sure but fairly expensive way to travel to Winter Park. U.S. 40 over the switchback, 11,300-foot Berthoud Pass can be closed at times and a hair-raising experience much of the rest of the winter.

Six other national forests received over 500,000 recreation visitor days in 1992 in "winter sports." The sixth-ranked, jointly administered Grand Mesa–Gunnison–Uncompaghre National Forests in western Colorado received 0.76 million RVDs in 1992 with 86 percent of the use occurring in downhill skiing and 9 percent in cross-

country skiing. Crested Butte and Powderhorn are the major ski areas. Crested Butte has the best ski deal in the world, with free skiing from Thanksgiving until Christmas. The seventh-ranked Inyo National Forest has 0.71 million RVDs and is located on the eastern side of the Sierra Nevada in east-central California and extends slightly into Nevada; 85 percent of the use occurrs in downhil skiing. The principal ski area is Mammoth Mountain, which is usually among the three leading ski areas in the United States in terms of tickets sold. June Mountain is located nearby. The White Mountain National Forest (New Hampshire and Maine) was ranked 27th in total recreational use in 1992 but jumped to number 8 in the "winter sports" ranking. Seventy-nine percent of the use was downhill skiing, but a relatively high 19 percent was related to cross-country skiing. The two major ski areas with the most use are Waterville Valley and Loon Mountain. The ninth-ranked Routt National Forest (Colorado) is the location of Steamboat Springs, one of the country's largest ski areas; 86 percent of the "winter sports" recreation visitor days are attributable to downhill skiing and 13 percent to cross-country skiing. Eighty-five percent of the recreation visitor days at the 10th-ranked Mt. Baker–Snoqualmie National Forest (Washington) was related to downhill skiing. An extremely high 94 percent of the recreation visitor days (0.515 million) in the San Bernardino National Forest were accounted for by downhill skiing. The 11th-ranked Angeles National Forest's use of 0.489 million RVDs was just slightly below that of the San Bernardino. The popularity of both the Angeles and the San Bernardino is related to their location immediately next to the Los Angeles metropolitan area. In the Angeles National Forest downhill skiing accounted for 49 percent of the recreation visitor days, while snow play accounted for a very high 37 percent and sledding and tobogganing for another 12 percent.

The lower half of Table 9.11 identifies the national forests for which an exceptionally high percentage of the total recreational use is attributed to "winter sports." This category accounted for 6.27 percent of the total recreation visitor days for the entire National Forest System. The median value was 1.4 percent. The following is a breakdown of the number of national forests in different intervals of percentage of use related to "winter sports": over 50 percent, 1; 30 to 40 percent, 1; 20 to 30 percent, 3; 10 to 20 percent, 11; 5 to 10 percent, 23; 1 to 5 percent, 40; 0.01 to 1 percent, 35; and 0 percent, 30. Clearly, in only a relatively few national forests does most of the winter sports use occur and the relative importance is extremely important in only a few forests. In only the Green Mountain National Forest is over 50 percent of the recreational use related to winter sports, while the White River National Forest (Colorado) is a close second at 47 percent. Then a drop of 20 points occurs from the White River to the third-ranking Routt National Forest, where winter sports accounts for 28 percent of the use. The Tahoe and the White Mountain National Forests are in close third and fourth places at 20 percent each. National forests in which winter sports play a significantly above average role and yet their total "winter sports" RVDs are not high are the Flathead (Montana) and the Lincoln (N. Mexico). The Flathead's 114,500 RVDs ranks it 33rd in terms of RVDs, but it jumps to the 12th position in terms of percent of total recreational use related to winter sports. The Big Mountain is a major ski center, with plenty of elbow room, located in the Flathead National Forest west of Glacier National Park. The Lincoln National Forest jumps from 26th place to 14th place for the comparable statistics. Its major ski area, Ski Apache, is located on the Lincoln National Forest on land leased by the Mescalero Apache Na-

tive Americans. Many of the guests stay at their elaborate resort called the Inn of the Mountain Gods. This recreational area and resort will be featured in Chapter 13 as a case study in recreational use of Native American tribal resources. Quite clearly, the major conclusion that can be reached about the relative importance of "winter sports" is that they are nonexistent in 20 percent of the national forests and relatively insignificant in another 50 percent of them.

Resorts, Cabins, and Organization Camps   Table 9.12 summarizes the category of "resorts, cabins, and organization camps." The specific recreational activities included within this category are general day organization camping, night organization camping, general resort and commercial public service, resort lodging, and recreational cabin use. This is another one of the categories that the Forest Service should break into at least three categories for reporting purposes. The uses are quite different within the broader category and range from commercial resorts to private recreation residences to youth organization camps. The average number of recreation visitor days for the national forests in this category is 115,380, while the median is skewed to the low side at an extreme 38,700, RVDs. Following is a breakdown of use data into the number of forests receiving RVDs in this category: over 1 million RVDs, 2; 500,000 to 1 million, 4; 100,000 to 500,000, 45; 50,000 to 100,000, 50; 25,000 to 50,000, 17; under 25,000, 61. In 12 national forests there were no RVDs in this category. The "resorts, cabins, and organization camps" category is primarily a western—especially a West Coast—phenomenon. Of the 51 national forests receiving over 100,000 RVDs in this category, only three are in the Eastern Region (Superior, Chippewa, and White Mountain) and none are in the Southern Region. Among the lower-49 ranked national forests with fewer than 15,000 RVDs in this category, 26 are in the Southern Region and six are in the Eastern Region. Of the 12 national forests with no recreational use in this category, all are in the Southern Region, except for the Finger Lakes National

Table 9.12   Resorts, Cabins, and Organization Camps—1992

Leading National Forests in Category—RVDs (000s) and % of Use					
Angeles	1466.4	16.0%	Umpqua	370.1	19.6%
Inyo	1020.9	12.2%	Deschutes	330.5	8.9%
Sierra	792.8	17.0%	Tonto	328.2	3.5%
San Bernardino	669.4	12.2%	Sequoia	319.8	9.1%
Stanislaus	575.1	21.2%	Rogue River	295.3	22.4%
Wenatchee	519.9	13.4%	Columbia R. Gorge	283.3	8.6%
Los Padres	497.8	10.5%	Bighorn	271.6	14.4%
Cleveland	494.8	17.2%	Superior	254.9	6.3%
Eldorado	479.4	14.5%	Wasatch-Cache	248.6	5.1%
Lake Tahoe Basin	386.3	13.2%	Tahoe	221.5	4.3%
National Forests with High % of Use in Category					
Rogue River	22.4%	Angeles	16.0%	Shoshone	13.0%
Stanislaus	21.2%	Eldorado	14.5%	Targhee	12.9%
Umpqua	19.6%	Bighorn	14.4%	Lassen	12.5%
Cleveland	17.2%	Wenatchee	13.4%	Inyo	12.2%
Winema	17.0%	Fishlake	13.3%	San Bernardino	12.2%
Sierra	17.0%	Lake Tahoe Basin	13.2%	Chippewa	11.9%

Source: Forest Service.

Forest (New York) and the Wayne National Forest (Ohio), which are in the Eastern Region.

Nine of the top 10 national forests are in California (Pacific Southwest Region), and the recreational use in this category in these nine forests accounts for 39 percent of the national total. After California (7.6 million RVDs), Oregon has 1.33 million RVDs and Washington has 1.10 million RVDs. These three states account for 61 percent of the national total in this category. In most cases the leading subcategory is "recreation cabins," which typically accounts for half to two-thirds of the total recreation visitor days in this category. For the Pacific Southwest Region (California) the following is the breakdown in use by subcategories: "general day organization camping," 14 percent; "night organization camping," 17 percent; "general resort and commercial public service," 6 percent; "resort lodging," 15 percent; and "recreational cabin use," 48 percent. The same breakdown for the Pacific Northwest Region (Oregon and Washington) is "general day organization camping," 7 percent; "night organization camping," 12 percent; "general resort and commercial public service, 25 percent; "resort lodging," 26 percent; and "recreational cabin use," 29 percent.

In prominent first place in the ranking of recreation visitor days in this category is the Angeles National Forest (California) with 1.46 million RVDs, and it is ranked second in total recreation use. The Angeles borders the Los Angeles area on the north and east. "Recreation cabin use" is the leading subcategory, accounting for 57 percent of its use attributed to "resorts, cabins, and organization camps." The second-ranking Inyo National Forest in east-central California and Nevada is similarly ranked at number 3 in overall use. This forest is unlike many of the others in that "recreation cabin use" represents only a very low 15 percent of the use in this category, while seventy-four percent of the recreational use is related to "resort lodging." Most of the latter is concentrated in the Mammoth/June Mountain area with the ski areas of the same names as the focal points. The Sierra National Forest (California) is ranked third in this listing but a lower 15th in overall use; "recreation cabin use" accounts for 69 percent of the use in this category. This forest is located in the Sierra Nevada south of Yosemite National Park and north of Sequoia–Kings Canyon National Parks.

The fourth-ranked San Bernardino National Forest (California) ranks ninth in total recreational use; it is located east of Los Angeles and next to San Bernardino and Palm Springs. "Recreation cabin use" again is the leading subcategory with 45 percent of the use, but "general day organization camping" is a strong second at 28 percent and "night organization camping" is a strong third at 24 percent. The fifth-ranked Stanislaus National Forest (California), located in the Sierra Nevada west and north of Yosemite National Park, is especially prominent in this class, for it jumped from 35th place in overall recreation use. The 380-acre Calaveras Bigtree National Forest, the smallest national forest in the system, is surrounded by the Stanislaus and is administered jointly with it. It contains no facilities, and its main feature is a grove of giant sequoias. The Stanislaus is unlike many national forests in this category in that "recreation cabin use" accounts for a relatively small 20 percent of the use in this category. "Night organization camping" is the leading subcategory with 29 percent of the use, followed by "resort lodging" with 23 percent and "general day organization camping" with 20 percent of the use.

The sixth-ranked Wenatchee National Forest (Washington) is the only one in the Pacific Northwest Region ranking in the top 10 in this category. It is located on the

east side of the Cascade Range and received 0.52 million RVDs in 1992. It ranks number 20 in terms of total recreational use. "Recreation cabin use" is the leading subcategory with 61 percent of the recreational use. Other prominently ranked national forests in this category and in the Pacific Northwest Region are the Umpqua, the Deschutes, the Rogue River, and the Columbia River Gorge National Scenic Area, all in Oregon. The Umpqua National Forest is ranked number 11 in this category, a dramatic move from number 54 in total recreational use. The Umpqua lies on the west side of the Cascade Range in southern Oregon and borders Crater Lake National Forest on the north. Its use by subcategories differs greatly from the rest of the country: "Resort lodging" accounts for 56 percent and "general resort and commercial public service" for another 34 percent, while "recreation cabin use" is responsible for only 10 percent. A similar use pattern exists in the 15th-ranked Rogue River National Forest, located west of the Cascade Range in southern Oregon. An even more striking 86 percent of the use is for "resort lodging;" 10 percent is for "general resort and commercial public service," and only 3 percent is for "recreation cabin use." The Rogue River jumps from number 77 in total recreational use. The Deschutes National Forest, in central Oregon on the eastern side of the Cascade Range, ranks number 12 in this category, up from number 22 in total recreational use. "General resort and commercial public service" at 36 percent of the use in the category leads both "recreation cabin use" (29 percent) and "resort lodging" (23 percent). The Columbia River Gorge National Scenic Area receives all 283,333 RVDs in the subcategory of "general resort and commercial public service." Besides the Columbia River Gorge, there is no "recreation cabin use" in the Malheur, the Olympic, and the Siuslaw National Forests in the Pacific Northwest Region.

The seventh-ranked Los Padres National Forest, the eighth-ranked Cleveland National Forest, and the ninth-ranked Eldorado National Forest are all in California. The Los Padres stretches for over 200 miles north and northwest of Los Angeles to Big Sur along the Coast Range. The Cleveland is located just east of San Diego, and the Eldorado is located on the western slope of the Sierra Nevada and is bordered by the Tahoe National Forest on the north and the Stanislaus National Forest on the south. In all three, two-thirds to three-quarters of the use in the "recreation cabin use" subcategory.

In the Southwest Region (Arizona and N. Mexico) the Tonto is the most heavily used in this category but is ranked 13th, a drop from its number 1 ranking in total recreational use. This is the closest national forest to Phoenix, and the use in this category accounts for 27 percent of the use in this category in the region. In three other forests another 44 percent of the region's use occurs in this category: the Coronado (Arizona and N. Mexico), the Santa Fe (N. Mexico), and the Kaibab (Arizona). Only in the Coronado National Forest does "recreation cabin use" account for over 50 percent of the use in this category. In the Kaibab, located north and south of Grand Canyon National Park, 74 percent of the use in this category is related to "resort lodging" and another 25 percent to "general resort and commercial public service."

In Region 4 (Intermountain) the Wasatch-Cache (Utah, Wyoming, and Idaho) is the leading national forest, with a number 19 ranking, and "recreation cabin use" is 55 percent of the total use in the category. These forests are located east and north of Salt Lake City. The other important Forests in this category in the region are the Sawtooth (Idaho and Utah) and the Targhee (Wyoming and Idaho); only about one-

third of the use in these two is for "recreation cabin use." In Region 2 (Rocky Mountain) "recreation cabin use" accounts for the most use in most forests, but "general resort and commercial public service" is the leading subcategory in the Pike and San Isabel National Forests and the Grand Mesa–Gunnison–Uncompaghre National Forests (all in Colorado). "Resort lodging" is the leading category in the San Juan National Forest (Colorado) and the Shoshone National Forest (Wyoming). A low 3 percent of the use in Region 1 (Northern) is measured in this category. In Region 10 (Alaska) "recreation cabin use" account for 79 percent of the total in this category in the Tongass National Forest but only 46 percent in the Chugach National Forest.

In the Eastern Region (Region 9) only 5 percent of the national total recreation visitor days in this category are tallied. The leading subcategory is "recreation cabin use" with 44 percent of the use, followed by "resort lodging" with 25 percent of the use and "general resort and commercial public service" with 17 percent of the use. Two-thirds of all the recreation visitor days in this region are contributed by just three national forests: the Superior (Minnesota, 254,900 RVDs), the Chippewa (Minnesota, 204,100 RVDs), and the White Mountain (N. Hampshire and Maine, 120,300 RVDs). In both the Superior and Chippewa National Forests "recreation cabin use" accounts for 50 percent of the use in this category, but in the White Mountain National Forest it is 0 percent. "Resort lodging" accounts for 63 percent and "general resort and commercial public service" for 35 percent in the White Mountain National Forest.

The Southern Region (Region 8) accounts for only 4 percent of the national total of recreation visitor days in this category. Four national forests contribute two-thirds of the recreation visitor days for the entire region in this category: the Ocala (Florida, 179,200 RVDs), the Cherokee (Tennessee, 94,100 RVDs), the Nantahala (N. Carolina, 60,900 RVDs), and the Chattahoochee (Georgia, 44,900 RVDs). In the Ocala, "recreation cabin use" accounts for 37 percent, "resort lodging" for 28 percent and "night organization camping" for 26 percent of the use. In the Cherokee, "recreation cabin use," "night organization camping," and "general resort and commercial public service" each account for 25 percent of the use. In the Nantahala, "night organization camping" accounts for an impressive 80 percent of the use. In the Chattahoochee, "recreation cabin use" has a slight lead at 35 percent, and "general day organization camping" and "night organization camping" each account for another 30 percent.

The lower portion of Table 9.12 identifies the national forests in which an exceptionally high percentage of their total recreational use is related to the category of "resorts, cabins, and organization camps." For the entire National Forest System, 5.73 percent of the total recreational use is contributed by this category. The median value of 2.8 percent is significantly below this mean value and is the result of a large number of national forests in which this category is extremely small or, as in 16 cases, nonexistent. The intervals for this distribution are: over 20 percent, 2 forests; 15 to 20 percent, 5 forests; 10 to 15 percent, 16 forests; 5 to 10 percent, 20 forests; 1 to 5 percent, 65 forests; and under 1 percent, 36 forests. For 16 of the forests in the "under 1 percent" group, the value is zero. Two-thirds of the national forests listed in this table are also among those that have high RVD totals in this category. The Rogue River National Forest (Oregon) is the leader, with 22 percent of its total recreation use in this category, and the Stanislaus National Forest is a close second at 21 percent. The outstanding characteristic of the Rogue River National Forest in this category is the dominance of the "resort lodging" subcategory, which accounts for 86 percent of the

use within the broader category. In the Stanislaus an even contribution is made to the total by all subcategories. In the third-ranked Umpqua, a high percentage of its use (56 percent) is contributed by "resort lodging." The most dramatic shift in position is the Winema, which is ranked 55th in recreation visitor days in this category but jumps to number 5 in terms of percentage in importance to its total recreational use. The Winema National Forest is located on the east side of the Cascade Range, and Crater Lake National Park borders it on the west.

Hunting   Table 9.13 summarizes the category "hunting." There are four types of hunting tallied in subcategories within the main one: (1) big-game hunting, (2) small-game hunting, (3) upland bird hunting, and (4) waterfowl hunting. The mean number of recreation visitor days in this classification is 117,935 per national forests. The median of 96,000 is skewed to the low side of the mean, due to a large number of forests with low usage. The intervals of use and the numbers of forests in each interval are as follows: over 500,000, 2; 100,000 to 500,000, 67; 50,000 to 100,000, 40; 25,000 to 50,000, 18; and under 25,000, 15. In only two national forests—the Caribbean (Puerto Rico) and Choctawhatchee (Florida)—is there no hunting. Table 9.2 identified the relative importance of hunting, and the other major recreational activities, by Forest Service regions. The dominance of the Southern Region is a major geographic characteristic. While the Southern Region accounted for only 10.5 percent of the total recreational use, it accounted for an extremely high 25.6 percent of the nation's hunt-

Table 9.13   Hunting—1992

Leading National Forests in Category—RVDs (000s) and % of Use					
George Washington	578.4	23.7%	Coconino	240.5	4.2%
Grand Mesa–Gunnison–Uncompaghre	556.7	12.0%	Cherokee	237.3	8.0%
			Wayne	231.9	34.5%
White River	455.6	5.5%	Bridger-Teton	230.2	7.8%
Huron-Manistee	355.9	17.6%	Dixie	213.3	3.5%
Routt	341.6	15.6%	Gallatin	210.6	7.5%
Jefferson	336.3	15.5%	Lincoln	207.9	16.1%
Ouachita	281.8	21.9%	Idaho Panhandle	207.1	8.5%
Ozark	280.3	24.7%	Daniel Boone	206.4	9.8%
Chattahoochee	274.5	10.5%	Nantahala	205.4	10.1%
Mark Twain	266.9	14.8%	Allegheny	199.0	6.8%
Wasatch-Cache	249.7	5.1%			

National Forests with High % of Use in Category					
Delta	48.2%	Holly Springs	26.2%	Modoc	20.0%
Homochitto	46.5%	Tuskegee	26.1%	Beaverhead	19.3%
Bienville	42.4%	Ozark	24.7%	Apalachicola	18.2%
Conecuh	37.3%	George Washington	23.7%	Humboldt	18.1%
Wayne	34.5%	Helena	22.9%	Huron-Manistee	17.6%
Uwharrie	30.7%	Ouachita	21.9%	Lincoln	16.1%
Talladega	29.4%	Caddo-LBJ	21.0%	Custer	16.1%
Oconee	28.0%	Sumter	21.0%	Umatilla	15.6%
Davy Crockett	27.7%	St. Francis	20.9%	Routt	15.6%
Croatan	27.3%	DeSoto	20.9%	Jefferson	15.5%
Francis Marion	27.1%	Kisatchie	20.4%	Ochoco	15.2%

Source: Forest Service.

ing in national forests. The breakdown of hunting by types in the Southern Region is as follows: big-game hunting, 54 percent; small-game hunting, 34 percent; upland bird hunting, 10 percent; and waterfowl hunting, 2 percent. The Southern Region not only has several fairly large national forests where hunting is extremely significant but also a large number of small ones where this use plays an extraordinary role in the total number of recreational visitor days. Eight of the top-ranked 22 leading national forests in Table 9.13 are in this region.

The Eastern Region is ranked second in terms of recreation visitor days of hunting activity. Its 13.7 percent of the national total of recreational use in this category is way above its national percentage of total recreational use—8.7 percent. In the Eastern Region the breakdown by types of hunting is as follows: big-game hunting, 51 percent; small-game hunting, 24 percent; upland bird hunting, 19 percent; and waterfowl hunting, 7 percent. The third-ranking Rocky Mountain Region has about equal representation of hunting and total recreational use: 13.2 percent and 12.7 percent, respectively. Similar equal representation of hunting as a recreational activity occurs in the Intermountain Region, with 11.8 percent of the nation's hunting in the national forests within the region and 12.3 percent of the total recreational use. In the Northern Region hunting is extremely significant, accounting for 9.2 percent of the nation's participation in this activity but only 5.3 percent of the total recreational use. In the Pacific Southwest, hunting is of much less importance (9.2 percent of all hunting in national forests) than the total amount of recreational use the region contributes to the national total (23 percent). "Hunting" is the only recreational use category for which several of the California national forests are not among the leaders. Hunting plays a slight below average role in the Southwest Region and a much below average role in the Pacific Northwest and Alaska Regions. None of the forests in these last two regions is among the leaders.

In Table 9.13, which identifies the leading national forests in which hunting is extremely important, several national forests appear in the ranking that have relative low rankings in terms of total recreational use. Only two of the top 10 forests in terms of total recreational use are included in the top 22 national forests in terms of hunting. The White River (Colorado) is ranked third in terms of hunting and fourth in terms of total recreational use. The fifth-ranked Dixie National Forest (Utah) is number 16 in hunting. The top-ranked George Washington National Forest (Virginia and W. Virginia) is ranked 40th in total recreational use. It and the second-ranked Grand Mesa–Gunnison–Uncompaghre National Forests (Colorado) are the only ones with over 500,000 RVDs in this category. In the George Washington National Forest, small-game hunting accounts for 50 percent of the total and big-game hunting for 41 percent. These data contrast with most other eastern and western forests, where big game is the leading subcategory. In the high-ranked Grand Mesa–Gunnison–Uncompaghre (#2), Routt (Colorado, #5), White River (Colorado, #3), and Dixie (Utah, #16), over 90 percent of the hunting is big-game. The fourth-ranked Huron-Manistee National Forest (Michigan) is ranked 53rd in total recreational use; 67 percent of the hunting is big-game. The sixth-ranked Jefferson (W. Virginia, Kentucky, and Virginia) is ranked 46th in total use. The seventh-ranked Ouachita National Forest (Arkansas and Oklahoma) is ranked 78th in total use, and the eighth-ranked Ozark National Forest (Arkansas) is 84th. The most remarkable change in position is the Wayne National Forest (Ohio), which ranks 14th in recreation visitor days for hunting but 109th in

total recreational use. In the Wayne, small-game hunting accounts for 50 percent and big-game hunting for 33 percent of the use. Notably absent from the 22 leading national forests with over 200,000 RVDs related to hunting are those in California, Oregon, and Washington. In the Southwest Region the only forest ranked (18th) is the Lincoln (N. Mexico); 96 percent of the hunting is big-game. Small totals of recreational use for hunting are measured in the Lake Tahoe Basin (California and Nevada, 2100 RVDs), the Finger Lakes National Forest (New York, 4100 RVDs), the Columbia River Gorge (Oregon and Washington, 4800 RVDs), the Rogue River National Forest (10,300 RVDs), and the San Bernardino (California, 11,200 RVDs).

The lower portion of Table 9.13 identifies the national forests where hunting is responsible for a much above average portion of the total recreational use. Nationally, 5.9 percent of the total recreational use is related to hunting. The median value among national forests is 7.5 percent. Following is the distribution of numbers of forests by percentage of use related to hunting: over 40 percent, 3; 30 to 40 percent, 3; 20 to 30 percent, 17; 10 to 20 percent, 33; 5 to 10 percent, 41; and under 5 percent, 45. In two national forests—the Caribbean and Choctawhatchee—there is no hunting. Of the 22 national forests in which over 20 percent of total recreational use is accounted for by hunting, all are in the Southern Region except two—the Wayne and the Helena (Montana). Most of these forests are relatively small in geographic extent. The top-ranked Delta National Forest (in west-central Mississippi), with 48 percent of its recreational use in hunting, has only 59,534 acres. Its leading subcategories are big-game hunting, 65 percent, and small-game hunting, 21 percent. Its relatively small number of RVDs related to hunting (21,100) rank it a low 132nd. The second-ranked Homochitto National Forest has 189,899 acreas and is located in southwestern Mississippi south of the Delta National Forest. Its 84,800 RVDs rank it 86th among the national forests in hunting, and 47 percent of its recreational use is related to hunting. The third-ranked Bienville National Forest is also in Mississippi, and 42 percent of its total use is related to hunting. It ranks 66th in terms of RVDs in hunting (85,900). In these three leading national forests in Mississippi, 65, 72, and 83 percent of the hunting is accounted for by the big-game category. A very large portion of the national forests with an extremely low percentage of their recreational use occurring in hunting are in California, Oregon, and Washington. In addition to the Choctawhatchee and Caribbean, where the hunting use is zero, the national forests with under 1 percent of their total recreational use related to hunting are the Lake Tahoe Basin, the Columbia River Gorge, the San Bernardino, the Stanislaus, the Angeles, the Rogue River, and the Tahoe.

Fishing   Table 9.14 summarizes the category of fishing, which has four subcategories: (1) cold-water fishing; (2) warm-water fishing; (3) saltwater fishing; and (4) ice fishing. The mean number of recreation visitor days in this category per national forest is 110,511, and the median is 75,400. A larger number of national forests with relatively small amounts of fishing use causes this skewing of the median. The number of national forests in the following intervals of recreation visitor days are: 400,000 to 500,000, 4; 300,000 to 400,000, 6; 200,000 to 300,000, 18; 100,000 to 200,000, 32; 50,000 to 100,000, 27; 25,000 to 50,000, 26; and under 25,000, 31. The only national forest in which no fishing occurs is the Caribbean National Forest (Puerto Rico). As was the case with hunting, two regions—the Eastern and the Southern—have much more

Table 9.14   Fishing—1992

Leading National Forests in Category—RVDs (000s) and % of Use

Chippewa	468.7	27.2%	Plumas	267.0	10.4%
Pike and San Isabel	439.3	7.9%	Sierra	254.1	5.4%
Inyo	417.4	5.0%	Routt	252.8	11.5%
Superior	412.4	10.3%	Coconino	252.5	4.4%
Shasta-Trinity	398.0	8.3%	Arapaho-Roosevelt	248.6	4.6%
Grand Mesa–Gunnison–			Ashley	248.2	13.4%
Uncompaghre	351.9	7.6%	Gallatin	243.3	8.7%
Tonto	350.3	3.8%	Apache-Sitgreaves	242.9	9.8%
Sabine	350.0	49.9%	Eldorado	228.8	6.9%
Tongass	347.3	8.6%	Hiawatha	228.1	14.8%
Nicolet	302.4	26.8%	Kootenai	224.1	14.1%
Angelina	276.7	50.0%	Sequoia	220.7	6.3%
Toiyabe	271.0	7.2%			

National Forests with High % of Use in Category

Angelina	50.0%	Challis	15.6%	Ashley	13.4%
Sabine	49.9%	Hiawatha	14.8%	Payette	13.2%
Chippewa	27.2%	Hooiser	14.8%	Manti-Lasal	13.0%
Nicolet	26.8%	Holly Springs	14.7%	Tombigbee	12.3%
Sam Houston	19.1%	Kootenai	14.1%	Routt	11.5%
St. Francis	18.8%	Conecuh	13.5%	Delta	11.4%

Source: Forest Service.

than their share of fishing when compared with other regions. Region 9 (Eastern) accounts for 15 percent of the recreation visitor days of fishing in the national forests but only 9 percent of the total recreational use. Region 8 (Southern) has 16 percent of the fishing RVDs in the national forests but only 11 percent of the total recreational use. The Pacific Southwest Region's 2.9 million RVDs exceeds the Southern Region's 2.6 million RVDs and the Eastern Region's 2.4 million RVDs, but its percentage of fishing use (18 percent) is below its percentage of total recreational use (23 percent). Region 6's (Pacific Northwest) 9.3 percent of the fishing RVDs is below its 14 percent share of the total national recreational use. The same situation exists for Region 3 (Southwestern), with 8 percent of the fishing use but 12 percent of the total recreational use. Regions 2 (Rocky Mountain) and 4 (Intermountain) both have about equal 12 to 13 percent shares of fishing and total recreational use. Fishing is a little more significant than the overall recreational use in both the Northern and Alaska Regions: The former has 7 percent of the fishing but 5 percent of the total recreational use, and the latter has 3 percent and 2 percent, respectively, for the same categories.

For all regions in the entire National Forest System, cold-water fishing accounts for the largest portion of the fishing except for Region 10 (Alaska), where the saltwater and cold-water fishing are about equal in significance. Saltwater fishing is almost nonexistent except in Alaska and the Pacific Northwest Regions. Ice fishing plays a relatively minor role in all regions except the Eastern, where it is 10 percent of the total fishing use. Only in the Eastern and Southern Regions does warm-water fishing play a greater role—24 percent for cold-water and 66 percent for warm-water in the Eastern, and 32 percent for cold-water and 68 percent for warm-water in the Southern. In the Rocky Mountain Region cold-water fishing is over 90 percent of the

total in all forests except the Nebraska National Forest, where warm-water fishing is more important than cold-water. In the Southwestern Region fishing is almost exclusively cold-water except for in the Tonto National Forest (Arizona), which has 96 percent warm-water fishing. Warm-water fishing is also fairly important in the Coconino (Arizona, 31 percent), the Coronado (Arizona and N. Mexico, 42 percent), and the Prescott (Arizona, 46 percent). In the Intermountain Region fishing is over 90 percent cold-water in all forests except for 24 percent ice fishing in the Caribou (Utah, Idaho, and Wyoming) and 10 percent ice fishing in the Fishlake (Utah) National Forests. In the Pacific Southwest Region fishing is 79 percent cold-water and 18 percent warm-water. Fishing is also predominantly cold-water in the Pacific Northwest Region, except for two forests. In the Siuslaw (Oregon) the following breakdown in fishing exists: cold-water, 40 percent; saltwater, 27 percent; anadromous, 23 percent; and warm-water, 10 percent. In the Siskiyou (Oregon and California) the distribution is 55 percent anadromous and 45 percent cold-water fishing. Other, relatively minor amounts of anadromous fishing occurs in the Pacific Northwest Region. In Region 10 (Alaska) saltwater is 61 percent and cold-water is 39 percent of the total in the Tongass National Forest. In the Chugach National Forest cold-water is 86 percent and saltwater is 14 percent.

Many of the national forests that rank high for the number of recreation visitor days related to fishing occupy relatively low positions in terms of total recreational use. Forests from all regions of the country, except the Pacific Northwest, are represented in the 24 leading national forests listed in Table 9.14. The leading one is the Chippeawa (Minnesota, 468,700 RVDs); which ranks 60th in total recreational use. The second-ranked Pike–San Isabel National Forests (Colorado, 439,300 RVDs) and third-ranked Inyo (California and Nevada, 417,400 RVDs) rank seventh and third, respectively, in total recreational use. The Superior (Minnesota) ranks fourth in fishing but 19th in total recreational use. A similar ranking exists for the fifth-ranked Shasta-Trinity (California), the sixth-ranked Grand Mesa–Gunnison–Uncompaghre, and the ninth-ranked Tongass National Forests. The seventh-ranked Tonto National Forest (350,300 RVDs) is number 1 for total recreational use. The eighth-ranked Sabine National Forest (Texas) shows a distant 107th ranking for total recreational use. The 10th-ranked Nicolet National Forest (Wisconsin) has 302,400 RVDs of fishing and jumps from 85th place for total recreational use. The 11th-ranked Angelina National Forest is also a distant 112th in total recreational use. At the other end of the list are several national forests that had very low fishing use. Besides the Caribbean, which has no fishing use, exceptionally low values exist for the Finger Lakes (New York, 1300 RVDs), Lincoln (N. Mexico, 1500 RVDs), Choctawhatchee (Florida, 2000 RVDs), Tuskegee (Alabama, 2000), and Homochitto (Mississippi, 3700 RVDs).

The lower portion of Table 9.14 identifies the national forests in which fishing plays an especially prominent role. For the entire National Forest System, 5.65 percent of the recreation visitor days are related to fishing, and the median was a close 5.5 percent. The distribution of the national forests by percentage of fishing use shows a rather even pattern clustered to either side of the mean: 40 to 50 percent, 2; 30 to 40 percent, 0; 20 to 30 percent, 2; 10 to 20 percent, 20; 5 to 10 percent, 60; and under 5 percent, 60. Almost half of the national forests listed in the bottom of Table 9.14 are small ones in the Southern Region, and another quarter are in the Eastern Region. The Angelina and the Sabine National Forests, both in southeastern Texas, stand far

above all the other ones in that fishing accounts for 50 percent of their total recreational use. Other Southern Region forests with very high percentages of their total recreational use accounted for by fishing are the Sam Houston (Texas, 19 percent); the St. Francis (Arkansas, 19 percent); the Holly Springs (Mississippi, 15 percent), the Conecuh (Alabama, 14 percent), the Tombigbee (Mississippi, 12 percent), and the Delta (Mississippi, 11 percent). In the Eastern Region the Chippewa (Minnesota, 27 percent), the Nicolet (Wisconsin, 27 percent), the Hiawatha (Michigan, 15 percent), and the Hoosier (Indiana, 15 percent) fishing plays an especially prominent role. In seven national forests, under 1 percent of the recreational use is related to fishing: the Caribbean (none), the Lincoln (N. Mexico), the Cleveland (California), the Columbia River Gorge (Oregon and Washington), the Kaibab (Arizona), the San Bernardino (California), and the Cibola (N. Mexico).

Nonconsumptive Fish and Wildlife Use   Table 9.15 summarizes "nonconsumptive fish and wildlife use." This category involves nature study, and observation and photography of wildlife, birds, and fish. The focus is on observing fish and wildlife but not using them in a consumptive manner. Hunting is an example of a consumptive use of wildlife. This category accounts for the smallest percentage of recreational use in the national forests among all nine major categories of use. Only 0.87 percent, or 2.5 million RVDs, of all recreational use in the national forests, is related to "nonconsumptive fish and wildlife use." The mean for all forests is 17,617, with an extremely skewed median of 9800. Only 2 forests record over 100,000 RVDs. The distribution for the other Forests by intervals of use is as follows: 50,000 to 100,000, 4; 25,000 to 50,000, 24; 5000 to 25,000, 70; and under 5000, 44. Most of the recreation visitor days

Table 9.15   Nonconsumptive Fish and Wildlife Use—1992

Leading National Forests in Category—RVDs (000s) and % of Use					
Coronado	334.6	7.3%	Okanogan	35.3	3.0%
Inyo	166.3	2.0%	Sierra	34.8	0.7%
Deschutes	91.7	2.5%	Pike and San Isabel	34.2	0.6%
Cibola	72.0	4.8%	Siuslaw	33.3	1.5%
Toiyabe	63.6	1.7%	Arapaho-Roosevelt	32.2	0.6%
Wallowa-Whitman	52.9	2.5%	Tongass	32.1	0.8%
Angeles	49.9	0.5%	Santa Fe	32.1	1.2%
Los Padres	48.0	1.0%	Kootenai	31.9	2.0%
Gifford Pinchot	44.3	1.6%	Sequoia	31.7	0.9%
San Bernardino	38.9	0.7%	Green Mountain	30.9	2.0%

National Forests with High % of Use in Category					
Tombigbee	8.3%	Wallowa-Whitman	2.5%	Davy Crockett	1.9%
Coronado	7.3%	Tuskegee	2.2%	Deerlodge	1.8%
Holly Springs	6.2%	Modoc	2.1%	Kaibab	1.7%
Cibola	4.8%	Custer	2.1%	Toiyabe	1.7%
Francis Marion	3.5%	Fremont	2.0%	Payette	1.6%
Okanogan	3.0%	Kootenai	2.0%	Ouachita	1.6%
Oconee	2.9%	Inyo	2.0%	Ozark	1.6%
Medicine Bow	2.8%	Green Mountain	2.0%	Gifford Pinchot	1.6%
Umatilla	2.6%	Gila	1.9%	Shawnee	1.6%
Deschutes	2.5%	Finger Lakes	1.9%	Shoshone	1.6%

Source: Forest Service.

in this category are contributed by a relatively few number of national forests in Regions 3, 5, and 6. The leading national forest is the Coronado (Arizona and N. Mexico). Its 334,600 RVDs in this category account for an astounding 13 percent of the entire recreational use in this category for the entire National Forest System. The second-ranked Inyo National Forest accounts for another 7 percent and the Deschutes (Oregon) another 4 percent. These three national forests, along with the fourth-ranked Cibola (N. Mexico), fifth-ranked Toiyabe (California and Nevada), and the sixth-ranked Wallowa-Whitman (Oregon and Idaho), are the sites of one-third of the total National Forest System use in this category. The only Eastern national forest among the top 20 listed in Table 9.15 is the Green Mountain (Vermont), but its value is only 30,900 RVDs. In three forests there is no use in this category: the Osceola (Florida), the Olympic (Washington), and the William B. Bankhead (Alabama).

When the bottom portion of Table 9.15 is examined, the national forests in which the relative importance of "nonconsumptive fish and wildlife use" as a percentage of total use are listed, one finds a large number of forests that do not lead in the ranking in the upper portions. Nationally, 0.87 percent of the recreational use within the National Forest System is contributed by this category, and the median value is 0.70 percent. The breakdown into categories of percentage use by forests yields: over 5 percent, 3; 4 to 5 percent, 1; 3 to 4 percent, 2; 2 to 3 percent, 10; 1 to 2 percent, 34; and under 1 percent, 94. The Tombigbee National Forest (Mississippi) is a clear leader, with 8.3 percent of its recreational use related to this category, but only 10,000 RVDs yielded this value. The second-ranked Coronado National Forest has 7.3 percent of its use in this category, but it is the leader in terms of recreation visitor days with 334,600. The third-ranked Holly Springs National Forest (Mississippi), with 6.2 percent of its use in this category has only 13,000 recreation visitor days. In addition to the Osceola, the Olympic, and the William B. Bankhead National Forests, where no "nonconsumptive fish and wildlife use" was observed, exceptionally low percentages of use occur in the following national forests: the Columbia River Gorge (0.02 percent), the Bridger-Teton (Wyoming, 0.02 percent), the Eldorado (California, 0.06 percent), and Wenatchee (Washington, 0.09 percent).

Other Recreational Activities   Table 9.16 summarizes the category "other recreational activities," which contains 13 subcategories (only the category "mechanized travel and viewing scenery" is broken down into more subcategories for data collection.) The specific subcategories included within the broad category of "other recreation activities" are team sports, individual sports, games and play, gathering forest products, viewing interpretative exhibits, attending talks and programs, guided touring, unguided touring, guided walking, unguided walking, viewing interpretive signs, listening to audio programs, and general information. The average use is 107,298 RVDs for each forest. The median value of 67,400 RVDs is lower because of a large number of forests with low usage in the category. The number of forests in different RVD use intervals are: over 1,000,000, 1; 500,000 to 1,000,000, 2; 400,000 to 500,000, 2; 300,000 to 400,000, 5; 200,000 to 300,000, 6; 100,000 to 200,000, 34; 50,000 to 100,000, 38; and under 50,000, 56. Generally, the subcategory that accounts for the most recreation visitor days in most national forests is "gathering forest products" (30 to 75 percent of this category in most forests). General information is usually the second-ranked subcategory. There are some variations in this generalization. In Regions 1

Table 9.16 Other Recreational Activities—1992

Leading National Forests in Category—RVDs (000s) and % of Use

Coronado	1388.7	30.1%	Gallatin	283.6	10.1%
Dixie	734.4	11.9%	Grand Mesa–Gunnison–		
Inyo	565.7	6.8%	Uncompaghre	276.3	5.9%
Tongass	491.3	12.2%	Apache-Sitgreaves	239.7	9.7%
Angeles	401.4	4.4%	Sequoia	239.2	6.8%
Carson	372.5	21.9%	Idaho Panhandle	214.6	8.8%
Shasta-Trinity	341.8	7.1%	Plumas	212.4	8.3%
Coconino	331.0	5.7%	Pike and San Isabel	196.5	3.5%
Malheur	325.9	43.3%	Santa Fe	189.6	7.3%
Gifford Pinchot	318.3	11.3%	Targhee	189.1	11.6%
			Lolo	188.5	11.9%

National Forests with High % of Use in Category

Malheur	43.3%	Caribbean	16.6%	Cibola	11.4%
Coronado	30.1%	Six Rivers	12.6%	Gifford Pinchot	11.3%
Conecuh	28.8%	Tongass	12.2%	Challis	11.2%
Tuskegee	28.3%	Lolo	11.9%	Gallatin	10.1%
Carson	21.9%	Dixie	11.9%	Lassen	9.9%
Holly Springs	17.5%	Targhee	11.6%	Davy Crockett	9.8%

Source: Forest Service.

(Northern) and 10 (Alaska) this category is relatively more important than its share of total recreational use. The reverse is the case in the other seven regions. This lesser share of importance is especially great in Regions 3 (Southwestern), 4 (Intermountain), and 6 (Pacific Northwest).

In the Eastern Region (Region 9) the breakdown of use in the "other recreational activities" category in terms of the leading subcategories is "gathering forest products," 48 percent; "general information," 15 percent; and "unguided walking," 8 percent. The distribution of use in the Southern Region (Region 8) is "gathering forest products," 32 percent; "general information," 16 percent; "unguided walking," 10 percent; "attending talks and programs," 7 percent; and "viewing interpretive exhibits," 7 percent. The distribution of use in Region 10 (Alaska) is different. In the Chugach National Forest, 42 percent of the use is related to viewing interpretive exhibits, 17 percent to unguided walking, and 15 percent to viewing interpretive signs. The Tongass National Forest differs from the Chugach in that "guided touring" is the leading subcategory at 55 percent, followed by "viewing interpretive exhibits" (12 percent), "attending talks and programs" (10 percent), and "guided walking" (8 percent). In the Pacific Southwest Region, "general information" (25 percent) and "gathering forest products" (24 percent) are almost equally in the lead, followed by "unguided walking" (10 percent), "viewing interpretive exhibits" (10 percent), and "individual sports" (8 percent). In the Intermountain Region (Region 4) "gathering forest products" is the leading category in all forests except the Uinta (Utah) and ranges from a low of 36 percent in the Fishlake National Forest to a high of 95 percent in the Payette National Forest (Idaho). In the Uinta National Forest, general information gathering (22 percent) is just ahead of forest product gathering (20 percent), with team sports in third (19 percent). In the Wasatch-Cache National Forest (Utah and Wyoming), "gathering forest products" is in the lead at 35 percent and "team

sports," "individual sports," and "games and play" are tied for second each with 12 percent. In most national forests in the Southwestern Region "gathering forest products" is the leading subcategory and ranges from a low of 15 percent in the Coronado to a high of 82 percent in the Kaibab. In most forests in this region viewing interpretive signs and exhibits and general information are next in importance. In the Tonto National Forest "games and play" is the leading subcategory at 34 percent of the use. In the Pacific Northwest (Region 6) "gathering forest products" is the leading subcategory of use in most Forests, varying from 36 percent in the Deschutes to 88 percent in the Winema (Oregon). In only three Forests in this region are other subcategories more important: Mt. Hood National Forest (Oregon), where "unguided walking" is the leader at 41 percent, the Rogue River National Forest (Oregon), where "unguided walking is the leader" at 46 percent, and the Columbia River Gorge (Oregon and Washington) where "viewing interpretive exhibits" accounts for 98 percent. In the Gifford Pinchot National Forest (Washington) "viewing interpretive exhibits" with 28 percent is close to the leader of 32 percent for "gathering forest products." The Mt. St. Helen's National Volcanic Monument has become a national attraction in this forest. In most forests in the Rocky Mountain Region (Region 2) "gathering forests products" is the leading subcategory, except in the Arapaho-Roosevelt, San Juan, and White River (all in Colorado) National Forests, where "general information" is the leader at 21, 54, and 42 percent, respectively, and the Medicine Bow, (Wyoming) where "unguided touring" is the leader at 26 percent. The Nebraska National Forest is anomalous for this region in its distribution of recreational use in this category: team sports (30 percent), games and play (20 percent), individual sports (9 percent), attending talks and programs (7 percent), and guided touring (6 percent).

The Coronado National Forest is far ahead of the second-ranked national forest in this category in terms of number of recreation visitor days. The 1.39 million RVDs in this forest account for a very high 9.2 percent of all use in this category in the entire National Forest System. This category accounts for 30 percent of the total recreational use in the Coronado. The breakdown of use into subcategories for the Coronado National Forest yields an even distribution among the five leaders: "guided tours," 16 percent, "viewing interpretive signs," 16 percent, "unguided walking," 16 percent, "gathering forest products," 15 percent, and "general information," 14 percent. The second-ranked Dixie National Forest (Utah) has noticeably lower recreation visitor days than the top-ranked Coronado—0.734 million. "Gathering forest products" accounts for 39 percent of the use and "viewing interpretive exhibits" another 29 percent of the use in the Dixie. The third-ranked Inyo National Forest (California and Nevada) has 0.566 million RVDs in this category. "General information" is the leading subcategory in the Inyo. Much of this use occurs at the beautiful visitor center built above Mono Lake near Lee Vining, Calif. (Figure 9.9). "Gathering forest products" and "viewing interpretive exhibits" are tied for second. The next-ranked Tongass National Forest (Alaska) has 0.491 million RVDs, where guided touring accounts for 55 percent of the use in this category. In the fifth-ranked Angeles National Forest (California) "individual sports" is a decided leader, with one-third of the use in the category. These five leading national forests represent 24 percent of the total recreational use in the entire National Forest System for the category "other recreational activities." Several national forests have an extremely low number of recreation visitor days in this category: the Delta (Mississippi, 700), the Osceola (Florida, 1000), the

Figure 9.9 Visitor Center at Mono Basin National Scenic Area in the Inyo National Forest.

Finger Lakes (New York, 1400), Homochitto (Mississippi, 2100), the St. Francis (Arkansas, 2400), the Tombigbee (Mississippi, 2900), the Ochoco (Oregon, 3200), the Choctawhatchee (Florida, 3500), the Angelina (Texas, 5600), the William B. Bankhead (Alabama, 6300), and the Siskiyou (Oregon and California, 9600).

The lower portion of Table 9.16 identifies the national forests that have extremely high percentages of use in this category. The amount of recreational use attributed to "other recreational activities" for the entire National Forest System is 5.24 percent, and the median value is a slightly lower 4.7 percent. The number of national forests in the different percentage-of-use intervals are as follows: over 40 percent, 1; 30 to 40 percent, 1; 20 to 30 percent, 3; 10 to 20 percent, 11; 5 to 10 percent, 53; 1 to 5 percent, 71; and under 1 percent, 5. The Malheur National Forest in east-central Oregon is way above all others in terms of the total recreational use in this category—43 percent; 98 percent of this use occurs in the subcategory "gathering forest products." The breakdown into subcategories of use in the Coronado National Forest—where 30 percent of the total recreational use occurs in this category—was identified in the previous paragraph. Four of the next five-ranked national forests are in the Southern Region. In the third-ranked Conecuh National Forest (Alabama, 29 percent), the leading subcategories are "gathering forest products" and "general information," each accounting for 47 percent of the use. In the fourth-ranked Tuskegee National Forest (Alabama) 28 percent of the total recreational use occurs in this category, and the leading subcategory of use is general information at 69 percent. In the fifth-ranked Carson National Forest (N. Mexico), 22 percent of its use is in this category, and the leading subcategories are "gathering forest products" (51 percent) and "viewing interpretive exhibits" (29 percent). Exceptionally low percentages of total recreational use in this category have been calculated for the Osceola (Florida, 0.2 percent), the Routt (Colorado, 0.6 percent), the White Mountain (N. Hampshire and Maine, 0.9 percent), and the Wallowa-Whitman National Forests (Oregon and Idaho, 0.9 percent).

Wilderness Use   Table 9.17 identifies the national forests in which the greatest number of recreation visitor days and the largest percentage of total use occur in units that are designated part of the National Wilderness Preservation System. In 1992, there were 13,134,700 RVDs in National Forest wilderness areas. This resulted in an average of 93,154 RVDs/Forest with a very skewed median of 27,400 RVDs. The

Table 9.17 National Forest Wilderness Area Use—1992

Leading National Forests in Category—RVDs (000s) and % of Use					
Superior	1,404.0	34.94%	Santa Fe	285.5	11.00%
Tongass	797.0	19.82%	Tonto	246.7	2.67%
Bridger-Teton	543.5	18.36%	San Bernardino	244.9	4.45%
Shasta-Trinity	520.8	10.82%	Challis	234.6	31.35%
Stanislaus	520.8	19.23%	Sierra	222.7	4.77%
Inyo	511.6	6.11%	Coronado	210.1	4.56%
White River	451.8	5.49%	Grand Mesa–Gunnison–		
Wenatchee	414.1	10.66%	Uncompaghre	208.2	4.48%
Toiyabe	293.7	7.75%	Ashley	200.8	10.84%
Gallatin	291.8	10.43%	San Juan	188.6	11.00%
			Gifford Pinchot	182.5	6.48%

National Forests with High % of Use					
Superior	34.94%	Salmon	17.10%	Ashley	10.84%
Challis	31.35%	Klamath	16.53%	Shasta-Trinity	10.82%
Bitterroot	24.58%	Flathead	14.57%	Wenatchee	10.66%
Tongass	19.82%	Shoshone	14.34%	Gallatin	10.43%
Stanislaus	19.23%	Nez Perce	12.71%	Payette	9.48%
Custer	19.15%	San Juan	11.00%	Cibalo	9.18%
Bridger-Teton	18.36%	Santa Fe	11.00%	Gila	8.91%

Source: Forest Service.

distribution of national forests by intervals of recreation visitor days in wilderness areas is as follows: over 1 million, 1; 500,000 to 1,000,000, 5; 200,000 to 500,000, 12; 100,000 to 200,000, 23; 50,000 to 100,000, 16; 25,000 to 50,000, 17; 5000 to 25,000, 32; 1 to 5,000, 17; 0, 18. The number 1 Superior National Forest (Minnesota), has 1.4 million RVDs, which is almost double the figure for the second-ranked forest, the Tongass (Alaska) with 0.80 million RVDs. The one wilderness area in the Superior National Forest is the 803,050-acre Boundary Waters Canoe Area, established in 1964 as one of the initial 54 units of the National Wilderness Preservation System. Most heavily used of all the wilderness areas, it accounts for almost 11 percent of the total use of the National Wilderness Preservation System units located in national forests. The second-ranked Tongass National Forest has 19 wilderness areas on 5.8 million acres that range in size from the 4937-acre Maurelle Islands to the 2.1-million-acres Misty Fjords. Forty-four percent of the national forest wilderness area acreage is in the Tongass National Forest, but despite the large acreage, the degree of use there is surprisingly high. The third-ranked Bridger-Teton National Forest (Wyoming) has 0.54 million RVDs in its three large wilderness areas: the Bridger (428,078 acres), the Teton (585,238 acres), and the Gros Ventre (287,000 acres).

Three California national forests receive the fourth, fifth, and sixth most wilderness use: the Shasta-Trinity (0.52 million RVDs), the Stanislaus (0.52 million RVD), and the Inyo (0.51 million RVDs). The Shasta-Trinity National Forests are located in northern California and contain 394,881 acres of the Trinity Alps Wilderness Area. This wilderness area also extends into the Six Rivers and Klamath National Forests and onto Bureau of Land Management (BLM) land. Other wilderness areas in the Shasta-Trinity National Forests include the Castle Crags, Mt. Shasta, Chanchelulla, and part of the Yolla Bolly-Middle Eel Wilderness Areas. The Stanislaus National

Forest is located in the high country of the Sierra Nevada to the north and west of Yosemite National Park. Included within its boundary is the 112,277-acre Emigrant Wilderness Area and parts of the Carson-Iceberg (77,993 acres) and Mokelumne (22,267 acres) Wilderness Areas. The Carson-Iceberg Wilderness extends into the Toiyabe National Forest, and the Mokelumne extends into the Eldorado and Toiyabe National Forests. The Inyo National Forest is located on the crest and southeastern side of Yosemite National Park in the Sierra Nevada Range and in the White Mountains extending into Nevada. The Boundary Peak Wilderness Area (10,000 acres) surrounds the 13,140-foot peak of the same name on the California-Nevada border. Parts of five other wilderness areas are in the Inyo National Forest: the Ansel Adams (also in the Sierra National Forest); the Golden Trout (also in the Sequoia National Forest); the Hoover (also in the Toiyabe National Forest); the John Muir (also in the Sierra National Forest); and the South Sierra (also in the Sequoia National Forest).

The seventh-ranked White River National Forest (Colorado) has 0.45 million RVDs of recreational use in its seven wilderness areas, only one of which—the Hunter-Fryingpan—is located totally within its boundary. The Collegiate Peaks Wilderness Area is shared with the Gunnison and San Isabel National Forests, the Eagles Nest is shared with the Arapaho National Forest, the Flat Tops is shared with the Routt National Forest, the Holy Cross is shared with the San Isabel National Forest, and the Maroon Bells–Snowmass and Raggeds are shared with the Gunnison National Forest. The eighth-ranked Wenatchee National Forest (Washington), with 0.41 million RVDs, shares all four of its wilderness areas with other national forests: the Alpine Lakes with the Snoqualmie National Forest, the Glacier Peak with the Mt. Baker National Forest, the Henry M. Jackson with the Mt. Baker and Snoqualmie National Forests, and the Lake Chelan-Sawtooth with the Okanogan National Forest.

The Toiyabe National Forest is ninth-ranked (0.29 million RVDs) and lies along the California-Nevada border east of the Tahoe, Eldorado, and Stanislaus National Forests as well as occupying several mountain ranges several hundred miles to the east in Nevada. Totally on the Toiyabe National Forest are the Alta Toquima, the Mt. Charleston, the Mt. Rose, and the Table Mountain Wilderness Areas. The 11,919-foot Charleston Peak in the Spring Mountains, 35 miles west of Las Vegas, offers a stark contrast to the desert of Las Vegas. The Lee Canyon Ski Area is located here, outside of the Mt. Charleston Wilderness Area (Figure 9.10). Part of the Hoover Wilderness Area is shared with the Inyo National Forest, and part of the Mokelumne Wilderness Area is shared with the Stanislaus and Eldorado National Forests. Almost all of the 115,000-acre Arc Dome Wilderness Area is in the Toiyabe National Forest, except for 20 acres that is on BLM land. The Gallatin National Forest (Montana) is ranked 10th, very close in position to the Toiyabe National Forest. The Gallatin has 574,738 acres of the Absaroka-Beartooth Wilderness Area; the other 345,589 acres are in the Custer National Forest (Montana). Part of the Lee Metcalf Wilderness Area is also in the Gallatin National Forest, but another part is in the Beaverhead National Forest (Montana) and a small area on BLM land.

Eighteen national forests have no wilderness use: the Finger Lakes, the Delta, the Tuskegee, the Choctawhatchee, the St. Francis, the Tombigbee, the Conecuh, the Homochitto, the Holly Springs, the Bienville, the Caribbean, the Oconee, the Wayne, the Caribou, the Fishlake, the Chippewa, the Chugach, and the Boise. Seventeen other national forests have under 5000 RVDs each.

Figure 9.10   Only 35 miles west of Las Vegas, Nev., is the Lee Canyon Ski Area on the flank of 11,919-ft. Charleston Peak in the Spring Mountains of Toiyabe National Forest.

The lower portion of Table 9.17 identifies the national forests in which an extremely high percentage of their total recreational use is attributable to wilderness areas. The mean for all national forests is 4.66 percent, and the median is 2.1 percent. In terms of use intervals, two forests have over 30 percent of their use, one Forest has 20 to 30 percent, 15 forests have 10 to 20 percent, 19 forests have 5 to 10 percent, 60 forests have 1 to 5 percent, and 47 forests have under 1 percent of their use accounted for by wilderness areas, of which 18 have no wilderness use. The Superior (Minnesota) has 35 percent and the Challis (Idaho), has 31 percent of their total recreational use related to wilderness areas. Part of the Sawtooth Wilderness and Frank Church–River of No Return Wilderness Areas are on the Challis. In the Bitterroot National Forest (Idaho and Montana), 25 percent of its use is in the Anaconda-Pintlar and parts of the Selway-Bitterroot and Frank Church–River of No Return Wilderness Areas. The Selway-Bitterroot Wilderness Area lies on 270,321 acres in Idaho and 246,676 acres in Montana in the Bitterroot National Forest, as well as on 259,165 acres of the Clearwater National Forest (Idaho), 559,531 acres of the Nez Perce National Forest (Idaho), and 9767 acres of the Lolo National Forest (Montana). The Frank Church–River of No Return is a mammoth wilderness area and occupies parts of seven national forests on 2.4 million acres in Idaho; 802 acres are also on BLM land. Wilderness use accounts for a surprising 20 percent of the total recreational use on the Tongass National Forest.

Developed Recreation Sites

Nationwide   Earlier in this chapter it was stated that over half of the recreational use (56 percent) in the National Forest System occurs in dispersed sites. This dispersed recreational use includes mechanized travel and viewing scenery; hiking, horseback, and water travel; hunting; fishing; and nonconsumptive fish and wildlife

use. Because of the dispersed character of this recreation, the use cannot be tied to specific sites. However, 27 percent of the use takes place at developed sites, and another 12 percent takes place at private-sector facilities. Table 9.18 identifies the types of developed sites that exist in the National Forests: boating sites, swimming sites, campgrounds, picnic grounds, recreation residences, ski areas, major interpretive sites, and all other developed sites. This table also identifies the fee status, the number of sites, and the capacity (where PAOT = persons at one time) for each type of developed site. For the entire system the 19,428 developed sites can accommodate 1,844,821 persons at one time. Only 20 percent (3968) of these sites charge fees; the other 80 percent (15,460) do not. The 7547 recreation residences account for 39 percent of the number of developed sites but only 4 percent of the capacity. In contrast, the 188 ski areas account for only 1 percent of the developed sites but 35 percent of the total capacity. Campgrounds account for the other major portion of the total capacity at developed sites. The 4,530 campgrounds account for 23 percent of the number of developed recreation sites and 27.2 percent of the total capacity. Over half of the campgrounds charge fees.

Regional Differences   There are significant variations in both number and capacities of these developed recreation sites in different regions of the United States. Table 9.19 identifies the number of developed recreation sites and the capacities for

Table 9.18   National Forest Recreation Site and Area Information: National Summary—1992

Type of Developed Site	Fee Status	Number of Sites	Capacity (PAOT)
Boating sites	Fee	21	7,052
	Nonfee	1,195	112,740
Swimming sites	Fee	97	43,575
	Nonfee	226	33,814
Campgrounds	Fee	2,529	372,704
	Nonfee	2,000	129,049
Picnic grounds	Fee	59	8,059
	Nonfee	1,405	97,662
Recreation residences	Fee	922	8,561
	Nonfee	6,625	71,994
Ski areas	Fee	47	138,285
	Nonfee	141	508,325
Interpretive sites (major)	Fee	4	1,610
	Nonfee	341	28,235
All other developed sites	Fee	289	22,550
	Nonfee	3,527	260,606
Total	Fee	3,968	602,396
	Nonfee	15,460	1,242,425
Grand Total		19,428	1,844,821

Note: Each developed site and its PAOT capacity are inventoried only once in the appropriate site-type and fee-status category. Each developed site must be inventoried:
  1. In only one site-type category.
  2. As having either fee or nonfee status, but not in both. For example, a campground and its PAOT capacity are counted only once as either a fee or nonfee campground. Do not count the camping units on the campground as separate developed sites.
Source: Forest Service, Washington office.

Table 9.19 National Forest Recreation Sites and Areas: Information by Region—1992

	Boating Sites		Swimming Sites		Campgrounds		Picnic Grounds		Recreation Residences		Ski Areas		Interpretive Sites		All Other Developed		Total	
	No.	Capacity[1]	No.	Capacity	No.	Capacity	No.	Capacity	No.	Capacity	No.	Capacity	No.	Capacity	No.	Capacity	No.	Capacity
Region 1	106	6,464	34	2,220	367	28,017	121	7,340	630	4,734	17	22,445	16	810	348	12,037	1,639	84,067
Region 2	58	7,463	10	1,800	531	53,311	221	11,851	1,188	6,946	30	163,210	37	2,637	518	37,510	2,593	284,808
Region 3	67	19,420	4	1,485	290	35,435	130	11,751	710	5,724	19	24,970	33	1,941	191	22,736	1,444	123,462
Region 4	92	14,623	13	2,440	770	74,186	124	12,023	589	7,845	21	62,190	109	5,372	459	39,114	2,177	217,793
Region 5	104	16,187	30	10,825	878	113,660	223	15,470	3,379	32,383	33	234,428	92	4,618	577	59,441	5,316	487,012
Region 6	69	8,893	3	390	867	96,086	90	7,677	128	14,453	31	97,292	12	3,591	585	61,153	1,785	289,535
Region 8	227	24,223	106	33,311	388	50,593	260	21,870	291	3,262	2	450	10	5,125	351	23,790	1,635	162,264
Region 9	448	21,924	121	24,723	411	46,905	265	16,719	585	4,882	34	38,125	23	4,276	428	23,466	2,315	181,020
Region 10	45	595	2	115	28	3,560	30	1,020	47	326	1	3,500	13	1,475	359	3,909	525	14,500
Total	1,216	119,792	323	77,389	4,530	501,753	1,464	105,721	7,547	80,555	188	646,610	345	29,845	3,816	283,156	19,429	1,844,821

[1]Capacity in PAOT (persons at one time).
Source: Forest Service Washington Office.

each of the nine Forest Service regions. Region 5 (Pacific Southwest) is by far the leading region in terms of both number of developed sites and capacity; it has 27 percent of the number of developed sites and 26 percent of the total National Forest System capacity. It was shown earlier in the chapter that this region accounts for 23 percent of the total RVDs measured in the National Forest System in 1992. The next leading regions in terms of capacity at developed recreation sites are Region 6 (Pacific Northwest), 15.7 percent and Region 2 (Rocky Mountain), 15.4 percent. Region 10 (Alaska) contained only 3 percent of the number of developed recreation sites, with less than 1 percent of the total national capacity. Region 1 (Northern) also has less than 5 percent of the total national capacity.

Ski areas account for 35 percent of the total national capacity at developed recreation sites in the national forests, but the 188 ski areas represent only 1 percent of the total number of developed recreation sites. Two Forest Service regions account for over 60 percent of the national capacity for ski areas in the National Forests: Region 5 (Pacific Southwest, 36 percent), and Region 2 (Rocky Mountain, 25 percent). These regions contain many "mega" ski resorts, including Mammoth Mountain in California's Inyo National Forest and Vail in Colorado's White River National Forest. Region 6 (Pacific Northwest) was the third-ranking region, with 15 percent of the national capacity. On the other extreme, Region 8 (Southern) has only two ski areas that together have 0.06 percent of the national capacity. Region 10's (Alaska) one ski area accounts for only 0.5 percent of the national capacity. Region 9 (Eastern) has the most ski areas in the National Forest System (34, or 18.1 percent) but only contributed 6 percent of the national capacity. The national average capacity per ski area is 3439 PAOT (persons at one time), but this varies from 225 PAOT in Region 8 (Southern) to 5440 PAOT in Region 2 (Rocky Mountain) and 7104 PAOT in Region 5 (Pacific Southwest). The two most controversial recreational issues in the national forests have been the construction of new ski areas and the setting aside of land as wilderness in the National Wilderness Preservation System. The topics of ski areas and wilderness within the national forests are covered later in this chapter.

The 4530 campgrounds account for 23 percent of the developed recreation sites and 27 percent of the developed site capacity. Region 5 (Pacific Southwest) and Region 6 (Pacific Northwest) contain both the greatest capacity and the largest number of campgrounds. Region 5 has 19 percent of the total number of campgrounds and 23 percent of the capacity, and Region 6 has 19 percent for each category. Region 4 (Intermountain) ranks third in campgrounds, with 17 percent of the number and 15 percent of the capacity. Region 10 (Alaska, 0.7 percent), and Region 1 (Northern, 6 percent), have small percentages of the national campground capacities. The average PAOT capacity for the nation is 111 per campground, but this varies from a low of 76 in the Northern Region to a high of 130 in Regions 5, 8, and 9.

Boating sites account for about 6.5 percent of both the number of developed sites and the national capacity. Region 8 (Southern) is the leader in capacity (20 percent) followed by Region 9 (Eastern, 18 percent) and Region 3 (Southwestern, 16 percent). Region 9 has the greatest number of boating sites—448, or 37 percent of the total— but the average capacity of 49 PAOT per site is half the national average of 99. The average capacity of 290 per site for Region 3 is almost triple the national average. Alaska's 45 sites average a capacity of 13 each, making it significantly below the national average. These sites provide only 0.5 percent of the national capacity. Boating sites are conspicuously underrepresented in Regions 2 and 6.

Swimming sites represent less than 2 percent of the developed recreation sites and account for a little over 4 percent of the total capacity in national forests. Extreme geographic variation exists for this class of sites, with Region 8 (Southern) having 33 percent of the sites and 43 percent of the capacity, and Region 9 (Eastern) having 38 percent of the sites and 32 percent of the capacity. This results in 75 percent of the developed swimming capacity in the National Forest System being in the eastern half of the country. This eastern dominance contrasts greatly with the fact that most of national forest lands are in the western half. Only in Region 5 in the West is swimming a significant developed type of recreation site, with 9 percent of the sites and 13 percent of the capacity. Swimming sites are almost nonexistent in Region 6, whose three sites (1 percent) account for only 0.5 percent of the national capacity, and in Region 10, whose two sites account for 0.2 percent of the national capacity. Swimming sites are underrepresented also in Regions 1 (3 percent of national capacity), 2 (2 percent), 3 (2 percent), and 4 (3 percent). The lack of developed swimming sites is a surprise in Region 3 (Southwestern), but this region's four sites have the largest average capacity in the country (371 PAOT), compared with a national average of 239 PAOT. Regions 5 (average 361 PAOT) and 8 (314 PAOT) also had larger-than-average capacities. Regions 1 (average 65 PAOT) and Region 10 (average 58 PAOT) had significantly less capacity per developed swimming site.

Picnic grounds represent 8 percent of the number of developed recreation sites and 6 percent of the capacity for the National Forest System nationwide. As is the case with swimming sites, Regions 8 (Southern) and 9 (Eastern) are the leading regions in both numbers of picnic grounds (36 percent combined) and capacity of picnic grounds (37 percent combined). Region 5 is in a close third place, with 15 percent of each. But overall, picnic grounds are the type of developed recreation site that has the most even geographic distribution in the National Forest System; there is less regional variation for this type of recreation site than any other. The average for the system is a capacity of 72 PAOT, but this varies from 34 in Region 10 to 97 in Region 4. Assuming 3 to 4 users per table, this results in an average of 20 to 25 tables per picnic site.

Recreation residences are a declining use of the national forests. In 1992, 7547 recreation residences (39 percent of the developed recreation sites in the country) provided a PAOT capacity of 80,555 (4 percent of the national capacity for developed recreation sites). Numerically, this is the leading category for developed recreation sites. Forty-five percent of the number and 40 percent of the capacity for this type of recreation site are found in one region—Region 5 (Pacific Southwest). Another 18 percent of the capacity but just 2 percent of the number of sites are found in Region 6 (Pacific Northwest). The national average PAOT capacity for this type of site is extremely small—just 10.7, but this figure jumps to an extraordinary large average 113 PAOT for Region 6.[2] For the rest of the regions this average figure ranges from a low of 5.8 in Region 2 to a high of 13.3 in Region 4.

"Major interpretive sites" is the final category of developed recreation sites in national forests, accounting for a little under 2 percent of both the number of areas

---

[2]The author suspects that this figure for Region 6 is an error, but this is how it was reported by the Forest Service.

and the total national capacity. These sites are particularly prominent in Regions 4 (Intermountain) and 5 (Pacific Southwest). In Region 4 there are 109 sites (32 percent of the national total), which have 18 percent of the national total PAOT capacity, and in Region 5, 92 sites (27 percent of the national total) have 16 percent of the national total PAOT capacity. The 10 major sites of Region 8 (Southern) account for 17 percent of the national total capacity. The 3816 other developed sites (20 percent of national total) have a capacity of 283,156 PAOT (15 percent of national total).

Appendix XI identifies the specific recreational activities that are available in each of the 156 individual national forests. The availability of the following recreational activities is detailed in this appendix: boating, cabins, camping, fishing, hiking, hotel/lodge, hunting, picnicking, horseback riding, swimming, and winter sports. Camping, picnicking, and fishing are the most widely available recreational activities, found in all national forests except a very few.[3]

Roads and Other Infrastructure

Roads are a major recreational resource in the national forests. In themselves, they serve a major recreational purpose as the vehicles for mechanized travel and scenery viewing, which is the major category of recreational use in the system. Roads also serve as access points to campgrounds and picnic areas, hunting and fishing grounds, and trailheads. The Forest Service now manages 114 national scenic byways on 6000 miles of roads. The term *infrastructure* refers to the facilities, utilities, and transportation systems needed to meet public and administrative needs. In addition to roads, water and sanitation systems, recreational facilities, administrative buildings, and other constructed facilities comprise the infrastructure. The civil engineers on the staff of the Forest Service, who build these roads and other infrastructures, have been referred to as the world's largest construction company. Virtually all activities in the National Forest System depend to some extent on the Forest Development Road System. The system roads are managed in accordance with decisions reached during the land management planning process. These roads are constructed, operated, and maintained to the minimum standards necessary to provide safe, economical, and environmentally acceptable access. However, road construction has often been environmentally damaging—especially in stream situation cases.

Recreationists make up the majority of the users of Forest Development roads. Most recreational activities are dependent on the road system to access recreation destinations (Figure 9.11). The Forest Development Road System currently consists of 369,000 miles of arterial, collector, and local roads. During FY92, 25 percent of the road system was intended for use by passenger cars, 57 percent was intended for use by high-clearance vehicles (such as pick-up trucks and four-wheel drive vehicles), and 18 percent was closed to motorized traffic all year long. The Forest Service often imposes seasonal restrictions on road use when necessary to protect wildlife during

---

[3]The Forest Service was unable to provide individual site capacity data for each National Forest. The Chief's office promised to send this data but it never materialized. The lack of this data, again, reflects two basic problems with the Forest Service: (1) a poor information system and (2) poor cooperation by Forest Service employees, including the former chief, Dale Robertson, who has publicly stated that "public service" is a major function of the Forest Service.

Figure 9.11   Snowmobiles on Forest Road 228 (Shrine Pass Road) in Arapaho National Forest.

migration, mating, or rearing periods; to prevent fires; to prevent road damage when the road is unstable; and to provide for public safety during periods of high fire danger.

The 1990 RPA (Resources Planning Act) Program projects a decrease in new road construction. As new road construction has trended downward in this time period, the proportion of Forest Road Program funds spent on recreation and general-purpose roads (roads that serve all forest users) increased from 16 to 51 percent. These trends are consistent with a road system that is largely in place, with an increasing emphasis on recreation and general-purpose use. During FY92, the Forest Service constructed 1180 miles of road. Although the majority of new roads were initially constructed to access timber sales, these roads are also used to access areas for recreational opportunities such as hiking, hunting, camping, and fishing. Other national forest activities, such as fire fighting, wildlife habitat improvement projects, watershed projects, grazing allotments, and mineral activities benefit from the construction of new roads. The continuing decline in the amount of timber being hauled over Forest Development roads has resulted in a decrease in the amount of road maintenance done by timber purchasers. In FY92, reconstruction was required on 3259 miles of existing Forest Development roads, and 4000 miles of roads no longer needed to implement forest plans were obliterated and the land restored for the production of vegetation.

Other infrastructures in the national forests that have varying degrees of recreational significance includes bridges, buildings, and dams. The Forest Service has over 8000 road bridges in the Forest Development Road System, and approximately 3000 trail bridges for management of various resources. In FY92, 68 new bridges were constructed and 86 bridges were reconstructed or rehabilitated. The Forest Service owns or leases buildings providing approximately 26 million square feet of space located on 852 administrative units; 22 percent of the buildings are leased. Also

owned are over 1000 dams, and the Forest Service administers permits for another 2200 dams owned by others but located on the National Forest System.

Road construction in the national forests has been a controversial issue for almost three decades for two primary reasons. In the first place, when roads are extended into remote sections of national forests, these areas are precluded from being included in the National Wilderness Preservation System. This was the basis for the controversy in the RARE processes in the late 1960s and 1970s. Environmental groups believed the Forest Service's road building plans to be too aggressive. They feared this rapid expansion of the road system would seriously limit future additions to the National Wilderness Preservation System by rendering them "roaded." The second major controversy related to roads focuses on the major role road building expenses play in the deficit timber sales in many national forests. *Deficit timber sales* refers to the fact that selling and harvesting the timber costs the Forest Service, and thus the taxpayers, more than the revenue paid by the private sector for the stumpage. Road and bridge construction and reconstruction are major expenses in timber harvesting. While the timber purchasers build some of the roads and bridges, a significant number of these are built by the Forest Service. While critics of the economics of deficit timber sales have some good arguments against these sales, they sometimes fail to recognize the recreational value of the roads and bridges that remain after the timbering process is finished. If the recreational value of these roads and bridges were amortized over the longer time period, many of these timber sales would not be as deficit as some make them appear.

Trails

Trails are another major recreational resource in the National Forest System. Cross-country skiers, hikers, horseback riders, all-terrain vehicle (ATV) riders, motorcyclists, snowmobilers, bicyclers, and recreationists with disabilities use the 120,284 miles of the National Forest trail system. In FY92 the Forest Service constructed or reconstructed 1976 miles of trails, and an additional 128 miles were constructed through contributed funds in challenge cost-share projects and by volunteers. Table 9.20 lists the total mileage, constructed mileage, and maintained mileage of trails in the National Forest System by state in 1992. The states with the most mileage of trails are Idaho (19,045 miles), Montana (14,492 miles), California (13,973 miles), and Oregon (11,008 miles). Fifty percent of the total trail mileage is in these four states. The Forest Service has administrative responsibility for three national scenic trails and one national historic trail in the National Trails System: the Continental Divide National Scenic Trail, the Pacific Crest National Scenic Trail, the Florida National Scenic Trail, and the Nez Perce (Nee-Me-Poo) National Historic Trail. The Forest Service also has administrative responsibility for a number of national recreation trails in the National Trails System. The National Trails System will be detailed in Chapter 14.

Water Features

The National Forest System contains 83,000 miles of streams and 2.7 million acres of lakes and reservoirs (Frome, 1984, 140). Many of these water features (for example, Hungry Horse Reservoir in Montana's Flathead National Forest) are readily accessible

Table 9.20 Trail Miles in the National Forest System by State[1]

State, Commonwealth, or Terriitory[2]	Total	1992 Constructed[3]	1992 Maintained
Alabama	260.1	8.5	130.8
Alaska	833.3	9.7	492.4
Arizona	4,260.7	180.3	788.7
Arkansas	771.2	60.2	534.0
California	13,973.2	151.0	7,313.8
Colorado	9,358.0	131.1	4,746.6
Florida	350.8	6.0	223.1
Georgia	700.0	1.0	280.8
Idaho	19,044.6	175.5	10,396.4
Illinois	220.0	13.5	49.7
Indiana	146.0	0.0	146.0
Kansas	37.5	2.0	14.5
Kentucky	466.7	18.9	205.4
Louisiana	132.1	12.0	107.0
Maine	120.0	0.0	120.0
Michigan	2,920.8	99.0	2,497.4
Minnesota	2,649.0	53.5	2,649.0
Mississippi	298.4	32.0	182.9
Missouri	650.0	63.5	619.0
Montana	14,492.3	163.3	9,169.2
Nebraska	54.0	1.0	41.0
Nevada	1,639.9	9.0	654.0
New Hampshire	1,308.0	47.8	1,308.0
New Mexico	4,126.7	63.9	1,270.10
New York	31.0	0.3	31.0
North Carolina	1,500.1	26.1	369.5
North Dakota	34.9	1.5	32.6
Ohio	260.0	30.0	260.0
Oklahoma	148.8	17.0	10.7
Oregon	11,008.3	105.2	8,303.8
Pennsylvania	648.8	22.0	555.4
Puerto Rico	21.1	2.5	6.0
South Carolina	316.6	23.3	226.0
South Dakota	234.2	12.3	223.2
Tennessee	716.2	7.9	104.1
Texas	295.4	5.0	122.0
Utah	5,184.4	151.0	3,024.8
Vermont	965.2	20.4	769.9
Virginia	1,832.9	40.5	379.3
Washington	9,004.9	131.0	6,693.0
West Virginia	944.6	24.1	443.5
Wisconsin	1,684.6	31.0	1,349.2
Wyoming	6,638.2	21.8	2,988.1
Total[4]	120,283.50	1,975.6	69,831.9

[1]Includes work accomplished by Human Resource Programs and volunteers.
[2]States not listed have no Forest Service recreation program.
[3]Miles constructed include construction of new trails and reconstruction of existing trails.
The predominate activity is reconstruction. Funds used are appropriated, timber, and other receipts.
[4]Totals may not add due to rounding.
Source: Report of the Forest Service Fiscal Year 1992, February 1993.

by road and serve as valuable recreational attractions. Others are remotely located in high mountain areas, and it requires work to reach them. The National Wild and Scenic Rivers System now totals 10,410 miles, of which 4316 miles are managed by the Forest Service. Of the 153 rivers or segments of rivers in the system nationwide, 96 are managed by the Forest Service. In FY92, the 102nd Congress added 26 rivers totaling 899 miles in Pennsylvania, Michigan, Arkansas, and California to the National Forest System. Recommendations for another 121 National Forest System rivers have resulted from forest planning and special river studies. An additional 524 rivers have been identified as having outstanding resource values and free-flowing characteristics, making them eligible for the Wild and Scenic Rivers System; studies are presently in progress on some of these rivers. The Wild and Scenic Rivers System will be detailed in Chapter 14.

Wildlife, Fish, and Rare Plants

The National Forest System provides diverse habitats for more than 3000 species of birds, mammals, reptiles, fish, and amphibians, as well as for more than 3000 rare plant species. The Forest Service serves as a steward for these national biological resources, managing habitats to produce wildlife and fish; to protect threatened, endangered, and sensitive species; and to provide recreational opportunities for hunters, anglers, amateur naturalists, photographers, and all other national forest users. Many of these biological treasures are major recreational attractions; one example is the Ancient Bristlecone Pine Forest in the high elevations of the White Mountains in California's Inyo National Forest. In FY92, National Forest System lands provided an estimated 49.1 million activity days (averaging 4.3 hours of participation) of recreational fishing, with an economic value of more than $2 billion. Also in FY92, the National Forest System provided 26 million activity days (averaging 7.9 hours of participation) of sport hunting, at an economic value of $949.6 million. Photography, bird watching, and nature study are becoming increasingly popular, and in FY92 the National Forest System provided 30.1 million activity days (averaging 3.9 hours of participation) of such nonconsumptive recreational use, at a value of $784.4 million. The number of combined visits to fish, hunt, and view wildlife on the National Forest System is expected to increase by 183 percent in the next 50 years. These activities provide enjoyment to the forest user and employ 103,540 in jobs related to natural resource recreation and tourism goods and services, as well as generating $2.2 billion in local community income (Forest Service, Annual Report FY92, 1993, 30).

The National Forest System is home to 243 plant and animal species listed as either threatened or endangered by the United States Fish and Wildlife Service, which represents 33 percent of all federally listed species nationwide. The distribution of these 243 species is as follows: plants, 92; fishes, 50; mammals, 27; snails, mussels and crustaceans, 27; birds, 26; reptiles and amphibians, 13; and insects, 8. In addition, the Forest Service has identified 2200 sensitive species that are managed to prevent the need for federal listing.

Ski Areas

The construction of new ski areas on National Forest System land has at times been one of the most controversial resource management issues in the national forest plan-

ning process. This issue has particularly caused conflicts among recreationists—the alpine skier versus the backcountry wilderness user. The first major ski area issue arose in the early 1940s, when the Forest Service considered a proposal to build a ski resort in the San Gorgonio Primitive Area in California's San Bernardino National Forest. Wilderness advocates opposed the project, and after 5 years of hearings the Forest Service decided not to permit the development. In 1964, this 56,722-acre area became one of the initial 54 components of the new National Wilderness Preservation System. Since this time, however, the development of downhill ski areas have been encouraged by the Forest Service, for not only do they provide recreation, they also pay fees to the United States Treasury based on the number of skier visits. They also stimulate the local economy, and the Forest Service has traditionally been supportive of local economic development. In many cases, the land at the bottom of the mountain on which ski areas are constructed is in private ownership while the mountain slopes are National Forest System land. While most of the lodging and support facilities are built on the private land at the base of the mountain, the ski trails, lifts, on-mountain restaurants, warming shelters, and ski patrol shelters are constructed on the national forest portion. Such is the case at Vail Ski Area (Figure 9.12) in Colorado's White River National Forest and at Heavenly Valley Ski Area in the Lake Tahoe Basin of California's El Dorado National Forest (Figure 9.13). In the case of Crystal Mountain, which is located on the Snoqualmie National Forest just east of Mount Rainier National Park in Washington, the Forest Service went so far as to make public land available for private condominiums. This was done to make the project attractive to a group of developers and to "provide needed accommodations that seemed otherwise unavailable" (Frome, 1984, 150). The tremendous growth in the popularity of downhill skiing in the 1960s and 1970s was a contributing factor to the increased demands placed on national forests as the site for new alpine ski areas.

The most controversial ski area ever proposed for a national forest, however, was Mineral King. Mineral King became an important symbol of the contest over intensive recreational development of public lands and is an extremely interesting case study

Figure 9.12   The building at Eagles Nest, at the top of the Lionshead Gondola lift, at Vail Ski Area, houses a restaurant and bathrooms.

Figure 9.13 The tram at Heavenly Valley Ski Area is located on lands of the El Dorado National Forest in the Lake Tahoe Basin Management Unit.

in public land policy and the struggle between developers and preservationists. It not only generated intense controversy but also extensive litigation. Mineral King is a small valley surrounded by eight alpine bowls and a number of peaks over 12,000 feet in elevation, which rise over 4000 vertical feet above the valley floor. The valley is about 2 miles long and ¼ mile wide. It is located in the Sierra Nevada of south-central California, 225 miles northeast of Los Angeles and 275 miles southeast of San Francisco. Part of the reason for the controversy is the shape of the boundary of Sequoia National Park, which surrounded it on three sides—west, north and east. When Sequoia National Park was established in 1890, the valley was excluded be-cause of its mineral deposits and remnant developments from mining activity in the 1870s and 1880s. The 15,000-acre valley and its surrounding lands became part of Sequoia National Forest, and in 1926 the valley was declared the Sequoia National Game Refuge. While the valley was not a wilderness, it was relatively undisturbed. The only access road passed through the national park to the west. This seasonal road was very narrow, winding, and closed by snow for all but a few summer months. The resulting use was extremely seasonal, with limited use made of the valley in winter. The area served as the base for exploring the surrounding wilderness in addition to hiking, fishing, and camping. One-quarter of the recreation visitor days

were accounted for by use of recreation residences that were converted old mining shacks.

In response to inquiries, a forester sent into Mineral King in 1945 reported that the area would be desirable as a summer and winter recreation area. The high elevation of the valley and the surrounding eight bowls were deemed extremely desirable for skiing. In 1949 the Forest Service issued a prospectus soliciting development proposals for the area by private developers, but there were no takers. It was surmised that the cost of building a 25-mile all-weather road to the site would be too great. In 1953, a congressional hearing on the Mineral King ski area development was held, and the Sierra Club did not even object. It was the Sierra Club's position that if Mineral King was not developed, the San Gorgonio Primitive Area would be. The Forest Service issued a second prospectus in February 1965, this time much more ambitious than the first. In July 1965, the California State Highway Commission approved funding of an all-weather access road, which removed the economic obstacle to development. Six proposals were submitted, four of which met the Forest Service's minimum qualifications. In December 1965 the Forest Service selected the one submitted by Walt Disney Productions.

The Disney plan called for, in addition to the all-weather access road through Sequoia National Park, an "alpine village" that included a hotel complex and restaurants in the valley and at least one restaurant on a peak, a multilevel parking structure covering 4.5 acres that could park over 5000 cars, and the lifts and ski trails. It was planned that 2.5 million visitors would use the facility per year, with peak use bringing 16,000 persons at one time (Frome, 1984, 150). In October 1966, a preliminary permit for three years for planning was issued. After initial opposition to construction of the road across Sequoia National Park, the Secretary of the Interior in December 1967 approved the road. In January 1969 the Forest Service accepted Disney's master plan for development of the valley. In June 1969, before a 30-year permit was issued to Disney, the Sierra Club filed suit in a U.S. District Court in San Francisco against the Secretaries of Agriculture and the Interior. The Sierra Club obtained a temporary injunction in the District Court in July 1969, only to be reversed in September 1970 by the Ninth Circuit Court of Appeals, which stated that the Sierra Club had no standing to sue. The Supreme Court in April 1972 affirmed the Court of Appeals decision. The Sierra Club amended its complaint, alleging sufficient injury to local club members to conform to the Supreme Court's standards, and also added a further claim under the National Environmental Policy Act (NEPA).

The environmental impact statement (EIS) required by the 1969 passage of NEPA deferred the development decision, and the final EIS did not clear all the hurdles until February 1976. In the intervening years Walt Disney Productions had scaled down the scope of the project. There was still also opposition to the road across Sequoia National Park, for not only would the road cross the national park but it would also disturb a grove of giant sequoias. Finally, there was opposition to providing a road at public expense to a single private facility. The change in administration with Jimmy Carter's victory in November 1976 and taking office in January 1977 proved to be another major factor in the ultimate fate of Mineral King. In November 1978, President Carter signed Public Law 95-625, which transferred the Mineral King area from the Forest Service to the Park Service by making it part of Sequoia National Park. This law contained a section (313-h) stating that the development of

Figure 9.14   Beaver Creek Valley and elk wintering area in White River National Forest before development of hotels and ski area in 1976.

high-density, downhill skiing facilities would not be a compatible use. The Sierra Club, which did not initially oppose the development, played a crucial role in determining the ultimate fate of Mineral King, not only by bringing litigation, but also by lobbying for the legislation that added the area to Sequoia National Park.

New proposals for either expansion of existing ski areas or construction of new ski areas are still being submitted to the Forest Service. In the 1980s the Forest Service was presented with proposals for at least six new destination resorts in Colorado: Wolf Creek Valley, Adams Rib, Quail Mountain, East Fork, Lake Catamount, and Rifle. Also in Colorado, opposition to the Burnt Mountain expansion of the Snowmass Ski Area was partially based on the likely blockade of the last elk migration route in the area. The proposed Mt. Hood Ski Area expansion, which contemplates resort housing on federal lands, also raises some serious environmental issues.[4]

Just recently, a major proposed resort on the National Forest—the Early Winters Ski Area—was declared dead. This area was proposed for the Okanogan National

---

[4]The author can attest to the impact of ski areas on wildlife patterns. He has witnessed the disappearance of the elk from their wintering ground at the site of Beaver Creek Ski Area in Colorado. Beaver Creek Ski Area was built by Vail Associates, 10 miles west of Vail, in the White River National Forest of Colorado. It was to be the site for the 1976 Olympics—until the voters of Colorado rejected this. The author witnessed plentiful elk during a cross-coounry ski expedition in 1976, before development in the aspen groves where the village portion of the ski area is now located (Figure 9.14). Visits to the former elk wintering area in the mid and late 1980s and early 1990s revealed their absence. Luxurious hotels and residences are now located in the former "elk grove" (Figure 9.15). Beaver Creek is an extremely well-planned and attractive resort and ski area. The author recommends that skiers who become frustrated with the crowds at Vail give Beaver Creek a try, they won't regret it, especially if they don't like crowds. An extremely attractive cross-country ski area is located at the top of one of the lifts at Beaver Creek. The hustle and bustle of the alpine skiing at Beaver Creek, however, cannot replace the solitude the author experienced on his 1976 cross-country skiing expedition in the valley before any development occurred.

Figure 9.15 Hotels built in the elk wintering area (shown in Figure 9.14 before development) at Beaver Creek Ski Area and Resort in the White River National Forest.

Forest, on the eastern slope of the Cascade Range in northern Washington. A 1970 joint National Park Service/National Forest System study identified the Early Winters area (Sandy Butte) as having the highest potential of any site in the state for development as a major destination resort. The 1984 Washington Wilderness Act excluded the Sandy Butte area from wilderness designation. A special-use permit was issued to Methow Recreation Inc. in July 1986. Management direction for the northern spotted owl called for the creation of Category III Habitat Conservation Areas (HCAs) around all owl pairs identified on the Okanogan National Forest during the 5 years prior to 1990. This direction established eight category III HCAs in the forest, including one on Sandy Butte that includes the entire Early Winters permit area. The Forest Service proposed eliminating the Sandy Butte HCA and substituting it with one at Foggy Dew. In May 1992, the R. D. Merrill Company of Seattle began foreclosure proceedings because loans made to Early Winters Associates were in default. In August 1992, the R. D. Merrill Company obtained the 1200-acre land base associated with the proposed Early Winters Resort, the stock of Methow Recreation Inc. (the entity that held the permit issued by the Forest Service in 1986), and other assets of Early Winters Associates at a foreclosure auction. Harry Hosey, president of Early Winters Associates, has blamed the Forest Service for Early Winter's inability to make loan payments. He claimed that the Forest Service designation of Sandy Butte, the site of the proposed ski area, as a habitat conservation area for northern spotted owls was based on suspect survey data collected in 1988 and that this designation stopped him from being able to attract additional investors. Trying to develop a major alpine ski area in a national forest is a totally different task from the one it was in the 1960s, before NEPA and the National Forest Management Act (NFMA).

SPECIAL CLASSIFICATIONS

The National Forest System contains 42 legislatively established special recreation areas totaling more than 7 million acres: 17 national recreation areas, six national scenic areas, four national monuments, and 15 other areas. Two areas were added in FY92: Springer Mountain National Recreation Area and Coosa Bald National Scenic Area. The legislative basis and policy for these specially designated areas were discussed in Chapter 8.

"National recreation areas," as mentioned in Chapters 3 and 8, have outstanding combinations of outdoor recreation opportunities, aesthetic attractions, and proximity to potential users. They may have cultural, historical, archaeological, pastoral, wilderness, scientific, wildlife, and other values contributing to public enjoyment. Table 9.21 identifies our national recreation areas, which occupy 2.4 million acres of the National Forest System. Over half of this acreage is in Idaho and California. The largest national recreation area—the Sawtooth—covers 729,322 acres and parts of three different national forests in Idaho. The smallest is the 6600-acre Pine Ridge National Recreation Area in Nebraska National Forest. Some of the national recreation areas in the east are quite large, among them Mount Rogers (Virginia) and Spruce Knob–Seneca Rock (W. Virginia).

"National monuments" are areas of unique ecological, geological, historical, prehistoric, cultural, or scientific interests. Table 9.22 identifies the two national monuments in Alaska and Table 9.23 identifies the two national volcanic monuments. The 80,000-acre Mount St. Helens National Volcanic Monument in Washington's Gifford Pinchot National Forest has become a major recreational attraction. The landscape in this area was drastically changed by the eruption of Mt. St. Helens in 1980. Expansive vistas are offered by the scenic road that comes close to the north slope of Mt. St. Helens above the east side of Spirit Lake (Figure 9.16). These expansive, scenic views are the result of the obliteration of the forest by the explosive force of the 1980 eruption. "National scenic-research areas" are areas that contain outstanding scenic values for research, scientific, and recreational purposes. The 6619-acre Cascade Head National Scenic-Research Area is located in Oregon on the Siuslaw National Forest.

Four other classifications of National Forest System lands have recreational value. Two of these are "national game refuge" and "national wildlife preserve." Table 9.24 identifies these areas. Half of the 1.2 million acres classified in these categories is occupied by just one unit—the 613,000-acre Grand Canyon Preserve in Arizona's Kaibab National Forest. Most of the rest of these areas are in the eastern half of the United States. Also classified is one "national historic area," the 6540-acre Cradle of Forestry National Historical Area in the Pisgah National Forest in North Carolina. There is only one remaining "primitive area" in the National Forest System, the Blue Range (173,762 acres) in the Apache National Forest in Arizona. Many of the former primitive areas in national forests that have been around since the 1930s have been added to the National Wilderness Preservation System. The 1964 Wilderness Act designated the Forest Service primitive areas as the "study areas" to be reviewed for possible inclusion in the Wilderness System.

Table 9.21   National Forest System: National Recreation Areas by State—1992

State
  Recreation Area
    National Forest
	NFS Acreage	Other Acreage	Total Acreage

California			
Smith River			
Six Rivers NF	305,169	26,060	331,229
Whiskeytown-Shasta-Trinity			
Shasta NF	141,165	19,642	160,807
Trinity NF	35,202	7,578	42,780
State total	481,536	53,280	534,816
Colorado			
Arapaho			
Arapaho NF	30,690	4,241	34,931
State total	30,690	4,241	34,931
Georgia			
Springer Mountain*			
Chattahoochee NF	23,166	164	23,330
State total	23,166	164	23,330
Idaho			
Hells Canyon			
Nez Perce NF	103,660	440	104,100
Payette NF	29,211	0	29,211
Wallowa NF*	3,208	2,346	5,554
Sawtooth			
Boise NF	155,984	0	155,984
Challis NF	253,863	8,899	262,762
Sawtooth NF*	319,475	17,798	337,273
State total	865,401	29,483	894,884
Michigan			
Grand Island			
Hiawatha NF	12,957	0	12,957
State total	12,957	0	12,957
Montana			
Rattlesnake			
Lolo NF	59,119	1,881	61,000
State total	59,119	1,881	61,000
Nebraska			
Pine Ridge			
Nebraska NF	6,600	0	6,600
State total	6,600	0	6,600
Oklahoma			
Winding Stair Mountain			
Ouachita NF*	25,890	555	26,445
State total	25,890	555	26,445
Oregon			
Hells Canyon			
Wallowa NF*	355,109	0	355,109
Whitman NF	45,460	1,902	47,362
Oregon Dunes			
Siuslaw NF	25,698	5,868	31,566
State total	426,267	7,770	434,037
Pennsylvania			
Allegheny			
Allegheny NF	23,063	0	23,063
State total	23,063	0	23,063

Table 9.21 (continued)

State Recreation Area National Forest	NFS Acreage	Other Acreage	Total Acreage
Utah			
Flaming Gorge			
Ashley NF*	94,308	2,105	96,413
State total	94,308	2,105	96,413
Vermont			
White Rocks			
Green Mountain NF	36,400	0	36,400
State total	36,400	0	36,400
Virginia			
Mount Rogers			
Jefferson NF	114,071	40,745	154,816
State total	114,071	40.745	154,816
Washington			
Mount Baker			
Mt. Baker NF	8,473	0	8,473
State total	8,473	0	8,473
West Virginia			
Spruce Knob-Seneca Rocks			
Monogahela NF	56,968	43,032	100,000
State total	56,968	43,032	100,000
Wyoming			
Flaming Gorge			
Ashley NF*	95,517	9,184	104,701
State total	95,517	9,184	104,701
Grand total	2,360,426	192,440	2,552,866

*Unit is in 2 or more states.
Source: Forest Service. *Land Areas of the National Forest System as of Sept. 30, 1992,* February, 1993.

WILDERNESS

Recreation on lands classified as wilderness under the 1964 Wilderness Act accounted for 13.3 million recreation visitor days in FY92. Chapter 7 detailed how the National Wilderness Preservation System had its beginnings in 1924 in New Mexico's Gila National Forest, with the establishment of *de facto* wilderness by Forest Service administrative policy. The passage of the 1964 Wilderness Act established a *de jure* Wilderness System. It was pointed out in Chapter 7 that all of this initial system was on National Forest System lands. The Forest Service manages 395 units of the National Wilderness Preservation System in 36 states. This includes 34 million acres or approximately 18 percent of the National Forest System. Forest Service–managed wilderness is 74 percent of the National Wilderness Preservation System in the lower 49 states, and 36 percent of the entire system including Alaskan wilderness. In 1988, 76 percent of the total use of the National Wilderness Preservation System occurred in national forest wilderness areas. Among the three other federal land-managing agencies with land classified as part of the National Wilderness Preservation System,

Table 9.22   National Forest System: National Monument Areas by State—1992

State National Monument National Forest	NFS Acreage	Other Acreage	Total Acreage
Alaska Admiralty Island			
Tongass NF	955,810	32,161	987,971
Misty Fiords			
Tongass NF	2,293,428	1,311	2,294,739
State total	3,249,238	33,472	3,282,710
Grand Total	3,249,238	33,472	3,282,710

Source: Forest Service. *Land Areas of the National Forest System as of Sept. 30, 1992,* February, 1993.

Table 9.23   National Forest System: National Volcanic Monument Areas by State—1992

State Volcanic Monument National Forest	NFS Acreage	Other Acreage	Total Acreage
Oregon Newbery*			
Deschutes NF	54,822	678	55,500
State total	54,822	678	55,500
Washington Mount St. Helens*			
Gifford Pinchot NF	80,498	30,530	111,028
State total	80,498	30,530	111,028
Grand Total	135,320	31,208	166,528

*Acreage estimated pending final map compilation.
Source: Forest Service. *Land Areas of the National Forest System as of Sept. 30, 1992,* February, 1993.

Figure 9.16   View of the devastation from the 1980 eruption of Mt. St. Helens in Gifford Pinchot National Forest as seen from Windy Ridge looking west over Spirit Lake (here filled with dead trees). Spirit Lake was formerly a very popular recreation area.

the following percentages of use occurred: National Park Service, 14 percent; Fish and Wildlife Service, 5 percent; and Bureau of Land Management, 5 percent (Cordell et al., 1989, 39). Table 9.25 identifies the acreage by state in the National Wilderness Preservation System in the National Forest System. The leading states are Alaska (5.7 million acres), California (4.3 million acres), Idaho (4.0 million acres), Montana (3.4 million acres), and Wyoming (3.1 million acres). The National Wilderness Preservation System will be covered in greater detail in Chapter 14.

On December 11, 1991, the Chattahoochee Forest Protection Act was passed and signed into law by President Bush, adding 25,480 National Forest System acres in Georgia to the National Wilderness Preservation System. On June 19, 1992, the Pres-

Table 9.24   National Forest System: National Game Refuges and Wildlife Preserves by State—1992

State	National Game Refuge or Wildlife Preserve	Unit Name		NFS Acreage
Arizona	Grand Canyon Preserve	Kaibab NF		612,736
			Total	612,736
Arkansas	Ouachita #1 (Pigeon Creek)	Ouachita NF*		8,440
	Ouachita #2 (Oak Mountain)	Ouachita NF*		8,500
	Ouachita #4 (Caney Creek)	Ouachita NF*		8,300
	Ozark #2 (Barkshead)	Ozark NF		5,927
	Ozark #5 (Black Mountain)	Ozark NF		19,074
	Ozark #4 (Haw Creek)	Ozark NF		4,108
	Ozark #1 (Livingston)	Ozark NF		9,122
	Ozark #3 (Moccasin)	Ozark NF		3,932
	Ouachita Wildlife Preserve	Ouachita NF*		78,000
			Total	145,403
California	Tahquitz Game Preserve	San Bernardino NF		27,573
			Total	27,573
Florida	Ocala National Game Refuge	Ocala NF		79,735
			Total	79,735
Georgia	Noontootly Game Preserve	Chattahoochee NF		24,670
			Total	24,760
Louisiana	Red Dirt Wildlife Preserve	Kisatchie NF		40,112
	Catahoula Wildlife Preserve	Kisatchie NF		36,117
			Total	76,229
North Carolina	Pisgah National Game Refuge	Pisgah NF		97,408
			Total	97,408
South Carolina	Francis Marion Preserve	Francis Marion NF		50,600
			Total	50,600
South Dakota	Norbeck Wildlife Preserve	Black Hills NF*		33,656
			Total	33,656
Tennessee	Cherokee Game Refuge #1	Cherokee NF*		10,900
			Total	10,900
Virginia	Big Levels Game Refuge	George Washington NF*		31,725
			Total	31,725
Wyoming	Sheep Mountain Game Refuge	Medicine Bow NF		28,318
			Total	28,318
Grand Total				1,218,953

*Unit is in two or more states.
Source: Forest Service. *Land Areas of the National Forest System as of Sept. 30, 1992,* February, 1993.

Table 9.25   National Forest System: National Wilderness Areas Summary—1992

State	NFS Acreage	Other Acreage	Total Acreage
Alaska	5,753,106	35,531	5,788,637
California	4,302,461	60,141	4,362,602
Idaho	3,961,501	8,256	3,969,757
Montana	3,371,770	3,929	3,375,699
Wyoming	3,080,358	689	3,081,047
Colorado	2,586,835	13,707	2,600,542
Washington	2,575,500	13,808	2,589,308
Oregon	2,079,854	15,111	2,094,965
New Mexico	1,388,063	2,980	1,391,043
Arizona	1,344,970	132	1,345,102
Minnesota	803,050	283,904	1,086,954
Nevada	786,067	160	786,227
Utah	774,328	192	774,520
Arkansas	116,560	377	116,937
Georgia	113,455	404	113,859
North Carolina	103,262	592	103,854
New Hampshire	102,932	0	102,932
Michigan	91,891	1,594	93,485
Virginia	87,453	205	87,658
West Virginia	80,852	0	80,852
Florida	74,495	4	74,499
Tennessee	66,305	40	66,345
Missouri	63,198	429	63,627
Vermont	59,421	177	59,598
Wisconsin	42,294	2,153	44,447
Texas	34,712	1,638	36,350
Alabama	33,151	80	33,231
Illinois	25,549	717	26,266
Kentucky	16,415	1,022	17,437
South Carolina	16,847	0	16,847
Oklahoma	14,151	1,817	15,968
Indiana	12,935	18	12,953
Maine	12,000	0	12,000
South Dakota	9,826	0	9,826
Pennsylvania	8,938	0	8,938
Louisiana	8,679	0	8,679
Nebraska	7,794	0	7,794
Mississippi	6,046	0	6,046
Grand Total	34,017,024	449,807	34,466,831

Source: Forest Service. *Land Areas of the National Forest System as of Sept. 30, 1992*, February, 1993.

ident signed the Los Padres Condor Range and River Protection Act, adding another 400,450 National Forest System acres to the Wilderness System. The Forest Service was actively involved in congressional consideration of additional wilderness in North Carolina, Montana, and Colorado, but legislation designating more wilderness in these three states failed to pass the 102nd Congress.

The 103rd Congress passed the *Colorado Wilderness Act of 1993*. This was the first wilderness legislation signed by President Bill Clinton. It provided for eight new wilderness areas that totaled 405,360 acres and eight additions that totaled 141,750 acres on Colorado national forests. It also renamed the Big Blue Wilderness Area, the Uncompaghre Wilderness Area; this wilderness area was expanded by 815 acres on

National Forest land and also included 3390 acres of BLM-administered land. The act also established the Powderhorn Wilderness Area on BLM-administered land. As management regimes are being further refined for the wilderness administered by the Forest Service, the role of wilderness is being recognized as a key component of the ecosystem of which each wilderness is a part.

The Forest Service exchanged 38,574 acres of the National Forest System for 69,102 acres in nonfederal land in FY92. Much of the nonfederal land acquired through these land exchanges lies within classified wilderness areas, national recreation areas, wild and scenic rivers corridors, national trails, and other congressionally designated areas. These exchanges reduced National Forest property boundary lines by 773 miles, saving approximately $4.5 million in future landline location costs— more than half of the $8.4 million cost of the exchanges. Additional savings will also be realized from fewer trespass and rights-of-way cases and special-use permits.

References

Clawson, Marion, and Carlton Van Doren, *Statistics on Outdoor Recreation*. Washington, D.C.: Resources of the Future, 1984.

Cordell, H. Ken, John C. Bergstrom, Lawrence A. Hartman, and Donald B. K. English. *An Analysis of the Outdoor Recreation and Wilderness Situation in the United States: 1989– 2040. A Technical Document Supporting the 1989 USDA Forest Service RPA Assessment*, General Technical Report RM-189. Rocky Mountain Forest and Range Experiment Station, Forest Service, April, 1990.

Forest Service, *1992 Annual Report of the Forest Service*, February 1993.

Frome, Michael. *The Forest Service-2nd Ed.* Boulder, Colorado: Westview Press, 1984.

## CHAPTER 10

National Forest System: Case Studies

A clear stream, a long horizon, a forest wilderness and open sky—these are man's most ancient possessions. In a modern society, they are his most priceless.

Lyndon B. Johnson

This fourth and final chapter on the Forest Service and its role in providing recreation in the National Forest System will present 12 detailed case studies of individual national forests that are representative of the system. Geographic balance is well represented in their selection. As was done for the National Park System, special attention will be paid to Alaska in this chapter. Alaska only has two National Forests, the *Tongass* and the *Chugach,* but both are massive, being the two largest in the system. The impact of the Alaska National Interest Lands Conservation Act (ANILCA) on the National Forest System in Alaska will be covered here. Then, 10 National Forests and three national grasslands that are representative of the system in the lower 49 states will be discussed. The *White Mountain National Forest* (New Hampshire and Maine) will be used to represent the northeastern forests. The White Mountain is a very popular national forest and heavily used by the urbanites of the Northeast. The Chattahoochee and Oconee National Forests (Georgia) have been selected to represent the southeastern United States; because they are jointly administered, they will be considered as a single unit for case-study purposes. The Chattahoochee-Oconee is closely located to and an important recreational resource for the Atlanta urban area. Two greatly different national forests—the *Shawnee* (Illinois) and *Nebraska-Samuel R. McKelvie* (Nebraska)—have been selected to represent the heartland of the country. (As with the Chattahoochee-Oconee, the Nebraska and the Samuel R. McKelvie are separate forests but jointly administered and treated in a single case study.) The Shawnee in extreme southern Illinois presents a contrast to its surroundings. The Nebraska–Samuel R. McKelvie unit is probably the most unusual location of all the national forests and is the only human-made national forest. The forest supervisor for the Nebraska National Forest, Mary Peterson, also has administrative responsibility for three national grasslands: the *Oglala* (Nebraska), the *Buffalo Gap* (S. Dakota), and the *Fort Pierre* (S. Dakota). The topic of national grasslands and examples of recreational use on these three will serve as case studies. The *Superior National Forest*

(Minnesota) has been selected to represent the northern lake country of the United States. The Superior has the most heavily used unit of the National Wilderness Preservation System, the Boundary Waters Canoe Area.

Two forests have been selected to represent the Rocky Mountains, one in the northern part of the range and the other in the south. The *Flathead National Forest* (Montana) represents the Northern Rocky Mountains, and the *Lincoln National Forest* (N. Mexico) represents the Southern Rocky Mountains. The Flathead, located immediately south and west of Glacier National Park is a big forest; its use is quite light compared with Glacier. The Lincoln National Forest presents a contrast to the surrounding desert and steppe lands. The *Dixie National Forest* (Utah) has been selected to represent the Intermountain region, which lies between the Rocky Mountains and the Sierra Nevada and Cascade Range. The Dixie is one of the most heavily used national forests, and this use is based in part on its proximity to several very popular national parks in southern Utah and to the Grand Canyon National Park in northern Arizona. The *Gifford Pinchot National Forest* (Washington) was chosen from among the forests of the Pacific Northwest region. It is the location of a newly created National Volcanic Monument, which was established after Mt. St. Helens erupted in May 1980—it has become a major tourist attraction. Finally, the *Inyo National Forest* (California and Nevada) was chosen to represent the Pacific Southwest region. Like the Dixie, it is also one of the most heavily used national forests, despite being several hundred miles from major California population centers. The Inyo is a national forest in which recreation is the major resource. This more detailed coverage of a dozen carefully selected national forests and three national grasslands will contribute to a better understanding of the entire National Forest System.

ALASKA

In Alaska, the Forest Service administers the nation's two largest national forests, the Tongass and the Chugach. One of the first areas, in what is now the National Forest System, to be withdrawn was the Afognak Forest and Fish Culture Reserve, proclaimed by President Harrison on December 24, 1892 and located on Afognak Island, which is located near Kodiak Island. Alaska's first forest reserve came about through concerns for salmon conservation. Afognak's major significance is that it was the first forest reserve to be created in Alaska and the only one to be created for fisheries purposes (Rakestraw, 1981, 10). On July 23, 1907, portions of land totaling 4,960,000 acres bordering Prince William Sound on the west and north and extending east to the Copper River Delta, inland to the Chugach Mountains, and south to the southern tip of Montague Island, were the first areas to be proclaimed Chugach National Forest (Rakestraw, 1981, 44). In 1908, the Afognak Reserve was added to this withdrawal. On August 20, 1902, President Theodore Roosevelt proclaimed the Alexander Archipelago Forest Reserve, which would later become part of the Tongass National Forest. On September 10, 1907, despite objections to the creation of any new national forests in Alaska by Richard A. Ballinger, who was the commissioner of the General Land Office, the Tongass National Forest was proclaimed. On July 1, 1908, the Alexander

Archipelago and the Tongass were consolidated into a single National Forest, the Tongass, with a total area of 6,756,362 acres (Rakestraw, 1981, 23). "In 1909 the Forest Service made recommendations for withdrawal of the remaining islands, the mainland to the south of Skagway to Icy Strait, and the area from Dry Bay to the south shore of Yakutat Bay. On February 16, 1909, the second proclamation relating to the Tongass added 8,724,000 acres to its area" (Rakestraw, 1981, 24). It was Giffort Pinchot's role in advocating creation of national forests in Alaska that created the controversy with Richard Ballinger that led to his firing as chief of the Forest Service in 1910 by President Taft.

The role of the Alaska Statehood Act (1958), the Alaska Native Claims Settlement Act (ANCSA, 1971), and the Alaska National Interest Lands Conservation Act (ANILCA, 1980) in reallocating landownership and land management roles in Alaska has already been detailed in Chapter 4. Selections of land from both the Tongass and Chugach National Forests by the state of Alaska and by native corporations occurred as a result of the first two acts. The Alaska National Interest Lands Conservation Act (ANILCA) provided for extensive additions to the Chugach National Forest of lands previously in the public domain and managed by the Bureau of Land Management (BLM). These additions totaled 2,156,000 million acres and include the Nellie Juan area east of Seward, the College Fiord extension, the Copper/Rude Rivers addition, and a small extension at Controller Bay. The Nellie Juan addition, in western Prince William Sound, takes in the eastern portion of the Resurrection Peninsula along the coast to Puget Bay. The portion of the Sargent Icefield previously not part of the national forest, and Nellie Juan Lake and Nellie Juan River drainage were added to the Chugach National Forest. The College Fiord addition in northwestern Prince William Sound takes in all of the College Fiord drainage and Barry Glacier. The addition extends north to include Mt. Marcus Baker, at 13,176 feet the tallest peak in the Chugach Range. All of Harvard and Columbia Glaciers were also added to the Forest. Congress directed that this area be part of a 2-million-acre study unit known as The Nellie Juan-College Fiord Wilderness Study Unit and mandated 3 years for the study. As of December 1994, no areas within the Chugach National Forest had been added to the National Wilderness Preservation System. The Copper/Rude Rivers addition extended the boundary of the forest north and east of Cordova. The new boundary follows the Copper River to its confluence with the Wernicke River and then includes the Wernicke drainage and Wernicke Glacier. The addition's eastern boundary runs south from Wernicke Glacier to Martin River Glacier and includes Miles Glacier. The Copper/Rude area is to be managed for conservation of fish and wildlife and their habitat. A small addition at Controller Bay is a triangle-shaped area at the outlet of the Bering River north of Kayak Island.

ANILCA created nearly 5.5 million acres of designated wilderness within the nation's largest national forest, the 16.7-million-acre Tongass National Forest in southeastern Alaska. It also added three new areas to the forest: the Juneau Icefield, Kates Needle, and parts of the Brabazon Range. These additions totaled over 1 million acres. As part of this wilderness designation, two new national monuments were created, to be managed primarily as wilderness by the Forest Service: Admiralty Island National Monument and Misty Fiords National Monument. The 5.5 million acres of wilderness in the Tongass National Forest include 14 areas ranging in size from Maurelle Islands' 4937 acres to Misty Fiords 2,142,243 acres. The Kootznoowoo

Wilderness occupies almost all of Admiralty Island National Monument. ANILCA made special provisions in Alaska for uses that are prohibited in wilderness in the lower 49 states, due to the great distances and rugged terrain in Alaska. Mechanized vehicles, such as airplanes and motorboats, may be used to gain access to and within wilderness areas where such use is traditional (Figure 10.1). Also, because of the climate, preexisting shelter cabins were allowed to remain, and provisions were made for building other cabins for public safety. Fishing, hunting, and trapping are allowed to continue as on other national forest land, subject to state fish-and-game regulations. Subsistence use, including sport fishing and hunting, is given special attention on all national forest land including wilderness. Table 10.1 summarizes the allowable land uses in Alaskan national forests, before and after the enactment of ANILCA.

Chugach National Forest

The 5,469,226-acre Chugach National Forest is the second largest in the National Forest System. The gross acreage within its boundaries is 6,898,770 acres; 79.3 percent of this land is National Forest System land. There have been several major and minor boundary adjustments, and since its establishment in 1907 it has ranged in size from 11,360,000 acres to the present 5.47 million acres. It extends from Cape Suckling in the east to Seward and Afognak Island in the west and includes many of the islands and much of the land bordering Prince William Sound and the northeastern part of the Kenai Peninsula. The remaining acreage on Afognak Island that is national forest land is very small, a mere shadow of its former extent on the island. Along the coast, fingers of the sea probe into the mountains, forming secluded bays. The principal mountain range is the Chugach Range, with peaks up to 13,000 feet (Mt. Marcus Baker = 13,176 ft.). Glaciers are numerous, and there is little level land except on the

Figure 10.1 The Alaska National Interest Lands Conservation Act provided for mechanized vehicle access to wilderness areas in the Tongass National Forest. Shown is a float plane at Klackas Inlet in the Prince of Wales Wilderness. (Forest Service photo)

Table 10.1   National Forests in Alaska, Allowable Land Uses—1965 and 1985

| | | 1985 | |
	1965	Nonwilderness	Wilderness[a]
Total acreage	21 million acres	23 million	
		17.4 million	5.6 million
Sport fishing	All open	All open	All open
Sport hunting	All open	All open	All open
Subsistence hunting and fishing	All open	All open	All open
New mining claims	All open	Open	Closed
New petroleum leasing[b]	All potentially open	All potentially open	Closed
Settlement	All closed	Closed	Closed
Commercial timber harvest[c]	All open	15 million open[c]	Closed[c]
Recreation	All open	All open	All open
Motor access[d]	All open	All open	All open

[a]Includes areas within forests designated as monuments.
[b]National forest lands can be opened to petroleum leasing, but there are no lands currently under petroleum lease in either the Tongass or the Chugach National Forest.
[c]Wilderness areas of the national forests are closed to commercial timber harvest. Also closed are about 2.6 million acres in the Tongass National Forest under a special designation that emphasizes uses other than logging.
[d]Generally, motor vehicles can use any part of the national forests, including wilderness areas. The Alaska lands act specifically allows reasonable access through wilderness areas for inholders and for subsistence and recreational users, with traditional means of access-including planes, snow machines, and motorboats. Restrictions on use of off-road vehicles and other vehicles are in effect in certain areas.
Source: Linda Leask, "Changing Ownership and Management of Alaska Lands," Alaska Review of Social and Economic Conditions, 22(2):October 30, 1985.

narrow coastal plain and the floodplains of glaciers. The climate includes excessive rain in the summer and heavy snow in the winter. Except for the Kenai Peninsula, much of the Chugach National Forest is roadless, and most travel is by boat or plane. The forest supervisor is located in Anchorage, and the forest is divided into three ranger districts: (1) the Cordova Ranger District in the central and eastern area, with its office at Cordova; (2) the Glacier Ranger District, office at Girdwood, on Turnagain Arm; and (3) the Seward Ranger District, office at Seward.

The Chugach National Forest received 1,866,600 recreation visitor days (RVDs) of use in 1992, equal to 16,272,000 million recreation visits. This ranks the Chugach 56th in terms of recreation visitor days among the national forests. The Chugach is one of the least intensively used of national forests, having an intensity of use of 2.93 acres/RVD. None of the use occurred in wilderness, since there are no designated wilderness areas on the Forest. The category "mechanized travel and viewing scenery" accounted for 63 percent of the RVDs measured. The leading subcategories of use within the main category are viewing scenery (43 percent); automobile travel (35 percent); and tour boat, ship, and ferry (10 percent). The categories "camping, picnicking, and swimming" and "hiking, horseback riding, and water travel" each account for about another 8 percent of the RVD total. Camping is the leading subcategory in the first category, with 90 percent of the use; hiking is 75 percent, and canoeing 17 percent of the use in the second category. "Winter sports" and "fishing" each account for about 5 percent of the total use, with downhill skiing comprising two-thirds of the former category and cold-water fishing 86 percent of the latter category. "Hunting" (60 percent big-game) accounted for only 2 percent of the RVD total. "Resorts, cabins, and organization camps" comprised another 3 percent of the

RVD total, with most of this use equally distributed between recreational cabin use and general resort and commercial public service. Six percent of the recreational use in 1992 was classified "other recreational activities," with 40 percent of this in the subcategory "viewing interpretive exhibits" and about another 15 percent each in "unguided walking" and "viewing interpretive signs." "Nonconsumptive fish and wildlife use" accounted for a very low 0.3 percent of the total recreational use.

In 1984, when the Forest had 5,936,000 acres, the *Chugach National Forest Land and Resource Management Plan* (hereafter referred to as "the *Plan*") identified the following acreages in different land classifications: water, 66,768 acres; nonforest land, 4,764,376 acres; nonproductive (not capable) forest land, 757,367 acres; and productive (capable) forest land, 347,489 acres. *Forest land* is defined as land at least 10 percent occupied by forest trees of any size, or formerly having had such tree cover, and not currently developed for nonforest use. *Nonproductive forest land* is defined as forest land not capable of growing industrial crops of wood, at least at the minimum biological growth potential established in the RPA program of the regional guide.

The Chugach National Forest lies at the doorstep of Anchorage, Alaska's major city with a 1990 population of 226,338. It is the major entry point for nonresident visitors. A wide variety of recreational opportunities are available. Due to access and abundance of fish and wildlife, most recreational use occurs in a relatively small portion of the forest on the Kenai Peninsula. Tourism is projected to increase for the state as a whole, and this increase will also affect other areas of the forest. The *Plan* projects that the gap between developed and dispersed recreation use will narrow in the future. In 1985, developed recreation accounted for 37 percent of the RVDs, which is expected to increase to 48 percent in the period 2021–2030. Developed recreation includes campgrounds, cabins, interpretive services, and winter sports areas. The Portage Glacier Recreation Area and the Alyeska Ski Area are important recreational attractions in the forest. The 8600-acre Portage Glacier Recreation Area is located 5.5 miles from milepost 79 of the Seward-Anchorage Highway (AK 1). A clear view may be had across Portage Lake of chunks of glacial ice as much as 60 feet thick calving off Portage Glacier, which is 3 miles distant. A 1-hour narrated boat cruise may be taken from the Visitor Center across Portage Lake for a close-up view of this spectacular sight. The Begich-Boggs Visitor Center contains an observatory, orientation exhibit, and exhibit hall. This visitor center is the most-visited attraction in Alaska. There are campgrounds in the area. The Alyeska Resort and Ski Area is 40 miles south of Anchorage on AK 1. Alaska's major alpine ski area has three double chairs and two high-speed quad chairs. In addition to 15 road-accessible campgrounds, the Forest Service operates 40 cabins in remote areas near lakes, bays, and streams. Accessible by trail, boat, or float plane, the cabins are equipped with bunks, furniture, wood or oil stoves, and outhouses but not with electricity. Current demand is not being met in two important areas: the cabin system and some campgrounds. Cabins must be reserved months ahead of time. During salmon runs, some campgrounds fill to capacity, and visitors must be turned away. Kenai Lake is a popular camping site.

There is no shortage of dispersed recreation opportunities in the Chugach National Forest. Dispersed recreation includes driving, hiking, boating, cross-country skiing, primitive camping, and hunting and fishing. Water-oriented use and tourism in Prince William Sound are an important element in the dispersed recreation spectrum. This area was the site of the March 24, 1989 *Exxon Valdez* oil-spill disaster. This

is the worst oil spill in the United States so far, with 10.8 million gallons of crude oil released into the water of Prince William Sound. The Chugach is a paradise for hunters and fishermen. Hunters travel great distances to pursue Kenai moose, Dall sheep, brown and black bear, mountain goat, and elk. King salmon are plentiful in the fall and silver salmon in the summer, around Valdez and Cordova; halibut and red snapper fishing here is also excellent. Dolly Varden, rainbow, and cutthroat trout are found in most streams. The 700,000-acre Copper River Delta Wildlife Management Area just east of Cordova is a refuge for trumpeter swans, Canada geese, and other waterfowl.

The Chugach National Forest is an outstanding scenic and visual resource. Combinations of vegetation patterns, rugged mountains, fresh and salt water, glaciers and snowfields create a landscape of high scenic value. Three character types can be found within the forest, each with its own distinct combination of these elements. The Kenai Peninsula is the most viewed in the forest and perhaps exhibits the most visual variety of any national forest land in Alaska. A combination of U-shaped valleys, conifer and deciduous vegetation, glaciers and snowfields, and numerous rivers and lakes, create a landscape high in diversity and visual interest. The Anchorage to Seward Highway (AK 1) offers 127 miles of scenic driving near saltwater bays, mountains, glaciers, and valleys filled with wildlife. Prince William Sound exhibits many of the same qualities. A strong saltwater orientation with rugged ice-covered mountains as a backdrop creates a landscape of vast proportions and high contrast. The Copper River Delta area, extending from Cordova to the eastern forest boundary, is noted for its wildlife but is also rich in scenic qualities. This vast marshland is traversed with meandering streams and backed by rugged mountains.

While the maximum supply for dispersed recreation greatly exceeds the potential demand, the potential for developed recreation is projected to increase almost twice as rapidly as for dispersed recreation. Demand for fishing opportunities, particularly salmon fishing on the Kenai Peninsula, exceeds the supply. This same problem exists in accessible areas of Prince William Sound, but not to the same extent. Demand for water-oriented recreational activities is growing at a faster rate than for other activities, especially in saltwater areas and whitewater boating (Figure 10.2). Recreation cabins on the Kenai Peninsula are not meeting existing demand, and cabin use in Prince William Sound is near the saturation level. The Russian River campground does not meet existing demand during peak season. Other campgrounds along the Sterling Highway also fill to capacity early in the weekend when the Russian River red salmon run is in progress. Intermediate and beginner ski slopes are heavily used, and the demand for this type of skiing is not being met.

For purposes of forest planning, the land base of the Chugach National Forest is stratified at three levels of hierarchy. *Level I* areas are the most general and consist of the three major, contiguous geographic areas of the Forest. The Kenai Peninsula Area consists of steep glaciated mountains and valleys in which the use and management activities are primarily a result of the intensive use related to the road corridors in the major valleys. The Prince William Sound Area consists of coastal shorelines of the mainland and islands in which use and management activities are primarily related to the surrounding waterways. This is the area that suffered the most degradation after the *Exxon Valdez* oil spill in 1989. The Copper River Area includes a large delta, backed by glaciers and steep glaciated mountains, in which the use and man-

Figure 10.2 Sea kayaking along the rugged coast of the protected bays of the Chugach National Forest is a popular activity. (Forest Service photo)

agement activities are primarily related to the limited overall access and the large waterfowl populations. *Level II* consists of 9 *Management Areas*. These are related to the pattern and intensity of use and sensitivity to management conflicts. They are not contiguous and do not cross Level I boundaries. The Kenai Peninsula and Prince William Sound each have four Level II (Management) Areas. The Copper River Area has only one area in Level II, and it is identical to the Level I area. The management areas in the Kenai Peninsula (and their numbers) are Road Corridor (1), East Side (2), Resurrection Pass (3), and Crescent Lake (4). In the Prince William Sound area the management areas (and their numbers) are Nellie Juan (5), College Fiord (6), Gravina (7), and Big Islands (8). The Level I Copper River Area is also management area 9. The *Level III* areas represent further subdivision of the Level II areas into 22 noncontiguous *analysis areas*, which were arrived at by dividing the management areas according to four groups of associated landforms and vegetative types that express the capability of the land in relation to various management activities. These groups are the *alpine* (includes snow fields and glaciers), *timbered slopeside, coastal,* and *depositional valleys.*

The management areas on the Kenai Peninsula are Road Corridor, Resurrection Pass, Crescent Lake, and East Side. The Road Corridor area is generally in the valley bottoms and includes intensive recreational use, important visual sensitivity, major wildlife management programs and populations of moose, important timber stands and programs, intensively used sport fisheries, and placer mining activities. The Resurrection Pass area includes the activities related to the high-use Resurrection Pass trail system and includes cabins, wildlife management programs, and populations of moose, caribou, bear, and sheep. The Crescent Lake area includes important recreational trail systems and cabins, bear, sheep, and moose. The East Side area includes recreational trails, primitive fly-in cabins, bear, sheep, and moose. There are five management areas in Prince William Sound. The College Fiord area is accessible by boat

from Valdez and Whittier, and has the highest relative amount of boat-related activity and includes part of the Alaska Marine Highway System, major fisheries, many important commercial timber areas, and black bear. The Nellie Juan area includes major boat-related recreational activities, a ferry route, major fisheries, many important commercial timber areas, and some black bear and deer. The Gravina area includes the boat access from Valdez and some of the boat-related recreational activities adjacent to Forest Service land, a ferry route, some fisheries, important commercial timber areas, sheep, goat, and bear. The Big Island area (Montague, Hinchinbrook, and Hawkins Islands) includes a few major fisheries and deer-related recreational activities, major commercial fisheries, one of the more important commercial timber areas on the Forest, and major deer and brown bear populations.

Tongass National Forest

The 16,724,169-acre Tongass National Forest is the largest unit in the National Forest System. The gross area within its boundaries is 17,446,595 acres, 95.9 percent of which is national forest land. Its size has diminished slightly in recent years as the state of Alaska and Alaska natives have selected parcels allowed them by the Alaska Statehood Act and ANCSA. The forest is located in Southeast Alaska, includes part of the Alexander Archipelago, and occupies about 7 percent of the state's area. The Tongass extends from Dixon Entrance in the south to Yakutat in the north, and is bordered on the easy by Canada and on the west by the Gulf of Alaska. It extends 500 miles north to south and approximately 120 miles east to west at its widest point. The Tongass includes a narrow mainland strip of steep, rugged mountains and icefields, and over 1000 offshore islands. Together, the islands and mainland equal nearly 11,000 miles of meandering shoreline, with numerous bays and coves. A system of seaways separates the many islands and provides a protected waterway called the *Inside Passage*. Federal lands comprise about 95 percent of Southeast Alaska, with about 80 percent in the Tongass National Forest (and most of the rest in Glacier Bay National Park and Preserve). The remaining land is held in state, native, and private ownerships.

Most of the area of the Tongass National Forest is wild and undeveloped. About 65,000 people inhabit Southeast Alaska, most living in 33 communities on island or mainland coasts. Only eight of these communities have populations greater than 1000 persons, the largest being Juneau (the state capital), Ketchikan, Sitka, and Petersburg. Most of these communities are surrounded by, or adjacent to, National Forest System land. Only three towns are connected to other parts of the mainland by road: Haines and Skagway to the north, and Hyder to the south. The *Alaska Marine Highway* provides access from Bellingham, Wash., and Prince Rupert, B.C., to Ketchikan and through Southeast Alaska to as far north as Skagway and west to Sitka. It is operated by the state of Alaska. The Marine Highway serves the communities in the same way that land-based roads do elsewhere. The *State Ferry System* is widely used by tour groups and independent travelers to view the unique scenery. The economies of Southeast Alaska's communities are largely dependent on the Tongass National Forest to provide natural resources for uses such as fishing, timber harvesting, recreation, sightseeing, tourism, mining, and subsistence. Because of its immense size, the Tongass National Forest is divided into three administrative areas, each with its own

forest supervisor: the Chatham Area, with its supervisor's office at Sitka; the Stikine Area, with its supervisor's office at Petersburg; and the Ketchikan Area, with its supervisor's office in Ketchikan. There are nine ranger districts, each named after the town in which its town is located: Yakutat, Juneau, Hoonah, Sitka, Petersburg, Wrangell, Thorne Bay, Craig, and Ketchikan. There are also two national monuments, Admiralty Island and Misty Fiords, with offices in Juneau and Ketchikan. The Forest Service regional office is in Juneau.

The mainland and many of the islands of southeastern Alaska are mountainous, often rising from sea level to several thousand feet. Over 1 million years ago (and up to as recently as 15,000 years ago), glaciers covered all but the highest peaks. It is this modification by glaciers that gives Southeast Alaska's landscape its unique character of U-shaped valleys and fiords. Elevations of forested areas extend up to approximately 3000 feet in the southern section and up to 2500 feet farther north. The convoluted configuration of the coastline, the warm Japanese Current, abundant midlatitude low-pressure systems that originate in the "Aleutian Low," and the high coastal mountains are all factors in producing the abundant rainfall. The mean annual precipitation at sea level averages more than 100 inches throughout most of the area, decreasing from south to north, but ranging from 30 inches at Skagway to 220 inches at Little Port Walter. Elevation and exposure to prevailing winds play a major role in precipitation amounts received. It is estimated that as much as 400 inches per year may fall on the southern end of Baranof Island and about 260 inches a year on the Juneau Icefield. Southeast Alaska has complete cloud cover about 85 percent of the year. May through July are the drier months. Snowfall varies according to elevation and distance inland from the coast. In the southern half of the panhandle, snow accumulation in the winter below 500 feet in elevation is short-lived, but in the northern part low-elevation snowpack exists from December through March. The abundant moisture feeds the numerous streams, rivers, and lakes that dot the landscape.

The Pacific maritime influence holds daily and seasonal temperatures within a narrow range; temperatures average 32°F (high teens to low 40s) in the winter and 55–60°F (mid-40s to mid-60s) in the summer. The coastal forest of Southeast Alaska is part of the cool, temperate rain forest that extends along the Pacific Coast from northern California to Afognak Island in Alaska. Most of the forest is composed of old-growth conifers, primarily western hemlock and Sitka spruce, with a scattering of mountain hemlock, western red cedar (in the south) and Alaska yellow-cedar. The alpine zone usually lies above 2500 to 3000 feet. It occupies the area above the coastal forest and is separated from the forest by a subalpine or transition zone. The forests, shorelines, streams, and rivers provide habitat for over 300 species of birds and mammals, including both game and nongame animals such as brown and black bear, Sitka black-tailed deer, moose, wolf, mountain goat, beaver, marten, and otter. The coastline provides an ideal habitat for a large population of bald eagles, and wetlands provide nesting habitat for many waterfowl. A highly productive marine environment includes an abundance of marine mammals, halibut, herring, and shellfish. Both resident and anadromous fish are found, including all five species of Pacific salmon, as well as Dolly Varden, and other trout. Table 10.2 identifies and describes the geographic provinces of Southeast Alaska. These are seven large land areas that are distinguished by differences in ecological processes and defined by a combination of climatic and geographic features. The Forest Service has classified the land of the

Table 10.2   Southeast Alaska Geographic Provinces

Geographic Province	Description
Yakutat Forelands	Includes Glacier Bay north to Yakutat Bay. Recently uplifted beaches and active fluvial processes related to icefields, valley glaciers, and cold wet climate distinguish this region from the rest of southeastern Alaska.
Lynn Canal	The driest and one of the most continental environments in southeastern Alaska. Extreme rain shadow from the Chilkat and St. Elias Ranges allows extensive development of fire-dependent forests (lodgepole and birch) and the southern and westward extension of boreal forest and tundra plant species. Rugged, scored terrain with large vertical relief.
Coast Range	Ruggged, heavily glaciated terrain with extensive alpine and icefield environments. Productive forest land usually confined to river valleys and marine terraces. British Columbia batholith has major influence over the whole area. This province may be logically divided into two subzones, perhaps divided at the Bradfield Canal with more extensive alpine and active glaciation to the north and less extensive ice to the south.
Northern Outer Islands	Rugged, highly dissected topography in exposed, extremely wet, outer coastal environment, and extensive alpine environments with productive forested areas that are highly fragmented and usually concentrated on oversteepened slopes and on valley bottoms.
Northern Interior Islands	Includes eastern Chichagof and Admiralty Islands. Protected from full force of storms off the outer coast, but with colder climate and more rugged topography than in the Central Interior Islands province. Also, with distinctive fauna. Originally considered to be a subprovince of the Northern Outer Islands, but because of its contrast in climate and geology with the outer coast and Baranof Island, it was redefined as its own province.
Central Interior Islands	Includes Kupreanof Island lowlands and surrounding areas protected from storms off the outer coast and generally moderate in precipitation and temperature extremes. Includes several major rain-shadow areas such as northwest Kupreanof and parts of Etolin Island. Generally subdued rolling topography and extensive muskeg areas.
Southern Outer Islands	Rolling subdued topography to the north and localized rugged topography to the south. Includes many refugia, unique plant and animal populations at the northern extent of their natural range, and highly productive forests, especially on limestone and marble soils derived from ancient coral reefs.

Source: Forest Service, *Tongass Land Management Plan Revision—Part 1* (August 1991).

Tongass National Forest into the following categories: nonforested, 41.1 percent; non-productive forest, 25.0 percent; tentatively suitable productive forest land (84 percent of which is old-growth), 15.1 percent; withdrawn productive forest land, 13.5 percent; and nonsuitable productive forest land, 5.3 percent.

The Tongass National Forest received 4,020,450 RVDs in 1992, and the recreation visits were 1,003,470. This ratio of recreation visits to recreation visitor days indicates that the visitor comes to the Tongass for an extended period of time. The Tongass ranked 18th in terms of recreational use in the National Forest System, but it varies widely among the three administrative areas. The Chatham Area receives 74 percent

of the recreational use, and the Ketchikan Area receives 20 percent of the use. The Stikine Area receives only 6 percent of the use. The Tongass is used even less intensively than the lightly used Chugach National Forest and has an intensity of use of 4.14 acres per recreation visitor day. Only two national forests in Oregon, the Fremont (4.46 acres/recreation visitor day) and the Ochoco (4.26 acres/RVD), have lesser intensities of use. This index is not a good indicator of "crowding" in the Tongass, since most of the use is either on the water or immediately along the littoral (shoreline). The Tongass ranks as the second leading national forest in terms of wilderness use, with 797,000 RVDs, a figure exceeded only by the Superior National Forest's 1,404,000 RVDs. Eighty-five percent of the total wilderness use occurs in just three areas: Kootznoowoo (38 percent), Misty Fiords National Monument (27 percent), and West Chichagof-Yakobi (20 percent).

Like the Chugach, the leading category of recreational use in the Tongass is "mechanized travel and viewing scenery" at 62 percent of the total use. The leading subcategory is viewing scenery (49 percent), but a second major subcategory of use is tour boat, ship, and ferry use (35 percent). The second leading category of use is "other recreational activities," which accounts for 12 percent of the RVDs; "guided touring" contributes 55 percent of this category, "viewing interpretive exhibits" another 12 percent, and "attending talks and programs" another 9 percent. Within this category the 5 percent contributed by power boating represents the major recreational activity of the residents of Southeast Alaska. "Fishing" is the third-ranked category of use (9 percent of the RVD total), with saltwater fishing contributing 61 percent of the category and cold-water fishing another 39 percent. "Hiking, horseback riding, and water travel" is the fourth-ranked category at 6 percent of total recreational use; "hiking and walking" is the leading subcategory (54 percent of category use), and mountain climbing contributes another 23 percent of the use. "Canoeing" is also an important subcategory, with 13 percent of the category use. The category of "camping, picnicking, and swimming" is fifth-ranked at an extremely low 4 percent of the total recreational use: Camping contributes 62 percent, picnicking 33 percent, and swimming 4 percent of the use to this category. "Hunting" accounts for under 3 percent of the total recreational use, 60 percent of which is big-game hunting. Hunting, like power boats, is one of the major recreational activities of the residents. "Resorts, cabins, and organization camps" accounts for a low 3 percent of the total use, but 80 percent of this category use occurs at recreational cabins rented by the Forest Service. These cabins are usually located on water and are highly sought after as recreational destinations (Figure 10.3). The Forest Service rents these cabins for $25 per night (1994). "Winter sports" accounts for a very low 1 percent of the total use; 80 percent of this winter use is related to snowshoeing and cross-country skiing. Less than 2 percent of the winter sports use is downhill skiing at the Eaglecrest Winter Sports Center at Juneau. The final category, "nonconsumptive fish and wildlife use," accounts for less than 1 percent of the use. Most of the recreational use occurs in summer and fall and is related directly to cruise ships, which run from May through September.

Southeast Alaska, of which the Tongass National Forest makes up about 80 percent, possesses a remarkable and unique combination of features. These features include inland waterways with over 11,000 miles of shoreline and 646,000 acres of beach; 42,500 miles of perennial streams; 20,000 lakes and ponds; mountains, fiords,

Figure 10.3 A unique feature of Alaska's National Forests is the recreation cabins, which can be rented for $25 per night from the Forest Service. Shown here is the Shrode Lake Cabin in the Tongass National Forest. (Forest Service photo)

and glaciers; and large or unusual fish and wildlife populations. They provide opportunities for a wide range of excellent outdoor recreation experiences. The area imparts a feeling of vastness, wildness, and solitude. These feelings are enhanced by the small resident population and relative absence of development compared with most national forests. While the large acreages of federal land are impressive, they are also deceptive in that the amount of land actually available and usable for outdoor recreation is less than might be expected. The difficult and steep terrain, wetlands, icefields and glaciers, and heavy vegetation confine most of the recreation activities to the accessible shorelines, river and stream bottoms, and the areas around the many lakes within the Forest. Some use is made of certain parts of the icefields, and the alpine areas above treeline are popular for goat hunting, but access is usually by aircraft. Near the communities, residents and visitors alike use the developed camp and picnic grounds, beaches, and visitor centers. Community road systems are limited, but are heavily used for access to recreation sites and attractions near local communities. The Forest Development Road System includes 3355 miles of road and provides access to about 9 percent of the forest. Of the 2180 miles of road open to public motorized use, about 1150 miles are connected to communities. The remainder are isolated road systems that require chartered barge or ferry access. Except in a few cases, the Tongass has not experienced the kinds of resource damage typically associated with off-highway vehicles (ORVs and ATVs). Because of this, the Forest Travel Plan designates the entire forest accessible to OHVs, unless specifically designated closed in specific locations. The modes of travel constrain the potential demand somewhat since the ferry system can handle only so many people and vehicles and the communities can handly only so many cruise ships and aircraft. In 1990, the Forest Service, the states of Alaska and Washington, and the province of British Columbia entered into an agreement to develop a system of marine parks stretching from Southeast Alaska to Puget Sound.

The Tongass National Forest is made up of six distinct landscape character types (see Appendix XII). Each has unique characteristics of landforms, rock formations, water forms, and vegetative patterns. The visual condition of the Tongass varies by location and is dependent on a number of factors. In addition to the variety of natural aspects of the visual resource (geology, vegetation, landforms, water, and so on), visible, human-made developments affect the visual condition of some areas. These developments include roads, rock quarry sites, timber harvests, log transfer facilities, hydroelectric powerline clearings, recreational facilities, fish improvement projects, mariculture operations, and mining developments. Development activities on national forest lands are concentrated mostly in areas near the communities of Petersburg, Wrangell, Ketchikan, Hoonah, Sitka, and Juneau. Timber harvest activities on native corporation and state lands, and their associated development, are changing the appearance of parts of Southeast Alaska from predominantly natural-appearing to a more developed and altered visual setting.

Tourists, or nonresident recreationists, can be categorized into two major groupings: the adventure traveler and those passing through. The adventure travelers constitute a small but growing group and plan their itineraries largely by themselves. The spend more time in the Tongass National Forest and in the communities, and may secure the services of outfitters and guides, motels, and transportation services. The other group passing through consists of the cruise ship clients and many passengers on the ferries. This much larger group of tourists especially values the visual resource and use areas near communities. These visitors spend less time in the area, and often follow preplanned and regimented itineraries. The cruise-ship phenomenon has witnessed the most explosive growth in the national forest of all categories of recreational use. Usage increased from 46,279 total passengers aboard in 1979 to 240,000 total passengers aboard in 1990—a 519 percent increase. The adventure travelers compete more directly with residents for recreational opportunities, for recreation place capacity, facilities, and resources such as fish, game, and solitude. Tourists staying overnight do so in the following places: cruise ships (67 percent), hotels or motels (19 percent), and aboard ferries (13 percent) (Data Decisions Group, Inc., 1988).

The majority of the Forest is undeveloped and is primarily used for dispersed recreation. Access plays a key role in the nature of how the outdoor recreation resource is used. Access is typically by boat, or by vehicle on community road systems. The use of aircraft is limited by both cost and the small number of people that can be carried. Nearly 1400 recreation places, totaling approximately 4.4 million acres, have been inventoried by the Forest Service. Table 10.3 summarizes the geographic distribution, acreage, and capacities of these recreation places, and Table 10.4 identifies the acreage distribution of the setting of the recreation places according to the Recreation Opportunity Spectrum (ROS), previously discussed in Chapter 8. In terms of recreational use the largest component of recreation has been the "semiprimitive motorized" ROS category. These areas primarily include natural-appearing shorelines, lakes, and rivers that provide for semiprimitive experiences; however, due to motorized boat and/or float plane traffic, they are considered motorized. This category comprised 60 percent of the total recreational use between 1977 and 1987 and showed a 45 percent increase during this 10-year period. Resources in the Tongass that are assigned to this category will not have sufficient capacity to meet projected use. The next largest components of recreational use are the "primitive" and "semiprimitive nonmotorized" ROS classes. Recreational use in these classes utilizes a nat-

Table 10.3   Tongass National Forest: Summary of Recreation Places

	Number of Places	Acres (1000s)	Capacity PAOT (1000s)
Chatham Area			
Inside wilderness	151	542	497
Outside wilderness	361	1472	1918
Stikine Area			
Inside wilderness	54	316	125
Outside wilderness	337	646	397
Ketchikan Area			
Inside wilderness	73	510	122
Outside wilderness	418	845	969
Total Tongass			
Inside wilderness	278	1368	744
Outside wilderness	1116	2963	3284
Tongass-wide total	1394	4334	4031

Source: Forest Service, *Tongass Land Management Plan Revision—Part 1* (August 1991).

ural or natural-appearing setting with little evidence of humans and no motorized use. Use of these areas comprised 20 percent of the total recreational use between 1977 and 1987 and showed the largest percentage growth at 54 percent. The smallest component comes from the "roaded natural," "roaded modified," and "rural" ROS classes, comprising 18 percent of the use between 1977 and 1987 and increasing 39 percent during the same time period.

Recreation places can also be categorized into three broad, general groupings, according to their principal uses and attraction:

1. *Marine recreation* is where 34 percent of the recreation place acres and 41 percent of the individual recreation places occur. The family boat is used in the same manner as wheeled recreational vehicles in other places. The majority of the use originates in local community boat harbors or launching sites accessed by road systems, and typical day-use occurs within a 15- to 30-mile radius (University of Oregon, 1983). The most popular activities are beachcombing and hiking, fishing, motorboating, clamming and crabbing, onshore hunting, and canoeing and kayaking. For overnight use the activities remain the same with the addition of camping and cabin use.

Table 10.4   Tongass National Forest: Recreation Opportunity Spectrum Class Summary for Recreation Places

ROS Class	Acres
Primitive	1,968,502
Semiprimitive nonmotorized	1,114,204
Semiprimitive motorized	814,315
Roaded natural	149,591
Roaded modified	330,497
Rural	6,184
Urban	0

Source: Forest Service, *Tongass Land Management Plan Revision—Part 1* (August 1991).

2. *Freshwater recreation* accounts for 25 percent of the recreation place acres and 21 percent of the identified recreation places. Eighty-one of the 145 Forest Service recreational cabins are located on or near freshwater lakes or streams. These cabins can be rented for $25 a night, and most are only accessible by boat or plane.

3. *Land-based recreation* occupies 41 percent of the recreation place acres and accounts for 37 percent of the recreation places. The most popular activities are hunting, hiking, and driving for pleasure. Included within recreation places are developed recreation sites that can be used for concentrated visitor use. These facilities are identified in Table 10.5 and, with the exception of cabins, are generally accessible from community road systems. The largest campground in the Tongass is Mendenhall Lake with 33 tent sites and 28 recreational vehicle sites.

There are seven designated *special-interest areas* in the forest: The Mendenhall Glacier Recreation Area (5791 acres) is located 13 miles northwest of Juneau and is the only glacier in Southeast Alaska located on the road system. The Mendenhall Glacier flows from the Juneau Icefield. A visitor center has an observatory that offers spectacular views of the glacier. The six other special-interest areas are the Ward Lake Recreation Area (440 acres), the New Eddystone Rock Geological Area (1 acre), the

Table 10.5 Tongass National Forest: Recreational Facilities

Facilities	Chatham Area	Stikine Area	Ketchikan Area	Tongass NF Total
Anchor buoys	4	2	22	28
Campgrounds	3	1	10	14
# of sites	92	15	59	166
Fishing sites	0	0	0	0
Interpretive sites	1	1	3	5
Historic sites	0	0	1	1
Observation sites	1	3	3	7
Organized camps	1	1	1	3
Picnic areas	8	7	10	25
# of units	74	21	47	142
Recreation Cabins:				
Wilderness	19	16	18	53
Nonwilderness	33	26	34	93
On salt water	12	26	15	53
Total rec. cabins	54	39	52	145
Recreation Residences	17	27	4	48
Recreation road miles	143	258	837	1,238
Resorts and Lodges	2	0	2	4
Other concessions	0	0	0	0
Ski areas	0	0	0	0
Trails (# of miles):				
Nonwilderness	198.9	66.9	153.6	419.4
Wilderness	43.0	23.7	18.4	85.1
Total trail miles	241.9	90.6	172.0	504.5
Trail shelters	8	5	12	25
Trailheads	3	32	13	48
Visitor centers	2	0	1	3
Winter sports	0	1	0	1

Source: Forest Service, *Tongass Land Management Plan Revision—Part 1* (August 1991).

Hubbard Glacier Geological Area (46,000 acres), the Walker Cove–Rudyerd Bay Scenic Area (93,540 acres), the Admiralty Lakes Recreation Area (8,710 acres), and the Tracy Arm–Fords Terror Scenic Area (283,000 acres). The last three have been recently included within wildernesses and/or national monuments. Since the same values are promoted in these new areas, there are no proposals for declassification of the older terminology. Walker Cove–Rudyerd Bay is now in Misty Fiords National Monument and Wilderness, Admiralty Lakes is in Admiralty Island National Monument and Kootznoowoo Wilderness, and Tracy Arm–Fords Terror is now a designated wilderness of the same name.

ANILCA established two national monuments in the Tongass National Forest: Admiralty Island and Misty Fiords. Admiralty Island National Monument (955,810 acres) is 15 miles southwest of Juneau and accessible by boat or float plane. Its two major recreational attractions are Mitchell Bay and Admiralty Lakes Recreation Area. A 25-mile trail links the eight major lakes on the island. Canoeing and kayaking, hunting, fishing, and bird watching are popular activities. The small Tlingit village of Angoon (500 inhabitants) is the principal community on the island. In August 1990, Congress passed the *Admiralty Island National Monument Land Management Act,* which changed the name of the Admiralty Island Wilderness to the Kootznoowoo Wilderness Area and paved the way to clear up a land dispute with Kootznoowoo, Inc., a native corporation. The Kootznoowoo Wilderness occupies most of the island and most of the national monument. Misty Fiords National Monument (2,293,428 acres, 2,142,243 acres designated as wilderness) is located in the southeastern corner of the Forest. Behm Canal, a deep inlet, leads to the interior of the monument, where Walker Cove and Rudyerd Bay are surrounded by rock walls that rise 3000 feet. Recreational activities include backpacking, picnicking, bird watching, fishing, hunting, and crabbing. Forest Service cabins are available here.

The Tongass National Forest was the first to complete a *Land and Resource Management Plan* in 1979 under the provisions of the 1976 National Forest Management Act (NFMA). This *Plan* was amended in 1986 and again in 1990 by the *Tongass Timber Reform Act* (November 1990). This act accomplished several things. It amended ANILCA, designated five new wilderness areas (Chuck River, Karta, Kuiu, Pleasant-Lemusurier-Inian Islands, and South Etolin), and included an addition (Young Lake Addition) to the Kootznoowoo Wilderness Area. These six areas added another 299,697 acres to the National Wilderness Preservation System in the Tongass, increasing the total acreage to 5,753,106 acres in the 19 wilderness areas. The 14 wilderness areas established in the Tongass National Forest in 1980 by ANILA are Admiralty Island (955,921 acres, renamed Kootznoowoo and with Young Lake Addition added in 1990), Coronation Island (19,232 acres), Endicott River (98,729 acres), Maurelle Islands (4937 acres), Misty Fiords National Monument (2,142,243 acres), Petersburg Creek–Duncan Salt Chuck (46,777 acres), Russell Fiord (348,701 acres), South Prince of Wales (90,996 acres), Stikine-LeConte (448,881 acres), Tebenkof Bay (66,839 acres), Tracy Arm–Fords Terror (653,179 acres), Warren Island (11,181 acres), and West Chichagof–Yakobi (264,747 acres). Several other provisions of the Tongass Timber Reform Act affected timber harvesting and contracts. One provision eliminated the controversial ANILCA requirement of cutting 4.5 billion board feet per decade in the Tongass, replacing it with "the goal of seeking to supply an amount of timber to meet market demand."

A *Final Revised Plan* and EIS have been released (Forest Service, 1991c, d, e) that identified 10 major planning issues on the Tongass. They are:

- What areas of the Tongass National Forest should be managed to emphasize scenic resources?
- What areas should be managed to emphasize recreation?
- What methods should be used to protect resident and anadromous fish habitat?
- What amount of old-growth and undeveloped habitat should be managed for the protection of wildlife?
- What should the Forest Service do to continue providing subsistence opportunities?
- What areas of the Tongass should be managed to emphasize timber harvesting?
- What road system should be developed in the Tongass National Forest?
- What areas and accessibility should be emphasized for exploration, development, and production of mineral resources?
- What areas and what amount of roadless lands should be recommended for wilderness designation or other types of unroaded management?
- What ways should national forest lands be managed to provide for the local life-style of Southeast Alaska communities?

All land-use planning decisions in the Tongass revolve around timber cutting and road building and lead to the basic questions of what amount of timber to make available (or what amount of old growth to retain), and where? On one side are the concerns over scenic quality; recreation settings; fish and wildlife habitat (including old-growth); subsistence use; roadless areas; and wild, scenic and recreational rivers. On the other side is the concern over timber-related employment and its relationship to the economies of Southeast Alaska's communities. No significant industrial harvesting of timber occurred in the Tongass until the early 1950s and the opening of pulpmills and negotiation of long-term timber sale contracts. Since 1900, about 415,000 acres have had timber activities, with 88 percent of this since 1952. Since the 1979 *Tongass Land and Resource Management Plan* (Forest Service, 1979), 106,000 acres have been altered by logging. For the next several decades timber harvest is going to depend on old-growth timber. Ninety-one percent of the Tongass is roadless today. The only roads are through small areas around where communities are developing or where road construction is associated with timber harvesting. These developed areas total 1.6 million acres (9 percent) of the forest. Eighty-three percent of the non-wilderness national forest land is roadless.

The Forest Service has selected "Alternative P" (out of a total of five alternatives) in the ongoing land management planning process. The theme of this alternative is to enhance the balanced use of resources of the forest and provide a public timber supply to maintain the Southeast Alaska timber industry. Many of the most important wildlife habitats, recreational and subsistence opportunities, and scenic values will be maintained in a natural setting. Resources that will contribute to the local and regional economies of Southeast Alaska are emphasized. In 1954, there was an estimated 5.44 million acres of productive old-growth forest. Under Alternative P, this is expected to decrease to 3.8 million acres by the year 2050. The goal for recreation management under Alternative P is to "provide a range of recreation opportunities consistent with public demand, with emphasis on recreation places identified as being

popular with local users or important to the tourist industry." Recreation is predicted to increase over the next decade but will remain below the forest's current capacity of 4.7 million RVDs. Over time, the Forest will continue to shift toward the developed end of the ROS, bringing about increased opportunities associated with roads, and decreased opportunities associated with primitive forms of recreation. In Alternative P a higher proportion of the change will occur in the moderate or transitional settings than in the more developed ones. Despite the change in settings to more modification, the Forest still maintains 40 percent of the recreation place acres in areas protected through legislation. In the future the Forest will be managed to achieve the following degrees of modification of the environment:

- *Unmodified Environments*   The majority of Tongass National Forest land (about 60 percent) will be managed to emphasize natural values and to allow natural processes to determine future conditions.
- *Near-Natural Environments*   Another 8 percent of Tongass National Forest land will be managed to allow a wider range of human activities in an environment where natural values still predominate.
- *Modified Environments*   Twelve percent of Tongass National Forest land will be managed to allow a moderate amount of timber harvest that is either not visually evident to most visitors, or is designated to appear compatible with surrounding landscapes.
- *Highly Modified Environments*   Twenty percent of Tongass National Forest land will be managed to emphasize timber harvest or the potential for mineral development.

LOWER 49 STATES

Chattahoochee-Oconee National Forests

The Chattahoochee and Oconee are the only national forests in Georgia and are administered jointly under a single forest supervisor. The Chattahoochee National Forest was formally established in 1936 and is located in the extreme south of the Southern Appalachian Mountains in northern Georgia. It has a gross area of 1,515,885 acres, 749,072 acres or 49.4 percent of which are National Forest System land. Forest headquarters are at Gainesville, with the main section of the Forest lying east of Dalton and extending along the North Carolina boundary to South Carolina. There are six ranger districts in this larger part of the forest: Brasstown (office in Blairsville), Chattooga (Clarkesville), Chestatee (Dahlonega), Cohutta (Chatsworth), Tallulah (Clayton), and Toccoa (Blue Ridge). A smaller section of the Chattahoochee—the Armuchee Ranger District (Layfayette)—lies west of Dalton. The percentage of national forest land is considerably smaller in this ranger district.

The Oconee National Forest is located in the rolling Piedmont of central Georgia to the east and southeast of Atlanta. The Oconee National Forest is much smaller than the Chattahoochee, being only 111,060 acres, or 42.6 percent of its gross acreage of 260,884 acres. The Oconee shares the same forest headquarters at Gainesville. There is one ranger district in the Oconee—also called the Oconee—with its office at Mon-

ticello. The Oconee National Forest is divided into two sections with Interstate 20 passing between them offering ready access. The larger segment is located south of I-20 and north of Macon. The majority of the lands in the Oconee were originally purchased during the Depression years under the Resettlement Administration. The Soil Conservation Service administered these lands for a number of years until they were transferred to the Department of Agriculture in 1954; national forest status was acquired in 1959.

Most of the Chattahoochee National Forest is located within the Blue Ridge Physiographic Province, although the western portion is in the Ridge and Valley Province. In this smaller, western portion, the national forest land is located along the lineal ridges. The Oconee is located on the Lower Piedmont. The Chattahoochee ranges in altitude from 1000 feet to nearly 5000 feet and has many high mountains, including Georgia's highest—4,784 foot Brasstown Bald. Many visitors from throughout the Southeast, particularly from large urban areas such as Atlanta, are attracted to the mountains of northern Georgia and the Chattahoochee National Forest because of its scenic beauty. Mountain vistas and whitewater streams provide a scenic landscape not found elsewhere in Georgia. Because scenic qualities are highly valued in the forest, the public is sensitive to logging or other disturbances that cause major changes in the landscape. The situation is different in the Oconee. The Piedmont terrain is considered less scenic than the mountains of the Chattahoochee. Logging is more common because the private land is managed for timber and as a result, the public has less concern about visual change on the Oconee. The diversity of trees in the Chattahoochee is tremendous. About 48 percent of the forest today is in upland–mixed hardwood types, 16 percent in cove hardwoods, 28 percent in yellow pine, and 8 percent in white pine. The Oconee today is predominantly a pine forest, with 88 percent in yellow pine and the remainder split between upland and bottomland hardwoods. Although the Oconee is about one-seventh the size of the Chattahoochee, it generally generates about one-third the volume of timber sales in the two forests. The presence of Lake Sinclair and the recently completed Lake Oconee has increased interest in developed recreation sites on the Oconee National Forest. The following land classification exists for the forests: (1) nonforest land (includes streams), 6544 acres; (2) forest land, 839,276 acres; (3) nonproductive forest land, 858 acres; (4) forest land withdrawn from timber production, 62,346 acres; (5) unsuitable forest land, 0 acres; (6) tentatively suitable forest land (item 2 minus items 3, 4, and 5), 776,072 acres; (7) not appropriate forest land, 100,999 acres; (8) unsuitable forest land (items 3, 4, 5, and 7), 164,203 acres; (9) total suitable forest land (item 2 minus item 8), 675,073 acres; and (10) total national forest land (items 1 and 2), 845,820 acres.

The Oconee has a humid subtropical climate, which becomes more continental in the mountains of the Chattahoochee. In the Chattahoochee the summer days are warm to mild, and nights are comfortably cool. Winters in the area are quite cold, with snow and ice in the higher elevations. Precipitation varies from 40 inches in the Oconee to 75 inches in the mountains of the Chattahoochee. The frost-free season is 240 days in the Oconee and 170 days in the Chattahoochee. The Chattahoochee contains about 19,000 acres of lakes and 1900 miles of perennial streams that contain native or stocked trout. The Oconee contains about 34,000 acres of lakes and 240 miles of perennial streams that contain largemouth bass and bream. Over 500 wildlife species occur in both forests. Major game species include deer, turkey, squirrel, grouse

(only on Chattahoochee), quail, raccoon, fox, dove, woodcock, and bear. A wide variety of fur-bearing and nongame species exists, including such species as muskrat, mink, bobcat, otter, and beaver as well as numerous types of birds, reptiles, amphibians, and fish. The red-cockaded woodpecker, the bald eagle, and the bog turtle are the only endangered, threatened, or sensitive animal species confirmed residing in the forests.

The Chattahoochee National Forest receives much more recreational use than does the Oconee National Forest—2,614,900 RVDs versus 378,400 RVDs. The Chattahoochee National Forest is ranked 37th in total use and has an intensity of use index of 0.286 acres/RVD, which indicates considerable crowding. The Oconee has a similar intensity of use index (0.293) but ranks much lower in RVDs: 123rd among all of the national forests. The smaller size of the Oconee is a contributing factor. There are no wilderness areas in the Oconee National Forest, but there are 10 such areas in the Chattahoochee National Forest that cover 113,455 acres and received 100,200 RVDs in 1992 (3.8 percent of total use). These wilderness areas are Big Frog (80 acres in the Chattahoochee; 7986 acres in the Cherokee National Forest in Tennessee); Blood Mountain (7800 acres); Brasstown (12,338 acres); Cohutta (35,143 acres); Ellicott Rock (2181 acres in the Chattahoochee National Forest; 4022 acres in the Nantahala National Forest in N. Carolina); Mark Trail (16,400 acres); Raven Cliffs (8562 acres); Rich Mountain (9476 acres); Southern Nantahala (11,770 acres in the Chattahoochee and 11,703 acres in the Nantahala National Forest); and Tray Mountain (9702 acres).

In the Chattahoochee National Forest "camping, picnicking, and swimming" accounts for 32 percent of the RVDs. Camping (73 percent) is the major subcategory, with picnicking at 15 percent and swimming and diving at 10 percent. "Mechanized travel and viewing scenery" is in a close second at 31 percent of the total use, with "automobile travel" (53 percent) and "viewing scenery" (26 percent) the leading subcategories. "Hiking, horseback riding, and water travel" ranks third at 14 percent of use, with the subcategory "hiking" comprising 75 percent of this use, and horseback riding another 11 percent. "Hunting" accounts for 11 percent of the recreational use, with big-game hunting accounting for 64 percent of this category. "Fishing" accounts for another 7 percent of the RVDs, where three-quarters of the fishing is cold-water. The category "resorts, cabins, and organization camps" accounts for a low 2 percent of the use, with most of this category equally comprised of general day organization camping, night organization camping, and recreational cabin use. Winter sports are almost insignificant on the Chattahoochee, accounting for only 0.03 percent of the recreation visitor days, and most of this limited use is snow play. "Nonconsumptive fish and wildlife use" accounts for 1 percent of the recreational use, and "other recreational activities" for a little over 3 percent of the use. In the latter category the two main subcategories of use are "gathering forest products" and "attending talks and programs."

On the Oconee National Forest "mechanized travel and viewing scenery" is responsible for 41 percent of the use, and the leading subcategory is automobile travel (78 percent). "Hunting" is the second-ranked activity group at 28 percent, with 90 percent of this use in big-game hunting. "Hiking, horseback riding, and water travel" accounts for 5 percent of the use and "fishing" for 4 percent. All fishing is warm-

water on the Oconee. Of the 4 percent in the "other recreational activities" category, most of this use is related to gathering forest products. A relatively high 3 percent of the use is related to "nonconsumptive fish and wildlife use." There are no "winter sports" or "resorts, cabins, and organization camps" uses in the Oconee.

The Chattahoochee National Forest provides recreational opportunities ranging from modern campgrounds to wilderness. There are 34 developed recreation areas in the forest, varying from small roadside overlooks and picnic areas, to large campgrounds offering swimming, boating, picnicking, and camping. Dispersed recreation is also very popular, with 1017 miles of existing roads and over 600 miles of hiking trails. Table 10.6 summarizes the ROS categories of the forest, with "roaded natural-appearing" accounting for 83 percent of the total. The Appalachian National Scenic Trail originates at Springer Mountain and spans the forest for 79 miles before entering North Carolina. There are five national recreational trails in the forest totaling 87.4 miles, and the Chattooga National Wild and Scenic River is well known for its challenging whitewater and scenic beauty. Off-road-vehicle use is popular in the forest, and all system roads and 90 miles of trails are open to them. The Brasstown Bald Visitor Center is located on 4784-foot Brasstown Bald, the highest point in Georgia. It is open May through October and has a rooftop observatory deck; the summit also has picnic facilities and three hiking trails. A parking lot is located ¼ mile below the facilities at the summit, which may be accessed by trail or shuttle bus (for a small fee). A popular recreation area at Anna Ruby Falls is surrounded by the 1600-acre Anna Ruby Falls Scenic Area. Twin waterfalls merge at their base to form Smith Creek. The falls are reached by a ½ mile scenic walk from the parking lot. Another scenic waterfall is at DeSoto Falls Scenic Area, where camping, hiking and fishing opportunities exist. Excellent fishing, camping, picnicking, and hiking may be had at Cooper Creek Scenic Area. Scenic overlooks are located at Cohutta Overlook, Chestatee Overlook, and John's Mountain Overlook.

The Oconee National Forest offers both developed and dispersed recreation. There are five developed recreation areas, all of which are associated with one of three lakes in the forest or the Oconee River. The two most developed recreation areas provide boat ramp and picnicking facilities along the shoreline of Lake Oconee. ORV use is allowed only on system roads and designated trails. Hunting is the most popular form of dispersed recreation, as the Oconee is well known for its excellent deer population. All acreage in the forest falls into the "roaded natural-appearing"

Table 10.6 Recreational Opportunities in the Chattahoochee National Forest

ROS Category	Description	Acres	Percent of Total Forest Acreage
Semiprimitive nonmotorized	At least ½ mile from all roads or trails with motorized use, and at least 2500 acres in size.	89,349	12
Semiprimitive motorized	Within ½ mile from primitive roads and at least 2500 acres in size.	36,923	5
Roaded natural appearing	Within ½ mile of roads better than primitive, no size criteria.	615,128	83

Source: Forest Service, *Final Environmental Impact Statement: Chattahoochee-Oconee National Forests.*

category of the ROS. These two jointly administered forests offer over 500 developed campsites, over 200 picnicking sites, and six swimming beaches, in addition to numerous lakes and streams and 10 wilderness areas in the Chattahoochee.

One of the 12 major issues identified in the Land and Resource Management Planning process was "How much and of what types of recreational opportunities should be provided on national forest land?" Conflicts between recreation and other forest values were frequently mentioned. Potential solutions for dispersed recreation include: defining some areas as backcountry, building new trails, providing additional protection of scenic quality through visual quality objectives (VQOs), maintaining semiprimitive motorized and semiprimitive nonmotorized recreational opportunities, and providing rehabilitation and improved control in areas receiving heavy dispersed recreation use. Potential solutions for developed recreation include new construction (or expansion) if a need is indicated by demand data, shifting more emphasis to the private sector, changing the length of the recreation season, and increasing information services. Demand for developed recreation is expected to more than double in the next 50 years, with current capacity exceeding demand until 2025. Although capacity now exists for total demand, the demand for particular activities in certain areas may not be met. Demand for dispersed recreation will also double in the next 50 years, and current capacity will meet demand only until 2015.

Dixie National Forest

The Dixie National Forest is located in southwestern Utah and stretches for 160 miles from the Nevada border to Capitol Reef National Park. It is Utah's largest national forest at 1,883,955 acres. Within the gross area of the forest boundary there are 1,967,190 acres. An exceptionally high 96 percent of the total area within the boundaries of the forest is National Forest land. The Dixie National Forest had its beginnings as the Aquarius Forest Reserve and Sevier Forest Reserve in 1905. Various consolidations occurred until 1945, when the Dixie's current configuration was finally established. The warm-climate portions of the Dixie National Forest reminded Mormon settlers of the Deep South, which is how the Forest obtained its name. The Mormons grew cotton in the lower elevations of this region. The forest headquarters are at Cedar City, and there are five ranger districts. The westernmost ranger district is the Pine Valley (with district office at St. George), which extends from the Nevada border to near I-15 between Cedar City and St. George. The Cedar City Ranger District (office at Cedar City) lies east of Cedar City and west of Panguitch. The Pine Valley and Cedar City Ranger Districts receive the heaviest recreational use. The Powell Ranger District (Panguitch) lies east of Panguitch and, although only 17 miles from east to west at its greatest point, it is over 50 miles from north to south. While the first three ranger districts are noncontiguous, the last two, the Escalante and the Teasdale, border each other in the eastern part of the forest. The Escalante Ranger District (Escalante) lies in the southeastern corner of the forest and the Teasdale Ranger District (Teasdale) lies north of it in the northeastern corner of the forest.

Prominent in the geography of the Dixie National Forest is the location of several National Park System units in, or in close proximity to, the Forest. Cedar Breaks National Monument (6155 acres) is a major inholding in the Cedar City Ranger District. This ranger district has the largest amount of other inholdings, followed by the

Pine Valley Ranger District. Inholdings are extremely infrequent in the Powell, Escalante, and Teasdale Ranger Districts. Zion National Park lies 10 miles southwest of the Cedar City Ranger District and 3 miles east of the Pine Valley Ranger District. Bryce Canyon National Park borders the Powell Ranger District in the southeast and touches the southwestern corner of the Escalante Ranger District. For 8 miles the Powell Ranger District surrounds the southern extension of Bryce Canyon National Park; here, the main park road extends to Rainbow Point. Capitol Reef National Park borders both the Escalante and Teasdale Ranger Districts on the east. Glen Canyon National Recreation Area comes as close as 20 miles to the Dixie, where the Escalante River flows. Grand Canyon National Park is as close as 60 miles to the south of the forest in a straight line but is 110 miles by road. Extensive areas of BLM land border the forest on all sides.

The Dixie National Forest lies across the meeting place of two Physiographic Provinces—the Colorado Plateau Province and Basin and Range Province. The main portion of the forest is in the High Plateaus of Utah Section of the Colorado Plateau, but the Pine Valley Ranger District portion of the forest in the west lies within the Great Basin Section of the Basin and Range Province. This area is noted for its internal drainage characteristics and steep mountain ranges arising abruptly from valley floors. The Pine Valley Mountains, which rise 3000 feet above the valley floor, are the principal physiographic feature of this part of the forest. Elevations in the forest range from 2800 feet near St. George to 11,322 feet at Bluebell Knoll on Boulder Mountain. The southern rim of the Great Basin provides spectacular scenery, and the canyons of rivers flowing off the plateaus to the Colorado River present many colored cliffs and steep-walled gorges. The topography of most of the forest consists of broad plateaus bounded by receding escarpments and dissected by vast canyons. High-altitude forests found in gently rolling hills characterize the Markagunt, Paunsaugunt, and Aquarius Plateaus. Three major north-south trending lineal faults are found along these plateaus: the Hurricane, west of the Markagunt Plateau; the Sevier, west of the Sevier and Paunsaugunt Plateaus; and the Paunsaugunt, west of the Aquarius Plateau. Among the more colorful of the escarpments in the forest are the Pink Cliffs (Wasatch Formation of Eocene age) at the western edge of the Markagunt Plateau at Cedar Breaks National Monument and at the southern edge of the Paunsaugunt Plateau at Bryce Canyon National Park. There is evidence of Pleistocene glaciation on the Markagunt and Aquarius Plateaus (over 11,000 feet in elevation). Boulder Mountain, the northeastern part of the Aquarius Plateau, is one of the largest high-elevation plateaus in the United States and is dotted with hundreds of small lakes that lie 10,000 to over 11,000 feet above sea level. The summit area of Boulder Mountain has a lava cap and is a fairly flat area of about 70 square miles, with steep, bounding slopes, descending 6000 feet on the east (Figure 10.4). The numerous small lakes on the summit are evidence of glaciation.

Due to the large range in altitude in the forest from 2800 feet to 11,322 feet, a great range of climatic and vegetation diversity exists. Precipitation ranges from 10 inches in the lower elevations to over 40 inches per year near Brian Head. About a third of the precipitation falls as rain and the remainder as snow from October through April. Although most roads are open by April in the lower elevations and late May at the higher elevations, accumulated snow remains in some locations into June. Thunderstorms are common in July and August. Temperature extremes can be

Figure 10.4 Boulder Mountain (the northeastern part of the Aquarius Plateau) rises 6000 vertical feet to 11,000 ft. in elevation along its eastern side in the Dixie National Forest. The newly paved Utah Highway 12, which passes over the side of Boulder Mountain, here reaches an elevation of 9200 ft. and has been designated a National Forest Scenic Byway.

great, ranging from over 100°F near St. George to minus 30°F on the plateau tops, although in the summer the highland climate rarely exceeds 80°F. Vegetation types in the forest are determined largely by elevation, with desert-type plants at the lower elevations, to stands of pinyon pine and juniper in the middle elevations to about 8000 feet of elevation. Between 8000 and 10,000 feet, Ponderosa pine is the most common species, with a great deal of aspen interspersed. In the highlands over 10,000 feet, spruce, fir, and meadow types predominate. The percentages of the major vegetation type in the forest are: pinyon-juniper, 27.6 percent; sagebrush, 13.8 percent; Ponderosa pine, 13.1 percent; mixed conifer, 12.5 percent; grass-forb, 9.8 percent; mountain brush, 8.5 percent; spruce-fir, 7.0 percent; aspen, 6.6 percent; and riparian, 1.2 percent. More than 350 species of wildlife and fish inhabit the forest for at least part of their life. Important wildlife species include mule deer, elk, antelope, mountain lion, turkey, black bear, grouse, and rabbit. Game fish include brook, rainbow, cutthroat, and brown trout. There are over 3100 acres of lakes and reservoirs and 330 miles of streams. Domesticated animals that graze in the forest during the summer include about 20,000 cattle and 28,000 sheep, which belong to 350 farm and ranch families. The following land classification exists for the Dixie National Forest: (1) nonforest land (includes water), 1,204,900 acres; (2) forest land, 678,800 acres; (3) forest land withdrawn from timber production, 28,500 acres; (4) forest land not capable of producing crops of industrial wood, 236,600 acres; (5) forest land physically unsuitable, 82,500 acres; (6) tentatively suitable forest land (item 2 minus items 3, 4, and 5), 331,200 acres; (7) forest land not appropriate for timber production, 31,100 acres; (8) unsuitable forest land (items 3, 4, 5, and 7), 378,700 acres; (9) total suitable forest land (item 2 minus item 8), 300,100 acres; and (10) total national forest land (items 1 and 2), 1,883,700 acres.

The Dixie National Forest is one of the more heavily used national forests, ranking fifth nationally with 6,175,600 recreation visitor days in 1992. Its intensity of use

index of 0.305 acres/RVD ranks it in 31st place. In the same year, recreation visits totaled 8,483,000. Three areas in the forest have been designated units of the National Wilderness Preservation System (in 1984): Ashdown Gorge (7000 acres), Box-Death Hollow (25,751 acres), and Pine Valley Mountain (50,000 acres). The actual use of the three wilderness areas is quite light, with only 13,500 RVDs in 1992 (0.54 percent of the total recreational use). The Pine Valley Mountain is the most heavily used of the wilderness areas. The Dixie is an interesting study of the RVD concept, for its use increased from 2,518,200 RVDs in 1991 to 6,175,600 RVDs in 1992—an absolutely astounding 245 percent increase in one year. Virtually all of this increase in use occurred in just one category, "mechanized travel and viewing scenery." In 1991, 597,100 RVDs were reported in this category, which increased to 3,635,800 in 1992. The leading category of use in the Dixie is "mechanized travel and viewing scenery," which accounts for a very high 59 percent of the total use. Seventy-five percent of the use in this category is viewing scenery and another 19 percent is automobile travel. The close proximity of several national park units is responsible for this heavy use. Interstate 15 passes close to, but not through, the forest boundary and is thus not counted in this total. The next ranking category of use is "camping, picnicking, and swimming," contributing 16 percent of the total use; 87 percent of this use is camping and another 12 percent is picnicking. "Other recreational activities" is the third-ranked category, at 12 percent of the total recreational use. Over half of the use in this category is general information and another 16 percent each of the use is related to gathering forest products and viewing interpretive exhibits. Pinyon nuts are a highly sought after delicacy provided by the forest; 28 percent of the land area of the forest is in the pinyon-juniper vegetation category. "Hunting" ranks a distant fourth (3.5 percent of use), and 90 percent of this is big-game hunting. "Winter sports," "hiking, horseback riding, and water travel," "fishing," and "resorts, cabins, and organization camps" each account for between 2 and 3 percent of the total recreational use. Downhill skiing comprises 82 percent of the use of the first category, hiking and walking 57 percent and horseback riding another 38 percent of the second category, and coldwater fishing 97 percent of the use of the third category. The use among subcategories in "resorts, cabins, and organization camps" is more evenly distributed among day and night organization camping, general resort and commercial public service, resort lodging, and recreational cabin use. "Nonconsumptive fish and wildlife use" accounts for a low 0.33 percent of the total use.

The Dixie National Forest has unique recreational opportunities. It is adjacent to, or surrounds, three national parks and one national monument. These features draw people into the area from throughout the United States and other parts of the world (especially Europe). Once in the area, people often visit many parts of the forest and use the campgrounds for overnight accommodations. The principal communities within 1 hour's driving time of the forest are Cedar City, St. George, Panguitch, Enterprise, Hurricane, and Escalante. The population of these communities and others within a 1-hour driving time is 100,000. Larger, more-distant communities such as Las Vegas and those in southern California are the source of many users of the forest. Many of these people have summer homes on private land within and adjacent to the forest. The recreational opportunities across the forest are highly diverse. The primitive recreation areas provide opportunities for camping, hunting, viewing scenery, and horseback riding. Semiprimitive nonmotorized areas provide opportunities similar to those in primitive areas plus opportunities for small boats and cold-water

fishing. Motorized recreation areas have opportunities for camping, picnicking, resort lodging, recreation residence, sledding, alpine and cross-country skiing, hunting, gathering forest products, viewing interpretive exhibits, hiking, viewing scenery, driving for pleasure, snowmobiling, biking, horseback riding, canoeing, sailing, swimming, waterskiing, and fishing.

The forest has a persons-at-one-time (PAOT) capacity of 5895 for developed public recreation sites; 5455 of this total is at 26 campgrounds and 440 at five picnic areas. The Cedar City and Pine Valley Ranger Districts, which lie to the east and west of I-15, receive the heaviest recreational use and have the greatest developed recreation capacity. The Pine Valley Ranger District has seven campgrounds (1005 PAOT) and three picnic areas (390 PAOT) and the Cedar City Ranger District has 10 campgrounds (2790 PAOT) and one picnic area (20 PAOT). In the other ranger districts the similar values are as follows: Powell, two campgrounds (680 PAOT) and no picnic area; Escalante, three campgrounds (450 PAOT) and one picnic area (30 PAOT); and Teasdale, four campgrounds (530 PAOT) and no picnic area. Demand for developed public recreation will be met until 2015; the Forest Service will work with other government agencies and the private sector to help meet demand after 2015.

The only downhill ski area in the Forest is at Brian Head. The Brian Head Ski Resort is 29 miles east of Cedar City. It is the largest ski area in southern Utah and one of the fastest-growing areas in the entire state. It is an all-year resort, with downhill and cross-country skiing and snowmobiling in the winter and hiking, horseback riding, fishing, and boating during the summer. The proposed Crystal Mountain Ski Area on Navaho Ridge adjacent to Brian Head has never been built. Present capacity at Brian Head is 3200 *skiers at one time* (SAOT) with an additional 1324 SAOT planned within the ski-area boundaries. There is potential outside the present ski-area boundaries for an additional 2390 SAOT. On most weekends during the peak season the ski area nears capacity; conditions are even more crowded at holiday times. Brian Head, like most ski areas in Utah, is located up a narrow canyon, and access is often a problem during the winter months. Other developed private recreation includes recreation residences, group organization camps, and other recreational opportunities provided by private enterprises under special-use permit from the Forest Service. There are 43 recreation residences at two sites, Pine Valley and Navaho Lake, that provide 5600 RVDs. No new permits have been issued for recreation residences since 1959. Originally, they were used only in the summer, but snowmobiles and four-wheel-drive vehicles now make year-round access possible. Two lodge resorts account for 7400 RVDs, one organization camp for 5500 RVDs, and four boat marinas for 6000 RVDs. Recreational use in the private sector has not shown an increase other than in skiing. Private residences on private land have shown a great increase in number.

Driving for pleasure and viewing scenery is the most popular dispersed recreational activity, followed by camping, fishing, gathering forest products, hunting, and hiking. The scenic beauty of the forest is one of the major attractions to recreationists. Brian Head Peak, Strawberry Point, Zions Overlook, and The Point Overlook provide especially scenic views. The recent paving of the Boulder Mountain Highway, Utah 12, provides one of the most scenic drives in southern Utah. This highway was designated a national forest scenic byway and a Utah state scenic byway in 1990. (Figure 10.4). From overlooks along this highway on the eastern side of Boulder Mountain,

an expansive area, stretching east from I-70 north of the San Rafael Swell to the La Sal Mountains near Moab and south to Navaho Mountain on the far side of Lake Powell, may be viewed. The entirety of Capitol Reef National Park is below and immediately to the east of these vantage points. This highway climbs the eastern flank of Boulder Mountain, going from Pinon-juniper woodland at 7000 feet in elevation to aspen and spruce at the highway's high point of 9200 feet at Roundup Flat. The top of Boulder Mountain and the Aquarius Plateau, with its numerous lakes and fishing and primitive camping opportunities, still lies at a 2000-foot vertical rise above this point. This highway passes the Wildcat Visitor Information Center, which was built by the Civilian Conservation Corps in the 1930s. There are three easily accessible campgrounds along Highway 12 (Singletree, Pleasant Creek, and Oak Creek) and one primitive campground (no water) at Lower Browns Reservoir. Figure 10.5 shows the Singletree campground in the Teasdale Ranger District of the Dixie National Forest. In September 1992 every site at this campground was vacant, while just 20 miles away at the Fruita campground (Figure 10.6) in Capitol Reef National Park, there were no vacant sites. Visitor centers in other parts of the forest are found at Duck Creek, Panguitch Lake, and Red Canyon.

Spectacular views of the canyonland country open along the southern part of Boulder Mountain on Highway 12. The highway passes Anazazi Indian Village State Park at Boulder as it leaves the forest, and then reenters the forest for a little over a mile before exiting and passing through BLM land on a spectacular narrow ridge called "the Hogback." Calf Creek flows west of this Hogback, and there is a lovely BLM campground named Calf Creek immediately along the highway. Hiking trails may be taken to falls on Calf Creek. (This BLM area will be illustrated and discussed in more detail in Chapter 12.) The passage of the highway through the slickrock formations of the Navaho sandstone mazes of the Escalante River Canyons is breathtaking. Two other state parks, Escalante and Kodachrome Basin, are nearby as the

Figure 10.5 Singletree campground in Dixie National Forest. In September 1992 every site was vacant (contrast with Figure 10.6).

Figure 10.6 Fruita Campground in Capitol Reef National Park. There were no vacancies in September 1992, while just 20 miles to the southwest at the Singletree Campground in the Dixie National Forest (Figure 10.5), every site was vacant.

highway heads west toward Panguitch and passes through Bryce Canyon National Park.

The Dixie National Forest has over 2100 miles of Forest Development roads, including 527 miles of arterial roads, 615 miles of collector roads, and 984 miles of local or terminal roads. The forest currently has 181,840 acres closed to all types of motorized vehicle use and another 159,845 acres closed to all but snowmobiles. There are 637 miles of trails, the majority of which were originally constructed for fire access or livestock distribution. Only 175 of these miles are in good shape. Most trail use occurs in the summer but snowmobiling and cross-country skiing are increasing in winter use. Two trails—the Whipple Trail and the Cascade Falls Trail—have been designated national recreation trails. The Whipple Trail is one of the main access routes into the Pine Valley Mountain Wilderness.

Dispersed recreation areas receive intensive use on weekends and holidays, with areas near water being most popular. The current annual capacity for dispersed recreation in the Dixie National Forest is 5,668,300 RVDs, which breaks down into ROS classes and acreages as follows: primitive, 83,000 acres/25,800 RVDs; semiprimitive nonmotorized, 831,309 acres/748,200 RVDs; semiprimitive motorized, 645,797 acres/1,811,400 RVDs; roaded natural, 237,747 acres/2,948,100 RVDs; and rural, 10,869 acres/134,800 RVDs. Capacity for dispersed recreation is directly related to ease of access and facilities. The projected use for all types of dispersed recreation is predicted by the *Land and Resource Management Plan for the Dixie National Forest* (Forest Services, n.d.) to be 4,811,700 RVDs in 2030. Demand for dispersed recreation will never exceed the supply unless some unforeseen population explosion takes place.

Recreational Issues   In preparation of the *Land and Resource Management Plan for the Dixie National Forest* the following issues pertaining to recreation were identified:

- *Issue 10   How much emphasis should the Dixie National Forest place on coordinating or restricting forest activities in order to maintain or enhance scenic values along major roads,*

other travel corridors, and areas of outstanding scenic quality? Increased emphasis is placed by the *Plan* on scenic values through the use of management direction and standards and guidelines.

- *Issue 11 What should the balance be between accommodating increased recreational use and other resource uses?* Developed facilities should be located to take advantage of local attractions and to enhance dispersed recreation activities. Recreational facilities will be located to meet the needs of the public, unless there is a conflict with other resources that cannot be resolved.
- *Issue 12 Should the Dixie National Forest emphasize developed group sites over single family units when considering new recreation site construction?* The *Plan* provides for constructing primarily single-family units in new recreation sites because these will be located in areas not favored for group use. However, the *Plan* also provides for reconstructing existing group sites to accommodate heavier use.
- *Issue 13 What should be done to separate the recreational activities of conflicting user groups such as cross-country skiing and snowmobilers?* The *Plan* provides separate and distinct areas of the forest where the management direction will provide for recreational experiences ranging from primitive to rural. Conflict between recreational user groups will be minimized because there are sufficient areas of each experience type to accommodate the expected increase in user groups.

Recreational Goals   The goals for recreation as stated in the *Plan* are to:

- Provide a broad range of outdoor recreation opportunities for all segments of the public
- Allow the private sector to accomplish desired high-capital investment recreational opportunities to meet recreation demand after the year 2015
- Provide a broad spectrum of low-cost dispersed recreation opportunities
- Encourage other landowners to provide dispersed recreation opportunities
- Provide a trail system adequate to disperse recreational users and prevent overuse in popular areas, to provide safety for the user, and to provide for more year-round use of the forest
- Provide a system of managed cross-country ski and snowmobile trails with adequate trailhead facilities
- Provide opportunities for the use of off-road motor vehicles where they will not unacceptably impact forest resources or unnecessarily impact other forest users
- Provide a pleasing visual landscape
- Manage designated wilderness areas in accordance with the Wilderness Act of 1964 and the Utah Wilderness Act of 1984

Flathead National Forest

The Flathead National Forest contains 2,354,281 acres, which ranks it the 10th largest in the entire National Forest System. Among the 10 national forests in Montana, it is clearly the largest. The gross area within the boundaries is 2,629,088 acres, and 89.5 percent of this is National Forest System land. It is located in the northwestern corner of Montana and extends south from the Canadian border for 130 miles on the western side of the Continental Divide. In an east-west direction the forest extends for almost 100 miles, although a large area of private land north of Flathead Lake and around Kalispell separates sections of the forest. It borders the western and southern sides

of Glacier National Park. South of Glacier National Park the Lewis and Clark National Forest forms the eastern border of the Flathead and the Continental Divide. The Lolo National Forest borders the Flathead on the south, and the Flathead Indian Reservation borders it on the southwest and partly on the west. There is also a section of the Flathead Indian Reservation that lies between the southeastern side of Flathead Lake and the forest. The Kootenai National Forest borders the Flathead on the northwest. The 12-mile northern border of the forest is with British Columbia. The 100,000-acre Stillwater State Forest divides northern sections of the forest in the Rocky Mountain Trench, east of the Whitefish Range. There is also the 15,000-acre Coal Creek State Forest between the east side of the Whitefish Range and the North Fork of the Flathead River (south of Polebridge). The 40,000-acre Swan River State Forest lies in the forest east of the portion of the Flathead Indian Reservation that borders the southeastern side of Flathead Lake. The National Bison Range lies 12 miles west of the Mission Mountains.

Forest headquarters are at Kalispell, whose population of 12,000 makes it the largest community in the region. There are five ranger districts in the forest. The largest is the Spotted Bear Ranger District, located in the southeastern part of the Forest. Much of this ranger district consists of designated wilderness—the Bob Marshall over most of its extent but part of the Great Bear in the north. The Hungry Horse Ranger District is located north of the Spotted Bear Ranger District, surrounds most of the Hungry Horse Reservoir, and includes much of the Great Bear Wilderness on the eastern side of the reservior. It also borders Glacier National Park on the south. The administrative offices for both the Spotted Bear and Hungry Horse Ranger Districts are at Hungry Horse. The Continental Divide along the Lewis and Clark Range forms the eastern boundary of both the Hungry Horse and Spotted Bear Ranger Districts. The Swan Lake Ranger District consists of a larger portion east and southeast of Flathead Lake and a smaller portion west of Flathead Lake. The district ranger's administrative office is at Bigfork. The Mission Mountains Wilderness Area lies in the western portion of the larger unit of the ranger district. The Tally Lake Ranger District is located west and north of Kalispell with administrative offices at Whitefish. Northernmost is the Glacier View Ranger District with administrative offices at Columbia Falls. This ranger district borders Glacier National Park on the west and extends from Columbia Falls to the British Columbia border.

The Flathead National Forest is located in the Northern Rocky Mountain Physiographic Province. The topography consists of lineal north-south-trending mountain ranges with longitudinal valleys. Elevations range from the 2893-foot level of Flathead Lake to 9510 feet on Sphinx Peak on the Continental Divide. The major mountain ranges include the Lewis and Clark Range along the Continental Divide east of the South Fork of the Flathead River (Sphinx Peak, 9510 ft.), the Swan Range (Holland Peak, 9356 ft.) west of the South Fork of the Flathead River, the Mission Mountains (East St. Mary Peak, 9425 ft.) west of the Swan Range and the Swan River, and the Whitefish Range (Nasukoin Mountain, 8086 ft.) west of Glacier National Park and the North Fork of the Flathead River and east of the Rocky Mountain Trench. The northern portion of the forest that adjoins Glacier National Park shares much of the park's spectacular scenery, including a wild, glaciated landscape. A spectacular landform on the eastern border of the forest, in the heart of the Bob Marshall Wilderness Area, is the Chinese Wall. This 12-mile, 1000-foot limestone escarpment hugs the east

side of the Continental Divide on the common border of the Flathead and the Lewis and Clark National Forests. The high peaks in the Bob Marshall Wilderness are known as the Flathead Alps. The Mission Mountains are especially impressive as viewed from the west at the National Bison Range (Figure 10.7). This range rises precipitously from the valley floor at 3000 feet to elevations of over 9000 feet, an abrupt 6000-foot vertical rise. The Rocky Mountain Trench is a prominent physiographic feature of the region. It is a lowland that extends 800 miles to the northwest of Kalispell into Canada and for another 150 miles south along the Flathead and Bitterroot River Valleys. Very few peaks of the Flathead Mountains west and northwest of Kalispell exceed 6000 feet. The forest's principal rivers are the Swan, the Stillwater, and the North, Middle, and South Forks of the Flathead River. The three units of the Flathead River System are protected as components of the Wild and Scenic Rivers System. The other major water feature within the forest is the 34-mile-long Hungry Horse Reservoir, which exists behind a Bureau of Reclamation dam on the South Fork of the Flathead River.

The climate and vegetation of the Flathead National Forest vary tremendously with elevation and exposure. Average lows in the winter range from 4° to 12°F, and average highs in the summer range from 74° to 82°F. Precipitation ranges from a low of 18 inches in the Island Geographic Unit west of Flathead Lake to as high as 100 inches in the Upper Swan Geographic Unit. Snowfall ranges from 50 inches to 600–800 inches in the same places. Most of the major vegetative habitat types common to western Montana are located on significant acreage of the forest and range from the warm, dry ponderosa pine–bunchgrass type to the cool whitebark pine types. Ponderosa pine and western white pine are found primarily at the lower elevations along with western larch, Douglas fir, lodgepole pine, and spruce at many locations and in the middle elevations, and subalpine fir and whitebark pine at higher elevations to timberline. Subalpine fir is also found in some drainages at lower elevations. The forest provides habitat for approximately 250 species of wildlife and 22 species

Figure 10.7 The Mission Mountains in the Flathead National Forest rise abruptly over 1 mile in elevation (6000 ft. vertical) above the Flathead Valley. View is looking east across National Bison Range.

of fish. Elk, mule deer, and whitetail deer are important big-game animals in the forest. There are approximately 3400 miles of streams in the forest, about half of which support fish populations that includes native cutthroat, rainbow, and eastern brook trout and grayling. The Flathead National Forest provides habitat for three endangered species (gray wolf, bald eagle, and peregrine falcon) and one threatened species (grizzly bear). Eighty-seven percent of the forest is roamed by grizzlies. The number of grizzly bears that roam the Northern Continental Divide Ecosystem are estimated at 440 to 680 bears. Eighteen percent of this habitat is in Glacier National Park and another 59 percent is in the Flathead, Lewis and Clark, Lolo, Helena, and Kootenai National Forests. The 64,640-acre Trail Creek Geographic Unit in the extreme north of the Flathead National Forest is recognized as the finest grizzly bear habitat in the lower 49 states and is very important to recovering the grizzly bear from its threatened status. This area is administratively classified as the Trail Creek Grizzly Bear Management Area, and all management activities will be oriented toward maintaining or improving grizzly bear habitat. The gray wolf is also reinhabiting this area as part of its home range.

The *Forest Plan: Flathead National Forest* (Forest Service, 1985; hereafter *Forest Plan*) has classified the land of the Flathead National Forest as follows: (1) Nonforest land (including water), 222,450 acres; (2) forest land, 2,139,632 acres; (3) forest land withdrawn from timber production, 519,741 acres; (4) forest land not capable of producing crops of industrial wood, 784,144 acres; (5) tentatively suitable forest land (item 2 minus items 3 and 4), 835,747 acres; (6) forest land not appropriate for timber production, 165,077 acres; (7) unsuitable forest land (items 3, 4, and 6), 1,691,412 acres; (8) total suitable forest land (item 2 minus item 7), 670,670 acres; and (9) total national forest land (items 1 and 2), 2,362,082 acres. Within the exterior boundaries of the Flathead National Forest, there are 274,807 acres of nonnational forest ownership. Major owners of these inholdings are Plum Creek Timber Company, the state of Montana (mostly school trust lands), and Champion International. A major checkerboard landownership pattern exists in the Upper Swan Valley with Plum Creek Timber Company, and the state of Montana. Widespread subdivision for recreational and rural residential use over the last 15 years has resulted in thousands of other small ownerships.

Despite its enormous size, the Flathead is one of the least-used national forests. In 1992, its 881,500 recorded recreation visitor days ranked it 96th place in recreational use in the National Forest System. The number of recreation visits in 1992 totaled 2,289,000. The Flathead had an intensity of use index of 2.671 acres/RVD in 1992, ranking it ninth lowest in use intensity in the entire National Forest System. Only the Chugach (Alaska), Nez Perce (Idaho), Humboldt (Nevada), Challis (Idaho), Bitterroot (Idaho and Montana), Tongass (Alaska), Ochoco (Oregon), and Fremont (Oregon) National Forests had lower use intensities. Three wilderness areas cover 45 percent of the forest area: the Bob Marshall (709,356 acres), the Great Bear (286,700 acres), and the Mission Mountains (73,877 acres). A high 15 percent (128,400 RVDs) of the total recreational use for the forest occurred in these three wilderness areas. The Bob Marshall received the most use (78,400 RVDs) followed by the Great Bear (39,300 RVDs) and the Mission Mountains (10,700 RVDs). These wilderness areas are characterized by many rugged peaks, alpine lakes, mountain valleys with meadows and meandering streams, waterfalls, and abundant wildlife. In addition to grizzly

bear, elk, and mule and white-tailed deer, there are black bear and bighorn sheep. About 50 outfitter-guides serve the area. Another 300,000 acres of the Bob Marshall Wilderness Area lies in the adjacent Lewis and Clark National Forest on the eastern side of the Continental Divide. The 239,296-acre Scapegoat Wilderness Area borders the Bob Marshall on the south in the Lewis and Clark National Forest and continues into the Lolo and the Helena National Forests. It is about equally divided in area among these three national forests.

The leading category of recreational use in the Flathead National Forest is "mechanized travel and viewing scenery," comprising 29 percent of the recreation visitor days. Automobile travel is responsible for two-thirds of this total, and viewing scenery another 9 percent. "Camping, picnicking, and swimming" rank second with 24 percent of the use; camping is the leading subcategory at 75 percent of the use. "Hiking, horseback riding, and water travel" and "winter sports" play especially prominent roles in the Flathead, each contributing 13 percent of the RVDs. "Hiking" is the leading subcategory of the first category, with 38 percent of the use; "horseback riding" is another major contributor to this category, with another 33 percent. Virtually all of the hiking and horseback riding occur in the three wilderness areas. Outfitter-supplied horses provides a major means of access into the wilderness areas. Other watercraft (namely, powerboats on the Hungry Horse Reservoir) are the third major contributor to the broader category, with 25 percent of the use. Ninety-seven percent of the "winter sports" category is accounted for by downhill skiing at the one major winter sports resort—Big Mountain. "Fishing" (94 percent cold-water) and "hunting" (92 percent big-game) each account for an average of 5 percent of the total national recreational use. "Resorts, cabins, and organization camps" accounts for 4 percent of the total use, and the leading subcategories are "recreational cabin use" (67 percent), "resort lodging" (19 percent), and "general resort and commercial public service" (12 percent). "Other recreational activities" represents 6 percent of the use, with 69 percent of this use related to gathering forest products. "Nonconsumptive fish and wildlife use" contributes a very low 0.44 percent of the recreational use.

For management purposes, the Flathead National Forest has been divided into 22 management areas by the *Forest Plan*. Five of these management areas have special recreational significance:

1. *Management Area 18*   Wild, Scenic, and Recreational River Management under the 1968 Wild and Scenic Rivers Act (13,838 acres)
2. *Management Area 19*   Jewel Basin Hiking Area (15,368 acres)
3. *Management Area 20*   Big Mountain Winter Sports Area (3574 acres)
4. *Management Area 21*   Great Bear Wilderness Area and Flathead Portion of Bob Marshall Wilderness Area (996,381 acres)
5. *Management Area 22*   Mission Mountains Wilderness Area (73,573 acres)

The *Forest Plan* also identifies 31 geographic units distributed among the five ranger districts (Table 10.7).

Developed recreation of the Flathead National Forest includes both private and public facilities. Private facilities include 67 summer home sites, six resorts, and the Big Mountain Winter Sports Center, located on Big Mountain (6817 ft.) in the Whitefish Geographic Unit. It is located on both private and national forest land in the Whitefish Range, 8 miles north of Whitefish. During the summer a chairlift operates,

Table 10.7   Flathead National Forest: Geographic Units by Ranger District

Swan Lake Ranger District	Tally Lake Ranger District
Upper Swan Geographic Unit	Upper Whitefish Geographic Unit
Lower Swan Geographic Unit	Whitefish Geographic Unit
East Shore Geographic Unit	Olney-Martin Creek Geographic Unit
Noisy Face Geographic Unit	Upper Good Creek Geographic Unit
Island Geographic Unit	Sylvia Lake Geographic Unit
Spotted Bear Ranger District	Star Meadow–Logan Creek Geographic Unit
South Fork Geographic Unit	Tally Lake–Round Meadow Geographic Unit
Spotted Bear River Geographic Unit	Mountain Meadow–Rhodes Draw Geographic Unit
Bunker Creek Geographic Unit	Upper Griffin Geographic Unit
Sullivan Creek Geographic Unit	Ashley Lake Geographic Unit
Glacier View Ranger District	Hungry Horse Ranger District
Canyon-Teakettle Geographic Unit	West Side Geographic Unit
Big Creek Geographic Unit	Columbia Mountain Geographic Unit
North Fork Valley Geographic Unit	Lake Five–Desert Mountain Geographic Unit
Whale-Coal Geographic Unit	Emery Creek Geographic Unit
Trail Creek Geographic Unit	East Side Geographic Unit
	Bear Creek–Challenge Cabin Geographic Unit
	Middle Fork Geographic Unit

Source: Forest Service, *Forest Plan: Flathead National Forest* (December 1985).

affording easy access to outstanding views. The 5.6-mile Danny On Memorial Trail, a cooperative effort of the Forest Service and The Big Mountain Ski and Summer Resort, interprets the natural history of the area. This trail may be hiked in sections or its entirety. There are 23 developed camping areas with 310 sites, over half of which are on the shore of the Hungry Horse Reservoir. This reservoir was built by the Bureau of Reclamation (BOR) for the primary purpose of water storage, flood control, and power generation. The reservoir is located behind Hungry Horse Dam. There is a visitor center, and a self-guided tour may be taken. The reservoir is 34 miles long and 3.5 miles at its widest point with a maximum depth of 500 feet. There are developed picnic areas at six of these campgrounds. Nine of these campgrounds charge fees that range from $3 to $7; the rest are free. There is boat access at nine of the campgrounds. The West Side Geographic Unit receives more recreational use than the East Side Geographical Unit, probably because several trails provide access to the Swan Divide and the Jewel Basin Hiking Area. Murray Bay, on the east side of the Hungry Horse Reservoir, is the largest campground (46 sites) in the forest. Other, moderate size campgrounds on the Hungry Horse Reservoir include Lost Johnny Point (21 sites) and Lid Creek (23 sites). Other campgrounds are located at Big Creek (22 sites) in the Big Creek Geographic Unit in the northern part of the forest, Tally Lake (34 sites) in the Tally Lake–Round Meadow Geographic Unit, Swan Lake (42 sites) in the Lower Swan Geographic Unit, and at Holland Lake (40 sites) in the Upper Swan Geographic Unit. There is also the Round Meadows Cross-Country Ski Area in the Tally Lake–Round Meadow Geographic Unit. Other cross-country skiing opportunities are available at Glacier View/Cedar Trail, Lion Lake, and Essex Trail complexes, and at Blacktail Mountain.

About 77 percent of the dispersed recreation occurs in a roaded environment (including activities such as berry picking, snowmobiling, fishing, hunting, driving for pleasure, and roadside camping), while 23 percent occurs in an unroaded envi-

ronment (backpacking, hiking, fishing, and hunting). Use is unevenly distributed across ranger districts. There are 3146 miles of roads in the forest, including approximately 222 miles of arterial roads, 813 miles of collector roads, and 2111 miles of local roads. Two especially scenic drives in the Flathead National Forest are (1) along State Route 83 through the Swan River Valley between the Mission and Swan Mountains and (2) along State Route 486 and the gravel road through Polebridge along the North Fork of the Flathead River to the Canadian border. A 115-mile-loop road encircles the Hungry Horse Reservoir. Terrain, soils, and road and trail systems are generally not suitable for trail bikes or four-wheel-drive vehicles. More than 4000 miles of roads and most of the trails outside of wilderness areas are open to mountain bikes. There are over 100 miles of snowmobile trails laid out separate from routes used by cross-country skiers. Popular snowmobile trails include Crane Yew (37 miles), Canyon Creek (73 miles), Skyline Road (40 miles), and Emery Creek (30 miles). There are 2100 miles of foot and horse trails. An easily accessible 15,349-acre hiking-only unit (no horses or motorized equipment allowed), located on the north end of the Swan Range, is the Jewel Basin Hiking Area. This area includes 35 miles of trails and 27 lakes, with elevations ranging from 4240 feet on Graves Creek to 7542 feet on Big Hawk Mountain. Rangers have estimated that about 80 percent of the use is day use. The Danny On Memorial Trail on Big Mountain near Whitefish was discussed earlier. The Elk Mountain National Recreation Trail extends for 9 miles along the divide north and south of Elk Mountain in the Upper Good Creek Geographic Unit.

The three forks of the Flathead River comprise 219 miles (97.9 miles classified as wild, 40.7 miles classified as "scenic," and 80.4 miles as "recreational") of the National Wild and Scenic Rivers System. In the Middle Fork Geographic Unit, the Middle Fork of the Flathead River is classified as "recreational." A short section is classified as "wild" just below the Great Bear Wilderness Boundary and above the Bear Creek junction. This fork parallels U.S. 2 and the Burlington Northern Railroad in the canyon bottom. Floating down this portion of the river is growing in popularity. The Middle Fork is an important fish passage for migrating bull and cutthroat trout. The North Fork of the Flathead River flows along the eastern edge of the Glacier View Ranger District. It is classified as "scenic" in the Trail Creek Geographic Unit, the North Fork Valley Geographic Unit, and north of the Camas bridge in the Big Creek Geographic Unit; it is classified as "recreational" south of the Camas bridge in the Big Creek Geographic Unit and in the Canyon Teakettle Geographic Unit, where it joins the Middle Fork. The road along the North Fork leads to the most isolated community in the forest, Polebridge. The South Fork of the Flathead River is in the South Fork Geographic Unit and is classified as "wild" from the Bob Marshall Wilderness boundary to the Spotted Bear River and "recreational" from the Spotted Bear River to the Hungry Horse Reservoir. It becomes impounded as a reservoir by the Hungry Horse Dam, 34 miles farther downstream. River floating is popular on this stretch of the South Fork.

The three National Wilderness Preservation System units in the Flathead National Forest comprise over 45 percent of the forest's land. The Mission Mountains Wilderness, a 73,877-acre wilderness created in 1975, is located on the east side of the Mission Mountain Range. About 97 percent of the use is on foot, and the length of stay averages 1.7 days. Most of the users are from the forest's zone of influence. In two drainages where lakes are close to the road, these areas have been closed to forestall

further resource damage. Although portions of the wilderness are heavily used, other areas are rarely visited. On the west side of the range is the Confederated Salish and Kootenai Tribal Wilderness (Mission Mountains Tribal Wilderness), recently designated for preservation on Flathead Indian Reservation land. The Bob Marshall (709,356 acres) and Great Bear Wildernesses (286,700 acres) comprise the Flathead portion of the second-largest wilderness complex in the lower 49 states, as was discussed earlier in this section. The Bob Marshall Wilderness Area was established in 1964 to honor wilderness advocate Robert Marshall, and the Great Bear Wilderness Area was established in 1978. In contrast to the Mission Mountains, the Great Bear and the Bob Marshall attract more out-of-state visitors, particularly in the fall hunting season, when the use is heavy. Length of stay averages nearly 5 days in the Great Bear and 5.7 days in the Bob Marshall. Two of these wilderness areas have shown a decrease in use between 1980 and 1992. Use has decreased from 94,000 to 78,400 RVDs in the Bob Marshall, and from 15,000 to 10,700 RVDs in the Mission Mountains. In contrast, the Great Bear Wilderness Area increased from 23,000 RVDs in 1980 to 39,300 RVDs in 1992. About 50 outfitters operate in the Flathead National Forest portion of this wilderness complex. The Flathead National Forest presently has approximately 495,400 acres of inventoried roadless lands that qualify for inclusion into the National Wilderness Preservation System. In contrast, about 835,747 acres (35 percent of the forest) are tentatively suitable for producing commercial timber. This timberland is composed of 18 percent lodgepole pine and 82 percent mixed conifer stands.

Recreational Goals   The resource management objectives for recreation as stated in the *Forest Plan* are as follows:

- *Developed Recreation*   Bring all developed sites up to full-service level by 1995.
- *Trails*   Provide a system of trails in a variety of settings. Construct or reconstruct about 50 miles by 1995.
- *Wild and Scenic Rivers*   Implement visitor management for the Wild and Scenic River System of the Flathead National Forest.

Gifford Pinchot National Forest

The Gifford Pinchot National Forest is located in the Cascade Range in southwestern Washington. The gross area within its boundary is 1,395,728 acres, of which 1,305,267 (94 percent) are national forest land. It extends along the west slope and summit of the Middle Cascade Range for 75 miles from the Columbia River on the south to Mt. Rainier National Park on the north. It borders the Columbia River Gorge National Scenic Area on the south, the Yakima Indian Reservation and the portion of the Mt. Baker–Snoqualmie National Forest administered by the Wenatchee National Forest on the east, and Mt. Rainier National Park on the north. Included within its boundary, in the western part of the forest, is the 111,028-acre Mount St. Helens National Volcanic Monument. In addition to national forest lands, there are 114,300 acres in other ownerships within the administrative boundaries. The major landowners are the Weyerhaeuser Co., Murray Pacific Corp., and the state of Washington. The forest had its origin as Mt. Rainier Forest Reserve, initially proclaimed by President Cleveland in 1897, with additions in 1902, 1904, and 1906 made by President Theodore Roose-

velt. In 1908, President Roosevelt proclaimed the reserve the Columbia National Forest. The portion of the Mt. Rainier Forest Reserve around the mountain of the same name became Mt. Rainier National Forest, which was dissolved in 1933 when Mt. Rainier National Park was established. In 1949, the Columbia National Forest was renamed the Gifford Pinchot National Forest, to honor the former chief of the Forest Service. Forest headquarters are at Vancouver, Washington. The four ranger districts (and ranger district offices) are Packwood (Packwood), in the north; Randle (Randle), south of Packwood Ranger District; Mt. Adams (Trout Lake) in the southeast; and Wind River (Carson) in the southwest. The former Mt. St. Helens Ranger District, whose headquarters were at Cougar, is now designated the Mount St. Helens National Volcanic Monument, with headquarters at Amboy. Included among the 1,395,728 acres of the Gifford Pinchot's administrative boundary is the 75,784-acre Mineral District of the Snoqualmie National Forest, which is located 12 miles west of the forest's northwest corner.

This forest is located along the western slope of the Middle Cascades Mountain Section of the Cascade–Sierra Mountains Physiographic Province. This section is characterized by generally accordant summits, with high volcanic cones thrusting above the accordant level. Elevations in the forest range from 400 feet at the Mount St. Helens Visitor Center to 12,326 feet on the summit of Mt. Adams. Average elevation of the mountain ridges on the forest is between 3000 and 4000 feet, with several peaks in the northeast near the Goat Rocks section approaching 8000 feet. It is in this northeastern quarter of the forest that glacier-covered mountains form the steepest and most rugged section; it is also habitat for mountain goats. The two prominent snow-clad volcanic peaks within the forest are Mt. St. Helens (8363 ft.; 9677 ft. before the 1980 eruption) and Mt. Adams (12,326 ft.). Mt. Rainier (14,411 ft.) looms immediately north of the forest. Gentle-to-moderate slopes prevail in the southeastern portion, where the Big Lava Bed is located. The Big Lava Bed covers more than 21 square miles. Other lava beds and numerous *lava-tube caves* are found here. *Lahars,* including mud and debris flows, are common near the major volcanoes. The largest lahar is in the Kalama River drainage on the southwestern side of Mt. St. Helens. The topography along the western edge of the forest, including the Mt. St. Helens area, is more varied. The forces of glaciation and volcanic activity are evident all over the forest. The forest's western slope location results in heavy precipitation deposited from moist Pacific air masses. Portions of the headwaters of 11 rivers lie within the forest. From north to south they are the Nisqually, the Cowlitz, the Cispus, the Green, the Toutle, the Kalama, the Muddy, the North Fork of the Lewis, the Wind, the Little White Salmon, and the White Salmon Rivers. Several hundred lakes, most of them glacial in origin, dot the landscape. The majority are less than 20 acres in size, but several are substantially larger. Three of these are in the volcanic monument: Spirit Lake (2580 acres), Coldwater Lake (805 acres), and Castle Lake (315 acres). Packwood Lake (452 acres) and Walupt Lake (384 acres), are west and south of Goat Rocks.

Climatic conditions vary greatly between the west and east side of the Cascades. Average annual rainfall is 60 inches on the west side of the forest, in the Cowlitz Valley, and 120 inches at the summits of the ranges, but it lessens to 40 inches in the White Salmon Valley on the eastern boundary, and at Lyle, 15 miles east of White Salmon, it is only 25 inches per year. Temperatures vary considerably also, being milder and on the western side of the mountains, where they seldom reach zero, but

often reaching −10°F on the eastern side. Summers are pleasant in the west, hot in the east, and dry in all locations: Little or no rain falls during June, July, or August on either side of the range. The poleward shift of the Hawaiian Subtropical Anticyclone is responsible for this dry summer season. Average snowfall is 250 to 500 inches on the summits of the Cascades (4000-ft. elevation) and 30 to 60 inches in the lower valleys (like the Wind River, Little White Salmon, and valleys to the north).

Precipitation on the western side of the Cascades influences the heavier stands of timber found on the western slopes. Stands of conifers occupy about 84 percent of the forest. The western hemlock zone is found up to about 2300 feet. From there, Douglas-fir predominates up to about 3500 feet, although western hemlock and western red cedar are common associates. The Pacific silver fir zone, which includes grand fir, noble fir, and some subalpine fir, dominates from 3500 to 5000 feet. The mountain hemlock zone extends from about 4500–5000 feet to 6000 feet; some Englemann spruce is included in this zone, which becomes more parklike in its upper extent. On the eastern slope of the southern Washington Cascades a grand fir zone occurs as a midslope forest and is bounded by alpine fir on the upper limit and ponderosa pine on the lower limits. An alpine zone is found on the upper portion of all major volcanic peaks, such as Mt. Adams and Mt. St. Helens. Western white pine and western larch are scattered throughout the forest, and a 2800-acre tract of lodgepole pine is found just south of Mt. Adams. About 17 percent of the forest (198,000 acres) is old growth. The recently completed *Land and Resource Management Plan: Gifford Pinchot National Forest* (National Forest Service, 1990) calls for the retention of almost half of this acreage for over a century.

The Gifford Pinchot National Forest is home to hundreds of species of plants and animals, some threatened or endangered. The largest population of Roosevelt elk in the nation occupies this forest. It is also home to deer, mountain goat, black bear, eagles, peregrine falcon, and spotted owl. Currently, the habitat capability for northern spotted owls is estimated at 101 pairs for the entire forest. Timber harvest has historically reduced spotted owl habitat through the removal of mature and old-growth stands and the fragmentation of habitat areas. Resident fisheries are found throughout the forest. Anadromous fish are found in the Green River, the East Fork of the Lewis River, and the Wind River. Dams outside the forest halt anadromous runs on most of the other streams. The forest has 310 lakes and 660 miles of fishing streams.

The *Land and Resource Management Plan: Gifford Pinchot National Forest* (Forest Service, 1990d) has classified the timberland of the forest as follows:

1. Nonforest land (including water), 209,900 acres
2. Forest land, 1,161,800 acres
3. Forest land withdrawn from timber production, 195,500 acres
4. Forest land not capable of producing crops of industrial wood (acreage data not available)
5. Forest land physically unsuitable: irreversible damage likely to occur, 2300 acres; not restockable within 5 years, 17,100 acres
6. Forest land, inadequate information, 0 acres
7. Tentatively suitable forest land (item 2 minus items 3–6), 946,900 acres
8. Forest land not appropriate for timber production, 270,400 acres
9. Unsuitable forest land (items 3–6 and 8), 485,300 acres

10. Total suitable forest land (item 2 minus item 9), 676,500 acres
11. Total national forest land (items 1 and 2), 1,371,700 acres.

The Gifford Pinchot National Forest is considered a metropolitan forest, as are the Mt. Hood, the Willamette, the Mt. Baker–Snoqualmie, and the Olympic National Forests. Recreational visitors come primarily from the Portland-Vancouver, Yakima, and Tacoma metropolitan areas. It is fairly heavily used for recreation, ranking 32nd in the entire system with 2,816,257 RVDs in 1992. Its intensity of use index was 0.464 acres/RVD, which ranked it 56th among the more intensely used national forests. Over half the use occurs in the Mount St. Helens National Volcanic Monument and another 25 percent in the Randle Ranger District. The Wind River Ranger District receives the least recreational use. The forest's seven wilderness areas cover 179,101 acres and received 182,500 RVDs in 1992, which is 6.5 percent of the total use. The Wilderness Areas and their acreages are as follows: Glacier View (3123 acres); Goat Rocks (71,203 acres, with another 37,076 acres in the Snoqualmie National Forest); Indian Heaven (20,960 acres); Mt. Adams (46,626 acres); Tatoosh (15,750 acres); Trapper Creek (5970 acres); and William O. Douglas (15,469 acres, with another 152,688 acres in the Snoqualmie National Forest). The leading category of recreational use in the Gifford Pinchot National Forest is "mechanized travel and viewing scenery" (34 percent of use). The three major contributing subcategories are "viewing scenery" (55 percent), "automobile travel" (25 percent), and "bus touring" (14 percent). The major attraction of the forest, where much of this use occurs, is related to the Mount St. Helens National Volcanic Monument; much of the travel across the forest has this area as its primary destination. "Camping, picnicking and swimming" ranks second, with 26 percent of the use, 89 percent of which is related to camping and another 9 percent to picnicking. Both of the two leading categories of use mirror the national averages for the entire National Forest System. The third-ranking category of use in the Gifford Pinchot National Forest—"hiking, horseback riding, and water travel"— accounts for 19 percent of the use, which is considerably higher than the 8 percent national average. Over 90 percent of this category is attributed to day hiking and walking, 5 percent to horseback riding, and another 4 percent to mountain climbing. A high 11 percent of total use is accounted for by the "other recreational activities" category, where "gathering forest products" is the leading subcategory, with 32 percent of the category use. Berry picking (huckleberries and blackberries) is a very popular activity in the forest. Other major subcategories in this "other" category are "viewing interpretive signs" (28 percent), "attending talks and programs" (14 percent), and "general information" (10 percent). "Hunting" (96 percent big-game) and "fishing" (94 percent cold-water) each account for a below-average 3 percent of the recreational use. Each of the other three categories—"winter sports," "resorts, cabins, and organization camps," and "nonconsumptive fish and wildlife use"—accounts for a little over 1 percent of the use. Cross-country skiing is the main winter sport, with 83 percent of the total, while snow play accounts for another 17 percent. Recreation residences account for 58 percent of the "resorts, cabins, and organization camps" category, with "night organization camps" and "general resort commercial public service" each another 20 percent.

The range of recreation settings in the Gifford Pinchot National Forest is extremely broad. It varies from snow-covered peaks to low-elevation forest land, from remote backcountry wilderness areas to highly developed interpretive sites, and from

large lakes to small alpine lakes and streams. The forest is a year-round destination for recreationists. Winter snows bring cross-country skiing, snowmobiling, and winter-run steelhead fishing. Spring and summer offer camping, hiking, rafting, and fishing for salmon and summer steelhead. Fall is the time when many people hunt elk and deer or just enjoy the last warm days before cold and snow sets in. There are 55 campgrounds, seven picnic areas, and numerous viewpoints, trails, and caves. The trail system consists of 1068 miles, of which 317 are in the seven wilderness areas. There are 200,000 acres of roadless areas outside wilderness areas for those who desire solitude. Trails are available for the hiker, biker, horseback rider, or ORV user. Since the 1980 eruption of Mt. St. Helens, the Gifford Pinchot National Forest has become a major tourist attraction on the West Coast. The Mount St. Helens National Volcanic Monument entertains over a half million visitors a year. The visitor center offers guided tours, interpretive facilities, and many educational programs.

The forest's current capacity of developed recreation sites is about 11,923 PAOT. Most of the use at the developed sites occurs during the summer months, but additional facilities will be built to accommodate winter use. Over half of the increased PAOT capacity in the forest over the next decade will be associated with the Mount St. Helens National Volcanic Monument. The largest development is the Coldwater Lake–Johnston Ridge complex, which is expected to be open year-round. There are no developed ski areas administered by the Gifford Pinchot National Forest; the White Pass Ski Area is partly on the forest land but is administered by the Wenatchee National Forest. In the Mt. Adams Ranger District some of the larger campgrounds are Cultus Creek (51 sites), Goose Lake (25 sites), Little Goose (28 sites), Oklahoma (23 sites), Peterson Prairie (30 sites), and Tillicum (49 sites). In the Mount St. Helens National Volcanic Monument, Lower Lewis River Falls (42 sites) is the largest campsite, and Twin Falls has four sites. In the Packwood Ranger District is located the largest campsite on the Forest—La Wis Wis (100 sites). Other large campsites are at Big Creek (30 sites) and Walupt Lake (44 sites). Major campsites in the Randle Ranger District are Adams Fork (24 sites), Iron Creek (98 sites), North Fork (33 sites), Takhlakh (54 sites), and Tower Rock (22 sites). In the Wind River Ranger District major campsites include Beaver (24 sites), Panther Creek (33 sites), and Paradise Creek (42 sites). The Beaver Creek Group Camp can accommodate groups with a minimum size of 20 and a maximum size of 100.

Several day-use sites are especially noteworthy. Ape Cave is widely known as the longest intact lava tube in the United States and has a length of 12,810 feet. In 1979, Ape Cave was designated a national recreation trail due to the unusual experience it offers. The eruption that produced Ape Cave 1900 years ago was less explosive than more recent eruptions. The Big Lava Beds are 14 miles west of Trout Lake on Forest Road 60. The unusual formations here cover 21 square miles and originated from a 500-foot-deep crater in the northern part of the lava bed. Ice Cave, located 6 miles southwest of Trout Lake on Washington Highway 141, is one of numerous lava tubes in an area known as the Big Trench Cave System. The Mount St. Helens Visitor Center is located on Washington 504 east of the monument between Castle Rock and Toutle. Two information stations exist, one at Pine Creek on Forest Road 25 and the other at Woods Creek on Forest Road 90. There is a food concession with tables for customers at Cascade Peaks on Forest Road 99, which leads to Windy Ridge. From the 4000-foot elevation at Windy Ridge there is an excellent view of

Spirit Lake, which is covered with floating timber that drifts with the wind, and the northern side of Mt. St. Helens (Figure 9.16). This is currently the closest view of Mt. St. Helens from a drive-to site. There are interpretive programs, displays, and rest-rooms at Windy Ridge. There are seven picnic tables at the Bear Meadows Viewpoint on Forest Road 99, five picnic sites at the Lava Cast on Forest Road 8303, and three picnic sites at the Trail of Two Forests on the same road. On Ryan Lake off Forest Road 26, there are four picnic sites and an interpretive trail at a former popular camping site that was devastated by the eruption of Mt. St. Helens (Figure 10.8).

The opportunities for dispersed recreation are outstanding in the Gifford Pinchot National Forest. There are 4300 miles of roads, 1300 of which are designed for pas-senger vehicles. The biggest single attraction, and the site of over half of the total recreational use in the forest, is the Mount St. Helens National Volcanic Monument. This 111,028-acre area is administered as a separate unit of the forest. Mt. St. Helens is the smallest and youngest of Washington's five major stratovolcanoes. Even though the geological history of Mt. St. Helens goes back over 37,000 years, eruptions during the past 2500 years have been responsible for the mountain as viewed in 1980. Most of the visible cone was formed during the last 500 years. The last major eruption prior to the one in 1980 was in 1843. On March 20, 1980, an earthquake measuring 4.1 on the Richter scale occurred. This was the beginning of events leading up to the May 18, 1980, eruption. On this date at 8:32 A.M. a violent explosion devastated an area of 150 square miles to the northwest, north, and northeast of the mountain, sending an ash column 70,000 feet into the stratosphere. Within 15 minutes, 151,000 acres of forest and recreation land were devastated by the lateral blast of escaping gases. This blast blew down forests on 52,000 acres, and its heat killed trees and other plants but left them standing on another 24,000 acres. The blast resulted in 36 known casualties, 23 persons missing, and extensive damage to national forest, state, and private land. Mudflows and floods in the Toutle River valley destroyed or damaged 150 homes. The Spirit Lake Recreation Area, a major attraction of the forest, was totally destroyed. The surface of Spirit Lake was raised 200 feet. The mountain's

Figure 10.8 A former popular camping site in the Gifford Pinchot National Forest was at Ryan Lake. Today it is the site of a small picnic area and interpretive site.

Figure 10.9 The 1980 eruption of Mt. St. Helens in the Gifford Pinchot National Forest devastated 151,000 acres of forest and recreation land. The upper 1300 ft. of the mountain simply vanished. This area has been given special designation by Congress as the Mt. St. Helens National Volcanic Monument.

summit was reduced from 9677 feet to approximately 8300 feet—the upper 1300 feet of the mountain simply vanished, leaving a large, gaping hole on the north side of the mountain (Figure 10.9). The devastated area instantly became a major attraction in the Gifford National Forest. A quota system now limits the number of climbers above 4800 feet on Mt. St. Helens, and reservations for these limited permits should be made well in advance.

Scenic drives at two places offer especially good views of Mt. St. Helens and the devastated area. The new 22-mile Spirit Lake Memorial Highway (Washington 504) extends 22 miles to the Coldwater Ridge Visitor Service Center. This road will be extended to the future site of the Johnson Ridge Observatory on the north flank of the mountain. Forest Road 99, which runs west from the major Forest Road 25, offers an especially scenic drive and view. It is amazing to see where the groves of big Douglas firs simply stop and the devastated area opens up abruptly along this road; there is no zone of transition. This road culminates at Windy Ridge, which at 4000 feet of elevation is high above Spirit Lake and also offers a close-up view of Mt. St. Helens, only 4 miles distant. Be forewarned that gas pumps are few and far between in this part of the forest.[1]

There are 1068 miles of trails, including 317 miles within the seven wilderness areas; 49 miles allow hikers only; 467 miles allow horses and hikers; 84 miles allow hikers and mountain bikes; 292 miles allow hikers, horses, or mountain bikes; and 176 miles allow hikers, horses, ORVs, or mountain bikes. A total of 112 miles of the

[1]The author drove for 325 miles, running on vapors the last 25 miles, without finding a gas pump in the Gifford Pinchot National Forest or its environs. The one gas pump in Cougar was not open after Labor Day. It's a good thing Washington 503 is downhill to Woodland! On a 15,000-mile trip conducting research and taking pictures for this book in the fall of 1992, this was the closest the author came to running out of gas. Even Nevada had more plentiful gas pumps.

Pacific Crest National Scenic Trail traverses the forest. The Boundary Trail is designated a national recreation trail. Trail bike riding is offered on this trail over ridges and high mountain meadows, and the scenery is superb. A winter trail system provides opportunities for cross-country skiing and snowmobiling; 69 miles are for snowmobiles only, 95 miles are for snowmobiles and cross-country skiing, and 49 miles are for cross-country skiing only.

Currently, 180,600 acres (13 percent) of the forest are in seven wilderness areas. The Goat Rocks and Mount Adams areas were initial components (1964) of the National Wilderness Preservation System, and the Glacier View, Indian Heaven, Tatoosh, Trapper Creek, and William O. Douglas areas were added by Congress with passage of the Washington Wilderness Act (1984). The capacity of the wildernesses in the Gifford Pinchot is an estimated 181,000 RVD, which the use of 182,500 RVD in 1992 exceeded. The Mount Adams Wilderness Area receives the heaviest use, followed by the Indian Heaven and Goat Rocks Wilderness Areas. Snowgrass Flats in the Goat Rocks Wilderness and the south climb in the Mount Adams Wilderness are especially heavily used. Since 1992, permits have been required for all wilderness areas in the Gifford Pinchot except the William O. Douglas Wilderness Area. The purposes of these permits, which may be obtained at the trailheads, is primarily to gather use data. The Double LL Outfitters offer guided llama pack trips into the northern portion of the forest. Portions of four rivers on the forest have been proposed for congressional designation as wild and scenic rivers: the Lewis, the Cispus, the Muddy Fork of the Cowlitz, and the Clear Fork of the Cowlitz.

Recreational Issues   One of the *ICOs* (issues, concerns, and opportunities) in the recently completed *Land and Resource Management Plan: Gifford Pinchot National Forest* (Forest Service, 1990d, hereafter the *Plan*) was "How much and what kinds of recreation will be accommodated? Thirty-six percent of the RVDs occur in developed sites and 64 percent in dispersed sites. The present developed recreation capacity is expected to meet demands until about the turn of the century. The current annual capacity for dispersed recreation is 3,746,000 RVDs. It is expected that capacity for unroaded recreation will be adequate, but this does not mean that capacity will be adequate in every specific location. Popular areas may become overcrowded, and demand for primitive and semiprimitive nonmotorized recreational opportunities may exceed supplies; the same may be said for roaded recreation. Concerns exist about hiking trails being severed by timber harvest and road construction. Motorized use of trails is another concern of some visitors. In the proposed trail plan, motor vehicles are allowed on 27 percent of the trails outside of designated wilderness.

Recreational Goals   The goals for recreation of the *Plan* are to:

- Provide a diverse range of dispersed recreation, interpretive, and educational opportunities
- Provide a full range of trail experiences and difficulty levels, for a variety of users
- Provide safe, well-maintained facilities for developed recreation within a range of development levels
- Maintain the wild, scenic, or recreational river character of streams recommended for "wild and scenic rivers" designation

Inyo National Forest

The Inyo National Forest encompasses 2,003,110 acres within its gross boundary in the Eastern High Sierra Region, of which 1,900,543 acres (95 percent) is national forest land. These numbers rank it number 17 in size among the national forests, and it is the largest one in California. Ninety-seven percent of its area lies in east-central California, with the rest extending into adjacent Nevada. It is a long and narrow forest, extending for 165 miles from north to south and varying in width from 4 to 60 miles. On its northern border is the Toiyabe National Forest and on its west it borders—from north to south—Yosemite National Park, the Sierra National Forest, Kings Canyon National Park, Sequoia National Park, and Sequoia National Forest. Extensive holdings of land administered by the Bureau of Land Management (BLM) and land owned by the city of Los Angeles in the Owens Valley separate the section of the forest in the Sierra Nevada from the section in the White and Inyo Mountains. The BLM-administered land continues to divide sections of the forest north of Bishop along U.S. 6 to Benton. This BLM land continues northwest from Benton to west and north of Mono Lake. Extensive holdings by the BLM and the city of Los Angeles are also found around Lake Crowley and south of Mono Lake and Lee Vining. The Mono Basin National Forest Scenic Area was designated by the California Wilderness Act of 1984. There is a large, well-designed visitor center here. The scenic area totals about 116,000 acres, of which approximately 21,402 were national forest before receiving the "scenic area" designation. Congress transferred 24,430 additional acres from BLM administration to the national forest. The remaining nonfederal land includes the lake surface itself and some relict lands (lakeshore exposed during the past 40 years because of water diversion) administered by the state of California. The federal government owns approximately 60 percent of the relict lands, and the state owns approximately 40 percent. Figure 10.10 shows Mono Lake as seen from 35,000 feet. Table 10.8 identifies the distribution of the 758,876 acres of withdrawals by the Forest Service, by Congress, or by other federal agencies. Devils Postpile National Monument, administered by the National Park Service, is completely surrounded by the Inyo National Forest in the Reds Meadow–Fish Creek Management Unit. Death Valley National Monument, also administered by the National Park Service, is located only 10 air miles southeast of the Inyo Mountains Management Area of the Forest.

The Inyo National Forest, much of it along the floor of the Owens Valley, was proclaimed in 1907 by President Theodore Roosevelt for the purpose of protecting land needed to build the Los Angeles aqueduct. In 1908, President Roosevelt issued an Executive Order that reorganized the Sierra National Forest (originally established as the Sierra Forest Reserve in 1893) and transferred 1,521,107 acres of its "east side" to the fledgling Inyo National Forest. This included the portion in the White and Inyo Mountains. In 1912, President Taft rescinded the original withdrawal of public land along the Owens River, and the middle portion of the forest reached its current boundary configuration. In 1910 the Kern National Forest, consisting of 1,938,528 acres, was created from the southern end of the Sequoia National Forest, and in 1920 the major part of the present-day Mount Whitney Ranger District in the Inyo National Forest was transferred to the Inyo National Forest from its eastern slope. In the north the Mono National Forest, which included all of Mono Lake, was transferred to the Inyo National Forest in 1946. Forest headquarters are located in Bishop, Calif. There

Figure 10.10 Mono Lake (14 by 10 miles) is the central feature in the Mono Basin National Forest Scenic Area in the Inyo National Forest (California). This aerial photo was taken from 35,000 feet above.

are four ranger districts: Mono Lake in the north (office at Lee Vining), Mammoth Lakes in the middle (office at Mammoth Lakes), Mount Whitney in the south (office at Lone Pine), and White Mountain in the east (office at Bishop).

The Inyo National Forest straddles the boundary of two physiographic provinces: the Sierra Nevada Section of the Sierra-Cascades Province and the Great Basin Section of the Basin and Range Province. Few physiographic features on earth are more distinct than the dramatic eastern escarpment of the Sierra Nevada, especially in the area west of the Owens Valley between Lone Pine and Big Pine. Elevations range from 3680 feet near Owens Lake (which is dry) to the peak of Mt. Whitney at 14,495 feet. Mt. Whitney is the highest point in the lower 49 states. The Sierra Nevada is a

Table 10.8   Inyo National Forest: Withdrawals by Category

Area Name or Designation Type (Responsible Entity)	Acres
Ancient Bristlecone Pine Forest (Forest Service)	28,887
Mono Basin National Forest Scenic Area (Congress)	45,000
Developed recreation sites (Forest Service)	5,363
Administrative sites (Forest Service)	1,136
Research-natural areas (Forest Service)	8,946
Watershed and irrigation (various entities)	26,921
Power projects (FERC)	46,420
Power site reserves (FERC)	31,061
Wilderness (Congress)	565,142
Total	758,876

Source: Forest Service, *Inyo National Forest: Environmental Impact Statement for the Land and Resource Management Plan* (1988), 258.

block mountain range tilted west, whose boldest east-facing escarpment lies in the Inyo National Forest in the Mt. Whitney area. The Sierra Nevada is primarily composed of intrusive igneous rock that is 70 to 180 million years old, with the occasional remains of older sediments up to 400 million years old. Numerous peaks in the Sierra Nevada exceed 13,000 feet in elevation, and several glaciers occur under these lofty summits. The Palisades Glacier, beneath the 14,242-foot North Palisade, is the largest glacier. Besides the Sierra Nevada, the forest encompasses the Glass, White, and Inyo Mountains. The Glass Mountains (Glass Mountain, =11,123 ft.) were a historic source of obsidian for arrowheads. The White and Inyo Mountains are in the Basin and Range Province and are composed primarily of metamorphic sediments, some older than 600,000 years. Volcanic rocks (some as young as 500 years) and sand and gravel fill Mono Basin, the Long Valley Caldera, and Owens Valley. Boundary Peak (13,140 ft.) in the White Mountains is the highest point in Nevada, while White Mountain Peak (14,228 ft.) in the California portion, is the highest point in the range. Waucoba Mountain (11,123 ft.) is the highest point in the Inyo Mountains. The Owens Valley forms a major lowland (elevation about 4000 ft.) with high mountains rising abruptly on either side. It is non–National Forest land, owned either by the city of Los Angeles or administered by the BLM. The Owens River flows from Crowley Lake to the south, ending in Owens Lake. This essentially dry lake is the remnant of a Pleistocene lake that once drained to the south. Most of the national forest lands drain into the Mono Basin or Owens River; smaller portions drain westward into the San Joaquin and Kern Rivers. Mono Lake is projected to stabilize at 45 percent of its original volume (the volume it had before water diversions began in 1941) although this stabilization is still a major unresolved issue. Within the present forest boundary, nearly 50 miles of streams are dewatered, primarily for purposes of irrigation, municipal and domestic supplies, and hydroelectric power generation. Virtually every stream that flows into the Mono Basin and the Owens Valley is controlled either by the Los Angeles Department of Water and Power or the Southern California Edison Company. Internal drainage is characteristic of the Basin and Range Province.

The climate on the forest is as diverse as its topography. The higher elevations in the Sierra Nevada receive high levels of precipitation, most of which is snow during the winter. Mammoth Pass, for example, receives an average of 45 inches a year, most of which falls as snow between November and March, and Mammoth Mountain itself averages 335 inches of snow a year. Summer is very dry. Water production and storage are a major resource value of the forest, providing 70 percent of the water needs of the city of Los Angeles. There are 18 dams on Inyo National Forest land, three of which are owned by the Forest Service, four by the city of Los Angeles, and 11 by Southern California Edison. All of these dams provide water storage and regulation; 15 are also used for hydroelectric power; and 11 include impoundments with recreational use. The eastern portions and lower elevations of the forest are quite arid. The Sierra Nevada forms a classic rain shadow to its east in the prevailing westerlies. The principal city in the region, Bishop (population 3700), is located at 4147 feet of elevation and records an average of just 6 inches of rainfall, most of which falls during the winter months. The summer temperatures are extremely hot in these lower elevations.

The natural environment is noteworthy for its contrasts. Plant and animal habitats include such diverse elements as desert and wet meadow, and forest and alpine

tundra. Rugged, barren escarpments stand above forested hills, sagebrush flats, and grassy plateaus. In the lower elevations desert vegetation prevails, with pinyon-juniper woodland dominating from 5000 to 8000 feet in elevation. The most commercially valuable forest type, Jeffrey pine, grows between 7000 and 10,000 feet in elevation; lodgepole pine and red and/or white fir are intermixed and have commercial value. The *Forest Plan* (Forest Service, 1988b) states that the allowable sale quantity will be reduced to 7.1 million board feet per year from the present 10 million board feet. Lodgepole pine forest occurs from 7000 to 12,000 feet in elevation, and the red fir type occurs from 9000 to 11,000 feet. The subalpine forest grows above 12,000 feet and includes lodgepole pine, mountain hemlock, western white pine, whitebark pine, limber pine, and foxtail pine. *The Jeffrey pine in the Glass Mountain and Upper Owens River Management Areas of the forest make up the largest contiguous stand of pure Jeffrey pine in the world.* Tentatively suitable timber stands are found in two general locations in the forest: (1) on the north half of the forest (south of Mono Lake and north of Mammoth Lakes), and (2) at the south end of the forest (near Monache Meadows on the Kern Plateau). The vegetation in the White Mountains varies from sagebrush and desert scrub at the lower elevations through pinyon-juniper woodland to bristlecone and limber pine forests above the 10,000-foot elevation. This area has been set aside for special management as the Ancient Bristlecone Pine Forest Botanical Area. Found here is "Methuselah," at over 4600 years old the oldest-known living thing on earth, and the "Patriarch," the largest of the gnarled old bristlecone pines. A bristlecone pine found in what is now Great Basin National Park (the Humboldt National Forest until 1986) in the Snake Range in eastern Nevada was the world's oldest living tree until 1964. In this year "Prometheus," as the 4950-year-old tree was called, was cut to obtain an accurate reading of its growth rings. The Inyo National Forest provides habitat for approximately 400 terrestrial vertebrate species, including mule deer, red fox, pine marten, wolverine, Tule elk, Nelson (desert) mountain sheep, Sierra Nevada (California) mountain sheep, bald eagle, spotted owl, peregrine falcon, and sage and blue grouse. Special California Mountain Sheep Zoological Areas have been established in the Owens Valley Escarpment Management Area of the Sierra Nevada. The forest has about 1100 miles of streams and several hundred lakes, most of which are less than 100 acres. Fish habitat quality in most streams is rated medium or high. About 90 percent of the resident trout are in the lakes. Few streams and lakes in the forest supported fish prior to the arrival of Europeans. Only seven fish species are native to the area: Owens tui chub, Owens pupfish, Owens dace, Owens sucker, western sucker, rainbow trout (but only in the Kern River), and golden trout. Introduced species include the brown, brook, rainbow (outside the Kern River), Paiute cutthroat, Lahontan cutthroat, and Colorado cutthroat trout. Reproducing populations of brown, brook, and rainbow trout are common. Paiute and Lahontan cutthroat trout are federally listed as threatened.

Recreation is the primary resource value of the Inyo National Forest, and the majority of its users travel 6 to 8 hours from southern California population centers to use its resources (85 percent of the forest users are from southern California). San Francisco is the same driving distance in the summer, but this lengthens in the winter when some of the mountain passes are closed because of snow conditions. Inyo is the third most heavily used national forest in the entire National Forest System for recreation, recording 8,376,300 RVDs in 1992. Only the Tonto (Arizona) and the An-

geles (California) receive heavier recreation use. It is one of the most intensively used national forests with an intensity of use index of 0.227 acres/RVD. Only 14 forests receive a higher degree of intensity of use. The forest has six wilderness areas that total 551,278 acres (30 percent of the forest's acreage). Only one of these areas is totally within the forest—the Boundary Peak (Nevada, 10,000 acres). The others wilderness areas are shared with other national forests: Ansel Adams (78,775 acres in the Inyo National Forest; 151,483 acres in Sierra National Forest); Golden Trout (192,765 acres in the Inyo; 110,746 acres in the Sequoia National Forest); Hoover (9507 acres in the Inyo; 39,094 acres in the Toiyabe); John Muir (228,366 acres in the Inyo; 351,957 acres in the Sierra); and South Sierra (31,865 acres in the Inyo; 28,219 acres in the Sequoia). These wilderness areas are extremely heavily used, so a quota system has been implemented to protect both the resource and the quality of recreation experiences. In 1992, 511,600 RVDs were measured in these six wilderness areas in the Inyo National Forest. Only four other national forests received heavier wilderness use in 1992: the Superior (Minnesota, 1,404,000 RVDs), the Tongass (Alaska, 797,000 RVDs), the Bridger-Teton (Wyoming, 543,500 RVDs), and the Shasta-Trinity (California, 520,800 RVDs).

The leading category of recreational use in 1992 was "mechanized travel and viewing scenery," accounting for 40 percent of the total in the Inyo National Forest. "Automobile travel" was the principal subcategory, contributing 68 percent of the use, and "viewing scenery" was the other major subcategory, contributing 18 percent of the use. A significant number of these users pass through the forest in the Mono Lake Ranger District on U.S. 395 and California 120. The new visitor center, located just north of the junction of these roads, sits above Mono Lake. California 120 is the only entrance to Yosemite National Park from the east. This road through Tioga Pass closes for the winter. The second-ranking major category of use is "camping, picnicking, and swimming," accounting for 20 percent of the total recreational use; 83 percent of this is camping, and the remainder is evenly distributed between picnicking and swimming. The category "resorts, cabins, and organization camps" contributes a very high 12 percent of the total recreational use. The distribution among subcategories is as follows: "resort lodging," 71 percent; "recreational cabin use," 15 percent; and "general resort and commercial public service," 9 percent. Most of this use occurs in the resort industry in the Mammoth and June Lake Loop Management Areas. The two alpine ski areas in the forest, Mammoth Mountain and June Mountain, are located here. The summer resort business at June Lake is relatively more important than at Mammoth. The fourth-ranking category of recreation use is "winter sports," accounting for over 8 percent of the total recreational use; 85 percent of this use is related to downhill skiing at the two ski areas, Mammoth Mountain and June Mountain. Only two ski areas in the United States—Vail and Breckenridge (both in Colorado)—had more skiers than Mammoth Mountain in 1992–1993. Cross-country skiing and snow play each contribute 6 percent to the category's total. "Other recreational activities" ranks fifth in recreational use (7 percent of total use), with several important subcategories: "general information," 40 percent; "gathering forest products," 17 percent; "viewing interpretive exhibits," 16 percent; "unguided walking," 12 percent; and "viewing interpretive signs," 12 percent. "Hiking, horseback riding, and water travel" ranked sixth among the categories of recreational use, accounting for 6 percent of the use. The leading subcategories of use are: "hiking," 74 percent;

"horseback riding," 16 percent; "mountain climbing," 4 percent, and "other water-craft," 4 percent. "Fishing" was the seventh-ranked major category of use, of which 99.88 percent was cold-water fishing and the other 0.12 percent was ice fishing. "Non-consumptive fish and wildlife use" ranked eighth, with 2 percent of the recreational use, and "hunting" ranked ninth and last at a very low 1 percent of the recreational use. Seventy-eight percent of the hunting was big-game, 11 percent was small-game, 6 percent was upland birds, and 6 percent was waterfowl.

Recreation is the most significant resource on the Inyo National Forest and is expected to continue in that role into the foreseeable future. The economic stability of all Eastern Sierra communities rests heavily on recreation-based income. The at-tractions include more than a half million acres of designated wildernesses, hundreds of lakes and miles of streams with excellent trout fishing, 4000 developed campsites (both public and private), and two major ski areas with a long ski season. Most developed sites in the forest have historically been used only in the summer. How-ever, the growth of downhill skiing has generated an increase in other winter activ-ities as well (for example, cross-country skiing, winter camping, and organized snow play). The current trend in Forest Service recreation management is to encourage more dispersed use rather than construct more developed sites. However, the amount of dispersed recreation is closely associated with the amount of overnight capacity available on both public and private land in the area. Because the Eastern Sierra is located at least 4 to 5 hours from any major population center, most forest visitors require overnight accommodations. If developed recreation on the Inyo were de-emphasized, dispersed recreation would be deemphasized accordingly. The Inyo is already one of the most recreationally developed national forests nationwide, and there are many opportunities for additional development. These developed facilities are oriented toward overnight accommodations, day use, and interpretation.

Approximately 98 percent of public and private developed sites are located in *concentrated recreation areas*. The location of these areas and the total available recre-ational facilities and capacities for the forest are summarized in Table 10.9. Of the concentrated recreation areas, only the Inyo Craters–Deer Mountain, Shady Rest, and Cedar Flat–Schulman Grove areas are located away from water. All areas are located in the Sierra Nevada with the exception of Hot Creek and Cedar Flat–Schulman Grove. The concentrated recreation areas are listed from north to south in this table. These areas comprise approximately 47,000 acres, or 2 percent of the national forest land base. Figure 10.11 shows the Ellerly Lake campground along CA 120 in the Lee Vining Canyon–Tioga Pass Concentrated Recreation Area. Because developed sites are concentrated in these areas, 65 percent of the nonwilderness dispersed recreation in the forest takes place on the same acres. A combination of factors attracts recrea-tionists to these areas: outstanding scenery, the mountain environment, cool weather, lakes and streams with superb trout fisheries, a wide variety of recreational oppor-tunities, and ease of access on high-standard paved roads. Most concentrated recre-ation areas are water-oriented. Many parallel the main streams flowing from the Sierra Nevada crest, while others surround major lakes.

The two downhill ski areas that operate on the Inyo National Forest under spe-cial-use permit are Mammoth Mountain Ski Area and June Mountain Ski Area. Mam-moth Mountain Ski Area is located at Mammoth Lakes (Figure 10.12). The statistics for the ski area are as follows: 3500 skiable acres, a 3100-foot vertical drop, a 7953-

Table 10.9   Inyo National Forest: Recreation Summary

Recreation Facilities	
Camp and picnic sites (14,763 PAOT)	102
Interpretive sites	33
Major visitor centers	3
Wilderness trailheads	31
Resorts	22
Organizational campsites	5
Concessionaires	25
Recreation residences	410
Alpine ski areas (22,050 SAOT)	2
Nordic touring centers	2
Trail mileage	1,236
OHV route mileage	Over 5000 miles

Concentrated Recreation Areas (North to South)

Lundy Canyon	Convict Creek–Convict Lake
Lee Vining Canyon–Tioga Pass	Rock Creek
June Lake Loop	Bishop Creek
Glass Creek–Deadman Creek	Big Pine Creek
Inyo Craters–Deer Mountain	Independence Creek
Shady Rest–Sherwin Creek	Lone Pine Creek
Mammoth Lakes Basin	Hot Creek
Reds Meadow–San Joaquin River	Cedar Flat–Schulman Grove

Source: Forest Service, *Inyo National Forest: Environmental Impact Statement for the Land and Resource Management Plan* (1988), 275, 276.

Figure 10.11   The Ellerly Lake campground is located on California Route 120 in the Lee Vining Canyon-Tioga Pass Concentrated Recreation Area in the Inyo National Forest.

foot base elevation, an 11,053-foot top elevation, 30 lifts, 150 trails (30 percent begin-ner, 40 percent intermediate, 30 percent advanced), 22 snowmaking trails, longest run of 2.5 miles, a 335-inch average snowfall, and 70 percent sunny days. June Mountain Ski Area is located at June Lake. Its statistics are: 500 skiable acres, a 2590-foot vertical drop, a 7545-foot base elevation, a 10,135-foot top elevation, eight lifts, 35 trails (35 percent beginner, 45 percent intermediate, 20 percent advanced), longest run of 2.5 miles, a 250-inch average snowfall, and 70 percent sunny days. The approved Mam-moth Mountain development plan allows it to increase to 3600 acres and 31,000 SAOT, and total development at June Mountain could expand that area to 1500 acres and its capacity to 7000 SAOT, for a total of 38,000 SAOT at the two ski areas. An additional five sites totaling 12,500 acres and having an estimated capacity of 31,400 SAOT, all in the Mammoth area, are considered suitable for ski area development: Sherwin Bowl (2400 acres, 8000 SAOT); Minaret Summit (1300 acres, 3200 SAOT); Mammoth Knolls (3800 acres, 3200 SAOT); San Joaquin (3500 acres, 14,000 SAOT); and White Wing (1500 acres, 3000 SAOT).

The Inyo National Forest has a wide and varied range of dispersed recreation activities and includes those activities that occur outside of developed sites, such as hiking, fishing, public wood gathering, hunting, four-wheel driving, sightseeing, and cross-country skiing. There is competition between wilderness recreation and other dispersed activities, as certain lands now being used for four-wheel-drive and off-road vehicle (ORV) recreation are being considered for wilderness designation. For planning purposes the dispersed areas outside of concentrated recreation areas are subdivided into two categories: open national forest lands (roaded outside of con-centrated recreation areas) and unroaded lands (all nonwilderness lands of the forest that are not accessible by constructed and maintained public roads). Major summer activities in the "open" category are primitive camping, driving for pleasure, wood gathering, hunting, and motorbike use. Winter activities include snowmobiling and

Figure 10.12 Aerial view of Mammoth Mountain Ski Area looking south down the Sierra Nevada Range in the Inyo National Forest. (Mammoth Mountain Ski Area photo)

cross-country skiing. The forest has 32 miles of arterial roads, 201 miles of collector roads, and 741 miles of local roads. Total use in this category is about half that generated in concentrated recreation areas. The most popular areas in this category are the forested lands northeast of Mammoth Lakes, the Buttermilk area west of Bishop, the area east of Lake Crowley, and the roaded parts of the White and Inyo Mountains. Most of the unroaded lands are accessible only by foot, horseback, or four-wheel-drive vehicle. Hunting, hiking, backpacking, fishing, sightseeing, and ORV use are the major activities. This category includes most of the White and Inyo Mountains, Monache Meadows, portions of the Coyote Plateau, and most of the Glass and Excelsior Mountains.

Increases in dispersed recreation use are tied directly to the availability of overnight accommodations, both in the forest and in neighboring communities. The forest is capable of doubling dispersed use in concentrated recreation areas. In the open national forest and on unroaded lands, the potential for dispersed use exceeds the current demand. Recreational access for vehicle-based dispersed recreation is good. The forest road system is virtually complete, and most roads could accommodate more use than they do at present. There is, however, a major shortage of trails in dispersed areas. Cross-country skiing is the fastest-growing dispersed use on the forest. The amount of snowmobile use is minor. Table 10.10 identifies the acreage, capacity, and percent of use in the Inyo National Forest by ROS classes for developed and dispersed recreation. The original ROS system had only six classes. Managers of the Inyo have chosen to split the "roaded natural" class into two subparts: "roaded natural" (roaded with limited development) and "roaded modified" (roaded with moderate development). Heavily developed areas are classified as "Rural." Although

Table 10.10   Inyo National Forest: ROS Classes

ROS Class	Acres	Capacity (PAOTs)	% of Use
Developed Recreation			
Primitive	3	75	0.07
Semiprimitive nonmotorized	0	0	0.00
Semiprimitive motorized	2	50	0.035
Roaded natural	110	2,195	9.07
Roaded modified	870	18,100	46.47
Rural	3,730	25,750	43.15
Urban	15	310	1.20
Total	4,730	46,480	100.00
Dispersed Recreation			
Primitive	872,600	4,290	31.45
Semiprimitive nonmotorized	392,600	4,050	4.90
Semiprimitive motorized	189,200	2,500	1.36
Roaded natural	383,600	62,900	25.18
Roaded modified	35,100	34,900	31.54
Rural	11,600	15,050	5.57
Urban	2,000	0	0.00
Total	1,886,700	123,600	100.00

Source: Forest Service, *Inyo National Forest: Environmental Impact Statement for the Land and Resource Management Plan* (1988), 286.

46 percent of the forest is classified as "primitive," the recreational capacity of those areas is low because of steep, inaccessible terrain, a lack of water, and a lack of recreational attractions. Even the addition of trails in the Inyo and White Mountains would not generate great increases in use.

The Inyo National Forest trail system, encompassing 1236 miles of trails, provides hikers and equestrians access into (1) the Hoover, Ansel Adams, John Muir, Golden Trout, and South Sierra Wildernesses; (2) the Yosemite, Kings Canyon, and Sequoia National Park backcountry areas; and (3) large uncrowded portions of the White Mountains and the southern Sierra Nevada near Monache Meadows. The renowned John Muir Trail and 53 miles of the Pacific Crest National Scenic Trail traverse Inyo forest lands. The Discovery Trail (1.0 miles) and the Whitney Portal Trail (4.1 miles) are national recreation trails. Approximately 705 miles of the trails are located in wilderness areas. The demand for wilderness recreation in the forest is very high. Existing wildernesses are managed under a trailhead quota system so that use does not exceed established wilderness capacity limits. Quotas are essentially full during the summer peak-use season.

Recreational Issues and Goals   In the planning process that resulted in the recently completed *Inyo National Forest Land and Resource Management Plan* (Forest Service, 1988), the basic recreation issue/concern was: "What is the best recreational opportunity program for the Inyo (considering supply, demand, other resource management and development opportunities, and environmental protection needs)?" In this planning process, *Alternative PRF: Preferred Alternative* was selected. This plan protects and enhances the environmental and recreation benefits provided by the Inyo National Forest while providing moderate levels of grazing, minerals development, and timber harvest to support the local economy. Developed summer recreation will be managed with the objective of increasing opportunities in response to demand. Alpine skiing will increase at a rate that responds to demand within environmental, infrastructural, and social constraints. The management of dispersed summer and winter recreation will provide for an increase in use roughly proportional to the use of developed sites. And last, the wilderness land base will be increased.

Lincoln National Forest

The 1,103,636-acre Lincoln National Forest is located in the mountainous area of south-central New Mexico between the Tularosa Basin and the Pecos River drainage. The amount of national forest land represented is 86.8 percent of the land area within its gross boundaries of 1,271,064 acres. It extends north from the Texas border for 150 miles to the Jicarilla Mountains and includes the Guadalupe, Sacramento, Sierra Blanca, and Capitan Mountains. Its greatest east-west extent is 35 miles. The Guadalupe Mountains section is detached from the rest of the forest and borders Guadalupe Mountains National Park (Texas) and Carlsbad Caverns National Park (N. Mexico). The Mescalero Apache Indian Reservation divides the section of the forest in the Sacramento Mountains from the Sierra Blanca Mountains section. White Sands National Monument is 15 miles west of the forest, and an excellent view of this National Park unit may be had from the summit of the west escarpment of the Sacramento Mountains. The McGregor Range of the Fort Bliss Military Reservation bor-

ders the Cloudcroft Ranger District of the forest on the south. The land in what is today's Lincoln National Forest was initially set aside in 1902 as the Lincoln Forest Reserve in the Capitan and White Mountains to protect and conserve recreational and water values. Additions were made to the initial forest reserve in 1905, 1906, and 1907, which made it about the size of the present-day Smokey Bear Ranger District. In 1908 the Gallinas Forest Reserve, located west of Corona and surrounding Gallinas Peak, was added to the Lincoln. (In 1958 this portion of the forest was transferred to the Cibola National Forest.) In 1908 the Lincoln also gained national forest status. In 1917, the Alamo National Forest was transferred to the Lincoln. The Alamo National Forest had been created in 1908 by the merger of the Sacramento National Forest (created in 1907) and the Guadalupe National Forest (created in 1907).

Forest headquarters are located west of the forest boundary at Alamogordo (population 28,000). The forest is divided into four ranger districts: The Guadalupe Ranger District is a detached section located to the southeast, with ranger headquarters in Carlsbad; the Cloudcroft Ranger District is located in the Sacramento Mountains with ranger headquarters at Cloudcroft; the Mayhill Ranger District is located east of the Cloudcroft Ranger District with ranger headquarters at Mayhill; and the Smokey Bear Ranger District is the northernmost one, with ranger headquarters at Capitan. The Lincoln National Forest is known as the birthplace of the world-famous "Smokey Bear," the living symbol of the campaign to prevent forest fires. In 1950, a small black bear cub was found singed and badly frightened in the charred ruins of the Capitan fire, which burned 17,000 acres. Nicknamed Smokey by the firefighters who found him, he was nursed back to health and then flown to Washington, D.C., to live in the National Zoo as "Smokey Bear," the living symbol of the nation's campaign to prevent forest fires. The original "Smokey Bear" retired in 1975 and died a few years later and is buried in Smokey Bear State Park at Capitan, N. Mex. The scars of the fire around Capitan Gap may still be observed.

The Lincoln National Forest is located in the Sacramento Mountain Section of the Basin and Range Physiographic Province. The landscape varies from rugged canyons to gently sloping foothills. Elevations range from 4200 feet above sea level at the western base of the Sacramento Mountains to over 11,500 feet near Sierra Blanca Peak. (The summit of Sierra Blanca Peak is 11,973, but 1 mile outside of the forest boundary, on the Mescalero Indian Reservation.) The forest's western edge is a rugged escarpment that at one point plunges over 5000 feet to the floor of the Tularosa Basin. Most of the forest lies east of the escarpment and slopes gradually to the Pecos River, in the Pecos Valley Section of the Great Plains Physiographic Province. Four perennial streams (the Rio Bonito, the Rio Ruidoso, the Rio Penasco, and the Sacramento River) form near the escarpment and flow eastward to join the Pecos. The Guadalupe Mountains, consisting of sandstone, are the exposed portion of the Capitan Reef. This noteworthy geological feature is the youngest and best known of the Permian barrier reefs, which were once under sea level. The southern end forms 45 miles of reef front from Carlsbad to El Capitan Peak, the bold southern headland of the Reef Escarpment. This escarpment encompasses Carlsbad Caverns National Park and Guadalupe Mountains National Park.

The climate varies from warm and semiarid at lower elevations to cool and subhumid in the mountains. Elevation plays a major role in determining temperatures. Average annual temperatures range from about 60°F near the forest's borders (with

rainfall about 9 inches/year) to 40°F and 28 inches/year in the central parts. At higher elevations—7000 feet and up—summer nights are chilly (40°F) and days are warm (78°F), while winter temperatures can drop to −15°F at night and rise to 40–50°F during the day. At lower elevations—6000 to 7000 feet—winter temperatures rarely fall below 0°F and usually run from the teens to the 50s. Summer temperatures range from 50° to 85°F. At the lowest elevations—4000 to 6000 feet—temperatures are generally 10° higher throughout the year. Spring is the windy season, with high winds drying the forest to the point of extreme fire danger. Fire season usually begins in March or April and continues through mid-July. Over 50 percent of the precipitation falls during the "monsoon" months of July, August, and September. The first snow falls in late October or early November. Elevations of 4000 to 11,500 feet pass through five different life zones from Chihuahuan desert to subalpine forest. Vegetation ranges from rare cacti in the lower elevations, to pinyon-juniper woodland, aspen, ponderosa pine, Douglas fir, spruce, and fir and high-elevation grasses and forbs. The Guadalupe Mountains are not as high, ranging in elevation from 3500 to 7500 feet. Pinyon and juniper prevail in the northern part of the mountains along with grasses, brush and cacti. Vegetation in the southern portion is pinyon-juniper, oak, pine, fir, and Texas madrone trees with ground covers of grasses and cacti.

The Lincoln National Forest is the destination of more large- and small-game hunters than any national forest in New Mexico. Deer (whitetail and mule), elk, black bear, and turkey are large animals commonly observed and hunted. Other animals that may be viewed include mountain lions, desert bighorn sheep, coyote, raccoon, squirrel, bobcat, skunk, badger, porcupine, and gray fox. Five species of birds have crucial habitat in high-altitude wilderness areas. The Lincoln is a very dry forest, and fishing opportunities are rather limited. They are nonexistent in the Guadalupe Ranger District. The best fishing opportunities are for rainbow and native trout in Nogal and Benito Lakes and the Rio Ruidoso.

The land classification for the Lincoln National Forest is as follows:

1. Nonforest land (including water), 206,274 acres
2. Forest land, 897,221 acres
3. Forest land withdrawn from timber production, 82,879 acres
4. Forest land not capable of producing crops of industrial wood, 557,239 acres
5. Forest land physically unsuitable, 0 acres
6. Forest land—inadequate information, 0 acres
7. Tentatively suitable forest land (item 2 minus items 3–6), 257,103 acres
8. Forest land not appropriate for timber production—need for MMRs and multiple-use objectives (25,236 acres) and not cost-efficient (92,447 acres)
9. Unsuitable forest land (items 3–6 and 8), 757,801 acres
10. Total suitable forest land (item 2 minus item 9), 139,420 acres
11. Total national forest land (items 1 and 2), 1,103,495 acres.

The Lincoln National Forest received 1,289,400 RFDs of use in 1992, ranking it 78th among all national forests. The recreation visits for the forest in 1992 were 3,000,000. The intensity of use index is a relatively light 0.856 acres/RVD; 88 national forests had higher intensities of use. In the Lincoln, the use varies tremendously from very heavy in the Cloudcroft Ranger District to extremely light in the Guadalupe Ranger District. The forest has two units of the National Wilderness Preservation

System: The 48,208-acre White Mountain Wilderness Area was established as an initial component of the Wilderness System in 1964, and the 34,658-acre Capitan Mountains Wilderness Area was added in 1980. These two wilderness areas recorded 20,300 RVDs in 1992, which was 1.6 percent of the total recreational use of the forest.

The leading category of recreational use is "mechanized travel and viewing scenery" (35 percent), which is exactly the average for the entire National Forest System. The leading subcategory is "automobile travel" (67 percent), and "motorcycle and scooter use" accounts for another 18 percent. "Camping, picnicking, and swimming" is the second-ranking category of use, again being the same as the Systemwide average, 25 percent; "camping" is the leading subcategory at 74 percent, followed by picnicking at a high 25 percent and swimming at a low 1 percent. "Hunting," 96 percent of which is big-game, ranks third with a much-above-average 16 percent of the use. "Winter sports" also plays a much-above-average role in the Lincoln's recreational use, accounting for over 12 percent of the total. Ninety-five percent of this use is downhill skiing at the two alpine ski areas in the forest—Ski Apache and Ski Cloudcroft. "Hiking, horseback riding, and water travel" accounts for another 7 percent of the use, with "hiking" the major subcategory at 75 percent and the other 25 percent related to horseback riding. The "other recreational activities" category accounts for 3 percent of the recreational use. There are several specific subcategories that make contributions to this category's total: "gathering forest products" (34 percent); "unguided walking" (15 percent); "attending talks and programs" (13 percent); "team sports" (10 percent); "individual sports" (8 percent); and "viewing interpretive signs" (8 percent). Pinion nuts are a delicacy provided by the forest for gathering purposes. "Resorts, cabins, and organization camps" contributes a low 2 percent to the recreational use. The three subcategories contributing to this category are: "night organization camping" (46 percent); "general day organization camping" (37 percent); and "recreational cabin use" (17 percent). "Nonconsumptive fish and wildlife use" accounts for another 0.7 percent of the recreational use, and "fishing" an extremely low 0.12 percent (1500 RVDs, all cold-water). The Lincoln is an extremely dry forest, so fishing opportunities are limited.

The Lincoln is a valuable recreational resource in this section of New Mexico. Developed and dispersed camping and picnicking, big- and small-game hunting, caving (spelunking), wildlife viewing, skiing, hiking, photography, and pleasure driving are major recreational activities on the forest. The forest road system totals 2960 miles, of which 2270 miles are open for use. Most of the forest is open for dispersed camping and picnicking. Visitors should be cautioned that the Lincoln National Forest has developed a travel policy to help improve wildlife habitat and water quality, provide erosion control, insure public safety, and eliminate conflicts between types of use. The policy allows vehicular traffic on designated roads and trail routes only. All open routes are designated by route number signs. Trail routes are marked with a "T" before the number and are limited to 40-inch-wide vehicles. Absence of a route number sign means the road or trail is closed to motor vehicles. Vehicles are allowed to travel 300 feet off designated routes for direct access to campsites or parking locations. An especially scenic drive is U.S. 82, which passes through Cloudcroft, a major tourist center and a site of developed recreation facilities. Halfway between Cloudcroft and Alamogordo on U.S. 82 is the only highway tunnel in southern New

Mexico. A parking area just west of the tunnel offers a spectacular view of Fresnal Canyon, White Sands, and the Tularosa Basin. Closer to Cloudcroft is another pull-off area where the largest of 58 trestles of "The Cloudclimbing Railroad" that crosses Mexican Canyon may be viewed. This railroad operated from the 1890s until 1945. From Cloudcroft the 15-mile Sunspot Scenic Byway (New Mexico 6563) climbs to the Sacramento Peak Observatory, an area used for solar research. The observatory may be toured. The highway traverses the front rim of the Sacramento Mountains, with an elevation range of 8360 feet at its lowest elevation to a height of 9500 feet. The vistas of the Tularosa Basin are outstanding along this road.

The forest has 13 family campgrounds, four family picnic areas, and five group camp- and picnic grounds. The main concentration of campgrounds is in the Cloud-croft Ranger District near Cloudcroft and north of Ruidoso in the Smokey Bear Ranger District. There are over 300 miles of trails that offer opportunities for hiking, horseback riding, and motorcycling. Many of these trails are used by cross-country skiers and snowmobilers in the winter. Among the many trails on the forest are two national recreation trails: the Dog Canyon Trail and the Rim Trail. The Rim Trail is 13.5 miles long and parallels the Sunspot Scenic Byway. It begins near the Slide Group campground and affords outstanding views of the Tularosa Basin below. The Dog Canyon Trail gains 3130 vertical feet over 4.2 miles as it ascends the western face of the Sacramento Escarpment from the Oliver Lee Memorial State Park to Joplin Ridge. This old Apache Indian trail is one of the most popular trails on the forest, with spring and fall the best times to use it. There are no developed campgrounds in the Guadalupe District, but a picnic area and rare waterfall are found in this semiarid area at Sitting Bull Falls Picnic Area. This area is located in the East Guadalupe Management Area, 44 miles west of Carlsbad. There are also about 100 caves in this part of the forest that can be entered with a permit. The South Guadalupe Management Area is managed primarily for cave preservation and includes the Guadalupe Escarpment Wilderness Study Area. The Rim Road (Forest Road 540, not to be confused with the Rim Trail) is a maintained gravel road along the southern part of the district with spectacular views of Dog Canyon and the Brokeoff Mountains.

As mentioned earlier, two downhill ski areas are located in the Lincoln National Forest: Ski Apache, near Ruidoso and operated by the Mescalero Apache Tribe, and Ski Cloudcroft, located next to the village of the same name. Many visitors to Ski Apache stay at the elaborate Inn of the Mountain Gods Resort, located 2 miles south of Ruidoso (the ski area is 16 miles northwest of Ruidoso). The Inn of the Mountain Gods Resort is located on the Mescalero Apache Indian Reservation. It will serve as the case study of the recreational use of Native American Tribal lands in Chapter 13. Ski Apache is located primarily on national forest land and is operated under a special-use permit. This ski area has a base elevation of 9700 feet and receives 180 inches of snow per year. It has a four-passenger gondola, a quad-chair, five triple chairs, two double chairs, and one "mighty mite" tow that operates during a ski season from Thanksgiving through Easter. The ski area includes 1060 acres and has 45 trails with an even mix of beginner, intermediate, and advanced runs. The capacity of the ski area is 7000 skiers per day, and the uphill lift capacity is 15,300 skiers per hour. The *Lincoln National Forest Plan* (Forest Service, 1986a; hereafter the *Forest Plan*) has allocated land in Rice or Russia Canyon in the Upper Penasco Management Area

for future ski-area development with a capacity of 2000 PAOT. The plan also provides for expansion of the Ski Cloudcroft Ski Area, which is located in the Upper James Management Area.

The Capitan Mountains Wilderness Area (34,658 acres) is located in the north-eastern corner of the forest, and the White Mountain Wilderness Area (48,208 acres) is located in the northwestern corner of the forest; both lie in the Smokey Bear Ranger District. The Capitan Mountains Wilderness ranges in elevation from 5500 feet on the eastern side to 10,083 feet at Capitan Peak. The Capitan Mountain Range, in which Capitan Peak is located, is quite unique in that it trends from east to west. The lower stretches of this area are comprised of pinyon-juniper woodland, with ponderosa pine and pinyon on the middle slopes, and Douglas fir, Englemann spruce, corkbark fir, and ponderosa pine on the main ridgetop. There are also several good-sized aspen groves. There are 47 miles of trails in the Capitan Mountains Wilderness. The White Mountain Wilderness Area borders the northern side of the Mescalero Reservation. In 1933 it was set aside as a "primitive area," and became part of the Initial National Wilderness Preservation System in 1964. Elevations range from a low of 6500 feet at Three River campground on the western side to 11,580 feet near Lookout Mountain on the south. There are four different life zones from Three Rivers to the crest: pinyon-juniper, ponderosa pine, mixed conifer, and subalpine forest. Interspersed along the crest are several meadows as well as some oak-grass savannas that are the result of fires. During the winter months the higher elevations may be under 6 or more feet of snow. There is a developed and maintained trail system of 50 miles within the wilderness area.

An interesting area with a special classification in the *Forest Plan* is the William G. Telfer Research Natural Area. This 727-acre area was named in honor "of a loyal Forest Service employee who died in performance of his duty." It is located in the South Fork Bonito Management Area west of Buck Mountain and north of the Ski Apache Ski Area. The area consists of high mountain meadows and corkbark fir and spruce. William G. Telfer was a Forest Service entomologist who died in a 1984 plane crash doing aerial pest detection work.

Recreational Issues   In the planning process leading to the preparation of the *Lincoln National Forest Plan*, two principal recreation issues were raised:

- "Demand for motorized dispersed recreation is increasing. Off-road travel by vehicles is damaging resources. There are conflicts between motorized and non-motorized uses on roads and trails."
- "Current management of caves is not responding to demand. Unacceptable damage to caves is occurring."

Recreational Goals   The goals for recreation management, as stated in the *Forest Plan*, are to:

- Manage for a variety of developed and dispersed recreation experiences, while maintaining the current spectrum of opportunities
- Encourage opportunity for the private sector to meet part of the recreational demand
- Provide a system of roads and trails for motorized recreational use, while protecting other resources.

- Preserve and protect cave resources to provide a wild caving experience and to provide quality information and interpretive services related to this unique resource.
- Protect and manage historical and cultural resources.
- Emphasize visual resources through application of landscape management principles.
- Coordinate with the New Mexico Natural Resources Department to contribute to goals and objectives specified in the State Comprehensive Outdoor Recreation Plan.

Nebraska and Samuel R. McKelvie National Forests and Oglala, Buffalo Gap, and Fort Pierre National Grasslands

The administrative structure of the Nebraska National Forest is quite complex. The Forest Supervisor, headquartered in Chadron, Nebr., is responsible not only for the 141,547-acre Nebraska National Forest but also the 115,800-acre Samuel R. McKelvie National Forest, the 94,435-acre Oglala National Grassland, the 597,109-acre Buffalo Gap National Grassland, and the 115,999-acre Fort Pierre National Grassland. These separate units are spread over a very large geographic area in central and northwestern Nebraska and south-central and southwestern South Dakota. The *Nebraska National Forest* consists of two segments that are separated by 135 air miles. The Pine Ridge Ranger District is located in the northwestern corner of Nebraska south of Chadron, with ranger district headquarters in Chadron. The Pine Ridge Ranger District administers the *Oglala National Grassland,* which is located west of Chadron in the extreme northwestern corner of the state. The Bessey Ranger District of the Nebraska National Forest is located 135 miles to the southeast with headquarters at Halsey. The *Samuel R. McKelvie National Forest* is located 15 miles southwest of Valentine and 50 miles north of the Bessey District, and it is administered by the Bessey Ranger District. This is quite a unique arrangement, in which a ranger district of one national forest administers another, separate national forest. The Nebraska National Forest includes a National Forest within a National Forest, which is the Samuel R. McKelvie. The large *Buffalo Gap National Grassland* is located in the extreme southwestern corner of South Dakota west of the Pine Ridge Indian Reservation and extends to the east on the northern boundary of the reservation. It also surrounds Badlands National Park on all sides except for 6 miles on the northwestern side. Its border comes within 5 miles of Black Hills National Forest. The *Fort Pierre National Grassland* is located 55 miles east-northeast of the Buffalo Gap National Grassland in south-central South Dakota, 10 miles south of Pierre. The Buffalo Gap National Grassland has two ranger districts: Fall River (headquarters at Hot Springs, S.D.) in the west, and Wall (headquarters at Wall, S.D.) in the east. The Wall Ranger District is responsible for the Fort Pierre National Grassland.

The inholdings in these five units of the National Forest System vary considerably. The Nebraska National Forest has a gross size of 229,598 acres, of which 61.6 percent is national forest land. The national forest landownership, however, varies between the two units, from almost 100 percent in the Bessey Ranger District to well under 50 percent in the Pine Ridge Ranger District. In the Samuel R. McKelvie National Forest, 99.1 percent of its 116,885 gross acres is national forest land. Almost all

(91.1 percent) of the Oglala National Grassland's acreage is in federal ownership. The percentages in federal ownership of the two national grasslands in South Dakota are also quite high: 89.5 percent of the Buffalo Gap National Grassland's gross acreage of 667,021 acres, and 93 percent of the Fort Pierre National Grassland's 124,758 acres. The variation in percentage of federal lands is explained by the historical circumstances leading to their creation.

The Nebraska National Forest had its origins in the Niobrara and Dismal River Forest Reserves, which were proclaimed by President Theodore Roosevelt in 1902. In 1907 they were merged to become the Nebraska National Forest, with a Niobrara Ranger District and the Dismal River area, later named the Bessey Division in honor of Dr. Charles Bessey, professor of botany at the University of Nebraska. He pioneered the planting of jack pine, eastern red cedar, Scotch pine and ponderosa pine in the entire Bessey Division and 2300 acres of plantings in the Niobrara Division. *These plantings resulted in the Nebraska National Forest being the only human-made forest in the National Forest System and the largest human-made forest in the world.* In 1963, the Bessey Division and Niobrara Division were merged for administrative purposes, and in 1971 the Niobrara Division was renamed the Samuel R. McKelvie National Forest in honor of a former governor of Nebraska. In 1960, the Pine Ridge Land Utilization Project gained National Forest status and was named the Pine Ridge Division of the Nebraska National Forest. This district consisted of 58 percent natural forest, much of it ponderosa pine. On June 20, 1960, nearly 4 million acres of federal lands in the Great Plains states became national grasslands, to be managed as an integral part of the National Forest System. These lands included the present-day Buffalo Gap, Oglala, and Fort Pierre National Grasslands. The administrative order signed by the Secretary of Agriculture stipulated that "the National Grasslands shall be administered for outdoor recreation, range, timber, watershed, and wildlife and fish purposes." These lands were submarginal properties that the federal government started to acquire in the 1930s under President Franklin D. Roosevelt's "New Deal." The national grasslands are examples of progressive agriculture in semiarid grass country. They serve as demonstration areas to show how intermingled public and private lands can be managed to complement each other and to conserve the resources— grass, water, and wildlife habitat.

The forest lies entirely within the Great Plains Province, but it straddles two Sections where, in extreme northwestern Nebraska, the north-facing Pine Ridge delineates the division of the High Plains Section to the south from the Unglaciated Missouri Plateau Section to the north. The forest is comprised of three topographically distinct areas: (1) the Sand Hills in north-central Nebraska, (2) the Pine Ridge in northwest Nebraska, and the (3) Pierre Hills stretching from the northwestern corner of Nebraska across western and central South Dakota. Elevations across the forest range from 2000 feet in the Pierre Hills to 3000 feet in the Sand Hills, to over 4000 feet in the Pine Ridge. Major drainages are the Dismal River, the Middle and North Forks of the Loup River, the Snake River, and Niobrara River in the Sandhills; the White River in the Pine Ridge; and the White, Cheyenne, and Bad Rivers in the Pierre Hills. The forest rests on sedimentary bedrock that was deposited beginning about 130 million years ago. The land has undergone several periods of submersion and deposition under a vast inland sea followed by several periods of exposure and erosion. The climate of the forest is humid continental, characterized by hot summers

and cold winters. Large temperature swings in all seasons are common as Canadian cP (continental polar) air masses interact with Gulf mT (maritime tropical) air masses. Temperature can range from minus 30°F in winter to 110°F in summer, and precipitation ranges from 15 to 18 inches, with three-quarters of it coming during the 120- to 130-day growing season. Rainfall in summer thunderstorms can be torrential. Chadron (3300-ft. elevation) has a January mean of 24°F and a July mean of 75°F and an average of 16.8 inches of precipitation per year.

Several characteristic landscapes exist on the forest. The Bessey Ranger District and the Samuel R. McKelvie National Forest are located in choppy-to-rolling Sand Hill country. The Sand Hills cover 24,000 square miles and comprise the largest sand dune area in the Western Hemisphere and one of the largest areas of sand dunes in the world. The region lacks permanent surface streams in many places, and the intermittent streams flow into nearby, small lake basins or depressions. The landscape is dominated by mid- and tall-grass prairie. Tree cover is limited and occurs mainly as plantations on forest lands, as shelter belts around farms and ranches, and along drainages. All 22,000 acres of the forest in the Bessey District is human-planted, and 2300 acres in the Samuel R. McKelvie National Forest are human-planted. The tree species that were planted with success are ponderosa pine, eastern red cedar, jack pine, and Scotch pine. The species that have been planted unsuccessfully are white pine, red pine, and pinyon pine. The Bessey Nursery, 2 miles west of Halsey, has been the source of this stock. About 5 million tree seedlings are annually produced, at this, the oldest federally operated nursery in the United States. The Pine Ridge area of the forest is a mosaic of vegetation and topographic patterns (Figure 10.13). Vegetation patterns vary from dense natural ponderosa pine to open parks and grass meadows. The topography varies from flat ridgetops to rolling hills to steep side slopes with vertical rock outcroppings. *The Nebraska National Forest is not a timber-producing forest.* There are 53,000 acres of timber, including natural ponderosa pine in the Pine Ridge, and conifer plantations (mostly ponderosa pine, eastern red cedar,

Figure 10.13 The Pine Ridge area of the Nebraska National Forest has naturally occurring ponderosa pine forest. Shown is the area devastated by the Dead Horse fire of July 6, 1973, south of Chadron, Nebr.

and jack pine) in the Bessey District and the Samuel R. McKelvie National Forest. The Oglala, Buffalo Gap, and Fort Pierre National Grasslands are characterized by vast, sweeping, grassy landscapes. The vegetation varies from mid- and short-grass prairie on the Oglala and Buffalo Gap National Grasslands to mid-grass prairie on the Fort Pierre National Grassland. Visual diversity is provided by woody draws that intermingle with the grassland. Wildlife in the forest includes mule deer, whitetail deer, pronghorn antelope, turkey, sharptail grouse, prairie chicken, cottontail rabbits, porcupine, fox, badger, bobcat, coyote, and prairie dogs. Over 120 different nongame bird species are found, including American kestrel, red-tailed and Swainson's hawks, golden eagles, bald eagles, magpies, mountain bluebirds, pinon jay, and several warblers. Cold-water and warm-water fishing are available.

The Nebraska National Forest is one of the most lightly used of national forests, with 349,200 RVDs in 1992, which ranks it in 124th place. (Only 17 national forests had less use.) The intensity of use index was 0.737 acres/RVD; this resulted in the higher ranking of 79th place. The forest has one unit of the National Wilderness Preservation System—Soldier Creek (7794 acres)—which had 1700 RVDs in 1992, and was only 0.5 percent of the total recreational use. The leading category of recreation use in the forest is "mechanized travel and viewing scenery," which accounts for 53 percent of the use. "Viewing scenery" contributes 69 percent of the use in this category, and "automobile travel" another 17 percent. The second-ranking category of use is "camping, picnicking, and swimming," with 14 percent of the total. "Camping" is the leading subcategory, with 75 percent of the use, followed by "picnicking" (16 percent) and "swimming" (9 percent). The third-ranking category—"resorts, cabins, and organization camps"—receives 11 percent of the total use. The distribution of this use in the subcategories was fairly even: "general day organization camping" (23 percent), "night organization camping" (21 percent), "general resort commercial and public service" (21 percent), "resort lodging" (19 percent), and "recreation cabin use" (16 percent). "Other recreational activities" ranks fourth with 8 percent of the use; the leading contributors to this category are "team sports" (30 percent), "games and play" (20 percent), "general information" (10 percent), "individual sports" (9 percent), "gathering forest products" (7 percent), and "guided touring" (7 percent). "Hunting" ranks fifth, accounting for 7 percent of the total recreational use; 51 percent of this category is big-game hunting, 24 percent is upland bird hunting, and 22 percent is small-game hunting. "Hiking, horseback riding, and water travel" ranks sixth with 5 percent of the recreational use. "Hiking and walking" is the leading subcategory (59 percent), but "horseback riding" (23 percent) and "canoeing" (12 percent) receive substantial use. "Fishing" follows in seventh place with only 2 percent of the use; 54 percent is warm-water, 38 percent cold-water, and 9 percent ice fishing. Two categories receive the least recreational use, "winter sports" and "nonconsumptive fish and wildlife use," each receiving only 0.14 percent of the use.

The one developed recreation site in the Pine Ridge Division of the Nebraska National Forest is the 13-site Red Cloud Picnic Area, on Highway 385 approximately 9 miles south of Chadron. Those seeking developed campsites in this portion of the forest are well served by Chadron State Park, located just north of the Red Cloud Picnic Area on Highway 385, or Fort Robinson State Park, located 3 miles west of Crawford. The lovely Chadron State Park (840 acres) was Nebraska's first state park, established in 1921. It is exceptionally well designed and landscaped. Visitors will

find modern cabins, a developed campground, and swimming pool. Fort Robinson State Park (22,673 acres) includes Fort Robinson, established by the Sioux Expedition in 1874 and serving as an active military base until 1949. Numerous buildings have been reconstructed, and living history tours may be taken. The *Nebraska Wilderness Act* (1986) gave special designation to two areas: Soldier Creek Wilderness Area and Pine Ridge National Recreation Area. Soldier Creek Wilderness Area is located immediately west of Fort Robinson, of which it used to be a part before it became the 9600-acre Soldier Creek Management Unit of the Nebraska National Forest. It is named for the two creeks which bisect the area. This Wilderness is characterized by wide, flat hardwood draw bottoms adjacent to steep, grassy hillsides. The Soldier Creek trailhead has room for camping, and there are corrals, vault toilets, and water. There are two main hiking and horseback trails, the Boots and Saddles Trail and the Trooper Trail (designated a national recreation trail). Much of this wilderness area was burned in 1989 during the 48,000-acre Fort Robinson fire. Fire is a constant threat in the forest. A major fire burned much of the area around Chadron State Park in the Deadhorse fire (Figure 10.13). The Pine Ridge National Recreation Area (6600 acres) is located on the Pine Ridge Escarpment approximately halfway between Chadron and Crawford. This area was given special designation by Congress for its ability to provide a primitive-semiprimitive recreational opportunity in a natural environment. It was initially proposed as a wilderness area, but in the legislative process was changed to a national recreation area. Motorized vehicles are not allowed. Ponderosa pine trees cover the steep hillsides, and a mix of ponderosa pines and hardwoods grows in the draw bottoms. The Roberts Tract is the primary access point; it has corrals, vault toilets, water, tables, and room to camp. In 2.5 miles the Roberts Trail joins the Pine Ridge Trail. There is a small (six-unit) Toadstool campground and picnic area located 15 miles north of Crawford in the Oglala National Grassland. This area is noted for its unusual geological formations and fossil deposits.

The developed recreation facilities within the forest are primarily in the Bessey Recreation Complex. Facilities include the Bessey picnic ground, the Bessey swimming site (a large, modern swimming pool), Cedars campground, Claypit group camp, Hardwoods campground, Nebraska 4-H Organization Camp, and the Scott Lookout observation site, which provides a panoramic view of the human-made forest. The only developed site in the Samuel R. McKelvie National Forest is the 23-unit Steer Creek campground, located 19 miles south of Nenzel. The nearby Merritt Reservior State Recreation Area offers developed recreation facilities. There are two picnic areas in the Buffalo Gap National Grasslands: Pioneer roadside rest (9 miles south of Oelrichs, S.D., on U.S. 385) and French Creek picnic ground (13 miles east of Highway 79 on the Fairburn Road). There are no developed recreation facilities on the Fort Pierre National Grassland, but the area may be used for nature study, picnicking, camping, hiking, hunting, and fishing.

Recreational Issues   In the preparation of the *Land and Resource Management Plan: Nebraska National Forest* (Forest Service, 1984b; hereafter the *Plan*), three of the planning questions that arose pertaining to recreation were:

- How should off-road-vehicle use be managed on the Nebraska National Forest?
- How should the forest respond to the demand for recreational opportunities?
- How much wilderness should be designated in the forest?

Recreational Goals   In helping to determine management direction for recreation purposes, three Recreational Goals were identified by the *Plan*:

- Maintain or increase the land base of the forest.
- Identify and protect significant historic and archaeological sites.
- Improve usability of the forest resources by handicapped individuals.

Shawnee National Forest

The Shawnee National Forest is located in extreme southern Illinois in a part of the state that contrasts greatly with the rest of Illinois. It is a relatively small national forest—260,133 acres, which is only 36.4 percent of its gross proclamation boundary size of 714,890 acres. Only six other national forests have a lower percentage of national forest land within their proclamation boundaries: the Uwharrie (North Carolina), 22 percent; the Wayne (Ohio), 25 percent; the Hoosier (Indiana), 29 percent; the Holly Springs (Mississippi), 30 percent; the Sam Houston (Texas), 33 percent; and the Sabine (Texas), 36 percent. The Shawnee National Forest extends in an east-west direction for 88 miles and in a north-south direction for 47 miles. The 125,106-acre Shawnee Purchase Unit (only 7 percent, or 8309 acres, of which is national forest land) adjoins the larger eastern section with the smaller western section of the forest. The eastern portion of the forest borders the Ohio River along the border with Kentucky for most of its extent. The western portion is located on the bluffs from ½ to 5 miles east of the alluvial floodplain of the Mississippi River, although the forest borders the Mississippi for 3.5 miles in the vicinity of Brunkhorst Landing. Missouri lies on the other side of the Mississippi. Crab Orchard National Wildlife Refuge borders the forest on the north. Dixon Springs State Park lies within the forest's boundary in the eastern section, and Giant City State Park lies within the western section. Ferne Clyffe State Park lies within the Shawnee Purchase Unit. Forest headquarters and the supervisor are located at Harrisburg. For administrative purposes, the forest is divided into four ranger districts, with offices in cities of the same name: Elizabethtown and Vienna in the eastern section, and Jonesboro and Murphysboro in the western section. Large cities within a 1-hour drive to the forest are Cape Girardeau, Mo. (5 miles); Paducah, Ky. (20 miles); and Evansville, Ind. (50 miles). The closest major city is St. Louis, Mo. (110 miles).

Proponents of an Illinois national forest became active in the 1920s, and several areas of the state were proposed. Key players in the drive for a national forest were the *Chicago Tribune*, the Illinois Manufacturers' Association, the Izaak Walton League, and the University of Illinois. (The University of Illinois was searching for a research project area in southern Illinois.) Although the Forest Service was not enthusiastic about establishing a national forest in Illinois, the editorial interest of the *Chicago Tribune* forced the idea on the agency. In 1933 the Illini and Shawnee Purchase Units were approved with respective areas of 262,000 and 248,000 acres. The Shawnee National Forest was proclaimed by President Franklin D. Roosevelt in 1939. Later in the year the two purchase units were merged into one, and "Illini" was dropped from the name. In 1958, all lands were given Weeks Act status. When proclaimed a national forest in 1939, the Shawnee had a land base of 184,539 acres; by 1962 the acreage had become 211,021, and by 1992 it was 260,133 acres. The *Amended Forest Plan* (Forest

Service, 1992) estimates the ultimate size of the Shawnee will be approximately 300,000 acres. Except for only 460 acres, which were never in private ownership, the entire 268,442 acres of the Shawnee National Forest and Purchase Unit were formerly private land.

The Shawnee National Forest is located astride the meeting place of three major physiographic divisions of the country: the Interior Highlands, the Interior Plains, and the Atlantic Plains. The mosaic of hills, bluffs, valleys, unusual rock formations and trees contrasts with the level cropland of most of the rest of Illinois. The Salem Plateau Section of the Ozark Plateaus Province extends from Missouri into the extreme northwestern portion of the forest. The larger portion of the forest lies in the Shawnee Hills Section of the Interior Low Plateaus Province. This physiographic section possesses great diversity of topography because of its geologic variety. Two other characteristics of the Shawnee Hills Section are its intense faulting and widespread alluviation along major valleys and their larger tributaries (Thornbury, 1965, 202). The Shawnee Hills extend across the southern tip of Illinois from Fountain Bluff on the Mississippi River to the Shawneetown Hills near the mouth of the Wabash River. This unglaciated hill country is characterized by a high east-west escarpment of Pennsylvanian sandstone cliffs forming the Greater Shawnee Hills, which average 10 miles wide, and a series of lower hills underlain by Mississippian limestone and sandstone known as the Lesser Shawnee Hills. Sinkholes and caves are common features in the Lesser Shawnee Hills. The topography of the Shawnee Hills is very rugged, with many bluffs and ravines. The northern slopes of the Greater Shawnee Hills are relatively gentle; but the southern slopes consist of many escarpments, cliffs, and overhanging bluffs. Streams have eroded canyons in the sandstone. The Lesser Shawnee Hills are on average about 200 feet lower than the Greater Shawnee Hills. The highest elevation (1068 ft.) in the forest occurs at Williams Hill in this section. The East Gulf Coastal Plain Section (east) and the Mississippi Alluvial Plain Section (west) of the Coastal Plain Province extends into the extreme south of the forest. The coastal plains are a region of swampy forested bottomlands and low clay and gravel hills. Bald cypress–tupelo gum swamps are a unique feature of this region. The lowest elevation (340 ft.) is found in the southeastern corner of the forest on the Ohio River.

The climate is humid subtropical, which is characterized by hot, humid summers and short, moderate winters, although occasional invasions of polar air can result in very cold winter temperatures. Elizabethtown has a January mean of 37°F and a July mean of 79°F; the mean annual precipitation is 46 inches. The wettest month is March (4.9 inches), and the driest month is October (2.4 inches). Mean annual snowfall is 16 inches, but infrequent heavy snowfalls add to this mean value. The snow does not remain on the ground very long. The growing season is about 200 days. The percentage distribution of vegetation classes is as follows: upland forest (47 percent), crop and pasture lands (35 percent), pine (7 percent), glades (5 percent), bottomland forest (3 percent), swamps and wetlands (2 percent), and savannas and grasslands (1 percent). The "upland forest" category is dominated by oak and hickory (81 percent); the remainder is blackjack/post oak, and oak-pine (17 percent) and beech and maple (2 percent). The Shawnee National Forest is at the meeting place of three forest cover types: the northern forest region, the southern forest region, and the central forest region. The bottomland forest includes a diversity of tree species: pin oak, sweet gum, river birch, sycamore, red maple, silver maple, cherry bark oak, cottonwood, and box

elder. The acreage classified as suitable for timber production is 58,700 acres, or 22 percent of the forest's total acreage. Approximately 500 vertebrate species live in the Shawnee, and includes 48 mammals, 237 birds, 52 reptiles, 57 amphibians and 109 species of fish. Wildlife in the Shawnee National Forest is managed in cooperation with the Illinois Department of Conservation to develop habitat for game and non-game species. Within the forest one can find whitetail deer, fox and gray squirrels, Canada geese, bobwhite quail, ruffed grouse, mallard, widgeon, wood duck, and wild turkey. Federally listed threatened and endangered species on the Shawnee National Forest include the gray bat, Indiana bat, American peregrine falcon, American bald eagle, and least tern. Fish in and near the forest include large- and smallmouth bass, bluegill, catfish, and crappie. There are 15 lakes of over 10 acres and several hundred small walk-in ponds. These lakes and ponds provide 7500 acres of water surface.

Only 21 national forests received less use than the Shawnee's 899,500 RVDs in 1992. The number of recreation visits was 939,000 for the same time period. But an intensity of use index of 0.289 acres/RVD ranked it the 29th most intensively used national forest. This high intensity of use index is evidence of the regional importance of the Shawnee National Forest as a recreational resource. The *Illinois Wilderness Act* (1990) designated seven wilderness areas on 25,549 acres in the forest, as well as 4050 acres of wilderness in the Crab Orchard National Wildlife Refuge that borders the forest's northern boundary. The seven Wilderness Areas in the Shawnee National Forest are Bald Knob (5863 acres), Bay Creek (2866 acres), Burden Falls (3671 acres), Clear Springs (4730 acres), Garden of the Gods (3268 acres), Lusk Creek (4466 acres), and Panther Den (685 acres). These seven wilderness areas received 30,600 RVDs in 1992, which was 3.4 percent of the total recreational use in the forest.

The recreational use of the Shawnee National Forest pretty much mirrors the national averages for the National Forest System, with the exception that "winter sports" and "resorts, cabins, and organization camps" play a much-below-average role and "hunting" a much-above-average role. The leading category of use is "mechanized travel and viewing scenery," which accounts for 39 percent of the recreational use. The leading subcategory within this category is "automobile travel" (42 percent), closely followed by "viewing scenery" (34 percent); "motorcycle and scooter travel" accounts for another 11 percent of this category. The forest has a designated system of ATV trails. The second-ranking category of recreational use is "camping, picnicking, and swimming" (20 percent); "camping" is the leading subcategory (53 percent), but "picnicking" (27 percent) is a major contributor as well as "swimming and water play" and "waterskiing" (20 percent). The third-ranking category is "hiking, horseback riding, and water travel," accounting for 16 percent of the recreational use. "Horseback riding" is the leading subcategory (52 percent), followed by "hiking and walking" (41 percent). "Hunting" ranks a close fourth, with 14 percent of the recreational use. All four subcategories of types of hunting contribute to this total: "big-game" (37 percent); "small-game" (32 percent); "upland bird" (23 percent); and "waterfowl" (7 percent). The fifth-ranking category of use is "other recreational activities," which accounts for 5 percent of the recreational use. The leading subcategories are "gathering forest products" (32 percent), "general information" (22 percent), "viewing interpretive exhibits" (12 percent), "attending talks and programs" (7 percent), and "unguided walking" (5 percent). "Fishing" is the sixth-ranked major category of use (4 percent of total), with 99 percent being "warm-water." "Noncon-

sumptive fish and wildlife use" ranks seventh, with 2 percent of the total recreational use. The category "resorts, cabins, and organization camps" ranks eighth, with less than 1 percent of the recreational use; 68 percent of this small amount is "night organization camping," and the other 32 percent is "general day organization camping." In last place for recreational use is the category "winter sports." Only 0.09 percent of the total recreational use occurs in this category. The meager percentage is accounted for by only 400 RVDs of "snow play," 200 RVDs of "tobogganing and sledding," and 200 RVDs of "cross-country skiing and snowshoeing."

Recreational use in the forest is distributed among the following Recreation Opportunity Spectrum (ROS) categories: "roaded natural motorized" (43.4 percent), "roaded natural nonmotorized" (27.3 percent), "rural" (23.4 percent), "semiprimitive motorized" (3.6 percent), and "semiprimitive nonmotorized" (2.2 percent). A variety of recreational opportunities exist in the Shawnee National Forest, and the patterns of use change seasonally. In early spring (March and April) the primary activities are hiking, riding, camping, and fishing. In May, picnicking increases in popularity. The vacation months (June, July, and August) are months of peak water-oriented activities, with a great deal of swimming and boating due to hot, humid weather. Hiking, riding, and camping again become preeminent in September and October, and the colorful fall foliage attracts many pleasure-drivers and photographers. Outdoor activities are primarily limited to hunting during the winter, although winter camping is growing in popularity. The Shawnee National Forest has very little winter sports activity due to mild winters and light snowfall. Nature study occurs year-round. A network of public roads and trails provides ready access to all sections of the forest. Of the 1250-mile Forest Road System, about 323 miles are currently open to public motorized use year-round, another 407 miles have seasonal restrictions from mid-December to early May, and the remaining 520 miles are generally closed year-round. The Shawnee Hills on the Ohio National Scenic Byway is a scenic 70-mile route through the forest; access to some attractions from it are on gravel roads.

There are 1500 acres of designated developed recreation areas. Table 10.11 summarizes them by number of sites (62), capacity (8490 PAOT), and use (356,000 RVDs). All of the 62 developed recreation sites are within the "rural" ROS class. There are 12 developed forest service campgrounds, nine of which also have picnic grounds.

Table 10.11   Shawnee National Forest: Developed Recreation Sites

Kind of Site	No. of Sites	Capacity (PAOT)	Use (RVDs)
Observation	12	465	105,700
Boating site	6	1,040	36,800
Swimming site	4	2,860	42,400
Campground—family	14	1,935	116,700
Campground—group	3	390	6,200
Picnic ground—family	20	1,485	43,700
Picnic ground—group	2	245	4,800
Organization site	1	70	0
Forest total	62	8,490	356,000

Source: Forest Service, Shawnee National Forest: Amended Land and Resource Management Plan (1992).

The largest are at Pounds Hollow Recreation Area (76 camping and picnic sites), Johnson Creek (75 camping and 30 picnic sites), Lake Glendale (74 camping and 52 picnicking sites), Lake of Egypt (41 camping and 46 picnicking sites), Tower Rock (35 camping and 7 picnicking sites), and Bell Smith Springs (31 camping and 12 picnicking sites). Smaller camping and picnicking sites are located in the Ohio River Recreation Area, Garden of the Gods, and on the Grapevine Trail. Camping-only sites are located at Turkey Bayou, Pine Hills and Camp Cadiz. Other recreation areas where picnicking is available include Oakwood Bottoms Greentree Reservoir, Pomona Natural Bridge, McCann Spring, Iron Furnace, the Rimrock Trail, Buttermilk Hill, Winters Pond, McGee Hill, and Allens Flat. Hiking is available at the first six of these areas, swimming is available only at Buttermilk Hill, and fishing is available at Buttermilk Hill, Winters Pond, and Iron Furnace.

Canoeing is allowed on all lakes, ponds and streams. Popular canoeing streams are the Big Muddy, the Cache, and the Saline Rivers. Biking is becoming increasingly popular on the many back roads of the forest, and portions of the U.S. Bike Route 76 Trail wind through the forest. The forest has 286 miles of trails designated for ATV, hiker, and equestrian use, and 338 miles designated for hiker and equestrian use. One of the most popular trails suited for horseback riding includes the River-to-River Trail. Three national recreation trails are located in the Shawnee National Forest: the Rim Rock, the Little Grand Canyon, and the Inspiration Point. The Rim Rock National Recreation Trail is a 1-mile circuit through some of the state's geological wonders. The Little Grand Canyon National Recreation Trail is a 3.6-mile loop through steep-sided sandstone creek beds. The Inspiration Point National Recreation Trail is a 0.5-mile trail through a variety of forest plant communities in the LaRue–Pine Hills Ecological Area. These 1312 acres were set aside as a scenic area in 1939, the first "special area" designation on the Shawnee. It is managed as a research-natural area today and contains a greater diversity of plant and animal species than the entire Great Smoky Mountains area and about 39 percent of all the known species of plants and animals in Illinois.

There are 10 miles of interconnecting trails at Bell Smith Springs that pass by cliffs, a canyon with several caves, creeks, ponds, and a natural stone bridge. The 1.5-mile Lusk Creek Trail leads into the Lusk Creek Wilderness, and the Kincaid Hiking Trail offers more than 12 miles of trails with carry-in campsites. The Gardens of the Gods Recreation Area is bounded by the wilderness area of the same name on three sides. A ¼ mile Garden of the Gods Observation Trail leads to areas immediately above the cliffs, where there are outstanding views of the Shawnee Hills and the Garden of the Gods Wilderness Area. There are 8 miles of trails above and below the bluffs and fascinating rock formations. Erosion has transformed these bluffs into features named Camel Rock, Tower of Babel, Noah's Ark, and Anvil Rock. Pounds Hollow Recreation Area features a 25-acre lake constructed by the Civilian Conservation Corps; recreational opportunities here include picnicking, camping, boating, fishing, hiking, and swimming. The Greentree Reservoir Interpretive Trail at Oakwood Bottoms is designed for beginning hikers and the physically disabled, has a combination of short- and medium-length trails, and has an elevated boardwalk through a part of the Green Tree Reservoir. This atypical area is an unusual oak forest surrounded by levees that is flooded each fall and drained in March. A ½-mile trail

leads to the Illinois Iron Furnace, which was the first charcoal-fired iron furnace in Illinois and a principal source of iron during the Civil War. The restored 50-foot furnace features a nearby shelter house with information displays.

Issues and Concerns   A major change in the management of the Shawnee National Forest occurred in the 1992 *Shawnee National Forest Amended Land and Resource Management Plan* (Forest Service, 1992c; hereafter the *Amended Plan*). This amended plan replaced the 1986 *Plan*. Under both the *Amended Plan* and the 1986 *Plan*, 1500 acres was designated as developed recreation areas for camping, picnicking, and swimming under management prescription 7.1. An additional 52,900 acres adjacent to developed recreation sites, lakes, and other popular areas were designated for management under the *Amended Plan,* management prescription 6.6, which emphasizes recreation, wildlife, soil and water protection, and visual quality. This is a major change from the 1986 *Plan,* which did not include management prescription 6.6 and managed most of these areas for objectives that included timber production. Table 10.12 identifies the acreage for each of the 16 management area prescriptions. (Prescription 7.1 is listed ninth in Table 10.12, and prescription 6.6 is listed eighth.) Under the *Amended Plan* the largest acreage is in management prescription 2.1 (listed second in Table 10.12), described as "uneven hardwood forest. Suitable for timber production. Includes ATV/OHM travel ways." This prescription area contains 86,200 acres,

Table 10.12   Shawnee National Forest: Management Area Prescription

Description	Acres
Oakwood Bottoms Greentree Reservoir	4,100
Uneven-aged hardwood forest. Suitable for timber production. Includes ATV/OHM travelways.	86,200
Congressionally designated wilderness.	25,600
Congressionally designated special management areas that become wilderness after an opportunity for fluorspar exploration and mining.	2,700
Filter strips and riparian areas. Unsuitable for timber production.	29,400
Forest Interior management units. Unsuitable for timber production. ATV connector routes permitted.	7,600
Cave Valley nongame bird area. Emphasis on Swainson's warbler habitat. Unsuitable for timber production. ATV use prohibited.	1,700
Mature and old-growth hardwood forest with emphasis on wildlife and recreation. Unsuitable for timber production.	52,900
Developed recreation areas.	1,500
Areas used for manipulative research (Kaskaskia Experimental Forest; Dixon Spring Agricultural Center).	7,400
Natural areas.	12,400
Significant cultural resource sites, generally on the National Register of Historic Places.	4,200
Minimum-level management. Generally available for exchange. Unsuitable for timber production. ATV connector routes permitted.	10,700
Candidate wild and scenic rivers	11,600
Area recommended for wilderness study.	3,500
Camp Hutchins—managed to maintain ecological integrity and for study.	3,600
Total	265,100

Source: Forest Service, *Shawnee National Forest Amended Land and Resource Management Plan* (1992).

which is still one-third of the forest. Designated suitable for timber production are 58,700 acres (22 percent). This is a significant change from the 1986 *Plan,* which classified about 60 percent of the forest as suitable for timber production.

The third management prescription area in Table 10.12, number 5.1, is for 25,600 acres in seven congressionally designated wilderness areas. The fourth prescription area in Table 10.12, number 5.2, is for two areas—East Fork and Eagle Creek—totaling 2684 acres that are designated special management areas under the Illinois Wilderness Act of 1990. They will automatically become wilderness areas after an opportunity for exploration and development of fluorspar and associated minerals. Prospecting is allowed until November 28, 1998. If significant amounts of such minerals are found to exist, mining may be allowed until November 28, 2010. In the interim, these areas will be managed to protect their wilderness character to the extent possible, and will be managed under prescription 5.2.

The *Amended Plan* incorporated "Alternative 5." The intent of this alternative is to respond to the concerns from people who felt that the Forest should provide a mix of products and uses, but these uses should avoid sensitive areas, be closely controlled, and continue at about the same levels as provided for in the past. "Alternative 5" emphasizes a variety of motorized and nonmotorized recreational opportunities, including ATV/OHM use on 286 miles of travel ways and provides for broader use of ATVs during the firearms deer-hunting season. In addition to recommending Ripple Hollow for wilderness study, Hutchins Creek (7 miles) has been added as a candidate wild and scenic river under management prescription area 9.2 (11,600 acres). Other candidates for wild and scenic river status previously recommended are Bay Creek (24 miles), Big Creek (20 miles), Big Grande Pierre Creek (20 miles), Big Muddy Creek (21 miles), and Lusk Creek (28 miles). It is expected that the *Amended Plan*'s added emphasis on trails, ATV/OHM travel ways, and a pleasing, naturally appearing visual quality will enhance the Shawnee National Forest's contribution to tourism and rural development. It has been determined that "Alternative 5" provides the best mix of recreational opportunities because it gives special attention to visual quality and recreation in areas adjacent to the Shawnee's most popular recreation sites. Almost 53,000 acres that are near these popular sites have been removed from the land base classified as suitable for timber production. This assures that recreation, wildlife, soil and water protection, and visual quality remain the primary emphases in these areas.

Management Opportunities   The selection of "Alternative 5" in 1992 to become part of the *Amended Plan* was made because it best resolves conflicting public issues and management concerns. While not all constituencies were satisfied, the *Amended Plan* provides a balanced approach to meeting the various public desires for uses, products, and conditions on the Shawnee National Forest. Seven management opportunities are a consolidation of public issues and management concerns identified through the process of amending the *Forest Plan.* Each management opportunity describes an important consideration in the management of the Shawnee National Forest for today's and tomorrow's visitors. The development and analysis of alternatives, as documented in the *Shawnee National Forest Amended Plan* (Forest Service, 1992d) was based on responding to these management opportunities. These seven management opportunities are:

- Protecting water quality and riparian ecosystems.
- Providing biological diversity and wildlife habitat.
- Providing desirable forest settings and facilities for recreation.
- Providing timber products.
- Providing opportunities for mineral production.
- Providing additional wilderness.
- Contributing to the growth of the local economy.

Superior National Forest

The Superior National Forest is located in northeastern Minnesota between Lake Superior and the Canadian border (province of Ontario). It is the largest national forest in the eastern United States with 2,065,788 acres, which is 63.4 percent of the gross acreage (3,260,634 acres) within the proclamation boundary. It is also the 15th-largest forest in the National Forest System. It extends for 125 miles in a longitudinal direction along the Canadian border and for 75 miles in a latitudinal direction. Quetico Provincial Park, Canada, borders the forest on its entire northern side except for 12 miles in the extreme northwest where Voyageurs National Park separates the Forest from the Canadian border. The inholdings within the proclamation boundary (which total 36.6 percent of the area within the proclamation boundary) are most extensive in five areas of the forest: (1) in the extreme east, (2) in the south, (3) the area around Ely, (4) the northwest, and (5) within the detached southwestern unit of the forest. General Christopher C. Andrews, the first chief fire warden of Minnesota and later its forestry commissioner, lobbied for the creation of the Superior National forest at the turn of the century. As a result of his efforts, the commissioner of the General Land Office withdrew from entry the following amounts of land in the public domain in Lake and Cook Counties: 500,000 acres in 1902, 141,000 acres in 1905, and 518,700 acres in 1908. The initial forest proclamation by President Theodore Roosevelt established an area of 1,018,638 acres in 1909. In 1912 a second proclamation expanded the forest by 380,000 acres, and a third proclamation in 1927 further enlarged the forest by 360,000 acres. The forest supervisor's office is located 60 miles to the south in Duluth. The forest has five ranger districts: Gunflint, in the east (office in Grand Marais); Tofte, to the west of the Gunflint Ranger District (office in Tofte); Kawishiwi, in the center (Ely); Laurentian, in the southwest (Aurora); and LaCroix, in the west (Cook). There are two major population centers or corridors. The Iron Range area, from Ely to Virginia/Hibbing, has the largest population. The second corridor of population is along the northern shore of Lake Superior. There are smaller residential areas scattered throughout the forest. Minneapolis–St. Paul is over 3 hours' drive and 200 miles to the south.

The Superior National Forest is located in the Superior Upland Physiographic Province, which only elsewhere extends into the United States in the Adirondack Mountains (New York). The rocks of the Superior Upland are primarily Precambrian. Intrusive and extrusive igneous rocks, meta-igneous rocks, and meta-sedimentary rocks all occur in great variety. The structure here is as complex as any that will be found elsewhere in the world (Thornbury, 1965, 257). Folds and faults are common. Major structural trends in the forest and vicinity north of Lake Superior run northeast-southwest and are strikingly reflected in the alignment of homoclinal

ridges, escarpments, and valley lowlands. General altitudes of the highlands of St. Louis, Cook, and Lake Counties range between 1000 and 1700 feet above the Precambrian Canadian Shield, but certain erosional remnants rise 400 to 500 feet above this level. Eagle Mountain (2301 ft.) is the highest point in Minnesota and is found in the eastern part of the forest. The lowest elevation in the forest is along the shore of Lake Superior (602 ft.) (Figure 10.14). Near the Canadian border in what is called the Rove Slate Belt and Gunflint district are a series of east-west monoclinal ridges and valleys with linear lakes in the valleys. The ridge scarp faces north, giving a sawtooth type of topography. South of this belt of linear topography is the outcrop area of the Duluth Gabbro. Developed on it is an upland that is set off from the Rove Slate Belt to the north by an escarpment. West and north of the Duluth Gabbro upland is the St. Louis Plain, a poorly drained tract that extends northward to the Mesabi Iron Range. The Superior Upland has been repeatedly glaciated, but the present topography is primarily a product of the late Wisconsin glacial state. Topography varies from level and rolling in the southwest of the forest, to rough and rugged in many areas of the eastern and northern portions. The low hills and few isolated mountains are glacial rounded, and the soil is thin and unproductive. The morainal ground between these low hills is hummocky. The depressions are occupied by lakes and swamps, and many of the hillocks are kames, eskers, and drumlins. Much bedrock is exposed, especially in the north. There are two major drainage basins, Hudson Bay and the Great Lakes. Over 2000 lakes in the forest are over 10 acres in size. Over 445,000 acres, or 12 percent of the total forest area, is surface water. More than 1300 miles of cold-water streams and 950 miles of warm-water streams flow within the forest boundary. Lakes, streams, and wetlands are among the forest's most important assets, and they influence the management of timber, recreation, wildlife, and other resources. Figure 10.15 illustrates the Vermillion River.

The climate in the Superior National Forest is humid continental, with a short summer characterized by warm days (upper 70s) and cool nights (mid-50s), and with long, very cold, snowy winters. Temperatures in the forest as low as −50°F and as

Figure 10.14 The Superior National Forest adjoins Lake Superior, whose 602-ft. level is the lowest in the Forest. (Forest Service photo)

Figure 10.15 The Vermillion River is one of the many water features in the Superior National Forest. (Forest Service photo)

high as 98°F have been recorded. Precipitation ranges from about 26 to 31 inches. Most of the forest averages 60 inches of snow, which usually forms a durable cover from late November through April. Lake Superior moderates the nearby climate and is responsible for an increase in precipitation in the northeast. Grand Marais (elevation 622 ft.), on the shore of Lake Superior, has a January mean of 14.2°F and a July mean of 59.4°F, with 25.7 inches of precipitation. September is the wettest month with 3.3 inches, and February is the driest month with 1.0 inches. At Virginia (elevation 1445 ft.), and 75 miles inland from Lake Superior, the January mean is 6.5°F and the July mean is 67°F. Precipitation averages 27.3 inches; July is the wettest month (4.0 inches), and January is the driest month (0.89 inches).

The forest contains about equal amounts of softwoods (red, white, and Jack pine; black and white spruce; and balsam fir) and hardwoods (mostly aspen and birch, but some sugar maple, oak, and basswood are found). It represents the extension of the boreal forest into the United States and is known as the *southern boreal forest*. The southern boreal forest is transitional between two major biomes: the northern boreal forest and the temperate deciduous forest. There is also some influence from prairie ecosystems. There are six major forest communities within the forest: upland spruce–balsam fir, hardwood, pine, lowland black spruce–tamarack, white cedar, and wetlands. In the upland sites white and black spruce and balsam fir codominate; red maple, paper birch, and pines may be associated in places. The most numerous animals are migrant passerine birds and red-backed voles; the boreal owl is a unique species here. The principal hardwoods are trembling aspen and paper birch. Sugar maple predominates in the eastern part of the forest. The newly disturbed sites are the most productive in the food chains of the boreal forest. Animal species found include American kestrel, varying hare, red fox, white-tailed deer, and moose. Pole-sized trees are excellent habitat for ruffed grouse. In the pine community, Jack pine dominates, especially in the northern part of the forest. White and red pine often

occur within the spruce-fir community. Red squirrel and pine marten are found in mature pines, and bald eagle, osprey, and great blue heron favor old-growth pine forests for nesting. The lowland black spruce–tamarack community is often developed over peat, and some balsam fir and Jack pine may be found. The white cedar community is more common in the eastern part of the forest; codominants include black spruce, fir, tamarack, and black ash. This community is favored for yarding areas by white-tailed deer. The various classes of wetlands also occupy a significant segment of the forest. Over 300 animal species are found in the forest and include moose, white-tailed deer, black bear, lynx, ruffed grouse, fisher, mink, marten, river otter, red squirrel, porcupine, woodcock, osprey, loon, black duck, great grey owl, spruce grouse, gray jay, woodpeckers (black-backed, three-toed, and pileated), and northern goshawk. The forest also represents one of the last strongholds of the gray wolf; 300 to 400 of these large carnivores still roam the Superior National Forest. The peregrine falcon is endangered, and the bald eagle and the gray wolf are threatened. Fish include lake trout, brook trout, walleye, northern pike, smallmouth and largemouth bass, crappie, and bluegill.

The classification of the national forest land for timber production is as follows:

1. Total national forest land, 2,134,992 acres (nonforest land, 31,630 acres)
2. Total forest land, 2,103,362 acres
3. Land withdrawn from timber production: (a) congressionally withdrawn land, 750,183 acres; (b) land not capable of timber production, 109,243 acres; (c) physically unsuited, 33,204 acres; (d) total land withdrawn, 892,630 acres
4. Tentatively suited land, 1,210,732 acres
5. Land not appropriate: (a) wild and scenic rivers, 0 acres; (b) roadless areas, 0 acres; (c) recreation sites, 1474 acres; (d) special uses, 3996 acres; (e) water corridors, 62,000 acres; (f) economically not appropriate, 498,227 acres; (g) total land not appropriate, 565,697 acres
6. Total suitable forest land, 645,035 acres

The Superior National Forest ranks 19th in the National Forest System in terms of recreation visitor days of use—4,018,300 in 1992. The number of recreation visits for the same year was 1,069,000. The forest's large size helps absorb much of this use, resulting in a 59th-place ranking for intensity of use index (0.514 acres/RVD). The Boundary Waters Canoe Area is the only designated wilderness area within the forest. It is by far the most heavily used unit of the National Wilderness Preservation System, having received 1,404,000 RVDs in 1992. These 1,404,300 RVDs in this wilderness area are responsible for an exceptionally high 35 percent of the total recreational use in the Superior National Forest. This total is almost double the use of all wilderness areas in the second-ranked Tongass National Forest (797,000 RVDs) and triple the use in the third- and fourth-ranked Shasta-Trinity National Forests (520,800 RVDs) and Inyo National Forest (511,600 RVDs). Ninety-three percent of the present-day 803,050-acre wilderness was a component of the Initial Wilderness Preservation System in 1964. The *Boundary Waters Canoe Area Wilderness Act* (BWCA Wilderness Act, 1978) added 56,914 acres. This act also prohibited all logging and mining in the canoe area and established a mining protection area bordering the area where mining is also prohibited on federal land. The federal government was given cojurisdiction with the state of Minnesota to regulate the use of motorboats in the Boundary Waters

Canoe Area. The amount of surface water open to use by motorboats was immediately reduced from 60 to 33 percent, with eventual reduction to 24 percent by 1999. Large horsepower towboats and snowmobiles were phased out in 1984, except for two short snowmobile access routes to Canada that are to remain indefinitely. Maximum horsepower limits were imposed on motorboats using the lakes that remained open to their use. The legislation also directed the establishment of quotas for motorboat use. This act again illustrates the influence of Congress on resource management decisions in the National Forest System.

The recreational use in the Superior National Forest differs from other forests in the system in the low percentage of total recreational use accounted for by "mechanized travel and viewing scenery" and the high use accounted for by "hiking, horseback riding, and water travel," especially "canoeing." *The 653,400 RVDs in the one subcategory "canoeing" in the Superior National Forest exceeded the total recreational use in 31 national forests in 1992.* In the Superior National Forest the leading major category of recreational use is "camping, picnicking, and swimming," which accounts for 40 percent of the total use. Ninety-six percent of this category is accounted for by the four subcategories of camping: "general day camping" (46 percent), "automobile camping" (3 percent), "trailer camping" (4 percent), and "tent camping" (43 percent). Most of this last subcategory occurs in the Boundary Waters Canoe Area. Only 2 percent of the broad category of "camping, picnicking, and swimming" is contributed by "picnicking," and 1 percent is related to "swimming." The second-ranking category of recreational use is "hiking, horseback riding, and water travel," which is responsible for 20 percent of the recreational use in the forest. The overwhelming majority of this use is the 82 percent (653,400 RVDs) contributed by "canoeing." Another 17 percent is related to "hiking," much of which also occurs in the Boundary Waters Canoe Area. The third-ranking category of use—"mechanized travel and viewing scenery"—accounts for only 14 percent of the total recreational use in the forest. This contrasts with a value of 35 percent for this category for the entire National Forest System. The leading subcategory is "automobile travel," with 32 percent of the larger category. It is noteworthy that the use related to canoeing (653,400 RVDs) is 3½ times the amount (186,900 RVDs) related to automobile travel—a situation that exists in no other national forest. *The Superior National Forest is indeed canoe country!* The other major contributors to the broader category "mechanized travel and viewing scenery" are "power boating" (31 percent), "ice and snow travel" (19 percent), and "viewing scenery" (8 percent). Not surprisingly, the category "fishing" places high in fourth place, with 10 percent of the recreational use; 64 percent is warm-water, 27 percent is cold-water, and 9 percent is ice fishing. The fifth-ranking category of use is "resorts, cabins, and organization camps," with 6 percent of the use. The major subcategory contributors are: "recreational cabin use" (47 percent), "general resort and commercial public service" (26 percent), and "resort lodging" (25 percent). "Hunting" ranks in sixth place, with the following breakdown into subcategories: "big-game" (43 percent), "upland bird" (33 percent), "waterfowl" (19 percent), and "small-game" (5 percent). The seventh-ranking category of recreational use is "other recreational activities," with 3 percent of the total. The leading subcategories are "gathering forest products" (50 percent), "viewing interpretive signs" (12 percent), "general information" (11 percent), "unguided walking" (10 percent), and "attending talks and programs" (6 percent). "Winter sports" ranks eighth, with only 2 percent

of the total recreational use, most of which is related to "cross-country skiing" and "snowshoeing" (83 percent) and "snow play" (15 percent). It is important to note that snowmobiling and ice fishing are important winter recreational activities on the Superior National Forest, but they are tallied in with other categories by the Forest Service for statistical reporting. "Nonconsumptive fish and wildlife use" ranks ninth and last among the major categories of recreational use, accounting for only a very low 0.29 percent of the use.

The Superior National Forest provides a wide range of recreational opportunities and facilities. The Forest is unique in offering opportunities for four types of dispersed recreation experiences not generally available in eastern forests: (1) wilderness canoeing, (2) moose hunting, (3) lake trout fishing, and (4) viewing and hearing wildlife such as the bald eagle or wolf. Recreational opportunities for this forest will be discussed under two separate sections: first, the developed and dispersed recreational opportunities that exist in the 61 percent of the Forest that is not in the Boundary Waters Canoe Area and second, the recreational opportunities in the Boundary Waters Canoe Area. The amount of land in each ROS class outside the Boundary Waters Canoe Area is: (1) primitive, 0 percent; (2) semiprimitive, 511,000 acres (18.3 percent); (3) semiprimitive nonmotorized, 672,000 acres (24.2 percent); (4) roaded natural appearing, 1,228,000 acres (44.2 percent); (5) rural, 365,000 acres (13.1 percent); and (6) urban, 5000 acres (0.2 percent).

There are 1474 acres of developed sites, which include campgrounds, picnic areas, boat landings, and observation sites. Table 10.13 identifies the number of developed recreation sites (183) and their capacities (11,184 PAOT). The *Superior National Forest Land and Resource Management Plan* (Forest Service, 1986, hereafter the *Plan*) concluded from an analysis of the projected demand for use of recreational facilities that the capacity of existing facilities exceeds the estimated demand. If existing facilities are fully utilized, the forest can provide 827,000 RVDs per year, which is 55 percent above the estimated demand. Some of these sites need to be relocated to distribute recreational use better and to be more consistent with the desired recreational experience.

Table 10.14 identifies the specific recreational opportunities available at the Forest Service recreation sites. The 27 campgrounds on the forest range from fully developed to secluded sites with few or no facilities. The camping season is from mid-May through September, although at least one campground in each section of the forest

Table 10.13   Superior National Forest: Developed Recreation Site Capacities

Developed Sites	No. of Sites	Capacity (PAOT)
Boating sites	83	4,658
Swimming sites	10	500
Campgrounds	27	3,250
Picnicgrounds	21	792
Recreation residences (groups)	21	999
Other (lodges, resorts, etc.)	21	985
Total	183	11,184

Source: Dave Tucci, Superior National Forest (December 1993).

Table 10.14 Superior National Forest: Recreation Sites

Site Name	Camping	Day Use	Boat Launch	Swim	Fee	Handicap Access	Fishing/ Handicap
Baker Lake	5		X				
Birch Lake	30		X		X		
Bird Lake		2					
Cadotte Lake	27	4	X	X	X	X	X
Cascade River	4						
Crescent Lake	33*		X		X	X	X
Devil Track Lake	16		X		X	X	
Divide Lake	3				X		
Dumbbell Lake		3	X				
East Bearskin Lake	33		X		X	X	
Echo Lake	24*	4	X	X	X	X	
Echo River		1					
Fall Lake	65	3	X	X	X	X	
Fenske Lake	15	2	X	X	X	X	X
Flat Horn		5		X			
Flour Lake	35		X		X		
Hogback Lake		5	X				X
Iron Lake	7				X		
Kawishiwi Lake	5		X				
Kimball Lake	10		X		X		
Lake Jeanette	12		X		X	X	
Lake Leander		30		X		X	
Laurentian Divide		6				X	
Little Isabella River	11	3			X	X	
McDougal Lakes	21	2	X	X	X	X	
Meander Lake	3	3				X	X
Mink Lake						X	X
Ninemile Lake	24		X		X	X	
Norway Point		3	X				
Ojibway Lake		2	X				
Pfeiffer Lake	16	6	X	X	X	X	
Poplar River	4						
Salo Lake		2	X				
Sawbill Lake	50	3	X		X	X	X
South Kawishiwi River	32	2	X	X	X	X	
Temperance River	9				X		
Trails End	33	2	X		X	X	
Two Island Lake	36		X		X		
Vermillion Falls		5					
Whiteface Reservoir	53	12	X	X	X	X	X
White Pine		2				X	

*Group site also available.
X = available recreation opportunity.
Source: Forest Service, *Superior National Forest Map* (1992).

is left open during the winter, but the roads are not necessarily plowed. The number of sites at these campgrounds range from three at Meander Lake and Divide Lake to 65 at Fall Lake. Eight of the campgrounds have fewer than 10 sites, eight have 10 to 25 sites, eight have 25 to 50 sites, and two have over 50 sites. Group camping is available at Echo Lake and Crescent Lake. There are also 241 primitive sites that exist in the forest outside of the Boundary Waters Canoe Area; these can offer a degree of

solitude that can equal or exceed the experience obtained within the Canoe Area. There are 30 day-use areas available for picnicking; 18 of these are associated with camping areas and 12 are not. Most day-use sites are quite small, with two-thirds having five or fewer sites. The largest day-use area is Lake Leander. Fees are charged at 23 of the developed recreation sites. Twenty-six of these sites have boat launching sites and ramps, and 10 have swimming areas. Eight lakes have boat docks. A conscious effort has been made to provide recreational opportunities for the physically challenged. Twenty-one of the recreation sites are accessible to individuals with disabilities, and eight sites have fishing piers accessible for these individuals. Giant Ridge Ski Center is the one downhill ski area that operates under a Forest Service permit; there are two other alpine ski areas within the forest boundary on private land (Lookout Mountain and Lutsen). The Voyageurs Visitor Center at Ely has been turned into the International Wolf Center; the Forest Service operates its Kawishiwi Permit Center here also.

Dispersed recreation opportunities are many and varied in the Superior National Forest. There are 2140 miles of roads in the forest. Within much of the forest, travel is limited. The majority of high-standard roads run north-south; there are no major east-west roads that run across the forest. Roads provide moderate to good access to about 40 percent of the forest. Certain areas, such as the Boundary Waters Canoe Area, have no roads. About 45 percent of the forest has no roads at all; hiking and canoeing are the principal means of access in these areas. Nevertheless, some of the roads do provide scenic automobile routes. A particularly scenic drive, especially when fall colors are at their peak, is through the Sawtooth Mountains. The Sawtooth Mountain Range parallels Lake Superior's shoreline from East Beaver Bay to the Cascade River. The range is named for its ridges, which rise sharply like the teeth of a saw. Temperance Ridge Vista offers an outstanding view of the Temperance River, its valley, and Carlton Peak, which rises 900 feet above Lake Superior. The Forest Service has designated four scenic drives in this area: Beaver Dam Drive (31 miles/ 1 hr., 45 min.), Maple Leaf Drive (10 miles/30 min.), Mountain View Drive (6 miles/ 30 min.), and Moose Drive (12.5 miles/45 min.). Other scenic drives in the forest include the Gunflint Trail (extending 58 miles from Grand Marais to near the Canadian border), the Sawbill Trail (from Tofte on Lake Superior to the Boundary Waters Canoe Area), the Echo Trail (north and west from Ely to Echo Lake and Buyck), and Lakeshore Drive (U.S. 61).

Other forms of dispersed recreation in the forest outside the Boundary Waters Canoe Area that are popular includes hiking trails, canoe routes, cross-country ski trails, and ORV routes. The trail-and-road network is well developed with trailhead parking. There are 29 hiking trails that total 338.3 miles; some cover hilly terrain and lead to scenic overlooks, while others run through swamps, streams, and by the lakes. Twelve of these trails have portions inside the Boundary Waters Canoe Area. These trails range from the 0.3-mile Camp Four Trail to the 90-mile Superior Hiking Trail. The 9-mile Eagle Mountain Trail climbs to the highest point in Minnesota and offers a spectacular view of lakes and land. There are nine primitive canoe routes outside of the Boundary Waters Canoe Area that often offer solitude similar to remote portions of the wilderness. Other possible canoe routes offer a lesser degree of solitude. There are 65 boat launch sites outside of the canoe area. There are 10 hunter walking trails and 15 miles of dog-sledding trails. There are 28 designated cross-country ski

trails totaling 644.1 miles, of which 486.9 miles are groomed. These trails vary in length from the 2.4-mile George Washington Trail to the 53-mile Cascade Trail. Off-road opportunities exist in the Forest for ATVs, snowmobiles, motorized trail bikes, street-legal two- and four-wheel-drive vehicles, and mountain bikes. Fourteen designated snowmobile trails total 504 miles and range in length from the 9-mile X-Trail to the 59-mile Voyageur Trail and the Tomahawk Trail.

Perhaps the best-known recreational attraction in the Superior National Forest is the 803,050-acre Boundary Waters Canoe Area. Twenty percent of the surface area is water. Two sections of the canoe area are not contiguous and are separated by roads from the main section, one in the extreme east along the Canadian border and the other northwest of Ely. There are inholdings within the canoe area, especially in the detached western section northwest of Ely. The expansion of the area, the prohibition of logging and mining, and other new regulations for its management mandated by the 1978 BWCA Wilderness Act were discussed in earlier paragraphs. The Boundary Waters Canoe Area extends for 150 miles along the international boundary and is bordered on the north by Canada's Quetico Provincial Park and on the west by Voyageurs National Park. These areas sit astride the Voyageurs Highway, which was the canoe fur-trade route of French-Canadian voyageurs in the 17th and 18th centuries. The canoe area contains 1175 lakes over 10 acres in size, several hundred miles of streams, 1500 miles of canoe routes; 14 hiking trails; and nearly 2200 designated primitive campsites (Figure 10.16), each with a steel fire grate, a pit latrine, and a clearing for tents. There are no picnic tables or modern conveniences. The area was first set aside in 1926 to preserve its primitive character, and it became an initial component of the National Wilderness Preservation System in 1964. The Boundary Waters Canoe Area is the most heavily used unit of the National Wilderness Preservation System. In 1992, it received 1,404,000 RVDs, which is 35 percent of the total recreational use measured on the Superior National Forest. This wilderness use is 10

Figure 10.16 Typical primitive campsite in the Boundary Waters Canoe Area in the Superior National Forest; this site is located on Lake Insula. (Forest Service photo)

percent of the total wilderness use that occurs in the entire National Forest System. Each year, close to 200,000 people generate 1.4 million RVDs. One-third of the summer use is attributed to visitors from northeastern Minnesota, one-third to the rest of Minnesota (especially Minneapolis–St. Paul), and the remaining third to predominantly midwestern states. Seventy-five percent of the visitors are paddle canoeists, 20 percent use motorized watercraft, and the remaining 5 percent are hikers. The average group size is four people, and the average length of stay is just over 4 days. In 1992, there were 27,023 overnight permits issued and 6708 day-trip permits issued. The percentage distribution of the groups by entry month in 1992 for overnight use is: August (27.6 percent); July (22.5 percent); June (21.9 percent); May (15.1 percent); and September (12.8 percent). For day use the distribution is different (June, 26.2 percent; July, 24.9 percent; August, 20.3 percent; May, 19.4 percent; and September, 9.2 percent).

Through congressional acts (Wilderness Act of 1964, BWCA Wilderness Act of 1978), Executive Orders, and administrative directives, the Forest Service manages the Boundary Waters Canoe Area (1) to promote, perpetuate, and where necessary restore the wilderness character of the land and its specific values of solitude and physical and mental challenge; (2) to provide scientific study; (3) to enhance inspiration; and (4) to provide for primitive recreation. The challenge the resource managers face is allowing human use in an amount and manner consistent with the wilderness resource. A carrying capacity, based on the effects people have on the land and on the visitors around them, has been established. A visitor distribution program limiting the number of overnight groups allowed to enter the Boundary Waters Canoe Area at each access point per day assures that this capacity is not exceeded. While the distribution program has not substantially affected overall use, it has eliminated the extreme peak periods such as weekends, holidays, and traditionally popular weekdays. It has also helped to shift use away from some of the more heavily used access points. There have been several regulations in effect that help reduce the impact of users on wilderness: (1) Cans and bottles are prohibited; (2) camping is limited to designated campsites only; (3) group size is limited to 10 people, 9 after 1994; (4) motor-powered watercraft are permitted only on specific lakes named in P.L. 95-495 (the BWCA Wilderness Act); and (5) permits are required for each overnight party and day-use motor party from May 1 to September 30. Day-use hikers and paddlers do not need a permit, nor do day-use groups using a motor and entering the Crane Lake to Little Vermillion Lake entrance point 12.

On August 19, 1993, the *Superior National Forest Land and Resource Management Plan* (1986) was amended to replace the "Boundary Waters Canoe Area Wilderness Standards and Guidelines" with the *"Boundary Waters Canoe Area Wilderness Management Plan and Implementation Schedule"* (Forest Service, 1993). These changes will not be implemented until after the 1994 use season (except for overnight quotas, which were implemented for the 1994 use season). This *Amended Plan* adopted the following directives for the major resource management issues in the Boundary Waters Canoe Area:

- The number of campsites will be maintained at approximately 2000.
- Overnight quotas will be set at 280.5 daily (for permits, May to September).
- There will be a maximum of three watercraft per group.

- Group size will be a maximum of nine.
- 62 water-access entry points will be maintained.
- Overnight motor quotas will be set at 1976 annually (May to September).
- Day-use motor quotas will be set at 7902 annually (May to September).
- Visitor permits will be required year-round for all types of travel.
- Towboats will be permitted under special-use permits at 1992 levels.
- Special-use permits will be required for all guides, including day trips.
- 183 miles of hiking trails, including the Pow Wow, will be maintained.
- Rehabilitation of other trails will be at district ranger discretion.
- Dogs will be required to be under voice or leash control.
- Sailboats will be prohibited.
- Visitor education will be emphasized.
- Canoe rests will be removed.

In the planning process, "Alternative 6A," which allows a capacity of 2.17 million RVDs in the Boundary Waters Canoe Area, was selected.

In the preparation of the *Superior National Forest Land and Resource Management Plan* (1986), before the Boundary Waters Canoe Area Wilderness Amendment of 1993, six management problems guided the preparation of the original 1986 *Plan:*

- Balancing the recreational opportunities inside and outside the Boundary Waters Canoe Area
- Maintaining appropriate mix of aspen, pine, and spruce
- Maintaining desirable habitat for moose, deer, and grouse
- Developing appropriate recreational facilities
- Developing subsurface and surface resources
- Setting aside additional wilderness

This *Plan* zoned the forest into 15 management areas, three of which were for the Boundary Waters Canoe Area. The 1993 Amended Plan modified these management areas and reorganized the Boundary Waters Canoe Area into four management areas zones:

> *Management Area 5.1—Pristine* (124,118 acres)   Areas in this zone provide a pristine wilderness experience where human presence is almost nonexistent. Trails, portages, and campsites are not constructed or maintained. Leaving no trace of camping or travel techniques is stressed. Visitors will experience a high degree of freedom, challenge, and risk.
>
> *Management Area 5.2A—Primitive* (395,710 acres)   Areas in this zone provide visitors with primitive wilderness experiences in an unmodified environment. Areas in this zone are generally off main travel routes and are meant for those who seek a high degree of solitude and challenge but do not wish to, or are not capable of, traveling to a 5.1 area.
>
> *Management Area 5.2B—Semiprimitive Nonmotorized* (458,852 acres)   Areas in this zone provide visitors with semiprimitive wilderness experiences in a predominantly unmodified natural environment. Areas in this zone are generally located along the main travel routes, where visitors expect to encounter others more frequently and where solitude is not one of the highest priority. A lesser degree of challenge, risk, and freedom is provided here.

Management Area 5.3—Semiprimitive Motorized (105,425 acres)   Areas in this zone provide visitors with semiprimitive motorized experiences in a slightly modified natural environment. "Motor lakes" were designated by the 1978 BWCA Wilderness Act. Though not all travel in this area is by motorboat, visitors should expect to see a high number of boats with motors. These are generally lakes located on the periphery of the Boundary Waters Canoe Area Wilderness, with little portaging involved. Visitors will experience considerably less solitude, freedom, and challenge than are found in other management areas in the Boundary Waters Canoe Area Wilderness.

White Mountain National Forest

The White Mountain National Forest is located in north-central New Hampshire and western Maine. Ninety-three percent of the Forest's geographic extent lies in New Hampshire. It is fairly large for an eastern forest, with 739,325 acres of national forest land: 697,142 acres in New Hampshire and 42,183 acres in Maine. Eighty-seven percent of the area within the proclamation boundary is National Forest System land. The forest is in three noncontiguous but closely situated sections. The largest body of the forest extends east from I-93 and into Maine; the highest peaks of the White Mountains are located in this section. Mt. Washington State Park is located around the 6288-foot summit of the peak of the same name in the Presidential Range. This park may be reached by hiking trails through the surrounding national forest or through two unique, linear inholdings: the Mt. Washington Auto Road and the Mt. Washington Cog Railway. Both were constructed in the mid-19th century. The forest boundary excludes Crawford Notch State Park, which is on either side of U.S. 302 and the area to the west around Bretton Woods. The inholdings within this section of the forest are located primarily near major communities and transportation routes. The interior of this section is almost totally national forest land except for a major private inholding at Glen House, where the Mt. Washington Company operates the Mt. Washington Auto Road base station, restaurant, and support facilities. A section of the forest west of I-93 has larger inholdings: Franconia Notch State Park divides a portion of the forest at this location. This park was created by public action in 1924. To preserve the extreme beauty of Franconia Notch, which is perhaps the most famous mountain gap in the East and the site of the "Old Man of the Mountains" (also called the "Great Stone Face"), the Franconia Notch Parkway was developed as a scenic, limited-access route through the notch for a distance of 5 miles. The third and northernmost section of the forest lies north of U.S. 2 and west of Berlin, N.H.; Berlin is the site of a major paper mill. There are large inholdings in the southeastern corner of this section.

Forest headquarters and the supervisor's office are located 35 miles south of the forest at Laconia. There are five ranger districts: (1) Ammonoosuc (ranger station at Bethlehem, N.H.) in the northwest; (2) Androscoggin (Gorham, N.H.) in the northeast; (3) Evans Notch (Bethel, Maine) in the east; (4) Pemigewasset (Plymouth, N.H.) in the southwest; and (5) Saco (Conway, N.H.) in the southeast. Visitor information centers are located at Lincoln, Campton, and the Saco Ranger Station at the east end of the Kancamagus Highway (N.H. 112) near Conway. Interstate 93 provides a direct transportation route from Boston, Mass., which is 130 miles and 2 hours to the south.

The combination of this large area of public land that is especially scenic and unique with this direct and easy access to a major urban center is the principal reason for the heavy recreational use made of the White Mountain National Forest.

The White Mountains have historically been an important tourist destination since the early 19th century. In 1828, Allen Crawford opened one of the first guest houses. When the railroads came, grand hotels such as the Profile House, Fabyan's, Twin Mountain House, and Glen House and various inns and hotels sprang up in towns along the wayside, and the White Mountains became the playground of the wealthy of the East, especially the elite from Boston. The railroads also provided a fast, efficient way to move lumber and other wood products to market. This heavy use ravaged the landscape, and fires further deteriorated it. When the last public land was sold in the late 1860s, 650 timber companies were cutting in the White Mountains. By 1900 New Hamsphire was the most heavily logged state in the country. The slash left by logging set the stage for large forest fires, many of which were ignited by the sparks from locomotives. In 1888, 12,000 acres were lost to fire, and in 1907, 85,000 acres were lost. In the first years of the 20th century, conservation organizations and concerned individuals exerted pressure on Congress to establish a White Mountain Forest Reserve. Joining in this fight were the Appalachian Mountain Club (formed in 1876), the Society for the Protection of New Hampshire Forests (formed in 1901), and the grand hotel owners. Because the land in the White Mountains was not in the public domain, President Theodore Roosevelt could not proclaim the forest reserve as he did for many areas of the west. The states of New Hampshire and Maine passed the necessary legislation to authorize a national forest in 1903; in the same year a bill was introduced into the U.S. Senate *"for the purchase of a national forest reserve in the White Mountains, to be known as the National White Mountain Forest Reserve."* (Senate 327, Dec. 10, 1903) The Speaker of the House, Joe Cannon, delayed the process, declaring he would not *"spend one cent for scenery."* (The White Mountain National Forest: A Resource Unit, 4)

The passage of the Weeks Act in 1911 cleared the way for the purchase of forest lands at the head of navigable streams east of the Mississippi, and large sections of the White Mountains were acquired. By June 1912 the Forest Service had acquired 72,252 acres at an average price of $6.18 per acre. This area included Bean's Purchase and tracts in Franconia, Bethlehem, and the northern Presidential Range. In 1915 this total increased to 106,000 acres. The White Mountain National Forest was proclaimed on May 16, 1918, by President Wilson, and a second proclamation was made in 1929 by President Hoover. The land comprising the White Mountain National Forest was acquired by purchase or donation from private landowners; current law forbids the use of eminent domain. An average 1500 acres/year have been acquired over the last two decades.

The White Mountain National Forest is located in the New England Province of the Appalachian Highlands Division of the United States. The White Mountain Section of this physiographic province extends northeast and includes mountain ranges in Maine that extend to the Katahdin Range. The White Mountains are a somewhat irregular group of residual mountains that rise well above the New England Upland Section. The mountains are developed on a large granite pluton that is Paleozoic in age. Small areas of Paleozoic sedimentary and meta-sedimentary rocks are also found. The bases of most mountains lie above 1500 feet. The 15-mile Presidential Range

forms the backbone of the forest; the highest elevation in the forest is found in this range at Mt. Washington (6288 ft.), which is also the highest point in the Northeast. Seven other peaks in the Presidential Range exceed 5000 feet: Mt. Adams (5798 ft.), Mt. Jefferson (5715 ft.), Mt. Clay (5532 ft.), Mt. Quincy Adams (5400 ft.), Mt. Monroe (5385 ft.), Mt. Madison (5363 ft.), and Mt. Franklin (5004 ft.). Fifteen miles southwest of the Presidential Range are two peaks over 5000 feet: Mt. Lafayette (5249 ft.) and Mt. Lincoln (5089 ft.). Forty-seven peaks in the forest are over 4000 feet, and numerous other mountain ranges dominate the landscape. Elevations drop below 500 feet in the southwestern portion of the forest near Plymouth, and the lowest elevation in the forest is 440 feet, located south of Deer Hill near Colton Brook in the Pemigewasset Ranger District. The effects of mountain glaciation are prominent in the White Mountains, especially in the Presidential Range. Features known locally as "gulfs" or "ravines" are glacial cirques. The headwall of the Great Gulf is 1500 feet high. Tuckerman's Ravine is one of the best known of this cirques and is a major attraction for no-lift alpine skiing in the spring. Passes such as the Franconia, Dixville, Kinsman, Crawford, and Pinkham Notches provide scenic routes through the mountains. Many of the mountains in the southern section of the forest commemorate Native Americans: Mt. Chocorua, Mt. Passaconaway, and Mt. Kancamagus.

The northern hardwood forest is the dominant vegetation type up to about 2500 feet in elevation, the principal tree species being sugar maple, yellow and paper birch, and beech. From about 2500 to 3100 feet a mixed northern hardwood–spruce-fir forest occurs, becoming pure red spruce and balsam fir in the upper elevation range. A subalpine zone of dwarf spruce and fir is found from 3100 to 4000 feet, and the alpine zone above 4000 feet consists of krummholz and alpine plants. The forest has 8 square miles of land in this alpine zone. The present forest is composed as follows: northern hardwood (45 percent), northern hardwood–spruce (22 percent), paper birch (5 percent), aspen (5 percent), spruce-fir (15 percent), oak-pine (1 percent), permanent openings (1 percent), wetland (1 percent), and other (5 percent). The following land classification exists for the White Mountain National Forest:

1. water, 1400 acres
2. nonforest land, 17,600 acres
3. forest land, 732,000 acres
4. forest land withdrawn from timber production (designated wilderness areas, scenic areas, and experimental forests), 122,000 acres
5. forest lands not producing crops of industrial wood (data not available)
6. forest land physically not suitable: irreversible damage likely to occur or not restockable within 5 years, 51,000 acres
7. forest land (inadequate information), 67,000 acres
8. tentatively suitable forest land (item 3 minus items 4–7), 492,000 acres
9. forest land not appropriate for timber production, 147,000 acres
10. not suitable forest land (items 4–7 and 9), 387,000 acres
11. total suitable forest land (item 3 minus item 10), 345,000 acres
12. total net national forest area (items 1–3), 751,000 acres

There are two experimental forests: the Bartlett for timber research and the Hubbard Brook for watershed research. On December 3, 1993, Drs. Gene Likens and F. Herbert Bormann were jointly awarded the prestigious Tyler Prize for Environmental

Achievement for 30 years of pioneering forest ecosystem research at Hubbard Brook Experimental Forest. It was at Hubbard Brook in 1972 that they discovered acid rain. The Tyler Prize recognizes Hubbard Brook as a premier model for ecosystem studies in the world. Dr. Liken's experiments still continue here.

The climate in the White Mountain National Forest ranges from humid, continental, mild summer in the lower elevations to alpine tundra on the highest summits. A subarctic climatic zone occurs from about a little below 3000 feet to a little above 4000 feet elevation between these two zones. Summers are pleasant and mild in the valleys and lower elevations and winters are long, cold, and snowy. On the southern edge of the Forest, Campton (elevation 660 ft.) averages 18.5°F in January and 67.1°F in July and receives 42.5 inches of water equivalent per year; this precipitation is fairly evenly distributed but ranges from 2.8 inches in February to 4.3 inches in November. The weather conditions become much more severe in the higher elevations. Some have described the weather on the summit of Mt. Washington at the weather station (6262 ft.) as the worst of any inhabited place on earth. In April, 1934, the world's highest recorded surface wind speed of 231 miles per hour was measured here. The wind speed was so severe that it broke the anemometer. Two huge chains anchor that building to the summit of the mountain. The average annual wind speed averages 35 mph. The wind exceeds hurricane force (75 mph) about 104 days/year. The mean annual temperature on Mt. Washington is 27.1°F. February is the coldest month, averaging 5.7°F, and July is the warmest month, averaging 49.2°F. Temperatures rarely rise above 70°F in the summer (72°F is the highest temperature ever recorded). Precipitation averages a little over 6 inches per month, with a mean annual value of 73.6 inches; much of it is in the form of snow. Average annual snowfall is 244.7 inches, with a record snowfall of 566.4 inches in 1968–1969. Cloud cover prevails a great deal of the time on the summit of the mountain, with the summit in the clouds about 60 percent of the time, but when the weather is clear, the view from the summit is outstanding. The forest's 21 major watersheds make up all or part of the headwaters of the Androscoggin, Saco, Merrimack, and Connecticut River basins. The lands and waters of the White Mountain National Forest provide food, cover, and habitat for approximately 339 species of wildlife, including white-tailed deer, black bear, Canada lynx, gray and red squirrel, goshawk, and ruffed grouse. A small number of pine marten, listed in New Hamsphire as threatened, are found in the Forest. Bald eagles have been observed in the forest. The endangered peregrine falcon has been reintroduced to the forest. Several species of fish inhabit the streams and ponds of the forest. These include native fish such as brook trout and stocked fish such as rainbow trout. Atlantic salmon, plentiful prior to 1895, are being reintroduced in streams on the forest.

The White Mountain National Forest is one of the more heavily used in the National Forest System, ranking 27th in 1992 with 3,097,600 RVDs (with only 60,700 RVDs in the Maine part of the forest). For the same year, the number of recreation visits was 6,018,000 (with only 121,000 visits in the Maine part of the forest). The intensity of use index (0.239 acres/RVD) ranks it in 19th place. The forest has four areas designated as components of the National Wilderness Preservation System in New Hampshire and totaling 102,932 acres: Great Gulf Wilderness Area (5552 acres), Pemigewasset Wilderness Area (45,000 acres), Presidential Range–Dry River Wilderness Area (27,380 acres), and Sandwich Range Wilderness Area (25,000 acres). The

Great Gulf Wilderness Area is one of the 54 national forest areas that became the initial components of the National Wilderness Preservation System as soon as President Johnson signed the Wilderness Act in 1964. The Great Gulf and portions of the Pemigewasset are extremely heavily used. The Presidential Range–Dry River Wilderness Area was established in 1975 and 1984, and the Pemigewasset and Sandwich Range Wilderness Area were established in 1984. The wilderness use in the New Hampshire portion of the Forest totaled 116,900 RVDs in 1992, which was 3.85 percent of the total recreational use of the forest. There is one unit of the National Wilderness Preservation System in the Maine segment of the Forest—the 12,000-acre Caribou–Speckled Mountain Wilderness Area, which was established in 1990. This wilderness area is very lightly used, receiving only 500 RVDs in 1992, which is only 0.82 percent of the total recreational use of the part of the forest located in Maine. In 1988, 13.5 miles of Wildcat Creek and tributaries were designated "scenic" and 1 mile was designated "recreational" as components of the National Wild and Scenic Rivers System.

For purposes of summarizing the recreational use of the White Mountain National Forest, the New Hampshire totals have been aggregated here with the Maine totals. When compared to the rest of the National Forest System, the categories "hiking, horseback riding, and water travel" and "winter sports" are of much greater importance. The categories "hunting," "fishing," and "other recreational activities" are of much lesser importance. "Camping, picnicking, and swimming" and "mechanized travel and viewing scenery" are pretty close to the national norm. The leading major category of recreational use is "mechanized travel and viewing scenery," being responsible for 37 percent of the total recreational use. The leading subcategories are "automobile travel" (54 percent), and "viewing scenery" (28 percent). "Camping, picnicking, and swimming" is the second-ranking category, with 23 percent of the use. Eighty-seven percent of this use is camping, with "tent camping" accounting for over half of the use. Other subcategories contributing to the major category are "picnicking" (9 percent) and "swimming" and "water play" (4 percent). The third-ranking major category of use is "winter sports," accounting for a very high 20 percent of the total recreational use. The leading subcategory is "downhill skiing" (79 percent), with "snowshoeing" and "cross-country skiing" contributing another 20 percent. Only seven other national forests record a greater number of "winter sports" RVDs than the 630,900 in the White Mountain National Forest: White River (Colorado, 3,894,200), Tahoe (California, 1,072,000), Green Mountain (Vermont, 832,800), Wasatch-Cache (Utah and Wyoming, 824,900), Arapaho-Roosevelt (Colorado, 821,000), Grand Mesa–Uncompaghre–Gunnison (Colordo, 760,000), and Inyo (California and Nevada, 709,500). When the percentage of total recreational use attributed to "winter sports" is analyzed, in only four national forests does this category account for a higher percentage than the White Mountain National Forest's 20.4 percent: Green Mountain (53 percent), White River (47 percent), Routt (Colorado, 28 percent), and Tahoe (20.7 percent).

The fourth-ranking category of recreational use is "hiking, horseback riding, and water travel," 98.5 percent of which is "hiking." The Forest Service and the Appalachian Mountain Club have an extensive hiking trail and hut system in the White Mountain National Forest; the Appalachian Trail passes through the forest. The fifth-ranking category of use is "resorts, cabins, and organization camps," which accounts

for 4 percent of the total recreational use; the leading subcategories are "resort lodging" (62 percent) and "general resort and commercial public service" (34 percent). There are no private recreational cabins in the White Mountain National Forest. "Hunting" accounts for a little over 1 percent of the use and ranks sixth; the breakdown of "hunting" by subcategories is as follows: "big-game" (50 percent), "small-game" (27 percent), "upland bird" (18 percent), and "waterfowl" (6 percent). "Fishing" is the seventh-ranking category of recreational use with only 1 percent of the total; 90 percent is "cold-water fishing." "Other recreational activities" is especially insignificant in the White Mountain National Forest, contributing less than 1 percent of the recreational use. The leading subcategories are: "gathering forest products" (27 percent), "general information" (21 percent), "viewing interpretive signs" (16 percent), "attending talks and programs" (11 percent), and "viewing interpretive exhibits" (11 percent). "Nonconsumptive fish and wildlife use" ranks ninth and last with less than ½ percent of the recreational use.

The many recreational opportunities in the forest vary by altitudinal zones. The recreational opportunities unique to the White Mountain National Forest are (1) above-timberline backcountry recreation experiences, (2) a hut-and-shelter system coupled with a well-established trail system, and (3) quality downhill ski areas. On the lower mountain slopes below 2500 feet and valley bottoms, there is noticeable human activity from many uses. This part of the forest supports traditional uses such as timber harvesting, hunting and fishing, camping, picnicking, hiking, ski touring, snowmobiling, and pleasure driving. Numerous panoramic views and landscapes are provided. The steep mountain slopes above 2500 feet offer unique opportunities for recreational experiences not available in most parts of the East, including backcountry recreation above timberline, downhill skiing, high-country hiking, snowmobiling, and wilderness. The majority of the higher forest areas are free from evidence of human activities, except in the Presidential Range. Motorized use is permitted on a seasonal basis only in selected parts, but most of the area contains only foot trails and occasional camping facilities. The four existing downhill ski areas are the only other significant areas of the forest characterized by a substantially modified natural environment on the upper mountain slopes. The alpine portion of the forest above timberline is a distinctive geological, ecological, and visual resource in New England and in the eastern United States. Alpine areas are generally vegetated with tundralike plants or low-growing black spruce. These, coupled with shallow soils, provide a fragile environment easily disrupted by human impact. With the exception of the major intrusion into the alpine zone on Mt. Washington by the Auto Road, the Cog Railway, and various buildings on the summit, use on these summits is limited to hiking trails and some huts.

Developed recreation sites in the White Mountain National Forest account for 44 percent of the recreational use and include campgrounds, picnic areas, boat access sites, swimming sites, and downhill ski areas. The developed recreation sites occupy 1393 acres and have a capacity of 13,227 PAOT. The cross-country trails of the Jackson Ski Touring Foundation account for 4000 PAOT of this total capacity. Downhill ski areas are not included in these capacities. Table 10.15 identifies the recreational opportunities available at the Forest Service–operated recreation sites. There are 19 campgrounds that contain a total of 820 sites, and the two group campgrounds have a capacity of 594 (PAOT). These campgrounds range from the seven-site Crocker

Table 10.15 White Mountain National Forest: Recreation Sites

Site Name	Camping	Picnic	Trailer Space	Boat Access	Fishing	Swimming	Hiking	Interpretive Trails	Group Camping
Basin	21	4	X	X	X				
Beaver Brook		15							
Big Rock	28		X		X		X		
Blackberry Crossing	20		X		X		X		
Campton	58	9	X		X				X
C. L. Graham Wangan Ground		10							
Cold River	12	4	X		X		X		
Covered Bridge	49		X		X		X	X	
Crocker Pond	7		X	X	X		X		
Dolly Copp*	176	26	X		X		X	X	X
Dugway		18			X				
Gilead		12							
Glenn Ellis Falls		3			X		X	X	
Hancock	56				X		X		
Hastings	24		X		X		X		
Jigger Johnson	75		X		X				
Long Pond		3		X	X				
Lost River Road		5							
Lower Falls		10			X	X			
Passaconaway	33		X		X		X		
Passaconaway Historic Site*								X	
Peabody Field		6			X		X		
Rocky Gorge									
Russell Pond	87		X	X	X	X			
Sabbaday Falls		11					X	X	
Sawyer Rock		12							
South Pond		28			X	X	X		
Sugarloaf	63		X		X		X		
Waterville	27				X		X		
White Ledge	39	5	X				X		
Wild River	8		X		X		X		
Wildwood	26	8	X		X		X		
Zealand	11	9	X		X		X		

*Historical sites.
X = available recreation opportunity.
Source: Forest Service, *White Mountain National Forest Map* (1984).

Pond to 176-site Dolly Copp. Dolly Copp was the first campground constructed in the White Mountain National Forest (in 1921). Group camping is available at Dolly Copp and at Campton. Figure 10.17 shows a campsite at the Zealand campground. There are also 19 picnic areas with 198 sites, seven of which are associated with campgrounds and 12 of which are not. These picnic sites range in size from three to 28 sites. All of the picnic areas and all but two of the campgrounds fall within the "roaded natural" ROS class. Only two campgrounds (Wild River and Crocker Pond) are considered to be in the "semiprimitive motorized" ROS class. Campground and picnicking facilities also exist in Franconia Notch State Park and Crawford Notch State Park, both of which are surrounded by the White Mountain National Forest.

Figure 10.17   A typical site at the Zealand campground in the White Mountain National Forest.

Four downhill ski areas operate under special-use permit in the forest: Waterville Valley, Wildcat, Loon Mountain, and Attitash. These ski areas have 32 surface, chair, and gondola lifts with an estimated lift capacity of 35,750 people per hour. Wildcat and Waterville Valley are entirely on national forest land. Attitash uses national forest land only on the upper quarter of the mountain, and Loon is on national forest for the upper three-quarters of the ski area. The Mittersill Ski Area, which formerly operated under a special-use permit, has closed. A large downhill ski area is operated at Cannon Mountain on state land that borders the national forest. Other downhill ski areas on private land in or near the forest are Mt. Cranmore, Bretton Woods, and Black Mountain.

Dispersed recreation accounts for 56 percent of the recreational use on the White Mountain National Forest and includes pleasure driving, snowmobiling, backcountry camping and hiking, alpine and cross-country skiing, hunting, and fishing. There are 490 miles of Forest Service roads; 150 miles are open to public vehicular access. Paved highways provide scenic drives through several major "notches" in the forest. Outstanding scenery has been the basis for a major tourist industry in and near the forest. Major tourist centers that support this industry are located at Conway/North Conway, Gorham, Berlin, Twin Mountains, Jackson, Lincoln/North Woodstock, Waterville Valley, and Bartlett/Glen. I-93 passes through Franconia Notch between the Kinsman and Franconia Ranges. This notch, which is also the site of a state park of the same name, has more scenic attractions than any of the notches. The Profile ("Old Man of the Mountains" or "Great Stone Face") is on a mountainside 1200 feet above Echo Lake. An excellent bikeway has been developed as an alternative means of visiting the sights in the park. To preserve the scenic beauty through Franconia Notch, completion of the two-lane, divided I-93 was abandoned for 5 miles in favor of the limited access Franconia Notch Parkway. The aerial tram at Cannon Mountain Ski Area offers

rides to the 4060-foot summit of Cannon Mountain; all of this area is on state land, but it borders the national forest. The Flume is a natural gorge that may be toured for a fee at the southern end of the notch.

Crawford Notch is another glacier-carved gap through which U.S. 302 and the Saco River pass. It is also a New Hampshire State Park. A hiking trail leads to Arethusa Falls, at 200 feet one of the highest waterfalls in New Hampshire. The Silver and Flume Cascades are dramatic sheets of water plunging down bare granite along U.S. 302. New Hampshire Route 16 passes through the Pinkham Notch Scenic Area between the Presidential Range to the west and high peaks such as Mount Moriah, North Carter Mountain, Carter Dome, and Wildcat Mountain on the east. This is the site of the Appalachian Mountain Club Base Camp and Glen Ellis Falls and Picnic Area. The scenic area includes all of the gulfs and ravines on the eastern side of the Presidential Range south of the Mt. Washington Auto Road. Tuckerman Ravine is the most famous of these glacial cirques within the scenic area. Wildcat Mountain Ski Area operates under a Forest Service permit on the western side of 4422-foot Wildcat Mountain on the eastern side of Pinkham Notch. Crystal Cascades is found along the Tuckerman Ravine Trail.

Tuckerman Ravine Ski Area offers one of the most unique recreational experiences on the forest (Figure 10.18). It is a glacial cirque and its amphitheater-like basin collects the wind-blown snow of the Presidential Range, which may collect to a depth of 75 feet in the Bowl. It is famous for its spring skiing, which can be reached by hiking the 2.4-mile Tuckerman Ravine Trail from Pinkham Notch. You have to climb the ski slopes above this point where the trail ends. The Forest Service maintains Snow Rangers in the ravine to forecast avalanches and ice falls. The Forest Service is assisted by the Mt. Washington Volunteer Ski Patrol. The Appalachian Mountain Club maintains a caretaker in the ravine who oversees the camping shelters. Camping in

Figure 10.18 Tuckerman Ravine is a popular location for spring skiing in the White Mountain National Forest; there are no lifts. The "bowl" of the Ravine is in the center of the picture. Mt. Washington (6288 ft.), in the upper right corner, is the highest peak of the Presidential Range.

Table 10.16   Tuckerman Ravine Ski Area

Area	Length of Run	Vertical Drop	Maximum Pitch
Hillman Highway	0.5–0.6 mi.	1500 ft.	40°
Lower Snowfield	0.2–0.3 mi.	700 ft.	35°
Little Headwall	75 yd.	150 ft.	35°
Left Gully	¼ mi.	800 ft.	40°
Headwall	.1–.2 mi.	800 ft.	55°
Right Gully	¼ mi.	800 ft.	40°
Sherburne Trail	2.4 mi.	1900 ft.	35°
East Snowfield	200 yd.	400 ft.	30°

Source: Forest Service, *Tuckerman—White Mountains.*

the area is limited, and tickets must be bought at Pinkham Notch Base Camp. Facilities for those who wish to camp overnight are limited to eight Adirondack open-front shelters with a capacity of 86 people. No tent camping or wood or charcoal fires are permitted in the area. Tuckerman is for expert skiers only and for those in good physical shape. There are no lifts; it is necessary to hike upslope, which is very steep. The spring season in Tuckerman Ravine begins generally in late March and continues through Memorial Day; skiing lasts well into June and as late as July 4, but conditions are poor at this time. There are several slopes in the vicinity of Tuckerman Ravine where skiing is possible. Table 10.16 identifies these ski areas, length of run, vertical drop, and degree of slope. From the early part of the season to about May 1, conditions allow skiers to ski down to the Pinkham Notch Camp from Tuckerman Ravine on the John Sherburne Ski Trail. Later in the season it is necessary to hike down the Tuckerman Ravine Trail.

In addition to the numerous hiking trails that lead to the summit of Mt. Washington, there are two other alternatives for reaching the summit, where Mt. Washington State Park is located. The Mt. Washington Auto Road climbs 4725 feet in altitude in the 8 miles from Glen House up the east side of the Presidential Range to the summit. Built in the 1850s, it was long known as the Carriage Road. It was opened to the public in 1861, and the first automobile ascent was made in 1899 by F. O. Stanley and his "Stanley Steamer." The average grade is 12 percent, and the road can be quite frightening for those not accustomed to narrow, steep, no-shoulder or no–guard rail mountain roads. The author has driven most of the mountain roads of Colorado and deems none of these as exhilarating as the Mt. Washington Auto Road. Because of the narrow and curving nature of the road, wheel bases longer than 138 inches are not permitted.[2] The drive along the upper portion of this road above timberline is a rare treat in the East, the only place where such an experience is possible. For those who are timid about mountain driving, the Mt. Washington Company offers chauffeured "stages" (actually vans) to the summit. The Auto Road operates from mid-June to Labor Day, weather permitting.

Another alternative to the summit is on the west side on the Mt. Washington Cog Railway (Figure 10.19). Both the Cog Railway and Auto Road are narrow lineal

---

[2]This regulation is enforced. The first time the author tried to drive this road he was refused admittance due to the 155 inch wheel base of his Ford Supercab pickup truck.

Figure 10.19   The Mt. Washington Cog Railway is one way to reach the summit of Mt. Washington in the Presidential Range in the White Mountain National Forest. The Great Gulf Wilderness Area drops off in the ravine (the Great Gulf) beyond the Cog Railway and up the sides of other peaks of the Presidential Range.

private inholdings surrounded by national forest land. The Cog Railway was built in 1869 and climbs for 3 miles from the 2569-foot elevation at Marshfield Station to a few feet below the 6288-foot summit. This coal-fired, steam-powered, mountain-climbing railroad outputs a great deal of soot and pollution that can be seen from several miles away. The railway operates from mid-April to early November. There are fees for using both routes to the summit; the 3-hour Cog Railway trip is fairly expensive. Weather problems can close or cause delays on both routes. At the top of Mt. Washington is the Sherman Adams Summit Building. The Mt. Washington Museum, located in the basement of the Summit Building, is an educational facility of the Mt. Washington Observatory that features exhibits on the mountain's history and natural history. The Tip-Top House is the oldest building on the summit, built in 1853. It has been restored to the style of that time by the New Hampshire Division of Parks.

Another spectacular scenic drive in the forest is the Kancamagus Highway (N.H. 112) from near Conway to Lincoln. This scenic road passes through almost all national forest land for 34.5 miles along the Swift River Valley in the east and along the Pemigewasset River Valley in the west. The drainage divide between the two rivers and also the highest elevation on the road is Kancamagus Pass (2860 ft.). This highway did not become a through-road until 1959, when roads that ran up each valley were joined at Kancamagus Pass. There are six Forest Service campgrounds and five Forest Service picnic areas along the road, in addition to many scenic overlooks. No camping or fires are allowed on land within ½ mile of the Kancamagus Highway, except at campgrounds. Rocky Falls Gorge Scenic Area is an area along the highway where the Swift River has worn a narrow cleft in the solid rock. Half-day hikes lead

from the highway to two other scenic areas: Sawyer Pond Scenic Area and Greeley Ponds Scenic Area. No overnight camping is allowed at Greeley Pond. Camping is allowed at Sawyer Pond on platforms and in the shelter only. A 5-minute walk along the Sabbaday Brook National Recreation Trail leads to Sabbaday Falls. Other self-guided trails along the highway are the Rail 'n River Trail and the Boulder Loop Trail. In the western section of the forest a scenic drive along N.H. 12 passes through Kinsman Notch. Lost River Gorge is located here; it is privately operated, and there is a fee for entering.

The White Mountains are well known for hiking and backpacking opportunities. There are 1167 miles of trails available in the forest. Many of these trails were developed in the 1930s by the Civilian Conservation Corps. The Appalachian Trail winds across the major peaks for 102 miles in the forest. Hikers consider this section through the White Mountains the most scenic, yet most difficult, section of the entire trail from Maine to Georgia. An especially unique feature of backcountry recreation in the forest is the Appalachian Mountain Club hut system. This system began over 100 years ago, when the first hut (Madison Springs) was built in the col between Mt. Madison and Mt. Quincy Adams. Since then, a unique system of eight huts has developed that stretch for 56 miles by trail from Lonesome Lake Hut in the southwest to Carter Notch Hut in the east. Each of these huts are a day's hike apart along the Appalachian Trail in the forest. The highest-elevation and most popular hut is Lake-of-the-Clouds, located on the southern shoulder of Mt. Washington above timberline at 5000 feet. This hut has accommodations for 90 in eight bunkrooms. The other huts can accommodate 36 to 60 people. The Pinkham Lodge Camp has accommodations for 106 in the Joe Dodge Lodge. The hut system allows hikers to carry less cumbersome packs and provides homemade breakfasts and dinners during the full-service season. The huts are also centers for learning about the environment. In 1917 the Appalachian Mountain Club and the Forest Service signed an agreement that highlighted the beginning of the Forest Service's role in managing recreational activities in the White Mountains. This may be the longest-running active recreation partnership in the history of the Forest Service. There are also 43 Adirondack (3 sided) shelters and eight cabins along the hiking trails of the forest. National recreation trails in the forest are the Sabbaday Brook National Recreation Trail and Boulder Loop National Recreation Trail. Designated restricted-use areas (RUAs) protect portions of the forest that are particularly fragile or have been subjected to heavy use. Generally, all areas above timberline fall into this category. Fires and camping are allowed only at designated campsites in RUAs. Restricted use is in effect from May 1 through November 1.

Opportunities for ski touring exist on hiking trails, logging roads, and trails built and maintained specifically for skiing. There are over 100 miles of cross-country skiing on eight marked trails on the forest. The following areas charge a fee for using their groomed trails: Jackson Ski Touring Foundation, Jackson; Waterville Valley Ski Touring Area, Waterville Valley; and Bretton Woods Ski Touring Area, Bretton Woods. There are 372 miles of groomed and ungroomed snowmobile trails, and trails are available for minibikes, trail bikes, ATVs, and four-wheel-drive vehicles. Twin Mountains is a focal point for snowmobiling activities. Mountain biking is growing in popularity, and there are 22 miles of designated bike routes. Summer ORV use is limited to a few specific trails.

The Recreation Opportunity Spectrum (ROS) is used to manage the forest's recreational resources. The "primitive" class is not common in the White Mountain National Forest. Parts of "wilderness" (management area 5.1), "wilderness study area" (management area 9.1), and those management areas managed exclusively for nonmotorized recreation (management area 6.2) meet the criteria. The current on-the-ground situation is such that these areas are more semiprimitive nonmotorized than primitive. It is a goal of forest personnel to work toward the "primitive" class for management areas 5.1 and 9.1. The greatest number of acres in the forest fit into the "semiprimitive nonmotorized" ROS class. Management areas 5.1, 9.1, and 6.2 are managed exclusively for nonmotorized use. Management area 6.1 is prescribed semiprimitive with seasonal variation between motorized and nonmotorized. Snowmobile use is permitted on designated trails during the winter. Another large portion of the forest is in management area 3.1, which, although classified "semiprimitive motorized" provides semiprimitive nonmotorized experience opportunities when timber sales are not occurring, as well as some roaded natural opportunities. Timber sales occur on less than 1 percent of the forest each year. "Semiprimitive motorized" includes management areas 6.3 and 6.1, which are classified as "semiprimitive nonmotorized" but does allow for incidental motorized use in specific areas (for example, snowmobiles).

The "roaded natural" ROS class is closely associated with state, county, and town roads as well as Forest Service type III roads. This class usually extends ½ mile to either side of the roads. Most of these roads, because of their visually sensitive nature, are designated part of management area 2.1. A few places in management area 3.1 where type III roads are used for timber operations also meet the criteria for this class. The only part of the forest considered to be in the "rural" ROS class is management area 7.1, which is used for downhill ski areas. In some management areas the ROS class is a result of other objectives. Management area 8.1 describes "special areas." These can range from a heavily used and roaded experimental forest (ROS "Roaded Natural") to a low-use scenic area (ROS class "semiprimitive nonmotorized"). Nine areas totaling 15,639 acres in this management area are classified as "scenic" and are managed to protect outstanding scenery: Gibbs Brook, Greeley Ponds, Lafayette Brook, Lincoln Woods, Pinkham Notch, Rocky Gorge, Sawyer Pond, Snyder Brook, and Mt. Chocorua.

Another important aspect of the ROS is the seasonal variation in ROS class. For example, management area 6.3 is semiprimitive nonmotorized in summer, as almost all motorized use is snowmobile. The objective of resource management in the forest is to manage for the ROS class that represents the major use season in any particular land area because it would have the greatest potential to affect the ROS class. For example, the Great Gulf Wilderness is managed as semiprimitive nonmotorized because of the high summer use, even though in the winter months it may be closer to primitive.

Table 10.17 summarizes the management areas that are designated in the *White Mountain National Forest Land and Resource Management Plan* (Forest Service, 1986f). Over half (50.3 percent) of the acreage in the forest falls in just two of these 10 management prescriptions: management area 3.1 (227,000 acres) and management area 6.2 (151,000 acres). Both of these management areas allow timber harvesting. Of these acres open for potential timber harvesting, 345,000 (45.9 percent) are deemed

Table 10.17   White Mountain National Forest: Management Area Summary

Management Area	# of Acres
2.1 Emphasize visual quality. Even-aged and uneven-aged silviculture. Long harvest rotations. Optimum wildlife habitat diversity. Roaded-rural recreation.	118,000
3.1 Emphasize high-quality sawtimber. Primarily even-aged silviculture with long rotations. Increase in wildlife habitat diversity. Roaded-rural recreation.	227,000
5.1 Designated wilderness.	102,000
6.1 Emphasize nonmotorized semiprimitive recreation. Increase in old-growth wildlife habitat. Temporary roads only.	94,000
6.2 Emphasize nonmotorized semiprimitive recreation. No motorized use. No timber harvest or road construction. Limited recreational facilities.	151,000
6.3 Emphasize semiprimitive recreation with motorized use. No timber harvest or road construction. Limited recreational facilities.	14,000
7.1 Downhill ski permit area.	2,000
8.1 Protection of unique, scientific, and scenic areas.	26,000
9.1 A "holding area" for existing and recommended wilderness study areas.	12,000
9.2 A "holding area" for ski area expansion.	2,000
9.3 A "holding area" for candidates for research natural area status that are not classified as wilderness.	3,000
Total national forest acres	751,000

Source: Forest Service, *White Mountain National Forest Land and Resource Management Plan* (1986).

suitable for timber harvesting. The lands that are not managed for timber production total 406,000 acres, or 54 percent of the land area of the forest. The breakdown on this "unmanaged land" is: (1) alpine (23,000 acres, 3 percent), and (2) Other forested (383,000 acres, 51 percent). Management area 3.1 emphasizes high-quality sawtimber, employing even-age silvicultural practices with long rotations. This is expected to increase wildlife habitat diversity. A "roaded rural" recreational experience is provided. Management area 2.1 emphasizes visual quality, while practicing even-age and uneven-age silvicultural practices with long harvest rotations. This is projected to provide optimum wildlife habitat diversity and provide roaded rural recreational opportunities. The direction of this *Plan* seems to be counter to what is being done in other national forests that are also heavily used for recreation. While many of these other forests are deemphasizing timber production and emphasizing recreation, this does not seem to be the case in the White Mountain National Forest.

Management Issues   In the process of preparing the 1986 *Plan*, 13 basic issues were addressed:

- Minerals management
- Downhill skiing
- Developed recreation facilities
- Nonmotorized dispersed recreation
- Off-road vehicles
- Wilderness and roadless areas
- Roads
- Timber management
- Visual quality
- Wildlife and fish

- Economic efficiency
- Community well-being
- Research natural areas

In the planning process "Alternative 6" was chosen to become the *Plan*. This alternative provides for multiple use and sustained yield of goods and services in an environmentally sound manner. This choice had the third-highest present net value. It provides the mix of outputs that best meet net public benefits. It emphasizes a variety of recreational opportunities while maintaining the traditional uses and experiences. It is responsive to public comments on the draft EIS and was the preferred alternative.

Management Goals   The goals of this *Plan* are to:

- Conduct all management activities to protect soil and water resources.
- Conduct all management activities with full recognition of the appearance of the Forest, realizing the importance to society of a natural landscape distinct from the human-made environments otherwise dominant in the East.
- Feature high-quality recreational opportunities not likely to be provided elsewhere on other lands.
- Recognize the demand for and importance of day-use areas and driving for pleasure as part of the forest's total Recreation Opportunity Spectrum.
- Recognize the need for the forest user to bear a share of management costs through continued use of volunteer programs, payment for services, cooperative agreements, and voluntary contributions and donations.
- Use existing roads, trail, and utility corridors to the maximum extent possible. Plan and design access to serve multiple management purposes.
- Design and build any new access, regardless of type, according to standards and criteria that focus on minimum impact.
- Feature management for indigenous wildlife species including those that require old-growth habitat, those that are threatened or endangered, and those that are sensitive or unique species. Recognize the demand for nonconsumptive uses of wildlife, including opportunities to observe.
- Work with the research and academic communities to preserve unique portions of the forest through the Research Natural Area program.
- Use timber management as one of the tools available to achieve the desired future condition and integrated resource objectives of certain management areas.
- Feature the management of northern hardwoods over softwoods. Move toward the culturing of high-quality hardwoods that are in demand for specialty products. Assure a stable, reliable source of this raw material to support community stability.
- Involve the public in management decisions.

Specific Objectives   Some of the major objectives of this adopted *Plan* are as follows:

- An emphasis on nonmotorized dispersed recreation opportunities.
- Identification of land for potential downhill ski expansion pending site-specific investigations.
- Expansion of developed campgrounds to meet projected demand during the 10-year plan period.

- Timber volumes averaging 35 million board feet during the 10-year plan period.
- Seven miles of new Types I, II, and III road construction annually during the 10-year plan period.
- A 5700-acre area established around Mt. Chocorua.
- Ten candidate areas totaling approximately 5000 acres for evaluation as research natural areas.
- Protection of the Kilkenny and Caribou-Speckled roadless areas.
- Recommendation for wilderness study of approximately 12,000 acres of the Caribou-Speckled roadless area. (*Note:* In 1990, a 12,000-acre Caribou—Speckled Mountain Wilderness Area was established in the eastern portion of the White Mountain National Forest in Maine by P.L. 101-401.)
- Assignment of 22,000 acres in the Kilkenny area to roadless status (management area 6.1, which emphasizes nonmotorized dispersed recreation).

References

Appalachian Mountain Club. *The Guide to AMC Huts and Lodges.* Boston: Appalachian Mountain Club, 1991.

Chronological History of the Nebraska National Forest.

Colwell, Joseph. *Boulder Mountain: Throne of the Colorado Plateau.* Salt Lake City: Falcon Publishing, 1992.

Dixie National Forest. Cedar City, Utah: Blackner, no date.

Forest Service. *The Boundary Waters Canoe Area.*

Forest Service. *The Boundary Waters Canoe Area: A Synopsis of Historical Events.*

Forest Service, USDA. *Final Environmental Impact Statement: Chattahoochee-Oconee National Forests.*

Forest Service, USDA. *A Guide to Enjoying Lincoln National Forest.*

Forest Service, USDA. *Garden of the Gods Recreation Area.*

Forest Service, USDA. *Land and Resource Management Plan: Dixie National Forest.* No date.

Forest Service, USDA. *Onfoot in the White Mountain National Forest.*

Forest Service, USDA. *Rim Rock Pounds Hollow Recreation Complex.*

Forest Service, USDA. *Shawnee Hills of the Ohio National Scenic Byway.*

Forest Service. *Superior National Forest—Canoe Routes Outside the BWCA Wilderness.*

Forest Service, USDA. *Superior National Forest—Hiking.*

Forest Service. *Tuckerman—White Mountains.*

Forest Service. *Welcome to the Lincoln National Forest.*

Forest Service. *Tongass National Forest Map.* 1973 (revised 1990).

Forest Service, USDA. *Buffalo Gap National Grassland Map.* 1974.

Forest Service, USDA. *Chugach National Forest Map.* 1978a (revised 1989).

Forest Service, USDA. *Lincoln National Forest Map (Guadalupe District).* 1979b.

Forest Service, USDA. *Nebraska and Samuel R. McKelvie National Forests and Oglala National Grassland Map.* 1978c.

Forest Service, USDA. *Fort Pierre National Grassland Map.* 1980.

Forest Service, USDA. *Chattahoochee National Forest Map.* 1982a.

Forest Service, USDA. *Dixie National Forest Map (Pine Valley and Cedar City Ranger Districts).* 1982b.

Forest Service, USDA. *Dixie National Forest Map (Powell, Escalante, and Teasdale Ranger Districts).* 1982c.

Forest Service, USDA. *Chugach National Forest Land and Resource Management Plan.* July 1984.

Forest Service, USDA. *Land and Resource Management Plan: Nebraska National Forest (and Amendments).* 1984b.

Forest Service. *White Mountain National Forest Map.* 1984c.

Forest Service, USDA. *Forest Plan: Flathead National Forest.* December 1985.

Forest Service, USDA. *Lincoln National Forest Plan.* 1986a.

Forest Service. *Superior National Forest: Final Environmental Impact Statement Land and Resource Management Plan.* 1986b.

Forest Service. *Superior National Forest Land and Resource Management Plan (and Amendments).* May 1986c.

Forest Service. *Superior National Forest Record of Decision—Final Environmental Impact Statement Land and Resource Management Plan.* 1986d.

Forest Service. *White Mountain National Forest Final Environmental Impact Statement—Land and Resource Management Plan.* 1986e.

Forest Service. *White Mountain National Forest Land and Resource Management Plan.* 1986f.

Forest Service. *White Mountain National Forest Record of Decision: Final Environmental Impact Statement—Land and Resource Management Plan.* 1986g.

Forest Service, USDA. *Inyo National Forest Map.* 1987a.

Forest Service, USDA. *Land and Resource Management Plan: Chattahoochee-Oconee National Forests.* Revised. May 1987b.

Forest Service, USDA. *Directory: Chattahoochee-Oconee National Forest Recreational Areas.* 1988a.

Forest Service, USDA. *Inyo National Forest: Environmental Impact Statement for the Land and Resource Management Plan.* 1988b.

Forest Service, USDA. *Inyo National Forest: Land and Resource Management Plan.* 1988c.

Forest Service, USDA. *Lincoln National Forest Map (Smokey Bear, Cloudcroft, and Mayhill Ranger Districts).* 1988d.

Forest Service, USDA. *Record of Decision for the Inyo National Forest Land and Resource Management Plan.* 1988e.

Forest Service, USDA. *Shawnee National Forest (and Shawnee Purchase Unit) Map.* 1988f.

Forest Service, USDA. *Appendices A–O, Final Environmental Impact Statement: Land and Resource Management Plan—Gifford Pinchot National Forest.* 1990a.

Forest Service, USDA. *Appendix P, Final Environmental Impact Statement: Land and Resource Management Plan—Gifford Pinchot National Forest.* 1990b.

Forest Service, USDA. *Forest Facts—White Mountain National Forest.* 1990c.

Forest Service, USDA. *Land and Resource Management Plan: Gifford Pinchot National Forest.* 1990d.

Forest Service. *Superior National Forest—Cross Country Skiing.* December 3, 1990e.

Forest Service, USDA. *Flathead National Forest Map.* 1991a.

Forest Service, USDA. *1992 Key Issues Facing the Inyo National Forest.* December 1991.

Forest Service, USDA. *Land and Resource Management Plan—1990 and Beyond: Gifford Pinchot National Forest.* 1991b.

Forest Service. *Tongass Land Management Plan Revision (Parts 1 and 2): Supplement to the Draft Environmental Impact Statement.* August 1991c.

Forest Service. *Tongass Land Management Plan Revision: Supplement to the Draft Environmental Impact Statement—Proposed Revised Forest Plan.* August 1991d.

Forest Service. *Tongass Land Management Plan Revision: Supplement to the Draft Environmental Impact Statement—Summary.* August 1991e.

Forest Service, USDA. *Gifford Pinchot National Forest Map.* 1992a.

Forest Service, USDA. *Primitive Management Areas—Superior National Forest.* July 1992b.

Forest Service, USDA. *Shawnee National Forest Amended Land and Resource Management Plan.* 1992c.

Forest Service. *The Superior Experience.* Spring/Summer, 1992g.

Forest Service. *Superior National Forest Map.* 1992h.

Forest Service. *Superior National Forest—Off-Road Vehicles.* May 1992i.

Forest Service. *Volcano Review.* Summer/Fall 1992j.

Forest Service, USDA. *BWCA Wilderness Management Plan and Implementation Schedule.* August 1993a.

Forest Service, USDA. *Final Environmental Impact Statement for the BWCA Wilderness Management Plan and Implementation Schedule* (Amendment #3 to the Forest Land and Resource Management Plan.) August 1993b.

Forest Service, USDA. *Record of Decision: Final Environmental Impact Statement for the BWCA Wilderness Management Plan and Implementation Schedule.* August 1993c.

Forest Service, USDA. *Superior National Forest.* March 1993d.

Forest Service. *White Mountain National Forest—Monitoring Report 1993.* 1993e.

Forest Service. *White Mountain National Forest Guide.* 1993f.

Gebhardt, Carl. Forest Service. *1993 White Mountain National Forest Monitoring Report—Dispersed Recreation.* August, 1993.

Illinois Nature Preserves Commission. *Comprehensive Plan for the Illinois Nature Preserves System—Part 2—The Natural Divisions of Illinois.* 1973.

International Wolf Center. *International Wolf.* Fall 1993.

Kacprzynski, Fred. *White Mountain National Forest—Developed Recreation.* Forest Service, USDA.

Leask, Linda. "Changing Ownership and Management of Alaska Lands," *Alaska Review of Social and Economic Conditions,* Vol. 22, No. 2, October, 1985.

Martin, Emilie. *The History of the Inyo National Forest and Its Ranger District.*

Mason, Robert H. Shawnee National Forest Lands and Minerals Staff Officer. *History of the Shawnee National Forest.*

Plattsburgh Press-Republican. December 7, 1993.

Rakestraw, Lawrence W. *A History of the Forest Service in Alaska.* Anchorage: Alaska Historical Commission, et al., 1981.

Roenke, Karl. *Interpreting Historic Values of High Elevation Shelters and Cabins on the White Mountain National Forest: Past, Present, and Future.* Forest Service, USDA, May 1991.

Southern Illinois Regional Tourism Council and Forest Service. *Shawnee National Forest Guide.* July 1992.

Senate 327, December 10, 1903.

Spoerl, Patricia M. *A Brief History of the Early Years of the Lincoln National Forest.* February 1981.

The White Mountain National Forest: A Resource Unit.

Thornbury, William D. *Regional Geomorphology of the United States.* New York: Wiley, 1965.

## CHAPTER 11

National Wildlife Refuge System

We abuse land because we regard it as a commodity belonging to us. When we see land as a community to which we belong, we may begin to use it with love and respect.

Aldo Leopold (1949)

The National Wildlife Refuge System is a network of U.S. lands and waters that are managed specifically for wildlife, especially migratory birds and endangered species. Almost 500 refuges, 164 waterfowl production areas, and 51 coordination areas encompassing almost 91 million acres in all 50 states and five trust territories now comprise the system. These refuges range in size from the 0.6-acre Mille Lacs (Minnesota) to the 19.3-million-acre Arctic (Alaska). Small or large, each refuge provides vital habitat for at least a portion of America's wildlife populations. They support nearly all species of North American mammals. Most are year-round residents, but some, such as elk, antelope, deer, bats and caribou, may be migrants. Six hundred out of 813 bird species in the United States have been observed on the refuges. Refuges are found in every major ecosystem of the country, including desert and swamp, prairie and forest, and seashore and tundra. Most major topographic features of North America are represented in the system, with elevations ranging from 280 feet below sea level at the Salton Sea Refuge (California) to over 9000 feet in the Arctic National Wildlife Refuge (Alaska). Numerous refuges are located in the prairie pothole region of the north-central United States. Another important topographic type where refuges are located is the freshwater marshes and swamps and coastal-estuarine areas of the South. The western game ranges consist of arid Sonoran desert playas, rugged mountains, and alluvial outwash plains. In Alaska the refuges are measured in thousands of square miles and may encompass glaciers, rugged mountains, volcanoes, vast marshes, glacial lakes and streams, tidal lagoons, and Arctic tundra. Oceanic island refuges range from the tropical islands of Hawaii to the Aleutian Islands of Alaska. Geographically, they extend from Florida to Alaska to the South Pacific. Many are located along the routes of the major flyways, providing feeding and resting areas for the great semiannual migration of ducks, geese, and other birds.

The National Wildlife Refuge System is the home of many unusual or endangered species. The Aransas Refuge in Texas is the winter home of the whooping crane.

The Hawaiian Islands Refuge provides the only habitat for a number of endangered species including the Hawaiian monk seal and green sea turtle. The Red Rock Lakes Refuge in Montana serves as the year-round home of the trumpeter swan, and the Desert National Wildlife Refuge in Nevada is a unique area for desert bighorn sheep. Archaeological artifacts and areas of historic significance located on refuge land are preserved along with wildlife habitat. The DeSoto Refuge (Iowa), for example, maintains an impressive collection of items reclaimed from the historic steamship *Bertrand*, which sank in the Missouri River in 1865. The National Wildlife Refuge System is managed by the Division of Refuge Management of the U.S. Fish and Wildlife Service, which is a bureau within the Interior Department.

The National Wildlife Refuge System represents the most comprehensive wildlife resource management program in the world. The refuges are managed to maintain habitat, food supplies, and water for animals. While the preservation aspect of resource management dominates management decisions within the National Park System, the conservation or utilitarian aspect of resource management governs the National Wildlife Refuge System, just as it does for the National Forest System. One of the basic purposes of the National Wildlife Refuge System is to conserve wildlife for hunting. Hunting, growing agricultural crops, cutting hay, logging, and trapping are allowed. On many refuges it is necessary to manage lands to increase natural diversity and improve habitat for wildlife. At the Key Deer Refuge (Florida) woody undergrowth is burned to stimulate the growth of tender shoots to sustain its endangered Key Deer population. At the White River Refuge (Arkansas) and at other refuges, selective timber harvest encourages the development of mature oaks and other food-producing trees. Grains such as corn, sorghum, and millet are often planted as a source of food for migratory waterfowl. Water control is one of the most important activities on many refuges. Hundreds of miles of dikes have been built to create shallow marshes for waterfowl. Some marshes are drained in the spring to stimulate production of native natural foods and then reflooded in the fall to attract migrating ducks. Not all refuge lands are manipulated. Many areas, including units of the National Wilderness Preservation System and research-natural areas, are left in a wild or natural state. There are 75 congressionally designated units of the National Wilderness Preservation System, totaling 20.7 million acres, in the national wildlife refuges.

The National Wildlife Refuge System is not as well known to most Americans as the National Park System or the National Forest System. Although refuges are not managed specifically for recreation, a broad range of recreational opportunities is possible on many of them. An estimated 25 million people visit these lands annually. These 25 million recreation visits equaled 4.4 million recreation visitor days (RVDs) in 1991. This accounted for only 0.7 percent of the recreational use on the federal public lands overseen by the seven principal federal land-managing agencies. Although public uses are regulated so they do not interfere with the wildlife purposes of the refuge, many activities are available. Virtually all of these recreational opportunities evolve around wildlife, and 91 percent of this use is wildlife-oriented. Only 3 percent of the recreational use on the refuges is related to hunting and another 16 percent to fishing. Other recreational uses include photography, hiking, nature study, picnicking, swimming, camping, and boating. Activities vary with each refuge and may depend on the season of the year. It is advisable to check with the refuge personnel prior to a visit to determine which activities are allowed and what regulations

apply. Some refuges have no visitor facilities, but even in these, wildlife can be viewed while traveling on roads passing through or near the refuges. Some refuges are equipped to handle a large number of visitors and others are not. The Fish and Wildlife Service is in the business of managing wildlife—not providing recreation. Where feasible, recreational opportunities are provided. In some sections of the country the recreational opportunities in the National Wildlife Refuge System are often one of the primary recreational resources that are available.

Table 11.1 is a statistical summary of the lands under the jurisdiction of the Fish and Wildlife Service that pertain to wildlife management. To understand the National Wildlife Refuge System, it is imperative that each of these classifications be explained. The *National Wildlife Refuge System* is defined as "all lands, waters, and interests therein administered by the Fish and Wildlife Service for the protection and conservation of fish and wildlife including those that are threatened with extinction." There are five categories of land and area withing the National Wildlife Refuge System:

- *National Wildlife Refuge* "Any area of the National Wildlife Refuge System, except Coordination Areas."
- *Waterfowl Production Area* "Any wetland or pothole area acquired pursuant to the Migratory Bird Hunting and Conservation Stamp Act and administered as part of the National Wildlife Refuge System (identified by county designation)."
- *Coordination Area* "Any area administered as part of the National Wildlife Refuge System managed by the states under cooperative agreements between the Fish and Wildlife Service and one or more state fish and wildlife agency."
- *Wilderness Area* "Fish and Wildlife Service Land designated by Congress to be managed as part of the National Wilderness Preservation System, in accordance with the terms of the Wilderness Act of 1964. All Fish and Wildlife Service Wilderness Areas occur within National Wildlife Refuges with the exception of Mount Massive which is located at the Leadville National Fish Hatchery." (see table 11.3)
- *Migratory Waterfowl Refuge on a Federal Water Resource Project* "Federal land managed by the Fish and Wildlife Service to mitigate a federal water resource project for the benefit of mitigating waterfowl (and other wildlife) under the Fish and Wildlife Coordination Act of 1954 as amended."

Table 11.1 Lands under Control of U.S. Fish and Wildlife Service

Category	Number	Total Acres
National wildlife refuges	485	88,615,895.98
Waterfowl production areas	164	2,015,072.16
Coordination areas	51	315,797.17
Total	700	90,946,765.31
Wildlife research centers	6	647.41
Administrative sites	37	1,032.27
National fish hatcheries	84	19,753.87
Fishery research stations	17	2,574.75
Total	144	24,008.30
Grand Total	844	90,970,773.61

Source: Fish and Wildlife Service, *Annual Report of Lands under Control of the U.S. Fish and Wildlife Service*, September 30, 1992.

It is the 485 areas classified as National Wildlife Refuges that most people think of when the system is mentioned. These account for the bulk of the acreage administered by the Fish and Wildlife Service (97.4 percent, or 88,615,895.98 acres). Over 2 million acres on 164 waterfowl production areas and almost ⅓ million acres in 51 coordination areas are also part of the National Wildlife Refuge System. These three categories together comprise the National Wildlife Refuge System, with 700 areas on 90,946,765.31 acres in 1992.

The lower portion of Table 11.1 identifies the areas under the jurisdiction of the Fish and Wildlife Service that are not part of the National Wildlife Refuge System:

- *Wildlife Research Center and Field Station*   "Facility where the Fish and Wildlife Service conducts research to provide biological information on numbers, dynamics, ecological relationships, diseases, habitat requirements, and new population management methods."
- *Administrative Site*   "Land used to support administrative programs such as maintenance facilities or offices."
- *National Fish Hatchery*   "Facility where the Fish and Wildlife Service cultures warm, cool, and cold water fish species to various life stages. Hatchery objectives are to replenish depleted stocks, to mitigate federal water projects, to assist with the management of fishery resources on federal (primarily Fish and Wildlife Service) and Indian lands, and to enhance recreational fisheries."
- *National Fisheries Research Station and Its Field Station*   "Fish and Wildlife Service facility for scientific studies on fisheries resources. The Service is responsible for anadromous species and species which inhabit transboundary or federally managed water."

As Table 11.1 reveals, these last four categories not part of the National Wildlife Refuge System consist of 144 areas on 24,008.3 acres. In 1992, these combined areas placed a grand total of 844 areas on 90,970,773.61 acres under the jurisdiction of the Fish and Wildlife Service.

HISTORICAL BACKGROUND

Most individuals identify the establishment of the Pelican Island "preserve and breeding ground," by Executive Order of March 14, 1903, issued by President Theodore Roosevelt, as the start of the National Wildlife Refuge System. This small 5.5-acre island off the coast of Florida was reserved to protect a colony of brown pelicans. However, significant actions predated this event. The first documented U.S. wildlife refuge was created by the state of California in 1870 at Lake Merritt, in what is now downtown Oakland (Foss, 1971, 21). The earliest effort to set aside an area of federally owned land specifically for wildlife occurred when President Grant took action in 1868, and Congress acted in 1869, to protect the northern fur seal in the Pribilof Islands, Alaska. In 1881, President Harrison created, by Executive Order, the Afognak Island Forest and Fish Culture Reserve in Alaska. The second refuge proclaimed by President Roosevelt was in the Wichita Mountains Forest and Game Preserve (Oklahoma) in 1905. Roosevelt proclaimed another six refuges in 1906, and by the

time he left office in 1909, he had proclaimed a total of 53 refuges. The first use of congressionally appropriated funds to purchase a wildlife refuge, the National Bison Range, occurred in 1909, when 12,800 acres in Montana were bought from the Flathead Indians. The Izaak Walton League initiated the establishment of the National Elk Refuge (Wyoming), by donating 1760 acres as a nucleus for the refuge. This was the first unit of the present system to be referred to as a refuge. In 1913, President Taft set aside 2.7 million acres in the Aleutian Island chain for the system.

The first substantial funds appropriated by Congress for the purchase of a wildlife reservation from private owners was the *Upper Mississippi River Fish and Wildlife Act* (1924), which created the Upper Mississippi River Fish and Wildlife Refuge. This was the first refuge acquired specifically for management of waterfowl. The Bear River Migratory Bird Refuge (1928) in Utah was significant in that it was the first time Congress appropriated funds for the construction of dikes and other structures to develop and maintain a marsh. The *Migratory Bird Conservation Act* (1929), despite shortcomings because it did not provide for funding, provided the authority under which the National Wildlife Refuge System grew in the years that followed. The major stimulus for the Refuge System came in 1934 with the passage of the *Migratory Bird Hunting and Conservation Act* (also known as the *Duck Stamp Act*), which provided a funding mechanism for purchasing migratory bird habitat. The year 1934 also saw the passage of the *Fish and Wildlife Coordination Act*, which authorized most federal water resource agencies to acquire lands associated with water-use projects as mitigation and enhancement of fish and wildlife. It further provided for the management of these lands by the Fish and Wildlife Service or state agencies. The same year, President Roosevelt appointed a "blue ribbon panel" consisting of *J. N. "Ding" Darling* (chairman), Thomas Beck, and Aldo Leopold to advise him on waterfowl needs. In 1935 "Ding" Darling was appointed head of the Bureau of Biological Survey. He brought with him *J. Clark Salyer II* to manage the refuge program. By 1943 the system had grown to 272 refuges. Salyer has been referred to as the "father of the National Wildlife Refuge System," since he was the driving force behind expansion and protection of the system until his death in 1966.

The *Fish and Wildlife Act* (1956) established a comprehensive fish and wildlife policy that authorized the establishment of refuges for all kinds of wildlife. In 1958, Congress passed an amendment to the Duck Stamp Act that authorized the *Waterfowl Production Area Program*. The *Refuge Recreation Act* (1962) authorized the recreational use of refuges, when such uses did not interfere with the area's primary purposes and when sufficient funds were available to conduct recreational activities. While recreation visits to some refuges were permitted from the beginning, funds, facilities, and personnel were ordinarily not available to accommodate the visitors or to enhance the recreational experience. *This act clarified the appropriateness of public use on refuges and encouraged efforts to provide wildlife-oriented recreation, interpretation and environmental education activities.*

The Migratory Bird Hunting and Conservation Act has had a major impact on the growth of the system. A *Duck Stamp* must be affixed (and signed) to the state hunting license of anyone over the age of 16 hunting ducks, geese, brant, and swans. Since its inception in 1934, it has been the source of funding for (1) over 1 million acres purchased for refuges, (2) ½ million acres acquired as Waterfowl Production Areas, and (3) easements of over 1 million acres of private land that prohibit drainage.

Until 1949, when the price of a Duck Stamp was raised from $1 to $2, hunting had been allowed on only a few refuges. Hunting now became recognized as a management tool and a legitimate form of recreation, and its use expanded after this date. In 1982, over 50 percent of all refuges and most waterfowl production areas were open to hunting (Reed and Drabelle, 1984, 48). In 1994, the price of a Duck Stamp was $15.

The other law of great significance for the Wildlife Refuges is the *National Wildlife Refuge System Administration Act* (1966). It provides guidelines and directives for administration and management of all areas in the system, including "wildlife refuges, areas for the protection and conservation of fish and wildlife that are threatened with extinction, wildlife ranges, game ranges, wildlife management areas, and waterfowl production areas." In addition, this law established the standard of *compatibility*, requiring that uses of refuge lands must be determined to be compatible with the purpose for which individual refuges were established.

The Wilderness Act (1964) provided a mechanism that mandated review, for possible inclusion in the National Wilderness Preservation System, of all units of the National Wildlife Refuge System that were roadless and/or insular. Management emphasis has been changed on the 20.7 million acres of refuges that have been added to the Wilderness System. The Endangered Species Act (1973) also redirected management emphasis on some refuges. It is considered the world's foremost law protecting species faced with extinction, using such extensive means as penalties for harming endangered animals, review and compliance obligations for various federal agency programs, and the listing of species eligible for protection). Over 25 new refuges have been added to the system under this authority, including the Attwater Prairie Chicken (Texas), the Mississippi Sandhill Crane (Mississippi), the Columbian White-tailed Deer (Washington), and the Crocodile Lake (Florida). The Alaska Native Claims Settlement Act (ANCSA; 1971) authorized the addition of immense acreages of highly productive, internationally significant wildlife land to the National Wildlife Refuge System. Nine years later the Alaska National Interest Lands Conservation Act (ANILCA; 1980) added nine new refuges and expanded seven existing refuges. This one act added 53.7 million acres to the National Wildlife Refuge System, more than doubling the acreage of lands encompassed in the system.

HOW REFUGES ARE ESTABLISHED

Since 1903 refuges have usually been established by five different methods:

Executive Withdrawal   This was the method used by President Theodore Roosevelt to establish many refuges during the first decade of the century, starting with Pelican Island, Florida.

Acquisition Funded by the Migratory Bird Conservation Act Account   Funds from Duck Stamps are deposited into this account to serve as a basis of funding new migratory bird refuges.

Acquisition Funded by the Land and Water Conservation Fund   Since 1965, the Land and Water Conservation Fund has been used to establish refuges that support

endangered species and recreation purposes. Fifty percent of the funding is
provided by this act.

Act of Congress   The first occasion of Congress establishing a national wildlife
refuge was in 1905 in the Wichita Mountains of Oklahoma. Any refuges that
require land acquisition and are not primarily for migratory birds or endangered species must be established by Congress.

Donation   A recent example is the Sevilleta National Wildlife Refuge in New
Mexico, where in 1973 the Campbell Family Foundation donated 220,000 acres
(Reed and Drabelle, 1984, 24).

FISH AND WILDLIFE SERVICE

The U.S. Fish and Wildlife Service is the principal agency through which the federal
government carries out its responsibilities to conserve, protect, and enhance the nation's fish and wildlife and their habitats for continuing benefit of people. The service's major responsibilities are for migratory birds, endangered species, certain marine mammals, and freshwater and anadromous fish. The service's origins date back
to 1871, when Congress established a U.S. Fish Commission. In 1903 the commission
was placed under the Department of Commerce and renamed the Bureau of Fisheries.
In 1885, the Office of Economic Ornithology was established within the Department
of Agriculture to study the food habits and migratory patterns of birds. A number
of name changes occurred until it was renamed the Bureau of Biological Survey
(1905), which, among other activities, managed the first wildlife refuges. In 1939, the
Bureau of Biological Survey was transferred to the Department of the Interior from
the Agriculture Department, and the Bureau of Fisheries was transferred from the
Commerce Department to the Interior Department. In 1940 the two bureaus were
merged to form the Fish and Wildlife Service. The Service assumed its present form
with passage of the Fish and Wildlife Act (1956), which created the U.S. Fish and
Wildlife Service and established within the agency two separate bureaus, the Bureau
of Sport Fisheries and Wildlife (which included the Division of Wildlife Refuges) and
the Bureau of Commercial Fisheries. In 1970, the Bureau of Commercial Fisheries was
transferred to the Department of Commerce and became the National Marine Fisheries Service, while the Bureau of Sport Fisheries and Wildlife remained in the Interior
Department. In accordance with a 1974 act of Congress, "Bureau" has been dropped
from the name, and the agency is simply called the U.S. Fish and Wildlife Service.

Today the Fish and Wildlife Service employs approximately 6500 people at facilities all over the country. Office headquarters are in Washington, D.C., and there
are eight regional offices (including one for research) and over 700 field units and
installations. The service is headed by a director and a deputy director. There are five
associate directors (Research and Development, Environment, Federal Assistance,
Fishery Resources, and Wildlife Resources) and three assistant directors (Administration, Planning and Budget, and Public Affairs). Each region has a regional director.
Region names, headquarters locations, and states included are as follows:

Region 1 (Portland)—California, Idaho, Hawaii, Nevada, Oregon, Washington

Region 2 (Albuquerque)—Arizona, New Mexico, Oklahoma, Texas

Region 3 (Twin Cities, Minn.)—Illinois, Indiana, Iowa, Michigan, Minnesota, Missouri, Ohio, Wisconsin

Region 4 (Atlanta)—Arkansas, Alabama, Florida, Georgia, Kentucky, Louisiana, Mississippi, North Carolina, South Carolina, Tennessee, Puerto Rico

Region 5 (Newton Corner, Mass.)—Connecticut, Delaware, Massachusetts, Maryland, Maine, New Hampshire, New Jersey, New York, Pennsylvania, Virginia, Vermont, West Virginia

Region 6 (Denver)—Colorado, Kansas, Montana, Nebraska, North Dakota, South Dakota, Utah, Wyoming

Region 7 (Anchorage)—Alaska

Only about half of the refuges are managed on-site; the rest are managed by staff at nearby refuges.

The functions of the Fish and Wildlife Service are:

- Managing the national wildlife refuges
- Helping endangered species
- Conserving migratory birds
- Restoring the nation's fisheries
- Administering the federal aid programs
- Enforcing laws and managing wildlife populations
- Conducting research
- Providing biological information
- Conserving habitat through field operations
- Planning, administration, and other services

GEOGRAPHIC EXTENT

The National Wildlife Refuge System has the most geographically even distribution of all the public lands open for recreation. The only major voids, where there are no refuges, are in West Texas, the border areas of southern Utah and northern Arizona, eastern Colorado and western Kansas, and the Illinois-Indiana border area south of Lake Michigan. Regions with especially high numbers of refuges include the East Coast, the lower Mississippi Valley, North Dakota, the Columbia River Valley, and California's Central Valley. Table 11.2 summarizes the number of refuges and their acreages for the states and territories. Appendix XIII is a complete listing of all national wildlife refuges, their location (states), size, and recreational use. Figure 11.1 shows the location of these refuges and is keyed to Appendix XIII.

The principal geographic characteristic of the Wildlife Refuge System is the high percentage of the total acreage that is in Alaska: 42 refuges on 76,385,0047 acres, or

Table 11.2   State Summary of National Wildlife Refuges by State or Territory

State/Territory	Number	Total Acres	State/Territory	Number	Total Acres
Alabama	10	53,553.44	New Jersey	5	56,670.63
Alaska	42	76,385,046.64	New Mexico	11	384,984.80
Arizona	13	1,713,847.33	New York	11	25,452.48
Arkansas	12	238,139.60	North Carolina	13	414,194.54
California	41	366,683.32	North Dakota	108	1,349,120.38
Colorado	9	61,609.39	Ohio	4	8,432.55
Connecticut	1	346.58	Oklahoma	9	154,003.65
Delaware	3	25,405.16	Oregon	27	575,384.57
Florida	29	534,648.90	Pennsylvania	6	10,005.53
Georgia	12	477,315.97	Rhode Island	5	1,491.65
Hawaii	9	271,516.60	South Carolina	9	176,275.00
Idaho	17	87,991.17	South Dakota	51	682,462.88
Illinois	8	125,102.07	Tennessee	8	110,417.63
Indiana	1	8,055.53	Texas	20	416,969.73
Iowa	20	83,643.73	Utah	7	102,590.51
Kansas	5	56,669.33	Vermont	3	6,013.57
Kentucky	2	2,060.11	Virginia	12	119,926.12
Louisiana	18	442,593.74	West Virginia	4	1,700.30
Maine	11	44,547.69	Wisconsin	20	227,157.97
Maryland	6	37,335.49	Wyoming	14	81,271.53
Massachusetts	12	12,751.89	American Somoa	1	39,066.00
Michigan	15	117,087.72	Baker Island	1	31,736.89
Minnesota	37	500,784.13	Johnston Atoll	1	100.00
Mississippi	12	181,314.62	Midway Islands	1	90,096.85
Missouri	11	58,519.69	Puerto Rico	4	3,288.22
Montana	51	1,206,337.56	Swan Islands	1	32,550.25
Nebraska	14	167,050.46	Virgin Islands	3	385.65
Nevada	13	2,375,432.69	Jarvis Island	1	37,519.17
New Hampshire	5	2,917.20			
			Grand Total	844	90,970,773.61

Source: Fish & Wildlife Service. *Annual Report of Lands under Control of the U.S. Fish and Wildlife Service*, September 30, 1992.

84 percent of the total acreage in the entire system. Just three of these huge refuges in Alaska—the Arctic (19.3 million acres), the Yukon Delta (19.1 million acres), and the Yukon Flats (8.6 million acres)—account for over half (52 percent) of the total acreage of the National Wildlife Refuge System. In the lower 49 states only four states have over 1 million acres in the Refuge System. Nevada has the most acreage—2.4 million acres in 13 refuges—but just one refuge, the Desert, contains 1.6 million acres. Arizona ranks second in acreage for the system, with 1.7 million acres, and, like Nevada, a few large units dominate. In Arizona, the Cabeza Prieta (860,000 acres) and the Kofa (666,480 acres) account for most of the acreage. North Dakota has the largest number of refuges of any state (108) and ranks third in the lower 49 states, with 1.4 million acres. The largest refuge in North Dakota is the J. Clark Salyer (59,383 acres). The huge Charles M. Russell Wildlife Refuge (903,332 acres) dominates the 51 refuges on 1.2 million acres in Montana. States with between 500,000 and 1,000,000 acres in refuge land include South Dakota (682,463 acres), Oregon (575,385 acres), Florida (534,649 acres), and Minnesota (500,784 acres). Two very large refuges in Oregon are the Hart Mountain (251,295 acres) and the Malheur (185,412 acres). In

Florida, two large refuges are the Arthur R. Marshall Loxahatchee (145,665 acres) and the Merritt Island (138,263 acres). Very small numbers and acreages of refuges are found in Connecticut, Indiana, Kentucky, New Hampshire, Rhode Island, Ohio, Vermont, and West Virginia. U.S. territories in which refuges are found include Puerto Rico and the Virgin Islands in the Caribbean and American Samoa, Baker Island, Johnston Atoll, Swan Islands, and Jarvis Island in the South Pacific.

WILDERNESS

The initial Wilderness System established by the Wilderness Act in 1964 consisted of 54 national forest wilderness areas that covered 9.1 million acres. The act instructed that,

> Within ten years after the effective date of this Act the Secretary of the Interior shall review every roadless area of five thousand contiguous acres or more in the national parks, monuments and other units of the national park system and *every such area of, and every roadless island within, the national wildlife refuges and game ranges [author emphasis]* . . . and shall report to the President his recommendation as to the suitability or nonsuitability of each such area or island for the preservation of wilderness.

The first unit of the National Wildlife Refuge System to be added to the National Wilderness Preservation System was in 1968—the Great Swamp National Wildlife Refuge (New Jersey), which consisted of 3660 acres. New additions were made in 1970 (139,254 acres), 1972 (379 acres), 1974 (354,122 acres), 1975 (117,585 acres), 1976 (154,878 acres), and 1978 (459 acres). Even with these additions, the total acreage of wilderness in the Refuge System in 1978 was 770,337 acres, and almost half of this was in one wilderness area—the *Okefenokee National Wildlife Refuge* (Georgia) with 353,981 acres.

ANILCA (1980) caused a dramatic increase in wilderness area acreage among the national wildlife refuges. This legislation, among many other effects, created 10 wilderness areas in Alaska in existing and new national wildlife refuges that totaled 18,560,000 acres. Almost half of this total wilderness was in one refuge: 8 million acres in the Arctic National Wildlife Refuge. There were no other additions during the rest of the 1980s to the Wilderness System on any of the national wildlife refuges. The most recent national wildlife refuges in which new wilderness areas have been established (1990) are all in Arizona: the Cabeza Prieta (803,418 acres), the Havasu (14,606 acres), the Imperial (9,220 acres), and the Kofa (516,200 acres). There are currently 73 wilderness areas totaling 20,676,341 acres in 26 states in national wildlife refuges (Table 11.3). Ninety percent of the wilderness acreage is in refuges in Alaska, an even higher percentage than the 84 percent of the total Refuge System acreage that is in the state. In the lower 49 states three refuges are much larger than any of the others and contain 79 percent of the acreage: the Cabeza Prieta (Arizona, 803,418 acres), the Kofa (Arizona, 516,200 acres), and Okefenokee (Georgia, 353,981 acres). A dozen of the wilderness areas in the lower 49 states are under 100 acres in size, including the 6-acre Pelican Island (Florida).

Table 11.3   Wilderness Areas in the National Wildlife Refuge System

Wilderness Area	Refuge	State	Acres	Wilderness Area	Refuge	State	Acres
Aleutian Islands	Alaska Maritime NWR	AK	1,300,000	Wolf Island	Wolf Island NWR	GA	5,126
Bering Sea	Alaska Maritime NWR	AK	81,340	Crab Orchard	Crab Orchard NWR	IL	4,050
Bogoslof	Alaska Maritime NWR	AK	175	Breton	Breton NWR	LA	5,000
Chamisso	Alaska Maritime NWR	AK	455	Lacassine	Lacassine NWR	LA	3,346
Forrester Island	Alaska Maritime NWR	AK	2,832	Monomoy	Monomoy NWR	MA	2,420
Hazy Island	Alaska Maritime NWR	AK	32	Baring Unit	Moosehorn NWR	ME	4,680
Saint Lazaria	Alaska Maritime NWR	AK	65	Birch Islands Unit	Moosehorn NWR	ME	6
Semidi	Alaska Maritime NWR	AK	250,000	Edmunds Unit	Moosehorn NWR	ME	2,706
Simeonof	Alaska Maritime NWR	AK	25,855	Huron Islands	Huron NWR	MI	147
Tuxedni	Alaska Maritime NWR	AK	5,566	Michigan Islands	Michigan Islands NWR	MI	12
Unimak	Alaska Maritime NWR	AK	910,000	Seney	Seney NWR	MI	25,150
Arctic	Arctic NWR	AK	8,000,000	Agassiz	Agassiz NWR	MN	4,000
Becharof	Becharof NWR	AK	400,000	Tamarac	Tamarac NWR	MN	2,180
Innoko	Innoko NWR	AK	1,240,000	Mingo	Mingo NWR	MO	7,730
Izembek	Izembek NWR	AK	300,000	Medicine Lake	Medicine Lake NWR	MT	11,366
Kenai	Kenai NWR	AK	1,350,000	Red Rock Lakes	Red Rock Lakes NWR	MT	32,350
Koyukuk	Koyukuk NWR	AK	400,000	UL Bend	UL Bend NWR	MT	20,819
Selawik	Selawik NWR	AK	240,000	Swanquarter	Swanquarter NWR	NC	8,785
Togiak	Togiak NWR	AK	2,270,000	Chase Lake	Chase Lake NWR	ND	4,155
Andreafsky	Yukon Delta NWR	AK	1,300,000	Lostwood	Lostwood NWR	ND	5,577
Nunivak	Yukon Delta NWR	AK	600,000	Fort Niobrara	Fort Niobrara NWR	NE	4,635
Big Lake	Big Lake NWR	AR	2,144	Brigantine	Edwin B. Forsythe NWR	NJ	6,681
Cabeza Prieta	Cebeza Prieta NWR	AZ	803,418	Great Swamp	Great Swamp NWR	NJ	3,660
Havasu	Havasu NWR	AZ	14,606	Salt Creek	Bitter Lake NWR	NM	9,621
Imperial	Imperial NWR	AZ	9,220	Chupadera Unit	Bosque del Apache NWR	NM	5,289
Kofa	Kofa NWR	AZ	516,200	Indian Well Unit	Bosque del Apache NWR	NM	5,139
Farallon	Farallon NWR	CA	141	Little San Pascual Unit	Bosque del Apache NWR	NM	19,859
Mount Massive	Leadville NFH	CO	2,560	West Sister Island	West Sister Island NWR	OH	77
Cedar Keys	Cedar Keys NWR	FL	379	Charons Garden Unit	Wichita Mountains NWR	OK	5,723
Chassahowitzka	Chassahowitzka NWR	FL	23,580	North Mountain Unit	Wichita Mountains NWR	OK	2,847
Florida Keys	Great White Heron NWR	FL	1,900	Oregon Islands	Oregon Islands NWR	OR	21
Island Bay	Island Bay NWR	FL	20	Oregon Islands	Oregon Islands NWR	OR	459
J. N. "Ding" Darling	J. N. "Ding" Darling NWR	FL	2,619	Three Arch Rocks	Three Arch Rocks NWR	OR	15
Florida Keys	Key West NWR	FL	2,019	Cape Romain	Cape Romain NWR	SC	29,000
Lake Woodruff	Lake Woodruff NWR	FL	1,066	Washington Islands	Copalis NWR	WA	60
Florida Keys	National Key Deer Refuge	FL	2,278	Washington Islands	Flattery Rocks NWR	WA	125
Passage Key	Passage Key NWR	FL	36	Washington Islands	Quillayute Needles NWR	WA	300
Pelican Island	Pelican Island NWR	FL	6	San Juan Islands	San Juan Islands NWR	WA	353
St. Marks	St. Marks NWR	FL	17,350	Wisconsin Islands	Gravel Island NWR	WI	27
Blackbeard Island	Blackbeard Island NWR	GA	3,000	Wisconsin Islands	Green Bay NWR	WI	2

NWR = National Wildlife Refuge, NFH = National Fish Hatchery.
Source: Hal Hallett, Bureau of Land Managememt, personal communication, 1993.

MANAGEMENT AND PLANNING

Mission of the Fish and Wildlife Service

The mission of the U.S. Fish and Wildlife Service, which is responsible for wild birds, endangered species, certain marine mammals, inland sport fisheries, and specific fish-

ery and wildlife research activities, is to conserve, protect and enhance fish and wildlife and their habitats for the continuing benefit of the American people. Within this framework, the service (1) assists in the development of an environmental stewardship ethic for our society based on ecological principles, scientific knowledge of wildlife, and a sense of moral responsibility; (2) guides the conservation, development, and management of the nation's fish and wildlife resources; and (3) administers a national program that provides opportunities for the American public to understand, appreciate, and wisely use these resources.

Mission and Goals of the National Wildlife Refuge System

According to the *Refuge Manual,* Fish and Wildlife Service, 1985 the special mission of the National Wildlife Refuge System is

> "To provide, preserve, restore, and manage a national network of lands and waters sufficient in size, diversity and location to meet society's needs for areas where the widest possible spectrum of benefits associated with wildlife and wildlands is enhanced and made available."

Goals of the National Wildlife Refuge System

- To preserve, restore, and enhance in their natural ecosystems (when practicable) all species of animals and plants that are endangered or threatened with becoming endangered.
- To perpetuate the migratory bird resource.
- To preserve a natural diversity and abundance of fauna and flora on refuge lands.
- To provide an understanding and appreciation of fish and wildlife ecology and the human role in the environment, and to provide refuge visitors with high-quality, safe, wholesome, and enjoyable recreational experiences oriented toward wildlife to the extent these activities are compatible with the purpose for which the refuge was established.

The management of the wildlife refuges is a good example of *dominant use*. The primary function of the refuges is the conservation of wildlife. Other uses, such as recreation, environmental education, timber, grazing, oil and gas, and mining, are considered secondary uses. These secondary uses are allowed only if they are compatible with the primary use. The primary use is the purpose for which the refuge was established. Since refuges have been established for many different purposes, what is considered an acceptable secondary use on one refuge might not be an acceptable secondary use on another. It is with this management scheme that recreational use is governed within the National Wildlife Refuge System. This policy is based on the Refuge Recreation Act (1962), which authorized the recreational use on refuges as long as these uses do not interfere with the primary purpose, and on the National Wildlife Refuge System Administration Act (1966), which mandated the "compatibility requirement" for any secondary uses.

Public Use and Recreational Management

Basic Policies Regarding Recreational Use of Refuges

1 Any recreational activity permitted will be managed to ensure high-quality experiences.
2 Existing programs should be reviewed and adequacy of present funding determined before new efforts for public-use expansion begins.
3 Non-wildlife or wild lands–oriented recreational activities presently occurring on refuges will be deemphasized and eventually phased out, except when they are mandated by statute. Also, such recreational activities that fulfill a recognized societal need and cannot be provided at locations off the refuge may continue if sufficient operating funds are available, but they must pass the compatibility test. Their continuation must be justified and documented.
4 Reductions or phaseouts of any public-use activities must be justified and documented. Such documentation must demonstrate that these activities are incompatible with wildlife protection and management; are clearly unsafe and substandard and exceed budget constraints; or address an audience insufficient in size to warrant continuation. With the approval of the regional office, any activity that is discontinued may be replaced with a more appropriate wildlife or wild lands-oriented recreational activity.

The Objectives of Public Use Management on Refuges

1 To provide the public with wildlife and wild lands–related opportunities when compatible with the primary purpose of individual refuges
2 To provide visitors with the opportunity to enjoy appropriate activities on refuge lands and to learn about the relationships of plant and animal populations within the ecosystem
3 To enhance the public's understanding of natural resource management programs and ecological concepts
4 To encourage public participation

Legislation permits the Secretary of the Interior to permit hunting on any refuge where it is compatible with the major purpose for which the refuge was established and where funds are available to support the hunting program. The same situation pertains to sport fishing. There are limitations for hunting on "inviolate sanctuaries" and on easements where the landowner controls the rights. Alaskan refuges are open to hunting according to terms of ANILCA. Except in Alaska, all lands within the National Wildlife Refuge System are closed to off-road vehicles (ORVs) by the general public, unless specifically designated as open to ORV use.

It is the policy of the Fish and Wildlife Service to deemphasize non–wildlife wild lands–oriented recreation on most refuges. Examples of such recreation are swimming, surfing and sunbathing, waterskiing, motorized boating, jogging, bicycling, and horseback riding. These activities may be permitted where they are mandated by law, are found to be compatible uses, or support wildlife or wild lands–oriented recreational activities. No private cabins may be constructed on refuges, and private docks, floats, rafts, and piers are generally prohibited.

Wildlife wild lands–oriented recreational activities that are permissible include nature observation and study, photography, camping, picnicking, consumptive wildlife or wild lands–oriented activities (berry picking, clamming, mushroom gathering, etc.), hiking, canoeing, cross-country skiing, and snowshoeing. Camping and picnicking are permitted only where required to implement or sustain an approved wildlife or wild lands–oriented recreational activity where no other alternative is practical.

Planning

Two kinds of planning in the National Wildlife Refuge System are master planning and management planning. (There is also a third kind—budgetary planning—which will not be covered here.) The purpose of *master planning* is to provide long-range guidance for management of the national wildlife refuges. Through the master planning process, the objectives (outputs and objective levels) of a refuge are established and the type and extent of management and development necessary to meet those objectives are identified.

Major Objectives of Refuge Master Planning

- To ensure that national policy direction is incorporated into the management of individual refuges
- To determine the capability of individual refuges to further the goals, objectives, and long-range plans of the Fish and Wildlife Service, and to provide a means of evaluating accomplishments
- To provide a systematic process for making and documenting refuge decisions
- To establish broad management strategies to guide refuge management programs and activities
- To provide continuity in the management of individual refuges and of the Refuge System as a whole
- To provide a basis for budgeting requests to implement management programs leading to the achievement of refuge objectives

Management planning is the formulation of an integrated program of action for a field station to pursue in order to achieve, or move toward the achievement of, approved refuge objectives. The *refuge management plan* is the single document, prepared and maintained for each unit of the Refuge System, that sets forth and describes the management program to be followed. For refuges with approved master plans (or comprehensive conservation plans), the refuge management plan forms the basis for annual work planning and annual budgeting. In the absence of master planning, the refuge management plan also serves to identify long-term program needs and forms the basis for additional funding requests to meet refuge objectives. To have value, it is essential that the refuge management plan be viewed as a working document.

Objectives of Refuge Management Planning

- To provide a written program of action that leads toward the achievement of approved station objectives (outputs and objective levels)

- To ensure that management activities make efficient and effective use of refuge fiscal and personnel resources
- To ensure that all management activities are fully coordinated
- To communicate management decisions to higher levels of authority
- To provide management continuity by documenting management decisions and supporting information

Where a refuge master plan will be developed prior to management planning, master and management planning should be considered interrelated aspects of refuge planning. The relationship between the two is hierarchical. Management planning is an extension of, or step down from, master planning. Where the results of a planning needs assessment indicate that refuge programs and activities are stable and guided by sound objectives, requirements for master planning may be waived at the discretion of the regional director.

RECREATIONAL OPPORTUNITIES AND USE

While recreation visits to some refuges were permitted from the beginning, funds, facilities, and personnel were ordinarily not available to accommodate the visitors or to enhance the recreational experience. The Refuge Recreation Act (1962) changed this by giving official recognition and approval to recreation on the refuges and authorizing appropriations for that purpose. The most recent public-use report analyzing use patterns for the entire Refuge System was released in 1988. This report indicated that there were 25,307,000 visits to the National Wildlife Refuge System between October 1986 and September 1987. Total public use for the same period was identified as 30,794,000 visits; this figure is larger than the first, since people often participate in more than one activity during a visit to a refuge. *This report concluded that 91.3 percent of the total public use was wildlife-oriented and 8.7 percent was nonwildlife-oriented recreation.*

The following major categories of use accounted for the 91.3 percent of the total public use that is wildlife oriented:

Nonconsumptive wildlife-oriented recreation	(14,274,000 visits) =	42.3%
Interpretation	(9,271,000 visits) =	27.5%
Fishing	(5,384,000 visits) =	16.0%
Hunting	(1,100,000 visits) =	3.3%
Other consumptive wildlife-oriented recreation	(603,000 visits) =	1.8%
Environmental education	(159,000 visits) =	0.5%

The breakdown of the leading category, "nonconsumptive wildlife-oriented recreation" into subcategories is: "land vehicle wildlife or wild land observation" (59 percent), "foot wildlife or wild land observation" (20 percent), "boat wildlife or wild land observation" (7 percent), "picnicking" (6 percent), "photography" (4 percent), "camping" (2 percent), and "other wildlife or wild land observation" (2 percent).

The breakdown of the category "interpretation" which ranked second, into subcategories is: "self-guided interpretive exhibits or demonstrations" (23 percent), "self-

guided nonmotor wildlife trails" (17 percent), "visitor contact station" (15 percent), "self-guided wildlife motorized tour route" (14 percent), "conducted wildlife motorized tour route" (13 percent), "interpretive center" (9 percent), "conducted interpretive exhibits or demonstrations" (5 percent), and "other on-refuge program" (4 percent).

The breakdown among the 5,384,000 visits in the "fishing" category is: "warm-water" (73 percent), "saltwater" (11 percent), "cold-water (9 percent), and "clams, crabs, oysters" (6 percent). For the 1,100,000 visits in the "hunting" category, the breakdown is: "migratory birds" (34 percent), "upland game birds" (15 percent), "white-tailed deer—gun" (14 percent), "trapping" (13 percent), "small-game" (9 percent), and "white-tailed deer—bow" (9 percent).

Only 2,945,000 visits or 8.7 percent of the total public use was classified "non-wildlife-oriented recreation." The subcategories in this class are "boating" (27 percent), "swimming" (25 percent), "picnicking" (21 percent), "other" (18 percent), "waterskiing" (5 percent), and "camping" (3 percent).

Table 11.4 summarizes the recreational use of the National Wildlife Refuge System by state. Florida is clearly the leader with 3.7 million visits. Other leading states, each with over 1 million visits, are Oklahoma (1.8 million), Virginia (1.7 million), Wisconsin (1.5 million), North Carolina (1.5 million), Illinois (1.4 million), California (1.3 million), and Alabama (1.0 million). The preeminence of these states is accounted for by a few very heavily used refuges in each of the states. Four states—Connecticut, New Hampshire, Utah and Vermont—receive under 10,000 visits per year. There is

Table 11.4   Recreational Use of the National Wildlife Refuge System, by State

State	Visits	State	Visits
Alaska	141,244	Montana	236,709
Alabama	1,033,994	North Carolina	1,456,605
Arkansas	476,460	North Dakota	258,974
Arizona	383,498	Nebraska	77,943
California	1,334,627	New Hampshire	4,530
Colorado	19,612	New Jersey	376,853
Connecticut	4,000	New Mexico	182,083
Delaware	122,476	Nevada	181,509
Florida	3,680,483	New York	340,557
Georgia	524,189	Ohio	42,093
Hawaii	427,934	Oklahoma	1,821,225
Iowa	465,717	Oregon	396,770
Idaho	97,997	Pennsylvania	81,387
Illinois	1,362,500	Rhode Island	168,546
Indiana	89,479	South Carolina	358,960
Kansas	128,481	South Dakota	302,229
Louisiana	217,715	Tennessee	590,113
Massachusetts	494,116	Texas	770,374
Maryland	221,460	Utah	6,278
Maine	22,795	Virginia	1,703,419
Michigan	80,784	Vermont	7,773
Minnesota	426,839	Washington	813,811
Missouri	321,325	Wisconsin	1,487,659
Mississippi	144,770	Wyoming	535,233

Source: Fish and Wildlife Service, *National Wildlife Refuge System Public Use Report*, April 15, 1988.

no documented recreational use in two states, Kentucky and West Virginia and the District of Columbia.

Table 11.5 identifies the 25 most heavily used National Wildlife Refuges, and Appendix XIII provides the use data for all Refuges. Several of these most heavily used refuges are located on barrier islands, where national seashores administered by the National Park Service have been established. The Merritt Island National Wildlife Refuge is the most heavily visited refuge in the system, with 1.9 million visits. It is part of a barrier island system on the eastern coast of Florida that includes Canaveral National Seashore and the John F. Kennedy Space Center. This is a major tourist region of Florida, lying just 40 miles east of Orlando. The second most used refuge is the Chincoteague (Virginia and Maryland, 1.5 million visits). Chincoteague is located on another barrier island, Assateague Island, which also includes Assateague Island National Seashore. Assateague Island is a very popular recreational resource, attracting many visitors. While remotely located, it is easily accessible to several East Coast population centers. Ranked third is the Wichita Mountains (1.4 million visits). The unique environment of this refuge contrasts greatly with the rest of the surrounding Great Plains and is the reason for its popularity and use. It borders the Fort Sill Military Reservation and is located 90 miles southwest of Oklahoma City. The Dallas–Fort Worth urban area lies 200 miles south-southeast. The fourth most heavily used refuge, the Pea Island (North Carolina, 1.3 million visits), is located just south of Oregon Inlet on a barrier island (Hatteras Island) that includes another national

Table 11.5   Highest-Use National Wildlife Refuges

Refuge	State	Acres	Visits
Merritt Island	FL	138,262.70	1,904,974
Chincoteague	MD, VA	417.81	1,491,008
Wichita Mountains	OK	59,019.60	1,438,000
Pea Island	NC	5,834.20	1,304,268
Crab Orchard	IL	43,661.74	1,042,172
J. N. "Ding" Darling	FL	5,347.66	845,248
Yukon Delta	AK	19,131,644.67	620,416
Wheeler	AL	34,169.98	604,038
National Elk	WY	24,774.44	532,274
Havasu	AZ, CA	36,334.82	520,665
DeSoto	IA, NE	3,502.77	446,527
Tennessee	TN	51,357.97	401,688
Eufaula	AL, GA	7,953.19	401,559
Hanalei	HI	917.42	396,382
Horicon	WI	21,176.41	392,885
Okefenokee	FL, GA	3,678.14	351,152
Parker River	MA	4,652.41	346,708
Imperial	AZ, CA	17,809.76	330,246
Felsenthal	AR	64,902.12	289,137
San Francisco Bay	CA	18,560.46	275,224
Santa Ana	TX	2,087.50	260,132
Hagerman	TX	12,142.25	233,210
St. Marks	FL	65,400.37	194,001
Columbia	WA	29,596.83	184,503
Kenai	AK	1,904,752.00	183,494

Source: Fish and Wildlife Service, *National Wildlife Refuge System Public Use Report,* April 15, 1988.

seashore, Cape Hatteras. This very popular summer recreation region is on the part of Hatteras Island that is easily road-accessible. The fifth most visited refuge is the Crab Orchard (1.0 million visits), an extremely popular recreational resource in southern Illinois near Carbondale, the site of Southern Illinois University. The refuge is located 115 miles southeast of St. Louis. The J. N. "Ding" Darling National Wildlife Refuge receives 845,248 visits and is ranked sixth for recreational use among the refuges. It is located on Sanibel Island near Fort Myers on the "Gold Coast" of Florida.

Appendix XIV identifies the recreational opportunities available in the national wildlife refuges. One or more of 13 different categories of recreational use is/are permissible on 343 refuges. Hunting is the most widely occurring recreational use, being permitted in 240 refuges. Hunting is permitted on all of the refuges in Alaska. Foot trails are present on 165 refuges, and environmental study areas exist in 158 refuges. The fourth most common recreational use allowed is fishing, on 157 refuges. Nonmotorized boating is allowed in 130 refuges, and motorized boating is allowed in 110 refuges. Visitor centers, ranging in nature from very simple to elaborate, can be found in 109 refuges. The visitor center at the DeSoto National Wildlife Refuge (Iowa) is magnificent. Designated auto tours can be found in 95 refuges. Picnicking facilities exist in 80 refuges, and camping is permitted in 52 refuges. The public affairs specialist for the Fish and Wildlife Service in Washington, D.C., told this author to be sure to emphasize the nature of the camping permitted in refuges. The Fish and Wildlife Service continually receives inquiries from the public about camping opportunities in the National Wildlife Refuge System. The Fish and Wildlife Service sends a form letter to these individuals that states:

> Because of the wildlife conservation mission of the National Wildlife Refuge System, only a very small percentage of national wildlife refuges permit public camping. Where permitted, it is usually of a primitive type and associated with a hunting or fishing program or a wilderness activity. Few refuges can accommodate recreational vehicle camping. Many refuges, however, have private or State-operated campgrounds nearby. (personnel communication with Nancy Marx)

Bicycling and backcountry use opportunities can both be found in 48 refuges. Swimming is the least available outdoor recreation activity permitted in the National Wildlife Refuge System, being allowed in only 15 refuges. There is only one refuge at which all 13 recreational activities are permitted: the Kenai (Alaska). Twelve of the recreational uses are permitted at the Crab Orchard (Illinois). In the following refuges, 10 of the 13 recreational uses are possible: the Okefenokee (Georgia), the Alaska Peninsula Unit of the Alaska Maritime, the Imperial (California), the DeSoto (Iowa), the Kirwin (Kansas), the Seney (Michigan), the Wichita Mountains (Oklahoma), and the Lacreek (S. Dakota).

NATIONAL WILDLIFE REFUGES: CASE STUDIES

Alaska

The Alaska National Interest Lands Conservation Act (ANILCA) had a profound impact on the National Wildlife Refuge System in Alaska. Table 11.6 summarizes the

Table 11.6   National Wildlife Refuges in Alaska

Before 1971*		As of December 2, 1980**		
Name	Acreage	Name	Total Acreage (Includes acreage class as wilderness)	Wilderness Acreage (Lands within each NWR that are maintained as natural areas)
Aleutian Islands NWR	2,720,225	Alaska Maritime NWR	3,548,783+	2,460,000
Bering Sea NWR	81,340			
Bogoslof NWR	175			
Chamisso NWR	455			
Forrester Island NWR	2,832			
Hazy Islands NWR	32			
St. Lazaria NWR	65			
Semidi NWR	251,930			
Simeonof NWR	26,046			
Tuxedni NWR	5,683			
Total	3,088,783			
		Alaska Peninsula NWR	3,500,000	
Arctic National Wildlife Range (later changed to Wm. O. Douglas NWR)	8,894,624	Arctic NWR	18,054,624+	8,000,000
		Becharof NWR*	1,200,000	400,000
		Innoko NWR	3,850,000	1,240,000
Izembek NWR	320,893	Izembek NWR	320,893+	300,000
		Kanuti NWR	1,430,000	
Kenai National Moose Range	1,730,000	Kenai NWR	1,970,000+	1,350,000
Kodiak National Wildlife Range	1,815,000	Koliak NWR	1,865,000+	
		Koyukuk NWR	3,550,000	400,000
		Nowitna NWR	1,560,000	
		Selawik NWR	2,150,000	240,000
		Tetlin NWR	700,000	
Cape Newenham NWR	265,000	Togiak NWR	4,105,000+	2,270,000
Clarence Rhode NWR	2,887,026	Yukon Delta NWR	19,624,458	1,900,000
Hazen Bay NWR	6,800			
Nunivak NWR	3,330,632			
Total	6,224,458			
		Yukon Flats NWR*	8,630,000	
Total acreage	23,338,758		76,058,758	18,560,000

*1971-Section 17(d)(2) of the Alaska Native Claims Settlement Act (ANCSA) authorized the withdrawal of unreserved public lands by December 1978. However, Congress failed to meet the deadline, so late in 1978 these lands were withdrawn under emergency authority prescribed by the Federal Land Policy and Management Act of 1976. Becharof Lake and Yukon Flats were established at that time as national monuments by the president.
**In December 1980 the Alaska National Interest Lands Conservation Act (ANILCA) established these lands as national wildlife refuges.
+Includes pre-1971 acreage.
Source: Alaska Geographic Society, "Alaska National Interest Lands." *Alaska Geographic*, (Alaska National Interest Lands) 8(4), 1981.

status of the system in Alaska prior to passage of ANCSA (1971) and after ANILCA (1980). Prior to 1971, there were 18 refuges totaling 23,338,758 acres. After December 2, 1980, there were 16 refuges totaling 76,058,758 acres—a more-than-threefold increase in acreage in Alaska and a doubling of the acreage in the entire National Wildlife Refuge System. The smaller number of refuges in Alaska after 1980 is due to the consolidation of 10 refuges plus additional acreage into one large refuge, the *Alaska Maritime*.

Seven totally new refuges were established: the *Alaska Peninsula*, the *Innoko*, the *Kanuti*, the *Koyukuk*, the *Nowitna*, the *Selawik*, and the *Tetlin*. Two other new refuges, the *Becharof* and the *Yukon Flats*, were also established within two national monuments proclaimed in 1978. Section 17(d)(2) of ANCSA authorized the withdrawal of unreserved public lands by December 1978. However, Congress failed to meet the deadline, so late in 1978 these lands were withdrawn under emergency authority prescribed by the Federal Land Policy and Management Act (1976). Becharof Lake and Yukon Flats were established at that time as national monuments by President Carter; ANILCA later designated them national wildlife refuges. The Arctic National Wildlife Range was renamed the *Arctic National Wildlife Refuge* and expanded in size from 8.9 million to over 18 million acres. The Kenai National Moose Range was renamed the *Kenai National Wildlife Refuge* and increased in size by 240,000 acres, and the Kodiak National Wildlife Range was renamed the *Kodiak National Wildlife Refuge* and increased in size by 50,000 acres. The Cape Newenham was incorporated into the larger *Togiak* and the Clarence Rhode, the Hazen Bay, and the Nunivak were incorporated into the 19.6-million-acre *Yukon Delta National Wildlife Refuge*.

The National Wildlife Refuge acreage in Alaska increased over threefold with the passage of ANILCA. Concurrent with the signing of the legislation, Alaska was given full regional status in Fish and Wildlife Service administration, and the Anchorage office became a regional office. Areas now included within the Refuge System in Alaska contain a wide and nearly complete spectrum of ecosystems in Alaska. These lands are also large enough and diversified enough to maintain a representative sample of most of the various wildlife and habitats found there. Because refuges have been expanded to include areas previously in the public domain, a number of privately built and owned cabins for recreational and subsistence use are now within refuge boundaries. These cabins can continue to be occupied by the owners with special permits. Refuge visitors are permitted to possess, use, and transport firearms for hunting and personal protection. Subsistence living activities such as hunting, fishing, berry gathering, wood cutting, and cutting logs for buildings are all allowed by the legislation. Use of snowmobiles, motorboats, and other means of surface transportation traditionally relied on by local rural residents for subsistence are generally permitted under the new regulations. Aircraft access to refuges is allowed, and ORVs may be used on special routes and in areas designated by the refuge manager. In 10 of the refuges, 18.6 million acres were declared as wilderness areas and added to the National Wilderness Preservation System. Table 11.7 summarizes the allowable land uses in the National Wildlife Refuge System in Alaska for 1965 and in 1985.

The refuges in Alaska received 1,024,862 visits from October 1986 through September 1987. This represented 4 percent of the total 25,307,000 visits to the entire National Wildlife Refuge System. Use of the refuges in Alaska is very uneven, with just three refuges receiving 89 percent of the total use in the state: Yukon Delta (60.5 percent of state use), Kenai (17.9 percent), and Yukon Flats (10.1 percent). This high use in the Yukon Delta and Yukon Flats Refuges is explained by the subsistence use of Alaskan natives. Several of the Alaskan refuges receive extremely low use: the Innoko (150 visits), the Becharof (703 visits), the Alaska Peninsula (1125 visits), the Alaska Maritime (1469 visits), the Nowitna (2208 visits), the Arctic (3463 visits), and the Kanuti (3773 visits). The use patterns in Alaska differ in some significant ways from the entire Refuge System. The percentage of total use related to fishing is 29

Table 11.7   National Wildlife Refuges in Alaska: Allowable Land Uses—1965 and 1985

	1965	1985	
		Nonwilderness	Wilderness
Total acreage	22.2 million	75.4 million	
		56.4 million	19 million
Sport fishing	All open	All open	All open
Sport hunting	All open	All open	All open
Subsistence hunting and fishing	All open	All open	All open
New mining claims[a]	3.1 million open	Closed	Closed
New petroleum leasing[b]	All potentially open	Potentially open	Closed
Settlement	All closed	Closed	Closed
Timber harvest[c]	All potentially open[c]	Potentially open[c]	Closed
Recreation	All open	All open	All open
Motor access[d]	All open[d]	All open[d]	All open[d]

[a]Historically, most wildlife refuges in the United States have been closed to hard-rock mining; of the 18 refuges that existed in Alaska before 1980, all but two were closed to mining. The 1980 Alaska Lands Act closed newly created refuges to mining.

[b]Wildlife refuges can be opened to oil and gas leasing if the Fish and Wildlife Service judges such leasing to be compatible with wildlife protection. Some acreage in the Kenai National Moose Refuge in south-central Alaska has been under petroleum lease for a number of years. That is the only refuge with petroleum leases in Alaska today, but the Fish and Wildlife Service is preparing comprehensive plans for all Alaska refuges that will specify whether oil or gas leasing would be acceptable (compatible) in other refuges. Areas designated as wilderness—19 million of the 75 million refuge acres—are closed to petroleum leasing. A maximum of 56 million acres in refuges could be opened to oil and gas leasing, but the actual figure is likely to be much smaller. In addition, 19 million acres of the coastal plain of the Arctic National Wildlife Refuge are under a special oil or gas exploration program authorized in the Alaska Lands Act. Leasing and development there would have to be approved by Congress.

[c]Refuges (except areas designated as wilderness) can be opened for timber harvest if such harvest is for the benefit of the wildlife. For example, the Kenai National Moose Range has been opened in the past for harvesting older trees to allow growth of young, shrubby vegetation that moose feed on.

[d]Fixed-wing aircraft, motorboats, and snow machines are allowed in most areas of Alaska's wildlife refuges, including areas designated as wilderness, where these vehicles have been traditionally used. Certain areas of individual refuges have historically been closed to specific motorized vehicles, and these areas remain closed. Use of ORVs and helicopters is generally prohibited in the refuges unless specially permitted by the refuge manager.

Source: Leask, Linda. "Changing Ownership and Management of Alaska Lands." *Alaska Review of Social and Economic Conditions* 22(2): 1–32, October 1985.

percent in Alaskan refuges, compared with 16 percent for the entire Refuge System. The percentage of use related to hunting is 21 percent for the Alaskan refuges, compared with 3 percent for the entire Refuge System. Again, subsistence use by Alaskan natives and others plays a major role in use of the refuges in Alaska.

Alaska Maritime National Wildlife Refuge   This refuge consists of over 2400 parcels of land on islands and other features along Alaska's coastal waters that extend from Cape Lisburne in the Chukchi Sea to Forrester Island in Southeast Alaska. It includes most of the Aleutians (which account for the majority of the acreage). This new designation includes 10 refuges that previously existed. Most of this land is lonely, barren inaccessible tundra. The major purpose of this refuge is to protect marine birds and mammals. The refuge contains habitat for about 75 percent of Alaska's total marine bird population; eagles, hawks and falcons, and other nonmarine birds also use the refuge. A variety of mammals including foxes, otters, mink, brown/grizzly bears, wolves, and wolverines depend on the refuge's habitat. Several species of seal, sea lion, walrus, sea otter, and polar bear seek shelter here, and 16 whale species swim offshore. Wilderness areas have been established on 2,576,320 of the refuge's 3,435,639 acres. The individual wilderness areas in the refuge are the Aleutian Islands (1,300,000 acres), the Bering Sea (81,340 acres), the Bogoslof (175

acres), the Chamisso (455 acres), the Forrester Island (2832 acres), the Hazy Island (32 acres), the Saint Lazaria (65 acres), the Semidi (250,000 acres), the Simeonof (25,855 acres), the Tuxedni (5566 acres), and Unimak (910,000 acres).

Alaska Peninsula National Wildlife Refuge   This 3,500,000-acre refuge is located in southwestern Alaska on the Alaska Peninsula. It extends from the Becharof National Wildlife Refuge along the Pacific Coast side of the peninsula to False Pass but excludes Aniakchak National Monument. This refuge contains an unusual diversity of natural features: active volcanoes, lakes, rivers, and a rugged coastline. Rich waters offshore yield a valuable harvest of king crab and other species. This treeless area is often windy and overcast. The lakes and rivers support an extremely productive salmon fishery where brown/grizzly bears concentrate during the salmon-spawning season. Other large mammals found here are moose, caribou, wolves, and wolverines. The shoreline and offshore islands support large populations of sea lions, seals, and sea otters. Migratory birds are also common. The Alaska Peninsula has been a major big-game hunting area for many years—especially for the brown/grizzly bears.

Arctic National Wildlife Refuge   This refuge is located in extreme northeastern Alaska. It borders the Beaufort Sea on the north, Canada's Yukon Territory on the east, the Alaska pipeline corridor on the west, and Yukon Flats National Wildlife Refuge on the south. It is the largest unit in the National Wildlife Refuge System, covering 19,285,922 acres. This area is generally above tree line and consists of rugged, snow-capped glaciated peaks and a large number of streams that drain both to the north and south. This refuge preserves a large portion of the migration routes of the Porcupine caribou herd, which numbers about 120,000 in size and is one of the two largest herds in Alaska. This refuge also contains a virtually undisturbed wilderness that extends from the Canadian boundary through the Sheenjek Valley and across the eastern Brooks Range to the Arctic Ocean. Eight million acres have been added to the National Wilderness Preservation System. Until just recently, this refuge was under consideration for potential exploration for petroleum resources. In 1991, Congress overrode President Bush's proposed energy policy and prohibited any future exploration for oil in the refuge. Besides caribou, many other large mammals are found within the refuge that includes polar bear, brown/grizzly bear, black bear, Dall sheep, moose, wolf, wolverine, Arctic fox, and musk ox (which are gradually building up their numbers since being reintroduced in 1969). Ducks, geese, swans, and loons breed on the coastal tundra. Other avian species include snowy owl, peregrine falcon, hawks, golden eagle, and gyrfalcon. Arctic grayling are the most common sport fish, but Arctic char, lake trout, and northern pike are also found.

This refuge has seen an increase in recreational use in recent years. Major recreational activities include river kayaking and rafting and mountaineering on the refuge's two highest peaks—Mt. Chamberlin (9020 ft.) and Mt. Michelson (8855 ft.). Wildlife observation is always outstanding.

Becharof National Wildlife Refuge   This refuge is located in southwestern Alaska between Katmai National Park and Preserve on the north and Alaska Peninsula National Wildlife Refuge on the south; 400,000 acres of its 1,200,018 acres have

been classified as wilderness. The landscape is dominated by Becharof Lake, the surrounding low rolling hills and tundra wetlands in the northwest, and volcanic peaks to the southeast. One of the greatest concentrations of brown/grizzlies in Alaska is attracted to the salmon-spawning streams. Other mammals include wolves, wolverines, moose, and caribou. The large variety of salmon found in Becharof Lake and its tributaries form the basis of an important fishery. Sport fish include Arctic grayling, Dolly Varden trout, and rainbow trout. Sea otters, sea lions, and harbor seals inhabit the Pacific coastline. Nesting and migrant waterfowl can be found in the refuge's wetlands and lakes.

Innoko National Wildlife Refuge   The Innoko National Wildlife Refuge is located in the central Yukon River Valley in interior western Alaska and includes the Innoko River basin, some Yukon River islands, and the Kaiyuh Flats. The refuge contains 3,850,000 acres, of which 1,240,000 acres have been classified as wilderness. Eighty percent of the refuge, which is divided into two sections, is wetlands. It is a major nesting area for waterfowl—pintail, widgeon, scaup, and Canada geese breed here. Moose are abundant, especially along the Kaiyuh River, and caribou from the Beaver Mountain herd winter in the refuge. Many other fur bearers are found here.

Izembek National Wildlife Refuge   This is one of the older refuges in Alaska and lies at the extreme western tip of the Alaska Peninsula. Its size was not changed in 1980; 300,000 acres of the refuge's 303,094 acres are part of the National Wilderness Preservation System. It fronts on the Bering Sea side of the peninsula and adjoins Alaska Peninsula National Wildlife Refuge. One of the world's largest beds of eelgrass is found in Izembek Lagoon and is a haven for passing migratory waterfowl; some use it for a wintering habitat. The entire North American population of brant assembles here before migrating across the Pacific en masse. Bears, bald eagle, and caribou are also found here.

Kanuti National Wildlife Refuge   Kanuti National Wildlife Refuge consists of the Kanuti Flats, which are west of the Alaska pipeline and south of Bettles. It extends westward to the villages of Alatna and Allakaket. The refuge is characterized by the broad, rolling plain of the Kanuti and Koyukuk Rivers interspersed with lakes, ponds, and marshes. The Kanuti National Wildlife Refuge is an important subsistence resource for natives of the area. It is also a major waterfowl breeding area. Portions of the western Arctic caribou herd winter here. Black and brown/grizzly bear, wolves, and wolverine are also found within the refuge. The refuge contains 1,430,002 acres.

Kenai National Wildlife Refuge   This is the most accessible refuge in Alaska, located on the Kenai Peninsula across Turnagain Arm from Anchorage. It borders Kenai Fjords National Park and Kachemak Bay State Park; 1.35 million acres of the refuge's 1.9 million acres have been designated wilderness. The Kenai is located on both sides of the Sterling Highway, an all-year, all-weather paved road. A large part of this refuge was set aside in 1941 to protect the Kenai moose population. Within the refuge a variety of habitats and scenic and recreational resources are found ranging from high mountains and glaciers to uplands, forests, lowland lakes, rivers, and wetlands. Large numbers of beaver, mink, and otter are found in the waters, and

one-third of the salmon caught in Cook Outlet spawn in this refuge's streams. In the mountainous areas, Dall sheep and mountain goat are found, with caribou, black and brown/grizzly bears, lynx, wolf, and coyote in the lower foothill areas. Recreational use of the refuge is heavy because of its location a few hours' drive from Anchorage. A major attraction in the north is the Swanson Canoe Trail, and kayakers and canoeists are attracted to the lakes. The uplands provide excellent hiking opportunities, and horseback trips provide accessibility for hikers and hunters.

Kodiak National Wildlife Refuge   This 1.7-million-acre refuge is located on both Kodiak Island and Afognak Island, in the western Gulf of Alaska across Shelikof Strait from Katmai National Park and Preserve on the mainland. A portion of this refuge is one of the first areas in the country to be protected for wildlife management purposes; President Harrison proclaimed the Afognak Island Forest and Fish Culture Reserve in 1881. Many years ago the Kodiak Island portion of the Refuge was set aside to protect the Kodiak brown/grizzly bear population. On Afognak Island, an introduced band of elk share the refuge with the bears. The islands support substantial fish populations, and their coastlines shelter waterfowl and marine mammals.

Koyukuk National Wildlife Refuge   Koyukuk National Wildlife Refuge is located north of the Innoko National Wildlife Refuge and adjoins the Selawik National Wildlife Refuge at its northwestern corner; 400,000 acres of the Refuge's 3,550,000 acres have been added to the National Wilderness Preservation System. The refuge is heavily forested and lies in a circular floodplain, formed by the lower Koyukuk River, that is abundant with wetlands, sloughs, ponds, and lakes. The wetlands attract great numbers of waterfowl. Koyukuk is also the northwestern limit of the breeding range of the trumpeter swan. The western Arctic caribou herd winters in the refuge, and moose are common. Wolves are numerous, black bears occur in the forested areas, and brown/grizzly bears can be found in the open tundra. Fur bearers such as mink, beaver, marten, and muskrat are plentiful. A unique feature of the refuge is the 10,000-acre patch of shifting sand called the Nogahabara Sand Dunes.

Nowitna National Wildlife Refuge   The 1,560,00-acre Nowitna National Wildlife Refuge lies east of the Koyukuk and Innoko Refuges. It protects a lowland basin bordering the Nowitna and Yukon Rivers. A portion of the upper Nowitna River is classified a wild and scenic river. Forested lowlands provides wetland complexes with a diversity of habitats that support both fish and waterfowl. More than a quarter million birds, including trumpeter swans, breed within the refuge. A few small bands of caribou as well as black bears, brown/grizzly bears and numerous moose are found here. The Nowitna River contains important shellfish spawning grounds and nourishes several varieties of salmon.

Selawik National Wildlife Refuge   This refuge is located in northwestern Alaska; and its northern boundary adjoins Kobuk Valley National Park, and its southeastern corner adjoins the Koyukuk National Wildlife Refuge. The refuge includes an extensive area of estuaries and brackish lakes situated where the Kobuk and Selawik Rivers form deltas. Inland to the east are numerous pothole lakes, ponds, marshes, and streams. Higher points include the Waring Mountains in the north and the Se-

lawik Hills in the south. The major wildlife resource in the refuge is the western Arctic caribou herd, which often winters in the upland taiga (boreal forest) areas. It is also a crucial breeding ground for migratory waterbirds. The only reported nesting area of the Asiatic whooper swan is found here. A variety of mammals, including black and brown/grizzly bears, moose, beaver, wolves, and many small fur bearers is present. The Selawik River is classified a wild and scenic river. The refuge totals 2,150,001 acres, 240,000 of which are classified wilderness.

Tetlin National Wildlife Refuge   This 700,054-acre refuge is located along the Canadian border in eastern Alaska south of the Alaska Highway. It is an undulating plain interspersed with hills, forest, ponds, lakes, and extensive marshes. The Chisana and Nabesna Rivers meander through the refuge and join to form the Tanana River. The refuge's location near the Alaska Highway makes it one of the easier refuges in Alaska to visit. The nesting density of ducks here is second only to that at the Yukon Flats. Unusual species for Alaska, such as redheads, ring-necked ducks, and blue-winged teals, have been sighted here. Sandhill cranes nest in the open wetlands. Other birds include loons, grebes, osprey, bald eagle, grouse, and three varieties of ptarmigan. Other wildlife includes caribou from the Chisana herd, moose, black and brown/grizzly bears, wolves, wolverine, lynx, coyote, red fox, and smaller fur bearers.

Togiak National Wildlife Refuge   The Togiak National Wildlife Refuge is located in southwestern Alaska between Kuskokwim Bay on the west and Bristol Bay on the south and east. The Togiak is bordered on the north by the Yukon Delta National Wildlife Refuge and on the east by Wood-Tikchik State Park. This new (1980) 4.1-million-acre refuge absorbed the Cape Newenham National Wildlife Refuge and contains 2.3 million acres of wilderness in the northern portion. The entire refuge is roadless, and 80 percent of it is in the Ahklun Mountains where large expanses of tundra uplands are cut by several broad glacial valleys opening onto a coastal plain. Togiak is a breeding and resting area for such birds as old squaw, common scoter, greater scaup, and pintail. Millions of seabirds frequent the refuge's offshore waters and Capes Pierce and Newenham. Land-based mammals include brown/grizzly bear and moose, while marine mammals include sea lion, walrus, and four species of seal. The six native villages in the area use the refuge for subsistence activities.

Yukon Delta National Wildlife Refuge   This refuge is located in western Alaska in the deltas of the Yukon and Kuskokwim Rivers. At 19,131,645 acres in size, this immense unit of the National Wildlife Refuge System is almost as large as the Arctic National Wildlife Refuge. The large delta area is treeless and, except for the uplands of the Andreafsky and Kilbuck Hills, is a seemingly limitless expanse of wetlands. The extensive pothole lakes and the low elevation make this refuge prime habitat for waterfowl. On Nunivak Island the terrain consists of volcanic craters, sand dunes, sea cliffs, and tundra. The wetlands of the Yukon Delta National Wildlife Refuge are some of the most significant waterfowl breeding areas in North America. A total of 170 species of birds have been observed, and 136 species nest here. Nunivak Island harbors a transplanted musk ox herd and a reindeer herd. Large mammals on the mainland include moose, brown/grizzly bears, and caribou. The Andreafsky River

and its east tributary are designated wild and scenic rivers. Two wilderness areas that have been established on the refuge total 1,900,000 acres: the Andreafsky Wilderness Area (1,300,000 acres) and the Nunivak Wilderness Area (600,000 acres). Over 50 villages, many within the refuge, rely on this area for subsistence activities.

Yukon Flats National Wildlife Refuge   Yukon Flats National Wildlife Refuge is located in east-central Alaska near the Canadian border and about 100 miles north of Fairbanks. This large, 8,630,000-acre refuge is located in the vast interior basin known as the Yukon Flats. It is primarily a wetland complex that includes more than 40,000 lakes, ponds, and sloughs. Low hills almost completely surround the basin. Nesting densities for ducks are greater herein than any other large area in Alaska and are some of the highest on the continent. It is estimated that 15 percent of all canvasbacks ducks breed here. Major mammals include moose, caribou, wolves, and black and brown/grizzly bears.

Lower 49 States

Ten refuges have been selected to illustrate the characteristics of the National Wildlife Refuge System in the lower 49 states. These selections represent different geographic areas. They also represent the diversity of characteristics of the system. These selections range in geographic area from Vermont to Oregon and from Nevada to Florida. Some are very heavily used while others are very lightly used. Some are located near large population centers or major tourist destination areas, and others are remote from either. *Chincoteague National Wildlife Refuge* (Virginia and Maryland) is a very heavily used unit near large population centers on the Eastern Seaboard. It was established to protect migratory waterfowl and contains a unique species—a herd of wild ponies. Its Atlantic Ocean beach is a major attraction. *Desert National Wildlife Refuge* (Nevada) is located in the Basin and Range country and is relatively lightly used. It was established primarily to protect the desert bighorn sheep. *DeSoto National Wildlife Refuge* (Iowa and Nebraska) is located in the middle of the country and was established as a migratory waterfowl refuge. It is a valuable recreational resource in the midst of extensive farmland. *J. N. "Ding" Darling National Wildlife Refuge* (Florida) is a barrier island established to protect subtropical ecosystems and wildlife. It is very heavily used and is a major tourist attraction in southwestern Florida. *Malheur National Wildlife Refuge* (Oregon) is located in the middle of a desert and was established as a migratory bird refuge. Its use is fairly light. *Missisquoi* (Vermont) and *Montezuma* (New York) *National Wildlife Refuges* were both established as migratory bird refuges. Missisquoi receives extremely light use and Montezuma receives moderately heavy use. The *National Bison Range* (Montana) was established primarily to perpetuate one species—the American bison or buffalo—and receives moderately heavy use. *Okefenokee National Wildlife Refuge* (Georgia and Florida) was set aside primarily to preserve an entire ecosystem in the Okefenokee Swamp; it receives heavy use. *Wichita Mountains National Wildlife Refuge* (Oklahoma) was initially established to preserve the bison, but other protected species include elk and Texas longhorn cattle. It receives very heavy use and is managed for recreation, including camping, as a major focus.

Chincoteague National Wildlife Refuge   Chincoteague National Wildlife Refuge is located on the southern end of Assateague Island, a 37-mile barrier beach on the southeastern side of the Delmarva Peninsula and on other islands to the south. The refuge totals 13,870.4 acres, of which 13,452.6 acres are in Virginia and 417.8 acres are in Maryland. The northern end of the larger portion of the refuge on Assateague Island ends at the Virginia-Maryland border. The 418-acre section of the refuge in Maryland is detached and is located a few miles north of the state border, on the western side of the island within Assateague Island National Seashore. A proposal is made in the *Final Environmental Impact Statement for the Chincoteague National Wildlife Refuge Master Plan* (Fish and Wildlife Service, 1992) to exchange the 418-acre portion of the refuge in Maryland with 435.7 acres of National Park Service holdings in the Virginia portion of the refuge. The boundary of Assateague Island National Seashore, created in 1965, is drawn around all of Assateague Island and extends from Ocean City Inlet to the south end of the spit that encloses Tom's Cove. Assateague State Park is located toward the northern end of Assateague Island, with National Park–administered land to the north and south of the state park. This state park is 680 acres in size and is administered by the state of Maryland. It has camping facilities, bathhouses, a bait-and-tackle shop, and food service. Its beach offers separate swimming, surf fishing, and surfboarding areas. Three divisions of the refuge lie on islands to the south of Assateague Island: the Assawoman Island Division, the Metompkin Division, and the Cedar Island Division. The principal developed areas of Assateague Island are at the northern end around Assateague State Park and at the southern end in the refuge around Toms Cove. The National Park Service operates two campground south of Assateague State park: Oceanside and Bayside. There are also some oceanside and bayside walk-in sites (tents only) for hikers or canoeists. It is not possible to drive the entire length of the island, since the paved road that offers access to Assateague State Park ends at South Beach. There is a beach route (permit required) from this point south, but it ends at the Maryland-Virginia state line. Highway 175 offers paved access to the southern end of the island, but north of Toms Cove there are 10 miles of wild beach that extend to the state line; there is foot access only along this section of beach. The 50-mile road-distance between the northern and southern ends of the island, which is on the mainland of the Delmarva Peninsula, takes about 1¼ hours to drive.

Chincoteague National Wildlife Refuge was established in 1943 for use as "an inviolate sanctuary, or for any other management purpose, for migratory birds." The refuge was purchased with Duck Stamp revenues. At the time of the original acquisition, primary recognition was given to southern Assateague Island's value as an important habitat for migrating and wintering greater snow geese. While the refuge continues to provide important waterfowl habitat, the management emphasis has expanded over the years to address a variety of other wildlife needs. The primary function of the refuge, which is crucially located in the Atlantic Flyway, is to protect native and migratory species of wildlife and their habitat. Chincoteague is one of the top five shorebird migratory staging areas east of the Rocky Mountains in the United States. Today, Chincoteague National Wildlife Refuge supports breeding populations of the endangered Delmarva Peninsula fox squirrel and the threatened piping plover. A nesting tower on the refuge has supported a resident pair of peregrine falcons,

which are also an endangered species. Hundreds of peregrine falcons stop on the refuge during migration. Bird watchers rate Chincoteague one of the East's finest sites. More than 300 species of birds are known to use the refuge regularly; most conspicuous are seabirds, shorebirds, wading birds, raptors, and waterfowl. There are no freshwater streams or lakes on the refuge. Twelve freshwater impoundments covering 2623 acres were constructed to provide submergent and emergent wetland vegetation as forage for wildlife and habitat for other waterbirds. These freshwater impoundments combine with marshes to host a variety of herons, egrets, and other wading birds during the summer. Terns, gulls, and sandpipers are attracted to the beaches.

The refuge contains a diversity of habitat types that includes: beach and unvegetated dunes, dunegrass, upland scrub or shrub, wetland scrub or shrub, freshwater marsh, salt marsh, wetland forest, upland forest, sand flats and mud flats, seasonal open water, marine or estuarine open water, and agricultural lands. Visitors are surprised to find 1500 acres of upland forest, most of which are pure stands of loblolly pine. Whitetail deer and Sika deer are observed in these upland forests. The Sika "deer" are really oriental elk released here in 1923. Two herds of wild ponies make their home on Assateague Island. The herds are separated by a fence at the boundary between Maryland and Virginia. The Maryland herd is managed by the National Park Service; the Virginia herd is owned by the Chincoteague Volunteer Fire Company and allowed by permit to graze on Chincoteague National Wildlife Refuge. Each year the Fire Company rounds up the Virginia herd and sells some of the herd at the Pony Penning and auction, held on the last Wednesday and Thursday of July. The ponies are gathered into the corral off Beach Road and then herded to Assateague Channel, which they swim to Chincoteague Island. The entire herd is penned, and most yearlings and foals are auctioned. Proceeds benefit the town's ambulance and fire services. Following the auction, the remaining pony herd is returned to the refuge. Smaller than horses, these shaggy, sturdy wild ponies are descended from domesticated stock that were grazed on the island as early as the 17th century. Marsh and dune grass supply the bulk of their food. In Maryland, the ponies are often seen around roads and campgrounds. In Virginia, they may be observed in marshes off the Pony Trail observation platform. These ponies are wild animals and should be treated as such—do not feed, and maintain your distance. They can kick and bite and inflict serious injury.

The refuge is open to recreational uses centered around wildlife and wild land activities that are in harmony with this primary objective. Overall, Chincoteague is one of the most appealing refuges in the Northeast. As a barrier-island refuge, Chincoteague's relatively large size, variety of landscape types, accessibility and accommodation to visitor use, seasonal changes, viewing opportunities, and contrast with other nearby development combine to make the refuge an outstanding regional recreational and aesthetic resource. The beautiful beach and wildlife viewing opportunities are the prime recreational attractions of the refuge. Two factors have contributed to a sharp increase in use of the refuge since 1960: (1) the construction of a bridge from Chincoteague Island to Assateague Island in 1962, and (2) the establishment of Assateague Island National Seashore in 1965. The bridge construction opened the ocean beach to easy access, and the establishment of the National Seashore further encouraged the island's trend toward a tourist economy. These developments added

a dynamic new growth factor to land development on Chincoteague Island. Tourist accommodations have expanded from a few rooming houses and small hotels in the 1950s to enough motel and hotel rooms, cabins, and campsites to accommodate more than 15,000 summer visitors. In 1990, the Chincoteague chamber of commerce estimated that the year-round island population of 3600 swelled to over 19,000 visitors during the summer months. According to a 1985 survey conducted by the Chincoteague mayor and the Town Council's advisory committee on tourism, 71 percent of all business on Chincoteague Island is related to tourism. The town's major tourist attraction is Chincoteague National Wildlife Refuge.

According to refuge records, public use has increased from 100,000 visits in 1963 to 1.5 million visits in 1987. This use ranks Chincoteague National Wildlife Refuge the second most heavily used unit in the National Wildlife Refuge System. Chincoteague contrasts with many of the other units in the Refuge System in that a significant portion of the recreational use is nonwildlife-oriented recreation. The second-ranking category of use is "nonwildlife-oriented recreation" (31 percent of total use), almost equal to the first-ranked "nonconsumptive wildlife-oriented recreation" (32 percent of total use). "Other consumptive wildlife-oriented recreation" and "interpretation" rank next, with each contributing 15 percent of the total use. Clamming and crabbing are the other primary consumptive wildlife-oriented recreational activities. Fishing accounts for 6 percent of the total use (both warm-water and saltwater). Within the leading major category "nonconsumptive wildlife-oriented recreation" the breakdown of use into subcategories is: "land vehicle wildlife/wild lands observation" (61 percent), "picnicking" (21 percent) and "foot wildlife/wild lands observation" (17 percent). Within the close second-ranking category of use—"nonwildlife-oriented recreation"—the breakdown by subcategories is: "swimming" (54 percent) and "picnicking" (44 percent). More than 50 percent of the refuge's total annual visitation comes during summer vacation season. Although almost all summer visitors use the beach, surveys indicate that people choose Assateague Island beaches because of the wildlife viewing and wild lands experiences the refuge and national seashore provide. In fall, passerine bird and waterfowl migrations draw visitors who enjoy the Wildlife Drive and walking trails. Fall also yields some of the best saltwater fishing opportunities. Visitation declines during late fall and remains low during the winter but picks up again in the spring as people come to watch the spring migrations, nesting, foaling, and fishing.

The lifeguarded beach and picnic area at Toms Cove is the center of summer activity on the refuge. This area consists of an attractive beach, a narrow dune, several acres of asphalt, a number of substantial visitor facilities of modern design, and bayside marshes. Other developed sites and corridors on the refuge consist of visitor and management facilities, including trails. The Chincoteague Visitor Center complex, hidden in its dune-forest setting, provides information, descriptive leaflets, and schedules for interpretive activities, including guided walks and auditorium programs. A concessioner operates a series of wildlife and boat tours; reservations may be made at the visitor center. The bicycle and Wildlife Drive trails that stem off the site provide major links to areas with a strong wildlife focus, enhancing the image of the area as a refuge. Trails and associated trail development are particularly well designed. The boardwalks and overlooks are designed to match their forest–marsh edge settings. In general, the variety of landscapes through which the trails pass, the

range of trail lengths and types, trail maintenance, and the viewing opportunities give refuge trails a high aesthetic quality. The Wildlife Drive is reserved for hikers and bicyclists until 3 P.M. each day. The Pony Trail is usually a good place to see ponies. Beach hikers can enjoy miles of undisturbed beach north of the Toms Cove Visitor Center. A bike path leads from the town of Chincoteague to the Chincoteague Refuge Visitor Center and continues to the Toms Cove Visitor Center. The Pony Trail is also open for bikes. The only oversand vehicle route on the refuge is south for 2.5 miles from the Toms Cove Visitor Center; a permit is needed. The lighthouse at the end of Lighthouse Trail is the refuge's strongest cultural visual resource. The major corridor on the refuge is Beach Road, which passes through a variety of habitats and providing much viewing interest. Other corridors, with the exception of the Wildlife Drive, are more primitive and have similar qualities of diversity and wildlife viewing opportunities. Each year the refuge holds an open house during Waterfowl Week, generally around Thanksgiving, when large numbers of migratory birds use the refuge. Hunting is strictly prohibited on the refuge, except for an annual deer hunt and for waterfowl hunting in Wildcat Marsh. Pets are prohibited in the refuge, and landing a boat anywhere on the island's Virginia end is prohibited except at Fishing Point on the end of Toms Cove Hook. No camping is available in the refuge, but there are commercial campgrounds on nearby Chincoteague Island.

The legislation establishing Assateague Island National Seashore stipulated that Chincoteague National Wildlife Refuge be managed primarily for wildlife and secondarily for public use. A 1979 "Memorandum of Understanding" between the National Park Service and the Fish and Wildlife Service assigned administration of public use of the Refuge's Toms Cove Hook portion to the National Park Service, while the Fish and Wildlife Service retained wildlife management responsibility on the Hook. The Toms Cove Visitor Center offers exhibits, maps, and other publications and information on National Park Service naturalist, or beach-type recreational activities there. Swimming and picnicking are available at Toms Cove. In 1990, agency responsibilities were further refined in a revised interagency agreement. The 1974 Assateague Island Wilderness Study Summary indicated that approximately 8000 acres of federally owned lands on Assateague Island quality for wilderness designation, of which 1300 acres lie in Chincoteague National Wildlife Refuge.

To ensure that visitors have a safe high-quality experience, the Fish and Wildlife Service staff at Chincoteague National Wildlife Refuge have proposed the following public-use and facilities management actions for the future in their recently completed *Final Environmental Impact Statement for the Chincoteague National Wildlife Refuge Master Plan:*

- Emphasize wildlife-oriented recreation and educational opportunities
- Continue the migratory bird hunting programs. Manage ORV access to Toms Cove Hook, from September 1 through March 14, unless threatened or endangered species needs dictate a longer closure.
- Retain the current beach general recreation zone in the vicinity of parking lots 1–4. Establish a maximum beach-use capacity of 4400 beach visitors at any one time.
- Allow wildlife-oriented recreation, such as wildlife or wild lands observation, north of the current general beach recreation zone but not within critical shorebird nesting areas.

- Continue private vehicle beach access as long as beach parking areas remain, and allow the National Park Service to maintain existing parking at the beach as long as the land base remains, realizing that this area will be lost eventually to natural barrier island movement.
- Coordinate with the National Park Service and the Chincoteague community in identifying a suitable off-site parking area to be used once the existing beach parking is lost due to the lack of suitable land behind the dunes; jointly establish an alternate means of moving people to the beach.
- Implement a system to eliminate traffic backups at the beach when beach parking lots are full.
- Allow the National Park Service to maintain existing beach facilities until lost to natural causes; thereafter allow a minimum level of development in keeping with the unstable beach-dune system, to include a visitor contact station–first aid station and comfort station or bathhouses.
- Develop a new Fish and Wildlife Service Refuge headquarters and visitor center on a geologically stable portion of the island. The building will provide interpretive and educational areas, an auditorium, and office space. It was concluded that the site of the existing visitor center is the most desirable location.

Desert National Wildlife Refuge   The Desert National Wildlife Range (1,588,819 acres) is the largest unit of the National Wildlife Refuge System in the lower 49 states and is located in the Mohave Desert of southern Nevada. The refuge is located 20 miles north of Las Vegas and is bordered on the west by the Nellis Air Force Range, where entry is prohibited. Its most important objective is perpetuating the desert bighorn sheep. The range contains six major mountain ranges, the highest rising from 2500-foot-elevation valleys to nearly 10,000-foot peaks. Of the six major mountain ranges, the Sheep Range is the highest and most scenic and supports the greatest diversity of wildlife and vegetative types. Annual rainfall ranges from less than 4 inches in the valley floors to over 15 inches on the highest peaks. Staff working on the range actively improve habitats by developing new water sources and maintaining and improving existing ones. Dependable, year-round water sources located throughout bighorn habitat enables the sheep to use all available habitat; this reduces competition for food, cover, water, and space. Numerous other wildlife species share the refuge with bighorns. Mule deer, coyotes, badgers, foxes, and an occasional mountain lion are the larger mammals. Over 260 species of birds have been identified in the refuge.

An understanding of the vertical zonation of plant communities is crucial to successful viewing of specific wildlife species. Most of the communities can be seen when driving the Mormon Wells Road. Only the highest portions of the coniferous forest communities are inaccessible by car. In the desert shrub communities, creosote bush and white bursage dominate in the hottest, lowest elevation zone. A few thousand feet above the 2000-foot valley floor, Mohave yucca and cactus become dominant. Near 6000 feet elevation, at the upper edge of the desert shrub communities, blackbrush and Joshua tree are dominant. Desert bighorn often inhabit the upper range of this community, as do loggerhead shrikes, cactus wrens, and sage sparrows. An anomaly in these communities is Corn Creek, where springs turn the desert into an oasis attracting over 200 species of birds. The desert woodland communities start

above 6000 feet; here Joshua tree becomes scarce, replaced by single-leaf pinyon and Utah juniper. Big sagebrush is the most common shrub. Desert bighorns and mule deer inhabit the woodlands when springs are close by or vegetation is lush from recent rain. Pinyon jays, common bushtits, and broad-tailed hummingbirds are common in the desert woodlands. The coniferous forest communities exist from 7000 to 9000 feet, with ponderosa pine and white fir the dominant trees. Near 10,000 feet the only trees surviving are bristlecone pines. Desert bighorns and mule deer are found in this zone, especially at the lower ranges. Snow is common at these elevations.

A multitude of recreational opportunities are permissible in the Desert National Wildlife Range. Vehicles are permitted only on designated roads and must be street-legal. The roads are rough and unimproved and may be impassable for passenger cars. The major access point is through the Corn Creek Field Station, which can be reached by traveling north from Las Vegas approximately 23 miles, where a sign on the eastern side of the road marks the 4-mile gravel road to Corn Creek. The Mormon Well Road Truck Tour Route has several designated points of interest. The Corn Creek Field Station has trees, pasture, and spring-fed ponds. The ponds provide habitat for the endangered, transplanted Pahrump poolfish. At the Agave Roasting Pit one can see where ancient native people once slow-cooked meats and vegetables. There are interesting geological features at Peek-A-Boo Canyon. Camping and backpacking are permitted year-round in the refuge. All camps, except backpack camps, must be located within 100 feet of designated roads and are prohibited within sight or within ¼ mile of any waterhole. The most popular backpacking areas are Hidden Forest Canyon and Sawmill Canyon. The entire refuge, excluding the portion used by Nellis Air Force Base, is open to horseback riding and hiking year-round. Picnicking is permitted along designated roads. There are two small picnic areas with tables and grills, but no water, at Corn Creek Field Station and Mormon Well Pass. Limited hunting for bighorn sheep and mule deer is permitted; possession of firearms for all other purposes is prohibited. The western half of the refuge is used by Nellis Air Force Base as a bombing and gunnery range throughout the year. The Corn Creek headquarters area, including the interpretive exhibits and walking trails, is open daily from sunrise to sunset. All other areas of the refuge are open 24 hours a day subject to the restrictions mentioned above.

The Desert National Wildlife Range is a lightly used refuge, receiving only 23,150 visits annually. The leading category of use is "nonconsumptive wildlife-oriented recreation," which accounts for 76 percent of the annual use; 69 percent of this use is foot wildlife/wild lands observation and another 25 percent is land vehicle wildlife/wild lands observation. Almost all of the remaining recreational use is the 21 percent that occurs in nonwildlife-oriented recreation; 65 percent of this is picnicking and 32 percent is camping. Only 2 percent or 392 visits was for hunting.

DeSoto National Wildlife Refuge   DeSoto National Wildlife Refuge is 7827 acres in size and is located on the floodplain of the Missouri River in Iowa (3503 acres) and Nebraska (4324 acres). The open section of the refuge is accessible only from the Iowa side of the Missouri River. The principal feature of this open section is horseshoe-shaped DeSoto Lake, an old oxbow lake that was once the course of the Missouri River. The Iowa-Nebraska border is still in the center of DeSoto Lake. Established in 1958, DeSoto National Wildlife Refuge's primary wildlife management role is to serve as a stopover for migrating ducks and geese. During typical years

200,000 snow and blue geese utilize the refuge as a resting and feeding area during their fall migration between the Arctic nesting grounds and the Gulf Coast wintering area. Peak populations of 125,000 or more ducks, mostly mallards, are common in the refuge during the fall migration. October and November are the months of peak use; fewer numbers of ducks and geese return in March and early April. Bald eagles arrive with the ducks and geese in the fall, with many wintering until March. As many as 120 bald eagles have been seen at one time. An interesting assortment of warblers, gulls, shorebirds, and other bird life can be observed during fall and spring migration. White-tailed deer, cottontails, raccoons, coyotes, skunks, opossums, and fox squirrels are frequently observed. Backwater areas of DeSoto Lake and several wetlands in the refuge serve as habitat for beaver, muskrat, and an occasional mink. Woods, fields of native prairie grasses, and the multiflora rose hedges along roads attract a variety of songbirds and other wildlife, such as pheasants and bobwhite quail. Red-headed woodpeckers are common, and wood ducks may be seen in ponds throughout the refuge.

Neighboring farmers farm nearly 3000 of the refuge's 7827 acres, leaving a portion in food for the migrating ducks and geese: Both migrant and resident wildlife use farm crops to supplement their natural foods. Since 1965, several hundred acres of refuge fields have been reverted to native prairie grasses, which provide an important source of nesting habitat and winter shelter for wildlife. Wildlife managers use both fire and haying as management tools to maintain healthy stands of native grasses. Wood duck nest boxes have been installed to provide nesting sites for the refuge's principal resident duck species. One of DeSoto's most interesting programs involves the restoration of sandbar habitat to attract nesting piping plovers and Interior least terns, the latter an endangered species.

An extremely well designed and sited visitor center serves as the focal point for the refuge visitor. The 26,000-square-foot visitor center opened in 1981. Interior viewing galleries face large windows with views of DeSoto Lake, at the edge of which the visitor center was built (Figure 11.2). The natural and cultural history displays are outstanding and there is an auditorium for films, special exhibits, and programs. A 12-minute film introduces the visitor to the Missouri Basin. The visitor center is open from 9:00 A.M. until 4:30 P.M. daily, except for New Year's Day, Easter, Thanksgiving, and Christmas, when both the refuge and visitor center are closed. During the winter season, from December 1 until the second week in March, there is refuge access only to the visitor center and the adjacent Missouri Meander Nature Trail.

By the mid 1800s the Missouri River had become an artery for trade that opened the West. During the 19th and early 20th centuries more than 400 steamboats sank or were stranded between St. Louis, Mo. and Ft. Benton, Mont. One of these was the 1860-era sternwheeler *Bertrand*, which was discovered on the refuge in 1968 and unearthed the following year. Built in 1864 at Wheeling, W. Va., the *Bertrand* was a mountain packet sternwheeler 178 feet in length and designed for the shallow, narrow rivers of the West. On April 1, 1865, the vessel sank on its first voyage up the Missouri River. Many of the thousands of artifacts recovered from the hull of the *Bertrand* are exhibited in environmentally controlled chambers in the visitor center, along with a model of the steamship. This exhibit is the most fascinating one in the visitor center.

Auto touring and wildlife observation are encouraged in the refuge; vehicles are allowed on public roads and designated parking areas only. Twelve miles of all-weather roads traverse the refuge along DeSoto Lake, woods, grasslands, freshwater

Figure 11.2 A view inside the beautiful DeSoto National Wildlife Refuge Visitor Center overlooking DeSoto Lake.

ponds, and the Missouri River. During the Fall Auto Tour, numbered stops corresponding to a special interpretive brochure guides visitors and explains the annual migration. A short side trail from the main road around DeSoto Lake leads to the pond where the hull of the *Bertrand* lies buried. Displays explain its excavation and the historic significance of the Missouri River steamboat era. The refuge has three designated nature trails. The Bertrand Trail explores the old river channel and takes the visitor through grassland and marsh habitats. The ¾-mile Cottonwood Trail crosses Wood Duck Pond and leads through the woods and along the grassland edge. Visitors may observe wildlife management practices demonstrated nearby. The Missouri Meander Trail is adjacent to the visitor center and is a twin-looped trail open year-round. One loop provides a 900-foot paved trail accessible to those in wheelchairs or with walking difficulties (Figure 11.3). The other loop is a ⅞-mile wood-chipped trail that crosses a foot-bridge and meanders through woods and along DeSoto Lake.

Other recreational opportunities on DeSoto National Wildlife Refuge are picnicking, hunting, fishing, boating, and mushroom gathering. A number of picnic sites with grills are located in several sections of the refuge (Figure 11.4). While swimming is not permitted on the refuge, there are designated wading areas. Fishing and boating are permitted on DeSoto Lake during public-use season, April 15 to September 30. Boating is limited to no-wake speeds, not to exceed 5 mph (Figure 11.5). Fish species includes largemouth bass, bluegill, catfish, crappie, northern pike, and walleye. Much of the lakeshore is available for bank fishing, but some areas are accessible by boat only. Archery and spear fishing are allowed for nongame species. Ice fishing is available in January and February. Opportunities for archery and muzzleloader deer hunting, as well as waterfowl hunting, are available on a limited basis. Additional areas of the refuge are open to the public for mushroom picking during daylight hours from April 15 through May 31, when a profusion of morels usually emerge.

Figure 11.3 A paved 900-foot interpretive trail at DeSoto National Wildlife Refuge allows access by wheelchairs and for those with walking difficulties.

Figure 11.4 The main picnic area at DeSoto National Wildlife Refuge is one of the finest in this part of the country.

The DeSoto National Wildlife Refuge is a very popular Midwest recreational resource. It is one of the more heavily visited refuges, ranking 11th with 446,527 visits. Virtually all of the public use at DeSoto is wildlife-oriented, with the leading category of use being "interpretation," which accounts for 64 percent of the use. The breakdown of specific subcategories of use in the "interpretation category" is: "interpretive center" (37 percent); "self-guided interpretation exhibits and demonstrations" (36 percent); "self-guided motorized wildlife tour route" (13 percent); and "self-guided nonmotorized wildlife trails" (8 percent). The second-highest category of use is "nonconsumptive wildlife-oriented recreation" with 31 percent of the use. The major contributors to this category are "land vehicle wildlife/wild lands observation" (80 percent), "foot wildlife/wild lands observation" (10 percent), "picnicking" (8 percent), and "photography" (2 percent). Fishing is the third-ranking category of use, with 4 percent of the visits—all of it is warm water. The fourth-ranking category is "environmental education" with 1 percent of the use.

J. N. "Ding" Darling National Wildlife Refuge   This 5393-acre refuge is located on Sanibel Island and Buck Key, on the southwestern coast of Florida near Fort Myers. It was originally established in 1945 as the Sanibel National Wildlife Refuge and was a satellite of the former Everglades National Wildlife Refuge, before the latter became a national park. The refuge was renamed the J. N. "Ding" Darling National Wildlife Refuge in 1967 and dedicated to Darling in 1978. *Jay Norwood "Ding" Darling* was a Pulitzer Prize–winning syndicated political cartoonist at the *Des Moines Register* for 35 years and chief of the U.S. Biological Survey from 1934 to 1935. He is also credited with being one of the key people in establishing the National Wildlife Refuge System. In 1934, he initiated the Migratory Bird Hunting Stamp program and designed the first Duck Stamp. In 1976, 2619 acres of the refuge were designated a wilderness area in the National Wilderness Preservation System.

Figure 11.5   No-wake boating is permitted on DeSoto Lake at DeSoto National Wildlife Refuge.

This refuge protects subtropical barrier island habitats including mangrove eco-systems, tropical hardwood hammocks, beach, and interior freshwater marsh. The main tract is 4744 acres. Other tracts and their acreages are Bailey Tract (100 acres); Perry Tract (3 acres); Buck Key, where two-thirds are owned by the Fish and Wildlife Service (176 acres); Runyon Key (7 acres); Wulfert Point (180 acres); and State Botanical Site (183 acres). Four mangrove island refuges in Pine Island Sound and Charlotte Harbor are administered by the J. N. "Ding" Darling Refuge: Pine Island National Wildlife Refuge (16 islands/548 acres), Matlacha Pass National Wildlife Refuge (23 islands/512 acres), Caloosahatchee National Wildlife Refuge (3 islands/40 acres), and Island Bay National Wildlife Refuge (5 islands/20 acres). These areas are all nesting islands and reachable only by boat; therefore, wildlife observation has some seasonal restrictions.

The refuge provides a place for approximately 291 species of birds, over 50 species of reptiles and amphibians, and at least 32 different species of mammals. Year-round residents include osprey, raccoon, brown pelican, moorhen, and alligator. An extremely wide assortment of other birds and waterfowl may also be observed. One of the most beloved birds is the roseate spoonbill. In fall and spring, migrating songbirds may be observed, and during the winter a variety of migrating ducks may be seen. Endangered species present at the refuge include the American crocodile, Arctic peregrine falcon, Atlantic loggerhead turtle, Atlantic ridley turtle, bald eagle, Eastern indigo snake, West Indian manatee, and wood stork. The American alligator is listed as threatened. Management problems facing the refuge include wildlife habitat destruction due to urban growth, nonpoint source pollution, nonnative species encroachment, and intense popularity of the refuge to visitors.

The J. N. "Ding" Darling National Wildlife Refuge is a major tourist attraction in southwestern Florida and receives heavy use. A visitor center near the intersection of Sanibel-Captiva and Rabbit Roads has exhibits, an orientation video, book sales, and an information desk. There is no charge to enter the visitor center. It is open every day, except Friday, from 9:00 A.M. until 5:00 P.M., November through April. From May through October it is open from 9:00 A.M. until 4:00 P.M. every day except Friday and Sunday. A variety of naturalist programs are offered by refuge staff and volunteers. A schedule is available at the visitor center, and it is necessary to sign up ahead of time, since the number of participants is limited. A prime attraction at the refuge is the 5-mile, one-way Wildlife Drive. There are interpretive signs and an observation tower along the drive (Figure 11.6). The Wildlife Drive is closed on Friday. For better wildlife-viewing opportunities, visiting should be planned for early morning, late afternoon, or low tide, when wildlife is most active. The entrance fee is $4 per vehicle and $1 for hikers and bicycles. Golden Age, Golden Access, and Golden Eagle Passports, and current federal Duck Stamps are acceptable for admission.[1]

Picnicking, swimming, hunting, and camping are not permitted in the refuge, but there are excellent hiking and canoeing opportunities. There are six public beach

---

[1]One should be sure to cover the entrance fee with one of these four methods: Although payment of fees is based on the honor system, don't be surprised if along the middle of the one-way road Fish and Wildlife Service officers check to be sure the fee is covered. There are inclined spikes at the entrance, so retreat is not a possibility. The author has observed some red-faced visitors at these road checks who tried to save a few dollars.

Figure 11.6   Visitors observing wildlife along Wildlife Drive at J. N. "Ding" Darling National Wildlife Refuge (observation tower in the background).

access sites on Sanibel and Captiva Islands, and picnic sites are available off the refuge along these roads. The five designated hiking trails on the refuge are the Indigo (2 miles each way), the Cross Dike (0.25 mile), the Red Mangrove Overlook (0.1 mile), the Shell Mound (0.3 mile), and the Bailey Tract (1.75 miles). There are two canoe trails: the Commodore Creek (2 miles) and the Buck Key (4 miles). A concession, the Tarpon Bay Recreation Area, offers tram, canoe, and kayak tours and bicycle, canoe, and kayak rentals. Saltwater and freshwater fishing are available along the Wildlife Drive, at Tarpon Bay, and at the Bailey Tract. Crabbing is permitted except in closed areas. The Sanibel-Captiva Nature Center is located east of and across the road from the visitor center. This private center offers exhibits, walking trails and guided tours. Two percent of the use is related to environmental education.

The J. N. "Ding" Darling National Wildlife Refuge is one of the most popular in the country, receiving 845,248 visits annually; this ranks it in sixth place nationally. "Nonconsumptive wildlife-oriented recreation" is the major category of recreational use, with 71 percent of the total use. Fifty-nine percent of the use in this category is related to "land vehicle wildlife/wild lands observation," 16 percent to "foot wildlife/wild lands observation," 13 percent to "other wildlife/wild lands observation" and 11 percent to "photography." The second-ranking category of use is "interpretation," accounting for 26 percent of the total use; of which 41 percent occurs at the visitor center.

Malheur National Wildlife Refuge   The 185,412-acre Malheur National Wildlife Refuge is one of the largest refuges in the lower 49-states and is located in the high desert country of southeastern Oregon. Since prehistoric times, the Malheur-Harney Lakes Basin has been a major nesting and migration stopover area for migratory birds. The extensive marshes, wet meadows, and riparian areas, surrounded by hundreds of square miles of desert, attracted tremendous numbers of birds. In 1908, President Theodore Roosevelt protected Malheur, Harney, and Mud Lakes together as a migratory bird sanctuary to halt the slaughter of swans, egrets, herons, and

grebes for the millinery business. The drainage and reclamation of the Blitzen Valley posed an equally serious threat to nesting birds by reducing the water supply to Malheur Lake. In 1935 the Blitzen Valley and the P Ranch were added to the Malheur National Wildlife Refuge. Refuge headquarters are located on the southern shore of Malheur Lake, 40 miles south of Burns. This refuge is remotely located and is an arid land of shallow marshes, lakes, small ponds in the Blitzen Valley, flood-irrigated meadows, alkali flats, rim rocks, and grass- and sagebrush-covered hills. The refuge has an elevation of 4100 feet, so freezing temperatures are common from September through May. This is a dry area, with an average annual precipitation of only 9 inches.

The three largest lakes— Malheur, Harney, and Mud— lie in the Malheur-Harney Basin. There is no external drainage for these lakes, so evaporation is the only way water can escape. The Donner und Blitzen river system flows off Steens Mountain and brings water to Malheur Lake; 73 miles of this river system on Bureau of Land Management land southeast of the refuge was designated a component of the National Wild and Scenic Rivers System in 1988. Water drains south from the Ochoco and Malheur National Forests and provides water to all three lakes. Water in this desert environment is the critical factor for determining how much wildlife the refuge can support. In drought years, such as in the early 1930s, the lakes totally dried up, since all water was diverted from the rivers for irrigation. In contrast, 3 years of heavy snowpack in the early 1980s flooded the Malheur-Harney Lakes Basin. The three lakes expanded into one large inland sea covering an estimated 180,000 acres. The effects of this high water were dramatic. Emergent vegetation drowned and new islands were created by the rising water. Marsh wrens and diving ducks lost their nesting areas, but numbers of white-faced ibis, great egret, and doublecrested cormorant increased; white pelicans nested on islands in Malheur Lake for the first time in 25 years.

The Malheur National Wildlife Refuge has an amazing mix of habitat types that contrast with the surrounding desert. During high water, Malheur Lake is transformed from a large marsh to a huge lake. A total of 300 species of birds and 58 species of mammals have been observed in the refuge. Attracted birds include white pelican, terns, grebes, gulls, loons, osprey, and waterfowl. Ponds, sloughs, and marshes in the Blitzen Valley and on the Double O Ranch attract trumpeter swans; Canada geese; ducks; greater Sandhill cranes; white-faced ibis; great, snow and cattle egrets; black-crowned night-heron; and Franklin's gull. The Double O Ranch and Blitzen Valley have been intensively developed, with ponds, canals, dikes, and water-control structures manipulating the water to create wildlife habitat. In August, after the flood-irrigated meadows are drained, some are grazed, hayed or burned. Riparian areas, which contain trees and shrubs, are scattered throughout the refuge. These areas are among the most important for wildlife because they provide food, shelter from weather and predators, and water all in one place. Most of the upland vegetation consists of antelope bitterbush, sagebrush, western juniper, and at the high elevations, quaking aspen and mountain mahogany. They provide forage for grazing animals (deer and antelope), nesting sites for birds (sage grouse and quail), and minimize wind erosion. A distinct sequence of events characterizes wildlife activity at the Malheur. Spring waterfowl migration peaks in late March, most shorebirds arrive in April, and songbird numbers peak in mid-May. Fall migration peaks in

August for songbirds and in October for waterfowl. Rough-legged hawks and bald eagles feed in the Blitzen Valley in winter.

Motorized vehicles and bicycles are permitted on designated roads. An auto tour includes five stops that offer outstanding opportunities to view wildlife and their habitat. At Buena Vista Ponds and Overlook one can see Steen's Mountain and nesting trumpeter swans. At Benson Pond, tall cottonwood trees and water create an oasis in the desert, where great horned owls may be observed. Knox Ponds are closed March 1 through August 1 to protect nesting birds. At P Ranch a walk along a typical riparian habitat reveals a large number of birds. The only structures that remain from the Peter French cattle empire of the late 19th century at the P Ranch are the Long Barn, the beef wheel, and stockade fences. At the refuge office and visitor center, information on current road conditions, orientation and interpretive exhibits, refuge brochures, restrooms, and drinking water are available. The George M. Benson Memorial Museum contains nearly 200 mounted specimens of local birds. To minimize disturbance during the nesting season from March 1 to August 1, hiking is limited to roads open to motorized vehicles and to streams and canal banks in the public fishing area. During the remainder of the year, hiking is permitted everywhere in the refuge except for the Harney and Stinking Lake Research-Natural Areas. The Refuge does not have any marked or developed trails.

Regulated hunting and fishing are allowed in the refuge. Hunting is allowed in three sections. In the Malheur Lake Area, species that may be hunted include goose, duck, merganser, coot, common snipe, pheasant, and quail. Special-use permits are needed for everyone visiting the Malheur Lake Area at any time of the year. Boats and ATVs are not permitted. Temporary blinds may be constructed. Water levels can vary widely from year to year, occasionally making access to Malheur Lake difficult. In the Buena Vista Area, east of Highway 205, hunting is permitted for pheasant, quail, chukar, Hungarian partridge, and rabbit. In the Boundary Area, west of Highway 205, hunting is allowed for goose, duck, merganser, coot, common snipe, pheasant, quail, dove, pigeon, chukar, Hungarian partridge, antelope, deer, coyote and rabbit. Fishing is allowed in the following areas: Krumbo Reservoir and Krumbo Creek above the reservoir, Bridge and Mud Creeks, East Canal from Page Dam down to Bridge Creek, Blitzen River from Page Dam down to Bridge Creek, and West Canal from Page Dam down to P Lane. The species present are primarily rainbow trout and black bass. Motorless boats and boats with electric motors are permitted only on Krumbo Reservoir during the fishing season.

There is no overnight parking, camping, or swimming permitted on the refuge. Camping is available nearby at the BLM's Page Spring campground and Fish Lake campground and the privately owned Camper Corral. These areas are located south of the refuge. Camping is also available at Forest Service campgrounds that are located north of the refuge near Burns in the Ochoco and Malheur National Forests. Overnight accommodations are available at the Frenchglen Hotel, the Malheur Field Station, and motels in Burns and Hines.

The Malheur National Wildlife Refuge receives 37,850 visitors annually. All of the recreational use is wildlife-related. The leading categories of use are "interpretation" (43 percent) and "nonconsumptive wildlife-oriented recreation" (43 percent). In the second category, 67 percent of the use is "land vehicle wildlife/wild lands observation" and 32 percent of the use is "foot wildlife/wild lands observation."

Fishing, mostly cold-water, accounts for 11 percent of the total use and hunting accounts for 2 percent of the use.

Missisquoi National Wildlife Refuge   Missisquoi National Wildlife Refuge is located in northwestern Vermont on the eastern shore of Lake Champlain near the Canadian border. It was established in 1943, and the refuge headquarters are located 2 miles northwest of Swanton, Vt. The 5839-acre refuge includes most of the Missisquoi River delta where it flows into Missisquoi Bay of Lake Champlain. The refuge consists of calm waters and wetlands, which attract large flocks of migratory birds. Upland areas of the refuge are a hardwood mix of American elm, white ash, white oak, silver and red maple and open fields. Both provide habitat for migratory songbirds, resident mammals, and other wildlife; 201 species of birds and 34 mammals have been sighted. The refuge provides important feeding, resting, and breeding habitat for migratory birds, especially waterfowl, in the northern Lake Champlain section of the Atlantic Flyway. The refuge also protects the Shad Island great blue heron rookery, one of the largest in Vermont.

The Missisquoi River meanders through beds of wild rice and stands of wetland plants such as arrowhead, bullrush, and wild celery. In addition to 500 acres of natural marsh, the refuge includes 1800 acres of managed wetlands formed by three diked impoundments. While refuge waters attract waterfowl most of the year, peak use is in the fall, when large numbers of ring-necked ducks converge to feed along with green-winged teal, black ducks, and mallards. Water levels in impoundments are manipulated to encourage the growth of waterfowl food and cover plants, while also providing good ground-nesting habitat. There are 200 nesting structures (nest boxes, cones, and cylinders) located throughout the refuge to help wood ducks, common golden eyes, hooded mergansers, and black ducks increase their numbers. Haying, mowing, and controlled burning are methods used by wildlife managers to keep fields from reverting back to woodland. Limited raccoon trapping is used to control predation on waterfowl, and trapping is used to help protect dikes from muskrat and woodchuck burrowing.

Recreational and educational activities consistent with the primary goals of protecting and managing wildlife habitat are available throughout the year. The refuge is open daily from dawn to dusk. Missisquoi is a lightly used refuge, recording only 7773 visits per year. The period of heaviest use is April through October. Warm-water fishing accounts for 57 percent of the visits, followed by interpretation with 21 percent of the visits. Hunting accounts for 16 percent of the visits; migratory waterfowl made up 78 percent of the hunting. The Black Creek and Maquam Creek interpretive trails provide good opportunities for observation and photography of waterfowl and wading birds. These trails wind through 1.5 miles of wooded lowland. Visitors may also observe wildlife by walking along Mac's Bend Road next to the Missisquoi River. Boats and canoes may be launched from First Landing (Louie's Landing) all season. A second boat ramp, on Mac's Bend Road, is open only from September 1 until the end of the waterfowl season in December. Boating is permitted along the Missisquoi River and in Lake Champlain where it borders the refuge. Portions of the refuge are closed to boaters to protect wildlife habitat and are designated with "Closed Area" signs. Visitors may fish for bass, perch, landlocked salmon, and northern pike, from the banks of the Missisquoi River and from boats in the river and in Lake Champlain

in areas not posted or closed to public access. Portions of the refuge are open to waterfowl, deer, and small-game hunting in accordance with state and federal regulations. Blueberry picking is allowed in the bog off Tabor Road during July and August. Frog picking is allowed from July 15 to September 30 in the mowed refuge fields along Route 78 and Mac's Bend Road; the limit has been set at 12 frogs per person per day to avoid overharvesting. A valid Vermont hunting license or combination hunting-fishing license is required. Refuge nature trails are open for cross-country skiing in the winter. To protect wildlife and visitors, the following are prohibited: camping, open fires, cutting firewood, removing plants or animals, littering (state fine, $500), snowmobiling, leaving vehicles overnight, and abandoning wild or domestic animals in the refuge.

Montezuma National Wildlife Refuge Montezuma National Wildlife Refuge lies at the northern end of Cayuga Lake in the Finger Lakes region in the western part of New York. This 6446-acre refuge is located 5 miles east of Seneca Falls. The major east-west route across New York—the New York Thruway or I-90—passes through the center of the refuge. The Cayuga-Seneca Barge Canal forms the eastern boundary of the refuge and joins Cayuga Lake with the New York State Barge Canal, which borders the refuge on the northeastern side. Historically, Montezuma Marsh was one of the most productive marshes in North America. Prior to 1900, it extended north for 12 miles from Cayuga Lake and was up to 8 miles wide. By the early 1900s, all but a few hundred acres had been drained. In 1937, the Fish and Wildlife Service acquired the land and the Civilian Conservation Corps began work on a series of low dikes, to hold water and restore part of the once great marsh. Montezuma serves as a major resting area for waterfowl and other waterbirds on their journeys to and from nesting areas in northeastern and east-central Canada. Management of the refuge benefits wildlife and provides a place for people to visit and enjoy wildlife in their native habitat. The *Emergency Wetlands Act* (1986) allows the Fish and Wildlife Service to charge entrance fees for refuges such as Montezuma. Visitors may pay the daily entrance fee or purchase a Duck Stamp or Golden Eagle Passport, the latter two being good for 1 year.

The primary objective of the refuge is to provide resting, feeding, and nesting habitats for migratory birds. The refuge lies in the middle of one of the most active flight lanes of the Atlantic Flyway. The refuge has 3500 acres of diked pools, which are carefully managed to maintain the proper mix of emergent and underwater plants along with open water and mud flats to meet the specific requirements of various species in each season. A second important objective is to manage the refuge's diverse forest, grassland, and wetland habitats to provide healthy, self-sustaining populations of the many species of mammals, resident birds, reptiles, insects, and other animals normally found in central New York State. A third objective is to provide compatible wildlife-oriented educational and recreational opportunities for the 150,000 to 200,000 visitors who stop at the refuge each year. White-tailed deer, rabbits, foxes, and other wildlife may be seen throughout the year. During the summer, Canada geese and several duck species nest here, beginning in early March. Great blue herons nest in flooded trees in Tschache Pool. In the fall, from mid-September until freeze-up, Canada goose numbers peak at 50,000, and by mid-October duck numbers peak at 150,000. From late February through April, 85,000 Canada geese, 15,000 snow geese, and various ducks arrive, although the ducks are not as abundant as in the fall.

Recreational and educational opportunities are available year-round at Montezuma, from dawn to dusk. A visitor center is normally open on weekends from 9 A.M. to 5 P.M. that contains exhibits, leaflets, and restrooms (Figure 11.7). A short walking trail near the visitor center leads to an observation tower on the Main Pool. A 3-mile, one-way, self-guided auto tour route (on which it is necessary to double back) provides opportunities to observe and photograph wildlife from your car. There is another observation tower at the northern end of this route on Tschache Pool. During the winter, snow and ice generally keep the route closed. The 2-mile Esker Brook Trail is open year-round. This trail and the auto route are open for cross-country skiing and snowshoeing during the winter. Although fishing and boating are prohibited in refuge waters, the refuge maintains access to the state-owned Barge Canal. Three public fishing sites provide shore fishing opportunities. Public hunting, primarily for waterfowl and deer, is permitted under special regulations on portions of the refuge during the legal state seasons. With advance notice, educational programs are available to groups throughout the year. Teacher workshops are held at various times during the year. The refuge received 164,681 visits in 1987. "Nonconsumptive wildlife-oriented recreation" accounts for 53 percent of the use, "interpretation" for 40 percent, and "fishing" for 6 percent. Seventy-four percent of the first category is attributable to "land vehicle wildlife/wild lands observation," and 19 percent to "foot wildlife/wild lands observation." Only 0.8 percent of the visits are related to hunting.

National Bison Range   The National Bison Range is located in the Flathead Valley of western Montana, 35 miles north of Missoula. It protects one of the most important of the remaining herds of American bison or buffalo. Established in 1908, this refuge is one of the oldest big-game ranges in the country. Its 18,497 acres were purchased from the Flathead Indians. Here, 300 to 500 bison roam the grassland and parklike patches of timber. By 1883 bison were practically extinct, and by 1900 only 20 wild bison were known to exist in the United States. Fortunately, there were a few small, scattered bands of privately owned bison. The American Bison Society raised money to purchase these bison, and thus the Bison Range herd was started. This is

Figure 11.7 *Visitor center at Montezuma National Wildlife Refuge (New York).*

an area of steep hills and narrow canyons at the southern end of the Flathead Valley where the snow does not accumulate very deep. Besides the bison, the Range holds herds of whitetail and mule deer, elk, bighorn sheep, and pronghorns. There are also a few Rocky Mountain goats.

As Executive Order in 1912 established the range additionally as a federal bird reserve. Ring-necked pheasants and gray partridges are numerous, while lesser numbers of blue and ruffed grouse are present. In fall and winter, wild ducks congregate on Mission Creek in the northern portion of the range. Ninepipe National Wildlife Range, located 8 miles to the north, is administered by the Bison Range.

The range possesses several distinct plant-cover types, but it is primarily a grassland area composed of largely Palouse Prairie vegetation, with blue bunch wheat grass, rough fescue, and Idaho fescue as principal species. The upper hills contain small parklike stands of Douglas fir and western yellow pine. Creek bottoms are a thick mix of alder, juniper, aspen, birch, cottonwood, thorn apple, and willow, which are favored by whitetail deer. Mule deer frequent the higher slopes and ridges. A variety of wild flowers put on a dazzling display in May and June. Range condition, as governed by climate and use, determines the number of animals that can be supported. The herd varies in size from year to year, but generally contains 300 to 400 bison, 75 to 100 elk, 100 to 200 mule deer, 100 to 200 whitetails, 40 to 100 bighorn sheep, and 50 to 100 pronghorns. (Other animals that may be observed include badger, mink, beaver, muskrat, weasel, bobcat, coyote, black bear, and yellow-bellied marmots.) In order to keep the herds in balance with their food supply, a number from each species, approximately equal to the annual increase, must be removed each year. Surplus buffalo are removed in October. All animals are sold alive for exhibition, propagation, or meat.

A visitor center is located near the range's entrance on Route 212 (Figure 11.8). There are interpretive exhibits and information about the range. The highlight of a visit is the 2-hour, 19-mile Red Sleep Mountain self-guided drive. Five numbered

Figure 11.8 Visitor center at National Bison Range (Montana).

stops keyed to an interpretive tour guide along this route highlight: habitats, ecotones, glaciers and ducks, grasslands, and riparian zones. A short tour, the Buffalo Prairie Drive, is also available for those with less time (Figure 11.9). Both tours begin and end at the visitor center. The Red Sleep Mountain Scenic Drive is a one-way gravel road that has steep grades and switchbacks with no guardrails. This section of the road is closed in winter, and the less steep portion of the road becomes two-way. Motorcycles and bicycles are prohibited on all tour routes, and trailers or other towed units are not allowed on Red Sleep Mountain Drive. A picnic area with restrooms and a nature trail are available in the day use area near the visitor center. Public fishing is permitted along Mission Creek as posted and on the Jocko River where it flows through the southern edge of the range. Special tours are provided for organized groups when arrangements are made in advance. Otherwise, visitors are restricted from the open range.

The National Bison Range is a fairly popular refuge, recording 122,372 visits in 1986–1987. Fifty-five percent of the use is "noncomsumptive wildlife-oriented recreation"; 71 percent of this category is related to "land vehicle wildlife/wild lands observation" and 27 percent is related to "picnicking." The major category "interpretation" accounts for another 41 percent of the total use, 49 percent of which is at the interpretive center, 21 percent is "self-guided motorized wildlife tour route use, 15 percent is "other on-refuge programs," and 13 percent is "self-guided nonmotorized wildlife trails."

Okefenokee National Wildlife Refuge   The Okefenokee National Wildlife Refuge is located in southeastern Georgia and northern Florida. Of its total 395,080 acres, 391,402 acres are in Georgia and 3,678 acres are in Florida. Only five refuges in the lower 49 states are larger: the Desert (Nevada), the Charles M. Russell (Montana), the Cabeza Prieta (Arizona), the Kofa (Arizona), and the Sheldon (Nevada and Oregon). It was established in 1937 to preserve the 438,000-acre Okefenokee Swamp.

Figure 11.9   Buffalo Prairie Drive in National Bison Range.

Over 431 million board feet of timber—primarily cypress—were removed from the swamp from 1909 to 1927, when logging operations ceased. In 1974, 353,981 acres were designated a wilderness area. The swamp remains one of the oldest and most well preserved freshwater areas in the United States, extending 38 miles north to south and 25 miles east to west. Okefenokee is essentially a vast bog inside a huge, saucer-shaped depression that lies 103 to 128 feet above sea level. Peat deposits, as much as 15 feet thick in places, cover much of the swamp floor. The slow-moving waters of the Okefenokee are tea-colored due to the tannic acid released by decaying vegetation. The Suwanee River originates in the heart of, and is the principal outlet of, the swamp, and it drains southwest into the Gulf of Mexico. The swamp's south-eastern drainage is the St. Mary's River, which forms the Florida-Georgia boundary as it flows to the Atlantic. The swamp contains numerous islands and lakes, along with vast areas of nonforested terrain. Prairies cover about 60,000 acres of the swamp. Once forested, these expanses of marsh were created when fires burned out vegetation and the top layers of peat. The prairies harbor a variety of wading birds: herons, egrets, ibises, cranes, and bitterns. A variety of waterfowl, raptors, and songbirds inhabit the refuge. Large mammals in the refuge include black bear and whitetail deer.

Management activities within the refuge serve to preserve the natural qualities of the swamp, to support habitat for a variety of wildlife, and to provide recreational opportunities for visitors. The swamp's unique environmental qualities are preserved through protection, research, and progressive management. Endangered species that benefit from these management efforts include the red-cockaded woodpecker, American alligator, wood stork, and American bald eagle. Hunting, waterfowl banding, wildlife censuses, vegetative transects, and water-level recorders are used to monitor and manage wildlife populations and habitat conditions. Wildlife habitat is improved through the use of wildlife clearings, forest thinning and planting, and prescribed burning.

Although managed primarily for wildlife, public use is an important aspect of the refuge. Visitor facilities are provided on a portion of the refuge, creating a place where wildlife, wild lands, and people can interact in harmony. There are three entrances to the refuge: East, North, and West. The East Entrance is 8 miles southwest of Folkston, Ga., and another 3 miles west of State Route 23/121. This entrance offers visitors access to the core of the Okefenokee via the human-made historic Suwanee Canal. The swamp's most extensive open areas—Chesser, Grand, and Mizell Prairies—branch off the Canal. The small natural lakes and 'gator holes offer some of the best freshwater fishing in the refuge. The prairies are excellent for bird watching and are home of the Florida sandhill crane. The refuge's visitor center is located at this entry point, where concession facilities offer guided boat tours; snacks, souvenirs, and camping and fishing supplies; and boat, motor, canoe, and bicycle rentals. There are day-use shelters with restrooms on the Suwanee Canal. A picnic area is located near the visitor center. Other facilities at this location include the 0.55-mile Canal Digger's Trail and the entrance to the 4.5-mile wildlife observation drive to Chesser Island. Along this drive is located a prescribed burning exhibit and the 0.17-mile Peckerwood Trail. On Chesser Island there are three trails, two of which lead to observation towers: the 0.49-mile Chesser Island Homestead Trail, the 0.53-mile Deer-stand Trail and Tower, and the 1.5-mile round-trip Boardwalk to Tower.

The North Entrance to the refuge is south of Waycross, Ga. via Okefenokee Swamp Park, a private, nonprofit attraction that operates under a lease with the Fish and Wildlife Service. The moderate admission fee includes a 1.5-mile boat tour, all wildlife exhibits, wilderness walkways, an observation tower, Pioneer Island, the Swamp Creation Center, the Living Swamp Center, and wildlife shows. For an extra charge, a 10-mile tour can be taken or canoes can be rented. There are no overnight accommodations, so visitors have to stay in Waycross, Ga.

The West Entrance comes through the 82-acre Stephen C. Foster State Park, which is operated under a leasing agreement with the Fish and Wildlife Service and lies northeast of Fargo, Ga., on the Suwanee River. Overnight stays are possible here, with campsites and rental cottages. Boat tours are offered, and boats, motors, and bicycles may be rented.

It requires advanced planning to obtain the most from a visit to the Okefenokee National Wildlife Refuge, especially if one wants to camp and explore the interior. The only camping allowed is on overnight canoe trips and at designated areas in Stephen C. Foster State Park. Canoeing and motor boating are permitted year-round, but motors are limited to 10-horsepower or less. Fishing is permitted year-round, in accordance with Georgia laws. Swimming is prohibited in refuge waters—there are alligators here! Canoe trails through the Okefenokee may be traveled by campers holding permits for trips lasting 2 to 5 days. Very specialized regulations apply to this use, and any prospective visitor is recommended to request ahead of time and read the Fish and Wildlife Service pamphlet *Wilderness Canoeing in Okefenokee*. There are 15 designated canoe trails, one of which is closed. Water levels sometimes become too low to use certain canoe trails. There are limitations on use of the wilderness area. Each canoe trail is limited to one party daily. Due to seasonal peak use of trails and limited availability, all individuals and organizations or groups are limited to one trip per year during the months of March and April. Reservations to obtain permits for canoe travel into the Okefenokee Wilderness must be made by phone no earlier than 2 months in advance of the intended departure date. Lightening from summer thunderstorms is a greater hazard than either snakes or alligators.

The Okefenokee National Wildlife Refuge is one of the more heavily used refuges in the United States, ranking 16th nationally, with 351,152 annual visits. It is worth noting that the *total* public use is 945,205. This high ratio of visits to total public use (2.69) indicates that most visitors participate in almost three activities during each visit to the refuge. Most of the use at the refuge (97.1 percent) takes place in just two major categories of the seven that are employed: "interpretation" (61.4 percent) and "nonconsumptive wildlife-oriented recreation" (36.1 percent). The third-ranking category and only other major category where any significant use occurs, is "fishing" (2.1 percent). The use in the "interpretive" category is broadly spread over several subcategories: "self-guided interpretive exhibits and demonstrations" (32.3 percent), "visitor contact station" (17.3 percent, "self-guided motorized wildlife tour route" (9.8 percent), "other on refuge programs" (8.4 percent), "interpretive center" (6.2 percent), "conducted motorized wildlife tour route" (4.8 percent), and "conducted interpretive exhibits and demonstrations" (4.6 percent). Use in the "nonconsumptive wildlife-oriented recreation" category is distributed as follows: "land vehicle wildlife/wild lands observation" (68.2 percent), boat wildlife/wild lands observation" (10.6 percent), "camping" (9.3 percent), "picnicking" (4.9 percent), "photography"

(4.4 percent), and "foot wildlife/wild lands observation" (2.6 percent). Very limited, controlled big-game hunting for whitetail deer accounted for 195 visits for gun hunting and 194 visits for bow hunting.

Wichita Mountains National Wildlife Refuge   The 59,020 acre Wichita Mountains National Wildlife Refuge is located in southwestern Oklahoma in the Wichita Mountains, northwest of Lawton. Fort Sill Military Reservation borders it on the south. President McKinley designated the Wichita Forest Reserve in 1901, which became established as a game preserve (the Wichita Forest and Game Preserve) in 1905. A fence was built and in 1907 the New York Zoological Society donated 15 bison. In 1911–1912, 20 elk were brought from Jackson Hole, Wyo. to the area and in 1927 thirty head of Texas longhorns were introduced. In 1935, the area was redesignated the Wichita Mountains Wildlife Refuge and transferred from the Forest Service in the Agriculture Department to the Bureau of Biological Survey in the Interior Department, the predecessor of today's Fish and Wildlife Service. Careful management has resulted in a successful buffalo herd, which today is maintained at about 525 animals. Surplus animals are rounded up each fall and sold live at auction. The refuge now maintains about 300 longhorns. Management of elk and deer now includes a fall harvest to keep the herds within the carrying capacity of the range.

The Wichita Mountains trend east to west for almost 100 miles along an isolated fault line, and the refuge occupies the higher portions of the mountains. Spheroidal weathering has eroded the Wichita uplands' granite into domes and balanced boulders. Altitudes vary from a low of about 1350 feet near Lake Elmer to 2479 feet at the top of Mt. Pinchot. There are 20 lakes in the refuge over 2 acres in size, all of which were constructed primarily by the CCC in the 1930s. The refuge lies at a vegetation crossroads of the Great Plains. Excellent examples of the western shortgrass prairie consisting of buffalo and grama grasses can be found here along with bluestems, Indian grass, and switchgrass, which are more typical of the eastern tallgrass prairies. The oak timberlands, typical of the Cross Timbers, extend into the grasslands. Along the many streams, other trees such as cottonwood, walnut, pecan, and a few rare sugar maple exist. Although the Wichita Refuge is managed primarily for big-game animals, its lakes, woodlands, prairies, and granite outcrops provide habitat for a wide range of bird species at a mid-continent crossroads area for eastern and western species. The purpose of the refuge has been to perpetuate the environment in as pristine a condition as possible, consistent with the other objectives of maintaining representative populations of native wildlife (including longhorn cattle) while providing an opportunity for people to enjoy the natural setting.

The Wichita Mountains Wildlife Refuge offers as wide of a range of recreational opportunities as may be found at any other refuge. It is maintained in a natural and wild condition as open range with only a little over one-third of the area designated for public use; the rest is exclusively reserved for the animals, although a volunteer group known as the Association of the Friends of the Wichita's leads outings that often enter the restricted area. The Scenic Highway crosses the refuge. The Quanah Parker Visitor Center offers visitors a chance to learn more about the history behind the refuge and its wildlife. There are exhibits depicting the geology, flora, and fauna of the Wichita Mountains, and a 7-minute slide program introduces visitors to the refuge. The visitor center is open on weekends from March through November. A

self-guiding interpretive trail, with handicapped access, is located east of the visitor center parking area. Picnic areas are designated at Boulder, Lost Lake, Sunset, and Mount Scott. For group picnics of 20 to 60 people, the Boulder Cabin may be reserved. There are two campgrounds on the refuge. The Doris campground is located west of the Quanah Parker Visitor Center on Quanah Parker Lake and is fully developed, with water, fire grills and grates, picnic tables, a sanitary dump station, shower/restroom facilities, tent sites, limited electrical hookups, and trailer spaces. The Fawn Creek Reserved Youth campground is set aside for environmental education groups, scouts, and other youth programs. Camping facilities are tent sites, fire grills and grates, tables, and vault toilets. There are two units of the national Wilderness Preservation System in the refuge: Charons Garden Wilderness Area (5723 acres) and North Mountain Wilderness Area (2847 acres). Backcountry camping is allowed only in the Charons Garden Wilderness Area and is on a reservation-and-permit basis only. To protect the area, it is necessary to limit the number of permits to 10 at one time.

The refuge has 15 miles of good hiking trails for both novice and experienced hikers. The trails wind through scrub oak forest, across rocky mountains, and over grassy prairie lands. Wildlife abounds along these trails. The Dog Run Hollow Trail System—a national recreation trail—has trailheads at French Lake, Boulder, Lost Lake, and the Dog Run Hollow parking areas. Using the French Lake trailhead, visitors may choose between a 1-, 2-, or 4-hour hike through some of the more unique areas of the refuge. The Elk Mountain Trail System consists of two trails: One leads through the Charons Garden Wilderness Area and ends at the Post Oak–Treasure Lake parking area, and the other leads to the summit of Elk Mountain, from which a spectacular view of much of the refuge may be seen. Fishing is permitted in all of the refuge lakes in the public-use section. Largemouth bass, sunfish, crappie, and channel catfish are likely to be caught. A fishing pier with handicapped access is available near the visitor center. Hand-powered boats are permitted only on Jed Johnson, Quanah Parker, and French Lakes; electric trolling motors are permitted on boats 14 feet or less on these lakes.

The Wichita Mountains National Wildlife Refuge is the third most heavily used in the National Wildlife Refuge System: Public use totals 1,438,000 visits a year, a figure exceeded only by those for the Merritt Island (Florida) and Chincoteague (Virginia and Maryland) National Wildlife Refuges. Seventy-nine percent of this use is "nonconsumptive wildlife-oriented recreation," 62 percent of which is related to "land vehicle wildlife/wild lands observation" and another 25 percent to "foot wildlife/wild lands observation." "Picnicking" is the third subcategory, contributing 10 percent of the visits to the larger category. The second-ranking major category of use is "interpretation" (16 percent). Ninety-one percent of the interpretation is self-guided nonmotorized wildlife trails, and another 7 percent occurs at the interpretive center. Fishing accounts for 4 percent of the total use of the refuge.

References

Chadwick, Douglas H. "Mountain Refuge on the Prairie." *National Geographic Traveler.* September/October 1993, pp. 98–105.

Defenders of Wildlife. *A Report on the National Wildlife Refuge System.* Washington, D.C.: Defenders of Wildlife, 1977.

Fish and Wildlife Service. *Ash Meadows National Wildlife Refuge.* December 1990.

Fish and Wildlife Service. *Bertrand.* 1987.

Fish and Wildlife Service. *Birds—DeSoto National Wildlife Refuge.* 1985.

Fish and Wildlife Service. *Birds—Missisquoi National Wildlife Refuge.* June 1990.

Fish and Wildlife Service. *Birds of the J. N. "Ding" Darling National Wildlife Refuge, Sanibel and Captiva Islands and Surrounding Waters.* July 1993.

Fish and Wildlife Service. *Black Creek and Maquam Creek Trail.* May 1991.

Fish and Wildlife Service. *Desert National Wildlife Range—Nevada.* November 1992.

Fish and Wildlife Service. *DeSoto National Wildlife Refuge.*

Fish and Wildlife Service. *DeSoto National Wildlife Refuge—Cottonwood Nature Trail.* 1983.

Fish and Wildlife Service. *DeSoto National Wildlife Refuge—The Fall Migration of Snow Geese.*

Fish and Wildlife Service. *DeSoto National Wildlife Refuge—Fishery Management Program.* 1985.

Fish and Wildlife Service. *DeSoto National Wildlife Refuge—Wood Duck Nature Trail.* 1983.

Fish and Wildlife Service. *DeSoto National Wildlife Refuge Visitor Center.*

Fish and Wildlife Service. *Draft Environmental Impact Statement—Operation of the National Wildlife Refuge System.* 1975.

Fish and Wildlife Service. *Fact Sheet—J. N. "Ding" Darling National Wildlife Refuge.* June 1993.

Fish and Wildlife Service. *Final Environmental Impact Statement for the Chincoteague National Wildlife Refuge.* August 1992.

Fish and Wildlife Service. *Fishing on the Missisquoi Delta.* July 1992.

Fish and Wildlife Service. *J. N. "Ding" Darling National Wildlife Refuge.* April 1991.

Fish and Wildlife Service. *Malheur National Wildlife Refuge—Oregon.* January 1992.

Fish and Wildlife Service. *Malheur National Wildlife Refuge—Oregon: Hunting and Fishing.* September 1992.

Fish and Wildlife Service. *Mammals—Missisquoi National Wildlife Refuge.* July 1992.

Fish and Wildlife Service. *Map and Visitors Guide—National Bison Range.* Washington, D.C.: U.S. Government Printing Office, 1990.

Fish and Wildlife Service. *Missisquoi National Wildlife Refuge.* April 1991.

Fish and Wildlife Service. *Montezuma National Wildlife Refuge.* March 1988.

Fish and Wildlife Service. *National Bison Range—Self-Guided Auto Tour.* Washington, D.C.: U.S. Government Printing Office, 1990.

Fish and Wildlife Service. *National Wildlife Refuges—A Visitors Guide.*

Fish and Wildlife Service. *National Wildlife Refuge System.*

Fish and Wildlife Service. *National Wildlife Refuge System Public Use Report,* April 15, 1988.

Fish and Wildlife Service. *Okefenokee National Wildlife Refuge.*

Fish and Wildlife Service. *Pahranagat National Wildlife Range—Nevada.* 1991.

Fish and Wildlife Service. *Public Use Report.* 1988.

Fish and Wildlife Service. *Refuge Manual.* (Release 013), May 24, 1985.

Fish and Wildlife Service. *The U.S. Fish and Wildlife Service.*

Fish and Wildlife Service. *Wichita Mountains Wildlife Refuge.*

Fish and Wildlife Service. *Wilderness Camping in Okefenokee National Wildlife Refuge.*

Fisher, Ron. *Our Threatened Inheritance.* Washington, D.C.: National Geographic Society, 1984.

Foss, Phillip O. *Conservation in the United States: A Documentary History—Recreation.* New York: Chelsea House Publishers in association with Van Nostrand Reinhold, 1971.

Grove, Noel. *Wild Lands for Wildlife—America's National Refuges.* Washington, D.C.: National Geographic Society, 1984.

Laycock, George. *The Sign of the Flying Goose: A Guide to the National Wildlife Refuge System.* Garden City, N.Y.: Natural History Press, 1965.

Leask (see Table 11.7)

Leopold, Aldo. *A Sand County Almanac* and *Sketcher Here and There.* New York, Oxford University Press, 1949.

Riley, Laura, and William Riley. *Guide to the National Wildlife Refuges.* Garden City, N.Y.: Anchor Press/Doubleday, 1979.

National Park Service and Fish and Wildlife Service. *Assateague Island National Seashore/Chincoteague National Wildlife Refuge—Map and Guide.*

Okefenokee Swamp Park.

Reed, Nathaniel P., and Dennis Drabelle. *The United States Fish and Wildlife Service.* Boulder and London: Westview Press, 1984.

Stephen C. Foster State Park.

Suwanee Canal Recreation Concession. *Okefenokee National Wildlife Refuge.*

## CHAPTER 12

Bureau of Land Management

Transition from custodianship to action programs is part of the new direction by which BLM is putting the public lands to work in the public interest.

Stewart Udall (1966)

Much of the land under control of the Bureau of Land Management (BLM) is located in those areas of the western United States that are devoid of place names. No federal agency suffers more of an identity problem than the BLM. Out of ignorance, it has been lampooned by some as the "Bureau of Livestock and Mining." It is often difficult for the visitor to these lands to identify the boundary without a detailed map. There are few entry gates or signs indicating the location of the BLM lands. Despite this recognition problem, this one agency has more land under its jurisdiction— 268,976,599 acres—than the combined total of the National Forest System and National Park System. These lands are what remains of the once vast 1.8 million acres of public land originally acquired by the United States. Two-thirds of this original land went to individuals, industries, and states. Of that remaining, much was set aside for national parks, national forests, national wildlife refuges, and other public purposes. The remaining one-eighth (269 million acres) is left for the BLM to manage. Most of these lands are in the 11 western states and Alaska, although small parcels are scattered across the eastern United States. The BLM's mandate of multiple-use management and its responsibilities are varied and complex.

The *national resource lands* managed by the BLM are one of the best-kept secrets in the West, but it takes some work to locate them. Tour guides amply document the national parks and some of the national forests but do not highlight the recreational opportunities on those national resource lands administered by the BLM. It is true that recreational opportunities are scarce in places; this is due to three factors: (1) Many of the best sites have been transferred to other agencies, (2) many of these lands are remote from major population centers, and (3) the arid and semiarid nature of much of the environment is responsible for a shortage of water features. Despite the aridity of the BLM lands in the West, an endless number of recreational opportunities are possible. Recreational settings include desert mountain ranges, alpine tundra, evergreen forests, expanses of sagebrush, and red-rock canyons. In 1987 the

BLM started a new initiative entitled "Recreation 2000," which expands services and information to make the public aware of the recreational opportunities available on national resource lands.

HISTORICAL BACKGROUND

Among federal land-managing agencies, the BLM is a relative newcomer. It was established by President Harry Truman's *Reorganization Plan Number 3* (1946), which combined the *General Land Office* and the *Grazing Service* into a single agency. The General Land Office traces its origin back to 1812. It was established to handle the rapidly growing public land business as public land surveys, sales, and other transactions multiplied. Except for the period 1836–1841, when it was under the control of the president, the agency was in the Treasury Department until 1849. At this time it came under control of the new Department of the Interior, where it remained until its demise in 1946. The *Taylor Grazing Act*, passed in 1934, gave new responsibilities to the General Land Office and sought:

> to stop injury to the public grazing lands (excluding Alaska) by preventing overgrazing and soil deterioration; to provide for their orderly use, improvement, and development; to stabilize the livestock industry dependent upon the public range.

The previous function of the General Land Office had been primarily to dispose of public lands and minerals. Now the General Land Office had authority to manage these resources. The Taylor Grazing Act provided for a system of managing federal grazing resources through grazing districts (referred to as *Taylor grazing districts*) and limits on allowable grazing. The act also gave the Secretary of the Interior the authority to classify federal land according to the use for which it was best suited. A new Division of Grazing was created in the Interior Department and was renamed the *Grazing Service* in 1939. According to Marion Clawson, director of the BLM, "by June, 1946, the Grazing Service and the General Land Office had both been rendered ineffective, though in quite different ways" (Clawson, 37–38). By the 1920s the General Land Office ceased to be a real force in federal land management, and the Grazing Service was embroiled in controversy with Congress over grazing fees (Clawson, 1971, 33 and 37).

"The Bureau of Land Management from 1946 to 1960 was an agency in search of identity" (Muhn and Stewart, 1988, 54), although credit should be given to the strong role of Marion Clawson as director from 1948 to 1953. The 1960s brought rapid growth and change to the BLM. A multiple-use philosophy was endorsed for the public lands in the *Classification and Multiple-Use Act* (1964). The BLM was reorganized to reflect new programs and authorities under this mandate: Concerns for wildlife, recreation, soil, and water resources were integrated into traditional programs (range, forestry, lands, and minerals) through a land-use planning process. This act changed the BLM's land management process. No longer were lands classified on a case-by-case basis, evaluating petitions from land users; planning now occurred for the management of all lands and resources. One of the early classifications was for the Red Rocks Recreation Lands in the Spring Mountains near Las Vegas. This was

the first such designation made by Secretary of the Interior Udall in 1976 (Figure 12.1). Although the Classification and Multiple-Use Act was a temporary measure, the BLM in 1967 convinced the Interior Department that the classifications should be continued indefinitely. At the same time the BLM was classifying its lands, from 1964 to 1970 the *Public Land Law Review Commission* was studying the 3000 land laws and federal management of the public domain to identify problems and recommend new policy, programs, and legislation. Its chairman, Wayne Aspinall, had strong disagreements with the BLM over how the bureau was carrying out its responsibilities. The commission's 1970 report, *One Third of a Nation's Land* was the first comprehensive assessment of public land laws since the first law was implemented in 1792. The report made 137 numbered recommendations, one of which was ending the policy of disposing of unappropriated public-domain lands. Other issues arising at that time, such as wilderness debates, oil spills, and Alaska policies, plus the passage of the National Environmental Policy Act and other conservation legislation drew attention away from the commission's report.

In 1976, another act of Congress—the *Federal Land Policy and Management Act*—dramatically impacted the BLM by essentially repealing all public-land laws except the General Mining Act of 1872.

> Thirty years after its formation, the Bureau of Land Management was finally granted a mission. The Federal Land Policy and Management Act of 1976 (FLPMA) formally recognized what BLM had been doing on an interim basis for many years; managing the public lands under the principles of multiple use and sustained yield. FLMPA did much more though—it granted BLM new authorities and responsibilities, amended or repealed previous legislation, prescribed specific management techniques, and established BLM's California Desert Conservation Area. The Bureau was now in the big leagues (Muhn and Stewart, 1988, 158).

Figure 12.1   The Red Rocks Recreation Lands west of Las Vegas, were the first BLM lands classified in this category in 1967. Shown here is the Red Rock Canyon Scenic Backcountry Byway.

The major provisions of the Federal Land Policy and Management Act are as follows:

1. *Congressional Review of Land Withdrawals*   While FLPMA provided for the continuation of all classifications and withdrawals made under the Classification and Multiple-Use Act, Section 202 also required the BLM to review these actions when preparing new land-use plans. Congress was empowered to review sales of land in excess of 2500 acres or withdrawals of tracts of over 5000 acres, as well as decisions on principal uses of lands in areas greater than 100,000 acres.

By the end of the decade, the BLM had taken little action on reviewing existing withdrawals or classifications. It was preparing an inventory of these actions and implementing new land-use plans (resource management plans) in the field. Prior to FLPMA, 67 million acres of the public lands had been formally withdrawn from the public domain, including land for BLM and Forest Service recreation sites, land adjacent to national parks, land to protect watersheds, and land for Forest Service roadside zones. Under the Classification and Multiple-Use Act, the BLM had also classified more than 150 million acres of its own lands in the lower 49 states for retention, plus an additional 32 million acres in Alaska.

2. *Amendments to the Recreation and Public Purposes Act*   The original Recreation Act, passed in 1926, authorized transfer of "unreserved public lands" to states, counties, and municipalities for recreation purposes. This original act was amended in 1954 as the Recreation and Public Purposes Act; as amended in 1954, it included other public purposes and permitted nonprofit organizations to purchase or lease public lands for certain purposes. FLPMA amended the RPPA to increase the land the BLM could sell or lease to state and local governments, and it required public participation in all decisions to dispose of lands under the act.

3. *Law Enforcement*   FLPMA authorized the BLM to hire a force of uniformed rangers in the California Desert but required the bureau to rely on local officials as much as possible through cooperative agreements with local enforcement agencies.

4. *Finance and Budget*   FLPMA provided the BLM with long-needed authorities that made its work more efficient. FLPMA established the BLM's Working Capital Fund. It also allowed the BLM to accept contributions and donations for specific activities on BLM lands (such as wildlife habitat improvements or recreational developments) and allowed the BLM to establish service charges for applications and documents.

5. *Land Exchanges and Acquisitions*   FLPMA provided for cash payments from the government to equalize values of exchanged lands. It also gave the BLM authority for acquisition under its land-use plans but limited the government's power of eminent domain. The BLM was allowed to use Land and Water Conservation funds to acquire public recreation lands.

6. *Special Management Areas*   Section 202 of FLPMA authorized the BLM to identify *areas of critical environment concern* (ACECs) through its planning process. ACECs were defined as areas "within the public lands where special management attention is required" to protect "historic, cultural or scenic areas, fish and wildlife resources, or other natural systems or processes. . . ."

7. *Livestock Grazing*   FLPMA authorized a study of grazing fees but prohibited any increase in the fee in 1977. To assure long-term stability and use of BLM lands

by the livestock industry, it also authorized 10-year grazing permits and required 2-year notices of cancellation. BLM grazing advisory boards were directed to advise the BLM on the development of allotment management plans and the allocation of range improvement funds.

8. *Wilderness* Section 602 of FLPMA directed the BLM to review the public lands for wilderness potential as set forth in the 1964 Wilderness Act. The act also directed BLM to conduct early wilderness reviews on all lands designated as primitive or natural areas before November 1, 1975.

9. *Wild Horses and Burros* FLPMA amended the *Wild and Free-Roaming Horse and Burro Act* (1971) to authorize the use of helicopters in horse and burro roundups. Wild horse and burro populations had more than tripled since passage of the latter act. Horse numbers on BLM lands in the West were estimated at more than 60,000 compared with 17,000 in the late 1960s.

10. *Minerals Management* FLPMA modified the formulas for distribution of funds collected under the *Mineral Leasing Act* (1920) and the *Geothermal Steam Act* (1970). It also required persons holding claims under the *General Mining Law* (1872) to record their claims with the BLM within 3 years. FLPMA authorized loans to state and local governments to relieve social and economic impacts of mineral development and directed the Secretary of the Interior to develop stipulations that would prevent unnecessary or undue degradation of the land.

11. *Other Provisions* FLPMA established the California Desert Conservation Area and directed the BLM to develop a land allocation plan for the area by 1980. FLPMA (in 1976) also repealed the *Homestead Act* (except in Alaska, where it was given a 10-year life) and other settlement acts. The act also decided how future directors of the BLM would be selected—by the president, with approval from the Senate.

The role of the Alaska Native Claims Settlement Act (ANCSA, 1971) in resolving the claims of Alaskan natives and paving the way for the construction of the Alaskan pipeline has been documented in earlier chapters of this book. The Alaska National Interest Lands Conservation Act (ANILCA, 1980) and its impact on land management agency jurisdiction was a major topic in Chapter 4. In 1958, over 80 percent of Alaska's 375 million acres were open public domain, under the jurisdiction of the BLM. The Alaska Statehood Act (1958) marked the beginning of transfer of large portions of BLM-administered lands to the state of Alaska. In this massive transfer of real estate in Alaska, which still continues today, the BLM lost vast acreages under its jurisdiction, while the other three major federal land-managing agencies gained: BLM lands have decreased from 309 million acres in 1958 to an ultimate entitlement of 47 million acres. The gainers in Alaska at the expense of the BLM are the Fish and Wildlife Service (53.2 million acres), the National Park Service (44.5 million acres), the Forest Service (2.3 million acres), the state of Alaska (105 million acres), and Alaskan natives (44 million acres).

ANILCA also designated two new types of special areas for BLM-administered lands in Alaska: the 1-million-acre White Mountain National Recreation Area and the 1.2-million-acre Steese National Conservation Area. These areas were given special classification and protection because they include representative landforms, wildlife habitat, and vegetation complexes peculiar to the interior Alaska uplands, ranging

from spruce and birch to willow, alder, and alpine tundra. These classifications still permit mining of existing valid claims, but in the recreation area, no additional mining claims may be made. The Steese National Conservation Area consists of two portions. One part is on the northern side of the Steese Highway and adjacent to and east of the White Mountains National Recreation Area; the other part lies south and east within the drainage of Birch Creek, a designated wild river. The Steese National Conservation Area has excellent caribou habitat, and there are 125 miles of recreation trails. The White Mountains National Recreation Area lies west of the northern unit of the Steese National Conservation Area and north of the Steese Highway. It encloses the Beaver Creek drainage and some high peaks of the White Mountains. Beaver Creek is designated a wild river, and there are two recreation trails.

BUREAU OF LAND MANAGEMENT TODAY

Mission of the BLM

The Bureau of Land Management is an agency within the Department of the Interior that is responsible for managing the nation's public lands and resources in a combination of ways that best serves the needs of the American people. Management is based on the principles of multiple use and sustained yield—a combination of uses that balances the needs of future generations for renewable and nonrenewable resources. These resources include not only the subject of this chapter—recreation—but also range; timber; minerals; watershed; fish and wildlife; wilderness; and natural scenic, scientific and cultural values.

Organization of the Bureau of Land Management

The BLM's national office is in the Interior Department at Washington, D.C., where the director resides. In addition, there are 12 state offices, 58 district offices, and 140 resource area offices. The state offices are Alaska (Anchorage), Arizona (Phoenix), California (Sacramento), Colorado (Denver), Eastern states (Alexandria, Va.), Idaho (Boise), Montana (Billings), Nevada (Reno), New Mexico (Santa Fe), Oregon (Portland), Utah (Salt Lake City), and Wyoming (Cheyenne). Other administrative centers are the Boise Interagency Fire Center (Boise, Idaho) and the Service Center (Denver, Colo.). Table 12.1 identifies the districts by state, and Table 12.2 identifies the resource areas by state. Figure 12.2 delineates the geographic extent of the districts and resource areas and shows the locations of the state and district offices. The numbers in Table 12.2 identify the resource areas in Figure 12.2. The BLM has about 9650 employees, most of whom work in field offices in the West. Multiple-use management requires many skills and talents. Foresters, range conservationists, wildlife biologists, archaeologists, cadastral surveyors, engineers, recreation specialists, and many other professionals are needed to carry out the mission of today's Bureau of Land Management.

Table 12.1   BLM-State and Districts

State	District	State	District
Alaska	Anchorage	Nevada	Elko
	Glennallen		Winnemucca
	Artic		Carson City
	Kobuk		Ely
	Steese/White Mountains		Las Vegas
Arizona	Arizona Strip		Battle Mountain
	Phoenix	New Mexico	Albuquerque
	Safford		Las Cruces
	Yuma		Roswell
California	Bakersfield	Oregon	Lakeview
	Susanville		Burns
	Ukiah		Vale
	California Desert District		Prineville
Colorado	Craig		Salem
	Montrose		Eugene
	Canyon City		Roseberg
	Grand Junction		Medford
Idaho	Boise		Coos Bay
	Burley		Spokane, Wash.
	Idaho Falls	Utah	Salt Lake
	Salmon		Cedar City
	Shoshone		Richfield
	Coeur d'Alene		Moab
Montana	Miles City		Vernal
	Dickinson, N.D.	Wyoming	Worland
	Lewiston		Rawlins
	Butte		Rock Springs
			Casper

Source: Bureau of Land Management.

BLM Programs

Although the major function of this chapter is to highlight the recreational use of BLM land, a brief overview of the programs of the agency will first be undertaken. These programs cover four major areas: (1) lands and renewable resources, (2) minerals, (3) support services, and (4) management services. Understanding the recreation mission of the Bureau of Land Management is much more easily understood if all of the other programs are also understood.

Lands and Renewable Resources Programs

Recreation   The BLM manages a full range of recreational activities and accommodates about 73 million recreation visits to public lands each year. This includes national conservation areas, one national recreation area, about 2000 miles of the Wild and Scenic River System, and about 2200 miles of national trails. In addition, the BLM manages 85,000 miles of streams containing trout, salmon, and other sport fish; more than 4 million acres of lakes and reservoirs; more than 765 developed recreation sites; and thousands of areas open to a wide variety of dispersed types of recreational uses.

Table 12.2   BLM Resource Areas

Arizona	40. Bruneau	74. Tonopah	109. Tillamook
1. Gila	41. Cascade	26. Walker (CA)	110. Tioga
2. Havasu	42. Challis	75. Wells	111. Umpqua
3. Kingman (NV)	43. Cottonwood		112. Yamhill
4. Lower Gila	44. Deep Creek	New Mexico	
5. Phoenix	45. Emerald Empire	76. Carlsbad (TX)	South Dakota
6. San Simon (NM)	46. Jarbridge	77. Farmington	113. South Dakota
7. Shivwits	47. Lemhi	78. Mimbres	
8. Vermillion	48. Medicine Lodge	79. Rio Puerco	Texas
9. Yuma	49. Monument	80. Roswell	76. Carlsbad (NM)
	50. Owyhee	6. San Simon (AZ)	53. Oklahoma (OK, KS)
California	51. Pocatello	81. Socorro	
10. Alturas	52. Snake River	82. Taos	Utah
11. Arcata		83. White Sands	114. Bear River
12. Barstow	Kansas		115. Beaver River
13. Bishop	53. Oklahoma (OK, TX)	North Dakota	116. Book Cliffs
14. Caliente		84. Dickinson	117. Diamond Mountain
15. Cedarville (NV)	Montana		118. Dixie
16. Clear Lake	54. Big Dry	Oklahoma	119. Escalante
17. Eagle Lake (NV)	55. Billings	53. Oklahoma (TX, KS)	120. Grand
18. El Centro	56. Dillion		121. Henry Mountain
19. Folsom	57. Garnet	Oregon	122. House Range
20. Hollister	58. Great Falls	85. Alsea	123. Kanab
21. Indio	59. Havre	86. Andrews	124. Pony Express
22. Lamontan (NV)	60. Headwaters	87. Ashland	125. Price River
23. Needles	61. Judith	88. Baker	34. San Juan (CO)
24. Redding	62. Phillips	89. Butte Falls	126. San Rafael
25. Ridgecrest	63. Powder River	90. Central Oregon	127. Sevier River
26. Walker (NV)	64. Valley	91. Clackamas	128. Warm Springs
		92. Coast Range	
Colorado	Nebraska	93. Deschutes	Washington
27. Glenwood Springs	65. Newcastle (WY)	94. Dillard	129. Border
28. Grand Junction		95. Drain	130. Wenatchee
29. Gunnison	Nevada	96. Glendale	
30. Kremmling	66. Caliente	97. Grant Pass	Wyoming
31. Little Snake	15. Cedarville (CA)	98. Jordan	131. Buffalo
32. Northeast	17. Eagle Lake (CA)	99. Klamath	132. Cody
33. Royal Gorge	67. Egan	100. Lakeview	133. Grass Creek
34. San Juan (UT)	68. Elko	101. Malheur	134. Great Divide
35. San Luis	3. Kingman (AR)	102. McKenzie	135. Green River
36. Uncompahgre Basin	22. Lahontan (CA)	103. Myrtlewood	136. Kemmerer
37. White River	69. Paradise-Denio	104. North Umpqua	137. Lander
	70. Schell	105. Santiam	65. Newcastle (NE)
Idaho	71. Shoshone-Eureka	106. South Umpqua	138. Pinedale
38. Bennett Hills	72. Sonoma-Gerlach	107. South Valley	139. Platte River
39. Big Butte	73. State-Line	108. Three Rivers	140. Washakie

Note: Numbers refer to Fig. 12.2.
Source: Bureau of Land Management.

Forestry   The BLM administers 90 million acres of forested lands. Most of these lands are in Alaska; however, some 26 million acres lie within the lower 49 states, including 21 million acres of woodlands and 5 million acres of commercial forest lands. The most valuable commercial timber resources on BLM lands are those of the *Oregon and California Revested Lands* (O & C Lands). These revested lands had been granted in 1866 to the Oregon and California (O & C) Railroad Company for con-

struction of a line from Portland to the California border. Congress in 1869 placed certain stipulations on the sale of these lands, which totaled 3.7 million acres. The company ignored the conditions, and in 1916 the federal government revoked title to more than 2 million acres. In 1919, the government reclaimed another 93,000 acres from the nearby Coos Bay Wagon Road Grant. The *Oregon and California Revested Lands Sustained Yield Management Act* (1937) specified management directions for these lands by the General Land Office. These lands, which came under the jurisdiction of the BLM in 1946, exist in a checkerboard pattern of private, state, and federal ownership and are 85 percent old-growth Douglas fir–covered. It is from these Douglas fir forests on the western slope of the Cascade Range in western Oregon that most of the timber receipts in the Bureau of Land Management are derived. Table 12.3 identifies the value of timber and nontimber sales by state. Ninety-three percent of the total revenues brought in on BLM timbered lands comes from western Oregon, and this valuable timberland is the revested O & C lands.

Wilderness   The BLM, as mandated by the FLPMA (1976), has developed a wilderness review process for its lands. In 1994 there are 67 wilderness areas in nine states and covering 1.6 million acres. In addition, there are currently 777 wilderness study areas covering 26 million acres; along with 2.7 million acres of wilderness recommended to Congress as suitable for designation as wilderness.

Range   The BLM manages livestock grazing on 165 million acres of public lands. About 18,800 ranchers and farmers graze livestock on BLM-administered lands. About 90 percent of these permittees have small (less than 100 head) or medium (100 to 500 head) livestock operations. The issue of grazing fees continues to be the most controversial publicly debated issue.

Table 12.3   BLM-Summary of Total Timber and Nontimber Forest Product Sales—FY91

Administrative State	Timber Sales	Nontimber Forest Product Sales[a]	Grand Total
Alaska	$ 7,867.00		$ 7,867.00
Arizona	6,207.80	$ 4,711.00	10,919.30
California	1,605,388.60	1,807.00	1,607,195.60
Colorado	63,037.17	52,537.90	115,575.07
Idaho	846,512.58	821.50	847,334.08
Montana	406,888.49	15,973.05	422,861.54
Nevada	55,954.60	51,482.00	107,436.60
New Mexico	38,063.00	8,321.00	46,384.00
Oregon:			
Eastern[b]	8,214,966.05	6,782.00	8,221,748.05
Western[c]	151,231,558.74	58,380.47	151,289,939.21
Utah	49,095.90	32,517.00	81,612.90
Wyoming	30,015.34	7,020.00	37,035.34
Total	$162,555,555.27	$240,353.42	$162,795,908.69

[a]This heading includes "negotiated nontimber forest product sales less than $1,000," which were reported in this table in a separate column prior to the 1986 edition.
[b]Eastern Oregon comprises public lands that include, and extend eastward from, Range 9, East, Willamette Meridian, and public lands in the state of Washington.
[c]Western Oregon comprises the revested Oregon and California (O&C) lands, the reconveyed Coos Bay Wagon Road lands, and other public lands that include, and extend westward from, Range 8 East, Willamette Meridian.
Source: BLM, *Public Land Statistics—1991*, Washington, D.C.: Government Printing Office, September 1992.

Cultural Resources   The BLM evaluates and protects the government's largest, most varied body of cultural resources. Of the 150,000 cultural properties identified, 350 archaeological and cultural properties are entered in the National Register of Historic Places, and an additional 1200 are considered to have nationally significant values. These range from campsites of the Hemisphere's earliest inhabitants to physical reminders of the historic setting of the West.

Wildlife   Wildlife habitat is managed for more than 3000 plant and animal species, including 140 that are threatened or endangered. The BLM manages and protects key riparian habitat along 85,000 miles of streams. The BLM manages habitats for one out of every five big-game animals in the United States, including caribou, brown/grizzly bears, desert bighorn sheep, moose, mule deer, and antelope.

Wild Horses and Burros   The BLM manages more than 43,000 wild horses and burros on public lands.

Lands   The BLM issues leases, rights-of-way, and use permits for a wide variety of uses of public land including parks, power transmission and distribution lines, petroleum products collection and transmission systems, advertising and motion picture filming, and recreational events.

Minerals Programs

Fluid Minerals Leasing   The BLM manages onshore oil, gas, and geothermal resources; conducts lease sales; issues leases; and administers operations on about 80,000 onshore oil and gas leases on 70 million acres.

Coal Leasing   The BLM conducts lease sales, issues leases, and administers operations on approximately 550 coal leases on 800,000 acres. Public lands provide nearly 20 percent of the nation's coal production.

Mineral Materials   For many communities in the West, public lands continue to be the only source for sand, gravel and other common stone, which are sold by the BLM for such uses as construction of transportation systems and expansion of communities.

Other Minerals Activity   Nonenergy minerals are managed through leasing and mining claims programs. Lease sales and operations for nonenergy leasable minerals are administered under this program. About 50 percent of the nation's potash, 45 percent of its sodium compounds, and 70 percent of its lead are mined on public lands. The BLM also administers about 2.4 million mining claims. Public lands in the West, particularly Nevada, are supporting a major new gold rush; 14 of the top 25 U.S. gold mines are on public lands.

Support Services Programs

Law Enforcement   This program protects against unauthorized uses of public lands and enforces public land laws through the use of special agents and rangers.

Land Information Systems   The Bureau of Land Management operates Land Information Systems to manage data and information about public lands including survey records, ownership status, and resources for the BLM and other users.

Hazardous Materials   This program identifies and arranges the cleanup of hazardous material sites on public lands.

Cadastral Survey   This program conducts federal surveys and provides maintenance of all official Public Land Survey System records covering 30 states.

Fire   This program manages prescribed fires and aggressively suppresses an average of 2350 wildfires.

Management Services Programs   Revenues and receipts are collected and disbursed. The BLM is a primary generator of revenues for the federal government. The development and use of BLM lands and resources generate more than $800 million annually from a variety of sources, including timber sales, sale of public lands, grazing leases, right-of-way leases, permits, and mineral receipts. In the period 1980–1990, state and local governments received nearly $4 billion as their share of revenues collected from the lease or sale of public land resources and as payments for federal tax-exempt lands. In addition, management services provides a variety of services such as personnel, employee development, management research, program evaluations and procurement, and budget development.

GEOGRAPHIC DISTRIBUTION OF BLM LANDS

Figure 12.3 shows the distribution of the lands under the control of the BLM. This map clearly indicates that these lands are exclusively a Western phenomenon, being located in the 11 western states and Alaska. Despite the large jurisdictional losses in Alaska to other federal agencies, the state of Alaska, and the Alaskan natives, there is still 90 million acres in Alaska (25 percent of the state) under the BLM's control. This is still one-third of the total BLM-administered land. Most of this land in Alaska is in interior and northwestern Alaska. Table 12.4 summarizes the geographic distribution of public lands under the exclusive jurisdiction of the BLM. Nevada ranks second in acreage and first percentage-wise among the states in BLM dominance—48 million acres, or 69 percent of the total state area. It is no wonder that the short-lived Sagebrush Rebellion had its start in the Nevada legislature in 1979. Utah ranks third, with 22 million acres of BLM land, or 42 percent of the state's area. Nevada is clearly the leader in acreage of grazing districts—45 million acres—followed by Utah's 20 million acres. Wyoming has 18 million acres of BLM land, which is 30 percent of the state's geographic base. The western state with the least amount of BLM-administered land is Washington—327,284 acres, located mainly in the northeastern corner of the state.

NATURE OF BLM LANDS

The land administered by the BLM has been referred to as the "residue (or leftover) land that no one else wanted." It is a geographic fact that most BLM lands are dry

Table 12.4 Public Lands under Exclusive Jurisdiction of the BLM (in acres)—FY91

State	Vacant Public Lands			Reserved Lands		Grand Total
	Outside Grazing Districts	Within Grazing Districts	Total	LU	Other	
Alabama	3,157	—	3,157	—	107,846	111,003
Alaska	90,437,842	—	90,437,842	—	—	90,437,842
Arizona	1,435,601	10,093,191	11,528,792	32,321	2,696,510	14,257,623
Arkansas	2,059	—	2,059	—	289,107	291,166
California	12,936,771	2,479,947	15,416,718	—	1,823,557	17,240,275
Colorado	497,920	6,788,274	7,286,194	37,248	986,086	8,309,528
Florida	1,512	—	1,512	—	23,765	25,277
Idaho	427,389	10,731,053	11,158,442	72,276	628,705	11,859,423
Illinois	3	—	3	—	5,000	5,003
Indiana	—	—	—	—	200	200
Iowa	—	—	—	—	1,400	1,400
Kansas	42	—	42	—	—	42
Louisiana	4,376	—	4,376	—	305,260	309,636
Michigan	47	—	47	—	74,807	74,854
Minnesota	8,198	—	8,198	—	145,211	153,409
Mississippi	2,206	—	2,206	—	55,971	58,177
Missouri	400	—	400	—	2,175	2,575
Montana	1,151,270	4,936,210	6,087,480	1,808,896	170,551	8,066,927
Nebraska	7,613	—	7,613	—	—	7,613
Nevada	3,136,944	44,651,455	47,788,399	3,127	207,299	47,998,825
New Mexico	1,369,070	11,146,242	12,515,312	229,500	134,014	12,878,826
North Dakota	66,303	—	66,303	—	181	66,484
Oklahoma	2,630	—	2,630	—	—	2,630
Oregon	577,352	12,458,733	13,036,085	80,101	2,598,050	15,714,236
South Dakota	271,558	—	271,558	—	7,592	279,150
Utah	—	20,214,644	20,214,644	45,033	1,677,596	21,937,273
Washington	324,707	—	324,707	—	2,577	327,284
Wisconsin	2,577	—	2,577	—	157,631	160,208
Wyoming	3,925,428	11,274,844	15,200,272	10,434	3,189,004	18,399,710
Total	116,592,975	134,774,593	251,367,568	2,318,936	15,290,095	268,976,599

Source: BLM, *Public Land Statistics—1991*, Washington, D.C.: U.S. Government Printing Office, September 1992.

and rather barren. A high percentage of these lands are governed by steppe and desert climate, and most receive only 5 to 12 inches of precipitation per year. These lands were not selected in the homesteading process of the 19th century since they were not generally suited for cultivation. This is due to both lack of rainfall and rough topography. Many of the desert valleys are interior *bolsons* (basins of interior drainage) with outwash and playas with excess alkalis in them. Limited grazing is the best agricultural use on some of these lands. The most extensive major type of vegetation is northern desert shrub, and sagebrush is the most common plant. This vegetation is found in most of Nevada, much of Utah and western Wyoming, southern Idaho, and southeastern Oregon. In the drier and hotter climate of southern California, southern Arizona, and southern Nevada, southern desert shrub dominates; these are woody plants such as the Joshua tree, yuccas, and creosote bush. In parts of Arizona, the saguaro makes a stately appearance. Pinyon-juniper woodland

dominates in the foothills of the mountains, and short grasses appear in the Great Plains. Where mountains rise high enough to intercept more moisture, forests appear. Many of these mountainous, forested areas have been set aside as national forests; for example, the Inyo, Humboldt, Dixie, and Wasatch. The best forest resources on BLM lands are found on the western slope of the Cascade Range in western Oregon in the O & C lands. Extensive areas of forest occur in interior Alaska, but these are mainly pole-sized trees.

Scattered throughout these dry western lands are streams, lakes, and artificial water bodies that have recreational potential. These "oases" in the dry West are ideal for camping and fishing opportunities. The Calf Creek Recreation Area in southern Utah is an example of such an area (Figure 12.4). Big-game animals are plentiful in these lands for both consumptive and nonconsumptive use. The geology in many places offers outstanding features, such as the red-rock country and the slickrock country. Exquisite landforms and canyons have been carved in these areas. Mountains can offer altitudinal zonation and cooler temperatures and environments. These lands also contain many historic sites such as old mining towns and historic forts. There are also many cave dwellings and petroglyphs. To many, the most valuable "resource" of these lands is the wide-open spaces.

PLANNING

Multiple-use, sustained-yield goals and land-use planning are the cornerstones of managing BLM lands. In the 1970s, systematic land-use planning was implemented in the field. *Management framework plans* (MFPs) were prepared for 80 to 85 percent of BLM lands in the lower 49 states by 1976. Data from resource inventories were

Figure 12.4   The Calf Creek Recreation Area in the BLM's Escalante Resource Area (Utah) is a delightful oasis of green that is extremely attractive for camping and picnicking.

considered together with economic and social information to develop and compare management alternatives. After holding a series of public meetings, BLM resource areas reviewed and finalized the MFPs, and implemented them as management tools. Ironically, the National Environmental Policy Act (NEPA) had much to do with the demise of the BLM's first successful, agency-wide planning system. Court decisions had made Environmental Impact Statements (EISs) the BLM's primary tool for analyzing resources, impacts, and management alternatives on the ground—especially for BLM's range activities. MFPs were becoming duplicative. Also, Section 202 of FLPMA required the BLM to develop a more comprehensive land-use planning system for "developing, displaying, and assessing" management alternatives. It also directed the Bureau to strengthen its coordination with state and local governments.

Starting in 1977, the BLM began developing *resource management plans* (RMPs), which were to be prepared in the field in conjunction with EISs. In 1979, the BLM phased in a transition from MFPs to RMPs, whereby scheduled updates of MFPs would be replaced by RMPs. By 1988, 61 RMPs were completed, which are about half of the RMPs that will eventually be prepared. The BLM has scheduled replacement of all its MFPs by 1994.

Basic Steps in Completing a Resource Management Plan

1   Develop a plan for public participation.
2   Identify issues.
3   Develop planning criteria (set standards for data collection and formulation of management alternatives).
4   Gather information and inventory resources.
5   Analyze the management situation.
6   Formulate management alternatives.
7   Estimate the effects of alternatives.
8   Select a preferred alternative.
9   Publish a draft RMP/EIS (with a 90-day comment period).
10   Publish the final RMP/EIS (with a 30-day protest period).
11   Monitor and evaluate the overall plan.
12   Prepare activity plans.

Public meetings conducted by the employees developing the plan are required during issue identification, development of planning criteria, and publication of both the draft and final RMP/EIS. Once the RMP is approved, the BLM prepares more specific activity plans for specific programs (for example, allotment management plans or habitat management plans); the activities proposed in these plans must conform to the RMP. For actions that do not, the district manager prepares a plan amendment, again with participation from the public.

SPECIAL MANAGEMENT AREAS

Beginning in the 1960s, the BLM identified and designated millions of acres of the public lands in the lower 49 states as special management areas to recognize unique or threatened resources on the public lands. In 1965, Secretary of the Interior Udall

and BLM director Stoddard proposed that the BLM designate 130 natural areas on BLM lands, totaling about 500,000 acres. These lands, categorized as ecological or geological areas, were set aside for research and educational use through BLM's classification process. In the late 1960s, the BLM began to designate recreation lands and other areas, such as *national natural landmarks*. One of the early designations was the Red Rocks Recreation Lands in the Spring Mountains near Las Vegas, the first such designation made by Udall in 1967. This protection of lands for their amenity resource value marked a new trend in resource management.

Special management areas were designated in two ways: by congressional and administrative action. Congress established national trails, wild and scenic rivers, and national conservation areas. The BLM and the Interior Department designated recreation areas, primitive areas, natural areas (including outstanding natural areas and research natural areas), resource conservation areas, and other areas, such as the Little Book Cliffs Wild Horse Range. After FLPMA passed, the BLM also designated areas of critical environmental concern (ACECs). In the early 1970s, under Director Silcock, the BLM began to set aside major amounts of public lands. About 27,000 acres of land in the Organ Mountains in southern New Mexico were dedicated in 1971 as a recreation area. In Montana, Humbug Spires, Bear Trap Canyon, and the Centennial Mountains were designated as primitive areas. Bear Trap Canyon was subsequently designated the BLM's first wilderness area in 1983, as part of the Lee Metcalf Wilderness. The BLM's Boise District had recognized for many years that the canyon country along the Snake River provided a unique and valuable nesting area for birds of prey. Here, 500-foot cliffs along 80 miles of the river attract a large assortment of hawks, eagles, osprey, vultures, and falcons. In 1971, Secretary of the Interior Morton withdrew 26,000 acres of land along the Snake River in Idaho for management as a natural area. The area was renamed the Snake River Birds of Prey Area by Secretary Andrus, who enlarged it to 482,640 acres in 1980.

The nation's first conservation area, the King Range National Conservation Area, was established by Congress in 1970 on 54,000 acres of public lands along the northern coast of California. Congress required the BLM to develop a management plan before it was officially designated in 1974. The *King Range Act* (1970) provided for land acquisition, and exchanges, with private owners and the state of California and established a program of multiple use and sustained yield for the area. Because private and state lands were intermixed with public lands, the BLM set up seven management zones in the area to designate primary uses (three zones were for recreational uses, two were for residential uses, one was for forest management, and one was for wildlife habitat).

The Classification and Multiple Use Act (CMUA) of 1964 specifically called for an inventory of BLM lands in the California Desert to determine what areas should remain in federal ownership. This represented a real challenge to the BLM due to the rapidly increasing public use of the area. Almost all of the BLM's 12.5 million acres—which represented just half of the desert's total area—were classified for retention and multiple-use management. In 1971, Secretary Morton designated 19 areas on 2.7 million acres as *national recreation land*, and recreational use in the area doubled after this special designation. In 1976, FLPMA established the California Desert Conservation Area in a large area of southeastern California. Through a series of public meetings, the BLM developed a management plan that was approved in December

1980. The plan classified allocated desert land into four categories according to their primary uses. The largest classification was "Class L (Limited Use)," applied to 48.5 percent, or 5.9 million acres, of the geographic area. This category allowed only low-intensity multiple land uses in order to protect resource values. "Class M (Moderate Use)" lands struck a balance between use and preservation, allowing a variety of uses on 3.3 million acres (28 percent of the area). "Class C (Controlled Use)" areas totaled 2.1 million acres (17 percent of area). Most of these lands—45 sites totaling 2.0 million acres—were designated areas of critical environmental concern and proposed for inclusion into the National Wilderness Preservation System. "Class I (Intensive Use)" allowed a diversity of concentrated uses on 500,000 acres. The plan designated most of this acreage as off-road vehicle (ORV) areas.

RECREATION 2000

From the late 1970s through the mid-1980s the BLM was not able to focus much attention on its recreation program because of other national priorities specified by FLPMA (1976). This was unfortunate, since the recreational use on the public lands was increasing rapidly. To remedy this situation, BLM Director Robert Burford initiated *Recreation 2000*. The release of the report of President Reagan's Commission on Americans Outdoors served as a major catalyst for this initiative. (This report and its findings and recommendations were discussed in Chapter 2.) Recreation 2000 is a long-term strategic plan for the management of outdoor recreation opportunities on public lands. It presents an overview of the BLM's recreation and wilderness programs and provides policy for future efforts, including visitor information and interpretation; resource protection and monitoring; landownership and access adjustments; partnerships and volunteer programs; and facilities, permits, fees, and concessions.

On the opening page of *Recreation 2000: A Strategic Plan* (BLM, 1990), Director Robert Burford made the following statement to the people of the BLM:

> . . . While the Public Lands represent a national system similar to the National Forest system, they are unique in providing opportunities to the public from a broader spectrum of resource-dependent outdoor recreation experiences and activities. We in the BLM have the challenge of managing for the optimum use of the Public Lands while protecting their resource values.
>
> Recreation is an important part of the economic base of this country. The January 1987 report of the President's Commission on Americans Outdoors has shown us how important outdoor recreation is to our national economy and to the health and well-being of our bodies and minds. The report calls for all Americans to become involved—to start a grass roots effort to improve opportunities for participation in outdoor recreation.
>
> Recreation is one of many uses of the Public Lands; an equal partner within the family of multiple-use management. We in BLM are serious about our responsibility to manage and enhance recreational opportunities. Because of this commitment, we have prepared *RECREATION 2000: A STRATEGIC PLAN*. The purpose of the Plan is to provide a clear statement of BLM recreation management policies and goals. It describes the policies that will guide the BLM and the issues facing both our Agency and Public Land users. It also highlights where we will concentrate our

efforts in Agency programs related to recreation. Through the RECREATION 2000 plan, we hope to create a better awareness and understanding of the importance of outdoor recreation resources and the role the Public Lands play in providing recreation opportunities. . . ."

In addition to general and specific recreation policy statements, *Recreation 2000* identifies eight specific challenges facing the BLM and Public Land users and lists objectives for resolution of these issues. All of these items are summarized in the following sections.

Policies The *general recreation policy* states that

The BLM will ensure the continued availability of Public Land for a diversity of resource-dependent outdoor recreation opportunities while maintaining its commitment to managing the Public Lands as a national resource in harmony with the principle of balanced multiple use.

Specific policy statements address the following issues:

- *Diversity* The BLM will provide and maintain a wide diversity of recreational opportunities on the public lands.
- *Resource Dependency* The BLM will provide recreational opportunities that are resource-dependent.
- *Resource Monitoring and Protection* The BLM will manage and monitor the basic natural, cultural, and scenic resources found on the public lands in a manner that assures protection of sensitive resources and the continued availability of quality outdoor recreation opportunities and experiences.
- *Visitor Service* The BLM will place a priority on providing for a variety of public recreation opportunities and experiences through visitor awareness, information, interpretation, and protection, emphasizing an on-the-ground presence where appropriate and reasonable.
- *Partnerships* The BLM will expand and strengthen cooperative partnerships with federal, state, and local agencies and the private sector to enhance the outdoor recreation opportunities offered on, and adjacent to, the public lands.
- *Maintenance* The BLM will maintain recreational facilities to a standard that protects the resource, the public, and the public investment and that fosters pride of public ownership.
- *Construction* The BLM will develop appropriate recreational facilities, balancing public demand, protection of public-land resources, and fiscal responsibility.
- *Planning* The BLM will plan for all outdoor recreation activities through the Bureau Planning System. BLM recreation planning efforts will assure public awareness and encourage public participation, and the BLM will assist and cooperate in federal, state, local, and private planning efforts.
- *Use Limits and Allocation* Recreational resource use may have to be limited or allocated. As necessary, use limitations and allocations will be established through the Bureau Planning System.
- *Special Recreation Permits* The BLM will issue special recreation permits in an equitable manner for specific recreational uses of the public lands and related waters as a means to control visitor use, to protect recreational resources, and to provide for private and commercial recreation use.

- *Fees for the Use of the Public Lands* To assure that recreational users assume an appropriate share of the cost of maintaining recreational facilities and of protecting the resources, the BLM will establish and assess equitable fees at appropriate facilities and for certain uses of the public lands.
- *Landownership and Access Adjustments* The BLM will enhance recreational opportunities through landownership adjustments, increased and improved access, and other adjustments.
- *Tourism* The BLM will develop and maintain cooperative relationships with national, state, and local tourism entities.
- *Professional Development* The BLM will support professionalism and career development of recreation and resource management specialists.

Challenges   *Recreation 2000* identifies a number of challenges faced in the recreation management program, and lists one or more objectives for resolving each of them.

Overall Challenge and Objective   The Plan recognizes an overall challenge dealing with program emphasis:

> The public has an inaccurate perception of the Bureau of Land Management and its role in providing recreation opportunities.

To meet this challenge, the objective is to:

> Improve service to the recreation-seeking public by placing more emphasis on our recreation program and other programs supporting recreation.

Other Challenges and Their Objectives   Eight additional challenges, and the objectives to meet them, are listed in *Recreation 2000*:

1. *Visitor Information and Interpretation* "How can the BLM provide for public awareness of the extent of its management responsibilities and the magnitude of the resources the Agency manages?" Except in a few areas, the BLM has not provided a well coordinated public information program regarding the types and location of recreation opportunities. The BLM also does not consistently provide on-the-ground public contact in areas where public use and resource values warrant such a presence.

Objectives

- Maintain an appropriate on-the-ground presence of professional, well-trained personnel who are identifiable as BLM employees.
- Expand efforts to give the public an opportunity for a better awareness and understanding of, and appreciation for, the public-land resources and accompanying recreational opportunities, and assist the public in its quest for increased knowledge and a quality outdoor recreation experience. This will include the development of specific and suitable information about the public lands through signs, brochures, maps, and quality public contact on-the-ground.
- Use visitor information programs as a primary tool to direct users to those public lands that can accommodate additional recreational use.
- Use visitor information and interpretation as a primary tool to protect sensitive resources, discourage vandalism, and encourage the visitor to "Use, Share, and Appreciate" the public lands and to "Take Pride in America."

- Develop visitor information distribution centers at each district office which will have, at a minimum, information and brochures on federal and state recreation opportunities within that state.
- In outreach and good neighbor programs, provide accurate recreation information to federal, state, and local agencies and private entities for use in their programs and publications.
- Develop a signing strategy to effectively identify the public lands (Figure 12.5).

2. *Resource Protection and Monitoring*   "How can BLM assure the protection of the vast resources under its stewardship?"

Objectives

- Provide an appropriate on-the-ground presence of professional, well-trained personnel who are identifiable as BLM employees.
- Manage recreational resource uses on the public lands where significant recreational, cultural, and natural values have been identified through the planning system.
- Actively pursue implementation of an on-the-ground management presence and a resource monitoring program that begins with the highest-priority areas (for example, wilderness and wilderness study areas, wild and scenic rivers, historic and scenic trails, national conservation and recreation areas, and so on) to assure that the basic natural, cultural, and scenic resources are properly protected as directed in the land-use planning documents and legislative mandates.
- Establish optimum carrying-capacity levels, using techniques such as *limits of acceptable change* (LAC), in all areas where visitor use has reached, or could reach in the foreseeable future, a level that could adversely impact significant resource values and/or the quality of visitor experiences.
- Continually assess visitor use trends, new recreation technologies, and public attitudes in order to be aware of how use will or may affect resources. Any

Figure 12.5   One of the objectives of the BLM's Recreation 2000 initiative was to provide a better awareness of public lands. Shown is a sign for Utah's Henry Mountains Resource Area.

change in provision of recreational opportunities must go through the process of reevaluating the specific area goals.

- Seek additional law-enforcement capability as needed to increase the effectiveness of resource protection efforts.

3. *Landownership and Access Adjustments*   "How can public needs be best met in areas where there are vast acreages of scattered or fragmented public lands and an ownership pattern that makes their management very difficult and limits or precludes public use of land- and water-based recreation resources?"

Objectives

- Identify exchange opportunities to enhance management and meet public needs through a coordinated, cooperative program of aligning public and private landownership.
- Identify access needs in conjunction with transportation plans, with due consideration of constraints to recreational opportunities, and begin implementation of these plan recommendations on a priority basis.
- Be an active participant in the Land and Water Conservation Fund (LWCF) for acquisition of appropriate recreation lands or interest in lands.
- Work with private landowners in establishing partnership relationships to accomplish improved public-land management where acquisition or exchanges are not desirable.

4. *Partnerships*   "How can the BLM maximize effective use of partnerships to provide for basic user needs and resource protection?"

Objectives

- Maximize effective use of active partnerships with volunteers and volunteer groups, private landowners, user groups, individuals, state and local governments, and other federal land-managing agencies to enhance resource management and improve the quality of recreational opportunities on the public lands.
- Increase opportunities for public participation in the management of recreational resources and facilities in alignment with the "Take Pride in America" campaign, and provide greater recognition and acknowledgment of individuals and groups contributing to public-land management.
- Encourage greater state and local government and private sector participation in the management of recreational activities on public lands, and, where appropriate, assist those agencies and private individuals in providing recreational opportunities on nonpublic lands.
- Develop a recreation concession policy to guide the development of recreational opportunities through concession partnerships.

5. *Volunteers*   "Although volunteer contributions to BLM efforts have been highly visible and successful in nearly half of the districts, how can the BLM maximize effective use of the volunteer resource?"

Objectives

- Encourage and recognize volunteers as working partners within the recreation program bureau-wide.

- Expand and enhance visitor services through the appropriate use of volunteers, and seek removal of current constraints on effective use of volunteers in assisting in the collection of recreation fees.
- Expand resource protection capabilities through the appropriate use of volunteers. Although volunteers may not be used in hazardous work without special legislative authority, they may assist in nonhazardous recreation-related aspects.

6. *Tourism Programs* "How can the BLM work more effectively with tourism organizations and the travel industry?"

Objective

- Develop and maintain working relationships with local, regional, and state tourism agencies and organizations to complement the development and promotional programs that identify the role of outdoor recreation on public lands.

7. *Facilities* "Is there a need to reevaluate the BLM recreation investment in infrastructure in terms of current and future visitor needs, protection of the resource and public investments, and reduction of maintenance costs?"

Objectives

- Assess the need and ability to operate and maintain existing recreation sites and related facilities based on policies established in *Recreation 2000.*
- Assess the status and condition of existing recreation access roads and trails, and develop a strategy for their repair and maintenance commensurate with planning documents and public use.
- Assure that all future recreation-related facility investments will be in accordance with established recreation construction and maintenance policies and land-use planning decisions.
- Assess the status and condition of existing recreation sites to determine which sites should continue to be managed, which should be redesigned and reconstructed or expanded, and which should be transferred, closed, or removed.

8. *Permits, Fees, and Concessions* "How can BLM manage recreation permit programs and fee and concession policies to assure adequate protection and management of resource values, as well as the return of fair market value for the use of the public lands?"

Objectives

- Continue to use the Special Recreation Permit Program to manage visitor use on the public lands to protect resource values, reduce use conflicts, and provide increased opportunities for safe and enjoyable recreational experiences.
- Seek to recover the fair market value from commercial recreation permittees, concessionaires, and sponsors of events for use of the public lands.
- Implement user fees at developed sites subject to criteria of the LWCF and consistent with fees being charged by other land management agencies and the private sector.
- Continually analyze the Special Recreation Permit and Concession Programs in order to strengthen them and to assure that appropriate user fees are charged.

Examples   The following examples demonstrate some of the ways the BLM is meeting the challenge of managing natural resources with its relatively modest financial and personnel resources:

- Cooperative management agreements are being used in many locations to share administrative costs with other entities to keep open recreation sites that otherwise would be closed. One example is the Angle Peak Recreation Site in New Mexico. When the site was scheduled to be closed, the county asked to enter into an agreement to maintain the facility, thus avoiding a potential loss of revenue.
- In Montana two recreational opportunities, Garnet National Winter Recreation Trail and Garnet Ghost Town, are available only because of cooperative management approaches. Through cooperative management, snowmobile trails are groomed as a joint venture with the Montana Department of Fish, Wildlife and Parks. Thanks to a cooperative management agreement with the Garnet Preservation Association, a nonprofit organization based in Missoula, the public has access, use, and enjoyment of a historic ghost town.
- Development of a visitor service contract agreement with a Billings, Mont. motorcycle club has allowed OHV (off-highway vehicle) use of 1200 acres of public land. The club manages and maintains the area. Through the club's efforts, fencing, water bars, and signs have been installed, controlling use within the area and preventing trespass onto contiguous private property.
- The Oregon office has managed to implement a variety of recreation planning decisions by using various state funding sources: state all-terrain vehicle (ATV) funds, state Marine Board funds, and Deschutes River boater pass revenues.
- Utah has been working with local groups to design local tourism brochures. This saves the BLM costs, enables it to present recreation within a multiple-use framework, and assists the community by providing secondary attractions that encourage visitors to stay in the area longer.
- Arizona became the first BLM office to obtain California Boating and Waterways funding to improve facilities at Squaw Lake Recreation Site. Approximately $490,000 has been approved, while another $700,000 grant is pending for the Parker Strip.
- In Nevada, staff for the Red Rock Canyon Recreation Lands initiated the formation of the Natural Resource Environmental Education Committee, composed of federal and state agency personnel and interested organizations and citizens. The primary purpose of the committee is to act as a clearinghouse for the dissemination of environmental education information and materials to the public. Additionally, the committee works closely with the Project Wild and Project Learning Tree programs and coordinates teacher workshops.
- In Alaska, the BLM has expanded the popular recreation cabin program. This program provides the public with the opportunity to visit national recreation areas during the winter by renting rustic, weatherproof cabins for $15 per night.
- Hunting opportunities for elk, deer, and antelope in Montana have increased due to a cooperative effort between the BLM, ranchers, private landowners, and the state to establish 14 walk-in hunting areas totaling 230,000 acres across the state. These areas are on lands with intermingled private and public ownership and have been opened to the public in exchange for increased management and enforcement

patrols by the state and the BLM. Hunters do not need permission to enter private land in these designated areas as long as access is gained on foot or horseback. Vandalism has been reduced, gates have not been left open as often, there has been less livestock damage, and less of landowners' time has been spent responding to requests for hunting privileges. These areas have also had an increase in game available, wildlife benefits, and better road protection.

- California's *Chappie-Z'Berg OHV Law* (1971), as amended, authorizes the state's Department of Parks and Recreation to enter into cooperative agreements with federal agencies. Funding for this program is supported by OHV registration fees and the gas tax. These user-generated revenues are spent for the enhancement of OHV opportunities and resource management. These funds have been used since 1979–1980 as one tool to implement OHV-related needs of the recreation program. Projects range from planning, acquisition, development of needed support, access, resource management, and site management, including operations and maintenance. More than 90 projects are being considered or are being implemented at this time within California BLM's priority-intensive recreation management areas. Total funding approved by the state of California is more than $13 million.

- The BLM, the Friends of the Mojave Road, and the California Four Wheel Drive Clubs Association have entered into a cooperative agreement to research, mark, and interpret one of the unique wagon routes of the California Desert National Conservation Area. In cooperation with this volunteer group, the route has been marked to facilitate public travel. In addition, volunteers developed a detailed, mile-by-mile guide to aid travelers—both hikers and OHV users.

- New Mexico has an active program for training volunteers for developing trails and other site development and maintenance programs through a cooperative effort with "Volunteers for the Outdoors."

- The Arizona and California offices joined forces to manage the burgeoning winter "snowbird" use on public lands. By requiring a permit to camp in *long-term visitor areas* (LTVAs), the BLM allows long-term use in certain areas and protects fragile desert resources in other areas. Currently there are 10 LTVAs, and in 1986–1987, 7790 visitors bought 4040 permits.

- Colorado BLM is cooperating with the Forest Service, the National Park Service, the state of Colorado's Division of Wildlife and Parks and Outdoor Recreation, the Colorado Parks and Recreation Association, the Center for Public-Private Sector Cooperation, the Colorado Board of Tourism, and several chief executive officers from the private sector on the Colorado Outdoor Recreation Resource Project (CORRP). The project's purpose is to communicate the public value and resulting management needs of Colorado's diverse outdoor recreation resources in such a way that their intrinsic and economic values are maintained for future generations. Project efforts in 1986 resulted in development of a private-sector business plan for the Arkansas River Special Recreation Management Area. Efforts are presently underway to produce a statewide intergovernmental natural resources recreation opportunity guide as a joint effort of the Colorado Tourism Board and CORRP.

- In Arizona, the BLM has entered into a cooperative management agreement for a 60-mile Black Canyon Hiking and Equestrian Trail, with the BLM providing the land and the counties maintaining the trail. This trail provides a vital link to the 100-mile Sun Circle Trail and the Prescott National Forest.

RECREATIONAL USE OF BLM LANDS

In 1991, BLM-administered lands received 44,981,600 recreation visitor days (RVDs). This accounted for 7 percent of the total RVDs on federal lands and made the BLM the fourth-ranking federal land management agency in recreational use, behind the Forest Service (42 percent of use), the Army Corps of Engineers (29 percent of use), and the National Park Service (17 percent of use). The BLM is a newcomer both as a federal land-managing agency and as a provider of outdoor recreation on an organized basis. The O & C Act of 1937 allowed recreational development on BLM land, but recreational development did not really start until 1960. "Facilities for camping and picnicking were first constructed on BLM land in western Oregon in 1960" (Clawson and Van Doren, 1984, 223). Camping and picnicking have been the primary outdoor recreation facilities on BLM land. Outdoor recreation on these lands has generally been of the dispersed and resource-dependent types. In 1967 there were 160 developed camping and picnicking areas with a capacity of 2600 family units at once (Clawson and Van Doren, 1984, 115). Recreational use on public lands rose steadily in the 1970s, approaching 50 million visitor-use days each year. By 1972, the bureau hired an additional 30 outdoor recreation planners so that virtually all district offices were staffed with these positions. By the mid-1970s, the BLM was maintaining more than 400 developed recreation sites (Muhn and Stewart, 1988, 203). It was during the 1970s that the BLM experienced its greatest growth. Because of other national priorities, the BLM was not able to focus much attention on its recreation program through the early and mid-1980s. This situation has changed dramatically since the late 1980s and the initiation of Recreation 2000.

Recreational Resources and Facilities

Recreation management is focused on 355 areas, comprising approximately 10 percent of BLM-administered land. These more intensively used areas require direct supervision of recreational activities and of cooperative commercial and BLM-regulated recreation operations. High-use areas include 32 national wild and scenic rivers; 22 designated recreational, historic, and scenic trails (2300 miles); the White Mountains National Recreation Area; designated OHV areas; and major portions of the California Desert, King Range, San Pedro, Steese, and El Malpais National Conservation Areas. The BLM makes recreational opportunities available to the public by issuing permits to private individuals, commercial operators, and concessionaires.

Table 12.5 presents a summary of the recreational resources and facilities that exist on BLM lands. Note that just about every possible outdoor recreational opportunity is available except for downhill skiing. One of the most valuable resources on BLM land—a high percentage of sunshine—is not listed here. The arid and semiarid climates that dominate much of the BLM land in the lower 49 states are responsible for these sunny conditions. Since the late 1980s, it has been the intent of the BLM to make the public better aware of the great variety of recreational opportunities available on BLM land.

A summary of developed recreation sites by states is given in Table 12.6. There is a total of 726 developed recreation sites on 34,142 acres in the 11 states. On these

Table 12.5 BLM Recreation Resources and Facilities

72,541,000	Visits in FY91
539,779,000	Visitor hours in FY91
94,376	Recreation use permits issued in FY91
14,839	Special recreation permits issued in FY91
355	Special recreation management areas
161	Extensive recreation management areas
765	Developed recreation sites
2,381	Day-use units and 22,366 family camp units
3,150	Undeveloped recreation sites
41	Visitor information centers (including 8 major facilities, field contact stations, and cooperative exhibit centers)
21	Concessions (Lower Colorado River)
65,000	Miles of roads suitable for travel by normal vehicles, and thousands of miles of primitive roads used for backcountry exploring, hunting, fishing, etc.
2,254	Miles of 46 designated national backcountry byways in 11 states
9,203	Miles of floatable rivers, with 746 river segments
4,138,078	Acres of lakes and reservoirs
156,328	Miles of fishable streams
533	Boating access points
5,948	Miles of hiking trails
163	Miles of 15 national recreation trails
955	Caves
28,390,000	Acres of waterfowl habitat
235,716,000	Acres of small-game habitat
206,000,000	Acres of big-game habitat
4,240,000	Acres of lakes and reservoirs
26,642,753	Acres under wilderness study
2,433,000	Acres in established natural areas (162 acres)
3,130,000	Acres in areas of critical environmental concern (245 acres)
129,000	Historic and archaeological sites
2,000	Miles of 32 rivers (5 states: Alaska, California, Montana, New Mexico, Oregon) in the National Wild and Scenic Rivers System
1,730	Miles of national historic trails (5: Lewis & Clark, Iditarod, Oregon, Mormon Pioneer, and Nez Perce)
502	Miles of national scenic trails (2: Continental Divide and Pacific Crest)
1,610,995	Acres in 66 national wilderness areas
14,203,121	Acres in 13 national conservation areas (Steese, San Pedro and Gila Box Riparian, King Range, 7 in the California Desert, Red Rock Canyon, and El Malpais)
1,000,000	Acres in 1 national recreation area (White Mountain)
80	Acres in 1 national outstanding natural area (Yaquina Head)

Source: BLM

developed acres are found 2318 picnic units and 22,366 camping units. In terms of number of developed sites, Oregon is the leader with 171, but in terms of developed site acres and capacity, Arizona is clearly the leader. Arizona has three-quarters of the developed acreage and two-thirds of the camping-unit capacity on BLM land. Alaska and Nevada have the lowest number of camping and picnicking units. Appendix XV identifies the recreational opportunities at the different recreation sites and is keyed to Figure 12.6, which shows their precise geographic locations.

Appendix XVI is a more detailed summary of recreational resources. In this appendix, the number of recreation management areas (RMAs) by type—extensive or special—is identified for each district. An *extensive recreation management area* is an

Table 12.6   Developed Recreation Sites Administered by the BLM

Administrative State	Number of Developed Sites	Acres	Picnic Units (day use)	Camping Units	Total Units
Alaska	25	538	5	236	241
Arizona	47	16,358	246	16,572	16,818
California	79	3,394	136	2,276	2,412
Colorado	58	304	209	214	423
Idaho	104	2,289	212	513	725
Montana[a]	28	227	175	253	428
New Mexico	58	522	355	246	601
Nevada	26	689	109	144	253
Oregon[b]	171	5,346	541	1,169	1,710
Utah	74	1,528	156	483	639
Wyoming	56	2,947	174	260	434
Total	726	34,142	2,318	22,366	24,684

[a]Includes North and South Dakota
[b]Includes Washington
Source: BLM; *Public Land Statistics—1991*, Vol. 176. Washington, D.C.: U.S. Government Printing Office, September 1992.

area where recreation management is only one of several management objectives and where limited commitment of resources is required to provide extensive and unstructured types of recreational activities. Such areas may contain recreation sites. These areas consist of the remainder of the land areas not included in special recreation management areas within a resource area or district. A *special recreation management area* is an area where a commitment has been made, within the parameters of multiple use, to provide specific recreational activity and experience opportunities on a sustained-yield basis. These areas usually require a high level of recreation investment and/or management. The following recreational resources by district are summarized for both extensive and special recreation management areas: count, acres, motorized access points, nonmotorized access points, boat access points, miles of improved access road, developed recreation sites, undeveloped recreation sites, visitor centers, river segments, river miles, number of caves, and number of managed caves.

Nationally, 151 recreation management areas are classified as extensive, and 344 are classified as special. The numbers reverse for the two categories in terms of acreage: 244,025,000 acres are classified as extensive, and 27,071,000 acres are classified as special. There are 200 developed and 1308 undeveloped recreation sites in the extensive recreation management areas, and 565 developed and 1842 undeveloped recreation sites in the special recreation management areas. Oregon is the clear leader among the states, with a total of 173 developed and 649 undeveloped recreation sites. New Mexico has 9 of the 41 visitor centers. The states with over 1000 miles of BLM rivers are Alaska (2582 miles), Oregon (1419 miles), Idaho (1297 miles), and Utah (1060 miles). Of the known 955 caves on BLM land, 495 are in New Mexico, and 203 are in Idaho.

A tremendous diversity of wildlife habitats may be found on the public lands, and these are summarized in Table 12.7. Alaska clearly has the greater portion of all classes of habitat except for reservoirs, for which it has none. The numbers of big-

Table 12.7   Types of Wildlife Habitats (Acres) on Public Lands—FY91

Administrative State	Lakes	Reservoirs	Fishable Streams (Miles)	Riparian Land	Wetlands	Big Game[b]	Small Game[b]	Waterfowl[b]
Alaska	2,269,000		135,311	6,046,000	22,663,000	72,243,000	71,355,000	22,239,000
Arizona	1,164	10,554	1,220	42,200	12,510	14,487,360	14,499,970	32,209
California	41,000	9,000	738	118,000	219,000	8,964,000	15,971,000	209,000
Colorado	560	17,845	2,505	59,318	15,512	9,034,721	9,382,378	55,125
Eastern states				286	4,019	3,105	2,780	5,860
Idaho	10,433	36,924	8,639	81,338	9,324	9,244,600	11,897,144	79,470
Montana	26,000	33,420	1,296	66,849	148,801	7,483,251	5,648,550	191,000
Nevada	24,570	11,300	2,463	98,310	55,971	25,380,977	34,277,582	43,954
New Mexico	1,690	381	332	9,995	5,790	7,945,433	10,135,291	10,900
Oregon	50,617	9,219	5,428	64,972	40,149	8,853,000	8,822,300	76,549
Utah[a]	2,900	6,631	5,905	161,192	45,532	22,195,113	20,398,818	122,200
Wyoming	4,716	31,628	7,330	137,615	33,206	18,000,436	18,671,509	89,949
Total	2,432,650	166,902	171,167	6,886,075	23,249,814	203,834,996	221,062,322	23,155,216

[a]Changes in value over the previous year are attributed to a change in classification procedures.
[b]Acreages shown for big-game, small-game, and waterfowl habitats are nonexclusive and are estimates only.
Source: BLM, *Public Land Statistics—1991*, Washington, D.C.: U.S. Government Printing Office, September 1992.

game animals that live on the public lands administered by the BLM are summarized in Table 12.8. For the entire country, deer are most numerous, followed by caribou. Caribou are found exclusively in Alaska, and ibex are found exclusively in New Mexico.

Recreational Use

National Use   The Bureau of Land Management uses the *visit* and the *visitor hour* for its basic statistical measurement units. All of the summaries in this section use these units. It is quite easy to convert visitor hours to visitor days: Divide the number of visitor hours by 12, since 12 visitor hours equals 1 visitor day. Table 12.9 summarizes the recreation visits to public lands under the jurisdiction of the BLM. Nationally, a total of 72,541,000 recreation visits are estimated to have occurred on BLM land in 1991. It is estimated that the actual use was 539,779,000 recreation visitor hours, which is equivalent to 44,981,583 RVDs. The leading category of use is "camping," which accounts for 36.4 percent of the visitor hours of recreational use. The next-ranking categories of use (and their percentages of total use) are "other site-based activities" (11.1 percent), "other motorized travel" (10.3 percent), "OHV travel" (9.4 percent), "hunting" (9.2 percent), "site-based nonmotorized travel" (8.2 percent), "fishing" (3.9 percent), "boating" (3.7 percent), "other water-based recreational activities" (1.6 percent), "winter sports" (0.5 percent), and "snowmobiling" (0.2 percent).

Table 12.10 summarizes the recreational use-for-fee sites, permit areas, and concessions on public lands. There are 134 fee sites, where 14,534,609 recreation visitor hours of use occurred in 1991; this represents only 2.7 percent of the total use that occurs on BLM-administered land. There were 14,860 special recreation permits issued, accounting for another 34,247,554 recreation visitor hours of use, which rep-

Table 12.8 Estimated Number of Big-Game Animals on Public Lands—FY91

Administrative State	Antelope	Barbary Sheep	Bear[a]	Bighorn Sheep[b]	Buffalo	Caribou	Deer[c]	Elk	Ibex	Javelina Wild Boar	Moose	Mountain Goat	Turkey
Alaska	—	—	9,000	5,890	550	785,000	625	—	—	—	47,400	350	—
Arizona	2,430	—	154	5,980	1	—	63,880	100	—	16,820	—	—	820
California	6,270	—	385	3,320	—	—	101,000	920	—	3,400	—	—	1,650
Colorado	13,369	68	2,190	1,765	2	—	309,193	84,893	—	—	26	2	2,700
Idaho	17,940	—	1,120	2,285	—	—	112,500	15,500	—	—	1,625	90	740
Montana	49,000	—	650	1,347	—	—	127,700	20,000	—	—	490	210	3,580
Nevada	8,957	—	1	4,763	—	—	183,358	2,007	—	—	1	—	—
New Mexico	6,980	410	146	125	—	—	36,500	3,270	510	3,060	—	—	960
Oregon	10,750	200	1,895	1,210	—	—	163,000	7,890	—	—	15	50	2,550
Utah	12,972	—	539	1,183	435	—	256,616	15,902	—	—	92	70	395
Wyoming	30,436	—	535	1,328	10	—	250,692	34,887	—	—	2,503	—	1,140
Total	159,104	678	16,615	29,196	998	785,000	1,605,064	185,369	510	23,280	52,152	772	14,535

[a]Includes black, grizzly, and brown bears.
[b]Includes Rocky Mountain, Dall, California, and Desert bighorn sheep.
[c]Includes whitetail, blacktail, and mule deer.
Source: BLM, Public Land Statistics—1991, Washington, D.C.: U.S. Government Printing Office, September 1992.

Table 12.9 Estimated Recreational Visitation to Public Lands under Jurisdiction of the BLM—1991

		Amount and Type of Recreation Used (thousands of visitor hours)										
		Land-Based Recreational Activities						Water-Based Recreational Activities			Snow/Ice-Based Recreational Activities		
		Motorized Travel			Site Based								
Administrative State	Number of Visits[a] (thousands)	Off-highway vehicle travel	Other motorized travel	Non-motorized travel	Camping	Hunting	Other	Fishing	Boating	Other	Winter Sports	Snow-mobiling	Total
Alaska	224	53	375	91	3,976	384	157	335	179	4	21	74	5,649
Arizona[b]	10,413	720	474	2,563	42,669	2,679	10,430	895	5,704	2,239	1		68,374
California	29,105	35,085	48,688	25,378	93,007	12,677	28,565	3,261	3,074	2,567	180	84	252,566
Colorado	2,901	1,271	5,114	922	4,991	7,020	1,492	1,403	1,536	52	176	101	24,078
Idaho	2,446	1,041	1,274	598	5,208	2,771	1,539	2,100	1,384	536	1,376	302	18,129
Montana[c]	2,300	1,923	1,641	495	3,168	2,796	375	1,744	456	55	182	132	12,967
Nevada	1,901	3,048	5,035	2,603	5,147	2,972	2,501	1,636	225	165	51	53	23,436
New Mexico	2,758	2,561	1,390	1,285	3,642	5,671	3,808	967	696	65	2	1	20,088
Oregon[d]	14,421	1,436	11,900	5,593	17,782	4,894	6,724	7,029	3,467	2,181	531	140	61,679
Utah	4,820	3,363	8,889	4,582	14,812	4,663	2,848	397	2,657	436	60	59	42,766
Wyoming	1,252	348	1,055	288	1,908	3,066	1,489	1,172	298	51	137	235	10,047
Total	72,541	50,849	55,835	44,398	196,310	49,593	59,928	20,939	19,676	8,353	2,717	1,181	539,779

[a]Rounded to the nearest thousand.
[b]Includes concession visitation data.
[c]Includes North and South Dakota.
[d]Includes Washington.
Source: BLM, *Public Land Statistics—1991*, Vol. 176. Washington, D.C.: U.S. Government Printing Office, September 1992.

Table 12.10 Recreational Use-for-Fee Sites, Permit Areas, and Concessions on Public Lands under the Jurisdiction of BLM—1991

Administrative State	Fee Sites					Special Recreation Permits				Recreation Concession/Vendors				Total Revenue Collected
	No. Fee Sites	Number of Visits	Visitor Hours	No. of Permits Issued	Revenue Collected	Number of Visits	Visitor Hours	No. of Permits Issued	Revenue Collected	Number Visits	Visitor Hours	No. of Permits Issued	Revenue Collected	
Alaska	10	2,619	18,400	297	$ 5,325	1,567	62,453	73	$ 21,451					$ 26,776
Arizona	4	201,107	1,733,774	10,657	38,076	2,482,997	19,447,906	6,764	113,900	8,124,559	38,518,714	16	$229,568	381,544
California	20	124,838	1,668,374	12,744	52,022	527,030	4,732,078	1,533	128,424					180,446
Colorado	3	42,700	180,400	950	4,500	146,800	740,326	319	84,602					89,102
Idaho	7	88,239	370,926	2,191	8,165	318,392	1,947,582	168	101,534					109,699
Montana[a]	5	77,330	1,146,360	6,107	26,356	313,829	252,844	125	22,811					49,167
Nevada	2	5,490	163,900	1,360	11,074	59,687	631,625	140	39,283					50,357
New Mexico	17	277,093	2,086,360	17,911	67,823	18,935	93,905	84	35,057					102,880
Oregon[b]	46	612,248	5,683,600	26,217	182,967	449,034	1,423,708	462	284,443					467,410
Utah	12	149,993	1,279,617	12,867	54,098	388,228	4,549,076	4,845	252,724					306,822
Wyoming	8	32,724	202,898	3,075	14,340	40,072	366,051	347	24,890					39,230
Total	134	1,614,381	14,534,609	94,376	$464,746	4,740,571	34,247,554	14,860	$1,109,119	8,124,559	38,518,714	16	$229,568	$1,803,433

[a]Includes North and South Dakota.
[b]Includes Washington.

Source: BLM, *Public Land Statistics—1991*, Vol. 176. Washington, D.C.: U.S. Government Printing Office, September 1992.

resents 6.3 percent of the total use. Finally, 38,518,714 recreation visitor hours of use occurred at 16 recreation concessionaires or vendors; this represents 7.1 percent of the total use. All 16 of these recreation concessionaires or vendors are in Arizona.

State Use   Tables 12.9 and 12.10 also summarize the use by states. Here the data for North and South Dakota are included in with Montana's and the data for Washington are included in with Oregon's figures. *Almost half (46.8 percent) of all recreational use on BLM land in the entire country occurs in California.* Much of this use is in the California Desert, and this heavy use was the reason for establishing the California Desert Conservation Area through FLPMA in 1976. Another 12.7 percent occurs in Arizona, and 11.4 percent in Oregon and Washington. Utah ranks a more distant fourth, with 7.9 percent of the total use. The percentages of the total national use that occur in the other states are Colorado (4.5 percent), Nevada (4.3 percent), New Mexico (3.7 percent), Idaho (3.4 percent), Montana (2.4 percent), Wyoming (1.9 percent), and Alaska (1.1 percent). California is also a clear leader in all categories of use except boating (where Oregon has more use) and winter sports and snowmobiles (where Idaho is the leader). A close study of Table 12.9 will reveal other use patterns.

District Use   Appendix XVII presents a more detailed breakdown of the recreational use on BLM lands by district and by activity based on 1992 data.[1] For 1992, there were 69,417,123 recreation visits and 518,689,233 recreation visitor hours. Both of these figures showed a decrease from 1991, which had 72,541,000 recreation visits and 539,779,000 recreation visitor hours. Both the number of participants and the total visitor hours of use are given for each district, for 11 categories of recreational use. Table 12.11 ranks the districts for total recreational use. *The California Desert District commands an impressive lead*, with 188,605,000 recreation visitor hours, or 36.3 percent of the total use. Ranking second is the Yuma District (Arizona), with 53,589,861 recreation visitor hours, or 10.3 percent of the total use. The rest of the districts each have less than 5 percent of the national use. The Dickinson District (N.D.) has the least number of recreation visitor hours, with only 16,060.

Table 12.12 through Table 12.22 identify the 10 leading districts for each of the 11 categories of recreational use. While the California Desert District is clearly the leading district in terms of total recreational use, it does not lead in all categories. It is the leader in five categories of use: "ORV travel," "other motorized travel," "non-motorized travel," "other site-based," and "camping." "Camping" is only one of two categories in which an Alaskan district—the Glennallen—ranks among the top 10 in recreational use. In the "hunting" category the Las Cruces District (New Mexico) is the leader, followed by the California Desert District. Twenty-six districts receive more fishing use than the California Desert District—the Vale District (Oregon) is clearly the leader in fishing use. The California Desert District is one of only five districts where no boating use occurs. The Yuma District (Arizona) is the prominent leader for boating use. The Yuma District is also the leader for other water-based recreational use; the California Desert District ranks fourth but receives only one-fifth

---

[1]The author is deeply indebted to David Wickstrom (National Recreation Program Leader) of the California Office in Sacramento of the BLM for providing them.

Table 12.11   BLM Districts: Total Visitor Hours of Recreational Use—1992

District	State	Visitor Hours	District	State	Visitor Hours
California Desert	CA	188,605,000	Boise	ID	3,696,350
Yuma	AZ	53,589,861	Rawlins	WY	3,261,375
Moab	UT	22,464,100	Worland	WY	3,071,250
Bakersfield	CA	19,149,900	Idaho Falls	ID	2,989,500
Las Vegas	NV	14,327,700	Shoshone	ID	2,799,630
Richfield	UT	14,093,300	Grand Junction	CO	2,734,560
Cedar City	UT	14,075,714	Burley	ID	2,290,500
Vale	OR	13,345,300	Salt Lake	UT	2,009,000
Susanville	CA	11,262,900	Lewiston	MT	1,988,100
Albuquerque	NM	9,695,250	Vernal	UT	1,952,860
Butte	MT	9,433,780	Burns	OR	1,875,967
Canon City	CO	8,419,700	Miles City	MT	1,746,719
Salem	OR	8,104,670	Lakeview	OR	1,690,860
Ukiah	CA	8,077,300	Rock Springs	WY	1,636,288
Prineville	OR	7,921,773	Roswell	NM	1,465,850
Montrose	CO	7,607,800	Winnemucca	NV	1,430,650
Las Cruces	NM	7,595,870	Casper	WY	1,104,225
Coos Bay	OR	7,049,407	Salmon	ID	937,210
Medford	OR	6,521,765	Safford	AZ	876,424
Coeur d'Alene	ID	5,851,300	Arizona Strip	AZ	871,298
Elko	NV	5,650,030	Battle Mountain	NV	704,300
Craig	CO	5,460,600	Steese/White Mountains	AK	693,550
Eugene	OR	5,419,780	Ely	NV	676,400
Phoenix	AZ	4,901,100	Arctic	AK	281,460
Glennallen	AK	4,748,661	Anchorage	AK	125,615
Spokane, Wash.	OR	4,574,971	Kobuk	AK	52,100
Roseberg	OR	4,007,400	Dickinson, N.D.	MT	16,060
Carson City	NV	3,756,200			

Source: David Wickstrom, BLM, personal communication, 1993.

Table 12.12   Top 10 BLM Districts: ORV Travel (Visitor Hours)—1992

District	State	Visitor Hours	District	State	Visitor Hours
California Desert	CA	25,718,500	Bakersfield	CA	1,559,300
Albuquerque	NM	2,366,400	Richfield	UT	1,547,900
Ukiah	CA	1,786,500	Moab	UT	933,700
Butte	MT	1,742,780	Grand Junction	CO	823,540
Cedar City	UT	1,704,420	Miles City	MT	759,400

Source: David Wickstrom, BLM, personal communication, 1993.

Table 12.13   Top 10 BLM Districts: Other Motorized Travel (Visitor Hours)—1992

District	State	Visitor Hours	District	State	Visitor Hours
California Desert	CA	42,180,000	Canon City	CO	2,785,300
Las Vegas	NV	9,965,000	Bakersfield	CA	2,146,700
Cedar City	UT	8,994,290	Medford	OR	1,825,960
Moab	UT	4,223,400	Richfield	UT	1,681,600
Montrose	CO	3,013,100	Susanville	CA	1,595,000

Source: David Wickstrom, BLM, personal communication, 1993.

Table 12.14   Top 10 BLM Districts: Nonmotorized Travel (Visitor Hours)—1992

District	State	Visitor Hours	District	State	Visitor Hours
California Desert	CA	21,208,700	Coos Bay	OR	1,243,363
Moab	UT	3,630,200	Cedar City	UT	1,089,194
Yuma	AZ	2,205,080	Salem	OR	969,370
Las Vegas	NV	1,813,500	Eugene	OR	930,800
Bakersfield	CA	1,643,900	Ukiah	CA	844,900

Source: David Wickstrom, BLM, personal communication, 1993.

Table 12.15   Top 10 BLM Districts: Camping (Visitor Hours)—1992

District	State	Visitor Hours	District	State	Visitor Hours
California Desert	CA	72,323,900	Vale	OR	4,369,800
Yuma	AZ	32,171,555	Susanville	CA	4,361,100
Moab	UT	8,901,800	Glennallen	AK	3,724,657
Bakersfield	CA	8,770,100	Albuquerque	NM	3,090,500
Richfield	UT	5,922,300	Prineville	OR	3,045,760

Source: David Wickstrom, BLM, personal communication, 1993.

Table 12.16   Top 10 BLM Districts: Hunting (Visitor Hours)—1992

District	State	Visitor Hours	District	State	Visitor Hours
Las Cruces	NM	4,454,440	Richfield	UT	2,044,700
California Desert	CA	3,616,200	Spokane, Wash.	OR	1,767,468
Susanville	CA	3,409,300	Vale	OR	1,628,000
Craig	CO	2,949,000	Montrose	CO	1,531,900
Phoenix	AZ	2,105,000	Lewiston	MT	1,408,400

Source: David Wickstrom, BLM, personal communication, 1993.

Table 12.17   Top 10 BLM Districts: Other Site-Based (Visitor Hours)—1992

District	State	Visitor Hours	District	State	Visitor Hours
California Desert	CA	22,898,500	Prineville	OR	1,548,620
Yuma	AZ	9,425,229	Richfield	UT	1,358,900
Salem	OR	2,851,600	Cedar City	UT	1,071,628
Medford	OR	1,689,900	Spokane, Wash.	OR	1,045,912
Las Vegas	NV	1,618,900	Las Cruces	NM	987,700

Source: David Wickstrom, BLM, personal communication, 1993.

Table 12.18   Top 10 BLM Districts: Fishing (Visitor Hours)—1992

District	State	Visitor Hours	District	State	Visitor Hours
Vale	OR	3,476,600	Ukiah	CA	951,200
Butte	MT	1,561,400	Yuma	AZ	921,997
Elko	NV	1,120,500	Eugene	OR	853,100
Bakersfield	CA	1,035,500	Idaho Falls	ID	703,500
Albuquerque	NM	1,016,100	Coos Bay	OR	699,018

Source: David Wickstrom, BLM, personal communication, 1993.

Table 12.19   Top 10 BLM Districts: Boating (Visitor Hours)—1992

District	State	Visitor Hours	District	State	Visitor Hours
Yuma	AZ	6,308,005	Coeur d'Alene	ID	872,800
Moab	UT	2,271,300	Albuquerque	NM	760,600
Vale	OR	1,097,000	Richfield	UT	531,000
Canon City	CO	973,400	Prineville	OR	505,292
Bakersfield	CA	968,900	Ukiah	CA	483,500

Source: David Wickstrom, BLM, personal communication, 1993.

Table 12.20   Top 10 BLM Districts: Other Water-Based Recreation (Visitor Hours)—1992

District	State	Visitor Hours	District	State	Visitor Hours
Yuma	AZ	2,420,919	Richfield	UT	439,900
Bakersfield	CA	1,114,700	Vale	OR	278,000
Medford	OR	863,500	Ukiah	CA	269,400
California Desert	CA	480,500	Salem	OR	158,100
Coeur d'Alene	ID	444,400	Eugene	OR	143,700

Source: David Wickstrom, BLM, personal communication, 1993.

Table 12.21   Top 10 BLM Districts: Winter Sports (Visitor Hours)—1992

District	State	Visitor Hours	District	State	Visitor Hours
Shoshone	ID	1,034,800	Worland	WY	77,000
Vale	OR	192,800	Canon City	CO	76,000
Butte	MT	168,500	Boise	ID	73,600
Medford	OR	99,420	Ukiah	CA	73,000
Idaho Falls	ID	92,700	Bakersfield	CA	71,600

Source: David Wickstrom, BLM, personal communication, 1993.

Table 12.22   Top 10 BLM Districts: Snowmobiling (Visitor Hours)—1992

District	State	Visitor Hours	District	State	Visitor Hours
Butte	MT	123,900	Idaho Falls	ID	66,800
Rawlins	WY	101,675	Burley	ID	63,900
Vale	OR	86,000	Rock Springs	WY	61,064
Bakersfield	CA	74,100	Steese/White Mountains	AK	57,400
Shoshone	ID	68,200	Craig	CO	55,700

Source: David Wickstrom, BLM, personal communication, 1993.

of the use of the Yuma District. In the snow-based sports—winter sports and snow-mobiling—extremely small amounts of use occur in many districts. As would be expected, most of the snow-based recreation occurs in the more northerly districts. For winter sports, the Shoshone District (Idaho) is the clear leader, receiving five times as much use as the second-ranked Vale District (Oregon). Thirty districts receive

under 10,000 recreation visitor hours of winter sports use, of which seven have none. Snowmobiling accounts for the smallest amount of recreational use on BLM land. Thirty-three districts receive less than 10,000 recreation visitor hours of snowmobiling use, with 14 of these receiving none. The leading two districts in snowmobile use, and the only districts with over 100,000 recreation visitor hours, are the Butte District (Montana) and the Rawlins District (Wyoming). Snowmobiling is one of only two categories of use where one of the Alaska districts ranks high: The Steese/White Mountains District ranks ninth.

Economic Studies   The BLM has estimated the economic value of both consumptive and nonconsumptive recreational use on public lands. Considerable economic value can be associated with these uses. Table 12.23 summarizes the number of days and estimated net value of hunting trips on public lands. Deer hunting provides the greatest net economic value ($122,376,172), followed by elk hunting ($50,524,252). Waterfowl hunting provides a net economic value of $18,185,720. The greatest net economic value for deer hunting is in Utah ($28,904,126), Oregon ($20,169,396), and California ($16,100,068). For elk hunting the greatest net economic value is in Colorado ($10,764,538), Idaho ($9,075,864), Montana ($8,236,990), and Oregon ($7,884,930). The net economic value for waterfowl hunting in California ($12,044,094) far surpasses the other states. Table 12.24 summarizes the number of days and estimated net value for primary nonconsumptive trips to public lands. *Net economic value* is defined as the amount a person is willing to spend above the current trip costs. The allowable maximums represent the greatest amounts above current costs a person would be willing to pay for a primary nonconsumptive trip. For an allowable maximum of $500, California ($42,424,444) is the leader, followed by Idaho ($17,061,556) and Arizona ($11,299,912).

WILDERNESS

The original Wilderness Act of 1964 made no provision for adding lands administered by the Bureau of Land Management to the National Wilderness Preservation System. This changed with the passage of the Federal Land Policy and Management Act (FLPMA) in 1976. Sections 202 and 603 of FLPMA set up BLM's wilderness review process for lands outside of Alaska. Within 15 years, the Secretary of the Interior was to review roadless areas of 5000 acres or more, or islands, on the public lands and report to the president as to the suitability or nonsuitability of each area for preservation as wilderness. Areas under 5000 acres could be considered under certain circumstances. The Wilderness Act identifies the criteria for evaluating public lands for wilderness. Sections 1001 and 1004 of the Alaska National Interest Lands Conservation Act (ANILCA) established a special wilderness study program for BLM lands in the Central Arctic Management Area of Alaska. Future studies of lands in Alaska will be conducted under the provisions of Section 202 of FLPMA as provided by section 1320 of ANILCA. The BLM established a review process consisting of three phases: inventory, study, and reporting to Congress. During the inventory phase, the BLM identified wilderness study areas. The inventory required by section 603 was

Table 12.23   Estimated Number of Days and Estimated Net Value of Hunting Trips on Public Lands—FY91

Administrative State	Deer		Elk		Waterfowl		Small Game		Other Game	
	Hunter Days[a]	Net Economic Value[b]	Hunter Days[a]	Net Economic Value[b]	Hunter Days[a]	Net Economic Value[b]	Hunter Days[a]	Net Economic Value[b]	Hunter Days[a]	Net Economic Value[b]
Alaska	NA	NA	NA	NA	NA	NA	NA	NA	NA	NA
Arizona	345,584	$ 1,428,994	24,913	$ 1,204,288	NA	NA	519,616	NA	212,071	NA
California	504,639	16,100,068	(c)	(c)	232,828	$12,044,094	481,072	NA	NA	NA
Colorado	212,097	9,222,758	226,906	10,764,538	NA	NA	94,868	NA	26,606	NA
Eastern States[d]	5,873	241,586	(c)	(c)	3,974	145,680	7,988	NA	1,905	NA
Idaho	319,864	12,569,756	182,785	9,075,864	67,934	1,924,190	159,447	NA	33,357	NA
Montana	251,313	7,864,292	169,975	8,236,990	NA	NA	87,299	NA	67,867	NA
Nevada	147,413	7,673,694	NA	NA	NA	NA	549,277	NA	62,067	NA
New Mexico	196,144	8,243,060	17,347	579,078	NA	NA	88,677	NA	30,295	NA
Oregon	597,764	20,169,396	236,789	7,884,930	48,966	2,016,454	187,621	NA	148,120	NA
Utah	742,164	28,904,126	75,916	2,732,714	91,078	2,055,302	193,907	NA	83,485	NA
Wyoming	248,303	9,958,442	187,817	10,045,850	NA	NA	148,877	NA	103,101	NA
Total	3,571,158	$122,376,172	1,122,448	$50,524,252	444,780	$18,185,720	2,518,649	NA	768,874	NA

[a]Hunter days are based on figures from *The 1985 National Survey of Fishing, Hunting, and Wildlife-associated Recreation.*
[b]These figures are updated from the *1985 Survey* by using the 1985 figures as a base and adjusting those figures by the consumer price index (CPI) through 1990.
[c]Species does not occur on public lands in this administrative state.
[d]All of these figures are for Minnesota, as it is the only one among the eastern states area that has more than 9000 acres of public land.
NA, not available: The sample size was considered too small for an accurate estimate.
Source: U.S. Fish and Wildlife Service, *The 1985 National Survey of Fishing, Hunting, and Wildlife-Associated Recreation.* Washington, D.C.: 1986.

Table 12.24   Estimated Number of Days and Estimated Net Value of Primary Nonconsumptive Trips to Public Lands—FY91

Administrative State	Number of Visitor Days[a]	Allowable Maximum of $300[b]	Allowable Maximum of $500[b]
Alaska	73,372	832,804	1,176,366
Arizona	368,327	7,285,214	11,299,912
California	896,051	33,908,234	42,424,444
Colorado	191,814	5,714,298	7,871,576
Eastern States[c]	502	14,568	14,568
Idaho	291,012	13,315,152	17,061,556
Montana	30,515	564,510	1,051,324
Nevada	101,882	3,018,004	3,635,930
New Mexico	68,974	2,419,502	2,707,220
Oregon	184,397	5,697,302	6,647,864
Utah	108,018	3,637,144	4,440,812
Wyoming	47,656	1,227,354	1,810,074
Total	2,362,520	77,634,086	100,141,646

[a]Visitor days are taken from *The 1985 National Survey of Fishing, Hunting, and Wildlife-associated Recreation*, U.S. Fish and Wildlife Service, Dept. of the Interior. The BLM feels that there has been no significant increase or decrease in the figures since 1985.
[b]*Net economic value* is defined as the amount a person is willing to spend above their current trip costs. The allowable maximums represent the greatest amount above current costs a person would be willing to pay for a primary nonconsumptive trip.
[c]All of these figures are for Minnesota, as it is the only one among the eastern states that has more than 9000 acres of public land.
Source: N. A. Connelly and T. L. Brown, *Estimates of Nonconsumptive Wildlife Use on Forest Service and BLM Lands.* Ithaca, N.Y.: Cornell University, 1988.

completed in 1980 in the lower 49 states. It identified more than 24 million acres of public lands as wilderness study areas and eliminated approximately 150 million acres from further consideration. It was mandated that reports on all wilderness study areas reach the president no later than October 1991 and Congress by October 1993. In the early 1980s, Secretary of the Interior James Watt ordered that no further wilderness studies be conducted on BLM land in Alaska. As of January, 1995, this order still stood.

Since this process began, Congress has designated 67 separate wilderness areas on 1,653,529 acres of BLM land in 10 states. The first BLM wilderness area designated by Congress was the Santa Lucia Wilderness Area (February 2, 1978). This 1733-acre wilderness in the Bakersfield District adjoins a 18,679-acre wilderness of the same name, established at the same time, in the Los Padres National Forest. Later in the same year (October 11) the second wilderness on BLM land was established on 5 acres in the Coos Bay District. This addition represented a 5-acre enlargement of the preexisting Oregon Islands Wilderness Area; concurrently, an additional 459 acres of the Oregon Islands National Wildlife Refuge were added to the original 21-acre wilderness area (that was originally established in 1970). Bear Trap Canyon, in the Lee Metcalf Wilderness in Montana, was added as the third BLM wilderness in 1983. This wilderness is in the Butte District and consists of 6000 acres. The BLM's first wilderness management plan was completed for Bear Trap Canyon in 1984. Table 12.25 identifies the BLM wilderness areas. Today, 47 out of 67 of them are located in Arizona, and almost 90 percent of the total BLM wilderness acreage is in that state. New Mexico (128,900 acres) is the only other state that has over 100,000 acres of BLM

Table 12.25 BLM Wilderness Areas

Wilderness	District	State	Acres
Aravaipa Canyon	Safford	AZ	19,700
Arc Dome	Battle Mountain	NV	20
Arrastra Mountain	Phoenix	AZ	129,800
Aubrey Peak	Phoenix	AZ	15,400
Baboquivari Peak	Safford	AZ	2,040
Beaver Dam Mountains	Arizona Strip	AZ	15,000
Beaver Dam Mountains	Cedar City	UT	3,630
Big Horn Mountains	Phoenix	AZ	21,000
Bisti	Albuquerque	NM	3,946
Cebolla	Albuquerque	NM	62,800
Cottonwood Point	Arizona Strip	AZ	6,860
Coyote Mountains	Safford	AZ	5,100
Currant Mountain	Ely	NV	3
De-na-zin	Albuquerque	NM	22,454
Dos Cabezas Mountains	Safford	AZ	11,700
Eagletail Mountains	Yuma	AZ	100,600
East Cactus Plain	Yuma	AZ	14,630
Fishhooks	Safford	AZ	10,500
Frank Church–River of No Return	Coeur d'Alene	ID	802
Gibraltar Mountain	Yuma	AZ	18,790
Grand Wash Cliffs	Arizona Strip	AZ	37,030
Harcuvar Mountains	Yuma	AZ	25,050
Harquahala Mountains	Phoenix	AZ	22,880
Hassayampa River Canyon	Phoenix	AZ	12,300
Hells Canyon	Phoenix	AZ	10,600
Hells Canyon	Vale	OR	968
Hummingbird Springs	Phoenix	AZ	31,200
Ishi	Ukiah	CA	240
Juniper Dunes	Spokane	WA	6,900
Kanab Creek	Arizona Strip	AZ	6,700
Lee Metcalf	Butte	MT	6,000
Machesna Mountain	Bakersfield	CA	120
Mount Logan	Arizona Strip	AZ	14,650
Mount Moriah	Ely	NV	6,435
Mount Nutt	Phoenix	AZ	27,660
Mount Tipton	Phoenix	AZ	32,760
Mount Trumbull	Arizona Strip	AZ	7,880
Mount Wilson	Phoenix	AZ	23,900
Muggins Mountains	Yuma	AZ	7,640
Needle's Eye	Phoenix	AZ	8,760
New Water Mountains	Yuma	AZ	24,600
North Maricopa Mountains	Phoenix	AZ	63,200
North Santa Teresa	Safford	AZ	5,800
Oregon Islands	Coos Bay	OR	5
Paiute	Arizona Strip	AZ	87,900
Paria Canyon–Vermilion Cliffs	Arizona Strip	AZ	89,400
Paria Canyon–Vermilion Cliffs	Cedar City	UT	23,000
Peloncillo Mountains	Safford	AZ	19,440
Powderhorn	Montrose	CO	48,115
Rawhide Mountains	Yuma	AZ	38,470
Redfield Canyon	Safford	AZ	9,930
Santa Lucia	Bakersfield	CA	1,733
Sierra Estrella	Phoenix	AZ	14,400
Signal Mountain	Phoenix	AZ	13,350
South Maricopa Mountains	Phoenix	AZ	60,100
Swansea	Yuma	AZ	16,400
Table Rock	Salem	OR	5,750
Table Top	Phoenix	AZ	34,400
Tres Alamos	Phoenix	AZ	8,300
Trigo Mountains	Yuma	AZ	30,300
Trinity Alps	Ukiah	CA	4,623
Uncompahgre	Montrose	CO	3,390
Upper Burro Creek	Phoenix	AZ	27,440
Wabayuma Peak	Phoenix	AZ	40,000
Warm Springs	Phoenix	AZ	112,400
West Malpais	Albuquerque	NM	39,700
White Canyon	Phoenix	AZ	5,790
Woolsey Peak	Phoenix	AZ	64,000
Yolla Bolly–Middle Eel	Ukiah	CA	7,145

Source: Rob Hellie, BLM, personal communication, January 3, 1994.

wilderness areas. The largest BLM wilderness areas are in Arizona: the Arrastra Mountain Wilderness Area (Phoenix District, 129,800 acres), the Warm Springs Wilderness Area (Phoenix District, 112,400 acres), and the Eagletail Mountains (Yuma District, 100,600 acres). The smallest BLM wilderness area (3 acres) is Currant Mountain, which is in the Ely District of Nevada, and adjoins a larger Forest Service wilderness area of the same name in the Humboldt National Forest. Several other small BLM wilderness areas are also adjacent to national forest wilderness areas with the same name: Arc Dome, Frank Church–River of No Return, Hell's Canyon, Ishi, Machesna Mountain, Santa Lucia, Trinity Alps, and Uncompaghre. The landownership and management pattern is responsible for these occurrences. Their character is similar to the adjacent national forests, but these areas by circumstance are on BLM land.

The *Colorado Wilderness Act* (1993) established the first BLM wilderness areas in Colorado: the 3390-acre Uncompaghre Wilderness Area and the 48,115-acre Powderhorn Wilderness Area. Both adjoin Forest Service wilderness areas with the same name. The Uncompaghre Wilderness Area contains 98,516 acres of the former Big Blue Wilderness Area (renamed the Uncompaghre by the Colorado Wilderness Act), the 3390 acres of BLM wilderness, plus an 815-acre expansion; the Forest Service wilderness is in the Uncompaghre National Forest. In addition to the 48,115 acres of BLM land in the new Powderhorn Wilderness, there are also 11,985 acres of the wilderness in the Gunnison National Forest. Besides these changes, the Colorado Wilderness Act of 1993 also established eight new wilderness areas on 405,360 acres and additions to eight other wilderness areas totaling 141,750 acres. The largest of these new Forest Service wilderness areas is the 226,455-acre Sangre de Cristo Wilderness in the Rio Grande National Forest.

From 1977 to 1993, the BLM evaluated 860 roadless areas, called *wilderness study areas* (WSAs), that encompass 27 million acres in Alaska, Arizona, California, Colorado, Idaho, Montana, Nevada, New Mexico, Oregon, Utah, Washington, and Wyoming. Table 12.26 summarizes the study area status of potential BLM wilderness areas. As of January 4, 1994, there were 770 WSAs and *instant study areas* (ISAs) covering about 26.6 million acres administered by the BLM in the 11 western states plus Alaska. California and Nevada have the greatest potential for future wilderness areas. The BLM has recommended that Congress designate 326 WSAs, which comprise 9,645,015 acres, as wilderness areas and release all or part of 654 WSAs comprising 16.9 million acres, for other uses. Until Congress passes laws to these effects, however, the BLM must protect the wilderness character of all the WSAs. Table 12.27 summarizes the BLM wilderness recommendations that were pending before Congress as of January 3, 1994. Of the total 9.7 million acres recommended for wilderness status, 2.3 million acres are in California, 2.0 million are in Utah, 1.9 million acres are in Nevada, and 1.3 million are in Oregon. Only 41,000 out of 3.6 million acres in Alaska were recommended as suitable for wilderness status.

Legislation is pending in Congress (as of May 1994) that, if passed, "could change the way BLM does business in California (Rob Hellie, BLM Washington office, personal communication)." Senate 21 (*California Desert Protection Act*) initially introduced by Alan Cranston almost a decade ago, was later sponsored by Diane Feinstein and passed the Senate on April 13, 1994. The companion bill in the House of Representatives is H.R. 580. The Senate bill establishes a new, 1,181,521-acre Mohave Desert National Park and enlarges and upgrades to national park status both Death Valley

Table 12.26 BLM Wilderness: Instant Study Area Status as of January 3, 1994

| | Wilderness Study Areas[a] | | | | | | | | | |
| State | FLPMA Sec. 202 | | FLPMA Sec. 603 | | ANILCA Sec. 1001 | | Instant Study Areas[b] | | Total | |
	Number	Acres	Number	Acres	Number	Acres	Number	Acres	Number	Acres
Alaska					1	3,680,000			1	3,680,000
Arizona	1	4,812	1	59,118					2	63,930
California	44	108,412	179	7,049,236			4	9,736	227	7,167,384
Colorado	17	29,899	37	680,906			5	9,016	59	719,819
Idaho	10	22,483	54	1,367,900			2	380,360	66	1,770,743
Montana	10	21,883	27	389,867			3	40,813	40	452,563
Nevada	3	11,878	99	5,077,171			10	37,419	112	5,126,468
New Mexico	8	27,101	42	894,300			2	4,507	52	925,908
Oregon	8	16,740	79	2,780,378			5	9,480	92	2,806,598
Utah	14	21,754	71	2,896,351			10	340,145	95	3,258,250
Washington			1	5,518					1	5,518
Wyoming	7	15,764	34	554,104			1	7,636	42	577,504
Total[c]	121	280,724	606	21,754,849	1	3,680,000	42	839,112	770	26,554,685

[a]FLPMA, Federal Land Policy and Management Act of October 21, 1976 (P.L. 94-579, 90 Stat. 2743); ANILCA, Alaska National Interest Lands Conservation Act of December 2, 1980 (P.L. 96-487, 94 Stat. 2371).

[b]Instant study areas (ISAs) are special study areas mandated by Congress in FLPMA.

[c]Figures in the number columns for FLPMA will not add to the total shown at the bottom because wilderness study areas cross state lines and are reported in the count for each state. The figures "121" and "606" represent the total numbers of FLPMA wilderness study areas. The figure "770" is the number of wilderness study areas (WSAs) and instant study areas (ISAs) on public lands administered by the BLM in the states listed. These acreage figures do add to the totals shown at the bottom.

Note: The wilderness/instant study areas (WSA/ISAs) listed in this table include the areas pending before Congress. The reported acreage includes all acreage under wilderness study. In certain cases adjoining acreage outside a WSA/ISA has been studied in conjunction with the WSA/ISA.

Source: Rob Hellie, BLM, personal communication, January 3, 1994.

Table 12.27   BLM Wilderness Recommendations Pending Before Congress as of January 3, 1994

State	Wilderness Study Areas Pending (number)	Instant Study Areas Pending (number)	Total Area Pending (acres)	Area Recommended to Congress as Suitable (acres)	Area Recommended to Congress as Nonsuitable (acres)
Alaska	1		3,680,000	41,000	3,639,000
California	208	4	7,130,025	2,278,024	4,852,001
Colorado	48	5	713,629	338,435	375,194
Idaho	64	2	1,770,743	972,239	798,504
Montana	33	3	447,327	173,499	273,828
Nevada	102	10	5,126,468	1,877,856	3,248,612
New Mexico	48	2	907,586	487,186	420,400
Oregon	87	5	2,806,598	1,278,073	1,528,525
Utah	85	10	3,258,250	1,958,339	1,299,911
Washington	1		5,518		5,518
Wyoming	41	1	577,504	240,364	337,140
Total[a]	699	42	26,423,648	9,645,015	16,778,633

[a]Figures in the "Wilderness Study Areas Pending" column do not add to the total shown at the bottom because wilderness areas cross state lines and are reported in the count for each state. The figure of "699" is the total number of pending wilderness study areas. Acreage figures do add to the totals shown at the bottom.
Source: Rob Hellie, BLM, personal communication, January 3, 1994.

and Joshua Tree National Monuments. The bill establishes 3,183,438 acres of wilderness in the new Death Valley National Park, 695,056 acres of wilderness in the new Mohave Desert National Park, and 131,780 acres of wilderness in the new Joshua Tree National Park. It would also create 76 new wilderness areas—two within national wildlife refuges, one in a national forest, and 74 on BLM lands. The acreage to be included in the three new national parks would be transferred from the BLM to the National Park Service. Although there has not been much action on H.R. 580 recently, this situation should change since S. 21 has passed the Senate.

NOTE: The California Desert Protection Act became law when President Clinton signed a compromise bill on October 31, 1994 (See Epilogue for details).

BACKCOUNTRY BYWAYS

The BLM's *Backcountry Byways program* offers an outstanding opportunity to discover the scenic grandeur of the American West. This program is BLM's contribution to the larger *National Scenic Byways program*. Both are the result of findings of the President's Commission on Americans Outdoors, which found 43 percent of American adults identified driving for pleasure as a favorite pastime. In 1990 the BLM dedicated Gold Butte Road in southeastern Nevada as the first of more than 44 backcountry byways in the 11 western states where the BLM operates. These byways are designated only if there is local community involvement and support. The BLM works to create partnerships to involve the private sector in the program. In cooperation with members

from the business community, the BLM is erecting signs to help motorists find the byways, distributing maps and promotional materials, and posting interpretive markers. Table 12.28 identifies the BLM backcountry byways.

National backcountry byways are designated by the type of road and the vehicle needed to travel it safely. There are four types of road:

Type I   Roads paved with an all-weather surface and with grades that are negotiable by a normal touring car. These roads are usually narrow, slow-speed, secondary roads.

Table 12.28   BLM Backcountry Byways

Byway Name	Length (miles)	BLM District	Byway Name	Length (miles)	BLM District
Arizona			Mount Wilson	62	Ely
Hualapai Mountain	47	Phoenix	Red Rocks	13	Las Vegas
			New Mexico		
California			Quebrandas	23	Las Cruces
Barrel Spring	20	Susanville	Wild Rivers	13	Albuquerque
Buckhorn	31	Susanville			
East Mojave Scenic Area			Oregon		
*Black Canyon	20	Calif. Desert	Christmas Valley	93	Lakeview
*Cedar Canyon	25	Calif. Desert	*Diamond Loop	75	Burns
*Cima	17	Calif. Desert	Galice-Hellgate	39	Medford
*Essex	20	Calif. Desert	Grave Creek to Marial	33	Medford
*Kelbaker	60	Calif. Desert	Lakeview–Steens Mountain	90	Lakeview-Burns
*Kelso-Cima	20	Calif. Desert	Leslie Gulch–Succor Creek	52	Vale
*Lanfair-Ivanpah	55	Calif. Desert	Lower Crooked River	43	Prineville
*Wild Horse Canyon	12	Calif. Desert	Lower Deschutes River	36	Prineville
			Nestucca River	48	Salem
Colorado			North Umpqua River	8	Roseburg
Alpine Loop	63	Montrose	*Snake River–Mormon Basin	130	Vale
Gold Belt	122	Canon City	Steens Mountain	66	Burns
Unaweep/Tabequache	138	Grand Junction	South Fork Alsea River	11	Salem
			South Fork John Day River	50	Prineville
Idaho					
Lewis and Clark	39	Salmon	South Dakota		
Owyhee Uplands	101	Boise	Fort Meade	5	Miles City
Montana			Utah		
Big Sheep Creek	51	Butte	Bull Creek Pass	68	Richfield
Garnet Range	24	Butte	Nine Mile Canyon	78	Moab
Missouri Breaks	73	Lewiston	Smithsonian Butte	9	Cedar City
Nevada			Wyoming		
Bitter Springs	28	Las Vegas	Red Gulch–Alkali	32	Worland
*California Trail	74	Elko	Seminoe to Alcova	64	Rawlins
Fort Churchill–Wellington	67	Carson City	South Bighorn–Red Wall	102	Casper
Gold Butte	61	Las Vegas			

*Newest byways.
Source: Farmers Insurance Group. "Rediscovering America: Back Country Byways," *Friendly Exchange*, Number 2, Fall 1992.

Type II   Roads requiring high-clearance vehicles such as trucks or four-wheel drives. These roads are usually not paved but may have some type of surfacing. Grades, curves, and road surfaces may be negotiated with a two-wheel drive high-clearance vehicle without undue difficulty.

Type III   Roads requiring four-wheel drive vehicles or other specialized vehicles such as dirt bikes, ATVs, and so on. These roads are usually not surfaced but are managed to provide for safety considerations and protect resource needs. They have grades, tread surfaces, and other characteristics that require specialized vehicles to negotiate.

Type IV   Trails managed specifically to accommodate dirt bike, mountain bike, snowmobile, or ATV use. These are usually single-track trails.

Following are a few examples of some byways:

- *Wild Rivers Byway*   This 13-mile-long byway is located in the Wild Rivers Recreation of the Albuquerque District, 26 miles north of Taos, N.M. The key feature is the 800-foot gorge carved by the Rio Grande and the Red River. There is a visitor center and camping and picnicking facilities.

- *Lower Deschutes River*   This 36-mile byway, in the Prineville District of central Oregon, is rough in places since it follows the Deschutes River as it drops rapidly over many falls. There are many primitive campgrounds and the more developed Beavertail campground. This byway is heavily used in the summer.

- *South Bighorn–Red Wall*   This 102-mile byway, on country roads in central Wyoming in the Casper District, follows historic stock trails through the scenic Red Wall country. There is a shorter loop where passenger cars can negotiate the roads without difficulty, but on the upper reaches of the longer route, high-clearance vehicles are advised. There are two campgrounds along the route. Travel is not recommended in wet weather or winter.

- *Buckhorn*   This 31-mile byway meanders across the Nevada–northern California border in the Susanville District. There is a wild horse population of 200–300 that may be viewed. There are no facilities, and the road is a high-clearance dirt and gravel road that is closed in winter.

- *Garnet Range*   This unique 24-mile byway in the Butte District is located 30 miles east of Missoula. It leads to one of Montana's best-preserved mining ghost towns in the Garnet Range, and in the winter travel is limited to snowmobiles or skis. Lodging is available, but sleeping bags and food must be brought. The town's cabins and houses are authentic and have been preserved.

- *Gold Belt*   This 122-mile byway is made up of three routes in the pinon-, sage-, and cactus-studded Colorado high country between Canon City and Cripple Creek. It is located in the Canon City District and encompasses steep, forested canyons, high-mountain meadows, agricultural flatlands, fossil digs, and modern and historic gold-mining districts. The entire byway is accessible year-round in a two-wheel-drive vehicle, although four-wheel drive is recommended in rainy or snowy weather. Each third of the route takes about 2 hours.

OTHER EXAMPLES OF BLM RECREATION AREAS

Alaska

The BLM provides an important role as a major provider of recreational opportunities in Alaska. In 1988, the BLM provided roadside developed recreation opportunities at 14 campgrounds and eight public-use cabins, totaling 221 use units serving 1100 visitors. In addition to standard campground facilities, the BLM manages one-third of the Wild and Scenic River mileage in Alaska and 630 miles of summer and winter trails. The Anchorage District manages 16 million acres in southwestern and south-central Alaska. The Iditarod National Historic Trail traverses much of the district. The Campbell Tract in Anchorage is a recreation playground for half of the state's population. The Glennallen District manages approximately 5.5 million acres in east-central Alaska. The 135-mile Denali Highway provides summer visitors with access to spectacular scenery and prime wildlife habitat. The Gulkana and Delta Wild and Scenic Rivers offer excellent floating opportunities. The Tangle Lakes Archaeological District near Paxson preserves hundreds of cultural sites. The Kobuk District in west-central Alaska manages 17 million acres of public land. The Squirrel River and the Kigkluaik Mountains provide first-rate recreation. The hugh Arctic District covers 34 million acres of surface public lands across Alaska's North Slope. Major resource values on these remote lands include internationally important waterfowl habitat, calving and summer habitat for Alaska's largest caribou herd, high-density nesting habitat for raptors, internationally significant archaeological and paleontological sites, unlimited potential for recreational activities, and extensive reserves of oil, gas, coal, and other minerals. Much of the district supports traditional subsistence lifestyles of local residents.

The Steese–White Mountains District is responsible for 7.5 million acres of public lands in the interior of eastern Alaska. The Steese National Conservation Area and White Mountains National Recreation Area, each over 1 million acres, offer outstanding opportunities for river floating, fishing, hiking, photography, wildlife observation, and cross-country skiing. Fort Egbert is a restored historic site dating to 1899 that sits on the Yukon River. The 27-mile Pinnell Mountain National Recreation Trail traverses a series of alpine ridgetops that offer outstanding views and is closed to motorized vehicles. The district is also responsible for the management of more than 620 miles of national wild and scenic river corridors including Birch and Beaver Creeks.

Arizona

Arizona's 14.2 million acres of BLM public lands offer a wide range of temperatures, elevations, and topography to suit various recreational activities. The Arevaipa Canyon Wilderness is 120 miles southwest of Phoenix and contains 19,410 acres, including the 11-mile-long Arevaipa Canyon, surrounding tablelands, and nine side canyons. Within the colorful 1000-foot canyon walls are outstanding scenery, wildlife, and rich history. The Gila Box Riparian National Conservation Area is located 15 miles east of Safford. The two main features of the area are Bonita Creek, where informal camping, picnicking, hiking, and bird watching occur, and the Gila Box, a

desert canyon where seasonal boating, fishing, and hiking are popular. The San Pedro Riparian National Conservation Area contains 40 miles of the upper San Pedro River between the U.S.-Mexican border and St. David, Ariz. Dispersed recreational opportunities include bird watching, wildlife viewing, photography, hiking, camping, hunting, horseback riding, and nature study. Sailing, swimming, and fishing are possible in the Colorado River in the Parker Strip Recreational Lands and the Squaw Lake Recreation Lands. Due to the popularity of desert camping in the winter, the BLM has set up campgrounds in the Yuma District called "long-term visitor areas"; these designated areas allow visitors to camp from September 15 to April 30 for a minimal fee.

California

BLM lands in California cover 17.2 million acres and range from desert to snow-capped mountains. Among these lands are America's first two national conservation areas: the 12-million-acre California Desert and the 60,000-acre King Range on the Pacific Coast. The California Desert National Conservation Area offers a great diversity of recreational opportunities, including exploring on ORVs, camping, hiking, rock hounding, and nature study. America's first national scenic area—the East Mohave National Scenic Area—encompasses 1.5 million acres in the California Desert National Conservation Area. This area has extraordinary beauty and contrasts, including geological oddities, gardens of cacti and stone, historic places, and an overall Old West flavor. Improved campgrounds are located at Hole in the Wall and Mid-Hills. In the Bishop Resource Area in the Alabama Hills, camping opportunities are available, with Mt. Whitney and other high peaks of the Sierra Escarpment rising a few

Figure 12.7 The BLM's Tuttle Creek campground is in the Bishop Resource Area in California in the Alabama Hills Recreation Lands. The eastern escarpment of the Sierra Nevada Range, near Mt. Whitney, rises in the background.

miles to the west (Figure 12.7). Don't bother stopping at the nearby Interagency Visitor Center on U.S. 395.[2]

Colorado

The Colorado State BLM office is to be commended for the exceptionally fine little guidebook and map they provide to the visitor entitled *BLM Colorado Recreation Opportunities* (BLM, 1991). This guide focuses on recreational opportunities in the recreation management areas of the state. The Arkansas Headwaters Recreation Area extends downstream on the Arkansas River for 148 miles, from south of Leadville to near Canon City. Outstanding kayaking and whitewater rafting, primarily for day trips, include challenging rapids over an 80-mile stretch of the river. The Powderhorn Wilderness Area, in the San Juan Mountains south of Gunnison, encompasses one of the largest and least-disturbed, relatively flat alpine tundra areas in the United States. This is an important elk breeding ground and a peripheral-use area for Rocky Mountain bighorn sheep. A system of trails provides nonmotorized access into good hunting and fishing areas. North Sand Hills is an area of sand dunes northeast of Walden that is still open to OHVs. Dune buggies, trail bikes, ATVs, and other ORVs are restricted to active sand dunes and existing routes in this 700-acre area.

Idaho

There are 12 million acres of BLM lands in Idaho, which offer mountains, canyons, lakes, whitewater rivers, desert and sand dunes. Some of the traditional recreational opportunities include camping, fishing, and rock hounding. Other opportunities include mountain biking, hang gliding, rock climbing, and cave exploring. Wagon ruts from the original Oregon and California Trails are still visible, and historic 19th-century mining towns such as Silver City and Elk City remain. Whitewater rafting on such famous streams as the Bruneau, Owyhee, and lower Salmon is possible. The Snake River Birds of Prey Area features the largest known density of nesting raptors in the world. Also, a BLM wildlife management area in the St. Anthony Sand Dunes hosts the biggest high-desert wintering elk herd in the United States.

Montana

A 149-mile stretch of the Upper Missouri River Wild and Scenic River flows through central Montana and is managed to preserve the scenic and historic values of the Missouri River corridor; the White Rocks area is exceptionally scenic. The Bear Trap Canyon Unit of the Lee Metcalf Wilderness—among the first BLM wilderness areas—is located 15 miles northeast of Ennis. The Holter Lake–Sleeping Giant Recreation Area, located 30 miles north of Helena, is a popular camping, boating, and fishing area with a spectacular mountain setting. The Pryor Mountain Wild Horse Range,

---

[2]The employees at this site are of no help to the visitor—at least in November 1993, when the author stopped here. They appear annoyed as soon as one arrives. The author of this book bestows upon this visitor center his award for "undeservedly poor public service," among the hundreds of visitor centers in the United States.

accessible from Lovell, Wyo., was the first nationally designated area established to provide a home for free-roaming wild horses. In this unique geological setting a band of approximately 120 wild horses roams the rugged expanses of the Pryor Mountains along with bands of bighorn sheep, mule deer, and other wildlife. The Humbug Spires Recreation Area is located 15 miles south of Butte in southwestern Montana. Rock formations are unique in this area, as boulder outcrops have weathered into fascinating columns. Recreational activities include fishing, sightseeing, hiking, backpacking, horseback riding, hunting, and photography.

Nevada

Red Rock Canyon National Conservation Area is located at the eastern edge of the Spring Mountains, 20 miles west of Las Vegas. This 83,100-acre area provides a 13-mile scenic drive, more than 20 miles of hiking trails, and a visitor center with exhibit rooms and a bookstore (Figure 12.8). The unique geological features, plants, and animals of Red Rock Canyon represent some of the best examples of the Mohave Desert. The 13-mile scenic drive is a one-way road and is well suited for bicycles as well as automobiles. A number of hiking trails of different lengths and difficulties are available from the designated pullouts and parking areas. There is a picnic area at Willow Spring along the drive. The most significant geological feature is the Keystone Thrust Fault. Here, gray carbonate rocks have been thrust on top of the younger tan and red sandstone. The Keystone Thrust Fault extends from the Cottonwood Fault along State Route 160 north for 13 miles along the crest of the Red Rock escarpment. It then curves east along the base of Le Madre Mountain before being obscured by very complex faulting north of the Calico Hills. The conservation area is extremely popular among rock climbers. There is a primitive campground at Oak Creek that is scheduled to be closed in the fall of 1994. Due to serious problems of resource damage

Figure 12.8 BLM Visitor Center at Red Rock Canyon National Conservation Area, 20 miles west of Las Vegas.

from off-road travel, cutting of vegetation for fuel, improper disposal of wastes, illegal ground fires, and trampling of vegetation, the number of sites has been reduced and sites have been designated. There are 14 designated sites (Figure 12.9). The BLM has acquired a parcel of land a few miles south of Oak Creek known as the Oliver Ranch that will be developed as a campground. The new campground will contain more sites, sites will be more attractive with greater privacy, and there will be running water, permanent restrooms, telephone access, and possibly showers.

Salmon Falls Creek Special Recreation Management Area, located just west of Jackpot, Nev., contains 2180 acres. It adjoins the Salmon Falls Reservoir Special Recreation Management Area in Idaho and includes 6 miles of Salmon Falls Creek. The primary recreational activities are for floating, fishing, and sightseeing. Other recreational opportunities include primitive camping, hiking, backpacking, and hunting. There are only three access locations for vehicles, which allows the stream to be maintained in a primitive setting.

New Mexico

The El Malpais National Conservation Area has been preserved in its natural state. It has cinder cones, lava tubes, ice caves, sculptured sandstone features, and a pine forest. Whitewater boaters, campers, and picnickers can experience the Rio Grande Wild and Scenic River; there is also a visitor center northwest of Taos. Some of the most impressive archaeological resources in the United States are located on BLM land in New Mexico and include the prehistoric petroglyphs at the Three Rivers Recreation Area, petrified logs and stumps at the Fossil Forest, and fossilized tracks and remains of dinosaurs at the Paleo Trackways.

Figure 12.9 Oak Creek primitive campground in the BLM's Red Rock Canyon National Conservation Area

Oregon

More contrasts exist on BLM lands in Oregon than in any other state. The most valuable forests on BLM land are located in western Oregon in the revested O & C lands. The landscape in eastern Oregon is more wide open and sparsely vegetated due to the rain-shadow effect of the Cascade Range. In southeastern Oregon in the Burns District is the Steens Mountain Complex, a geographic area that includes Steens Mountain and Diamond Craters, with the Malheur National Wildlife Refuge located between these two features. Steens Mountain is a 30-mile fault block that rises almost 5000 feet above the Alvord Desert. The steep side of the mountain faces east, and the west side rises more gradually. The summit of Steens Mountain is 9733 feet—the highest point in Oregon that can be reached by vehicle. Outstanding features of the area includes alpine areas, glaciated areas, and abundant wildlife. Steens Mountain was designated by the BLM as Steens Mountain Recreation Lands in 1971, with recreational resources recognized as a primary value of the area. The recreation lands consist of approximately 200,000 acres and include five research natural areas, one area of critical environmental concern, and portions of six wilderness study areas. The Donner und Blitzen River System (72.7 miles) was designated a component of the National Wild and Scenic River System in 1988. There are 24 camping sites at Fish Lake and a smaller six-unit campground at Jackman Park. Diamond Craters is a 6-mile-diameter shield volcano. It is an area of recreational, educational, geological, and biological significance. An Auto Tour Guide describes geological features at 12 stops along a 40-mile auto tour.

The Rogue Wild and Scenic River is located in the Medford District of southwest Oregon. It is jointly administered by the BLM and the Forest Service and was one of the eight initial components of the National Wild and Scenic Rivers System in 1968. The BLM administers the upper 47 miles, and the Forest Service administers the lower 37 miles. Twenty miles of the river, from Graves Creek to Mule Creek, are classified "wild." In this section the river flows through an essentially natural canyon environment with many outstanding scenic areas. Canyon walls are very sheer in some areas, rising 2,000 feet from the water's edge to the ridgetop above. The river gradient averages 12.5 feet of vertical drop per river mile, providing whitewater rapids interspersed with gently flowing sections. The 27-mile segment from Hellgate Canyon to Grave Creek is classified "recreational." This section flows through a rural setting, is narrow with steep topography, and there is some residential development on the left bank. Recreational opportunities vary along each section of the river. The wild segment's primary attraction is whitewater rafting and primitive camping. During the summer season, recreational use is limited to allow a wild recreational experience. A paved road parallels most of the river's recreational segment. This augments sightseeing opportunities and provides convenient access to a variety of other recreational opportunities on a year-round basis. Recreational opportunities include swimming, picnicking, camping, rafting, hiking, and fishing. Jet boat trips on the recreational segment are available in summer.

Utah

A wide variety of recreational opportunities abounds on the 22 million acres of BLM land in Utah. Calf Creek Recreation Area, near Escalante in south-central Utah, is an

area of contrasts within the surrounding eroded canyonlands. The canyon of Calf Creek, viewed from Route 12 high above on the narrow upland called the Hogback or Hell's Backbone, is a vivid sight. This canyon is the site of the recreation complex and is an oasis of greenery set amidst a dry desert (Figures 12.10 and 12.11). At the entrance to the recreation area there is a shaded picnic area and a developed campground alongside Calf Creek. Calf Creek is a crystal-clear stream with headwaters 7 miles north of the entrance to the recreation complex. A 5.5-mile round-trip interpretive trail leads to Lower Calf Creek Falls. The falls are 126 feet high, and Calf Creek runs year-round. This trail winds between mineral-streaked cliffs of Navaho Sandstone; along the way are beaver ponds, remains of Indian living quarters and granaries, and prehistoric rock art sites. There is little elevation change encountered along the trail, but most of it is sandy and can be strenuous walking—especially in warm weather. However, the falls area, once reached, is a delightfully cool, shady haven worth the effort. The Upper Falls are located farther upstream and can be reached by a difficult 1-mile hike over sandstone slickrock from the Escalante-Boulder Highway (Route 12), 5.5 miles north of the campground road intersection.

The Little Sahara Recreation Area is located 115 miles south of Salt Lake City. The area contains 60,000 acres of sagebrush flats, juniper-covered hills, and free-moving sand dunes. The main attraction is the dunes, which cover about one-third of the area. Two-thirds of the area is designated for ORV use: The dunes provide an ideal sand-buggy playground, while the sagebrush flats and the Black Mountains are challenging for motorcycles and four-wheel-drive vehicles. Camping and picnic areas have been developed, and the Rockwell Natural Area provides an undisturbed site for nature study.

The Canyon Rims Recreation Area lies along the eastern and southern boundary of Canyonlands National Park. The Manti–La Sal National Forest lies to its south. Within this vast area visitors may tour scenic overlooks by automobile, camp, explore off-highway vehicle trails, hike, backpack, ride bikes, and rock climb. Most of Canyon Rims Recreation Area is primitive and undeveloped. Developed facilities include three public campgrounds, two overlooks, and a commercial resort.

The Moab Slickrock Bike Trial extends from 2 miles north of Moab, Utah, to the Colorado River on a scenic and rugged expanse of rolling Navaho Sandstone. The bike trail is ideal for use by mountain bikes and motorcycles designed for off-road use. It is not suitable for three- and four-wheel ATVs since it crosses steep slopes and narrow sections above drop-offs. For inexperienced riders there is a 2.3-mile practice loop. For more experienced riders, the main trail has many steep hills and requires advanced riding skills and endurance. The main-loop trail, including the side trail to Panorama Point, is 10.3 miles long and takes most people about 5 hours to ride.

Parowan Gap, located 10 miles west of Parowan and Interstate 15, has two features of distinction, one natural and the other human-made. The pass or gap is a classic example of a *wind gap,* an unusual geological landform in which an ancient river has cut a 600-foot-deep notch through the Red Hills. The other, the Parowan Gap Petroglyphs, is a nationally recognized extravaganza of Native American rock art. These features are set amidst the vast panoramas of the Escalante Desert and are easily accessible.

Figure 12.10 View of Calf Creek from the Hogback in the BLM's Escalante Resource Area in south-central Utah

Wyoming

The public lands in Wyoming includes a full spectrum of terrain and vegetative types. These range from the strangely beautiful badlands at Adobe Town, McCullough Peaks, and Dubois, to the forested peaks in the Raymond Mountains and the Ferris Mountains. There are many outfitters who guide the visitors to bountiful hunting

Figure 12.11 Entrance to the BLM's Calf Creek Recreation Area

and fishing opportunities on the public lands. The Oregon and Mormon National Historic Trails cross 345 miles of public lands. These two trails coincide for most of their distance across Wyoming. The Continental Divide Trail crosses 200 miles of public land in the Rawlins District. For the motorist, there are many scenic routes, which include several backcountry byways. The Sand Dunes Play Area in the Rock Springs District and the Bentonite Pit Area near Casper provide special opportunities for trail bikes, dirt bikes, dune buggies, and ATVs. The Worland District has one of the largest concentrations of caves in BLM lands, in the Worland Caves Special Recreation Management Area; over 40 caves, with 24 miles of cave passageways, have been surveyed to date. Natural Trap Cave, which has a vertical entrance and contains an accumulation of animal remains, is of considerable interest in the scientific community. Other caves include Horsethief, Great X, Tres Charros, Spirit Mountain, Holy Sheep, Great Expectation, and Titan. The West Slope Special Recreation Management Area is located on the western slope of the Big Horn Mountains in north-central Wyoming. The most frequent recreational pursuits there are hunting, fishing, picnicking, camping, and snowmobiling. Developed opportunities include Five Springs Falls campground, Middle Fork of the Powder River campground, and three hiking trails.

References

"BLM Backcountry Hikeways and Bikeways," *Backpacker Magazine* Special Supplement, pp. 47–65, June 1993.
Bureau of Land Management. *Alaska River Adventures.*
Bureau of Land Management. *Arevaipa Canyon Wilderness.*
Bureau of Land Management. *Arkansas Headwaters Recreation Area.*
Bureau of Land Management. *Back Country Byway.*
Bureau of Land Management. *BLM—Meeting the Challenge in 1991.*
Bureau of Land Management. *BLM Alaska.* 1990.
Bureau of Land Management. *BLM California—Recreation 2000 Opportunities Map.* 1991.
Bureau of Land Management. *BLM California Camping.* 1991.
Bureau of Land Management. *BLM California Trails and Rivers.* 1991.
Bureau of Land Management. *BLM Colorado Recreation Opportunities.* 1991.
Bureau of Land Management. *BLM Colorado River Adventures.* 1991.
Bureau of Land Management. *BLM in California.*
Bureau of Land Management. *BLM in Colorado.* 1992.
Bureau of Land Management. *BLM National Recreation Guide.*
Bureau of Land Management. *BLM Nevada Wilderness Program.* September 1991.
Bureau of Land Management. *BLM Oregon Recreation Map.* 1991.
Bureau of Land Management. *BLM Oregon/Washington Watchable Wildlife.*
Bureau of Land Management. *BLM Recreation Users Guide—Carson City District.*
Bureau of Land Management. *BLM Recreation Users Guide—Ely District.*
Bureau of Land Management. *BLM Recreation Users Guide—Winnemucca District.*
Bureau of Land Management. *BLM Utah: Calf Creek Falls Trail Guide.* 1992.
Bureau of Land Management. *BLM Wilderness.*
Bureau of Land Management. *BLM Wyoming Back Country Byways.* 1991.
Bureau of Land Management. *BLM Wyoming Fishing Opportunities: Big Horn River.* 1992.

Bureau of Land Management. *BLM Wyoming Fishing Opportunities: Northeast and Central.* 1991.

Bureau of Land Management. *BLM Wyoming Recreation Guide.* 1990.

Bureau of Land Management. *BLM Wyoming Wilderness.* 1992.

Bureau of Land Management. *Camping on the Public Lands.*

Bureau of Land Management. *Canyon Rims Recreation Area.*

Bureau of Land Management. *Desert Conservation—A Management Showcase.* 1991.

Bureau of Land Management. *Garnet—Snowmobile to a Ghost Town.*

Bureau of Land Management. *Gila Box Riparian National Conservation Area.*

Bureau of Land Management. *In the Meantime—Protecting Your Wilderness Study Areas.*

Bureau of Land Management. *Little Sahara Recreation Area.* July 1990.

Bureau of Land Management. *Missouri Breaks Historic Trails.*

Bureau of Land Management. *Moab Slickrock Bike Trail.*

Bureau of Land Management. *Montana BLM Recreation Opportunities.*

Bureau of Land Management. *Nevada Back Country Byway—Mt. Wilson.* April 1990.

Bureau of Land Management. *Nevada Back Country Byway—Red Rock Canyon.* April 1990.

Bureau of Land Management. *Nevada Back Country Byway—The California Trail.* April 1990.

Bureau of Land Management. *Nevada Back Country Byways.* 1990.

Bureau of Land Management. *Nevada Backcountry Byway—Gold Butte.* April 1990.

Bureau of Land Management. *Nevada Recreation Management Strategy and Implementation Plan.* 1990.

Bureau of Land Management. *Newsbeat—BLM California.* August 1993.

Bureau of Land Management. *Oregon National Back Country Byways.*

Bureau of Land Management. *Parowan Gap Petroglyphs.* 1992.

Bureau of Land Management. *Pinnell Mountain National Recreation Trail.* 1990.

Bureau of Land Management. *Public Land Statistics—1991.* Washington, D.C.: U.S. Government Printing Office, September 1992.

Bureau of Land Management. *Recreation 2000 Tri-State Strategy—Volume I: The Plan.* May 1990.

Bureau of Land Management. *Recreation 2000 Tri-State Strategy—Volume II: Special Recreation Management Areas.* May 1990.

Bureau of Land Management. *Recreation 2000 Tri-State Strategy—Volume III: Background and References.* May 1990.

Bureau of Land Management. *Recreation 2000: A Strategic Plan.* Washington, D.C.: U.S. Government Printing Office, 1990.

Bureau of Land Management. *Recreation 2000: Alaska.* May 1989.

Bureau of Land Management. *Recreation and Vehicle Guide to Beaver River Resource Area.* May 1988.

Bureau of Land Management. *Recreation Futures for Colorado.* 1989.

Bureau of Land Management. *Red Rock Canyon National Conservation Area.*

Bureau of Land Management. *Red Rock Canyon National Conservation Area—Geology.* 1992.

Bureau of Land Management. *Red Rock Canyon National Conservation Area—Hiking.* 1991.

Bureau of Land Management. *Red Rock Canyon National Conservation Area—Mammals.* 1992.

Bureau of Land Management. *Red Rock Canyon National Conservation Area—Plants.* 1992.

Bureau of Land Management. *Red Rock Canyon National Conservation Area—Birds.* 1992.

Bureau of Land Management. *Red Rock Canyon National Conservation Area—Bicycling.*

Bureau of Land Management. *Royal Gorge Resource Area—Draft Resource Management Plan and Environmental Impact Statement.* September 1993.

Bureau of Land Management. *San Luis Resource Area—Record of Decision and Approved Resource Management Plan.* December 1991.

Bureau of Land Management. *San Pedro Riparian National Conservation Area.*

Bureau of Land Management. *Supplement—Public Lands Recreation: Extensive Recreation Management Areas—Oregon and Washington.* June 1989.

Bureau of Land Management. *The Bureau of Land Management.*

Bureau of Land Management. *The Gold Belt Tour—A National Back Country Byway.*

Bureau of Land Management. *The New BLM: 1989–1992.*

Bureau of Land Management. *Public Lands Recreation—Volume 1: A Special Management Strategy for Special Recreation Management Areas in Oregon and Washington.* June 1989.

Bureau of Land Management. *Public Lands Recreation—Volume II: Special Recreation Management Area Narratives.* June 1989.

Bureau of Land Management. *Wyoming—Guiding and Outfitting on BLM Administered Public Lands.* 1991.

Bureau of Land Management. *Wyoming BLM—Recreation 2000 Implementation Plan.* 1989.

Bureau of Land Management. *Wyoming Public Land Access.* 1990.

Clawson, Marion. *The Bureau of Land Management.* New York: Praeger Publishers, 1971.

Clawson, Marion. *Man and Land in the United States.* Lincoln: University of Nebraska Press, 1964.

Clawson, Marion, and Carlton Van Doren. *Statistics on Outdoor Recreation.* Washington, D.C.: Resources of the Future, 1984.

Connelly, Nancy A., and Tommy L. Brown. *Estimates of Nonconsumptive Wildlife Use of Forest Service and BLM Lands.* Series No. 88-2. Ithaca, N.Y.: Cornell University, April 1988.

Connelly, Nancy A., and Tommy L. Brown. *Estimates of the Use of Bureau of Land Management Lands for Hunting.* HDRU Series 90-10. Ithaca, N.Y.: Cornell University, October 1990.

Culhane, Paul J. *Public Lands Politics.* Baltimore: Published for Resources for the Future by Johns Hopkins University Press, 1981.

Farmers Insurance Group. "Rediscovering America—Back Country Byways." *Friendly Exchange,* No. 2, Fall 1992.

Muhn, James, and Hanson R. Stuart. *Opportunity and Challenge: The Story of BLM.* Washington, D.C.: U.S. Government Printing Office, September 1988.

Zeveloff, Samuel I., and Cyrus M. McKell, Editors. *Wilderness Issues in the Arid Lands of the Western United States.* Albuquerque: University of New Mexico Press, 1992.

## CHAPTER 13

Army Corps of Engineers, Bureau of Reclamation, Tennessee Valley Authority, and Indian Lands

Man has too long forgotten that the earth was given to him for usufruct alone, not for consumption, still less for profligate waste.

George P. Marsh (1864)

It is not the intent of this last and final chapter on federal land-managing agencies to go into the depth that Chapters 3 through 12 have done for the National Park Service, the Forest Service, the Fish and Wildlife Service, and the Bureau of Land Management. The intent of this chapter is to present a broad overview of the recreational opportunities that are available on projects and lands managed by the Army Corps of Engineers, the Bureau of Reclamation, and the Tennessee Valley Authority and on federal Indian lands. One of the major contributions of this chapter are the maps, which identify the geographic location of the lands, projects, reservoirs, and existing recreational facilities. Another major contribution is the appendices (at back of book) and tables (within the chapter) keyed to this series of maps. These appendices and tables identify the recreational opportunities that are available on the various lands. Much of the information contained in this chapter can be obtained from these tables, maps, and appendices.

Practically all of the recreational opportunities available on Bureau of Reclamation (BUREC) and Tennessee Valley Authority (TVA) projects are located on reservoirs. The same may be said about the Army Corps of Engineers. But in addition to the reservoirs that this agency has constructed, there are also many other projects that have recreational benefits, for example, the Intracoastal Waterway, stream channel or depth improvements, canals, locks, and harbor projects. The interesting aspect regarding the management of the recreational facilities at the three reservoir-provid-

ing agencies is that in many cases the land and facilities are transferred over to other jurisdictions for management purposes. In many cases, therefore, it is standard practice for other agencies (such as state and local government) to actively manage and develop the recreational facilities. The primary function of the BUREC or the Army Corps of Engineers is to regulate the water level in the reservoirs and to maintain the dams.

Virtually all of the large reservoirs that exist in the United States have been built by the BUREC, the Corps, or the TVA. Although the reservoirs built by these agencies have always had recreational values, it was not until 1965 that specific recreational responsibilities at these reservoirs were addressed by Congress. The *Federal Water Project Recreation Act* (1965) specified that "any federal navigation, flood control, reclamation, hydroelectric, or multiple-purpose water resource project should give full consideration to outdoor recreation and wildlife enhancement." The act also provided limited authority to expand existing projects. Recreation benefits have been the leader in benefit-cost analysis at many projects.

The construction of reservoirs has had a variety of impacts, some positive and some negative, depending on differences of interpretation. The construction of reservoirs is a classic example of an *irreversible natural resource decision*. Simply put, this means that once a reservoir is constructed and filled with water, changes are set in motion that are incapable of being reversed. When reservoirs are constructed, wildlife and cultural features, including humans, are displaced or lost. The water table is altered, being raised upstream and lowered downstream. The loss from evaporation greatly increases in a reservoir with its larger surface area. This evaporative loss is especially severe in the arid West. The migration of anadromous fish is disrupted. Stream temperature and turbidity are changed. While the sediment carried by the streams is deposited in the reservoirs, the cool, clear tailwater releases support new cold-water species, such as trout. Even the fish species in the reservoir change. The nature of the recreational use changes dramatically from whitewater recreation to flatwater recreation. Before reservoir construction, recreational use is often very light, with perhaps only a few canoers, kayakers, rafters, hikers, backpackers or fishermen using the stream. These recreational uses change drastically once a reservoir is constructed. The recreational carrying capacity of the larger reservoir increases. Large campgrounds and resorts are often built on the reservoirs, and the associated tourist and commercial development increases. Some towns have arisen, and remained, to serve as housing for the construction workers needed to build the dams; witness Page, Ariz., and Boulder City, Nev. Powerboats replace hand-propelled boats, and waterskiing is now possible. The visual character of the area is changed. A major change in the visual landscape is the presence of power lines, which carry the low-cost electricity generated by the turbines in the dams; they are now dominant visual features, especially in the barren West, where trees are unavailable to screen them. Many of the major dams have become recreational attractions.

The construction of new federal water projects slowed drastically in the late 1970s when President Carter eliminated the construction of a number of projects. Many controversial natural resource issues evolved around the construction of new dams by the Army Corps of Engineers, the BUREC, and the TVA. Perhaps none is more famous than the Tellico Dam, proposed by the TVA on the Little Tennessee River (Figure 13.1). This dam gained a great deal of prominence regarding the snail darter (a 3-inch fish) and the Endangered Species Act. In fact, the controversy almost caused

Figure 13.1   The TVA's Tellico Dam, on the Little Tennessee River, is one of the most controversial dams ever constructed in the United States. The issue here was the role of the Endangered Species Act in protection of the snail darter (a 3 inch fish). (Tennessee Valley Authority photo)

Congress not to renew the Endangered Species Act. A ruling of the Supreme Court in 1978 (Hill *v.* TVA) stopped the 80 percent–complete Tellico Dam. After many attempts at having the Tellico Dam project exempted from the Endangered Species Act, proponents attached an amendment to a major $10 billion water projects appropriation bill. This amendment exempted the Tellico Dam project from any laws that would prohibit it. President Carter could not veto such a major bill, and shortly after he signed it the reservoir behind the Tellico Dam started to fill. The snail darter survives today and is no longer "endangered" due to a successful relocation process by the Fish and Wildlife Service. In Missouri, a major controversy arose over the Corps-proposed Meramec Park Lake project. The reservoir formed behind the dam on the Meramec River in south-central Missouri would have, among other things, flooded several caverns. The Meramec River is also a major recreational resource for canoe or jon (small, flat bottomed) boat floats.[1] The issue of dam construction was so controversial that its future was placed on the ballot for the voters of Missouri to decide its future—and they voted no. The dam was never built. The passage of the Wild and Scenic Rivers Act in 1968 placed a new national priority on valuing free-flowing rivers and has been responsible for keeping many proposed future Army Corps of Engineers and BUREC dams and reservoirs from being constructed.

The topic of federal Native American lands is included in this chapter for lack of a better location. Indian lands are essentially private property that are held in trust or restricted status by the Bureau of Indian Affairs (BIA) in the Interior Department.

---

[1]The author began his development as a potential recreational geographer by spending the finest days of his youth floating, fishing, spelunking, and camping on the Meramec River, and he knows the area for the proposed dam extremely well. The construction of this dam would have destroyed a unique recreational resource.

They may be regarded as private or quasi-federal lands, since they are jointly administered by the Indian tribes and the BIA. The BIA has encouraged recreational developments because of their economic potential. Indoor recreation, such as bingo and gambling, has been a fairly common occurrence on Indian lands. The outdoor recreational potential of Native American lands is just beginning to be realized. On some reservations, such as the Warm Springs Reservation (Oregon) or the Mescalero Reservation (N. Mexico), the Native Americans have developed very sophisticated resorts that include a multitude of outdoor recreation opportunities. At many reservations, however, the outdoor recreation potential is either untapped or is just beginning to be developed. This recreational potential for outsiders is purposely not allowed in certain cases since the Indians want to keep the land for their exclusive use for personal and/or spiritual reasons.

ARMY CORPS OF ENGINEERS

The Army Corps of Engineers is the second-ranking provider of outdoor recreation opportunities among the seven major federal land-managing agencies. In 1991 the Corps registered 192,166,500 recreation visitor days, which accounted for 29 percent of all recreation visitor days on federal lands. Only the Forest Service tallied greater use—278,849,000 recreation visitor days, for 42 percent of the federal total. The land base of Corps projects is small, but the use is high. Several factors explain this high amount of recreational use that occurs on Corps projects: (1) Many Corps projects are located close to large cities. About 80 percent of Corps lakes are within 50 miles of major metropolitan areas, and 94 percent are within a 2-hour drive. (2) In many parts of the country, Corps-created reservoirs are the only recreational resource within many miles. (3) Also, water has always been a focal point and major attraction for outdoor recreation, and water is a principal feature at Corps projects. Corps projects that have recreational value usually occur in one of the following type of areas: reservoirs and stabilizing pools, harbors, waterways, locks and dams, or improvement of coastal beaches.

The U.S. Army Corps of Engineers has been in existence far longer than any of the other federal land-managing agencies discussed in this book. The Corps traces its beginning to June 16, 1775. At this time, successfully engineered defenses were constructed under the direction of General George Washington's first chief engineer, Colonel Richard Gridley, at the Battle of Bunker Hill. Congress officially established the agency on March 11, 1779. Early Corps missions were military in nature, but the civil works mission of the Corps began in 1824 with the passage of the first *Rivers and Harbors Act,* when Congress provided the first appropriations for work in navigable waters. The Corps protected Yellowstone and Yosemite National Parks until the National Park Service was created in 1916. Flood-control activities were added to Corps responsibilities in the 1920s and 1930s. "Reservoir development expanded the scope of public service of the Corps" (Army Corps of Engineers, 1990, 5). The development of Corps lakes nationwide for a variety of purposes attracted so many

visitors that Congress passed the *Flood Control Act* (1944), which gave the Corps specific authority to provide public outdoor recreation facilities at its projects. Section 4 of this act states:

> The Chief of Engineers . . . is authorized to construct, maintain, and operate public park and recreational facilities in reservoir areas under control of (the Department of the Army), and to permit the construction, maintenance and operation of such facilities.

During the 1940s and the 1950s, provision of recreational facilities for the general public was limited to basic facilities, including roads and restrooms. This was because land acquisition was limited to a very narrow ribbon surrounding the lakes, and public access was very limited. While many of the Corps projects were initially rural in nature, cities grew out to meet the once-rural property. Many people began to purchase property adjacent to Corps projects, and these people began to assume rights of private ownership right to the water's edge. Facilities, including private boathouses, launching ramps, and picnic areas, were constructed on public lands by adjacent landowners for their own private use. During the 1950s and early 1960s these uses did not receive much opposition from the Corps. This situation changed and regulations were issued in 1971 that discouraged exclusive private use of public lands. Regulations adopted in 1974 stated that "any private docks or vegetation modification previously developed on Corps projects be covered by a Lakeshore [Now "Shoreline"] Use Permit and that such development not be permitted on new projects or on existing projects where such facilities did not exist in 1974." (U.S. Army Corps of Engineers, 1990, p. 6) Currently, about 50,000 private facilities and areas of vegetation modification are under permit at 100 Corps lakes.

Although state and local partnerships through leases and licenses under authority of the 1944 act had been very successful, an accelerated program was initiated with implementation of the *Code 712 Program*. This program entailed construction of recreational facilities at 100 percent federal expense with subsequent turnover to nonfederal public agencies for continued operation and maintenance. The objective was to achieve a turnover to state and local agencies of as many Corps recreation areas as possible in a 5-year period beginning July 1, 1967. The program was initiated in 1969. The Code 712 Program was not successful, and several of the nonfederal agencies began returning facilitates to the Corps due to their own funding problems. Significant changes in the Corps recreation program were initiated with the passage by Congress of the Federal Water Project Recreation Act (1965) and the Land and Water Conservation Fund (1965). A 1974 amendment to the Land and Water Conservation Fund Act required the Corps to provide at least one free primitive campground at Corps projects where camping is permitted.

It is important to stress that Corps projects cannot be constructed primarily for recreational purposes. Navigation, maintenance, and improvement of navigable waters and flood control have been the primary purposes for Corps projects (Figure 13.2). Some Corps projects are used for water supply and power generation. The Corps of Engineers is the fourth-largest producer of power in the United States, with an installed capacity of 20,625,900 kW. Only the TVA, Commonwealth Edison, and Georgia Power have greater capacities. Recreation is given full consideration in plan-

Figure 13.2 The Army Corps of Engineers' W. P. Franklin Lock and Dam on the Caloosahatchee River near Fort Myers, Fla., allows recreational boating access to Lake Okeechobee and continuation to the eastern coast of Florida. Shown here is a sternwheeler tour boat passing through the lock.

ning and development today. It is interesting to note that in the benefit-cost analysis process, recreation represents the largest dollar amount of benefits for some projects. Such was the case for the now-defunct Meramec Park Lake project in Missouri.

As one of the nation's largest providers of outdoor recreation, the Corps of Engineers plays an important role in the U.S. tourism industry. Recent studies undertaken by the Corps indicate that significant economic activity is generated by recreational opportunities provided at Corps projects. Visitors to Corps projects in 1988 spent more than $10 billion for such nondurable goods and services as food, fuel, bait, restaurant meals, and lodging. This trip spending generated an estimated $8 billion of income and over 265,000 jobs for local economies. Trip spending alone by visitors to Corps projects accounted for approximately 3.5 percent of all tourism spending and resulted in about 5 percent of all tourism employment. This does not include the spending on such durable items as boats and camping equipment, which also results from Corps recreation projects. In 1988 the economic impact performance indicator used by the Corps averaged $33 of visitor spending for each operation and maintenance dollar spent (Army Corps of Engineers, 1990, 21).

The Army Corps of Engineers is allowed, by law, to charge fees for the public use of specialized recreation sites, facilities, services, and special-event permits. The Corps is prohibited, by law, from charging entrance fees or for charging for such day-use activities as sightseeing and use of the water. The Corps is the only federal agency that must provide at least one free campground at each project where it provides camping facilities. Recreational boaters may use navigation locks free of charge. All revenue from recreation fees is returned to the Corps for use in operating, maintaining and in some cases, enhancing existing recreation areas.

Geographic Location of Corps Projects

Army Corps of Engineer projects show a closer spatial relationship with population distribution than do those of any other federal land-managing agency. These projects

are generally absent in the more sparsely populated sections of the country, especially in the Rocky Mountains, the Great Basin, and Alaska. Of course, many of the BUREC's dams and reservoirs are located in the Intermountain West. High numbers of Corps projects are located in the eastern Great Plains and adjacent Midwest, the Northeast, and the West Coast. There is an especially dense concentration of Corps projects on the Upper Mississippi River. Providing a safe channel for shipping on the Mississippi was one of the Corps of Engineers' first civil-works missions. Today, much of the region's commerce moves through the chain of 29 locks and dams from Minneapolis to St. Louis. The Illinois Waterway, another Corps project, links the Mississippi near St. Louis with the Great Lakes–St. Lawrence Seaway at Chicago. Another especially dense concentration of Corps projects extends from Pennsylvania through Ohio and West Virginia to Kentucky. A third major concentration of Corps projects occurs in East Texas, eastern Oklahoma, and Arkansas. Several states have a disproportionately high number of Corps projects: Pennsylvania (39), Illinois (37), Ohio (33), Texas (29), Oklahoma (28), Kentucky (27), Arkansas (23), and California (22). Many Corps projects are on waterways that serve as the boundary between two states. Figure 13.3 shows the location of Corps projects and is keyed to Appendix XVIII, which also identifies the recreational opportunities available at each project. The only states that do not have major Corps projects are Delaware, Maine, Nevada, New Jersey, Utah, and Wyoming. Alaska has only one Corps project: Chena River Lakes. Other states with only a few Corps projects are Arizona (2), Hawaii (1), Idaho (3), Louisiana (3), Maryland (1), Michigan (2), Montana (2), New York (4), and South Carolina (3). The Corps' largest reservoir, and one of six built to control recurrent flooding on the Missouri River, is Lake Sakakawea, behind the Garrison Dam in North Dakota.

Recreational Use

Recreation is a major use at virtually all Corps projects today. Table 13.1 presents a statistical summary of recreation-related data for the Army Corps of Engineers. In 1992, there were 4382 recreation areas on 461 Corps projects. Fifty-seven percent of the recreation areas were managed directly by the Corps. The remaining 43 percent were managed by other federal agencies (1.4 percent), state governments (13.1 percent), local governments (13.3 percent), concessionaires (3.7 percent), and quasi-public agencies (11.5 percent). Figure 13.4 identifies the relative importance of the management of recreation areas. Corps projects cover 11,897,449 acres and have 40,647 miles of shoreline. The Corps has issued a total of 53,504 lakeshore use permits, 58 percent of which are for private boat docks. The basic facilities are usually built by the Corps. These include access roads, water supply, sanitary facilities, overlooks, signs, and simple picnicking and camping areas. Further developments are provided by cooperating governmental agencies or nonprofit organizations under long-term leases. Recreation lands not required for public use may be leased to private individuals or organizations for commercial development. Appendix XVIII, which is keyed to Figure 13.3, identifies 518 Corps projects and the recreational facilities that are available. Restrooms are provided at 457, or 88 percent, of the projects, and drinking water and picnic/day-use facilities are located at 430 (83 percent). Boat launching ramps are very common, existing at 395 (76 percent). Camping without electricity is available at 324 (63 percent) of the projects, and camping with electricity is available at 250 (48

Table 13.1   U.S. Army Corps of Engineers: Nationwide Statistical Data—1992

Visitation (visitor hours)		2,441,207,673
Corps of Engineer projects		461
Number of recreation areas:		4,382
Number managed by the Corps of Engineers		2,500
Number managed by other agencies		1,882
By other federal agencies	61	
By state government	572	
By local government	583	
By concessionaire	160	
By quasi-public agencies	506	
Project lands owned in fee (acres)		8,059,514
Fee acres above conservation pool		4,295,069
Water surface acres at conservation pool		5,581,707
Total acres (fee, easement, riverbed)		11,897,449
Total shoreline miles in fee		40,647
Rangers:		
Permanent (full time)	904	
Permanent (part time)	133	
Temporary	569	
Total		1,606
Lakeshore use permits:		
Land-based	17,785	
Private boat docks	30,740	
Community boat docks	3,333	
Other floating facilities	1,646	
Total		53,504
Volunteer data:		
Number of volunteers		82,511
Volunteer hours worked		628,135
Value of volunteer hours worked		$4,437,598

Source: Cori Brown, Army Corps of Engineers, Baltimore, Md., personal communication, 1993.

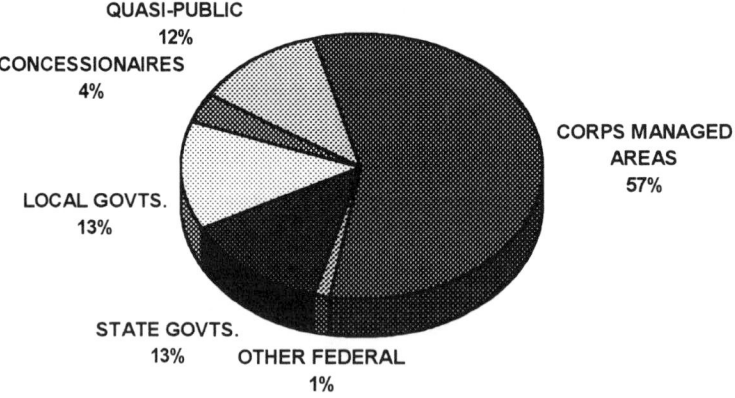

Figure 13.4   Management responsibility for Corps of Engineers recreation areas, 1992. (*Source:* Cori Brown, Army Corps of Engineers, Baltimore, MD.)

percent) of the projects. There are visitor centers at 225 (43 percent) of the projects and marinas at 215 (42 percent). The Corps has estimated the percentage distribution of recreational use at its projects among the following categories: sightseeing (34 percent), fishing (26 percent), boating (18 percent), picnicking (16 percent), camping (11 percent), swimming (10 percent), waterskiing (4 percent), and hunting (3 percent).

Table 13.2 summarizes the visitation and number of projects and recreation areas by Corps division. The Corps uses the *recreation visitor hour* as its unit of measurement. Recreation visitor hours can be easily converted to recreation visitor days by dividing the number of recreation visitor hours by 12. The leading Corps divisions in terms of recreational use are the Southwestern (29 percent of use), the South Atlantic (23 percent), and the Ohio River Divisions (22 percent). Relatively low percentages of total recreational use occur in the New England (1 percent), the North Atlantic (1 percent), the South Pacific (2 percent), and the North Pacific Divisions (3 percent). The largest number of Corps projects are located in the Ohio River (27 percent of projects) and the Southwestern Divisions (21 percent). The greatest number of Corps recreation areas are located in the following divisions: Southwestern (665, or 27 percent), South Atlantic (469, or 19 percent), and Ohio River (457, or 19 percent). The same three divisions have the largest number of non-Corps recreation areas: Southwestern (623, or 34 percent), Ohio River (366, or 20 percent), and South Atlantic (341, or 18 percent). Divisions with the least number of recreation projects are the North Atlantic (42, or 1.7 percent, of Corps and 13, or 0.7 percent, of non-Corps recreation areas) and the New England Divisions (59, or 2.4 percent of Corps and 22, or 1.2 percent of non-Corps recreation areas).

Table 13.3 summarizes the distribution of recreation visits by visitation level and by division. At Corps recreation areas, the most common level of use is between 100,000 and 499,999 visitor hours, occurring at 39 percent of the recreation areas. The second most common level of use is 5000 to 99,999 visitor hours, occurring at 32 percent of the recreation areas. At non-Corps recreation areas the two leading levels are reversed: 42 percent of areas receive 5000 to 99,999 visitor hours, and 29 percent receive 100,000 to 499,999.

Table 13.2   Army Corps of Engineers: Visitation, Projects, and Recreation Areas by Division—1989

Division	Visitation (million visitor hours)	Number of Projects	Number of Recreation Areas (Corps)	Number of Recreation Areas (Non-Corps)
Lower Mississippi Valley (LMVD)	148.8	25	197	91
Missouri River (MRD)	163.5	44	221	184
New England (NED)	22.0	32	59	22
North Atlantic (NAD)	21.6	18	42	13
North Central (NCD)	115.6	29	130	120
North Pacific (NPD)	62.0	32	97	70
Ohio River (ORD)	512.0	122	457	366
South Atlantic (SAD)	535.4	33	469	341
South Pacific (SPD)	45.6	26	99	24
Southwestern (SWD)	669.4	98	665	623
Total	2,295.9	459	2,436	1,854

Source: U.S. Army Corps of Engineers Natural Resources Management System, 1989.

Table 13.3   Distribution of Visitation at Corps and non-Corps Recreation Areas by Division—1989

Visitation Level (in visitor hours)	LMV	MRD	NED	NAD	NCD	NPD	ORD	SAD	SPD	SWD	Total
				Number of Corps Recreation Areas							
Under 5,000	1	21	4	1	7	0	28	7	19	14	102
5,000–99,999	48	78	29	22	60	41	146	153	33	166	776
100,000–499,999	90	74	23	13	40	39	182	203	25	253	942
500,000–1,000,000	30	34	1	3	15	13	58	47	15	114	330
Over 1,000,000	28	14	2	3	8	4	43	59	7	118	286
Total	197	221	59	42	130	97	457	469	99	665	2436
				Number of Non-Corps Recreation Areas							
Under 5,000	1	17	0	1	4	0	12	13	1	82	131
5,000–99,999	18	85	13	0	76	26	94	119	6	350	787
100,000–499,999	46	40	4	7	30	30	160	109	8	107	541
500,000–1,000,000	14	15	3	2	9	11	46	44	2	28	174
Over 1,000,000	12	27	2	3	1	3	54	56	77	56	221
Total	91	184	22	13	120	70	366	341	94	623	1854

Note: LMV, Lower Mississippi Valley Division; MRD, Missouri River Division; NED, New England Division; NAD, North Atlantic Division; NCD, North Central Division; NPD, North Pacific Division; ORD, Ohio River Division; SAD, South Atlantic Division; SPD, South Pacific Division; SWD, Southwestern Division

Source: U.S. Army Corps of Engineers Natural Resources Management System (in house database), 1989.

Table 13.4 identifies the 10 most heavily visited Corps projects. Lake Texoma, (Texas and Oklahoma, 83,808,300 visitor hours) and Lake Sidney Lanier (Georgia, 82,526,900 visitor hours) are the clear leaders followed by Allatoona Lake (Georgia, 66,381,000 visitor hours) and Hartwell Lake (Georgia and S. Carolina, 64,424,800 visitor hours). Lake Texoma is formed by the Denison Dam on the Red River, and the reservoir straddles two states (Texas and Oklahoma). It is located north of Dallas–Fort Worth and south of Oklahoma City. In 1946, the National Park Service assumed management of Lake Texoma but 1 year later returned it to the Corps. The Park Service stated that management of multipurpose reservoirs requires some unique skills it did not possess and that it did not believe such projects fit the mission of preservation of the service. The proximity of Lake Sidney Lanier a short distance northeast of Atlanta contributes to its heavy recreational use. Buford Dam backs up the Chattahoochee River, and the lake encompasses 38,000 surface acres of water with

Table 13.4   Army Corps of Engineers: 10 Most Visited Projects—1992

Project Name	Visitor Hours
Texoma Lake, OK and TX	83,808,300
Lake Sidney Lanier, GA	82,526,900
Allatoona Lake, GA	66,381,000
Hartwell Lake, GA and SC	64,424,800
J. Strom Thurmond Lake, GA and SC	52,966,612
Wolf Creek Dam–Lake Cumberland, KY	49,264,100
Old Hickory Lock and Dam, TN	48,416,800
Mississippi River Rock Island District, IL	45,869,500
John H. Kerr Dam and Reservoir, NC and VA	38,441,445
Table Rock Lake, AR and MO	38,335,308

Source: Cori Brown, Army Corps of Engineers, Baltimore, Md., personal communication, 1993.

540 miles of shoreline. The Corps has developed numerous park areas around the lake for camping and day-use activities. Lake Lanier Islands, a development by the Corps and the state of Georgia, is the major resort area on the lake. The islands complex provides picnicking, camping, beach areas, a water theme park, tennis courts, golf courses, rental boats, and hotel accommodations. Allatoona Lake is located in the foothills of the Blue Ridge Mountains, just 30 miles north of Atlanta. The reservoir is formed behind a dam on the Etowah River and has a surface area of 12,010 acres and a shoreline of 270 miles. This is the oldest Corps lake in the Southeast and is heavily used for recreation. Camping, hiking, marinas, and cabins are available. Hartwell Lake, in the upstate region of Georgia and South Carolina on the Savannah River, has an excellent reputation for all types of outdoor recreation activity. The area adjoins Clemson University and is rich in historical lore.

The fifth-ranked J. Strom Thurmond Lake (52,966,612 visitor hours) is the largest Corps lake east of the Mississippi River and is located downstream from Hartwell Lake on the Savannah River. Like Hartwell Lake, it straddles the Georgia–South Carolina border. J. Strom Thurmond Lake is especially noted for its excellent striper and black bass fishing, and its large wildlife management areas offer some of the South's best hunting and wildlife observation opportunities. Wolf Creek Dam–Lake Cumberland ranks sixth in use (49,264,100 visits) and is located in southeastern Kentucky on the Cumberland River. This large deepwater lake offers a variety of attractions and activities, including the Lake Cumberland State Resort Park. Old Hickory Lake ranks seventh in use (48,416,800 visits) and is located on the Cumberland River a few miles northeast of Nashville. This lake is extensively developed and is noted for sailing and yachting; numerous regattas are held on the lake. The Old Hickory Nature Trail, a part of the National Trail System, provides interesting features for all age groups. Most of the surface area of the John H. Kerr Reservoir (38,441,445 visits) lies in Virginia, but it also extends into North Carolina. The John H. Kerr Dam is on the Roanoke River, and the 50,000-acre reservoir behind it is one of the largest human-made lakes in the east. It is noted for its camping facilities and striped bass fishing. Table Rock Lake (38,335,308 visits), on the White River in southwestern Missouri on the Arkansas border, is located in a highly developed resort area with many caves, museums, and resorts in the vicinity. The 800 miles of shoreline on the lake harbor many recreational opportunities. The small town of Branson, Mo., has grown into a major country music mecca, with the numbers of country music theaters and shows here rivaling those in Nashville.

Case Study: Canyon Dam and Lake

Canyon Dam and Lake is located on the Guadalupe River in South Texas, 48 miles north of San Antonio and 16 miles northwest of New Braunfels; Austin lies 56 miles to the northeast, and San Marcos is 24 miles to the east. Interest in constructing a flood-control structure heightened after major floods on the Guadalupe River in 1932, 1935, and 1936. Field studies were conducted between 1935 and 1939 on the feasibility of a Guadalupe River Dam. In 1939 the Corps of Engineers presented a study to Congress recommending the construction of a flood-control structure. Congress passed the *Rivers and Harbors Act* of 1945, which authorized construction of the dam, and in 1949 the project site was selected. The *Flood Control Act* of 1954 gave local

agencies rights for water conservation control. In 1955, the first planning and construction funds were appropriated by Congress for Canyon Dam, and in 1958 additional funds were appropriated. In 1958 construction began, and in 1964 the impoundment of water was started. The project was dedicated in 1966, and in 1968 the lake reached conservation pool level. The cost of the project was approximately $20,745,000.

The primary purpose of the Canyon Dam is for flood control and water conservation on the 1432 square miles of watershed above the dam. The *conservation pool* covers an area of 8231 acres with 80 miles of shoreline. The top elevation of the conservation pool is 909 feet above mean sea level, with the elevation of the streambed at 750 feet above mean sea level. The capacity of the conservation pool is 382,000 acre-feet. The *flood-control pool* has an elevation of 943 feet above mean sea level, with an area of 12,890 acres and a capacity of 346,400 acre-feet. The lowest elevation of the water level since reaching the conservation pool level has been 899.7 feet above mean sea level in December 1984. During major floods in 1978 and 1991 the lake elevation reached 930.6 and 937 feet, respectively, above mean sea level. A flood of record occurred in July 1987, when an elevation of 942.67 feet was reached. The dam is a rolled earth fill type; its overall length is 6830 feet with a crown width of 20 feet. The height of the dam is 224 feet above stream bed. The spillway is a broadcrested, uncontrolled type with a length of 1260 feet and a crest elevation 943 feet above mean sea level. The Guadalupe–Blanco River Authority, an agency of the state of Texas, has agreed to contribute an amount, not to exceed 42.9 percent of the total cost of the construction of the project, in return for rights to use the conservation storage space provided in the project. Water stored in the conservation pool is under complete control of the state of Texas and is available for municipal and other beneficial uses.

The Army Corps of Engineers has referred to recreation and favorable fish and wildlife habitats as "extra dividends" derived from the project. In 1993, there were 1,146,907 recreation visits, which equaled 6,185,049 recreation visitor hours. The lake lands are open to all, and there are many attractive areas for outdoor recreation, water sports, camping, fishing, and boating. Other popular activities include jet skiing, sailing, and scuba diving. Swimming areas are unsupervised (no lifeguards). There is also a private yacht club, Lake Canyon Yacht Club, located just east of Jacob Park. The management of fish and wildlife resources is being conducted in cooperation with the Texas Parks and Wildlife Commission. Hunting is prohibited at Canyon Lake. Species that may be caught in the lake include crappie, white bass, yellow catfish, walleye, and largemouth and smallmouth bass. Rainbow trout have been stocked in the cold tailwater release from the dam into the Guadalupe River.

Eight "parks" have been established on all sides of the lake that serve as the shore-based areas for outdoor recreation. Three of these parks are located at the dam site. Immediately below the dam is 92-acre Guadalupe Park. There are no developed facilities here, and the area is kept as open space. There is a trail along the river here, and trout fishermen are among the principal users of the river. Immediately on the south side of the dam at the headquarters area is the 36-acre Overlook Park, which is primarily an observation area, offering views of the lake and the dam; there is also a restroom facility here. North Park is located on the small peninsula at the north end of the dam. North Park is 45 acres, and there are 20 free multiple-purpose sites

that may be used for picnicking or camping. Most of these sites are suited only for tent camping due to lack of parking space. There is one restroom here.

Away from the dam site, on the north shore of the lake, are three additional parks: Jacobs Creek Park, Canyon Park, and Potters Creek Park. Jacobs Creek Park is 102 acres and differs from the other parks in that two sections are held for exclusive military use. On much of the northern side of the peninsula a special permit is held by Fort Sam Houston, and on part of the southern side of the peninsula a special permit is held by Randolph Air Force Base. The only users permitted in these two areas are active military, retired, or reserve military personnel. In the remainder of Jacob Creek Park there are 58 free multiple-purpose sites for public camping or picnicking. A few sites here are for recreational vehicles or trailers, but there are no hookups. There is a swimming beach on the southern side of the outermost part of the peninsula.

Canyon Park is considered a model park. It encompasses 428 acres of land on the northeastern side of the lake. The nature of the park site as a peninsula gives the area adequate access to water with occasional cover and a jagged shoreline. Facilities include roads, parking areas, water supply and other utilities, sanitary facilities, public camping and picnic areas, swimming, boat launching ramps, information signs, safety measures, and concessions. Trailer areas are available, and there is a group picnic shelter. Shortly after entering the Canyon Park area there are two day-use beaches and picnic sites—one on the western side of the road and the other on the eastern side. There are 46 picnic-only sites at these two beaches, and no fee is charged for use. A short distance past the day-use areas there is a private concession on the western side of the peninsula called Canyon Park Marina Concession (Figure 13.5). Here are located boat slips, covered boat storage, other features associated with marinas, and a restaurant. On the eastern side of the road across from the marina is a

Figure 13.5 The Canyon Park Marina Concession is operated by the private sector under permit from the Army Corps of Engineers at Canyon Lake, Texas. Shown is a picnic site in the foreground and the marina in the background.

closed former camping area. Where the peninsula broadens out past the marina area there is a fee house and traffic-control gate. Within this gated area, on the remainder of the peninsula there are 202 multiple-use sites. Most of the public-use sites at Canyon Park are multiple-use and may be used for picnicking or camping. What is unique about this section of Canyon Lake is that day users or campers must each pay a fee ($6 per day) to use this area. There are two boat dock-and-launch areas within this pay zone, but one has been closed.

Potters Creek Park, the westernmost park on the northern shore of the lake, covers 375 acres and is slightly more developed than the other parks. There are 109 multiple-use sites, of which 17 have electrical and water hookups. The regular camp-sites are $6 per night; the 17 electrical sites are $2 extra per night. There is no charge for day use at these sites. There is one swimming area and two boat dock-and-launching sites. There is also an earth-and-rock fishing pier.

There are two major parks on the south shore of the lake: Cranes Mill and Comal. Cranes Mill Park, the westernmost park on the southern shore, is situated on a 229-acre peninsula. There are 80 multiple-use sites, which permit both camping and picnicking on a first-come-first-served basis, and the entrance to this area is gated. The charge for camping is $6 per night, but there is no charge for day use. A private concessionaire operates here the second marina on the lake, Cranes Mill Park Marina. There are two separate boat docks-and-launch areas, one designated swimming area, and a handicapped-accessible fishing pier. The 115-acre Comal Park lies to the east of Cranes Mill Park on the southern shore. There are 63 multiple-use sites, which are free for day use, but camping is $6 a night. There are two boat dock-and-launching sites and a swimming beach. Comal Park tends to attract more day use while Canyon Park and Potters Creek Park attract more overnight use.

BUREAU OF RECLAMATION

The Bureau of Reclamation, an agency in the Interior Department, is the fifth-ranking provider of outdoor recreation opportunities among the seven major federal land-managing agencies. In 1991 the Bureau recorded 23,365,200 recreation visitor days (RVDs) according to the *Federal Recreation Fee Report to Congress—1991*. This use accounted for 4 percent of all recreational use occurring on federal land. The recreational use at Bureau projects is actually 2½ times this amount, but much of this use is reported under the agency responsible for administering the recreation area. For example, major national recreation areas such as Lake Mead, Glen Canyon, or Flaming Gorge are Bureau projects. Their recreational use is tallied under the National Park Service for the first two areas and the Forest Service for the third in the Federal Fee Reporting System. It is the Bureau's policy to transfer recreation management responsibilities to other agencies.

The Bureau is responsible for the development and conservation of the nation's water resources in the western United States. The Bureau's original purpose "to provide for the reclamation of arid and semi-arid lands in the West" today covers a wide range of interrelated functions. These include providing municipal and industrial

water supplies; hydroelectric power generation; irrigation water for agriculture; water-quality improvement; flood control; river navigation; river regulation and control; fish and wildlife enhancement; outdoor recreation; and research on water-related design, construction, materials, atmospheric management, and wind and solar power. Bureau programs most frequently are the result of close cooperation with the Congress, other federal agencies, state and local governments, academic institutions, water user organizations, and other concerned groups.

The *Reclamation Act* (1902) established the agency that became known as the Bureau of Reclamation. The original purpose of this act was to apply receipts from the sale and disposal of public lands toward the location, construction, operation, and maintenance of projects for storage, diversion, and development of waters in order to reclaim arid and semiarid lands in 17 western states. The water for agriculture was meant for family farms. Water for a single-person farm could be applied to 160 acres, and for a husband and wife to 320 acres. For the first 5 years after the passage of the Reclamation Act, the U.S. Geological Survey carried out the mandates of the law. In 1907 the Reclamation Service was established, and it took over the tasks that the Geological Survey had been handling. The Reclamation Service was renamed the Bureau of Reclamation in 1923. Early reservoirs were constructed for a single purpose—the storage of irrigation waters. Gradually, other purposes were added to the water projects: power, municipal and industrial water, flood control, and most recently fish and wildlife, and recreation. Figure 13.6 shows the Bureau of Reclamation's Jackson Lake Dam on the Snake River in Grand Teton National Park (Wyoming) with the Teton Range in the background. Jackson Lake serves as a storage reservoir for irrigated farms downstream in Idaho. Sometimes a large amount of drawdown is necessary to meet these water needs, as illustrated in Figure 3.7.

Facilities in operation on Bureau of Reclamation projects today include 355 storage reservoirs, 254 diversion dams, 16,047 miles of canals, 1509 miles of pipelines, 278 miles of tunnels, 37,193 miles of laterals, 17,002 miles of project drains, 249 pumping stations over 1000 horsepower, and 51 hydroelectric power plants. Completed

Figure 13.6 Bureau of Reclamation's Jackson Lake Dam on the Snake River in Grand Teton National Park, Wyoming.

water services facilities are transferred to local water-user organizations for operation and maintenance as soon as the organizations become capable of assuming these functions. The Bureau operates and maintains hydroelectric power plants and some water storage and supply works on multipurpose projects. Some highlights of 1989 operations include:

- *Water Deliveries*   Totaled 30.3 million acre-feet (9898.4 billion gallons), including 25.7 million acre-feet for irrigation, 3.5 million acre-feet for municipal and industrial use, and 1.1 million acre-feet for other nonagricultural uses. The "below-cost" water sales of the Bureau of Reclamation have been an issue of major contention in Congress.
- *Population Served*   28.4 million people. Of this total, 24.7 million people received municipal and industrial water, 2.9 million people received irrigation service on urban and suburban land, and 0.8 million people received irrigation service on full- or part-time farms.
- *Gross Value of All Crops Produced* $8.9 billion.
- *Acreage Irrigated*   9,432,000 acres.
- *Food, Fiber, and Forage Production*   Totaled 61.4 million tons, which fed 39 million people.
- *Irrigated Farms*   Totaled 137,700, of which full-time farms represented 57 percent of the total number of farms and 87 percent of the irrigable land in farms.
- *Electricity Generated*   51 power plants produced 40.4 billion kilowatt hours. The Bureau of Reclamation is the 11th-largest producer of electricity in the nation and produces 25 percent of the total western hydropower and 16 percent of the nation's total. In Wyoming, 100 percent of the state's hydropower is derived from the Bureau and over 75 percent of the hydropower in Nevada and Arizona is produced by the Bureau. The Bureau's greatest hydropower generating capacity is in Washington.
- *Flood-Control Benefits*   Totaled $40.2 million.

Some of the proposed Bureau of Reclamation projects have been extremely controversial, starting in the 1950s with the Echo Park Dam, which was proposed for the Green River in Dinosaur National Monument (Colorado). A national campaign of public opposition killed the Echo Park project, but saving Dinosaur National Monument paved the way for construction of the Glen Canyon Dam (Arizona). Farther downstream on the Colorado River, the Green River joins the Colorado River above Glen Canyon. While Lake Powell, the reservoir behind the Glen Canyon Dam, is probably the most scenic reservoir in the world, many irreplaceable natural and cultural features were lost in the flooding process. The Glen Canyon Dam (Figure 13.7) is an excellent example of an irreversible natural resource decision. Some of the least-known and most spectacular canyons in the country were inundated behind the dam, and ancient Indian ruins and artwork were lost. In the 1960s the Bureau proposed dams for Grand Canyon National Park, Grand Canyon National Monument, and Marble Canyon National Monument. Public opposition to these proposed dams were responsible for enlarging Grand Canyon National Park so that it would protect the entire area of the Colorado River from the Lake Mead to the Glen Canyon National Recreation Areas.

In recent years, the Bureau's primary role as the developer of large, federally financed agricultural projects has declined. No major new reclamation project has

Figure 13.7   Glen Canyon Dam (Arizona) was built by the Bureau of Reclamation on the Colorado River. Jurisdiction over the land surrounding Lake Powell (Glen Canyon National Recreation Area) was given to the National Park Service.

been authorized by Congress since 1968. Environmental concerns, a farm economy no longer capable of sustaining the burden of increasingly costly projects, a revised public perception of Reclamation's mission, and budgetary constraints at all levels of government have combined to make major agricultural water and power projects increasingly difficult to justify. The passage of the Wild and Scenic Rivers Act has played a major role in this change in focus, by protecting from dam construction many of the remaining free-flowing rivers. By the mid-1990s, construction of federally funded water and power projects is no longer a priority in Bureau activities. The Bureau plans to focus on efficiency in total resource management and more effective use of existing facilities. Bureau of Reclamation water and power systems on the average are 30 to 40 years old, and some are becoming obsolete. There is a need to renovate, rehabilitate, and in some cases, rebuild these facilities. The Bureau projects that by the year 2000 its order of priorities is likely to be as follows:

1. Operation and maintenance
2. Water quality and environmental enhancement
3. Groundwater management
4. Total system optimization
5. Dam safety

Amazing changes are occurring in the manner in which the contemporary Bureau of Reclamation is doing business. For example, in January 1994 it announced a major change in its management practices at the Glen Canyon Dam (Arizona). The Bureau's release of water from the dam will give priority to amenity resource values (such as wildlife and recreation) over power production. The Bureau will strive to allow no

more than a 3- to 4-foot variation in the water level below the dam as water is released to generate electricity. (Previously, the release of water for power production caused fluctuation of up to 13 feet in the water level in the Colorado River below the dam.) This new standard will result in less power generation from the dam, but recreational opportunities and wildlife will be enhanced. Although the only announced plans for such a change in water releases are at the Glen Canyon Dam, the Bureau has said this policy will be extended to other dams.

Geographic Location of Bureau of Reclamation Projects

The geographic location of Bureau of Reclamation recreation areas is randomly scattered about the western half of the country. There are 300 recreation areas located on projects that total 4.7 million acres of land and 1.7 million acres of water with 12,994 miles of shoreline. Especially dense concentrations of Bureau recreation areas are found in the Central Valley of California, on the Columbia River System in Washington, in southern Idaho, in northeastern Utah, on the western slope of Colorado, in Wyoming, in the Great Plains of Kansas and Nebraska, and in southern Arizona around Phoenix. Bureau recreation areas are noticeably sparse in Texas, which has just three. This pattern is explained by the active role the Army Corps of Engineers has assumed in Texas. A large portion of Nevada is devoid of Bureau recreation areas; only in southern Nevada near Las Vegas and in northwestern Nevada near Reno are they found. The states with the most recreation areas are California (51), Washington (35), Colorado (31), Oregon (24), Utah (20), Wyoming (20), and Idaho (18). Figure 13.8 shows the locations of the 300 Bureau of Reclamation recreation areas and is keyed to Appendix XIX, which lists them in detail. This appendix identifies for each of the 300 recreation areas: the project; the acres of land; the acres of water; the administering agency; the number of recreation visitor days; and the primary recreation activities.

Recreational Use

Bureau of Reclamation reservoirs and project lands across the West provide a wide variety of recreational facilities and opportunities. While the primary purpose of early Bureau projects was the storage of irrigation water, the recreational value of these projects was discovered early. An example of this recreational attraction is the Theodore Roosevelt Dam, located 76 miles northeast of Phoenix on the Salt River Project and completed in 1911. The new reservoir proved an attraction for boating and swimming, and a hotel was built. As interest in the recreational attraction of Bureau projects heightened, arrangements started to be made by the Bureau to transfer recreational responsibility to other agencies. The first of these involvements came at Lake Mead, which was created by the Hoover Dam in 1935. In 1936, the National Park Service assumed responsibility for all recreational activities on its reservoir at what was first titled the Boulder Dam National Recreation Area. The second such agreement was at the Grand Coulee Dam (Washington), which was completed in 1941 and created Franklin D. Roosevelt Lake. In 1946, the National Park Service assumed recreational responsibility for the Coulee Dam National Recreation Area.

Today's Bureau of Reclamation is much less involved in recreation management than the other federal land-managing agencies. Bureau of Reclamation policy is to transfer management of recreation areas on its project lands to other federal and nonfederal governmental entities. In 1989 Reclamation was the sole managing agency at only 31 recreation areas and shared in the management of only 17 out of a total of 300 recreation areas on its projects. Most of these 17 recreation areas are small. State and local agencies managed all or part of 181 areas, followed by other federal agencies with 95, water-user organizations with 16, and other organizations with 3 areas. The Forest Service is the federal agency with the most recreation areas on Bureau of Reclamation projects. This is because most of them were on land already in the National Forest System. Figure 13.9 identifies the relative importance of recreation-managing agencies on Reclamation projects.

The amount of recreational use at Bureau of Reclamation projects is reported in different ways. The *Federal Recreation Fee Report to Congress—1991* (National Park Service, 1992) reported a total of 23,365,200 recreation visitor days for the Bureau of Reclamation. This figure is less than the 56.3 million RVDs reported by the Bureau in its *1989 Summary Statistics—Water, Land and Related Data*. The reason for the larger figure reported by the Bureau is that the 56.3-million-RVD value is the total at all 300 recreation areas on Bureau projects for all administering agencies. While the Bureau of Reclamation counts such high-use areas as the Lake Mead National Recreation Area (7.0 million RVDs) and the Glen Canyon National Recreation Area (6.4 million RVDs) in its reporting system, the Federal Fee Reporting System credits this use to the National Park System. The 56.3 million RVDs reported by the Bureau of Reclamation in 1989 represented a 3 percent increase over the 54.5 million RVDs in 1988, despite lower water levels and drought conditions that persisted throughout much of the West. The Bureau reported 79.2 million recreation visits for 1989.

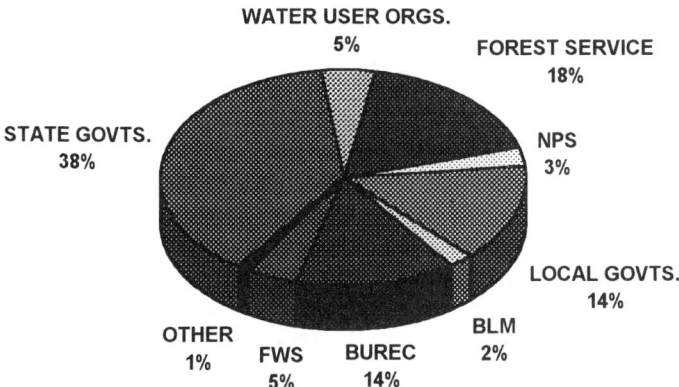

Figure 13.9 Recreation managing agencies on Bureau of Reclamation Projects, 1989. BLM, Bureau of Land Management; BUREC, Bureau of Reclamation; FWS, Fish and Wildlife Service, NPS, National Park Service. (*Source:* Bureau of Reclamation, 1989 Summary Statistics: Water, Land, and Related Data.)

The most popular Reclamation project recreation area for many years has been the Lake Mead National Recreation Area (Arizona and Nevada), Boulder Canyon Project, which surrounds the Hoover Dam and its reservoir. More than 8.8 million people visited Lake Mead, accounting for 7.0 million recreation visitor days. Another 1.8 million visitors toured the Hoover Dam itself, accounting for 74,517 visitor days. Of the 300 recreation areas on Reclamation projects, seven areas reported over 1 million RVDs in 1989, and another 15 areas reported between 500,000 and 1 million RVDs. Together, these 22 popular areas accounted for 59 percent of the total visitation to recreation areas on Reclamation project lands. By contrast, the 201 areas with less than 100,000 RVDs accounted for only 10 percent of the total use. Table 13.5 identifies the 10 most heavily used recreation areas. Appendix XIX is a complete listing of all recreation areas, the administering agency, the land and water acreage, the number of recreation visitor days, and the primary recreational activities. This appendix provides a wealth of information for Bureau of Reclamation recreation areas. California's 10.7 million RVDs of use at Bureau of Reclamation projects was far greater than for any other state.

In 1989, recreation areas on Reclamation-constructed projects provided 4.7 million acres of land, 1.7 million acres of water surface, and 12,994 miles of shoreline for public recreation areas; 3.2 million acres were open for public hunting. Some wildlife species have benefited from Bureau projects; for example, fish and waterfowl are now found for the first time in the marshes below Lake Mead. In 1989, public-use facilities in these areas included:

- 990 campgrounds with 29,000 campsites
- 835 picnic areas with 20,700 picnic tables
- 730 boat launch ramps with 1375 ramp lanes
- 60 mobile home or trailer parks with 5275 spaces
- 147 swimming beaches

Table 13.5   Bureau of Reclamation: 10 Most Visited Projects—1989

Recreation Area	Project	Administering Agency	Recreation Visitor Days
Lake Mead National Recreation Area	Boulder Canyon, AZ and NV	National Park Service	6,997,356
Glen Canyon National Recreation Area (Lake Powell)	Colorado River Storage AZ, UT	National Park Service	6,380,074
Lake Havasu Area	Parker-Davis, AZ and CA	BLM	3,513,455
Shasta Lake	Central Valley, CA	Forest Service, Bureau of Reclamation	2,421,650
Lake Berryessa	Solano, CA	Bureau of Reclamation	1,671,637
Lake Thunderbird	Norman, OK	Okla. Tourism & Rec. Dept.	1,266,595
Theodore Roosevelt Reservoir	Salt River, AZ	Forest Service	1,056,000
Elephant Butte Reservoir	Rio Grande, NM	N.M. Energy, Min. and NRD	876,978
Cheney Reservoir	Pick-Sloan MBP, KS	Kans. Dept. Wildlife and Parks	851,608
Jackson Lake	Minidoka-Palisades, WY	National Park Service	817,284

Source: Bureau of Reclamation, *1989 Summary Statistics—Water, Land, and Related Data.* Bureau of Reclamation: Denver, Colorado (no date).

Various private concessions on Reclamation projects—such as cafes, golf courses, marinas, lodges and resorts, campgrounds, and trailer parks—numbered 253 in 1989.

Applying an average value of $13.26 per RVD, the value of recreation on Reclamation project lands in 1989 totaled $746 million. This value is based on current measures used in National Economic Development (NED) benefit evaluation procedures. These procedures assign values ranging from $2.06 to $24.46 per RVD unit, depending on the ratings assigned to each area. The rating criteria and the associated measuring standards used for NED evaluation reflect differences in quality, relative scarcity, activities available, accessibility, and aesthetic features of the recreation area.

Case Study: Flaming Gorge Dam and Reservoir

The Flaming Gorge Dam and Reservoir is located on the Green River and straddles the border where the northeastern corner of Utah meets the southwestern corner of Wyoming. The reservoir is 91 miles long and occupies Flaming Gorge and Red Canyons. The dam is in Utah near the small community of Dutch John. Rock Springs, Wyo., is 60 miles north of the dam, and Vernal, Utah, is 40 miles to the south of the dam. The landscape of the reservoir area varies between Utah and Wyoming. In Utah, the Green River has cut through the Uinta Mountains. Differences in elevation cause climatic variations in this mountainous southern section. This southern section consists of benches, canyons and forest inhabited by deer, elk, and eagles. The northern section in Wyoming is composed of low hills, shale badlands, and desert shrubs. Pronghorn antelope and prairie dogs inhabit this part of Flaming Gorge country. It was a few miles above the northern end of the reservoir, near Green River, Wyo., that Maj. John Wesley Powell and nine men in 1869 embarked on their daring exploration of the Green and Colorado Rivers. On May 26, 1869, Major Powell named the Flaming Gorge after seeing the sun reflecting off the red rocks.

Construction of the Flaming Gorge Dam was authorized, along with three other units, in 1956 under the *Colorado River Storage Project Act*. Other units of the Colorado River Storage Project are the Glen Canyon Dam, on the Colorado River in northern Arizona; the Navaho Unit, on the San Juan River in northwestern New Mexico; and the Wayne N. Aspinall Unit, on the Gunnison River in west-central Colorado, which contains the Blue Mesa, Morrow Point, and Crystal Dams. Construction of the Flaming Gorge Dam was begun in 1958 and completed in 1964 at a cost of $65 million. The function of this dam is to store water to meet downstream water commitments and to produce hydroelectric power. Flaming Gorge Dam rises 502 feet above bedrock and 455 feet above the original river channel. The dam is a thin-arch concrete type that varies in thickness from 151 feet at the base to 27 feet at the crest. The reservoir, which extends 91 miles west and then north from the dam, has a total capacity of 3,788,900 acre-feet. At its full elevation of 6045 feet, the surface area is 42,020 acres. The power plant has three generators that produce an average of 533,000 megawatt-hours annually. The total installed capacity of the three generating units is approximately 152 megawatts.

The Flaming Gorge National Recreation Area was established by Congress on October 1, 1968, under P.L. 90-540. The act added approximately 123,000 acres to the Ashley National Forest and assigned management of the entire national recreation area to the Forest Service. The area contains 207,363 acres of land and water that are almost equally divided between Utah and Wyoming. The Flaming Gorge National Recreation Area is managed by the Forest Service in Vernal, Utah, as part of the Ashley National Forest. The district ranger's office is in Manila, Utah, near the Utah-Wyoming border on the western side of the reservoir. The Bureau of Reclamation administers the dam, the power plant, the reservoir, and the housing area of Dutch John, Utah.

A large number of recreational opportunities abound at the Flaming Gorge National Recreation Area. The Flaming Gorge Dam Visitor Center is located at the dam, and free guided tours of the dam are given. The Red Canyon Visitors Center is located 8 miles west of the dam and offers a spectacular view from 1400 feet above Red Canyon and Flaming Gorge Reservoir. Slide programs, movies, displays, and interpretive literature are available. Sheep Creek Canyon, located southwest of Manila, has been designated by the Forest Service as a geological area and presents a lavish display of twisted and upturned rock. Sheep Creek has been eroding this canyon for millions of years, since the uplift of the Uinta Mountains began. A paved road now runs through this narrow canyon, making a loop that connects with Utah 44. There are 20 campgrounds, of which four are accessible only by boat, and there are picnicking facilities at 27 areas. There are 14 boat launches and four marinas. On the western side of the reservoir at Buckboard and Lucerne Valley there are major recreational facilities, including marinas, campgrounds, picnic facilities, and boat launch ramps. The marinas provide boat rentals and supplies. On the eastern side at Mustang Ridge (north side of reservoir) there are facilities for camping, picnicking, and boat launching, and at Cedar Springs (south side of reservoir) there are campgrounds, picnic facilities, a boat launching ramp, and a marina with boat rentals and supplies.

The recreation area is open year-round, but most facilities are closed during the winter months. The reservoir is noted for trophy trout fishing. The following Utah records have been caught at Flaming Gorge Reservoir: brown trout (33 lbs. 10 oz.), rainbow trout (26 lbs. 2 oz.), lake trout (51 lbs. 8 oz.), and kokanee salmon (5 lbs. 5 oz.). Smallmouth bass are also caught in the reservoir. Flaming Gorge Reservoir and the Green River are open to year-round fishing, but periods of closure are established to protect salmon during the spawning season in some streams flowing into the reservoir. Ice fishing is popular during the winter. Hunting is permitted away from public use areas. There are hiking trails within the recreation area, and cross-country ski trails are available in winter.

The Green River in Red Canyon below the dam is noted for fine river rafting and fishing opportunities. The water that flows from the dam is cold—55°F or lower—and river levels may vary due to power generation. An excellent half-day float is from the dam to Little Hole. This float takes a leisurely pace, with occasional wilder rapids, which provide excitement. A float trip to Brown's Park takes all day. On this longer trip some may want to portage around Red Creek Rapids. No motors are permitted between the dam and Indian Crossing. Permits are needed for those floating beyond the Gates of Lodore. People wishing to travel farther need to obtain a permit in advance from the Dinosaur National Monument.

TENNESSEE VALLEY AUTHORITY

The Tennessee Valley Authority (TVA) is a U.S. government–owned corporation created by Congress in 1933 to integrate development of the basin of the Tennessee River. It is a New Deal regional resource development agency, charged with long-range planning for the region. As an independent public corporation, it was authorized to build dams and power plants to control the flood-prone Tennessee River. Economic and social improvement of an impoverished region was a principal goal of the legislation. Senator George Norris of Nebraska proposed the plan and guided it through Congress. The TVA is based on the concept that all of the resources of a river basin are interrelated and should be developed under one unified plan for maximum effectiveness. It is a classic example of using the most natural division that exists for planning purposes—that of a river basin. The TVA is an independent agency of the Executive Branch and is administered by a board of three officials who are appointed by the president for 9-year terms. The appointments are staggered and subject to approval by the Senate. The TVA employs over 19,000, and the main offices are in Knoxville, Tenn.

The TVA region in which 5 million people live, covers a drainage basin of about 40,910 square miles and extends from the western slope of the Southern Appalachian Mountains to the Ohio River. The drainage basin of the 650-mile Tennessee River, the principal stream of the region, extends into seven southeastern states: Virginia; western North Carolina; eastern, southern, and western Tennessee; northwest Georgia; northern Alabama; the extreme northeastern corner of Mississippi; and western Kentucky. Major tributary streams include the Little Tennessee, the French Broad, the Holston, the Clinch, and the Hiwassee Rivers. The Tennessee River system is the nation's fifth largest. The headwater streams of the Tennessee River meet near Knoxville in eastern Tennessee, and the river then flows southwest into northern Alabama. At Guntersville, Ala., the river then flows west-northwest and serves as the Alabama-Mississippi border in the extreme northwestern corner of Alabama. From this point the river flows north through western Tennessee and Kentucky and joins the Ohio River near Paducah, Ky. Portions of several national forests and one national park are included within the TVA region. The Little Tennessee River forms the southern boundary of Great Smoky Mountains National Park. Along much of this boundary is located Fontana Lake, formed behind the Fontana Dam. The Appalachian Trail crosses from the Nantahala National Forest to the Great Smoky Mountains National Park at Fontana Dam. Other national forests within the TVA region are the Cherokee, the Chattahoochee, the Pisgah, the Jefferson, and the Bankhead National Forests.

The primary purposes of the Tennessee Valley Authority are flood control, power production, and navigation. To accomplish all three of these goals it was necessary for the TVA to build a series of dams. Related activities, based on the original legislation and subsequent enactments, include reforestation, industrial and community development, test-demonstration farming, and establishing recreational facilities. A preexisting dam the TVA was directed to operate was the Wilson Dam at Muscle Shoals, Ala., for national defense and for the development of new types of fertilizers. Today, there are 39 multi-purpose major dams in the TVA Water Control System.

(There are also other smaller dams on tributaries that are not part of the TVA Water Control System.) The most recently completed (1979), and most controversial, dam is the Tellico Dam on the Little Tennessee River. The controversy over this dam was addressed in the introduction to this chapter. There are nine major dams that form a continuous 650-mile navigable channel on the Tennessee River. These dams, moving upstream, are the Kentucky, the Pickwick, the Wilson, the Wheeler, the Guntersville, the Nickajack, the Chicamauga, the Watts Bar, and the Fort Loudon Dams. Near Paducah, Ky., the channel connects with the Ohio River and the 21-state Inland Waterways System. The Tennessee River is linked to the Tombigbee River and the Gulf of Mexico by the Tennessee-Tombigbee Waterway. The other 24 dams are on tributaries of the Tennessee River. Figure 13.10 illustrates the Chicamauga Dam and lock.

All of the dams generate electricity, and in addition the TVA operates 12 large coal-burning steam-generating plants and two nuclear plants (with two nuclear plants still under construction). In 1978 the Environmental Protection Agency took the TVA to court over the emission of sulfur dioxide from these coal-burning plants—and won. Most TVA activities are financed largely through appropriations by Congress, although the TVA power program is self-supporting. The TVA is the nation's largest "utility," with an installed capacity of 30,930,900 kilowatts. The availability of low-cost power has attracted businesses to the area, and the TVA is credited with improving the economic climate of the area and changing Tennessee's economy from an agricultural to a diversified industrial economy.

There are more than 600,000 acres of water surface and 11,000 miles of shoreline on TVA reservoirs. The TVA has acquired in fee 1,389,058 acres. Of this total, 1,087,642 acres were acquired for reservoir projects, and 301,416 acres were acquired for nonreservoir projects including steam plants, other electric plants, general plants, and chemical operations. Of the lands acquired, a total of 174,226 acres has been sold and

Figure 13.10   The TVA's Chickamauga Dam and lock is one of the reasons the Tennessee River is navigable for 650 miles. (TVA photo)

182,239 acres have been transferred. Of the latter, 123,891 acres have been transferred to other federal agencies, as follows: Department of the Army, 5784 acres; the Atomic Energy Commission, 1286 acres; the Fish and Wildlife Service, 8319 acres; the Forest Service, 64,285 acres; and the National Park Service, 44,216 acres. The remaining 58,348 acres were transferred to state and local agencies, principally for public recreation use (TVA, *The TVA Handbook,* 1988, 227).

Recreational Use

From its beginning, the TVA has worked to encourage a wide range of outdoor recreation facilities and opportunities, especially on TVA lakes and shorelines. Although recreation was not a specific charge of the original act, it did call for a comprehensive approach to planning to ensure the orderly development of resources. Initially, the TVA did not develop or operate recreational facilities and services, but transferred land to other government agencies or nonprofit organizations. In 1937 the first lease of reservoir land to a public agency for recreational development was made to the State of Tennessee for Cave Lake State Park. In 1945 the first transfer of reservoir land to a state for public recreation development was made to the state of Tennessee for Paris Landing State Park. Some lands have been sold at public auction for private or commercial development. Today, the TVA builds and operates recreational facilities at selected reservoir locations to help meet public needs. The recreation policy of the TVA today is

> . . . to identify the recreation resources available throughout the Valley (especially those associated with TVA lakes), to encourage development by other public agencies and private investors, to provide technical assistance where needed to achieve this development, and to provide basic facilities where needed to assure safe access to the lakes and to protect the shoreline from misuse. (TVA, 1988, p. 184)

In 1966, recreation was recognized for the first time as a significant benefit (56 percent) in the economic justification of one TVA project, Tim's Ford, and in 1967 the Recreation Resources Program was established by TVA. Since 1969, the TVA has been providing basic recreational improvements such as picnic facilities, boat launching ramps, access roads, and sanitary facilities along its reservoir shorelines where such public use indicated a need for such facilities. By 1978 the use of these shoreline facilities had grown to such an extent that it became evident to the TVA board of directors that a new policy for facility management was needed. During 1979 the TVA began implementing the new policy. Community meetings were held throughout the region to be sure local conditions were taken into account. Based on these comments, specific management plans were developed for management of TVA facilities on reservoir properties.

The new policy basically maintained the TVA's long-standing recreational goals: (1) to provide a quality outdoor experience for citizens of the Valley and for visitors to the area, (2) to encourage state and local government agencies to develop parks and other recreational facilities wherever feasible, and (3) to assist in the growth and development of quality private recreational opportunities in the Valley. In managing its own facilities, TVA designated certain areas for specific uses (day use; overnight camping; informal use, including a combination of camping and day use; boat

launching). The TVA began employing onsite, resident caretakers for key areas, and a modest fee was charged for overnight camping at developed campgrounds.

Through planning and technical assistance, the TVA furnishes guidance to all types of parks and recreation programs as well as to development of lake-oriented facilities. This program also furnishes information about recreational use and development of the region's resources for TVA and other planners to use in analyzing and evaluating recreational opportunities and needs. One of the most effective ways the TVA supports its overall recreation commitment has been to make suitable portions of its shoreline lands available to others for development. Land and land rights have been transferred or conveyed for a nominal consideration to federal, state, and local governmental agencies for the development of public parks and access areas. Lands have been leased, licensed, and sold to quasi-public groups and organizations for group camps. In addition to these activities on reservoir lands, the TVA has provided a wide range of technical assistance to communities, counties, municipalities, and state agencies to help them improve their own recreation programs.

Recreation has grown to be an increasingly important benefit of TVA lakes. The only measurement of current recreational use is the 1,069,800 RVDs for TVA fee management units in 1991 (National Park Service, *Federal Fee Report*, 1992). This accounts for only 0.2 percent of the recreational use among the seven major federal land-managing agencies and ranks the TVA in last place. However, a much greater amount of recreational use is actually made of the TVA system. This figure does not include the use made of TVA-managed facilities such as dams, reservoirs, boat launches, and day-use areas where no fee is charged. And it does not include the large amount of use of lands under other jurisdictions on the TVA reservoirs. Robert Marker, recreation manager of the TVA, has estimated (January 10, 1994) that there are probably at least 10 million visits annually to TVA-administered nonfee areas and dam reservations (Marker, personal communication, January 10, 1994). Unfortunately, the TVA stopped collecting use data in 1980 for all recreational use that occurs on its projects. In 1980 the total recreational use at all recreation areas, including TVA dam reservations and Land Between the Lakes, was 70,857,000 recreation visits. The most popular reservoirs or projects were Kentucky (16.6 million visits), Guntersville (7.5 million visits), Chickamauga (6.6 million visits), Pickwick (6.3 million visits), Wilson (3.9 million visits), Wheeler (3.4 million visits), Watts Bar (3.4 million visits), Norris (3.4 million visits), Fontana (3.2 million visits), and Cherokee (2.6 million visits).

Table 13.6 summarizes the nature of the recreation lands in the TVA region. A total of 227,643 acres have been transferred or conveyed by other methods to other jurisdictions for public recreation. The largest amount of acreage has been transferred or conveyed by other methods to four national forests (61,992 acres), 28 state wildlife management areas (61,291 acres), Great Smoky Mountain National Park (44,217 acres), and 118 public parks (36,358 acres). The acreages for TVA recreation lands are not given in Table 13.6, since this amounts to only about 2000 out of the 250,000 acres retained by the TVA (exclusive of Land Between the Lakes, where the TVA manages another 170,000 acres). Appendix XX is a more detailed listing of recreation areas by reservoirs on TVA land, former TVA land, tributary area association land, and private land.

Table 13.7 is keyed to Figure 13.11, which is a map of the TVA area and identifies the 44 TVA recreation areas, the reservoirs, and the recreational opportunities avail-

Table 13.6   Tennessee Valley Authority: Recreation Summary

Items		Acres[a]
118 public parks:		36,358
21 state	25,963	
37 county	3,995	
55 municipal (1 on phosphate land)	6,107	
3 county-municipal	249	
1 fair association	44	
455 public access areas and roadside parks:		4,926
7 federal (USFS)	89	
346 state	4,525	
48 local	312	
140 TVA-improved public recreation areas		—
34 tributary area authority public access areas		—
2 environmental study areas		—
28 state wildlife management areas:		61,291
2 national wildlife refuges		18,428
1 national park		44,217
1 national parkway		431
4 national forests (12 reservoirs)		61,992[b]
Total		227,643[c]

55 group camps and clubs
298 commercial recreation areas
37,000 number of boats and houseboats moored on lakes

[a]Acreage reported is principally land above the maximum shoreline contour. Considerably more land is available and used for public recreation because rights are granted to use the land between this contour and the water's edge; e.g., Federal and state wildlife agencies use thousands of additional acres subject to permanent or periodic flooding in connection with their wildlife development programs.
[b]Includes 3,756 acres which are also reported under state wildlife management areas, public access areas, and county parks.
[c]Does not add because some national forest land is also reported under other specific uses.
Source: TVA, The TVA Handbook, Knoxville, Tenn., 1988, p. 186

able at each of them. Among these facilities, the TVA operates 32 major campgrounds with a total of 2323 camping units, and 32 picnic areas with 1363 picnic units. There are 35 pavilions at these picnic areas. The TVA operates swimming beaches at 29 of these recreation areas, and there are boat launching facilities at 39 of them.

A wide range of recreational opportunities are available including picnicking, boating, fishing, swimming, camping, hiking, nature study, photography, and hunting. Facilities to accommodate these activities are managed by national, state, and local agencies. Private interests operate commercial boat docks and resorts. In addition, thousands of acres of undeveloped TVA lands are available for informal recreation. The system of improved channels, dams, and locks provides a tremendous variety of pleasure boat cruising choices. There is no charge for recreational boats passing through the navigation locks at dams. A bell rope on each end of the lock wall allows the boater to signal the lock operator that a boat is ready to pass through. Many TVA reservoirs have one or more trails for backpacking, hiking, jogging, and bicycling, as well as quiet paths for walking and nature study. Several trails are interpretive. Special *small wild areas* have been established to preserve and protect areas of scenic or scientific beauty; the first 18 of these areas were identified in 1974.

Table 13.7 TVA Recreation Areas

Reservoir	Map Number	Area	Boat Launch	Beach	Camping	Restroom	Showers	Dump	Picnic	Fish Pier	Pavillion	Trails	Play Area	Court
Boone	1	Dam Reservation	X	X		H		H	H					
Cherokee	2	Dam Reservation	X	X		H								
	3	May Springs			X	Ha	Ha	X	X		H			
	4	Fall Creek	X		X	Ha	Ha							
Chickamauga	5	Dam Reservation	X	X		H			H					
	6	Possum Creek	X	X		H	H		H	H	H	X		
	7	Sale Creek	X	Xa	X	Ha	Ha	X	X	H				X
	8	Agency Creek		X	X	X								
	9	Armstrong Ferry	X	X	X	X								
	10	Grasshopper Creek	X	X	X	H	H	X	X		X			
	11	Skull Island	X	Xa	X	Ha	Ha	X						
Douglas	12	Dam Reservation Headwater	X	X	X	H	H	X	X					
	13	Dam Reservation Tailwater	X		Xb	H	Ha			H	X			
Fort Loudoun	14	Dam Reservation	X	X		X	X	X						
	15	Yarberry Peninsula	X	X	X	Ha	Ha	X	X	X				
	16	Poland Creek	X		X	Ha	Ha	X	X					
Guntersville	17	Dam Reservation	X		H	H	Ha		H	H	H	X		
	18	Seibold Creek	X	X	X	Ha		X		H			Xa	
Kentucky	19	Dam Reservation			H	H	H							
	20	Barge Island	X	Xa	X	H	H	X						
	21	Thoroughbred	X	X	H	H	H	X	X				X	
	22	Big Eagle	X	X	X	X	X		X		H			
	23	Beech Bend	X		H	H	H	X	X		H	X	X	X

#	Reservoir	Recreation Area										
24	Melton Hill	Dam Reservation	X	X	X	H		H	H		H	X X
25	Nickajack	Dam Reservation	X	X	X	H	X	H	X	H	H X	X
26		Maple View	X	X		H		X	X		X	
27	Normandy	Barton Springs	X	X	X	H	X	H	H	H	H X	X
28		Cedar Point	X	X	X	H	X	H	X	H	H	X
29	Norris	Dam Reservation	X		X	H		X	X	H	X X	
30		Loyston Point	X	H	X	H	Xa	X	H		X X	
31	Nottely	Poteete Creek	X	X	X	H	X	H	H		H	X
32	Pickwick	Dam Reservation	X	H		H	H	X	H	X		
33		Goat Island	X	H		H	H	H	H			X
34	Tellico	Dam Reservation	X			H						
35	Watauga	Dam Reservation	X			H		X	X	H	X	X
36	Watts Bar	Dam Reservation	X	X	X	H	H		H	H	H H	X
37		Rhea Springs	X	X	X	H	X	H	H	X	H X	
38		Riley Creek	X	X	X	H	X	X		H	X	
39		Hornsby Hollow	X	H	X	H	H	X	H	X	H	X
40		Fooshee Pass	X	X	X	H	H	X	H	H	H	
41	Wheeler	Dam Reservation	X	X	X	H	X	X	X	X	X	
42		Mallard Creek	X	Hb		H	X	X	X	H	X	X
43	Wilson	Dam Reservation	X	H		H	H	X	H	X	X X	
44		Muscle Shoals Reservation				H		X	H	H	X X	

H, handicap; a, available to campers only; b, electrical hookups available.
Source: TVA, *Guide to TVA Reservoir Recreation Areas*, 1992.

Canoeing, river fishing, hiking, and biking have grown tremendously in popularity, and the TVA is working with various groups to promote protection of streams while providing for their use (Figure 13.12). During 1978, the TVA began acquisition of some 250 stream access sites on 40 scenic streams in the Valley. The TVA is providing assistance to commercial river outfitters and is deeply involved in public information related to stream recreation. The TVA is concentrating trail development on agency lands near population centers and developed recreation clusters. Nine trails have been designated national recreation trails. Planning activities are carried out on a regional basis to assure that trail development meets the larger goals of state and national programs. The *Natural Heritage* project is directed toward classification, identification, and inventory of sensitive natural resource features.

The TVA has set aside large tracts of reservoir shoreline for wildlife management and hunting areas, for wildlife refuges, and for duck and geese feeding areas to be managed by the states' fish and game agencies and the U.S. Fish and Wildlife Service. Fishing is permitted all year in TVA lakes. Principal game fish are largemouth, smallmouth, spotted, white, and striped bass; crappie; walleye; sauger; and sunfish. Rainbow trout are present in several of the deep tributary lakes and below some of the dams. "Fish attractors," which are piles of brush anchored to the bottoms of lakes, have been installed in 21 of the reservoirs. The fish-attractor program, initiated in 1977 as a joint project between the TVA and the states' fish and game agencies, was started because vegetation is sparse or totally lacking in many reservoirs. A population study conducted on Barkley Lake indicated that brush fish attractors harbored 19 times the weight of harvestable crappies found in open water areas without the attractors, as well as 9 times more harvestable largemouth bass.

Of all the TVA lakes, Kentucky Lake is the largest, most popular, and most developed. This lake is the first impoundment on the downstream end of the Tennessee

Figure 13.12   Not all boating in the TVA system is flatwater. Shown is a stretch of the Ocoee River with kayakers enjoying its whitewaters. (TVA photo)

River and straddles the Tennessee-Kentucky border. It extends for 180 miles and is located on the western side of Land Between the Lakes. It is possible to boat from Kentucky Lake to the Army Corps of Engineers' Barkley Lake through the Barkley Canal. Lake Barkley is on the Cumberland River—not a part of TVA's jurisdiction—and borders Land Between the Lakes on its eastern side. The western shore of Kentucky Lake is a major recreation area with 80 resorts and five state parks. Shiloh National Military Park is also located here.

Norris Dam was the first dam built by the TVA. Its construction was begun only a few months after the agency was formed in 1933 (Figure 13.13). Norris Lake extends 72 miles up the Clinch River and 56 miles up the Powell River. It has 800 miles of shoreline and a surface area of 34,200 acres. The TVA acquired the entire shoreline of the reservoir that is dedicated to public recreation; 35,300 acres have been transferred or leased to the state of Tennessee and the various counties for public recreation. The state administers two large-game management areas, three state parks, 59 public-access areas, and there are three county parks. The TVA retains about 22,000 acres for future recreational development. The recreational use of Norris Lake exceeds that of any other tributary lake.

The Fontana Dam on the Little Tennessee River is the highest dam in the East at 480 feet. It is a major attraction, and Fontana Lake has exceptional recreational opportunities in a beautiful setting. It was built from 1942 to 1944 and is located in a spectacular setting amid the 6000-foot peaks of the Great Smoky Mountains. The lake is 29 miles in length, has a shoreline of 248 miles, and an area of 10,530 acres at full pool. The TVA has transferred 44,204 acres to Great Smoky Mountains National Park (on the north shore) and 11,667 acres to the Nantahala National Forest (on the south shore). Recreational opportunities are available in both of these units. The Appalachian Trail crosses the Fontana Dam, and the TVA provides a shelter, with sleeping platforms for up to 20 people, on a side road, ½ mile south of the dam.

Figure 13.13 Norris Dam on the Clinch River was the first dam constructed by the Tennessee Valley Authority; construction was started in 1933. (TVA photo)

The Clinch River Floatway is a 13-mile scenic stretch of the Clinch River from below Norris Dam to the backwater of Melton Hill Lake. Hills rise 200 to 500 feet above the streambed. With the power units operating at Norris Dam there is a steady current but no rapids. This is a good stream for beginning canoeists. The usual float trip will take about 4 to 6 hours. Canoes and similar boats are the most-used crafts, although flat-bottomed boats with small motors are used by people fishing. The river supports a variety of fish, including rainbow trout. The Grand Canyon of Tennessee occupies that stretch on Nickajack Lake from Little Cedar Mountain to the base of Lookout Mountain. The mountains rise so steeply that little human encroachment is noticeable. The diverse hardwood forest extends for 30 miles and is the main attraction of Chattanooga's Annual Fall Color Cruise.

Case Study: Land Between the Lakes

Land Between the Lakes is a 170,000-acre regional development program of the Tennessee Valley Authority on a peninsula in western Kentucky and Tennessee. This peninsula was previously known as "between the rivers" because the Cumberland and Tennessee Rivers almost encircled it. The TVA dammed the western river, the Tennessee, in 1944 to create Kentucky Lake. In 1959, when the Army Corps of Engineers began building the Barkley Dam on the Cumberland River, the TVA investigated the potential for the recreational development of the peninsula between what was to become two lakes. The 40-mile-long peninsula varies from 6 to 12 miles in width and has a shoreline of 300 miles. Two-thirds of the peninsula is in Kentucky, and the remainder is in Tennessee. In 1961, the TVA proposed to President John F. Kennedy that the lower Cumberland and Tennessee Rivers be established as a national recreation area. In June 1963, President Kennedy announced the approval of the 170,000-acre project and made recommendations to Congress for budget appropriations. The *Public Works Appropriation Act* (1964), which was signed by President Lyndon B. Johnson, provided funding for partial planning, land acquisition, and development of Land Between the Lakes. In 1965 the Army Corps of Engineers filled Lake Barkley. The federal government already owned 67,000 acres but 103,000 acres had to be purchased from residents and companies, for there were to be no private inholdings. This was the first time that an area of this size, all in federal land, could be managed and cultivated to provide the most favorable environment for outdoor recreation and environmental education. The area is kept in an undeveloped state except for facilities that help meet the Land Between the Lakes' primary goals of (1) supplying a quality outdoor recreation setting for current and future generations, and (2) providing opportunities for visitors to learn about the environment.

There are four entrances to Land Between the Lakes. U.S. 79 serves as the southern boundary of the area, and access is provided off this road at the Fort Henry Road and The Trace. Highway 453 provides access from the north, on a bridge over the Barkley Canal that connects the two lakes. U.S. 68 runs east-west through the central portion of the peninsula and offers easy access from each side. Interstate 24 passes immediately north of both dams. The Trace is the major 40-mile-long north-south road through the Land Between the Lakes. It passes both North and South Welcome Stations at the northern and southern ends. In the middle it intersects with U.S. 68, where the Golden Pond Visitor Center is located. Located at the visitor center is the

Golden Pond Planetarium, the Golden Pond Observatory, and the Gift Shoppe. The Homeplace is located on The Trace between the South Welcome Center and the Golden Pond Visitor Center. It is a 19th-century working farm that consists of 16 log structures from the region. Dressed in period clothing, interpreters carry out the daily and seasonal work of the farm. Daily programs vary with the seasons but typically include activities such as butter making, fall plowing, tobacco firing, bread making, spinning, dyeing, weaving, and oxen working. Across the road from The Homeplace is the 200-acre Buffalo Range and the largest publicly owned herd of buffalo (American bison) east of the Mississippi. Kentucky Lake Drive is a 3.2-mile-loop off The Trace that provides vistas of Kentucky Lake and the Barkley canal. The Woodlands Loop is 16 miles long and one of the most scenic drives in Land Between the Lakes. It offers excellent views of Lake Barkley and Honker Lake. The environmental education area is in this part of the project, and the Woodlands Nature Center is the focal point. There are many exhibits and species of wildlife to observe. The Wranglers Loop is a 10-mile road that winds through forest and fields and past Wranglers Campground. The Fort Henry Drive is a 6.5-mile road that passes the Fort Henry Hiking Trails.

There are five developed campgrounds. The most complete facilities, with swimming areas, are located at Hillman Ferry, Piney, and Energy Lake. The first two are open from March to November, and Energy Lake, a subimpoundment of Lake Barkley, is open year-round. Piney has 382 sites, 322 of them with electrical hookups. There is a popular fishing pier at Piney. Energy Lake has 34 sites with electrical hookups. Rushing Creek campground is not as developed. Wranglers campground is especially suited to horseback riders. In addition to campsites it has barns, hitching and tethering posts, and 24 miles of trails. For those interested in less developed camping, there are 10 fee sites scattered at various locations along the 300-mile shoreline. Backcountry camping is permitted throughout Land Between the Lakes, except in posted areas.

A large variety of trail types meet the differing recreational needs. The longest hiking trail is the 65-mile North-South Trail. Along this trail spaced 15 miles apart are metal open-air shelters. The 26-mile Fort Henry Trail is another major trail. It consists of a series of interconnected loops. The 5-mile Honker Trail leads to Honker Lake and sightings of the resident flock of Canadian geese. The nearby Hematite Trail offers possible sighting of muskrat, beaver, and migratory waterfowl on Hematite Lake. The 14-mile Canal Loop Trail includes Barkley Trail (9 miles) and four short connectors, all of which link the Barkley Trail with the North-South Trail. Touring bikes can use any of the scenic drives and mountain bikes can ride on any of the numbered roads. Biking is prohibited on all foot trails except a 2.2-mile biking/ hiking trail located between Hillman Ferry campground and the North Welcome Station. At the Wrangler campground there are 24 miles of riding trails designated especially for horses. The 2350-acre Turkey Bay ORV Area provides opportunities for trail bikes and all-terrain vehicles (ATVs).

Kentucky Lake and Lake Barkley cover more than 220,000 acres and provide excellent fishing for crappie, bass, sauger, catfish, and bluegill. Anglers can also fish in ponds and on four small lakes within Land Between the Lakes. There are dozens of boat ramps, and many marinas surround Land Between the Lakes. Hunters can pursue the abundant populations of white-tailed deer and wild turkey as well as small game and waterfowl.

Each year over 7000 students (mostly grades 4 through 6) participate in structured environmental education programs at Land Between the Lakes' two resident camps, Brandon Springs and the Youth Station (Figure 13.14). Thousands more visit for day field trips to participate in environmental activities. Groups of university students meet to study environmental issues. Over 40 research projects are conducted annually, and Land Between the Lakes is a testing and demonstration site for recreation and resource management.

In 1987 a major study was undertaken at Land Between the Lakes to determine the primary reasons for which visitors were being attracted to the area. The main reasons were identified as sightseeing (34.1 percent), developed camping (25.5 percent), fishing (14.4 percent), other (9.1 percent), hunting (6.7 percent), primitive camping (4.1 percent), water sports (2.6 percent), relaxing (2.2 percent), and riding (1.2 percent). The study identified the sightseers as "grazers," people looking for something to do; they are not likely to stay very long at one activity. Scenic beauty was identified as the main reason for choosing Land Between the Lakes for sightseeing. About half the family campground users come primarily to camp, while the other half camps as a means to enjoy other activities. A high number of the campers at Land Between the Lakes are demanding more electrical sites. Those surveyed said that if any improvements are made in the campgrounds, the first should be in the swimming and boating area. The most popular game sought by hunters is deer, which accounts for almost three-quarters of the hunting. Small game and turkey each account for another 10 percent of the hunting. Those who come primarily for swimming gave the lowest satisfaction rating of all Land Between the Lakes user groups. Those who identified "relaxing" as the primary reason for coming comprised the user group not tied directly to any particular activity or facility. They walk and drive for pleasure, visit facilities, and spend money. The "riders" are the highest-risk users group and fall into two groups—ORV users and wranglers. The average group size for Wranglers Camp visitors is 5.35, the highest of any user type at Land Between

Figure 13.14 Canoes on the shoreline of Lake Barkley at Brandon Springs group campsite, Land Between the Lakes. (TVA photo)

the Lakes. Another segment of the visitors are those who come to be part of an organized group. This segment consists of group campers, day-use groups, and adult tour groups. In addition, there are three main group-camper subgroups: primitive campers, developed area campers, and residential camping. Colson Hollow is a key facility for the primitive group campers. Group camping is allowed at Energy Lake Campground. Little market information is available on resident facility users. Day-use school groups behave much like the sightseeing segment. Most tour groups come to the area on bus, with retirees accounting for a significant percentage of the use.

The Land Between the Lakes mission mandates that it must contribute to economic development of the region. The typical visitor party spends about $150 per trip, but some segments spend more than others. The following is the rank order of expenditures grouped according to the main reason for coming to Land Between the Lakes: relaxing ($354), water sports ($353), fishing ($284), sightseeing ($177), developed camping ($160), primitive camping ($148), hunting ($142), and horseback riding ($57). The study has suggested three ways the economic impact can be increased: (1) by attracting more visitors, (2) by holding visitors longer, and (3) by changing the "mix" to increase the numbers of tourists who stay overnight.

FEDERAL INDIAN LANDS

The topic of Native American lands is briefly covered here because of the large amount of geographic space they occupy, especially in the West. There is a tremendous amount of potential for outdoor recreation opportunities on these lands. Typically, most recreational use of Native American lands has been for high-stakes bingo and gambling, public ceremonies and powwows, and museums and exhibits. While hunting and fishing are allowable recreational uses, for a fee, on some lands, these have not been very developed with support facilities. There have been some exceptions to this generalization, but in general the vast recreational resources on Indian lands remains a potential to be tapped. The physical character of these Indian lands most closely approximates that of BLM lands, due to the arid and semiarid nature of the climate in much of the West.

Most of these Indian lands are held in trust by the federal government and are administered by the Bureau of Indian Affairs (BIA). Indian lands should be treated as private property, and all proper permissions and / or fees must be given or paid before the land is entered. The BIA is currently part of the Interior Department and is directed by an assistant secretary appointed by the president. This agency has had many name changes and is one of the oldest in the federal government. It was formed in 1824 as part of the War Department and moved to the Interior Department in 1849. Under a U.S. policy of Indian self-determination, the BIA's main goal is to support tribal efforts to govern their own reservation communities by providing them with technical assistance, as well as programs and services, through 12 area offices and 109 agencies and special offices. Education, social services, law enforcement, mineral and water rights, and land leasing are important caretaking responsibilities assumed by the BIA on some reservations. On other reservations, these functions are now entirely or in part administered by tribal governments. In the 1970s the American

Indian Movement and other Indian groups began to actively express dissatisfaction with the work of the BIA. Since this time the BIA has changed its objectives to include encouragement and training of Indians to manage their own affairs; improvement of their educational opportunities and social services; and the economic advancement of Native Americans. It is important to emphasize that the BIA does not run Indian reservations. Elected tribal governments run them, working with the BIA whenever trust resources or BIA programs are involved. As of 1988, the federal government recognized and acknowledged that it had a special relationship with, and a trust responsibility for, 307 federally recognized Indian "entities" in the lower 49 states, plus 200 tribal "entities" in Alaska. The term *Indian entity* includes Indian tribes, bands, villages, groups, pueblos, Eskimos, and Aleuts. A number of Indian tribes and groups in the United States do not have federally recognized status, although some are state-recognized.

Figure 13.15 shows the location of the federal Indian reservations in the lower 49 states and the native corporation boundaries for Alaska. This map is keyed to Appendix XXI, which lists these lands. A number of different names are used for some of these reservations—*pueblo, rancheria,* and *community*. Federal Indian reservations are primarily a western phenomena, with the exception of several large reservations in Minnesota and Wisconsin. Reservation lands total 54,688,111 acres; 44,400,791 acres are tribally owned, and 10,287,320 acres are individually owned. A sizable portion of this acreage lies in just four states: Arizona (20.1 million acres), New Mexico (7.9 million acres), Montana (5.6 million acres), and South Dakota (4.5 million acres). Fifteen reservations are 1 million acres or larger in size: Navaho (Arizona, N. Mexico, Utah; 17.5 million acres), Crow (Montana; 2.5 million acres), Fort Peck (Montana; 2.1 million acres), Wind River (Wyoming; 2.0 million acres), Uintah and Ouray (Utah, 2.0 million acres), San Carlos (Arizona, 1.8 million acres), Fort Apache (Arizona; 1.6 million acres), Blackfeet (Montana; 1.6 million acres), Hopi (Arizona; 1.5 million acres), Cheyenne River Sioux (South Dakota; 1.4 million acres), Colville (Washington, 1.3 million acres), Flathead (Montana; 1.2 million acres), Osage (Oklahoma, 1.0 million acres), and Fort Berthold (N. Dakota, 1.0 million acres). The greatest number of reservations is in California—96—but the acreage is relatively small. The number of Native Americans is 1,750,000, with the most living in Oklahoma (252,420), California (242,164), and Arizona (203,527).

It is far beyond the scope of this book, and is not its purpose, to detail *all* of the recreational opportunities available on Native American lands; this book can only make the reader aware of a few. This will be accomplished by briefly discussing several reservations and then detailing the Mescalero Apache Reservation as a case study.[2]

The Navaho Reservation is located in northeastern Arizona, northwestern New Mexico, and southern Utah, and its 17.5 million acres cover an area larger than New England. The Navaho Tourism Department oversees recreation and tourism on this

---

[2]It has been the general policy of the author not to recommend any of the various guide books that detail specific recreational opportunities. This policy is being waived due to an exceptionally good guide that provides a wealth of details on the recreational opportunities available on Indian reservations: *Discover Indian Reservations USA*, edited by Veronica E. Tiller 1992, 402 pp. It may be obtained from Council Publications, 1999 Broadway, Suite 2600, Denver, CO 80202-5726. This book covers only the lower 49 states but includes state as well as federal reservations.

huge reservation. There are a number of campgrounds, and a major attraction is the 14-mile drive through Monument Valley Tribal Park. This drive passes through a wonderland of unique rock spires and other erosional features. The 1.5-million-acre Hopi Reservation is completely surrounded by the Navaho Reservation. The 188,077-acre Havasupai Reservation (Arizona) borders the southern edge of Grand Canyon National Park. Here, 430 tribal members live in Havasupai Canyon, a tributary of the Grand Canyon. This pastoral scenic area has numerous waterfalls and a trading company and tourist enterprise has been recently opened to welcome visitors. The Hualapai Reservation (Arizona) covers 1 million acres west of the Havasupai Reservation and comes very close to the Colorado River on the south side. Camping, fishing, and trophy game hunts are available. There is a small visitor center at Grand Canyon West. Guided bus tours with a barbecue lunch are given. On the 1.6-million-acre Fort Apache Reservation in east-central Arizona, the White Mountain Apaches operate a resort, the Sunrise Park Resort, and Ski Sunrise, a major alpine ski area. Ski Sunrise has 65 trails and 11 lifts on three mountains with a vertical drop of 1800 feet. A base elevation of 9200 feet assures a long ski season from December 1 until April 1. There are also cross-country ski trails, snowmobile tours, and sledding. The 100-room Sunrise Park Hotel is nearby with a restaurant and lounge, an indoor pool, spa, and sauna. To the south on the 1.8-million-acre San Carlos Reservation, fishing, hunting, and camping are available.

In Montana, outdoor activities for the adventurous who do not demand developed facilities may be had at several large reservations. The 1.6-million-acre Blackfeet Reservation spreads east from the Rocky Mountains and offers primitive fishing and camping. The 2.5-million-acre Crow Reservation in southern Montana surrounds much of the Bighorn National Recreation Area, and many recreational activities are possible. On the western slope of the Rockies in Montana the 1.2-million-acre Flathead Reservation offers camping, hunting, and fishing. A new resort, Kwataqnuk, features 112 guest rooms, restaurants, a lounge, a casino, a convention center, a banquet hall, gift shops, a gallery, and a wide range of recreational activities. A major resort area has been built at the 640,000-acre Warm Springs Reservation in north-central Oregon on the eastern slope of the Cascade Range. At Kah-Nee-Ta Resort there are deluxe rooms and suites; cottages; recreational vehicle, trailer, and other camping; teepee rentals; two restaurants; a lounge; two gift shops; two swimming pools; an 18-hole golf course; miniature golf; a riding stable; bike paths; river rafting; and fishing. Many special events are scheduled throughout the year.

In the East, different types of recreation are offered at reservations. A major tourist industry has evolved since the 1940s on the Cherokee Reservation in western North Carolina, and it is the mainstay of the economy today. This reservation is located next to the southeastern entrance to Great Smoky Mountains National Park. There is a Museum of the Cherokee Indian, and a famous drama, Unto These Hills, is performed nearby. In Florida, bordering Everglades National Park on the north is the Miccosukee Reservation. A major attraction along U.S. 41 is the Miccosukee Culture Center and Indian Village. This is a living museum, and alligator wrestling may be viewed. Airboat rides on the Everglades (outside the national park) are available nearby. An interesting stop on these airboat rides is an isolated island camp. (The author advises anyone who takes these airboat rides to bring hearing protectors. The noise from the big motors, which have no mufflers, is deafening.) In the Northeast,

in eastern Connecticut, is the 214-acre Mashantucket Pequot Reservation, whose main attraction is the Foxwoods High Stakes Bingo and Casino. There is seating for 2400 patrons, and table games are available. The casino opened in February 1992, and within 1 year it had 4500 workers and a yearly payroll of over $100 million. The Oneida Indian Reservation in nearby central New York saw the success of the Foxwoods operation and in July 1993 opened the Turning Stone Casino. Most of their tribal lands had been sold, and only 35 acres remained. They did have a bingo operation prior to opening the casino. This is the first legal gambling casino in New York's 206-year history.

Case Study: Mescalero Apache Reservation

The Mescalero Apache Indian Reservation is located in the mountains of south-central New Mexico. It was established in 1873 and contains 460,661 acres. The reservation is 27 miles from north to south and 36 miles from east to west. It lies on both the eastern and western slopes of the northern Sacramento Mountains. The eastern slope drains into the Pecos River, and the western slope drains into the Tularosa Basin where White Sands National Monument is located. The Lincoln National Forest lies both to the north and south of the reservation. The highest point on the reservation is Sierra Blanca Peak (12,003 ft.), the site of Ski Apache. The lowest point is the Three Rivers, northwest of Mescalero, where the elevation is 5450 feet. Almost all the reservation is covered with timber—pine, spruce, fir, aspen, white oak, pinon, and juniper—in contrast with the lower desert surrounding the Sacramento Range. The principal settlement on the reservation is Mescalero, located on U.S. 70, which runs through the reservation. The resort and tourist center of Ruidoso is located a few miles north of the reservation, Alamogordo is located 25 miles to the southwest, and Roswell is 75 miles to the east. In 1991 the BIA identified 3511 Indians living on or adjacent to the reservation. Most of the tribal families live in or near the community of Mescalero, but there are also settlements at Three Rivers, Elk Silver, Carrizo, Whitetail, and Mudd Canyon. The tribal economy is based on timber, cattle, tourism, and outdoor recreation. The varied and beautiful terrain provides a variety of year-round recreational opportunities.

The recreational and tourism activities on the reservation are focused at two locations: Sierra Blanca Peak and the Inn of the Mountain Gods. Sierra Blanca Peak is the location of Ski Apache, and the Inn of the Mountain Gods is the heart of the resort. Ski Apache is 20 miles northwest of Ruidoso, and the Inn of the Mountain Gods is a few miles south of Ruidoso. Ski Apache is located primarily on national forest land on the northern side of Sierra Blanca Peak and is operated under a special-use permit. The 12,003-foot summit of Sierra Blanca Peak is in the northern portion of the reservation. This ski area has a base elevation of 9700 feet and receives 180 inches of snow per year. It has a four-passenger gondola, a quad-chair, five triple chairs, two double chairs, and one "mighty mite" tow that operates during a ski season from Thanksgiving through Easter. The ski area includes 1060 acres and has 45 trails with an even mix of beginner, intermediate, and advanced runs. There are 25 miles of ski trails, with runs as long as 2 miles. The capacity of the ski area is 7000 skiers a day and the uphill lift capacity is 15,300 skiers per hour. Ski Apache is a full-service ski area with ski school, equipment rentals, and restaurants, one of

which is on top of the mountain at the gondola terminal. Lodging and lift packages are available through the Inn of the Mountain Gods.

The Inn of the Mountain Gods is a luxurious mountain resort situated at 7200 feet of elevation (Figure 13.16). Since the inn opened in July 1975, it has gained a reputation as one of the finest resort facilities in the Southwest. The Inn of the Mountain Gods is a first-class operation.[3] The inn has 250 spacious guest rooms, including 20 suites, with spectacular views of lakes, forests, and mountains. There is a large outdoor swimming pool and whirlpool plus men's and women's saunas. There are conference facilities and an assortment of dining and meeting rooms. The convention center with its Wendell Chino Ballroom can handle conventions of up to 650 people. The inn is set on a 150-acre human-made lake that is available for boating and trout fishing. Boats available for rent include canoes, rowboats, and pedal boats. There is a complete bait-and-tackle shop. Lake Mescalero is stocked with rainbow and cut-throat trout from the Mescalero fish hatchery. There are two indoor tennis courts plus six outdoor courts beside the lake for day or night playing. A challenging 18-hole golf course is located at the inn. There is a stable for horseback riding with an Indian guide. For those who do not want to take advantage of the outdoor activities there is a casino on the premises. High-stakes bingo is available at Mescalero Bingo, 1.5 miles from the inn on U.S. 70. There is horse racing during the summer at Ruidoso Downs.

The big-game hunts are a very sophisticated operation. A trap-and-skeet range, an archery range, and the hunting center are located a short distance from the main inn buildings. A Mescalero Indian guide is required for bull elk hunts and recom-mended for cow elk and bear hunts. In 1992 a 5-day bull elk hunt package cost $8500. This includes meals and six nights' lodging at the Inn of the Mountain Gods, field lunches, a horse, and meat processing. A variety of lower-priced hunts are available. In 1992, there were 25 permits for bull elk hunts for $4200. There were two cow elk hunts, with 100 permits per hunt, each for $375. Native elk (the Merriam variety) became extinct about 1900. In 1966 and 1967, 162 Rocky Mountain elk were released and have successfully reproduced. The tribe brags that hunter success is 98 percent. There is a special bear hunt during the last week in August for which 50 permits (at $350 each) are granted. Any bear may be shot as long as it is not a female either with cubs or under 1 year old. In the spring there are two gobbler turkey hunts for which 50 permits are sold (at $150 each).

The visitor is advised to bring either a full wallet or a well-backed credit card, as there are charges for virtually every activity at the resort. This is not a cheap resort and if the Mescalero Apaches can be criticized for anything it would be their recre-ational activity charges. The following are some examples of prices charged for rec-reational activities in 1992: archery, $8 per hour; basketball and volleyball, $3 per hour; bicycles, $6 per hour; canoe, $8 per hour; rowboat, $8 per hour; pedal boat, $12 per hour; hotel guest daily 18-hole green fee, $32; hotel guest 18-hole cart fee, $20; club rentals for 18 holes, $15; 1-hour horseback ride, $10; outdoor tennis—day, $10 per hour (singles) and $20 per hour (doubles); outdoor tennis—night, $20 per hour

---

[3]The author testifies that the food is exquisite. During an extended western trip doing research for this book during the fall of 1992, the author had his most superb—and most expensive—meal on this excursion at the Inn of the Mountain Gods.

Figure 13.16 Inn of the Mountain Gods Resort on the Mescalero Apache Reservation (N. Mexico). Sierra Blanca Peak, the location of Ski Apache, rises in the horizon.

(singles) and $40 per hour (doubles); and regular trap and skeet shooting (25 targets with gun rental), $16. However, fishing is a real bargain at $8 per day. Don't plan to recoup some of your expenses in the casino on the slots, for they are not "loose."

References

Army Corps of Engineers. *Allatoona Lake.*

Army Corps of Engineers. *Lake Sidney Lanier.*

Army Corps of Engineers. *Canyon Lake and Dam.* 1986.

Army Corps of Engineers. *U.S. Army Corps of Engineers Recreation Study—Volume I: Main Report.* September 1990.

Army Corps of Engineers. *Lakeside Recreation in New England.* August 1992a.

Army Corps of Engineers. *Lakeside Recreation in the Central States.* August 1992b.

Army Corps of Engineers. *Lakeside Recreation in the Great Lakes States.* August 1992c.

Army Corps of Engineers. *Lakeside Recreation in the Great Plains.* August 1992d.

Army Corps of Engineers. *Lakeside Recreation in the Mid-Atlantic States.* August 1992e.

Army Corps of Engineers. *Lakeside Recreation in the Northwest.* August 1992f.

Army Corps of Engineers. *Lakeside Recreation in the South Central States.* August 1992g.

Army Corps of Engineers. *Lakeside Recreation in the Southeast.* August 1992h.

Army Corps of Engineers. *Lakeside Recreation in the Southwest.* August 1992i.

Army Corps of Engineers. *Lakeside Recreation in the Upper Mississippi Basin.* August 1992j.

Bureau of Reclamation. *Reclamation Faces the Future.*

Bureau of Reclamation. *1989 Summary Statistics—Water, Land and Related Data.* Bureau of Reclamation, Denver, Colorado.

Bureau of Indian Affairs. *Indian Land Areas* (map). 1989.

Bureau of Reclamation. *Colorado River Storage Project Information Sheet—Flaming Gorge Dam and Powerplant, Flaming Gorge Reservoir.* April 1990.

Bureau of Indian Affairs. *American Indians Today*. Third edition. 1991a.

Bureau of Reclamation. *Flaming Gorge Dam and Reservoir*. 1991b.

Mescalero Apaches. *Mescalero Indian Reservation—General Information*.

Mescalero Apaches. *Various Inn of the Mountain Gods Publications*.

National Park Service. *Federal Recreation Fee Report to Congress 1991*. Washington, D.C.: U.S. Department of the Interior, National Park Service, 1992.

Tennessee Valley Authority. *Guntersville Lake Recreation Map*. 1970.

Tennessee Valley Authority. *Nickajack Lake Recreation Map*. 1977.

Tennessee Valley Authority. *Upper Holston Lakes Recreation Map*. 1979.

Tennessee Valley Authority. *Chickamauga Lake Recreation Map*. 1980.

Tennessee Valley Authority. *Melton Hill Lake Recreation Map*. 1982a.

Tennessee Valley Authority. *Cherokee–Douglas Lakes Recreation Map*. 1982b.

Tennessee Valley Authority. *Fontana Lake Recreation Map*. 1982c.

Tennessee Valley Authority. *Fort Loundon Lake Recreation Map*. 1982d.

Tennessee Valley Authority. *Tims Ford Lake Area*. 1983.

Tennessee Valley Authority. *Upper Hiwassee Lakes Recreation Map*. 1983.

Tennessee Valley Authority. *Pickwick Lake Recreation Map*. 1985a.

Tennessee Valley Authority. *Wheeler and Wilson Lakes Recreation Map*. 1985b.

Tennessee Valley Authority. *Kentucky Lake Recreation Map*. 1986.

Tennessee Valley Authority. *Land Between the Lakes Constituent Needs Assessment*. Marketing and Planning Group, June 12, 1987a.

Tennessee Valley Authority. *Watts Bar Lake Recreation Map*. 1987b.

Tennessee Valley Authority. *The TVA Handbook*. TVA: Knoxville, Tenn., 1988.

Tennessee Valley Authority. *Land Between the Lakes—It's a Natural*. 1989.

Tennessee Valley Authority. *Norris Lake Recreation Map*. 1991.

Tennessee Valley Authority. *Recreation on TVA Lakes—Great Lakes of the South*. 1991.

Tennessee Valley Authority. *A Guide to Land Between the Lakes*. 1992a.

Tennessee Valley Authority. *Guide to TVA Reservoir Recreation Areas*. 1992b.

Tiller, Veronica E., editor. *Discover Indian Reservations USA*. Denver: Council Publications, 1992.

## CHAPTER 14

Amenity Resources: Wilderness, Rivers, Trails, Seashores and Lakeshores

In wilderness is the preservation of the world.

Henry David Thoreau

This final chapter is devoted to a major theme of this book, the preservation of natural resources for their *amenity value.* This concept was introduced early in Chapter 1 and elaborated on in Chapter 2. The legislative role of Congress as the ultimate resource manager has been emphasized. Chapters 3 through 12 repeatedly discussed and gave examples of amenity resource valuation by the four large federal land-managing agencies: the National Park Service, the Forest Service, the Fish and Wildlife Service, and the Bureau of Land Management. The other three federal land-managing agencies—the Army Corps of Engineers, the Bureau of Reclamation, and the Tennessee Valley Authority—have not been significantly involved in the preservation of amenity resources. If anything, through their dam and reservoir building programs they have destroyed large amounts of amenity resources. The pros and cons of dam and reservoir construction and the impacts on recreational land use were emphasized in Chapter 13. The concept of *irreversible natural resource decisions* was discussed in several earlier chapters, especially in Chapter 13.

Starting in the 1960s, Congress established new directions for the use of the public lands by passing legislation such as the Wilderness Act (1964), the Wild and Scenic Rivers Act (1968), and the National Trails System Act (1968). This legislation actually caused the dam-building agencies such as the Army Corps of Engineers, the Bureau of Reclamation, and the Tennessee Valley Authority to virtually halt the building of new dams, since most of the remaining prime dam sites were now protected by this legislation. This legislation was passed on the heels of the Outdoor Recreation Resources Review Commission's report, *Outdoor Recreation for America,* which was released in 1962. At this time the country was in the middle of an outdoor recreation "explosion." With increased amounts of leisure time and extra discretionary purchasing power, Americans were increasing their participation in outdoor recreation activities at almost exponential rates. The completion of the interstate highway system

brought many resource-based areas much closer to visitors' homes in terms of driving times. As participation in outdoor recreation increased, a large number of Americans started realizing the value of preserving "nature for nature's sake." They started to develop a new relationship with the land, akin to Aldo Leopold's land ethic. The membership rosters of environmental interest groups such as the Sierra Club and the Wilderness Society grew, and they pressed Congress for the protection of more amenity resources. As these memberships grew, the organizations had greater political clout to push for expansion of the amenity protection systems. The National Environmental Policy Act (1969) mandated that environmental impact statements (EISs) be prepared, and this opened a new avenue for public participation in the resource allocation process. Citizen and environmental interest groups began to question the land-use policies of the public land-managing agencies.

The preservation of seashores and lakeshores has occurred a little differently than in the case of wilderness, rivers, and trails. There was a separate piece of legislation for each of these categories of wilderness, rivers, and trails. Our first national seashore—Cape Hatteras (North Carolina)—was established in 1937 as a unit of the National Park System. Although the concept developed in the 1930s, it was in the 1960s before any additional national seashores or national lakeshores were established through several different acts of Congress. Unlike wilderness, rivers, and trails, national seashores and lakeshores are exclusively administered by the National Park Service.

WILDERNESS

Background

As early as the 19th century, individuals such as American essayist and poet Henry David Thoreau and Scottish-born American naturalist John Muir extolled the value of wilderness. Then the country was more interested in taming wilderness than in preserving it. The *Yosemite Grant* (1864) and the creation of Yellowstone National Park (1872) were significant events in the "twilight of the conservation movement," but they were not established primarily for wilderness values. In fact, the passage of the *National Park Service Act* (1916) actually hastened the development of roads and support facilities so that the national parks could be used. The mandate of the National Park System Act was to "conserve but allow use." It was not until the post–World War I era that the allocation of public land specifically for wilderness values occurred, largely through the efforts of three employees of the Forest Service: Arthur Carhart, Aldo Leopold, and Robert Marshall.

The Forest Service conducted a survey of recreational resources and their possibilities in 1917 and 1918, which determined that national forests should be opened, summer home site rentals should be encouraged, and landscape architects should be hired. In 1919, *Arthur Carhart* was hired as a landscape architect by the Forest Service. His first assignment was at *Trapper Lake* in Colorado's White River National Forest, about 30 miles from Glenwood Springs. He was told to design a road to, and plan a

vacation home settlement on, the 300-acre lake. He was taken aback by the spectacular setting of the lake and the 11,000-foot mountain peaks surrounding it. The only access to the lake was a 5-mile trail. After spending a summer in the area he decided that the best use for the area was to preserve it in its pristine condition and not to develop it or build a road. Surprisingly, the Denver office of the Forest Service approved Carhart's suggestion. *This was the first time public land in the United States, or the world, was allocated specifically for its wilderness value.* Carhart continued to work for the Forest Service from 1919 to 1922 and recommended similar areas be set aside for wilderness values in the Superior National Forest of Minnesota. After 1922, he retired from the Forest Service and moved on to a career in conservation writing and city planning.

Carhart's ideas of wilderness preservation attracted the attention of *Aldo Leopold*, who had joined the Forest Service in 1909 in the Southwest region. When Leopold first came to the Southwest, there were six roadless areas of 1 million acres or more. By 1922, New Mexico's Gila National Forest, which was created in 1906, was the only large tract left. In 1924, through the efforts of Leopold, the Forest Service designated the 574,000-acre *Gila Primitive Area* for wilderness purposes. Leopold left the Forest Service in 1926, the same year Chief Greeley formulated a policy for wilderness stating that commercial use (grazing and logging) could continue but campsites, meadows, and scenic spots would be protected. Greeley also instructed his associate forester, L. F. Kneipp, to make an inventory of roadless areas over 230,400 acres. This first roadless area review discovered 74 roadless areas on 5 million acres. In 1929, Kneipp wrote Forest Service *Regulations L-20*, which was an agency policy that standardized the term *primitive area* for a decade. By 1939, some 14 million acres of national forests had been designated "primitive" (Roth 1988, 3).

Another wilderness supporter was *Robert Marshall*. Marshall grew to love the wilderness of New York's Adirondack Mountains, as his family had their Camp Knollwood on Upper Saranac Lake. He was trained as a plant pathologist and worked for the Forest Service in Wyoming's Wind River Mountains. Even though the L-20 Regulations were in effect, he worried about the depletion of wilderness. His classic article, "The Problem of the Wilderness," published in *Scientific Monthly* in 1930, is regarded as the "Magna Carta of wilderness." In this article Marshall denoted *wilderness* as

> . . . a region which contains no permanent inhabitants, possesses no possibility of conveyance by any mechanical means and is sufficiently spacious that a person in crossing it must have the experience of sleeping out. The dominant attributes of such an area are: first, that it requires any one who exists in it to depend exclusively on his own effort for survival; and second, that it preserves as nearly as possible the primitive environment. This means that all roads, power transportation and settlements are barred. But trails and temporary shelters, which were common long before the advent of the white race, are entirely permissible.

Marshall urged that "A thorough study should forthwith be undertaken to determine the probable wilderness needs of the country." In the early 1930s Marshall, as director of the Forestry Division of the U.S. Office of Indian Affairs, helped established a system of Indian wildernesses. An extremely strong hiker, Marshall is probably best known for his explorations of the Brooks Range in northern Alaska. Here he named the "Gates of the Arctic." Marshall recommended in his book *The People's Forests*,

published in 1933, that a countrywide web of primeval reservations be located in all sections of the country. The *Wilderness Society* grew out of a meeting between Marshall, Benton MacKaye (of Appalachian Trail fame), Harvey Broome, and Bernard Frank in October 1934 as a "friends of the wilderness group." In January 1935 the Society was formally formed; other charter members included Aldo Leopold and Howard Zahniser. The wilderness concept now had an organized voice.

In 1937, Marshall became the chief of the Division of Recreation and Lands in the Forest Service. In 1939, largely through the work of Marshall, dissatisfaction with the L-20 Regulations led to its replacement with the *U Regulations,* which tightened protection on 14 million acres of wilderness in the national forests. Under the U Regulations, three land-use designations were defined. *Regulation U-1* established *wilderness areas* on lands over 100,000 acres; only the Secretary of Agriculture could authorize any modification or elimination of a wilderness area. *Regulation U-2* defined *wild areas* as those between 5,000 and 100,000 acres; they could be established, modified, or eliminated only by the chief. *Regulation U-3(a)* established *roadless areas.* These areas were to be used primarily for recreation and were substantially in their natural condition. Roadless areas over 100,000 acres could only be established or modified by the Interior Secretary, and roadless areas under 100,000 acres could be established or modified by the chief. "The only areas ever classified under this regulation were three separate tracts in the Superior National Forest in Minnesota that were consolidated in 1958 to form what is now the Boundary Waters Canoe Area Wilderness" (Hendee et al., 1990, 101). Robert Marshall died in November 1939 at the age of 38, just 2 months after the U Regulations became effective. In 1940 the Forest Service created the Bob Marshall Wilderness in the Montana Rocky Mountains in recognition of the many contributions to wilderness he made.

The Wilderness Act

The L-20 and U Regulations of the Forest Service were only administrative designations, implemented at the discretion of the Secretary of Agriculture or the chief of the Forest Service. They only created and applied to *de facto* wilderness, which could be deleted at any time by administrative policy. *Howard Zahniser,* charter member and executive director of the Wilderness Society, became one of the most powerful supporters of a *de jure* (legal) national wilderness system. After World War II, Zahniser continued where Bob Marshall left off. He was one of the most effective opponents of the dams proposed for the Green and Yampa Rivers in Dinosaur National Monument in the mid-1950s. He believed that unless there was an effective, strong national program of wilderness protection, the conservation community would exhaust itself repulsing project after project. Like Bob Marshall, Zahniser learned to love wilderness as a result of his experiences with the wild country in the forest preserve in New York's Adirondack Mountains and Park. He was a journalist by trade and worked for the U.S. Biological Survey until 1945, when he went to work for the Wilderness Society. In 1955, Zahniser suggested the protection of wilderness by law in the speech he delivered on behalf of the Wilderness Society to the National Citizens Planning Conference on Parks and Open Space for the American People.

With the defeat of the dams proposed for the Dinosaur National Monument in 1956, Zahniser turned his attention to drafting a wilderness bill. He outlined his

proposal in a speech to the American Civic Planners Association. Zahniser gave the proposal to Sen. Hubert Humphrey, who introduced it in Congress in 1956. It took 8 years for the final Wilderness Act to emerge from Congress, during which time 65 different wilderness bills were introduced, 18 hearings were held across the country, and thousands of pages of testimony were put in print. On September 3, 1964, President Lyndon Johnson signed the Wilderness Act (P.L. 88-577).

> Many supporters of wilderness legislation were disappointed with the discrepancy between the act as passed and the original conception as proposed by Zahniser. The Wilderness Act was clearly a compromise, yet unless it had been, it is unlikely the bill would have every passed (Hendee et al., 1990, 106).

Some major changes are revealed when contrasting the Wilderness Act with the original 1956 bill:

- Lands from the Bureau of Indian Affairs were omitted.
- The National Wilderness Advisory Council was dropped.
- The "primitive areas" in the national forests were not included in the initial Wilderness System, and their classification as such required affirmation by Congress.
- The restrictions on uses of Wilderness were not as severe (especially for mining).

Section 2 of the Wilderness Act states the purpose and policy of the Act:

> In order to assure that an increasing population, accompanied by expanding settlement and growing mechanization, does not occupy and modify all areas within the United States and its possessions, leaving no lands designated for preservation and protection in their natural condition, it is hereby declared to be the policy of the Congress to secure for the American people of present and future generations the benefits of an enduring resource of wilderness. For this purpose there is hereby established a *National Wilderness Preservation System* [emphasis by the author] to be composed of federally owned areas designated by Congress as "wilderness areas", and these shall be administered for the use and enjoyment of the American people in such manner as will leave them unimpaired for future use and enjoyment as wilderness, and so as to provide for the protection of these areas, the preservation of their wilderness character, and for the gathering and dissemination of information regarding their use and enjoyment as wilderness; and no Federal lands shall be designated as "wilderness areas" except as provided for in this Act or by a subsequent Act.

The definition of *wilderness* as defined in Section 2(c) of the Wilderness Act is as follows:

> A wilderness, in contrast with those areas where man and his own works dominate the landscape, is hereby recognized as an area where the earth and its community of life are *untrammeled* [emphasis by the author] by man, where man himself is a visitor who does not remain. An area of wilderness is further defined to mean in this Act an area of undeveloped Federal land retaining its primeval character and influence, without permanent improvements or human habitation, which is protected and managed so as to preserve its natural conditions and which (1) generally appears to have been affected primarily by the forces of nature, with the imprint of man's work substantially unnoticeable; (2) has outstanding opportunities for solitude or a primitive and unconfined type of recreation; (3) has at least five thousand acres of land or is of sufficient size as to make practicable its preservation and use in an unimpaired condition; and (4) may also contain ecological, geological, or other features of scientific, educational, scenic, or historical value.

Howard Zahniser insisted, successfully, that the word *untrammeled* be included as part of the definition of wilderness. Not to be confused with *untrampled*, *untrammeled* means "not subject to human controls and manipulations that hamper the free play of natural forces."

The Wilderness Act prohibited, as per Section 4(c), certain uses, as follows:

> Except as specifically provided for in this Act, and subject to existing private rights, there shall be no commercial enterprise and no permanent road within any wilderness area designated by this Act and, except as necessary to meet minimum requirements for the administration of the area for the purpose of this Act (including measures required in emergencies involving the health and safety of persons within the area), there shall be no temporary road, no use of motor vehicles, motorized equipment or motorboats, no landing of aircraft, no other form of mechanical transport, and no structure or installation within any such area.

Zahniser and other conservationists were dismayed by some of the Special Provisions of Section 4(d) of the Wilderness Act, among them, those pertaining to motorized vehicles and the mining of the exploration for minerals:

> (1) Within wilderness areas designated by this Act the use of aircraft or motorboats, where these uses have already become established, may be permitted to continue subject to such restrictions as the Secretary of Agriculture deems desirable. In addition, such measures may be taken as may be necessary in the control of fire, insects, and diseases, subject to such conditions as the Secretary deems desirable.
> (2) Nothing in this Act shall prevent within national forest wilderness areas any activity, including prospecting, for the purpose of gathering information about mineral or other resources, if such activity is carried on in a manner compatible with the preservation of the wilderness environment.

Other uses that were permitted include water resource development (if the president thought the national interest would be best served), fewer restrictions for the Boundary Waters Canoe Area (tightened by later legislation in 1978, as was discussed in Chapter 10 in the section on the Superior National Forest), and commercial enterprises that are necessary for appropriate wilderness activities (for example, guiding and outfitting).

Despite its shortcomings, the passage of the Wilderness Act has been one of the greatest victories of American conservationists in the 20th century. For the first time, legal status was given to wilderness. Also for the first time, the Wilderness Act stated in the United States that the preservation of wilderness was a high priority national goal. The act went beyond just making a statement; it provided a mechanism for the system to grow. The successful lobbying by the conservationists that resulted in passage of the Wilderness Act marked the maturation of the modern environmental movement.[1] During the remainder of the 1960s many significant pieces of environmental legislation were adopted by Congress and signed into law by the president, including the Rare and Endangered Species Act, the Clean Water Restoration Act, the Air Quality Act, the Wild and Scenic Rivers Act, the National Trails System Act, and the National Environmental Policy Act.

---

[1]While many point to Earth Day in April 1970 as the beginning of the environmental movement, this author concludes that the movement really gained momentum in 1964 with the enactment of the Wilderness Act.

The new law immediately designated 54 wilderness areas on 9.1 million acres of national forests. This *initial Wilderness System* consisted of National Forest areas designated as "wilderness," "wild," or "canoe." The one canoe area was the Boundary Waters Canoe Area in the Superior National Forest (Minnesota). The remaining 34 "primitive" areas on national forest lands, which covered 5.5 million acres, were to be reviewed for inclusion into the system by September 4, 1974. Figure 14.1 identifies the 54 initial wilderness areas and their geographic location. The numbers in the figure are keyed to Appendix XXII, which is a complete summary of the entire current National Wilderness Preservation System. A study of Figure 14.1 reveals one major point: Most of the areas were located in 10 western states. California had the most areas at 13, followed by Oregon with nine. Utah was the one western state with no wilderness areas. There were also no initial wilderness areas in Alaska. Nevada had one, the Jarbridge Wilderness Area. Idaho's one wilderness area—the huge Selway-Bitterroot—extended into Montana. Montana, Arizona, New Mexico, and Colorado each had five wilderness areas, and Washington and Wyoming each had four. There were four initial wilderness areas in the East. One of these—the 5552-acre Great Gulf Wilderness Area in the White Mountain National Forest (N. Hampshire)—had the distinction of being the smallest unit of the initial System. The Linville Gorge Wilderness Area (11,786 acres) and the Shining Rock Wilderness Area (18,483 acres) were both in the Pisgah National Forest in North Carolina. The other eastern wilderness area—Minnesota's Boundary Waters Canoe Area—covered 801,829 acres, which ranked it the third largest in the initial system. The largest initial wilderness area was the Selway-Bitterroot, extending across 1,340,460 acres in four national forests in Idaho and Montana. The Bob Marshall Wilderness ranked second in size, with 1,009,356 acres in the Flathead and the Lewis and Clark National Forests (Montana). Only two other wilderness areas were over 500,000 acres: the John Muir Wilderness (580,323 acres) in the Inyo and Sierra National Forests of the Sierra Nevada Range (California), and the Gila Wilderness Area (557,873 acres) in the Gila National Forest (N. Mexico). The smallest wilderness area in the West was the 8581-acre Cucamonga Wilderness Area in California's San Bernardino National Forest.

In addition to mandating that the Forest Service review the 34 areas classified as "primitive" within a 10-year period, the Wilderness Act also established a 10-year period of review for lands under the jurisdiction of the two Interior Department agencies—the National Park Service and the Fish and Wildlife Service. This portion of the Wilderness Act in Section 3(c) states:

> Within ten years after the effective date of this Act the Secretary of the Interior shall review every roadless area of five thousand contiguous acres or more in the national parks, monuments and other units of the national park system and every such area of, and every roadless island within, the national wildlife refuges and game ranges, under his jurisdiction on the effective date of this Act and shall report to the President his recommendation as to the suitability or non suitability of each such area or island for preservation as wilderness.

The Wilderness Act did not mention that the Bureau of Land Management (BLM) could add lands (under its jurisdiction) to the system. The Federal Land Policy and Management Act (FLPMA, 1976) provided the authorization for BLM land to be reviewed and added to the National Wilderness Preservation System. The law and this process were discussed in Chapter 12. Another major group of potential wilder-

ness lands that the Wilderness Act did not mention were those roadless and undeveloped areas in the National Forest System that lacked explicit classification as wilderness. Since 1964, these Forest Service lands and their relationship to the Wilderness Act have been a subject of considerable controversy.

Despite all the criticisms that have been levied against the Wilderness Act, it did accomplish three things: (1) it established an initial Wilderness Preservation System, (2) it described a procedure for adding lands to the system, and (3) it gave broad guidelines on the kinds of land suitable for wilderness designation. It is indeed a monumental work of environmental legislation that has served, and will serve in the future, as the vehicle for preserving wild, roadless, and undeveloped lands.

Growth of the National Wilderness Preservation System

When the federal agencies began the task of implementing the Wilderness Act's directives regarding allocation of wilderness, three problems immediately surfaced: (1) What criteria should be used when making recommendations about the wilderness character of lands and the need for wilderness? (2) What lands should be considered? (3) Who should be the primary force in the process to complete and round out the system—agencies or interest groups? *For almost 15 years after passage of the act most of the controversy centered on national forest lands.* In late 1964 the Forest Service established a special task force of experienced wilderness managers to write policy and guidelines in accordance with the act. The task force took a "pure," or "strict constructionist," approach to wilderness policy. As the Forest Service developed its guidelines and reviewed the 34 primitive areas for possible inclusion in the system, environmental groups and the public began to demand a greater role in the wilderness allocation process—and their definition of wilderness was not always as pure as that of the Forest Service (Hendee et al., 1990, 124).

The Forest Service developed three criteria to guide the process of identifying potential additions to the Wilderness System: suitability, availability, and need. In 1973 the Forest Service completed an initial inventory that identified 1449 roadless areas with wilderness potential, containing 56 million acres; *only two of these were in the East*, and one was in Puerto Rico. Just how to go about the review and evaluation of potential wilderness additions proved a major question. A controversy in 1972 between the Forest Service and a citizens group in Montana demonstrated the need for an immediate and comprehensive review of roadless areas. The area involved was to become on August 20, 1972, the 239,296-acre Scapegoat Wilderness Area, the first Forest Service area classified under the Wilderness Act that was not a primitive area. The Chief assembled an interdisciplinary team to complete review of the 1449 potential wilderness, and the procedures used by the team became the analytical tool identified as the *Roadless Area Review and Evaluation* (RARE). As a result of the RARE process, the Forest Service in October 1973 recommended only 274 of these areas for wilderness designation, which represented only 19 percent of the total number of roadless areas inventoried and 23 percent of the acreage. The application of the Forest Service's "purity principle" eliminated such areas as Lone Peak (Utah), Sandia Mountains (N. Mexico), and Pusch Ridge (Arizona) because they were within sight and sound of the cities of Salt Lake City, Albuquerque, and Tucson, respectively.

It was 4 years after the passage of the Wilderness Act in 1964 before any additional wilderness areas were added to the system. In March 1968, the first new area was the San Rafael Wilderness Area in the Los Padres National Forest (California). Two months later the San Gabriel Wilderness Area in the Angeles National Forest (California) was added. In September 1968 the first Fish and Wildlife Service unit to be added to the system occurred—the Great Swamp Wilderness Area in the Great Swamp National Wildlife Refuge (N. Jersey). In 1968 the Glacier Peak (Mt. Baker and Wenatchee National Forests) and Pasayten (Mt. Baker and Okanogan National Forests) Wilderness Areas in Washington and the Mount Jefferson Wilderness Area (Deschutes, Mt. Hood, and Willamette National Forests) in Oregon were added. Two wilderness areas in California—the Ventana (Los Padres National Forest) and the Desolation (Eldorado National Forest)—were the only ones added in 1970. In 1970 there were 25 new wilderness areas most of which were Fish and Wildlife Service lands, including the first wilderness areas in Alaska. The year 1970 marked the first of the National Park Service lands to be added to the system—Craters of the Moon Wilderness Area (Craters of the Moon National Monument, Idaho), and Petrified Forest Wilderness Area (Petrified Forest National Park, Arizona). One Forest Service unit was added in 1970, the Mount Baldy Wilderness Area in the Apache National Forest (Arizona). There were no additions to the system in 1971. Nine wilderness areas were added in 1972 that included six in national forests, two in national parks, and one in a national wildlife refuge. One of the Forest Service areas in this year was the controversial Scapegoat Wilderness Area (Helena, Lewis and Clark, and Lolo National Forests, Montana), which was the first Forest Service area not designated "primitive" to be added to the National Wilderness Preservation System. In 1974, the only additions were two Fish and Wildlife Service refuges: the Okefenokee Wilderness Area (Okefenokee National Wildlife Refuge, Georgia) and the Farallon Wilderness Area (Farallon National Wildlife Refuge, California).

As these areas were added to the National Wilderness Preservation System between 1968 and 1974, a controversy over what to do about national forest lands in the East was heating up. In 1972, President Nixon directed Congress to make a greater effort to identify and protect wilderness values in the portions of the country where most of the people lived. Congress responded by passing the *Eastern Wilderness Act*, which was signed by President Gerald Ford on January 3, 1975. This act, Public Law 93-632, added 16 national forest wilderness areas in the East. In addition, it added another 15 national wildlife refuge wilderness areas to the system, most of which were in the East, and another four national forest areas in the West. The Eastern Wilderness Act was a statement by Congress that wilderness areas should be located near population centers on smaller areas showing evidence of past human use. Three of the Forest Service areas added by the Eastern Wilderness Act were under 5000 acres. In the next session of Congress in 1975, two additional Forest Service areas were added to the system—the Flat Tops Wilderness Area (in the Routt and White River National Forests, Colorado), and the Hells Canyon Wilderness Area (in the Nez Perce and Payette National Forests, Idaho, and the Wallowa and Whitman National Forests, Oregon)—and one National Park Service area—the Indian Peaks Wilderness Area (Rocky Mountain National Park, Colorado) by P.L. 94-146.

In 1976, P.L. 94-557 added an additional 12 national park wilderness areas, along with more national wildlife refuge and national forest areas. Among the national

forest areas added was the controversial Eagles Nest Wilderness Area in Colorado's Gore Range in the Arapaho and White River National Forests (Figure 14.2). Another Eastern National Forest Wilderness Area was also among these—the Hercules-Glades in the Mark Twain National Forest of Missouri. There were no additions to the system in 1977.

The RARE process of the Forest Service had been criticized not only for omitting eastern areas but also for omitting western areas that were near cities. Again, Congress addressed the issue by passing P.L. 95-237—the *Endangered American Wilderness Act*. This legislation was the first wilderness addition signed by President Jimmy Carter (February 24, 1978) and was the largest single addition to the National Wilderness Preservation System since the Wilderness Act of 1964 was passed. It added 17 new wilderness areas on 1.3 million acres in Arizona, California, Colorado, Idaho, New Mexico, Oregon, Utah, Washington, and Wyoming. Included in these additions were the Lone Peak Wilderness Area (Uinta and Wasatch National Forests, Utah), the Pusch Ridge Wilderness Area (Coronado National Forest, Arizona), and the Sandia Mountain Wilderness Area (Cibola National Forest, N. Mexico). The "lone" western state that had previously had no wilderness area (Utah) now had its first one—Lone Peak. The Endangered American Wilderness Act also established the first BLM wilderness areas in the system: the Santa Lucia Wilderness Area (Bakersfield District, California) and the Wild Rogue Wilderness Area (Medford District, Oregon). It is important to stress that each of these BLM areas was adjacent to a larger National Forest wilderness area with the same name. In 1993 the BLM lost jurisdiction over its section of the Wild Rogue Wilderness Area, which was transferred to the Forest Service. "In one sense [the Endangered American Wilderness Act] repudiated the RARE since some of the areas that the RARE process had ignored in the inventory,

Figure 14.2 In 1976, after a great deal of controversy, the Eagle's Nest Wilderness Area (in Colorado's Gore Range in the Arapaho and White River National Forests) was added to the National Wilderness Preservation System. Shown here is the White River National Forest portion of the wilderness area.

or had not recommended for wilderness study, were now wilderness" (Roth, 1984, in Hendee et al., 1990, 134)."

The Forest Service commenced a second RARE (RARE II) in mid-1977. President Carter's Assistant Secretary of Agriculture, *Rupert Cutler,* played a pivotal role in the process, since he believed the original RARE to be flawed. The basic objective of RARE II was to accelerate the planning process mandated by the Forest and Rangeland Renewable Resources Planning Act of 1974 and the National Forest Management Act of 1976. As a result of public comments in the RARE II process, the number of roadless areas to be considered for addition to the Wilderness System rose to 1921 areas and 65.7 million acres. The final RARE II environmental impact statement was published on January 4, 1979. It called for allocating 624 wilderness areas totaling 15,008,838 acres, 1981 nonwilderness areas totaling 36,151,558 acres, and further planning for 314 areas totaling 10,796,508 acres (Hendee et al., 1990, 138).

A controversy in the Shasta-Trinity National Forest became a test of the RARE II process. The director of the California Natural Resources Agency sued the Forest Service and sought a court injunction against the release of 46 California study areas to nonwilderness uses. The district court on January 8, 1980, sided with the state of California, enjoining the 46 areas from development, saying that an EIS would have to be prepared for each area before its status could change. In October 1982, the Ninth Circuit Court of Appeals upheld the lower court ruling (Hendee et al., 1990, 139). At this time neither the Forest Service nor environmentalists wanted to start a third RARE, so the RARE process ended. Two additional public laws in 1978 added eight additional national park wilderness areas (including the 1,296,500-acre Everglades Wilderness Area in Everglades National Park, Florida), four other national forests wilderness areas, one Fish and Wildlife Service wilderness area, and one BLM wilderness area.

There were no additions to the National Wilderness Preservation System in 1979, but the massive additions of 1980 made up for this. In July 1980, P.L. 96-312 added the huge Frank Church–River of No Return Wilderness to the system. This wilderness area covers 2,366,623 acres in central Idaho and extends into six national forests: the Bitterroot, the Boise, the Challis, the Nez Perce, the Payette, and the Salmon. This wilderness area also includes 802 acres of BLM land in the Coeur d'Alene District. The largest addition ever made to the National Wilderness Preservation System— and the largest addition that will ever be made—was accomplished by P.L. 96-487, the Alaska National Interest Lands Conservation Act (ANILCA). This one act added 56,275,000 acres to the National Wilderness Preservation System. The breakdown by agency of this wilderness acreage added in Alaska is Forest Service, 5,360,000 acres; National Park Service, 32,355,000 acres; and Fish and Wildlife Service, 18,560,000 acres. The Alaskan land situation was discussed in detail in Chapter 4 and elaborated on in Chapters 5 through 12, so despite its tremendous significance, it will not be reviewed at this point. It is worth noting that seven of these Alaskan wilderness areas exceed the size of the largest wilderness area in the lower 49 states—the 2,366,623-acre Frank Church–River of No Return. These Alaskan wilderness areas are the Wrangell–St. Elias (in the Wrangell–St. Elias National Park and Preserve), 9,078,675 acres; the Arctic (Arctic National Wildlife Refuge), 8,000,000 acres; the Gates of the Arctic (Gates of the Arctic National Park), 7,167,192 acres; Noatak (Noatak National Preserve), 5,765,427 acres; the Katmai (Katmai National Park and Preserve), 3,384,358

acres; Glacier Bay (Glacier Bay National Park and Preserve), 2,664,840 acres; and Lake Clark (Lake Clark National Park), 2,619,550 acres.

At the end of 1980, P.L. 96-560 added a large number of Forest Service wilderness areas. Most of them were in Colorado and New Mexico, but there were also eight areas in Missouri, four in South Carolina, and one in Louisiana. The largest wilderness areas established by this law are the Aldo Leopold (in the Gila National Forest, N. Mexico), 202,016 acres; the Holy Cross (San Isabel and White River National Forests, Colorado), 122,388 acres; the Lost Creek (Pike National Forest, Colorado), 105,090 acres; and the Big Blue (Uncompahgre National Forest, Colorado), 98,516 acres. (The Colorado Wilderness Act of 1993 renamed the Big Blue Wilderness Area the Uncompahgre Wilderness Area and enlarged it.) In 1980, P.L. 96-585 created the 1363-acre Fire Island Wilderness Area in Fire Island National Seashore, (New York), an area not far from New York City.

The years 1981 through 1983 saw the creation of a few new wilderness areas; in 1981 there were none. Only two were created in 1982: the Cumberland Island Wilderness Area (Cumberland Island National Seashore, Georgia) and the Charles C. Deam Wilderness Area (Hoosier National Forest, Indiana). In 1983, six wilderness areas were established: the Paddy Creek (Mark Twain National Forest, Missouri); the Cheaha (Talladega National Forest, Alabama); the Cranberry, Laurel Fork North, and Laurel Fork South (Monongahela National Forest, W. Virginia); and the Lee Metcalf (Beaverhead and Gallatin National Forests and the BLM's Butte District, Montana).

The year 1984 saw more additions to the National Wilderness Preservation System than any other year since the passage of the Wilderness Act, with the exception of 1980. Twenty-one wilderness bills passed Congress in 1984 adding 7,320,143 acres to the system. The national forests saw the greatest amount of the acreage—5,541,667 acres. Many of these new national forest wilderness areas were in eastern states such as Arkansas, Florida, Georgia, Missouri, Mississippi, New Hampshire, North Carolina, Pennsylvania, Tennessee, Vermont, Virginia, and Wisconsin. Among the western states, large numbers of wilderness areas were added to the national forests of California, Oregon, Washington, Arizona, Utah, and Wyoming. One of the author's favoriate wilderness areas, the Gros Ventre in Wyoming's Teton National Forest, was added in 1984 (Figure 14.3). The year 1984 also saw the first significant addition of BLM lands to the Wilderness System. Nineteen new BLM wilderness areas were created in Arizona, California, New Mexico, Oregon, Utah, and Washington and they totaled 363,896 acres. In 1984 there were only two additions to the Wilderness System from National Park lands, but they were large ones. The two new national park wilderness areas were the Sequoia–Kings Canyon (Sequoia–Kings Canyon National Park, California), 736,980 acres; and the Yosemite (Yosemite National Park, California), 677,600 acres.

The only addition to the system in 1985 was the Clifty Wilderness Area (11,662 acres) in the Daniel Boone National Forest (Kentucky). In 1986, several wilderness areas were added to the system from the national forests. Four areas were added to the Cherokee National Forest (Tennessee); four were added to the Chattahoochee National Forest (Georgia); three were added to the Olympic National Forest (Washington); two were added to the Angelina National Forest (Texas); and one each was added to the Sam Houston National Forest (Texas), the Sabine National Forest (Texas), and the Nebraska National Forest. In 1987, nine new wilderness areas were added

Figure 14.3   The Gros Ventre Wilderness Area in the Teton National Forest (Wyoming).

to Michigan national forests (five to the Hiawatha, three to the Ottawa, and one to the Manistee), and two were added to BLM land in the Albuquerque District. Among the additions in 1988 were some large ones on units of the National Park System. The largest of these were three in Washington: the Olympic Wilderness Area (Olympic National Park), 876,669 acres; the Stephen Mather Wilderness Area (North Cascades National Park), 634,614 acres; and the Mount Rainier Wilderness Area (Mount Rainier National Park), 228,488 acres. The other National Park System addition was the Congaree Swamp Wilderness Area (15,010 acres) in the Congaree Swamp National Monument (S. Carolina). Other additions were made in the George Washington and Jefferson National Forests of Virginia and West Virginia (five areas) and in the Ouachita National Forest of Oklahoma (two areas).

All of the additions to the National Wilderness Preservation System in 1989 were made in the state of Nevada and totaled 679,358 acres in the Humboldt (seven areas), Toiyabe (five areas) and Inyo (one area) National Forests. The largest of these was the Arc Dome Wilderness Area (115,000 acres) in the Toiyabe. Three BLM areas were included in the 1989 legislation, all of which are small and adjacent to national forest wilderness areas of the same name: Arc Dome (20 acres), Currant Mountain (3 acres), and Mount Moriah (6435 acres).

The major additions made to the Wilderness System in 1990 totaled 2,782,838 acres. Four of these areas (1,343,444 acres) were units of the National Wildlife Refuge System in Arizona and included the Cabeza Prieta Wilderness Area (Cabeza Prieta National Wildlife Refuge), 803,418 acres, and the Kofa Wilderness Area (Kofa National Wildlife Refuge), 516,200 acres. Forest Service wilderness areas totaled 318,764 acres, which included seven areas in the Shawnee National Forest (Illinois) and six areas in the Tongass National Forest (Alaska). In 1990, 38 new BLM wilderness areas—all in Arizona—were added to the system and totaled 1,120,630 acres. Three of these were over 100,000 acres: the Arastra Mountain Wilderness Area (129,800

acres) and the Warm Springs Wilderness Area (112,400 acres) in the Phoenix District, and the Eagletail Mountains (100,600 acres) in the Yuma District.

In 1991, only minor additions were made to the National Wilderness Preservation System, all of which were in the Chattahoochee National Forest (Georgia). The two new areas were: the Blood Mountain Wilderness Area (7800 acres) and the Mark Trail Wilderness Area (16,400 acres). There was also a 1160-acre addition to the Brasstown Wilderness Area.

All of the additions in 1992, which totaled 400,450 acres, were made in the Los Padres National Forest (California). Five new wilderness areas were established by P.L. 102-301, and additions were made to two others. The new wilderness areas are the Chumash (38,150 acres), the Garcia (14,100 acres), the Matilija (29,600) acres), the Sespe (219,700 acres), and the Silver Peak (14,500 acres). Additions were made to the San Rafael Wilderness Area (46,400 acres) and the Ventana Wilderness Area (38,000 acres).

The Colorado Wilderness Act (P.L. 103-77), which added 611,730 acres to the system, was signed by President Bill Clinton on August 13, 1993. These were the first additions to the system made during the Clinton Presidency. Nine new wilderness areas accounted for 465,775 of these acres. The largest new area was the Sangre de Cristo Wilderness Area (266,455 acres) in the Rio Grande National Forest. The second-largest area added was the 60,100-acre Powderhorn Wilderness Area, which is comprised of 48,115 acres of BLM land in the Montrose District and 11,985 acres in the Gunnison National Forest. Additions to nine other preexisting wilderness areas totaled 145,955 acres. A special note should be made about the effect of the Colorado Wilderness Act's creation of the Uncompahgre Wilderness Area, a new area that presently consists of 102,721 acres. It has three components: (1) 98,516 acres of the former Big Blue Wilderness Area (name discontinued), which was originally created in 1980; (2) 3390 acres of BLM land in the Montrose District; and (3) 815 additional acres in the Uncompahgre National Forest.

Present Extent of the National Wilderness Preservation System

The National Wilderness Preservation System has grown from an initial system of 9.1 million acres in 54 national forest areas in 1964, to 96,056,113 acres on 579 wilderness areas in national forests, national parks, national wildlife refuges, and national resource lands in 1994.[1] This Wilderness System is distributed as follows among the four federal land-managing agencies: National Park Service, 39,140,023 acres; Forest Serivce, 34,586,220 acres; Fish and Wildlife Service, 20,676,341 acres; and Bureau of Land Management, 1,653,529 acres. Figure 14.4 graphically illustrates the distribution of the acreage in the system among the administering agencies. In terms of numbers of wilderness areas under its jurisdiction, the Forest Service is the leader with 396 out of 579 areas (68 percent). The Fish and Wildlife Service has 74 areas (13 percent), the BLM has 67 areas (12 percent), and the National Park Service has 42 areas (7 percent). In terms of average size per wilderness area the ranking changes.

---

[1] See Epilogue for additions made by the California Desert Protection Act of October 31, 1994.

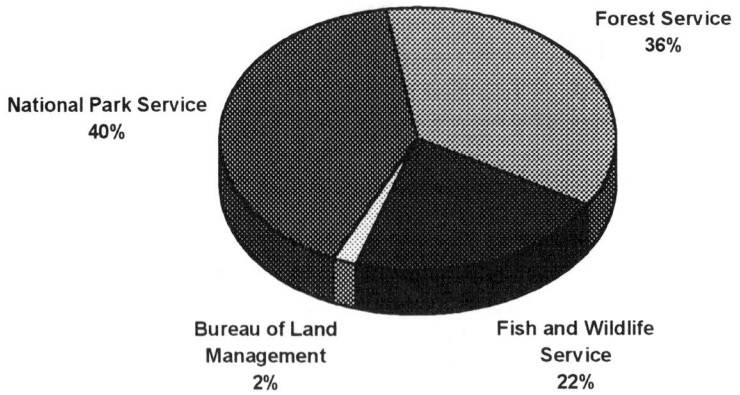

Figure 14.4   National Wilderness Preservation System, 1994: percentage of acreage administered by each agency. (*Source:* Rob Hellie, Bureau of Land Management, January, 1994.)

The average size for the entire system is 165,900 acres; for the BLM it is 24,680 acres; for the Forest Service it is 87,339 acres; for the Fish and Wildlife Service it is 279,410 acres; and for the National Park Service it is 931,905 acres. The large size of the National Park System wilderness areas and the National Wildlife Refuge System wilderness areas in Alaska greatly influences these average values.

Because of the large size of many of the Alaskan Wilderness Areas, it is more instructive to compare the Wilderness System in Alaska to the Wilderness System in the lower 49 states. Ninety-two percent of the 579 wilderness areas are in the lower 49 states but only 38,647,317 acres (40.2 percent of the acreage) is in the lower 49 states. Alaska has only 8 percent of the total number of wilderness areas but 57,408,796 acres (59.8 percent). The size of the average wilderness area in Alaska is 1,196,017 acres, while the comparable figure for the lower 49 states is 72,782 acres. Figure 14.5 graphically illustrates these differences by agency.

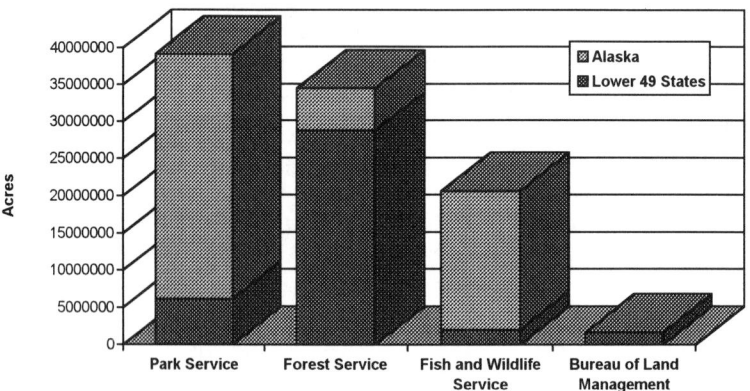

Figure 14.5   National Wilderness Preservation System, 1994: acreages administered by each agency, for Alaska and the lower 49 states. (*Source:* Rob Hellie, Bureau of Land Management, January, 1994.)

Figure 14.6 identifies and locates the units of the National Wilderness Preservation System. It is keyed to Appendix XXII, which is a complete database of information on the entire National Wilderness Preservation System. This appendix identifies the administering agency, the administrative unit, the state, the public law, the date established, and the size in acres. Figure 14.6 shows that most of the wilderness areas are in the West and that there is a disparity between population distribution and wilderness areas. Table 14.1 ranks the states by acreage in the National Wilderness Preservation System. Alaska's 57.4 million acres account for 60 percent of the acreage of the entire National Wilderness Preservation System. California ranks second with 6.3 million acres (6.6 percent of the total), followed by Arizona with 4.5 million acres (4.7 percent), Washington with 4.3 million acres (4.5 percent), Idaho with 4.0 million acres (4.2 percent), Montana with 3.4 million acres (3.5 percent), Colorado with 3.3 million acres (3.4 percent), and Wyoming with 3.1 million acres (3.2 percent). These eight states have 90 percent of the total acreage in the system, and half of them have very small populations. There are wilderness areas in 44 states; the only states with none are Connecticut, Delaware, Iowa, Kansas, Maryland, and Rhode Island. Some of the states have very small acreage of wilderness, including Ohio with 77 acres, New York with 1363 acres, and Massachusetts with 2420 acres.

The wilderness areas range in size from the Pelican Island Wilderness Area (Florida) with 6 acres to the Wrangell–St. Elias Wilderness Area (Alaska) with 9,078,675 acres. The largest wilderness areas are identified in Table 14.2. Of the 18 wilderness

Table 14.1   National Wilderness Preservation System: Acreage by State—1994

State	Wilderness Acreage	State	Wilderness Acreage
Alaska	57,408,796	West Virginia	80,852
California	6,306,497	South Dakota	74,076
Arizona	4,537,864	Missouri	70,928
Washington	4,323,009	Tennessee	66,305
Idaho	4,005,546	South Carolina	60,857
Montana	3,442,305	Vermont	59,421
Colorado	3,256,772	Wisconsin	42,323
Wyoming	3,080,358	North Dakota	39,652
Oregon	2,096,043	Alabama	33,151
New Mexico	1,613,263	Illinois	29,599
Florida	1,422,248	Oklahoma	22,721
Minnesota	809,230	Maine	19,392
Utah	800,958	Louisiana	17,025
Nevada	792,525	Kentucky	16,415
Georgia	484,402	Indiana	12,935
Michigan	249,218	Nebraska	12,429
Virginia	167,032	Mississippi	10,683
Hawaii	142,370	New Jersey	10,341
Arkansas	129,233	Pennsylvania	8,938
North Carolina	112,047	Massachusetts	2,420
New Hampshire	102,932	New York	1,363
Texas	81,562	Ohio	77
Total			96,056,113

Source: Rob Hellie, Bureau of Land Management, personal communication, January 1994.

Table 14.2   Largest Wilderness Areas—1994

Wilderness Area	Administrative Unit[a]	State	Acreage
Wrangell–St. Elias	Wrangell–St. Elias NP and Preserve	AK	9,078,675
Arctic	Arctic NWR	AK	8,000,000
Gates of the Arctic	Gates of the Arctic NP	AK	7,167,192
Noatak	Noatak Nat'l Preserve	AK	5,765,427
Katmai	Katmai NP and Preserve	AK	3,384,358
Glacier Bay	Glacier Bay NP and Preserve	AK	2,664,840
Lake Clark	Lake Clark NP	AK	2,619,550
Frank Church–River of No Return	Payette NF, Coeur d'Alene Dist., Bitterroot NF, Boise NF, Challis NF, Nez Perce NF, Salmon NF	ID	2,366,623
Togiak	Togiak NWR	AK	2,270,000
Misty Fjords	Tongass NF	AK	2,142,243
Denali	Denali NP	AK	2,124,783
Kenai	Kenai NWR	AK	1,350,000
Selway-Bitterroot	Nez Perce NF, Bitterroot NF, Clearwater NF, Lolo NF	ID, MT	1,340,460
Aleutian Islands	Alaska Maritime NWR	AK	1,300,000
Andreafsky	Yukon Delta NWR	AK	1,300,000
Everglades	Everglades NP	FL	1,296,500
Innoko	Innoko NWR	AK	1,240,000
Bob Marshall	Flathead NF, Lewis and Clark NF	MT	1,009,356
Kootznoowoo	Tongass NF	AK	955,921
Absaroka-Beartooth	Gallatin NF, Custer NF, Shoshone NF	MT, WY	943,610
Unimak	Alaska Maritime NWR	AK	910,000
Olympic	Olympic NP	WA	876,669
Cabeza Prieta	Cabeza Prieta NWR	AZ	803,418
Boundary Waters Canoe Area	Superior NF	MN	803,050
Sequoia–Kings Canyon	Sequoia–Kings Canyon NP	CA	736,980
Washakie	Shoshone NF	WY	704,274
Yosemite	Yosemite NP	CA	677,600
Tracy Arm–Fords Terror	Tongass NF	AK	653,179
Stephen Mather	North Cascades NP	WA	634,614
Nunivak	Yukon Delta NWR	AK	600,000
Teton	Teton NF	WY	585,238
John Muir	Sierra NF, Inyo NF	CA	580,323
Gila	Gila NF	NM	557,873
Pasayten	Okanogan NF, Mt. Baker NF	WA	530,031
Kofa	Kofa NWR	AZ	516,200
Trinity Alps	Trinity NF, Six Rivers NF, Ukiah District; BLM, Shasta NF, Klamath NF	CA	502,764
Weminuche	San Juan NF, Rio Grande NF	CO	488,344
High Uintas	Ashley NF, Wasatch NF	UT	456,705

[a]NF, national forest; NP, national park; NWR, national wildlife refuge
Source: Rob Hellie, Bureau of Land Management, personal communication, January 1994.

areas that are over 1 million acres, only four are in the lower 49 states: the Frank Church–River of No Return (Idaho), the Selway-Bitterroot (Idaho and Montana), the Everglades (Florida), and the Bob Marshall (Montana). Other large wilderness areas in the lower 49 states include the Absaroka-Beartooth (Montana and Wyoming), the Olympic (Washington), the Cabeza Prieta (Arizona), the Boundary Waters Canoe Area (Minnesota), the Sequoia–Kings Canyon (California), the Washakie (Wyoming), the Yosemite (California), the Stephen Mather (Washington), the Teton (Wyoming), the John Muir (California), the Pasayten (Washington), the Kofa (Arizona), the Weminuche (Colorado), and the High Uintas (Utah).

The 1964 Wilderness Act pertains only to federal lands. A number of state-developed wilderness systems also exist. Most states have modeled their wilderness programs on the federal legislation. Table 14.3 summarizes the acreage in the nine state wilderness preservation programs. Almost two-thirds of the state wilderness acreage is in New York. Wilderness preservation in New York traces its origin to 1885, when Article 14, Section 1, of the state constitution established the forest preserve to be "forever kept as wild forest land." Most of New York's over 1 million acres of wilderness are located in the Adirondack Park, where this wilderness has been so designated since the Adirondack Park State Land Master Plan was adopted in 1972. There are also smaller amounts of wilderness in the Catskill Park in New York. California has another 23 percent of the state wilderness in its system, and Minnesota has 6 percent of the state wilderness. All of Minnesota's wilderness is located within the boundary of the Boundary Waters Canoe Area. Three additional states have designated individual wilderness, but they are not part of a formal wilderness program. In Maine, much of 200,000-acre Baxter State Park is kept in its natural state. The Oklahoma Department of Wildlife Conservation manages the 14,000-acre McCurtain County Wilderness Area. In Hawaii, the Department of Land and Natural Resources has established the Alakai Wilderness Preserve on the Island of Kauai (Hendee et al., 1990, 173).

Recreational Use of the National Wilderness Preservation System

Measuring the use of wilderness areas is one of the most difficult types of recreational land usage to assess. The Fish and Wildlife Service and the BLM do not currently measure the use of their wilderness areas. The National Park Service does not have an active program of reporting wilderness use. Of the four federal land-managing agencies, only the Forest Service has an active program of reporting the use of its wilderness areas. The National Park Service has a permit system that reports back-

Table 14.3   State Wilderness Preservation Programs—1984

State	No. of Areas	No. of Acres
Alaska	n.g.	n.g.
California	6	419,410
Florida	10	56,864
Maryland	4	8,870
Michigan[1]	2	46,492
Minnesota[2]	n.g.	106,360
Missouri	10	16,159
New York[3]	20	1,156,935
Wisconsin	n.g.	29,772
Total	52	1,840,862

n.g. = not given
[1]Includes only those areas designated as wilderness or wild under the Michigan Wilderness and Natural Areas Act of 1972.
[2]Includes only state lands lying within the federally protected Boundary Waters Canoe Area Wilderness.
[3]Information from December 1989, courtesy of the Adirondack Park Agency.
Source: John C. Hendee, George H. Stankey, and Robert C. Lucas, *Wilderness Management,* Golden, Colo.: North American Press, 1990, 172.

country overnight use but makes no attempt to distinguish between the use that occurs inside and outside the wilderness boundaries. Moreover, the National Park Service does not measure the day use that occurs inside the wilderness areas. The National Park Service uses the recreation visit as the statistical unit, while the Forest Service uses the recreation visitor day (RVD). Especially in the larger wilderness areas, there are often many access points, and it is prohibitively expensive to accurately measure this use. Therefore, a variety of indirect ways of estimating or measuring wilderness use have been undertaken, including sample observations, electronic counters, automatic cameras, estimates based on data from trail registers or mandatory permits, and just guessing. The most accurate, useful wilderness use data probably come from mandatory visitor permit systems (Hendee et al., 1990, 363).

The most current study that sheds light on the relative amount of recreational use in the wilderness areas of the national parks, national forests, national wildlife refuges, and BLM lands was done in 1988. Figure 14.7 shows that an estimated 75 percent of all recreational use in the National Wilderness Preservation System in 1988 occurred on national forest wilderness areas. The percentages of recreational use occurring in wilderness areas on the other agency lands are as follows: National Park Service wilderness areas, 15 percent; Fish and Wildlife Service wilderness areas, 5 percent; and BLM wilderness areas, 5 percent. The data for estimating these percentages came from a nationwide telephone survey of managers (P.C. Reed in Cordell et al., 1990).

People behave much like cattle when it comes to the use of wilderness areas—they favor a few select "cool shady places." Certain sections of some wilderness areas are used much more heavily than others. Chapter 9 discussed the topic of recreational use in national forest wilderness areas. In 1992, there were 13,134,700 RVDs spent in these areas. By far, the most heavily used national forest wilderness area—as well as the most heavily used in the entire National Wilderness Preservation System—is the

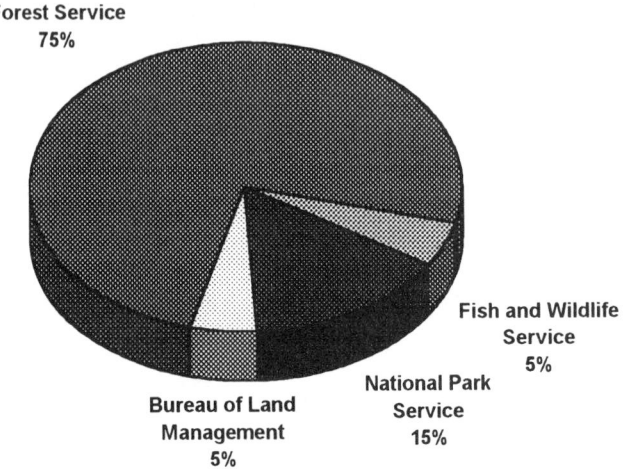

Figure 14.7 Estimated distribution of total recreational use in the National Wilderness Preservation System. (*Source:* Reed in H. Ken Cordell, et al. *An Analysis of the Outdoor Recreation and Wilderness Situation in the United States: 1989–2040,* April, 1990.)

Boundary Waters Canoe Area. The only wilderness area in the Superior National Forest, the Boundary Waters received 1,404,000 RVDs in 1992 (Figure 14.8). There were no data available for Fish and Wildlife Service or BLM wilderness areas to compare with this figure.

The author did conduct a mail survey of the superintendents of the 42 National Park System units that had wilderness areas, to determine the recreational use in these areas. This survey was conducted during the fall of 1993, and responses were received from 32 of the 42 superintendents surveyed. From these data, it was estimated that 583,233 RVDs occurred in 1992 on these 32 wilderness areas. Responses were not received from the following national park wilderness areas: Buffalo National River, Everglades, Glacier Bay, Haleakala, Hawaiian Volcanoes, Joshua Tree, Katmai, Lava Beds, Pinnacles, and Yosemite. To obtain proxy values for the nonrespondents, the author combined the number of National Park Service backcountry overnight stays for 1986 listed in Hendee et al (1990)—188,517—with the survey results to get a total of 771,750 RVDs in national park wilderness areas. It is noteworthy that in both the 1986 study and the author's 1992 survey, the most heavily used national park wilderness area was the Sequoia–Kings Canyon (165,656 RVDs) followed by the Yosemite (105,614 RVDs). The next most heavily used national park wilderness areas were the Philip Burton (Point Reyes National Seashore, California) 99,799 RVDs; the Olympic (Washington), 93,947 RVDs; the Mount Rainier (Washington), 40,509 RVDs; and the Denali (Alaska), 34,664 RVDs. The number of RVDs reported for the Philip Burton Wilderness Area is suspect, as it shows a considerable increase from the use reported in Hendee et al (1990).

It can be concluded that 15 national forest wilderness areas receive heavier use than any of the national park wilderness areas. Some of the latter receive very light use. The unit of the National Wilderness Preservation System with the lightest use is

Figure 14.8 The Boundary Waters Canoe Area in Minnesota's Superior National Forest is the most heavily used unit of the National Wilderness Preservation System.

Mesa Verde—none. Here is the reply the author received from the chief park ranger at Mesa Verde National Park:

> The recreation visitor days for the portion of Mesa Verde National Park that is classified as wilderness is zero. The park's backcountry is closed to visitor use to protect the cultural resources. (Personal communication with Howard L. Dimont, Chief Park Ranger, October 13, 1993).

Other national park wilderness areas with very light use are the Badlands (S. Dakota, 300 RVDs), the Craters of the Moon (Idaho, 146 RVDs), and the Great Sand Dunes (Colorado, 665 RVDs).

Several superintendents or chief park rangers have pointed out why the wilderness area use is not measured. The superintendent of Mount Rainier National Park made the following comment:

> We do not have the recreation visitor day use information for our legislated wilderness portion of Mount Rainier National Park. Because of the many access points we have not found a practical, economical way to count the day use of the wilderness. The total overnight camping use for the wilderness for 1992 was 40,509. (Personal communication with William J. Briggle, Superintendent, October 14, 1993).

The chief park ranger at Shenandoah National Park had these comments to make:

> Unfortunately, we do not maintain statistics on wilderness use. We do maintain a count for the number of backcountry campers, but this count is for the entire backcountry area of the park including wilderness. This count includes overnight campers only. The number of day users is not recorded in any format. (Personal communication with Larry L. Hakel, Chief Park Ranger, October 26, 1993).

The answer to the survey by the superintendent of Theodore Roosevelt National Park demonstrated a great deal of reflection on the question and the problems that are faced in assessing wilderness use in national parks where designated wilderness occupies only a portion of the area:

> At Theodore Roosevelt National Park, the only wilderness use figures that are precise are those for overnight backcountry campers. These backpackers are required to register and the majority of them [are] overnight in the wilderness. Overnight wilderness camping for the entire park in calendar year 1992 totaled 997 persons for approximately 2,500 user days.
>
> Most of the 24,000 acre north unit of the park is designated wilderness. There are approximately 5,000 acres, consisting of the development zone near the entrance and the road corridor through the unit, that were excluded from wilderness designation. It is our opinion, therefore, that the majority of the visitors to this unit, if they leave their vehicles and venture even a short distance from the road, are entering designated wilderness. We would estimate that of the total 1992 visitor count of 48,500 persons to this unit, not less than 60% must have spent some time in the wilderness. The exact length of time they spend would be even harder to determine, but if each spent at least one hour in the wilderness it would calculate out to 1,200 wilderness use days.
>
> Wilderness use in the 46,000 acre south unit of the park is even more difficult to determine. Only a 10,000 acre block in the northwest corner of this unit is designated wilderness. Visitors hike and ride into this area at will. There are trail registers, but day users are not required to register and we have no way of knowing what percentage do log in. Additionally, riders and hikers are not required to use only marked trails and may travel cross-country at will. Any wilderness use figures for the south unit would be a rough estimate at best.

Our estimate is that the south unit experiences somewhere in the neighborhood of 1,500 wilderness use days each year. Therefore the total estimated number of wilderness use days for Theodore Roosevelt National Park is 5,200." (Personal communication with Pete Hurt, Superintendent, October 14, 1993).

Based on a number of factors and assumptions the author estimates the use of the National Wilderness Preservation System to be approximately 17.7 million RVDs / year. The Forest Service maintains the best wilderness use data, and for 1992 reported the total recreational use in all national forest wilderness areas as 13.3 million RVDs. The author estimates the recreational use on national park wilderness areas as 2.7 million RVDs / year. This number is triple that of his survey but it does recognize day use which is not reflected in the National Park reporting system. The estimate for the recreational use on both Fish and Wildlife Service and BLM wilderness areas is 0.9 million RVDs for each. These estimates of use are based on two very important assumptions. The first assumption accepts Reed's estimate of the distribution of use among agencies in 1988 (Forest Service, 75 percent; National Park Service, 15 percent; Fish and Wildlife Service, 5 percent; and BLM, 5 percent. The second assumption accepts the Forest Service's value of 13.3 million RVDs for 1992.

The last subject to be covered in this section is the identification of the most heavily used wilderness areas. It must be emphasized here that these rankings are approximate for many wilderness areas. From one year to the next the use of a particular wilderness area can change greatly. For example, in the Alpine Lakes Wilderness Area (Washington) in 1991 the use reported was 406,959 RVDs. The following year—1992—the use was reported as 295,797 RVDs. All too often the author has watched Forest Service personnel make major changes in use data in a matter of a few seconds. This does make one question the reliability and validity of the data. However, there is no one better equipped to make these changes than the professionals in the offices and field near the wilderness areas. It is the job of the researcher to strive to obtain the best available data. Weather can also play a major role in recreational participation. The author has used a variety of sources to rank the wilderness areas in order of use in the following paragraphs.

The Boundary Waters Canoe Area (Minnesota, 1.4 million RVDs) is the undisputed leader in recreational use among all areas in the National Wilderness Preservation System. The second most used unit is the John Muir Wilderness Area (California, 0.51 million RVDs). Figure 14.9 shows the entrance road at the Whitney Portal, a popular means of access to the John Muir Wilderness Area in the Inyo National Forest. Entry permits are required for overnight use. The Frank Church–River of No Return Wilderness Area (Idaho, 0.41 million RVDs) ranks third in use, followed by the Kootznoowoo (Alaska, 0.31 million RVDs). The fifth-, sixth-, seventh-, and eighth-ranked wilderness areas are all close: Absaroka-Beartooth (Montana and Wyoming, 0.30 million RVDs); Alpine Lakes (Washington, 0.30 million RVDs); Pecos (N. Mexico, 0.27 million RVDs); and Desolation (California, 0.26 million RVDs). Misty Fjords (Alaska, 0.22 million RVDs) ranks ninth, and the Bridger (Wyoming) and the High Uintas (Utah) are virtually tied at tenth place with 0.20 million RVDs each. All 11 of these most heavily used wilderness areas are in national forest.

The following wilderness areas are, in rank order, the next most heavily used: San Gorgonio (California, 0.19 million RVDs), Three Sisters (Oregon, 0.18 million RVDs), Eagle Cap (Oregon, 0.18 million RVDs), Weminuche (Colorado, 0.18 million

Figure 14.9 A permit is required for overnight use in the John Muir Wilderness Area in the Inyo National Forest. Shown here is the Whitney Portal access road near Lone Pine, Calif.

RVDs), Sequoia–Kings Canyon (California, 0.17 million RVDs), Selway-Bitterroot (Montana and Idaho, 0.16 million RVDs), West Chichagof–Yakobi (Alaska, 0.16 million RVDs), Ansel Adams (California, 0.16 million RVDs), Bob Marshall (Montana, 0.15 million RVDs), Trinity Alps (California, 0.15 million RVDs), Collegiate Peaks (Colorado, 0.15 million RVDs), Holy Cross (Colorado, 0.13 million RVDs), Flat Tops (Colorado, 0.12 million RVDs), Yosemite (California, 0.11 million RVDs), and Granite Chief (California, 0.11 million RVDs). Twenty-four of the 26 wilderness areas ranked top in terms of use are in national forests. Only two National Park Service areas are listed here—Sequoia–Kings Canyon (16th place) and Yosemite (25th place).

It is important to emphasize, however, that the total amount of use is only one of the factors that can impact the quality of a wilderness experience. The use is spread over wilderness areas unequally, with some sections receiving very heavy use and others receiving light use. The principal reason for only having a limited number of permits available at each entry point is to spread the use around. It is usually the choice areas close to a trailhead that receive the most use. The use of many wilderness areas is seasonal, with the summer having the heaviest use. For example, in the Sequoia–Kings Canyon Wilderness Area 95 percent of the use occurs from May to November, with the heaviest use in August. This use pattern, which is common across much of the country, is related to both vacation patterns and the nature of the snow cover. In some of the southwestern wilderness areas, July and August—at least in the lower elevations—can be the slow months. At Everglades Wilderness Area (Florida) the winter is the heavier used period.

Another way to measure wilderness use is to calculate the number of RVDs per acre. This was the methodology used by Hendee, Stankey, and Lucas (1990). This is an excellent way to compare the relative intensities of use at wilderness areas because it relates the amount of use to the size of an area. Using 1986 data, they calculated RVDs / acre for the national forest wilderness areas. The average RVDs / acre for all national forest wilderness areas was 0.35. The most heavily used national forest wilderness area—the Boundary Waters Canoe Area—has 0.95 RVDs per acre and the

second ranked John Muir has 0.78 RVDs per acre. The third ranked Frank Church-River of No Return Wilderness Area has 0.17 RVDs per acre, which is well below the national average. Some of the relatively small wilderness areas that do not have very high total amounts of use, do have RVD/acre values which indicate crowding. Extreme examples of this crowding would be the Devils Backbone Wilderness Area, Missouri (12.05 RVD/acre) and the Glacier View Wilderness Area, Washington (9.15 RVD/acre). Other national forest wilderness areas with higher intensities of use include: Mount Timpanogos, Utah (4.45 RVD/acre); Great Gulf, New Hampshire (4.23 RVD/acre); Joyce Kilmer-Slickrock, North Carolina (4.23 RVD/acre); Lewis Fork, Virginia (4.05 RVD/acre); Shining Rock, North Carolina (3.70 RVD/acre); Black Elk, South Dakota (3.68 RVD/acre); Desolation, California (3.58 RVD/acre); San Gorgonio, California (3.36 RVD/acre); Jennie Lakes, California (2.93 RVD/acre); Peters Mountain, Virginia (2.77 RVD/acre); and Granite Chief, California (2.18 RVD/acre).

RIVERS

This section will focus primarily on the federal Wild and Scenic Rivers System, which is based upon the Wild and Scenic Rivers Act of 1968 (P.L. 90-542). (Other river protection programs will be covered briefly at the end of this section.) The passage of this act by Congress reaffirmed the growing trend, initiated with passage of the Wilderness Act in 1964, to protect natural resources for their amenity value. The Wild and Scenic Rivers Act states that certain selected rivers of the United States, "which, with their immediate environments, possess outstandingly remarkable scenic, recreational, geologic, fish and wildlife, historic, cultural, or other similar values, shall be preserved in free-flowing condition, and that they and their immediate environments shall be protected for the benefit and enjoyment of present and future generations." With this act, Congress declared that the established national policy of allowing dams and other construction at appropriate sections of U.S. rivers needs to be complemented by a policy that preserves other selected rivers or sections of them in a free-flowing state in order to protect their water quality and to fulfill other vital national conservation purposes. This act implements this policy by instituting a National Wild and Scenic Rivers System, by designating the initial components of that system, and by prescribing the methods by which and standards according to which additional components may be added to system from time to time.

The Wild and Scenic Rivers Act is an extraordinary piece of legislation in that, for the first time, value was assigned to rivers in their free-flowing state and protection was given to this value. The act placed new rules on single-purpose agencies, such as the Bureau of Reclamation and the Army Corps of Engineers, that were absorbed in continually finding new dam sites on just about every free-flowing stream in the country. The act has been a major factor in virtually bringing to a halt the era of dam construction that began at the beginning of the century. The act is a major influence on the types of recreational possibilities that currently are available or will be available on rivers in the future. The act assures that "whitewater" recreational opportunities, as opposed to the "flatwater" recreational opportunities exist-

ing on reservoirs, are and will be available as a recreational choice for Americans and others. The Outdoor Recreation Resources Review Commission reports in 1962 generated a great deal of interest in river preservation. The Craighead brothers—John and Frank—played a major role in stimulating interest in river preservation. They produced a film about the Middle Fork of the Salmon River and publicized the term *wild river*. In addition to their effort on behalf of wild rivers, they are also noted scientists for work with grizzly bears in Montana and Wyoming. Stewart Udall, the Secretary of the Interior in the 1960s, was also a crucial supporter of the concept. The first wild-and-scenic-rivers bill was introduced in 1964, and 16 different bills were introduced before passage of P.L. 90-542 in 1968.

Wild and Scenic Rivers Act

President Lyndon B. Johnson signed the Wild and Scenic Rivers Act on October 2, 1968. Section 2(a) of this act states:

> The national wild and scenic rivers system shall comprise rivers (i) that are authorized for inclusion therein by Act of Congress, or (ii) that are designated as wild, scenic or recreational rivers by or pursuant to an act of the legislature of the State or States through which they flow, that are to be permanently administered as wild, scenic or recreational rivers by an agency or political subdivision of the State or States concerned without expense to the United States, that are found by the Secretary of the Interior, upon application of the Governor to the State or the Governors of the States concerned, or a person or persons thereunto duly appointed by him or them, to meet the cirteria established in this Act and such criteria supplementary thereto as he may prescribe, and that are approved by him for inclusion in the system, including, upon application of the Governor to the State concerned, the Allagash Wilderness Waterway, Maine, and that segment of the Wolf River, Wisconsin, which flows through Langlade County.

Section 2(b) addressed the eligibility requirement and defined the terms *wild river, scenic river,* and *recreational river:*

> A wild, scenic or recreational river area eligible to be included in the system is a free-flowing stream and the related adjacent land area that possesses one or more of the values referred to in section 1, subsection (b) of this Act. Every wild, scenic or recreational river in its free-flowing condition, or upon restoration to this condition, shall be considered eligible for inclusion in the national wild and scenic rivers system and, if included, shall be classified, designated and administered as one of the following:
>   (1) *Wild river areas*—Those rivers or sections of rivers that are free of impoundments and generally inaccessible except by trail, with watersheds or shorelines essentially primitive and waters unpolluted. These represent vestiges of primitive America.
>   (2) *Scenic river areas*—Those rivers or sections of rivers that are free of impoundments, with shorelines or watersheds still largely primitive and shorelines largely undeveloped, but accessible in places by roads.
>   (3) *Recreational river areas*—Those rivers or sections of rivers that are readily accessible by road or railroad, that may have some development along their shorelines, and that may have undergone some impoundment or diversion in the past.

Section 3(a) designated the following rivers as the *initial components* of the National Wild and Scenic Rivers System:

- *Clearwater River, Middle Fork*   Idaho, 185 miles (includes the Lochsa and Selway tributaries)
- *Eleven Point*   Missouri, 44.4 miles
- *Feather, Middle Fork*   California, 77.6 miles
- *Rio Grande*   New Mexico, 53 miles (includes 4 miles of the Red River)
- *Rogue*   Oregon, 84.5 miles
- *Saint Croix*   Minnesota and Wisconsin, 200 miles (includes the Namekagon River)
- *Salmon, Middle Fork*   Idaho, 104 miles
- *Wolf*   Wisconsin, 25 miles

The act also identified 27 additional rivers to be studied as potential additions to the system and mandated that within 10 years the studies should be completed. In addition, it encouraged states to develop state programs for rivers to be included within the system or to develop their own state systems. The act also specified that the "boundaries shall include an average of not more than three hundred and twenty acres per mile on both sides of the river" and that no more than $17 million could be appropriated for the acquisition of lands and interests in lands.

Table 14.4 summarizes the classification criteria for the different categories of rivers. There can be no dams or impoundments on wild rivers or scenic rivers, but some low dams or impoundments are permissible on recreational rivers. No shoreline development is allowed in the "wild" category, but occasional buildings are permissible in the "scenic" category. There may be some development along the shorelines in the "recreational" category. Wild rivers are accessible only by trails. Roads may occasionally reach or bridge scenic rivers. Recreational rivers may be readily accessible by road or railroad.

Growth of the System

By the 10th anniversary of the Wild and Scenic Rivers System, in 1978, the system had grown to include 43 rivers and 2299 miles (Palmer, 1993, 32). The initial system in 1968 included eight rivers on 773.5 miles. In 1970, the Allagash Wilderness Waterway (92.5 miles) in Maine became the first state-protected river to be added to the national system. A major gain was the *Hells Canyon National Recreation Act*, which passed Congress December 31, 1975. This act "deauthorized" the Asotin Dam, which would have inundated the lower half of Hells Canyon. The upper half of Hells Canyon was already dammed. This act also added the Snake River (66.9 miles) in Idaho and Oregon and the Rapid River (26.8 miles) with its West Fork in Idaho to the Wild and Scenic Rivers System. In 1976, the designation of the North, Middle, and South Forks of the Flathead River (219 miles) in Montana eliminated dams that had been proposed for three sites at Glacier View, Spruce Park, and Smoky Range. In 1978, 191.2 miles of the Rio Grande along the Texas-Mexican border were added to the Wild and Scenic Rivers System; 107 of these miles forms Big Bend National Park's southern boundary (Figure 14.10). A major addition came in 1980 with the passage of the Alaska National Interest Lands Conservation Act (ANILCA). This single act added to the system 25 rivers in Alaska that included 3210 miles of river. In 1988, P.L. 100-557 added 40 rivers in Oregon totaling 1,437.25 miles. Most recently,

Table 14.4 Classification Criteria for Wild and Scenic Rivers

Attribute	Wild	Scenic	Recreational
Dams, reservoirs	Free of impoundment.	Free of impoundment.	Some existing impoundment for diversion. The existence of low dams, diversions, or other modifications of the waterway is acceptable, provided the waterway remains generally natural.
Shoreline development	Essentially primitive. Little or no evidence of human activity. The presence of a few inconspicuous structures, particularly those of historical or cultural value, is acceptable. A limited amount of domestic livestock grazing or hay production is acceptable. Little or no evidence of past timber harvest. No ongoing timber harvest.	Largely primitive and undeveloped. No substantial evidence of human activity. The presence of small communities or dispersed dwellings or farm structures is acceptable. The presence of grazing, hay production, or row crops is acceptable. Evidence of past or ongoing timber harvest is acceptable, provided the forest appears natural from the riverbank.	Some development. Substantial evidence of human activity. The presence of extensive residential development and a few commercial structures is acceptable. Lands may have been developed for the full range of agricultural and forestry uses. May show evidence of past and ongoing timber harvest.
Accessibility	Generally inaccessible except by trail. No roads, railroads, or other provision for vehicular travel within the river area. A few existing roads leading to the boundary of the river area are acceptable.	Accessible in places by road. Roads may occasionally reach or bridge the river. The existence of the short stretches of conspicuous or longer stretches of inconspicuous roads or railroads is acceptable.	Readily accessible by road or railroad. The existence of parallel roads or railroads on one or both banks as well as bridge crossing and other river access points is acceptable.
Water quality	Meets or exceeds federal criteria or federally approved state standards for aesthetics, for propagation of fish and wildlife normally adapted to the habitat of the river, and for primary contact recreation (swimming) except where exceeded by natural conditions.	No criteria prescribed by the Wild and Scenic Rivers Act. The Federal Water Pollution Control Act Amendments of 1972 have made it a national goal that all waters of the United States be made fishable and swimmable. Therefore, rivers will not be precluded from scenic or recreational classification because of poor water quality at the time of their study provided a water-quality improvement plan exists and is being developed in compliance with applicable federal and state laws.	

Source: Department of the Interior, *National Wild and Scenic Rivers System: Revised Guidelines for Eligibility, Classification, and Management of River Areas,* Washington, D.C., 1982.

Figure 14.10 Two sections of the Rio Grande are part of the Wild and Scenic Rivers System. Shown here is a portion of the 191.2-mile section along the Texas-Mexican boundary in Big Bend National Park.

five public laws in 1992 added 27 rivers totaling 1,043.4 miles in Michigan (14 rivers), Arkansas (eight rivers), California (three rivers), Pennsylvania (one river), and New Jersey (one river).

In 1993 the National Wild and Scenic Rivers System consisted of 152 river units on a total of 10,516.35 miles: "wild" 5263.9 miles; "scenic," 2136.15 miles; and "recreational," 3109.1 miles. Over half (2955 miles or 56 percent) of the wild rivers are located in Alaska. Figure 14.11 shows the location of each river in the National Wild and Scenic Rivers System and is keyed to Appendix XXIII, which is a complete listing of all rivers in the National Wild and Scenic Rivers System. The appendix also identifies the administering agency, the public law or secretarial designation, a breakdown of the mileage in each category, and the total number of miles on each river. The numbers in this appendix are keyed to Figure 14.11. A look at Figure 14.11 reveals that although national wild and scenic rivers are found in 34 different states, there are large voids of the United States where no designated rivers are located; the great void in the Great Basin Intermountain region can be explained by a lack of rivers altogether.

Certain geographic areas have dense concentrations of rivers. Alaska has more mileage than any other state with 3210 miles (31 percent of total). Most of these rivers are in the interior. In Alaska, 330 miles of the Noatak River (Figure 14.12) and 392 miles of the Fortymile River are the longest units in the entire National Wild and Scenic Rivers System. California has 1872.3 miles, or 18 percent of the total mileage in the System. Most of these rivers are in the Sierra Nevada or in the extreme northwestern corner of the state. Oregon has 1,692.2 miles or 16 percent of the total mileage. These rivers are widely scattered in all areas of the state except the extreme northwestern section. Michigan has 624.8 miles, or 6 percent of the total, all of which were added to the system in 1992, and most are in the Upper Peninsula. Idaho has

Figure 14.12 The Noatak River is one of the wildest rivers in the Wild and Scenic Rivers System, with 330 miles classified as "wild." Shown are rafters in the Grand Canyon of the Noatak in Noatak National Preserve. (National Park Service photo)

574 miles, or 5.5 percent of the system total, most of which are in the central portion of the state. Montana has 368 miles in just two river systems, the Flathead and the Missouri. The northwestern corner of Arkansas has the final major cluster of rivers with 210 miles on eight rivers in the system.

Table 14.5 summarizes the jurisdiction by miles by agency for the National Wild and Scenic Rivers System. The Forest Service has the greatest amount of river mileage under its jurisdiction—4270.6 miles or 41 percent of the total system. The National Park Service has 2609.3 miles, or 25 percent of the total, followed by the Bureau of Land Management with 1998.6 miles, or 19 percent. The Fish and Wildlife Service has 1043 miles, or 10 percent, and the states have 773.2 miles, or 7 percent. Indians are responsible for administering 65 miles, or 0.6 percent, and the Army Corps of

Table 14.5 Agency Jurisdiction over Wild and Scenic Rivers—1993

Agency	Miles
U.S. Forest Service	4,270.6
Fish and Wildlife Service	1,043.0
National Park Service	2,609.3
Bureau of Land Management	1,998.6
Corps of Engineers	4.6
States	773.2
Indian Reservations	65
Total	10,764.4

Source: National Park Service, Division of Park Planning and Protection, November 1992.

Engineers is responsible for only 4.6 miles, on the Cossatot River (Arkansas). None of the Forest Service rivers are in Alaska, but a large number are in Oregon. Almost half of National Park Service and BLM mileage is in Alaska, while all of the Fish and Wildlife Service mileage is in Alaska. Over half of the state mileage of 773.3 miles lies in California; 309 of which are part of one California river—the Eel. Of the 65 miles on Indian reservations, 29 miles of the Klamath River and 14 miles of the Trinity River are on the Hoopa Valley Indian Reservation, and 22 miles of the Eel River are on the Round Valley Indian Reservation.

Other River Protection Programs

There are two additional mechanisms for specifically protecting rivers: adding river units to the National Park System and developing state river protection programs. There are currently five of these "rivers" in the National Park System. The National Park units are generally called "national rivers," although the term is not used for the first one established—Ozark National Scenic Riverways (Missouri; authorized 1964, established 1972). The Buffalo National River (Arkansas; authorized 1972) includes 10,529 acres designated part of the National Wilderness Preservation System. In 1978, the Missouri National River (Nebraska and S. Dakota), and the New River Gorge National River (W. Virginia), were established and added to the National Park System. The most recent "river" addition to the National Park System is the Bluestone National Scenic River (W. Virginia). A variety of different programs protect rivers in varying degrees in 32 different states. Table 14.6 summarizes the state river programs. There are 13,552 miles of rivers on 303 rivers in these programs. The largest systems are in Michigan (1698 miles), Maine (1500 miles), California (1365 miles), Louisiana (1260 miles), and New York (1248 miles). New York enacted the New York State Wild and Scenic Rivers Act in 1972, modeling it after the 1968 federal legislation by using the same classifications and definitions. Virtually all of the mileage in New York's system is within the Adirondack Park, where strict land-use regulations apply. It is a model program for the rest of the nation to emulate.

TRAILS

Trails have played a vital part in America's history. Walking for pleasure and other trail-related activities are among the favorite outdoor recreation pursuits of Americans. Trails are needed for such recreational activities as walking, hiking, bicycling, horseback riding, snowmobiling and motorcycling. Trails also provide access routes that enhance opportunities for other activities such as camping in remote areas, fishing, hunting, and bird watching. This section will focus on the establishment of a National Trails System. It is important to note that there are a wide variety of other trail systems across the country. In February 1965, President Lyndon Johnson, in his "Natural Beauty Message" to Congress, called for development and protection of a national system of trails, including metropolitan trails. In April 1965, Interior Secretary Stewart Udall asked the Bureau of Outdoor Recreation (BOR) to take the lead in a nationwide trail study. In the fall of 1966, its detailed, comprehensive study

Table 14.6   State Scenic Rivers System

State	Date	Number of Rivers	Miles of Rivers	Status of State Inventory
Alaska	1987	6	350	None
Arkansas	1979	4	250	Ongoing
California	1972	8	1,365	None
Connecticut	1984	0	0	Ongoing
Florida	1972	1	5	Final for 50 rivers
Georgia	1969	4	74	None
Idaho	1988	13	581	Final
Indiana	1973	3	108	None
Iowa	1984	5	315	None
Kentucky	1972	9	114	Final
Louisiana	1970	47	1,260	Final for 48 rivers
Maine	1983	18	1,500	Final
Maryland	1968	9	441	Ongoing
Massachusetts	1971	4	86	None
Michigan	1970	14	1,698	None
Minnesota	1973	8	955	Final
New Hampshire	1988	4	120	Final for some rivers
New Jersey	1977	1	14	None
New York	1972	55	1,248	Ongoing
North Carolina	1971	3	142	None
Ohio	1968	10	629	Final
Oklahoma	1977	5	151	None
Oregon	1969	17	580	Final
Pennsylvania	1972	10	393	Final
South Carolina	1974	1	5	Final
South Dakota	1972	0	0	None
Tennessee	1968	10	318	Ongoing
Vermont	1987	0	0	Final
Virginia	1970	15	169	None
Washington	1977	4	74	Final
West Virginia	1969	5	236	Ongoing
Wisconsin	1965	10	371	None
Total (32 states)		303	13,552	Final for 13 states

Source: Tim Palmer, *The Wild and Scenic Rivers of America*, Washington, D.C.: Island Press, 1993.

entitled *Trails for America*, was printed. The report recommended the Appalachian Trail as the initial unit of the system, and when studies were completed, *Trails for America* urged that three other national scenic trails be designated: the Pacific Crest Trail, the Potomac Heritage Trail, and the Continental Divide Trail.

National Trails System Act and Amendments

In 1968, to provide assistance in maintaining the Appalachian Trail and to establish a national system of trails, Congress passed the National Trails System Act (P.L. 90-543), signed into law by President Johnson on October 2, 1968–the same day the Wild and Scenic Rivers Act was signed. The system came into being almost 20 months after Senator Henry Jackson introduced S.827. President Johnson had a great deal of personal interest in the passage of the National Trails System Act. The "Statement of Policy" of the act, as given in Section 2(a), is as follows:

In order to provide for the ever-increasing outdoor recreation needs of an expanding population and in order to promote public access to, travel within, and enjoyment and appreciation of the open-air, outdoor areas of the Nation, trails should be established (i) primarily, near the urban areas of the Nation, and (ii) secondarily, within established scenic areas more remotely located.

The purpose of the act, as stated in Section 2(b) is

. . . to provide the means for attaining these objectives by instituting a national system of recreation and scenic trails, by designating the Appalachian Trail and the Pacific Crest Trail as the initial components of that system, and by prescribing the methods by which, and standards according to which, additional components may be added to the system.

The National Trails System was initially to be composed of three types of components:

1 *National recreation trails,* which would provide a variety of outdoor recreation uses in or reasonably accessible to urban areas
2 *National scenic trails,* which would be extended trails located to provide for maximum outdoor recreation potential and for the conservation and enjoyment of the nationally significant scenic, historic, natural, or cultural qualities of the areas through which such trails might pass.
3 *Connecting or side trails,* which will provide additional points of public access to national research or national scenic trails or which will provide connections between such trails.

NOTE: Public Law 95-625 (passed November 10, 1978) added the new category *national historic trail.*

The Secretaries of the Interior and of Agriculture, in consultation with appropriate governmental agencies and public and private organizations, were authorized to establish a uniform marker for the National Trails System.

National Recreation Trails   Section 4(a) authorizes the Secretary of the Interior, or the Secretary of Agriculture, where lands are administered by them, to establish and designate national recreation trails, with the consent of the federal agency, state, or political subdivision having jurisdiction over the lands involved, upon finding that:

● Such trails are reasonably accessible to urban areas and/or
● Such trails meet the criteria established in the act.

Section 4(b) provides that trails within park, forest, and other recreation areas administered by the Secretary of the Interior or the Secretary of Agriculture or in other federally administered areas may be established and designated as "national recreation trails" by the appropriate Secretary and, when no federal land acquisition is involved:

● Trails in or reasonably accessible to urban areas may be designated "national recreation trails" by the Secretary of the Interior with the consent of the states, their political subdivisions, or other appropriate administering agencies.

• Trails within park, forest, and other recreation areas owned or administered by states may be designated "national recreation trails" by the Secretary of the Interior with the consent of the state.

National Scenic Trails   Section 5(a) provides that National Scenic Trails be authorized and designated only by act of Congress. Two trails were established as the *initial national scenic trails:*

1 *Appalachian Trail,* a trail of approximately 2000 miles extending generally along the Appalachian Mountains from Mount Katahdin (Maine) to Springer Mountain (Georgia). The Appalachian Trail is to be administered primarily as a footpath by the Secretary of the Interior, in consultation with the Secretary of Agriculture. (The Appalachian Trail was detailed in a case study in Chapter 6.)
2 *Pacific Crest Trail,* a trail of approximately 2350 miles, extending from the Mexican-California border northward generally along the mountain ranges of the West Coast states to the Canadian-Washington border near Lake Ross. The Pacific Crest Trail is to be administered by the Secretary of Agriculture, in consultation with the Secretary of the Interior.

The following trails are designated by Section 5(c) of the act to be studied as *potential additions* to the National Trail System as national scenic trails:

1 *Continental Divide Trail,* a 3100-mile trail extending from near the Mexican border in southwestern New Mexico northward generally along the Continental Divide to the Canadian border in Glacier National Park
2 *Potomac Heritage Trail,* an 825-mile trail extending generally from the mouth of the Potomac River to its sources in Pennsylvania and West Virginia, including the 170-mile Chesapeake and Ohio Canal towpath
3 *Old Cattle Trails* of the Southwest from the Vicinity of San Antonio, Tex., approximately 800-miles through Oklahoma via Baxter Springs and Chetopa, Kans., to Fort Scott, Kans., including the Chisholm Trail, from the vicinity of San Antonio or Cuero, Tex., approximately 800 north through Oklahoma to Abilene, Kansas
4 *Lewis and Clark Trail,* from Wood River, Illinois, to the Pacific Ocean in Oregon, following both the outbound and inbound routes of the Lewis and Clark Expedition
5 *Natchez Trace,* from Nashville, Tenn., approximately 600 miles to Natchez, Miss.
6 *North Country Trail,* from the Appalachian Trail in Vermont, approximately 3200 miles through New York, Pennsylvania, Ohio, Michigan, Wisconsin, and Minnesota, to the Lewis and Clark Trail in North Dakota
7 *Kittanning Trail* from Shirleysburg in Huntingdon County to Kittanning, Armstrong County, Pa.
8 *Oregon Trail,* from Independence, Mo., approximately 2000 miles to near Fort Vancouver, Washington
9 *Santa Fe Trail,* from Independence, Mo., approximately 800 miles to Santa Fe, N.M.
10 *Long Trail,* extending 255 miles from the Massachusetts border northward through Vermont to the Canadian border

11 *Mormon Trail*, extending from Nauvoo, Ill., to Salt Lake City, Utah, through Iowa, Nebraska, and Wyoming

12 *Gold Rush Trails* in Alaska.

13 *Mormon Battalion Trail*, extending 2000 miles from Mount Pisgah, Iowa, through Kansas, Colorado, New Mexico, and Arizona to Los Angeles, Calif.

14 *El Camino Real* from St. Augustine to San Mateo, Fla., approximately 20 miles along the southern boundary of the St. Johns River from Fort Caroline National Memorial to the St. Augustine National Park Monument

Public Law 94-527 (October 17, 1976) amended the National Trails System Act to add the following eight study trails to Section 5(c):

15 *Bartram Trail*, extending through Georgia, North Carolina, South Carolina, Alabama, Florida, Louisiana, Mississippi, and Tennessee.

16 *Daniel Boone Trail*, extending from the vicinity of Statesville, N.C., to Forth Boonesborough State Park, Ky.

17 *Desert Trail*, extending from the Canadian border through parts of Idaho, Washington, Oregon, Nevada, California, and Arizona, to the Mexican border.

18 *Dominguez-Escalante Trail*, extending approximately 2000 miles along the route of the 1776 expedition led by Fathers Francisco Atanasio Dominguez and Silvestre Velez de Escalante; trail originates in Santa Fe, N.M.; proceeds northwest along the San Juan, Dolores, Gunnison, and White Rivers in Colorado; thence moves westward to Utah Lake; thence turns southward to Arizona and returns to Santa Fe.

19 *Florida Trail*, extending north from Everglades National Park, including the Big Cypress Swamp, the Kissimme Prairie, the Withlacoochee State Forest, the Ocala National Forest, the Osceola National Forest, and the Black Water River State Forest; completed trail is to be approximately 1300 miles long of which over 400 miles of trail have already been built.

20 *Indian Nations Trail*, extending from the Red River in Oklahoma approximately 200 miles northward through the former Indian nations to the Oklahoma-Kansas borderline.

21 *Nez Perce Trail*, extending from the vicinity of Wallowa Lake (Oregon) to Bear Paw Mountain (Montana).

22 *Pacific Northwest Trail*, extending approximately 1000 miles from the Continental Divide in Glacier National Park (Montana) to the Pacific Ocean beach of Olympic National Park (Washington), by way of:

    A The Flathead and Kootenai National Forests in Montana;

    B The Kaniksu National Forest in Idaho; and

    C The Colville and Okanogan National Forests, the Pasayten Wilderness Area, the Ross Lake National Recreation Area, North Cascades National Park, Mount Baker, the Skagit River, Deception Pass, Whidbey Island, the Olympic National Forest, and Olympic National Park—all in Washington.

Public Law 95-625 (passed November 10, 1978) added a 23rd trail to the study list:

23 *Overmountain Victory Trail*, extending from the vicinity of Elizabethton, Tenn., to Kings Mountain National Military Park (South Carolina).

Connecting or Side Trails   Section 6 of P.L. 90-543 also provides that Connecting or Side Trails within national park, national forest, and other recreation areas administered by the Secretary of the Interior or Secretary of Agriculture be established, designated, and marked as components of a national recreation or national scenic trail. When no federal land acquisition is involved, connecting or side trails may be located across lands administered by interstate, state, or local governmental agencies with their consent as long as such trails provide additional points of public access to national recreation or scenic trails.

National Historic Trails   In addition to adding a 23rd trail to the list of potential national scenic trails P.L. 95-625 made another significant amendment to the National Trails System Act by adding a new category:

> *National historic trails,* which will be extended trails which follow as closely as possible and practicable the original trails or routes of travel of national historical significance. Designation of such trails or routes shall be continuous, but the established or developed trail, and the acquisition thereof, need not be continuous onsite. National historic trails shall have as their purpose the identification and protection of the historic route and its historic remnants and artifacts for public use and enjoyment. Only those selected land and water based components of an historic trail which are on federally owned lands and which meet the national historic trail criteria established in this Act, are established as initial Federal protection components of a national historic trail. The appropriate Secretary may subsequently certify other lands as protected segments of an historic trail upon application from State or local governmental agencies or private interests involved if such segments meet the national historic trail criteria established in this Act and such criteria supplementary thereto as the appropriate Secretary may prescribe, and are administered by such agencies or interests without expense to the United States.

National Trails System Today

Today the National Trails System consists of congressionally designated national scenic trails, which are protected scenic corridors for outdoor recreation, and national historic trails, which recognize prominent past routes of exploration, migration, and military action. The historic trails generally consist of remnant sites and trail segments and thus are not necessarily continuous. Although both types are administered by federal agencies, landownership may be in public or private hands. Of the 17 national scenic and national historic trails so far established, 12 are administered by the National Park Service, four by the Forest Service, and one by the Bureau of Land Management. Figure 14.13 shows the location of the national scenic and historic trails. National Recreation Trails, a third category, are existing trails recognized by the federal government as contributing to the National Trails System. They vary in length, terrain, difficulty, and accessibility. These trails are managed by public and private agencies at the local, state, and national levels and include nature trails, river routes, and historic tours.

Besides administering and coordinating the national trails, the National Park Service conducts a variety of programs to enhance and build a national system of trails available to all. Trail system planning occurs at the metropolitan, state, and regional levels to fulfill the requirement for a National Trail Plan. Through its Rivers, Trails, and Conservation Assistance Program, the National Park Service provides

technical assistance to local and state public agencies and private organizations working on river and trail corridor projects. Some of these involve establishing trails on abandoned railroad rights-of-way. An example of an ongoing 1994 National Park Service–sponsored trail project is the effort to develop a system of bike trails in the Champlain Valley of New York and Vermont.

National Scenic Trails There are currently eight national scenic trails, whose locations are shown in Figure 14.13. For each of these trails addresses (for obtaining further information) and descriptions follow.

Appalachian National Scenic Trail National Park Service; established 1968; 2144 miles.

The Appalachian Trail (the A.T.) was first envisioned in 1921 by Benton MacKaye as a greenway from Maine to Georgia. The trail hugs the crests of the Appalachian Mountains and is open only to hikers. Shelters are spaced for convenient overnight stays. The Appalachian Trail Conference, established in 1925, developed the trail and maintains it today through 32 affiliated volunteer trail clubs. Only 65 miles still need protection through public ownership. Almost 175 people each year hike the entire trail, while millions find inspiration and adventure on shorter trips along the A.T.

Appalachian Trail Conference *P.O. Box 807* *Harpers Ferry, WV 25425* *304-535-6331*	*National Park Service, Appalachian Trail* *Project Office* *c/o Harpers Ferry Center* *Harpers Ferry, WV 25425* *304-535-6278*

Continental Divide National Scenic Trail Forest Service; established 1978; 3200 miles.

The Continental Divide Trail provides spectacular backcountry travel the length of the Rocky Mountains from Mexico to Canada. It is the most rugged of the long-distance trails. The only section officially designated runs for 795 miles from Canada through Montana and Idaho to Yellowstone National Park. It is open to hikers, pack and saddle animals, and in some places, off-road motorized vehicles. Some segments are open for use in other states.

Continental Divide Trail Society *P.O. Box 30002* *Bethesda, MD 20814* *Forest Service, Northern Region* *Federal Building* *P.O. Box 7669* *Missoula, MT 59807* *406-329-3150 (Montana and Idaho)*	*Forest Service, Rocky Mountain Region* *11177 West 8th Avenue* *Box 25127* *Lakewood, CO 80225* *303-236-9501 (Wyoming, Colorado,* *and New Mexico)*

Florida National Scenic Trail Forest Service; established 1983; 1300 miles.

The Florida Trail was conceived and initiated by James A. Kern, who formed the Florida Trail Association in 1964. The trail will eventually extend from Big Cypress National Preserve in South Florida through Florida's three national forests to Gulf Islands National Seashore in the western panhandle. It is especially delightful for winter hiking and camping, passing through the United States' only subtropical land-

scape. Side-loop trails connect to nearby historic sites and other points of interest. More than 1000 miles are completed, and some 300 miles are officially open to public use.

Florida Trail Association
P.O. Box 13708
Gainesville, FL 32604
904-378-8823 or (Florida only)
  800-343-1882

Forest Service, National Forests in Florida
227 North Bronough Street
Suite 4061
Tallahassee, FL 32301
904-681-7293

Ice Age National Scenic Trail   National Park Service; established 1980; 1000 miles.

At the end of the Ice Age, about 10,000 years ago, glaciers retreated from North America and left behind a chain of moraine hills that defined their southern edge. In Wisconsin, this band of hills zigzag across the state for 1000 miles from Lake Michigan to the Saint Croix River. A trail along these hills was conceived by Ray Zillmer in the 1950s and publicized by Rep. Henry Reuss in his book, *On the Trail of the Ice Age.* Today, with help from the State of Wisconsin and the Ice Age Park and Trail Foundation, almost half of the trail is open to public use. Certain sections are popular for marathons, ski races, and ultrarunning.

Ice Age Park and Trail Foundation
P.O. Box 422
Sheboygan, WI 53082

National Park Service
Ice Age National Scenic Trail
700 Rayovac Drive
Suite 100
Madison, WI 53771
608-264-5610

Natchez Trace National Scenic Trail   National Park Service; established 1983; 110 miles.

The Natchez Trace National Scenic Trail lies within the boundaries of the Natchez Trace Parkway, extending for 450 miles from Natchez, Miss., to Nashville, Tenn. The parkway commemorates the historic Natchez Trace, an ancient path that began as a series of animal tracks and Native American trails. It was later used by early explorers, "Kaintuck" boatmen, post riders, and military men, including General Andrew Jackson after his victory at the Battle of New Orleans. In the trail's 1987 comprehensive plan, four segments near Nashville, Jackson, and Natchez totaling 110 miles were selected for development as hiking and horseback trails.

National Park Service
Natchez Trace Parkway
Rural Route 1, NT-143
Tupelo, MS 38801
601-842-1572

Natchez Trace Trail Conference
P.O. Box 6579
Jackson, MS 39282
601-373-1447

North Country National Scenic Trail   National Park Service; established 1980; 3200 miles.

Conceived in the mid-1960s, the North Country National Scenic Trail links New York's Adirondack Mountains with the Missouri River in North Dakota. The trail journeys through a variety of environments: The grandeur of the Adirondacks; Pennsylvania's hardwood forests; the farmlands and canals of Ohio; the Great Lakes shore-

lines of Michigan; the glacier-carved forests, lakes, and streams of northern Wisconsin and Minnesota; and the vast plains of North Dakota. Today almost half of this trail is open for public use. Some of the longer segments cross nine national forests and two national park areas along the route.

North Country Trail Association
P.O. Box 311
White Cloud, MI 49349
616-689-1912

National Park Service
North Country National Scenic Trail
700 Rayovac Drive
Suite 100
Madison WI 53771
608-264-5610

Pacific Crest National Scenic Trail   Forest Service; established 1968; 2638 miles.

Lying along the spectacular shoulders of the Cascade Mountains and the Sierra Nevada from Canada to Mexico, the Pacific Crest is the West Coast counterpart of the Appalachian Trail. Inspired in the 1930s by the idea of a long-distance mountain trail, citizen activists worked with the Forest Service to establish the trail. It passes through 25 national forests and seven national parks. The trail was completed in Oregon and Washington in 1987. Today only 30 miles in California are not protected.

Pacific Crest Trail Conference
P.O. Box 2514
Lynnwood, WA 98036-2514

Forest Service, Pacific Northwest Region
P.O. Box 3623
Portland, OR 97208
503-326-3644

Forest Service, Pacific Southwest Region
630 Sansome Street
San Francisco, CA 94111
415-705-2889

Potomac Heritage National Scenic Trail   National Park Service; established 1983; 700 miles.

The Potomac Heritage Trail recognizes and commemorates the unique mix of history and recreation along the Potomac River. Much is already in place: the 184-mile towpath of the Chesapeake and Ohio Canal in the District of Columbia and Maryland, the 18-mile Mount Vernon Trail in Virginia, and the 75-mile Laurel Highlands Trail in Pennsylvania. In western Maryland, members of the Potomac Heritage Trail Association have recommended a 55-mile hiking path from Cumberland, Md., north to Pennsylvania's Mount Davis and on to the Laurel Highlands.

Potomac Heritage Trail Association
5229 Benson Avenue
Baltimore, MD 21227

National Park Service, National
    Capital Region
Land Use Coordination
1100 Ohio Drive SW
Washington, DC 20242
202-619-7027

National Historic Trails   There are currently 11 national historic trails, whose locations are shown in Figure 14.13. For nine of these trails, descriptions and addresses follow.

Iditarod National Historic Trail   Bureau of Land Management; established 1978; 2450 miles, main route 900.

The Iditarod is a system of historic trails made famous by Alaskan gold prospectors and their dog teams during the late 19th- and early 20th-century gold rush. Most of the trail is usable only during Alaska' 6-month winter, when rivers and tundra are frozen. Each year the renowned 1150-mile Iditarod Sled Dog Race is run along the trail from Anchorage to Nome. Other events include the 210-mile Iditasport race for skiers, mountain bikers, and snowshoers, and the Alaska Gold Rush Classic Snowmachine Race. A network of shelters is being installed by the BLM and the Iditarod Trail Committee.

*Anchorage District, Bureau of
  Land Management
6881 Abbott Loop Road
Anchorage, AK 99507
907-267-1246*

*Iditarod Trail Committee
P.O. Box 870800
Wasilla, AK 99687
907-376-5155*

Juan Bautista de Anza National Historic Trail   National Park Service; established 1990; 1200 miles.

In 1775 a party of Spanish colonists led by Col. Juan Bautista de Anza set out from Mexico to establish an overland route to California. They sought to build *a presidio* and mission overlooking the Golden Gate (the entrance to San Francisco Bay) and secure it from threats by the Russians and British. This party of 30 families, a dozen soldiers, and 1000 cattle, horses, and mules spent 3 months traversing the deserts of the Southwest before reaching the missions of the California coast. Another 3 months were spent traveling up the Pacific coast to the Golden Gate where the city of San Francisco now stands. In 1975 and 1976, an expedition reenactment took place from Horcasitas, Mexico, to San Francisco.

*National Park Service, Western Region
Planning, Grants, and Environmental Quality
600 Harrison Street
Suite 600
San Francisco, CA 94107-1372
415-744-3975*

Lewis and Clark National Historic Trail   National Park Service; established 1978; 3700 miles.

In 1804, President Thomas Jefferson commissioned Meriwether Lewis and William Clark to explore the newly acquired Louisiana Territory and the "Oregon Country." Setting out in boats from what is today Wood River (Illinois), and following the Missouri River upstream, their expedition eventually reached the Pacific Ocean at the mouth of the Columbia River in 1805 and returned east the next year. In Idaho and western Montana, the route follows roads and trails as it crosses the Rocky Mountain passes. Along the route, state, local, and private interests have established motor routes, roadside interpretive markers, and museums exhibits telling the Lewis and Clark story.

Lewis and Clark Trail Heritage Foundation
P.O. Box 3434
Great Falls, MT 59403

National Park Service
Lewis and Clark National Historic Trail
700 Rayovac Drive
Suite 100
Madison, WI 53711
608-264-5610

Mormon Pioneer National Historic Trail   National Park Service; established 1978; 1300 miles.

Mormon emigration was one of the principal forces of settlement of the West. Departing from Nauvoo, Ill., in February 1846, thousands of Mormons crossed into Iowa seeking refuge from religious persecution. They spent the next winter in the Council Bluffs, Iowa, and Omaha, Neb., area. Early in 1847, Brigham Young led an advance party west along the Platte River, paralleling the Oregon Trail, to Fort Bridger, Wyo., where they turned southwest and eventually came to the Great Salt Lake. The 1624-mile auto tour route in five states is generally marked with the trail logo and closely follows the trail's historic route.

National Park Service, Rocky Mountain Region
Planning and Compliance Division
12795 West Alameda Parkway
Lakewood, CO 80225
303-969-2830

Nez Perce (Nee-Me-Poo) National Historic Trail   Forest Service; established 1986; 1170 miles.

This trail route honors the heroic and poignant attempt by the Nez Perce Indians to escape capture by the U.S. Army. In 1877 the Nez Perce were forced to leave their ancestral homelands in southeastern Washington and northeastern Oregon and move to a reservation east of Lewiston, Idaho. During this journey, hostilities broke out between white settlers and some groups of the Nez Perce. The U.S. Army was called in. The resisting bands headed east and crossed the Rocky Mountains, hoping to find refuge in Canada. Led by several commanders, including Chief Joseph, they eluded capture for months, traveling through the newly established Yellowstone National Park and out onto the Great Plains. Just short of reaching the Canadian border in Montana, most of the party were overtaken near the Bearpaw Mountains.

Forest Service, Northern Region
Federal Building
P.O. Box 7669
Missoula, MT 59807
406-329-3582

Oregon National Historic Trail   National Park Service; established 1978; 2170 miles.

As the harbinger of America's westward expansion, the Oregon Trail was the pathway to the Pacific for fur traders, gold seekers, missionaries, and emigrants. Beginning in 1841 and enduring for more than 20 years, an estimated 300,000 emi-

grants followed this route from the Midwest to Oregon on a trip that took 5 months to complete. Today the trail corridor contains some 300 miles of discernible wagon ruts and 125 historic sites. The approximate route can still be followed by automobile, and opportunities are available to travel by foot, horse, or mountain bike in many places.

Oregon-California Trails Association
P.O. Box 1019
Independence, MO 64051-0519
816-252-2276

National Park Service, Pacific
Northwest Region
Oregon National Historic Trail
83 South King Street
Suite 212
Seattle, WA 98104
206-553-5366

Overmountain Victory National Historic Trail   National Park Service; established 1980; 300 miles.

In the fall of 1780, upcountry patriots from Virginia, Tennessee, and North Carolina formed a militia to drive the British from the southern colonies. This trail marks their 14-day trek across the Appalachians to the Piedmont region of the Carolinas. There they defeated British troops at the Battle of Kings Mountain, setting in motion events that led to the British surrender at Yorktown and the end of the Revolutionary War. Each year history buffs commemorate this patriotic event. Much of the trail has become road and highway; only a small 20-mile portion remains as a foot trail across the mountains. In most places roadside signs indicate proximity to the trail. A guide to the seven walking sections of the trail is available.

Overmountain Victory Trail Association
c/o Sycamore Shoals State Historic Area
11651 West Elk Avenue
Elizabethton, TN 37643
615-543-5808

National Park Service
Southeast Region Planning and
Compliance Division
75 Spring Street SW
Atlanta, GA 30303
404-331-5465

Santa Fe National Historic Trail   National Park Service; established 1987; 1203 miles.

After Mexican independence in 1821, U.S. and Mexican traders developed the Santa Fe Trail, using American Indian travel and trade routes. It quickly became a commercial and cultural link between the two countries. It also became a road of conquest during the Mexican and Civil wars. With the building of the railroad to Santa Fe in 1880, the trail was largely abandoned. Of the 1203 miles of trail route between Old Franklin, Mo., and Santa Fe., N.M., more than 200 miles of ruts and trace remain visible; some 30 miles of these are protected on federal lands.

Santa Fe Trail Association
Santa Fe Trail Center
Route 3
Larned, KS 67550
316-285-2054

National Park Service, Southwest Region
Branch of Long Distance Trails
P.O. Box 728
Santa Fe, NM 87504-0728
505-988-6888

Trail of Tears National Historic Trail   National Park Service; established 1987; 2052 miles.

After many years of pressure from white settlers, 16,000 Cherokee Indians from the southeastern states were moved by the U.S. Army in the 1830s to lands west of the Mississippi River. Various detachments followed different routes west to the Oklahoma Territory. Thousands died along the way. Today, the designated trail follows two of the principal routes: (1) a water trail (1226 miles) along the Tennessee, Ohio, Mississippi, and Arkansas rivers, and (2) and overland route (826 miles) from Chattanooga, Tennessee, to Tahlequah, Oklahoma.

> *National Park Service, Southwest Region*
> *Branch of Long Distance Trails*
> *P.O. Box 728*
> *Santa Fe, NM 87504-0728*
> *505-988-6888*

Detailed information was not available for two national historic trails—the California and the Pony Express. Both trails are shown on Figure 14.13.

National Recreation Trails   National Recreation Trails today include a wide variety of trail types, uses, lengths, topography, history, and physical challenge. While national scenic and national historic trails can only be designated by Congress, national recreation trails are designated by the Secretaries of Agriculture and the Interior. Such designation carries with it the prestige and recognition of being considered a component of the National Trails System. This may result in favorable publicity, community benefits, increased public opportunity for prime outdoor recreation, and even added protection for the trail corridor. The process for designating a national recreation trail begins with the submission of an application form by the agency, group, or company with jurisdiction over the trail. For trails within the national forests, application is made to the district office. For all other trails, submission is made to the relevant National Park Service regional office. The application must follow the format and criteria found in the National Park Service called *National Recreation Trails: Information and Application Procedures for Designation*. The application is processed within the National Park Service, with recommendations then made to the Secretary of the Interior.

There are currently 801 national scenic trails that cover 9372.4 miles. Figure 14.14 identifies the number of national recreation trails in each state. All 50 states and Puerto Rico have at least one trail designated as a national recreation trail. This varies from one trail in Puerto Rico, Rhode Island, and Maryland to 77 trails in California. In terms of mileage, New York is the leader with 751.1 miles on 18 trails. But 365 miles of New York's total are on the Seaway National Recreation Trail and another 94 miles are on the Seaway Extension. This is the longest national recreation trail. Other leading states in terms of mileage are California (674.3 miles), Oregon (630.9 miles), Kentucky (604.3 miles), Idaho (518.7 miles), Montana (512.3 miles), Arkansas (389.9 miles), Arizona (379.5 miles), Pennsylvania (364.6 miles), and Washington

(332.4 miles). The average trail is 11.7 miles long, but length ranges from the 0.1-mile Buckeye National Recreation Trail (Army Corps of Engineers; Arkansas) and the 0.1-mile Discovery National Recreation Trail (Apalachicola National Forest; Florida) to the 365-mile Seaway National Recreation Trail (Seaway Trail, Inc.; New York). Only seven national recreation trails are over 100 miles long: the Seaway, the Sheltowee Trace (Kentucky, 337 miles), the Jenny Wiley (Kentucky, 213 miles), the Ouachita (Arkansas, 175 miles), the Oregon High Desert (Oregon, 150 miles), the Ozark Highlands (Arkansas, 140 miles), and the Okefenokee Wilderness Canoe (Georgia, 102 miles). A considerable number of trails are under $\frac{1}{2}$ mile. Figure 14.15 illustrates the 0.3-mile Desert Ecology National Recreation Trail at Saguaro National Monument, and Figure 14.16 shows the 7.3-mile Wilkinson National Recreation Trail at Saratoga National Historical Park.

Appendix XXIV summarizes the main characteristics of the 801 national recreation trails. The following information is supplied for each trail: state, administering agency, date created, trail number (for administrative purposes), season open, uses permitted, surface type, and length. A large number of these trails and their recreational uses have been discussed throughout this book, since many of the them are located in units of the National Park System, the National Forest System, the National Wildlife Refuge System, on Bureau of Land Management lands, and on Army Corps of Engineers projects. Different trails have been established for the following categories of use: foot, bicycle, snowmobile, handicapped, water, horse, ski, interpretive, underground, and motorized. Some trails are restricted to trail use only, while others permit a combination of uses. The locations of the trails vary from the hearts of cities (for example, the San Antonio River National Recreation Trail, San Antonio, Tex.), where only foot and bicycle use is permitted, to rural areas (such as the Headquarters National Recreation Trail, Medicine Bow National Forest, Wyo.), where the permitted uses are foot, horse, motorized, snowmobile, and ski. The reader is urged to carefully

Figure 14.15 The 0.3-mile, handicap-accessible Desert Ecology National Recreation Trail at Saguaro National Monument (Arizona)

Figure 14.16 The 7.3-mile Wilkinson National Recreation Trail at Saratoga National Historical Park (New York)

study Appendix XXIV to gain a better comprehension of the scope of the national recreation trails.

NATIONAL SEASHORES AND LAKESHORES

A fourth type of natural resource that has recreational value and has been protected for their amenity value is found along the Atlantic coast, the Gulf coast, and the Pacific coast and the shorelines of the Great Lakes. National Seashores and National Lakeshores preserve shorelines and offshore islands while at the same time providing water-oriented recreation. National seashores and national lakeshores are different from the other three types of amenity resources discussed previously in this chapter— wilderness, rivers, and trails—in that they are exclusively units of the National Park System. (National seashores and national lakeshores and their recreational use were highlighted in Chapter 6; however, because they represent significant protection of amenity resource values, a short discussion on them is included in this final chapter focusing on amenity natural resource protection.) There are currently 10 national seashores and four national lakeshores that are protected from development and thus preserved for open-space, beach-oriented recreation. These 14 units are listed in Table 14.7 and shown in Figure 14.17.

The purpose of national seashores is to preserve the natural values of shoreline areas and offshore islands, while at the same time providing water-oriented recreation. In 1934 the National Park Service surveyed the Atlantic and Gulf coasts and

Table 14.7   National Seashores and Lakeshores

	State	Size (Acres)
National Seashores		
Padre Island National Seashore	TX	130,355.50
Gulf Islands National Seashore	FL, MS	98,125.80
Point Reyes National Seashore	CA	64,505.10
Canaveral National Seashore	FL	57,626.70
Cape Hatteras National Seashore	NC	30,318.90
Cape Cod National Seashore	MA	27,386.40
Cape Lookout National Seashore	NC	25,173.60
Cumberland Island National Seashore	GA	18,698.10
Assateague Island National Seashore	MD, VA	17,774.90
Fire Island National Seashore	NY	6,220.60
Total		476,185.60
National Lakeshores		
Sleeping Bear Dunes National Lakeshore	MI	56,868.5
Apostle Islands National Lakeshore	WI	42,124.2
Pictured Rocks National Lakeshore	MI	35,791.4
Indiana Dunes National Lakeshore	IN	9,705.4
Total		144,489.5

Source: National Park Service. *The National Parks: Index 1991.* Washington, D.C.: U.S. Government Printing Office, 1991.

identified 12 significant areas deserving federal protection. Among them was Cape Hatteras (North Carolina), which Congress authorized as the first National Seashore in 1937. Land acquisition lagged until after World War II; the Mellon family foundations then made substantial grants to help North Carolina purchase and donate the needed lands. The seashore encompasses almost 100 miles of barrier islands and beaches and provides an outstanding natural resource base for swimming, surfing, sunbathing, sportfishing, nature study, and other recreational activities.

The further development of national seashores did not take place until a revival of the concept in 1961, when Congress authorized part of Cape Cod Massachusetts; it was 1966 before the land was acquired and the seashore was established. Cape Cod was the first large natural or recreational area for which Congress at the outset permitted the use of appropriated funds for land acquisition. The legislation that established Cape Cod National Seashore prohibited the Secretary of the Interior from using eminent-domain condemnation proceedings for private improved properties, once the local jurisdictions had approved zoning ordinances. Private development was closing out many Americans from ocean access. The Outdoor Recreation Resources Review Commission recognized this and recommended that additional national seashores and national lakeshores be added to the National Park System. In the 1960s Congress authorized the following national seashores: Point Reyes (California; authorized 1962, established 1972), Padre Island (Texas; authorized 1962, established 1968), Fire Island (New York; 1964), Assateague (Maryland and Virginia; 1965), and Cape Lookout (N. Carolina; 1966). In the 1970s the last three national seashores were established: Gulf Islands (Florida and Mississippi; 1971), Cumberland Island (Georgia; 1972), and Canaveral (Florida; 1975). Point Reyes is the only national seashore on the Pacific coast.

All the national seashores are on barrier islands except for Point Reyes, which is on a peninsula. Some of them (for example, the Mississippi portion of Gulf Islands and Cumberland Island) have no road access. Even those with road access have long stretches of beach that are distant from the nearest road. Units of the National Wilderness Preservation System are located on three of the seashores: Gulf Islands (1800 acres), Cumberland Island (8840 acres), and Fire Island (1363 acres).

The same concern about the loss of public access to the oceanfront that resulted in the revival of the national seashore concept in the 1960s also existed with the loss of public access to the Great Lakes' shoreline. As a result, the four national lakeshores were authorized in 1966 and 1970 generally followed the seashore pattern. Our first national lakeshore was Pictured Rocks (Michigan, 1966). Multicolored sandstone cliffs, broad beaches, dunes, waterfalls, inland lakes, ponds, and marshes, and hardwood and coniferous forests with a multitude of wildlife comprise this scenic area on the Upper Peninsula of Michigan on Lake Superior. Two months later in the same year (1966), Indiana Dunes became a national lakeshore. On the southern shore of Lake Michigan between Gary and Michigan City, Ind., it had been proposed as a national park as early as 1917. Here dunes rise as much as 180 feet above Lake Michigan's southern shore, with beaches, bogs, marshes, swamps, prairie remnants, and historic sites. It is the most urban of the national lakeshores. In 1970, Apostle Islands (Wisconsin) became the third national lakeshore. Here, 21 picturesque islands and an 11-mile strip of adjacent Bayfield Peninsula along the southern shore of Lake Superior comprise this lakeshore. Five days later our fourth, and most recent, national lakeshore was established on 34 miles of shoreline and islands at Sleeping Bear Dunes (Michigan).

References

Bureau of Land Management. Wilderness Database (computer file). December 21, 1993.

Bureau of Outdoor Recreation. "America's Trail." *Outdoor Recreation Action*, No. 42, Winter 1976.

Cordell, H. Ken, John C. Bergstrom, Lawrence A. Hartman, and Donald B. K. English. *An Analysis of the Outdoor Recreation and Wilderness Situation in the United States 1989–2040, A Technical Document Supporting the 1989 USDA Forest Service RPA Assessment.* General Technical Report RM-189. Fort Collins, Colo.: Rocky Mountain Forest and Range Experiment Station, Forest Service, USDA, 1990.

Frome, Michael. *Battle for the Wilderness.* New York: Praeger Publishers, 1974.

Hendee, John C., George H. Stankey, and Robert C. Lucas. *Wilderness Management.* Golden, Colo.: North American Press, 1990.

Marshall, Robert. "The Problem of the Wilderness." *Scientific Monthly.* February 1930, pp. 141–149.

National Geographic Society. *America's Wild and Scenic Rivers.* Washington, D.C.: National Geographic Society, 1983.

National Geographic Society. *Trails West.* Washington, D.C.: National Geographic Society, 1979.

National Park Service. *National Trails System.* Map and Guide.

National Park Service. Division of Park Planning and Protection. *River Mileage Classifications for Components of the National Wild and Scenic Rivers System.* November 1992.

National Park Service. Division of Park Planning and Protection. *The Wild and Scenic Rivers Act through December 31, 1992* (102nd Congress).

National Park Service. *Register of National Recreation Trails.* January 1993.

National Trails System Act. Statutes at Large. Vol. 82 (1968).

Palmer, Tim. *The Wild and Scenic Rivers of America.* Washington, D.C.: Island Press, 1993.

Roth, Dennis M. *The Wilderness Movement and the National Forests.* College Station, Tex.: Intaglio Press, 1988.

Wilderness Act. Statutes at Large. Vol. 768 (1964).

Epilogue

Anyone who has conducted research that deals with the U.S. public lands becomes aware of the dynamic nature of these public lands. The National Park System is continually expanding, and existing units are continually being reclassified. New inholdings within existing national forest boundaries are acquired and added to the National Forest System. New refuges are continually being added to the National Wildlife Refuge System. Transfers of land under the administration of the Bureau of Land Management (BLM) are continuously occurring. The National Wilderness Preservation System, Wild and Scenic Rivers System, and National Trails System are continuing to expand. It has been a major task for me to keep abreast of all of these changes. I have done my best to provide the most recent information available as of January 1994. I revised it in May 1994 in order to incorporate new information that became available. The material contained throughout the text, therefore, is the most recent data available as of May 1994. Another 10 months has passed since May 1994, and some additional major changes have occurred in the public lands. This last and final brief chapter provides additional information that will update and supplement the text that is current as of February 1, 1995.

Two major events occurred in October and November 1994 that will have a major impact on the use of public lands. During a rare Saturday session on October 8, as the Senate raced to wind up the 103rd Congress, the Senate agreed by a voice vote of 68 to 23 to approve the California Desert Protection Act of 1994. This bill was sent to the White House, and on October 31, 1994 Public Law 103-433 was signed by President Bill Clinton. The California Desert Protection Act of 1994 is the only major environmental protection bill to pass the 103rd Congress and, with the exception of the 1964 Wilderness Act, the largest land protection act ever passed by Congress for the lower 49 states. The second major event was the outcome of the elections of November 8, 1994: the Repubicans scored stunning victories and, for the first time in 40 years, gained control of both the House of Representatives and the Senate on January 4, 1995. While the people voted primarily on crime, the economy, and discontent with the existing political structure, environmentalists are predicting trouble ahead for important environmental laws now under consideration for reauthorization, such as the Endangered Species Act and the Clean Water Act. With the Republicans gaining control of both houses of Congress, they have promised a revolution to get government off the backs of the people by cutting taxes, spending, and unnecessary laws and regulations. The new Senate Majority Leader, Bob Dole of Kansas, has stated: "We will roll back federal programs, laws and regulations from A to Z—from Amtrak to zoological studies—working our way through the alphabet soup." As the federal government is downsized, I project that the protection of natural re-

sources for their amenity values on the public lands will suffer many setbacks. It is highly unlikely that the 104th Congress will enact strong forest protection laws or reform legislation.

The California Desert Protection Act of 1994 will drastically change the recreational use patterns on public land in California. The act upgraded Death Valley National Monument to a national park, transferring 1.3 million acres of BLM lands to the existing 2,067,627-acre Death Valley National Monument, for a new size of 3,367,627 acres. The act also upgraded Joshua Tree National Monument to national park status, transferring 234,000 acres of BLM lands to the existing 559,995-acre Joshua Tree National Monument; this made the new national park 793,995 acres in size. A totally new National Park System unit, Mohave National Preserve, comprising 1,419,800 acres, was created within the former BLM East Mohave Scenic Area. The act also designates 69 BLM/Forest Service wilderness areas totaling 3,667,020 acres. The majority of the acreage (3,571,520 acres) is on BLM land; 95,500 acres is Forest Service wilderness in the Inyo, Sequoia, and San Bernardino National Forests. The act released approximately 900,000 acres of BLM lands from further wilderness study and established 8 new BLM wilderness study areas totaling 326,430 acres. The act further designated nearly 4 million acres of wilderness in the three new National Park Service units: 3,162,000 acres in Death Valley National Park; an additional 132,000 acres added to the already existing 429,690 acres in Joshua Tree National Park; and 695,000 acres in the Mohave National Preserve. The act also designated new units in the National Wilderness Preservation System in two Fish and Wildlife Service areas—the Imperial National Wildlife Refuge (5,836 acres of wilderness) and the Havasu National Wildlife Refuge (3,195 acres of wilderness). Federal wilderness in California has expanded from 6,306,000 acres before the act to 13,971,548 acres after October 31, 1994. Special designations of the act created a 2,040-acre Desert Lily Sanctuary and a 590-acre Dinosaur Trackway Area of Critical Environmental Concern on BLM land. The act also transferred 20,500 acres from the BLM to the State of California's Red Rock Canyon Park and withdrew 6,000 acres in the BLM Bodie Bowl adjacent to the Bodie State Historic Park from mining and mineral leasing. Finally, the act clarifies Department of Defense withdrawals for Chocolate Mountains, China Lake, and other military lands. Prior to the passage of the act, off-road motor vehicle use was a major recreational activity of these 7,665,051 acres of new wilderness. Motorized access will be prohibited in these new wilderness areas. These additions bring the size of the National Wilderness Preservation System to approximately 103,721,164 acres as of February 1, 1995.

In addition to the new Death Valley National Park, the new Joshua Tree National Park, and the new Mohave National Preserve established by the California Desert Protection Act of 1994, other changes have occurred in the National Park System since the data for this book were gathered. The most recent edition of the *National Park Index* (1993) indicates that the National Park System consists of 367 units on 80,663,217.42 acres—an increase of 10 units and 507,233.24 acres since the previous *National Parks Index* (1991) was published. Dry Tortugas National Park, Florida, became the 51st national park on October 26, 1992. This park subsumed Fort Jefferson National Monument. On October 14, 1994, Saguaro National Monument was upgraded to national park status and expanded by 3,500 acres. Most of the other areas added to the National Park System, which are not included in the statistical data in

the text, tables, and appendices of this book, are historic in nature: Manzamar National Historic Site, California; Mary McLeod Bethune Council House National Historic Site, District of Columbia; Brown versus Board of Education National Historic Site, Kansas; Keweenaw National Historical Park, Michigan; Dayton Aviation National Historical Park, Michigan; Marsh-Billings National Historical Park, Vermont; Salt River Bay National Historical Park and Ecological Reserve, St. Croix, U.S. Virgin Islands; Ebey's Landing National Historical Reserve, Washington; and New Orleans Jazz National Historical Park, Louisiana. Three new natural areas added are Little River Canyon National Preserve, Alabama; Niobrara National Scenic Riverway, Nebraska; and Great Egg Harbor Scenic and Recreational River, New Jersey. Among the most recent additions to the National Park System are Cane River National Historic Site and the Presidio, California. Two areas recently have been deleted from the National Park System: the John F. Kennedy Center for the Performing Arts, District of Columbia, and Zuni-Cibola National Historical Park, New Mexico.

Administratively, the National Park Service will undergo a system-wide shakeup. In response to the Clinton administration's efforts to streamline the federal government, the National Park Service released during the summer of 1994 a broad plan to restructure its organization. This reorganization plan was approved in September 1994 by Interior Secretary Bruce Babbitt. It reduces the number of employees in administrative offices and transfers more authority and responsibility to park-level employees. The 367 national park units would be grouped into 16 clusters (10–35 units each) based on cultural and ecological associations. Each park cluster would be assisted by a systems support office. Seven field directors would replace the 10 currently in place, with each managing up to 3 clusters.

On August 11, 1994, the 500th refuge was added to the National Wildlife Refuge System in West Virginia's Canaan Valley and is 85.78 acres in size. Eventually, the Canaan Valley National Wildlife Refuge will include 20,000 acres and will be the first refuge entirely within West Virginia. Three new refuges were added to the system by September 30, 1994; Number 501, Cossatot National Wildlife Refuge (506.11 acres), Arkansas; Number 502, Patoka River National Wildlife Refuge (9.10 acres), Indiana; and Number 503, Rocky Mountain Arsenal National Wildlife Refuge (17,000 acres), Colorado. The Fish and Wildlife Service only has secondary jurisdiction over the Rocky Mountain Arsenal National Wildlife Refuge and will not receive primary jurisdiction until the contamination clean-up is completed. Other new refuges that have been added to the system during FY 1993 and FY 1994 and that are not included in Chapter 12 of this book are; Number 486, Lake Umbagog, New Hampshire; Number 487, Tualatin River, Oregon; Number 488, Kealia Pond, Hawaii; Number 489, Handy Break, Louisiana; Number 490, Bill Williams, Arizona (*note:* this acreage was split out from existing Havasu National Wildlife Refuge to form the new refuge); Number 491, Leslie Canyon, Arizona (*note:* this acreage was split out from existing San Bernardino National Wildlife Refuge to form the new refuge); Number 492, Crane Meadows, Minnesota; Number 493, Bald Knob, Arkansas; Number 494, Deep Fork, Oklahoma; Number 495, Guam, Guam; Number 496, Emiquon, Illinois; Number 497, Cokeville, Wyoming; Number 498, Trinity River, Texas; and Number 499, Lake Wales Ridge, Florida. The total acreage of the National Wildlife Refuge System was 91,775,636.05 acres as of September 30, 1994, which comprised the bulk of the grand total of 91,799,355.62 acres under control of the Fish and Wildlife Service.

The most recent data (1993) for the National Forest System shows an increase of 100,010 acres of National Forest System lands—from 191,453,345 acres to 191,553,355 acres. There was a smaller 51,090-acre increase from 1992 until 1993 in the gross acreage total—from 231,501,923 acres to 231,553,013 acres.

Changes also have occurred in other federal systems, which are protected for their amenity resource value. The addition of 7,665,051 acres to the National Wilderness Preservation System brought about by the California Desert Protection Act of 1994 has been covered earlier in this epilogue. The Wild and Scenic Rivers System has been expanded to 10,750 miles. Additions to the Wild and Scenic Rivers System that were not included in Chapter 14 and Appendix XXIII are the Red River, Kentucky (19.4 miles); Maurice River, New Jersey (35.4 miles); Westfield River, Massachusetts (43.3 miles); another section of the Rio Grande River, New Mexico (12 miles); West Branch of the Farmington River, Connecticut (14 miles); and Big Darby and Little Darby Creeks, Ohio (85.9 miles). There are two new national historic trails in the National Trails System that are not discussed in Chapter 14. The Pony Express National Historic Trail extends for 1800 miles from St. Joseph, Missouri, to Sacramento, California. The California National Historic Trail consists of 5600 miles of overland routes that start at five points along the Missouri River and end at many locations in California and Oregon. Eleven trails classified as "national recreation trails" totaling 715.1 miles have been added to the National Trails System. They are Nassau-Suffolk County Greenbelt, New York (22.0 miles); Paintsville Lake Kiwanis, Kentucky (1.25 miles); George O. Lapham Jr., Kansas (4.3 miles); Beach-to-Bay Indian Trail, Maryland (100.0 miles); Philadelphia to Valley Forge Bikeway, Pennsylvania (11.0 miles); Devil's Orchard, Idaho (0.5 miles); Nancy Dillard Lyon, Texas (1.8 miles); Walker Creek, Ohio (13.0 miles); US Route 6-Grand Army of the Republic Highway, Pennsylvania (410 miles); Old Growth Ridge Trail, Oregon (1.25 miles); and Cascadia Marine Trail, Washington (150 miles). A coast-to-coast "National Discovery Trail," which would run from Point Reyes, California, to Cape Henelopen, Delaware, is in the planning stage. Fourteen national recreation trails totaling 178.7 miles have been deleted from the National Trails System. All of these deleted trails, except one, are on national forest lands. The deleted Stiner's Woods National Recreation Trail, Tennessee (1.2 miles), was administered by the Tennessee Valley Authority. Eight of the deleted trails are on national forest land in Oregon: Badger Creek (11.0 miles), Billie Creek Nature (1.0 miles), Buck Canyon (13.5 miles), Cherry Creek (5.0 miles), Nee-Me-Poo (3.7 miles), North Fork John Day River (26.2 miles), Twin Pillars (8.5 miles), and Winom Creek-Big Creek (5.6 miles). The other national recreation trails in the national forest that have been deleted are Bartram, Alabama (1.0 miles); Ocala, Florida (68.0 miles); Bartram, Georgia (22.0 miles); Agonikak Snowmobile, Michigan (11.0); and Pine Mountain, Virginia (1.0 miles).

Such is the nature of the public lands and their recreational resources. The geographic extent of these national parks, forests, and other public lands and their amenity resource values will continue to change every year, because these lands and their protection for amenity resource values are far from static. Congress will be the resource manager that will determine the outcome of these changes.

Recommendations of the President's Commission on Americans Outdoors 1987

- That community by community, across America, we form coalitions for action. We must organize to invest in recreational opportunities for the future and to protect our outdoors heritage.
- That mayors and other local officials lead your communities by building a plan of action. Define a vision for the future, list your recreational assets, and identify your tools. Then decide what needs to be done, and go to work.
- That governors create Governor's Councils to promote outdoor recreation. Find out what people in your state will want to do in the outdoors 20 years in the future, or 50. Explore what needs to be done, to make sure they will have appropriate places to do those things. Draw a blueprint for action to meet tomorrow's needs.
- That the President launch a nationwide celebration of Americans Outdoors, a program that looks forward for Americans Outdoors of the future.
- That each geographic community and community of interest develop an outdoor ethic and work toward reflecting that ethic in personal and organizational actions.
- That educators make the environment an integral part of each child's basic education.
- That the president recognize the importance of an outdoor ethic to the health of the country in the annual State of the Union message.
- That as part of the prairie fire (the term used for an action program), local coalitions encourage school boards to provide education programs about our natural environment in schools. Curricula should reflect the 4 R's—Reading, 'Riting, 'Rithmetic, and Resources.
- That local, state, and federal recreational and natural resource agencies engage in educational activities through teaching in school classrooms, providing incentives to bring school children to the resource, and offering educational activities for visitors to their areas.

- That physical education programs include outdoor activity skills and proper use of the natural resource to ensure its protection.
- That mayors, county officials, governors, and state legislatures establish outdoor corps programs to encourage youth and citizens of all ages to dedicate a period of their lives to the stewardship of natural resources.
- That conservation and volunteer organizations provide technical and financial assistance to support local, state, and nonprofit outdoor corps.
- That local officials, mayors, governors, and private-sector managers support volunteering, develop incentives, and remove barriers to encourage Americans to volunteer in outdoor recreation. The goal is to double volunteer efforts in conservation and recreation by the year 2000.
- That current laws and regulations be reviewed to enhance mechanisms for using volunteers in national parks, national forests, and all federal agencies.
- That public recreation providers develop visitor service plans that integrate all visitor services, including information, activity programs, and health and safety, and that incorporate feedback from visitors to ensure quality.
- That public recreation services be improved through development of partnerships.
- That state recreation information clearinghouses be created to provide the public with information on recreational opportunities.
- That planning and design of recreation areas and programs be sensitive to the needs of special populations, and that action be taken to provide information, access, and other services.
- That a Recreation Quality Index be established and published annually to provide continuing information on the quality of recreational and natural resources for the American public.
- That strong local, state, and federal environmental quality laws, regulations, and policies be strictly enforced. Recreation should be explicitly recognized as a beneficiary of clear air, clean water, pleasing landscapes, and abundant and diverse wildlife.
- That citizens, businesses, and urban officials recognize the value of recreation in meeting community goals for livability, economic development, and healthy citizens. All Americans should have access to the outdoors close to home.
- That local governments place particular emphasis on meeting the needs of less mobile people, who are often concentrated in urban areas, including those with physical and mental disabilities, the elderly, minorities, new immigrants, and others who cannot easily leave their neighborhoods.
- That communities devote more time, money, and expertise to developing strong partnerships with neighborhood, corporate, and nonprofit groups to improve recreational resources in cities and to plan for future recreational needs. We must encourage Americans to discover and support their parks.
- That communities establish greenways, corridors of private and public recreation lands and waters, to provide people with access to open spaces close to where they live, and to link together the rural and urban spaces in the American landscape.
- That a "2000 by 2000" program be established in which, through local initiative, and with state and federal support where appropriate, 2000 river and stream seg-

ments are protected by the year 2000. Cities and towns should clean up and revitalize their stream corridors and states should set up or enhance river protection programs to complement local action.

- That the federal government consider ending subsidies for new development within floodplains, following the model of the Coastal Barriers Resources Act.
- That cooperative efforts among private, local, state, and federal interests increase in order to protect and enhance wetlands.
- That local coalitions, private organizations, and states, as part of the prairie fire, conduct public awareness efforts to educate Americans about the many values of wetlands.
- That states conduct or update inventories of relatively undeveloped shoreline areas and developed sites where public access is allowed.
- That local and state governments create a network of scenic byways, composed of scenic roadways and thoroughfares throughout the nation, and take action to protect these resources.
- That Congress establish an incentive program of matching grants to local and state governments to encourage scenic byway designations.
- That information concerning scenic byways be made available through partnerships between the private sector and all levels of government.
- That an annual report, "State of the Federal Estate: Resources and Recreation," be developed from reports prepared by the seven principal federal land-managing agencies and be submitted to the president and to Congress.
- That federal agencies and Congress place greater emphasis on long-term conservation of natural, cultural, and historic resources and the quality of recreational opportunities and experiences. The federal multiple-use agencies should assure that recreation has equal priority with other uses in budgets, staffing, and planning.
- That federal land management agencies embrace opportunities for partnerships with other government agencies and with for-profit businesses and not-for-profit organizations.
- That federal land management agencies encourage and stimulate innovation and experimentation.
- That congressionally authorized land acquisitions be expedited, making full use of alternative land protection techniques, and that exchange procedures be streamlined.
- That existing laws and regulations be reviewed to monitor visitor needs and satisfaction, improve public participation in the planning process, effectively utilize volunteers, facilitate acceptance of donations of real property and easements, collect recreation fees, and stimulate regional ecosystem planning.
- That federal land management be reviewed periodically.
- That partnerships be formed among private for-profit and nonprofit entities and public agencies to enhance recreational resources, services, and facilities.
- That public policy and planning actions consider, where appropriate, private recreational investments at public places.
- That communities study the development of desirable support services in areas adjacent to public recreational resources, balancing conservation and economic needs.

- That private developers, in cooperation with public agencies, plan for and include recreational space and outdoor amenities in capital projects, with particular attention to connecting their projects to recreation areas though greenways.
- That private landowners recognize the opportunity to provide expanded recreational resources and services to the public.
- That local, state, and federal governments consider incentives to private landowners to increase public access, and review existing statutes, policies, regulations, and practices to assure that impediments to providing public recreation on private lands are removed.
- That recreational organizations actively encourage respect for private property rights and assist in managing use of private lands.
- That recreation providers (both public and private entities) improve risk management practices through better training and sharing of information.
- That federal and state governments enact or improve recreational use statutes to provide greater protection to governmental entities and private providers who allow the public to use their land for recreation.
- That communities target key parts of their local heritage, including open space and natural, cultural, scenic, and wildlife resources, and build prairie fires of action to encourage that growth occur in appropriate areas and away from sensitive resources.
- That all governments and the private sector make imaginative use of a wide range of growth-shaping tools to identify and protect prime assets in growth planning processes, which also define areas most appropriate for more intensive development.
- That states help lead the way by establishing registries of outdoor resources with statewide significance, such as rivers, wildlife areas, historic sites, unique ecological areas, coastal lands, and scenic countrysides; and that states assist localities to develop and implement growth-shaping plans and policies.
- That the federal government coordinate its public investment decisions with state recreation priorities and local growth plans to avoid conflicts and encourage private-public partnerships in protecting key areas.
- That local, state, and federal officials plan and budget for systematic renovation and replacement of existing recreational facilities.
- That older facilities, where practical, be redesigned and adapted to allow access by people with physical disabilities.
- That local, state, and federal governments include recreational facilities in any overall considerations of their public works improvement needs.
- That people and private organizations who benefit from public recreational facilities be encouraged to volunteer their labor and dollars to help maintain and repair them.
- That a national recreational resource futures workshop be convened to assess professional outdoor recreation education and training needs.
- That partnerships be formed between the private sector and local, state, and federal agencies to ensure that college curricular requirements match professional skills needed in the field and are reflected in current accreditation evaluations.

- That states and the federal government compile and publish annual reports on the "State of the Outdoors" that describe the condition of our natural resources for recreation.
- That private-sector, governmental, and academic interests work jointly to establish a National Recreation Accounts network to facilitate collection, analysis, and sharing of statistical data and information.
- That a uniform system of National Biological Accounts be established, which compiles, analyzes, and disseminates data on critical natural areas, plant and animal species, key geological features, and threats to these resources. Where appropriate, this system would utilize existing information sources such as the state heritage programs.
- That researchers and practitioners meet to discuss how to direct research talents toward needed management information and how to support these efforts.
- That all private and public interests in recreation data and information come together to examine existing information and data gaps and determine what needs to be done and by whom.
- That a congressionally authorized, private, nonprofit outdoor institution be created to stimulate grass-roots leadership and to promote innovation and excellence.
- That each state establish an entity to encourage innovation and investment in outdoor recreation.
- That Congress and the Executive branch develop mechanisms to facilitate discussion and planning of national outdoor policy, such as a congressional caucus and a presidential subcabinet council.
- That local, state, and federal recreation and resources management agencies charge visitors fees to supplement regular appropriations, with the objective of recovering a reasonable portion of operations and maintenance costs.
- That Congress strengthen existing laws that contribute to outdoor recreation in order to increase opportunities available to the public.
- That the Land and Water Conservation Fund be succeeded by a dedicated trust—providing a minimum of $1 billion a year—to help pay for federal, state, and local land acquisition and for state and local facility development and rehabilitation. Congress should consider creating an endowed trust that, over time, would be self-sustaining.
- That states establish similar dedicated trusts to help meet their recreational and open-space needs.

Source: Adapted from the President's Commission on Americans Outdoors. *Americans Outdoors: The Legacy, the Challenge.* Washington, D.C.: Island Press, 1987.

National Park System: A Chronology[a]

LEGISLATIVE AND EXECUTIVE ACTIONS RELATING TO AREAS MANAGED BY THE DEPARTMENT OF THE INTERIOR THROUGH 1916

1832	April 20	Hot Springs Reservation, Arkansas (redesignated Hot Springs NP, 1921)
1864	June 30	Yosemite State Park, California (incorporated in Yosemite NP, 1906)
1872	March 1	Yellowstone NP, Wyoming, Montana, and Idaho
1889	March 2	Casa Grande Ruin Reservation, Arizona (redesignated Casa Grande NM, 1918)
1890	Sept. 25	Sequoia NP, California
	Oct. 1	General Grant NP, California (incorporated in Kings Canyon NP, 1940)
	Oct. 1	Yosemite NP, California
1899	March 22	Mount Rainier NP, Washington
1902	May 22	Crater Lake NP, Oregon
	July 1	Sulphur Springs Reservation, Oklahoma (redesignated Platt NP, 1906; incorporated in Chickasaw NRA, 1976)
1903	Jan. 9	Wind Cave NP, South Dakota
1904	April 27	Sullys Hill NP, North Dakota (transferred to Agriculture Dept. as game preserve, 1931)
1906	June 8	Antiquities Act
	June 29	Mesa Verde NP, Colorado
	Sept. 24	Devils Tower NM, Wyoming
	Dec. 8	El Morro NM, New Mexico
	Dec. 8	Montezuma Castle NM, Arizona
	Dec. 8	Petrified Forest NM, Arizona (redesignated a NP, 1962)
1907	March 11	Chaco Canyon NM, New Mexico (incorporated in Chaco Culture NHP, 1980)

1908	Jan. 9	Muir Woods NM, California
	Jan. 16	Pinnacles NM, California (under Agriculture Dept.; transferred to Interior, December 12, 1910)
	April 16	Natural Bridges NM, Utah
	May 11	Lewis and Clark Cavern NM, Montana (abolished 1937)
	Sept. 15	Tumacacori NM, Arizona (incorporated in Tumacacori NHP, 1990)
1909	March 20	Navajo NM, Arizona
	July 31	Mukuntuweap NM, Utah (incorporated in Zion NP, 1919)
	Sept. 21	Shoshone Cavern NM, Wyoming (abolished 1954)
	Nov. 1	Gran Quivira NM, New Mexico (incorporated in Salinas NM, 1980)
1910	March 23	Sitka NM, Alaska (redesignated a NHP, 1972)
	May 11	Glacier NP, Montana
	May 30	Rainbow Bridge NM, Utah
1911	May 24	Colorado NM, Colorado
1914	Jan. 31	Papago Saguaro NM, Arizona (abolished 1930)
1915	Jan. 26	Rocky Mountain NP, Colorado
	Oct. 4	Dinosaur NM, Colorado and Utah
1916	July 8	Sieur de Monts NM, Maine (incorporated in Lafayette NP, 1919; redesignated Acadia NP, 1929)
	Aug. 1	Hawaii NP, Hawaii (split into Haleakala NP and Hawaii NP, 1960; latter redesignated Hawaii Volcanoes NP, 1961)
	Aug. 9	Capulin Mountain NM, New Mexico (redesignated Capulin Volcano NM, 1987)
	Aug. 9	Lassen Volcanic NP, California (incorporated 1907 Cinder Cone and Lassen Peaks NMs from Agriculture Dept.)
	Aug. 25	National Park Service Act

NATIONAL PARK SYSTEM ADDITIONS
1917–1933

1917	Feb. 26	Mount McKinley NP, Alaska (incorporated in Denali NP and NPres, 1980)
	June 29	Verendrye NM, North Dakota (abolished 1956)
1918	Aug. 3	Casa Grande NM, Arizona (Casa Grande Ruin Reservation redesignated and transferred from General Land Office)
	Sept. 24	Katmai NM, Alaska (incorporated in Katmai NP and NPres, 1980)
1919	Feb. 26	Grand Canyon NP, Arizona (incorporated the 1908 Grand Canyon NM from Agriculture Dept.)
	Feb. 26	Lafayette NP, Maine (incorporated Sieur de Monts NM; redesignated Acadia NP, 1929)
	Nov. 19	Zion NP, Utah (incorporated Mukuntuweap NM)
	Dec. 12	Scotts Bluff NM, Nebraska
	Dec. 12	Yucca House NM, Colorado
1922	Oct. 21	Fossil Cycad NM, South Dakota (abolished 1956)

1923   Jan. 24   Aztec Ruins NM, New Mexico
        March 2   Hovenweep NM, Colorado and Utah
        May 31   Pipe Spring NM, Arizona
        Oct. 25   Carlsbad Cave NM, New Mexico (redesignated Carlsbad Caverns
                   NP, 1930)

1924   May 2   Craters of the Moon NM, Idaho
        Dec. 9   Wupatki NM, Arizona

1925   Feb. 26   Glacier Bay NM, Alaska (incorporated in Glacier Bay NP and NPres,
                   1980)
        Nov. 21   Lava Beds NM, California

1926   May 22   Great Smoky Mountains NP, North Carolina and Tennessee
        May 22   Shenandoah NP, Virginia
        May 25   Mammoth Cave NP, Kentucky

1928   Feb. 25   Bryce Canyon NP, Utah (incorporated 1923 Bryce Canyon NM from
                   Agriculture Dept.)

1929   Feb. 26   Grand Teton NP, Wyoming
        March 4   Badlands NM, South Dakota (redesignated a NP, 1978)
        April 12   Arches NM, Utah (redesignated a NP, 1971)

1930   Jan. 23   George Washington Birthplace NM, Virginia
        July 3   Colonial NM, Virginia (redesignated a NHP, 1936)

1931   Feb. 14   Canyon de Chelly NM, Arizona
        March 3   Isle Royale NP, Michigan

1932   Feb. 25   Bandelier NM, New Mexico (date transferred from Agriculture
                   Dept., where proclaimed 1916)
        March 17   Great Sand Dunes NM, Colorado
        Dec. 22   Grand Canyon NM, Arizona (incorporated in Grand Canyon NP,
                   1975)

1933   Jan. 18   White Sands NM, New Mexico
        Feb. 11   Death Valley NM, California and Nevada
        March 2   Black Canyon of the Gunnison NM, Colorado
        March 2   Morristown NHP, New Jersey
        Aug. 10   Reorganization

BACKGROUND TO THE REORGANIZATION OF 1933

National Capital Parks, 1790–1933

1790   July 16   District of Columbia authorized, including National Capital Parks,
                   National Mall, and White House

1866   April 7   Ford's Theatre, District of Columbia (date acquisition authorized;
                   designated a NHS, 1970)

1890   Sept. 27   Rock Creek Park, District of Columbia

1896   June 11   House Where Lincoln Died, District of Columbia (date acquisition authorized; incorporated in Ford's Theatre NHS, 1970)

1897   March 3   Potomac Park, District of Columbia (component of National Capital Parks)

1928   May 23   Mount Vernon Memorial Highway, Virginia (incorporated in George Washington Memorial Parkway, 1930)

1930   May 29   George Washington Memorial Parkway, Virginia and Maryland

National Memorials, 1876–1933

1876   August 2   Washington Monument, District of Columbia (date accepted by United States; dedicated 1885)

1877   March 3   Statue of Liberty, New York (date accepted by United States; dedicated 1886; also listed with "Other War Department Properties" below)

1911   Feb. 9   Lincoln Memorial, District of Columbia (dedicated 1922)

1913   Oct. 14   Cavrillo NM, California (also listed with Other War Department Properties below)

1916   July 17   Abraham Lincoln NP, Kentucky (also listed with Other War Department Properties below)

1925   March 23   Mount Rushmore NMem, South Dakota

1927   March 2   Kill Devil Hill Monument, North Carolina (redesignated Wright Brothers NMem 1953; also listed with Other War Department Properties below)

1928   May 23   George Rogers Clark Memorial, Indiana (incorporated in George Rogers Clark NHP, 1966)

1932   May 21   Theodore Roosevelt Island, District of Columbia

National Battlefield Areas, 1890–1933

1890   Aug. 19   Chickamauga and Chattanooga NMP, Georgia and Tennessee
       Aug. 30   Antietam NBS, Maryland (redesignated a NB, 1978)

1894   Dec. 27   Shiloh NMP, Tennessee

1895   Feb. 11   Gettysburg NMP, Pennsylvania

1899   Feb. 21   Vicksburg NMP, Mississippi

1907   March 4   Chalmette Monument and Grounds, Louisiana (redesignated Chalmette NHP,1939; incorporated in Jean Lafitte NHP and Preserve, 1978)

1917   Feb. 8   Kennesaw Mountain NBS, Georgia (redesignated a NBP, 1935)
       March 2   Guilford Courthouse NMP, North Carolina

1926   June 2   Moores Creeek NMP, North Carolina (redesignated a NB, 1980)
        July 3   Petersburg NMP, Virginia (redesignated a NB, 1962)

1927   Feb. 14   Fredericksburg and Spotsylvania County Battlefields Memorial NMP,
                    Virginia
        March 3   Stones River NMP, Tennessee (redesignated a NB, 1980)

1928   March 26   Fort Donelson NMP, Tennessee (redesignated a NB, 1985)

1929   Feb. 21   Brices Cross Roads NBS, Mississippi
        Feb. 21   Tupelo NBS, Mississippi (redesignated a NB, 1961)
        March 4   Cowpens NBS, South Carolina (redesignated a NB, 1972)

1930   June 18   Appomattox Court House monument, Virginia (designated
                    Appomattox Court House National Historical Monument, 1935;
                    redesignated Appomattox Court House NHP, 1954)

1931   March 4   Fort Necessity NMP, Pennsylvania (redesignated a NB, 1961)
        March 4   Kings Mountain NMP, South Carolina

Other War Department Properties, 1910–1933

1910   June 23   Big Hole Battlefield NM, Montana (redesignated Big Hole NB, 1963)

1913   Oct. 14   Cabrillo NM, California (also listed with National Memorials above)

1916   July 17   Abraham Lincoln NP, Kentucky (redesignated a NHP 1939;
                    redesignated Abraham Lincoln Birthplace NHS 1959; also listed
                    with National Memorials above)

1923   March 2   Mound City Group NM, Ohio

1924   Oct. 15   Castle Pinckney NM, South Carolina (abolished 1956)
        Oct. 15   Fort Marion NM, Florida (redesignated Castillo de San Marcos NM,
                    1942)
        Oct. 15   Fort Matanzas NM, Florida
        Oct. 15   Fort Pulaski NM, Georgia
        Oct. 15   Statue of Liberty NM, New York (also listed with National
                    Memorials above)

1925   Feb. 6   Meriwether Lewis NM, Tennessee (incorporated in Natchez Trace
                    Parkway, 1961)
        March 3   Fort McHenry NP, Maryland (redesignated Fort McHenry NM and
                    Historic Shrine, 1939)
        March 4   Custis-Lee Mansion, Virginia (date restoration authorized;
                    designated Arlington House, The Robert E. Lee Memorial, 1972)
        Sept. 5   Father Millet Cross NM, New York (abolished 1949)

1927   March 2   Kill Devil Hill Monument, North Carolina (redesignated Wright
                    Brothers NMem, 1953; also listed with National Memorials above)

1930   May 29   Fort Washington, Maryland (date transfer to George Washington
                    Memorial Parkway authorized; transferred 1940)

Agriculture Department National
Monuments, 1907–1933

1907	May 6	Cinder Cone NM, California (incorporated in Lassen Volcanic NP, 1916)
	May 6	Lassen Peak NM, California (incorporated in Lassen Volcanic NP, 1916)
	Nov. 16	Gila Cliff Dwellings NM, New Mexico
	Dec. 19	Tonto NM, Arizona
1908	Jan. 11	Grand Canyon NM, Arizona (incorporated in Grand Canyon NP, 1919)
	Jan. 16	Pinnacles NM, California (transferred to Interior Dept., 1910)
	Feb. 7	Jewel Cave NM, South Dakota
	Dec. 7	Wheeler NM, Colorado (abolished 1950)
1909	March 2	Mount Olympus NM, Washington (incorporated in Olympic NP, 1938)
	July 12	Oregon Caves NM, Oregon
1911	July 6	Devils Postpile NM, California
1915	Nov. 30	Walnut Canyon NM, Arizona
1916	Feb. 11	Bandelier NM, New Mexico (transferred to Interior Dept., 1932)
	Oct. 25	Old Kasaan NM, Alaska (abolished 1955)
1922	Jan. 24	Lehman Caves NM, Nevada (incorporated in Great Basin NP, 1986)
	Oct. 14	Timpanogos Cave NM, Utah
1923	June 8	Bryce Canyon NM, Utah (incorporated in Bryce Canyon NP, 1928)
1924	April 18	Chiricahua NM, Arizona
1929	May 11	Holy Cross NM, Colorado (abolished 1950)
1930	May 26	Sunset Crater NM, Arizona (redesignated Sunset Crater Volcano NM, 1990)
1933	March 1	Saguaro NM, Arizona

PRESENT-DAY NPS AREAS FROM THE 1933 REORGANIZATION

Abraham Lincoln Birthplace NHS, Kentucky
Antietam NB, Maryland
Appomattox Court House NHP, Virginia
Arlington House, The Robert E. Lee Memorial, Virginia
Big Hole NB, Montana
Brices Cross Roads NBS, Mississippi
Cabrillo NM, California
Castillo de San Marcos NM, Florida
Chickamauga and Chattanooga NMP, Georgia and Tennessee

Chiricahua NM, Arizona
Colonial NHP, Virginia—Yorktown National Cemetery
Cowpens NB, South Carolina
Devils Postpile NM, California
Ford's Theatre NHS, District of Columbia
Fort Donelson NB, Tennessee
Fort McHenry NM and Historic Shrine, Maryland
Fort Matanzas NM, Florida
Fort Necessity NB, Pennsylvania
Fort Pulaski NM, Georgia
Fredericksburg and Spotsylvania County Battlefields Memorial NMP, Virginia
George Washington Memorial Parkway, Virginia and Maryland
Gettysburg NMP, Pennsylvania
Gila Cliff Dwellings NM, New Mexico
Great Basin NP, Nevada—Lehman Caves NM portion
Guilford Courthouse NMP, North Carolina
Jean Lafitte NHP and Preserve, Louisiana—Chalmette Unit
Jewel Cave NM, South Dakota
Kennesaw Mountain NBP, Georgia
Kings Mountain NMP, South Carolina
Lincoln Memorial, District of Columbia
Moores Creek NB, North Carolina
Mound City Group NM, Ohio
Natchez Trace Parkway, Mississippi—Meriwether Lewis Park
National Capital Parks, District of Columbia and Maryland
National Mall, District of Columbia
Olympic NP, Washington—Mount Olympus NM portion
Oregon Caves NM, Oregon
Petersburg NB, Virginia
Rock Creek Park, District of Columbia
Saguaro NM, Arizona
Shiloh NMP, Tennessee
Statue of Liberty NM, New York and New Jersey
Stones River NB, Tennessee
Sunset Crater Volcano NM, Arizona
Theodore Roosevelt Island, District of Columbia
Timpanogos Cave NM, Utah
Tonto NM, Arizona
Tupelo NB, Mississippi
Vicksburg NMP, Mississippi
Walnut Canyon NM, Arizona
Washington Monument, District of Columbia
White House, District of Columbia
Wright Brothers NMem, North Carolina

NATIONAL PARK SYSTEM ADDITIONS
1933–1951

1933	June 16	Blue Ridge Parkway, North Carolina and Virginia (acquired 1936)
	Aug. 22	Cedar Breaks NM, Utah
1934	May 30	Everglades NP, Florida
	June 14	Ocmulgee NM, Georgia
	June 19	Natchez Trace Parkway, Mississippi, Alabama, and Tennessee (acquired 1938)
	June 21	Monocacy NMP, Maryland (reauthorized and redesignated a NB, 1976)
	June 26	Thomas Jefferson Memorial, District of Columbia (dedicated 1943)
1935	Jan. 4	Fort Jefferson NM, Florida
	June 20	Big Bend NP, Texas
	Aug. 21	Historic Sites Act
	Aug. 21	Fort Stanwix NM, New York (acquired 1973)
	Aug. 29	Andrew Johnson NM, Tennessee (redesignated a NHS, 1963)
	Dec. 20	Jefferson National Expansion Memorial, Missouri (Gateway Arch authorized 1954, dedicated 1968)
1936	March 2	Richmond NBP, Virginia
	March 19	Homestead NM of America, Nebraska
	May 26	Fort Frederica NM, Georgia
	June 2	Perry's Victory and International Peace Memorial NM, Ohio (redesignated Perry's Victory and International Peace Memorial 1972)
	June 23	Park, Parkway, and Recreation Area Study Act
	June 29	Whitman Mission NM, Washington (redesignated a NHS, 1963)
	Aug. 16	Joshua Tree NM, California
	Oct. 13	Boulder Dam NRA, Nevada and Arizona (redesignated Lake Mead NRA, 1974)
	Nov. 14	Catoctin Recreational Demonstration Area, Maryland (redesignated Catoctin Mountain Park 1954)
	Nov. 14	Chopawamsic Recreational Demonstration Area, Virginia (redesignated Prince William Forest Park 1948)
1937	Jan. 22	Zion NM, Utah (incorporated in Zion NP, 1956)
	April 13	Organ Pipe Cactus NM, Arizona
	Aug. 2	Capitol Reef NM, Utah (redesignated a NP, 1971)
	Aug. 17	Cape Hatteras NS, North Carolina
	Aug. 25	Pipestone NM, Minnesota
1938	March 17	Salem Maritime NHS, Massachusetts
	April 26	Channel Islands NM, California (incorporated in Channel Islands NP, 1980)
	June 1	Saratoga NHP, New York
	June 29	Olympic NP, Washington (incorporated Mount Olympus NM)
	July 16	Fort Laramie NM, Wyoming (redesignated a NHS, 1960)
	Aug. 3	Hopewell Village NHS, Pennsylvania (redesignated Hopewell Furnace NHS, 1985)

	Sept. 23	Chesapeake and Ohio Canal, District of Columbia, Maryland, and West Virginia (date acquired; designated a NM, 1961; incorporated in Chesapeake and Ohio Canal NHP, 1971)
	Oct. 25	Ackia Battleground NM, Mississippi (incorporated in Natchez Trace Parkway, 1961)
1939	May 17	Santa Rosa Island NM, Florida (abolished 1946; island included in Gulf Islands NS, 1971)
	May 26	Federal Hall Memorial NHS, New York (redesignated Federal Hall NMem, 1955)
	May 26	Philadelphia Custom House NHS, Pennsylvania (incorporated in Independence NHP, 1959)
	July 1	Mount Rushmore NMem, South Dakota (date acquired)
	July 25	Tuzigoot NM, Arizona
1940	March 4	Kings Canyon NP, California (incorporated General Grant NP)
	May 10	Manassas NBP, Virginia
	June 11	Cumberland Gap NHP, Kentucky, Virginia, and Tennessee
	July 1	National Cemetery of Custer's Battlefield Reservation, Montana (date acquired; redesignated Custer Battlefield NM, 1946)
	Aug. 12	Fort Washington Park, Maryland
	Dec. 18	Vanderbilt Mansion NHS, New York
1941	April 5	Fort Raleigh NHS, North Carolina
1943	March 15	Jackson Hole NM, Wyoming (incorporated in Grand Teton NP, 1950)
	July 14	George Washington Carver NM, Missouri
1944	Jan. 15	Home of Franklin D. Roosevelt NHS, New York
	June 30	Harpers Ferry NM, West Virginia and Maryland (redesignated a NHP, 1963)
	Oct. 13	Atlanta Campaign NHS, Georgia (abolished 1950)
1946	Aug. 12	Castle Clinton NM, New York
	Dec. 9	Adams Mansion NHS, Massachusetts (redesignated Adams NHS, 1952)
	Dec. 18	Coulee Dam NRA, Washington
1947	April 25	Theodore Roosevelt National Memorial Park, North Dakota (redesignated a NP, 1978)
1948	March 11	DeSoto NMem, Florida
	April 28	Fort Sumter NM, South Carolina
	June 19	Fort Vancouver NM, Washington (redesignated a NHS, 1961)
	June 22	Hampton NHS, Maryland
	June 28	Independence NHP, Pennsylvania
1949	Feb. 14	San Juan NHS, Puerto Rico
	June 8	Saint Croix Island NM, Maine (redesignated an international historic site, 1984)
	Aug. 17	Suitland Parkway, Maryland and District of Columbia (date acquired; incorporated in National Capital Parks, 1975)
	Oct. 25	Effigy Mounds NM, Iowa
1950	Aug. 3	Baltimore-Washington Parkway, Maryland (date acquired; incorporated in National Capital Parks, 1975)
	Aug. 3	Greenbelt Park, Maryland

	Sept. 14	Grand Teton NP, Wyoming (incorporated 1929 NP and Jackson Hole NM)
	Sept. 21	Fort Caroline NMem, Florida
1951	Sept. 15	Grand Portage NHS, Minnesota (redesignated a NM, 1958)

NATIONAL PARK SYSTEM ADDITIONS
1952–1972

1952	March 4	Virgin Islands NHS, Virgin Islands (redesignated Christiansted NHS, 1961)
	June 27	Shadow Mountain NRA, Colorado (transferred to Forest Service, 1978)
	July 9	Coronado NMem, Arizona
1954	June 28	Fort Union NM, New Mexico
1955	July 26	City of Refuge NHP, Hawaii (redesignated Pu'uhonua o Honaunau NHP, 1978)
	Dec. 6	Edison Home NHS, New Jersey (incorporated in Edison NHS, 1962)
1956	April 2	Booker T. Washington NM, Virginia
	July 14	Edison Laboratory NM, New Jersey (incorporated in Edison NHS, 1962)
	July 20	Pea Ridge NMP, Arkansas
	July 25	Horseshoe Bend NMP, Alabama
	Aug. 2	Virgin Islands NP, Virgin Islands
1958	April 18	Glen Canyon NRA, Utah and Arizona
	May 29	Fort Clatsop NMem, Oregon
	Aug. 14	General Grant NMem, New York
1959	April 14	Minute Man NHS, Massachusetts (redesignated a NHP, September 21)
1960	April 22	Wilson's Creek NBP, Missouri (redesignated a NB, 1970)
	June 3	Bent's Old Fort NHS, Colorado
	July 6	Arkansas Post NMem, Arkansas
	Sept. 13	Haleakala NP, Hawaii (detached from Hawaii NP)
	Dec. 24	St. Thomas NHS, Virgin Islands (abolished 1975)
1961	May 11	Russell Cave NM, Alabama
	Aug. 7	Cape Cod NS, Massachusetts
	Sept. 8	Fort Davis NHS, Texas
	Sept. 13	Fort Smith NHS, Arkansas
	Oct. 4	Piscataway Park, Maryland
	Dec. 28	Buck Island Reef NM, Virgin Islands
1962	Feb. 19	Lincoln Boyhood NMem, Indiana
	April 27	Hamilton Grange NMem, New York
	May 31	Whiskeytown-Shasta-Trinity NRA, California (Whiskeytown Unit)
	July 25	Sagamore Hill NHS, New York
	July 25	Theodore Roosevelt Birthplace NHS, New York
	Sept. 5	Edison NHS, New Jersey (incorporated Edison Home NHS and Edison Laboratory NM)

	Sept. 5	Frederick Douglass Home, District of Columbia (redesignated Frederick Douglass NHS, 1988)
	Sept. 13	Point Reyes NS, California
	Sept. 28	Padre Island NS, Texas
1963	July 22	Flaming Gorge NRA, Utah and Wyoming (transferred to Forest Service, 1968)
1964	Aug. 27	Ozark NSR, Missouri
	Aug. 30	Fort Bowie NHS, Arizona
	Aug. 31	Allegheny Portage Railroad NHS, Pennsylvania
	Aug. 31	Fort Larned NHS, Kansas
	Aug. 31	John Muir NHS, California
	Aug. 31	Johnstown Flood NMem, Pennsylvania
	Aug. 31	Saint-Gaudens NHS, New Hampshire
	Sept. 3	Land and Water Conservation Fund Act of 1965
	Sept. 3	Wilderness Act
	Sept. 11	Fire Island NS, New York
	Sept. 12	Canyonlands NP, Utah
	Dec. 31	Bighorn Canyon NRA, Wyoming and Montana
1965	Feb. 1	Arbuckle NRA, Oklahoma (incorporated in Chickasaw NRA, 1976)
	Feb. 11	Curecanti NRA, Colorado
	March 15	Sanford NRA, Texas (redesignated Lake Meredith Recreation Area, 1972; redesignated Lake Meredith NRA, 1990)
	May 15	Nez Perce NHP, Idaho
	June 5	Agate Fossil Beds NM, Nebraska
	June 28	Pecos NM, New Mexico (incorporated in Pecos NHP, 1990)
	July 30	Golden Spike NHS, Utah (designated 1957)
	Aug. 12	Herbert Hoover NHS, Iowa
	Aug. 28	Hubbell Trading Post NHS, Arizona
	Aug. 31	Alibates Flint Quarries and Texas Panhandle Pueblo Culture NM, Texas (redesignated Alibates Flint Quarries NM, 1978)
	Sept. 1	Delaware Water Gap NRA, Pennsylvania and New Jersey
	Sept. 21	Assateague Island NS, Maryland and Virginia
	Oct. 22	Roger Williams NMem, Rhode Island
	Nov. 11	Amistad Recreation Area, Texas (redesignated Amistad NRA, 1990)
1966	March 10	Cape Lookout NS, North Carolina
	June 20	Fort Union Trading Post NHS, North Dakota and Montana
	June 30	Chamizal NMem, Texas
	July 23	George Rogers Clark NHP, Indiana
	Sept. 9	San Juan Island NHP, Washington
	Oct. 15	National Historic Preservation Act
	Oct. 15	Guadalupe Mountains NP, Texas
	Oct. 15	Pictured Rocks NL, Michigan
	Oct. 15	Wolf Trap Farm Park for the Performing Arts, Virginia
	Nov. 2	Theodore Roosevelt Inaugural NHS, New York
	Nov. 5	Indiana Dunes NL, Indiana
1967	May 26	John Fitzgerald Kennedy NHS, Massachusetts
	Nov. 27	Eisenhower NHS, Pennsylvania
1968	March 12	National Visitor Center, District of Columbia (abolished 1981)
	April 5	Saugus Iron Works NHS, Massachusetts

	Oct. 2	National Trails System Act
	Oct. 2	Wild and Scenic Rivers Act
	Oct. 2	Appalachian NST, Maine, New Hampshire, Vermont, Massachusetts, Connecticut, New York, New Jersey, Pennsylvania, Maryland, West Virginia, Virginia, Tennessee, North Carolina, Georgia
	Oct. 2	Lake Chelan NRA, Washington
	Oct. 2	North Cascades NP, Washington
	Oct. 2	Redwood NP, California
	Oct. 2	Ross Lake NRA, Washington
	Oct. 2	St. Croix NSR, Minnesota and Wisconsin
	Oct. 17	Carl Sandburg Home NHS, North Carolina
	Oct. 18	Biscayne NM, Florida (incorporated in Biscayne NP, 1980)
1969	Jan. 16	Mar-A-Lago NHS, Florida (abolished 1980)
	Jan. 20	Marble Canyon NM, Arizona (incorporated in Grand Canyon NP, 1975)
	Aug. 20	Florissant Fossil Beds NM, Colorado
	Dec. 2	Lyndon B. Johnson NHS, Texas (redesignated a NHP, 1980)
	Dec. 2	William Howard Taft NHS, Ohio
1970	Sept. 26	Apostle Islands NL, Wisconsin
	Oct. 10	Fort Point NHS, California
	Oct. 16	Andersonville NHS, Georgia
	Oct. 21	Sleeping Bear Dunes NL, Michigan
1971	Jan. 8	Chesapeake and Ohio Canal NHP, District of Columbia, Maryland, and West Virginia (incorporated Chesapeake and Ohio Canal NM)
	Jan. 8	Gulf Islands NS, Florida and Mississippi
	Jan. 8	Voyageurs NP, Minnesota
	Aug. 18	Lincoln Home NHS, Illinois
1972	March 1	Buffalo NR, Arkansas
	June 16	John F. Kennedy Center for the Performing Arts, District of Columbia (date acquired)
	Aug. 17	Puukohola Heiau NHS, Hawaii
	Aug. 25	Grant-Kohrs Ranch NHS, Montana
	Aug. 25	John D. Rockefeller, Jr., Memorial Parkway, Wyoming
	Oct. 9	Longfellow NHS, Massachusetts
	Oct. 21	Hohokam Pima NM, Arizona
	Oct. 21	Thaddeus Kosciuszko NMem, Pennsylvania
	Oct. 23	Cumberland Island NS, Georgia
	Oct. 23	Fossil Butte NM, Wyoming
	Oct. 25	Lower St. Croix NSR, Minnesota and Wisconsin
	Oct. 27	Gateway NRA, New York and New Jersey
	Oct. 27	Golden Gate NRA, California

NATIONAL PARK SYSTEM ADDITIONS
1973–1990

1973	Dec. 28	Lyndon Baines Johnson Memorial Grove on the Potomac, District of Columbia

1974	March 7	Big South Fork NR and Recreation Area, Kentucky and Tennessee (assigned to National Park Service, 1976)
	Oct. 1	Boston NHP, Massachusetts
	Oct. 11	Big Cypress NPres, Florida
	Oct. 11	Big Thicket NPres, Texas
	Oct. 26	Clara Barton NHS, Maryland
	Oct. 26	John Day Fossil Beds NM, Oregon
	Oct. 26	Knife River Indian Villages NHS, North Dakota
	Oct. 26	Martin Van Buren NHS, New York
	Oct. 26	Springfield Armory NHS, Massachusetts
	Oct. 26	Tuskegee Institute NHS, Alabama
	Dec. 27	Cuyahoga Valley NRA, Ohio
1975	Jan. 3	Canaveral NS, Florida
1976	March 17	Chickasaw NRA, Oklahoma (incorporated Platt NP and Arbuckle NRA)
	June 30	Klondike Gold Rush NHP, Alaska and Washington
	July 4	Valley Forge NHP, Pennsylvania
	Aug. 19	Ninety Six NHS, South Carolina
	Oct. 12	Obed WSR, Tennessee
	Oct. 18	Congaree Swamp NM, South Carolina
	Oct. 18	Eugene O'Neill NHS, California
	Oct. 21	Monocacy NB, Maryland (reauthorization and redesignation of Monocacy NMP)
1977	May 26	Eleanor Roosevelt NHS, New York
1978	April 17	Constitution Gardens, District of Columbia
	June 5	Lowell NHP, Massachusetts
	Aug. 15	Chattahoochee River NRA, Georgia
	Aug. 18	War in the Pacific NHP, Guam
	Oct. 19	Fort Scott NHS, Kansas
	Nov. 10	Delaware NSR, Pennsylvania and New Jersey
	Nov. 10	Edgar Allan Poe NHS, Pennsylvania
	Nov. 10	Friendship Hill NHS, Pennsylvania
	Nov. 10	Jean Lafitte NHP and Preserve, Louisiana (incorporated Chalmette NHP)
	Nov. 10	Kaloko-Honokohau NHP, Hawaii
	Nov. 10	Maggie L. Walker NHS, Virginia
	Nov. 10	Missouri National Recreational River, Nebraska and South Dakota
	Nov. 10	New River Gorge NR, West Virginia
	Nov. 10	Palo Alto Battlefield NHS, Texas
	Nov. 10	Rio Grande WSR, Texas
	Nov. 10	St. Paul's Church NHS, New York (designated 1934)
	Nov. 10	San Antonio Missions NHP, Texas
	Nov. 10	Santa Monica Mountains NRA, California
	Nov. 10	Thomas Stone NHS, Maryland
	Nov. 10	Upper Delaware Scenic and Recreational River, Pennsylvania and New York
	Dec. 1	Aniakchak NM, Alaska (incorporated in legislated Aniakchak NM and NPres by ANILCA, 1980)
	Dec. 1	Bering Land Bridge NM, Alaska (redesignated a NPres by ANILCA, 1980)

	Dec. 1	Cape Krusenstern NM, Alaska
	Dec. 1	Denali NM, Alaska (incorporated with Mount McKinley NP in Denali NP and NPres by ANILCA, 1980)
	Dec. 1	Gates of the Arctic NM, Alaska (incorporated in Gates of the Arctic NP and NPres by ANILCA, 1980)
	Dec. 1	Glacier Bay NM, Alaska (addition to existing NM; total incorporated in Glacier Bay NP and NPres by ANILCA, 1980)
	Dec. 1	Katmai NM, Alaska (addition to existing NM; total incorporated in Katmai NP and NPres by ANILCA, 1980)
	Dec. 1	Kenai Fjords NM, Alaska (redesignated a NP by ANILCA, 1980)
	Dec. 1	Kobuk Valley NM, Alaska (redesignated a NP by ANILCA, 1980)
	Dec. 1	Lake Clark NM, Alaska (incorporated in Lake Clark NP and NPres by ANILCA, 1980)
	Dec. 1	Noatak NM, Alaska (incorporated in Noatak NPres by ANILCA, 1980)
	Dec. 1	Wrangell–St. Elias NM, Alaska (incorporated in Wrangell–St. Elias NP and NPres by ANILCA, 1980)
	Dec. 1	Yukon-Charley NM, Alaska (redesignated Yukon-Charley Rivers NPres by ANILCA, 1980)
1979	Oct. 12	Frederick Law Olmsted NHS, Massachusetts
1980	March 5	Channel Islands NP, California (incorporated Channel Islands NM)
	June 28	Biscayne NP, Florida (incorporated Biscayne NM)
	July 1	Vietnam Veterans Memorial, District of Columbia
	Sept. 9	USS *Arizona* Memorial, Hawaii
	Oct. 10	Boston African American NHS, Massachusetts
	Oct. 10	Martin Luther King, Jr., NHS, Georgia
	Dec. 2	Alaska National Interest Lands Conservation Act (ANILCA)
	Dec. 2	Alagnak Wild River, Alaska
	Dec. 19	Chaco Culture NHP, New Mexico (incorporated Chaco Canyon NM)
	Dec. 19	Salinas NM, New Mexico (incorporated Gran Quivira NM; redesignated Salinas Pueblo Missions NM, 1988)
	Dec. 22	Kalaupapa NHP, Hawaii
	Dec. 28	James A. Garfield NHS, Ohio
	Dec. 28	Women's Rights NHP, New York
1983	March 28	Natchez Trace NST, Mississippi, Alabama, and Tennessee
	March 28	Potomac Heritage NST, Maryland, District of Columbia, Virginia, and Pennsylvania
	May 23	Harry S. Truman NHS, Missouri (designated 1982)
1986	Oct. 21	Steamtown NHS, Pennsylvania
	Oct. 27	Great Basin NP, Nevada (incorporated Lehman Caves NM)
1987	June 25	Pennsylvania Avenue NHS, District of Columbia (designated 1965)
	Dec. 23	Jimmy Carter NHS, Georgia
	Dec. 31	El Malpais NM, New Mexico
1988	Feb. 16	Timucuan Ecological and Historic Preserve, Florida
	June 27	San Francisco Maritime NHP, California (formerly part of Golden Gate NRA)
	Sept. 8	Charles Pinckney NHS, South Carolina
	Oct. 7	Natchez NHP, Mississippi
	Oct. 31	National Park of American Samoa, American Samoa

	Oct. 31	Poverty Point NM, Louisiana
	Oct. 31	Zuni-Cibola NHP, New Mexico
	Nov. 18	City of Rocks National Reserve, Idaho
	Nov. 18	Hagerman Fossil Beds NM, Idaho
	Nov. 18	Mississippi NR and Recreation Area, Minnesota
	Dec. 26	Bluestone National Scenic River, West Virginia
	Dec. 26	Gauley River NRA, West Virginia
1989	Oct. 2	Ullysses S. Grant NHS, Missouri
1990	June 27	Pecos NHP, New Mexico (incorporated Pecos NM)
	June 27	Petroglyph NM, New Mexico
	Aug. 6	Tumacacori NHP, Arizona (incorporated Tumacacori NM)
	Oct. 31	Weir Farm NHS, Connecticut

AFFILIATED AREAS

As of 1990 there were 32 areas with which the National Park Service had particular connections but which it did not administer. These "affiliated areas," designated by Congress or by Secretaries of the Interior under the Historic Sites Act, may receive technical or financial assistance in accordance with the legislation or cooperative agreements defining their relationships with the Park Service.

American Memorial Park, Saipan; August 18, 1978
Benjamin Franklin National Memorial, Pennsylvania; October 25, 1972
Blackstone River Valley National Heritage Corridor, Massachusetts and Rhode Island; November 10, 1986
Chicago Portage National Historic Site, Illinois; January 3, 1952
Chimney Rock National Historic Site, Nebraska; August 2, 1956
David Berger National Memorial, Ohio; March 5, 1980
Delaware and Lehigh Navigation Canal National Heritage Corridor, Pennsylvania; November 18, 1988
Ebey's Landing National Historical Reserve, Washington; November 10, 1978
Father Marquette National Memorial, Michigan; December 20, 1975
Gloria Dei (Old Swedes') Church National Historic Site, Pennsylvania; November 17, 1942
Green Springs Historic District, Virginia; December 12, 1977
Historic Camden, South Carolina; May 24, 1982
Ice Age National Scenic Trail, Wisconsin; October 3, 1980
Ice Age National Scientific Reserve, Wisconsin; October 13, 1964
Iditarod National Historic Trail, Alaska; November 10, 1978
Illinois and Michigan Canal National Heritage Corridor, Illinois; August 24, 1984
International Peace Garden, North Dakota and Manitoba; October 25, 1949
Jamestown National Historic Site, Virginia; December 18, 1940
Lewis and Clark National Historic Trail, Illinois to Oregon; November 10, 1978
Mary McLeod Bethune Council House National Historic Site, District of Columbia; October 15, 1982

McLoughlin House National Historic Site, Oregon; June 27, 1941

Mormon Pioneer National Historic Trail, Illinois to Utah; November 10, 1978

North Country National Scenic Trail, New York to North Dakota; March 5, 1980

Oregon National Historic Trail, Missouri to Oregon; November 10, 1978

Overmountain Victory National Historic Trail, Virginia to South Carolina; September 8, 1980

Pinelands National Reserve, New Jersey; November 10, 1978

Red Hill Patrick Henry National Memorial, Virginia; May 13, 1986

Roosevelt Campobello International Park, New Brunswick; July 7, 1964

Santa Fe National Historic Trail, Missouri to New Mexico; May 8, 1987

Sewall-Belmont House National Historic Site, District of Columbia; October 26, 1974

Touro Synagogue National Historic Site, Rhode Island; March 5, 1946

Trail of Tears National Historic Trail, North Carolina to Oklahoma; December 16, 1987

[a]Abbreviations used in this appendix:

NB	National battlefield	NM	National monument	NRA	National recreation area
NBP	National battlefield park	NMem	National memorial	NS	National seashore
NBS	National battlefield site	NMP	National military park	NSR	National scenic riverway
NHP	National historical park	NP	National park	NST	National scenic trail
NHS	National historic site	NPres	National preserve	WSR	Wild and scenic river
NL	National lakeshore	NR	National river		

Source: National Park Service, *The National Parks: Shaping the System,* 1991.

National Park System: Areas, Acreages, and Use

Unit	State	Fig. 3.5 Map No.	Gross Area	NPS Lands	% Park Land	1991 Recreation Visits (thousands)	1991 Non-Recreation Visits (thousands)	1991 Recreation Visitor Days (thousands)	1991 Non-Recreation Visitor Days (thousands)
Alagnak Wild River	AK	4	24,038.0	24,038.0	100.00	Not reporting			0.0
Aniakchak National Monument	AK	5	137,176.0	137,176.0	100.00	1.5	0.0	2.6	
Aniakchak National Preserve	AK	5	465,603.0	454,151.0	97.54	Included in Aniakchak National Monument			
Bering Land Bridge National Preserve	AK	6	2,784,960.0	2,690,179.0	96.60	Not reporting			
Cape Krusenstern National Monument	AK	7	659,807.0	621,592.0	94.21	2.9	10.2	1.7	5.6
Denali National Park	AK	8	4,716,726.0	4,715,200.1	99.97	558.9	838.3	276.2	20.3
Denali National Preserve	AK	8	1,311,365.0	1,310,565.0	99.94	Included in national park	Included in national park		
Gates of the Arctic National Park	AK	9	7,523,888.0	7,281,654.5	96.78	1.2	1.0	11.7	3.5
Gates of the Arctic National Preserve	AK	9	948,629.0	948,504.0	99.99	Included in national park	Included in national park		
Glacier Bay National Park	AK	10	3,225,284.0	3,224,938.0	99.99	203.7	2.8	245.5	28.2
Glacier Bay National Preserve	AK	10	57,884.0	55,439.0	95.78	Included in national park	Included in national park		
Katmai National Park	AK	11	3,716,000.0	3,575,000.0	96.21	41.4	0.2	45.0	0.2
Katmai National Preserve	AK	11	374,000.0	374,000.0	100.00	Included in national park	Included in national park		
Kenai Fjords National Park	AK	12	669,541.0	649,946.0	97.07	107.0	0.9	53.8	0.5
Kobuk Valley National Park	AK	14	1,750,421.0	1,726,463.0	98.63	2.8	4.8	1.8	3.4
Lake Clark National Park	AK	15	2,636,839.0	2,573,724.0	97.61	4.1	0.1	2.6	0.3
Lake Clark National Preserve	AK	15	1,407,293.0	1,288,259.6	91.54	Included in national park	Included in national park		
Noatak National Preserve	AK	16	6,574,481.0	6,569,710.0	99.93	5.6	5.9	7.1	5.8
Sitka National Historical Park	AK	17	106.8	106.2	99.44	136.1	4.2	5.5	0.3
Wrangell–St. Elias National Park	AK	18	9,141,604.0	8,905,970.0	97.42	39.0	1.5	39.0	1.5
Wrangell–St. Elias National Preserve	AK	18	4,856,721.0	4,349,564.0	89.56	Included in national park	Included in national park		
Yukon-Charley Rivers National Preserve	AK	19	2,523,509.0	2,249,071.0	89.12	2.1	1.8	3.9	3.2
Klondike Gold Rush National Historic Park[1]	AK, WA	13	13,191.4	2,721.3	20.63	218.8	1.1	20.5	0.2
Horseshoe Bend National Military Park	AL	1	2,040.0	2,040.0	100.00	58.5	572.8	11.0	2.4
Russell Cave National Monument	AL	2	310.5	310.5	100.00	20.8	0.7	4.1	0.1
Tuskegee Institute National Historic Site	AL	3	57.6	8.3	14.41	402.5	0.0	24.4	0.0
Natchez Trace National Scenic Trail	AL, MS, TN	177	10,995.0	0.0	0.00	Not reporting			
Natchez Trace Parkway	AL, MS, TN	178	51,742.1	51,651.1	99.82	5,832.7	6,986.3	1,958.4	582.2
Arkansas Post National Memorial	AR	41	389.2	389.2	100.00	81.4	0.0	10.2	0.0
Buffalo National River	AR	42	94,218.5	91,788.3	97.42	981.8	0.0	493.9	0.0
Hot Springs National Park	AR	44	5,839.2	4,853.1	83.11	1,203.9	4,289.7	69.0	35.7
Pea Ridge National Military Park	AR	45	4,300.4	4,278.8	99.50	103.0	0.0	6.6	0.0
Fort Smith National Historic Site	AR, OK	43	75.0	34.9	46.53	75.7	0.0	8.4	0.0
The National Park of American Samoa	AS	20	9,000.0	0.0	0.00	Not reporting			
Canyon de Chelly National Monument	AZ	21	83,840.0	0.0	0.00	728.3	995.9	467.4	79.3
Casa Grande National Monument	AZ	22	472.5	472.5	100.00	176.9	2.2	12.5	0.0
Chiricahua National Monument	AZ	23	11,984.8	11,982.4	99.98	83.7	1.4	37.9	0.0

Unit	State	Fig. 3.5 Map No.	Gross Area	NPS Lands	% Park Land	1991 Recreation Visits (thousands)	1991 Non-Recreation Visits (thousands)	1991 Recreation Visitor Days (thousands)	1991 Non-Recreation Visitor Days (thousands)
Coronado National Monument	AZ	24	4,750.2	4,748.2	99.96	61.9	1.9	3.9	0.1
Fort Bowie National Historic Site	AZ	25	1,000.0	1,000.0	100.00	8.2	0.0	1.4	0.0
Grand Canyon National Park[2]	AZ	26	1,218,375.2	1,179,194.1	96.78	3,886.0	336.4	5,703.7	28.0
Hohokam Pima National Monument	AZ	27	1,690.0	0.0	0.00	Not reporting			
Hubbell Trading Post National Historic Site	AZ	28	160.1	160.1	100.00	208.4	4.6	9.0	0.1
Montezuma Castle National Monument	AZ	29	857.7	840.9	98.04	876.1	0.4	72.2	0.0
Navajo National Monument	AZ	30	360.0	360.0	100.00	81.5	26.6	25.4	0.6
Organ Pipe Cactus National Monument	AZ	31	330,688.9	329,316.3	99.58	228.8	2.4	101.2	0.3
Petrified Forest National Park	AZ	32	93,532.6	93,532.6	100.00	874.5	13.4	111.8	4.2
Pipe Spring National Monument	AZ	33	40.0	40.0	100.00	55.3	0.1	4.8	0.0
Saguaro National Monument	AZ	34	83,573.9	81,958.2	98.07	679.0	1,451.9	74.2	30.2
Sunset Crater Volcano National Monument	AZ	35	3,040.0	3,040.0	100.00	520.5	10.2	53.2	0.3
Tonto National Monument	AZ	36	1,120.0	1,120.0	100.00	62.6	0.0	6.4	0.0
Tumacacori National Historical Park	AZ	37	16.5	15.9	96.36	58.3	0.0	3.2	0.0
Tuzigoot National Monument	AZ	38	800.6	57.8	7.22	136.1	0.3	8.5	0.0
Walnut Canyon National Monument	AZ	39	2,249.5	2,011.6	89.42	157.1	0.5	17.0	0.0
Wupatki National Monument	AZ	40	35,253.2	35,253.2	100.00	234.1	6.5	24.0	0.3
Lake Mead National Recreation Area	AZ, NV	197	1,495,665.5	1,468,952.2	98.21	8,445.0	306.3	6,761.1	153.1
Glen Canyon National Recreation Area	AZ, UT	307	1,236,880.0	1,193,671.0	96.51	3,181.1	29.7	5,706.4	29.0
Cabrillo National Monument	CA	46	137.1	137.1	100.00	1,234.8	81.8	144.1	1.7
Channel Islands National Park	CA	47	249,353.8	64,254.6	25.77	149.3	46.7	127.7	93.5
Devils Postpile National Monument	CA	49	798.5	798.5	100.00	145.4	0.0	49.9	0.0
Eugene O'Neill National Historic Site	CA	50	13.2	13.2	100.00	3.3	0.3	0.7	0.0
Fort Point National Historic Site	CA	51	29.0	29.0	100.00	1,351.5	0.0	72.8	0.0
Golden Gate National Recreation Area[3]	CA	52	73,121.8	28,749.7	39.32	Suspended—see footnote 3			
John Muir National Historic Site	CA	53	340.0	8.9	2.62	22.7	1.0	3.4	0.0
Joshua Tree National Monument	CA	54	559,954.5	549,669.7	98.16	1,145.5	4.6	1,334.1	0.8
Kings Canyon National Park	CA	55	461,901.2	461,845.0	99.99	1,071.0	3.1	2,963.1	1.0
Lassen Volcanic National Park[2]	CA	56	106,372.4	106,366.5	99.99	463.2	0.0	454.6	0.0
Lava Beds National Monument	CA	57	46,559.9	46,559.9	100.00	76.2	33.1	21.7	1.4
Muir Woods National Monument	CA	58	553.6	523.0	94.47	1,518.9	6.0	168.7	0.7
Pinnacles National Monument	CA	59	16,265.4	16,254.6	99.93	192.6	0.0	51.4	0.0
Point Reyes National Seashore	CA	60	71,049.6	64,505.1	90.79	2,396.9	25.8	896.7	2.1
Redwood National Park	CA	61	110,132.4	75,341.8	68.41	366.3	0.0	219.4	0.0
San Francisco Maritime National Historical Park	CA	62	50.0	0.0	0.00	4,317.6	0.0	373.4	0.0
Santa Monica Mountains National Recreation Area[2]	CA	63	150,050.0	16,667.4	11.11	334.3	35.4	99.0	3.0
Sequoia National Park	CA	64	402,482.4	402,298.7	99.95	1,120.3	0.4	3,099.6	0.1
Whiskeytown-Shasta-Trinity National Recreation Area[2]	CA	65	42,503.5	42,448.2	99.87	1,537.1	7.1	468.6	1.0

Name	State	#							
Yosemite National Park	CA	66	761,170.2	759,463.7	99.78	3,423.1	124.1	7,675.3	269.9
Death Valley National Monument	CA, NV	48	2,067,627.7	2,048,928.9	99.10	743.6	31.0	603.1	3.9
Bent's Old Fort National Historic Site	CO	67	799.8	736.6	92.10	47.2	0.0	4.9	0.0
Black Canyon of the Gunnison National Monument	CO	68	20,766.1	20,646.1	99.42	316.3	0.0	70.2	0.0
Colorado National Monument	CO	69	20,454.0	20,454.0	100.00	373.0	574.5	90.8	24.1
Curecanti National Recreation Area	CO	70	42,114.5	42,114.5	100.00	1,090.9	0.0	459.5	0.0
Florissant Fossil Beds National Monument	CO	72	5,998.1	5,992.3	99.90	73.1	0.0	7.5	0.0
Great Sand Dunes National Monument	CO	73	38,662.2	36,426.2	94.22	295.1	0.4	93.4	0.0
Mesa Verde National Park	CO	75	52,121.7	51,890.7	99.56	678.1	4.0	504.7	2.0
Rocky Mountain National Park	CO	76	265,197.9	264,747.1	99.83	2,751.8	152.0	1,663.1	3.0
Yucca House National Monument	CO	77	10.0	10.0	100.00	Not reporting			
Dinosaur National Monument	CO, UT	71	210,844.0	204,160.3	96.83	447.8	20.6	168.9	5.2
Hovenweep National Monument	CO, UT	74	784.9	784.9	100.00	26.9	0.2	10.1	0.0
Appalachian National Scenic Trail	CT[4]	141	161,381.6	100,333.7	62.17	Not reporting			
Weir Farm National Historic Site	CT	78	62.0	0.0	0.00	Not reporting			
Constitution Gardens[5]	DC	79	52.0	52.0	100.00	Included in national park			
Ford's Theatre National Historic Site	DC	80	0.3	0.3	100.00	853.5	0.4	81.3	0.1
Frederick Douglass National Historic Site	DC	81	8.5	8.1	95.29	45.5	0.0	3.8	0.0
John F. Kennedy Center for the Performing Arts	DC	82	17.5	17.5	100.00	3,401.9	0.0	547.0	0.0
Lincoln Memorial	DC	83	109.6	109.6	100.00	1,141.3	0.0	47.6	0.0
Lyndon Baines Johnson Memorial Grove on the Potomac	DC	84	17.0	17.0	100.00	660.7	0.0	27.5	0.0
National Capital Parks[5]	DC	85	6,467.9	6,467.9	100.00	7,530.4	0.0	969.1	0.0
National Mall	DC	86	146.4	146.4	100.00				
Pennsylvania Avenue National Historic Site	DC	87	(undet.)			230.6	0.0	6.3	0.0
Rock Creek Park	DC	88	1,754.4	1,754.4	100.00	2,155.8	12,369.7	319.4	515.4
Theodore Roosevelt Island	DC	89	88.5	88.5	100.00	50.7	0.0	7.6	0.0
Thomas Jefferson Memorial	DC	90	18.4	18.4	100.00	655.4	0.0	27.3	0.0
Vietnam Veterans Memorial	DC	91	2.0	2.0	100.00	1,615.9	0.0	67.3	0.0
Washington Monument	DC	92	106.0	106.0	100.00	1,168.7	0.0	97.4	0.0
White House	DC	93	18.1	18.1	100.00	978.6	0.0	59.4	0.0
Potomac Heritage National Scenic Trail	DC, MD, PA, VA	154	(undet.)[6]			Not reporting			
Chesapeake and Ohio Canal National Historical Park	DC, MD, WV	146	19,236.6	14,068.9	73.14	1,945.2	15.0	451.4	1.2
Big Cypress National Preserve	FL	94	716,000.0	535,190.9	74.75	159.2	0.0	37.8	0.0
Biscayne National Park[2]	FL	95	173,467.4	169,345.3	97.62	488.1	0.0	172.5	0.0
Canaveral National Seashore	FL	96	57,661.7	57,626.7	99.94	1,159.0	0.0	244.4	0.0
Castillo de San Marcos National Monument	FL	97	20.5	19.9	97.07	794.4	15.9	49.6	0.3
De Soto National Memorial	FL	98	26.8	24.8	92.54	181.0	0.0	25.0	0.0
Everglades National Park[2]	FL	99	1,506,499.4	1,398,613.6	92.84	1,292.0	55.6	704.9	20.9
Fort Caroline National Memorial	FL	100	138.4	133.1	96.17	132.4	0.0	11.0	0.0
Fort Jefferson National Monument	FL	101	64,700.0	61,480.0	95.02	18.2	8.6	38.7	28.6
Fort Matanzas National Monument	FL	102	227.8	227.8	100.00	343.9	0.0	27.3	0.0

697

Unit	State	Fig. 3.5 Map No.	Gross Area	NPS Lands	% Park Land	1991 Recreation Visits (thousands)	1991 Non-Recreation Visits (thousands)	1991 Recreation Visitor Days (thousands)	1991 Non-Recreation Visitor Days (thousands)
Gulf Islands National Seashore	FL	103	65,816.6	28,975.8	44.03	4,988.0	139.7	1,285.7	34.6
Timucuan Ecological and Historic Preserve	FL	104	46,000.0	1,984.0	4.31	Not reporting			
Andersonville National Historic Site	GA	105	494.6	474.3	95.90	151.4	0.0	25.2	0.0
Appalachian National Scenic Trail	GA[4]	141	161,381.6	100,333.7	62.17	Not reporting			
Chattahoochee River National Recreation Area	GA	106	9,256.7	4,005.0	43.27	1,660.6	0.0	553.5	0.0
Cumberland Island National Seashore	GA	108	36,415.1	18,698.1	51.35	36.5	0.0	68.9	0.0
Fort Frederica National Monument	GA	109	216.4	210.7	97.37	322.4	1.8	27.2	0.0
Fort Pulaski National Monument	GA	110	5,623.1	5,365.1	95.41	373.8	28.8	85.1	0.6
Jimmy Carter National Historic Site	GA	111	69.6	0.0	0.00	34.3	0.0	1.4	0.0
Kennesaw Mountain National Battlefield Park[2]	GA	112	2,884.5	2,880.0	99.84	787.4	10,133.6	98.7	135.1
Martin Luther King, Jr., National Historic Site[2]	GA	113	23.2	4.8	20.69	2,870.6	0.0	179.4	0.0
Ocmulgee National Monument	GA	114	683.5	683.5	100.00	127.8	0.0	16.0	0.0
Chickamauga and Chattanooga National Military Park	GA, TN	107	8,106.0	8,089.3	99.79	1,002.3	7,306.3	148.4	91.3
War in the Pacific National Historical Park	Guam	115	1,960.2	915.7	46.71	60.0	0.5	4.9	0.0
Haleakala National Park	HI	116	28,655.3	27,468.3	95.86	1,228.3	33.0	240.5	2.8
Hawaii Volcanoes National Park	HI	117	229,177.0	217,298.1	94.82	1,238.7	1,337.7	689.7	36.8
Kalaupapa National Historical Park	HI	118	10,778.9	22.9	0.21	Not reporting			
Kaloko-Honokohau National Historical Park[2]	HI	119	1,160.9	321.6	27.70	46.8	0.0	12.7	0.0
Pu'uhonua o Honaunau National Historical Park	HI	120	181.8	181.8	100.00	401.5	0.0	33.5	0.0
Puukohola Heiau National Historic Site	HI	121	80.5	34.4	42.73	70.5	0.0	2.9	0.0
USS Arizona Memorial	HI	122	0.0			1,489.0	8.0	248.2	1.3
Effigy Mounds National Monument	IA	131	1,481.4	1,481.4	100.00	125.7	1.5	19.5	0.0
Herbert Hoover National Historic Site	IA	132	186.8	181.1	96.95	298.1	18.0	24.8	0.1
City of Rocks National Reserve	ID	123	14,407.2	7,001.2	48.60	Not reporting			
Craters of the Moon National Monument	ID	124	53,545.1	53,545.1	100.00	217.9	0.0	55.6	0.0
Hagerman Fossil Beds National Monument	ID	125	4,280.0	3,787.6	88.50	Not reporting			
Nez Perce National Historical Park	ID	126	2,108.9	1,833.2	86.93	242.1	11.9	38.5	0.1
Yellowstone National Park	ID, MT, WY	350	2,219,790.7	2,219,772.7	100.00	2,920.5	37.3	8,435.4	12.4
Lincoln Home National Historic Site[2]	IL	127	12.2	12.0	98.36	509.5	50.2	37.8	3.2
George Rogers Clark National Historical Park	IN	128	26.2	26.2	100.00	128.1	0.0	14.2	0.0
Indiana Dunes National Lakeshore	IN	129	13,844.8	9,705.4	70.10	2,058.8	342.5	343.1	14.3
Lincoln Boyhood National Memorial	IN	130	199.7	180.8	90.54	209.2	16.1	19.6	0.2
Fort Larned National Historical Site	KS	133	718.4	679.7	94.61	46.8	0.0	7.8	0.0
Fort Scott National Historic Site	KS	134	16.7	16.7	100.00	74.5	1.4	9.3	0.0
Abraham Lincoln Birthplace National Historic Site	KY	135	116.5	116.5	100.00	316.9	0.0	26.4	0.0
Mammoth Cave National Park	KY	137	52,419.0	51,592.1	98.42	2,158.2	173.1	332.3	7.2
Big South Fork National River & Recreation Area	KY, TN	282	122,960.0	16,860.0	13.71	860.0	0.0	468.6	0.0

Unit	State	No.							
Cumberland Gap National Historical Park	KY, TN, VA	136	20,274.4	20,270.6	99.98	951.7	259.6	154.9	14.6
Jean Lafitte National Historic Park and Preserve	LA	138	20,020.0	9,651.0	48.21	875.4	449.3	133.8	9.2
Poverty Point National Monument	LA	139	910.9	0.0	0.00	27.0	Not reporting	Not reporting	0.0
Adams National Historic Site	MA	156	9.8	9.2	93.88	232.1	0.4	1.7	0.0
Appalachian National Scenic Trail	MA[4]	141	(undet.)[6]						
Boston African American National Historic Site	MA	157	(undet.)[6]				0.0	8.9	0.7
Boston National Historical Park	MA	158	41.0	35.2	85.85	2,020.6	48.2	147.5	15.1
Cape Cod National Seashore	MA	159	43,557.2	27,386.4	62.87	5,442.4	30.1	898.6	0.0
Frederick Law Olmsted National Historic Site	MA	160	1.8	1.8	100.00	4.0	0.2	0.7	0.0
John Fitzgerald Kennedy National Historic Site	MA	161	0.1	0.1	100.00	13.5	0.0	0.6	0.0
Longfellow National Historic Site	MA	162	2.0	2.0	100.00	15.3	0.0	1.3	0.0
Lowell National Historical Park	MA	163	136.9	7.9	5.77	711.7	0.0	82.3	0.0
Minute Man National Historical Park	MA	164	810.4	665.3	82.10	769.7	0.0	32.1	0.0
Salem Maritime National Historic Site	MA	165	9.0	8.9	98.89	786.9	3.3	28.9	0.2
Saugus Iron Works National Historic Site	MA	166	8.5	8.5	100.00	47.6	49.6	5.2	0.4
Springfield Armory National Historic Site	MA	167	54.9	20.6	37.52	17.0	0.0	2.8	0.0
Antietam National Battlefield	MD	143	3,244.1	2,381.8	73.42	263.1	Not reporting	Not reporting	
Appalachian National Scenic Trail	MD[4]	141	161,381.6	100,333.7	62.17		0.0	57.8	0.0
Catoctin Mountain Park	MD	145	5,770.2	5,770.2	100.00	581.4	209.0	199.3	2.0
Clara Barton National Historic Site	MD	147	8.6	8.6	100.00	16.6	0.0	1.4	0.0
Fort McHenry National Monument and Historic Shrine	MD	148	43.3	43.3	100.00	563.0	0.7	70.4	0.0
Fort Washington Park	MD	149	341.0	341.0	100.00	349.7	0.0	111.1	0.0
Greenbelt Park	MD	150	1,176.0	1,176.0	100.00	249.2	10.7	80.3	0.2
Hampton National Historic Site	MD	151	62.0	59.4	95.81	30.1	0.6	3.3	0.0
Monocacy National Battlefield	MD	152	1,647.0	1,014.5	61.60		Not reporting	Not reporting	
Piscataway Park	MD	153	4,262.5	4,216.5	98.92	164.5	0.0	27.4	0.0
Thomas Stone National Historic Site	MD	155	328.3	322.0	98.08		Not reporting	Not reporting	
Potomac Heritage National Scenic Trail	MD, DC, PA, VA	154	(undet.)[6]				Not reporting	Not reporting	
Chesapeake and Ohio Canal National Historical Park	MD, DC, WV	146	19,236.6	14,068.9	73.14	1,945.2	15.0	451.4	1.2
Assateague Island National Seashore	MD, VA	144	36,630.8	17,774.9	48.52	2,087.5	3.6	1,539.6	0.3
George Washington Memorial Parkway	MD, VA	318	7,159.5	7,088.6	99.01	5,004.7	0.0	598.1	0.0
Harpers Ferry National Historical Park	MD, VA, WV	340	2,260.7	2,133.5	94.37	489.9	0.0	163.3	0.0
Acadia National Park[2]	ME	140	41,888.0	40,728.1	97.23	2,475.5	252.6	1,099.9	21.0
Appalachian National Scenic Trail	ME[4]	141	161,381.6	100,333.7	62.17		Not reporting	Not reporting	
Saint Croix Island International Historic Site	ME	142	35.4	22.2	62.71		Not reporting	Not reporting	
Isle Royale National Park	MI	168	571,790.1	539,281.9	94.31	22.0	0.2	114.3	1.8
Pictured Rocks National Lakeshore	MI	169	72,902.5	35,791.4	49.09	704.9	1.9	287.8	0.1
Sleeping Bear Dunes National Lakeshore	MI	170	71,187.5	56,868.5	79.89	1,246.3	0.0	504.0	0.0
Grand Portage National Monument	MN	171	710.0	710.0	100.00	67.6	0.0	3.6	0.0
Mississippi National River and Recreation Area	MN	172	(undet.)[6]				Not reporting	Not reporting	
Pipestone National Monument	MN	173	281.8	281.8	100.00	120.4	0.0	25.1	0.0

Unit	State	Fig. 3.5 Map No.	Gross Area	NPS Lands	% Park Land	1991 Recreation Visits (thousands)	1991 Non-Recreation Visits (thousands)	1991 Recreation Visitor Days (thousands)	1991 Non-Recreation Visitor Days (thousands)
Voyageurs National Park	MN	174	218,035.3	131,900.9	60.50	221.9	19.1	137.6	0.8
Lower Saint Croix National Scenic Riverway	MN, WI	343	25,278.9	8,143.4	32.21		Not reporting		
Saint Croix National Scenic Riverway	MN, WI	344	67,379.3	27,144.5	40.29	468.8	0.0	583.6	0.0
George Washington Carver National Monument	MO	181	210.0	210.0	100.00	34.3	0.0	3.7	0.0
Harry S. Truman National Historic Site	MO	182	1.4	1.2	85.71	115.2	0.0	6.9	0.0
Jefferson National Expansion Memorial	MO	183	190.6	91.0	47.74	2,622.4	184.1	218.5	2.6
Ozark National Scenic Riverways[2]	MO	184	80,790.8	61,368.4	75.96	2,304.8	0.0	396.6	0.0
Ulysses S. Grant National Historic Site[7]	MO	185	(undet.)[6]			0.5	0.0	0.1	0.0
Wilson's Creek National Battlefield	MO	186	1,749.9	1,749.4	99.97	146.9	0.0	25.4	0.0
Brices Cross Roads National Battlefield Site	MS	175	1.0	1.0	100.00		Not reporting		
Gulf Islands National Seashore	MS, FL	103	73,958.8	69,150.0	93.50				
Natchez National Historical Park	MS	176	78.7	78.7	100.00		Not reporting		
Tupelo National Battlefield	MS	179	1.0	1.0	100.00		Not reporting		
Vicksburg National Military Park[2]	MS	180	1,619.9	1,613.1	99.58	864.8	0.0	162.6	0.0
Natchez Trace National Scenic Trail	MS, AL, TN	177	10,995.0	0.0	0.00		Not reporting		
Natchez Trace Parkway[2]	MS, AL, TN	178	51,742.1	51,651.1	99.82	5,832.7	6,986.3	1,958.4	582.2
Big Hole National Battlefield	MT	187	655.6	655.6	100.00	54.1	0.0	7.2	0.0
Custer Battlefield National Monument[8]	MT	189	765.3	765.3	100.00				
Glacier National Park	MT	190	1,013,572.4	1,012,995.7	99.94	2,097.0	7.5	1,481.3	5.4
Grant-Kohrs Ranch National Historic Site	MT	191	1,498.4	1,371.5	91.53	26.9	0.0	2.8	0.0
Yellowstone National Park	MT, ID, WY	350	2,219,790.7	2,219,772.7	100.00	2,920.5	37.3	8,435.4	12.4
Fort Union Trading Post National Historic Site	MT, ND	241	442.5	392.2	88.63	29.9	0.7	3.1	0.0
Bighorn Canyon National Recreation Area	MT, WY	188	120,296.2	68,484.6	56.93	481.1	30.8	247.3	2.6
Appalachian National Scenic Trail	NC[4]	141	161,381.6	100,333.7	62.17		Not reporting		
Cape Hatteras National Seashore	NC	234	30,319.4	30,318.9	100.00	2,098.9	123.7	949.7	37.4
Cape Lookout National Seashore[2]	NC	235	28,243.4	25,173.6	89.13	320.2	4.8	178.6	1.2
Carl Sandburg Home National Historic Site	NC	236	263.5	263.5	100.00	65.2	0.0	7.5	0.0
Fort Raleigh National Historic Site	NC	237	157.3	153.1	97.33	282.5	1.3	45.9	0.1
Guilford Courthouse National Military Park	NC	238	220.3	220.3	100.00	199.6	3,394.6	10.4	2.4
Moores Creek National Battlefield	NC	239	86.5	86.5	100.00	68.5	0.0	3.6	0.0
Wright Brothers National Memorial	NC	240	431.4	424.8	98.47	461.5	2.2	34.9	0.1
Great Smoky Mountains National Park	NC, TN	284	520,003.8	520,003.8	99.95	8,654.5	9,267.0	5,539.5	386.1
Blue Ridge Parkway	NC, VA	233	85,954.8	78,837.8	91.72	16,414.3	1,942.3	8,677.7	80.9
Knife River Indian Villages National Historic Site	ND	242	1,293.4	1,293.4	100.00	13.8	0.9	1.9	0.0
Theodore Roosevelt National Park	ND	243	70,446.6	69,701.7	98.94	468.9	6.5	110.6	0.2
Fort Union Trading Post National Historic Site	ND, MT	241	442.5	392.2	88.63	29.9	0.7	3.1	0.0
Agate Fossil Beds National Monument	NE	192	3,055.2	2,737.5	89.60	13.9	9.0	1.4	0.1

Area	State	No.							
Homestead National Monument of America	NE	193	195.1	180.4	92.47	40.4	0.0	3.6	0.0
Scotts Bluff National Monument	NE	195	2,997.1	2,936.0	97.96	186.8	0.0	15.6	0.0
Missouri National Recreational River	NE, SD	194	(undet.)[6]			Not reporting	Not reporting	Not reporting	
Appalachian National Scenic Trail	NH[4]	141	161,381.6	100,333.7	62.17	Not reporting	Not reporting	Not reporting	
Saint-Gaudens National Historic Site	NH	198	148.2	141.2	95.28	39.8	0.5	4.9	0.1
Appalachian National Scenic Trail	NJ[4]	141	161,381.6	100,333.7	62.17	Not reporting	Not reporting	Not reporting	
Edison National Historic Site	NJ	199	21.3	21.3	100.00	63.2	0.0	9.1	0.0
Morristown National Historical Park	NJ	200	1,670.6	1,669.8	99.95	686.0	0.0	102.0	0.0
Gateway National Recreation Area	NJ, NY	220	26,310.9	20,375.9	77.44	6,643.9	82.0	1,822.3	1.7
Statue of Liberty National Monument	NJ, NY	228	58.4	58.4	100.00	4,343.0	0.0	1,085.8	0.0
Delaware National Scenic River	NJ, NY, PA	255	1,973.3	0.0	0.00	Included in Delaware Water Gap NRA			
Delaware Water Gap National Recreation Area[2]	NJ, PA	256	66,651.9	54,600.8	81.92	4,275.8	279.7	1,556.2	11.7
Aztec Ruins National Monument	NM	201	319.5	27.1	8.48	89.2	1.3	11.2	0.2
Bandelier National Monument	NM	202	32,737.2	32,737.2	100.00	345.7	0.8	126.6	0.0
Capulin Volcano National Monument	NM	203	792.8	792.8	100.00	62.2	0.3	7.5	0.0
Carlsbad Caverns National Park	NM	204	46,774.5	46,435.3	99.27	679.5	0.0	199.8	0.0
Chaco Culture National Historical Park	NM	205	33,974.3	23,248.2	68.43	72.2	5.3	82.6	0.4
El Malpais National Monument	NM	206	114,335.4	96,443.4	84.35	69.1	0.4	23.5	0.0
El Morro National Monument	NM	207	1,278.7	1,039.9	81.32	69.4	14.2	17.8	0.4
Fort Union National Monument	NM	208	720.6	720.6	100.00	22.3	0.3	2.2	0.0
Gila Cliff Dwellings National Monument	NM	209	533.1	533.1	100.00	53.0	0.0	4.4	0.0
Pecos National Historical Park	NM	210	364.8	364.8	100.00	47.1	0.0	4.4	0.0
Petroglyph National Monument	NM	211	5,207.8	0.0	0.00	Not reporting	Not reporting	Not reporting	
Salinas Pueblo Missions National Monument	NM	212	1,076.9	884.6	82.14	41.2	0.0	5.7	0.0
White Sands National Monument	NM	213	143,732.9	143,322.8	99.71	588.5	2.3	64.8	2.2
Zuni-Cibola National Historical Park	NM	214	800.0	0.0	0.00	Not reporting	Not reporting	Not reporting	
Great Basin National Park	NV	196	77,100.0	77,100.0	100.00	63.9	1.5	66.3	0.1
Lake Mead National Recreation Area	NV, AZ	197	1,495,665.5	1,468,952.2	98.21	8,445.0	306.3	6,761.1	153.1
Death Valley National Monument	NV, CA	48	2,067,627.7	2,048,928.9	99.10	743.6	31.0	603.1	3.9
Appalachian National Scenic Trail	NY[4]	141	161,381.6	100,333.7	62.17	Not reporting	Not reporting	Not reporting	
Castle Clinton National Monument	NY	215	1.0	1.0	100.00	3,344.1	98.4	139.4	32.5
Eleanor Roosevelt National Historic Site	NY	216	180.5	180.5	100.00	77.6	0.0	9.7	0.0
Federal Hall National Memorial	NY	217	0.5	0.5	100.00	179.2	12.3	7.0	2.3
Fire Island National Seashore	NY	218	19,578.6	6,220.6	31.77	763.2	118.2	241.9	29.5
Fort Stanwix National Monument	NY	219	15.5	15.5	100.00	57.2	0.0	7.1	0.0
General Grant National Memorial	NY	221	0.8	0.8	100.00	89.2	33.1	3.7	6.1
Hamilton Grange National Memorial	NY	222	0.1	0.0	0.00	40.5	0.8	2.5	0.1
Home of Franklin D. Roosevelt National Historic Site	NY	223	290.3	290.3	100.00	165.8	0.0	29.8	0.0
Martin Van Buren National Historic Site	NY	224	39.6	38.5	97.22	15.4	0.8	1.3	0.0
Sagamore Hill National Historic Site	NY	225	83.0	83.0	100.00	115.2	0.0	14.4	0.0
Saint Paul's Church National Historic Site[7]	NY	226	6.1	6.1	100.00	6.0	1.0	0.8	0.1
Saratoga National Historical Park	NY	227	3,392.8	2,847.7	83.93	169.9	343.3	23.7	2.0

Unit	State	Fig. 3.5 Map No.	Gross Area	NPS Lands	% Park Land	1991 Recreation Visits (thousands)	1991 Non-Recreation Visits (thousands)	1991 Recreation Visitor Days (thousands)	1991 Non-Recreation Visitor Days (thousands)
Theodore Roosevelt Birthplace National Historic Site	NY	229	0.1	0.1	100.00	13.2	0.7	1.5	0.0
Theodore Roosevelt Inaugural National Historic Site	NY	230	1.0	1.0	100.00	26.9	14.4	3.4	2.4
Vanderbilt Mansion National Historic Site	NY	231	211.7	211.7	100.00	434.8	0.0	54.1	0.0
Women's Rights National Historical Park	NY	232	5.5	3.0	54.55	17.3	1.7	1.7	0.2
Gateway National Recreation Area	NY, NJ	220	26,310.9	20,375.9	77.44	6,643.9	82.0	1,822.3	1.7
Statue of Liberty National Monument	NY, NJ	228	58.4	58.4	100.00	4,343.0	0.0	1,085.8	0.0
Delaware National Scenic River	NY, NJ, PA	255	1,973.3	0.0	0.00	Included in Delaware Water Gap NRA			
Upper Delaware Scenic and Recreational River	NY, PA	267	75,000.0	14.5	0.02	222.6	1.5	89.9	0.0
Cuyahoga Valley National Recreation Area	OH	244	32,524.8	16,544.3	50.87	1,359.0	9.7	233.9	0.4
James A. Garfield National Historic Site	OH	245	7.8	7.8	100.00	Not reporting			
Mound City Group National Monument	OH	246	270.2	178.1	65.91	42.3	0.0	2.5	0.0
Perry's Victory and International Peace Memorial	OH	247	25.4	25.0	98.43	195.0	0.0	12.4	0.0
William Howard Taft National Historic Site	OH	248	3.1	1.7	54.84	8.3	0.0	0.7	0.0
Chickasaw National Recreation Area	OK	249	9,521.9	9,517.4	99.95	1,453.0	1,373.9	399.1	4.6
Fort Smith National Historic Site	OK, AR	43	75.0	34.9	46.53	75.7	0.0	8.4	0.0
Crater Lake National Park	OR	250	183,224.1	183,223.8	100.00	456.9	68.5	218.6	2.9
Fort Clatsop National Memorial	OR	251	125.2	125.0	99.84	279.8	0.3	28.4	0.0
John Day Fossil Beds National Monument	OR	252	14,014.1	10,883.0	77.66	103.9	0.8	11.0	0.0
Oregon Caves National Monument	OR	253	488.0	484.0	99.18	99.1	0.5	25.6	0.1
Allegheny Portage Railroad National Historic Site	PA	254	1,247.0	955.9	76.66	154.8	1.5	15.7	0.1
Appalachian National Scenic Trail	PA[4]	141	161,381.6	100,333.7	62.17	Not reporting			
Edgar Allan Poe National Historic Site	PA	257	0.5	0.5	100.00	13.0	0.0	1.1	0.0
Eisenhower National Historic Site	PA	258	690.5	690.5	100.00	109.3	0.0	18.5	0.0
Fort Necessity National Battlefield	PA	259	902.8	894.5	99.08	209.4	0.1	21.9	0.0
Friendship Hill National Historic Site	PA	260	674.6	661.4	98.04	13.5	0.0	1.3	0.0
Gettysburg National Military Park	PA	261	3,942.1	3,699.2	93.84	1,415.8	74.4	356.4	1.0
Hopewell Furnace National Historic Site	PA	262	848.1	848.1	100.00	107.2	0.6	10.7	0.0
Independence National Historical Park	PA	263	44.9	41.9	93.32	3,200.4	0.0	412.8	0.0
Johnstown Flood National Memorial	PA	264	164.1	155.4	94.70	154.6	42.1	23.7	0.1
Steamtown National Historic Site	PA	265	44.4	0.0	0.00	91.4	2.4	16.4	0.1
Thaddeus Kosciuszko National Memorial	PA	266	0.0	0.0	100.00	5.8	0.0	0.1	0.0
Valley Forge National Historical Park[2]	PA	268	3,468.1 (undet.)[6]	2,950.6	85.08	1,687.2	5,639.9	210.9	94.0
Potomac Heritage National Scenic Trail	PA, DC, MD, VA	154				Not reporting			
Delaware Water Gap National Recreation Area[2]	PA, NJ	256	66,651.9	54,600.8	81.92	4,275.8	279.7	1,556.20	11.7
Delaware National Scenic River	PA, NJ, NY	255	1,973.3	0.0	0.00	Included in Delaware Water Gap NRA			
Upper Delaware Scenic and Recreational River	PA, NY	267	75,000.0	14.5	0.02	222.6	1.5	89.9	0.0
San Juan National Historic Site	PR	269	75.1	53.2	70.84	2,345.3	0.0	433.8	0.0

Name	State	No.							
Roger Williams National Memorial[2]	RI	270	4.6	4.6	100.00	107.4	7.9	3.7	0.1
Charles Pinckney National Historic Site	SC	271	25.0	21.4	85.60	Not reporting	Not reporting	Not reporting	Not reporting
Congaree Swamp National Monument	SC	272	22,200.0	19,275.2	86.83	31.0	0.0	6.5	0.0
Cowpens National Battlefield	SC	273	841.6	788.7	93.71	147.6	0.0	7.6	0.0
Fort Sumter National Monument	SC	274	194.4	194.4	100.00	309.9	233.9	29.5	0.0
Kings Mountain National Military Park	SC	275	3,945.3	3,945.3	100.00	233.9	0.0	17.2	3.2
Ninety Six National Historic Site	SC	276	989.1	989.1	100.00	30.0	12.0	3.3	0.0
Badlands National Park	SD	277	242,755.9	232,742.2	95.87	1,518.4	0.4	510.1	0.5
Jewel Cave National Monument	SD	278	1,273.5	1,273.5	100.00	152.3	637.4	20.5	0.0
Mount Rushmore National Memorial	SD	279	1,278.5	1,238.5	96.87	2,044.5	584.2	224.3	51.0
Wind Cave National Park	SD	280	28,295.0	28,295.0	100.00	597.1		51.5	16.2
Missouri National Recreational River	SD, NE	194	(undet.)[6]			Not reporting	Not reporting	Not reporting	Not reporting
Andrew Johnson National Historic Site	TN	281	16.7	16.7	100.00	82.1	0.0	2.4	0.0
Appalachian National Scenic Trail	TN[4]	141	161,381.6	100,333.7	62.17	Not reporting	Not reporting	Not reporting	Not reporting
Fort Donelson National Battlefield[2]	TN	283	536.4	524.6	97.80	206.5	556.4	11.8	1.5
Obed Wild and Scenic River[2]	TN	285	5,074.9	3,109.0	61.26	86.4	0.0	32.9	0.0
Shiloh National Military Park	TN	286	3,837.5	3,782.5	98.57	401.0	279.7	65.3	4.7
Stones River National Battlefield	TN	287	402.9	350.2	86.92	222.6	0.9	14.9	0.0
Natchez Trace National Scenic Trail	TN, AL, MS	177	10,995.0			Not reporting	Not reporting	Not reporting	Not reporting
Natchez Trace Parkway[2]	TN, AL, MS	178	51,742.1	51,651.1	99.82	5,832.7	6,986.3	1,958.4	582.2
Chickamauga and Chattanooga National Military Park	TN, GA	107	8,106.0	8,089.3	99.79	1,002.3	7,306.3	148.4	91.3
Big South Fork National River and Recreation Area	TN, KY	282	122,960.0	16,860.0	13.71	860.0	0.0	468.6	0.0
Cumberland Gap National Historical Park	TN, KY, VA	136	20,274.4	20,270.6	99.98	951.7	259.6	154.9	14.6
Great Smoky Mountains National Park	TN, NC	284	520,269.4	520,003.8	99.95	8,654.5	9,267.0	5,539.5	386.1
Alibates Flint Quarries National Monument	TX	288	1,371.0	1,079.2	78.72	3.8	0.0	0.8	0.0
Amistad National Recreation Area	TX	289	57,292.4	57,292.4	100.00	1,215.7	1.1	761.9	0.1
Big Bend National Park	TX	290	801,163.0	764,608.1	95.44	296.5	2.4	745.5	0.6
Big Thicket National Preserve	TX	291	85,736.4	83,270.3	97.12	64.1	0.0	19.0	0.0
Chamizal National Memorial	TX	292	54.9	54.9	100.00	220.3	6.1	54.3	1.8
Fort Davis National Historic Site	TX	293	460.0	460.0	100.00	66.7	0.3	9.2	0.0
Guadalupe Mountains National Park	TX	294	86,415.9	76,293.0	88.29	200.4	0.0	54.1	0.0
Lake Meredith National Recreation Area	TX	295	44,977.6	44,977.6	100.00	1,280.0	0.0	414.5	0.0
Lyndon B. Johnson National Historical Park	TX	296	1,571.9	550.1	35.00	194.2	10.8	45.5	3.6
Padre Island National Seashore[2]	TX	297	130,434.3	130,355.5	99.94	972.1	1.7	541.1	1.1
Palo Alto Battlefield National Historic Site	TX	298	50.0	0.0	0.00	Not reporting	Not reporting	Not reporting	Not reporting
Rio Grande Wild and Scenic River	TX	299	9,600.0	0.0	0.00	0.6	0.0	9.4	0.0
San Antonio Missions National Historical Park	TX	300	492.7	250.2	50.78	290.5	0.0	22.3	0.0
Arches National Park	UT	301	73,379.0	66,343.5	90.41	705.9	395.9	292.3	0.0
Bryce Canyon National Park	UT	302	35,835.1	35,832.6	99.99	929.1	3.4	571.5	9.9
Canyonlands National Park	UT	303	337,570.4	337,570.4	100.00	339.3	50.8	309.0	3.1
Capitol Reef National Park	UT	304	241,904.3	222,753.4	92.08	618.1	13.1	86.4	0.7
Cedar Breaks National Monument	UT	305	6,154.6	6,154.6	100.00	456.0		76.0	2.2

Unit	State	Fig. 3.5 Map No.	Gross Area	NPS Lands	% Park Land	1991 Recreation Visits (thousands)	1991 Non-Recreation Visits (thousands)	1991 Recreation Visitor Days (thousands)	1991 Non-Recreation Visitor Days (thousands)
Golden Spike National Historic Site	UT	307	2,735.3	2,203.2	80.55	57.2	206.5	11.2	8.6
Natural Bridges National Monument	UT	308	7,636.5	7,636.5	100.00	124.6	0.8	50.9	0.3
Rainbow Bridge National Monument	UT	309	160.0	160.0	100.00	258.3	0.0	32.3	0.0
Timpanogos Cave National Monument	UT	310	250.0	250.0	100.00	104.7	0.0	20.1	0.0
Zion National Park	UT	311	146,597.6	143,040.4	97.57	2,237.0	266.1	868.7	22.2
Glen Canyon National Recreation Area	UT, AZ	306	1,236,880.0	1,193,671.0	96.51	3,181.1	29.7	5,706.4	29.0
Dinosaur National Monument	UT, CO	71	210,844.0	204,160.3	96.83	447.8	20.6	168.9	5.2
Hovenweep National Monument	UT, CO	74	784.9	784.9	100.00	26.9	0.2	10.1	0.0
Appalachian National Scenic Trail	VA[4]	141	161,381,6	100,333.7	62.17	Not reporting			
Appomattox Court House National Historical Park	VA	312	1,325.1	1,322.8	99.83	321.7	0.0	21.7	0.0
Arlington House, The Robert E. Lee Memorial	VA	313	27.9	27.9	100.00	483.4	0.0	20.1	0.0
Booker T. Washington National Monument	VA	314	223.9	223.9	100.00	20.9	0.1	2.6	0.0
Colonial National Historical Park	VA	315	9,327.4	9,253.9	99.21	2,197.9	6,432.4	126.7	268.0
Fredericksburg and Spotsylvania County Battlefields Memorial National Monument	VA	316	7,687.6	5,976.0	77.74	471.3	1,390.1	48.3	12.8
George Washington Birthplace National Monument	VA	317	538.2	538.2	100.00	152.3	3.7	25.4	0.3
Maggie L. Walker National Historic Site	VA	319	1.3	0.4	30.77	5.2	0.1	0.2	0.0
Manassas National Battlefield Park	VA	320	5,071.6	4,356.2	85.89	905.5	0.5	56.6	0.0
Petersburg National Battlefield	VA	321	2,735.4	1,529.4	55.91	293.9	165.2	26.1	3.4
Prince William Forest Park	VA	322	18,571.6	17,410.3	93.75	290.7	0.5	217.3	0.1
Richmond National Battlefield Park	VA	323	769.2	769.2	100.00	475.8	77.1	27.7	1.0
Shenandoah National Park	VA	324	196,039.1	195,403.7	99.68	1,939.5	44.7	1,319.9	0.9
Wolf Trap Farm Park for the Performing Arts	VA	325	130.3	130.3	100.00	597.5	1.6	170.3	0.0
Potomac Heritage National Scenic Trail	VA, DC, MD, PA	154	(undet.)[6]			Not reporting			
Cumberland Gap National Historical Park	VA, KY, TN	136	20,274.4	20,270.6	99.98	951.7	259.6	154.9	14.6
Assateague Island National Seashore	VA, MD	144	36,630.8	17,774.9	48.52	2,087.5	3.6	1,539.6	0.3
George Washington Memorial Parkway	VA, MD	318	7,159.5	7,088.6	99.01	5,004.7	0.0	598.1	0.0
Harpers Ferry National Historical Park	VA, MD, WV	340	2,260.7	2,133.5	94.37	489.9	0.0	163.3	0.0
Blue Ridge Parkway	VA, NC	233	85,954.8	78,831.8	91.72	16,414.3	1,942.3	8,677.7	80.9
Buck Island Reef National Monument	VI	326	880.0	880.0	100.00	51.5	0.0	22.8	0.0
Christiansted National Historic Site	VI	327	27.2	26.2	96.32	110.6	0.0	5.2	0.0
Virgin Islands National Park	VI	328	14,688.9	12,909.6	87.89	710.2	286.1	367.3	37.8
Appalachian National Scenic Trail	VT[4]	141	161,381,6	100,333.7	62.17	Not reporting			
Coulee Dam National Recreation Area	WA	329	100,390.3	100,390.3	100.00	1,771.4	18.0	587.6	0.8
Fort Vancouver National Historic Park	WA	330	208.9	201.7	96.55	245.4	27.6	30.0	0.1
Lake Chelan National Recreation Area[2,7]	WA	331	61,882.8	59,293.9	95.82	58.1	0.0	47.6	0.0
Mount Rainier National Park	WA	332	235,612.5	235,612.5	100.00	1,549.4	686.2	1,875.5	57.2

North Cascades National Park[2,7]	WA	333	504,780.9	504,554.8	99.96	22.8	0.0	30.1	0.0
Olympic National Park	WA	334	922,654.0	912,870.0	98.94	2,759.7	608.5	1,217.4	17.0
Ross Lake National Recreation Area[2,7]	WA	335	117,574.6	115,857.4	98.54	298.9	0.7	157.9	0.1
San Juan Island National Historical Park	WA	336	1,752.0	1,725.5	98.49	359.2	0.0	23.5	0.0
Whitman Mission National Historic Site	WA	337	98.2	98.2	100.00	83.9	0.9	7.0	0.0
Klondike Gold Rush National Historical Park[1]	WA, AK	13	13,191.4	2,721.3	20.63	218.8	1.1	20.5	0.2
Apostle Islands National Lakeshore	WI	342	69,371.9	42,124.2	60.72	141.0	0.8	62.6	0.0
Lower Saint Croix National Scenic Riverway	WI, MN	343	25,278.9	8,143.4	32.21		Not reporting		
Saint Croix National Scenic Riverway	WI, MN	344	67,379.3	27,144.5	40.29	468.8	0.0	583.6	0.0
Appalachian National Scenic Trail	WV[4]	141	161,381.6	100,333.7	62.17		Not reporting		
Bluestone National Scenic River	WV	338	4,268.0	3,032.0	71.04		Not reporting		
Gauley River National Recreation Area	WV	339	10,300.0	0.0	0.00		Not reporting		
New River Gorge National River[2]	WV	341	62,143.7	34,103.2	54.88	772.2	1.5	77.4	0.2
Chesapeake and Ohio Canal National Historical Park	WV, DC, MD	146	19,236.6	14,068.9	73.14	1,945.2	15.0	451.4	1.2
Harpers Ferry National Historical Park	WV, MD, VA	340	2,260.7	2,133.5	94.37	489.9	0.0	163.3	0.0
Devils Tower National Monument	WY	345	1,346.9	1,346.9	100.00	456.7	2.8	91.3	0.1
Fort Laramie National Historic Site	WY	346	832.9	831.1	99.78	66.1	0.4	8.3	0.0
Fossil Butte National Monument	WY	347	8,198.0	8,198.0	100.00	22.7	0.6	2.9	0.0
Grand Teton National Park	WY	348	309,993.1	307,616.6	99.23	1,625.8	1,236.4	1,366.3	106.4
John D. Rockefeller, Jr., Memorial Parkway	WY	349	23,777.2	23,777.2	100.00	1,576.8	16.3	226.1	0.3
Yellowstone National Park	WY, ID, MT	350	2,219,790.7	2,219,772.7	100.00	2,920.5	37.3	8,435.4	12.4
Bighorn Canyon National Recreation Area	WY, MT	188	120,296.2	68,484.6	56.93	481.1	30.8	247.3	2.6

[1] The following parks are combined as Klondike Gold Rush National Historical Park; breakdown is available; Klondike Gold Rush National Historical Park—Alaska and Klondike Gold Rush—Washington.

[2] Due to changes in 1991 counting procedures in one or more types of data reported, the figures for this unit require special adjustments to be comparable with earlier data.

[3] Reporting data suspended pending completion of studies to verify validity of data for this unit.

[4] NOTE: Appalachian Trail runs through the following states: CT,GA, MA, MD, ME, NH, NJ, NY, NC, PA, TN, VT, VA, WV.

[5] The following parks are combined as National Capital Parks; breakdown is available: Constitution Gardens, National Capital Parks—East, National Capital Parks—Central, and President's Park.

[6] (undet.) = undetermined.

[7] This unit is either reporting for the first time or reporting separately in 1991.

[8] Redesignated in 1991 to Bighorn Battlefield National Monument.

Note: Due to the opening of additional areas, programs, or facilities, the following areas may require special adjustments to be comparable with earlier data: none in 1991; due to partial or temporary closing, the figures for the following areas may require special adjustments to be comparable with earlier data: none in 1991; due to unusual events (anniversaries, civic fairs, significant natural disasters, storm damage,e tc.), the following may require special adjustments to be comparable with earlier data: none in 1991. New areas named but not reporting: Mary McLeod Bethune Council House National Historic Site, Niobrara Wild and Scenic River.
Source: National Park Service, 1991 Statistical Abstract.
National Park Service, The National Parks: Index 1991.

Overnight Stays in National Park Service Areas by Type of Accommodation—1991

	Concession		NPS Campground		NPS Back Country	NPS Group & Misc.	Total Rec. Overnight Stays	Non-Rec. Overnight Stays
	Lodging	Camping	Tents	RVs				
Acadia National Park[1]	0	0	140,760	30,222	0	9,581	180,563	0
Amistad National Recreation Area	0	0	3,981	11,586	3,541	3,255	22,363	0
Aniakchak National Monument and Preserve	0	0	0	0	913	0	913	0
Antietam National Battlefield	0	0	0	0	0	3,362	3,362	0
Apostle Islands National Lakeshore	0	0	0	0	8,669	17,692	26,361	0
Arches National Park	0	0	29,698	17,871	2,850	7,835	58,254	0
Arkansas Post National Memorial	0	0	0	0	197	197	197	0
Assateague Island National Seashore	0	0	24,565	22,358	2,444	9,646	59,013	0
Badlands National Park	8,112	0	5,602	4,576	220	0	18,510	0
Bandelier National Monument	0	11,808	10,952	7,861	3,746	0	22,559	0
Big Bend National Park	49,206	0	63,362	36,662	40,476	22,993	224,507	0
Big Cypress National Preserve	0	0	2,897	15,714	477	4,790	23,878	0
Big Hole National Battlefield	0	0	0	0	0	0	0	109
Big South Fork National River and Recreation Area	1,847	0	11,416	15,808	0	2,867	31,938	0
Big Thicket National Preserve	0	0	0	0	1,565	0	1,565	0
Bighorn Canyon National Recreation Area	0	0	4,350	10,121	946	1,125	16,542	0
Biscayne National Park[1]	0	0	1,092	0	0	8,115	9,207	0
Black Canyon of the Gunnison National Monument	0	0	10,069	9,929	693	0	20,691	0
Blue Ridge Parkway	62,086	32,015	62,436	72,619	4,809	1,294	235,259	0
Bryce Canyon National Park	45,471	0	54,404	43,384	3,452	2,697	149,408	0
Buck Island Reef National Monument	0	0	0	0	1,796	1,796	1,796	0
Buffalo National River	7,703	0	53,525	22,490	20,595	23,084	127,397	0
Canaveral National Seashore	0	0	0	0	965	0	965	0
Canyon de Chelly National Monument	41,992	0	28,515	31,644	1,489	2,845	106,485	0
Canyonlands National Park	0	0	12,035	4,405	67,469	7,609	91,518	951
Cape Cod National Seashore	4,230	0	0	0	0	25,922	30,152	0
Cape Hatteras National Seashore	0	0	91,902	51,556	0	11,732	155,190	9,553
Cape Krusenstern National Monument	0	0	0	0	142	0	142	161
Cape Lookout National Seashore[1]	21,298	0	0	0	9,538	0	30,836	0
Capitol Reef National Park	0	0	16,965	24,986	2,165	2,553	46,669	0
Carlsbad Caverns National Park	0	0	0	0	161	0	161	0
Catoctin Mountain Park	0	0	8,441	1,852	97	36,087	46,477	0
Cedar Breaks National Monument	0	0	1,655	1,541	0	0	3,196	0
Chaco Culture National Historical Park	0	0	23,495	4,908	0	4,149	32,552	0
Channel Islands National Park	0	0	0	0	1,437	30,324	31,761	22,981
Chesapeake and Ohio Canal National Historical Park	0	0	11,334	2,068	27,924	0	41,326	0
Chickamauga and Chattanooga National Military Park	0	0	0	0	0	1,584	1,584	0
Chickasaw National Recreation Area	0	0	35,816	17,290	0	25,688	78,794	0
Chiricahua National Monument	0	0	7,214	7,433	0	672	15,319	0

	Concession		NPS Campground		NPS Back Country	NPS Group & Misc.	Total Rec. Overnight Stays	Non-Rec. Overnight Stays
	Lodging	Camping	Tents	RVs				
Colorado National Monument	0	0	8,353	10,516	88	0	18,957	150
Congaree Swamp National Monument	0	0	0	0	167	382	549	0
Coulee Dam National Recreation Area	0	0	58,908	90,568	0	0	149,476	0
Cowpens National Battlefield	0	0	0	0	0	69	69	0
Crater Lake National Park	10,711	39,899	963	0	1,775	0	53,348	0
Craters of the Moon National Monument	0	0	6,917	9,024	75	567	16,583	0
Cumberland Gap National Historical Park	0	0	2,840	3,508	1,634	1,236	9,218	0
Cumberland Island National Seashore	0	0	16,081	0	7,811	0	23,892	0
Curecanti National Recreation Area	0	0	15,196	87,716	720	848	104,480	0
Cuyahoga Valley National Recreation Area	1,352	0	0	0	0	2,582	3,934	0
Death Valley National Monument	28,008	5,495	67,361	184,757	0	2,983	288,604	0
Delaware Water Gap National Recreation Area[1]	0	6,257	0	0	53,253	18,353	77,863	0
Denali National Park and Preserve	24,311	0	26,824	35,715	29,798	2,683	119,331	0
Devils Postpile National Monument	0	0	4,350	1,874	0	0	6,224	0
Devils Tower National Monument	0	0	6,807	8,861	0	0	15,668	0
Dinosaur National Monument	0	0	25,467	16,607	24,646	2,378	69,098	0
El Malpais National Monument	0	0	0	0	275	0	275	0
El Morro National Monument	0	0	2,354	1,667	0	358	4,379	0
Everglades National Park[1]	46,268	0	16,330	34,652	12,813	2,783	112,846	0
Fire Island National Seashore	0	0	7,825	0	0	53,573	61,398	0
Fort Donelson National Battlefield[1]	0	0	0	0	0	184	184	0
Fort Jefferson National Monument	0	0	2,238	0	0	24,104	26,342	19,975
Fort Necessity National Battlefield	0	0	0	0	0	159	159	0
Fort Point National Historic Site	0	0	0	0	0	1,150	1,150	0
Fort Pulaski National Monument	0	0	0	0	465	104	569	0
Fort Stanwix National Monument	0	0	0	0	0	0	0	0
Gates of the Arctic National Park and Preserve	0	0	0	0	5,841	0	5,841	97
Gateway National Recreation Area	0	0	0	0	0	3,769	3,769	1,167
Gettysburg National Military Park	0	0	0	0	0	25,413	25,413	0
Glacier Bay National Park and Preserve	10,977	0	1,250	0	9,657	14,431	36,315	14,004
Glacier National Park	105,823	0	111,380	121,967	22,909	0	362,079	0
Glen Canyon National Recreation Area	185,027	88,244	102,231	81,068	16,902	1,706,150	2,179,622	9,551
Golden Gate National Recreation Area[2]	68,459	0	2,328	0	619	44,486	115,892	10,416
Grand Canyon National Park[1]	629,133	43,729	142,087	107,841	225,781	37,667	1,186,238	0
Grand Portage National Monument	0	0	0	0	116	0	116	0
Grand Teton National Park	205,409	53,726	126,501	108,226	27,114	25,540	546,516	0
Great Basin National Park	0	0	18,688	15,710	292	0	34,690	0
Great Sand Dunes National Monument	0	0	22,570	15,698	505	4,952	43,725	0
Great Smoky Mountains National Park	10,499	0	190,879	170,014	77,207	31,153	479,752	0

Park							
Greenbelt Park	0	0	13,309	11,025	0	0	24,334	0
Guadalupe Mountains National Park	0	0	10,854	6,426	3,069	0	20,349	0
Guilford Courthouse National Military Park	0	0	0	0	0	2,566	0	51
Gulf Islands National Seashore	0	0	39,881	116,269	8,172	3,978	166,888	21,763
Haleakala National Park	0	0	16,570	30	3,384	66,073	23,962	0
Hawaii Volcanoes National Park	30,806	0	9,221	328	4,596	0	111,024	0
Hot Springs National Park	0	0	3,338	6,904	0	0	10,242	0
Hoverweep National Monument	0	0	2,880	1,507	0	3,239	4,387	876
Isle Royale National Park	5,850	1,852	6,902	0	38,148	876	55,991	0
John D. Rockerfeller, Jr., Memorial Parkway	27,310	26,050	4,083	0	452	951	58,771	0
John Day Fossil Beds National Monument	0	0	0	0	951	0	951	0
Joshua Tree National Monument	0	0	138,444	50,355	6,196	56,578	251,573	0
Katmai National Park and Preserve	3,678	0	3,564	0	5,327	0	12,569	56
Kenai Fjords National Park	0	0	712	222	1,098	34	2,066	196
Kennesaw Mountain National Battlefield Park[1]	0	0	0	0	0	96	96	0
Kings Canyon National Park	30,806	0	116,295	62,776	65,050	0	274,927	0
Kings Mountain National Military Park	0	0	0	0	56	0	56	0
Klondike Gold Rush National Historic Park[3]	0	0	1,669	997	3,095	0	5,761	0
Knife River Indian Villages National Historic Site	0	0	0	0	0	0	0	14
Kobuk Valley National Park	0	0	0	0	243	0	243	518
Lake Chelan National Recreation Area[1,4]	7,604	0	0	0	5,776	38	13,418	0
Lake Clark National Park and Preserve	0	0	0	0	859	0	859	22
Lake Mead National Recreation Area	79,468	239,052	112,447	348,070	504,972	166,429	1,450,438	285,430
Lake Meredith National Recreation Area	0	0	0	0	13,478	155,665	169,143	0
Lassen Volcanic National Park[1]	5,402	0	76,683	37,488	8,440	950	128,963	0
Lava Beds National Monument	0	0	3,867	2,301	254	11	6,433	128
Mammoth Cave National Park	30,159	0	39,171	29,119	3,331	5,261	107,041	0
Mesa Verde National Park	55,536	0	80,923	24,522	0	6,686	167,667	0
Moores Creek National Battlefield	0	0	0	0	132	0	132	0
Mount Rainier National Park	42,862	0	72,678	50,637	35,383	10,623	212,183	0
Natchez Trace Parkway[1]	0	0	5,808	9,666	0	0	15,474	0
Natural Bridges National Monument	0	0	1,880	1,361	0	0	3,241	0
Navajo National Monument	0	0	5,524	4,163	449	2,567	12,703	0
New River Gorge National River[1]	0	0	709	538	0	0	1,247	0
Noatak National Preserve	0	0	0	0	3,033	0	3,033	0
North Cascades National Park[1,4]	0	0	0	0	16,514	0	16,514	384
Obed Wild and Scenic River[1]	0	0	0	0	0	6,892	6,892	0
Olympic National Park	80,510	14,968	118,191	96,843	77,801	1,573	389,886	0
Oregon Caves National Monument	3,738	0	0	0	0	0	3,738	0
Organ Pipe Cactus National Monument	0	0	8,621	44,846	4,072	3,888	61,427	0
Ozark National Scenic Riverways[1]	4,082	0	106,204	25,744	22,534	46,912	205,476	0
Padre Island National Seashore[1]	0	0	25,263	41,496	19,773	5,504	92,036	0
Perry's Victory and International Peace Memorial	0	0	0	0	0	920	920	0
Petrified Forest National Park	0	0	0	0	924	0	924	503
Pictured Rocks National Lakeshore	0	0	13,689	4,127	11,218	0	29,034	0

	Concession		NPS Campground		NPS Back Country	NPS Group & Misc.	Total Rec. Overnight Stays	Non-Rec. Overnight Stays
	Lodging	Camping	Tents	RVs				
Pinnacles National Monument	0	0	4,117	606	0	0	4,723	0
Point Reyes National Seashore	9,023	0	0	0	22,049	0	31,072	0
Prince William Forest Park	0	21,431	14,860	1,603	222	38,778	76,894	0
Pu'uhonua o Honaunau National Historical Park	0	0	0	0	0	1,159	1,159	0
Redwood National Park	5,653	0	2,261	49,304	878	8,752	66,848	0
Rio Grande Wild and Scenic River	0	0	0	0	5,182	0	5,182	0
Rocky Mountain National Park	0	0	92,110	72,217	39,172	11,892	215,391	0
Ross Lake National Recreation Area[1,4]	13,982	0	23,699	21,040	7,156	619	66,496	0
Saguaro National Monument	0	0	0	0	1,516	0	1,516	0
Saint Croix National Scenic Riverway	0	0	0	0	33,312	0	33,312	0
Salinas Pueblo Missions National Monument	0	0	0	0	0	74	74	0
San Francisco Maritime National Historical Park	0	0	0	0	0	5,545	5,545	0
Santa Monica Mountains National Recreation Area[1]	0	0	4,447	83	75	417	5,022	0
Sequoia National Park	126,789	0	134,270	60,445	70,291	0	391,795	0
Shenandoah National Park	133,925	0	102,086	63,057	39,130	3,413	341,611	0
Shiloh National Military Park	0	0	0	0	0	2,481	2,481	0
Sleeping Bear Dunes National Lakeshore	0	33,217	21,981	7,992	23,062	0	86,252	0
Theodore Roosevelt National Park	0	0	9,268	15,506	682	1,732	27,188	0
Vicksburg National Military Park[1]	0	0	0	0	0	254	254	0
Virgin Islands National Park	17,099	18,254	0	0	0	131,119	166,472	20,163
Voyageurs National Park	0	0	9,101	0	7,034	25,939	42,074	0
Whiskeytown-Shasta-Trinity National Recreation Area[1]	0	25,908	0	4,503	6,021	20,272	56,704	0
White Sands National Monument	0	0	0	0	1,184	0	1,184	0
Wind Cave National Park	0	0	8,148	3,507	165	0	11,820	0
Wrangell–St. Elias National Park and Preserve	0	0	0	0	1,681	0	1,681	0
Wupatki National Monument	0	0	0	0	170	0	170	0
Yellowstone National Park	638,242	112,397	257,824	312,592	41,476	13,918	1,376,449	0
Yosemite National Park	1,028,088	0	647,698	355,184	121,913	0	2,152,883	0
Yukon-Charley Rivers National Preserve	0	0	0	0	1,793	0	1,793	234
Zion National Park	64,251	0	130,285	101,314	13,140	15,828	324,818	0
Total	4,012,785	774,302	4,204,744	3,621,586	2,032,379	3,108,053	17,753,849	419,453

[1]Due to changes in 1991 counting procedures in one or more types of data reported, the figures for this unit require special adjustments to be comparable with earlier data.

[2]Reporting data suspended pending completion of studies to verify validity of data for this unit.

[3]The following parks are combined as Klondike Gold Rush National Historical Park—Alaska and Klondike Gold Rush—Washington.

[4]This unit is either reporting for the first time or reporting separately in 1991.

[5]The following parks are combined as National Capital Parks; breakdown is available: Constitution Gardens, National Capital Parks—East, National Capital Parks—Central, and President's Park.

Note: Due to the opening of additional areas, programs, or facilities, the following areas may require special adjustments to be comparable with earlier data: none in 1991; due to partial or temporary closing, the figures for the following areas may require special adjustments to be comparable with earlier data: none in 1991; due to unusual events (anniversaries, civic fairs, significant natural disasters, storm damage, e tc.), the following may require special adjustments to be comparable with earlier data: none in 1991. New areas named but not reporting: Mary McLeod Bethune Council House National Historic Site, Niobrara Wild and Scenic River.

Source: National Park Service, Socio-Economic Studies Division, *1991 Statistical Abstract*, Denver, Colorado.

National Park Facilities

State/Park	Fig 3.5 Map No.	Entrance Fee	Visitor Center	Museum/Exhibit	Picnic Area	Campground	Hiking	Mountain Climbing	Horseback Riding	Swimming	Bathhouse	Boating	Boat Rental	Fishing	Hunting	Bicycle Trail	Snowmobile Route	Cross-Country Ski Trail	Cabin Rental	Hotel/Motel/Lodge
Alabama																				
Horseshoe Bend Natl. Military Park	1		X	X	X		X					X		X						
Russell Cave Natl. Monument	2		X	X	X		X		X											
Tuskegee Institute Natl. Historic Site	3		X	X																
Alaska																				
Aniakchak Natl. Monument and Preserve	5						X					X		X	X					
Bering Land Bridge Natl. Preserve	6						X							X	X		X			
Cape Krunsenstern Natl. Monument	7		X				X	X				X		X			X			X
Denali Natl. Park & Preserve*	8	X	X			X	X	X						X						X
Gates of the Arctic Natl. Park and Preserve*	9						X	X				X		X	X					
Glacier Bay Natl. Park and Preserve*	10					X	X	X				X		X	X					X
Katmai Natl. Park and Preserve	11		X		X	X	X	X				X	X	X	X					X
Kenai Fjords Natl. Park	12		X		X		X	X				X		X			X	X		
Klondike Gold Rush Natl. Historical Park	13		X	X	X	X	X					X		X						·X
Kobuk Valley Natl. Park	14		X				X	X				X		X			X			X
Lake Clark Natl. Park and Preserve	15						X	X				X		X	X		X	X	X	X
Noatak Natl. Preserve*	16		X				X	X				X		X	X		X			X
Sitka Natl. Historical Park	17		X	X	X		X							X						
Wrangell–St. Elias Natl. Park and Preserve	18		X				X	X	X			X	X	X	X		X			X
Yukon-Charley Rivers Natl. Preserve	19		X				X	X				X		X	X					
Arizona																				
Canyon de Chelly Natl. Monument	21		X	X	X	X	X		X											X
Casa Grande Natl. Monument	22	X	X	X	X															
Chiricahua Natl. Monument	23	X	X	X	X	X	X													
Coronado Natl. Memorial	24		X	X	X		X													
Fort Bowie Natl. Historic Site	25		X				X													
Grand Canyon Natl. Park†	26	X	X	X	X	X	X		X					X					X	X
Hubbell Trading Post Natl. Historic Site	28		X	X	X															
Montezuma Castle Natl. Monument	29	X	X	X	X															
Navajo Natl. Monument	30		X	X	X	X			X											
Organ Pipe Cactus Natl. Monument*	31	X	X	X	X	X	X													
Petrified Forest Natl. Park	32	X	X	X	X		X													
Pipe Spring Natl. Monument	33	X	X	X																
Saguaro Natl. Monument	34	X	X	X	X		X													
Sunset Crater Natl. Monument	35	X	X	X	X	X	X													
Tonto Natl. Monument	36	X	X	X	X															
Tumacacori Natl. Monument	37	X	X	X	X															

State/Park	Fig 3.5 Map No.	Entrance Fee	Visitor Center	Museum/Exhibit	Picnic Area	Campground	Hiking	Mountain Climbing	Horseback Riding	Swimming	Bathhouse	Boating	Boat Rental	Fishing	Hunting	Bicycle Trail	Snowmobile Route	Cross-Country Ski Trail	Cabin Rental	Hotel/Motel/Lodge
Tuzigoot Natl. Monument	38	X	X	X																
Walnut Canyon Natl. Monument	39	X	X	X	X															
Wupatki Natl. Monument	40	X	X	X	X		X													
Arkansas																				
Arkansas Post Natl. Memorial	41		X	X	X		X							X		X				
Buffalo Natl. River	42		X	X	X	X	X		X	X			X	X	X	X				X	
Fort Smith Natl. Historic Site	43	X	X	X	X															
Hot Springs Natl. Park	44		X	X	X	X	X		X		X									
Pea Ridge Natl. Military Park	45	X	X	X	X		X													
California																				
Cabrillo Natl. Monument	46	X	X	X			X							X						
Channel Islands Natl. Park*	47		X	X	X	X	X		X			X		X						
Death Valley Natl. Monument*	48	X	X	X	X	X	X		X	X	X					X			X	X
Devils Postpile Natl. Monument	49		X		X	X	X		X	X				X						
Fort Point Natl. Historic Site	51		X	X	X									X						
Golden Gate Natl. Recreation Area	52		X	X	X	X	X		X	X	X			X		X				
John Muir Natl. Historic Site	53	X	X	X	X															
Joshua Tree Natl. Monument*	54	X	X	X	X	X	X	X	X											
Kings Canyon Natl. Park*	55	X	X	X	X	X	X	X	X					X				X	X	X
Lassen Volcanic Natl. Park	56	X	X		X	X	X	X	X	X		X		X				X	X	
Lava Beds Natl. Monument	57	X	X	X	X	X	X													
Muir Woods Natl. Monument	58		X	X			X													
Pinnacles Natl. Monument	59	X	X	X	X	X	X	X												
Point Reyes Natl. Seashore	60		X	X	X	X	X		X	X				X		X				
Redwood Natl. Park*†	61		X	X	X	X	X		X	X				X						
Santa Monica Mountains Natl. Rec. Area	63		X	X	X	X	X		X	X		X		X		X				
Sequoia Natl. Park*	64	X	X	X	X	X	X	X	X					X				X	X	X
Whiskeytown-Shasta-Trinity Natl. Rec. Area	65		X		X	X	X		X	X	X	X	X	X	X					
Yosemite Natl. Park†	66	X	X	X	X	X	X	X	X	X		X	X	X		X		X	X	X
Colorado																				
Bent's Old Fort Natl. Historic Site	67	X		X	X															
Black Canyon of the Gunnison Natl. Monument	68	X	X	X	X	X	X	X						X				X		
Colorado Natl. Monument	69	X	X	X	X	X	X	X	X							X		X		
Curecanti Natl. Recreation Area	70		X	X	X	X	X		X			X	X	X	X			X	X	
Dinosaur Natl. Monument	71	X	X	X	X	X	X					X		X						
Florissant Fossil Beds Natl. Monument	72	X	X	X	X		X											X		
Great Sand Dunes Natl. Monument	73	X	X	X	X	X	X							X						
Hovenweep Natl. Monument	74		X	X	X	X	X													
Mesa Verde Natl. Park†	75	X	X	X	X	X														X
Rocky Mountain Natl. Park*	76	X	X	X	X	X	X	X	X					X				X	X	
District of Columbia																				
Constitution Gardens	79				X															
Ford's Theatre Natl. Historic Site	80		X	X																
Frederick Douglass Natl. Historic Site	81		X	X	X											X				
John F. Kennedy Center for the Performing Arts	82		X																	

State/Park	Fig 3.5 Map No.	Entrance Fee	Visitor Center	Museum/Exhibit	Picnic Area	Campground	Hiking	Mountain Climbing	Horseback Riding	Swimming	Bathhouse	Boating	Boat Rental	Fishing	Hunting	Bicycle Trail	Snowmobile Route	Cross-Country Ski Trail	Cabin Rental	Hotel/Motel/Lodge
Lincoln Memorial	83																			
L.B.J. Memorial Grove on the Potomac	84				X							X		X						
Rock Creek Park	88		X	X	X		X		X					X		X				
Theodore Roosevelt Island	89						X							X						
Thomas Jefferson Memorial and Tidal Basin	90		X	X																
Vietnam Veterans Memorial	91																			
Washington Monument	92			X												X				
White House	93			X																
Florida																				
Big Cypress Natl. Preserve	94		X	X	X	X	X							X	X					
Biscayne Natl. Park	95		X	X	X	X	X			X		X		X						
Canaveral Natl. Seashore	96		X	X	X		X			X		X		X						
Castillo de San Marcos Natl. Monument	97	X		X																
De Soto Natl. Memorial	98	X	X	X										X						
Everglades Natl. Park*†	99	X	X	X	X	X	X					X	X	X		X			X	X
Fort Caroline Natl. Memorial	100		X	X	X		X													
Fort Jefferson Natl. Monument	101		X	X	X	X				X		X		X						
Fort Matanzas Natl. Monument	102		X	X						X				X						
Gulf Islands Natl. Seashore	103	X	X	X	X	X	X			X	X	X		X		X				
Georgia																				
Andersonville Natl. Historic Site	105	X	X	X	X															
Chattahoochee River Natl. Recreation Area	106			X		X						X	X	X						
Chickamauga and Chattanooga Natl. Military Park	107	X	X	X	X		X		X											
Cumberland Island Natl. Seashore*	108		X	X	X	X	X			X	X			X						
Fort Frederica Natl. Monument	109	X	X	X																
Fort Pulaski Natl. Monument	110	X	X	X	X		X					X		X						
Kennesaw Mountain Natl. Battlefield Park	112		X	X	X		X		X											
Martin Luther King, Jr., Natl. Historic Site	113		X	X																
Ocmulgee Natl. Monument	114	X	X	X	X		X							X						
Guam																				
War in the Pacific Natl. Historical Park	115		X	X	X		X			X	X		X	X						
Hawaii																				
Haleakala Natl. Park*	116	X	X	X	X	X	X		X							X			X	
Hawaii Volcanoes Natl. Park*	117	X	X	X	X	X	X	X											X	X
Kalaupapa Natl. Historical Park	118			X																
Pu'uhonua o Honaunau Natl. Historical Park	120	X	X	X	X		X			X	X			X						
Puukohola Heiau Natl. Historic Site	121		X																	
USS *Arizona* Memorial	122		X	X																
Idaho																				
Craters of the Moon Natl. Monument	124	X	X	X	X	X	X											X		
Nez Perce Natl. Historical Park	126		X	X	X									X						
Illinois																				
Lincoln Home Natl. Historic Site	127		X	X	X															

State/Park	Fig 3.5 Map No.	Entrance Fee	Visitor Center	Museum/Exhibit	Picnic Area	Campground	Hiking	Mountain Climbing	Horseback Riding	Swimming	Bathhouse	Boating	Boat Rental	Fishing	Hunting	Bicycle Trail	Snowmobile Route	Cross-Country Ski Trail	Cabin Rental	Hotel/Motel/Lodge
Indiana																				
George Rogers Clark Natl. Historical Park	128	X	X	X																
Indiana Dunes Natl. Lakeshore	129		X	X	X		X		X	X	X	X		X		X		X		
Lincoln Boyhood Natl. Memorial	130	X	X	X			X													
Iowa																				
Effigy Mounds Natl. Monument	131	X	X	X			X											X		
Herbert Hoover Natl. Historic Site	132	X	X	X	X		X											X		
Kansas																				
Fort Larned Natl. Historic Site	133	X	X	X	X									X						
Fort Scott Natl. Historic Site	134	X	X	X	X															
Kentucky																				
Abraham Lincoln Birthplace Natl. Historic Site	135		X	X	X		X													
Cumberland Gap Natl. Historical Park	136		X	X	X	X	X													
Mammoth Cave Natl. Park†	137		X	X	X	X	X			X		X		X						X	X
Louisiana																				
Jean Lafitte Natl. Historic Park and Preserve	138		X	X	X		X					X		X	X	X					
Maine																				
Acadia Natl. Park	140	X	X	X	X	X	X	X	X	X		X	X	X		X	X	X		X
Saint Croix Island International Historic Site	142			X			X													
Maryland																				
Antietam Natl. Battlefield	143	X	X	X			X							X		X				
Assateague Island Natl. Seashore	144	X	X	X	X	X	X			X	X	X		X	X					
Catoctin Mountain Park	145		X	X	X	X	X	X						X				X	X	
Chesapeake and Ohio Canal Natl. Historical Park	146		X	X	X	X	X		X			X	X	X		X				
Clara Barton Natl. Historic Site	147		X	X												X				
Fort McHenry Natl. Monument and Historic Shrine	148	X	X	X	X															
Fort Washington Park	149	X	X	X	X		X							X		X				
Greenbelt Park	150			X	X	X														
Hampton Natl. Historic Site	151		X	X																
Piscataway Park	153				X		X							X						
Massachusetts																				
Adams Natl. Historic Site	156	X		X																
Boston Natl. Historical Park	158		X	X	X															
Cape Cod Natl. Seashore	159	X	X	X	X		X			X	X			X	X	X				X
Frederick Law Olmsted Natl. Historic Site	160			X																
John Fitzgerald Kennedy Natl. Historic Site	161	X	X	X																
Longfellow Natl. Historic Site	162	X	X	X																
Lowell Natl. Historical Park	163		X	X	X							X		X						X
Minute Man Natl. Historical Park	164	X	X	X																
Salem Maritime Natl. Historic Site	165		X	X	X		X					X		X		X				

State/Park	Fig 3.5 Map No.	Entrance Fee	Visitor Center	Museum/Exhibit	Picnic Area	Campground	Hiking	Mountain Climbing	Horseback Riding	Swimming	Bathhouse	Boating	Boat Rental	Fishing	Hunting	Bicycle Trail	Snowmobile Route	Cross-Country Ski Trail	Cabin Rental	Hotel/Motel/Lodge
Saugus Iron Works Natl. Historic Site	166		X	X	X															
Springfield Armory Natl. Historic Site	167			X																
Michigan																				
Isle Royale Natl. Park*	168		X		X	X	X			X		X	X	X					X	X
Pictured Rocks Natl. Lakeshore	169		X	X	X	X	X			X		X		X	X		X	X		
Sleeping Bear Dunes Natl. Lakeshore	170		X	X	X	X	X			X	X	X	X	X	X			X		
Minnesota																				
Grand Portage Natl. Monument	171	X	X	X	X		X							X				X		
Pipestone Natl. Monument	173	X	X	X	X															
Voyageurs Natl. Park	174		X	X	X	X	X			X		X	X	X			X	X	X	
Mississippi																				
Brices Cross Roads Natl. Battlefield Site	175			X																
Gulf Islands Natl. Seashore	103	X	X	X	X	X	X			X	X	X		X						
Natchez Trace Parkway	178		X	X	X	X	X		X	X		X		X						
Tupelo Natl. Battlefield	179			X																
Vicksburg Natl. Military Park	180	X	X	X	X															
Missouri																				
George Washington Carver Natl. Monument	181	X	X	X	X															
Harry S. Truman Natl. Historic Site	182	X	X	X																
Jefferson Natl. Expansion Memorial	183	X	X	X																
Ozark Natl. Scenic Riverways	184			X	X	X	X		X	X		X	X	X	X				X	
Wilson's Creek Natl. Battlefield	186	X	X	X	X		X		X					X		X				
Montana																				
Big Hole Natl. Battlefield	187	X	X	X	X									X						
Bighorn Canyon Natl. Recreation Area	188		X	X	X	X	X			X		X	X	X	X			X		
Custer Battlefield Natl. Monument	189	X	X	X																
Glacier Natl. Park*	190	X	X	X	X	X	X	X	X	X		X	X	X				X	X	X
Grant-Kohrs Ranch Natl. Historic Site	191	X	X	X																
Nebraska																				
Agate Fossil Beds Natl. Monument	192		X	X	X		X							X						
Homestead Natl. Monument of America	193		X	X	X		X												X	
Scotts Bluff Natl. Monument	195	X	X	X			X									X				
Nevada																				
Great Basin Natl. Park	196		X	X	X	X	X	X	X					X					X	
Lake Mead Natl. Recreation Area	197		X	X	X	X	X			X	X	X	X	X	X					X
New Hampshire																				
Saint-Gaudens Natl. Historic Site	198	X		X	X		X												X	
New Jersey																				
Edison Natl. Historic Site	199	X	X	X																
Morristown Natl. Historical Park	200	X	X	X			X												X	
New Mexico																				
Aztec Ruins Natl. Monument	201	X	X	X	X															
Bandelier Natl. Monument	202	X	X	X	X	X	X							X						
Capulin Volcano Natl. Monument	203	X	X	X	X		X													
Carlsbad Caverns Natl. Park	204		X	X	X		X													

State/Park	Fig 3.5 Map No.	Entrance Fee	Visitor Center	Museum/Exhibit	Picnic Area	Campground	Hiking	Mountain Climbing	Horseback Riding	Swimming	Bathhouse	Boating	Boat Rental	Fishing	Hunting	Bicycle Trail	Snowmobile Route	Cross-Country Ski Trail	Cabin Rental	Hotel/Motel/Lodge
Chaco Culture Natl. Historical Park	205	X	X	X	X	X	X									X				
El Malpais Natl. Monument	206		X				X													
El Morro Natl. Monument	207	X	X	X	X	X	X													
Fort Union Natl. Monument	208	X	X	X	X															
Gila Cliff Dwellings Natl. Monument	209		X	X										X						
Pecos Natl. Historical Park	210	X	X	X	X															
Salinas Pueblo Missions Natl. Monument	212	X	X	X	X															
White Sands Natl. Monument	213	X	X	X	X		X													
New York																				
Castle Clinton Natl. Monument	215		X	X																
Eleanor Roosevelt Natl. Historic Site	216			X																
Federal Hall Natl. Memorial	217		X																	
Fire Island Natl. Seashore	218		X	X	X	X	X			X	X	X		X	X					
Fort Stanwix Natl. Monument	219	X	X	X																
Gateway Natl. Recreation Area	220		X	X	X		X			X	X	X	X	X		X		X		
General Grant Natl. Memorial	221		X																	
Hamilton Grange Natl. Memorial	222		X	X																
Home of F.D.R. Natl. Historic Site	223	X	X	X	X															
Martin Van Buren Natl. Historic Site	224	X	X	X																
Sagamore Hill Natl. Historic Site	225	X	X	X																
Saint Paul's Church Natl. Historic Site	226		X	X																
Saratoga Natl. Historical Park	227	X	X	X	X		X									X		X		
Statue of Liberty Natl. Monument†	228		X	X																
Theodore Roosevelt Birthplace Natl. Historic Site	229	X		X																
Theodore Roosevelt Inaugural Natl. Historic Site	230		X	X																
Vanderbilt Mansion Natl. Historic Site	231	X	X	X	X															
Women's Rights Natl. Historical Park	232		X	X																
North Carolina																				
Blue Ridge Parkway	233		X	X	X	X	X		X			X	X	X			X	X	X	X
Cape Hatteras Natl. Seashore	234		X	X	X	X	X			X	X	X		X	X					
Cape Lookout Natl. Seashore*	235		X	X	X		X			X		X		X	X				X	
Carl Sandburg Home Natl. Historic Site	236	X	X	X			X													
Fort Raleigh Natl. Historic Site	237		X	X																
Guilford Courthouse Natl. Military Park	238		X	X												X				
Moores Creek Natl. Battlefield	239		X	X	X									X						
Wright Brothers Natl. Memorial	240	X	X	X																
North Dakota																				
Fort Union Trading Post Natl. Historic Site	241		X	X			X							X				X		
Knife River Indian Villages Natl. Historic Site	242		X	X	X		X							X				X		
Theodore Roosevelt Natl. Park	243	X	X	X	X	X	X		X			X		X				X		
Ohio																				
Cuyahoga Valley Natl. Recreation Area	244		X	X	X		X		X	X				X		X		X		X
James A. Garfield Natl. Historic Site	245		X	X	X															

State/Park	Fig 3.5 Map No.	Entrance Fee	Visitor Center	Museum/Exhibit	Picnic Area	Campground	Hiking	Mountain Climbing	Horseback Riding	Swimming	Bathhouse	Boating	Boat Rental	Fishing	Hunting	Bicycle Trail	Snowmobile Route	Cross-Country Ski Trail	Cabin Rental	Hotel/Motel/Lodge
Mound City Group Natl. Monument	246	X	X	X	X		X							X						
Perry's Victory and International Peace Memorial	247	X		X										X				X		
William Howard Taft Natl. Historic Site	248		X	X																
Oklahoma																				
Chickasaw Natl. Recreation Area	249		X	X	X	X	X			X		X		X	X					
Oregon																				
Crater Lake Natl. Park	250	X	X	X	X	X	X							X				X	X	X
Fort Clatsop Natl. Memorial	251	X	X	X	X															
John Day Fossil Beds Natl. Monument	252		X	X	X		X							X						
Oregon Caves Natl. Monument	253				X		X													X
Pennsylvania																				
Allegheny Portage Railroad Natl. Historic Site	254		X	X	X		X											X		
Delaware Water Gap Natl. Recreation Area	256		X	X	X	X	X	X	X	X		X	X	X	X		X	X		
Edgar Allan Poe Natl. Historic Site	257		X																	
Eisenhower Natl. Historic Site	258	X	X	X																
Fort Necessity Natl. Battlefield	259	X	X	X	X		X											X		
Friendship Hill Natl. Historic Site	260		X	X	X		X						X					X		
Gettysburg Natl. Military Park	261		X	X	X											X				
Hopewell Furnace Natl. Historic Site	262	X	X	X			X													
Independence Natl. Historical Park†	263		X	X																
Johnstown Flood Natl. Memorial	264		X	X	X		X													
Thaddeus Kosciuszko Natl. Memorial	266			X																
Upper Delaware Scenic and Recreational River	267		X	X		X			X	X		X	X	X	X				X	X
Valley Forge Natl. Historical Park	268	X	X	X	X		X		X			X		X		X		X		
Puerto Rico																				
San Juan Natl. Historic Site†	269		X	X																
Rhode Island																				
Roger Williams Natl. Memorial	270		X	X																
South Carolina																				
Congaree Swamp Natl. Monument*	272		X				X					X		X						
Cowpens Natl. Battlefield	273	X	X	X	X		X									X				
Fort Sumter Natl. Monument	274		X	X									X							
Kings Mountain Natl. Military Park	275		X	X			X		X											
Ninety Six Natl. Historic Site	276		X	X	X		X		X					X						
South Dakota																				
Badlands Natl. Park	277	X	X	X	X	X	X												X	
Jewel Cave Natl. Monument	278		X	X	X															
Mount Rushmore Natl. Memorial	279		X	X																
Wind Cave Natl. Park	280		X	X	X	X	X													
Tennessee																				
Andrew Johnson Natl. Historic Site	281	X	X	X																
Big South Fork Natl. River and Recreation Area	282		X	X	X	X	X		X			X		X	X					

State/Park	Fig 3.5 Map No.	Entrance Fee	Visitor Center	Museum/Exhibit	Picnic Area	Campground	Hiking	Mountain Climbing	Horseback Riding	Swimming	Bathhouse	Boating	Boat Rental	Fishing	Hunting	Bicycle Trail	Snowmobile Route	Cross-Country Ski Trail	Cabin Rental	Hotel/Motel/Lodge
Fort Donelson Natl. Battlefield	283	X	X	X	X		X													
Great Smoky Mountains Natl. Park*†	284		X	X	X	X	X		X					X		X			X	X
Obed Wild and Scenic River	285		X	X	X					X		X		X	X					
Shiloh Natl. Military Park	286	X	X	X	X											X				
Stones River Natl. Battlefield	287	X	X	X	X		X									X				
Texas																				
Alibates Flint Quarries Natl. Monument	288		X	X																
Amistad Natl. Recreation Area	289			X	X	X			X	X		X	X	X	X					
Big Bend Natl. Park*	290	X	X	X	X	X	X		X			X		X						X
Big Thicket Natl. Preserve*	291		X		X		X					X		X	X					
Chamizal Natl. Memorial	292		X	X	X															
Fort Davis Natl. Historic Site	293	X	X	X	X		X													
Guadalupe Mountains Natl. Park	294		X	X	X	X	X													
Lake Meredith Natl. Recreation Area	295			X	X	X				X		X		X	X					
Lyndon B. Johnson Natl. Historical Park	296		X	X																
Padre Island Natl. Seashore	297	X	X	X		X	X			X	X	X	X	X	X					
Palo Alto Battlefield Natl. Historic Site	298																			
San Antonio Missions Natl. Historical Park	300			X			X									X				
Utah																				
Arches Natl. Park	301	X	X	X	X	X	X													
Bryce Canyon Natl. Park	302	X	X	X	X	X	X		X									X	X	X
Canyonlands Natl. Park	303	X	X		X	X	X		X			X								
Capitol Reef Natl. Park	304	X	X	X	X	X	X	X	X											
Cedar Breaks Natl. Monument	305	X	X	X	X	X	X										X	X		
Glen Canyon Natl. Recreation Area	306		X	X	X	X	X		X			X	X	X	X					X
Golden Spike Natl. Historic Site	307	X	X	X	X															
Natural Bridges Natl. Monument	308	X	X	X	X	X	X													
Rainbow Bridge Natl. Monument	309						X					X	X	X						
Timpanogos Cave Natl. Monument	310		X	X	X															
Zion Natl. Park	311	X	X	X	X	X	X	X	X								X	X	X	X
Virginia																				
Appomattox Court House Natl. Historical Park	312	X	X	X	X		X													
Arlington House, The Robert E. Lee Memorial	313		X	X												X				
Booker T. Washington Natl. Monument	314	X	X	X	X		X													
Colonial Natl. Historical Park	315	X	X	X	X		X									X				
Fredericksburg and Spotsylvania County Battlefields Memorial Natl. Military Park	316		X	X	X		X							X		X				X
George Washington Birthplace Natl. Monument	317	X	X	X	X		X							X						
George Washington Memorial Parkway	318		X	X	X		X		X			X		X		X				
Great Falls Park		X	X	X	X		X	X						X				X		
Maggie L. Walker Natl. Historic Site	319			X																
Manassas Natl. Battlefield Park	320	X	X	X	X		X		X					X						
Petersburg Natl. Battlefield	321	X	X	X	X		X		X							X				

State/Park	Fig 3.5 Map No.	Entrance Fee	Visitor Center	Museum/Exhibit	Picnic Area	Campground	Hiking	Mountain Climbing	Horseback Riding	Swimming	Bathhouse	Boating	Boat Rental	Fishing	Hunting	Bicycle Trail	Snowmobile Route	Cross-Country Ski Trail	Cabin Rental	Hotel/Motel/Lodge
Prince William Forest Park	322	X	X	X	X	X	X							X		X			X	
Richmond Natl. Battlefield Park	323		X	X	X															
Shenandoah Natl. Park	324	X	X	X	X	X	X	X	X					X					X	X	X
Wolf Trap Farm Park for the Performing Arts	325				X															
Virgin Islands																				
Buck Island Reef Natl. Monument	326				X		X			X	X	X		X						
Christiansted Natl. Historic Site	327	X	X	X	X															
Virgin Islands Natl. Park*	328		X	X	X	X	X			X	X	X	X	X						X
Washington																				
Coulee Dam Natl. Recreation Area	329		X	X	X	X				X	X	X		X	X					
Fort Vancouver Natl. Historic Park	330	X	X	X	X															
Klondike Gold Rush Natl. Historical Park	13		X	X																
Lake Chelan Natl. Recreation Area	331		X		X	X	X	X	X			X	X	X	X				X	X	X
Mount Rainier Natl. Park	332	X	X	X	X	X	X	X						X			X	X		X
North Cascades Natl. Park	333					X	X	X						X						
Olympic Natl. Park*†	334	X	X	X	X	X	X	X	X	X		X	X	X				X	X	X
Ross Lake Natl. Recreation Area	335				X	X	X	X	X			X	X	X	X			X		X
San Juan Island Natl. Historical Park	336		X	X	X		X													
Whitman Mission Natl. Historic Site	337	X	X	X	X															
West Virginia																				
Appalachian Natl. Scenic Trail	141		X	X	X	X	X	X											X	
Harpers Ferry Natl. Historical Park	340	X	X	X			X	X						X						
New River Gorge Natl. River	341		X	X	X	X	X			X	X		X		X	X				X	
Wisconsin																				
Apostle Islands Natl. Lakeshore	342		X	X	X	X	X			X		X		X	X					
Saint Croix and Lower Saint Croix Natl. Scenic Riverway	343,344		X	X	X	X	X			X		X	X	X	X				X	X	X
Wyoming																				
Devils Tower Natl. Monument	345	X	X	X	X	X	X	X						X						
Fort Laramie Natl. Historic Site	346	X	X	X	X									X						
Fossil Butte Natl. Monument	347		X	X	X		X		X											
Grand Teton Natl. Park	348	X	X	X	X	X	X	X	X	X		X	X	X			X	X	X	X
John D. Rockefeller, Jr., Memorial Parkway	349				X	X			X			X		X	X		X	X	X	X
Yellowstone Natl. Park*†	350	X	X	X	X	X	X		X			X	X	X			X	X	X	X

*Parks that are designated as Man and the Biosphere reserves by another United Nations group, that preserve examples of the world's major ecosystem for scientific and educational purposes, and that play an important role in maintaining the Earth's diversity of life.
†U.S. national parks that have been specially recognized for their worldwide significance. Some are designated as World Heritage Sites by an international commission of the United States, are outstanding works of man or natural wonders that have universal value.
Source: National Park Service, *National Park System Map and Guide*, 1992.

National Park Service: Regional Offices

Alaska Region
National Park Service
2525 Gambell Street
Anchorage, AK 99503
Alaska

Mid-Atlantic Region
National Park Service
143 South Third Street
Philadelphia, PA 19106
*Delaware, Maryland, Pennsylvania,
    Virginia, and West Virginia*

Midwest Region
National Park Service
1709 Jackson Street
Omaha, NE 68102
*Illinois, Indiana, Iowa, Kansas, Michigan,
    Minnesota, Missouri, Nebraska, Ohio, and
    Wisconsin*

National Capital Region
National Park Service
1100 Ohio Drive SW
Washington, D.C. 20242
*Metropolitan area of Washington, D.C. with
    some units in Maryland, Virginia, and
    West Virginia*

North Atlantic Region
National Park Service
15 State Street
Boston, MA 02109
*Connecticut, Maine, Massachusetts, New
    Hampshire, New Jersey, New York, Rhode
    Island, and Vermont*

Pacific Northwest Region
National Park Service
83 South King Street
Suite 212
Seattle, WA 98104
Idaho, Oregon, and Washington

Rocky Mountain Region
National Park Service
12795 West Alameda Parkway
P.O. Box 25287
Denver, CO 80225
*Colorado, Montana, North Dakota, South
    Dakota, Utah, and Wyoming*

Southeast Region
National Park Service
75 Spring Street, SW
Atlanta, GA 30303
*Alabama, Florida, Georgia, Kentucky,
    Mississippi, North Carolina, Puerto Rico,
    South Carolina, Tennessee, and the Virgin
    Islands*

Southwest Region
National Park Service
P.O. Box 728
Santa Fe, NM 87504
*Arizona (northeast corner), Arkansas,
    Louisiana, New Mexico, Oklahoma, and
    Texas*

Western Region
National Park Service
600 Harrison Street
Suite 600
San Francisco, CA 94170
*Arizona (all but northeast corner),
    California, Hawaii, and Nevada*

Source: National Park Service, *Criteria for Parklands.*

National Forest System: Regional Offices

Northern Region (R-1)
Federal Building
P.O. Box 7669
Missoula, MT 59807
406-329-3511

Rocky Mountain Region (R-2)
11177 West 8th Avenue
P.O. Box 25127
Lakewood, CO 80225
303-236-9431

Southwestern Region (R-3)
Federal Building
517 Gold Avenue, S.W.
Albuquerque, NM 87102
505-842-3292

Intermountain Region (R-4)
Federal Building
324 25th Street
Ogden, UT 84401
801-625-5352

Pacific Southwest Region (R-5)
630 Sansome Street
San Francisco, CA 94111
415-705-2874

Pacific Northwest Region (R-6)
333 S.W. 1st Avenue
P.O. Box 3623 (97208-3623)
Portland, OR 97204
503-326-2971

Southern Region (R-8)
1720 Peachtree Road, N.W.
Atlanta, GA 30367
404-347-2384

Eastern Region (R-9)
310 West Wisconsin Ave., Rm. 500
Milwaukee, WI 53203
414-297-3693

Alaska Region (R-10)
Federal Building
P.O. Box 21628
Juneau, AK 99802-1628
907-586-8863

National Forest System: Areas, Acreages, and Use—1992

Unit	Class[a]	State	Fig. 7.7 Map No.	Gross Acreage	NFS Acreage	% NFS Acreage	Visitor RVDs (thousands)	Wilderness RVDs (thousands)	Acre/ RVD
Conecuh	NF	AL	1	171,177	83,037	48.5	137.1	0.0	0.606
Talladega	NF	AL	2	740,295	384,591	52.0	269.2	15.8	1.429
Tuskegee	NF	AL	3	15,628	11,073	70.9	46.0	0.0	0.241
William B. Bankhead	NF	AL	4	348,917	180,054	51.6	248.3	14.7	0.725
Chugach	NF	AK	5	6,898,770	5,469,226	79.3	1,866.6	0.0	2.930
Tongass	NF	AK	6	17,446,595	16,724,169	95.9	4,020.5	797.0	4.160
Apache	NF	AZ, NM	7	1,226,672	1,194,255	97.4	2,482.9	28.1	1.057
Coconino	NF	AZ	8	2,010,797	1,845,659	91.8	5,788.4	105.0	0.319
Coronado	NF	AZ, NM	9	1,788,259	1,719,109	96.1	4,607.5	210.1	0.388
Kaibab	NF	AZ	10	1,600,061	1,557,580	97.3	1,585.3	3.2	0.983
Prescott	NF	AZ	11	1,407,611	1,238,154	88.0	1,832.3	27.8	0.676
Sitgreaves	NF	AZ	12	884,495	817,015	92.4	Included in Apache		
Tonto	NF	AZ	13	2,969,542	2,874,896	96.8	9,247.4	246.7	0.311
Ouachita	NF	AR, OK	14	1,963,312	1,384,156	70.5	1,284.7	27.4	1.275
Ozark	NF	AR	15	1,497,000	1,123,549	75.1	1,134.2	14.5	0.991
St. Francis	NF	AR	16	29,729	21,201	71.3	95.7	0.0	0.222
Angeles	NF	CA	17	693,667	654,723	94.4	9,158.0	32.4	0.071
Calaveras Bigtree	NF	CA	18	380	380	100.0	Included in Stanislaus		
Cleveland	NF	CA	19	566,850	421,974	74.4	2,875.0	12.6	0.147
Eldorado	NF	CA, NV	20	884,635	676,998	76.5	3,304.9	126.1	0.205
Inyo	NF	CA, NV	21	1,940,762	1,839,887	94.8	8,376.3	511.6	0.227
Klamath	NF	CA, OR	22	1,886,725	1,682,402	89.2	1,000.5	165.4	1.708
Lassen	NF	CA	23	1,374,945	1,059,596	77.1	1,596.5	25.0	0.664
Los Padres	NF	CA	24	1,962,743	1,753,865	89.4	4,749.1	95.3	0.369
Mendocino	NF	CA	25	1,079,971	886,048	82.0	1,488.5	19.9	0.595
Modoc	NF	CA	26	1,979,327	1,663,536	84.0	834.4	16.8	1.994
Plumas	NF	CA	27	1,400,895	1,171,093	83.6	2,562.9	6.9	0.457
Rogue River	NF	CA, OR	28	61,031	53,796	88.1	Included in Oregon		
San Bernardino	NF	CA	29	818,999	670,100	81.8	5,501.1	244.9	0.122
Sequoia	NF	CA	30	1,192,680	1,141,734	95.7	3,530.9	132.3	0.323
Shasta	NF	CA	31	1,634,896	1,160,004	71.0	4,814.2	520.8	0.458

Unit	Class[a]	State	Fig. 7.7 Map No.	Gross Acreage	NFS Acreage	% NFS Acreage	Visitor RVDs (thousands)	Wilderness RVDs (thousands)	Acre/ RVD
Sierra	NF	CA	32	1,412,801	1,308,853	92.6	4,671.1	222.7	0.280
Siskiyou	NF	CA, OR	33	39,574	33,260	84.0	Included in Oregon		
Six Rivers	NF	CA	34	1,118,247	988,951	88.4	1,161.5	10.2	0.851
Stanislaus	NF	CA	35	1,090,039	897,712	82.4	2,707.8	520.8	0.332
Tahoe	NF	CA	36	1,211,425	830,094	68.5	5,175.4	17.4	0.160
Toiyabe	NF	CA, NV	37	696,373	645,767	92.7	Included in Nevada		
Trinity	NF	CA	38	1,179,098	1,043,677	88.5	Included in Shasta		
Butte Valley	NGL	CA	39	18,425	18,425	100.0	Not available		
Arapaho	NF	CO	40	1,155,470	1,020,461	88.3	5,437.7	155.4	0.387
Grand Mesa	NF	CO	41	351,704	346,219	98.4	4,644.8	208.2	0.636
Gunnison	NF	CO	42	1,766,945	1,665,121	94.2	Included in Grand Mesa		
Manti-La Sal	NF	CO, UT	43	27,145	27,105	99.9	Included in Utah		
Pike	NF	CO	44	1,288,371	1,110,091	86.2	5,590.3	180.9	0.398
Rio Grande	NF	CO	45	1,958,787	1,855,196	94.7	1,295.8	113.0	1.432
Roosevelt	NF	CO	46	1,082,050	789,512	73.0	Included in Arapaho		
Routt	NF	CO	47	1,247,292	1,125,740	90.3	2,189.6	85.6	0.514
San Isabel	NF	CO	48	1,245,304	1,117,131	89.7	Included in Pike		
San Juan	NF	CO	49	2,107,592	1,875,877	89.0	1,713.9	188.6	1.095
Uncompahgre	NF	CO	50	1,043,660	944,113	90.5	Included in Grand Mesa		
White River	NF	CO	51	2,088,227	1,961,667	93.9	8,232.3	451.8	0.238
Comanche	NGL	CO	52	460,211	435,319	94.6	Not available		
Pawnee	NGL	CO	53	214,328	193,060	90.1	Not available		
Apalachicola	NF	FL	54	631,260	563,986	89.3	436.2	4.1	1.293
Choctawhatchee	NF	FL	55	1,199	1,199	100.0	94.9	0.0	0.013
Ocala	NF	FL	56	430,446	383,166	89.0	2,122.4	21.9	0.181
Osceola	NF	FL	57	190,932	186,955	97.9	450.9	2.0	0.415
Chattahoochee	NF	GA	58	1,515,885	749,072	49.4	2,614.9	100.2	0.286
Oconee	NF	GA	59	260,884	111,060	42.6	378.4	0.0	0.293
Bitterroot	NF	ID, MT	60	464,037	463,985	100.0	Included in Montana		
Boise	NF	ID	61	2,958,665	2,648,636	89.5	2,093.0	0.0	1.265
Cache	NF	ID, UT	62	264,441	263,941	99.8	Included in Wasatch		
Caribou	NF	ID, UT, WY	63	1,067,409	972,567	91.1	860.7	0.0	1.147
Challis	NF	ID	64	2,488,105	2,464,679	99.1	748.4	234.6	3.293
Clearwater	NF	ID	65	1,739,353	1,668,573	95.9	898.8	31.0	1.856
Coeur d'Alene	NF	ID	66	804,897	724,289	90.0	Included in Idaho Panhandle		
Kaniksu	NF	ID, MT, WA	67	1,051,175	905,837	86.2	Included in Idaho Panhandle		
Kootenai	NF	ID, MT	68	46,480	46,480	100.0	Included in Montana		
Nez Perce	NF	ID	69	2,258,542	2,223,993	98.5	748.1	95.1	2.973
Payette	NF	ID	70	2,424,892	2,323,195	95.8	897.3	85.1	2.589
Salmon	NF	ID	71	1,795,241	1,772,114	98.7	667.1	114.1	2.656
Sawtooth	NF	ID, UT	72	1,802,376	1,732,419	96.1	2,291.1	64.1	0.787
St. Joe	NF	ID	73	1,072,301	866,354	80.8	Included in Idaho Panhandle		
Targhee	NF	ID, WY	74	1,355,073	1,312,545	96.9	1,627.0	45.1	1.010
Wallowa	NF	ID, OR	75	5,554	3,208	57.8	Included in Oregon		
Curlew	NGL	ID	76	75,248	47,749	63.5	Not available		
Idaho Panhandle	NF	ID, MT, WA	[b]	3,716,238	3,210,791	86.3	2,424.9	0.8	1.324
Shawnee	NF	IL	77	714,890	260,133	36.4	899.5	30.6	0.289
Hoosier	NF	IN	78	644,128	189,166	29.4	551.8	31.6	0.343
Cimarron	NGL	KS	79	116,319	108,175	93.0	Not available		
Daniel Boone	NF	KY	80	1,360,692	528,998	38.9	2,111.1	25.1	0.251
Jefferson	NF	KY, VA, WV	81	54,614	961	1.8	Included in Virginia		
Kisatchie	NF	LA	82	1,022,373	601,398	58.8	507.1	6.0	1.186

Unit	Class[a]	State	Fig. 7.7 Map No.	Gross Acreage	NFS Acreage	% NFS Acreage	Visitor RVDs (thousands)	Wilderness RVDs (thousands)	Acre/ RVD
White Mountain	NF	ME, NH	83	53,561	42,183	78.8	Included in New Hampshire		
Hiawatha	NF	MI	84	1,294,642	893,348	69.0	1,542.2	15.2	0.579
Huron	NF	MI	85	694,057	433,116	62.4	2,021.9	15.1	0.477
Manistee	NF	MI	86	1,331,669	531,594	39.9	Included in Huron		
Ottawa	NF	MI	87	1,559,906	980,910	62.9	1,201.1	73.1	0.817
Chippewa	NF	MN	88	1,599,650	664,225	41.5	1,720.3	0.0	0.386
Superior	NF	MN	89	3,260,634	2,065,788	63.4	4,018.3	1,404.0	0.514
Bienville	NF	MS	90	382,821	178,338	46.6	243.9	0.0	0.731
Delta	NF	MS	91	118,150	59,534	50.4	43.8	0.0	1.359
DeSoto	NF	MS	92	796,072	504,054	63.3	494.6	17.1	1.019
Holly Springs	NF	MS	93	519,943	154,065	29.6	211.2	0.0	0.729
Homochitto	NF	MS	94	373,497	189,899	50.8	182.3	0.0	1.042
Tombigbee	NF	MS	95	119,155	66,576	55.9	121.7	0.0	0.547
Mark Twain	NF	MO	96	2,943,952	1,462,348	49.7	1,803.4	57.6	0.811
Beaverhead	NF	MT	97	2,198,815	2,128,753	96.8	800.3	45.0	2.660
Bitterroot	NF	MT, ID	60	1,191,513	1,115,668	93.6	401.1	98.6	2.782
Custer	NF	MT, SD	98	1,200,437	1,112,379	92.7	738.9	141.5	1.605
Deerlodge	NF	MT	99	1,358,183	1,194,124	87.9	1,092.1	10.9	1.093
Flathead	NF	MT	100	2,629,088	2,354,281	89.5	881.5	128.4	2.671
Gallatin	NF	MT	101	2,150,613	1,744,772	81.1	2,797.9	291.8	0.624
Helena	NF	MT	102	1,164,581	976,656	83.9	394.0	6.1	2.479
Kaniksu	NF	MT, ID, WA	67	489,752	447,120	91.3	Included in Idaho		
Kootenai	NF	MT, ID	68	2,098,377	1,776,803	84.7	1,593.8	24.5	1.144
Lewis and Clark	NF	MT	103	1,999,229	1,843,286	92.2	1,009.4	58.6	1.826
Lolo	NF	MT	104	2,621,695	2,112,127	80.6	1,577.6	5.4	1.339
Nebraska	NF	NE	105	229,598	141,547	61.6	349.2	1.7	0.737
Samuel R. McKelvie	NF	NE	106	116,885	115,800	99.1	Included in Nebraska		
Oglala	NGL	NE	107	95,263	94,435	99.1	Not available		
Eldorado	NF	NV, CA	20	53	53	100.0	Included in California		
Humboldt	NF	NV	108	2,618,166	2,477,904	94.6	755.0	62.1	3.282
Inyo	NF	NV, CA	21	62,348	60,656	97.3	Included in California		
Toiyabe	NF	NV, CA	37	2,668,880	2,560,704	95.9	3,789.9	293.7	0.846
White Mountain	NF	NH, ME	83	798,405	697,142	87.3	3,097.6	117.4	0.239
Apache	NF	NM, AZ	7	650,219	614,202	94.5	Included in Arizona		
Carson	NF	NM	109	1,490,468	1,391,494	93.4	1,704.7	25.6	0.816
Cibalo	NF	NM	110	2,103,528	1,630,221	77.5	1,495.3	137.3	1.090
Coronado	NF	NM, AZ	9	71,541	68,936	96.4	Included in Arizona		
Gila	NF	NM	111	2,797,628	2,704,814	96.7	1,517.9	135.2	1.782
Lincoln	NF	NM	112	1,271,064	1,103,636	86.8	1,289.4	20.3	0.856
Santa Fe	NF	NM	113	1,734,800	1,568,892	90.4	2,595.3	285.5	0.605
Kiowa	NGL	NM	114	143,497	136,417	95.1	Not available		
Finger Lakes	NF	NY	115	13,327	13,327	100.0	31.2	0.0	0.427
Cherokee	NF	NC	116	327	327	100.0	Included in Tennessee		
Croatan	NF	NC	117	308,234	157,849	51.2	394.1	2.5	0.401
Nantahala	NF	NC	118	1,349,000	525,292	38.9	2,034.0	170.2	0.258
Pisgah	NF	NC	119	1,076,511	501,692	46.6	2,757.3	77.1	0.182
Uwharrie	NF	NC	120	219,757	47,954	21.8	590.6	17.6	0.081
Cedar River	NGL	ND	121	6,717	6,717	100.0	Not available		
Little Missouri	NGL	ND	122	1,028,058	1,028,058	100.0	Not available		
Sheyenne	NGL	ND	123	70,268	70,268	100.0	Not available		
Wayne	NF	OH	124	832,147	210,783	25.3	671.7	0.0	0.314
Ouachita	NF	OK, AR	14	416,590	254,257	61.0	Included in Arkansas		

Unit	Class[a]	State	Fig. 7.7 Map No.	Gross Acreage	NFS Acreage	% NFS Acreage	Visitor RVDs (thousands)	Wilderness RVDs (thousands)	Acre/ RVD
Black Kettle	NGL	OK, TX	125	32,537	30,710	94.4	Not available		
Rita Blanca	NGL	OK, TX	126	15,816	15,576	98.5	Not available		
Deschutes	NF	OR	127	1,852,497	1,605,196	86.7	3,728.4	113.0	0.431
Fremont	NF	OR	128	1,714,533	1,200,679	70.0	269.3	0.9	4.459
Klamath	NF	OR, CA	22	26,539	26,334	99.2	Included in California		
Malheur	NF	OR	129	1,541,082	1,465,396	95.1	752.6	29.9	1.947
Mt. Hood	NF	OR	130	1,113,387	1,065,467	95.7	1,688.7	65.2	0.631
Ochoco	NF	OR	131	978,987	847,898	86.6	199.1	2.1	4.259
Rogue River	NF	OR, CA	28	624,955	575,445	92.1	1,316.2	17.5	0.478
Siskiyou	NF	OR, CA	33	1,124,412	1,060,987	94.4	498.5	12.8	2.195
Siuslaw	NF	OR	132	835,699	628,403	75.2	2,235.1	4.5	0.281
Umatilla	NF	OR, WA	133	1,193,439	1,094,981	91.8	1,045.0	56.4	1.346
Umpqua	NF	OR	134	1,028,870	984,602	95.7	1,883.8	19.8	0.523
Wallowa	NF	OR, ID	75	1,073,723	994,906	92.7	Included in Whitman		
Whitman	NF	OR	135	1,317,357	1,266,256	96.1	2,153.5	171.2	1.051
Willamette	NF	OR	136	1,800,381	1,686,289	93.7	2,172.1	27.2	0.776
Winema	NF	OR	137	1,096,863	1,039,093	94.7	462.2	4.6	2.248
Crooked River	NGL	OR	138	173,629	111,352	64.1	Not available		
Allegheny	NF	PA	139	742,693	511,838	68.9	2,942.0	2.3	0.174
Francis Marion	NF	SC	140	414,700	249,870	60.3	155.2	1.2	1.610
Sumter	NF	SC	141	960,805	358,840	37.3	795.1	10.0	0.451
Black Hills	NF	SD, WY	142	1,326,839	1,071,258	80.7	3,137.5	20.8	0.397
Custer	NF	SD, MT	98	77,833	73,535	94.5	Included in Montana		
Buffalo Gap	NGL	SD	143	667,021	597,109	89.5	Not available		
Fort Pierre	NGL	SD	144	124,758	115,997	93.0	Not available		
Grand River	NGL	SD	145	155,075	155,075	100.0	Not available		
Cherokee	NF	TN	116	1,204,520	627,405	52.1	2,977.5	46.1	2.109
Angelina	NF	TX	146	402,231	153,098	38.1	553.3	6.0	0.277
Davy Crockett	NF	TX	147	394,200	161,942	41.1	226.7	2.0	0.714
Sabine	NF	TX	148	442,705	160,603	36.3	701.6	2.5	0.229
Sam Houston	NF	TX	149	491,800	161,446	32.8	689.2	0.5	0.234
Black Kettle	NGL	TX, OK	125	576	576	100.0	Not available		
Caddo	NGL	TX	150	68,661	17,784	25.9	Not available		
Lyndon B. Johnson	NGL	TX	151	115,438	20,309	17.6	Not available		
McClelland Creek	NGL	TX	152	1,449	1,449	100.0	Not available		
Rita Blanca	NGL	TX, OK	126	77,413	77,413	100.0	Not available		
Ashley	NF	UT, WY	153	1,300,388	1,287,909	99.0	1,852.5	200.8	0.121
Cache	NF	UT, ID	62	952,343	411,121	43.2	Included in Wasatch		
Caribou	NF	UT, ID, WY	63	8,940	6,955	77.8	Included in Idaho		
Dixie	NF	UT	154	1,967,190	1,883,955	95.8	6,175.6	16.2	0.305
Fishlake	NF	UT	155	1,525,656	1,424,830	93.4	1,275.8	0.0	1.117
Manti–La Sal	NF	UT, CO	43	1,310,921	1,238,425	94.5	865.0	5.5	1.463
Sawtooth	NF	UT, ID	72	92,404	71,183	77.0	Included in Idaho		
Uinta	NF	UT	156	947,390	870,506	91.9	3,532.1	138.4	0.246
Wasatch	NF	UT, WY	157	1,024,739	848,090	82.8	4,866.0	137.0	0.321
Green Mountain	NF	VT	158	815,000	344,482	42.3	1,564.7	20.2	0.220
George Washington	NF	VA, WV	159	1,635,566	959,392	58.7	2,444.1	14.2	0.435
Jefferson	NF	VA, KY, WV	81	1,586,343	688,278	43.4	2,174.5	72.5	3.255
Colville	NF	WA	160	1,030,742	952,651	92.4	1,488.4	2.9	0.640
Gifford Pinchot	NF	WA	161	1,395,728	1,305,267	93.5	2,816.3	182.5	0.463
Kaniksu	NF	WA, ID, MT	67	298,113	267,191	89.6	Included in Idaho		
Mt. Baker	NF	WA	162	1,312,698	1,281,976	97.7	5,511.3	160.6	0.457

Unit	Class[a]	State	Fig. 7.7 Map No.	Gross Acreage	NFS Acreage	% NFS Acreage	Visitor RVDs (thousands)	Wilderness RVDs (thousands)	Acre/ RVD
Okanogan	NF	WA	163	1,536,958	1,499,866	97.6	1,158.7	41.5	1.294
Olympic	NF	WA	164	692,688	627,213	90.5	2,230.7	42.6	0.281
Snoqualmie	NF	WA	165	1,560,288	1,239,408	79.4	Included in Mt. Baker		
Umatilla	NF	WA, OR	133	319,349	311,197	97.4	Included in Oregon		
Wenatchee	NF	WA	166	1,908,053	1,668,675	87.5	3,885.9	414.1	0.429
George Washington	NF	WV, VA	159	159,519	104,866	65.7	Included in Virginia		
Jefferson	NF	WV, KY, VA	81	29,888	18,497	61.9	Included in Virginia		
Monongahela	NF	WV	167	1,650,951	895,788	54.3	915.7	51.6	0.978
Chequamegon	NF	WI	168	1,049,539	856,938	81.6	1,056.4	2.2	0.811
Nicolet	NF	WI	169	973,402	661,202	67.9	1,128.7	15.5	0.586
Ashley	NF	WY, UT	153	104,701	96,223	91.9	Included in Utah		
Bighorn	NF	WY	170	1,115,161	1,107,671	99.3	1,880.7	85.6	0.589
Black Hills	NF	WY, SD	142	201,135	175,402	87.2	Included in South Dakota		
Bridger	NF	WY	171	1,744,705	1,733,629	99.4	2,960.4	543.5	1.148
Caribou	NF	WY, ID, UT	63	9,612	7,831	81.5	Included in Idaho		
Medicine Bow	NF	WY	172	1,402,623	1,093,618	78.0	905.7	11.8	1.207
Shoshone	NF	WY	173	2,466,555	2,432,990	98.6	1,210.4	173.6	2.010
Targhee	NF	WY, ID	74	333,704	331,249	99.3	Included in Idaho		
Teton	NF	WY	174	1,694,531	1,666,151	98.3	Included in Bridger		
Wasatch	NF	WY, UT	157	47,704	37,762	79.2	Included in Utah		
Thunder Basin	NGL	WY	175	583,116	572,211	98.1	Not available		
Caribbean	NF	PR	176	55,665	27,831	50.0	289.3	0.0	0.096

[a]NF, national forest; NGL, national grassland.
[b]The administrative unit—Panhandle National Forest—consists of 3 congressionally designated national forests (St. Joe NF, Kaniksu NF, Coeur d'Alene NF); see these 3 national forests for location of Panhandle National Forest.
Source: Forest Service.

Recreation Opportunity Spectrum Setting Indicator Matrices

	ACCESS				
ROS Class	Cross-Country Travel	Nonmotorized Trails	Motorized Trails and Primitive Roads (Traffic Ser. D)	Controlled TSL B&C Roads[1]	Full Access
Primitive	Norm	Norm	Unacceptable	Unacceptable	Unacceptable
Semiprimitive nonmotorized	Fully compatible	Norm	Inconsistent	Unacceptable	Unacceptable
Semiprimitive motorized	Fully compatible	Fully compatible	Norm	Inconsistent	Unacceptable
Roaded natural	Fully compatible	Fully compatible	Fully compatible	Norm[2]	Norm
Rural	Fully compatible	Fully compatible	Fully compatible	Fully compatible	Norm
Urban	Fully compatible	Fully compatible	Fully compatible	Fully compatible	Norm

[1]TSL = traffic service level. In TSL-D primitive roads should provide challenge to four-wheel drive and high-clearance vehicles but discourage use by highway vehicles. By definition they are single-use controlled traffic roads, the surface is rough, and they are stable during dry weather. Rutting is controlled for protection of water only.
[2]Roaded natural may be prescribed in certain circumstances with roads partially or fully closed.

	REMOTENESS			
ROS Class	Out of Sight and Sound of Human Activity; More than 1½-hr. walk[1]	Distant Sight and/or Sound of Human Activity; More than ½-hr. walk from Any Motorized Travel	Distant Sight and/or Sound of Human activity; More than ½-hr. walk from any Better-than- Primitive Roads.	Remoteness of Little Relevance
Primitive	Norm	Inconsistent	Unacceptable	Unacceptable
Semiprimitive nonmotorized	Fully compatible	Norm	Inconsistent	Unacceptable
Semiprimitive motorized	Fully compatible	Fully compatible	Norm	Inconsistent
Roaded natural	Fully compatible	Fully compatible	Norm	Norm
Rural	Fully compatible	Fully compatible	Fully compatible	Norm
Urban	Fully compatible	Fully compatible	Fully compatible	Norm

[1]Legislative direction (e.g., the Wilderness Act) may require primitive management on lands less remote than this.

	SOCIAL ENCOUNTERS				
ROS Class	6 Parties or Less Met per Day; Fewer than 3 Visible Parties per Campsite[1]	6–15 Parties Met per Day; 6 or Fewer Parties Seen at Campsite	Moderate to High Contact on Roads; Moderate to Low on Trails and Developed Sites	Moderate to High Contact in Developed Sites on Roads and Trails	Large numbers of Users on Site and In Nearby Areas; High Number of Social Encounters
Primitive	Norm	Inconsistent	Unacceptable	Unacceptable	Unacceptable
Semiprimitive nonmotorized	Fully compatible	Norm	Inconsistent	Unacceptable	Unacceptable
Semiprimitive motorized	Fully compatible	Norm	Inconsistent	Unacceptable	Unacceptable
Roaded natural	Fully compatible	Fully compatible	Norm	Inconsistent	Unacceptable
Rural	Fully compatible	Fully compatible	Fully compatible	Norm	Inconsistent
Urban	Fully compatible	Fully compatible	Fully compatible	Fully compatible	Norm

[1]See regional supplements for party size limitations.

	VISITOR MANAGEMENT				
ROS Class	Low Regimentation; No One-Site Controls or Information Facilities	Subtle On-site Regimentation and Controls; Very Limited Information Facilities	On-site Regimentation and Controls Noticeable but Harmonize with Natural Environment; Simple Information Facilities	Regimentation and Controls Obvious and Numerous; but harmonize; More Complex Information Facilities	Regimentation and Controls Obvious and Numerous; Sophisticated Information Exhibits
Primitive	Norm	Inconsistent	Unacceptable	Unacceptable	Unacceptable
Semiprimitive nonmotorized	Fully compatible	Norm	Inconsistent	Unacceptable	Unacceptable
Semiprimitive motorized	Fully compatible	Norm	Inconsistent	Unacceptable	Unacceptable
Roaded natural	Fully compatible	Fully compatible	Norm	Inconsistent	Unacceptable
Rural	Fully compatible	Fully compatible	Fully compatible	Norm	Inconsistent
Urban	Fully compatible	Fully compatible	Fully compatible	Fully compatible	Norm

	VISITOR IMPACTS				
ROS Class	Unnoticeable Impacts; No Site Hardening	Subordinate Impacts; No Site Hardening	Subordinate Impacts; Limited Site Hardening	Subtle Site Hardening	Site Hardening May Be Dominant but in Harmony
Primitive	Norm	Inconsistent	Unacceptable	Unacceptable	Unacceptable
Semiprimitive nonmotorized	Fully compatible	Norm	Inconsistent	Unacceptable	Unacceptable
Semiprimitive motorized	Fully compatible	Fully compatible	Norm	Inconsistent	Unacceptable
Roaded natural	Fully compatible	Fully compatible	Fully compatible	Norm	Inconsistent
Rural	Fully compatible	Fully compatible	Fully compatible	Fully compatible	Norm
Urban	Fully compatible	Fully compatible	Fully compatible	Fully compatible	Fully compatible

	NATURALNESS				
ROS Class	Preservation	Retention	Partial Retention	Modification	Maximum Modification
Primitive	Norm	Inconsistent	Unacceptable	Unacceptable	Unacceptable
Semiprimitive nonmotorized	Fully compatible	Norm	Inconsistent	Unacceptable	Unacceptable
Semiprimitive motorized	Fully compatible	Fully compatible	Norm[1]	Inconsistent	Unacceptable
Roaded natural	Fully compatible	Norm	Norm	Norm[2]	Inconsistent[3]
Rural	Fully compatible	Fully compatible	Norm	Norm[2]	Inconsistent[3]
Urban	Fully compatible	Fully compatible	Fully compatible	Fully compatible	NA

[1]Norm from sensitive roads and trails (see *USDA Handbook 462*.)
[2]Norm only in MG2 where "roaded modified" subclass is used (See *USDA Handbook 462*).
[3]Unacceptable where "roaded modified" subclass is used.

ON-SITE DEVELOPMENT

ROS Class	No Facilities for User Comfort Rustic and Rudimentary Ones for Site Protection Only Use Undiminished Native Materials Only	Rustic and Rudimentary Facilities Primarily for Site Protection No Evidence of Synthetic Materials Used Un-Dimensioned Native Materials	Rustic Facilities Providing Some Comfort for The User As Well As Site Protection Use Native Materials But With More Refinement in Design Synthetic Materials Should Not Be Evident	Some Facilities Designed Primarily for User Comfort and Convenience Some Synthetic But Harmonious Materials May Be Incorporated Design May Be More Complex and Refined	Facilities Mostly Designed for User Comfort and Convenience Synthetic Materials are Commonly Used Facility Design May Be Highly Complex and Refined but in Harmony or Complimentary to the Site
Primitive	Norm	Inconsistent	Unacceptable	Unacceptable	Unacceptable
Semiprimitive nonmotorized	Fully compatible	Norm	Inconsistent	Unacceptable	Unacceptable
Semiprimitive motorized	Fully compatible	Norm	Inconsistent	Unacceptable	Unacceptable
Roaded natural	Fully compatible	Fully compatible	Norm	Inconsistent	Unacceptable
Rural	Fully compatible	Fully compatible	Fully compatible	Norm	Inconsistent
Urban	Fully compatible	Fully compatible	Fully compatible	Fully compatible	Norm

Source: Forest Service, *ROS Primer and Field Guide,* April 1990.

National Forests: Recreational Use by Activity—1992 Recreation Visitor Days (000s)

National Forest	Region	State	Camp, Picnic Swim	Mechn. Travel, Viewing Scenery	Hiking, Horse Riding, Water Travel	Winter Sports	Resort, Cabins, Organiz. Camps	Hunting	Fishing	Nonconsumptive Fish and Wildlife	Other Recreational Activities	Total	Wilderness Use
Clearwater	1	ID	259.4	298.8	112.9	12.7	18.6	89.3	49.2	7.1	50.8	898.8	31.0
Idaho Panhandle	1	ID	641.4	856.8	138.4	77.4	110.2	207.1	152.5	26.5	214.6	2,424.9	0.8
Nez Perce	1	ID	241.9	202.7	89.7	13.4	7.6	95.2	33.7	3.3	60.6	748.1	95.1
Beaverhead	1	MT	194.5	193.0	86.9	27.6	33.3	154.3	61.6	6.3	42.8	800.3	45.0
Deerlodge	1	MT	217.2	395.5	85.7	47.3	39.9	128.9	97.3	20.1	60.2	1,092.1	10.9
Flathead	1	MT	208.9	259.1	112.9	114.5	37.9	45.6	44.8	3.9	53.9	881.5	128.4
Gallatin	1	MT	425.9	858.5	453.7	192.7	113.6	210.6	243.3	16.0	283.6	2,797.9	291.8
Helena	1	MT	98.3	86.5	35.5	22.5	21.6	90.4	12.2	2.3	24.7	394.0	6.1
Lewis and Clark	1	MT	239.3	309.8	153.3	44.2	51.7	84.6	40.6	9.2	76.7	1,009.4	58.6
Lolo	1	MT	280.2	532.0	188.0	93.0	14.7	181.0	82.8	17.4	188.5	1,577.6	5.4
Bitterroot	1	MT, ID	114.7	88.4	86.1	22.5	3.0	39.1	27.7	5.7	13.9	401.1	98.6
Kootenai	1	MT, ID	295.4	644.1	91.2	35.8	23.0	121.2	224.1	31.9	127.1	1,593.8	24.5
Custer	1	MT, SD	195.3	143.8	94.7	64.6	31.1	118.9	50.7	15.6	24.2	738.9	141.5
Arapaho-Roosevelt	2	CO	1,515.1	2,244.9	299.6	821.0	98.5	75.2	248.6	32.2	102.6	5,437.7	155.4
Grand Mesa, Uncompahgre, and Gunnison	2	CO	827.5	1,299.2	449.5	760.0	110.7	556.7	351.9	13.0	276.3	4,644.8	208.2
Rio Grande	2	CO	370.9	289.6	155.3	144.4	47.5	94.5	113.5	11.9	68.2	1,295.8	113.0
Routt	2	CO	359.6	426.4	168.9	603.7	10.2	341.6	252.8	12.3	14.1	2,189.6	85.6
Pike and San Isabel	2	CO	1,399.3	2,190.9	672.5	289.0	210.9	157.6	439.3	34.2	196.5	5,590.3	180.9
San Juan	2	CO	382.4	460.2	224.3	119.5	162.6	116.5	123.1	20.4	104.9	1,713.9	188.6
White River	2	CO	1,327.2	1,708.4	436.1	3,894.2	106.1	455.6	129.0	16.2	159.5	8,232.3	451.8
Nebraska-Sam. R. McKelvie	2	NE	47.6	185.9	16.8	0.5	38.7	24.2	5.6	0.5	29.4	349.2	1.7
Bighorn	2	WY	374.9	590.6	177.3	56.5	271.6	133.4	157.0	13.9	105.5	1,880.7	85.6
Medicine Bow	2	WY	203.8	273.2	53.4	59.5	51.9	111.3	67.4	25.6	59.6	905.7	11.8
Shoshone	2	WY	332.3	393.0	97.8	16.3	157.8	84.7	78.6	18.9	31.0	1,210.4	173.6
Blackhills	2	WY, SD	204.8	2,343.7	165.2	17.1	115.8	84.5	64.3	7.0	135.1	3,137.5	20.8
Coconino	3	AZ	864.0	3,355.2	292.6	318.1	115.1	240.5	252.5	19.4	331.0	5,788.4	105.0
Coronado	3	AZ	739.8	1,376.0	382.0	44.7	185.8	103.1	52.8	334.6	1,388.7	4,607.5	210.1
Kaibab	3	AZ	266.1	868.9	16.0	10.1	168.5	116.0	6.7	27.1	105.9	1,585.3	3.2
Prescott	3	AZ	377.0	1,000.1	109.5	13.5	35.7	101.5	32.0	7.9	155.1	1,832.3	27.8
Tonto	3	AZ	3,565.3	4,076.4	526.3	2.6	328.2	193.6	350.3	26.5	178.2	9,247.4	246.7
Apache-Sitgreaves	3	AZ, NM	814.2	737.0	124.8	32.9	110.4	162.0	242.9	19.1	239.7	2,482.9	28.1
Cibola	3	AZ, NM	363.0	498.9	165.0	97.2	57.0	76.5	10.6	72.0	172.2	1,512.3	137.3
Carson	3	NM	388.8	400.3	63.4	272.5	11.0	112.1	75.2	8.9	372.5	1,704.7	25.6
Gila	3	NM	580.1	325.3	237.2	11.5	0.6	137.0	83.7	29.2	113.3	1,517.9	135.2
Lincoln	3	NM	313.7	449.5	85.3	158.9	25.5	207.9	1.5	8.5	38.6	1,289.4	20.3
Santa Fe	3	NM	1,107.6	345.9	243.7	238.8	184.4	102.0	151.2	32.1	189.6	2,595.3	285.5

Forest	Region	State											
Manti-La Sal	4	CO, UT	276.9	244.2	37.4	14.5	25.6	108.8	112.5	2.5	42.6	865.0	5.5
Boise	4	ID	596.5	678.9	109.6	233.8	140.3	83.5	104.2	8.9	137.3	2,093.0	0.0
Challis	4	ID	206.6	108.9	126.9	6.0	14.1	80.9	116.5	4.5	84.0	748.4	234.6
Payette	4	ID	193.2	266.8	136.3	53.3	0.7	59.0	118.5	14.4	55.1	897.3	85.1
Salmon	4	ID	214.3	123.2	141.8	12.4	14.0	72.7	67.3	3.4	18.0	667.1	114.1
Sawtooth	4	ID, UT	671.3	599.5	166.8	283.2	211.5	117.3	117.9	18.8	104.8	2,291.1	64.1
Humboldt	4	NV	155.7	244.8	102.1	21.3	9.8	136.3	32.6	9.2	43.2	755.0	62.1
Toiyabe	4	NV, CA	1,428.7	1,125.4	331.6	148.6	170.3	91.2	271.0	63.6	159.6	3,790.0	293.7
Dixie	4	UT	986.0	3,635.8	151.1	184.9	109.9	213.3	139.8	20.4	734.4	6,175.6	16.2
Fishlake	4	UT	525.5	301.8	60.7	7.0	169.1	96.6	56.6	4.7	53.8	1,275.8	0.0
Uinta	4	UT	1,418.6	948.5	498.4	24.9	167.6	140.1	177.3	5.9	150.8	3,532.1	138.4
Bridger-Teton	4	WY	766.9	804.4	756.9	134.9	67.1	230.2	120.9	0.6	78.6	2,960.5	543.5
Targhee	4	WY, ID	462.6	329.1	99.6	116.2	210.6	119.0	90.0	10.8	189.1	1,627.0	45.1
Caribou	4	WY, ID, UT	367.0	156.5	54.6	29.8	14.7	114.0	35.1	6.2	82.8	860.7	0.0
Ashley	4	WY, UT	762.2	426.0	152.9	17.1	69.1	87.0	248.2	6.0	84.0	1,852.5	200.8
Wasatch-Cache	4	WY, UT	1,232.1	1,679.4	276.1	824.9	248.6	249.7	196.6	18.1	140.5	4,866.0	137.0
Angeles	5	CA	2,378.1	3,373.1	736.8	488.8	1,466.4	59.1	204.4	49.9	401.4	9,158.0	32.4
Cleveland	5	CA	370.1	1,532.4	308.4	8.7	494.8	40.6	6.1	13.9	100.0	2,875.0	12.6
Lassen	5	CA	506.9	461.3	55.4	25.4	199.8	76.9	104.2	8.0	158.6	1,596.5	25.0
Los Padres	5	CA	1,074.7	2,044.1	539.3	66.3	497.8	184.2	150.6	48.0	144.1	4,749.1	95.3
Mendocino	5	CA	648.1	351.2	113.5	18.7	122.7	91.5	73.4	3.5	65.9	1,488.5	19.9
Modoc	5	CA	317.0	178.7	43.0	10.4	2.2	166.9	29.0	17.9	69.3	834.4	16.8
Six Rivers	5	CA	293.0	362.8	105.0	63.3	21.9	65.5	99.5	4.6	145.9	1,161.5	10.2
Plumas	5	CA	866.1	818.2	124.6	35.5	152.1	72.3	267.0	14.7	212.4	2,562.9	6.9
San Bernardino	5	CA	993.2	2,771.6	333.7	517.0	669.4	11.2	28.8	38.9	137.3	5,501.1	244.9
Sequoia	5	CA	1,650.9	816.8	174.8	30.8	319.8	46.2	220.7	31.7	239.2	3,530.9	132.3
Shasta-Trinity	5	CA	1,468.8	1,979.6	196.6	64.8	163.2	194.4	398.0	7.0	341.8	4,814.2	520.8
Sierra	5	CA	1,466.2	1,270.4	512.2	111.3	792.8	91.4	254.1	34.8	137.9	4,671.1	222.7
Stanislaus	5	CA	934.5	753.0	109.4	154.7	575.1	16.2	111.4	4.2	49.3	2,707.8	115.3
Tahoe	5	CA	909.8	2,402.3	191.4	1,072.0	221.5	47.9	186.0	17.7	126.8	5,175.4	17.4
Lake Tahoe Basin	5	CA	887.3	918.1	176.1	412.4	386.3	2.1	66.3	4.3	67.4	2,920.3	196.5
Eldorado	5	CA	856.1	925.0	219.4	296.5	479.4	167.7	228.8	2.0	130.0	3,304.9	126.1
Inyo	5	CA, NV	1,625.5	3,328.2	461.4	709.5	1,020.9	81.4	417.4	166.3	565.7	8,376.3	511.6
Klamath	5	CA, NV	400.8	170.5	135.3	13.9	7.3	139.2	65.8	14.0	53.7	1,000.5	165.4
Deschutes	6	CA, OR	1,187.0	1,167.8	286.8	292.1	330.5	56.6	156.7	91.7	159.2	3,728.4	113.0
Fremont	6	OR	114.3	56.7	10.5	1.7	5.9	34.8	21.6	5.5	18.3	269.3	0.9
Malheur	6	OR	212.6	44.5	25.2	2.9	15.6	112.5	10.8	2.6	325.9	752.6	29.9
Mt. Hood	6	OR	761.2	219.5	115.1	273.5	175.0	40.8	48.8	1.8	53.0	1,688.7	65.2
Ochoco	6	OR	111.6	27.1	4.9	0.5	9.2	30.3	11.0	1.3	3.2	199.1	2.1
Rogue River	6	OR	219.1	654.9	37.1	19.5	295.3	10.3	30.3	18.5	31.2	1,316.2	17.5
Siskiyou	6	OR	205.7	163.8	59.0	4.5	11.0	18.5	22.9	3.5	9.6	498.5	12.8

National Forest	Region	State	Camp, Picnic Swim	Mechn. Travel, Viewing Scenery	Hiking, Horse Riding, Water Travel	Winter Sports	Resort, Cabins, Organiz. Camps	Hunting	Fishing	Nonconsumptive Fish and Wildlife	Other Recreational Activities	Total	Wilderness Use
Siuslaw	6	OR	622.5	1,061.3	190.3	6.4	16.0	45.2	149.9	33.3	110.2	2,235.1	4.5
Umatilla	6	OR	496.4	129.6	75.6	24.9	36.1	163.4	33.1	26.7	59.2	1,045.0	56.4
Umpqua	6	OR	614.3	564.8	121.7	43.3	370.1	49.4	74.4	18.5	27.3	1,883.8	19.8
Wallowa-Whitman	6	OR	1,157.2	449.2	254.1	33.5	28.8	87.6	70.6	52.9	19.6	2,153.5	171.2
Willamette	6	OR	856.9	517.4	288.2	57.4	136.1	74.6	207.3	8.7	25.5	2,172.1	27.2
Winema	6	OR	226.5	65.2	16.2	5.6	78.5	36.8	15.2	5.9	12.3	462.2	4.6
Columbia R. Gorge	6	OR, WA	63.1	2,106.4	789.5	0.0	283.3	4.8	8.1	0.5	49.2	3,304.9	0.0
Colville	6	WA	306.6	783.1	152.3	78.3	12.8	40.1	70.8	22.7	21.7	1,488.4	2.9
Gifford Pinchot	6	WA	721.6	957.7	528.5	38.9	32.4	98.6	75.8	44.3	318.3	2,816.1	182.5
Mt. Baker–Snoqualmie	6	WA	770.7	3,536.4	292.3	541.0	104.3	96.0	63.8	29.1	77.7	5,511.3	160.6
Okanogan	6	WA	250.3	608.9	99.3	16.3	60.9	40.6	13.5	35.3	33.6	1,158.7	41.5
Olympic	6	WA	610.2	1,320.5	113.7	10.0	47.2	53.6	41.5	0.0	34.0	2,230.7	42.6
Wenatchee	6	WA	1,567.3	781.3	466.0	200.3	519.9	169.9	39.9	3.3	138.0	3,885.9	414.1
William B. Bankhead	8	AL	143.4	26.4	24.5	0.0	0.0	24.2	23.5	0.0	6.3	248.3	14.7
Conecuh	8	AL	4.8	18.5	3.7	0.0	0.4	51.1	18.5	0.6	39.5	137.1	0.0
Talladega	8	AL	52.8	58.7	32.8	0.0	0.0	79.2	26.4	3.8	15.5	269.2	15.8
Tuskegee	8	AL	3.0	11.0	4.0	0.0	0.0	12.0	2.0	1.0	13.0	46.0	0.0
Ouachita	8	AR	270.6	439.3	128.6	0.2	0.6	281.8	75.4	20.4	67.8	1,284.7	27.4
Ozark	8	AR	366.2	246.4	98.3	0.1	13.6	280.3	36.5	18.0	74.8	1,134.2	14.5
St. Francis	8	AR	20.9	20.8	2.6	0.0	10.0	20.0	18.0	1.0	2.4	95.7	0.0
Apalachicola	8	FL	194.7	58.5	22.3	0.0	2.0	79.6	39.8	6.4	32.9	436.2	4.1
Ocala	8	FL	1,131.5	375.6	126.6	0.0	179.2	132.1	114.3	13.9	49.2	2,122.4	21.9
Osceola	8	FL	336.5	14.5	24.0	0.0	32.6	21.3	21.0	0.0	1.0	450.9	2.0
Choctawhatchee	8	FL	55.5	30.2	2.1	0.0	1.5	0.0	2.0	0.1	3.5	94.9	0.0
Chattahoochee	8	GA	840.3	801.7	366.3	0.8	44.9	274.5	176.7	25.8	83.9	2,614.9	100.2
Oconee	8	GA	59.4	154.2	18.6	0.0	0.0	106.0	15.7	11.0	13.5	378.4	0.0
Daniel Boone	8	KY	644.3	666.2	259.7	2.3	21.4	206.4	206.6	9.8	94.4	2,111.1	25.1
Kisatchie	8	LA	152.2	130.9	16.1	0.0	26.7	103.6	39.0	1.5	37.1	507.1	6.0
Bienville	8	MS	31.2	43.9	34.8	0.0	1.7	103.3	9.8	2.7	16.5	243.9	0.0
Delta	8	MS	11.4	4.1	1.2	0.0	0.0	21.1	5.0	0.3	0.7	43.8	0.0
DeSoto	8	MS	125.4	158.8	55.5	0.0	0.0	103.2	21.9	3.0	26.8	494.6	17.1
Holly Springs	8	MS	24.9	25.4	18.3	0.0	6.2	55.4	31.0	13.0	37.0	211.2	0.0
Homochitto	8	MS	24.8	60.7	5.7	0.0	0.1	84.8	3.7	0.4	2.1	182.3	0.0
Tombigbee	8	MS	27.5	44.8	5.9	0.0	0.3	15.2	15.0	10.1	2.9	121.7	0.0
Croatan	8	NC	127.0	49.5	36.0	0.0	10.0	107.1	41.9	1.4	20.6	394.1	2.5
Nantahala	8	NC	492.0	669.1	375.7	2.5	60.9	205.4	127.0	22.2	79.2	2,034.0	170.2

Forest	Region	State										
Pisgah	8	NC	736.0	1,216.5	358.9	5.5	17.6	197.0	121.8	9.7	94.3	2,757.3	77.1
Uwharrie	8	NC	116.6	155.7	71.5	0.0	8.5	181.4	40.0	1.4	15.5	590.6	17.6
Caribbean	8	PR, VI	109.1	100.1	23.3	0.0	7.0	0.0	0.0	1.9	47.9	289.3	0.0
Francis Marion	8	SC	29.6	48.1	5.9	0.0	0.0	42.1	10.0	5.4	14.1	155.2	1.2
Sumter	8	SC	224.5	171.7	129.2	0.0	0.4	166.6	42.2	10.4	50.1	795.1	10.0
Cherokee	8	TN	1,176.7	865.9	325.7	4.9	94.1	237.3	180.2	27.4	65.3	2,977.5	46.1
Angelina	8	TX	165.2	61.1	7.1	0.0	0.0	34.3	276.7	3.3	5.6	553.3	6.0
Davy Crockett	8	TX	73.4	33.5	15.3	0.0	0.0	62.8	15.2	4.3	22.2	226.7	2.0
Sabine	8	TX	134.4	119.5	28.3	0.0	3.0	41.4	350.0	3.7	21.3	701.6	2.5
Sam Houston	8	TX	212.6	188.1	41.0	0.0	16.8	72.5	131.6	5.0	21.6	689.2	0.5
Caddo-L.B.J.	8	TX	32.5	21.7	6.1	0.0	2.5	19.5	9.9	0.6	0.0	92.8	0.0
George Washington	8	VA	470.4	779.6	213.1	4.7	21.8	578.4	204.2	21.2	150.7	2,444.1	14.2
Jefferson	8	VA	637.6	677.6	242.8	4.6	0.9	336.3	163.8	21.1	89.8	2,174.5	72.5
Shawnee	9	IL	180.9	348.9	140.8	0.8	7.5	123.3	40.0	14.1	43.2	899.5	30.6
Hoosier	9	IN	242.9	69.4	66.1	0.0	0.0	69.1	81.4	5.2	17.7	551.8	31.6
Hiawatha	9	MI	407.4	565.3	53.3	13.3	63.2	153.2	228.1	5.7	52.9	1,542.2	15.2
Huron-Manistee	9	MI	604.0	524.8	187.3	33.3	71.3	355.9	161.2	4.3	79.8	2,021.9	15.1
Ottawa	9	MI	218.8	572.5	75.2	25.8	16.2	114.8	101.4	5.7	70.7	1,201.1	73.1
Chippewa	9	MN	269.1	425.4	86.2	12.3	204.1	189.7	468.7	25.8	38.9	1,720.2	0.0
Superior	9	MN	1,619.1	579.0	797.6	69.8	254.9	159.3	412.4	11.8	114.4	4,018.3	1,404.0
Mark Twain	9	MO	524.2	532.5	239.3	0.0	10.6	266.9	112.4	19.3	98.2	1,803.4	57.6
White Mountain	9	NH, ME	717.8	1,148.1	359.6	630.9	122.7	44.8	32.0	14.2	27.5	3,097.6	117.4
Finger Lakes	9	NY	16.2	2.5	3.6	1.5	0.0	4.1	1.3	0.6	1.4	31.2	0.0
Wayne	9	OH	109.7	145.3	73.8	0.8	0.0	231.9	48.5	5.0	56.7	671.7	0.0
Allegheny	9	PA	843.7	1,310.2	258.8	9.3	68.8	199.0	156.9	21.3	74.0	2,942.0	2.3
Green Mountain	9	VT	107.5	284.6	68.5	832.8	58.1	87.3	21.3	30.9	73.7	1,564.7	20.2
Chequamegon	9	WI	268.0	453.6	49.4	9.7	19.9	95.2	93.6	3.0	64.0	1,056.4	2.2
Monongahela	9	WV	443.5	118.9	81.8	1.7	45.6	96.1	96.9	3.4	27.8	915.7	51.6
Nicolet	9	WV	263.6	293.6	37.3	19.1	0.4	133.3	302.4	5.3	73.7	1,128.7	15.5
Chugach	10	AK	152.4	1,168.4	148.0	91.9	61.7	36.4	98.0	5.2	104.6	1,866.6	0.0
Tongass	10	AK	168.5	2,483.4	233.4	43.9	109.0	111.6	347.3	32.1	491.3	4,020.5	797.0

Source: Forest Service.

735

Recreation Facilities in the National Forests

Facility	State	Boating	Cabins	Camping	Fishing	Hiking	Hotel/Lodge	Hunting	Picnicking	Riding	Swimming	Winter Sports
Allegheny NF	PA	X		X	X	X	X	X	X	X	X	X
Angeles NF	CA	X	X	X	X	X	X	X	X	X	X	
Angelina NF	TX	X	X	X	X	X	X	X	X	X	X	
Apache NF	AZ	X		X	X	X	X	X	X	X	X	X
Apalachicola NF	FL	X		X	X	X		X	X	X	X	
Arapaho NF	CO	X	X	X	X	X	X	X	X	X	X	X
Ashley NF	UT	X		X	X	X		X	X	X	X	X
Beaverhead NF	MT	X	X	X	X	X	X	X	X	X	X	X
Bienville NF	MS	X		X	X	X		X	X	X	X	
Bighorn NF	WY	X	X	X	X	X	X	X	X	X	X	X
Bitterroot NF	MT	X	X	X	X	X	X	X	X	X	X	X
Black Hills NF	SD	X	X	X	X	X	X	X	X	X	X	X
Boise NF	ID	X	X	X	X	X	X	X	X	X	X	X
Bridger NF	WY	X	X	X	X	X	X	X	X	X	X	X
Cache NF	UT			X	X	X		X	X	X	X	X
Caribou NF	ID	X	X	X	X	X	X	X	X	X	X	X
Carson NF	NM	X	X	X	X	X	X	X	X	X	X	X
Challis NF	ID	X		X	X	X	X	X	X	X	X	X
Chattahoochee NF	GA	X	X	X	X	X	X	X	X	X	X	
Chequamegon NF	WI	X		X	X	X	X	X	X		X	
Cherokee NF	TN	X	X	X	X	X	X	X	X	X	X	X
Chippewa NF	MN	X	X	X	X	X	X	X	X	X	X	
Chugach NF	AK	X	X	X	X	X	X	X	X		X	X
Cibola NF	NM			X	X	X		X	X	X		X
Clearwater NF	ID	X		X	X	X	X	X	X	X	X	X
Cleveland NF	CA		X	X	X	X	X	X	X	X	X	
Coconino NF	AZ	X	X	X	X	X	X	X	X	X	X	X
Coeur d'Alene NF	ID	X		X	X	X	X	X	X	X	X	X
Colville NF	WA	X		X	X	X	X	X	X	X	X	X
Conecuh NF	AL	X		X	X	X		X	X		X	
Coronado NF	AZ	X	X	X	X	X	X	X	X	X	X	X
Croatan NF	NC	X		X	X	X		X	X	X	X	
Custer NF	MT, SD	X	X	X	X	X	X	X	X	X	X	X
Daniel Boone NF	KY	X		X	X	X	X	X	X	X	X	
Davy Crockett NF	TX	X		X	X	X	X	X	X	X	X	
Deerlodge	MT	X	X	X	X	X	X	X	X	X	X	X
Delta NF	MS	X		X	X	X		X	X		X	

Facility	State	Boating	Cabins	Camping	Fishing	Hiking	Hotel/Lodge	Hunting	Picnicking	Riding	Swimming	Winter Sports
Deschutes NF	OR	X	X	X	X	X	X	X	X	X	X	X
DeSoto NF	MS	X		X	X	X	X	X	X	X	X	
Dixie NF	UT	X	X	X	X	X	X	X	X	X	X	X
Eldorado NF	CA	X	X	X	X	X	X	X	X	X	X	X
Fishlake NF	UT	X	X	X	X	X	X	X	X	X	X	X
Flathead NF	MT	X		X	X	X	X	X	X	X	X	X
Francis Marion NF	SC	X		X	X	X		X	X	X	X	
Fremont NF	OR	X	X	X	X	X		X	X	X		X
Gallatin NF	MT	X	X	X	X	X	X	X	X	X	X	X
George Washington NF	VA	X		X	X	X	X	X	X	X	X	X
Gifford Pinchot NF	WA	X	X	X	X	X	X	X	X	X	X	X
Gila NF	NM	X		X	X	X	X	X	X	X		X
Grand Mesa NF	CO	X	X	X	X	X	X	X	X	X	X	X
Green Mountain NF	VT	X		X	X	X	X	X	X	X	X	X
Gunnison NF	CO	X	X	X	X	X	X	X	X	X	X	X
Helena NF	MT	X	X	X	X	X	X	X	X	X	X	X
Hiawatha NF	MI	X		X	X	X	X	X	X	X	X	X
Holly Springs NF	MS	X		X	X	X		X	X	X	X	
Homochitto NF	MS	X		X	X	X		X	X	X	X	
Hoosier NF	IN	X		X	X	X		X	X	X	X	
Humboldt NF	NV	X	X	X	X	X	X	X	X	X	X	X
Huron NF	MI	X		X	X	X	X	X	X	X	X	X
Inyo NF	CA	X	X	X	X	X	X	X	X	X	X	X
Jefferson NF	VA	X		X	X	X	X	X	X	X	X	X
Kaibab NF	AZ	X	X	X	X	X	X	X	X	X		X
Kaniksu NF	ID, WA	X	X	X	X	X	X	X	X	X	X	X
Kisatchie NF	LA	X		X	X	X		X	X	X	X	
Klamath NF	CA	X	X	X	X	X	X	X	X	X	X	X
Kootenai NF	MT	X	X	X	X	X	X	X	X	X	X	X
Lassen NF	CA	X	X	X	X	X		X	X	X	X	X
Lewis and Clark NF	MT	X	X	X	X	X	X	X	X	X	X	X
Lincoln NF	NM			X	X	X	X	X	X	X		X
Lolo NF	MT	X	X	X	X	X	X	X	X	X	X	X
Los Padres NF	CA	X	X	X	X	X	X	X	X	X	X	
Malheur NF	OR	X	X	X	X	X	X	X	X	X	X	X
Manistee NF	MI	X	X	X	X	X	X	X	X	X	X	X
Manti-La Sal NF	UT	X	X	X	X	X	X	X	X	X	X	X

Facility	State	Boating	Cabins	Camping	Fishing	Hiking	Hotel/Lodge	Hunting	Picnicking	Riding	Swimming	Winter Sports
Mark Twain NF	MO	x	x	x	x	x	x	x	x	x	x	
Medicine Bow NF	WY	x		x	x	x	x	x	x	x		x
Mendocino NF	CA	x	x	x	x	x	x	x	x	x	x	
Modoc NF	CA	x		x	x	x	x	x	x	x	x	
Monongahela NF	WV	x	x	x	x	x	x	x	x	x	x	
Mount Baker NF	WA	x	x	x	x	x	x	x	x	x	x	x
Mount Hood NF	OR	x		x	x	x	x	x	x	x	x	x
Nantahala NF	NC	x		x	x	x	x	x	x		x	
Nebraska NF	NE		x	x	x	x	x	x	x	x	x	
Nez Perce NF	ID	x	x	x	x	x	x	x	x		x	
Nicolet NF	WI	x		x	x	x	x	x	x	x	x	x
Ocala NF	FL	x	x	x	x	x	x	x	x	x	x	
Ochoco NF	OR	x	x	x	x	x	x	x	x	x	x	x
Oconee NF	GA	x		x	x	x	x	x	x	x	x	
Okanogan NF	WA	x	x	x	x	x	x	x	x	x	x	x
Olympic NF	WA	x	x	x	x	x	x	x	x	x	x	x
Osceola NF	FL	x		x	x	x	x	x	x	x	x	
Ottawa NF	MI	x	x	x	x	x	x	x	x	x	x	x
Ouachita NF	AR, OK	x		x	x	x	x	x	x	x	x	
Ozark NF	AR	x		x	x	x	x	x	x	x	x	
Payette NF	ID	x	x	x	x	x	x	x	x	x	x	x
Pike NF	CO	x	x	x	x	x	x	x	x	x	x	x
Pisgah NF	NC	x		x	x	x	x	x	x	x	x	
Plumas NF	CA	x	x	x	x	x	x	x	x	x	x	x
Prescott NF	AZ		x	x	x	x	x	x	x	x	x	
Rio Grande NF	CO	x	x	x	x	x	x	x	x	x	x	x
Rogue River NF	OR, CA	x	x	x	x	x	x	x	x	x		x
Roosevelt NF	CO	x	x	x	x	x	x	x	x	x	x	x
Routt NF	CO	x	x	x	x	x	x	x	x	x	x	x
Sabine NF	TX	x		x	x	x	x	x	x	x	x	
Salmon NF	ID	x	x	x	x	x	x	x	x	x	x	x
Sam Houston NF	TX	x		x	x	x	x	x	x	x	x	
San Bernardino NF	CA	x	x	x	x	x	x	x	x	x	x	x
San Isabel NF	CO	x	x	x	x	x	x	x	x	x	x	x
San Juan NF	CO	x	x	x	x	x	x	x	x	x	x	x
Santa Fe NF	NM		x	x	x	x	x	x	x	x	x	x
Sawtooth NF	ID	x	x	x	x	x	x	x	x	x	x	x
Sequoia NF	CA	x	x	x	x	x	x	x	x	x	x	x
Shasta NF	CA	x	x	x	x	x	x	x	x	x	x	x

Facility	State	Boating	Cabins	Camping	Fishing	Hiking	Hotel/Lodge	Hunting	Picnicking	Riding	Swimming	Winter Sports
Shawnee NF	IL	x		x	x	x	x	x	x	x	x	x
Shoshone NF	WY	x	x	x	x	x	x	x	x	x		x
Sierra NF	CA	x	x	x	x	x	x	x	x	x	x	x
Siskiyou NF	OR, CA	x	x	x	x	x	x	x	x	x	x	
Sitgreaves NF	AZ	x		x	x	x	x	x	x	x	x	x
Siuslaw NF	OR	x		x	x	x	x	x	x	x	x	
Six Rivers NF	CA	x		x	x	x	x	x	x		x	
Snoqualmie NF	WA	x	x	x	x	x	x	x	x	x	x	x
Stanislaus NF	CA	x	x	x	x	x	x	x	x	x	x	x
St. Francis NF	AR	x		x	x	x	x	x	x			
St. Joe NF	ID	x	x	x	x	x	x	x	x	x	x	x
Sumter NF	SC	x		x	x	x	x	x	x	x	x	x
Superior NF	MN	x	x	x	x	x	x	x	x	x	x	x
Tahoe NF	CA	x	x	x	x	x	x	x	x	x	x	x
Talladega NF	AL	x	x	x	x	x	x	x	x	x	x	
Targhee NF	ID, WY	x	x	x	x	x	x	x	x	x	x	x
Teton NF	WY	x	x	x	x	x	x	x	x	x	x	x
Toiyabe NF	NV, CA	x	x	x	x	x	x	x	x	x	x	x
Tombigbee NF	MS	x		x	x	x	x	x	x		x	
North Tongass NF	AK	x	x	x	x	x	x	x	x		x	x
South Tongass NF	AK	x		x	x	x	x	x	x		x	x
Tonto NF	AZ	x	x	x	x	x	x	x	x	x	x	
Trinity NF	CA	x		x	x	x	x	x	x		x	
Tuskegee NF	AL						x	x	x			
Uinta NF	UT	x		x	x	x	x	x	x	x	x	x
Umatilla NF	OR		x	x	x	x	x	x	x	x		x
Umpqua NF	OR	x	x	x	x	x	x	x	x	x	x	x
Uncompahgre NF	CO		x	x	x	x	x	x	x			
Uwharrie NF	NC	x		x	x	x	x	x	x	x		
Wallowa-Whitman NF	OR	x	x	x	x	x	x	x	x	x	x	x
Wasatch NF	UT	x	x	x	x	x	x	x	x	x	x	x
Wayne NF	OH	x		x	x	x	x	x	x	x	x	
Wenatchee NF	WA	x	x	x	x	x	x	x	x	x	x	x
White Mountain NF	NH, ME	x	x	x	x	x	x	x	x	x	x	x
White River NF	CO	x	x	x	x	x	x	x	x	x	x	x
Willamette NF	OR	x	x	x	x	x	x	x	x	x	x	x
William B. Bankhead NF	AL	x		x	x	x	x	x	x		x	x
Winema NF	OR	x		x	x	x	x	x	x	x	x	x

738

Tongass National Forest: Landscape Character Types

ADMIRALTY-CHICHAGOF

In the Admiralty-Chichagof visual character type, landforms are generally rounded, except for mountainous terrain, which is rugged and snow-covered most of the year. Rocky islands, reefs, and rock bluffs are found frequently on the outer coast of Chichagof Island, the Mitchell Bay and Kootznahoo area, and along the southern tip of Admiralty Island. Saltwater bays and estuaries are numerous. Much of this character type exists in a natural-appearing condition.

Small communities such as Hoonah, Tenakee Springs, Pelican, Elfin Cove, and Angoon are located within this character type. The West Chichagof–Yakobi Wilderness and the Admiralty National Monument are located here as well. Timber harvest activities are presently occurring on Chichagof Island from Icy Strait to Peril Strait on both private and national forest lands. On Admiralty Island, mining operations are occurring on public lands, and timber harvest on private lands.

KUPREANOF LOWLAND

The Kupreanof Lowland visual character type encompasses the central portion of the Inside Passage, including the Wrangell Narrows; the Chatham, Sumner and Stikine Straits; Duncan Canal; Salmon Bay Lake; and Frederick Sound. The area is made up of islands with rolling terrain and topographic relief varying from 300 to 1500 feet, and is separated by an intricate network of waterways. Mountains are scattered and blocklike, rising to 3500 feet above the lowlands. The shoreline is made up of many small bays, rock reefs, and occasional small gravel beaches. The spruce-hemlock forest dominates this character type, except for areas of higher elevations where alpine ecosystems are present.

The communities of Kake, Rowan Bay, Port Protection, and Point Baker as well as the Tebenkof Bay, Kuiu, and Petersburg–Duncan Salt Chuck Wildernesses are within this character type. The southern portions of Kuiu and Kupreanof Islands, Rocky Pass, and south Lindenburg Peninsula are in a natural condition. The northern portions of Prince of Wales and Kuiu Islands are heavily modified due to timber harvest and road development activities.

BARANOF HIGHLAND

The Baranof Highland character type reflects the unique qualities of Baranof Island, with elevations reaching 3000 to 5000 feet. Shoreline forms are very rugged with steep-sided fiords on both eastern and western coasts. The Sergius Narrows, Chatham and Peril Straits and the South Baranof Wilderness Area are included in this area.

The majority of this character type remains in a natural-appearing condition. The communities of Sitka, Baranof Warm Springs, and Port Alexander as well as the South Baranof Wilderness Area are located on Baranof Island. Timber harvest activities have occurred on the northern reaches of Baranof Island from Sitka Sound to Peril Strait to Chatham Strait, as well as on Kruzof Island.

CORDOVA-YAKUTAT

The Cordova-Yakutat visual character type runs east to west, spanning from Yakutat to the Malaspina Glacier to Icy Bay to Cordova. The Chugach Mountains to the north and the Wrangell–St. Elias Mountain Ranges to the south act as visual backdrops to this character type, which includes the second-tallest peak in North America. The Yakutat Forelands dominate scenes adjacent to Yakutat and Russell Fiords which includes the community of Yakutat.

Past logging activities are evident near Yakutat. Small fish camps are visible along the rivers and beaches. Large expanses of sand beaches stretching for miles make this a unique area on the Tongass. The Russell Fiord Wilderness is in this character type.

COASTAL HILL

The southern reaches of the forest are represented by the Coastal Hill visual character type, whose islands offer an extensive landform variety with elevations ranging from 1000 to 4500 feet. Areas with elevations of less than 3500 feet were glaciated and have rounded hummocky summits, knobs, and ridges. Marine travel routes of significance include Clarence, Stikine and Zimovia Straits, Behm Canal, and Chomly Sound.

The communities of Wrangell, Petersburg, Thorne Bay, Ketchikan, Craig, Klawock, and Hydaburg are within this character type. The area is substantially developed, with timber harvest activities evident on central Prince of Wales Island, north and central Revilla Island, Mitkof, Wrangell, Deer and North Etolin Islands. The Alaska Marine Highway (ferry) and cruiseship traffic pass through this area.

COAST-RANGE

The Coast-Range visual character type encompasses the mainland from Dixon Entrance to the south and Lynn Canal to the north. The scale of the landforms is large and massive, generally ranging from 5000 to 7000 feet in elevation with occasional rock formations reaching to 9000 feet. Geological features abound in this character type—cliffs, rock escarpments with jagged peaks, and spires at higher elevations. Glacial streams are generally braided and originate in British Columbia.

This character type offers numerous opportunities to view spectacular scenery, and includes the Stikine-LeConte, Endicott River, and Tracy Arm–Fords Terror Wilderness Areas; the Misty Fiords National Monument; and the communities of Juneau, Skagway, and Haines. The majority of areas with this character type are natural-appearing; however, there is evidence of past and current mining and timber harvest on both private and public lands. Significant travel routes of interest are Frederick Sound, Stephens Passage, Lynn Canal (north to Skagway), the Eastern Passage / Back Channel, and Behm Canal. Commercial sightseeing ventures are promoting the scenic attractions found in this area.

Source: Forest Service, *Tongass Land Management Plan Revision—Part 1.* August 1991.

National Wildlife Refuge System: Areas, Acreages, and Use

Refuge	State(s)	Fig. 11.1 Map #	Acres	Visits**
Blowing Wind Caves	AL	1	264.00	
Bon Secour	AL	2	4,628.74	10,977
Choctaw	AL	3	4,218.00	17,420
Eufaula	AL, GA	4	7,953.19	401,559
Fern Cave	AL	5	199.23	
Grand Bay	AL, MS	6	839.56	
Watercress Darter	AL	7	7.10	
Wheeler	AL	8	34,169.98	604,038
FH Interest*	AL		605.07	
Alaska Maritime	AK	9	3,435,639.27	1,469
Alaska Peninsula	AK	10	3,500,000.00	1,125
Arctic	AK	11	19,285,922.34	3,463
Becharof	AK	12	1,200,017.75	703
Innoko	AK	13	3,850,000.20	150
Inzembek	AK	14	303,094.00	6,305
Kanuti	AK	15	1,430,001.74	3,773
Kenai	AK	16	1,904,752.00	183,494
Kodiak	AK	17	1,656,362.71	20,192
Koyukuk	AK	18	3,550,000.30	14,580
Nowitna	AK	19	1,560,000.25	2,208
Selawik	AK	20	2,150,000.86	
Tetlin	AK	21	700,053.54	28,801
Togiak	AK	22	4,097,430.00	7,332
Yukon Delta	AK	23	19,131,644.67	620,416
Yukon Flats	AK	24	8,630,000.00	103,103
Buenos Aires	AZ	25	113,940.03	1,470
Cabeza Prieta	AZ	26	860,000.00	10,282
Cibola	AZ, CA	27	8,606.04	45,441
Havasu	AZ, CA	28	36,334.82	520,665
Imperial	AZ, CA	29	17,809.76	330,246
Kofa	AZ	30	666,480.00	41,500
San Bernardino	AZ	31	3,608.57	
Big Lake	AR	32	11,036.10	63,841
Cache River	AR	33	21,873.35	
Felsenthal	AR	34	64,902.12	289,137
Holla Bend	AR	35	6,077.38	24,120
Logan Cave	AR	36	123.59	
Overflow	AR	37	11,403.57	10,865
Wapanocca	AR	38	5,484.17	37,653

Refuge	State(s)	Fig. 11.1 Map #	Acres	Visits**
White River	AR	39	113,230.04	50,844
FH Interest*	AR		3,458.67	
Antioch Dunes	CA	40	55.38	4,911
Bitter Creek	CA	41	13,977.45	
Blue Ridge	CA	42	897.08	
Butte Sink	CA	43	9,163.91	
Castle Rock	CA	44	13.89	
Cibola	CA, AZ	27	3,646.52	Incl. in AZ
Clear Lake	CA	45	33,440.00	130
Coachella Valley	CA	46	3,074.10	
Colusa	CA	47	4,039.98	6,099
Delevan	CA	48	5,633.54	7,223
Ellicott Slough	CA	49	127.46	
Farallon	CA	50	211.00	1,646
Grasslands	CA	51	42,517.72	
Havasu	CA, AZ	28	7,235.34	Incl. in AZ
Hopper Mountain	CA	52	2,471.00	
Humboldt Bay	CA	53	2,109.51	
Imperial	CA, AZ	29	7,958.19	Incl. in AZ
Kern	CA	54	10,618.17	2,996
Kesterson	CA	55	11,500.00	1,253
Lower Klamath	CA, OR	56	40,294.44	135,621
Marin Islands	CA		8.70	
Merced	CA	57	2,563.30	2,119
Modoc	CA	58	6,386.38	8,874
North Central Valley	CA		7,126.41	
Pixley	CA	59	6,192.47	
Sacramento	CA	60	10,783.34	49,421
Sacramento River	CA	61	5,639.59	
Salinas River	CA	62	367.43	2,953
Salton Sea	CA	63	37,578.87	42,714
San Francisco Bay	CA	64	18,560.46	275,224
San Joaquin River	CA	65	777.00	
San Luis	CA	66	8,133.41	15,489
San Pablo Bay	CA	67	13,189.72	1,460
Seal Beach	CA	68	910.71	
Sutter	CA	69	2,590.16	2,949
Sweetwater Marsh	CA	70	315.80	
Tijuana Slough	CA	71	1,023.42	28,870
Tule Lake	CA	72	39,119.28	178,569
Willow Creek-Lurline	CA	73	4,596.32	
FH Interest*	CA		80.00	
Alamosa	CO	74	11,169.11	3,125
Arapaho	CO	75	18,253.67	5,816
Browns Park	CO	76	13,455.30	4,220
Monte Vista	CO	77	14,188.95	6,220
Two Ponds Wetland Preserve	CO		23.24	
FH Interest*	CO		159.00	
Stewart B McKinney	CT	78	346.58	
Bombay Hook	DE	79	15,121.66	79,043
Prime Hook	DE	80	9,700.90	43,433
FH Interest*	DE		2.60	
Archie Carr	FL	81	12.98	
Arthur R. Marshall Loxahatchee	FL	82	145,665.37	357,095

		Fig. 11.1		
Refuge	**State(s)**	**Map #**	**Acres**	**Visits****
Caloosahatchee	FL	83	40.00	
Cedar Keys	FL	84	721.15	4,433
Chassahowitzka	FL	85	30,436.34	19,010
Crocodile Lake	FL	86	6,558.93	
Crystal River	FL	87	46.34	46,538
Egmont Key	FL	88	328.30	
Florida Panther	FL	39	23,379.04	
Great White Heron	FL	90	7,407.53	
Hobe Sound	FL	91	979.87	133,000
Island Bay	FL	92	20.24	
J. N. "Ding" Darling	FL	93	5,347.66	845,248
Key West	FL	94	2,019.17	
Lake Woodruff	FL	95	19,545.02	26,661
Lower Suwanee	FL	96	50,138.59	14,023
Matlacha Pass	FL	97	511.61	
Merritt Island	FL	98	138,262.70	1,904,974
National Key Deer	FL	99	8,109.60	61,145
Okefenokee	FL, GA	100	3,678.14	351,152
Passage Key	FL	101	63.87	
Pelican Island	FL	102	4,425.70	13,050
Pine Island	FL	103	548.24	
Pinellas	FL	104	391.55	
St. Johns	FL	105	6,254.95	
St. Marks	FL	106	65,400.37	194,001
St. Vincent	FL	107	12,489.93	3,703
FH Interest*	FL		1,455.67	
Banks Lake	GA	108	4,049.00	22,332
Blackbeard Island	GA	109	5,617.64	3,580
Bond Swamp	GA	110	4,596.25	
Eufaula	GA, AL	4	3,231.00	Incl. in AL
Harris Neck	GA	111	2,761.83	2,535
Okefenokee	GA, FL	100	391,401.99	Incl. in AL
Piedmont	GA	112	34,903.10	118,610
Savannah	GA, SC	113	11,323.75	95,477
Tybee	GA	114	100.00	
Wassaw	GA	115	10,069.87	25,980
Wolf Island	GA	116	5,125.82	
FH Interest*	GA		3,907.70	
Hakalau Forest	HI	117	15,480.96	
Hanalei	HI	118	917.42	396,382
Hawaiian Islands	HI	119	254,418.10	
Huleia	HI	120	241.12	29,152
James C. Campbell	HI	121	165.51	353
Kakahaia	HI	122	44.61	2,025
Kilauea Point	HI	123	187.50	
Pearl Harbor	HI	124	61.15	22
Bear Lake	ID	125	18,068.18	1,827
Camas	ID	126	10,578.34	1,870
Deer Flat	ID, OR	127	11,265.39	86,179
Grays Lake	ID	128	16,579.02	1,260
Kootenai	ID	129	2,774.29	5,945
Minidoka	ID	130	20,723.69	916
Chautauqua	IL	131	6,445.57	27,982
Crab Orchard	IL	132	43,661.74	1,042,172

Refuge	State(s)	Fig. 11.1 Map #	Acres	Visits**
Cypress Creek	IL	133	5,443.04	
Mark Twain	IL, IA, MO	134	16,578.69	
Meredosia	IL	135	2,188.49	
Mississippi River Caue	IL, IA, MN, WI	136	20,120.00	
Upper Mississippi River	IL, IA, MN, WI	137	3,299.98	90
FH Interest*	IL		738.56	
Muscatatuck	IN	138	7,802.22	89,479
FH Interest*	IN		253.31	
DeSoto	IA, NE	139	3,502.77	446,527
Driftless Area	IA	140	506.55	
Mark Twain	IA, IL, MO	134	10,471.44	Incl. in IL
Mississippi River Cave***	IA, IL, MN, WI	136	30,315.00	Incl. in IL
Union Slough	IA	141	2,915.94	6,457
Upper Mississippi River	IA, IL, MN, WI	137	20,668.73	Incl. in IL
Walnut Creek	IA	142	4,115.52	
FH Interest*	IA		92.31	
Flint Hills	KS	143	18,463.36	40,650
Kirwin	KS	144	10,778.00	85,056
Marais Des Cygnes	KS		5,101.04	
Quivira	KS	145	21,820.10	2,775
FH Interest*	KS		116.50	
Reelfoot	KY, TN	146	2,039.64	
Atchafalaya	LA	147	15,255.23	
Bayou Cocodrie	LA		4,932.36	
Bayou Sauvage	LA	148	18,000.00	
Bogue Chitto	LA, MS	149	28,670.99	13,575
Breton	LA	150	9,047.00	
Cameron Prairie	LA	151	9,621.30	
Catahoula	LA	152	5,318.51	33,276
D'Arbonne	LA	153	17,419.63	50,140
Delta	LA	154	48,799.10	1,524
Grand Cote	LA		6,077.00	
Lacassine	LA	155	32,624.77	8,681
Lake Ophelia	LA	156	14,476.56	
Sabine	LA	157	139,436.81	85,644
Shell Keys	LA	158	8.00	
Tensas River	LA	159	59,023.11	22,590
Upper Ouachita	LA	160	20,890.25	24,875
FH Interest*	LA		12,881.63	
Cross Island	ME	161	1,703.10	
Franklin Island	ME	162	11.94	
Moosehorn	ME	163	23,914.30	13,339
Petit Manan	ME	164	3,334.62	
Pond Island	ME	165	10.00	
Rachel Carson	ME	166	4,216.48	8,585
Seal Island	ME	167	65.00	
Sunkhaze Meadows	ME	168	9,337.40	
FH Interest*	ME		622.08	
Blackwater	MD	169	17,860.26	150,415
Chincoteague	MD, VA	170	417.81	1,491,008
Eastern Neck	MD	171	2,286.28	65,784
Martin	MD	172	4,423.43	5,261
Patuxent	MD	173	12,275.98	
Susquehanna	MD	174	3.79	

Refuge	State(s)	Fig. 11.1 Map #	Acres	Visits**
FH Interest*	MD		67.94	
Great Meadows	MA	175	3,370.03	138,100
Massasoit	MA	176	184.00	
Monomoy	MA	177	2,701.85	7,932
Nantucket	MA	178	39.80	
Nomans Land Island	MA	179	620.00	
Oxbow	MA	180	711.03	1,376
Parker River	MA	181	4,652.41	346,708
Thacher Island	MA	182	22.00	
Harbor Island	MI	183	695.00	
Huron	MI	184	147.50	
Kirtlands Warbler	MI	185	6,310.43	
Michigan Island	MI	186	363.34	
Seney	MI	187	95,455.48	62,127
Shiawassee	MI	188	8,984.41	18,657
Wyandotte	MI	189	304.47	
FH Interest*	MI		2,520.09	
Agassiz	MN	190	61,500.93	22,188
Big Stone	MN	191	11,274.63	36,853
Hamden Slough	MN	192	2,196.83	
Mid Continent WMP	MN	193	5,076.89	
Mille Lacs	MN	194	0.60	
Minnesota Valley	MN	195	7,949.44	55,944
Mississippi River Cave***	MN, IL, IA, WI	136	15,420.77	Incl. in IL
Rice Lake	MN	196	16,371.48	13,903
Rydell	MN		2,070.00	
Sherburne	MN	197	29,605.89	49,070
Tamarac	MN	198	35,167.41	50,691
Upper Mississippi River	MN, IL, IA, WI	137	18,083.38	Incl. in IL
FH Interest*	MN		1,521.37	
Bogue Chitto	MS, LA	149	6,808.08	Incl. in LA
Dahomey	MS	199	4,849.80	
Grand Bay	MS, AL	6	2,649.13	Incl. in AL
Hillside	MS	200	15,405.87	6,733
Mathews Brake	MS	201	2,418.74	
Mississippi Sandhill Crane	MS	202	19,303.23	1,612
Morgan Brake	MS	203	4,864.86	2,608
Noxubee	MS	204	46,672.94	89,411
Panther Swamp	MS	205	28,599.78	6,716
St. Catherine Creek	MS	206	13,034.55	
Tallahatchie	MS	207	3,898.00	
Yazoo	MS	208	12,940.43	15,100
FH Interest*	MS		19,734.95	
Clarence Cannon	MO	209	3,749.98	702
Mark Twain	MO, IL, IA	134	1,352.32	Incl. in IL
Mingo	MO	210	21,745.64	121,118
Ozark Cavefish	MO		40.00	
Pilot Knob	MO	211	90.00	
Squaw Creek	MO	212	7,245.53	121,500
Swan Lake	MO	213	11,347.70	77,725
FH Interest*	MO		567.31	
Benton Lake	MT	214	12,453.01	8,435
Black Coulee	MT	215	1,308.88	
Bowdoin	MT	216	15,551.97	3,320

Refuge	State(s)	Fig. 11.1 Map #	Acres	Visits**
Charles M. Russell	MT	217	903,331.54	59,022
Creedman Coulee	MT	218	2,728.00	
Hailstone	MT	219	920.00	78
Halfbreed Lake	MT	220	4,318.24	25
Hewitt Lake	MT	221	1,360.92	
Lake Mason	MT	222	16,659.92	103
Lake Thibadeau	MT	223	3,868.48	
Lamesteer	MT	224	800.00	
Lee Metcalf	MT	225	2,792.52	19,950
Medicine Lake	MT	226	31,484.01	3,805
National Bison Range	MT	227	18,497.35	122,372
Nine-Pipe	MT	228	2,021.95	6,375
Pablo	MT	229	2,541.95	980
Red Rock Lakes	MT	230	44,157.92	4,941
Swan River	MT	231	1,568.81	410
UL Bend	MT	232	56,049.56	
War Horse	MT	233	3,192.24	11
FH Interest*	MT		510.62	
Crescent Lake	NE	234	45,849.48	16,817
DeSoto	NE, IA	139	4,324.20	Incl. in IA
Fort Niobrara	NE	235	19,132.53	34,717
Karl E. Munot	NE, SD	236	19.39	
North Platte	NE	237	5,047.00	3,251
Valentine	NE	238	71,517.09	11,336
FH Interest*	NE		790.00	
Anaho Island	NV	239	247.73	
Ash Meadows	NV	240	13,231.03	2,845
Desert	NV	241	1,588,818.55	23,150
Fallon	NV	242	17,901.94	
Moapa Valley	NV	243	32.41	
Pahranagat	NV	244	5,382.74	26,713
Ruby Lake	NV	245	37,631.26	68,083
Sheldon	NV, OR	246	570,461.24	18,200
Stillwater	NV	247	78,085.70	42,518
Great Bay	NH	248	1,054.00	
John Hay	NH	249	143.80	
Wapack	NH		1,672.00	4,530
Cape May	NJ	250	5,687.60	
Edwin B. Forsythe	NJ	251	39,460.94	
Great Swamp	NJ	252	7,238.24	133,989
Supawna Meadows	NJ	253	2,856.86	
Wallkill River	NJ		538.93	
Bitter Lake	NM		24,526.27	43,814
Bosque del Apache	NM	255	57,191.10	84,434
Grulla	NM, TX	256	3,230.55	89
Las Vegas	NM	257	8,672.08	37,823
Maxwell	NM	258	3,698.59	15,821
San Andres	NM	259	57,215.48	
Sevilleta	NM	260	229,673.57	102
Amagansett	NY	261	35.84	
Conscience Point	NY	262	60.40	13
Elizabeth A. Morton	NY	263	187.19	28,807
Iroquois	NY	264	10,821.53	83,647
Montezuma	NY	265	6,446.45	164,681

Refuge	State(s)	Fig. 11.1 Map #	Acres	Visits**
Oyster Bay	NY	266	3,204.08	12,575
Seatuck	NY	267	209.23	
Target Rock	NY	268	80.09	29,069
Wertheim	NY	269	2,424.25	18,405
FH Interest*	NY		1,855.90	
Alligator River	NC	270	141,595.51	7,292
Cedar Island	NC	271	14,482.04	41,620
Currituck	NC	272	2,045.72	20,900
Great Dismal Swamp	NC, VA	273	49,624.20	14,543
MacKay Island	NC, VA	274	6,996.64	29,209
Mattamuskeet	NC	275	50,180.18	51,044
Pea Island	NC	276	5,834.20	1,304,268
Pee Dee	NC	277	8,438.94	11,476
Pocosin Lake	NC	278	107,718.75	
Roanoke River	NC	279	6,058.00	
Swanquarter	NC	280	16,411.11	6,375
FH Interest*	NC		4,323.39	
Appert Lake	ND	281	907.75	
Ardoch	ND	282	2,696.13	
Arrowwood	ND	283	15,934.42	6,928
Audubon	ND	284	14,739.19	4,285
Bone Hill	ND	285	640.00	
Brumba	ND	286	1,977.48	
Buffalo Lake	ND	287	2,096.36	
Camp Lake	ND	288	584.70	
Canfield Lake	ND	289	313.23	
Chase Lake	ND	290	4,384.65	461
Cottonwood	ND	291	1,013.47	
Dakota Lake	ND	292	2,799.78	
Des Lacs	ND	293	19,547.14	5,279
Florence Lake	ND	294	1,888.20	
Half-Way Lake	ND	295	160.00	
Hiddenwood	ND	296	568.35	
Hobart Lake	ND	297	2,077.10	
Hutchinson Lake	ND	298	478.90	
J. Clark Salyer	ND	299	59,383.04	16,299
Johnson Lake	ND	300	2,007.91	
Kellys Slough	ND	301	1,269.50	
Lake Alice	ND	302	11,354.59	
Lake Elsie	ND	303	634.70	
Lake George	ND	304	3,118.81	
Lake Ilo	ND	305	4,034.50	2,870
Lake Nettie	ND	306	3,054.90	
Lake Otis	ND	307	320.00	
Lake Zahl	ND	308	3,823.19	
Lambs Lake	ND	309	1,206.67	
Little Goose	ND	310	288.41	
Long Lake	ND	311	22,498.50	5,902
Lords Lake	ND	312	1,915.29	
Lost Lake	ND	313	960.21	
Lostwood	ND	314	26,903.99	926
Maple River	ND	315	712.00	
McLean	ND	316	760.00	
Pleasant Lake	ND	317	897.80	

Refuge	State(s)	Fig. 11.1 Map #	Acres	Visits**
Pretty Rock	ND	318	800.00	
Rabb Lake	ND	319	260.80	
Rock Lake	ND	320	5,505.96	
Rose Lake	ND	321	836.30	
School Section Lake	ND	322	680.00	
Shell Lake	ND	323	1,835.10	
Sheyenne Lake	ND	324	797.30	
Sibley Lake	ND	325	1,077.40	
Silver Lake	ND	326	3,347.64	
Slade	ND	327	3,000.20	2,298
Snyder Lake	ND	328	1,550.18	
Springwater	ND	329	640.00	
Stewart Lake	ND	330	2,230.40	
Stoney Slough	ND	331	880.00	
Storm Lake	ND	332	685.90	
Stump Lake	ND	333	27.39	
Sullys Hill	ND	334	1,675.14	
Sunburst Lake	ND	335	327.51	
Tewaukon	ND	336	8,363.62	10,230
Tomahawk	ND	337	440.00	
Upper Souris	ND		32,302.25	79,045
White Lake	ND	339	1,040.00	
Wild Rice Lake	ND	340	778.80	
Willow Lake	ND	341	2,620.38	
Wintering River	ND	342	239.26	
Wood Lake	ND	343	280.00	
FH Interest*	ND		44.00	
Cedar Point	OH	344	2,445.42	1,568
Ottawa	OH	345	5,793.28	40,525
West Sister Island	OH	346	80.13	
Little River	OK	347	12,028.85	
Oklahoma Bat Caves	OK	348	593.22	
Optima	OK	349	4,332.81	626
Salt Plains	OK	350	32,057.12	149,639
Sequoyah	OK	351	20,800.00	79,243
Tishomingo	OK	352	16,464.18	122,600
Washita	OK	353	8,075.37	31,117
Wichita Mountains	OK	354	59,019.60	1,438,000
Ankeny	OR	355	2,796.33	6,566
Bandon Marsh	OR	356	306.78	
Baskett Slough	OR	357	2,492.33	22,763
Bear Valley	OR	358	4,178.34	875
Cape Meares	OR	359	138.51	26,287
Cold Springs	OR	360	3,116.83	51,226
Deer Flats	OR, ID	127	162.44	Incl. in ID
Hart Mountain	OR	361	251,295.23	
Julia Butler Hansen	OR, WA	362	1,978.42	
Klamath Forest	OR	363	37,686.05	1,200
Lewis and Clark	OR	364	38,172.46	6,685
Lower Klamath	OR, CA	56	6,618.13	Incl. in CA
Malheur	OR	365	185,411.59	37,850
McKay Creek	OR	366	1,836.50	60,259
Nestucca Bay	OR	367	369.25	
Oregon Islands	OR	368	611.03	

Refuge	State(s)	Fig. 11.1 Map #	Acres	Visits**
Sheldon	OR, NV	246	627.48	Incl. in NV
Siletz	OR		39.84	
Three Arch Rocks	OR	369	15.00	
Umatilla	OR, WA	370	8,879.77	139,768
Upper Klamath	OR	371	14,966.16	19,734
William L. Finley	OR	372	5,332.11	23,557
FH Interest*	OR		358.05	
Erie	PA	373	8,750.01	37,833
John Heinz	PA	375	922.67	
Ohio River Islands	PA, WV	374	55.20	
Block Island	RI	376	46.30	11,890
Ninigret	RI	377	407.83	6,124
Pettaquamscutt Cove	RI	378	153.90	
Sachuest Point	RI	379	241.90	34,517
Trustom Pond	RI	380	641.72	116,015
Ace Basin	SC	381	2,860.82	
Cape Romain	SC	382	65,224.94	59,535
Caroline Sandhills	SC	383	45,348.43	27,994
Pinckney Island	SC	384	4,052.70	61,330
Santee	SC	385	43,636.44	114,624
Savannah	SC, GA	113	14,284.55	Incl. in GA
FH Interest*	SC		500.67	
Bear Butte	SD	386	374.90	
Karl E. Mundt	SD, NE	236	1,063.21	Incl. in NE
Lacreek	SD	387	16,855.33	34,896
Lake Andes	SD	388	939.43	16,257
Pocasse	SD	389	2,584.51	
Sand Lake	SD	390	21,818.19	92,420
Waubay	SD	391	4,740.22	13,213
FH Interest*	SD		35.20	
Chickasaw	TN	392	21,939.36	41,470
Cross Creeks	TN	393	8,861.49	21,088
Hatchie	TN	394	13,049.10	35,850
Lake Isom	TN	395	1,845.96	5,390
Lower Hatchie	TN	396	4,342.48	6,511
Reelfoot	TN, KY	146	8,408.98	Incl. in KY
Tennessee	TN	397	51,357.97	401,688
FH Interest*	TN		541.53	
Anahuac	TX	398	28,559.84	23,748
Aransas	TX	399	112,422.30	72,603
Attwater Prairie Chicken	TX	400	7,984.18	7,277
Balcones Canyonlands	TX		3,535.77	
Big Boggy	TX	401	4,526.17	12,059
Brazoria	TX	402	42,338.41	15,177
Buffalo Lake	TX	403	7,664.16	9,913
Grulla	TX, NM	265	4.97	Incl. in NM
Hagerman	TX	404	12,142.25	233,210
Laguna Atascosa	TX	405	45,187.03	78,183
Little Sandy	TX	406	3,802.00	
Lower Rio Grande Valley	TX	407	60,708.71	
McFaddin	TX	408	42,955.73	10,944
Moody	TX	409	3,516.87	
Muleshoe	TX	410	5,809.10	21,615
San Bernard	TX	411	24,453.99	17,488

Refuge	State(s)	Fig. 11.1 Map #	Acres	Visits**
Santa Ana	TX	412	2,087.50	260,132
Texas Point	TX	413	8,952.02	8,025
Bear River	UT	414	65,163.08	211
Fish Springs	UT	415	17,992.24	3,502
Ouray	UT	416	12,138.24	
Missisquoi	VT	417	5,838.98	7,773
FH Interest*	VT		71.00	
Back Bay	VA	418	5,567.82	140,127
Chincoteague	VA, MD	170	13,452.57	Incl. in MD
Eastern Shore of Virginia	VA	419	651.02	
Featherstone	VA	420	325.82	
Fisherman Island	VA	421	1,025.00	
Great Dismal Swamp	VA, NC	273	82,150.04	Incl. in NC
James River	VA	422	4,146.50	
MacKay Island	VA, NC	274	874.40	Incl. in NC
Marumsco	VA	423	62.83	13,574
Mason Neck	VA	424	2,275.99	12,421
Nansemond	VA	425	207.51	
Plum Tree Island	VA	426	3,275.60	
Presquile	VA	427	1,328.92	2,537
Wallops Island	VA	428	3,373.00	
FH Interest*	VA		133.70	
Columbia	WA	429	29,596.83	184,503
Conboy Lake	WA	430	5,813.96	1,695
Copalis	WA	431	60.80	
Dungeness	WA	432	762.32	168,500
Flattery Rocks	WA	433	125.00	
Franz Lake	WA	434	530.88	
Grays Harbor	WA	435	73.37	
Julia Butler Hansen	WA, OR	382	2,776.89	Incl. in OR
Little Pend Oreille	WA	436	39,998.57	
McNary	WA	437	3,630.70	18,816
Nisqually	WA	438	2,846.88	70,350
Pierce	WA	439	329.38	
Protection Island	WA	440	319.31	
Quillayute Needles	WA	441	300.20	
Ridgefield	WA	442	5,150.20	27,808
Saddle Mountain	WA	443	30,810.00	
San Juan Island	WA	444	448.53	11,250
Steigerwald Lake	WA	445	626.91	
Toppenish	WA	446	1,978.84	8,668
Turnbull	WA	447	17,824.17	43,299
Umatilla	WA, OR	390	14,675.83	Incl. in OR
Willapa	WA	448	14,393.83	20,790
FH Interest*	WA		244.68	
Ohio River Islands	WV, PA	374	310.60	Incl. in PA
Fox River	WI	449	837.84	
Gravel Island	WI	450	27.00	
Green Bay	WI	451	2.00	
Horicon	WI	452	21,176.41	392,885
MIssissippi River Cave	WI, IA, IL, MN	136	40,341.00	Incl. in IL
Necedah	WI	453	43,655.86	90,750
Trempealeau	WI	454	5,616.94	48,050
Upper Mississippi River	WI, IA, IL, MN	137	48,206.26	Incl. in IL

Refuge	State(s)	Fig. 11.1 Map #	Acres	Visits**
FH Interest*	WI		1,611.11	
Bamforth	WY	455	1,166.03	
Hutton Lake	WY	456	1,968.34	231
Mortenson Lake	WY		1,776.34	
National Elk	WY	457	24,774.44	532,274
Pathfinder	WY	458	16,806.90	
Seedskadee	WY	459	15,723.05	2,959
FH Interest*	WY		2,000.00	
Rose Atoll	American Samoa	460	39,066.00	
Baker Island	Baker Island	461	31,736.89	
Johnston Island	Johnston Atoll	462	100.00	
Midway Atoll	Midway Island	463	90,096.85	
Cabo Rojo	PR	464	587.33	
Culebra	PR	465	1,568.00	
Desched	PR	466	360.00	
Laguna Cartagena	PR	467	772.89	
Howland Island	Swan Islands	468	32,550.25	
Buck Island	VI	469	45.15	
Green Cay	VI	470	13.77	
Sandy Point	VI	471	326.73	
Jarvis Island	Jarvis Island	472	37,519.17	

*Summary by state of all other acres, both fee and less than fee acquired from the Farmer's Home Administration, not reported within an existing project. Summary may contain one or more ownerships. FmHA state summary acres are included in the total acres for each state but are not counted as separate units in the national wildlife refuge state totals.

**Data not available where left blank.

***Corps of Engineers, Department of the Army, within reach of Upper Mississippi River Wildlife and Fish Refuge.

Sources: Fish and Wildlife Service, *Annual Report of Lands under Control of the U.S. Fish & Wildlife Service,* September 30, 1992; Fish and Wildlife Service, *National Wildlife Refuge System—Public Use Reports,* April 15, 1988.

National Wildlife Refuge System: Recreational Opportunities

State/Refuge listing of recreational activities by National Wildlife Refuge.

Alabama / Alaska / Arizona

State/Refuge	Visitor Center	Foot Trails	Auto Tour	Bicycling	Boating, Nonmotorized	Boating, Motorized	Environmental Study Area	Backcountry Use	Hunting	Fishing	Camping	Picnicking	Swimming
Alabama													
Bon Secour	x	x	x	x			x			x			
Choctaw		x	x	x	x		x		x	x		x	
Eufaula (AL and GA)	x	x	x	x	x	x	x		x	x	x	x	
Wheeler	x	x	x	x	x	x	x		x	x	x	x	
Alaska													
Alaska Maritime	x	x				x	x	x	x		x	x	
Alaska Peninsula Unit					x	x	x	x	x	x	x	x	
Aleutian Islands Unit	x	x			x	x	x	x	x	x	x	x	
Bering Sea Unit						x	x	x	x	x	x	x	
Chukchi Sea Unit						x	x	x	x	x	x	x	
Gulf of Alaska Unit					x	x	x	x	x	x	x	x	
Alaska Peninsula					x	x	x	x	x	x	x	x	
Becharof	x				x	x	x	x	x	x	x	x	
Arctic					x	x		x	x	x	x	x	
Innoko	x	x	x		x	x		x	x	x	x	x	
Izembek	x	x	x	x	x	x		x	x	x	x	x	
Kanuti					x	x		x	x	x	x	x	
Kenai	x	x	x	x	x	x	x	x	x	x	x	x	
Kodiak	x	x	x		x	x	x	x	x	x	x	x	
Koyukuk					x	x		x	x	x	x	x	
Nowitna					x	x		x	x	x	x	x	
Selawik	x				x	x		x	x	x	x	x	
Tetlin	x	x	x		x	x	x	x	x	x	x	x	
Togiak	x				x	x		x	x	x	x	x	
Yukon Delta					x	x		x	x	x	x	x	
Yukon Flats					x	x		x	x	x	x	x	
Arizona													
Buenos Aires	x	x	x	x			x	x	x		x	x	
Cabeza Prieta	x						x	x			x	x	
Cibola (AZ and CA)				x	x	x		x	x	x	x	x	x
Havasu (AZ and CA)					x	x	x	x	x	x	x	x	x
Imperial (AZ and CA)	x	x		x	x	x	x	x	x	x	x	x	x
Kofa	x	x			x	x		x	x	x	x	x	x
San Bernardino									x				

Arkansas / California / Colorado

State/Refuge	Visitor Center	Foot Trails	Auto Tour	Bicycling	Boating, Nonmotorized	Boating, Motorized	Environmental Study Area	Backcountry Use	Hunting	Fishing	Camping	Picnicking	Swimming
Arkansas													
Felsenthal	x	x			x	x	x		x	x			
Holla Bend		x	x	x	x	x	x		x	x			
Wapanocca	x		x	x	x	x	x		x	x			
Big Lake			x	x	x	x	x		x	x			
Cache River									x	x			
White River		x	x				x		x	x			
California													
Cibola, Havasu, Imperial (AZ)													
Kern		x	x				x		x				
Klamath Basin Refuges													
Clear Lake									x				
Lower Klamath (OR and CA)				x					x				
Tule Lake	x		x	x					x				
Modoc		x	x		x	x			x	x		x	
Sacramento Valley Refuges													
Colusa	x		x						x	x			
Delevan									x	x			
Sacramento	x		x						x	x			
Sutter									x				
Salton Sea		x		x					x	x			
Coachella Valley		x											
Tijuana Slough		x											
San Francisco Bay	x	x	x		x	x	x		x				
Antioch Dunes													
Humboldt Bay									x	x			
Salinas River		x							x				
San Pablo Bay		x			x	x	x		x	x			
San Luis			x	x	x	x	x		x	x			
Kesterson													
Merced			x						x				
Colorado													
Alamosa			x	x			x		x	x			
Monte Vista			x				x		x	x			
Arapaho			x						x	x			

754

State/Refuge	Visitor Center	Foot Trails	Auto Tour	Bicycling	Boating, Nonmotorized	Boating, Motorized	Environmental Study Area	Backcountry Use	Hunting	Fishing	Camping	Picnicking	Swimming
Browns Park	x	x		x			x			x	x	x	x
Connecticut													
Salt Meadow			x										
Stewart B. McKinney													
Delaware													
Bombay Hook	x	x	x	x		x		x		x			
Prime Hook	x	x	x	x	x	x	x			x	x	x	x
Florida													
Arthur R. Marshall Loxahatchee	x	x	x	x	x	x	x	x		x	x	x	x
Hobe Sound			x				x	x			x		
Chassahowitzka			x		x	x	x	x		x	x		
Cedar Keys						x	x	x		x	x		
Crystal River						x	x	x			x		
Egmont Key		x	x			x	x	x					
Lower Suwannee		x	x			x	x	x		x	x		
Passage Key							x	x					
Pinellas						x	x	x			x		
J. N. "Ding" Darling	x	x	x	x	x	x	x	x		x	x	x	x
Caloosahatchee							x	x					
Island Bay							x	x					
Matlacha Pass							x	x					
Pine Island							x	x					
Lake Woodruff		x	x		x	x	x	x		x	x		
Merritt Island	x	x	x	x	x	x	x	x		x	x		
Pelican Island							x	x					
National Key Deer		x	x		x		x	x	x				
Crocodile Lake							x	x					
Great White Heron		x	x		x	x	x	x		x	x		
Key West		x	x		x	x	x	x	x	x			
Georgia													
Eufaula (AL)	x	x			x	x	x	x	x	x	x		
Savannah Coastal Refuges													
Blackbeard Island		x	x				x	x		x	x	x	x

State/Refuge	Visitor Center	Foot Trails	Auto Tour	Bicycling	Boating, Nonmotorized	Boating, Motorized	Environmental Study Area	Backcountry Use	Hunting	Fishing	Camping	Picnicking	Swimming
Harris Neck	x	x	x	x			x		x	x			
Savannah (GA and SC)	x	x	x	x			x		x	x			
Tybee							x		x				
Wassaw		x					x						
Wolf Island							x	x					
Okefenokee	x	x	x	x	x	x	x	x	x	x			
Piedmont	x	x	x	x	x	x	x		x	x			
Hawaii													
Hawaiian and Pacific Islands Refuges													
Hawaiian Islands							x						
James C. Campbell							x						
Kakahaia							x						
Kilauea Point	x		x				x						
Hanalei							x						
Idaho													
Deer Flat	x	x			x	x	x		x	x		x	x
Snake River Islands					x	x			x	x			
Kootenai		x	x				x		x	x			
Southeast Idaho Refuges													
Bear Lake									x	x			
Camas									x				
Grays Lake									x				
Minidoka					x	x			x	x			
Oxford Slough					x				x	x			
Illinois													
Chautauqua		x	x	x	x	x			x	x			
Crab Orchard	x	x	x	x	x	x	x	x	x	x	x	x	x
Mark Twain	x		x	x									
Batchtown Division					x	x				x			
Calhoun Division	x	x			x	x				x			
Gardner Division					x	x				x			
Gilbert Lake Division						x			x	x			
Keithsburg Division					x	x							
Upper Mississippi River Wild and Fish Refuge (MN)				x	x	x		x	x	x	x	x	

State / Refuge	Visitor Center	Foot Trails	Auto Tour	Bicycling	Boating, Nonmotorized	Boating, Motorized	Environmental Study Area	Backcountry Use	Hunting	Fishing	Camping	Picnicking	Swimming
Savanna District	x				x	x		x	x	x	x	x	x
Indiana													
Muscatatuck	x	x	x	x	x		x		x	x		x	
Iowa													
De Soto (IA & NE)	x	x	x	x	x	x	x		x	x	x	x	
Mark Twain (IL)													
Big Timber Division													
Louisa Division	x	x			x	x	x		x	x			
Union Slough		x					x		x	x		x	
Upper Mississippi River Wildlife and Fish Refuge (MN)													
McGregor District	x					x		x	x	x	x		x
Kansas													
Flint Hills	x	x	x		x	x	x	x	x	x	x	x	
Kirwin	x	x	x		x	x		x	x	x	x	x	
Quivira	x	x					x		x	x	x		
Louisiana													
Bogue Chitto					x		x	x	x	x	x		
Catahoula		x	x				x	x	x	x			
D'Arbonne			x		x	x	x	x	x	x			
Upper Ouachita							x	x	x	x			
Delta-Breton							x	x	x	x			
Lacassine	x	x			x	x	x		x	x	x	x	
Sabine	x	x	x		x	x	x		x	x	x	x	
Tensas River	x		x				x	x	x	x	x	x	x
Maine													
Moosehorn	x	x		x	x		x		x	x	x		
Cross Island													
Franklin Island													
Petit Manan		x			x		x		x	x			
Rachel Carson		x					x			x			
Maryland													
Blackwater	x	x	x	x	x	x	x		x	x			
Eastern Neck	x	x	x	x	x	x	x		x	x			x

State / Refuge	Visitor Center	Foot Trails	Auto Tour	Bicycling	Boating, Nonmotorized	Boating, Motorized	Environmental Study Area	Backcountry Use	Hunting	Fishing	Camping	Picnicking	Swimming
Massachusetts													
Great Meadows	x	x		x	x	x							
Oxbow					x	x	x		x	x			
Parker River		x		x		x			x	x	x		
Monomoy							x	x		x	x		
Nantucket								x		x			
Michigan													
Seney	x	x	x	x			x	x	x	x			
Shiawassee		x	x	x		x	x	x	x	x		x	
Minnesota													
Agassiz		x		x	x		x		x				
Big Stone		x		x	x		x			x	x		
Minnesota Valley		x		x	x		x		x	x			
Minnesota Wetlands Complex													
Morris Wildlife Management District	x								x				
Detroit Lakes Wildlife Management District													
Fergus Falls Wildlife Management District									x				
Litchfield Wildlife Management District									x				
Rice Lake		x	x		x		x	x		x			
Sherburne		x	x		x	x	x	x	x	x			
Tamarac	x	x	x		x	x	x		x	x		x	
Upper Mississippi River Wildlife and Fish Refuge (IL, IA, MN, WI)								x	x	x	x	x	x
Winona District	x	x			x	x			x	x	x	x	x
Mississippi													
Mississippi Sandhill Crane	x	x					x						
Noxubee	x	x					x		x	x			
Yazoo		x	x				x		x				
Hillside					x	x	x		x	x	x	x	x
Morgan Brake					x	x	x		x	x	x	x	x

State/Refuge	Visitor Center	Foot Trails	Auto Tour	Bicycling	Boating, Nonmotorized	Boating, Motorized	Environmental Study Area	Backcountry Use	Hunting	Fishing	Camping	Picnicking	Swimming
Panther Swamp							x		x	x			
Missouri													
Mark Twain (IL)													
Clarence Cannon	x						x						
Mingo	x	x	x		x		x	x	x	x		x	
Squaw Creek	x	x	x	x					x	x		x	
Swan Lake	x	x		x	x	x				x	x		
Montana													
Benton Lake		x	x						x				
Bowdoin	x		x						x				
Charles M. Russell			x		x	x		x	x	x	x	x	x
Lee Metcalf	x	x	x						x	x		x	
Medicine Lake	x		x		x				x	x		x	
National Bison Range	x	x	x				x			x		x	
Red Rock Lakes	x				x				x	x	x		
Nebraska													
Crescent Lake	x	x			x		x		x	x		x	
Fort Niobrara	x	x	x		x		x	x				x	
Valentine					x		x	x	x	x		x	
Rainwater Basin Wetland Manag. Dist.									x				
Nevada													
Desert National Wildlife Range		x						x			x	x	
Ash Meadows							x		x				
Pahranagat					x				x	x	x	x	
Ruby Lake					x	x			x	x			
Sheldon								x	x	x	x	x	
Stillwater			x		x	x			x	x	x	x	x
Fallon									x				
New Hampshire													
Wapack		x											
New Jersey													
Edwin B. Forsythe													
Brigantine	x	x	x	x	x	x	x		x	x			
Barnegat					x	x			x	x			

State/Refuge	Visitor Center	Foot Trails	Auto Tour	Bicycling	Boating, Nonmotorized	Boating, Motorized	Environmental Study Area	Backcountry Use	Hunting	Fishing	Camping	Picnicking	Swimming
Great Swamp		x					x		x				
New Mexico													
Bitter Lake	x		x				x	x	x	x		x	
Bosque del Apache	x	x	x				x	x	x	x			
Sevilleta									x				
Las Vegas	x	x	x						x				
Maxwell	x				x	x				x	x	x	
New York													
Iroquois	x	x		x	x				x	x			
Montezuma	x	x	x				x		x	x			
Wertheim		x			x		x			x			
Morton		x					x			x			
Target Rock		x					x			x			
North Carolina													
Alligator River									x	x			
Currituck													
Pea Island	x	x					x			x			
MacKay Island (NC and VA)		x					x		x	x			
Mattamuskeet			x				x		x	x			
Cedar Island							x		x	x			
Pungo							x		x				
Swanquarter							x		x	x			
Pee Dee		x	x				x		x	x			
North Dakota													
Arrowwood	x	x	x		x	x			x	x		x	
Long Lake	x								x	x		x	
Valley City Wetland Management District									x				
Audubon	x		x						x				
Lake Ilo					x	x				x		x	
Des Lacs	x	x	x				x		x	x		x	
Crosby Wetland Management District									x				
Lostwood		x	x						x				
Devils Lake Wetland Management District		x	x						x			x	

Left Table

State/Refuge	Visitor Center	Foot Trails	Auto Tour	Bicycling	Boating, Nonmotorized	Boating, Motorized	Environmental Study Area	Backcountry Use	Hunting	Fishing	Camping	Picnicking	Swimming
Lake Alice	×	×	×										
Sullys Hill National Game Preserve		×	×						×		×	×	×
J. Clark Salyer	×	×	×		×					×		×	
Kulm Wetland Management District									×				
Tewaukon	×	×	×		×	×			×	×		×	
Upper Souris	×	×	×		×	×	×		×	×	×	×	
Ohio													
Ottawa		×					×		×	×		×	
Oklahoma													
Little River	×	×			×	×			×	×	×	×	
Salt Plains	×	×	×		×	×	×		×	×	×	×	
Sequoyah	×	×			×	×			×	×	×		
Tishomingo	×	×	×		×	×			×	×	×	×	
Washita	×	×			×				×	×	×		
Optima									×	×			
Wichita Mountains	×	×	×		×		×	×	×	×	×	×	×
Oregon													
Hart Mountain National Antelope Refuge	×							×	×	×	×	×	
Klamath Basin Refuges													
Bear Valley													
Klamath Forest		×	×	×					×	×			
Lower Klamath (OR and CA)		×	×		×	×			×		×		
Upper Klamath		×	×		×	×			×	×			
Malheur	×	×	×		×	×	×		×	×		×	
Umatilla (OR and WA)	×	×	×		×	×			×	×	×	×	
Cold Springs													
McKay Creek													
Western Oregon Refuges													
Ankeny	×						×		×				
Bandon Marsh													
Basket Slough	×	×							×				×

Right Table

State/Refuge	Visitor Center	Foot Trails	Auto Tour	Bicycling	Boating, Nonmotorized	Boating, Motorized	Environmental Study Area	Backcountry Use	Hunting	Fishing	Camping	Picnicking	Swimming
Cape Meares	×	×								×	×		
William L. Finley (OR and WA)	×	×					×		×	×	×		
Willapa (WA)									×	×	×		
Columbian White-tailed Deer (OR and WA)		×											
Lewis and Clark					×	×			×	×			
Pennsylvania													
Erie				×	×				×	×	×		
Tinicum National Environmental Center	×	×		×	×		×			×	×		
Puerto Rico													
Caribbean Islands													
Buck Island (VI)	×	×					×						
Cabo Rojo (PR)		×					×						
Culebra (PR)							×						
Desecheo (PR)							×						
Green Cay (VI)							×						
Sandy Point (VI)							×						
Rhode Island													
Ninigret	×	×								×			
Block Island	×									×			
Sachuest Point		×								×			
Trustom Pond		×								×			
South Carolina													
Cape Romain	×	×	×	×	×	×	×		×	×			
Carolina Sandhills		×	×	×			×		×	×			
Pinckney Island		×		×			×		×				
Santee	×	×		×	×	×	×		×	×			
South Dakota													
Lacreek	×	×	×	×	×	×	×		×	×	×	×	×
Lake Andes		×			×	×	×		×	×	×	×	×
Karl E. Mundt													
Madison Wetland Management District		×							×	×			
Sandy Lake	×	×	×	×			×		×	×	×	×	

Source: Fish and Wildlife Service, *National Wildlife Refuges Map*, March 1988.

State/Refuge	Visitor Center	Foot Trails	Auto Tour	Bicycling	Boating, Nonmotorized	Boating, Motorized	Environmental Study Area	Backcountry Use	Hunting	Fishing	Camping	Picnicking	Swimming
Waubay	x	x	x				x		x			x	x
Tennessee													
Cross Creeks	x	x	x	x					x	x			
Hatchie		x					x		x	x			
Chickasaw									x	x			
Lower Hatchie									x	x			
Reelfoot	x				x		x		x	x			
Lake Isom					x		x		x	x			
Tennessee		x			x	x	x		x	x			
Texas													
Anahuac	x				x		x		x	x			
McFaddin					x	x			x	x	x		
Texas Point					x	x			x				
Aransas	x	x	x		x		x		x	x		x	
Attwater Prairie Chicken	x		x	x					x				
Brazoria		x			x	x			x	x			
Big Boggy		x			x	x			x				
San Bernard		x	x		x	x			x	x		x	
Buffalo Lake	x	x	x						x	x	x	x	x
Grulla (NM and TX)													
Muleshoe	x										x	x	
Hagerman	x	x	x		x		x		x	x		x	
Laguna Atascosa	x	x	x		x	x			x	x		x	
Santa Ana	x	x			x	x	x					x	
Rio Grande Valley													
Utah													
Bear River Migratory Bird Refuge									x				
Fish Springs			x						x	x			
Ouray			x						x	x			x
Vermont													
Missisquoi	x	x							x	x			
Virginia													

State/Refuge	Visitor Center	Foot Trails	Auto Tour	Bicycling	Boating, Nonmotorized	Boating, Motorized	Environmental Study Area	Backcountry Use	Hunting	Fishing	Camping	Picnicking	Swimming
Back Bay	x	x	x	x			x		x	x			x
Chincoteague	x	x	x	x			x	x	x	x		x	x
Eastern Shore of Virginia		x					x	x	x	x			
Great Dismal Swamp (NC and VA)		x		x				x	x	x			
Mason Neck		x					x		x				
Presquile		x					x		x				
Washington													
Columbia					x	x	x	x			x		
Nisqually		x			x	x		x	x	x			
Dungeness		x			x	x		x	x	x		x	
San Juan Islands					x	x		x			x	x	
Ridgefield		x	x				x	x	x	x			
Conboy Lake		x	x	x			x	x	x	x			
Turnbull	x	x		x			x		x	x			
Umatilla (OR and WA)	x				x	x		x	x	x			
McNary		x			x		x	x	x	x			
Toppenish	x	x						x	x	x			
Willapa		x					x	x	x	x	x		
Columbian White-tailed Deer (OR and WA)		x							x	x			
Lewis and Clark (OR)									x	x			
Wisconsin													
Horicon	x	x	x		x		x	x	x	x	x	x	
Necedah	x	x	x		x		x	x	x	x	x		
Upper Mississippi River Wildlife and Fish Refuge (MN)								x	x	x			
La Crosse District		x		x	x			x	x	x	x	x	x
Trempealeau		x		x	x			x	x	x		x	
Wyoming													
National Elk Refuge	x			x		x	x		x	x	x	x	x
Seedskadee					x			x	x	x	x	x	

Bureau of Land Management: Recreational Opportunities

Point of Interest[a]	Site # on Fig. 12.6	Boating, Rafting	Sight, Nature	Mtn. Biking	Hiking	Winter Sports	Touring	Fishing	Picnic Sites	Camp Sites
Alaska										
White Mountain NRA	1	x	x		x	x	x	x		
Steese NCA	2	x	x		x	x				
Fort Egbert NHS	3		x				x		x	
Iditarod NHT	4		x		x	x				
Tangle Lakes RA	5	x	x		x	x	x	x		x
Beaver Creek NWSR	6	x	x		x			x		
Birch Creek NWSR	7		x					x		
Delta NWSR	8	x	x					x		
Fortymile NWSR	9	x	x					x		
Gulkana NWSR	10	x	x					x		
Unalakleet NWSR	11	x	x					x		
Dalton Scenic Highway	12	x	x	x	x	x	x		x	x
Denali Scenic Highway	13	x	x	x	x	x	x	x	x	x
Taylor Scenic Highway	14	x	x	x			x	x	x	x
Pinnell Mountain Trail	15		x		x					
Squirrel River	16	x						x		
Kigluaik Mountains	17		x				x			x
Campbell Tract	18	x	x	x	x	x				
Rental Recreation Cabins/Trails	19		x			x				
Arctic Circle	20		x				x			
Arizona										
San Pedro Riparian NCA	21		x		x		x	x		
Gila Box Riparian NCA	22	x	x		x		x		x	
Aravaipa Canyon NWA	23		x		x				x	x
Paria Canyon–Vermillion Cliffs	24		x		x					
Parker Strip RA	25	x	x				x		x	
Imperial Dam RA	26	x	x				x		x	x
Virgin River Gorge RA	27	x	x		x				x	x
Burro Creek RA	28		x						x	x
Empire-Cienega Area	29		x				x			
Betty's Kitchen WVA	30		x		x		x			
Painted Rocks RA	31		x						x	x
Little Black Mountain Petroglyphs	32		x		x		x			
Murray Springs Clovis Site	33		x		x					
Blythe Intaglios	34		x				x			
Hot Well Dunes	35						x		x	x
Cross Roads–Copper Basin Dunes	36	x					x			
La Posa LTVA	37									x
Black Canyon Trail	38		x		x		x			
Safford Morenci Trail	39		x	x	x		x			
Historic Route 66 RA	40		x					x		
California										
Santa Rosa Mountains NSA	41		x	x	x					
Pacific Crest NST	42		x		x				x	x
American NWSR	43	x	x		x			x		
Coachella Valley	44		x		x					
Cosumnes River	45		x							
King Range NCA	46		x	x	x			x	x	x
Carrizo Plains	47		x	x	x				x	x
East Mojave NSA	48		x	x	x		x		x	x
Imperial Sand Dunes	49		x		x				x	x
Rainbow Basin Natural Area	50		x						x	x
Sacramento River	51	x	x		x			x	x	x
Samoa Dunes	52		x	x				x	x	
Eagle Lake	53	x	x	x				x	x	x
Bizz Johnson Trail	54		x	x	x	x		x	x	
Cow Mountain	55		x	x	x				x	x
Cache Creek	56		x	x	x				x	x
Merced NWSR	57	x	x	x	x			x	x	x
Trinity NWSR	58	x	x					x	x	x
Kelso Dunes	59		x							
Skeddadle Mountain	60		x							
Colorado										
Arkansas River RA	61	x	x				x	x	x	x
Alpine Loop RA	62		x	x	x	x	x	x	x	x
Gold Belt RA	63		x	x	x		x		x	
Ruby Canyon–Bl Ridge RA	64	x	x		x			x	x	x
Gunnison Gorge RA	65	x	x	x	x			x	x	x
Anasazi RA	66		x	x	x		x		x	
Upper Colorado River RA	67	x	x	x	x		x	x	x	x
Dolores River RA	68	x	x	x	x		x	x	x	x

Left table:

Point of Interest[a]	Site # on Fig. 12.6	Boating, Rafting	Sight, Nature	Mtn. Biking	Hiking	Winter Sports	Touring	Fishing	Picnic Sites	Camp Sites
Little Yampa Canyon RA	69	x	x	x				x	x	x
Grand Valley RA	70	x	x	x				x	x	x
Powderhorn Primitive Area	71		x	x	x	x	x	x	x	x
San Miguel RA	72	x	x	x	x		x	x	x	x
North Sand Hills RA	73		x	x		x		x		x
Rio Grande River RA	74	x	x					x	x	x
Dominguez RA	75	x	x					x	x	x
Gateway RA	76	x	x	x			x	x	x	x
Penetente RA	77		x		x					x
Eagle River RA	78	x	x	x	x		x	x	x	x
Deep Creek RA	79		x	x	x			x	x	x
Bookcliffs Wildhorse Area	80		x		x		x			x
Idaho										
Blackfoot River	81	x	x	x				x		x
Boise Front	82		x	x	x	x	x			
Bruneau-Jarbridge Rivers	83	x	x		x		x	x	x	
C. J. Strike Reservoir	84	x	x	x		x	x	x	x	x
Clearwater River	85	x	x		x		x	x	x	
Great Rift	86		x		x		x			
Ketchum–Sun Valley	87	x	x	x	x	x	x	x	x	x
Lewis and Clark NHT	88		x	x	x	x	x		x	x
Lower Coeur d'Alene River	89	x	x	x	x		x	x	x	x
Lower Salmon River	90	x	x	x	x		x	x	x	x
MacKay Reservoir WVA	91	x	x		x			x	x	x
Magic Reservoir	92	x	x			x		x	x	x
Middle Snake River	93	x	x		x		x	x	x	x
Mineral Ridge RA	94		x		x		x		x	x
Oregon NHT	95		x	x			x			
Salmon Falls Creek	96	x	x			x	x	x	x	x
Snake River Birds of Prey	97	x	x	x			x	x	x	x
South Fork Snake River	98	x	x		x	x	x	x	x	x
St. Anthony Sand Dunes	99		x	x		x	x			
Upper Salmon River	100	x	x		x	x	x	x	x	x
Montana, N. Dakota, and S. Dakota										
Upper Missouri NWSR	101	x	x					x		
Fort Benton Visitor Center	102		x				x			x

Right table:

Point of Interest[a]	Site # on Fig. 12.6	Boating, Rafting	Sight, Nature	Mtn. Biking	Hiking	Winter Sports	Touring	Fishing	Picnic Sites	Camp Sites
Pompeys Pillar NHS	103		x						x	
Pryor Mountain Wild Horse Range	104		x		x		x			x
Divide Bridge Campground	105	x		x			x	x	x	x
Missouri Breaks NBCB	106		x	x			x			
Centennial Mountains	107		x		x	x	x			
Bear Trap Canyon	108	x	x		x			x		x
Upper Madison River	109	x	x		x			x	x	x
Garnet Range NBCB	110	x	x							x
Garnet Ghost Town	111		x			x				
Holter RA–Sleeping Giant	112	x	x		x			x	x	x
Humbug Spires	113		x		x					
Terry Badlands	114		x		x		x			
East Bank Campground	115	x						x	x	x
Rocky Mountain Front	116		x		x			x		
Faraasen Park RA	117		x		x	x			x	x
Fort Meade RA	118	x	x	x	x		x	x	x	x
Fort Meade NBCB	119			x			x	x	x	x
Centennial Trail	120		x		x		x			
Nevada										
Red Rock Canyon NCA	121		x	x	x		x	x	x	x
Marietta Wild Burro Range	122		x	x	x		x			x
Fort Churchill–Wellington NBCB	123		x	x	x		x		x	x
California Trail NBCB	124		x	x	x		x		x	x
Mt. Wilson NBCB	125	x	x	x	x		x	x	x	x
Gold Butte NBCB	126	x	x	x	x		x		x	x
Bitter Springs Trail NBCB	127		x	x	x		x		x	x
Grimes Point–Hidden Cave	128		x	x	x		x			
Mt. Moriah NWA	129		x		x					
Indian Creek RA	130	x	x	x	x		x	x	x	x
Walker Lake RA	131	x	x	x	x		x	x	x	x
Wilson Reservoir RA	132	x	x	x	x	x	x	x	x	x
Clark County ORV Areas	133			x		x	x		x	x
Pony Express NHT	134		x	x	x		x	x		
Black Rock Desert	135		x	x						x
Pine Forest RA	136		x		x			x	x	x
Hickison Smt. Petroglyphs	137		x					x	x	x

Point of Interest[a]	Site # on Fig. 12.6	Boating, Rafting	Sight, Nature	Mtn. Biking	Hiking	Winter Sports	Touring	Fishing	Picnic Sites	Camp Sites
Wildhorse RA	138		×	×	×				×	×
Sand Mountain RA	139		×	×			×		×	×
Railroad Valley WVA	140		×				×	×		
New Mexico										
Organ Mountains RA	141		×	×	×		×		×	×
Valley of Fires	142		×	×	×				×	×
Fort Stanton	143		×	×	×		×		×	×
Navajo Pueblitos	144		×		×				×	×
Simon Canyon	145		×				×	×	×	×
Santa Cruz Lake	146	×	×		×				×	×
McKittrick Hill Caves	147		×	×	×					
El Malpais NCA	148		×	×			×		×	×
El Malpais Ranger Station	149			×	×		×		×	×
Datil Well	150		×	×	×		×		×	×
Three Rivers Petroglyphs	151		×	×					×	×
Angel Peak	152		×	×			×		×	×
Mescalero Sands RA	153		×				×		×	×
Aguirre Springs	154		×		×				×	×
Tent Rocks RA	155		×		×				×	
Fort Craig	156			×			×			
Wild Rivers RA	157	×	×	×	×		×	×	×	×
Orilla Verde RA	158	×	×	×	×		×	×	×	×
Dripping Springs	159		×	×	×		×	×	×	×
Rio Grande NWSR	160	×	×	×				×	×	×
Oregon and Washington										
Yaquina Head ONA	161		×				×			
Fishermen's Bend RA	162	×						×	×	×
Shotgun RA	163				×				×	
North Umpqua NWSR	164	×	×	×	×		×	×	×	×
Rogue NWSR	165	×	×	×	×		×	×	×	×
Hyatt Lake RA	166	×	×			×		×	×	×
Dean Creek WVA	167		×				×			
Loon Lake RA	168	×	×		×			×	×	×
New River	169		×					×		
Deschutes NWSR	170	×	×	×	×		×	×	×	×
John Day NWSR	171	×	×	×	×		×	×	×	×
Steens Mountain RA	172		×	×	×		×	×	×	×
Diamond Craters Natural Area	173		×	×	×		×		×	×
Warner Wetlands	174		×		×		×	×		×
Klamath River	175	×	×		×			×		×
Flagstaff Hill Visitor Center	176		×	×	×		×		×	×
Owyhee NWSR	177	×	×					×		
Grande Ronde NWSR	178	×	×		×			×		×
Yakima River Canyon	179	×	×	×	×		×	×	×	×
Saddle Mountains	180		×							
Utah										
Little Sahara	181		×	×	×				×	×
Colorado River	182	×	×	×	×		×	×	×	×
Grand Gulch Archaeological Area	183		×	×	×				×	×
Pony Express Trail NBCB	184		×	×	×		×		×	×
Canyons of the Escalante	185		×	×	×				×	×
Canyon Rim RA	186	×	×	×	×		×	×	×	×
San Rafael Swell	187	×	×	×	×		×		×	×
Green River	188	×	×	×	×			×	×	×
San Juan River	189	×	×	×	×			×	×	×
Cleveland–Lloyd Dinosaur	190		×	×	×				×	
Bonneville Salt Flats	191	×	×	×	×		×			×
Brown's Park Historic Area	192		×	×	×			×	×	×
Yuba Lake RA	193	×	×	×	×			×	×	×
CP Historic Railroad Grade	194		×	×	×		×			
Kokopelli's Mountain Bike Trail	195		×	×	×					
Red Cliffs RA	196		×	×	×				×	×
Pelican Lake RA	197	×	×	×	×			×	×	×
Price Canyon RA	198		×	×	×				×	×
Moquith Mountain RA	199		×	×	×					
Joshua Tree Natural Area	200		×		×		×			
Wyoming										
North Platte River	201	×	×	×	×		×	×	×	×
Seminoe-Alcova NBCB	202		×	×	×		×	×	×	×
Red Canyon	203		×	×	×		×			
Oregon Mormon Pioneer NHTs	204		×	×	×		×		×	×
South Pass Historic Mining Area	205		×	×	×		×		×	×

763

Point of Interest[a]	Site # on Fig. 12.6	Boating, Rafting	Sight, Nature	Mtn. Biking	Hiking	Winter Sports	Touring	Fishing	Picnic Sites	Camp Sites
Outlaw Cave	206		x	x	x	x	x	x	x	x
Muddy Mountain	207		x	x	x	x	x		x	x
South Bighorn Red Wall NBCB	208		x	x	x		x		x	x
Golden Eye RA	209	x	x		x			x	x	
Killpecker Sand Dunes	210		x	x	x		x			x
Wind River Front	211		x	x	x	x	x	x	x	x
Green River	212	x	x	x	x			x	x	x
Continental Divide Snowmobile Trail	213		x			x	x			x

Point of Interest[a]	Site # on Fig. 12.6	Boating, Rafting	Sight, Nature	Mtn. Biking	Hiking	Winter Sports	Touring	Fishing	Picnic Sites	Camp Sites
Worland Caves	214		x		x					
Red Gulch–Alkali NBCB	215		x	x	x					
Big Horn River	216	x		x	x		x	x		
West Slope	217		x	x	x	x	x	x	x	x
Duck Swamp WVA	218		x		x	x		x	x	
Scab Creek RA	219		x		x				x	x
Mile Wild Horse Herd	220		x				x			x

[a]LTVA, Long Term Visitor Area; NBCB, National Backcountry Byway; NCA, National Conservation Area; NHS, National Historic Site; NHT, National Historic Trail; NSA, National Scenic Area; NWA, National Wilderness Area; NWSR, National Wild and Scenic River; ORV, off-road vehicle; ONA, Outstanding Natural Area; RA, Recreation Area; WVA, Wildlife Viewing Area.
Source: BLM, *BLM National Recreation Guide.*

Bureau of Land Management: Recreational Resources

| District | RMA Count[a] | | | Acres (thousands) | | | Access Points[b] | | | | | | | | |
| | | | | | | | Motorized | | | Nonmotor | | | Boat | | |
	Extensive	Special	Total	Extensive	Special	Total	Extensive	Special	Total	Extensive	Special	Total	Extensive	Special	Total
Alaska															
Anchorage	1	3	4	16,000	310	16,310	0	6	6	0	6	6	0	1	1
Glennallen	2	3	5	3,849	4,152	8,001	31	28	59	54	54	108	7	15	22
Arctic	2	1	3	31,680	786	32,466	0	6	6	0	10	10	0	0	0
Kobuk	2	1	3	25,856	944	26,800	0	0	0	0	0	0	1	0	1
Steese–White Mt.	1	4	5	5,276	2,444	7,720	0	10	10	0	8	8	0	7	7
State Total	8	12	20	82,661	8,635	91,296	31	50	81	54	78	132	8	23	31
Arizona															
Arizona Strip	2	6	8	2,184	620	2,805	8	1	9	1	15	16	0	0	0
Phoenix	3	6	9	6,458	148	6,606	1	5	6	1	1	2	0	0	0
Safford	3	2	5	1,549	78	1,627	12	6	18	3	8	11	4	0	4
Yuma	4	7	11	1,619	1,438	3,056	4	36	40	0	2	2	1	22	23
State Total	12	21	33	11,810	2,284	14,094	25	48	73	5	26	31	5	22	27
California															
Bakersfield	4	11	15	1,697	307	2,004	17	20	37	2	51	53	1	21	22
Susanville	3	4	7	2,816	61	2,877	0	1	1	0	3	3	0	0	0
Ukiah	3	8	11	417	197	614	50	38	88	15	20	35	9	13	22
Calif. Desert District	6	25	31	9,670	3,768	13,438	4	30	34	1	8	9	0	0	0
State Total	16	48	64	14,600	4,333	18,933	71	89	160	18	82	100	10	34	44
Colorado															
Craig	3	3	6	3,134	31	3,165	9	4	13	18	2	20	2	4	6
Montrose	3	8	11	1,655	502	2,157	30	26	56	41	28	69	1	12	13
Canon City	2	5	7	903	263	1,166	3	21	24	1	8	9	0	16	16
Grand Junction	2	8	10	1,440	406	1,846	56	31	87	24	19	43	8	22	30
State Total	10	24	34	7,132	1,202	8,333	98	82	180	84	57	141	11	54	65
Idaho															
Boise	5	19	24	4,984	593	5,577	0	15	15	0	14	14	0	8	8
Burley	2	7	9	1,310	75	1,385	16	18	34	2	4	6	3	9	12
Idaho Falls	3	13	16	2,264	146	2,410	1	21	22	1	5	6	0	15	15
Salmon	2	4	6	1,267	34	1,301	0	0	0	3	0	3	3	10	13
Shoshone	2	8	10	2,027	42	2,069	8	24	32	6	4	10	2	15	17
Coeur d'Alene	2	5	7	221	33	254	1	3	4	6	3	9	1	12	13
State Total	16	56	72	12,072	924	12,996	26	81	107	18	30	48	9	69	78
Montana															
Miles City	4	10	14	3,145	400	3,545	1	25	26	2	4	6	0	5	5
Dickinson ND.	1	1	2	43	24	67	0	0	0	0	0	0	0	0	0
Lewiston	5	15	20	2,098	1,511	3,608	5	23	28	2	10	12	1	21	22
Butte	3	17	20	1,239	155	1,394	18	24	42	6	8	14	2	16	18
State Total	13	43	56	6,525	2,089	8,614	24	72	96	10	22	32	3	42	45

| Miles of Improved Access Rds.[c] | | | Sites[d] | | | | | | Visitor Centers[e] | | | River Segments[f] | | | River Miles[g] | | | Caves[h] | |
| | | | Developed | | | Undeveloped | | | | | | | | | | | | | |
Extensive	Special	Total	Extensive	Special	Total	Extensive	Special	Total	Extensive	Special	Total	Extensive	Special	Total	Extensive	Special	Total	No.	Man.
0	0	0	0	4	4	0	1	1	0	0	0	11	1	12	480	81	561	0	0
56	18	74	0	5	5	60	234	294	0	0	0	0	6	6	0	243	243	0	0
0	0.5	1	0	1	1	0	20	20	0	1	1	5	0	5	332	0	332	0	0
0	0	0	2	0	2	0	0	0	0	0	0	12	3	15	662	155	817	0	0
0	11	11	0	16	16	0	11	11	0	1	1	0	21	21	0	629	629	0	0
56	29	85	2	26	28	60	266	326	0	2	2	28	31	59	1,474	1,108	2,582	0	0
0	4	4	1	5	6	1	6	7	0	0	0	1	3	4	22	80	102	14	3
27	37	64	3	2	5	1	0	1	0	0	0	2	1	3	17	22	39	0	0
3	6	9	9	11	20	8	5	13	0	0	0	8	3	11	63	52	115	5	1
6	23	29	1	24	25	12	38	50	0	0	0	2	5	7	41	98	139	0	0
36	70	106	14	42	56	22	49	71	0	0	0	13	12	25	143	252	395	19	4
35	43	78	5	13	18	9	6	15	1	2	3	19	19	38	45	84	129	7	0
0	0	0	3	4	7	3	3	6	0	0	0	0	0	0	0	0	0	0	0
170	66	236	9	33	42	9	32	41	0	0	0	12	4	16	128	63	191	0	0
3	110	112	1	18	19	32	56	88	0	4	4	0	0	0	0	0	0	0	0
208	219	426	18	68	86	53	97	150	1	6	7	31	23	54	173	147	320	7	0
60	1	66	7	7	14	300	55	355	0	0	0	11	4	15	12	55	66	1	0
400	17	417	4	25	29	33	92	125	0	2	2	12	14	26	120	230	350	0	0
4	30	34	1	16	17	0	17	17	0	0	0	1	10	11	25	205	230	3	0
38	9	47	2	14	16	29	78	107	0	0	0	5	7	12	51	141	192	4	0
502	61	564	14	62	76	362	242	604	0	2	2	29	35	64	208	630	838	8	0
0	13	13	1	17	18	13	23	36	0	0	0	2	31	33	21	375	396	37	5
25	30	55	6	13	19	17	16	33	0	0	0	4	4	8	3	47	50	11	3
0	59	59	4	17	21	30	22	52	1	0	1	3	24	27	137	172	309	11	1
1	1	2	11	10	21	4	2	6	1	1	2	3	1	4	53	112	165	0	0
3	41	44	5	14	19	5	10	15	0	0	0	5	8	13	56	45	100	143	20
46	28	74	6	12	18	9	81	90	0	0	0	1	5	6	50	227	277	1	1
75	172	247	33	83	116	78	154	232	2	1	3	18	73	91	320	977	1,297	203	30
15	28	43	1	4	5	3	8	11	1	0	1	5	113	118	17	88	105	5	1
0	0	0	0	0	0	0	0	0	0	0	0	0	0	0	0	0	0	0	0
81	214	295	0	16	16	39	53	92	0	1	1	0	13	13	0	315	315	6	4
1	45	46	1	12	13	120	184	304	0	2	2	12	39	51	11	107	118	0	0
97	287	384	2	32	34	162	245	407	1	3	4	17	165	182	28	510	538	11	5

District	RMA Count[a]			Acres (thousands)			Access Points[b] Motorized			Nonmotor			Boat		
	Extensive	Special	Total	Extensive	Special	Total	Extensive	Special	Total	Extensive	Special	Total	Extensive	Special	Total
Nevada															
Elko	2	6	8	7,248	32	7,279	0	8	8	4	7	11	5	6	11
Winnemucca	2	2	4	8,271	125	8,395	0	2	2	0	1	1	0	0	0
Carson City	2	3	5	4,710	82	4,792	2	4	6	2	6	8	1	5	6
Ely	2	1	3	8,081	19	8,100	0	0	0	0	0	0	0	0	0
Las Vegas	2	3	5	4,952	2,157	7,109	12	11	23	2	11	13	0	0	0
Battle Mt.	2	0	2	10,341	0	10,341	3	0	3	0	0	0	0	0	0
State Total	12	15	27	43,603	2,413	46,016	17	25	42	8	25	33	6	11	17
New Mexico															
Albuquerque	3	12	15	2,968	303	3,271	38	14	52	8	19	27	0	8	8
Las Cruces	3	8	11	6,377	85	6,462	5	6	11	0	6	6	0	1	1
Roswell	3	12	15	4,004	117	4,121	3	19	22	0	10	10	0	0	0
State Total	9	32	41	13,349	505	13,854	46	39	85	8	35	43	0	9	9
Oregon															
Lakeview	2	2	4	3,346	56	3,402	3	1	4	1	1	2	4	3	7
Burns	2	2	4	3,103	197	3,300	5	0	5	4	0	4	3	1	4
Vale	3	8	11	4,949	95	5,044	23	20	43	10	14	24	11	12	23
Prineville	2	5	7	1,530	143	1,672	15	30	45	0	3	3	1	18	19
Salem	5	7	12	379	143	394	5	9	14	4	6	10	0	0	0
Eugene	3	5	8	294	22	317	0	10	10	0	9	9	3	4	7
Roseberg	4	1	5	422	2	424	0	0	0	3	4	7	1	1	2
Medford	4	3	7	830	43	873	6	10	16	12	22	34	0	14	14
Coos Bay	3	5	8	329	4	333	3	3	6	0	11	11	2	3	5
Spokane, WA	2	3	5	291	57	348	7	7	14	6	7	13	0	3	3
State Total	30	41	71	15,474	633	16,106	67	90	157	40	77	117	25	59	84
Utah															
Salt Lake	2	5	7	3,084	119	3,203	8	4	12	1	6	7	0	0	0
Cedar City	4	5	9	4,884	860	5,744	6	3	9	6	17	23	0	1	1
Richfield	4	11	15	6,164	632	6,796	51	2	53	0	1	1	0	0	0
Moab	4	9	13	4,343	1,813	6,156	1	5	6	9	16	25	1	14	15
Vernal	2	2	4	1,768	21	1,789	3	9	12	0	1	1	0	5	5
State Total	16	32	48	20,243	3,444	23,687	69	23	92	16	41	57	1	20	21

| Miles of Improved Access Rds.[c] | | | Sites[d] | | | | | | Visitor Centers[e] | | | River Segments[f] | | | River Miles[g] | | | Caves[h] | |
| | | | Developed | | | Undeveloped | | | | | | | | | | | | | |
Extensive	Special	Total	Extensive	Special	Total	Extensive	Special	Total	Extensive	Special	Total	Extensive	Special	Total	Extensive	Special	Total	No.	Man.
1	8	9	2	3	5	2	3	5	0	0	0	6	3	9	36	35	71	1	0
0	0	0	0	1	1	0	0	0	0	0	0	2	0	2	72	0	72	22	1
0	8	8	0	5	5	9	7	16	0	0	0	3	1	4	7	4	11	6	4
0	3	3	4	2	6	19	2	21	0	0	0	0	0	0	0	0	0	34	7
107	32	139	3	7	10	3	2	5	0	1	1	13	0	13	57	0	57	12	5
9	0	9	0	0	0	5	0	5	0	0	0	0	0	0	0	0	0	6	0
117	51	168	9	18	27	38	14	52	0	1	1	24	4	28	172	39	211	81	17
12	31	43	3	31	34	41	58	99	1	6	7	40	8	48	114	93	206	4	0
70	42	112	0	8	8	21	10	31	0	2	2	2	1	3	8	6	14	12	3
3	17	20	1	12	13	10	214	224	0	0	0	0	4	4	0	8	8	479	38
85	90	175	4	51	55	72	282	354	1	8	9	42	13	55	122	107	228	495	41
3	4	7	18	5	23	8	6	14	0	0	0	0	2	2	0	18	18	5	2
62	59	121	2	3	5	1	4	5	0	1	1	1	1	2	4	75	79	0	0
17	5	22	14	16	30	37	146	183	1	1	2	11	7	18	203	364	567	31	21
45	61	106	0	13	13	3	8	11	0	0	0	7	22	29	29	506	535	8	3
1	4	5	4	9	13	0	1	1	0	0	0	0	6	6	0	46	46	0	0
1	9	10	1	6	7	21	24	45	0	0	0	16	8	24	49	44	93	0	0
2	0.6	3	7	5	12	4	2	6	0	0	0	7	1	8	11	8	19	0	0
1,907	117	2,024	11	40	51	15	84	99	1	2	3	0	2	2	0	47	47	4	0
0	1	1	9	3	12	215	56	271	0	0	0	0	3	3	0	7	7	0	0
13	15	28	4	3	7	6	8	14	1	0	1	0	2	2	0	9	9	0	0
2,052	275	2,326	70	103	173	310	339	649	3	4	7	42	54	96	296	1,123	1,419	48	26
11	13	24	1	1	2	1	3	4	0	0	0	0	0	0	0	0	0	3	3
2	13	15	6	11	17	5	10	15	0	2	2	7	5	12	24	146	170	1	1
7	17	24	9	7	16	22	6	28	0	1	1	1	1	2	62	7	69	14	2
3	34	37	4	25	29	23	90	113	0	3	3	4	22	26	134	458	592	0	0
2	5	7	2	8	10	53	8	61	0	0	0	5	1	6	211	18	229	0	0
25	81	106	22	52	74	104	117	221	0	6	6	17	29	46	431	629	1,060	18	6

| District | RMA Count[a] | | | Acres (thousands) | | | Access Points[b] | | | | | | | | |
| | | | | | | | Motorized | | | Nonmotor | | | Boat | | |
	Extensive	Special	Total	Extensive	Special	Total	Extensive	Special	Total	Extensive	Special	Total	Extensive	Special	Total
Wyoming															
Worland	3	5	8	2,789	369	3,158	2	10	12	9	8	17	42	28	70
Rawlins	2	5	7	6,251	93	6,344	14	5	19	1	1	2	1	6	7
Rock Springs	3	6	9	6,116	130	6,246	19	26	45	1	1	2	6	15	21
Casper	1	4	5	1,400	18	1,418	1	11	12	0	7	7	5	4	9
State Total	9	20	29	16,556	610	17,166	36	52	88	11	17	28	54	53	107
National Total	151	344	495	244,025	27,071	271,095	510	651	1,161	272	490	762	132	396	528

[a]RMA (Recreation Management Area) type: *Extensive.*—An area where recreation management is only one of several management objectives and where limited commitment of resources is required to provide extensive and unstructured types of recreational activities. May contain recreation sites. These areas consist of the remainder of the land areas not included in special recreation management areas within a resource area or a district.

Special.—An area where a commitment has been made, within the parameters of multiple use, to provide specific recreational activity and experience opportunities on a sustained-yield basis. These areas usually require a high level of recreational investment and/or management. They include recreation sites, but recreation sites alone do not constitute a special management area.

[b]Access Points: *Motorized.*—The number of physical locations (not sites) where the BLM recreation program (management, construction, and maintenance) has made or is making a capital management, or maintenance investment to allow motorized use.

Nonmotorized.—Same definition as motorized, but for nonmotorized uses such as hiking, walking, horseback riding, and bicycling.

Boat.—Same definition as motorized except these points are to provide access to BLM administrated water-related recreation resources.

Miles of Improved Access Rds.[c]			Sites[d] Developed			Undeveloped			Visitor Centers[e]			River Segments[f]			River Miles[g]			Caves[h]	
Extensive	Special	Total	Extensive	Special	Total	Extensive	Special	Total	Extensive	Special	Total	Extensive	Special	Total	Extensive	Special	Total	No.	Man.
2	4	6	1	6	7	9	12	21	0	0	0	6	81	87	362	210	572	63	32
29	33	62	5	8	13	1	2	3	0	0	0	5	21	26	21	15	36	2	2
20	32	52	4	4	8	31	13	44	0	0	0	3	2	5	39	14	53	0	0
0	7	7	2	10	12	6	10	16	0	0	0	0	12	12	0	5	5	0	0
51	76	127	12	28	40	47	37	84	0	0	0	14	116	130	422	244	666	65	34
3,304	1,409	4,713	200	565	765	1,308	1,842	3,150	8	33	41	275	555	830	3,788	5,766	9,553	955	163

[c]Miles of Improved Access Roads:—Any road primarily constructed or maintained for the recreation program. (e.g., road to Red Rock Recreation Lands in Nevada).

[d]Sites: Developed:—A site developed primarily to accommodate specific intensive recreational use activities or groupings of activities such as camping, picnicking, boating, swimming, winter sports, interpretative, etc. These sites include permanent facilities such as roads, trails, toilets, interpretative facilities, and other facilities needed to accommodate the specific use intended for the site.

Undeveloped:—A site used for intensive activities such as camping or picnicking but is not specifically developed for that purpose. The facilities are usually temporary in nature, designed to minimize resource damage and provide for short-term use.

[e]Visitor Centers: A visitor center is a building (or a cluster of buildings compromising one complex) whose primary purpose is to provide information and interpretation for the visitor (e.g., Flagstaff Hill). Does not include kiosks.

[f]River Segments: Any length of river managed as a unit. The same river may have more than one segment.

[g]BLM River Miles: Number BLM managed miles among all the river segments.

[h]Caves: Number:—The known number of caves on public land.

Man.—The number of caves where BLM has taken some direct action to protect or manage the use of the cave.

Source: Dept. of the Interior, BLM, 1992.

Bureau of Land Management Districts: Annual Visitor Use— 1992

District	State	ORV Travel	Other Motorized	Nonmotorized	Camping	Hunting	Site-Based	Fishing	Boating	Other Water-Based	Winter Sports	Snow-mobiling	Totals
Anchorage	AK												
No. of participants		1,000	0	10,000	1,700	1,600	3,000	1,515	1,500	0	11,000	3,200	34,515
Total visitor hours		4,000	0	14,000	24,000	12,800	13,500	12,015	12,000	0	16,500	16,800	125,615
Glennallen	AK												
No. of participants		4,732	39,846	2,086	90,455	3,715	6,434	7,475	2,245	331	1,126	1,259	159,704
Total visitor hours		92,982	180,842	40,624	3,724,657	253,810	99,784	253,486	87,452	2,541	5,761	6,722	4,748,661
Arctic	AK												
No. of participants		80	6,620	630	3,085	1,575	15,030	4,410	230	25	120	220	32,025
Total visitor hours		520	39,700	6,700	72,900	55,900	90,100	8,900	4,980	100	560	1,100	281,460
Kobuk	AK												
No. of participants		700	100	1,000	800	550	700	800	300	0	20	400	5,370
Total visitor hours		2,800	800	8,000	18,000	4,100	3,800	1,600	9,500	0	300	3,200	52,100
Steese/White Mnt.	AK												
No. of participants		3,150	63,350	1,400	5,147	8,500	8,900	4,500	1,350	350	1,550	3,350	101,547
Total visitor hours		38,000	287,300	11,600	69,500	125,000	26,200	22,750	50,200	1,300	4,300	57,400	693,550
Arizona Strip	AZ												
No. of participants		10,160	36,895	12,030	20,096	1,050	84,828	0	30	2,000	300	0	167,389
Total visitor hours		61,000	218,970	108,720	264,552	29,880	182,196	0	180	4,000	1,800	0	871,298
Phoenix	AZ												
No. of participants		174,200	110,000	62,100	63,600	333,000	233,650	600	400	2,200	1,000	0	980,750
Total visitor hours		459,000	280,000	239,400	1,181,700	2,105,000	626,000	2,300	700	4,400	2,600	0	4,901,100
Safford	AZ												
No. of participants		11,000	8,200	9,926	6,700	33,300	34,000	6,600	200	5,500	0	0	115,426
Total visitor hours		90,000	22,600	174,824	200,000	225,000	118,100	27,500	4,400	14,000	0	0	876,424
Yuma	AZ												
No. of participants		36,296	0	676,192	2,960,714	7,061	3,261,871	199,799	1,477,253	822,299	0	0	9,441,485
Total visitor hours		105,252	0	2,205,080	32,171,555	31,824	9,425,229	921,997	6,308,005	2,420,919	0	0	53,589,861
Bakersfield	CA												
No. of participants		246,200	871,000	721,600	201,500	156,600	222,500	212,300	79,900	212,400	15,400	13,000	2,952,400
Total visitor hours		1,559,300	2,146,700	1,643,900	8,770,100	1,108,600	656,500	1,035,500	968,900	1,114,700	71,600	74,100	19,149,900
Susanville	CA												
No. of participants		255,500	683,500	47,000	456,000	549,500	263,800	45,100	2,700	0	900	0	2,304,000
Total visitor hours		750,100	1,595,000	122,300	4,361,100	3,409,300	813,500	188,200	19,800	0	3,600	0	11,262,900
Ukiah	CA												
No. of participants		374,600	246,900	158,900	49,400	84,700	303,800	158,800	26,400	96,200	23,900	100	1,523,700
Total visitor hours		1,786,500	912,300	844,900	929,500	968,200	858,500	951,200	483,500	269,400	73,000	300	8,077,300

District	State	ORV Travel	Other Motorized	Nonmotorized	Camping	Hunting	Site-Based	Fishing	Boating	Other Water-Based	Winter Sports	Snow-mobiling	Totals
Calif. Desert District	CA												
No. of participants		4,325,500	2,577,200	1,702,000	4,866,200	567,200	2,056,500	32,500	0	97,400	3,800	0	16,228,300
Total visitor hours		25,718,500	42,180,000	21,208,700	72,323,900	3,616,200	22,898,500	168,800	0	480,500	9,900	0	188,605,000
Craig	CO												
No. of participants		37,000	36,000	29,750	92,000	213,500	34,250	14,200	48,400	3,100	9,800	13,200	531,200
Total visitor hours		352,500	200,000	120,500	1,084,000	2,949,000	135,500	78,000	407,000	9,600	68,800	55,700	5,460,600
Montrose	CO												
No. of participants		16,500	667,200	30,350	40,200	114,850	121,450	61,850	13,700	1,600	11,200	5,455	1,084,355
Total visitor hours		61,000	3,013,100	227,100	1,664,000	1,531,900	498,700	330,750	200,200	5,850	51,100	24,100	7,607,800
Canon City	CO												
No. of participants		72,900	954,800	77,150	125,600	56,700	153,000	71,300	244,200	8,300	15,800	8,000	1,787,750
Total visitor hours		198,650	2,785,300	267,450	2,591,400	443,600	718,800	296,200	973,400	32,800	76,000	36,100	8,419,700
Grand Junction	CO												
No. of participants		207,550	76,570	67,625	34,010	17,835	68,965	14,130	20,440	3,705	5,465	2,322	518,617
Total visitor hours		823,540	312,945	329,950	562,232	133,085	273,525	56,370	193,560	17,070	22,440	9,843	2,734,560
Boise	ID												
No. of participants		43,220	150,100	39,550	45,325	41,650	50,900	46,850	15,200	6,300	11,200	7,300	457,595
Total visitor hours		234,800	705,450	170,950	1,011,100	753,400	250,000	275,050	130,300	46,400	73,600	45,300	3,696,350
Burley	ID												
No. of participants		72,000	8,100	33,700	43,000	115,600	65,100	91,000	35,700	12,200	10,100	12,900	499,400
Total visitor hours		261,300	15,100	73,100	443,400	600,300	202,200	427,800	140,800	36,600	26,000	63,900	2,290,500
Idaho Falls	ID												
No. of participants		72,750	33,050	16,200	65,900	69,900	21,250	140,700	35,200	8,500	21,925	11,250	496,625
Total visitor hours		359,350	171,950	77,100	792,900	420,000	43,000	703,500	244,200	18,000	92,700	66,800	2,989,500
Salmon	ID												
No. of participants		7,425	45,850	12,475	20,800	20,025	6,300	28,375	7,060	3,590	1,600	5,750	159,250
Total visitor hours		22,700	187,000	100,225	298,950	56,800	12,200	198,775	19,950	13,660	5,900	21,050	937,210
Shoshone	ID												
No. of participants		30,800	22,200	64,900	27,050	45,300	62,000	95,900	14,480	4,900	249,750	9,300	626,580
Total visitor hours		123,100	73,700	104,700	387,100	270,600	269,000	392,150	58,780	17,500	1,034,800	68,200	2,799,630
Coeur d'Alene	ID												
No. of participants		8,800	34,800	41,300	73,600	28,400	212,000	88,100	40,700	113,400	3,100	1,300	645,500
Total visitor hours		67,400	181,200	184,700	2,451,200	382,400	786,400	454,600	872,800	444,400	18,600	7,600	5,851,300
Miles City	MT												
No. of participants		44,500	109,791	21,769	7,495	60,915	52,115	13,420	1,865	1,260	1,500	100	314,730
Total visitor hours		759,400	339,436	52,338	107,600	302,260	130,580	41,735	5,695	3,020	4,055	600	1,746,719

Location	State		C1	C2	C3	C4	C5	C6	C7	C8	C9	C10	C11	Total
Dickinson ND.	MT	No. of participants	240	0	0	320	1,000	800	0	0	0	40	180	2,580
		Total visitor hours	720	0	0	3,840	4,500	6,400	0	0	0	160	440	16,060
Lewiston	MT	No. of participants	5,100	27,600	10,100	12,100	59,400	64,100	14,500	8,200	700	1,900	1,800	205,500
		Total visitor hours	20,300	64,200	40,400	145,200	1,408,400	128,200	117,200	47,200	1,400	8,000	7,600	1,988,100
Butte	MT	No. of participants	229,320	356,900	56,550	277,850	156,000	52,000	363,100	179,000	13,400	34,500	30,100	1,748,720
		Total visitor hours	1,742,780	765,600	401,400	2,918,600	1,147,200	167,800	1,561,400	386,000	50,600	168,500	123,900	9,433,780
Elko	NV	No. of participants	81,300	159,000	61,600	77,710	108,690	31,000	208,800	35,500	38,200	7,000	8,600	817,400
		Total visitor hours	247,700	655,500	261,800	2,006,630	855,550	144,400	1,120,500	177,250	122,500	19,300	38,900	5,650,030
Winnemucca	NV	No. of participants	18,200	48,700	5,700	29,200	24,500	5,000	6,300	300	0	300	200	138,400
		Total visitor hours	197,250	492,200	39,800	505,800	101,000	27,300	63,200	2,000	0	1,200	900	1,430,650
Carson City	NV	No. of participants	110,400	30,800	240,800	47,900	50,300	289,600	20,900	11,900	8,100	600	100	811,400
		Total visitor hours	425,900	16,900	623,000	1,320,600	611,200	580,600	93,900	46,600	34,800	2,300	400	3,756,200
Ely	NV	No. of participants	21,500	16,900	6,200	10,700	33,800	24,100	11,000	400	1,900	5,100	2,500	134,100
		Total visitor hours	53,900	41,700	27,700	117,500	241,100	101,200	47,900	1,200	3,700	27,700	12,800	676,400
Las Vegas	NV	No. of participants	71,500	1,377,500	360,200	18,050	33,025	726,600	100	0	400	0	0	2,587,375
		Total visitor hours	488,200	9,965,000	1,813,500	224,800	215,900	1,618,900	200	0	1,200	0	0	14,327,700
Battle Mnt.	NV	No. of participants	7,400	11,000	1,200	12,800	24,800	8,000	1,300	0	0	3,100	600	70,200
		Total visitor hours	57,500	64,000	8,800	220,200	175,700	150,000	6,500	0	0	18,300	3,300	704,300
Albuquerque	NM	No. of participants	587,400	228,300	86,200	130,050	126,320	615,100	258,200	133,700	28,900	400	200	2,194,770
		Total visitor hours	2,366,400	509,500	611,600	3,090,500	526,000	744,000	1,016,100	760,600	67,450	2,100	1,000	9,695,250
Las Cruces	NM	No. of participants	14,000	38,750	113,200	25,870	132,310	177,100	5,600	200	100	100	0	507,230
		Total visitor hours	180,000	852,250	652,200	414,080	4,454,440	987,700	50,800	2,400	1,600	400	0	7,595,870
Roswell	NM	No. of participants	5,400	9,600	6,410	19,525	141,625	61,462	900	0	0	0	0	244,922
		Total visitor hours	27,000	40,700	33,400	310,200	695,900	354,150	4,500	0	0	0	0	1,465,850

District	State	ORV Travel	Other Motorized	Nonmotorized	Camping	Hunting	Site-Based	Fishing	Boating	Other Water-Based	Winter Sports	Snowmobiling	Totals
Lakeview	OR												
No. of participants		32,450	135,700	29,300	55,000	24,600	42,600	30,400	13,530	14,720	5,200	3,700	387,200
Total visitor hours		134,450	345,900	108,800	605,000	135,500	116,330	130,700	48,580	32,400	20,500	12,700	1,690,860
Burns	OR												
No. of participants		12,364	75,660	13,200	101,350	18,035	32,100	33,400	1,000	200	1,325	700	289,334
Total visitor hours		39,292	241,364	51,718	1,206,582	95,755	87,350	143,949	2,500	500	4,757	2,200	1,875,967
Vale	OR												
No. of participants		32,000	209,500	94,100	152,400	149,900	225,000	325,600	110,500	60,500	35,100	21,000	1,415,600
Total visitor hours		171,000	647,300	513,800	4,369,800	1,628,000	885,000	3,476,600	1,097,000	278,000	192,800	86,000	13,345,300
Prineville	OR												
No. of participants		23,400	302,557	233,465	248,300	118,850	166,845	93,900	135,922	14,740	0	0	1,337,979
Total visitor hours		42,460	351,289	827,100	3,045,760	861,100	1,548,620	690,760	505,292	49,392	0	0	7,921,773
Salem	OR												
No. of participants		53,800	806,400	281,600	152,500	50,900	1,589,000	112,900	29,100	75,300	18,500	1,500	3,171,500
Total visitor hours		172,200	1,376,900	969,370	1,677,500	264,500	2,851,600	485,500	81,400	158,100	62,900	4,700	8,104,670
Eugene	OR												
No. of participants		150,400	197,250	262,150	78,700	80,400	258,600	198,350	60,500	67,150	2,000	0	1,355,500
Total visitor hours		466,300	631,180	930,800	865,700	628,300	840,200	853,100	54,800	143,700	5,700	0	5,419,780
Roseberg	OR												
No. of participants		63,000	100,900	116,900	56,400	47,200	114,300	66,800	17,600	21,900	0	0	605,000
Total visitor hours		378,000	605,400	467,600	902,400	330,400	685,800	400,800	105,600	131,400	0	0	4,007,400
Medford	OR												
No. of participants		21,200	570,000	73,300	68,820	23,000	530,600	68,700	152,800	392,500	25,200	2,200	1,928,320
Total visitor hours		63,600	1,825,960	277,295	757,020	179,300	1,689,900	295,470	462,200	863,500	99,420	8,100	6,521,765
Coos Bay	OR												
No. of participants		109,467	302,453	241,903	134,902	54,053	552,682	166,416	66,721	59,963	7,746	0	1,696,306
Total visitor hours		328,402	907,359	1,243,363	2,158,069	421,600	742,231	699,018	400,403	131,920	17,042	0	7,049,407
Spokane, WA	OR												
No. of participants		7,970	400,720	8,950	4,742	221,478	400,496	6,018	48,000	5,860	0	0	1,104,234
Total visitor hours		16,500	1,283,295	41,660	242,380	1,767,468	1,045,912	22,956	134,000	20,800	0	0	4,574,971
Salt Lake	UT												
No. of participants		45,100	51,300	20,000	38,500	36,000	147,000	4,000	500	300	6,000	3,000	351,700
Total visitor hours		297,200	486,400	143,000	462,000	255,800	297,000	20,000	2,000	600	30,000	15,000	2,009,000
Cedar City	UT												
No. of participants		461,550	3,842,706	164,534	71,410	45,080	456,683	15,875	715	1,000	1,250	561	5,061,364
Total visitor hours		1,704,420	8,994,290	1,089,194	855,466	278,230	1,071,628	68,300	3,520	2,000	4,700	3,966	14,075,714
Richfield	UT												
No. of participants		220,100	185,100	93,200	312,900	267,600	384,800	38,900	172,500	153,100	3,200	2,200	1,833,600
Total visitor hours		1,547,900	1,681,600	369,800	5,922,300	2,044,700	1,358,900	158,100	531,000	439,900	7,200	31,900	14,093,300

Moab	UT												
No. of participants		82,000	558,400	207,100	290,100	69,900	345,355	14,900	81,900	10,500	2,600	1,000	1,663,755
Total visitor hours		933,700	4,223,400	3,630,200	8,901,800	1,401,200	971,600	78,200	2,271,300	40,600	8,300	3,800	22,464,100
Vernal	UT												
No. of participants		11,020	12,000	3,940	36,720	69,110	20,530	24,700	14,820	40	2,040	540	195,460
Total visitor hours		43,800	43,800	16,240	775,920	822,000	70,300	110,600	64,400	400	4,200	1,200	1,952,860
Worland	WY												
No. of participants		20,800	50,200	16,400	39,100	191,900	140,800	84,800	31,300	4,200	22,800	11,500	613,800
Total visitor hours		59,900	147,100	69,950	340,500	1,292,300	511,200	395,000	126,500	16,800	77,000	35,000	3,071,250
Rawlins	WY												
No. of participants		32,300	58,300	22,400	81,900	140,000	127,750	30,300	6,600	200	7,175	29,050	535,975
Total visitor hours		93,300	203,050	103,600	830,800	980,000	763,250	136,350	13,200	300	35,850	101,675	3,261,375
Rock Springs	WY												
No. of participants		29,344	177,585	22,588	32,282	199,029	26,130	40,690	57,023	12,410	12,328	15,024	624,433
Total visitor hours		105,695	111,602	102,229	329,402	421,810	56,624	190,609	203,444	30,447	23,362	61,064	1,636,288
Casper	WY												
No. of participants		12,500	14,750	4,500	20,500	41,150	27,250	70,200	1,525	1,500	1,100	7,000	201,975
Total visitor hours		37,500	33,250	20,750	251,400	241,750	78,250	410,600	4,075	3,250	3,400	20,000	1,104,225

Source: David Wickstrom, BLM, 1993.

Army Corps of Engineers Projects

779

Fig. 13.3 No.	Name	State	Camp with electricity	Camp w/o electricity	Showers	Restrooms	Drinking Water	Sanitary Dump	Picnic/Day Use	Launch Ramp	Marina	Visitor Center
57	Stanislaus River Parks	CA		o	x	x	x	x	x			x
58	Success Lake	CA		x	x	x	x	x	x		x	x
59	Whittier Narrows Dam	CA	x		x	x	x	x	x			x
		Colorado										
60	Bear Creek Lake	CO	x			x	x	x	x	x		x
61	Chatfield Lake	CO	x	x	x	x	x	x	x	x	x	
62	Cherry Creek Lake	CO	x		x		x	x	x	x	x	
63	John Martin Reservoir	CO		x			x	x	x	x		
64	Trinidad Lake	CO	x		x	x	x	x	x	x		
		Connecticut										
65	Black Rock Lake	CT										
66	Colebrook River Lake	CT				x				x		
67	Hancock Brook Lake	CT							x			
68	Hop Brook Lake	CT				x	x		x			
69	Mansfield Hollow Lake	CT				x	x		x	x		
70	Northfield Brook Lake	CT				x	x		x			
71	Thomaston Dam	CT				x	x		x			
72	West Thompson Lake	CT	x			x	x		x	x		
		Florida										
73	Inglis Lock–Lake Rousseau	FL				x	x		x	x		x
74	Lake Ocklawaha	FL				x	x		x	x		x
75	Moore Haven Lock	FL	x			x	x		x			
76	Ortona Lock	FL	x	x		x	x		x	x		
77	Port Mayaca Lock	FL					x		x			
78	St. Lucie Lock	FL	x	x	x	x	x	x	x	x	x	x
79	W. P. Franklin Lock	FL	x	x	x	x	x	x	x	x	x	x
		Georgia										
80	Allatoona Lake	GA	x	x	x	x	x	x	x	x	x	x
81	Carters Lake	GA	x	x	x	x	x	x	x	x	x	x
82	George W. Andrews Lake	GA	x		x	x	x	x	x	x		x
83	Lake Seminole	GA	x	x	x	x	x	x	x	x	x	x
84	Lake Sidney Lanier	GA	x	x	x	x	x	x	x	x	x	x
85	Walter F. George Lake	GA	x	x	x	x	x	x	x	x	x	x
86	West Point Lake	GA	x	x	x	x	x	x	x	x	x	x

Fig. 13.3 No.	Name	State	Camp with electricity	Camp w/o electricity	Showers	Restrooms	Drinking Water	Sanitary Dump	Picnic/Day Use	Launch Ramp	Marina	Visitor Center
		Hawaii										
87	PDO Regional Visitor Center	HI										x
		Iowa										
88	Bulgers Hollow	IA		x					x	x		
89	Clark's Ferry	IA	x	x		x	x	x	x	x	x	x
90	Coralville Lake	IA	x	x	x	x	x	x	x	x	x	x
91	Ferry Landing	IA								x		
92	Kilpeck Landing	IA								x		x
93	Lake Red Rock	IA	x	x		x	x	x	x	x	x	x
94	Pleasant Creek	IA		x					x	x		
95	Rathbun Lake	IA	x	x		x	x	x	x	x	x	x
96	Saylorville Lake	IA	x	x		x	x	x	x	x	x	x
97	Shady Creek	IA	x							x		x
		Idaho										
98	Albeni Falls Dam–Lake Pend Oreille	ID	x	x		x	x	x	x	x	x	x
99	Dworshak Dam and Reservoir	ID	x	x		x	x		x	x	x	x
100	Lucky Peak Lake	ID		x		x	x		x	x	x	
		Illinois										
101	Andalusia	IL		x					x	x		
102	Bear Creek	IL	x	x		x	x		x	x		
103	Big Slough	IL				x			x	x		
104	Blanchard Island	IL		x					x	x		
105	Blanding Landing	IL	x			x	x		x	x		
106	Brandon Road	IL							x	x		
107	Canton Chute	IL								x		
108	Carlyle Lake	IL	x	x		x	x	x	x	x	x	x
109	Cattail Slough	IL		x		x			x	x		
110	Dresden Island	IL		x			x		x	x		x
111	Ellis Island Access Area	IL								x		x
112	Environmental Demo Area	IL							x			x
113	Fisherman's Corner	IL	x			x	x	x	x	x		x
114	John Hay	IL				x	x		x	x		x

780

Fig. 13.3 No.	Name	State	Camp with electricity	Camp w/o electricity	Showers	Restrooms	Drinking Water	Sanitary Dump	Picnic/Day Use	Launch Ramp	Marina	Visitor Center
115	Kaskasia Lock and Dam	IL				x			x			
116	LaGrange	IL										
117	Lake Shelbyville	IL	x	x	x	x		x	x	x	x	x
118	Lock and Dam 12	IL										
119	Lock and Dam 13	IL		x		x	x		x	x		
120	Lock and Dam 14	IL				x	x	x	x	x		
121	Lock and Dam 15, Visitor Center	IL				x		x				x
122	Lock and Dam 16	IL				x	x		x			
123	Lock and Dam 17	IL							x			
124	Lock and Dam 18	IL										
125	Lock and Dam 19	IL										
126	Lock and Dam 52	IL										
127	Lock and Dam 53	IL										
128	Lockport	IL										
129	Lock 27, Visitor Center	IL				x						x
130	Marseilles	IL										
131	O'Brien	IL				x	x					
132	Park 'n' Fish	IL		x		x	x		x	x		
133	Peoria	IL								x		
134	Rend Lake	IL	x	x	x	x	x	x	x	x	x	x
135	Smithland Lock and Dam	IL			x	x	x	x	x	x	x	x
136	Starved Rock and Visitor Center	IL				x				x		x
137	Thompson Causeway	IL			x	x	x	x	x	x		
	Indiana											
138	Brookville Lake	IN	x	x	x	x	x	x	x	x	x	
139	Monroe Lake	IN	x	x	x	x	x			x	x	
140	Cannelton Lock and Dam	IN	x		x	x	x	x	x	x	x	x
141	Cecil M. Harden Lake	IN	x	x	x	x	x	x	x	x	x	
142	Falls of the Ohio WCA	IN										*
143	Huntington Lake	IN	x	x	x	x	x	x	x	x	x	
144	Mississinewa Lake	IN	x	x	x	x	x	x	x	x	x	
145	Cagles Mill Lake	IN	x	x	x	x	x	x	x	x	x	
146	Newburgh Lock and Dam	IN				x	x	x	x	x	x	x
147	Patoka Lake	IN	x	x	x	x	x	x	x	x	x	x
148	Salamonie Lake	IN	x	x	x	x	x	x	x	x	x	
149	Uniontown Lock and Dam	IN	x	x	x	x	x	x	x	x	x	x
	Kansas											
150	Clinton Lake	KS	x	x	x	x	x	x	x	x	x	
151	Council Grove Lake	KS	x	x	x	x	x	x	x	x	x	x
152	El Dorado Lake	KS	x	x	x	x	x	x	x	x	x	
153	Elk City Lake	KS	x	x	x	x	x	x	x	x	x	
154	Fall River Lake	KS		x				x	x	x	x	
155	Hillsdale Lake	KS		x	x	x		x	x	x		x
156	John Redmond Reservoir	KS		x		x	x	x	x	x	x	
157	Kanopolis Lake	KS	x	x	x	x	x	x	x	x	x	x
158	Marion Lake	KS	x	x	x	x	x	x	x	x	x	
159	Melvern Lake	KS	x	x	x	x	x	x	x	x	x	
160	Milford Lake	KS	x	x	x	x	x	x	x	x	x	x
161	Pearson-Skubitz/Big Hill Lake	KS	x	x	x	x	x	x	x	x	x	x
162	Perry Lake	KS	x	x	x	x	x	x	x	x	x	x
163	Pomona Lake	KS	x	x	x	x	x	x	x	x	x	x
164	Toronto Lake	KS	x	x	x	x	x	x	x	x		
165	Tuttle Creek Lake	KS	x	x	x	x	x	x	x	x	x	x
166	Wilson Lake	KS	x	x	x	x	x	x	x	x	x	x
	Kentucky											
167	Barren River Lake	KY	x	x	x	x	x	x	x	x	x	x
168	Buckhorn Lake	KY	x	x	x	x	x	x	x	x	x	x
169	Carr Fork Lake	KY	x	x	x	x	x	x	x	x	x	x
170	Cave Run Lake	KY	x	x	x	x	x	x	x	x	x	x
171	Dale Hollow Lake	KY	x	x	x	x	x	x	x	x	x	x
172	Dewey Lake	KY		x	x	x	x	x	x	x	x	
173	Fishtrap Lake	KY		x	x	x	x	x	x	x	x	
174	Grayson Lake	KY	x	x	x	x	x	x	x	x	x	
175	Green River Lake	KY	x	x	x	x	x	x	x	x	x	x
176	Green River Lock and Dam 1	KY	x	x	x	x	x	x	x	x	x	x

Fig. 13.3 No.	Name	State	Camp with electricity	Camp w/o electricity	Showers	Restrooms	Drinking Water	Sanitary Dump	Picnic/Day Use	Launch Ramp	Marina	Visitor Center
231	Lock and Dam 20	MO					x		x			
232	Lock and Dam 21	MO							x	x		
233	Lock and Dam 22	MO					x		x	x		
234	Lock and Dam 24	MO					x			x		
235	Lock and Dam 25	MO				x	x		x	x	x	x
236	Lock and Dam 27	MO	x		x	x	x	x	x	x	x	x
237	Long Branch Lake	MO	x			x	x	x	x	x	x	
238	Melvin Price Lock and Dam	MO			x	x	x	x	x	x	x	x
239	Pomme de Terre Lake	MO	x	x	x	x	x	x	x	x	x	x
240	Smithville Lake	MO	x	x	x	x	x	x	x	x	x	x
241	Stockton Lake	MO	x	x	x	x	x	x	x	x	x	x
242	Table Rock Lake	MO	x	x	x	x	x	x	x	x	x	x
243	Wappapello Lake	MO	x	x	x	x	x	x	x	x	x	
Mississippi												
244	Aberdeen Lake	MS	x	x	x	x	x	x	x	x	x	x
245	Arkabutla Lake	MS	x	x	x	x	x	x	x	x		x
246	Bay Springs Lake	MS	x	x	x	x	x	x	x	x	x	x
247	Canal Section Locks and Dams	MS	x	x	x	x	x	x	x	x	x	x
248	Columbus Lake	MS	x	x	x	x	x	x	x	x	x	x
249	Enid Lake	MS	x	x	x	x	x	x	x	x	x	x
250	Grenada Lake	MS	x	x	x	x	x	x	x	x	x	x
251	Okatibbee Lake	MS	x	x	x	x	x	x	x	x	x	x
252	Sardis Lake	MS	x	x	x	x	x	x	x	x	x	x
Montana												
253	Ford Peck Lake	MT	x	x	x	x	x	x	x	x	x	x
254	Libby Dam	MT	x	x	x	x	x	x	x	x	x	x
North Carolina												
255	B. Everett Jordan Dam and Reservoir	NC	x	x	x	x	x	x	x	x	x	x
256	Falls Lake	NC	x	x	x	x	x	x	x	x	x	x
257	John H. Kerr Reservoir	NC	x	x	x	x	x	x	x	x	x	x
258	Lock and Dam 1	NC				x	x		x	x		
259	Lock and Dam 2	NC				x	x		x	x		

Fig. 13.3 No.	Name	State	Camp with electricity	Camp w/o electricity	Showers	Restrooms	Drinking Water	Sanitary Dump	Picnic/Day Use	Launch Ramp	Marina	Visitor Center
260	W. Kerr Scott Dam and Reservoir	NC	x	x	x		x	x		x	x	x
261	Wm. O. Huske Lock and Dam	NC				x	x		x	x	x	
North Dakota												
262	Ashtabula Lake	ND	x	x	x	x	x	x	x	x	x	x
263	Bowman-Haley Lake	ND	x	x	x	x	x		x	x	x	x
264	Garrison Dam–Lake Sakakawea	ND	x	x	x	x	x	x	x	x	x	x
265	Homme Lake	ND	x			x	x		x	x		
266	Pipestem	ND	x	x	x	x	x	x	x	x	x	x
Nebraska												
267	Bluestem Lake	NE	x	x		x	x		x	x	x	
268	Branched Oak	NE	x	x	x	x	x	x	x	x	x	
269	Conestoga Lake	NE	x	x		x	x		x	x		
270	Glenn Cunningham Lake	NE	x	x		x	x		x	x	x	
271	Harlan County Lake	NE	x	x	x	x	x	x	x	x	x	x
272	Holmes Park Lake	NE		x		x	x		x	x		
273	Olive Creek Lake	NE		x		x	x		x	x		
274	Pawnee Lake	NE	x	x	x	x	x	x	x	x	x	
275	Stage Coach Lake	NE	x	x	x	x	x		x	x		
276	Standing Bear Lake	NE				x	x		x	x		
277	Twin Lakes	NE					x		x	x		
278	Wagon Train Lake	NE		x		x	x	x	x	x	x	x
279	Wehrspann Lake	NE				x	x		x	x	x	
280	Yankee Hill Lake	NE	x	x		x	x		x	x	x	
281	Zorinsky Lake and Recreation Area	NE								x	x	
New Hampshire												
282	Blackwater Dam	NH										
283	Edward MacDowell Lake	NH				x	x		x	x		
284	Everett Lake	NH				x	x		x	x		
285	Franklin Falls Dam	NH										
286	Hopkinton Lake	NH				x	x		x	x		

Fig. 13.3 No.	Name	State	Camp with electricity	Camp w/o electricity	Showers	Restrooms	Drinking Water	Sanitary Dump	Picnic/Day Use	Launch Ramp	Marina	Visitor Center
347	Keystone Lake	OK	x	x	x	x	x	x	x	x	x	x
348	Lake Texoma (Denison Dam)	OK	x	x	x	x	x	x	x	x	x	x
349	Newt Graham Lock and Dam	OK	x	x	x	x	x	x	x	x		x
350	Oologah Lake	OK	x	x	x	x	x	x	x	x	x	
351	Optima Lake	OK	x	x	x	x	x	x	x	x		x
352	Pine Creek Lake	OK	x	x	x	x	x	x	x	x	x	
353	Robert S. Kerr Lake	OK	x	x	x	x	x	x	x	x	x	x
354	Sardis Lake	OK	x	x	x	x	x	x	x	x		
355	Skiatook Lake	OK	x	x	x	x	x	x	x	x	x	x
356	Tenkiller Ferry Lake	OK	x	x	x	x	x	x	x	x	x	x
357	W. D. Mayo Lock and Dam	OK	x	x	x	x	x	x	x	x		x
358	Waurika Lake	OK	x	x	x	x	x	x	x	x	x	x
359	Webbers Falls Lock and Dam	OK	x	x	x	x	x	x	x	x		x
360	Wister Lake	OK	x	x	x	x	x	x	x	x		x
	Oregon											
361	Applegate Lake	OR	x	x	x	x	x	x	x	x		
362	Blue River Lake	OR	x	x	x	x	x	x	x	x	x	
363	Bonneville Lock, Dam and Lock	OR	x	x	x	x	x	x	x	x	x	x
364	Cottage Grove Lake	OR	x	x	x	x	x	x	x	x		
365	Cougar Lake	OR	x	x	x	x	x	x	x	x		
366	Detroit Lake	OR	x	x	x	x	x	x	x	x	x	x
367	Dexter Lake	OR	x	x	x	x	x	x	x	x	x	
368	Dorena Lake	OR	x	x	x	x	x	x	x	x	x	x
369	Fall Creek Lake	OR	x	x	x	x	x	x	x	x	x	x
370	Fern Ridge Lake	OR	x	x	x	x	x	x	x	x	x	x
371	Foster Lake	OR	x	x	x	x	x	x	x	x		
372	Green Peter Lake	OR	x	x	x	x	x	x	x	x	x	
373	Hills Creek Lake	OR	x	x	x	x	x	x	x	x	x	
374	John Day Lock and Dam–Lake Umatilla	OR	x	x	x	x	x	x	x	x	x	x
375	Lookout Point Lake	OR		x	x	x	x	x	x	x	x	x

Fig. 13.3 No.	Name	State	Camp with electricity	Camp w/o electricity	Showers	Restrooms	Drinking Water	Sanitary Dump	Picnic/Day Use	Launch Ramp	Marina	Visitor Center
376	Lost Creek Lake	OR	x	x	x	x	x	x	x	x	x	x
377	McNary Lock and Dam–Lake Wallula	OR	x	x	x	x	x	x	x	x	x	x
378	Dalles Lock and Dam–Lake Celilo	OR	x	x	x	x	x	x	x	x	x	x
379	Willow Creek Lake	OR				x	x		x	x		
	Pennsylvania											
380	Allegheny Lock and Dam 2	PA										
381	Allegheny Lock and Dam 3	PA										
382	Allegheny Lock and Dam 4	PA										
383	Allegheny Lock and Dam 5	PA										
384	Allegheny Lock and Dam 6	PA										
385	Allegheny Lock and Dam 7	PA										
386	Allegheny Lock and Dam 8	PA										
387	Allegheny Lock and Dam 9	PA										
388	Alvin R. Bush Dam	PA	x	x				x		x		x
389	Aylesworth Lake	PA				x			x			x
390	Beltzville Lake	PA			x	x	x	x	x	x		x
391	Blue Marsh Lake	PA			x	x	x	x	x	x		x
392	Conemaugh River Lake	PA				x	x	x	x	x		x
393	Cowanesque Lake	PA	x	x		x	x	x	x	x		x
394	Crooked Creek Lake	PA		x	x	x	x	x	x	x		x
395	Curwensville Lake	PA		x	x	x	x	x	x	x		x
396	Dashields Lock and Dam	PA										
397	East Branch Clarion R. Lake	PA	x	x	x	x	x	x	x	x		x
398	Emsworth Lock and Dam	PA										
399	Foster J. Sayers Dam	PA	x	x		x	x	x	x	x	x	x
400	Francis E. Walter Dam	PA				x	x	x	x	x		x
401	Kinzua Dam	PA	x	x	x	x	x	x	x	x		x
402	Loyalhanna Lake	PA	x	x	x	x	x	x	x	x		x
403	Mohoning Creek Lake	PA	x	x	x	x	x	x	x	x	x	x
404	Maxwell Lock and Dam	PA				x	x	x	x	x	x	x
405	Monongahela Lock and Dam 7	PA										

Fig. 13.3 No.	Name	State	Camp with electricity	Camp w/o electricity	Showers	Restrooms	Drinking Water	Sanitary Dump	Picnic/Day Use	Launch Ramp	Marina	Visitor Center
406	Monongahela Lock and Dam 2	PA										
407	Monongahela Lock and Dam 3	PA										
408	Monongahela Lock and Dam 4	PA										
409	Montgomery Lock and Dam	PA										
410	P. T. Marion Lock and Dam 8	PA										
411	Prompton Lake	PA					x		x	x		
412	Raystown Lake	PA	x	x	x	x	x	x	x	x		
413	Shenango River Lake	PA	x	x	x	x	x	x	x	x		
414	Tioga-Hammond Lakes	PA	x	x	x	x	x	x	x	x		
415	Tionesta Lake	PA	x	x	x	x	x	x	x	x		
416	Union City Dam	PA							x			
417	Woodcock Creek Lake	PA	x	x	x	x	x	x	x	x	x	x
418	Youghiogheny River Lake	PA		x				x	x	x	x	x
	South Carolina											
419	Hartwell Lake	SC	x	x	x	x	x	x	x	x	x	x
420	J. Strom Thurmond Lake	SC	x	x	x	x	x	x	x	x	x	x
421	Richard B. Russell Lake	SC	x	x	x	x	x	x	x	x	x	x
	South Dakota											
422	Big Bend Dam–Lake Sharpe	SD	x	x	x	x	x	x	x	x		x
423	Cold Brook Lake	SD	x	x	x	x	x	x	x	x		
424	Cottonwood Springs Lake	SD	x	x	x	x	x	x	x			
425	Ft. Randall Dam–Lake Francis Case	SD		x	x	x	x	x	x	x	x	x
426	Gavins Point Dam–Lewis and Clark Lake	SD	x	x	x	x	x	x	x	x	x	x
427	Lake Oahe	SD		x	x	x	x	x	x	x	x	x
	Tennessee											
428	Center Hill Lake	TN	x	x	x	x	x	x	x	x	x	x
429	Cheatham Lake	TN	x	x	x	x	x	x	x	x	x	x
430	Cordell Hull Lake	TN	x	x	x	x	x	x	x	x	x	x
431	Dale Hollow Lake	TN	x	x	x	x	x	x	x	x	x	x

Fig. 13.3 No.	Name	State	Camp with electricity	Camp w/o electricity	Showers	Restrooms	Drinking Water	Sanitary Dump	Picnic/Day Use	Launch Ramp	Marina	Visitor Center
432	J. Percy Priest Lake	TN	x	x	x	x	x	x	x	x	x	x
433	Lake Barkley	TN	x	x	x	x	x	x	x	x	x	x
434	Old Hickory Lake	TN	x	x	x	x	x	x	x	x	x	x
	Texas											
435	Addicks Reservoir	TX				x	x	x	x	x		x
436	Aquilla Lake	TX		x		x	x	x		x		
437	Bardwell Lake	TX	x	x	x	x	x	x	x	x	x	x
438	Barker Reservoir	TX					x		x			
439	Benbrook Lake	TX	x	x	x	x	x	x	x	x	x	x
440	Belton Lake	TX	x	x	x	x	x	x	x	x	x	x
441	Canyon Lake	TX	x	x	x	x	x	x	x	x	x	x
442	Cooper Lake	TX	x	x	x	x	x	x	x	x		x
443	Denison Dam–Lake Texoma	TX	x	x	x	x	x	x	x	x	x	x
444	Granger Lake	TX	x	x	x	x	x	x	x	x		x
445	Grapevine Lake	TX	x	x	x	x	x	x	x	x	x	x
446	Hords Creek Lake	TX	x	x	x	x	x	x	x	x	x	x
447	Joe Pool Lake	TX	x	x	x	x	x	x	x	x	x	x
448	Lake Georgetown	TX	x	x	x	x	x	x	x	x		x
449	Lake o' the Pines	TX	x	x	x	x	x	x	x	x	x	x
450	Lavon Lake	TX	x	x	x	x	x	x	x	x	x	x
451	Lewisville Lake	TX	x	x	x	x	x	x	x	x	x	x
452	Navarro Mills Lake	TX	x	x	x	x	x	x	x	x		x
453	O. C. Fisher Lake	TX	x	x	x	x	x	x	x	x	x	x
454	Pat Mayse Lake	TX	x	x	x	x	x	x	x	x	x	x
455	Proctor Lake	TX	x	x	x	x	x	x	x	x	x	x
456	Ray Roberts Lake	TX	x	x	x	x	x	x	x	x		x
457	Sam Rayburn Reservoir	TX	x	x		x	x	x	x	x	x	x
458	Somerville Lake	TX	x	x	x	x	x	x	x	x	x	x
459	Stillhouse Hollow Lake	TX	x	x	x	x	x	x	x	x	x	x
460	Town Bluff Dam–B. A. Steinhagen Lake	TX	x	x	x	x	x	x	x	x	x	x
461	Waco Lake	TX	x	x	x	x	x	x	x	x	x	x
462	Whitney Lake	TX	x	x	x	x	x	x	x	x	x	x
463	Wright Patman Lake	TX	x	x	x	x	x	x	x	x	x	x

Virginia

Fig. 13.3 No.	Name	State	Camp with electricity	Camp w/o electricity	Showers	Restrooms	Drinking Water	Sanitary Dump	Picnic/Day Use	Launch Ramp	Marina	Visitor Center
464	Atlantic Intracoastal Waterway	VA							x	x		
465	Gathright Dam (Lake Moomaw)	VA	x		x	x	x	x	x	x	x	x
466	John H. Kerr Reservoir	VA	x	x	x	x	x	x	x	x	x	x
467	John W. Flannagan Reservoir	VA	*		x	x	x	x	x	x	x	x
468	North Fork of Pound Lake	VA	x	x	x	x	x	x	x	x	x	
469	Philpott Lake	VA	x	x	x	x	x	x	x	x	x	x

Vermont

Fig. 13.3 No.	Name	State	Camp with electricity	Camp w/o electricity	Showers	Restrooms	Drinking Water	Sanitary Dump	Picnic/Day Use	Launch Ramp	Marina	Visitor Center
470	Ball Mountain Lake	VT		x	x	x	x	x	x			
471	North Hartland Lake	VT	x	x	x	x	x	x	x	x		
472	North Springfield Lake	VT		x		x	x	x	x	x		
473	Townshend Lake	VT	x	x	x	x	x	x	x	x		
474	Union Village Dam	VT				x	x	x	x	x		

Washington

Fig. 13.3 No.	Name	State	Camp with electricity	Camp w/o electricity	Showers	Restrooms	Drinking Water	Sanitary Dump	Picnic/Day Use	Launch Ramp	Marina	Visitor Center
475	Chief Joseph Dam–Rufus Woods Lake	WA	x	x	x	x	x	x	x	x	x	x
476	Ice Harbor Lock and Dam–Lake Sacajawea	WA	x	x	x	x	x	x	x	x	x	x
477	Lake Washington Ship Canal	WA			x	x	x	x	x	x	x	x
478	Little Goose Lock and Dam–Lake Bryan	WA	x	x	x	x	x	x	x	x	x	x
479	Lower Granite Lock and Dam	WA	x	x	x	x	x	x	x	x	x	x
480	Lower Monumental Lock and Dam–Lake West	WA	x	x	x	x	x	x	x	x	x	x
481	Mill Creek Lake	WA				x	x	x	x			
482	Mud Mountain Dam	WA				x	x	x	x			
483	Wynoochee Lake	WA		x	x	x	x	x	x	x		

Wisconsin

Fig. 13.3 No.	Name	State	Camp with electricity	Camp w/o electricity	Showers	Restrooms	Drinking Water	Sanitary Dump	Picnic/Day Use	Launch Ramp	Marina	Visitor Center
484	Bad Axe Landing	WI				x	x	x	x	x		
485	Blackhawk Park	WI	x	x	x	x	x	x	x	x		
486	Eau Galle Lake	WI	x	x	x	x	x	x	x	x		

Fig. 13.3 No.	Name	State	Camp with electricity	Camp w/o electricity	Showers	Restrooms	Drinking Water	Sanitary Dump	Picnic/Day Use	Launch Ramp	Marina	Visitor Center
487	Grant River	WI	x		x	x	x	x	x	x		
488	Jays Lake	WI			x	x	x	x	x	x		
489	Lock and Dam 10	WI					x					
490	Lock and Dam 11	WI				x	x					
491	Lock and Dam 3	WI					x					
492	Lock and Dam 4	WI				x	x					
493	Lock and Dam 5	WI					x					
494	Lock and Dam 5A	WI				x	x					
495	Lock and Dam 6	WI					x					
496	Lock and Dam 7	WI					x					
497	Lock and Dam 8	WI				x	x					
498	Lock and Dam 9	WI					x					
499	Sturgeon Bay	WI										

West Virginia

Fig. 13.3 No.	Name	State	Camp with electricity	Camp w/o electricity	Showers	Restrooms	Drinking Water	Sanitary Dump	Picnic/Day Use	Launch Ramp	Marina	Visitor Center
500	Beech Fork Lake	WV	x	x	x	x	x	x	x	x		
501	Bluestone Lake	WV	x	x	x	x	x	x	x	x		x
502	Burnsville Lake	WV	x	x	x	x	x	x	x	x	x	x
503	East Lynn Lake	WV	x	x	x	x	x	x	x	x		x
504	Gallipolis Lock and Dam	WV					x		x	x		
505	Hildebrand Lock and Dam	WV										
506	Jennings Randolph Lake	WV	x		x	x	x	x	x	x	x	x
507	London Lock and Dam	WV					x					
508	Marmet Lock and Dam	WV							x	x		
509	Morgantown Lock and Dam	WV							x	x	x	
510	Opekiska Lock and Dam	WV							x	x	x	
511	Pike Island Lock and Dam	WV							x	x	x	
512	R. D. Bailey Lake	WV	x	x	x	x	x	x	x	x	x	x
513	Racine Lock and Dam	WV								x	x	
514	Stonewall Jackson Lake	WV	x	x	x	x	x	x	x	x	x	x
515	Summersville Lake	WV	x	x	x	x	x	x	x	x	x	x
516	Sutton Lake	WV	x	x	x	x	x	x	x	x	x	x
517	Tygart Lake	WV	x	x	x	x	x	x	x	x	x	x
518	Winfield Lock and Dam	WV							x	x	x	x

Note: o, boat access camping only; *, future.
Sources: Army Corps of Engineers, *Lakeside Recreation in the Southeast,* August 1992; Army Corps of Engineers, *Lakeside Recreation in the Great Lakes States,* August 1992; Army Corps of Engineers, *Lakeside Recreation in New England,* August 1992; Army Corps of Engineers, *Lakeside Recreation in the Northwest,* August 1992; Army Corps of Engineers, *Lakeside Recreation in the South Central States,* August 1992; Army Corps of Engineers, *Lakeside Recreation in the Southwest,* August 1992; Army Corps of Engineers, *Lakeside Recreation in the Upper Mississippi Basin,* August 1992; Army Corps of Engineers, *Lakeside Recreation in the Great Plains,* August 1992; Army Corps of Engineers, *Lakeside Recreation in the Central States,* August 1992; Army Corps of Engineers, *Lakeside Recreation in the Mid-Atlantic States,* August 1992.

APPENDIX XIX

Bureau of Reclamation: Projects and Recreation Areas—1989

State(s)/Project	Recreation Area	Fig. 13.8 No.	Acres of Land	Acres of Water	Agency	Visitor Days	Primary Activity*
	Arizona						
Central Arizona	Horsemen's Park	1	359	0	City of Scottsdale	87,500	O, R, M
	Phoenix Reach 11 Recreation Area	2	1,500	0	City of Phoenix	3,478	I, O, A
	Scottsdale Golf Complex	3	330	0	City of Scottsdale	487,500	P
Salt River	Apache Lake	4	11,288	2,620	Forest Service	311,667	D, G, K
	Bartlett Reservoir	5	9,000	2,690	Forest Service	76,208	K, G, F
	Canyon Lake	6	12,490	930	Forest Service	329,833	G, C, D
	Horseshoe Reservoir	7	16,260	2,720	Forest Service	16,000	K, D, A
	Saguaro Lake	8	6,420	1,260	Forest Service	200,000	G, C, E
	Salt River Project Canals	9	1,100	0	Salt River Valley Water Users Assoc.	9,125	C, I, M
Yuma	Theodore Roosevelt Reservoir	10	28,079	16,990	Forest Service	1,056,000	D, G, K
	Mittry Lake Wildlife Area	11	3,450	400	AZ Game and Fish Dept.	117,862	K, L, G
Total: Arizona			90,276	27,610		2,695,173	
	Arizona–California						
Boulder Canyon	Imperial Natl. Wildlife Refuge	12	20,440	5,325	Fish and Wildlife Service	139,977	G, K, A
	Imperial Reservoir Area[1]	13	23,668	4,523	BLM	271,998	D, G, K
CO River Front Work–Levee System	Cibola Natl. Wildlife Refuge	14	16,667	1,913	Fish and Wildlife Service	22,633	M, K, A
Parker-Davis	Havasu Natl. Wildlife Refuge	15	41,075	11,039	Fish and Wildlife Service	169,155	K, G, F
	Lake Havasu Area[2]	16	21,887	15,026	BLM	3,513,455	D, G, K
Total: Arizona–California			123,737	37,826		4,117,218	
	Arizona–Nevada						
Boulder Canyon	Hoover Dam	17	0	0	Bureau of Reclamation	74,517	A, M
	Lake Mead Natl. Recreation Area[3]	18	1,496,626	191,477	National Park Service	6,997,356	A, G, K
Parker-Davis	Davis Dam[4]	19	76	0	Bureau of Reclamation	231,027	D, A, K
					Clark County Parks and Rec.		
					Mohave County Parks Dept.		
Total: Arizona–Nevada			1,496,702	191,477		7,302,900	
	Arizona–Utah						
Colorado River Storage	Glen Canyon Natl. Recreation Area (L. Powell)	20	1,245,855	162,628	National Park Service	6,380,074	G, K, A
	California						
Boulder Canyon	Lake Cahuilla	21	65	135	County of Riverside	127,362	C, E, K
	Salton Sea Natl. Wildlife Refuge	22	2,456	33,086	Fish and Wildlife Service	8,333	A, K, L
	Salton Sea State Recreation Area	23	4,584	3,220	CA Dept. of Parks and Rec.	183,424	K, D, C
Cachuma	Cachuma Lake Recreation Area	24	6,090	2,950	Santa Barbara County Parks Dept.	510,571	D, K, G

State(s)/Project	Recreation Area	Fig. 13.8 No.	Acres of Land	Acres of Water	Agency	Visitor Days	Primary Activity*
Central Valley	Auburn Reservoir	25	31,000	642	CA State Dept. of Parks and Rec.	319,937	E, C, D
	Avenal Cut-Off Fishing Access	26	1	1	Kings County Dept. of Parks and Rec.	917	K
	Canyon Road Angling Site	27	1	1	Merced County Parks and Rec. Division	583	K
	Clair Engle Lake (Trinity)[5]	28	5,220	16,500	Forest Service	716,733	D, G, H
	Contra Costa Canal Trail	29	169	0	E. Bay Regional Park District	33,333	M, M, M
	Contra Loma Reservoir	30	771	87	E. Bay Regional Park District	34,249	E, C, K
	Delta-Mendota Canal Site 2A	31	87	31	Stanislaus County Pks. and Facilities Dept.	75	K, A, I
	Delta-Mendota Canal Site 5	32	570	230	Fresno County Parks Division	7,683	K
	FairFax Fishing Access Area	33	1	1	Fresno County Parks Division	2,017	K, A
	Folsom Lake State Recreation Area	34	4,875	11,500	CA Dept. of Parks and Rec.	520,833	E, G, C
	Folsom South Canal Recreation Trail	35	70	0	Bureau of Reclamation	500	M, I, B
	Huron Fishing Access Area	36	1	1	Fresno County Parks Division	1,383	K
	Jenkinson Lake (Sly Park)	37	1,489	640	El Dorado Irrigation District	200,000	K, G, D
	Kesterson Reservoir	38	4,600	925	Fish and Wildlife Service	733	L, B, A
	Keswick Reservoir	39	570	630	Shasta County Rec. Commission	1,983	K, G, A
	Lake Natoma	40	783	500	CA Dept. Parks and Rec.	125,052	H, K, A
	Lake Woollomes (Delano)	41	145	300	Kern County Parks and Recreation	84,841	C, A, E
	Lewiston Lake	42	576	750	Forest Service	82,467	G, K, D
	Little Panoche Reservoir Wildlife Area	43	750	30	CA Dept. of Fish and Game	753	K, L, A
	Los Banos Detention Reservoir	44	1,702	470	CA Dept. of Fish and Game	69,690	K, H, D
	Mervel Angling Site	45	1	1	Merced Co. Parks and Rec. Div.	1,121	K
	Millerton Lake (Friant)	46	8,175	4,915	CA Dept. of Parks and Rec. BLM	568,661	G, F, D
	New Melones Lake	47	25,124	9,705	BLM	523,606	K, F, G
	Nimbus Fish Hatchery	48	20	0	CA Dept. of Fish and Game	28,306	A, K, B
	Nimbus Dam Shoals Fishing Access Site	49	20	0	CA Dept. of Parks and Rec.	21,750	K, A, B
	O'Neill Forebay	50	3,346	2,300	CA Dept. of Parks and Rec.	280,828	K, C, D
	Red Bluff Diversion Reservoir	51	350	575	BLM Forest Service	75,000	K, D, C
	San Luis Reservoir	52	9,184	13,000	CA Dept. of Parks and Rec.	163,963	K, D, C
	Shasta Lake[5]	53	13,500	30,000	Forest Service Bureau of Reclamation	2,421,650	G, D, F
	Squaw Leap	54	4,320	153	BLM	2,667	A, I, L
	Sugar Pine Reservoir	55	1,734	160	Forest Service	52,350	D, C, K
	Three Rocks Angling Site	56	1	2	Fresno County Parks Division	1,700	K, A, B

Project	No.	Facility	Managing Agency				Codes
	57	Trinity River Fish Hatchery	CA Dept. of Fish and Game	13	0	757	A, B, K
	58	Volta Wildlife Area	CA Dept. of Fish and Game	2,847	0	2,531	L, K, A
Klamath	59	Whiskeytown Reservoir[5]	National Park Service	42,397	3,250	452,656	E, G, A
	60	Clear Lake Natl. Wildlife Refuge	Fish and Wildlife Service	12,520	8,000	592	A, L
	61	Lower Klamath Natl. Wildlife Refuge	Fish and Wildlife Service	23,868	22,725	6,560	A, L
	62	Tule Lake Natl. Wildlife Refuge	Fish and Wildlife Service	25,373	5,640	7,951	A, L
Orland	63	East Park Reservoir	Bureau of Reclamation / Forest Service	2,468	1,820	50,729	K, D, F
	64	Stony Gorge Reservoir	Bureau of Reclamation / Forest Service	1,161	1,275	17,562	K, D, C
Solano	65	Lake Berryessa	Bureau of Reclamation	8,958	19,200	1,671,637	G, K, F
	66	Lake Solano	Solano County Parks Dept. / Lake Solano County Park	135	110	84,350	C, E, D
	67	Putah Creek Angling Access Site	CA Dept. of Fish and Game Wildlife Conservation	30	2	775	A, K
Truckee Storage	68	Boca Reservoir	Forest Service	2,912	980	215,833	K, D, F
Ventura River	69	Lake Casitas Recreation Area	Casitas Municipal Water District	6,200	1,590	575,025	A, K, D
Washoe	70	Prosser Creek Reservoir	Forest Service	2,030	740	116,917	K, G, C
	71	Stampede Reservoir	Forest Service	10,560	3,440	350,000	K, D, G
Total: California				273,823	202,075	10,728,929	
Colorado							
Bostwick Park	72	Silver Jack Reservoir	Forest Service	468	307	15,254	A, K, I
Colbran	73	Vega Reservoir	CO Div. of Parks and Rec.	925	898	117,278	K, D, G
CO River Basin Salinity Co.	74	Horsethief Canyon State Recreation Area	CO Div. of Wildlife	1,063	0	125	L, K, B
CO River Storage	75	Curecanti Natl. Recreation Area[6]	National Park Service	32,014	9,170	453,076	A, K, G
Colorado–Big Thompson	76	Carter Lake	Larimer County Parks Dept.	910	1,144	128,706	K, D, G
	77	East Portal Reservoir	Estes Valley Rec. & Parks District	70	2	11,300	D, A, C
	78	Flatiron Reservoir	Larimer County Parks Dept.	173	47	6,250	K, D, C
	79	Green Mountain Reservoir	Forest Service	1,998	2,125	62,850	K, D, G
	80	Horsetooth Reservoir	Larimer County Parks Dept.	1,978	1,899	89,167	K, G, D
	81	Lake Estes	Estes Valley Rec. and Park Dist.	118	145	23,004	M, H, C
	82	Lake Granby	Forest Service	10,831	7,258	225,000	G, K, D
	83	Marys Lake	Estes Valley Rec. and Park Dist.	138	42	37,920	D, K, C
	84	Pinewood Lake	Larimer County Pks. Dept.	142	96	12,500	K, D, G
	85	Shadow Mountain Lake	Forest Service	1,102	1,346	175,000	D, K, G
	86	Willow Creek Reservoir	Forest Service	665	303	60,000	K, D, C
Dallas Creek	87	Ridgway State Recreation Area	CO Div. of Parks and Outdoor Rec.	3,060	1,028	21,192	A, K, D
Delores	88	McPhee Reservoir	Forest Service / BLM	11,100	4,470	144,904	G, K, D
Florida	89	Lemon Reservoir	Forest Service	1,419	620	21,400	D, K, A
Fruitgrowers Dam	90	Fruitgrowers Reservoir	Bureau of Reclamation	184	444	42	C, K, B

State(s)/Project	Recreation Area	Fig. 13.8 No.	Acres of Land	Acres of Water	Agency	Visitor Days	Primary Activity*
Fryingpan-Arkansas	Pueblo Reservoir	91	12,744	4,646	CO Div. of Parks and Outdoor Rec.	659,017	A, K, G
	Ruedi Reservoir	92	1,407	997	Forest Service	89,909	D, H, K
	Turquoise Lake	93	4,894	1,780	Forest Service	175,373	A, D, K
	Twin Lakes Reservoir	94	5,600	2,440	Forest Service	151,833	K, A, D
Mancos	Jackson Gulch Reservoir	95	337	216	CO Div. of Parks and Outdoor Rec.	13,463	K, D, C
Paonia	Paonia Reservoir	96	1,165	322	CO Div. of Parks and Outdoor Rec.	7,826	A, F, G
Pick-Sloan MBP	Bonny Reservoir	97	5,187	2,042	CO Div. of Parks and Outdoor Rec.	94,750	D, K, E
Pine River	Vallecito Reservoir	98	961	2,720	Pine River Irrigation District	308,047	D, K, C
San Luis Valley	Platoro Reservoir	99	1,403	947	Forest Service	4,208	A, K, G
Silt	Rifle Gap Reservoir	100	1,305	348	CO Div. of Parks and Outdoor Rec.	58,080	A, G, K
Smith Fork	Crawford Reservoir	101	379	394	CO Div. of Parks and Outdoor Rec.	57,549	K, A, E
Uncompahgre	Taylor Park Reservoir	102	4,133	2,040	Forest Service	33,492	A, D, K
Total: Colorado			107,423	50,234		3,256,515	

Colorado–New Mexico

State(s)/Project	Recreation Area	Fig. 13.8 No.	Acres of Land	Acres of Water	Agency	Visitor Days	Primary Activity*
Colorado River Storage	Navajo Reservoir	103	22,376	15,590	NM State Park and Rec. Div. CO Div. of Parks and Outdoor Rec.	335,485	K, G, D

Idaho

State(s)/Project	Recreation Area	Fig. 13.8 No.	Acres of Land	Acres of Water	Agency	Visitor Days	Primary Activity*
Boise	Anderson Ranch Reservoir	104	6,668	4,730	Forest Service	40,950	K, D, A
	Arrowrock Reservoir	105	4,032	3,017	Forest Service	4,792	K, G, A
	Black Canyon Reservoir	106	1,264	1,100	Bureau of Reclamation	45,667	F, G, E
	Boise River Diversion Dam	107	1,280	0	Bureau of Reclamation	83	A
	Cascade Reservoir	108	6,238	27,550	Bureau of Reclamation	257,725	K, D, G
	Deadwood Reservoir	109	2,665	3,000	Forest Service	11,650	D, K, L
	Lake Lowell	110	788	9,560	Fish and Wildlife Service	28,549	A, K, G
Lewiston Orchards	Lake Waha	111	20	180	Lewiston Orchards Irrigation District	7,197	K, C, A
	Reservoir A (Mann Lake)	112	20	146	Lewiston Orchards Irrigation District	1,785	K, A, C
	Soldiers Meadow Reservoir	113	25	124	Lewiston Orchards Irrigation District	1,785	K, D, A
Little Wood River	Little Wood River Reservoir	114	612	364	Bureau of Reclamation	219,316	D, K, C
Mann Creek	Mann Creek Reservoir	115	653	283	Bureau of Reclamation	3,350	K, D, C
Minidoka-Palisades	American Falls Reservoir	116	2,224	57,669	Bureau of Reclamation Bingham County City of American Falls	99,794	K, G, A
	Cartier Slough	117	984	50	Bureau of Reclamation	347	B, K, L
	Island Park Reservoir	118	4,653	7,794	Forest Service	57,688	K, D, G
	Lake Walcott[7]	119	11,417	4,400	Fish and Wildlife Service	26,726	C, K, A

792

Project	Feature	No.			Managing Entity		Codes
Ririe	Ririe Lake	120	4,636	1,470	Bureau of Reclamation	62,959	K, G, C
Teton Basin	Tex Creek	121	9,113	5	Bureau of Reclamation	1,667	L, A, O
Total: Idaho			57,292	121,442		872,230	
					Idaho–Wyoming		
Minidoka-Palisades	Palisades Reservoir	122	11,695	16,150	Forest Service / Bureau of Reclamation	187,762	D, G, K
					Kansas		
Pick-Sloan MBP	Almena Diversion Dam	123	117	12	KS Dept. of Wildlife and Parks	640	A, L, M
	Cedar Bluff Reservoir	124	7,760	1,504	KS Dept. of Wildlife and Parks	267,193	G, D, F
	Keith Sebelius Reservoir	125	5,053	587	KS Dept. of Wildlife and Parks	96,273	G, D, F
	Kirwin Reservoir	126	6,623	1,355	Fish and Wildlife Service	76,144	A, K, C
	Lovewell Reservoir	127	3,155	2,986	KS Dept. of Wildlife and Parks	232,041	G, D, A
	Waconda Lake	128	15,307	12,602	KS Dept. of Wildlife and Parks	318,343	G, D, A
	Webster Reservoir	129	3,164	1,530	KS Dept. of Wildlife and Parks	101,640	G, D, A
	Woodston Diversion Dam	130	200	10	KS Dept. of Wildlife and Parks	1,400	A, L, K
Wichita	Cheney Reservoir	131	7,162	9,537	KS Dept. of Wildlife and Parks	851,608	G, D, A
Total: Kansas			48,541	30,123		1,945,282	
					Montana		
Hungry Horse	Hungry Horse Dam and Reservoir	132	6,836	23,780	Forest Service	71,667	A, D, M
Huntley	Anita Reservoir	133	148	32	Bureau of Reclamation	21	E, C, H
Lower Yellowstone	Lower Yellowstone Diversion Dam	134	1,431	200	MT Dept. of Fish, Wildlife, and Parks / Dawson County	17,467	K, C, G
Milk River	Fresno Reservoir	135	25,618	7,388	Bureau of Reclamation	8,333	E, G, F
	Lake Sherburne	136	222	1,601	National Park Service	144,536	A, K, S
	Milk River Wildlife Management Area	137	862	450	MT Dept. of Fish, Wildlife, and Parks / Malta and Glasgow Irrigation District	1,667	L, M, A
	Nelson Reservoir	138	7,702	4,320	Nelson Reservoir Rec. Assoc.	12,500	C, D, K
Pick-Sloan MBP	Barretts Diversion Dam	139	35	2	Bureau of Reclamation	16,782	C, K, D
	Canyon Ferry Lake	140	7,710	35,181	MT Dept. of Fish, Wildlife, and Parks	474,683	K, D, C
	Clark Canyon Reservoir	141	3,839	4,935	Bureau of Reclamation	75,264	K, D, H
	Helena Valley Reservoir	142	477	518	MT Dept. of Fish, Wildlife, and Parks	4,778	K, C, B
	Lake Elwell	143	21,244	17,678	Bureau of Reclamation	28,441	K, D, G
Sun River	Freezeout Lake	144	3,041	1,500	MT Dept. of Fish, Wildlife, and Parks	838	L, B, M
	Gibson Reservoir	145	8,253	1,296	Forest Service	81,312	L, D, M
	Pishkun Reservoir	146	2,683	1,550	MT Dept. of Fish, Wildlife, and Parks	1,542	K, G, D
	Willow Creek Reservoir	147	3,069	1,530	MT Dept. of Fish, Wildlife, and Parks	2,662	K, G, D
Total: Montana			93,170	101,961		942,493	
					Montana–Wyoming		
Pick-Sloan MBP	Bighorn Canyon Natl. Recreation Area	148	107,458	12,700	National Park Service	240,824	K, G, A

State(s)/Project	Recreation Area	Fig. 13.8 No.	Acres of Land	Acres of Water	Agency	Visitor Days	Primary Activity*
Nebraska							
Mirage Flats	Box Butte Reservoir	149	613	1,600	NE Game and Parks Commission	75,900	K, C, G
North Platte	Lake Minatare	150	2,078	2,158	NE Game and Parks Commission	212,000	K, G, E
Pick-Sloan MBP	Arcadia Diversion Dam	151	838	109	NE Game and Parks Commission	7,020	K, C, L
	Calamus Reservoir	152	6,484	5,124	NE Game and Parks Commission	320,657	K, G, A
	Enders Reservoir	153	3,690	1,707	NE Game and Parks Commission	45,720	K, C, D
	Harry Strunk Lake	154	6,644	1,850	NE Game and Parks Commission	45,120	K, L, G
	Hugh Butler Lake	155	4,320	1,629	NE Game and Parks Commission	77,625	K, D, L
	Merritt Reservoir	156	6,034	2,906	NE Game and Parks Commission	103,699	K, D, G
	Milburn Diversion Dam	157	317	355	NE Game and Parks Commission	2,370	K, L, C
	Sherman Reservoir	158	4,725	2,868	NE Game and Parks Commission	166,651	K, G, D
	Swanson Lake	159	4,651	4,974	NE Game and Parks Commission	99,740	K, D, C
Total: Nebraska			40,314	25,280		1,156,502	
Nevada							
Humboldt	Humboldt Toulon Sink	160	18,179	15,000	NV Dept. of Wildlife	2,021	L, A, G
	Rye Patch Reservoir	161	9,417	12,000	NV Div. of State Parks	193,333	K, E, A
Newlands	Fernley Wildlife Management Area	162	7,727	6,450	NV Dept. of Wildlife	667	L, B, A
	Lahontan Reservoir	163	22,814	11,200	NV Div. of State Parks / Truckee Carson Irrigation District	262,842	D, G, K
	Stillwater Wildlife Management Area	164	161,710	19,000	NV Dept. of Wildlife / Fish and Wildlife Service	17,834	K, L, C
Total: Nevada			219,847	63,650		476,697	
New Mexico							
Brantley	Brantley Reservoir	165	33,100	3,057	NM Energy, Minerals, and Natural Resources Department	1,667	G, D, K
Carlsbad	Avalon and McMillan Reservoirs	166	38,271	1,000	Carlsbad Irrigation District	1,000	D, B, A
	Lake Sumner	167	6,667	4,506	NM Energy, Minerals, and Natural Resources Department	39,258	K, D, G
Middle Rio Grande	El Vado Reservoir	168	1,728	3,220	NM Energy, Minerals, and Natural Resources Department	21,762	K, D, G
Rio Grande	Caballo Reservoir	169	5,326	11,500	NM Energy, Minerals, and Natural Resources Department	123,260	K, D, G
	Elephant Butte Reservoir	170	24,251	36,558	NM Energy, Minerals, and Natural Resources Department	876,978	K, G, D
	Leasburg Diversion Dam	171	290	0	NM Energy, Minerals, and Natural Resources Department	16,194	C, D, K
	Percha Diversion Dam	172	84	0	NM Energy, Minerals, and Natural Resources Department	7,091	C, K, D

System	Feature	No.			Agency		Codes
San Juan–Chama	Heron Reservoir	173	4,107	5,905	NM Energy, Minerals, and Natural Resources Department	56,288	D, H, K
Vermejo	Nambe Falls Reservoir	174	191	56	Office of the Governor	8,781	C, K, D
	Reservoir No. 13	175	109	329	Fish and Wildlife Service	3,333	K, A, B
	Stubblefield and No. 2 Reservoirs	176	821	1,290	NM Energy, Minerals, and Natural Resources Department	321	K, B, L
Total: New Mexico			114,945	67,421		1,155,933	
North Dakota							
Pick-Sloan MBP	Devils and Stump Lakes[8]	177	17,778	44,600	ND Parks and Rec. Dept.	111,236	K, D, G
	Edward Arthur Patterson Lake	178	1,278	1,191	Dickinson Parks and Rec. District	86,667	E, G, C
	Jamestown Reservoir	179	2,492	2,095	Stutsman County Park Board	62,500	G, K, E
	Lake Brekken–Holmes	180	620	675	Turtle Lake City Park Board	667	K, T, C
	Lake Tschida	181	7,361	3,397	Bureau of Reclamation	81,477	D, G, C
	McClusky Canal	182	10,060	2,605	Bureau of Reclamation	16,173	K, L, D
Total: North Dakota			39,587	54,563		358,720	
Oklahoma							
Arbuckle, OK	Chickasaw Natl. Recreation Area	183	4,455	2,346	National Park Service	555,211	D, K, E
McGee Creek	McGee Creek Reservoir	184	26,375	3,797	OK Tourism and Rec. Dept.	23,970	L, A, D
Mountain Park	Tom Steed Reservoir	185	4,000	7,400	OK Tourism and Rec. Dept.	98,549	G, K, D
Norman	Lake Thunderbird	186	6,753	6,070	OK Tourism and Rec. Dept.	1,266,595	G, C, D
W. C. Austin	Altus Reservoir	187	3,832	6,575	OK Tourism and Rec. Dept.	254,668	D, M
Washita Basin	Fort Cobb Reservoir	188	3,922	4,098	OK Tourism and Rec. Dept.	278,759	D, G, K
	Foss Reservoir	189	6,831	8,800	OK Tourism and Rec. Dept.	89,992	K, F, G
Total: Oklahoma			56,168	39,086		2,567,744	
Oregon							
Baker	Phillips Lake	190	2,803	2,235	Forest Service	791,983	K, D, C
	Thief Valley Reservoir	191	169	740	Union County Oregon	2,017	K, D, L
Burnt River	Unity Reservoir	192	610	928	Oregon State Parks Dept.; Bureau of Reclamation	30,479	K, E, D
Crescent Lake Dam	Crescent Lake	193	1,985	4,008	Forest Service	109,600	D, K, G
Crooked River	Ochoco Reservoir	194	20	1,100	Ochoco Irrigation District	64,564	K, D, G
	Prineville Reservoir	195	5,728	3,010	Crook County; OR Dept. of Fish and Wildlife	92,255	D, K, F
Deschutes	Crane Prairie Reservoir	196	2,200	4,940	Forest Service	133,500	D, K, G
	Haystack Reservoir	197	287	233	Forest Service	29,600	K, G, F
	Wickiup Reservoir	198	5,717	11,200	Forest Service	128,800	D, K, G
Klamath	A Canal Bike Path	199	158	0	Klamath County Park Board	1,000	M
	Gerber Reservoir	200	5,511	3,830	BLM	15,487	D, K, L
	Wilson Reservoir	201	284	240	Klamath County Park Board	3,333	K, A, C
Owyhee	Lake Owyhee	202	20,322	13,900	OR State Highway Commission; Bureau of Reclamation; BLM	14,333	K, G, L

State(s)/Project	Recreation Area	Fig. 13.8 No.	Acres of Land	Acres of Water	Agency	Visitor Days	Primary Activity*
Rogue River Basin	Agate Reservoir	203	476	216	Jackson County Parks and Rec. Dept.	35,248	K, M, E
	Emigrant Lake	204	531	806	Jackson County Parks and Rec. Dept.	149,380	C, G, F
	Howard Prairie Lake	205	1,946	1,990	Jackson County Parks and Rec. Dept.	308,100	K, D, C
	Hyatt Reservoir	206	180	880	Talent Irrigation District BLM	84,783	K, D, C
Tualatin	Henry Hagg Lake	207	1,449	1,132	Washington County	197,000	K, C, E
Umatilla	Cold Springs Reservoir	208	1,059	1,610	Fish and Wildlife Service	10,000	K, B, L
	McKay Reservoir	209	515	1,200	Fish and Wildlife Service	50,000	K, L, B
Vale	Beulah Reservoir	210	1,428	1,900	Malheur County	2,817	K, D, L
	Bully Creek Reservoir	211	1,083	985	Malheur County	5,292	K, F
	Warm Springs Reservoir	212	2,424	4,600	Bureau of Reclamation	2,317	K, D, L
Wapinitia	Clear Lake	213	1,374	557	Forest Service	27,250	D, K, G
Total: Oregon			58,259	62,238		2,289,118	
South Dakota							
Pick-Sloan MBP	Angostura Reservoir	214	3,494	4,706	SD Dept. of Game, Fish and Parks	194,968	K, E, D
	Belle Fourche Reservoir	215	6,694	8,040	SD Dept. of Game, Fish and Parks Belle Fourche Irrigation District	26,858	K, D, G
	James Diversion Reservoir	216	154	960	SD Dept. of Game, Fish and Parks	3,000	K, L, H
	Pactola Reservoir	217	5,970	860	Forest Service	15,622	A, K, D
	Shadehill Reservoir	218	8,358	4,800	SD Dept. of Game, Fish and Parks	54,917	D, C, K
Rapid Valley	Deerfield Reservoir	219	1,845	414	Forest Service	21,861	K, D, C
Total: S. Dakota			25,515	19,780		317,226	
Texas							
Canadian River	Lake Meredith Recreation Area[9]	220	28,433	16,518	National Park Service	408,283	A, E, G
Nueces River	Choke Canyon Reservoir	221	9,127	25,733	Texas Parks and Wildlife Dept.	306,195	K, G, D
Palmetto Bend	Lake Texana	222	6,585	10,400	Lavaca Navidad River Authority Texas Parks and Wildlife Dept.	220,883	A, K, D
San Angelo	Twin Buttes Reservoir	223	3,219	9,079	City of San Angelo	1,756	K, D, G
Total: Texas			47,364	61,730		937,117	
Utah							
Central Utah	Currant Creek	224	1,285	300	Uinta NF	83,314	D, K, C
	Red Fleet Reservoir	225	1,973	520	Bureau of Reclamation Red Fleet State Park	17,571	G, K, E
	Starvation Reservoir	226	3,310	3,445	Utah Div. of Parks and Rec.	57,523	D, K, G
	Steinaker Reservoir	227	2,283	795	Utah Div. of Parks and Rec.	10,793	G, K, D
	Strawberry Reservoir	228	55,608	8,752	Uinta NF	251,400	K, D, G
Emery County	Huntington North Reservoir	229	115	237	Utah Div. of Parks and Rec.	10,770	G, D, E
	Joes Valley Reservoir	230	1,553	1,160	Forest Service	178,891	K, D, A

	No.	Reservoir			Manager		Codes
Hyrum	231	Hyrum Reservoir	252	475	Utah Div. of Parks and Rec.	83,352	E, F, G
Lyman	232	Stateline Reservoir	710	280	Forest Service	16,800	D, K, A
Moon Lake	233	Moon Lake Reservoir	1,908	773	Ashley NF	33,333	D, K, A
Newton	234	Newton Reservoir	202	288	Cache County	5,125	G, K, D
Provo River	235	Deer Creek Reservoir	3,260	2,435	UT Div. of Parks and Rec.	107,842	K, G, H
Scofield	236	Scofield Reservoir	403	2,804	UT Div. of Parks and Rec.	32,917	K, G, D
Weber Basin	237	Causey Reservoir	407	140	Forest Service	5,906	K, E, D
	238	East Canyon Reservoir	277	681	UT Div. of Parks and Rec.	78,977	K, D, C
	239	Lost Creek Reservoir	693	345	UT Div. of Parks and Rec.	24,917	K, D, C
	240	Pineview Reservoir	470	2,789	Forest Service	240,375	C, D, G
	241	Rockport Lake	551	1,080	UT Div. of Parks and Rec.	195,843	K, D, G
	242	Willard Reservoir	2,673	9,920	UT Div. of Parks and Rec.	87,235	E, G, F
Weber River	243	Echo Reservoir	395	1,470	Weber River Water Users Assoc. Echo Resort Inc.	58,778	G, D, C
Total: Utah			**78,328**	**38,689**		**1,581,662**	
				Utah–Wyoming			
Colorado River Storage	244	Flaming Gorge Natl. Recreation Area	95,380	42,020	Forest Service	648,655	A, D, G
Lyman	245	Meeks Cabin Reservoir	589	477	Forest Service	4,920	D, C, G
Total: Utah–Wyoming			**95,969**	**42,497**		**653,575**	
				Washington			
Chief Joseph Dam	246	Spectacle Lake	6	340	WA State Dept. of Game Bureau of Reclamation	5,250	K, A, I
Columbia Basin	247	Babcock Ridge Lake	16	20	WA State Dept. of Wildlife	36	K, L, M
	248	Banks Lake	17,700	27,000	WA State Dept. of Wildlife WA State Parks and Rec. Commission	114,308	D, K, A
	249	Billy Clapp Lake (Long Lake Reservoir)	2,699	1,010	WA State Dept. of Wildlife WA State Parks and Rec. Commission	11,095	A, C, K
	250	Canal, Heart, Windmill, Virgin, and Susan Lakes	3,642	340	WA State Dept. of Wildlife	6,285	K, L, D
	251	Clark Lake	408	100	WA State Dept. of Wildlife	264	L, K, A
	252	Columbia Natl. Wildlife Refuge	1,388	50	Fish and Wildlife Service	65,116	K, C, D
	253	Crab Creek, Wanapum and Corfu Areas	7,225	50	WA State Dept. of Wildlife	1,365	L, K, A
	254	Desert Wildlife Rec. Area[10]	24,533	2,712	WA State Dept. of Wildlife	11,250	A, L, K
	255	Esquatzel Coulee Wasteway	1,727	5	WA State Dept. of Wildlife	653	L, A, C
	256	Franklin D. Roosevelt Lake[11]	15,750	60,450	National Park Service	422,917	C, D, A
	257	Gloyd Seeps Wildlife Rec. Area	3,170	100	WA State Dept. of Wildlife	1,139	L, K, M
	258	Goose Lake Area	3,476	150	WA State Dept. of Wildlife	2,215	K, L, D
	259	Grand Coulee Dam	95		Bureau of Reclamation	77,467	A, C
	260	Lake Linda	223	77	WA State Dept. of Wildlife	132	L, K, A
	261	Lyle Lake	452	23	WA State Dept. of Wildlife	479	K, B, L

State(s)/Project	Recreation Area	Fig. 13.8 No.	Acres of Land	Acres of Water	Agency	Visitor Days	Primary Activity*
	Mesa Lake	262	67	57	WA State Dept. of Wildlife	198	K, L, A
	Potholes Reservoir	263	14,500	18,000	WA State Parks and Rec. Commission WA State Dept. of Wildlife	348,489	K, D, G
	Quincy Wildlife Recreation Area	264	5,281	700	WA State Dept. of Wildlife	5,600	K, D, L
	Scooteney Reservoir	265	1,980	925	Bureau of Reclamation	8,401	K, D, C
	Warden Lake	266	20	60	WA State Dept. of Wildlife	2,634	K, D, L
	WB 10 Wasteway and Ringold Segment	267	1,823	48	WA State Dept. of Wildlife	515	K, L, A
	Winchester Wasteway Reservoir	268	930	1,020	WA State Dept. of Wildlife	2,541	K, D, L
	Worth Lake	269	68	10	WA State Dept. of Wildlife	204	L, K, A
Okanogan	Conconully Lake (Salmon)	270	768	310	Forest Service Okanogan Irrigation District	5,542	K, D
Yakima	Conconully Reservoir	271	200	450	WA, State Parks and Rec. Commission	187,572	C, D, K
	Bumping Lake	272	6,067	1,300	Forest Service	34,083	D, K, G
	Cle Elum Lake	273	1,006	4,812	Forest Service	176,603	D, E, C
	Easton Diversion Dam	274	112	240	WA State Parks and Rec. Commission	673,345	C, D, A
	Kachess Lake	275	1,119	4,535	Forest Service	225,048	D, C, A
	Keechelus Lake	276	1,108	2,560	Forest Service	141,049	A, G, K
	Prosser Diversion Dam	277	3	100	Bureau of Reclamation	438	K, E
	Rimrock–Clear Lake	278	4,129	2,790	Forest Service (Rimrock) Forest Service (Clear Lake)	94,667	D, K, G
	Roza Diversion Dam	279	100	100	Bureau of Reclamation	1,500	F, K, E
	Sunnyside Diversion Dam	280	2	5	Bureau of Reclamation	3,300	K, L, E
Total: Washington			121,793	130,449		2,631,700	
			Wyoming				
Eden	Big Sandy Reservoir	281	3,085	2,498	WY Rec. Commission	2,500	D, G, M
Kendrick	Alcova Reservoir	282	2,548	2,471	Natrona County Pks. and Pleasure Grounds WY Game and Fish Dept.	118,373	D, K, G
	Seminoe Reservoir	283	22,696	20,291	WY Rec. Commission WY Game and Fish Dept.	201,730	K, M, A
Minidoka-Palisades	Grassy Lake	284	1,477	310	Forest Service	975	K, G, D
	Jackson Lake[12]	285	7,555	23,970	National Park Service	817,284	A, I, D
North Platt	Guernsey Reservoir	286	5,713	2,382	WY Rec. Commission	431,417	M, E, A
	Pathfinder Reservoir	287	25,956	22,012	Natrona County Pks. & Pleasure Grounds WY Game and Fish Dept.	7,385	K, G, D
Pick-Sloan MBP	Anchor Reservoir	288	1,362		Bureau of Reclamation	134	C, K, I

798

Name	No.				Managing agency	Activities
Boysen Reservoir	289	15,145	19,560	497,553	WY Rec. Commission	D, E, C
Glendo Reservoir	290	9,101	12,365	571,088	WY Rec. Commission	E, C, G
Gray Reef Reservoir	291	43	182	4,317	WY Game and Fish Dept. Natrona County Pks. and Pleasure Grounds	L, H, D
Keyhole Reservoir	292	6,676	9,394	435,635	WY Rec. Commission	M, E, C
Kortes Reservoir–Miracle Mile	293	2,662	131	9,934	WY Game and Fish Dept.	K, L, D
Lake Cameahwait	294	1,057	365	19,818	Bureau of Reclamation	K, C, E
Ocean Lake	295	2,745	6,248	18,742	Bureau of Reclamation	K, C, E
Pilot Butte Reservoir	296	59	900	20,927	Bureau of Reclamation	C, E, G
Fontenelle Reservoir (Seedskadee)	297	16,452	2,312	3,750	Bureau of Reclamation	K, D, L
Buffalo Bill Reservoir (Shoshone)	298	4,889	6,720		WY Rec. Commission / Bureau of Reclamation	M, A, C
Deaver Reservoir	299	128	80	3,639	Bureau of Reclamation	K, C, D
Newton Lakes	300	554	60	8,700	WY Game and Fish Dept. / Bureau of Reclamation	K, E, C
Total: Wyoming		129,903	132,251	3,173,901		
Total: All Regions and States		4,707,340	1,707,450	56,304,780		

*A, sightseeing; B, nature study and photography; C, picnicking; D, camping; E, swimming; F, waterskiing; G, boating/motorized; H, boating/nonmotorized; I, hiking/backpacking; J, off-road-vehicle use; K, fishing; L, hunting; M, other; N, jogging; O, horseback riding; P, golf; Q, bicycling; R, special events; S, windsurfing; T, field activities; U, water sports.

[1]Includes Picacho State Recreation Area, Senator Wash Reservoir, and Squaw Lake.
[2]Included Parker Dam, Havasu State Recreation Area, Park Moabi Marina, Buckskin Unit, Needles Marina, Needles Park, La Paz County Park, and Mohave County Park.
[3]Includes Lake Mead, Lake Mohave, and Overton Wildlife Management Area.
[4]Includes Davis Camp and Sportsmen's Park.
[5]Part of Whiskeytown-Shasta-Trinty National Recreation Area.
[6]Includes Blue Mesa and Morrow Point Reservoirs.
[7]Includes Sightseeing Reported for Minidoka Powerplant.
[8]Includes Ziebach Pass and Highway No. 2 Site Recreation Areas.
[9]Includes Sanford National Recreation Area.
[10]Includes Frenchman Hills Wasteway and Winchester Extension.
[11]Coulee Dam National Recreation Area.
[12]Part of Grand Teton National Park.
Source: Bureau of Reclamation, *Summary Statistics,* 1989.

Recreation Areas by Reservoirs on TVA Land, Former TVA Land, Tributary Area Association Land, and Private Land

Kentucky
  1 national wildlife refuge
  5 state parks
 41 public-access areas
  4 county parks
  5 municipal parks
  2 state wildlife management areas
 10 group camps and clubs
 75 commercial recreation areas
  7 natural areas
 25 trails

Marion County
  2 natural areas

Pickwick
Natchez Trace Parkway
  2 state parks
  8 public-access areas
  2 county parks
  3 municipal parks
  1 tributary area association park
  4 state wildlife management areas
  1 club
 11 commercial recreation areas
  3 natural areas
  6 trails

Wilson
  3 public-access areas
  1 municipal park
  2 group camps and clubs
  8 commercial recreation areas

Wheeler
  1 national wildlife refuge
  1 state park
  9 public-access areas
  2 county parks
  4 municipal parks
  2 state wildlife management areas
  2 group camps
  9 commercial recreation areas

Guntersville
  2 state parks
 24 public-acces areas
  3 county parks
  8 municipal parks
  4 state wildlife management areas
  9 group camps and clubs
 22 commercial recreation areas
  7 natural areas
  2 trails

Nickajack
  2 county parks
  3 public-access areas
  4 commercial recreation areas
  1 natural area
  1 trail

Normandy
  6 public access areas

Chickamauga
2 state parks
72 public-access areas
1 county park
4 municipal parks
2 state wildlife management areas
9 group camps and clubs
24 commercial recreation areas

Watts Bar
60 public-access areas
2 county parks
5 municipal parks
2 state wildlife management areas
1 environmental study area
6 group camps and clubs
25 commercial recreation areas
2 natural areas
3 trails

Ft. Loudoun
32 public-access areas
6 county parks
3 municipal parks
6 group camps and clubs
10 commercial recreation areas

Apalachia
Nantahala and Cherokee National Forests
1 public access area

Bear Creek
4 public access areas

Little Bear Creek
4 public-access areas

Upper Bear Creek
3 public-access areas

Cedar Creek
4 public-access areas

Beech River Projects
1 state park
6 public-access areas

Blue Ridge
Chattahoochee National Forest
1 roadside park
3 camping areas
1 commercial recreation area
3 public-access areas

Boone
13 public-access areas
1 municipal park
1 group camp and club
8 commercial recreation areas
1 group camp

Bristol Flood Control Projects
Clear and Beaver Creeks
1 municipal park

Chatuge
Chattahoochee and Nantahala National Forests
3 public-access areas
3 county parks
1 municipal park
1 group camp
14 commercial recreation areas

Cherokee
1 state park
32 public-access areas
4 county parks
2 municipal parks
1 state wildlife management area
14 commercial recreation areas
1 trail (horse)
1 natural area

Davy Crockett (Nolichucky)
1 county-municipal park
2 trails

Douglas
11 public-access areas
1 county park
1 municipal park
2 state wildlife management areas
17 commercial recreation areas

Fontana
Great Smoky Mountain National Park
Nantahala National Forest
1 county park
2 camping areas
1 public-access area
1 municipal park
7 commercial recreation areas
1 trail shelter (Appalachian Trail)

Fort Patrick Henry
1 state park
3 public-access areas

Great Falls
1 state park

Hiwassee
Nantahala National Forest
2 camping areas
1 county-municipal park
3 commercial recreation areas
4 public-access areas

Hiwassee River
Hiwassee Recreation Riverway
1 public-access area

Melton Hill
4 county parks
2 municipal marinas
3 municipal parks
5 public-access areas
2 clubs
2 commercial recreation areas

Norris
3 state parks
59 public-access areas
4 county parks
3 municipal parks
2 state wildlife management areas
5 group camps and clubs
24 commercial recreation areas
6 natural areas
6 trails

Nottely
Chattahoochee National Forest
4 public-access areas
4 commercial recreation areas
2 group camps and clubs

Ocoee No. 2
Cherokee National Forest

Ocoee No. 3
Cherokee National Forest

Phosphate Source Land
1 municipal park

Parksville (Ocoee No. 1)
Cherokee National Forest
4 public-access areas
2 group camps
1 camping area
2 swimming areas
1 commercial recreation area
1 wildlife management area

South Holston
Cherokee and Jefferson National Forests
1 state wildlife management area
2 county parks
4 public-access areas
1 group camp
7 commercial recreation areas
1 natural area

Tellico
2 municipal park
12 public-access areas
1 state park
1 natural area

Tims Ford
1 state park
1 municipal park
7 public-access areas
1 group camp and club
3 commercial recreation areas

Watauga
Cherokee National Forest
9 public-access areas
6 commercial recreation areas

Wilbur
Cherokee National Forest

Source: TVA, *The TVA Handbook*, Knoxville, Tenn: TVA 1988.

Federal Indian Reservations

(Numbers Keyed to Figure 13.15)

Alabama
 1 Poarch Creek Indian Reservation

Alaska
 2 Annette Island Indian Reservation

Arizona
 3 Camp Verde Indian Reservation
 4 Cocopah Indian Reservation
 5 Colorado River Indian Reservation
 6 Fort Apache Indian Reservation
 7 Fort McDowell Indian Reservation
 8 Fort Mohave Indian Reservation
 9 Gila Bend Indian Reservation
 10 Gila River Indian Reservation
 11 Havasupai Indian Reservation
 12 Hopi Indian Reservation
 13 Hualapai Indian Reservation
 14 Kaibab Indian Reservation
 15 Maricopa Indian Reservation
 16 Navajo Indian Reservation (also in NM, UT)
 17 Papago Indian Reservation
 18 Pascua Yaqui Indian Reservation
 19 Payson Community Indian Reservation
 20 Salt River Indian Reservation
 21 San Carlos Indian Reservation

 22 San Xavier Indian Reservation
 23 Yavapai Indian Reservation

California
 24 Agua Caliente Indian Reservation
 25 Alturus Rancheria
 26 Augustine Rancheria
 27 Barona Rancheria
 28 Benton Paiute Indian Reservation
 29 Berry Creek Rancheria
 30 Big Bend Rancheria
 31 Big Lagoon Rancheria
 32 Big Pine Rancheria
 33 Big Sandy Rancheria
 34 Big Valley Rancheria
 35 Bishop Rancheria
 36 Blue Lake Rancheria
 37 Bridgeport Rancheria
 38 Cabazon Indian Reservation
 39 Cahuilla Indian Reservation
 40 Campo Indian Reservation
 41 Capitan Grande Indian Reservation
 42 Cedarville Rancheria
 43 Chemehuevi Indian Reservation
 44 Chicken Ranch Rancheria
 45 Cold Springs Rancheria
 46 Colusa Rancheria
 47 Cortina Rancheria

48 Coyote Valley Rancheria
49 Cuyapaipe Indian Reservation
50 Dry Creek Rancheria
51 Enterprise Rancheria
52 Fort Bidwell Indian Reservation
53 Fort Independence Indian
    Reservation
54 Fort Yuma Indian Reservation
55 Greenville Rancheria
56 Grindstone Creek Rancheria
57 Hoopa Valley Indian Reservation
58 Hopland Rancheria
59 Inaja-Cosmit Indian Reservation
60 Jackson Rancheria
61 Jamul Indian Village
62 Karok Indian Reservation
63 La Jolla Indian Reservation
64 La Posta Indian Reservation
65 Laytonville Rancheria
66 Likely Rancheria
67 Lone Pine Rancheria
68 Lookout Rancheria
69 Los Coyotes Indian Reservation
70 Manchester Rancheria
71 Manzanita Indian Reservation
72 Mesa Grande Indian Reservation
73 Middletown Rancheria
74 Montgomery Creek Rancheria
75 Morongo Indian Reservation
76 Northfork Rancheria
77 Pala Indian Reservation
78 Pauma Indian Reservation
79 Pechanga Indian Reservation
80 Pinoleville Rancheria
81 Ramona Indian Reservation
82 Redwood Valley Rancheria
83 Resighini Rancheria
84 Rincon Indian Reservation
85 Roaring Creek Rancheria
86 Robinson Rancheria
87 Rohnerville Rancheria
88 Round Valley Indian Reservation
89 Rumsey Rancheria
90 San Manuel Indian Reservation
91 San Pasqual Indian Reservation
92 Santa Isabel Indian Reservation
93 Santa Rosa Indian Reservation

94 Santa Rosa Rancheria
95 Santa Ynez Indian Reservation
96 Sheep Ranch Rancheria
97 Sherwood Valley Rancheria
98 Shingle Springs Rancheria
99 Smith River Rancheria
100 Soboba Indian Reservation
101 Stewarts Point Rancheria
102 Sulphur Bank Rancheria
103 Susanville Rancheria
104 Sycuan Indian Reservation
105 Table Bluff Rancheria
106 Table Mountain Rancheria
107 Torres-Martinez Indian
    Reservation
108 Trinidad Rancheria
109 Tule River Indian Reservation
110 Tuolumne Rancheria
111 Twentynine Palms Indian
    Reservation
112 Upper Lake Rancheria
113 Viejas Indian Reservation
114 Woodfords Indian Community
115 XL Rancheria
116 Yurok Indian Reservation

Colorado
117 Southern Ute Indian Reservation
118 Ute Mountain Indian Reservation
    (NM)

Connecticut
119 Mashantucket Pequot Indian
    Reservation

Florida
120 Big Cypress Indian Reservation
121 Brighton Indian Reservation
122 Hollywood Indian Reservation
123 Miccosukee Indian Reservation

Idaho
124 Coeur d'Alene Indian Reservation
125 Duck Valley Indian Reservation
    (also in NV)
126 Fort Hall Indian Reservation
127 Kootenai Indian Reservation
128 Nez Perce Indian Reservation

Iowa
129   Sac and Fox Indian Reservation
      (also in KS, NE)

Kansas
130   Kickapoo Indian Reservation
131   Potawatomi Indian Reservation
129   Sac and Fox Indian Reservation
      (also in IA, NE)

Louisiana
132   Chitimacha Indian Reservation
133   Coushatta Indian Reservation
134   Tunica-Biloxi Indian Reservation

Maine
135   Passamaquoddy Indian
      Reservation
136   Penobscot Indian Reservation

Massachusetts
137   Wampanoag Indian Reservation

Michigan
138   Bay Mills Indian Reservation
139   Grand Traverse Indian
      Reservation
140   Hannahville Indian Reservation
141   Isabella Indian Reservation
142   Lac Vieux Desert Indian
      Reservation
143   L'Anse Indian Reservation
144   Ontonagon Indian Reservation
145   Sault Ste. Marie Indian
      Reservation

Minnesota
146   Bois Forte Indian Reservation
147   Deer Creek Indian Reservation
148   Fond du Lac Indian Reservation
149   Grand Portage Indian Reservation
150   Leech Lake Indian Reservation
151   Lower Sioux Indian Reservation
152   Mille Lacs Indian Reservation
153   Prairie Island Indian Reservation
154   Red Lake Indian Reservation
155   Sandy Lake Indian Reservation
156   Shakopee Indian Reservation
157   Upper Sioux Indian Reservation
158   Vermillion Lake Indian
      Reservation
159   White Earth Indian Reservation

Mississippi
160   Mississippi Choctaw Indian
      Reservation

Montana
161   Blackfeet Indian Reservation
162   Crow Indian Reservation
163   Flathead Indian Reservation
164   Fort Belknap Indian Reservation
165   Fort Peck Indian Reservation
166   Northern Cheyenne Indian
      Reservation
167   Rocky Boys Indian Reservation

Nebraska
168   Omaha Indian Reservation
129   Sac and Fox Indian Reservation
      (also in KS, IA)
169   Santee Sioux Indian Reservation
170   Winnebago Indian Reservation

Nevada
171   Dresslerville Colony Indian
      Reservation
125   Duck Valley Indian Reservation
      (also in ID)
172   Duckwater Indian Reservation
173   Ely Colony Indian Reservation
174   Fallon Colony Indian Reservation
175   Fort McDermitt Indian
      Reservation (also in OR)
176   Goshute Indian Reservation (also
      in UT)
177   Las Vegas Colony Indian
      Reservation
178   Lovelock Colony Indian
      Reservation
179   Moapa River Indian Reservation
180   Pyramid Lake Indian Reservation
181   Reno Sparks Indian Reservation
182   Summit Lake Indian Reservation
183   Te-Moak Indian Reservation
184   Walker River Indian Reservation
185   Washoe Indian Reservation
186   Winnemucca Colony Indian
      Reservation
187   Yerington Indian Reservation
188   Yomba Indian Reservation

New Mexico
189 Acoma Indian Reservation
190 Alamo Navajo Indian Reservation
191 Canoncito Indian Reservation
192 Cochiti Indian Reservation
193 Isleta Indian Reservation
194 Jemez Indian Reservation
195 Jicarilla Apache Indian
     Reservation
196 Laguna Indian Reservation
197 Mescalero Indian Reservation
198 Nambe Indian Reservation
 16 Navajo Indian Reservation (also
     in AZ, UT)
199 Picuris Indian Reservation
200 Pojoaque Indian Reservation
201 Ramah Navajo Indian Reservation
202 San Felipe Indian Reservation
203 San Ildefonso Indian Reservation
204 San Juan Indian Reservation
205 Sandia Indian Reservation
206 Santa Ana Indian Reservation
207 Santa Clara Indian Reservation
208 Santo Domingo Indian
     Reservation
209 Taos Indian Reservation
210 Tesuque Indian Reservation
118 Ute Mountain Indian Reservation
     (CO)
211 Zia Indian Reservation
212 Zuni Indian Reservation

New York
213 Allegany Indian Reservation
214 Cattaraugus Indian Reservation
215 Oil Springs Indian Reservation
216 Oneida Indian Reservation
217 Onondaga Indian Reservation
218 St. Regis Indian Reservation
219 Tonawanda Indian Reservation
220 Tuscarora Indian Reservation

North Carolina
221 Cherokee Indian Reservation

North Dakota
222 Devis Lake Indian Reservation
223 Fort Berthold Indian Reservation
224 Lake Traverse Indian Reservation
     (also in SD)

225 Standing Rock Indian Reservation
     (also in SD)
226 Turtle Mountain Indian
     Reservation

Oklahoma
227 Osage Indian Reservation

Oregon
228 Burns Paiute Colony Indian
     Reservation
229 Coos, Lower Umpqua, and
     Siuslaw Indian Reservation
230 Cow Creek of Umpqua Indian
     Reservation
175 Fort McDermitt Indian
     Reservation (also in NV)
231 Grand Ronde Indian Reservation
232 Siletz Indian Reservation
233 Umatilla Indian Reservation
234 Warm Springs Indian Reservation

Rhode Island
235 Narragansett Indian Reservation

South Dakota
236 Cheyenne River Indian
     Reservation
237 Crow Creek Indian Reservation
238 Flandreau Indian Reservation
224 Lake Traverse Indian Reservation
     (also in ND)
239 Lower Brule Indian Reservation
240 Pine Ridge Indian Reservation
241 Rosebud Indian Reservation
225 Standing Rock Indian Reservation
     (also in ND)
242 Yankton Indian Reservation

Texas
243 Alabama-Coushatta Indian
     Reservation
244 Ysleta Del Sur Indian Reservation

Utah
173 Goshute Indian Reservation (NV)
 16 Navajo Indian Reservation (AZ,
     NM)
245 Paiute Indian Reservation
246 Skull Valley Indian Reservation
247 Uintah and Ouray Indian
     Reservation

Washington
248 Chehalis Indian Reservation
249 Colville Indian Reservation
250 Hoh Indian Reservation
251 Jamestown Klallam Indian
    Reservation
252 Kalispel Indian Reservation
253 Lower Elwha Indian Reservation
254 Lummi Indian Reservation
255 Makah Indian Reservation
256 Muckleshoot Indian Reservation
257 Nisqually Indian Reservation
258 Nooksack Indian Reservation
259 Ozette Indian Reservation
260 Port Gamble Indian Reservation
261 Port Madison Indian Reservation
262 Puyallup Indian Reservation
263 Quileute Indian Reservation
264 Quinault Indian Reservation
265 Sauk Suiattle Indian Reservation
266 Shoalwater Bay Indian
    Reservation
267 Skokomish Indian Reservation
268 Spokane Indian Reservation
269 Squaxin Island Indian Reservation

270 Stillaguamish Indian Reservation
271 Swinomish Indian Reservation
272 Tulalip Indian Reservation
273 Upper Skagit Indian Reservation
274 Yakima Indian Reservation

Wisconsin
275 Bad River Indian Reservation
276 Lac Courte Oreilles Indian
    Reservation
277 Lac Du Flambeau Indian
    Reservation
278 Menominee Indian Reservation
279 Oneida Indian Reservation
280 Potawatomi Indian Reservation
281 Red Cliff Indian Reservation
282 Sokaogon Chippewa Indian
    Reservation
283 St. Croix Indian Reservation
284 Stockbridge Indian Reservation
285 Winnebago Indian Reservation

Wyoming
286 Wind River Indian Reservation

NOTE: Numbers refer to location on Figure 13.15.
Source: Bureau of Indian Affairs, *Indian Land Areas (Map)*, Washington, D.C. 1989.

National Wilderness Preservation System— 1994

Map No. (Figs. 14.1, 14.6)	Wilderness Area	Agency*	Administrative Unit**	State	Public Law	Date	Acreage
	Alaska						
1	Aleutian Islands	FWS	Alaska Maritime NWR	AK	96-487	12/20/80	1,300,000
2	Andreafsky	FWS	Yukon Delta NWR	AK	96-487	12/20/80	1,300,000
3	Arctic	FWS	Arctic NWR	AK	96-487	12/20/80	8,000,000
4	Becharof	FWS	Becharof NWR	AK	96-487	12/20/80	400,000
5	Bering Sea	FWS	Alaska Maritime NWR	AK	91-504	10/23/70	81,340
6	Bogoslof	FWS	Alaska Maritime NWR	AK	91-504	10/23/70	175
7	Chamisso	FWS	Alaska Maritime NWR	AK	93-632	1/3/75	455
8	Chuck River	FS	Tongass NF	AK	101-626	11/28/90	74,278
9	Coronation Island	FS	Tongass NF	AK	96-487	12/20/80	19,232
10	Denali	NPS	Denali NP	AK	96-487	12/20/80	2,124,783
11	Endicott River	FS	Tongass NF	AK	96-487	12/20/80	98,729
12	Forrester Island	FWS	Alaska Maritime NWR	AK	91-504	10/23/70	2,832
13	Gates of the Arctic	NPS	Gates of the Arctic NP	AK	96-487	12/20/80	7,167,192
14	Glacier Bay	NPS	Glacier Bay NPPres	AK	96-487	12/20/80	2,664,840
15	Hazy Island	FWS	Alaska Maritime NWR	AK	91-504	10/23/70	32
16	Innoko	FWS	Innoko NWR	AK	96-487	12/20/80	1,240,000
17	Izembek	FWS	Izembek NWR	AK	96-487	12/20/80	300,000
18	Karta River	FS	Tongass NF	AK	101-626	11/28/90	39,889
19	Katmai	NPS	Katmai NPPres	AK	96-487	12/20/80	3,384,358
20	Kenai	FWS	Kenai NWR	AK	96-487	12/20/80	1,350,000
21	Kobuk Valley	NPS	Kobuk Valley NP	AK	96-487	12/20/80	174,545
22	Kootznoowoo	FS	Tongass NF	AK	96-487	12/20/80	955,921
22	Kootznoowoo	FS	Tongass NF	AK	101-626	11/28/90	0
23	Koyukuk	FWS	Koyukuk NWR	AK	96-487	12/20/80	400,000
24	Kuiu	FS	Tongass NF	AK	101-626	11/28/90	60,581
25	Lake Clark	NPS	Lake Clark NP	AK	96-487	12/20/80	2,619,550
26	Maurelle Islands	FS	Tongass NF	AK	96-487	12/20/80	4,937
27	Misty Fjords	FS	Tongass NF	AK	96-487	12/20/80	2,142,243
28	Noatak	NPS	Noatak NPres	AK	96-487	12/20/80	5,765,427
29	Nunivak	FWS	Yukon Delta NWR	AK	96-487	12/20/80	600,000
30	Petersburg Creek–Duncan Salt Chuck	FS	Tongass NF	AK	96-487	12/20/80	46,777
31	Pleasant, Lemusurier, Inian Islands	FS	Tongass NF	AK	101-626	11/28/90	23,096
32	Russell Fjord	FS	Tongass NF	AK	96-487	12/20/80	348,701
33	Saint Lazaria	FWS	Alaska Maritime NWR	AK	91-504	10/23/70	65
34	Selawik	FWS	Selawik NWR	AK	96-487	12/20/80	240,000
35	Semidi	FWS	Alaska Maritime NWR	AK	96-487	12/20/80	250,000

Map No. (Figs. 14.1, 14.6)	Wilderness Area	Agency*	Administrative Unit**	State	Public Law	Date	Acreage
36	Simeonof	FWS	Alaska Maritime NWR	AK	94-557	10/19/76	25,855
37	South Baranof	FS	Tongass NF	AK	96-487	12/20/80	319,568
38	South Etolin	FS	Tongass NF	AK	101-626	11/28/90	83,371
39	South Prince of Wales	FS	Tongass NF	AK	96-487	12/20/80	90,996
40	Stikine-LeConte	FS	Tongass NF	AK	96-487	12/20/80	448,841
41	Tebenkof Bay	FS	Tongass NF	AK	96-487	12/20/80	66,839
42	Togiak	FWS	Togiak NWR	AK	96-487	12/20/80	2,270,000
43	Tracy Arm-Fords Terror	FS	Tongass NF	AK	96-487	12/20/80	653,179
44	Tuxedni	FWS	Alaska Maritime NWR	AK	91-504	10/23/70	5,566
45	Unimak	FWS	Alaska Maritime NWR	AK	96-487	12/20/80	910,000
46	Warren Island	FS	Tongass NF	AK	96-487	12/20/80	11,181
47	West Chichagof-Yakobi	FS	Tongass NF	AK	96-487	12/20/80	264,747
48	Wrangell-St. Elias	NPS	Wrangell-St. Elias NPPres	AK	96-487	12/20/80	9,078,675
Total							57,408,796
	Alabama						
49	Cheaha	FS	Talladega NF	AL	97-411	1/3/83	7,245
	Cheaha	FS	Talladega NF	AL	100-547	10/28/88	0
50	Sipsey	FS	William B. Bankhead NF	AL	93-622	1/3/75	25,906
	Sipsey	FS	William B. Bankhead NF	AL	100-547	10/28/88	0
Total							33,151
	Arkansas						
51	Big Lake	FWS	Big Lake NWR	AR	94-557	10/19/76	2,144
52	Black Fork Mountain	FS	Ouachita NF	AR	98-508	10/19/84	8,350
53	Buffalo National River	NPS	Buffalo National River	AR	95-625	11/10/78	10,529
54	Caney Creek	FS	Ouachita NF	AR	93-622	1/3/75	14,460
55	Dry Creek	FS	Ouachita NF	AR	98-508	10/19/84	6,310
56	East Fork	FS	Ozark NF	AR	98-508	10/19/84	10,688
57	Flatside	FS	Ouachita NF	AR	98-508	10/19/84	9,507
58	Hurricane Creek	FS	Ozark NF	AR	98-508	10/19/84	15,307
59	Leatherwood	FS	Ozark NF	AR	98-508	10/19/84	16,838
60	Poteau Mountain	FS	Ouachita NF	AR	98-508	10/19/84	11,299
61	Richland Creek	FS	Ozark NF	AR	98-508	10/19/84	11,801
62	Upper Buffalo	FS	Ozark NF	AR	93-622	1/3/75	12,000
Total							129,233
	Arizona						
63	Apache Creek	FS	Prescott NF	AZ	98-406	8/28/84	5,666
64	Aravaipa Canyon	BLM	Safford District	AZ	98-406	8/28/84	19,700
	Aravaipa Canyon	BLM	Safford District	AZ	101-628	11/28/90	0

No.	Name	Agency	District	State	Code	Date	Acreage
65	Arrastra Mountain	BLM	Phoenix District	AZ	101-628	11/28/90	129,800
66	Aubrey Peak	BLM	Phoenix District	AZ	101-628	11/28/90	15,400
67	Baboquivari Peak	BLM	Safford District	AZ	101-628	11/28/90	2,040
68	Bear Wallow	FS	Apache NF	AZ	98-406	8/28/84	11,080
69	Beaver Dam Mountains	BLM	Arizona Strip District	AZ	98-406	8/28/84	15,000
70	Big Horn Mountains	BLM	Phoenix District	AZ	101-628	11/28/90	21,000
71	Cabeza Prieta	FWS	Cabeza Prieta NWR	AZ	101-628	11/28/90	803,418
72	Castle Creek	FS	Prescott NF	AZ	98-406	8/28/84	25,215
73	Cedar Bench	FS	Prescott NF	AZ	98-406	8/28/84	14,950
74	Chiricahua	FS	Coronado NF	AZ	88-577	9/3/64	87,700
	Chiricahua	FS	Coronado NF	AZ	98-406	8/28/84	0
	Chiricahua NM	NPS	Chiricahua NM	AZ	94-567	10/20/76	9,440
75	Cottonwood Point	BLM	Arizona Strip District	AZ	98-406	8/28/84	6,860
76	Coyote Mountains	BLM	Safford District	AZ	101-628	11/28/90	5,100
77	Dos Cabezas Mountains	BLM	Safford District	AZ	101-628	11/28/90	11,700
78	Eagletail Mountains	BLM	Yuma District	AZ	101-628	11/28/90	100,600
79	East Cactus Plain	BLM	Yuma District	AZ	101-628	11/28/90	14,630
80	Escudilla	FS	Apache NF	AZ	98-406	8/28/84	5,200
81	Fishhooks	BLM	Safford District	AZ	101-628	11/28/90	10,500
82	Fossil Springs	FS	Coconino NF	AZ	98-406	8/28/84	22,149
83	Four Peaks	FS	Tonto NF	AZ	98-406	8/28/84	61,074
84	Galiuro	FS	Coronado NF	AZ	88-577	9/3/64	76,317
	Galiuro	FS	Coronado NF	AZ	98-406	8/28/84	0
85	Gibraltar Mountain	BLM	Yuma District	AZ	101-628	11/28/90	18,790
86	Grand Wash Cliffs	BLM	Arizona Strip District	AZ	98-406	8/28/84	37,030
87	Granite Mountain	FS	Prescott NF	AZ	98-406	8/28/84	9,762
88	Harcuvar Mountains	BLM	Yuma District	AZ	101-628	11/28/90	25,050
89	Harquahala Mountains	BLM	Phoenix District	AZ	101-628	11/28/90	22,880
90	Hassayampa River Canyon	BLM	Phoenix District	AZ	101-628	11/28/90	12,300
91	Havasu	FWS	Havasu NWR	AZ	101-628	11/28/90	14,606
92	Hells Canyon	BLM	Phoenix District	AZ	101-628	11/28/90	10,600
93	Hellsgate	FS	Tonto NF	AZ	98-406	8/28/84	37,440
94	Hummingbird Springs	BLM	Phoenix District	AZ	101-628	11/28/90	31,200
95	Imperial	FWS	Imperial NWR	AZ	101-628	11/28/90	9,220
96	Juniper Mesa	FS	Prescott NF	AZ	98-406	8/28/84	7,406
97	Kachina Peaks	FS	Coconino NF	AZ	98-406	8/28/84	18,616
98	Kanab Creek	BLM	Arizona Strip District	AZ	98-406	8/28/84	6,700
	Kanab Creek	FS	Kaibab NF	AZ	98-406	8/28/84	63,760
99	Kendrick Mountain	FS	Coconino NF	AZ	98-406	8/28/84	1,510
	Kendrick Mountain	FS	Kaibab NF	AZ	98-406	8/28/84	5,000
100	Kofa	FWS	Kofa NWR	AZ	101-628	11/28/90	516,200

Map No. (Figs. 14.1, 14.6)	Wilderness Area	Agency*	Administrative Unit**	State	Public Law	Date	Acreage
101	Mazatzal	FS	Coconino NF	AZ	98-406	8/28/84	4,275
	Mazatzal	FS	Tonto NF	AZ	88-577	9/3/64	248,115
	Mazatzal	FS	Tonto NF	AZ	98-406	8/28/84	0
102	Miller Peak	FS	Coronado NF	AZ	98-406	8/28/84	20,190
103	Mount Baldy	FS	Apache NF	AZ	91-504	10/23/70	7,079
104	Mount Logan	BLM	Arizona Strip District	AZ	98-406	8/28/84	14,650
105	Mount Nutt	BLM	Phoenix District	AZ	101-628	11/28/90	27,660
106	Mount Tipton	BLM	Phoenix District	AZ	101-628	11/28/90	32,760
107	Mount Trumbull	BLM	Arizona Strip District	AZ	98-406	8/28/84	7,880
108	Mount Wilson	BLM	Phoenix District	AZ	101-628	11/28/90	23,900
109	Mount Wrightson	FS	Coronado NF	AZ	98-406	8/28/84	25,260
110	Muggins Mountains	BLM	Yuma District	AZ	101-628	11/28/90	7,640
111	Munds Mountain	FS	Coconino NF	AZ	98-406	8/28/84	24,411
112	Needle's Eye	BLM	Phoenix District	AZ	101-628	11/28/90	8,760
113	New Water Mountains	BLM	Yuma District	AZ	101-628	11/28/90	24,600
114	North Maricopa Mountains	BLM	Phoenix District	AZ	101-628	11/28/90	63,200
115	North Santa Teresa	BLM	Safford District	AZ	101-628	11/28/90	5,800
116	Organ Pipe Cactus	NPS	Organ Pipe Cactus NM	AZ	95-625	11/10/78	312,600
117	Paiute	BLM	Arizona Strip District	AZ	98-406	8/28/84	87,900
118	Pajarita	FS	Coronado NF	AZ	98-406	8/28/84	7,553
119	Paria Canyon–Vermillion Cliffs	BLM	Arizona Strip District	AZ	98-406	8/28/84	89,400
120	Peloncillo Mountains	BLM	Safford District	AZ	101-628	11/28/90	19,440
121	Petrified Forest	NPS	Petrified Forest NP	AZ	91-504	10/23/70	50,260
122	Pine Mountain	FS	Prescott NF	AZ	92-230	2/15/72	8,609
	Pine Mountain	FS	Tonto NF	AZ	92-230	2/15/72	11,452
123	Pusch Ridge	FS	Coronado NF	AZ	95-237	2/24/78	56,933
124	Rawhide Mountains	BLM	Yuma District	AZ	101-628	11/28/90	38,470
125	Red Rock–Secret Mountain	FS	Coconino NF	AZ	98-406	8/28/84	47,194
126	Redfield Canyon	BLM	Safford District	AZ	101-628	11/28/90	9,930
127	Rincon Mountain	FS	Coronado NF	AZ	98-406	8/28/84	38,590
128	Saddle Mountain	FS	Kaibab NF	AZ	98-406	8/28/84	40,539
129	Saguaro	NPS	Saguaro NM	AZ	94-567	10/20/76	71,400
130	Salome	FS	Tonto NF	AZ	98-406	8/28/84	18,531
131	Salt River Canyon	FS	Tonto NF	AZ	98-406	8/28/84	32,101
132	Santa Teresa	FS	Coronado NF	AZ	98-406	8/28/84	26,780
133	Sierra Ancha	FS	Tonto NF	AZ	88-577	9/3/64	20,850
134	Sierra Estrella	BLM	Phoenix District	AZ	101-628	11/28/90	14,400
135	Signal Mountain	BLM	Phoenix District	AZ	101-628	11/28/90	13,350

#	Name	Agency	Unit	State	Public Law	Date	Acres
136	South Maricopa Mountains	BLM	Phoenix District	AZ	101-628	11/28/90	60,100
137	Strawberry Crater	FS	Coconino NF	AZ	98-406	8/28/84	10,743
138	Superstition	FS	Tonto NF	AZ	88-577	9/3/64	159,757
	Superstition	FS	Tonto NF	AZ	98-406	8/28/84	0
139	Swansea	BLM	Yuma District	AZ	101-628	11/28/90	16,400
140	Sycamore Canyon	FS	Coconino NF	AZ	92-241	3/6/72	23,325
	Sycamore Canyon	FS	Coconino NF	AZ	98-406	8/28/84	0
	Sycamore Canyon	FS	Kaibab NF	AZ	92-241	3/6/72	7,125
	Sycamore Canyon	FS	Prescott NF	AZ	92-241	3/6/72	25,487
	Sycamore Canyon	FS	Prescott NF	AZ	98-406	8/28/84	0
141	Table Top	BLM	Phoenix District	AZ	101-628	11/28/90	34,400
142	Tres Alamos	BLM	Phoenix District	AZ	101-628	11/28/90	8,300
143	Trigo Mountains	BLM	Yuma District	AZ	101-628	11/28/90	30,300
144	Upper Burro Creek	BLM	Phoenix District	AZ	101-628	11/28/90	27,440
145	Wabayuma Peak	BLM	Phoenix District	AZ	101-628	11/28/90	40,000
146	Warm Springs	BLM	Phoenix District	AZ	101-628	11/28/90	112,400
147	West Clear Creek	FS	Coconino NF	AZ	98-406	8/28/84	15,238
148	Wet Beaver	FS	Coconino NF	AZ	98-406	8/28/84	6,155
149	White Canyon	BLM	Phoenix District	AZ	101-628	11/28/90	5,790
150	Woodchute	FS	Prescott NF	AZ	98-406	8/28/84	5,833
151	Woolsey Peak	BLM	Phoenix District	AZ	101-628	11/28/90	64,000
Total							4,537,864
	California						
152	Agua Tibia	FS	Cleveland NF	CA	93-632	1/3/75	15,933
153	Ansel Adams	FS	Inyo NF	CA	88-577	9/3/64	78,775
	Ansel Adams	FS	Sierra NF	CA	88-577	9/3/64	151,483
	Ansel Adams	FS	Sierra NF	CA	98-425	9/28/84	0
154	Bucks Lake	FS	Plumas NF	CA	98-425	9/28/84	21,000
155	Caribou	FS	Lassen NF	CA	88-577	9/3/64	20,546
	Caribou	FS	Lassen NF	CA	98-425	9/28/84	0
156	Carson-Iceberg	FS	Stanislaus NF	CA	98-425	9/28/84	77,993
	Carson-Iceberg	FS	Toiyabe NF	CA	98-425	9/28/84	83,188
157	Castle Crags	FS	Shasta NF	CA	98-425	9/28/84	8,627
158	Chanchelulla	FS	Trinity NF	CA	98-425	9/28/84	8,200
159	Chumash	FS	Los Padres NF	CA	102-301	6/19/92	38,150
160	Cucamonga	FS	Angeles NF	CA	98-425	9/28/84	4,200
	Cucamonga	FS	San Bernardino NF	CA	88-577	9/3/64	8,581
161	Desolation	FS	Eldorado NF	CA	91-82	10/10/69	63,475
162	Dick Smith	FS	Los Padres NF	CA	98-425	9/28/84	67,800
163	Dinkey Lakes	FS	Sierra NF	CA	98-425	9/28/84	30,000
164	Dome Land	FS	Sequoia NF	CA	88-577	9/3/64	93,781
	Dome Land	FS	Sequoia NF	CA	98-425	9/28/84	0

**Map No.
(Figs. 14.1,
14.6)**

Map No. (Figs. 14.1, 14.6)	Wilderness Area	Agency*	Administrative Unit**	State	Public Law	Date	Acreage
165	Emigrant	FS	Stanislaus NF	CA	93-632	1/3/75	112,277
	Emigrant	FS	Stanislaus NF	CA	98-425	9/28/84	0
166	Farallon	FWS	Farallon NWR	CA	93-550	12/26/74	141
167	Garcia	FS	Los Padres NF	CA	102-301	6/19/92	14,100
168	Golden Trout	FS	Inyo NF	CA	95-237	2/24/78	192,765
	Golden Trout	FS	Sequoia NF	CA	95-237	2/24/78	110,746
169	Granite Chief	FS	Tahoe NF	CA	98-425	9/28/84	19,048
170	Hauser	FS	Cleveland NF	CA	98-425	9/28/84	7,547
171	Hoover	FS	Inyo NF	CA	88-577	9/3/64	9,507
	Hoover	FS	Toiyabe NF	CA	88-577	9/3/64	39,094
172	Ishi	BLM	Ukiah District	CA	98-425	9/28/84	240
	Ishi	FS	Lassen NF	CA	98-425	9/28/84	41,099
173	Jennie Lakes	FS	Sequoia NF	CA	98-425	9/28/84	10,289
174	John Muir	FS	Inyo NF	CA	88-577	9/3/64	228,366
	John Muir	FS	Sierra NF	CA	88-577	9/3/64	351,957
	John Muir	FS	Sierra NF	CA	98-425	9/28/84	0
175	Joshua Tree	NPS	Joshua Tree NM	CA	94-567	10/20/76	429,690
176	Kaiser	FS	Sierra NF	CA	94-557	10/19/76	22,700
177	Lassen Volcanic	NPS	Lassen Volcanic NP	CA	92-510	10/19/72	78,982
178	Lava Beds	NPS	Lava Beds NM	CA	92-493	10/13/72	28,460
179	Machesna Mountain	BLM	Bakersfield District	CA	98-425	9/28/84	120
	Machesna Mountain	FS	Los Padres NF	CA	98-425	9/28/84	19,760
180	Marble Mountain	FS	Klamath NF	CA	88-577	9/3/64	241,744
	Marble Mountain	FS	Klamath NF	CA	98-425	9/28/84	0
181	Matilija	FS	Los Padres NF	CA	102-301	6/19/92	29,600
182	Mokelumne	FS	Eldorado NF	CA	88-577	9/3/64	60,154
	Mokelumne	FS	Eldorado NF	CA	98-425	9/28/84	0
	Mokelumne	FS	Stanislaus NF	CA	88-577	9/3/64	22,267
	Mokelumne	FS	Stanislaus NF	CA	98-425	9/28/84	0
	Mokelumne	FS	Toiyabe NF	CA	98-425	9/28/84	16,740
183	Monarch	FS	Sequoia NF	CA	98-425	9/28/84	24,152
	Monarch	FS	Sierra NF	CA	98-425	9/28/84	20,744
184	Mount Shasta	FS	Shasta NF	CA	98-425	9/28/84	33,845
185	North Fork	FS	Six Rivers NF	CA	98-425	9/28/84	7,999
186	Philip Burton	NPS	Point Reyes NS	CA	94-544	10/18/76	16,740
	Philip Burton	NPS	Point Reyes NS	CA	94-567	10/20/76	25,370
	Philip Burton	NPS	Point Reyes NS	CA	99-68	7/19/85	0
187	Pine Creek	FS	Cleveland NF	CA	98-425	9/28/84	13,480

No.	Name	Unit	Agency	Code	State	Date	Acres
188	Pinnacles	Pinnacles NM	NPS	94-567	CA	10/20/76	12,952
189	Red Buttes	Rogue River NF	FS	98-425	CA	9/28/84	16,150
190	Russian	Klamath NF	FS	98-425	CA	9/28/84	12,000
191	San Gabriel	Angeles NF	FS	90-318	CA	5/24/68	36,118
192	San Gorgonio	San Bernardino NF	FS	88-577	CA	9/3/64	56,722
	San Gorgonio	San Bernardino NF	FS	98-425	CA	9/28/84	0
193	San Jacinto	San Bernardino NF	FS	88-577	CA	9/3/64	32,248
	San Jacinto	San Bernardino NF	FS	98-425	CA	9/28/84	0
194	San Mateo Canyon	Cleveland NF	FS	98-425	CA	9/28/84	38,484
195	San Rafael	Los Padres NF	FS	90-271	CA	3/21/68	150,980
	San Rafael	Los Padres NF	FS	98-425	CA	9/28/84	0
	San Rafael	Los Padres NF	FS	102-301	CA	6/19/92	46,400
196	Santa Lucia	Bakersfield District	BLM	95-237	CA	2/24/78	1,733
	Santa Lucia	Los Padres NF	FS	95-237	CA	2/24/78	18,679
197	Santa Rosa	San Bernardino NF	FS	98-425	CA	9/28/84	13,787
198	Sequoia-Kings Canyon	Sequoia-Kings Canyon NP	NPS	98-425	CA	9/28/84	736,980
199	Sespe	Angeles NF	FS	102-301	CA	6/19/92	0
	Sespe	Los Padres NF	FS	102-301	CA	6/19/92	219,700
200	Sheep Mountain	Angeles NF	FS	98-425	CA	9/28/84	39,482
	Sheep Mountain	San Bernardino NF	FS	98-425	CA	9/28/84	2,401
201	Silver Peak	Los Padres NF	FS	102-301	CA	6/19/92	14,500
202	Siskiyou	Klamath NF	FS	98-425	CA	9/28/84	75,680
	Siskiyou	Siskiyou NF	FS	98-425	CA	9/28/84	5,300
	Siskiyou	Six Rivers NF	FS	98-425	CA	9/28/84	71,700
203	Snow Mountain	Mendocino NF	FS	98-425	CA	9/28/84	36,370
204	South Sierra	Inyo NF	FS	98-425	CA	9/28/84	31,865
	South Sierra	Sequoia NF	FS	98-425	CA	9/28/84	28,219
205	South Warner	Modoc NF	FS	88-577	CA	9/3/64	70,614
	South Warner	Modoc NF	FS	98-425	CA	9/28/84	0
206	Thousand Lakes	Lassen NF	FS	88-577	CA	9/3/64	16,335
207	Trinity Alps	Ukiah District	BLM	98-425	CA	9/28/84	4,623
	Trinity Alps	Klamath NF	FS	98-425	CA	9/28/84	77,860
	Trinity Alps	Shasta NF	FS	98-425	CA	9/28/84	102,821
	Trinity Alps	Six Rivers NF	FS	98-425	CA	9/28/84	25,400
	Trinity Alps	Trinity NF	FS	98-425	CA	9/28/84	292,060
208	Ventana	Los Padres NF	FS	91-58	CA	8/16/69	164,178
	Ventana	Los Padres NF	FS	95-237	CA	2/24/78	0
	Ventana	Los Padres NF	FS	98-425	CA	9/28/84	0
	Ventana	Los Padres NF	FS	102-301	CA	6/19/92	38,000

Map No. (Figs. 14.1, 14.6)	Wilderness Area	Agency*	Administrative Unit**	State	Public Law	Date	Acreage
209	Yolla Bolly–Middle Eel	BLM	Ukiah District	CA	98-425	9/28/84	7,145
	Yolla Bolly–Middle Eel	FS	Mendocino NF	CA	88-577	9/3/64	98,323
	Yolla Bolly–Middle Eel	FS	Mendocino NF	CA	98-425	9/28/84	0
	Yolla Bolly–Middle Eel	FS	Six Rivers NF	CA	98-425	9/28/84	10,813
	Yolla Bolly–Middle Eel	FS	Trinity NF	CA	88-577	9/3/64	37,560
210	Yosemite	NPS	Yosemite NP	CA	98-425	9/28/84	677,600
Total							6,306,497
			Colorado				
212	Black Canyon of the Gunnison	NPS	Black Canyon of Gunnison NM	CO	94-567	10/20/76	11,180
	Buffalo Peaks	FS	Pike NF	CO	103-77	8/13/93	23,570
	Buffalo Peaks	FS	San Isabel NF	CO	103-77	8/13/93	19,840
	Byers Peak	FS	Arapaho NF	CO	103-77	8/13/93	8,095
213	Cache La Poudre	FS	Roosevelt NF	CO	96-560	12/22/80	9,238
214	Collegiate Peaks	FS	Gunnison NF	CO	96-560	12/22/80	48,986
	Collegiate Peaks	FS	San Isabel NF	CO	96-560	12/22/80	82,248
	Collegiate Peaks	FS	White River NF	CO	96-560	12/22/80	35,482
215	Comanche Peak	FS	Roosevelt NF	CO	96-560	12/22/80	66,791
216	Eagles Nest	FS	Arapaho NF	CO	94-352	7/12/76	82,324
	Eagles Nest	FS	White River NF	CO	94-352	7/12/76	50,582
217	Flat Tops	FS	Routt NF	CO	94-146	12/12/75	38,870
	Flat Tops	FS	White River NF	CO	94-146	12/12/75	196,165
	Fossil Ridge	FS	Gunnison NF	CO	103-77	8/13/93	33,060
218	Great Sand Dunes	NPS	Great Sand Dunes NM	CO	94-567	10/20/76	33,450
	Greenhorn Mountain	FS	San Isabel NF	CO	103-77	8/13/93	22,040
219	Holy Cross	FS	San Isabel NF	CO	96-560	12/22/80	9,489
	Holy Cross	FS	White River NF	CO	96-560	12/22/80	112,899
220	Hunter-Fryingpan	FS	White River NF	CO	95-237	2/24/78	74,399
	Hunter-Fryingpan	FS	White River NF	CO	103-77	8/13/93	8,330
221	Indian Peaks	FS	Arapaho NF	CO	94-450	10/11/78	40,109
	Indian Peaks	FS	Arapaho NF	CO	96-560	12/22/80	0
	Indian Peaks	FS	Roosevelt NF	CO	95-450	10/11/78	30,265
	Indian Peaks	FS	Roosevelt NF	CO	96-560	12/22/80	0
	Indian Peaks	NPS	Rocky Mountain NP	CO	94-146	12/12/75	2,917
222	La Garita	FS	Gunnison NF	CO	88-577	9/3/64	79,822
	La Garita	FS	Gunnison NF	CO	96-560	12/22/80	0
	La Garita	FS	Rio Grande NF	CO	88-577	9/3/64	24,164
	La Garita	FS	Rio Grande NF	CO	96-560	12/22/80	0
	La Garita	FS	Rio Grande NF	CO	103-77	8/13/93	25,640

No.	Name	Agency	Unit	Code	Date	Acres
223	Lizard Head	FS	San Juan NF	96-560	12/22/80	20,802
	Lizard Head	FS	Uncompahgre NF	96-560	12/22/80	20,391
224	Lost Creek	FS	Pike NF	96-560	12/22/80	105,090
	Lost Creek	FS	Pike NF	103-77	8/13/93	14,700
225	Maroon Bells–Snowmass	FS	Gunnison NF	96-560	12/22/80	19,194
	Maroon Bells–Snowmass	FS	White River NF	88-577	9/3/64	161,768
	Maroon Bells–Snowmass	FS	White River NF	96-560	12/22/80	0
226	Mesa Verde	NPS	Mesa Verde NP	94-567	10/20/76	8,100
227	Mount Evans	FS	Arapaho NF	96-560	12/22/80	40,274
	Mount Evans	FS	Pike NF	96-560	12/22/80	34,127
228	Mount Massive	FS	San Isabel NF	96-560	12/22/80	27,980
	Mount Massive	FWS	Leadville NFH	96-560	12/22/80	2,560
229	Mount Sneffels	FS	Uncompahgre NF	96-560	12/22/80	16,565
230	Mount Zirkel	FS	Routt NF	88-577	9/3/64	139,818
	Mount Zirkel	FS	Routt NF	96-560	12/22/80	0
	Mount Zirkel	FS	Routt NF	103-77	8/13/93	20,750
231	Neota	FS	Roosevelt NF	96-560	12/22/80	9,657
	Neota	FS	Routt NF	96-560	12/22/80	267
232	Never Summer	FS	Arapaho NF	96-560	12/22/80	7,098
	Never Summer	FS	Arapaho NF	103-77	8/13/93	6,990
	Never Summer	FS	Routt NF	96-560	12/22/80	6,659
233	Platte River	FS	Routt NF	98-550	10/30/84	743
	Powderhorn	BLM	Montrose District	103-77	8/13/93	48,115
	Powderhorn	FS	Gunnison NF	103-77	8/13/93	11,985
	Ptarmigan Peak	FS	Arapaho NF	103-77	8/13/93	13,175
234	Raggeds	FS	Grand Mesa NF	103-77	8/13/93	5,500
	Raggeds	FS	Gunnison NF	96-560	12/22/80	43,062
	Raggeds	FS	White River NF	96-560	12/22/80	16,457
235	Rawah	FS	Roosevelt NF	88-577	9/3/64	71,606
	Rawah	FS	Roosevelt NF	96-560	12/22/80	0
	Rawah	FS	Routt NF	96-560	12/22/80	1,462
	Sangre de Cristo	FS	Rio Grande NF	103-77	8/13/93	226,455
	Sarvis Creek	FS	Routt NF	103-77	8/13/93	47,140
236	South San Juan	FS	Rio Grande NF	95-560	12/22/80	87,847
	South San Juan	FS	San Juan NF	95-560	12/22/80	39,843
	South San Juan	FS	San Juan NF	103-77	8/13/93	31,100
211	Uncompahgre	BLM	Montrose District	103-77	8/13/93	3,390
	Uncompahgre	FS	Uncompahgre NF	96-560	12/22/80	98,516
	Uncompahgre	FS	Uncompahgre NF	103-77	8/13/93	815
	Vasquez Peak	FS	Arapaho NF	103-77	8/13/93	12,300

Map No. (Figs. 14.1, 14.6)	Wilderness Area	Agency*	Administrative Unit**	State	Public Law	Date	Acreage
237	Weminuche	FS	Rio Grande NF	CO	93-632	1/3/75	164,715
	Weminuche	FS	Rio Grande NF	CO	96-560	12/22/80	0
	Weminuche	FS	San Juan NF	CO	93-632	1/3/75	294,889
	Weminuche	FS	San Juan NF	CO	96-560	12/22/80	0
	Weminuche	FS	San Juan NF	CO	103-77	8/13/93	28,740
238	West Elk	FS	Gunnison NF	CO	88-577	9/3/64	176,172
	West Elk	FS	Gunnison NF	CO	96-560	12/22/80	0
Total							3,256,772
			Florida				
239	Alexander Springs	FS	Ocala NF	FL	98-430	9/28/84	7,941
240	Big Gum Swamp	FS	Osceola NF	FL	98-430	9/28/84	13,660
241	Billies Bay	FS	Ocala NF	FL	98-430	9/28/84	3,092
242	Bradwell Bay	FS	Apalachicola NF	FL	93-622	1/3/75	24,602
	Bradwell Bay	FS	Apalachicola NF	FL	98-430	9/28/84	0
243	Cedar Keys	FWS	Cedar Keys NWR	FL	92-364	8/7/72	379
244	Chassahowitzka	FWS	Chassahowitzka NWR	FL	94-557	10/19/76	23,580
245	Everglades	NPS	Everglades NP	FL	95-625	11/10/78	1,296,500
246	Florida Keys	FWS	Great White Heron NWR	FL	93-632	1/3/75	1,900
	Florida Keys	FWS	Key West NWR	FL	93-632	1/3/75	2,019
	Florida Keys	FWS	National Key Deer Refuge	FL	93-632	1/3/75	2,278
247	Island Bay	FWS	Island Bay NWR	FL	91-504	10/23/70	20
248	J. N. "Ding" Darling	FWS	J. N. "Ding" Darling NWR	FL	94-557	10/19/76	2,619
249	Juniper Prairie	FS	Ocala NF	FL	98-430	9/28/84	14,277
250	Lake Woodruff	FWS	Lake Woodruff NWR	FL	94-557	10/19/76	1,066
251	Little Lake George	FS	Ocala NF	FL	98-430	9/28/84	2,833
252	Mud Swamp–New River	FS	Apalachicola NF	FL	98-430	9/28/84	8,090
253	Passage Key	FWS	Passage Key NWR	FL	91-504	10/23/70	36
254	Pelican Island	FWS	Pelican Island NWR	FL	91-504	10/23/70	6
255	St. Marks	FWS	St. Marks NWR	FL	93-632	1/3/75	17,350
Total							1,422,248
			Georgia				
256	Big Frog	FS	Chattahoochee NF	GA	98-578	10/30/84	83
257	Blackbeard Island	FWS	Blackbeard Island NWR	GA	93-632	1/3/75	3,000
258	Blood Mountain	FS	Chattahoochee NF	GA	102-217	12/11/91	7,800
259	Brasstown	FS	Chattahoochee NF	GA	99-555	10/27/86	11,178
	Brasstown	FS	Chattahoochee NF	GA	102-217	12/11/91	1,160

No.	Name	Administering unit	Agency	State	Public Law	Date	Acres
260	Cohutta	Chattahoochee NF	FS	GA	93-622	1/3/75	35,143
	Cohutta	Chattahoochee NF	FS	GA	99-555	10/27/86	0
261	Cumberland Island	Cumberland Island NS	NPS	GA	97-250	9/8/82	8,840
262	Ellicott Rock	Chattahoochee NF	FS	GA	93-622	1/3/75	2,181
	Ellicott Rock	Chattahoochee NF	FS	GA	98-514	10/19/84	0
263	Mark Trail	Chattahoochee NF	FS	GA	102-217	12/11/91	16,400
264	Okefenokee	Okefenokee NWR	FWS	GA	93-429	10/1/74	353,981
265	Raven Cliffs	Chattahoochee NF	FS	GA	99-555	10/27/86	8,562
266	Rich Mountain	Chattahoochee NF	FS	GA	99-555	10/27/86	9,476
267	Southern Nantahala	Chattahoochee NF	FS	GA	98-514	10/19/84	11,770
268	Tray Mountain	Chattahoochee NF	FS	GA	99-555	10/27/86	9,702
269	Wolf Island	Wolf Island NWR	FWS	GA	93-632	1/3/75	5,126
Total							484,402
	Hawaii						
270	Haleakala	Haleakala NP	NPS	HI	94-567	10/20/76	19,270
271	Hawaii Volcanoes	Hawaii Volcanoes NP	NPS	HI	95-625	11/10/78	123,100
Total							142,370
	Idaho						
272	Craters of the Moon	Craters of the Moon NM	NPS	ID	91-504	10/23/70	43,243
273	Frank Church–River of No Return	Coeur d'Alene District	BLM	ID	96-312	7/23/80	802
	Frank Church–River of No Return	Coeur d'Alene District	BLM	ID	98-231	3/14/84	0
	Frank Church–River of No Return	Bitterroot NF	FS	ID	96-312	7/23/80	193,703
	Frank Church–River of No Return	Bitterroot NF	FS	ID	98-231	3/14/84	0
	Frank Church–River of No Return	Boise NF	FS	ID	96-312	7/23/80	332,891
	Frank Church–River of No Return	Boise NF	FS	ID	98-231	3/14/84	0
	Frank Church–River of No Return	Challis NF	FS	ID	96-312	7/23/80	515,421
	Frank Church–River of No Return	Challis NF	FS	ID	98-231	3/14/84	0
	Frank Church–River of No Return	Nez Perce NF	FS	ID	96-312	7/23/80	110,698
	Frank Church–River of No Return	Nez Perce NF	FS	ID	98-231	3/14/84	0
	Frank Church–River of No Return	Payette NF	FS	ID	96-312	7/23/80	791,675
	Frank Church–River of No Return	Payette NF	FS	ID	98-231	3/14/84	0
	Frank Church–River of No Return	Salmon NF	FS	ID	96-312	7/23/80	421,433
	Frank Church–River of No Return	Salmon NF	FS	ID	98-231	3/14/84	0
274	Gospel Hump	Nez Perce NF	FS	ID	95-237	2/24/78	205,764
275	Hells Canyon	Nez Perce NF	FS	ID	94-199	12/31/75	59,900
	Hells Canyon	Payette NF	FS	ID	94-199	12/31/75	23,911
276	Sawtooth	Boise NF	FS	ID	92-400	8/22/72	150,071
	Sawtooth	Challis NF	FS	ID	92-400	8/22/72	12,020
	Sawtooth	Sawtooth NF	FS	ID	92-400	8/22/72	54,997
277	Selway-Bitterroot	Bitterroot NF	FS	ID	88-577	9/3/64	270,321
	Selway-Bitterroot	Bitterroot NF	FS	ID	96-312	7/23/80	0

Map No. (Figs. 14.1, 14.6)	Wilderness Area	Agency*	Administrative Unit**	State	Public Law	Date	Acreage
	Selway-Bitterroot	FS	Clearwater NF	ID	88-577	9/3/64	259,165
	Selway-Bitterroot	FS	Nez Perce NF	ID	88-577	9/3/64	559,531
Total							4,005,546
			Illinois				
278	Bald Knob	FS	Shawnee NF	IL	101-633	11/28/90	5,863
279	Bay Creek	FS	Shawnee NF	IL	101-633	11/28/90	2,866
280	Burden Falls	FS	Shawnee NF	IL	101-633	11/28/90	3,671
281	Clear Springs	FS	Shawnee NF	IL	101-633	11/28/90	4,730
282	Crab Orchard	FWS	Crab Orchard NWR	IL	94-557	10/19/76	4,050
283	Garden of the Gods	FS	Shawnee NF	IL	101-633	11/28/90	3,268
284	Lusk Creek	FS	Shawnee NF	IL	101-633	11/28/90	4,466
285	Panther Den	FS	Shawnee NF	IL	101-633	11/28/90	685
Total							29,599
			Indiana				
286	Charles C. Deam	FS	Hoosier NF	IN	97-384	12/22/82	12,935
			Kentucky				
287	Beaver Creek	FS	Daniel Boone NF	KY	93-622	1/3/75	4,753
288	Clifty	FS	Daniel Boone NF	KY	99-197	12/23/85	11,662
Total							16,415
			Louisiana				
289	Breton	FWS	Breton NWR	LA	93-632	1/3/75	5,000
290	Kisatchie Hills	FS	Kisatchie NF	LA	96-560	12/22/80	8,679
291	Lacassine	FWS	Lacassine NWR	LA	94-557	10/19/76	3,346
Total							17,025
			Massachusetts				
292	Monomoy	FWS	Monomoy NWR	MA	91-504	10/23/70	2,420
			Maine				
293	Baring Unit	FWS	Moosehorn NWR	ME	93-632	1/3/75	4,680
294	Birch Islands Unit	FWS	Moosehorn NWR	ME	91-504	10/23/70	6
295	Caribou–Speckled Mountain	FS	White Mountain NF	ME	101-401	9/28/90	12,000
296	Edmunds Unit	FWS	Moosehorn NWR	ME	91-504	10/23/70	2,706
Total							19,392
			Michigan				
297	Big Island Lake	FS	Hiawatha NF	MI	100-184	12/8/87	5,856
298	Delirium	FS	Hiawatha NF	MI	100-184	12/8/87	11,870
299	Horseshoe Bay	FS	Hiawatha NF	MI	100-184	12/8/87	3,790
300	Huron Islands	FWS	Huron NWR	MI	91-504	10/23/70	147

#	Name	Unit	Agency	Public Law	Date	State	Acres
301	Isle Royale	Isle Royale NP	NPS	94-567	10/20/76	MI	132,018
302	Mackinac	Hiawatha NF	FS	100-184	12/8/87	MI	12,230
303	McCormick	Ottawa NF	FS	100-184	12/8/87	MI	16,850
304	Michigan Islands	Michigan Islands NWR	FWS	91-504	10/23/70	MI	12
305	Nordhouse Dunes	Manistee NF	FS	100-184	12/8/87	MI	3,450
306	Rock River Canyon	Hiawatha NF	FS	100-184	12/8/87	MI	4,640
307	Round Island	Hiawatha NF	FS	100-184	12/8/87	MI	378
308	Seney	Seney NWR	FWS	91-504	10/23/70	MI	25,150
309	Sturgeon River Gorge	Ottawa NF	FS	100-184	12/8/87	MI	14,500
310	Sylvania	Ottawa NF	FS	100-184	12/8/87	MI	18,327
Total							249,218
	Minnesota						
311	Agassiz	Agassiz NWR	FWS	94-557	10/19/76	MN	4,000
312	Boundary Waters Canoe Area	Superior NF	FS	88-577	9/3/64	MN	803,050
	Boundary Waters Canoe Area	Superior NF	FS	95-495	10/21/78	MN	0
313	Tamarac	Tamarac NWR	FWS	94-557	10/19/76	MN	2,180
Total							809,230
	Missouri						
314	Bell Mountain	Mark Twain NF	FS	96-560	12/22/80	MO	8,977
315	Devils Backbone	Mark Twain NF	FS	96-560	12/22/80	MO	6,595
316	Hercules-Glades	Mark Twain NF	FS	94-557	10/19/76	MO	12,314
317	Irish	Mark Twain NF	FS	98-289	5/21/84	MO	16,117
318	Mingo	Mingo NWR	FWS	94-557	10/19/76	MO	7,730
319	Paddy Creek	Mark Twain NF	FS	97-407	1/3/83	MO	7,019
320	Piney Creek	Mark Twain NF	FS	96-560	12/22/80	MO	8,087
321	Rockpile Mountain	Mark Twain NF	FS	96-560	12/22/80	MO	4,089
Total							70,928
	Mississippi						
322	Black Creek	DeSoto NF	FS	98-515	10/19/84	MS	5,052
323	Gulf Islands	Gulf Islands NS	NPS	95-625	11/10/78	MS	4,637
324	Leaf	DeSoto NF	FS	98-515	10/19/84	MS	994
Total							10,683
	Montana						
325	Absaroka-Beartooth	Custer NF	FS	95-249	3/27/78	MT	345,589
	Absaroka-Beartooth	Gallatin NF	FS	95-249	3/27/78	MT	574,738
	Absaroka-Beartooth	Gallatin NF	FS	98-140	10/31/83	MT	0
326	Anaconda-Pintlar	Beaverhead NF	FS	88-577	9/3/64	MT	72,677
	Anaconda-Pintlar	Bitterroot NF	FS	88-577	9/3/64	MT	41,162
	Anaconda-Pintlar	Deerlodge NF	FS	88-577	9/3/64	MT	44,175
327	Bob Marshall	Flathead NF	FS	88-577	9/3/64	MT	709,356
	Bob Marshall	Lewis and Clark NF	FS	88-577	9/3/64	MT	300,000
	Bob Marshall	Lewis and Clark NF	FS	95-546	10/28/78	MT	0

Map No. (Figs. 14.1, 14.6)	Wilderness Area	Agency*	Administrative Unit**	State	Public Law	Date	Acreage
328	Cabinet Mountains	FS	Kaniksu NF	MT	88-577	9/3/64	44,320
	Cabinet Mountains	FS	Kootenai NF	MT	88-577	9/3/64	49,952
329	Gates of the Mountains	FS	Helena NF	MT	88-577	9/3/64	28,562
330	Great Bear	FS	Flathead NF	MT	95-546	10/28/78	286,700
331	Lee Metcalf	BLM	Butte District	MT	98-140	10/31/83	6,000
	Lee Metcalf	FS	Beaverhead NF	MT	98-140	10/31/83	108,350
	Lee Metcalf	FS	Gallatin NF	MT	98-140	10/31/83	140,594
332	Medicine Lake	FWS	Medicine Lake NWR	MT	94-557	10/19/76	11,366
333	Mission Mountains	FS	Flathead NF	MT	93-632	1/3/75	73,877
334	Rattlesnake	FS	Lolo NF	MT	96-476	10/19/80	32,844
335	Red Rock Lakes	FWS	Red Rock Lakes NWR	MT	94-557	10/19/76	32,350
336	Scapegoat	FS	Helena NF	MT	92-395	8/20/72	80,697
	Scapegoat	FS	Lewis and Clark NF	MT	92-395	8/20/72	84,407
	Scapegoat	FS	Lolo NF	MT	92-395	8/20/72	74,192
277	Selway-Bitterroot	FS	Bitterroot NF	MT	88-577	9/3/64	241,676
	Selway-Bitterroot	FS	Lolo NF	MT	88-577	9/3/64	9,767
337	UL Bend	FWS	UL Bend NWR	MT	94-557	10/19/76	20,819
338	Welcome Creek	FS	Lolo NF	MT	95-237	2/24/78	28,135
Total							3,442,305
			North Carolina				
339	Birkhead Mountains	FS	Uwharrie NF	NC	98-324	6/19/84	5,025
340	Catfish Lake South	FS	Croatan NF	NC	98-324	6/19/84	8,530
262	Ellicott Rock	FS	Nantahala NF	NC	93-622	1/3/75	4,022
	Ellicott Rock	FS	Nantahala NF	NC	98-324	6/19/84	0
341	Joyce Kilmer–Slickrock	FS	Nantahala NF	NC	93-622	1/3/75	13,562
	Joyce Kilmer–Slickrock	FS	Nantahala NF	NC	98-324	6/19/84	0
342	Linville Gorge	FS	Pisgah NF	NC	88-577	9/3/64	11,786
	Linville Gorge	FS	Pisgah NF	NC	98-324	6/19/84	0
343	Middle Prong	FS	Pisgah NF	NC	98-324	6/19/84	7,460
344	Pocosin	FS	Croatan NF	NC	98-324	6/19/84	11,709
345	Pond Pine	FS	Croatan NF	NC	98-324	6/19/84	1,685
346	Sheep Ridge	FS	Croatan NF	NC	98-324	6/19/84	9,297
347	Shining Rock	FS	Pisgah NF	NC	88-577	9/3/64	18,483
	Shining Rock	FS	Pisgah NF	NC	98-324	6/19/84	0
267	Southern Nantahala	FS	Nantahala NF	NC	98-324	6/19/84	11,703
348	Swanquarter	FWS	Swanquarter NWR	NC	94-557	10/19/76	8,785
Total							112,047

No.	Area	Unit	Agency	State	Public Law	Date	Acres
	North Dakota						
349	Chase Lake	Chase Lake NWR	FWS	ND	93-632	1/3/75	4,155
350	Lostwood	Lostwood NWR	FWS	ND	93-632	1/3/75	5,577
351	Theodore Roosevelt	Theodore Roosevelt NP	NPS	ND	95-625	11/10/78	29,920
Total							39,652
	Nebraska						
352	Fort Niobrara	Fort Niobrara NWR	FWS	NE	94-557	10/19/76	4,635
353	Soldier Creek	Nebraska NF	FS	NE	99-504	10/20/86	7,794
Total							12,429
	New Hampshire						
354	Great Gulf	White Mountain NF	FS	NH	88-577	9/3/64	5,552
355	Pemigewasset	White Mountain NF	FS	NH	98-323	6/19/84	45,000
356	Presidential Range–Dry River	White Mountain NF	FS	NH	93-622	1/3/75	27,380
	Presidential Range–Dry River	White Mountain NF	FS	NH	98-323	6/19/84	0
357	Sandwich Range	White Mountain NF	FS	NH	98-323	6/19/84	25,000
Total							102,932
	New Jersey						
358	Brigantine	Edwin B. Forsythe NWR	FWS	NJ	93-632	1/3/75	6,681
359	Great Swamp	Great Swamp NWR	FWS	NJ	90-532	9/28/68	3,660
Total							10,341
	New Mexico						
360	Aldo Leopold	Gila NF	FS	NM	96-550	12/19/80	202,016
361	Apache Kid	Cibola NF	FS	NM	96-550	12/19/80	44,626
362	Bandelier	Bandelier NM	NPS	NM	94-567	10/20/76	23,267
363	Bisti	Albuquerque District	BLM	NM	98-603	10/30/84	3,946
364	Blue Range	Apache NF	FS	NM	96-550	12/19/80	28,104
	Blue Range	Gila NF	FS	NM	96-550	12/19/80	1,200
365	Capitan Mountains	Lincoln NF	FS	NM	96-550	12/19/80	34,658
366	Carlsbad Caverns	Carlsbad Caverns NP	NPS	NM	95-625	11/10/78	33,125
367	Cebolla	Albuquerque District	BLM	NM	100-225	12/31/87	62,800
368	Chama River Canyon	Carson NF	FS	NM	95-237	2/24/78	2,900
	Chama River Canyon	Santa Fe NF	FS	NM	95-237	2/24/78	47,400
369	Chupadera Unit	Bosque del Apache NWR	FWS	NM	93-632	1/3/75	5,289
370	Cruces Basin	Carson NF	FS	NM	96-550	12/19/80	18,000
371	De-na-zin	Albuquerque District	BLM	NM	98-603	10/30/84	22,454
372	Dome	Santa Fe NF	FS	NM	96-550	12/19/80	5,200
373	Gila	Gila NF	FS	NM	88-577	9/3/64	557,873
	Gila	Gila NF	FS	NM	96-550	12/19/80	0
374	Indian Well Unit	Bosque del Apache NWR	FWS	NM	93-632	1/3/75	5,139
375	Latir Peak	Carson NF	FS	NM	96-550	12/19/80	20,000
376	Little San Pascual Unit	Bosque del Apache NWR	FWS	NM	93-632	1/3/75	19,859

Map No. (Figs. 14.1, 14.6)	Wilderness Area	Agency*	Administrative Unit**	State	Public Law	Date	Acreage
377	Manzano Mountain	FS	Cibola NF	NM	95-237	2/24/78	36,875
378	Pecos	FS	Carson NF	NM	88-577	9/3/64	24,736
	Pecos	FS	Santa Fe NF	NM	88-577	9/3/64	198,597
	Pecos	FS	Santa Fe NF	NM	96-550	12/19/80	0
379	Salt Creek	FWS	Bitter Lake NWR	NM	91-504	10/23/70	9,621
380	San Pedro Parks	FS	Santa Fe NF	NM	88-577	9/3/64	41,132
381	Sandia Mountain	FS	Cibola NF	NM	95-237	2/24/78	37,877
	Sandia Mountain	FS	Cibola NF	NM	96-248	5/23/80	0
	Sandia Mountain	FS	Cibola NF	NM	98-603	10/30/84	0
382	West Malpais	BLM	Albuquerque District	NM	100-225	12/31/87	39,700
383	Wheeler Peak	FS	Carson NF	NM	88-577	9/3/64	19,661
	Wheeler Peak	FS	Carson NF	NM	96-550	12/19/80	0
384	White Mountain	FS	Lincoln NF	NM	88-577	9/3/64	48,208
	White Mountain	FS	Lincoln NF	NM	96-550	12/19/80	0
385	Withington	FS	Cibola NF	NM	96-550	12/19/80	19,000
Total							1,613,263
	Nevada						
386	Alta Toquima	FS	Toiyabe NF	NV	101-195	12/5/89	38,000
387	Arc Dome	BLM	Battle Mountain District	NV	101-195	12/5/89	20
	Arc Dome	FS	Toiyabe NF	NV	101-195	12/5/89	115,000
388	Boundary Peak	FS	Inyo NF	NV	101-195	12/5/89	10,000
389	Currant Mountain	BLM	Ely District	NV	101-195	12/5/89	3
	Currant Mountain	FS	Humboldt NF	NV	101-195	12/5/89	36,000
390	East Humboldts	FS	Humboldt NF	NV	101-195	12/5/89	36,900
391	Grant Range	FS	Humboldt NF	NV	101-195	12/5/89	50,000
392	Jarbidge	FS	Humboldt NF	NV	88-577	9/3/64	113,167
	Jarbidge	FS	Humboldt NF	NV	101-195	12/5/89	0
393	Mount Charleston	FS	Toiyabe NF	NV	101-195	12/5/89	43,000
394	Mount Moriah	BLM	Ely District	NV	101-195	12/5/89	6,435
	Mount Moriah	FS	Humboldt NF	NV	101-195	12/5/89	70,000
395	Mount Rose	FS	Toiyabe NF	NV	101-195	12/5/89	28,000
396	Quinn Canyon	FS	Humboldt NF	NV	101-195	12/5/89	27,000
397	Ruby Mountains	FS	Humboldt NF	NV	101-195	12/5/89	90,000
398	Santa Rosa–Paradise Peak	FS	Humboldt NF	NV	101-195	12/5/89	31,000
399	Table Mountain	FS	Toiyabe NF	NV	101-195	12/5/89	98,000
Total							792,525

	New York						
No.	Name	Agency	Unit	State	P.L.	Date	Acres
400	Fire Island	NPS	Fire Island NS	NY	96-585	12/23/80	1,363
	Ohio						
401	West Sister Island	FWS	West Sister Island NWR	OH	93-632	1/3/75	77
	Oklahoma						
402	Black Fork Mountain	FS	Ouachita NF	OK	100-499	10/18/88	4,549
403	Charons Garden Unit	FWS	Wichita Mountains NWR	OK	91-504	10/23/70	5,723
404	North Mountain Unit	FWS	Wichita Mountains NWR	OK	91-504	10/23/70	2,847
405	Upper Kiamichi River	FS	Ouachita NF	OK	100-499	10/18/88	9,602
Total							22,721
	Oregon						
406	Badger Creek	FS	Mt. Hood NF	OR	98-328	6/26/84	24,000
407	Black Canyon	FS	Ochoco NF	OR	98-328	6/26/84	13,400
408	Boulder Creek	FS	Umpqua NF	OR	98-328	6/26/84	19,100
409	Bridge Creek	FS	Ochoco NF	OR	98-328	6/26/84	5,400
410	Bull of the Woods	FS	Mt. Hood NF	OR	98-328	6/26/84	27,427
410	Bull of the Woods	FS	Willamette NF	OR	98-328	6/26/84	7,473
411	Columbia	FS	Mt. Hood NF	OR	98-328	6/26/84	39,000
412	Cummins Creek	FS	Siuslaw NF	OR	98-328	6/26/84	9,173
413	Diamond Peak	FS	Deschutes NF	OR	88-577	9/3/64	34,413
	Diamond Peak	FS	Deschutes NF	OR	98-328	6/26/84	0
	Diamond Peak	FS	Willamette NF	OR	88-577	9/3/64	19,772
	Diamond Peak	FS	Willamette NF	OR	98-328	6/26/84	0
414	Drift Creek	FS	Siuslaw NF	OR	98-328	6/26/84	5,798
415	Eagle Cap	FS	Wallowa NF	OR	88-577	9/3/64	212,699
	Eagle Cap	FS	Wallowa NF	OR	92-521	10/21/72	0
	Eagle Cap	FS	Wallowa NF	OR	98-328	6/26/84	0
	Eagle Cap	FS	Whitman NF	OR	88-577	9/3/64	145,762
	Eagle Cap	FS	Whitman NF	OR	92-521	10/21/72	0
	Eagle Cap	FS	Whitman NF	OR	98-328	6/26/84	0
416	Gearhart Mountain	FS	Fremont NF	OR	88-577	9/3/64	22,809
416	Gearhart Mountain	FS	Fremont NF	OR	98-328	6/26/84	0
417	Grassy Knob	FS	Siskiyou NF	OR	98-328	6/26/84	17,200
275	Hells Canyon	BLM	Vale District	OR	98-328	6/26/84	968
	Hells Canyon	FS	Wallowa NF	OR	94-199	12/31/75	118,247
	Hells Canyon	FS	Wallowa NF	OR	98-328	6/26/84	0
	Hells Canyon	FS	Whitman NF	OR	94-199	12/31/75	11,848
	Hells Canyon	FS	Whitman NF	OR	98-328	6/26/84	0
418	Kalmiopsis	FS	Siskiyou NF	OR	88-577	9/3/64	179,655
418	Kalmiopsis	FS	Siskiyou NF	OR	95-237	2/24/78	0
419	Menagerie	FS	Willamette NF	OR	98-328	6/26/84	4,800

Map No.
(Figs. 14.1, 14.6)

Map No. (Figs. 14.1, 14.6)	Wilderness Area	Agency*	Administrative Unit**	State	Public Law	Date	Acreage
420	Middle Santiam	FS	Willamette NF	OR	98-328	6/26/84	7,500
421	Mill Creek	FS	Ochoco NF	OR	98-328	6/26/84	17,400
422	Monument Rock	FS	Malheur NF	OR	98-328	6/26/84	12,620
	Monument Rock	FS	Whitman NF	OR	98-328	6/26/84	7,030
423	Mount Hood	FS	Mt. Hood NF	OR	88-577	9/3/64	46,520
	Mount Hood	FS	Mt. Hood NF	OR	95-237	2/24/78	0
424	Mount Jefferson	FS	Deschutes NF	OR	90-548	10/2/68	32,734
	Mount Jefferson	FS	Mt. Hood NF	OR	90-548	10/2/68	5,021
	Mount Jefferson	FS	Willamette NF	OR	90-548	10/2/68	69,253
	Mount Jefferson	FS	Willamette NF	OR	98-328	6/26/84	0
425	Mount Thielsen	FS	Deschutes NF	OR	98-328	6/26/84	7,107
	Mount Thielsen	FS	Umpqua NF	OR	98-328	6/26/84	21,593
	Mount Thielsen	FS	Winema NF	OR	98-328	6/26/84	25,567
426	Mount Washington	FS	Deschutes NF	OR	88-577	9/3/64	14,116
	Mount Washington	FS	Deschutes NF	OR	98-328	6/26/84	0
	Mount Washington	FS	Willamette NF	OR	88-577	9/3/64	38,622
	Mount Washington	FS	Willamette NF	OR	98-328	6/26/84	0
427	Mountain Lakes	FS	Winema NF	OR	88-577	9/3/64	23,071
428	North Fork John Day	FS	Umatilla NF	OR	98-328	6/26/84	107,058
	North Fork John Day	FS	Whitman NF	OR	98-328	6/26/84	14,294
429	North Fork Umatilla	FS	Umatilla NF	OR	98-328	6/26/84	20,435
430	Oregon Islands	BLM	Coos Bay District	OR	95-450	10/11/78	5
	Oregon Islands	FWS	Oregon Islands NWR	OR	91-504	10/23/70	21
	Oregon Islands	FWS	Oregon Islands NWR	OR	95-450	10/11/78	459
189	Red Buttes	FS	Rogue River NF	OR	98-425	9/28/84	350
	Red Buttes	FS	Siskiyou NF	OR	98-328	6/26/84	3,400
431	Rock Creek	FS	Siuslaw NF	OR	98-328	6/26/84	7,486
432	Rogue-Umpqua Divide	FS	Rogue River NF	OR	98-328	6/26/84	6,850
	Rogue-Umpqua Divide	FS	Umpqua NF	OR	98-328	6/26/84	26,350
433	Salmon-Huckleberry	FS	Mt. Hood NF	OR	98-328	6/26/84	44,560
434	Sky Lakes	FS	Rogue River NF	OR	98-328	6/26/84	75,695
	Sky Lakes	FS	Winema NF	OR	98-328	6/26/84	40,605
435	Strawberry Mountain	FS	Malheur NF	OR	88-577	9/3/64	68,700
	Strawberry Mountain	FS	Malheur NF	OR	98-328	6/26/84	0
436	Table Rock	BLM	Salem District	OR	98-328	6/26/84	5,750
437	Three Arch Rocks	FWS	Three Arch Rocks NWR	OR	91-504	10/23/70	15

826

No.	Unit Name	Agency	Site	PL	State	Date	Acreage
438	Three Sisters	FS	Deschutes NF	88-577	OR	9/3/64	94,370
	Three Sisters	FS	Deschutes NF	98-328	OR	6/26/84	0
	Three Sisters	FS	Willamette NF	88-577	OR	9/3/64	192,338
	Three Sisters	FS	Willamette NF	95-237	OR	2/24/78	0
	Three Sisters	FS	Willamette NF	98-328	OR	6/26/84	0
439	Waldo Lake	FS	Willamette NF	98-328	OR	6/26/84	39,200
440	Wenaha-Tucannon	FS	Umatilla NF	95-237	OR	2/24/78	66,375
441	Wild Rogue	FS	Siskiyou NF	95-237	OR	2/24/78	34,629
Total							2,096,043

Pennsylvania

No.	Unit Name	Agency	Site	PL	State	Date	Acreage
442	Allegheny Islands	FS	Allegheny NF	98-585	PA	10/30/84	368
443	Hickory Creek	FS	Allegheny NF	98-585	PA	10/30/84	8,570
Total							8,938

South Carolina

No.	Unit Name	Agency	Site	PL	State	Date	Acreage
444	Cape Romain	FWS	Cape Romain NWR	93-632	SC	1/3/75	29,000
445	Congaree Swamp	NPS	Congaree Swamp NM	100-524	SC	10/24/88	15,010
262	Ellicott Rock	FS	Sumter NF	93-622	SC	1/3/75	2,809
446	Hell Hole Bay	FS	Francis Marion NF	96-560	SC	12/22/80	2,180
447	Little Wambaw Swamp	FS	Francis Marion NF	96-560	SC	12/22/80	5,154
448	Wambaw Creek	FS	Francis Marion NF	96-560	SC	12/22/80	1,937
449	Wambaw Swamp	FS	Francis Marion NF	96-560	SC	12/22/80	4,767
Total							60,857

South Dakota

No.	Unit Name	Agency	Site	PL	State	Date	Acreage
450	Badlands	NPS	Badlands NM	94-567	SD	10/20/76	64,250
451	Black Elk	FS	Black Hills NF	96-560	SD	12/22/80	9,826
Total							74,076

Tennessee

No.	Unit Name	Agency	Site	PL	State	Date	Acreage
452	Bald River Gorge	FS	Cherokee NF	98-578	TN	10/30/84	3,721
256	Big Frog	FS	Cherokee NF	98-578	TN	10/30/84	7,986
	Big Frog	FS	Cherokee NF	99-490	TN	10/16/86	0
453	Big Laurel Branch	FS	Cherokee NF	99-490	TN	10/16/86	6,251
454	Citico Creek	FS	Cherokee NF	98-578	TN	10/30/84	16,226
260	Cohutta	FS	Cherokee NF	93-622	TN	1/3/75	1,795
455	Gee Creek	FS	Cherokee NF	93-622	TN	1/3/75	2,493
341	Joyce Kilmer-Slickrock	FS	Cherokee NF	93-622	TN	1/3/75	3,832
456	Little Frog Mountain	FS	Cherokee NF	99-490	TN	10/16/86	4,684
457	Pond Mountain	FS	Cherokee NF	99-490	TN	10/16/86	6,626
458	Sampson Mountain	FS	Cherokee NF	99-490	TN	10/16/86	7,991

Map No. (Figs. 14.1, 14.6)	Wilderness Area	Agency*	Administrative Unit**	State	Public Law	Date	Acreage
459	Unaka Mountain	FS	Cherokee NF	TN	99-490	10/16/86	4,700
Total							66,305
			Texas				
460	Big Slough	FS	Davy Crockett NF	TX	98-574	10/30/84	3,455
461	Guadalupe Mountains	NPS	Guadalupe Mountains NP	TX	95-625	11/10/78	46,850
462	Indian Mounds	FS	Sabine NF	TX	98-574	10/30/84	9,358
	Indian Mounds	FS	Sabine NF	TX	99-584	10/29/86	0
463	Little Lake Creek	FS	Sam Houston NF	TX	98-574	10/30/84	3,855
	Little Lake Creek	FS	Sam Houston NF	TX	99-584	10/29/86	0
464	Turkey Hill	FS	Angelina NF	TX	98-574	10/30/84	5,473
	Turkey Hill	FS	Angelina NF	TX	99-584	10/29/86	0
465	Upland Island	FS	Angelina NF	TX	98-574	10/30/84	12,571
	Upland Island	FS	Angelina NF	TX	99-584	10/29/86	0
Total							81,562
			Utah				
466	Ashdown Gorge	FS	Dixie NF	UT	98-428	9/18/84	7,000
69	Beaver Dam Mountains	BLM	Cedar City District	UT	98-406	8/28/84	3,630
467	Box-Death Hollow	FS	Dixie NF	UT	98-428	9/18/84	25,751
468	Dark Canyon	FS	Manti-La Sal NF	UT	98-428	9/18/84	45,000
469	Deseret Peak	FS	Wasatch NF	UT	98-428	9/18/84	25,500
470	High Uintas	FS	Ashley NF	UT	98-428	9/18/84	276,175
	High Uintas	FS	Wasatch NF	UT	98-428	9/18/84	180,530
471	Lone Peak	FS	Uinta NF	UT	95-237	2/24/78	21,166
	Lone Peak	FS	Wasatch NF	UT	95-237	2/24/78	8,922
472	Mount Naomi	FS	Cache NF	UT	98-428	9/18/84	44,350
473	Mount Nebo	FS	Uinta NF	UT	98-428	9/18/84	28,000
474	Mount Olympus	FS	Wasatch NF	UT	98-428	9/18/84	16,000
475	Mount Timpanogos	FS	Uinta NF	UT	98-428	9/18/84	10,750
119	Paria Canyon–Vermillion Cliffs	BLM	Cedar City District	UT	98-406	8/28/84	23,000
476	Pine Valley Mountain	FS	Dixie NF	UT	98-428	9/18/84	50,000
477	Twin Peaks	FS	Wasatch NF	UT	98-428	9/18/84	11,334
478	Wellsville Mountain	FS	Cache NF	UT	98-428	9/18/84	23,850
Total							800,958
			Virginia				
479	Barbours Creek	FS	George Washington NF	VA	100-326	6/7/88	5
	Barbours Creek	FS	Jefferson NF	VA	100-326	6/7/88	5,695
480	Beartown	FS	Jefferson NF	VA	98-586	10/30/84	5,609

No.	Name	Agency	Unit	State	Map	Date	Acreage
481	James River Face	FS	Jefferson NF	VA	93-622	1/3/75	8,886
	James River Face	FS	Jefferson NF	VA	98-586	10/30/84	0
482	Kimberling Creek	FS	Jefferson NF	VA	98-586	10/30/84	5,542
483	Lewis Fork	FS	Jefferson NF	VA	98-586	10/30/84	5,618
484	Little Dry Run	FS	Jefferson NF	VA	98-586	10/30/84	2,858
485	Little Wilson Creek	FS	Jefferson NF	VA	98-586	10/30/84	3,613
486	Mountain Lake	FS	Jefferson NF	VA	98-586	10/30/84	8,187
487	Peters Mountain	FS	Jefferson NF	VA	98-586	10/30/84	3,328
488	Ramseys Draft	FS	George Washington NF	VA	98-586	10/30/84	6,518
489	Rich Hole	FS	George Washington NF	VA	100-326	6/7/88	6,450
490	Rough Mountain	FS	George Washington NF	VA	100-326	6/7/88	9,300
491	Saint Mary's	FS	George Washington NF	VA	98-586	10/30/84	9,835
492	Shawers Run	FS	George Washington NF	VA	100-326	6/7/88	95
	Shawers Run	FS	Jefferson NF	VA	100-326	6/7/88	3,570
493	Shenandoah	NPS	Shenandoah NP	VA	94-567	10/20/76	79,579
494	Thunder Ridge	FS	Jefferson NF	VA	98-586	10/30/84	2,344
Total							167,032
	Vermont						
495	Big Branch	FS	Green Mountain NF	VT	98-322	6/19/84	6,720
496	Breadloaf	FS	Green Mountain NF	VT	98-322	6/19/84	21,480
497	Bristol Cliffs	FS	Green Mountain NF	VT	93-622	1/3/75	3,738
	Bristol Cliffs	FS	Green Mountain NF	VT	94-268	4/16/76	0
498	George D. Aiken	FS	Green Mountain NF	VT	98-322	6/19/84	5,060
499	Lye Brook	FS	Green Mountain NF	VT	93-622	1/3/75	15,503
	Lye Brook	FS	Green Mountain NF	VT	98-322	6/19/84	0
500	Peru Peak	FS	Green Mountain NF	VT	98-322	6/19/84	6,920
Total							59,421
	Washington						
501	Alpine Lakes	FS	Snoqualmie NF	WA	94-357	7/12/76	117,776
	Alpine Lakes	FS	Wenatchee NF	WA	94-357	7/12/76	244,845
502	Boulder River	FS	Mt. Baker NF	WA	98-339	7/3/84	48,674
503	Buckhorn	FS	Olympic NF	WA	98-339	7/3/84	44,258
	Buckhorn	FS	Olympic NF	WA	99-635	11/7/86	0
504	Clearwater	FS	Snoqualmie NF	WA	98-339	7/3/84	14,374
505	Colonel Bob	FS	Olympic NF	WA	98-339	7/3/84	11,961
506	Glacier Peak	FS	Mt. Baker NF	WA	88-577	9/3/64	283,252
	Glacier Peak	FS	Mt. Baker NF	WA	90-544	10/2/68	0
	Glacier Peak	FS	Mt. Baker NF	WA	98-339	7/3/84	0
	Glacier Peak	FS	Wenatchee NF	WA	88-577	9/3/64	289,086
	Glacier Peak	FS	Wenatchee NF	WA	90-544	10/2/68	0
	Glacier Peak	FS	Wenatchee NF	WA	98-339	7/3/84	0
507	Glacier View	FS	Gifford Pinchot NF	WA	98-339	7/3/84	3,123

Map No. (Figs. 14.1, 14.6)	Wilderness Area	Agency*	Administrative Unit**	State	Public Law	Date	Acreage
508	Goat Rocks	FS	Gifford Pinchot NF	WA	88-577	9/3/64	71,203
	Goat Rocks	FS	Gifford Pinchot NF	WA	98-339	7/3/84	0
	Goat Rocks	FS	Snoqualmie NF	WA	88-577	9/3/64	37,076
	Goat Rocks	FS	Snoqualmie NF	WA	98-339	7/3/84	0
509	Henry M. Jackson	FS	Mt. Baker NF	WA	98-339	7/3/84	27,985
	Henry M. Jackson	FS	Snoqualmie NF	WA	98-339	7/3/84	47,446
	Henry M. Jackson	FS	Wenatchee NF	WA	98-339	7/3/84	27,242
510	Indian Heaven	FS	Gifford Pinchot NF	WA	98-339	7/3/84	20,960
511	Juniper Dunes	BLM	Spokane District	WA	98-339	7/3/84	6,900
512	Lake Chelan–Sawtooth	FS	Okanogan NF	WA	98-339	7/3/84	95,021
	Lake Chelan–Sawtooth	FS	Wenatchee NF	WA	98-339	7/3/84	56,414
513	Mount Adams	FS	Gifford Pinchot NF	WA	88-577	9/3/64	46,626
	Mount Adams	FS	Gifford Pinchot NF	WA	98-339	7/3/84	0
514	Mount Baker	FS	Mt. Baker NF	WA	98-339	7/3/84	117,528
515	Mount Rainier	NPS	Mount Rainier NP	WA	100-668	11/16/88	228,488
516	Mount Skokomish	FS	Olympic NF	WA	98-339	7/3/84	13,015
	Mount Skokomish	FS	Olympic NF	WA	99-635	11/7/86	0
517	Noisy-Diobsud	FS	Mt. Baker NF	WA	98-339	7/3/84	14,133
518	Norse Peak	FS	Snoqualmie NF	WA	98-339	7/3/84	52,180
519	Olympic	NPS	Olympic NP	WA	100-668	11/16/88	876,669
520	Pasayten	FS	Mt. Baker NF	WA	90-544	10/2/68	107,039
	Pasayten	FS	Okanogan NF	WA	90-544	10/2/68	422,992
	Pasayten	FS	Okanogan NF	WA	98-339	7/3/84	0
521	Salmo-Priest	FS	Colville NF	WA	98-339	7/3/84	29,386
	Salmo-Priest	FS	Kaniksu NF	WA	98-339	7/3/84	11,949
522	San Juan Islands	FWS	San Juan Islands NWR	WA	94-557	10/19/76	353
523	Stephen Mather	NPS	North Cascades NP	WA	100-668	11/16/88	634,614
524	Tatoosh	FS	Gifford Pinchot NF	WA	98-339	7/3/84	15,750
525	The Brothers	FS	Olympic NF	WA	98-339	7/3/84	16,682
	The Brothers	FS	Olympic NF	WA	99-635	11/7/86	0
526	Trapper Creek	FS	Gifford Pinchot NF	WA	98-339	7/3/84	5,970
527	Washington Islands	FWS	Copalis NWR	WA	91-504	10/23/70	60
	Washington Islands	FWS	Flattery Rocks NWR	WA	91-504	10/23/70	125
	Washington Islands	FWS	Quillayute Needles NWR	WA	91-504	10/23/70	300
440	Wenaha-Tucannon	FS	Umatilla NF	WA	95-237	2/24/78	111,048
528	William O. Douglas	FS	Gifford Pinchot NF	WA	98-339	7/3/84	15,469
	William O. Douglas	FS	Snoqualmie NF	WA	98-339	7/3/84	152,688

No.	Name	Unit	Agency	State	Public Law	Date	Acreage
529	Wonder Mountain	Olympic NF	FS	WA	98-339	7/3/84	2,349
Total							4,323,009
	Wisconsin						
530	Blackjack Springs	Nicolet NF	FS	WI	95-494	10/21/78	5,886
531	Headwaters	Nicolet NF	FS	WI	98-321	6/19/84	18,188
532	Porcupine Lake	Chequamegon NF	FS	WI	98-321	6/19/84	4,292
533	Rainbow Lake	Chequamegon NF	FS	WI	93-622	1/3/75	6,583
534	Whisker Lake	Nicolet NF	FS	WI	95-494	10/21/78	7,345
535	Wisconsin Islands	Gravel Island NWR	FWS	WI	91-504	10/23/70	27
535	Wisconsin Islands	Green Bay NWR	FWS	WI	91-504	10/23/70	2
Total							42,323
	West Virginia						
536	Cranberry	Monongahela NF	FS	WV	97-466	1/13/83	35,864
536	Cranberry	Monongahela NF	FS	WV	101-512	11/5/80	0
537	Dolly Sods	Monongahela NF	FS	WV	93-622	1/3/75	10,215
538	Laurel Fork North	Monongahela NF	FS	WV	97-466	1/13/83	6,055
539	Laurel Fork South	Monongahela NF	FS	WV	97-466	1/13/83	5,997
486	Mountain Lake	Jefferson NF	FS	WV	100-326	6/7/88	2,721
540	Otter Creek	Monongahela NF	FS	WV	93-622	1/3/75	20,000
Total							80,852
	Wyoming						
325	Absaroka-Beartooth	Shoshone NF	FS	WY	98-550	10/30/84	23,283
541	Bridger	Bridger NF	FS	WY	88-577	9/3/64	428,087
541	Bridger	Bridger NF	FS	WY	98-550	10/30/84	0
542	Cloud Peak	Bighorn NF	FS	WY	98-550	10/30/84	189,039
543	Encampment River	Medicine Bow NF	FS	WY	98-550	10/30/84	10,124
544	Fitzpatrick	Shoshone NF	FS	WY	94-557	10/19/76	198,525
544	Fitzpatrick	Shoshone NF	FS	WY	94-567	10/20/76	0
544	Fitzpatrick	Shoshone NF	FS	WY	98-550	10/30/84	0
545	Gros Ventre	Teton NF	FS	WY	98-550	10/30/84	287,000
546	Huston Park	Medicine Bow NF	FS	WY	98-550	10/30/84	30,588
547	Jedediah Smith	Targhee NF	FS	WY	98-550	10/30/84	123,451
548	North Absaroka	Shoshone NF	FS	WY	88-577	9/3/64	350,488
233	Platte River	Medicine Bow NF	FS	WY	98-550	10/30/84	22,749
549	Popo Agie	Shoshone NF	FS	WY	98-550	10/30/84	101,870
550	Savage Run	Medicine Bow NF	FS	WY	95-237	2/24/78	14,927
551	Teton	Teton NF	FS	WY	88-577	9/3/64	585,238
551	Teton	Teton NF	FS	WY	98-550	10/30/84	0
552	Washakie	Shoshone NF	FS	WY	88-577	9/3/64	704,274
552	Washakie	Shoshone NF	FS	WY	92-476	10/9/72	0
552	Washakie	Shoshone NF	FS	WY	98-550	10/30/84	0

Map No. (Figs. 14.1, 14.6)	Wilderness Area	Agency*	Administrative Unit**	State	Public Law	Date	Acreage
553	Winegar Hole	FS	Targhee NF	WY	98-550	10/30/84	10,715
Total							3,080,358

*BLM, Bureau of Land Management; FS, Forest Service; FWS, Fish and Wildlife Service; NPS, National Park Service.
**NF, National Forest; NFH, National Fish Hatchery; NM, National Monument; NP, National Park; NPres, National Preserve; NPPres, National Park and Preserve; NS, National Seashore; NWR, National Wildlife Refuge.
Source: Rob Hellie, Bureau of Land Management, January 1994.

Wild and Scenic Rivers System: River Mileage Classifications—1993

Fig. 14.11

No.	River/Present Units	State	Public Law*	Date	Administering Agency**	Miles by Classification			
						Wild	Scenic	Recreational	Total Miles
1	Middle Fork, Clearwater	ID	90-542	10/2/68	FS	54.0		131.00	185.0
2	Eleven Point	MO	90-542	10/2/68	FS		44.4	35.00	44.4
3	Feather	CA	90-542	10/2/68	FS	32.9	9.7	0.25	77.6
4	Rio Grande	NM	90-542	10/2/68	BLM	43.9			44.2
4	Rio Grande	NM	90-542	10/2/68	FS	7.9		0.75	8.6
5	Rio Grande	TX	95-625	11/10/78	NPS	95.2	96.0		191.2
6	Rogue	OR	90-542	10/2/68	BLM	21.0		26.00	47.0
6	Rogue	OR	90-542	10/2/68	FS	13.0	7.5	17.00	37.5
7	St. Croix	MN, WI	90-542	10/2/68	NPS		181.0	19.00	200.0
8	St. Croix (Lower)	MN, WI	90-560	10/25/72	NPS		12.0	15.00	27.0
9	St. Croix (Lower)	MN, WI	SD	6/17/76	MN			25.00	25.0
9	St. Croix (Lower)	MN, WI	SD	6/17/76	WI			25.00	25.0
10	Middle Fork Salmon	ID	90-542	10/2/68	FS	103.0		1.00	104.0
11	Salmon	ID	96-312	7/23/80	FS	79.0		46.00	125.0
12	Wolf	WI	90-542	10/2/68	NPS		24.0		24.0
13	Allagash Wilderness Waterway	ME	SD	7/19/70	ME	92.5			92.5
14	Little Miami	OH	SD	8/20/73	OH		18.0	48.00	66.0
15	Little Miami	OH	SD	1/28/80	OH			28.00	28.0
16	Chattooga	NC, SC	93-279	5/10/74	FS	39.8	2.5	14.60	56.9
17	Little Beaver	OH	SD	10/23/75	OH		33.0		33.0
18	Snake	ID, OR	94-199	12/31/75	FS	32.5	34.4		66.9
19	Rapid	ID	94-199	12/31/75	FS	26.8			26.8
20	New	NC	SD	4/13/76	NC		26.5		26.5
21	Missouri	MT	94-486	10/12/76	BLM	64.0	26.0	59.00	149.0
22	Missouri	NE, SD	95-625	11/10/78	NPS			59.00	59.0
23	Missouri	NE, SD	102-50	5/24/91	NPS			39.00	39.0
24	Flathead	MT	94-486	10/12/76	FS	97.9	40.7	80.40	219.0
24	Flathead	MT	94-486	10/12/76	NPS	97.9	40.7	80.40	219.0
25	Obed	TN	94-486	10/12/76	NPS	45.2			45.2
26	Pere Marquette	MI	95-625	11/10/78	FS		66.4		66.4
27	Skagit	WA	95-625	11/10/78	FS		99.0	58.50	157.5
28	Delaware (Upper)	NY, PA	95-625	11/10/78	NPS		25.1	50.30	75.4
29	Delaware (Middle)	NY, NJ, PA	95-625	11/10/78	NPS		35.0		35.0
30	American (North Fork)	CA	94-486	11/10/78	FS	26.3			26.3
30	American (North Fork)	CA	95-625	11/10/78	BLM	12.0			12.0
31	American (Lower)	CA	SD	1/19/81	CA			23.00	23.0
32	Saint Joe	ID	95-625	11/10/78	FS	26.6		39.70	66.3
33	Alagnak	AK	96-487	12/2/80	NPS	67.0		39.70	67.0

No.	River	State	Ref.	Date	Agency				
34	Alatna	AK	96-487	12/2/80	NPS	83.0			83.0
35	Aniakchak	AK	96-487	12/2/80	NPS	63.0			63.0
36	Charley	AK	96-487	12/2/80	NPS	208.0			208.0
37	Chilikadrotna	AK	96-487	12/2/80	NPS	11.0			11.0
38	John	AK	96-487	12/2/80	NPS	52.0			52.0
39	Kobuk	AK	96-487	12/2/80	NPS	110.0			110.0
40	Mulchatna	AK	96-487	12/2/80	NPS	24.0			24.0
41	Koyukuk	AK	96-487	12/2/80	NPS	102.0			102.0
42	Noatak	AK	96-487	12/2/80	NPS	330.0			330.0
43	Salmon	AK	96-487	12/2/80	NPS	70.0			70.0
44	Tinayguk	AK	96-487	12/2/80	NPS	44.0			44.0
45	Tlikakila	AK	96-487	12/2/80	NPS	51.0			51.0
46	Andreafsky	AK	96-487	12/2/80	FWS	262.0			262.0
47	Ivishak	AK	96-487	12/2/80	FWS	80.0			80.0
48	Nowitna	AK	96-487	12/2/80	FWS	225.0			225.0
49	Selawik	AK	96-487	12/2/80	FWS	160.0			160.0
50	Sheenjek	AK	96-487	12/2/80	FWS	160.0			160.0
51	Wind	AK	96-487	12/2/80	FWS	140.0			140.0
52	Beaver Creek	AK	96-487	12/2/80	BLM	16.0			16.0
52	Beaver Creek	AK	96-487	12/2/80	BLM	111.0			111.0
53	Birch Creek	AK	96-487	12/2/80	BLM	126.0			126.0
54	Delta	AK	96-487	12/2/80	BLM	20.0	24.0	18.00	62.0
55	Fortymile	AK	96-487	12/2/80	BLM	179.0	203.0	10.00	392.0
56	Gulkana	AK	96-487	12/2/80	BLM	181.0			181.0
57	Unalakleet	AK	96-487	12/2/80	BLM	80.0			80.0
58	Klamath	CA	SD	1/19/81	CA		3.0	41.00	44.0
58	Klamath	CA	SD	1/19/81	FS	12.0	21.0	177.50	210.5
58	Klamath	CA	SD	1/19/81	BLM			1.50	1.5
58	Klamath	CA	SD	1/19/81	HVIR			29.00	29.0
58	Klamath	CA	SD	1/19/81	NPS			1.00	1.0
59	Trinity	CA	SD	1/19/81	CA	2.0	11.0	24.00	37.0
59	Trinity	CA	SD	1/19/81	FS	42.0	22.0	71.00	135.0
59	Trinity	CA	SD	1/19/81	BLM		6.0	17.00	17.0
59	Trinity	CA	SD	1/19/81	HVIR			8.00	14.0
60	Eel	CA	SD	1/19/81	CA	36.0	22.5	250.50	309.0
60	Eel	CA	SD	1/19/81	FS	35.0	4.5	6.50	35.0
60	Eel	CA	SD	1/19/81	BLM	21.0	1.0	16.00	32.0
60	Eel	CA	SD	1/19/81	RVIR	5.0	0.5	28.50	22.0
61	Smith	CA			CA				29.0
61	Smith	CA	101-612	11/16/90	FS	78.0	30.5	187.50	296.4
62	Verde	AZ	98-406	8/28/84	FS	18.5	22.0		40.5
63	Tuolumne	CA	98-425	9/28/84	FS	7.0	6.0	13.00	26.0

Fig. 14.11

No.	River/Present Units	State	Public Law*	Date	Administering Agency**	Miles by Classification			Total Miles
						Wild	Scenic	Recreational	
63	Tuolumne	CA	98-425	9/28/84	NPS	37.0	17.0		54.0
63	Tuolumne	CA	98-425	9/28/84	BLM	3.0			3.0
64	Au Sable	MI	98-444	10/4/84	FS		23.0		23.0
65	Owyhee	OR	98-494	10/19/84	BLM	120.0			120.0
66	Illinois	OR	98-494	10/19/84	FS	28.7	17.9	3.80	50.4
67	Loxahatchee	FL	SD	5/17/85	FL	1.3	5.8	0.50	7.5
68	Horsepasture	NC	99-530	10/26/86	FS		3.6	0.60	4.2
69	Cache La Poudre	CO	99-590	10/30/86	FS	18.0		46.00	64.0
69	Cache La Poudre	CO	99-590	10/30/86	NPS	12.0			12.0
70	Black Creek	MS	99-590	10/30/86	FS		21.0		21.0
71	Saline Bayou	LA	99-590	10/30/86	FS		19.0		19.0
72	Klickitat	WA	99-663	11/17/86	FS			10.00	10.0
73	White Salmon	WA	99-663	11/17/86	FS		9.0		9.0
74	Merced	CA	100-149	11/2/87	FS	15.0	2.0	12.50	29.5
74	Merced	CA	100-149	11/2/87	NPS	53.0	14.0	14.00	81.0
74	Merced	CA	102-432	10/23/92	BLM		4.0	7.50	11.5
75	Kings	CA	100-150	11/3/87	FS	16.5		9.00	25.5
75	Kings	CA	100-150	11/3/87	NPS	49.0		6.50	55.5
76	Kern	CA	100-174	11/24/87	NPS	96.1	20.9	7.00	124.0
76	Kern	CA	100-174	11/24/87	NPS	27.0			27.0
77	Wildcat Creek	NH	100-554	10/28/88	FS		13.5	1.00	14.5
78	Sipsey Fork of West Fork	AL	100-547	10/28/88	FS	36.4	25.0		61.4
79	Big Marsh Creek	OR	100-557	10/28/88	FS			15.00	15.0
80	Chetco	OR	100-557	10/28/88	FS	25.5	8.0	11.00	44.5
81	Clackamas	OR	100-557	10/28/88	FS		20.0	27.00	47.0
82	Crescent Creek	OR	100-557	10/28/88	FS			10.00	10.0
83	Crooked	OR	100-557	10/28/88	BLM			15.00	15.0
84	Deschutes	OR	100-557	10/28/88	BLM		19.0	100.00	119.0
84	Deschutes	OR	100-557	10/28/88	FS		11.0	43.40	54.4
85	Donner Und Blitzen	OR	100-557	10/28/88	BLM	72.7			72.7
86	Eagle Creek	OR	100-557	10/28/88	FS	4.0	6.0	17.00	27.0
87	Elk	OR	100-557	10/28/88	FS	2.0		17.00	19.0
88	Grand Ronde	OR	100-557	10/28/88	BLM	9.0		15.90	24.9
88	Grand Ronde	OR	100-557	10/28/88	FS	17.4		1.50	18.9
89	Imnaha	OR	100-557	10/28/88	FS	15.0	4.0	58.00	77.0
90	John Day	OR	100-557	10/28/88	BLM			147.50	147.5
91	Joseph Creek	OR	100-557	10/28/88	FS	8.6			8.6
92	Little Deschutes	OR	100-557	10/28/88	FS			12.00	12.0

No.	River	State	Code	Date	Agency				
93	Lostine	OR	100-557	10/28/88	FS	5.0		11.00	16.0
94	Malheur	OR	100-557	10/28/88	FS		7.0	6.70	13.7
95	McKenzie	OR	100-557	10/28/88	FS			12.70	12.7
96	Metolius	OR	100-557	10/28/88	FS		17.1	11.50	28.6
97	Minam	OR	100-557	10/28/88	FS	39.0			39.0
98	North Fork Crooked	OR	100-557	10/28/88	FS		8.0	6.70	14.7
98	North Fork Crooked	OR	100-557	10/28/88	BLM	11.1	1.5	5.00	17.6
99	North Fork John Day	OR	100-557	10/28/88	FS	27.8	10.5	15.80	54.1
100	North Fork Malheur	OR	100-557	10/28/88	FS		25.5		25.5
101	North Fork of the Middle Fork of Willamette	OR	100-557	10/28/88	FS	8.8	6.5	27.00	42.3
102	North Fork Owyhee	OR	100-557	10/28/88	BLM	9.6			9.6
103	North Fork Smith	OR	100-557	10/28/88	FS	8.5	4.5		13.0
104	North Fork Sprague	OR	100-557	10/28/88	FS		15.0		15.0
105	North Powder	OR	100-557	10/28/88	FS		6.0		6.0
106	North Umpqua	OR	100-557	10/28/88	BLM			8.40	8.4
106	North Umpqua	OR	100-557	10/28/88	FS			25.40	25.4
107	Powder	OR	100-557	10/28/88	BLM		11.7		11.7
108	Quartzville	OR	100-557	10/28/88	BLM			12.00	12.0
109	Roaring	OR	100-557	10/28/88	FS	13.5		0.20	13.7
110	Salmon	OR	100-557	10/28/88	FS	15.0		10.50	25.5
110	Salmon	OR	100-557	10/28/88	BLM		4.8	3.20	8.0
111	Sandy	OR	100-557	10/28/88	FS	4.5		7.90	12.4
111	Sandy	OR	100-557	10/28/88	BLM		3.8	8.70	12.5
112	South Fork John Day	OR	100-557	10/28/88	BLM			47.00	47.0
113	Squaw Creek	OR	100-557	10/28/88	FS	6.6	8.8		15.4
114	Sycan	OR	100-557	10/28/88	FS		50.4	8.60	59.0
115	Upper Rogue	OR	100-557	10/28/88	FS	6.1	34.2		40.3
116	Wenaha	OR	100-557	10/28/88	FS	18.7	2.7		21.6
117	West Little Owyhee	OR	100-557	10/28/88	BLM	57.6		0.15	57.6
118	White	OR	100-557	10/28/88	FS		6.5	15.60	22.1
118	White	OR	100-557	10/28/88	BLM		17.5	6.90	24.4
119	Bluestone	WV	100-534	10/26/88	NPS		17.0		17.0
120	Rio Chama	NM	100-633	11/7/88	BLM	21.5			21.5
120	Rio Chama	NM	100-633	11/7/88	FS		3.1		3.1
121	Middle Fork of Vermilion	IL	SD	5/11/89	IL		17.1		17.1
122	East Fork of Jemez	NM	101-306	6/6/90	FS	4.0	5.0	2.00	11.0
123	Pecos	NM	101-306	6/6/90	FS	13.5		7.00	20.5
124	Clarks Fork of Yellowstone	WY	101-628	11/28/90	FS	20.5			20.5
125	Niobrara	NE	102-50	5/24/91	NPS		70.0	33.00	103.0
126	Bear Creek	MI	102-249	3/3/92	FS		6.5		6.5
127	Black	MI	102-249	3/3/92	FS		14.0		14.0

Fig. 14.11

No.	River/Present Units	State	Public Law*	Date	Administering Agency**	Miles by Classification			Total Miles
						Wild	Scenic	Recreational	
128	Carp	MI	102-249	3/3/92	FS	12.4	9.3	6.10	27.8
129	Indian	MI	102-249	3/3/92	FS		12.0	39.00	51.0
130	Manistee	MI	102-249	3/3/92	FS			26.00	26.0
131	Ontonagon	MI	102-249	3/3/92	FS	42.9	41.0	73.50	157.4
132	Paint	MI	102-249	3/3/92	FS			51.00	51.0
133	Pine	MI	102-249	3/3/92	FS		25.0		25.0
134	Preque Isle	MI	102-249	3/3/92	FS		19.0	38.00	57.0
135	Sturgeon (Hiawatha National Forest)	MI	102-249	3/3/92	FS		21.7	22.20	43.9
136	Sturgeon (Ottawa National Forest)	MI	102-249	3/3/92	FS	16.5	8.5		25.0
137	Tahquamenon, East Branch	MI	102-249	3/3/92	FS	3.2		10.00	13.2
138	Whitefish	MI	102-249	3/3/92	FS		31.5	2.10	33.6
139	Yellow Dog	MI	102-249	3/3/92	FS	4.0			4.0
140	Allegheny	PA	102-271	4/20/92	FS			85.00	85.0
141	Big Piney	AR	102-275	4/22/92	FS		45.2		45.2
142	Buffalo River	AR	102-275	4/22/92	FS	9.4	6.4		15.8
143	Cossatot River	AR	102-275	4/22/92	FS		11.3		15.5
143	Cossatot River	AR	102-275	4/22/92	ACE			4.20	4.6
143	Cossatot River	AR	102-275	4/22/92	AR		4.6		10.7
144	Hurricane Creek	AR	102-275	4/22/92	FS	2.4	13.1		15.5
145	Little Missouri	AR	102-275	4/22/92	FS	4.4	11.3		15.7
146	Mulberry	AR	102-275	4/22/92	FS		19.4	36.60	56.0
147	North Sylamore Creek	AR	102-275	4/22/92	FS		14.5		14.5
148	Richland Creek	AR	102-275	4/22/92	FS	5.3	11.2		16.5
149	Sespe Creek	CA	102-301	6/19/92	FS	27.5	4.0		31.5
150	Sisquoc River	CA	102-301	6/19/92	FS	33.0			33.0
151	Big Sur River	CA	102-301	6/19/92	FS	19.5			19.5
152	Great Egg Harbor River	NJ	102-536	10/27/92	NPS		30.6	98.40	129.0
Totals						5,263.90	2,136.15	3,109.1	10,516.35†

*SD, secretarial designation.
**ACE, Army Corps of Engineers; BLM, Bureau of Land Management; FS, Forest Service; FWS, Fish and Wildlife Service; HVIR, Hoopa Valley Indian Reservation; NPS, National Park Service; RVIR, Round Valley Indian Reservation.
†Total miles are 10.7 more than the sum of Wild, Scenic and Recreational due to currently unclassified nature of State of Arkansas administered miles of the Cossatot River.
Source: National Park Service, Division of Park Planning and Protection, 1992.

National Recreation Trails—1993

Name	Trail No.	Date	Season[a]	Uses[b]	Surface[c]	Length (miles)	Administering Agency[d]
Alabama							
Bartram	74	12/1/75	0	F	N	1.0	Tuskegee NF
George Ward Park Exercise	154	4/14/78	0	F	N	1.5	Birmingham Park and Rec. Bd.
Muscle Shoals	649	11/27/81	0	F, B	N	9.3	TVA
Pinhoti	115	4/22/77	0	F	N	26.0	Talladega NF
Pinhoti	115	4/22/77	0	F	N	2.0	AL Div. of Parks
Total						39.8	
Alaska							
Crane Lake	267	6/29/79	0	F	N	0.3	Tongass NF
Deer Mountain–John Mountain	188	12/8/78	0	F	N	9.0	Tongass NF
Mendenhall Glacier	190	12/8/78	0	F, S, I	N	1.5	Tongass NF
Mt. Edgecombe	407	12/13/79	0	F	N	7.0	Tongass NF
Naha River	187	12/8/78	0	F	N	6.3	Tongass NF
Petersburg Lake	189	12/8/78	0	F	N	6.5	Tongass NF
Pinnell Mountain	1	6/1/71	0	F	N	24.0	BLM
Resurrection Pass	238	2/7/79	0	F, H, M, S	N	37.5	Chugach NF
Swan Lake Canoe Route	524	1/2/81	0	W	N	60.0	FWS
Swanson River Canoe Route	525	1/2/81	0	W	N	80.0	FWS
Williwaw	275	6/29/79	0	F, I	N	0.8	Chugach NF
Total						232.9	
Arizona							
Arcadia	362	11/27/79	0	F, H	N	6.0	Coronado NF
Benham and Bill Williams	232	6/20/78	0	F, H	N	7.4	Kiabab NF
Betty's Kitchen Interpretive	802	9/20/92	0	F	N	0.5	BLM
Blue Ridge	442	2/1/79	0	F, H, V	N	8.7	Apache-Sitgreaves NF
Bright Angel	548	3/20/81	0	F, H	A	7.8	Grand Canyon NP
Coronado Peak	641	11/19/81	0	F, H	A	0.4	Coronado NM
Desert Ecology	688	4/13/82	0	F, C	A	0.3	Saguaro NM
Eagle	331	10/19/79	0	F, H	N	28.5	Apache-Sitgreaves NF
Escudilla	191	12/8/78	0	F, H	N	3.3	Apache-Sitgreaves NF
General George Crook	296	10/5/79	0	F, H, S	N	138.0	Coconino–Apache Sitgreaves
Granite Mountain	201	12/18/78	0	F, H	N	4.0	Prescott NF
Highline	180	11/3/78	0	F, H, V	N	40.0	Tonto NF
Hunter	50	9/12/74	0	F	N	2.3	Arizona State Parks Board
Joe's Canyon	640	11/19/81	0	F, H	N	3.1	Coronado NM

Name							
Kaibab	550	3/20/81	0	F, H	N	6.3	Grand Canyon NP
North Kaibab	551	3/20/81	0	F, H	N	14.2	Grand Canyon NP
North Mountain	44	1/7/74	0	F, H	N	0.9	Phoenix Parks and Rec. Dept.
Old Baldy Super Loop	203	12/18/78	0	F, H	N	12.9	Coronado NF
Parks Rest Area	317	10/5/79	0	F, I, C	N	0.5	Kiabab NF
River	549	3/20/81	0	F, H	N	1.7	Grand Canyon NP
Sixshooter Canyon	342	11/16/79	0	F, H	N	4.9	Tonto NF
South Mountain Park	10	6/1/71	0	B, F, H	N	14.0	Phoenix Parks and Rec. Dept.
Squaw Peak	43	1/7/74	0	F, H	N	1.2	Phoenix Parks and Rec. Dept.
Sun Circle	107	3/25/77	0	F, H, B	N	68.0	Maricopa County Parks
Wilson Mountain	304	10/5/79	0	F, H, V	N	4.6	Coconino NF
Total						379.5	
			Arkansas				
Alum Cove Natural Bridge	353	11/16/79	0	F	N	1.1	Ozark–St. Francis NF
Bona Dea	738	4/12/84	0	F, I	N	5.6	ACE
Bridge Rock	140	3/8/78	0	F	N	1.0	ACE
Buckeye	141	3/8/78	0	F, C	A	0.1	ACE
Buckskin Nature	449	4/9/80	0	F	N	0.5	ACE
Cedar Creek Self-Guiding	55	1/16/75	0	F	N	1.5	Arkansas Dept. of Parks
Cedar Falls	137	3/8/78	0	F	N	2.2	Petit Jean State Park
Dam Mountain	146	3/8/78	0	F	N	4.5	Lake Catherine State Park
Devil's Den Self-Guided	144	3/8/78	0	F	N	1.5	Little Rock Dept. Parks and Tourism
Dripstone	176	8/22/78	0	F	N	0.7	Ozark–St. Francis NF
Falls Branch	148	3/8/78	0	F	N	2.0	Lake Catherine State Park
Feaster	742	6/29/84	0	F, B	A	1.4	Arkadelphia Parks and Rec.
Forest Hills	138	3/8/78	0	F	N	1.5	ACE
Grand Promenade	699	4/13/82	0	F, C	A	0.5	Hot Springs NP
Horseshoe Mountain	147	3/8/78	0	F, C	N	3.5	Lake Catherine State Park
Kingfisher	447	4/9/80	0	F, C	N	0.5	Pinnacle Mountain State Park
Levi Wilcoxon Forest	96	10/5/76	0	F	N	0.8	Georgia-Pacific Corp.
Lost Bridge Hiking	629	11/19/81	0	F	N	5.0	ACE
Louisiana Purchase	602	6/8/81	0	F, C	A	0.2	Little Rock Dept. Parks and Tourism
Mossy Bluff	142	3/8/78	0	F	N	0.7	ACE
Ouachita	178	8/30/78	0	F	N	175.0	Ouachita NF
Ouachita Go-Float	484	9/4/80	0	W	N	16.0	Lake Catherine State Park
Ozark Highlands	745	4/11/84	0	F	N	140.0	Ozark–St. Francis NF
Prairie Creek Jogging	135	3/8/78	0	F	N	1.0	ACE
River Bluff Nature	601	6/8/81	0	F	N	1.0	ACE
Robinson Point Nature	145	3/8/78	0	F	N	3.0	ACE
Rocky Valley	642	11/19/81	0	F	N	2.0	Pinnacle Mountain State Park
Seven Hollows	56	1/16/75	0	F	N	3.5	AR Dept. of Parks
Sugar Loaf Mountain Nature	18	6/1/71	0	F	N	1.0	ACE

Name	Trail No.	Date	Season[a]	Uses[b]	Surface[c]	Length (miles)	Administering Agency[d]
Summit Park Self-Guided	139	3/8/78	O	F	N	1.7	Mount Nebo State Park
Tollantusky	136	3/8/78	O	F, C	A	1.4	ACE
Village Creek Hiking	603	6/8/81	O	F	N	7.0	Village Creek State Park
Woodpecker Hollow Nature	448	4/9/80	O	F, C	A	0.5	ACE
Yellow Rock	143	3/8/78	O	F	N	2.0	Little Rock Dept. of Parks
Total						389.9	
California							
Bayside	737	4/12/84	O	F	A	2.0	Cabrillo NM
Bear Valley	556	3/20/81	O	F, H, B	N	4.2	Point Reyes National Seashore
Big Trees	382	12/13/79	O	F	N	1.4	Tahoe NF
Bizz Johnson Trail	792	9/20/92	O	F, B, M, H, S, I	N	25.7	BLM, Eagle Lake Resource Area
Black Point	385	12/13/79	O	F, H	N	0.6	Sierra NF
Blue Lake	381	12/13/79	O	F	N	1.5	Modoc NF
Boundary Trail–Kangaroo	380	12/13/79	O	F, H, V	N	19.5	Klamath NF
Bumpess Hell	553	3/20/81	O	F	N	1.5	Lassen Volcanic NP
California Aqueduct	46	3/21/74	O	B, F	N	67.0	California Dept. of Water Resources
Camp Creek	283	8/17/79	O	F	N	3.6	San Bernardino NF
Cannell Meadow	302	10/5/79	O	F, H, V	N	9.0	Sequoia NF
Clear Creek	372	11/28/79	O	F, H	N	19.3	Klamath NF
Coalinga Mineral Spring	705	7/9/82	O	F, H	N	2.5	BLM
Coastal	539	3/20/81	O	F	N	4.0	Redwood NP
Columns of the Giants	359	11/16/79	O	F, I	N	0.6	Stanislaus NF
Congress	669	2/5/82	O	F, S	N	2.0	Sequoia and King's Canyon NP
Crystal Cave	670	2/5/82	O	F	N	0.8	Sequoia and King's Canyon NP
Discovery	312	10/5/79	O	F, I	N	1.0	Inyo NF
Donner Camp	383	12/13/79	O	F, I	N	0.4	Tahoe NF
East Bay Skyline	8	6/1/71	O	F, H	N	14.0	East Bay Regional Park District
Emigrant Summit	467	5/6/80	O	F, H, S, V	N	18.0	Eldorado NF
Feather Falls	182	11/22/78	O	F, H, V	N	3.5	Plumas NF
Gabriellino	9	5/18/70	O	F, H	N	28.0	Angeles NF
Hartman Bar	423	12/13/79	O	F, H, V	N	7.5	Plumas NF
Hawley Grade	388	12/13/79	O	F, H	N	1.5	Lake Tahoe NF
Heart Lake	369	11/16/79	O	F, H	N	3.5	Lassen NF
High Desert	536	3/4/81	O	F, H	N	27.0	Angeles NF
High Grade	468	5/6/80	O	F, H, V	N	5.5	Modoc NF
Horse Trail Ridge	316	10/5/79	O	F, H	N	15.0	Six Rivers NF
Ides Cove Loop	386	12/13/79	O	F, H	N	7.8	Mendocino NF

Name	No.	Date		Facilities		Miles	Administering Agency
Inaja Memorial Nature	357	11/16/79	0	F, I	N	0.5	Cleveland NF
Jackass Creek	417	12/13/79	0	F, H, M	N	3.0	Sequoia NF
Jedediah Smith	45	3/21/74	0	B, F, H	N	26.0	Sacramento County Parks
King Range	6	6/1/71	0	F, H	N	10.0	BLM
Kings River	365	11/27/79	0	F, H	N	3.0	Sierra NF
Lake Tahoe Bicycle	389	12/13/79	0	F, B	N	3.5	Lake Tahoe NF
Lake Tahoe Bike and Pedestrian	78	2/23/76	0	B, F	A	5.0	Placer County Dept. of Parks
Lassen Peak	554	3/20/81	0	F	N	2.5	Lassen Volcanic NP
Lewis Creek	687	3/29/82	0	F	N	3.7	Sierra NF
Lost Lake Nature	69	10/1/75	0	F	N	2.0	Fresno County Dept.
McGowen	656	10/11/81	0	S	A	11.0	Lassen NF
Methuselah	720	1/28/83	0	F	N	4.2	Inyo NF
Middle Fork Applegate	579	5/18/81	0	F, H, M	N	6.1	Rogue River NF
Muir Woods Interpretive	83	3/1/76	0	F, C	A	0.9	Muir Woods NM
Noble Canyon	685	3/29/82	0	F, H	N	8.0	Cleveland NF
North Shore	306	10/5/79	0	F, H, V	N	5.2	San Bernardino NF
Observatory	371	11/27/79	0	F	N	2.1	Cleveland NF
Penitencia Creek	42	10/31/74	0	C	A	5.5	San Jose Dept. of Rec. and Parks
Piedra Blanca	132	12/23/77	0	F, H	N	18.2	Los Padres NF
Pine Crest Lake	358	11/16/79	0	F	N	3.6	Stanislaus NF
Pony Express	370	11/27/79	0	F, H, S	N	10.0	Eldorado NF
Rancheria Falls	522	12/16/80	0	F	N	1.0	Sierra NF
Salmon Summit	410	12/13/79	0	F, H	N	5.2	Six Rivers NF
Santa Ana River	100	11/3/76	0	F, H	N	10.0	Riverside County Parks Dept.
Santa Ana River	80	3/12/76	0	F, B, H	N	15.7	Orange County Admin. Bldg.
Santa Cruz–Aliso	387	12/13/79	0	F, H	N	12.5	Los Padres NF
Shadow of the Giants	210	12/18/79	0	F, I	N	1.0	Sierra NF
Silver Moccassin	279	8/17/79	0	F, H	N	15.5	Angeles NF
Sisson-Callahan	384	12/13/79	0	F, H	N	9.0	Shasta-Trinity NF
Sled Ridge	429	2/1/80	0	F, V	N	8.9	Mendocino NF
South Fork Trinity River	469	5/6/80	0	F, H, V	N	8.0	Shasta-Trinity NF
South Kelsey	315	10/5/79	0	F, H, S	N	14.0	Six Rivers NF
South Yuba	7	6/1/71	0	F, H	N	10.5	BLM
Spencer Meadow	368	11/27/79	0	F, H	N	6.0	Lassen NF
Squaw Leap	591	6/8/81	0	F, H	N	10.5	BLM
Sugarloaf	284	8/17/79	0	F	N	4.0	San Bernardino NF
Summit	327	10/5/79	0	F, H, V, S	N	12.0	Sequoia NF
Tidelands	639	8/12/81	0	F, B	N	1.3	FWS
Tomales Point	555	3/20/81	0	F, H, B	A	4.1	Point Reyes NS
Toro Riding and Hiking	61	6/16/75	0	F, H	N	6.0	Monterey County Parks
Traveler's Home	367	11/27/79	0	F, H	N	9.5	Mendocino NF
Twenty Mule Team	59	6/16/75	0	F, C	A	12.0	CA City Park

843

Name	Trail No.	Date	Season[a]	Uses[b]	Surface[c]	Length (miles)	Administering Agency[d]
West Fork	517	12/4/80	0	F, B	N	6.8	Angeles NF
Western States Pioneer	70	12/5/75	0	F, H	N	50.0	CA Dept. of Parks
Whitney Portal	360	11/16/79	0	F	N	3.9	Inyo NF
York	49	8/22/74	0	F, H	N	3.5	Oakland Office of Parks and Rec.
Zumwalt Meadow	671	2/5/82	0	F	N	1.5	Sequoia and King's Canyon NP
Total						674.3	
				Colorado			
Apex	181	11/13/78	0	F, H	N	3.3	Jefferson County Open Space
Barr	346	11/16/79	0	F, H	N	13.0	Pike–San Isabel NF
Bear Creek	347	11/16/79	0	F	N	4.2	Uncompahgre NF
Calico	349	11/16/79	0	F, H, V, M	N	6.5	San Juan NF
Crag Crest	150	3/14/78	0	F, H	N	11.0	Grand Mesa NF
Crag Crest	727	7/19/83	1	M, S	N	7.5	Grand Mesa NF
Devil's Head	352	11/16/79	0	F, H	N	1.3	Pike–San Isabel NF
Fish Creek	398	12/13/79	0	F, H	N	10.5	Routt NF
Grays Peak	402	12/13/79	0	F	N	5.0	Arapaho–Roosevelt NF
Greyrock	403	12/13/79	0	F	N	3.3	Arapaho–Roosevelt NF
Highline Canal	11	6/1/71	0	F, B, S, H	N	18.0	South Suburban Metro
Highline Canal	31	1/2/72	0	F, B, S, H	N, A	13.0	Aurora Parks and Rec.
Highline Canal	149	8/9/78	0	H, F, B, S	N	17.0	Colorado Div. of Parks
Highline Canal	171	3/8/78	0	F, B	A	13.2	Denver Parks and Rec.
Highline Loop	350	11/16/79	0	F, H, M	N	20.0	San Juan NF
Lake Fork	344	11/16/79	0	F, H, V	N	7.1	Rio Grande NF
Mount Evans	395	12/13/79	0	F	N	0.3	Arapaho–Roosevelt NF
Mount McConnel	611	7/20/81	0	F	N	3.3	Arapaho–Roosevelt NF
Petroglyph Point	692	4/13/82	0	F	N	2.3	Mesa Verde NP
Platte River Greenway	156	4/25/78	0	F, B	A	7.0	Colorado Div. of Parks
Round Mountain	479	3/2/81	0	F	N	4.5	Arapaho–Roosevelt NF
Swamp Park	466	5/6/80	0	F, H, V	N	17.0	Routt NF
Two Elk	397	12/13/79	0	F, H, V	N	7.0	White River NF
Vail Pass	474	7/29/80	0	B, F, S, C, M	A, N	21.0	White River NF
West Lost Trail Creek	345	11/16/79	0	F, H, V	N	7.5	Rio Grande NF
Wheeler Tenmile	396	12/13/79	0	F, H	N	10.0	White River NF
White House Ranch Nature	495	10/3/80	0	S, C, F	A	22.0	CO Springs Park and Rec. Dept.
Total						255.8	

Name	Number	Date					Agency
Connecticut							
Sleeping Giant	106	3/23/77	0	F	N	25.0	CT Dept. of Environmental Protection
Southern New England Trunk Line	610	7/20/81	0	H, V, F, S, B	N	28.0	Southern New England Trail Conference
Total						53.0	
Delaware							
Hagley Museum Trail System	755	9/11/85	0	F	C, N	0.8	Hagley Museum and Library
Pinelands Nature	578	5/23/81	0	F	N, W	1.2	DE Div. of Parks and Rec.
Total						2.0	
District of Columbia							
Black History	766	2/13/87	0	F, B, I	C	7.0	NPS, Capitol Region
Fort Circle Parks	25	6/1/71	0	B, F	A, N	19.5	NPS, Capitol Region
Total						26.5	
Florida							
Apalachicola Bluffs	95	9/14/76	0	F	N	0.8	FL Dept. of Natural Resources
Discovery	435	10/5/79	0	F, I, C	N	0.1	Apalachicola NF
Felix Lake Nature	594	6/8/81	0	F	N	1.6	Tyndall Air Force Base HQ
Hell's Bay Canoe	541	3/20/81	0	W	N	8.0	Everglades NP
Jackson	91	6/15/76	0	F	N	21.0	FL Dept. of Agriculture
Lake Arbuckle Hiking	593	6/8/81	0	F	N	16.0	Avon Park Air Force Range
Ocala	110	3/1/77	0	F	N	68.0	Ocala NF
Rice Creek	85	4/28/76	0	F	N	3.0	Hudson Pulp and Paper Co.
University Nature	159	5/19/78	0	F, C	A	12.0	University of N. Florida
Upper Ben's Lake Nature	595	6/8/81	0	F	N	0.7	Dir. of Civil Engineering
Wilderness Waterway	540	3/20/81	0	W	N	99.0	Everglades NP
Total						230.2	
Georgia							
Anna Ruby Falls	257	5/8/79	0	F, I	N	0.4	Chattahoochee-Oconee NF
Arkaquah	301	10/5/79	0	F	N	5.5	Chattahoochee-Oconee NF
Bartram	124	11/23/75	0	F	N	22.0	Chattahoochee-Oconee NF
Bluff	617	11/19/81	0	F	N	4.5	Chickamauga and Chattanooga NMP
Bush Mountain	165	6/23/79	0	F	N	0.8	Atlanta Bureau Parks and Rec. Outdoor Activity Center
Callaway Gardens	451	4/28/80	0	F	N	9.9	Ida Cason Callaway Foundation
Cason J. Callaway	452	4/28/80	0	F	N	8.0	Mrs. Carson J. Callaway; SR
Duncan Ridge	480	8/18/80	0	F	N	30.6	Chattahoochee-Oconee NF
Jacks Knob	465	5/6/80	1	F	N	4.5	Chattahoochee-Oconee NF

Name	Trail No.	Date	Season[a]	Uses[b]	Surface[c]	Length (miles)	Administering Agency[d]
Okefenokee Wilderness Canoe	600	6/8/81	O	W	N	102.0	FWS
Stone Mountain	24	6/1/71	O	F	N	6.5	Stone Mt. Memorial Park Assn.
Tumbling Waters Nature	596	6/8/81	O	F	N	1.0	ACE
Total						195.7	
				Hawaii			
Crater Rim	664	2/5/82	O	F	N	11.3	Hawaii Volcanoes NP
Halemau'u	667	2/5/82	O	F, H	N	10.2	Haleakala NP
Kaupo	668	2/5/82	O	F, H	N	3.5	Haleakala NP
Ke Ala Kahiko	665	2/5/82	O	F	N	1.0	Hawaii Volcanoes NP
Sliding Sands	666	2/5/82	O	F, H	N	7.5	Haleakala NP
Total						33.5	
				Idaho			
Anderson Butte	308	10/5/79	O	F, H, V	N	12.0	Nez Perce NF
Bald Mountain Trail	793	9/20/92	O	F, B, S	N	5.0	BLM, Shoshone District
Bear Valley	281	8/17/79	O	F, H, V	N	7.0	Salmon NF
Big Creek	329	10/18/79	O	F, H	N	41.0	ID Panhandle NF
Big Springs Water	532	1/8/81	O	C, W	N	5.0	Targhee NF
Big Wood River	282	8/17/79	O	F, H, S	N	5.0	Sawtooth NF
Big Wood River	282	8/17/79	O	F, H, S	N	0.5	BLM
Caribou Ridge	731	7/19/83	O	F	N	4.9	ID Panhandle NF
Chilco Mountain	716	10/25/82	O	M, H, F	N	6.3	ID Panhandle NF
Chipmunk Rapids	506	10/24/80	O	F, H, V	N	12.7	ID Panhandle NF
Coeur d'Alene River	161	6/5/78	O	F, H, V	N	14.0	Coeur d'Alene NF
Colgate Licks Nature	289	9/14/79	O	F, I	N	0.6	Clearwater NF
Crawford–Yellow Pine	364	11/27/79	O	M	N	65.0	Boise NF
Divide–Twin Creek	286	9/14/79	O	F, H, V	N	11.0	Salmon NF
East Boyd–Glover	311	10/5/79	O	F, H, V	N	14.5	Nez Perce NF
English Point	472	6/13/80	O	F, S, H, V	N	5.2	Coeur d'Alene NF
Fishhook Creek Nature	293	9/14/79	O	F, I	N	0.2	Sawtooth NF
Hanna Flat	129	12/22/77	O	F, C, S, I	A	0.3	ID Panhandle NF
Heaven's Gate	209	12/18/78	O	F, I	N	0.2	Nez Perce NF
High Line	254	5/8/79	O	F, H, V	N	48.0	Caribou NF
Hulls Gulch Environmental	489	5/2/80	O	F	N	3.5	Boise NF; BLM
Independence Creek	418	12/13/79	O	F, H, V	N	13.7	ID Panhandle NF
Jackass Ridge Snowmobile	471	6/13/80	O	S, M	N	41.0	Coeur d'Alene NF
Knapp Creek–Loon Creek	278	8/17/79	O	F, H	N	15.0	Challis NF
Lakeshore	164	6/7/78	O	F, C, S	A	7.0	ID Panhandle NF

Name	No.	Date		Use		Miles	Agency
Lava Ridge	413	12/13/79	0	F, H, V	N	7.0	Payette NF
Major Fenn	134	1/31/78	0	F	N	0.6	Clearwater NF
Marble Creek	748	4/5/84	3, 4	F, H	N	26.7	ID Panhandle NF
Meadow Creek	470	6/13/80	0	F, H	N	15.0	Nez Perce NF
Mill Creek-Main Fork	241	3/6/79	0	F, H	N	1.8	Challis NF
Mineral Ridge	691	4/1/82	0	F	N	3.0	BLM
Nelson Ridge	208	12/18/78	0	F, H, V	N	18.0	ID Panhandle NF
Palisades	240	3/6/79	0	F, H	N	7.9	Targhee NF
Sheep Creek	292	9/14/79	0	F, H	N	12.0	Boise NF
Sheeprock Overlook	239	3/6/79	0	F, I	N	0.6	Payette NF
Snake River	533	1/28/81	0	F, H	N	21.0	Wallowa-Whitman NF
Two Top Snowmobile	392	12/13/79	0	F, M	N	48.5	Targhee NF
White Pine	379	12/13/79	0	F, H, V	N	3.5	Clearwater NF
Whoop-Um-Up Ski	392a	12/13/79	0	F, S	N	2.5	Boise NF
Wright's Creek	310	10/5/79	0	F, H, V	N	12.0	Caribou NF
Total						518.7	

Illinois

Name	No.	Date		Use		Miles	Agency
Camp Camfield Nature	631	11/19/81	0	F, I	N	3.0	ACE
Chief Illini	781	7/2/90	2, 3, 4	F, N	N	12.0	ACE
Eberley Park Fitness	674	2/5/82	0	F	N	1.5	Sterling Park District
Great Western Nature	712	8/6/82	0	F, B, M, H, S	N, A	14.5	Forest Preserve Dist. of Kane County
Greenbelt Bikeway	496	10/9/80	0	B, F	N	1.6	Champaign Park District
Illinois Prairie Path	21	6/2/71	0	B, F, H	N	27.8	Illinois Prairie Path, Inc.
Inspiration Point	431	2/1/80	0	F	N	0.8	Shawnee NF
Lake Forest Bike	675	2/5/82	0	B, F	A, C	3.4	Lake Forest Parks and Forestry Dept.
Red Cedar Hiking	592	6/8/81	0	F	N	16.0	Giant City State Park
Rim Rock	409	12/13/79	0	F	N	0.9	Shawnee NF
Roby Recreation	637	11/19/81	0	F, B	C	1.3	Champaign Park District
Shag Bark Nature Preserve	711	8/6/82	0	F	N, W	1.1	Round Lake Area Park District
Starved Rock State Park	527	1/12/81	0	F	N	11.0	Starved Rock State Park
Virgil Gilman Nature	526	1/12/81	0	F, B, H, S	N	3.5	Fox Valley Park District
Total						98.4	

Indiana

Name	No.	Date		Use		Miles	Agency
Adventure	337	11/21/79	0	F	N	30.0	IN Dept. of Natural Resources
Calmut	89	5/28/76	0	B, F	N	9.2	IN Dept. of Natural Resources
Dobbs Park System	709	8/6/82	0	F, I	N	2.5	Terre Haute Park and Rec. Dept.
Lincoln Boyhood	626	11/19/81	0	F	N	1.9	Lincoln Boyhood NM
Two Lakes Loop	415	12/13/79	0	F	N	12.2	Wayne-Hoosier NF
Wabash Heritage	490	9/8/80	0	F, S	N	2.0	Tippecanoe County Park and Rec. Board

Name	Trail No.	Date	Season[a]	Uses[b]	Surface[c]	Length (miles)	Administering Agency[d]
Wabash Heritage	767	7/15/87	0	F, W, S	N	5.9	Tippecanoe County Park and Rec. Board
Whitewater Gorge	708	8/6/82	0	F, I	N, W	3.5	Richmond Dept. of Parks and Rec.
Witmer Trace	725	11/22/83	0	F, I	N	1.1	Elkhart Park and Rec. Dept.
Total						68.3	
Iowa							
Blackhawk	486	9/4/80	0	F	N	0.5	Burlington Parks Dept.
Cedar Greenbelt	450	4/24/80	0	F, S	N	2.3	Indian Creek Nature
Cedar Valley Nature	749	10/13/84	0	F, B, S, I	N	42.0	Linn County Conservation Bd.; Black Hawk County Conservation Bd.
Des Moines River	784	11/16/90	0	F, B, M, S	A	7.8	IA Dept. of Natural Resources
Des Moines R.–Saylorville Lake	784	11/26/90	0	F, B, M, S	A	13.7	ACE
Herbert Hoover Prairie	609	7/21/81	0	F, S	N	1.0	Herbert Hoover Natl. Historic Site
Heritage	758	5/27/85	0	F, B, M, C, W, S	N, W	25.7	Heritage Trail, IA Rails to Trails
Mad Creek Greenbelt	498	10/9/80	0	B, F	N	1.2	Muscatine Parks and Rec. Dept.
Matsell Bridge	647	11/1/81	0	F, H, C	N	8.4	Linn County Conservation Bd.
Sac Fox	54	4/1/75	0	F, B, H, S	N, A	5.0	Indian Creek Center
Total						107.6	
Kansas							
Buffalo Track Canyon	529	1/12/81	0	F	N	0.5	KS Park and Resources Authority
Bur Oak Nature	723	8/12/83	2, 3	F	N	0.7	ACE
Dornwood Park Nature	184	11/22/78	0	F	N	1.0	Topeka Parks and Rec.
Elk River Hiking	632	11/19/81	0	F	N	9.5	ACE
Fort Leavenworth–Gateway	570	5/5/81	0	F, H	N	52.3	U.S. Army Arms. Center; Ft. Leavenworth
International Forest	93	6/1/76	0	F, C	N	0.6	Atchison City Hall
Kaw River	499	1/9/80	0	F	N	4.0	Lawrence Parks and Rec. Dept.
Perry Lake	114	6/29/77	0	F	N	10.0	ACE
Post Oak Nature	252	3/28/78	0	F	N	0.7	KS State Park Authority
Table Mound Hiking	251	3/28/78	0	F	N	2.8	KS Dept. of Wildlife and Parks
Webster and S. Solomon	530	1/12/81	0	F	N	10.0	KS Park and Resources Authority
Woodard Nature	170	8/9/78	0	F	N	0.5	Dillion Nature Center
Total						92.6	

Kentucky

Name	No.	Date		Use		Miles	Manager
Anderson Woodland	335	11/21/79	0	F	N	0.3	ACE
Eagle Falls	695	4/13/82	0	F	N	1.0	Frankfort Dept. of Parks
Grayson Lake Shoreline	174	8/14/78	0	F	N	1.8	ACE
Hillman Heritage	72	11/1/75	0	F	N	10.0	TVA
Jenny Wiley	475	7/29/80	0	F, C	A	213.0	Fivco Area Development District; Jenny Wiley Trails Conference
Kleber Wildlife Management Area	599	6/8/81	0	F	N	2.0	Dept. of Fish and Wildlife Resources
Long Creek	22	6/1/71	0	F, C	A	0.3	TVA
Natural Bridge	724	11/30/83	0	F	N	0.5	KY Dept. of Parks
Red River Gorge	183	11/17/78	0	F	N	34.0	Daniel Boone NF
Redbird Fitness	390	12/13/79	0	F	N	0.2	Daniel Boone NF
Sheltowee Trace	261	6/22/79	0	F	N	137.0	Daniel Boone NF
Sheltowee Trace	261	6/22/79	0	F	N	200.0	KY Dept. of Parks
Tioga Falls Historic Nature	585	6/1/81	0	F	N	2.0	U.S. Army Armor Center and Ft. Knox
Wilderness Road	694	4/13/82	0	F	N	2.2	Frankford Dept. of Parks
Total						604.3	

Louisiana

Name	No.	Date		Use		Miles	Manager
Acadiana Park	445	2/26/80	0	F	N	3.0	Lafayette Dept. of Rec., Education, and Culture
Chicot Nature	643	11/19/80	0	F	N	10.2	Baton Rouge Office State Parks
Cypress Nature	253	4/4/79	0	F, C, S	A	4.0	Cypress-Black Bayou Rec. Area
Jefferson Linear	698	4/13/82	0	F, B, C	A	8.2	Baton Rouge Dept. Parks and Rec.
John James Audubon	444	2/26/80	0	F, H, B	N	2.8	City of New Orleans
Red River	92	6/18/76	0	B, F	N	5.3	City of Shreveport Parks
Scotlandville Bike	488	9/4/80	0	B, F	N	3.5	Baton Rouge Rec. and Park Commission
Sugar Cane	355	12/16/79	0	F	N	4.8	Kisatchie NF
Wild Azalea	163	6/7/78	0	F	N	30.0	Kisatchie NF
Total						71.8	

Maine

Name	No.	Date		Use		Miles	Manager
Dorr Mountain	623	11/19/81	3, 4	F	N	3.5	Acadia NP
Sargent Mountain	658	2/5/82	0	F, S, B, H	N	4.5	Acadia NP
Total						8.0	

Maryland

Name	No.	Date		Use		Miles	Manager
Touch of Nature	47	5/1/74	0	C	N	0.3	Maryland Park Service

Name	Trail No.	Date	Season[a]	Uses[b]	Surface[c]	Length (miles)	Administering Agency[d]
Massachusetts							
Atlantic White Cedar Swamp	659	2/5/82	O	F	N	1.2	Cape Cod National Seashore
Caratunk Wildlife Refuge	514	11/28/80	O	F, S	N	5.0	Audubon Society R.I.
Derby Wharf	660	2/5/82	O	F, B, C	C	0.5	Salem Maritime Natl. Historic Site
Dr. Paul Dudley White	75	1/14/76	O	F, B	A, C	6.5	Boston Metropolitan Dist. Comm.
Freedom	76	1/14/76	O	F	C	2.5	Boston Natl. Historic Park
Lowell Canal Heritage	584	6/1/81	O	F, W	N	2.6	Lowell Natl. Historic Park
Northfield Mountain	88	5/18/76	O	H, F, S	N	30.0	Northeast Utilities Service Co.
Quincy Presidential	625	11/19/81	O	F, B, C	A	10.5	City of Quincy
Saugus Iron Works Nature	775	6/22/89	O	F	N	0.5	Saugus Iron Works Natl. Historic Site
Southern New England Trunkline	610	7/1/81	O	H, V, F, S, B	N	3.0	Southern New England Trail Conference
Total						62.3	
Michigan							
Agonikak Snowmobile	195	12/8/78	1	M	N	11.0	Ottawa NF
Bay De Noc–Grand Island	461	5/6/80	O	F, H	N	40.0	Hiawatha NF
Belle Isle Bicycle	33	1/2/72	2, 3, 4	B	A	0.9	Detroit Parks and Rec. Dept.
Binder Winter Park Nordic	672	2/5/82	1	F, S	N	4.4	Binder Winter Park, Inc.
Caberfae Way Snowmobile	198	12/8/78	1	M, F	N	36.0	Huron-Manistee NF
Driggs River Nature	706	7/9/82	O	F	N, W	1.3	FWS
For-Mar Nature Reserve	500	10/9/80	O	F, S, I	N, A	3.7	Genesee County Parks and Rec. Commission
Gallup Park	673	2/5/82	O	B, F, S	A, N	4.5	Ann Arbor Parks and Rec. Dept.
Jordan River Pathway	501	10/9/80	O	F, I	N	18.0	MI Dept. of Natural Resources
Mackenzie Touring	197	12/8/78	O	F, S	N	8.3	Huron-Manistee NF
Mackinac Island Trail System	491	9/8/80	O	B, F, H	N, A	15.0	MI Dept. of Natural Resources
Munising Cross Country Ski	736	3/30/84	1	S	N	9.7	Pictured Rocks Natl. Lakeshore
Pine Ridge Nature	707	7/9/82	O	F, S	N, W	1.9	FWS
Potawatomi-Gorge Falls	196	12/8/78	O	F, S	N	0.6	Ottawa NF
Rapid River Cross-Country	456	5/6/80	1	S	N	9.0	Hiawatha NF
Riverfront	628	11/19/81	O	F, B	A, W	1.8	Lansing Dept. of Parks and Rec.
Saline River	485	9/8/80	O	F, B, S, I	N	1.2	Saline Parks and Beautification Commission
Shiawassee Wildlife	546	3/20/81	2, 3, 4	F, I	N	5.0	Shiawassee NWR
State Line-Mile Post Zero	411	12/13/79	O	F	N	0.4	Ottawa NF
Wildwood Pathway	502	10/9/80	O	F, S, I	N	2.6	Isabella Parks and Rec. Dept.
Total						175.3	

Trail name	No.	Date		Activities	Access	Miles	Managing agency
Minnesota							
Congdon Creek Park	67	8/22/75	0	F, S	N	0.8	Duluth Parks and Rec. Dept.
Cut Foot Sioux	441	2/1/80	0	F, S, H	N	22.3	Chippewa NF
Heartland State	785	7/3/91	0	H, S, F, M, B	A, N	28.0	Trails and Waterways Unit; MN Dept. of Natural Resources
Lester Park Nature	68	9/22/75	0	F, S	N	0.8	Duluth Parks and Rec. Dept.
Mahnomen Wildlife	552	3/20/81	0	F, S, I	N	3.0	Sherburne NWR
Oakdale Park Nature	722	8/12/83	0	F, S	N	5.0	City of Oakdale
Ritter Farm Park	493	9/10/80	0	F, S	N	15.0	Lakeville Park and Rec. Dept.
Riverside Park	682	2/5/82	0	S, F	N	1.3	St. Cloud Park and Rec. Dept.
Shingobee	684	3/29/82	0	S, F	N	6.0	Chippewa NF
South Washington	492	9/10/80	0	F, S	N	5.3	Washington County Parks
Superior Hiking	457	5/6/80	0	F	N	4.3	Superior NF
Taconite	376	12/13/79	0	F, M	N	11.5	Superior NF
Total						103.3	
Mississippi							
Black Creek	615	1/28/85	0	F	N	41.0	DeSoto NF
Burnside Park Nature	151	4/4/78	0	F	N	2.0	Philadelphia Parks and Rec. Commission
Riverside Park Nature	152	4/4/78	0	F	N	2.0	Jackson Parks and Rec. Dept.
Rocky Ridge Horse	741	6/29/84	0	H, B	A	8.0	Vicksburg District
Schockaloe	37	2/14/69	0	F, H	N	23.0	Bienville NF
Tuxachanie	307	10/5/79	0	F	N	20.0	DeSoto NF
Total						96.0	
Missouri							
Berryman	434	2/1/80	0	F, H	N	24.0	Mark Twain NF
Crane Lake	432	2/1/80	0	F	N	5.0	Mark Twain NF
Elephant Rocks Braille	41	10/12/73	0	F, C	A	1.0	Jefferson City Div. of Parks and Rec.
Johnson Tract	782	10/30/90	0	F	N, A	5.0	ACE
Lost Creek	679	2/5/82	0	F	N	1.0	ACE
Mingo Boardwalk Nature	566	4/23/81	0	F, C	A	1.0	Mingo NWR
Mudlick	503	10/9/80	0	F, H	N	10.2	Jefferson City Dept. of Natural Resources
Pine Ridge	678	2/5/82	0	F	N	0.5	ACE
Ridge Runner	433	2/1/80	0	F, H	N	23.0	Mark Twain NF
Total						70.7	

Name	Trail No.	Date	Season[a]	Uses[b]	Surface[c]	Length (miles)	Administering Agency[d]
				Montana			
Baldy Lookout-Lake	606	5/15/81	O	F, H, V	N	3.0	Lolo NF
Basin Lakes	374	11/27/79	O	F, H	N	3.8	Custer NF
Bear Trap	794	9/20/92	2, 3, 4	F, W	N	9.0	Dillion Resource Area; BLM
Big Hole	509	10/24/80	O	F, H	N	3.8	Bitterroot NF
Big Hole Battlefield	117	8/8/77	O	F, H	A	0.5	Big Hole National Battlefield
Blacktail–Wild Bill	219	1/5/79	O	M	N	13.5	Flathead NF
Blue Mountain Equestrian	157	4/21/78	O	F, H	N	6.0	Lolo NF
Blue Mountain Nature	158	4/21/78	O	F, I	N	0.2	Lolo NF
Boulder River Natural Bridge and Falls	534	3/5/81	O	F	N	0.2	Dept. of Fish, Wildlife, and Parks; Gallatin NF
Bridger Mountains	200	12/18/78	O	F	N	24.0	Gallatin NF
Cascade Falls Nature	427	2/1/80	O	F, I	N	0.7	Lolo NF
Como Lake Loop	233	2/7/79	O	F, H, V, S	N	7.0	Bitterroot NF
Crown Mountain	581	5/18/81	O	F, H, V, S	N	7.6	Lewis and Clark NF
Crystal Lake Shoreline	175	8/22/78	O	F	N	1.7	Lewis and Clark NF
Danny On Memorial	583	5/18/81	O	F, H, V	N	6.4	Flathead NF
Deep Creek "Figure 8" Loop	378	12/13/79	O	F, H, V, S, M	N	18.5	Lewis and Clark NF
Elk Mountain	217	1/5/79	O	F, H, V, S, M	N	9.0	Flathead NF
Gallatin Riverside	419	10/19/79	O	F, H	N	3.2	Gallatin NF
Garnet Mountain	420	10/19/79	O	F, H	N	4.0	Gallatin NF
Garnet Winter	746	5/11/84	O	S, M	N	30.3	BLM
Grasshopper Ridge	462	5/6/80	O	S, F	N	3.5	Beaverhead NF
Griffin Creek	205	12/18/78	O	F, H, V, S, M	N	10.5	Flathead NF
Hanging Valley and Vigilante	214	1/5/79	O	F, H, S	N	7.0	Helena NF
Haystack Mountain	377	12/13/79	O	F	N	3.0	Deerlodge NF
Holland Falls	730	7/19/83	O	F	N	1.5	Flathead NF
Ingalls Mountain–Sylvia Lake	204	12/18/78	O	F, H, V	N	3.3	Flathead NF
Jones Creek	582	5/18/81	O	F, H, V	N	7.5	Lewis and Clark NF
Little North Fork	747	7/5/84	O	F	N	0.1	Kootenai NF
Lodgepole Ski-Touring	437	11/5/79	O	S	N	3.5	Deerlodge NF
Lost Cabin Lake	421	12/13/79	O	F, H, V	N	5.0	Deerlodge NF
Louise Lake	515	11/10/80	O	F, H, M	N	2.9	Deerlodge NF
Lupine Lake	220	1/5/79	O	F, H, V, S, M	N	3.0	Flathead NF
May Creek	523	12/16/80	O	F, H, S	N	7.0	Beaverhead NF
Morrell Falls	507	10/24/80	O	F, M, V, S, H	N	2.5	Lolo NF

Name	No.	Date		Activities	Type	Miles	Agency
Mt. Helena	250	3/16/79	0	F, S, M	N	7.0	Helena Parks and Rec. Dept.
Palisade Falls	131	12/1/77	0	F, C	N	0.3	Gallatin NF
Palisade Mountain	477	8/18/80	0	F, H, S, V	N	6.0	Bitterroot NF
Parkside Ski	520	12/16/80	0	S	N	8.1	Custer NF
Pattee Canyon	428	2/1/80	0	S, F	N	6.5	Lolo NF
Pioneer Loop	416	12/13/79	0	F, V, M, S	N	35.0	Beaverhead NF
Pulpit Mountain	717	5/15/81	0	F, C, M	A	5.0	Kootenai NF
Ralph L. Thayer Memorial	740	4/17/84	0	F, I	N	18.0	Flathead NF
Refuge Pt. Cross Country Ski	508	12/16/80	0	S	N	2.6	Gallatin NF
S. Fork Teton and Blacktail	234	2/7/79	0	F, H, M, V	N	28.0	Lewis and Clark NF
Silver Run Ski	521	12/16/80	0	S, F	N	6.8	Custer NF
Skookum Butte	430	2/1/80	0	F, H	N	1.0	Lolo NF
Skyline	728	7/19/83	0	F, H	N	22.0	Kootenai NF
State Line	510	10/24/80	0	F, B, H	N	18.3	Lolo NF
Tally Mountain–Bill Creek	453	5/6/80	0	F, C	A	7.0	Flathead NF
Trout Creek Loop	718	10/25/82	0	F	N	22.2	Kootenai NF
Two Medicine–Elk Calf	235	2/7/79	0	F, H, V, M, S	N	18.2	Lewis and Clark NF
Two Top Snowmobile	216	1/5/79	0	F, M	N	28.0	Gallatin NF
Vinal Creek	729	7/19/83	0	F	N	25.0	Kootenai NF
Whitefish Divide–Smokey	218	1/5/79	0	F, S, M	N	11.0	Flathead NF
Wild Bill's Lake	375	9/20/79	0	F, C	N	0.5	Custer NF
Wise River–Elkhorn	614	9/14/81	0	M	N	23.1	Beaverhead NF
Total						512.3	
Nebraska							
Fontenelle Forest	16	6/1/71	0	F	N	3.9	Fontenelle Forest Nature Center
Schramm Park	263	7/6/79	0	F	N	3.0	NE Game and Parks
Scott Lookout	393	9/25/79	0	F	N	3.0	NE NF
Trooper	394	12/13/79	0	F, H	N	4.5	NE NF
Wilderness Park	104	2/16/77	0	F, S	N	13.0	Lincoln Parks and Rec.
Total						27.4	
Nevada							
Grimes Point	162	6/13/78	0	F	N	0.6	BLM
Mount Charleston	339	11/16/79	0	F, H	N	10.0	Toiyabe NF
Ruby Crest	244	5/6/79	0	F, H, M, S	N	40.0	Humboldt NF
Toiyabe Crest	242	3/6/79	0	F, H	N	72.0	Toiyabe NF
Wheeler Peak	245	3/5/79	0	F, H, M	N	10.0	Humboldt NF
Total						132.6	

Name	Trail No.	Date	Season[a]	Uses[b]	Surface[c]	Length (miles)	Administering Agency[d]
New Hampshire							
Boulder Loop	454	5/6/80	3	F	N	2.8	White Mountain NF
Sabbaday Brook	455	5/6/80	0	F, C	N	0.4	White Mountain NF
Total						3.2	
New Jersey							
Delaware and Raritan Canal	789	5/22/92	0	F, B, H, S, W	N	60.0	Trenton Dept. of Environmental Protection
Palisades Long Path	27	6/1/71	0	F	N	11.2	Palisades Interstate Park Commission
Palisades Shore	28	6/1/71	0	F	N	11.2	Palisades Interstate Park Commission
Patriots Path	476	8/21/80	0	F, B, H, S	A	20.2	Morris County Park Commission
Total						102.6	
New Mexico							
Bandelier Backcountry	703	4/13/82	0	F	N	30.0	Bandelier NM
Canones Creek	340	11/16/79	0	F, H, V	N	12.5	Santa Fe NF
Carlsbad Caverns	700	4/13/83	0	F, C	A	3.0	Carlsbad Cavern NP
Carolino Canyon Nature	567	4/23/81	0	F, C	A	0.5	Albuquerque Parks and General Services
Catwalk	206	12/18/78	0	F	N	2.2	Gila NF
Cienega Nature	202	12/18/78	0	F, I, C	A	0.2	Cibola NF
Columbine-Twining	207	12/18/78	0	F, H, S	N	14.0	Carson NF
Dog Canyon	528	1/21/81	0	F, H	N	4.2	Lincoln NF
Dripping Springs	795	9/20/92	0	F, I	N	1.5	BLM, Las Cruces
El Morro	701	4/13/83	0	F, C	A, N	2.0	El Morro NM
Fort Bayard Wood Haul	333	10/19/79	0	F, H	N	11.5	Gila NF
Frijoles Canyon	702	4/13/83	0	F, C	A, N	9.0	Bandelier NM
Jicarita Peak	305	10/5/79	0	F, H, V	N	23.0	Carson NF
Mount Taylor	440	2/1/80	0	F, H	N	4.0	Cibola NF
Organ Mountain	12	6/1/71	0	F, H	N	8.7	BLM
Paseo del Bosque Bicycle	155	4/14/78	0	B, F	A	5.0	Albuquerque Parks and General Services
Paseo del Nordeste Bike	683	2/5/82	0	B, F, C	A	6.2	Albuquerque Parks and General Services
Rim	179	11/3/78	0	F, M, S, V	N	13.0	Lincoln NF
Rio Bonito Petroglyph	796	9/20/92	0	F	N	1.4	BLM, Roswell District Office
Rio Grande	588	6/8/81	0	F, H	N	12.0	BLM
Santa Cruz Lake	589	6/8/81	0	F	N	6.4	BLM
Sawmill Brook	332	10/19/79	0	F, H	N	8.5	Gila NF
South Boundary	704	5/10/82	0	F, H, V	N	20.0	Carson NF
Tent Rocks Trail	797	9/20/92	0	F	N	2.0	BLM, Albuquerque District
Winsor	341	11/16/79	0	F, H, V, M, S	N	9.0	Santa Fe NF
Total						209.8	

New York

Name	No.	Date		Type	Mgmt	Miles	Administering Agency
Beaver Lake Nature Center	483	9/4/80	0	F, S, C, W	N, W	8.3	Beaver Lake Nature Center
Cassadaga-Conewango	663	2/5/82	0	W	N	53.0	Chautauqua County Parks Commission
Central Park Heritage	334	11/19/79	0	F, B	N, A	3.7	N.Y.C. Dept. of Parks and Rec.
Crandall Park Ski	77	2/1/76	0	S, F, B	N	2.2	Glen Falls Rec. Dept.
Erie Canal Heritage	743	7/17/84	0	F, B, S	A, C	65.3	Albany Dept. of Transportation
Harriman Long Path	29	6/1/71	0	F	N	16.0	Palisades Interstate Park Commission
Hudson-Mohawk Urban Cultural	719	5/16/74	0	F, B, V	N	28.0	Hudson-Mohawk Urban Cultural Park Commission
Interloken	226	2/7/79	0	F, M, V, S	N	12.0	Finger Lakes NF
Kings Highway–Pine Bush	754	9/11/85	0	F, H, S, I	N	4.0	Albany Dept. of Parks and Rec.
Long Island Greenbelt	662	2/5/82	0	F	N	34.0	Long Is. Greenbelt Trail Conference; Long Is. State Parks and Rec. Commission
Old Erie Canal State Park	654	11/27/81	0	F, B, W, C, M	A	35.0	N.Y. State Parks and Rec.
Robert Frost	273	6/29/79	0	F, S	N	0.8	Green Mountain NF
Roosevelt Woods	661	2/5/82	0	F	N	3.0	Roosevelt-Vanderbilt NHS
Seaway	733	12/12/83	0	F, B, M, V	A, C	365.0	Seaway Trail, Inc.
Seaway Extension	764	12/20/86	2, 3, 4	F, B, V	A, C	94.0	Seaway Trail, Inc.
Smith Point West Nature	624	11/19/81	0	F, C	W, N	0.9	Fire Island NS
Westside Overland	655	11/27/81	0	F, S	N	25.9	Chautauqua County Parks Commission
Wilkerson	769	9/16/87	0	F	N	7.3	Saratoga National Historical Park
Total						751.1	

North Carolina

Name	No.	Date		Type	Mgmt	Miles	Administering Agency
Art Loeb	298	10/5/79	0	F	N	34.0	Pisgah NF
Bartram Nature	756	5/12/85	0	F	N	18.0	FS
Big Glassy	564	4/23/81	0	F	N	2.0	Carl Sandburg Home NHS
Biltmore Campus	79	2/1/76	0	F, I	N	1.0	Pisgah NF
Bob's Creek	52	10/1/74	0	F	N	8.0	Bowaters Carolina Corp.
Cedar Point Tideland	249	3/6/79	0	F	N	1.5	Croatan NF
Cherokee Arboretum	597	6/8/81	0	F	N	0.5	Cherokee Historical Assn.
Daniel Boone Scout	714	8/17/82	0	F	N	3.2	Grandfather Mountain, Inc.
Elizabeth City	753	7/31/85	0	F, B, S	A, C	1.6	City of Elizabeth City
Grandfather	713	8/17/82	0	F	N	3.5	Grandfather Mountain, Inc.
Historic Edenton	113	6/29/77	0	F	N	1.9	Town of Edenton
Historic Salisbury	750	10/15/84	0	F, B	C	4.0	City of Salisbury
Historic Tarboro	258	5/21/79	0	F	N	2.0	Uwharrie NF

Name	Trail No.	Date	Season[a]	Uses[b]	Surface[c]	Length (miles)	Administering Agency[d]
Joyce Kilmer	248	3/6/79	0	F	N	2.0	Nantahala NF
Linville Falls	645	11/27/81	0	F	N	1.2	NPS, Blue Ridge Parkway
Lumber River	512	11/10/80	0	W	N	60.0	Scotland County Parks and Rec. Commission
Pisgah Ecology	459	8/6/79	0	F	N	0.6	Pisgah NF
Roan Mountain Gardens	460	5/6/80	0	F, C	N	1.4	Pisgah NF
Shelley Lake	224	1/25/79	0	F, B, C	A	2.0	Raleigh Parks and Rec. Dept.
Shut-In	644	11/27/81	0	F	N	6.5	Pisgah NF
Shut-In	644	11/27/81	0	F	N	9.8	NPS, Blue Ridge Parkway
Uwharrie	436	2/1/80	0	F	N	20.0	Uwharrie NP
Washington National	734	12/12/84	0	F	C	1.9	City of Washington
Whiteside Mountain	221	8/7/78	0	F	N	2.0	Nantahala NF
Total						188.6	
North Dakota							
Gunlogson Aboretum	167	7/14/78	0	F, S	N	3.0	ND Parks and Rec.
J. Clark Salyer Canoe	560	3/20/81	0	W	N	13.0	FWS
Old Oak	84	4/6/76	0	F, M, S	N	3.0	ND Parks and Rec.
Roughrider	443	2/26/80	0	F, H, M	N	17.0	ND Parks and Rec.
Total						36.0	
Ohio							
Black Creek System	634	11/19/81	0	F, S, I	N, W	3.0	Holmes Park District
Buttercup Valley	285	9/18/79	0	F	N	1.0	Cincinnati Park Board
Caldwell Park	425	1/4/80	0	F	N	1.5	Cincinnati Park Board
California Junction	773	11/10/88	0	F	N	1.0	Cincinnati Rec. Commission
Cuyahoga Valley Towpath	128	12/29/77	0	F, H	N	2.8	NPS, Cuyahoga Valley NRA
Dayton River Bikeway	173	8/14/78	0	B, F	A	8.2	Miami Conservancy District
Grandma Gatewood	446	2/26/80	0	F	N	6.0	OH Dept. of Natural Resources
Harriet L. Keeler Woodland	48	5/16/74	2, 3, 4	F, C	A	0.5	Cleveland Metroparks
Little Pond	487	9/8/80	0	F, I	N	1.5	ACE
Mt. Airy Forest Explorers	690	4/13/82	0	F	N	10.0	Cincinnati Park Board
Olentangy/Scioto	636	11/19/81	0	B, F	A, C	10.9	Columbus Rec. and Parks Dept.
Ottawa Wildlife Interpretive	545	3/20/81	0	F, I	N	7.0	Ottawa NWR
Rocky River Bicycle	66	8/19/75	2, 3, 4	B	A	5.0	Cleveland Metroparks
Sells Nature Park	710	8/6/82	0	F	N	4.0	Athens Parks and Rec. Dept.
Stanbery Creek	424	1/4/80	0	F	N	1.8	Cincinnati Park Board
Towner's Woods	336	11/21/79	0	F, B, S	N	6.0	Portage County Parks and Rec. Dept.

Name	No.	Date		Use		Miles	Administered By
Trillium Valley	635	11/19/81	0	F, I	N	0.8	Cincinnati Rec. Commission
Vesuvius Backpack	412	12/13/79	0	F	N	16.0	Wayne-Hoosier NF
Total						87.0	

Oklahoma

Name	No.	Date		Use		Miles	Administered By
Dog Run Hollow	587	6/8/81	0	F	N	7.0	FWS
Frank Raab Nature	780	4/6/90	0	F	N	2.8	ACE
Indian Nations	121	11/27/77	0	F	N	20.0	Oklahoma City Tourism and Rec. Dept.
Jean Pierre Choteau Hiking	511	11/13/80	0	F, H	N	64.0	ACE
Murrell Home Nature	177	9/20/78	0	C, S, F	A	0.5	Oklahoma City Tourism and Rec. Dept.
Oxley Nature Center	586	6/8/81	0	F, C	A	7.0	Tulsa Park and Rec. Dept.
Pathfinder Parkway	111	6/22/77	0	F, B	N	4.7	City of Bartlesville
Red Stick	57	4/18/75	0	F	N	1.5	OK City Parks
Riverside	276	7/25/77	0	F, B	N	6.0	Tulsa River Parks Authority
Struggle For Survival	354	11/16/79	0	F, C, I	N	0.7	Ouachita NF
Trail Across The Water	739	4/12/84	0	F, B	A	2.5	City of Cleveland
Trestle Pond	776	6/22/89	0	F, I	N	2.4	ACE
Wintersmith Park Jogging	630	11/19/81	0	F, B, C	A	2.3	Ada City Hall
Total						121.4	

Oregon

Name	No.	Date		Use		Miles	Administered By
Acker Divide	686	3/29/82	0	F, H, V	N	5.4	Umpqua NF
Arch Rock	613	7/20/81	0	F	N	0.4	Malheur NF
Badger Creek	243	3/6/79	0	F, H, S, V	N	11.0	Mount Hood NF
Bear Creek Bikeway	81	3/9/76	0	B, F	N	3.4	Medford Parks Division
Billie Creek Nature	563	4/2/81	0	F, H	N	1.0	Winema NF
Bohemia	537	3/4/81	0	F, H, S, M, V	N	2.5	Umpqua NF
Boundary	303	10/5/79	0	F, H, V	N	17.0	Siskiyou NF
Buck Canyon	580	5/18/81	0	F, M, V	N	13.5	Rogue River NF
Cedar Grove	231	2/7/79	0	F	N	1.0	Malheur NF
Cherry Creek	319	10/5/79	0	F, H	N	5.0	Winema NF
Cow Creek	605	5/15/81	0	H, F, S, V, M	N	6.5	Umpqua NF
Crane Mountain	321	10/5/79	0	F, H, V	N	7.0	Fremont NF
Elkhorn Crest	314	10/5/79	0	F, H, V	N	15.6	Wallowa-Whitman NF
Fall Creek	228	2/7/79	0	F	N	9.0	Willamette NF
Fall Creek Falls	193	12/8/78	0	F	N	0.9	Umpqua NF
Fish Lake	535	3/2/81	0	F, H	N	8.0	Umpqua NF

Name	Trail No.	Date	Season[a]	Uses[b]	Surface[c]	Length (miles)	Administering Agency[d]
Fremont	320	10/5/79	O	F, H, V	N	8.0	Fremont NF
Gin Lin	313	10/5/79	O	F, H, V	N	17.0	Rogue River NF
High Wallowa	562	4/2/81	O	F	N	2.0	Wallowa-Whitman NF
Illinois River	366	11/27/79	O	F	N	3.0	Siskiyou NF
Jubilee Lake	538	3/4/81	O	F	N	3.0	Umatilla NF
Lava Cast Forest	607	5/15/81	O	F	N	0.9	Deschutes NF
Lava River	482	8/18/80	O	F	N	0.5	Willamette NF
Link River	82	3/15/76	O	F	N	0.8	Pacific Power & Light Co.
Maidu Lake	322	10/5/79	O	F, H	N	2.7	Winema NF
Maidu Lake	726	7/19/83	O	F, H	N	10.0	Umpqua NF
Malheur River	230	2/7/79	O	F, H, V, M, S	N	9.0	Malheur NF
McKenzie River	116	4/1/77	O	F	N	13.0	Willamette NF
Metolius-Windigo	481	5/18/80	O	F, H, S, M	N	35.0	Deschutes NF
Mt. Bailey	518	1/10/80	O	F, H, S, M, V	N	2.0	Umpqua NF
Nee-Me-Poo	295	10/5/79	O	F	N	3.7	Wallowa-Whitman NF
North Fork John Day River	330	10/19/79	O	F, H, V	N	26.2	Umatilla NF
North Umpqua—Mott Section	194	12/8/78	O	F, H	N	5.5	Umpqua NF
North Umpqua—Tioga Section	798	9/20/92	O	F, B, C	N	11.0	BLM, Roseburg District
Oregon High Desert Trail	799	9/20/92	O	F, H, V	N	150.0	BLM
Peter Skene Ogden	270	6/29/79	O	F, H	N	9.5	Deschutes NF
Riverside	229	2/7/79	O	F	N	4.6	Mount Hood NF
Rogue River	575	5/5/81	O	F, C	N	40.0	BLM; Salem State Parks and Rec. Div.
Rogue River	608	5/21/81	O	F	N	16.0	Siskiyou NF
Rogue-Umpqua Divide	478	8/18/80	O	F, H, V, S	N	26.0	Rogue River–Umpqua NF
Round Mountain	328	10/19/79	O	F, H, V	N	6.5	Ochoco NF
Saint Perpetua	519	12/16/80	O	F	N	1.7	Siuslaw NF
Salmon River	406	12/13/79	O	F	N	14.6	Mt. Hood NF
Silver Creek Canyon	223	1/25/79	O	F	N	6.5	Silver Falls State Park
South Breitenbush Gorge	516	11/10/80	O	F, V, H	N	2.4	Willamette NF
Tahkenitch Dunes	227	2/7/79	O	F, I	N	1.6	Siuslaw NF
Tillamook Head	5	6/1/71	O	F	N	6.0	Salem State Parks and Rec. Div.
Trail of the Molten Land	269	6/29/79	O	F, I	N	0.5	Deschutes NF
Trail of the Restless Waters	192	12/8/78	O	F, I	N	0.4	Siuslaw NF
Twin Pillars	318	10/5/79	O	F, H	N	8.5	Ochoco NF
Upper Rogue River	215	1/5/79	O	F	N	45.5	Rogue River NF
Wildwood	62	6/24/75	O	F, H	N	26.3	Portland Park Bureau

858

Name	No.	Date		Activities		Miles	Agency
Willamette River	30	6/1/71	0	F	N	3.8	Eugene Parks and Rec. Dept.
Winom Creek–Big Creek	375	11/29/79	0	F, H, V	N	5.6	Umatilla NF
Total						630.9	
				Pennsylvania			
Baptism Creek	619	11/19/81	0	F, H, S	N	0.8	Hopewell Village NHS
Bear Run Nature Reserve	732	12/12/83	0	F, S	N	20.0	Bear Run Nature Reserve
Black Cherry	213	12/18/78	0	F	N	1.2	Alleghany NF
Black Willow Water	752	3/7/85	0	W	N	3.1	ACE
Bossard Nature	646	11/27/81	0	F, C	N, W	1.5	ACE
Delaware Canal Heritage	778	4/6/90	0	B, F, S	N	60.0	Harrisburg Bureau State Parks
East Impoundment	676	2/5/82	0	F, B	N	3.0	FWS
Fairmount Park Bike Path	26	6/1/71	0	B, F	A	8.2	Fairmount Park Commission
Flour Sak Battle	64	6/1/75	0	C	N, W	1.0	PA Historic and Museum Commission
Friendship Hill Loop	744	6/19/84	0	F, S, I	N	5.4	Friendship Hill NHS
Harrisburg Riverfront	118	9/18/77	0	B, F	A	4.0	Harrisburg Dept. of Parks and Rec.
John Bartrams Garden	751	3/7/85	0	F	N	1.0	John Bartrams Association
Kellys Run–Pinnacle System	99	10/1/76	0	F, H	N	7.6	PA Power & Light Co.
Laurel Highlands Hiking	759	2/25/86	0	F, S, M	N	70.0	Rockwood Dept. of Environmental Resources
Laurel Hill Cemetery Victorian	779	4/2/90	0	F	A	25.0	Laurel Hill Cemetery Co.
Lehigh Canal Heritage	262	6/26/79	0	F, H, B, S	N	31.6	Northampton Parks and Rec.; Lehigh Canal Rec. Commission
Lehigh Parkway Heritage	689	4/13/82	0	B, F, H	N	7.0	Allentown Bureau of Parks
Pennsylvania Seaway	783	12/13/90	0	V, B, F	A	46.0	PA Dept. of Transportation
Presque Isle State Park	777	12/5/89	0	F, B, H, S	A, C	5.8	Presque Isle State Park
River	620	11/19/81	0	F, H	N	3.0	Valley Forge NHP
Seth Meyers Nature	677	2/5/82	0	F	N	0.5	ACE
Summit Nature	618	11/19/81	0	F	N, W	1.3	Allegheny Portage R.R. NHS
Switchback Railroad	513	11/10/80	0	F, S, B, C	N	15.0	Carbon County Rec. Authority
Towpath Bike	638	11/19/81	0	F, B	A	7.8	Town of Palmer; Township of Bethleham
Tracy Ridge	225	2/7/79	0	F, S	N	4.2	Allegheny NF
Union Canal Walk and Bike	73	10/27/76	0	F, B	N	4.2	Berks County Parks and Rec. Dept.
Wissahickon	58	4/1/75	0	F, H, B	N	5.4	Fairmount Park Commission
Woodlands Heritage	774	1/20/89	0	F, I	A	10.0	University City Historical Society; Woodlands Cemetery Co.
Youghiogheny River	772	5/5/88	0	F, B, S, W	A	11.0	Ohiopyle State Park
Total						364.6	

Name	Trail No.	Date	Season[a]	Uses[b]	Surface[c]	Length (miles)	Administering Agency[d]
				Puerto Rico			
El Toro	438	2/1/80	O	F	N	2.6	Caribbean NF
Tradewinds	439	2/1/80	O	F	N	5.0	Caribbean NF
Total						7.6	
				Rhode Island			
Cliff Walk	65	8/1/75	O	F	A, C	3.5	City of Newport
				South Carolina			
Bulls Island Wildlife	680	2/5/82	O	F	N	2.0	FWS
Edisto Nature	126	12/28/77	O	F	N	1.5	Westvaco Corporation
Foothills	300	10/5/79	O	F	N	23.0	Sumter NF
Francis Beidler Forest	735	4/12/84	O	F	W	1.7	National Audubon Society
Hunting Island Marsh	127	12/28/77	O	F	W	0.3	Columbia Dept. of Parks
Jones Gap	790		O	F	N	5.3	Columbia Div. of State Parks
Kings Mountain Hiking	598	6/8/81	O	F	N	9.0	King's Mt. NMP; SC Div. of Parks
Swampfox	391	12/13/79	O	F	N	24.0	Francis Marion NF
Table Rock	86	5/6/76	O	F	N	9.0	SC Div. of Parks
Total						75.8	
				South Dakota			
Bear Butte	13	6/1/71	O	F	N	3.5	Pierre Div. of Parks and Rec.
Farm Island System	633	11/19/81	O	F, C	N	4.1	Pierre Div. of Parks and Rec.
Flume	405	12/13/79	O	F, C	N	6.5	Black Hills NF
Fossil Exhibit	504	10/22/80	O	F, C	A	0.3	Badlands NM
Laframboise Island	577	5/5/81	O	F, C	A	8.0	ACE
Lake Oahe Nature	576	5/5/81	O	F, S, C	A	1.5	ACE
Lost Cabin	348	11/16/79	O	F	N	5.1	Black Hills NF
Rankin Ridge	693	4/3/82	O	F	N	1.0	Wind Cave NP
Sunday Gulch	14	6/1/71	O	F	N	4.0	Pierre Div. of Parks and Rec.
Trail of the Spirits	15	6/1/71	O	F	N	0.5	Pierre Div. of Parks and Rec.
Woodland	102	12/8/76	O	F, M, S	N	1.3	Pierre Div. of Parks and Rec.
Total						35.8	
				Tennessee			
Anderson Road Exercise	573	5/5/81	O	F, B	N	1.0	J. Percy Priest Lake
Bearwaller Gap Hiking	160	6/1/78	O	F	N	6.0	ACE
Big Hill Pond	260	5/21/79	O	F	N	8.3	Nashville Dept. of Conservation
Blue Beaver	108	3/28/77	O	F, H	N	10.5	Chickamauga and Chattanooga NMP
Chickasaw Nature	653	11/27/81	O	F	N	1.1	FWS
Cordell Hull Lake	561	4/7/81	O	H, F	N	22.0	ACE
Dale Hollow Dam Area	572	5/5/81	O	F, B, C	A	0.6	ACE
Forest City	652	11/27/81	O	C, F, I	A	0.1	TVA

Name	Number	Date		Activities		Code	Amount	Agency
Fort Henry Hiking	97	10/21/76	0	F		N	26.0	TVA
Hemlock Bluff	651	11/27/81	0	F		N	5.0	TVA
Honey Creek	38	6/1/73	0	F		N	5.0	Bowaters Southern Paper Co.
Honeysuckle	40	7/1/73	0	F		N	0.5	TN Dept. of Conservation
John Muir	361	11/27/79	0	F		N	14.0	Cherokee NF
Lady Finger Bluff	125	12/28/77	0	F		N	2.7	TVA
Laurel-Snow	23	6/1/71	0	F, M		N	8.0	Bowaters Southern Paper Co.
North Ridge	36	3/1/73	0	F, B		N	7.5	City of Oak Ridge
Obey River Canoe	715	8/17/82	0	W		N	6.0	ACE
Old Hickory	94	9/14/76	0	F		N	1.7	ACE
Piney River	153	4/12/78	0	F		N	10.0	Bowaters Southern Paper Co.
River Bluff	90	6/10/76	0	F		N	3.1	TVA
South Cumberland	294	10/11/79	0	F		N	60.0	TN Dept. of Conservation
Stiner's Woods	650	11/27/81	0	F		N	1.2	TVA
Third Creek Bicycle	112	6/22/77	0	B, F		N	2.3	Knoxville Rec. Dept.
Three Hickories Nature	574	5/5/81	0	F		N	1.8	ACE
Turkey Creek Nature	571	5/5/81	0	F		N	2.8	ACE
Twin Arches	760	5/20/86	0	F, H		N	6.0	South Big Fork NRA
Virgin Falls	39	6/1/73	0	F		N	8.0	Bowaters Southern Paper Co.
Warriors Passage	422	12/13/79	0	F		N	2.8	Cherokee NF
Total							224.0	
				Texas				
Baker Park Nature	569	4/4/81	0	F, C		A	2.2	Sherman City Manager
Benbrook Lake Horseback	568	3/4/81	0	F, H		N	7.3	ACE
Cargill Long Park	32	6/2/72	0	F, B, C		A	2.5	Longview Parks and Rec. Dept.
Chisolm-Bluebonnet	627	11/19/81	0	F, B		N	8.5	City of Plano
Four C's	274	6/29/79	0	F		N	19.0	Davy Crockett NF
Greer Island Nature	17	6/1/71	0	F		N	3.0	Fort Worth Parks and Rec.
Lone Star	169	7/14/78	0	F		N	26.0	Sam Houston NF
Northshore	787	8/20/91	0	B, F		N	7.0	ACE, Ft. Worth District
San Antonio River	105	3/18/77	0	F, B		N	8.0	San Antonio Parks and Rec.
Town Lake Walk and Bikeway	71	12/2/75	0	F, B		N	9.8	Austin Parks
Walnut Grove	788	8/20/91	0	H, F, B		N	7.0	ACE, Ft. Worth District
Total							100.3	
				Utah				
Bald Mountain	363	11/17/79	0	F		N	1.5	Wasatch NF
Bicentennial	648	11/27/81	0	F, H		N	3.2	Weber Co. Planning Comm.
Cascade Falls	338	11/16/79	0	F		W	1.0	Dixie NF
Cascade Nature	186	11/29/78	0	F, C, I		N	0.6	Uinta NF
Fish Creek	287	9/14/79	0	F, H		N	6.0	Ashley NF
Fish Creek	290	9/14/79	0	F, H		N	10.0	Manti-La Sal NF

Name	Trail No.	Date	Season[a]	Uses[b]	Surface[c]	Length (miles)	Administering Agency[d]
Lakeshore	325	10/5/79	O	F	N	1.4	Fishlake NF
Left Fork Huntington Creek	291	9/14/79	O	F, H	N	4.0	Manti-La Sal NF
Little Hole	264	6/29/79	O	F	N	7.3	Ashley NF
Moab Slickrock Bike Trail	800	9/20/92	O	B, V	N	12.1	BLM, Moab District
Mount Naomi Peak	414	12/13/79	O	F, H, S	N	9.0	Wasatch NF
Mount Timpanogos	309	10/5/79	O	F, H	N	18.0	Uinta NF
Skyline	326	10/5/79	O	F, H, M	N	8.8	Fishlake NF
Whipple	266	6/29/79	O	F, H	N	6.5	Dixie NF
Total						89.4	
Vermont							
Long	763	10/15/86	O	F, H	N	72.4	Green Mountain NF
Stowe Recreation Path	786	11/15/90	O	F, B, S, M	A	5.3	Town of Stowe
Total						77.7	
Virginia							
Blackwater Creek	531	1/12/81	O	F, B	C, A	8.6	City of Lynchburg
Booker T. Washington	622	11/19/81	O	F	N	3.0	Booker T. Washington NM
Cascades	98	10/12/76	O	F	N	4.0	Jefferson NF
Flat Top-Falling Water Cascade	696	4/13/82	O	F	N	5.4	Blue Ridge Parkway
Little Stony	765	2/6/87	O	F	N	2.8	Jefferson NF
Mount Rogers	268	6/29/79	O	F	N	4.5	Jefferson NF
Mount Laurel	770	9/30/87	O	F, C	A	0.5	National Wildlife Federation
Petersburg Battlefield	621	11/19/81	O	F, B, H, C	A, N	7.2	Petersburg National Battlefield
Pine Mountain	505	10/22/80	2, 3, 4	F	N	1.0	Jefferson NF
Rock Castle Gorge	697	4/13/82	O	F	N	10.6	NPS, Blue Ridge Parkway
Seashore State Park	109	4/14/77	O	F, B	N	23.0	Virginia Div. of Parks
Spotsylvania Battlefield	721	4/25/83	O	F	N	7.0	Fredericksburg and Spotsylvania Natl. Battlefield Park
The Lion's Tale	356	11/16/79	2, 3, 4	F, C	W	0.2	George Washington NF
Virginia Creeper	757	9/8/85	O	F, H, S	A	32.0	Jefferson NF
Washington and Old Dominion	768	8/21/87	O	F, B, H	A	44.0	N. Virginia Regional Park Authority
Wild Oak	280	8/17/79	O	F, H, M	N	25.6	George Washington NF
Total						179.4	
Washington							
Ape Cave	265	6/29/79	O	F	N	2.0	Gifford Pinchot NF
Ape Cave	761	5/20/86	O	F	N	3.5	Gifford Pinchot NF
Bayside Greenbelt	120	10/12/75	O	F	N	2.5	Tacoma Dept. of Public Works

Name	No.	Date					Agency
Blue Lake	458	5/6/80	0	F	N	2.2	Okanogan NF
Boulder Cave	464	5/6/80	0	F	N	0.8	Wenatchee NF
Boundary	222	1/5/79	0	F, H, V	N	45.0	Gifford Pinchot NF
Brown Farm Dike	590	6/8/81	0	F	N	5.0	FWS
Cape Alava	557	3/20/81	0	F	N	3.3	Olympic NP
Cedar Creek	463	5/6/80	0	F, H, V	N	9.6	Okanogan NF
Clearwater and Snake	771	3/2/88	0	F, B, W	A	16.0	ACE
Cutthroat Creek	604	5/15/81	0	F	N	5.5	Okanogan NF
Deception Falls Nature	288	9/14/79	0	F, I	N	0.5	Mt. Baker–Snoqualmie NF
Diablo Lake	558	3/20/81	0	F	N	3.8	North Cascades NP
Discovery Park Loop	60	6/24/75	0	F, B	N	2.8	Seattle Parks and Rec.
Domke Lake	256	5/8/79	0	F	N	0.4	Wenatchee NF
Eagle Lake	271	6/29/79	0	F	N	0.8	Okanogan NF
Fred Cleator Interpretive	4	6/1/71	0	F, F, I	N	1.3	Washington State Parks
Ice Caves	133	1/31/78	0	F, H, S	N	0.9	Mt. Baker–Snoqualmie NF
Kettle Crest	247	3/6/79	0	B, F	N	33.0	Colville NF
Lake Washington Bike	2	6/1/71	0	F	N	3.2	Seattle Dept. of Parks and Rec.
Lake Washington Ship Canal	3	6/1/71	0		N	0.3	ACE
Lena Lake	185	11/29/78	0	F, S	N	20.8	Olympic NF
Log Flume	299	10/5/79	0	F, I	N	0.5	Colville NF
Meta Lake	762	5/20/86	3, 4	F, I	N	0.3	Gifford Pinchot NF
Pass Creek–Grassy Top	616	9/24/81	0	F, H, V	N	29.7	Colville NF
Pine Ridge	426	1/4/80	0	F, S	A	3.5	Whitman County Parks and Rec. Dept.
Quinault Rain Forest	237	2/7/79	0	F, I	N	0.4	Olympic NF
Quinault Loop	236	2/7/79	0	F, C	N	4.1	Olympic NF
Rainy Lake	130	10/22/77	0	F, I	N	0.2	Okanogan NF
Shadow of the Sentinels	323	10/5/79	0	F	N	0.5	Mt. Baker–Snoqualmie NF
Silver Falls	272	6/29/79	0	F	N	7.0	Wenatchee NF
Skookum Flats	297	10/05/79	0	F, B, C, H	N	7.6	Mt. Baker–Snoqualmie NF
Snohomish County Centennial	791	9/20/92	0	F	A, N	7.0	Snohomish County Parks and Rec.
Sullivan Lake	246	9/11/78	0	F	N	3.5	Colville NF
Washington Pass Overlook	168	7/14/78	0	F, C	N	0.2	Okanogan NF
Wonderland	559	3/20/81	0	F, H	N	90.0	Mt. Rainier NP
Wynoochee Lake Shore	277	8/23/79	0	F, H, V	N	10.0	Olympic NF; ACE
Yakima Greenway Pathway	803	10/29/92	0	F, B, C	A	4.7	Yakima Greenway Foundation
Total						332.4	

West Virginia

Name	No.	Date					Agency
Huntington Museum of Art System	53	12/1/84	0	F, C	N	0.4	Huntington Museum of Art
North Bend Rail-Trail	803	10/29/92	0	F, B, C	N	60.5	North Bend State Park
Whispering Spruce	473	6/12/80	2, 3	F	N	0.5	Monongahela NF
Total						61.4	

Name	Trail No.	Date	Season[a]	Uses[b]	Surface[c]	Length (miles)	Administering Agency[d]
Wisconsin							
Ahnapee State Park	63	6/24/75	O	F, B, M	N	15.0	WI Dept. of Natural Resources
Anvil	199	12/8/78	O	F, S	N	11.0	Nicolet NF
Bearskin State Park	172	8/9/78	O	B, F, M	N	16.5	WI Dept. of Natural Resources
Ed's Lake	612	7/20/81	O	F, S	N	6.2	Nicolet NF
Elroy-Sparta	19	6/1/71	O	B, F, M	N	30.0	WI Dept. of Natural Resources
Ice Age	20	6/1/71	O	F	N	25.0	WI Dept. of Natural Resources
Ice Age	103	1/11/77	O	F, S, M	N	62.5	Ice Age Park and Trail Foundation
Ice Age	119	10/6/77	O	F, S, M	N	15.0	Ice Age Park and Trail Foundation
Ice Age	122	10/21/77	O	F	N	40.0	Chequamegon NF
Janesville School Outdoor Lab	497	10/9/80	O	F, S	N	4.8	School District of Janesville
Jordon Park Nature	681	2/5/82	O	F, S, I	N	2.0	Portage County Park Commission
Kiwanis	565	4/23/81	O	F, B	N	1.0	City of Janesville
Lake Park Bicycle	34	3/8/73	O	F, B	A	3.1	Milwaukee County Dept. of Parks
Lauterman	408	12/13/79	O	F, S	N	8.0	Nicolet NF
Rock Lake	657	11/18/81	O	F, S	N	13.6	Chequamegon NF
Sugar River State	51	9/18/74	O	B, F, M	N	23.0	WI Dept. of Natural Resources
Warnimont Park Bicycle	35	3/8/73	O	F, B	A	1.5	Milwaukee County Dept. of Parks, Rec., and Culture
Total						278.2	
Wyoming							
Beartooth Loop	343	11/16/79	O	F, H, V	N	14.4	Shoshone NF
Blackwater Fire Memorial	404	12/13/79	O	F, H	N	5.0	Shoshone NF
Bucking Mule Falls	351	11/16/79	O	F, H	N	11.0	Bighorn NF
Grassroots	101	5/1/76	O	B, F	A	0.9	Torrington Parks Dept.
Headquarters	399	12/13/79	O	F, H, V, M, S	N	5.0	Medicine Bow NF
Horsethief Cave Underground	801	9/20/92	2, 3, 4	U	N	1.2	BLM, Worland District
Le McCune Braille	87	5/11/76	O	F	N	0.3	Natrona County Parks
Morning Glory	544	3/20/81	O	F, S	A	1.5	Yellowstone NP
Rock Creek–Deep Creek	400	12/13/79	O	F, H, V	N	14.0	Medicine Bow NF
Shell Falls	401	12/13/79	O	F, C, I	N	0.2	Bighorn NF
Sheridan	324	10/5/79	O	F, H	N	16.0	Bridger-Teton NF
South Rim	542	3/20/81	O	F	A	9.0	Yellowstone NP
Three Senses	543	3/20/81	O	F	W	0.2	Yellowstone NP

| Wyoming Range | 255 | 5/8/79 | O | F, V | N | 70.0 | Bridger-Teton NF |
| Total | | | | | | 148.7 | |

[a]Seasons Open: O, all year; 1, December, January, February; 2, March, April, May; 3, June, July, August; 4, September, October, November.
[b]Types of Uses: B, bicycle; C, handicapped; F, foot; H, horse; I, interpretive; M, snowmobile; S, ski; U, underground; V, motorized; W, water.
[c]Types of Surfaces: A, asphalt; C, concrete; N, natural of native material; W, wood.
[d]Abbreviations: ACE, Army Corps of Engineers; BLM, Bureau of Land Management; FWS, Fish and Wildlife Service; NF, National Forest; NHP, National Historical Park; NHS, National Historic Site; NM, National Monument; NMP, National Military Park; NP, National Park; NPS, National Park Service; NS, National Seashore; NRA, National Recreation Area; NWR, National Wildlife Refuge; SR, Scenic River; TVA, Tennessee Valley Authority.
Source: Register of National Recreation Trails, Washington, DC: U.S. Dept. of Interior. January 1993.

Index

Note: References in **boldface** indicate maps in back envelope.

Note: References in **boldface** indicate maps in back envelope.

Note: References in **boldface** indicate maps in back envelope.

Note: References in **boldface** indicate maps in back envelope.

Note: References in **boldface** indicate maps in back envelope.

Note: References in **boldface** indicate maps in back envelope.

Note: References in **boldface** indicate maps in back envelope.

Note: References in **boldface** indicate maps in back envelope.

Note: References in **boldface** indicate maps in back envelope.

Note: References in **boldface** indicate maps in back envelope.

Note: References in **boldface** indicate maps in back envelope.

Note: References in **boldface** indicate maps in back envelope.

Note: References in **boldface** indicate maps in back envelope.

Note: References in **boldface** indicate maps in back envelope.

Note: References in **boldface** indicate maps in back envelope.

Note: References in **boldface** indicate maps in back envelope.

Note: References in **boldface** indicate maps in back envelope.

Note: References in **boldface** indicate maps in back envelope.

Note: References in **boldface** indicate maps in back envelope.

Note: References in **boldface** indicate maps in back envelope.

Note: References in **boldface** indicate maps in back envelope.

Note: References in **boldface** indicate maps in back envelope.

Note: References in **boldface** indicate maps in back envelope.

Note: References in **boldface** indicate maps in back envelope.

Note: References in **boldface** indicate maps in back envelope.

Note: References in **boldface** indicate maps in back envelope.

Note: References in **boldface** indicate maps in back envelope.

Note: References in **boldface** indicate maps in back envelope.

Note: References in **boldface** indicate maps in back envelope.

Note: References in **boldface** indicate maps in back envelope.

Note: References in **boldface** indicate maps in back envelope.